MW01050114

Remedies

Remedies

A Practical Approach

David Hricik
PROFESSOR OF LAW
MERCER UNIVERSITY SCHOOL OF LAW

CAROLINA ACADEMIC PRESS
Durham, North Carolina

ISBN 978-1-5310-1389-9
eISBN 978-1-5310-1390-5
LCCN 2020934161

Carolina Academic Press
700 Kent Street
Durham, North Carolina 27701
Telephone (919) 489-7486
Fax (919) 493-5668
E-mail: cap@cap-press.com
www.cap-press.com

Printed in the United States of America

This is dedicated to the many teachers and professors I have had who helped me to become a better reader and writer, to the lawyers and judges who mentored me to learn to simplify and organize complex material, and to Lisa and my family — who put up with me while I tried to use the skills that I have been given to write this book. I am grateful as well to Mercer University for grants which helped make this possible and to students who "test drove" earlier versions — and who helped me turn this course into something both practical and which can help pass the bar!

Contents

Online Materials

Additional content for *Remedies: A Practical Approach* is available on Carolina Academic Press's Core Knowledge for Lawyers (CKL) website.

Core Knowledge for Lawyers is an online teaching and testing platform that hosts practice questions and additional content for both instructors and students.

To learn more, please visit:

coreknowledgeforlawyers.com

Instructors may request complimentary access through the "Faculty & Instructors" link.

Table of Principal Cases

Acknowledgments

Note on Case Editing

Because this is book is designed for upper-level students, all of the materials used have been edited for ease of reading and understanding, and often without indicating an omission or minor alteration. For example, many footnotes, citations, and quotation marks have been deleted. In addition, most cases begin with a summary of the facts, and contained within brackets. All of this was done to shorten the text, to focus on remedies, and to increase readability. In no instance was the meaning of a case altered.

Remedies

Chapter 1

Introduction

1. The Structure of the Book

This section describes the broad analytical framework needed to determine what, if any, remedies are available to a plaintiff. At a most general level, there are two types of remedies: (a) specific relief, typically taking the form of order from the court either compelling the defendant to do, or not do, something needed to make the plaintiff whole; and (b) substitutionary relief, most commonly in the form of a judgment for an amount of money to make the plaintiff whole. Substitutionary remedies are the most common. Substitutionary relief—money—is often described as the "remedy at law," and specific relief is often referred to as the "equitable remedy." Equitable remedies most frequently take the form of injunctions. There are, of course, other forms of relief, but relief in the form of a monetary award or an injunction is, by far, the most common.

Remedies are available only to a plaintiff who prevails on a claim. As you recall, courts decide claims, not "disputes," "lawsuits," "civil actions," or even "cases." Some lawyers and opinions in this book refer to a claim as a "cause of action," a "right of action," or a "count." These are synonyms for "claim." Because of *res judicata* and the "single action rule," a plaintiff typically pleads more than one claim in its complaint, but courts adjudicate lawsuits on a claim-by-claim basis, and remedies are determined on a claim-by-claim basis.

Over the history of the common law, courts have recognized claims to provide a remedy for different types of harm. But, even including negligence, each claim requires a certain type of harm or no remedy is available. The most common forms of harm are: *harm to person* (e.g., personal injury, including pain and suffering inherently caused by a physical injury, and the ultimate form of personal injury, death), *harm to property or to rights in property* (e.g., destroyed personal items or trespassing on land), *psychic harm* (e.g., mental anguish or distress caused by something other than a physical impact, say by being put in fear of being injured but not actually being injured), harm to *dignity* (e.g., defamation), and *economic harm* (e.g., losses caused by a breach of contract or fraud). Of course, there are other harms, such as being unlawfully detained (false imprisonment) or being humiliated by an unjustified criminal prosecution (malicious prosecution).

Each claim has "elements," including a required type of harm. To obtain any relief whatsoever, a plaintiff must establish each element, including the type of harm that the particular claim requires as "damage." For example, the elements of assault are typically: (a) the defendant (b) intentionally (c) acted (d) and that act caused (e) *the plaintiff to apprehend imminent and serious bodily harm.* Without proof of the type of harm required for the damage element, the plaintiff has no claim upon which relief can be granted. Thus, just as a defendant sued for assault should move to dismiss if the complaint fails to allege the defendant acted intentionally, so too should the defendant if the plaintiff does not allege the *particular type* of "damage" required by the claim. In both instances, the court should grant the defendant's motion.

This book approaches remedies by identifying the claim, or claims, for which a particular harm is sufficient to be the "damage" required by that claim. Of the common claims, courts disagree the most on the meaning of "damage" for negligence claims. Yet the elements are probably the most familiar: (a) the defendant owed the plaintiff a duty, (b) the defendant breached that duty, (c) that breach of duty both as a matter of fact and proximately (i.e., there is a legally sufficient connection) caused plaintiff (d) *damages.*

In your Torts course, you read many cases, but likely did not even notice that, almost invariably, the plaintiff had suffered a physical impact. Plaintiffs constantly slipped on bananas, were hit by trains, or had strange objects fall from hotels during wild parties. There is a reason for that: with exceptions, most courts hold that "damages" for a negligence claim requires there be a physical impact on the plaintiff's person or property. Yet, just like the cases you read in Torts seldom mentioned that fact, neither do courts. The court in *Henry v. Dow Chem. Co.*, 701 N.W.2d 684 (Mich. 2005), explained why courts rarely discuss "damage" required by negligence, even though its meaning severely limits negligence claims:

> While the courts of this state may not have always clearly articulated this injury requirement, nor finely delineated the distinction between an "injury" and the "damages" flowing therefrom, the injury requirement has always been present in our negligence analysis. It has simply always been the case in our jurisprudence that plaintiffs alleging negligence claims have also shown that their claims arise from present physical injuries. We are not aware of any Michigan cases in which a plaintiff has recovered on a negligence theory without demonstrating some present physical injury. Thus, in all known cases in Michigan in which a plaintiff has satisfied the "damages" element of a negligence claim, he has also satisfied the "injury" requirement.

The key initial point is that every claim requires a certain type of harm or the law allows no recovery. For example, mental anguish, alone, is insufficient to constitute the damage element for breach of contract or fraud, and with some exceptions is insufficient to constitute the damage element of a negligence claim. It is important to always consider what types of harm the plaintiff suffered because unless that harm constitutes the type of "damage" required by a claim, no remedy is available — at all.

After Chapter 2 describes declaratory judgments and begins discussion of injunctions, the book focuses on remedies for typical tort and contract claims — those on which bar exams focus and that lawyers address in daily practice. This book discusses claims in a deliberate order, starting with claims that — to satisfy the damage element of the claim — require physical harm, then claims that require less tangible harms, such as mental anguish, freedom of movement, and reputation. It then turns to claims that remedy harm to personal or real property and, finally, claims that require "damage" in the form of pure economic harm, first examining the claim of breach of contract and then the very few tort claims for which economic harm is sufficient to constitute "damage."

If a plaintiff does not suffer the type of harm required to constitute damage for a claim, that claim is not one upon which *any* relief can be granted. Thus, a critical step is to determine whether, given the harms suffered, any relief is available, which is the focus of the first chapters of this book. Each chapters then turns to the measure of damages for each harm and describes "consequential damages" that may be available. In addition, after addressing monetary damages, the chapters address how courts determine whether money is "adequate" or if, instead, equitable relief (usually in the form of an injunction) is available. With some exceptions, only a plaintiff whose "remedy at law" — money — is "inadequate" may obtain equitable relief.

This structure accomplishes several things. First, by focusing on the required harm for a claim, the book helps prepare for the bar, which often makes the correct answer to a multiple-choice question turn on whether the plaintiff suffered the "damage" required for a particular claim. Further, the case law in this book is generally the law that bar exams apply and that most states follow. This book helps with both bar and practice. The book also intentionally uses spaced repetition: chapters discuss both the legal and equitable remedies for each claim, thus repeating equitable principles — which are often bar-tested but not often covered fully in other law school courses.

To see how critical identifying the harm required by the "damages" element of a claim is, consider two simple hypotheticals. In this book, you will learn in detail the law providing the answer to each of them, but you should be able to understand the first one from what you learned in Torts.

First, consider the difference between the type of harm for which damages may be recovered for a negligence claim compared to an assault claim. Hopefully you recall that negligence generally requires physical harm, and assault requires apprehending imminent serious physical harm. Suppose a plaintiff walking on a sidewalk suffers mental distress when she perceives the defendant's car veering toward her at high speed, but at the last second, it heads back down the roadway. If the defendant had intentionally veered toward plaintiff, the plaintiff will recover damages for an assault, but if the defendant *negligently* did so, she will (in most states) recover nothing — even if the defendant clearly caused severe anguish.

Second, imagine a plaintiff who, because of the defendant's conduct, has suffered both economic losses and severe emotional anguish. We will see that whether damages are available for either type of harm turns on the meaning of the "damage" element of a claim. For example, if those harms were caused by the defendant's breach of a typical contract, the plaintiff would recover damages for the economic loss, but not for the emotional distress; if, instead, the harms were caused by the defendant punching the plaintiff in the nose, she would recover damages to compensate for her pain and suffering — her mental anguish — and, if they were the "consequence" of the battery, for those economic losses (e.g., medical expenses).

It may be helpful to think of the type of harm required to constitute "damage" for a claim as that claim's "trigger" harm. Without it, a plaintiff has no claim upon which relief can be granted. With it, a plaintiff will recover damages for that harm. In addition, the claim may permit the plaintiff to recover "consequential damages" for other harms caused by the defendant.

Stripped to a misleadingly simple general rule, but one that puts remedies in context, the harm, or harms, suffered by a client is the basis for determining which claim, or claims, a lawyer must assert to recover all available damages for a client, or to obtain equitable relief (like an injunction). A client may have suffered a harm for which only one claim will permit relief; or no claim may. The client may have suffered a harm for which multiple claims permit recovery. Or it may be that to obtain recovery for each type of harm suffered by a client, a lawyer must assert multiple claims. This chapter concludes with simple examples of this process.

2. The Three Steps to the Broad Analytical Framework

A. What Is the Required Harm and the Measure of Damages?

Usually, the measure of damages for a particular harm is the same for each claim for which it is recoverable as "damage," whether as direct or consequential damages. So, for example, the jury instruction on the amount of "pain and suffering" damages it should award to a plaintiff who had been intentionally punched by a defendant is the same as a jury instruction for a plaintiff who was negligently injured by a defendant. However, in certain circumstances the measure of damages depends on the claim. Interesting problems arise, for example, where the plaintiff suffered only economic harm and the plaintiff has both a contract and a tort claim.

Sometimes the measure of damages for a particular harm is objective and, relatively speaking, straightforward to apply. A plaintiff whose car was destroyed will be entitled to recover its fair market value at the time and place of the injury. Even that "objective" determination requires a lawyer to gather and present critical, and not necessarily intuitive, evidence. And even the simplest measure can be difficult to apply to simple fact patterns. For example, if the plaintiff's restaurant equipment had been destroyed in a fire, is it the value of the equipment in an "undestroyed" restaurant, or the value after cost to remove it and sell it to a third party? Other measures of damage are simple to state, but highly subjective and difficult to apply in an objective manner. For example, how should a jury be instructed to determine the monetary value of being injured, or of being threatened with assault? How much is too much for a jury to award? Should a court compare a jury's award to awards in other cases?

B. If the Plaintiff Suffered the Required Harm and Other Harms, Are Damages for Those Other Harms "Consequential Damages" for That Claim?

If the plaintiff suffered other harms — in addition to the type of harm required to trigger any remedy for the claim — damages for those other harms may be recoverable as "consequential damages" for that claim. For example, as a consequence of a car wreck, a plaintiff may incur medical bills. A harm suffered as a consequence of the damage element of a claim *may* be recoverable as "consequential damages" for that claim. If, however, an additional harm was not suffered as a consequence of the required form of damage, then the plaintiff may need to determine if another claim will allow the plaintiff to recover damages for that harm. Simple examples are below, but just like the scope of the damage element varies for each claim, so does the scope of "consequential damages." For example, suppose a driver collides with a car being driven by a mother with her daughter as passenger and she becomes distraught at seeing her daughter suffer in pain. Is that a consequence of the mother's injuries in the same way that medical bills the mother incurs to heal her own injuries are?

Further, some harms are readily recoverable as consequential damages for one tort claim, but not another, and consequential damages are generally more limited for breach of contract than for tort claims. For example, if a defendant breaches a contract that causes the plaintiff economic loss, the plaintiff can recover damages for those economic losses. However, even if the breach caused severe emotional distress, with very narrow exceptions, contract law does not permit their recovery as consequential damages. Just like "damage" for each claim is circumscribed, so too are "consequential damages."

C. If the Plaintiff Has a Claim Upon Which Relief Can Be Granted and Wants Equitable Relief, Are Money Damages "Inadequate"?

Equitable relief usually means an injunction. Although a few courts treat the adequacy of the legal remedy as merely one factor in whether injunctive relief is proper, generally they are granted only if the "remedy at law"—money—is "inadequate." To know whether money is inadequate, one must know: (a) if *any* relief is available (i.e., does the plaintiff have a claim upon which *any* relief can be awarded?) and (b) if so, whether the "remedy at law" is "adequate" (is money, and its amount, sufficient?). Without knowing a claim's elements, including the required harm and measure of damages for that harm and the scope of recoverable consequential damages for that claim, it is impossible to gauge the "adequacy" of the legal remedy.

Chapter 2 addresses injunctions in significant detail, but this book returns to equitable remedies repeatedly—and does so on purpose. This is because a key factor in whether money is an adequate remedy is the type of harm the plaintiff has or will suffer. For example, the remedy at law for the economic losses caused by breach of an ordinary commercial contract is almost always adequate; but when it is not, a court may order an injunction—in the form of what is referred to as an order of "specific performance." On the other hand, if the defendant likely will continue to trespass on plaintiff's land, or continue to cause noise that interrupts plaintiff's sleep to intrude on plaintiff's land, money will more likely be inadequate. Critically, however, a plaintiff in either circumstance must be able to establish a claim upon which relief can be granted—including the damage element—or *no remedy* is available, let alone injunctive relief. As one court put it, no injunction is proper unless "the plaintiff has a cause of action against the defendant." *Harbor Perfusion, Inc. v. Floyd*, 45 S.W.3d 713 (Ct. App. Tex. 2001). Thus, again, this book is organized on the basis of identifying the harm, the claims that remedy that harm, the measure of damages for that claim, and then determining when courts will hold money damages inadequate and, if sought, award injunctive relief.

3. A Diagram of the Analytical Framework for Damages

Below is a diagram of the process. It requires you to use the law of assault (which includes a defendant who causes the plaintiff the harm of fear of imminent bodily injury) and battery (which includes a defendant who intentionally causes physical harm to the plaintiff). However, you should use this approach for every chapter to analyze monetary remedies.

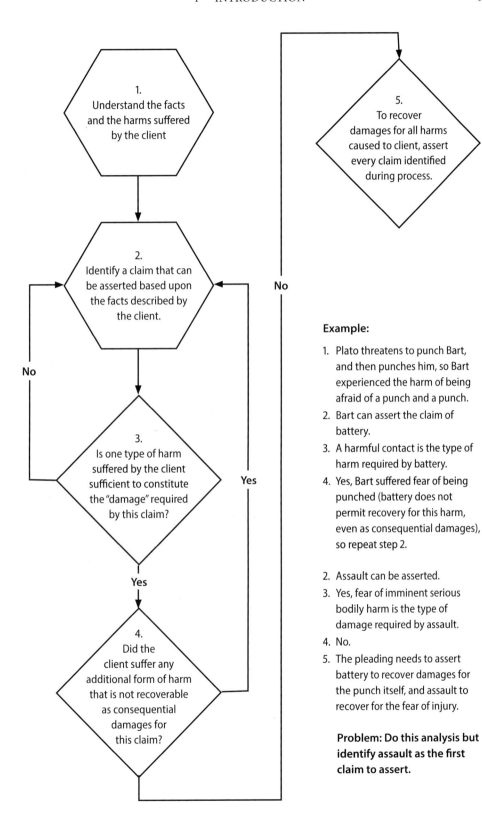

Example:

1. Plato threatens to punch Bart, and then punches him, so Bart experienced the harm of being afraid of a punch and a punch.
2. Bart can assert the claim of battery.
3. A harmful contact is the type of harm required by battery.
4. Yes, Bart suffered fear of being punched (battery does not permit recovery for this harm, even as consequential damages), so repeat step 2.

2. Assault can be asserted.
3. Yes, fear of imminent serious bodily harm is the type of damage required by assault.
4. No.
5. The pleading needs to assert battery to recover damages for the punch itself, and assault to recover for the fear of injury.

Problem: Do this analysis but identify assault as the first claim to assert.

Thus, determining monetary damages requires identifying the harm and a claim for which that type of harm satisfies the "damage" element. If the plaintiff suffered only one form of harm (e.g., Plato threatened but did not punch Bart), the analysis is over. If the plaintiff suffered other harms, damages for those may be recoverable as consequential damages for that claim. (For example, and as we will see, if Plato's punch caused Bart to incur medical expenses, those would be recoverable consequential damages.) If damage for an additional harm is not recoverable as consequential damage for that claim, there may be another claim for which that type of harm is the required form of damage.

Two additional examples illustrate this point. A plaintiff pleading a breach of contract claim who asserts the breach caused *only* emotional distress has not (with narrow exceptions) asserted the kind of "damage" required by a breach of contract claim. Conversely, a plaintiff asserting a negligence claim who pleads the defendant's negligence caused *only* "economic loss" (e.g., medical bills) has not (with narrow exceptions) asserted the type of "damage" for that element of a negligence claim. Those plaintiffs will receive no remedy.

The word "damage," when used as an element of a claim, is perhaps more intuitive if understood as a type of harm for which "damages" (in the form of money) are recoverable. Each claim requires a specific form of harm before *any* remedy is available. If the harm required by the damage element for a claim is satisfied, then a remedy for that harm, and for consequential damages to the extent the claim permits it, are available. A combination of historical accident and logic led us to the system we have, but under it, the type of harm often dictates whether a plaintiff has a claim upon which *any* relief can be granted.

Problems

1. <u>Paula Kisses David in the Break Room</u>. Suppose Paula and David are co-workers. Paula is attracted to David, who is uninterested and has told Paula that he does not want a romantic relationship with her. One day, Paula and David are alone in the coffee break room at work. As David is pouring coffee, Paula pushes a table blocking the only door out of the break room, blocking David's exit. David asks, "Hey, what's going on, I want to leave." Instead of moving the table back and out of the way, Paula said "Shhhh" and walked toward him. David feared she was going to kiss him. He began to say "Please don't" but then, without otherwise touching him, she kissed him gently on the cheek. David turned, gently pushed her away, moved the table, and left the room. Suppose David sues Paula. What claims does he have? Which allow recovery for what harm(s)?

2. <u>Bart Fails to Help Marge Get off the Mall Floor, Then Threatens Her</u>. Imagine that because of her own clumsiness, Marge has fallen down while shopping at a mall. Another shopper, Bart, sees Marge on the floor, but does nothing. In your Torts course, you probably learned that there is generally no duty to rescue. A plaintiff injured by a defendant's failure to take action to help the plaintiff has no claim

because the plaintiff cannot satisfy the *duty* element of the tort of negligence. As a result, if Marge sued Bart and asserted a claim for negligence, Bart could move to dismiss for failure to state a claim upon which relief can be granted because he owed her no duty to rescue. Most courts would grant that motion, and do so even if Marge had pled that Bart laughed when she had begged for help and his laughter and callously walking away from her caused her severe mental distress. You learned in Torts that virtually all courts hold Bart owed Marge no duty. In this book, you will also see that almost all courts would also hold that her mental distress is insufficient to show the harm required before a court will award damages for a negligence claim. Generally, if all the plaintiff experienced is mental distress, that is not the type of harm recognized as sufficient to impose liability for a negligence claim.

But some claims do allow recovery solely for mental distress. Suppose that Marge had fallen and was sitting on the floor after her fall when Bart approached her, menacingly gesturing at her, had said: "If you don't move right now I will beat you up." From Torts, you probably recall that a person who is put in imminent apprehension of bodily harm has an assault claim. Even if Marge's fear of being hit was minimal, she would have an assault claim for which a jury could award damages. Fear of injury—a specific type of mental distress—is the type of harm recognized as sufficient to impose liability for an assault claim.

Because each claim has different elements, and not every claim allows for recovery of damages for each type of harm, most lawsuits involve more than one claim. Part of the job of creative plaintiffs' lawyers is to plead as many claims as the law might reasonably recognize. Part of the job of diligent defense lawyers is to examine each claim to see if it has weaknesses, and those weaknesses include assessing whether the claim permits recovery of any damages for the type of harm alleged. So, the plaintiff's lawyer in *Marge v. Bart* might plead two claims in her complaint and not be explicit about what damages were caused by Bart failing to help Marge get up, and what were caused by threatening her if she did not move.

Assume Marge pled both claims, and Bart moved to dismiss both claims. Why should the court deny the motion to dismiss the assault claim, but grant dismissal of the negligence claim? With respect to the assault claim, why would it be improper for the jury to award Marge damages for the anguish she suffered because of Bart's failure to help her? What anguish is compensable for her assault claim—the anguish of being left by him on the floor, or the anguish of the threat? Consider what happens if she testifies at her deposition that it is hard for her to separate out the anguish caused solely by the threat from that caused by Bart having left her on the floor? Finally, and just slightly differently, suppose instead she testified: "Had Bart not left me on the floor before threatening me, I am sure I wouldn't have been as frightened by his threat."

While these hypotheticals may seem trivial, they raise real-world problems that lawyers must address in practical and efficient ways. Now, think about what motions in limine and jury instructions you would request for both parties in each case.

Chapter 2

The Remedies of Declaratory Judgments and Injunctions

The most common remedy is a substitutionary remedy in the form of a money judgment to compensate for harms suffered by a plaintiff. But a party may obtain a declaratory judgment without having been harmed or even been threatened with any harm. In contrast, an injunction is available on if money is inadequate, such as when the defendant is continuing conduct that will likely harm the plaintiff in the future and money is inadequate to remedy that harm.

This chapter contains the book's full discussion of declaratory judgments. It only begins the analysis of injunctions because injunctions are generally available if monetary remedies are "inadequate" and either the plaintiff *has prevailed* on a claim or, for preliminary injunctions, is *likely to prevail on a claim*. Subsequent chapters provide the elements of each claim, and thus the necessary information to determine whether the plaintiff can obtain any remedy (and so provide the knowledge to determine whether a plaintiff likely will prevail on a claim), and the monetary remedies available if the plaintiff does so (and so provide the knowledge to determine whether the monetary remedy is adequate). In other words, this chapter merely starts to explain injunctions, but fully discusses declaratory judgments, because, for a declaratory judgment, no harm is required.

1. The Remedy of a Declaratory Judgment

The Declaratory Judgment Act, 28 U.S.C.A. § 2201, creates a statutory remedy:

> In a case of actual controversy within its jurisdiction . . . any court of the United States, upon the filing of an appropriate pleading, may declare the rights and other legal relations of any interested party seeking such declaration, whether or not further relief is or could be sought. Any such declaration shall have the force and effect of a final judgment or decree and shall be reviewable as such.

Article III of the Constitution limits federal courts to deciding "actual cases or controversies." A "case" exists after a plaintiff files suit. However, a "controversy" can exist before then that allows a federal court to have jurisdiction to issue a declaratory judgment.

ABS Global, Inc. v. Inguran, LLC

No. 14-cv-503-wmc, 2015 WL 1486638 (W.D. Wis. Mar. 31, 2015) (Conley, J.)

[ABS Global, Inc., and Inguran, LLC were competitors in the field of sexed bovine semen—semen processed so that when used to impregnate a cow, the resulting calf will be female. (Female dairy cows are obviously more desirable.) A clause in a contract between ABS Global and Inguran prevented ABS Global from marketing certain products. ABS Global had secretly developed a newer technology and wanted to market it. Concerned that Inguran might sue it for breach of the contract, ABS Global sued, seeking a declaration that marketing the newer technology would not breach the contract, and that the contract was invalid or unenforceable. Inguran moved to dismiss the claims for declaratory relief, asserting there was no controversy.]

As the Supreme Court has recognized, case law has not drawn "the brightest of lines between those declaratory-judgment actions that satisfy the case-or-controversy requirement and those that do not." *MedImmune, Inc. v. Genentech, Inc.*, 549 U.S. 118 (2007). Generally, the Court has "required that the dispute be definite and concrete, touching the legal relations of parties having adverse legal interests; and that it be real and substantial and admit of specific relief through a decree of a conclusive character, as distinguished from an opinion advising what the law would be upon a hypothetical state of facts." *Id.* At the same time, a plaintiff need not expose itself to liability to create a justiciable controversy. *See Id.* (plaintiff not constitutionally required to breach or terminate license agreement before seeking a declaratory judgment that the underlying patent was invalid, unenforceable or not infringed). The essential question is "whether the facts alleged, under all the circumstances, show that there is a substantial controversy, between parties having adverse legal interests, of sufficient immediacy and reality to warrant the issuance of a declaratory judgment." *Id.*

Applying these principles, the court agrees with ABS Global that its declaratory judgment claims present an Article III case or controversy sufficient to establish subject matter jurisdiction. ABS Global has presented sworn testimony that it has developed and field-tested a technology it now wishes to commercialize. ABS Global believes that the technology falls outside the terms of the contract but wishes to avoid the real potential for liability that the Agreement expressly imposes should it be proved wrong, including liquidated damages of $1.5 million plus $7.50 per unpurchased straw of sexed bovine semen that remains under the minimum purchase requirements of the Agreement as of the termination date. In this way, the present case fits easily into what the Seventh Circuit described as the "usual declaratory judgment pattern," one "under which the 'natural' defendant wants to proceed with a business opportunity—*e.g.,* the production of widgets—but it is impeded because of a lack of clarity as to its legal rights, fearing something like a possible patent infringement suit." *Hyatt Int'l Corp. v. Coco,* 302 F.3d 707 (7th Cir. 2002).

Even if this were not enough, ABS Global has amply documented Inguran's litigious history through its wholly-owned subsidiary XY, LLC, including against parties with whom it has an existing or had a previous contractual relationship. At minimum, this makes ABS Global's apprehension of suit more plausible. Viewing this history in combination with ABS Global's preparations to enter the market, the court is persuaded that an Article III case or controversy existed at the time ABS Global filed this lawsuit.

Additional support for this conclusion is found in *MedImmune,* a relatively recent Supreme Court case addressing Article III justiciability in declaratory judgment actions brought against private parties. In *MedImmune,* the plaintiff entered into a patent license agreement with defendant Genentech, requiring it to pay royalties on products covered by Genentech's patents, including an application that later matured into the "Cabilly II" patent. Upon its issuance, Genentech wrote to MedImmune to advise that one of MedImmune's drugs was covered by the Cabilly II patent and express "its expectation that petitioner would pay royalties beginning March 1, 2002." *MedImmune,* 549 U.S. at 121. MedImmune believed the Cabilly II patent was invalid and that its drug did not infringe even if the patent *was* valid, but it paid the demanded royalties under protest, unwilling to risk the possibility of treble damages, attorney's fees and an injunction. MedImmune then sued for a declaratory judgment that it did not owe royalties under the license agreement, which the Supreme Court interpreted as a claim seeking an interpretation of its contractual obligations.

The Supreme Court held that there existed a live "case or controversy" within the meaning of Article III, and that MedImmune was "not required, insofar as Article III is concerned, to break or terminate its 1997 license agreement before seeking a declaratory judgment in federal court that the underlying patent is invalid, unenforceable, or not infringed." *Id.* While the Supreme Court acknowledged that its own jurisprudence is somewhat sparse on the application of the Declaratory Judgment Act to situations in which a plaintiff self-avoids imminent injury due to threatened enforcement from a private party, it noted that "lower federal courts have long accepted jurisdiction in such cases." *Id.* The Court went on to reject its earlier decision in *Willing v. Chicago Auditorium Association,* 277 U.S. 274 (1928), which had held there was no case or controversy where a lessee wanted to demolish an antiquated auditorium, believed it could do so without the lessors' consent, but "was unwilling to drop the wrecking ball first and test its belief later." *MedImmune,* 549 U.S. at 133.

In particular, the Court stated, "Had *Willing* been decided after the enactment (and our upholding) of the Declaratory Judgment Act, and had the legal disagreement between the parties been as lively as this one, we are confident a different result would have [been] obtained." *Id.* "The rule that a plaintiff must destroy a large building, bet the farm, or (as here) risk treble damages and the loss of 80 percent of its business before seeking a declaration of its actively contested legal rights finds no support in Article III." *Id.* Likewise here. ABS Global need not risk breaching its contract with the only supplier of sexed bovine semen in the United States (and incur significant financial penalties under the terms of that contract) before seeking a declaration that it may launch its competing technology. Admittedly, this case differs from *MedImmune* in one significant way that Inguran seeks to exploit. Unlike the defendant in *MedImmune,* who knew of the plaintiff's drug and unequivocally expressed its expectation of royalty payments, Inguran has repeatedly professed its ignorance of ABS Global's new laser-sorting technology. This has prevented Inguran from making the sort of direct threat that was present in *MedImmune,* at least as regards the laser-sorting technology at issue here.

Nevertheless, the court concludes that it would be unfair or inefficient to require the parties to wait for a decision at this point. ABS Global is prepared to launch a new technology that may violate the stringent non-compete terms of the Agreement and could expose ABS Global to more than $1.5 million in damages. Inguran has previously engaged in activity rendering ABS Global's fear of suit reasonable. Accordingly, the court concludes that the controversy between the parties is of sufficient immediacy and reality to warrant the issuance of a declaratory judgment. It will, therefore, deny Inguran's motion to dismiss.

Notes and Questions

1. <u>First-to-File</u>. When a declaratory judgment is filed, either the defendant files a counterclaim for affirmative relief—the mirror image of the declaratory judgment claim—or the declaratory judgment defendant files a second suit, in its preferred forum, and the parties dispute which court should proceed. In the principal case, because Inguran had not known of ABS Global's new technology, ABS was able to sue in Wisconsin. In response to being sued in Wisconsin, Inguran sued in Texas for breach of contract. The Texas district court transferred that suit to Wisconsin, consolidated the two cases, and then denied Inguran's motion to dismiss in the opinion above. This effort to choose a forum implicates the "first to file" rule. In determining whether a first-filed declaratory judgment claim should proceed over a later-filed suit for affirmative relief, the plaintiff in the declaratory judgment suit must persuade the court why its suit should not be transferred to the jurisdiction where the affirmative case is pending, or stayed until that case is resolved, as *QFO Labs, Inc. v. Best Buy Stores, L.P.*, 2018 WL 3966313 (D. Minn. Aug. 17, 2018) explained:

> When cases involving substantially overlapping issues are pending before two federal district courts, there is a strong preference to avoid duplicative litigation. The first-to-file rule stands for the common sense proposition that, when two cases are the same or very similar, efficiency concerns dictate that only one court decide both cases. The purpose of the rule is to avoid conflicting decisions and promote judicial efficiency. It generally favors pursuing only the first-filed action when multiple lawsuits involving the same claims are filed in different jurisdictions. Under the first-to-file rule, a district court may—in its discretion—dismiss, transfer, or stay a duplicative, later-filed action if the two actions substantially overlap.

See also H-D Mich., LLC v. Hellenic Duty Free Shops S.A., 694 F.3d 827 (7th Cir. 2012) (district court properly limited its injunction of related suit only to acts that would "contradict, impair, or otherwise affect this court's rulings" but did not enjoin defendant from defending itself if the foreign court did not stay that case).

2. Discretion. Even if a justiciable "controversy" exists, courts have discretion to decline to proceed to the merits of the dispute after considering these factors:

(1) whether the judgment would settle the controversy;

(2) whether the declaratory judgment action would serve a useful purpose in clarifying the legal relations at issue;

(3) whether the declaratory remedy is being used merely for the purpose of procedural fencing or to provide an arena for a race for res judicata;

(4) whether the use of a declaratory action would increase the friction between our federal and state courts and improperly encroach on state jurisdiction; and

(5) whether there is an alternative remedy that is better or more effective.

AmSouth Bank v. Dale, 386 F.3d 763 (6th Cir. 2004). If, for example, a declaratory judgment requires deciding a novel or matter of first impression of state law, federal courts may decline to proceed to the merits. *See Westport Ins. Corp. v. Atchley, Russell, Waldrop & Hlavinka, LLP,* 267 F. Supp. 3d 601 (E.D. Tex. 2003) (characterizing declaratory judgment suit as an "end run" around letting state courts decide issue).

3. Abstention. Somewhat analogous to the question of when courts will not enjoin ongoing criminal proceedings, discussed later in this book, federal courts may, or must, abstain from issuing a declaratory judgment. Reasons for abstaining from issuing a declaratory judgment include when a federal decision would interfere with a state's effort to establish a coherent policy on a matter of public concern; when a suit on the same issue between the same parties was already pending in state court; or if the declaratory judgment plaintiff lost a case in state court and is effectively using the federal proceeding to attack it. *See State Farm Mut. Auto. Ins. Co. v. Physicians Grp. of Sarasota, L.L.C.,* 9 F. Supp. 3d 1303 (M.D. Fla. 2014).

4. Jury Right. Whether a party is entitled to a jury trial in a declaratory judgment action turns on whether a right to a jury trial exists on the underlying claim. *Chan v. Schatz,* 280 F. Supp. 3d 546 (S.D.N.Y. 2017).

5. Amount in Controversy. In a declaratory judgment action, "the amount in controversy is measured by the value of the object of the litigation." *Carpet Super Mart, Inc. v. Benchmark Intl. Co. Sales Specialist, LLC,* 2019 WL 1244086 (M.D.N.C. Mar. 18, 2019) (amount in controversy satisfied where plaintiff sought declaration it did not owe defendant $180,000) (quoting *Hunt v. Wash. State Apple Advert. Comm'n,* 432 U.S. 333 (1977)).

6. Title to Out-of-State Property. Courts have no subject matter jurisdiction to adjudicate title to realty, including interests in oil and gas leases, located outside the forum state. *Devon Energy Prod. Co., L.P. v. KCS Resources, LLC,* 450 S.W.3d 203 (Ct.

App. Tex. 2014). But a court with jurisdiction over the parties may enforce a party's personal or contractual obligation that indirectly involves property in another state. *Id.* For example, a court may compel a party over whom it has jurisdiction to execute a conveyance of a real property interest situated in another state. *Id.* Some courts have described the distinction as whether the case involves a "naked question of title." *Id.*

2. Three Types of Injunctions

Like Federal Rule of Civil Procedure 65, most states authorize: (a) temporary restraining orders ("TRO"); (b) preliminary injunctions, and (c) permanent injunctions. Rule 65 addresses TROs in subsection (b) and preliminary injunctions in subsection (a) even though, almost invariably, a TRO is sought before a preliminary injunction. The following examines the procedural requirements, and then the "substantive" aspects, of each form of injunction.

A. The Different Procedural Requirements for Injunctions

Only a TRO may be issued without notice to opposing parties, and only if:

(A) specific facts in an affidavit or a verified complaint clearly show that immediate and irreparable injury, loss, or damage will result to the movant before the adverse party can be heard in opposition; and

(B) the movant's attorney certifies in writing any efforts made to give notice and the reasons why it should not be required.[1]

To obtain a TRO or preliminary injunction, the movant must provide "security," typically a bond, "in an amount that the court considers proper to pay the costs and damages sustained by any party found to have been wrongfully enjoined or restrained." Fed. R. Civ. P. 65(c). The purpose of security is "to ensure that the enjoined party may readily be compensated for the costs incurred as a result of the injunction should it later be determined that it was wrongfully enjoined" and "to provide notice to the moving party as to the maximum extent of its potential

---

1. Fed. R. Civ. P. 65. A TRO issued without notice can last no longer than 14 days (unless extended for good cause up to an additional 14 days), must state the time it expires and must: "state the date and hour it was issued; describe the injury and state why it is irreparable; state why the order was issued without notice; and be promptly filed in the clerk's office and entered in the record." *Id.* Likewise, a court issuing a TRO without notice must set a hearing on a preliminary injunction at the earliest possible time. A party subject to a TRO may move to dissolve it by giving 2 days' notice to the opponent. *Id.*

In every *ex parte* proceeding, attorneys have heightened obligations to the court which include disclosing all material facts, even if adverse to their client. *See Goodsell v. The Miss. Bar,* 667 So. 2d 7 (Miss. 1996) (suspending for six months an attorney who in a TRO hearing had stated that an affidavit had been signed by client, when in fact lawyer had signed it).

liability, since the amount of the bond is the limit of the damages the enjoined party can obtain for a wrongful injunction." *Axia NetMedia Corp. v. Mass. Tech. Park Corp.*, 889 F.3d 1 (1st Cir. 2018); *but see Takeda Pharma., U.S.A., Inc. v. West-Ward Pharma. Corp.*, 2018 WL 6529289 (D. Del. Nov. 12, 2018) (a wrongfully enjoined party may recover more than the bond amount if the injunction was obtained in bad faith or through fraud).

Although security is required, the amount is highly discretionary. *See Static Control Components, Inc. v. Lexmark Int'l, Inc.*, 697 F.3d 387 (6th Cir. 2012) ($250,000 bond not an abuse of discretion despite evidence that injunction would cost $17 million in lost sales). For example, in *Jennings Guest House v. Gibson*, 971 So. 2d 506 (Ct. App. La. 2007), the defendant had been fired from working at the plaintiff's retirement home because the defendant believed the plaintiff had stolen residents' medication and physically and verbally abused them. The trial court enjoined the plaintiff from returning to the home but had not required a bond. The appellate court affirmed but wrote: "the trial judge stated at the hearing that she thought about this issue but could think of no financial loss involved in simply staying away from a certain place. Such may be true in this case. However, the posting of security is a statutory requirement, and the trial court erred in not requiring security in some amount."

The foregoing applies only to prejudgment injunctions (TROs and preliminary injunctions). The other aspects of Rule 65 discussed next apply to all forms of injunctions.

First, an injunction must "(A) state the reasons why it issued; (B) state its terms specifically; and (C) describe in reasonable detail—and not by referring to the complaint or other document—the act or acts restrained or required." *Id.* "Reasonable detail" is a low threshold. In *Axia NetMedia Corp. v. Mass. Tech. Park Corp.*, 889 F.3d 1 (1st Cir. 2018), Axia appealed a preliminary injunction that required it to continue to provide "the same level of service that those affiliates are currently providing" as stated in the parties' 32-page agreement. The court affirmed:

> The specificity requirements are not merely technical but are designed to prevent uncertainty and confusion and to avoid basing a contempt citation on a decree too vague to be understood. The purpose of the specificity requirement is to protect the elementary due process requirement of notice. An injunction must simply be framed so that those enjoined will know what conduct the court has prohibited. Thus, an order that "judgment is entered in accordance" with an opinion that merely states that the plaintiff is "entitled to injunctive relief," without more, fails the test. But, conversely, elaborate detail is unnecessary.

> This order passes muster. We see no reason why Axia does not know, or could not readily discern, the precise level of services its affiliates had been providing. Nor has Axia advanced any reason as to why it may be in the dark. Further, we note that the affiliates' responsibilities to KCST are

spelled out in a thirty-two page "Transitional Services Agreement." And, to the degree that Axia's concern stems from a worry that its good faith attempts to comply with the order nevertheless render it vulnerable to contempt proceedings, our case law accounts for such concerns by cautioning courts against finding contempt when faced with genuine ambiguities about an order's scope.

What language in Rule 65(d) undermines the court's reliance on the contract? Given that requirement, consider *Supreme Fuels Trading FZE v. Sargeant*, 689 F.3d 1244 (11th Cir. 2012):

> When a district court denominates its order as an injunction, we have jurisdiction to entertain an appeal from that order even if the district court fails to comply with the requirements of Rule 65(d). And when a district court fails to denominate its order as an injunction, but otherwise complies with the requirements of Rule 65(d), we will treat its order as an appealable injunction. Rule 65(d) requires that the order (1) "state the reasons why it issued," (2) "state its terms specifically," and (3) "describe in reasonable detail—and not by referring to the complaint or other document—the act or acts restrained or required." When the order is injunctive in nature, requiring the defendant to perform enumerated steps under threat of the contempt power, the order is an injunction subject to appellate review under section 1292(a)(2). But the absence of any semblance of effort by the District Court to comply with Rule 65(d) is evidence that the district court did not intend to enter an order granting an injunction.

Does this suggest the order in *Axia* was not appealable? *See Petrello v. White*, 533 F.3d 110 (2d Cir. 2008) (to be appealable as an injunction, an order of specific performance must meet Rule 65).

B. The Different Standards for Injunctive Relief

TROs last a very short time and are available only in extraordinary circumstances. Preliminary injunctions generally are sought only after discovery has been completed and last through trial (if the preliminary injunction hearing is not consolidated with trial on the merits and the request for a permanent injunction). Permanent injunctions can be entered only after resolution of the merits and a finding of liability. A permanent injunction can be entered only after a liability finding on a claim after trial or a final hearing on the merits. *Livingston v. Livingston*, 537 S.W.3d 578 (Ct. App. Tex. 2017) (affirming entry of permanent injunction after jury verdict of no damages). Thus, TROs and preliminary injunctions differ from permanent injunctions because each is issued before a court decides whether the plaintiff in fact is entitled to *any* relief on the merits. So a plaintiff can obtain a TRO or preliminary injunction but lose at trial; a plaintiff who loses at trial cannot obtain a permanent injunction.

A permanent injunction is available only to: (A) a prevailing party, and (B) only if: (1) the remedy at law is inadequate; (2) the injury to the prevailing party that the injunction will likely prevent outweighs harm the injunction will likely cause to the losing party; and (3) the injunction would not be contrary to the public interest. TROs and preliminary injunctions are issued before a party has prevailed, and that fact changes the requirements in two ways.

First, for either a TRO or a preliminary injunction, the plaintiff must show it is reasonably likely to prevail on the merits. This requirement replaces the first requirement of a permanent injunction, that the plaintiff has prevailed. A party "is not required to prove his case in full at a preliminary injunction hearing," but "must show more than a mere possibility of success" and instead show a "strong probability of success on the merits." *F.S. Sperry Co., Inc. v. Schopmann*, 304 F. Supp. 3d 694, 701 (E.D. Tenn. 2018). Courts state that it is not a question of whether there is "a greater than fifty percent likelihood" the plaintiff will prevail, but instead requires showing the plaintiff has a "fair chance of prevailing" on a claim. *CPI Card Grp., Inc. v. Dwyer*, 294 F. Supp. 3d 791, 807 (D. Minn. 2017).

Second, TROs or preliminary injunctions added an element: the plaintiff must show that, without issuance, it will suffer "irreparable harm." Thus, the general requirements for preliminary injunctions or TROs are: (1) there is a substantial likelihood the movant will prevail on the merits; (2) the movant will suffer irreparable harm without the TRO or preliminary injunction; (3) the threatened injury to the movant outweighs harm the TRO or preliminary injunction will cause the opposing party; and (4) any TRO or injunction would not be contrary to the public interest.

For a TRO or preliminary injunction, the plaintiff *must* show "that irreparable injury is likely in the absence of an injunction." *Winter v. Nat. Resources Def. Council, Inc.*, 555 U.S. 7 (2008). Irreparable harm is "potential harm which cannot be redressed by a legal or an equitable remedy following a trial," and so a pre-trial "injunction must be the only way of protecting the plaintiff from harm and may not be granted to relieve purely economic harm." *ACE Am. Ins. Co. v. Wachovia Ins. Agency Inc.*, 306 F. App'x 727, 731 (3d Cir. 2009).

As noted in Chapter 1, courts continue to disagree on whether the other issues are elements, factors, or some hybrid. A 2008 Supreme Court decision appears to have made clear these are elements, not factors, but courts apply a "sliding scale" approach: so long as some evidence favoring an injunction is available, a stronger showing of one of the four factors can assist a weaker showing on another. The court in *Robert Half Intl. Inc. v. Billingham*, 315 F. Supp. 3d 419, 426 (D.D.C. 2018), explained the requirement of irreparable harm and the "sliding scale" approach to the other four elements (not "factors," despite its statement) this way:

> Courts in this Circuit traditionally have evaluated these four factors on
> a "sliding scale" — if a movant makes an unusually strong showing on one

of the factors, then it does not necessarily have to make as strong a showing on another factor. The Supreme Court's decision in *Winter*, however, called that approach into question and sparked disagreement over whether the "sliding scale" framework continues to apply, or whether a movant must make a positive showing on all four factors without discounting the importance of a factor simply because one or more other factors is convincingly established. *Compare Davis v. Billington*, 76 F.Supp.3d 59 (D.D.C. 2014) ("Because it remains the law of this Circuit, the Court must employ the sliding-scale analysis here."), *with ABA, Inc. v. District of Columbia*, 40 F. Supp.3d 153 (D.D.C. 2014) ("The D.C. Circuit has interpreted *Winter* to require a positive showing on all four preliminary injunction factors." (*citing Davis*, 571 F.3d at 1296 (Kavanaugh, J., concurring)).

Regardless of whether the sliding scale framework applies, it remains clear that a movant must demonstrate irreparable harm, which "always" has been "the basis of injunctive relief in the federal courts." *Sampson v. Murray*, 415 U.S. 61 (1974). "A movant's failure to show any irreparable harm is therefore grounds for refusing to issue a preliminary injunction, even if the other three factors entering the calculus merit such relief." *Chaplaincy of Full Gospel Churches v. England*, 454 F.3d 290 (D.C. Cir. 2006). Indeed, if a court concludes that a movant has not demonstrated irreparable harm, it need not even consider the remaining factors.

It is important to stop to consider the practicalities of these issues, whether they are factors, elements, or some hybrid. In all forms, one issue is harm to the opposing party: will a *movant* try very hard to show any injunction will harm the *opponent*? Consider, instead, whether this passage from *Girl Scouts of Manitou Council, Inc. v. Girl Scouts of the U.S. Inc.*, 549 F.3d 1079 (7th Cir. 2008), gives a more pragmatic explanation of the burdens:

> To determine whether a situation warrants such a remedy, a district court engages in an analysis that proceeds in two distinct phases: a threshold phase and a balancing phase.
>
> To survive the threshold phase, a party seeking a preliminary injunction must satisfy three requirements. First, that absent a preliminary injunction, it will suffer irreparable harm in the interim period prior to final resolution of its claims. Second, that traditional legal remedies would be inadequate. And third, that its claim has some likelihood of succeeding on the merits. If the court determines that the moving party has failed to demonstrate any one of these three threshold requirements, it must deny the injunction. If, however, the court finds that the moving party has passed this initial threshold, it then proceeds to the balancing phase of the analysis.
>
> In this second phase, the court, in an attempt to minimize the cost of potential error, must somehow balance the nature and degree of the

plaintiff's injury, the likelihood of prevailing at trial, the possible injury to the defendant if the injunction is granted, and the wild card that is the public interest. Specifically, the court weighs the irreparable harm that the moving party would endure without the protection of the preliminary injunction against any irreparable harm the nonmoving party would suffer if the court were to grant the requested relief. In so doing, the court employs a sliding scale approach: the more likely the plaintiff is to win, the less heavily need the balance of harms weigh in his favor; the less likely he is to win, the more need it weigh in his favor. Where appropriate, this balancing process should also encompass any effects that granting or denying the preliminary injunction would have on nonparties (something courts have termed the "public interest"). Taking into account all these considerations, the district court must exercise its discretion to arrive at a decision based on a subjective evaluation of the import of the various factors and a personal, intuitive sense about the nature of the case.

Thus, while the movant must establish irreparable harm and persuade that there is some evidence of each of the four elements that, on balance, weigh in favor of injunctive relief, as a practical matter the opponent must produce evidence that it, and the public, will suffer.

Throughout this book, chapters will return to injunctive relief, examining when courts find the particular harm in issue and the facts of the case warrant holding that the remedy at law is inadequate, and the factors indicate an injunction is proper. The following opinion grants in part a motion for a preliminary injunction to enjoin a breach of a contract, a form of "mandatory injunction" usually called an order of "specific performance."

Guidance Endodontics, LLC v. Dentsply Int'l, Inc.

633 F. Supp. 2d 1257 (D.N.M. 2008) (Browning, J.)

[Guidance Endodontics, LLC, and Densply International, Inc., both made endodontic equipment (used in specialized dental procedures). They had sued each other previously and had settled that case with an agreement whereby Dentsply became the exclusive supplier to Guidance of products it needed. Another dispute between the parties developed after Dentsply accused Guidance of breaching the settlement agreement, and Dentsply stopped providing products to Guidance.

Guidance sued and moved for a TRO and preliminary injunctive relief to compel Dentsply to provide two products and introduced evidence that without performance it faced financial ruin. One product was the V2, and the other, the Obturator. Dentsply had provided the Obturator product for a long time, but the V2 was still under development. In the court's opinion below, the court addressed the preliminary injunction and the TRO as a single issue, calling it a request for a TRO.]

To establish its right to preliminary relief, a moving party must demonstrate: (1) the movant will suffer irreparable harm unless the injunction issues; (2) there is a substantial likelihood the movant ultimately will prevail on the merits; (3) the threatened injury to the movant outweighs any harm the proposed injunction may cause the opposing party; and (4) the injunction would not be contrary to the public interest. If the moving party demonstrates that the first, third, and fourth factors tip strongly in his favor, the test is modified, and the moving party may meet the requirement for showing success on the merits by showing that questions going to the merits are so serious, substantial, difficult, and doubtful as to make the issue for litigation and deserving of more deliberate investigation.

There are, however,

> three types of specifically disfavored preliminary injunctions for which a movant must satisfy an even heavier burden of showing that the four preliminary injunction factors weigh heavily and compellingly in movant's favor before such an injunction may be issued: (1) preliminary injunctions that alter the status quo; (2) mandatory preliminary injunctions; and (3) preliminary injunctions that afford the movant all the relief that it could recover at the conclusion of a full trial on the merits.

O Centro Espirita Beneficiente Uniao do Vegetal v. Ashcroft, 389 F.3d 973 (10th Cir. 2004) (en banc) ("*O Centro Espirita*"), *aff'd* 546 U.S. 418 (2006). Any preliminary injunction fitting within one of the disfavored categories must be more closely scrutinized to assure that the exigencies of the case support the granting of a remedy that is extraordinary even in the normal course. Movants seeking such an injunction are not entitled to rely on this Circuit's modified-likelihood-of-success-on-the-merits standard. Instead, a party seeking such an injunction must make a strong showing both with regard to the likelihood of success on the merits and with regard to the balance of harms.

Of the three classes of disfavored injunctions in the Tenth Circuit, two are relevant here: (i) status-quo altering injunctions and (ii) mandatory injunctions. The TRO that Guidance seeks with respect to the V2 Order would both change the status quo and would be a mandatory injunction. The TRO with respect to the Obturator Order, in contrast, would preserve the status quo and would be a prohibitory injunction. Accordingly, the Court will analyze Guidance's request for a TRO regarding the V2 Order as a disfavored form of relief, but will consider the request for a TRO regarding the Obturator Order under the usual standard or the modified success-on-the-merits standard.

Ordering the Defendants to begin production, and later shipment, of the V2 would upset the status quo. The status quo is the last uncontested status between the parties which preceded the controversy until the outcome of the final hearing. In determining the status quo for preliminary injunctions, a court looks to the reality of the existing status and relationship between the parties and not solely to the parties' legal rights. The reality of the situation between the parties on the V2 is that it remains at a pre-production stage and that, at best for Guidance, there is a dispute whether manufacturing can immediately commence.

In addition to disturbing the status quo, a TRO aimed at the V2 Order would also be a mandatory injunction. Mandatory injunctions affirmatively require the nonmovant to act in a particular way, and as a result they place the issuing court in a position where it may have to provide ongoing supervision to assure that the non-movant is abiding by the injunction. The degree and number of affirmative actions that would be required of the Defendants, and the concomitant possibility that the Court would need to engage in substantial oversight to ensure compliance with the TRO, lead the Court to conclude that the TRO would be mandatory with respect to the V2 Order.

The fundamental disagreement between the parties regarding the status of the V2 and the amount of additional work necessary to bring the V2 to the point where it can be manufactured poses a significant possibility of entangling the Court in a number of different disputes. The Court might well, should a TRO issue, be required to resolve what the final design of the V2 is, whether more work is needed, who should be responsible for different tasks, whether safety concerns have been met, how long production will take, and a host of other issues large and small. This situation is not one where the TRO would obligate a party to continue a series of discrete, simple tasks that the defendant has long performed.

A TRO that applied to the V2 Order would thus be disfavored on two separate grounds. Because the TRO, in this respect, has landed in the disfavored category, that portion of the TRO must be more closely scrutinized to assure that the exigencies of the case support granting the TRO. Guidance will also be barred from the benefit of the Tenth Circuit's modified-likelihood-of-success-on-the-merits standard. Instead, Guidance must make a strong showing with regard to the likelihood of success on the merits.

The requested TRO presents a different story regarding the Obturator Order. Granting the TRO with respect to the Obturator Order would not upend the status quo the way granting it with respect to the V2 Order would. The Defendants have supplied Guidance with this product. No further design work must be finished; no new modifications are necessary.

Although the TRO escapes being disfavored as altering the status quo, it must also not be mandatory in nature. That point is more complicated, but ultimately the TRO with respect to the Obturator Order is also not mandatory. A TRO or injunction that prohibits the breach of an existing contract—or stated differently, one that enforces a contract—is not automatically within or outside of the disfavored classification. That the Defendants would be required to perform some specific acts is thus not, as the Defendants suggest, dispositive of the issue. The Court must instead undertake a more nuanced inquiry.

Enforcing a contract tends to be mandatory when the nature of the breach can only be remedied by the performance of actions different than those provided in the contract. Here, by contrast, no new duties must be imposed on the Defendants to ensure compliance with the contract. Only the exact same contractual obligations they were previously performing is required. There is something more essentially prohibitory about directing compliance with existing duties than with imposing new duties.

The most important factor in this situation, however, is the negligible chance that the Court will find itself having to constantly supervise the TRO. The importance of this factor is great. Simply filling and shipping an order for an existing product, however, is a routine business activity.

Because this portion of the TRO is neither mandatory nor disruptive of the status quo, the Court will evaluate it under the normal standard of review, and Guidance will be able to rely on the modified-likelihood-of-success-on-the-merits standard for the request related to the Obturator Order.

The first element of the test for injunctive relief is whether Guidance is in danger of irreparable harm if the Court does not grant a TRO or preliminary injunction. Economic damage to a business can be a basis for preliminary relief. The evidence reveals that Guidance is in a precarious financial situation and that it is unlikely to obtain needed supply from any source other than the Defendants. This evidence sufficiently demonstrates that Guidance is threatened with irreparable injury.

Guidance paints a dire picture about its situation and raises a number of reasons why it will suffer irreparable harm absent injunctive relief: (i) loss of goodwill; (ii) loss of unique economic opportunities; (iii) loss of customers; (iv) loss of future profits; (v) diminishment of competitive advantage in the marketplace; and (vi) impending bankruptcy. Guidance contends that the Defendants are the only reasonable source of supply and that, unless Guidance receives more product soon, it will begin to suffer the six consequences laid out. The evidence strongly favors Guidance's position.

Loss of goodwill, unique opportunities, competitive position, and customers are all damaging losses for a business. They all also essentially mean that Guidance is threatened with lost profits. As the Tenth Circuit has acknowledged, however, what makes such harms irreparable is not a loss of, for instance, goodwill specifically, or profits more generally. Most economic harms can be remedied with money. What makes these harms irreparable is that they are difficult to calculate with much certainty. Losses such as those of which Guidance has presented evidence are generally difficult to quantify. Moreover, Guidance's status as a fledgling company on the verge of expansion, with a minimal track record, makes it more difficult to estimate with a reasonable degree of accuracy the extent of the harm in areas such as lost goodwill and lost profits.

Guidance has presented evidence that, not only does it risk significant, hard to quantify losses of various future opportunities and profits, it faces the possibility of bankruptcy. Where a business would suffer a substantial loss of business and perhaps even bankruptcy the latter type of injury sufficiently meets the standards for granting interim relief, for otherwise a favorable final judgment might well be useless.

The next prong of the test is whether the threatened injury to Guidance outweighs whatever damage the TRO may inflict on the Defendants. Guidance has already demonstrated that it faces irreparable harm and stands on the brink of bankruptcy and going out of business. The scales thus already tip in Guidance's favor. Any harm flowing to the Defendants, however, is minimal. The damage that requiring the Defendants to fill the orders, and even to continue design work on the V2, will cause is likely to be small, given that the TRO would only require the Defendants to continue observing a contract that they had negotiated and freely entered into. Additionally, the Defendants are successful and dominant players in the endodontic market specifically and in the dental supply market more generally. When the slight damage that the Defendants might incur is compared with the significant and irreparable harm confronting Guidance, it becomes clear that the balance of harms tilts in Guidance's favor.

The only real injury that the Defendants have advanced so far is the harm they assert resulted from Guidance's alleged breach of the confidentiality provision of the Supply Agreement. Even if the Court credits this contention as correct, it does not alter the balance of hardships. Much of the harm from any disclosure has already occurred. As the Defendants themselves argue, the breach is incurable. Moreover, the TRO itself would not inflict any additional harm.

Guidance must also show that the TRO it is seeking would not be adverse to the public interest. TRO in this case would not be adverse to the public interest. Guidance is seeking a TRO to enforce the terms of a contract. The strong public policy favoring the enforcement of contracts and upholding the right of freedom of contract is widely recognized. The temporary restraining order will also serve the overriding public policy in favor of competition.

The Defendants have not argued that the relief that Guidance is pursuing would be contrary to the public interest. Moreover, Guidance has shown that its requested TRO would not be adverse to the public interest clearly and compellingly. Guidance has thus shown that the irreparable harm, balance of hardships, and not adverse to the public interest prongs of the test all favor Guidance. The Court also concludes that these three factors tip strongly in its favor and thus Guidance, with respect to that part of the TRO covering the Obturator Order, may meet the requirement for showing success on the merits by showing that questions going to the merits are so serious, substantial, difficult, and doubtful as to make the issue ripe for litigation and deserving of more deliberate investigation. Because the TRO with respect to the V2 Order is disfavored, however, Guidance must still show a substantial likelihood of success on the merits before the Court will grant that part of the TRO.

Guidance asserts a number of causes of action against the Defendants in its Complaint. Guidance, in its application for the TRO, however, attempts only to prove three claims: (i) the two breach of contract claims; and (ii) and the claim for breach of the covenant of good faith and fair dealing. Guidance need not prove that it is likely to succeed on all of its claims.

The merits of this case are complicated, both legally and factually. With respect to the TRO for the Obturator Order, the Court has no trouble concluding that Guidance has met its burden under the modified standard. With respect to the V2, however, Guidance is unable to make a clear enough showing that the Defendants are in breach. Because Guidance has not made that showing and is, for the V2 Order, seeking disfavored relief, Guidance has not met its burden on the TRO with respect to the V2 Order.

Notes and Questions

1. <u>Why Two Standards</u>? Why are certain injunctions disfavored? Can you change the facts regarding the Obturator that would make it disfavored?

2. <u>Irreparable Harm</u>? As explained in Chapter 1, most chapters in this book address the measure of damage for a particular harm and then turn to whether the remedy at law is adequate or whether, for preliminary injunctive relief, the harm is irreparable. Courts are more likely to find irreparable harm when an injunction will prevent physical harm, prevent interference with enjoyment or use of land, prevent the disclosure of confidential information, or where the amount of damages is uncertain and thus undercompensation is a risk. So, for example, it includes:

- disclosure of trade secrets, "because such information, once disclosed, loses its confidential nature." *Trump v. Comm. on Oversight and Reform of U.S. H.R.,* 380 F. Supp. 3d 76 (D.D.C. 2019); *Motion Control Sys., Inc. v. East,* 546 S.E.2d 424 (Va. 2001).

- misuse of proprietary business information that will likely cause loss of consumer goodwill or loss of business opportunities. *F.S. Sperry Co., Inc. v. Schopmann,* 304 F. Supp. 3d 694 (E.D. Tenn. 2018).

- breach of a noncompete or nonsolicitation provision by a former employee. *E.g., CPI Card Group, Inc. v. Dwyer,* 294 F. Supp. 3d 791 (D. Minn. 2018).

3. <u>Balancing the Scope of Injunctive Relief</u>. Even if the facts warrant injunctive relief, courts consider the parties' and the public's interests and other factors in determining the scope of an injunction. For example, while the threatened breach of a former employee's noncompete clause often serves as the basis for finding irreparable harm, courts carefully weigh the former employee's right to earn a living in determining the *scope* of any injunction. *E.g., Motion Control Sys., Inc. v. East,* 546 S.E.2d 424 (Va. 2001); *see also Harbor Perfusion, Inc. v. Floyd,* 45 S.W.3d 713 (Ct. App. Tex. 2001) (holding courts cannot impose injunction broader than parties' noncompete clause).

4. <u>Injunctions and the Amount in Controversy</u>. For diversity subject matter jurisdiction, the amount in controversy must exceed $75,000. If a plaintiff seeks only injunctive relief and sues in federal court, or sues in state court and the defendant removes, courts must determine whether that requirement is met. Although there is a split, many courts require the party asserting subject matter jurisdiction to prove

the requirement is met by showing the larger of two figures — the injunction's value to the plaintiff or its cost to the defendant. *JTH Tax, Inc. v. Frashier*, 624 F.3d 635 (4th Cir. 2010).

5. <u>Interlocutory Appeals</u>. An order granting, denying, dissolving, or modifying an injunction (other than a TRO) is immediately appealable. 28 U.S.C. § 1292(b) (a party may appeal "interlocutory orders of the district courts . . . granting, continuing, modifying, refusing or dissolving injunctions.") *But cf. Ala. Legis. Black Caucus v. Ala.*, 2013 WL 1397139 (M.D. Ala. Apr. 5, 2013) ("an order denying summary judgment to a plaintiff who has requested injunctive relief, but who has taken no practical step toward obtaining such relief" is not appealable). On the other hand, an order granting or denying a motion for a TRO is not appealable, with a narrow exception for orders that will have a "serious, perhaps irreparable, consequence," that can be "effectually challenged" only by immediate appeal. *Ross v. Rell*, 398 F.3d 203 (2d Cir. 2005) (father could appeal denial of TRO to stop execution of son). However, if a TRO is extended beyond the 28-day limit without the enjoined party's consent, "it comes in effect a preliminary injunction that is appealable, but the order remains effective." *H-D Mich., LLC v. Hellenic Duty Free Shops, S.A.*, 694 F.3d 827 (7th Cir. 2012). Can you see why these are, or are not, appealable?

C. Who Is Bound by — and the Remedies for Violating — an Injunction

An injunction "binds only the following who receive actual notice of it by personal service or otherwise: (A) the parties; (B) the parties' officers, agents, servants, employees, and attorneys; and (C) other persons who are in active concert or participation with anyone described in Rule 65(d)(2)(A) or (B)." Fed. R. Civ. P. 65(d)(2). If a court finds that a person covered by an injunction has violated it, the party who obtained the injunction can move for contempt.

Courts have discretion to determine the appropriate remedy that can both *compensate* for damages caused by the violation and *coerce* the person who violated the injunction to comply with it. Compensation furthers the interest of the injured party, and coercion furthers the interest of that party and the court, as *Avery v. Medina*, 163 A.3d 1271 (Conn. App. 2017), emphasized: "Having found noncompliance, the court, in the exercise of its equitable powers, necessarily has the authority to fashion whatever orders are required to protect the integrity of its original judgment." A court may also find it appropriate to hold the violator in criminal or civil contempt. The dividing line is critical but sometimes not bright. An order sending a person to jail obviously is criminal contempt, but whether a monetary award is civil or criminal turns on the purpose of the award: "civil contempt is coercive or compensatory, whereas the purpose of criminal contempt is punitive." *Koninklijke Philips Elecs., N.V. v. KXD Tech., Inc.*, 539 F.3d 1039 (9th Cir. 2008). The following case also tries to clarify the forms of contempt.

Porter v. Porter

776 N.W.2d 377 (Ct. App. Mich. 2009) (Markey, J.)

[Defendant and plaintiff were in a child custody dispute. The plaintiff mother failed to provide visitation in the summer as ordered, and the trial court issued a show cause order as to why she should not be held in contempt. After a hearing, the court found her in contempt and ordered her to pay $1,000 as a sanction and ordered her to permit visitation later in the summer and at Thanksgiving, but did not award plaintiff attorney fees. Plaintiff did not pay the sanction to the court or permit either visitation. In December, defendant moved for another finding of contempt and sought attorneys' fees, and the trial court ordered plaintiff to pay the $1,000 and $3,100 in defendant's attorney fees, and ordered plaintiff to attend counseling, warning that another $2,000 would be imposed if she failed to attend, and ordered visitation at Christmas. She did not comply with any aspect of the order. In January, the defendant again moved for contempt, and at the February hearing the judge awarded a total of $4,100 in fees and warned plaintiff that she would be jailed if she did not pay and did not provide visitation. Plaintiff appealed all of the orders.]

First, we reject plaintiff's argument that the contempt proceedings at issue here were criminal. Criminal contempt differs from civil contempt in that the sanctions are punitive rather than remedial. Criminal contempt is a crime in the ordinary sense; it is a violation of the law, a public wrong which is punishable by fine or imprisonment or both. Criminal contempt is intended to punish the contemnor for past conduct that affronts the dignity of the court. Thus, when a court exercises its criminal contempt power it is not attempting to force the contemnor to comply with an order, but is simply punishing the contemnor for past misconduct that was an affront to the court's dignity. On the other hand, if the court employs its contempt power to coerce compliance with a present or future obligation or to reimburse the complainant for costs incurred by the contemptuous behavior, including attorney fees, the proceedings are civil. Thus, there are two types of civil contempt sanctions, coercive and compensatory. Nevertheless, civil sanctions primarily intended to compel the contemnor to comply with the court's order may also have a punitive effect. If the contempt consists in the refusal of a party to do something which he is ordered to do for the benefit or advantage of the opposite party, the process is civil. The order in such a case is not in the nature of a punishment, but is coercive, to compel him to act in accordance with the order of the court.

Differentiating between civil contempt and criminal contempt is not easy because both forms of contempt might result in the contemnor's being imprisoned for willfully failing to comply with an order of the court. Thus, all contempt proceedings are referred to as "quasi-criminal" or "criminal in nature." The distinction between civil and criminal contempt is important because a criminal contempt proceeding requires some, but not all, of the due process safeguards of an ordinary criminal trial. A party charged with criminal contempt is presumed innocent, enjoys the right against self-incrimination, and the contempt must be proven beyond a reasonable doubt. Further, a party accused of criminal contempt must be informed of the nature of the charge against him or her and be given adequate opportunity to prepare a defense and to secure the assistance of counsel. In contrast, in a civil contempt proceeding, the accused must be accorded rudimentary due process, i.e., notice and an opportunity to present a defense, and the party seeking enforcement of the court's order bears the burden of proving by a preponderance of the evidence that the order was violated.

Our review of the record in this case convinces us that by invoking its contempt power, the trial court was not trying to punish plaintiff for past misconduct because its dignity had been offended; it was instead attempting to coerce plaintiff into complying with its orders for parenting time and related orders intended to facilitate defendant's right to parenting time with his son. At the time of the July 27, 2007, show cause hearing, plaintiff was in violation of the trial court's past and then-current orders to provide defendant with two weeks of summer visitation "commencing June 30, 2007," and was then still under a future duty to provide defendant his two weeks of summer visitation and comply with other provisions of the court's parenting time order. On entry of the contempt order of July 27, 2007, plaintiff could purge herself of contempt by paying the $1,000 sanction and complying with the order for specific makeup visitation. A party's parenting time rights might become meaningless if a court cannot enforce a visitation schedule through the use of its contempt powers.

Notes and Questions

1. <u>From Compensatory to Coercive</u>. In *Shell Offshore, Inc. v. Greenpeace, Inc.,* 815 F.3d 623 (9th Cir. 2016), Greenpeace activists had violated the court's injunction prohibiting blocking the plaintiff's ships from oil-drilling activities, and the district court found contempt and imposed a fine of $2,500 per hour the first 24-hour period, and then incrementally increased daily until a $10,000 per hour maximum. The general rule is that "per diem fines like this one are generally coercive." *Id.* Can you explain why? That court also noted that "it is possible for sanctions that were initially imposed for a civil, coercive purpose to change over time; indeed, civil coercive contempt may eventually evolve into criminal contempt." *Id.* Significantly, an order of criminal contempt is immediately appealable, but appeal of an order of civil contempt must await final judgment. *Koninklijke Philips Elecs., N.V. v. KSD Tech., Inc.,* 539 F.3d 1039 (9th Cir. 2008).

2. <u>Expired Injunctions and Coercive Contempt Orders</u>. Suppose a court holds a defendant in contempt and appeals that order, but while the appeal is pending the underlying injunction expires. In the *Greenpeace* case, the court held that if a contempt order was coercive, then once the underlying injunction expired, "there is no longer anything left to coerce," and "enforcing the sanctions could only serve to punish the contemnor." As a result, "the coercive contempt proceeding must be vacated" because awarding any damages would only serve to punish past actions, and, as they were civil, they were not accompanied by necessary due process concerns associated

with criminal contempt. "Enforcing the fee-schedule monetary sanction would only serve to punish Greenpeace for its past contumacious actions" and so the appellate court ordered the district court to vacate its order.

Problems

1. <u>What's Wrong</u>? Your client has asked you to serve as appellate counsel. As you review the trial record, which consisted of typical discovery and a live hearing, the record supports these facts: Your clients had agreed to buy land from the defendants, who refused to sell, likely because from the time of the closing date of September 2016 set in the parties' agreement to the time of the hearing in early 2018, the land had increased in value from an appraisal of $2.1 million to between $14.5 and $16 million. Your client's real estate attorney had sent the closing documents repeatedly, but each time they were returned unsigned. Your client's trial counsel had moved for summary judgment, and the trial court had issued a one-sentence order that stated: "Plaintiff's motion for summary judgment is granted. The Court orders specific performance of the August 2016 Contract of Sale." The other side has filed a notice of appeal. What issues do you see that may prevent your client from obtaining its desired remedy?

2. <u>First-Filed Declaratory Judgment Action</u>. Why should a court not be required to dismiss a declaratory judgment action filed before the substantive one? Think about the purpose of such actions, and why a rigid rule might permit strategic behavior. On the other hand, if the declaratory judgment plaintiff hid its actions, should that be a factor? Courts state, in making the analysis of which should proceed, that the second suit can proceed when "equity so demands" and look to factors such as extraordinary circumstances, inequitable conduct, bad faith, anticipatory suits, and forum shopping. How do those factors apply to *ABS Global*?

3. <u>Declaration or Injunction</u>? Suppose that in a case exactly like *Guidance*, a plaintiff seeks not injunctive relief, but a declaratory judgment that if the defendant failed to provide the two products, it would be in breach of the parties' agreement. What argument would you as the defendant make that such relief should be analyzed the same as injunctive relief?

4. <u>Why Criminal versus Civil Contempt Matters</u>. Think back on what you have learned about criminal law—the Sixth Amendment, the right to a jury, Due Process—and list reasons why courts are careful to categorize contempt orders.

5. <u>Landlord in Contempt</u>? A landowner leased its land to a tenant who used it as a nursery to raise and sell plants. A neighbor sued the landowner, arguing the landowner was permitting the tenant to dump toxic waste into the sewer system and showed that some of the waste was entering the neighbor's land, trespassing and creating a nuisance. The district court issued an injunction ordering the landowner to stop allowing dumping of certain waste on the property. The landowner, however, did not inform the tenant of the injunction, and the tenant continued to dump waste. The neighbor has moved for contempt against the landowner. The

landowner has defended by asserting it has not violated the injunction. How should the court rule?

6. <u>Loud Rooftop Bar</u>. Party A owns a 120-unit 12-story apartment building in a crowded downtown. It has existed there for years. Recently, the restaurant owned by Party B on the sixth floor of the building located across the alley, which has also existed for years, opened an outdoor deck. Since then, the apartment residents have complained to Party A of loud noise, cigar smoke, and loud talking and laughing until the late hours of the night. Assume that a court will likely hold that, as a matter of law, the deck is a "nuisance," <u>which is an unreasonable interference</u> with <u>use and enjoyment of property</u>. Given the discussion so far, describe whether and to what extent a court likely will enter a preliminary injunction against its operation. Would it permit some use, or prohibit all? If the former, what would the injunction state? If the latter, why?

7. <u>Amount in Controversy</u>. As noted, courts generally require the party asserting subject matter jurisdiction to show that the amount in controversy requirement (exceeding $75,000) has been met, and a common approach is to use the higher of the cost of compliance or the value to the plaintiff. However, some courts instead find the amount in controversy is met only if the cost exceeds $75,000 or the benefit exceeds $75,000. Suppose, for example, in the case above involving the restaurant, the cost to the defendant would be $50,000 a year in lost revenue by having to close the deck or limit its operation, but the benefit to the apartment owner would be $1,000,000. If it were to pick only one, why does the cost to the defendant matter since the "payment" by any injunction will be the benefit to the plaintiff? Why should a court not consider both numbers?

Chapter 3

Remedies Triggered by Harm to the Plaintiff's Body or Mind

1. Orientation to This Chapter

This chapter begins with claims that require "damage" to be harm to a plaintiff's body (which causes "pain and suffering") or mind (as "mental distress" or "mental anguish"). This includes what are commonly thought of as "personal injury" damages, such as those that result from a typical car wreck or bar fight. An "impact" to the plaintiff that causes "pain and suffering" satisfies the "damage" of a negligence claim, for example, and some states define "damage" for negligence claims to include mental distress not caused by an impact ("negligent infliction of emotional distress"). As noted in the introduction, the damage required by negligence is perhaps the most challenging (with breach of contract damages probably a close second).

The terms "mental anguish," "mental distress," and "pain and suffering" are sometimes used interchangeably. This book uses "pain and suffering" to refer to mental anguish caused by a physical injury, such as from a car wreck or fight. The book uses the phrases "emotional distress" or "mental anguish" to refer to mental harm *not* caused by a physical injury. The cases do not always keep the terminology clear, but be sure to read them with that distinction in mind.

Critically, if the plaintiff does not suffer the harm required by the "damage" element of a claim, no remedy is available. So, for example, in a few states the "damage" for a negligence claim requires an "impact." In those states, there is no remedy for mental anguish not caused by an impact. Similarly, a plaintiff who suffers only economic loss caused by the negligence of the defendant will, with some exceptions, recover nothing because economic harm ordinarily does not constitute the "damage" required for negligence. Note that *if* the plaintiff suffers an impact, then economic losses, such as lost income, are recoverable as consequential damages.

In addition to claims that require physical impact, this chapter includes claims that define "damage" to include only mental anguish, including battery—for which a *harmful* or *offensive* contact is sufficient, and no personal injury is required—as well as those caused by a plaintiff being put in fear of her own safety, or seeing the defendant injure another person. Thus, battery does not require an impact, and some of these claims do not require even a contact. *See* Restatement (Second) of Torts § 905 cmt. c (1979) ("The principal element of damages in actions for battery, assault or false imprisonment is frequently the disagreeable emotion experienced by the plaintiff."). Each claim defines the required "damage" to be distress caused by, and so limited to, particular conduct. For example, an assault plaintiff must experience fear of imminent bodily harm. Without that form of harm, no remedy is available.

Under the majority approach, the degree of physical harm required for a claim turns on the "degree of the defendant's culpability." *Schmidt v. Boardman Co.,* 11 A.3d 924, 951 (Pa. 2011). Thus, "damages for pure emotional distress should not be available under a negligent infliction theory but may be awarded under an intentional infliction theory where there is outrageous conduct." *Id.* (citing Restatement (Torts) Second § 313 cmt. a (1965)). "More generally, as a defendant's culpability increases (on the scale of faultless to negligent to intentional), the range of available damages tends to widen in light of the inherent connection between culpability and responsibility which was the traditional center of the law of torts." *Id.*

Significantly, the measure of damages for mental anguish, or pain and suffering, are typically the same — a jury should award an amount of money to compensate the plaintiff as determined in the enlightened conscience of the jury — but, again, each claim focuses on a distinct experience. For example, an award for assault is to compensate for the distress caused by the apprehension of imminent bodily injury, but an award of damages for assault is to compensate for the anguish caused by the offensive contact.

This chapter then turns to what are often called "derivative claims," available to a plaintiff when *another* person suffers an injury that satisfies the damage element of a claim that person could assert. For example, if one person is injured and can successfully assert a negligence claim against a defendant, another person may have a claim against that same defendant, even if that person did not suffer the type of harm required by negligence. The second person's claim derives from, and depends upon, the first.

The first derivative claim is loss of consortium. If a defendant injured the plaintiff's spouse (or in some states, other relatives of the plaintiff), a plaintiff may be able to recover damages if the injury to the spouse harmed their marriage (or, again, in some states, another familial relationship). Then the chapter discusses claims requiring physical injury to a person that causes distress to the plaintiff, either because: (a) the plaintiff had been in the "zone of danger" when the other person was injured or (b) was related to the injured person and saw the person injured — so-called "bystander" claims. Finally, this chapter turns to wrongful death claims, and shows that certain relatives have claims — both for their own mental suffering and to recover damages the decedent would have been entitled to recover for personal injury (including lost future wages, for example).

Many cases in the next few chapters address jury instructions and verdict forms. Lawyers must request proper, and object to improper, jury instructions and verdict forms. Juries must be properly instructed on: (a) whether damages for certain types of harm are recoverable; (b) the measure of such damages; (c) whether apportionment of damages applies; and (d) the substantive law, such as each element of a claim. The court in *Rosa-Rivera v. Dorado Health, Inc.*, 787 F.3d 614 (1st Cir. 2015) summarized the process:

> Federal Rule of Civil Procedure 51 requires the court to give parties the opportunity to object to its proposed jury instructions before closing arguments and the instructions are delivered. For an objection to be timely (except in circumstances not relevant here), it must be made at this point. Failure to do so means the objection is forfeited and reviewed for plain error only, the idea being that the trial judge should be afforded the opportunity to cure the alleged error and litigants stopped from ensuring a new trial in the event of an adverse verdict by covertly relying on the error.
>
> While a proper request (we have that) and a proper objection (we are missing that) is required for a party to assign error to the court's failure to give an instruction, the objection requirement does not apply when the court rejected the request in a definitive ruling on the record. In those instances, the challenge is deemed preserved and subject to de novo review.

Like jury instructions, the form of the verdict completed by the jury can be crucial. Because of the single action rule, plaintiffs often assert claims with overlapping, if not identical, damages. Lawyers must determine whether to request the judge submit a form of verdict with one blank for the amount of damages, or distinct interrogatories for different types of damage. If a lawyer does not request a special verdict form—one that requires the jury to associate a particular award of damages with each claim—review of awards is limited, as the court in *Free v. Baker,* 469 Fed. Appx. 786 (11th Cir. 2012) explained:

> We presume the jury followed its instructions, found actual damages, and awarded a lump sum for "medical expenses, pain and suffering, and permanent injury," or any combination of those things, or any one of them. The defendants did not request that the jury return a verdict breaking the damage award down into categories. In fact, they requested an instruction for a lump sum damages award. The jury's verdict is a general one; it does not divide the damages award into "categories;" it simply awards $483,750.00 as a lump sum. It makes no sense to contend, as the defendants do, that they are entitled to judgment as a matter of law on some categories of damages when there are no categories of damages in the award.

Apart from instructing juries on each claim—including the required "damage" and the measure for it—juries should be instructed not to award duplicative recoveries. A duplicative recovery can arise if the same harm is remedied by more than one claim. For example, "physical impairment" may overlap with "diminished capacity to work and earn money" and "loss of earning capacity," and "physical pain" may overlap with "mental anguish." *See Patel v. Hussain*, 485 S.W.3d 153 (Tex. App. Ct. 2016). Likewise, if different elements of damage for different claims potentially overlap, juries should be instructed not to "not award a recovery for an injury under one cause of action that was already compensated for by another." *Simuro v. Shedd*, 2016 WL 9526312 (D. Vt. Nov. 7, 2016). Courts assume that juries follow these instructions, as well as instructions that certain harms are compensable under one claim, but not another. *See LRX, Inc. v. Horizon Assocs. Joint Venture*, 922 So. 2d 984 (Ct. App. Fla. 2005).

Parties often disagree on whether the verdict form should have separate interrogatories for the measure of damages for each claim, or one aggregate amount. Generally, plaintiffs prefer a single verdict and defendants a claim-by-claim form, particularly where some harms are compensable under one claim but not the other. *See id.* (explaining that a new trial would be proper if a jury awarded the same damages for two claims that overlapped in part but only one of which permitted recovery of mental anguish damages).

This chapter then addresses injunctive relief, examining when courts will enjoin a defendant from committing future acts instead of simply requiring the plaintiff to sue the defendant again if it does so. Repetitive intentional acts or threats of violence can indicate that the remedy at law — suing and getting a money judgment — is inadequate. Ordinarily, no one *negligently* but repeatedly causes or threatens violence or physical harm, and a plaintiff can often simply avoid that defendant. As a result, injunctions involving negligent future harm to a plaintiff's health or safety are available only when the defendant is interfering with a plaintiff's use of its land. Chapter 7 thus contains additional insights into when courts will enter injunctions based upon physical or mental harm to a plaintiff.

2. Negligence or Products Liability Claims

A. Damages for the Harms of "Pain and Suffering" and "Mental Anguish"

All states permit recovery if a defendant's negligence or defective product caused an "impact" that resulted in a physical injury that caused the plaintiff to experience pain and suffering. *Schmidt v. Boardman Co.*, 11 A.3d 924 (Pa. 2011). Many states permit recovery without an impact, but only if the defendant's negligence or defective product caused plaintiff to suffer mental anguish because the plaintiff either: (1) saw the defendant severely injure a close relative ("bystander claims"); or (2) had been in the "zone of danger" when the defendant or its product physically injured another person, including but not limited to a relative ("zone-of-danger claims"). *See id.* Beyond that, and apart from a few specialized forms of negligence where physical harm of any kind is sufficient (discussed in the notes below), a few states permit recovery for mental anguish caused by a defendant's negligence — without any physical impact to anyone — based upon specific policies or, more commonly, because of long-standing case law, such as the "duty" of an innkeeper or common carrier not to cause mental anguish to business invitees.

The form of distress required for each claim is defined and so serves to limit the measure of damage. For example, in most states, a father driving a car with his daughter as a passenger when both were injured in a wreck caused by defendant's negligence can recover damages for: (a) pain and suffering caused by the impact and (b) mental anguish caused by having seen his daughter injured. In some states, a father who had been in the zone of danger and also had seen his daughter injured, but did not suffer any impact, could recover both for the fear of suffering the impact his daughter experienced *and* for the mental anguish he experienced by having seen his daughter injured. (And, again, with consequential damages.) Finally, in most states, a father who, from a safe distance away, only saw his daughter injured can recover only the latter, but in other states would recover nothing—even if the anguish was just as real and the consequential damages as significant. Where the required harm is present, the father could also recover consequential damages, such as medical bills or lost wages caused by the required form of distress.

B. Whether an Impact Is Required for Negligence

I. What Is an "Impact" and Why Require It?

All states hold that a defendant who negligently causes an "impact" with the plaintiff must compensate the plaintiff for the pain and suffering caused. "If the actor's negligent conduct has so caused *any* bodily harm to another as to make him liable for it, the actor is also subject to liability for *emotional disturbance resulting from the bodily harm*." *Werline v. CSX Transp., Inc.*, 2010 WL 5439770 (S.D. Ind. Dec. 28, 2010). While this is sufficient in all states, a few states require an impact. Those courts reason: "First, there is the fear, that absent impact, there will be a flood of litigation of claims for emotional distress. Second, is the concern for fraudulent claims. Third, there is the perception that, absent impact, there would be difficulty in proving the causal connection between the defendant's negligent conduct and claimed damages of emotional distress." *Lee v. State Farm Mut. Ins. Co.*, 533 S.E.2d 82 (Ga. 2000). In these states, without an impact, no damages are recoverable—not for the mental anguish and not for any consequential damages, such as medical bills or lost wages.

In determining whether the "impact rule" furthers public policy or might encourage equally unpalatable conduct, consider two cases that reached different results on whether the plaintiffs had suffered an "impact." In *Shores v. Modern Transp. Serv., Inc.*, 585 S.E.2d 664 (Ct. App. Ga. 2003), plaintiff Thomas Shores was on a train when he saw a tractor-trailer truck driven by defendant's employee racing to get through a crossing ahead of the train. Instead, it rammed into the train. Shores suffered post-traumatic stress disorder as a result of the incident. He asserted a negligence claim. The trial court granted the defendant's motion for summary judgment, and plaintiff appealed. The court affirmed because, although "he was moved in his seat by the collision, Shores was not physically impacted," did not seek medical treatment, but did suffer "post-traumatic stress syndrome, the result of seeing the accident develop, manifested by dreams, flashbacks, an episode of incontinence when passing through an intersection upon last operating a train following the accident, and panic attacks on contemplating returning to railroad work thereafter."

In contrast, in *Grizzle v. Norsworthy*, 664 S.E.2d 296 (Ct. App. Ga. 2008), plaintiff James Grizzle was the conductor of a train as it approached a crossing. He saw a car approach the crossing, and then slowed down and stopped on the track. After the train hit the car, Grizzle ran to the wreck to help, but its sole occupant, the driver, was unresponsive. Grizzle stayed with him until emergency personnel arrived five minutes later. The driver died at the scene. Grizzle sued the executrix of the driver's estate, Norsworthy, alleging the driver's negligence had caused him physical injury, anguish, medical expenses, lost wages, and had rendered him disabled. The trial court granted defendant summary judgment, but the court of appeals reversed, writing:

> Norsworthy's summary judgment motion concerned the second of these elements. She cited Grizzle's deposition testimony that the collision had caused his elbow and knee to strike the front console of the locomotive car, but that he had neither observed any physical injury nor sought medical treatment to his elbow or knee. When asked whether he had received "medical treatment for any physical ailment out of [the train collision] incident," Grizzle responded, "No physical ailment."

> Opposing Norsworthy's motion, Grizzle filed his own affidavit and the affidavits of those who had rendered him medical care. Grizzle averred that, although he did not seek medical attention the day of the accident, he was seen by his family doctor on December 8, 2003. He complained about increased irritable bowel syndrome, depression, anxiety, and experiencing flashbacks of images from the collision. A physician's assistant for Grizzle's doctor averred that during the December 8 clinical visit, Grizzle described the train accident and was noted to have suffered worsening shoulder and back pain, as well as post-traumatic stress disorder. She further recounted that later that month, Grizzle was seen for depression, anxiety, as well as "multiple orthopedic injuries and chronic pain." Grizzle's doctor averred that he had been treating Grizzle since June 2000 for various mental and physical conditions, including a shoulder injury; that on December 8, 2003, he determined that Grizzle's shoulder injury was worsening; and that it was his opinion that to a reasonable degree of medical certainty, the train/car accident that occurred in November 2003 had aggravated Grizzle's preexisting physical and mental conditions.

> The trial court expressly noted the doctor's and the physician's assistant's affidavits, but cited Grizzle's deposition testimony in concluding that it was

"not persuaded by the plaintiff's arguments that he has suffered physical injuries and mental anguish." Grizzle argues on appeal that the grant of summary judgment to Norsworthy was impermissibly based upon the trial court's resolution of a factual issue. We agree with Grizzle that, notwithstanding his deposition testimony, the affidavits created an issue of fact whether the physical impact he sustained during the collision caused him physical injury.

If you now think these cases show the impact rule is arbitrary or encourages strategic behavior by lawyers, or, on the other hand, if you believe it is a bright line that weeds out meritless clams, consider the following. The following case arose in a state that permits recovery for pain and suffering caused by an impact, and for mental anguish that causes a physical injury.

Majors v. Hillebrand

349 P.3d 1283 (Ct. App. Kan. 2015) (Gardner, J.)

[Plaintiff Jason Majors was driving with his six-year-old daughter in a rear car seat on the passenger side when defendant's 35-ton snowplow slammed into his car. Majors saw the plow just before it hit and saw it break through the passenger side window. It caused severe damage and his daughter suffered traumatic head injuries: her scalp was pushed back, she was bleeding and not breathing. After Majors pulled her from the car, she began to respond.

Majors was not physically injured and did not seek medical care. However, he filed suit, alleging that he began to have nightmares the night after the wreck, and starting a few months later and, as a result of the trauma of seeing his daughter and thinking she was dead, he began to suffer anxiety, post-traumatic stress disorder (PTSD), sleeping disorder, and hypertension, and these precluded him from working. He did not seek treatment until one year after the wreck, but then two mental health professionals examined him and found the wreck had caused his symptoms and opined healing would take three to five years. In granting defendant's motion for summary judgment, the trial court found Majors suffered from PTSD caused by the wreck, but held that it was insufficient to constitute "damage" for negligence under Kansas law. Plaintiff appealed.]

Kansas has consistently held that generalized physical symptoms of emotional distress, such as those associated with PTSD are insufficient to state a cause of action for a negligent infliction of emotional distress claim. And our court has recently held that the type of symptoms Majors experienced do not constitute physical injuries for purposes of a negligent infliction of emotional distress (NIED) claim:

> When determining if injuries may be classified as physical injuries under a NIED cause of action, Kansas courts have addressed various types of symptoms. *See, e.g., Reynolds v. Highland Manor, Inc.*, 24 Kan.App.2d 859 (1998) (plaintiff failed to meet physical injury requirement when she suffered

headaches, diarrhea, nausea, crying, shaking, sexual problems, and feelings of stress, all caused by anxiety); *Dill v. Barnett Funeral Home, Inc.,* 2004 WL 292124 (Kan.App.2004), *rev. denied* 278 Kan. 844 (2004) (lack of sleep, recurring dreams, and general fatigue not a compensable physical injury).

Williams v. Taco Tico, Inc., 2012 WL 2045369 (Kan. App. 2012) (finding "PTSD, depression, anxiety, insomnia, and nightmares do not qualify as physical injuries").

By his own admission, Majors suffered no emotional distress accompanied by or resulting in his physical injury. Majors' emotional distress manifested several months after the collision, with the exception of his nightmares which began the night after the collision. Under existing Kansas caselaw, Majors' symptoms of anxiety, sleeping disorder, hypertension, and those symptoms which led to his PTSD diagnosis are too remote and speculative for recovery as they did not appear within a short span of time after the emotional disturbance. Additionally, even if all of those symptoms had manifested closer in time to the accident, these were not accompanied by and did not result in physical injury to Majors. Thus, no genuine issue of material fact precluded summary judgment on plaintiff's claim of negligent infliction of emotional distress.

Majors argues that times have changed and that Kansas is now in the "very small minority" of states that continue to apply the physical injury rule. But we have no authority to overrule established precedent of the Kansas Supreme Court absent some indication that it is departing from its previous position. Majors cites no case indicating that the Kansas Supreme Court is tending to depart from the physical injury rule, and we find none.

Notes and Questions

1. <u>Does It Work?</u> Does the impact rule likely prevent a flood of fraudulent claims and difficult causal issues, or does requiring an impact result in dismissal of credible claims, as in *Majors?* Should juries decide if people like Majors are faking? What is the consequence of that view on litigation costs and "fake claims?"

2. <u>Facts and Circumstances.</u> Courts struggle and take different views of the boundaries, some relaxing it and others not. Consider the following cases. First, in *Higgins v. Metro-N.R.R. Co.,* 143 F. Supp. 2d 353 (S.D.N.Y. 2001), *aff'd sub nom. Higgins v. Metro-N.R.R. Co.,* 318 F.3d 422 (2d Cir. 2003), the plaintiff asserted a claim under the Federal Employers' Liability Act. She asserted she had suffered emotional distress caused by sexual harassment that included touching. For purposes of determining an issue under the FELA, the court analyzed whether an unwanted touching was sufficient to be an "impact" and wrote:

> The Supreme Court later clarified the meaning of the term "physical impact" in *Metro-North Commuter R.R. Co. v. Buckley,* 521 U.S. 424 (1997). In *Buckley,* the Supreme Court held that the mere exposure to a carcinogenic substance was not a physical impact if the only harm that was caused by the exposure was the increase of plaintiff's risk of cancer in the future.

Indeed, it held that the words 'physical impact' do not encompass every form of 'physical contact.' It applies only to those contacts "that caused, or might have caused, immediate traumatic harm." *Buckley,* 521 U.S. at 430. In sum, *Buckley* has restated the traditional rule that an event cannot constitute a physical impact, even if it entails contact, unless it has a physically harmful effect on the body.

In this case, although plaintiff testified that it "hurt" when she was slapped on the buttocks, she testified that she was never physically injured by the contacts and was never in apprehension of physical harm. According to plaintiff, she felt "demeaned," "offended" and "angry." Plaintiff felt that Militano was "emotionally abusing her, that's all. It was emotional abuse the whole time. That's what it was." Without any allegation of physical injury or apprehension thereof, these uninvited contacts, however emotionally repugnant, do not constitute physical impacts under FELA.

In *Allen v. National R.R. Passenger Corp.,* 90 F.Supp.2d 603 (E.D.Pa. 2000), the plaintiff alleged that she was the subject of sexual harassment and as a result felt "uneasy," "uncomfortable," "upset," "very nervous," "humiliated," "intimidated," and "afraid." Her emotional injuries caused her to suffer from "depression, chronic and acute anxiety, dry mouth, a lack of sleep and stress, as well as a gastro-intestinal problem." *Id.* Because the contacts with the plaintiff's ear and hand "neither caused physical injury nor could have resulted in physical harm," the court held that they were merely "harmless" and did not constitute a "physical impact" under *Gottshall. Id.* The court echoed the observations of *Buckley* and *Gottshall* respecting FELA's primary purpose of protecting railroad workers from "physical perils." *Id.*

The principle that a physical impact requires at least some physical injury was also applied in *Tongret v. Norfolk & Western Ry., Co.,* 980 F. Supp. 903 (N.D. Ohio 1997). In *Tongret,* a male employee claimed that he was harassed by male co-workers when he was hit in the back of the neck and placed in a headlock. In that case, the court held that the headlock, "while literally a physical impact," was nothing more than an uninvited touching because there was no infliction of injury. *See id.; see also McMillan v. National R.R. Passenger Corp.,* 648 A.2d 428 (1994) (upholding directed verdict for the defendant even though the victim alleged that he was punched in the shoulder and a lit blow torch was placed near the seat of his pants); *Visconti v. Consolidated Rail Corp.,* 801 F.Supp. 1200 (S.D.N.Y. 1992) (dismissing claim where plaintiff alleged that her supervisor "brushed close to her body, stood close to her for one or two minutes and put his hand on her back for less than a minute.").

In contrast, other courts have stated that the "essence of impact is that the outside force or substance, no matter how large or small, visible or invisible, and no matter that the effects are not immediately deleterious, touch or enter into the plaintiff's body." *Pipino v. Delta Air Lines, Inc.,* 196 F. Supp. 3d 1306 (S.D. Fla. 2016). For example, in *Willis v. Gami Golden Glades, LLC,* 967 So. 2d 846 (Fla. 2007), a hotel security worker told the plaintiff to park across the street from the hotel and refused to meet her there and escort her to the hotel. As she parked, someone put a gun to her head, gently touching her temple, and had her lift her dress and gently "patted" her body, either for sexual gratification or to search for valuables. The court held that both the touching of the gun and the patting were impacts. In contrast, the court in *Malphurs v. Cooling Tower Sys., Inc.,* 2016 WL 915191 (M.D. Ga. March 4, 2016), stated that an unwanted touching sufficient to support battery was insufficient to be an impact, but putting his hand down plaintiff's shirt and "squeezing her nipples" and "snatching her hair and pulling it back," so that her neck was sore, was sufficient to be an impact.

Could the *Malphurs* or *Willis* plaintiff assert an FELA claim? Do you believe Georgia or Florida courts allow fraudulent claims? Or does the FELA standard deny recovery to plaintiffs who were clearly harmed?

3. <u>When "Physical Harm" Is Sufficient</u>. While in all states an impact is sufficient to satisfy the damage element for negligence, every state also permits recovery for "physical harm" for certain negligence claims and some states permit recovery for products liability (i.e., strict liability) claims. As an example of the former, a defendant who undertakes "to render services to another which he should recognize as necessary for the protection of the other's person or things, is subject to liability to the other for *physical harm* resulting from his failure to exercise reasonable care to perform his undertaking, if (a) his failure to exercise such care increases the risk of such harm, or (b) the harm is suffered because of the other's reliance upon the undertaking." Restatement (Second) of Torts § 323 (1979) (emph. added). Thus, under that Restatement section a defendant is liable for "physical harm." As discussed more fully below, in products liability cases, some courts permit recovery for pure mental distress. *See Hagan v. Coca-Cola Bottling Co.,* 804 So. 2d 1234 (Fla. 2001) ("a plaintiff need not prove the existence of a physical injury in order to recover damages for emotional injuries caused by the consumption of a contaminated food or beverage").

II. The Measure of Damages for Pain and Suffering

Hendrix v. Burns

205 Md. App. 1 (2010) (Eyler, J.)

[Burns sped through a red light and injured Hendrix in a car wreck. Burns admitted liability. During the jury trial on damages, the judge excluded plaintiff's evidence that: (a) Burns had been drinking; (b) he had been speeding to catch up to a car as part of a road rage incident, and (c) he had tried to flee the scene of the wreck. The jury found for the plaintiff, who appealed the trial court's rulings as excluding evidence pertinent to her mental distress damages.]

In tort actions, damages may be recovered for emotional distress capable of objective determination. The emotional distress must have been proximately caused by the defendant's tortious conduct. In the case at bar, substantial evidence was adduced during the four-day trial about the emotional distress that Mrs. Hendrix experienced as a result of the accident. As noted, Mrs. Hendrix herself testified that, as the accident was happening, she thought she was going to die; that she was thinking, "oh, my God! This is not how this is supposed to end" and "am I going to die this way?" Captain Hahn testified that he heard the collision before he arrived at the scene, and that it sounded like a "loud screech, a biker boom" and that because of Mrs. Hendrix's injuries and the condition of her car he and his colleagues had to use the "jaws of death" to extract her from the vehicle. EMT Lay testified that Mrs. Hendrix was "moaning" in pain. Mrs. Hendrix's co-worker, neighbor, and daughter testified about the depression she experienced, and has continued to experience, as a result of the injuries she sustained in the accident. Mrs. Hendrix testified at length about the negative impact the injuries have had on her life, including forcing her to sleep in a recliner for months and not being able to raise her arms, and that she even now experiences "excruciating pain." The jurors were permitted to award Mrs. Hendrix damages for the fright she so vividly described experiencing during the accident and the emotional trauma her physical injuries caused her to endure.

What Mrs. Hendrix argues she was not allowed to recover, because of the court's *in limine* ruling, was emotional distress that she experienced upon learning, after the accident, that the person who struck her was a drunk driver, with a history of drunk driving, who had been in a "road rage" incident at the time of the collision and then tried to flee the scene. In other words, she maintains that she experienced additional emotional distress based upon information she learned, after the accident, about the person who hit her (Mr. Burns) and the conduct he had been and was engaging in prior to and after the accident; and that she should have been permitted to recover damages for that additional emotional distress. Accordingly, the excluded evidence was relevant to the issue of damages and should have been allowed.

We agree with the ruling of the trial court that, given the posture of the case—liability for negligence and negligent entrustment admitted and only the issue of damages to be decided by the jury—the fact that, after the accident, Mrs. Hendrix learned that the driver who hit her was drunk, was in a "road rage" incident, attempted to flee after the collision, and had a history of drunk driving convictions did not have a tendency to prove or disprove any fact that was of consequence to the determination of damages, any more than if she had learned, post-accident, that the driver was a pedophile attempting to evade the police or was a desperate husband attempting to get his wife to the hospital in time to deliver their baby.

Notes and Questions

1. <u>Causation of "Pain and Suffering."</u> A jury is typically instructed to award an amount of damages for pain and suffering in its enlightened conscience, with little additional guidance. The *Hendrix* court carefully defined this harm, but compare it to *Smith v. Borello*, 370 Md. 227 (2002), where a woman's injuries from a car wreck caused her to miscarry her pre-viable fetus. The court held she could recover

damages for anguish she felt upon losing her fetus because "if an actor's negligent conduct has so caused any bodily harm to another as to make the actor liable for it, the actor is also subject to liability for fright, shock, or other emotional disturbance resulting from the bodily injury or from the conduct which causes it." How is *Hendrix* different? If the *Smith* plaintiff's doctor had told her that her fetus was going to be stillborn, and that caused mental anguish, but then the baby was born healthy, does *Smith* allow recovery? Does *Hendrix*?

2. The Impact Rule and Damages for Pre-Impact Anguish. In "impact rule" states, the courts split on whether damages for the harm of pre-impact fear is recoverable. For example, in *Steel Techs., Inc. v. Congleton*, 234 S.W.3d 920 (Ky. 2007), *abrogated on other grounds by Osborne v. Keeney*, 399 S.W.3d 1 (Ky. 2012), the defendant was driving a tractor-trailer hauling a 37,000-pound steel coil. Because he had not properly secured the coil, when he was forced to suddenly stop, it flew off his truck and bounced into oncoming traffic. Plaintiff's wife was driving in oncoming traffic and the coil crushed her pickup, killing her. Plaintiff sued, seeking for the estate mental anguish damages his wife experienced before the crash. The jury found for the plaintiff, and the defendant appealed. The court, applying its strict impact rule, held damages for the harm of pre-impact fear were not compensable:

> It is not enough that emotional distress be accompanied by contact—it must be *caused* by the contact. This also means that any contact must precede the emotional distress before recovery is permissible under a negligence theory.

> The rationale for the current rule is that pre-impact fear, like other alleged negligently caused emotional distress, is possibly trivial and simply too speculative and difficult to measure unless is it directly linked to and caused by a physical harm. The proof of the fear in this case—the testimony of a person at the scene of the accident that the decedent's facial expression showed she saw the accident coming and was terrified—simply underscores the speculative nature of such harm. Mrs. Congleton's mental distress, if any, simply was caused not by the impact she suffered, but by fear of the impact. Under the impact rule as currently applied in Kentucky, her pre-impact fear and shock cannot serve as the basis of a claim, and any damages for such a claim are not recoverable.

On the other hand, the court in *Rutland v. S.C. Dept. of Transp.*, 734 S.E.2d 142 (S.C. 2012), reasoned it was "illogical to bar recovery for pre-impact distress when one can recover for post-impact suffering." Isn't it logical to do so? On the other hand, if there is an impact, is compensating for this fear likely to lead to fraudulent claims or open the floodgates of litigation?

3. Closing Arguments. Given the leeway courts afford to juries in deciding the amount of damages, lawyers use rhetorical devices that increase, or decrease, awards for pain and suffering. Two common methods are the "golden rule" and

"per diem" approaches. *Per diem* asks juries to pay the plaintiff on a per-day basis for pain and suffering. As for the golden rule, the court in *Ng-Wagner v. Hotchkiss,* 2018 WL 2277803 (Md. Spec. App. May 18, 2018) explained:

> A "golden rule" argument is one in which a litigant asks the jury to place themselves in the shoes of the victim, or in which an attorney appeals to the jury's own interests. Attorneys should not implore jurors to consider their own interests in violation of the prohibition against the 'golden rule' argument. The vice inherent in such argument is that it invites the jurors to disregard their oaths and to become non-objective viewers of the evidence which has been presented to them, or to go outside that evidence to bring to bear on the issue of damages purely subjective considerations.

A motion *in limine* often seeks to exclude evidence (such as estimates of value by property owners) or arguments (such as whether a jury should award damages for certain types of harm, like mental anguish, for particular claims). Litigators use motions *in limine* to regulate (and, at times, eliminate) remedies. Although common and important, most rules do not mention motions *in limine.* Typically, lawyers seek rulings on permissibility of arguments through a motion *in limine.* How do you think lawyers should be allowed to monetize pain?

4. <u>Judicial Review</u>. Review of an award of compensatory damages for emotional distress is deferential because the harm is subjective, and evaluation depends on the demeanor of witnesses. In some courts, a comparison to other cases is required because the jury verdict must be assessed to see if it "materially deviates" from awards in similar cases. In *Keenan v. Waldorf Carting Co.,* 2004 WL 1961592 (S.D.N.Y. Sept. 2, 2004), the plaintiff had been run over by a garbage truck and suffered a broken femur. The jury awarded $50,000 in past damages for pain and suffering and the court granted plaintiff's motion for new trial, writing:

> In addition to the cases cited by plaintiff, my own research of the law has led me to conclude that an award of $50,000 dollars for past pain and suffering for a fractured femur and ankle materially deviates from what the overwhelming weight of authority in New York has found to be reasonable compensation for similar injuries. *See Edwards v. Stamford Healthcare Soc'y Inc.,* 699 N.Y.S.2d 835 (3d Dep't 1999) (new trial on issue of damages ordered because $38,000 for past pain and suffering was inadequate for fractured pelvis, femur and wrist, abrasions on face and dislocated fingers); *Faulise v. Trout,* 678 N.Y.S.2d 211 (4th Dep't 1998) ($10,000 for past pain and suffering for broken femur is inadequate); *see also Villella v. New York City Hous. Auth.,* 2003 WL 23355282 (Unknown State Court, April 2003) (jury award of $10,000 for past pain and suffering for fractured tibia3 and fibula found to be inadequate; Trial Court increased the award to $450,000); *Seda v. City of New York,* 1990 WL 462078 (Sup. Ct. Kings Co., 1990) (jury award of $2,500 for past pain and suffering for fractured ankle found to be inadequate; Trial Court increased the award to $175,000).

Do these comparisons—injury and amount—illuminate the adequacy of the award? Shouldn't a full comparison include the susceptibility of each plaintiff to pain, for example?

5. <u>Consequential Damages</u>. As explained in Chapter 1, if a plaintiff establishes the harm required by a claim, then it may recover, not just for that harm—often called "general damages"—but also for consequential damages, including, most often, lost wages and medical bills. These are often called "special damages." The amount of economic consequential damages often far exceeds the amount of noneconomic pain and suffering damages. Federal Rule of Civil Procedure 9(g) and similar state rules require that pleadings allege more detail for damages that are "special" for a particular claim. As a result, parties who fail to comply may find special damages unrecoverable. *E.g., Norwest Properties, LLC v. Strebler,* 2018 WL 3636870 (Ct. App. S.C. Aug. 1, 2018) (reversing all but $350 of judgment of $40,000 because defendant had objected that those damages were not pled in accordance with Rule 9(g)). Conversely, failing to object to evidence of special damages when not pled waives the objection. *Lynn v. Soterra Inc.,* 802 So. 2d 162 (Ct. App. Miss. 2001) ("As with other pleading requirements, the need to plead special damages can be waived.").

C. Damages for Mental Anguish Not Caused by an Impact

All states recognize an impact is sufficient to satisfy the "damage" required for negligence. Some states expand the definition of "damage" to include "physical manifestations of emotional suffering, *i.e.,* depression, nightmares, stress, and anxiety." *Ramos v. United States,* 2017 WL 2812668 (M.D. Pa. June 28, 2017). These courts relax the "impact rule," but even so hold that "temporary fright, nervous shock, nausea, grief, rage, and humiliation if transitory are not compensable harm," but instead "long continued nausea or headaches, repeated hysterical attacks or mental aberration are compensable injuries." *Id.* The court in *Sawyer Bros., Inc. v. Island Transporter, LLC,* 887 F.3d 23 (1st Cir. 2018) elaborated on this:

> The term "physical" in the physical consequences requirement is not used in its ordinary sense. Its meaning includes both consequences of emotional distress that are traditionally "physical"—*e.g.,* heart attacks or ulcers—and other conditions that are susceptible of objective determination. For example, emotional distress may "physically" manifest as a psychological condition—*i.e.,* a nervous disorder or a stress disorder—so long as the condition is capable of objective determination. *Haught v. Maceluch,* 681 F.2d 291 (5th Cir. 1982) (noting that "physical injury" extends to nervous disorders, and deciding that "depression, nervousness, weight gain, and nightmares" were "sufficient to constitute physical injury" under Texas law). Whether a particular condition is a "physical" consequence presents a fact-intensive question, requiring case-by-case assessment.

In defining what "damage" is required by negligence, other courts consider not just the "manifestation," but its cause. For example, in *Jenson v. Arndt,* 2018 WL

1702408 (Ct. App. Minn. Apr. 9, 2018), a plaintiff had been in a rollover car accident that killed her fiancé, and the court explained its approach in this way:

> [A plaintiff in an earlier case, *Leaon*] alleged that he experienced emotional distress after being subjected to unwanted sexual contact with a nude female dancer at a bachelor party. Thereafter he lost weight (later regained), became depressed, and exhibited feelings of anger, fear, and bitterness. The supreme court rejected his NIED claim, stating, "These symptoms do not satisfy the physical manifestations test, a test designed to assure the genuineness of the alleged emotional distress." In the following sentence, the supreme court compared *Leaon's* evidence to the evidence in *Quill*, noting that the emotional distress in *Quill* was "undoubtedly attributable to a terrifying experience (the sudden, violent tailspin of a commercial airliner)" and "was under those circumstances sufficiently manifested by the objective, physical symptoms." The implication of *Leaon* is that the supreme court determined that the circumstances of that case were not disturbing enough or terrifying enough to guarantee the genuineness of the alleged emotional distress. The circumstances of this case, however, are unlike *Leaon* because Jensen's claim of emotional distress arises from a sudden and traumatic event, similar to the event in *Quill*. *See also Silberstein v. Cordie*, 474 N.W.2d 850 (Minn. App. 1991) (concluding that plaintiffs' evidence of physical symptoms was sufficient in light of home invasion and shotgun murder of plaintiffs' husband and father), *rev'd & remanded on other grounds*, 477 N.W.2d 713 (Minn. 1991).

Is this manifestation rule a better way than the impact rule to weed out meritless claims? In answering that, consider the following case.

Mower v. Baird

422 P.3d 837 (Utah 2018) (Himonas, J.)

[Plaintiff alleged a therapist had negligently caused his four-year-old daughter to falsely "remember" he had sexually molested her and sought mental anguish damages. The courts below dismissed the complaint. Plaintiff appealed.]

Under Restatement (Third) Torts §47(b), a plaintiff can recover for serious emotional harm if the harm "occurs in the course of specified categories of activities, undertakings, or relationships in which negligent conduct is especially likely to cause serious emotional harm." Restatement (Third) section 47(b) stems from cases around the country that recognized certain circumstances where a plaintiff should be allowed to recover for negligently inflicted emotional distress even when "the defendant [hasn't] created a risk of bodily harm to the plaintiff." *Id.* §47 cmt. f. Section 47(b) recognizes that some parties have a limited duty to exercise reasonable care when placing another at risk of serious emotional harm when engaged in certain conduct. *Id.* §47 cmt. g.

Courts originally recognized two types of cases that served as a predicate for the rule under section 47(b): "(1) delivering a telegram or other communication erroneously announcing death or illness; and (2) mishandling a corpse or bodily remains." *Id.* § 47 cmt. f. Courts around the country have expanded liability beyond those two types of cases, permitting recovery for claims such as a physician negligently diagnosing a patient with a dreaded or serious disease; a physician negligently causing the loss of a fetus; a hospital losing a newborn infant; a person injuring a fetus; a hospital (or another) exposing a patient to HIV infection; an employer mistreating an employee; or a spouse mentally abusing the other spouse.

Although different courts have adopted different approaches, the Restatement (Third) gives three suggested boundaries. First, foreseeability cannot appropriately be employed as the standard to limit liability for emotional harm. Second, the policy issues surrounding specific categories of undertakings, activities, and relationships must be examined to determine whether they merit inclusion among the exceptions to the general rule of no liability. Finally, the more general protection for emotional harm contained in section 47 should not be used to dilute or modify the requirements of those torts that protect specific aspects of emotional tranquility, such as defamation, invasion of privacy, false imprisonment, and malicious prosecution.

Based on the evolution of the law around the country, as well as the policy considerations at play, we believe that it's time to expand our recovery for negligent infliction of emotional distress in very limited circumstances. Specifically, we believe that there are certain types of relationships, activities, and undertakings that go to the core of another person's emotional well-being and security. Individuals who are engaged in such a relationship, activity, or undertaking have a duty to refrain from causing the other person severe emotional distress.

However, we're not prepared today to adopt section 47(b) wholesale. The rule we announce today deviates from section 47(b) in two key ways. First, we retain our "severe" emotional distress requirement—our limited adoption of section 47(b) does not include reducing this requirement to "serious" emotional distress. Second, we're not prepared to announce a duty to refrain from causing severe emotional distress when there wouldn't otherwise be a traditional duty of reasonable care.

This new, limited emotional distress duty analysis should still be completed in the same manner as a traditional duty analysis—on a categorical level. Therefore, in order to establish that a class of defendants would owe a limited emotional distress duty to a class of plaintiffs, the following two-step analysis is required: (1) Does the defendant owe a traditional duty of reasonable care to the plaintiff?; and (2) Is the relationship, activity, or undertaking of the type that warrants a special, limited duty to refrain from causing severe emotional distress?

The first prong of this test ensures that the relationship, activity, or undertaking is one that's fraught with the risk of emotional harm to the plaintiff. This prong can be met only in those very limited situations where the emotional well-being of others is at the core of, or is necessarily implicated by, the relationship, activity, or undertaking.

The second prong of this test recognizes that the imposition of a duty of care is not predicated on the existence of a highly emotional relationship alone. Not all negligence is very likely to cause severe emotional distress, and a duty of care to protect against emotional harm does not arise unless negligence is especially likely to cause severe emotional distress. It's necessary that it be not only foreseeable, but especially likely, that the defendant's negligence will cause severe emotional distress to the plaintiff.

An objective standard must be used in considering whether there's an especially likely risk of negligence causing emotional distress. To recover, a plaintiff must also establish that he or she did actually suffer severe emotional distress that manifested itself through severe mental or physical symptoms.

Finally, the third prong of the test recognizes that, as with traditional duties, public policy may weigh against recognizing a limited emotional distress duty.

This limited emotional distress duty shouldn't be viewed as an expansive mechanism for recovery. Any duty created under this analysis is limited to a duty to refrain from causing severe emotional distress. And, if a defendant breaches that duty, a defendant will only be liable for damages for the severe emotional harm that manifests itself through severe mental or physical symptoms. This duty "should not be used to dilute or modify the requirements of other torts that "protect specific aspects of emotional tranquility." Restatement § 47 cmt. o.

Notes and Questions

1. <u>On Remand</u>? The appellate court reversed for new trial. Do you believe the jury would likely find for plaintiff once properly instructed under the law? Does its hybrid test more likely avoid arbitrary results than the impact rule? Does it open the door to fraudulent claims?

2. <u>Other States</u>. As in the principal case, other courts permit recovery in negligence of mental anguish damages if plaintiff had a "special relationship" that gives rise to "a duty to care for the emotional well-being of the plaintiff," such as psychologists, mortuaries, physicians, or carriers transmitting telegrams announcing the death of close relatives. *Toney v. Chester County Hosp.*, 36 A.3d 83 (Pa. 2011). *See Maryott v. First Nat'l Bank of Eden*, 624 N.W.2d 96 (S.D. 2001) (courts split on whether damages for distress unaccompanied by physical manifestation may be awarded for wrongful dishonor of checks).

3. <u>Pre-Incident Fear in Physical Manifestation States</u>. In states permitting recovery without an impact but with physical manifestation, when should pre-impact fear be recoverable? *See Stephenson v. Honeywell Int'l, Inc.*, 669 F. Supp. 2d 1259 (D. Kan. 2009) (denying pre-impact fear that had only caused rapid heart rate, panic from dying, difficulty breathing, none of which were "physical manifestations"

under Kansas exceptions to the impact rule). In these states, does "manifestation" serve as the "impact" for this purpose?

D. Negligence Claims Where Mental Anguish Caused by Being in the Zone of Danger or by Having Been a Bystander

A majority of states allow "damage" for a negligence claim to consist of purely mental anguish, but only if the plaintiff had been a "bystander" or had been in the "zone of danger." The cases and notes below explore the common approaches further. A plaintiff in the "zone of danger" when a person was injured by a defendant's negligence can recover damages for the fear of also being injured. A plaintiff who was a bystander when a relative was injured can recover for the anguish caused by seeing the injury. The anguish a zone-of-danger plaintiff experiences is distinct from the harm the bystander plaintiff experiences. Of course, a relative can be in the zone of danger.

Only Nevada and Arkansas do not hold that "damage" for a negligence claim can consist of the distress caused by being in the "zone of danger" when a defendant causes an impact to another. In those states, a mother who sees her child killed by the defendant's negligence will recover nothing for her anguish because it was not caused by an impact. As *Mireles v. Infogroup/Opinion Research Corp.*, 2012 WL 78183 (D. Nev. Jan. 10, 2012) explained:

> To recover parasitic damages for emotional harm based on a simple negligence claim, a plaintiff must prove cognizable harm separate from the emotional harm itself. And although emotional harm is potentially available as a measure of damages if other claims in this case are established, recovery of this measure of damages in Nevada requires physical impact or objective evidence of physical manifestation of the emotional distress, and Plaintiff pleads neither.

In *Dowty v. Riggs*, 385 S.W.3d 117 (Ark. 2010), plaintiffs drove to visit the defendants at their home when the defendants' adult son, who was apparently mentally impaired, approached with a gun and shot the plaintiffs' son and shot at the plaintiffs, who sped off, unharmed. They brought a negligence claim against the parents. The court affirmed summary judgment for them: "Arkansas does not recognize the tort of negligent infliction of emotional distress." Until the decision below, Georgia was one of those strict states.

Lee v. State Farm Mut. Ins. Co.

533 S.E.2d 82 (Ga. 2000) (Hines, J.)

[Defendant was driving when he collided with a car carrying plaintiff and her daughter, seriously injuring them both. Pinned in the car with her daughter, the plaintiff witnessed her injuries and, an hour later, her death in the car. The plaintiff's insurance carriers, as part of uninsured motorist coverage, paid policy limits for the death of the daughter, but the plaintiff sued for damages for her own injuries and damages for the mental anguish experienced by watching her daughter suffer and die. The courts below held that that harm was not compensable because the mother was seeking recovery of damages that were not caused by the impact to her. Plaintiff appealed.]

The circumstances of this case clearly invite this Court to reject the impact approach. However, as has been discussed, the impact rule, even with its shortcomings, is not without benefit. And certainly, it would be imprudent to abandon over a hundred years of Georgia precedent. What is more, we decline to adopt any rule which might, in effect, create a separate tort allowing recovery of damages for the negligent infliction of emotional distress. Nor will we resort to artifice to make recovery possible to the plaintiff in this case by recasting the claim of emotional distress or otherwise attempting to fit the case into the parameters of the current rule.

But there is no meritorious reason to refuse to extend recovery for emotional distress to an incident in which the distress is the result of physical injury negligently inflicted on another. The circumstance of this case is such an appropriate and compelling situation. When, as here, a parent and child sustain a direct physical impact and physical injuries through the negligence of another, and the child dies as the result of such negligence, the parent may attempt to recover for serious emotional distress from witnessing the child's suffering and death without regard to whether the emotional trauma arises out of the physical injury to the parent. This is in accord with the precepts of the impact approach and appropriately restricts recovery to those directly affected by the defendant's negligent act or omission. Of course, the parent will be allowed to seek damages for the parent's own physical injuries and any mental suffering or emotional distress arising from those injuries. It will be for the finder of fact to determine whether the parent suffered emotional distress from witnessing the child's suffering and death apart from the grief which would naturally arise from a parent's loss of a child.

McDaniel v. Kidde Residential and Fire Co.

2015 WL 1326332 (W.D. Pa. Mar. 24, 2015) (Fischer, J.)

[Plaintiff was making donuts at home with her oldest daughter, Alaina, by filling a pot with canola oil and heating it on low on the stove. She went downstairs to put another daughter to bed and returned 10 minutes later. When she opened the pot's lid, the oil began to catch fire. She grabbed the fire extinguisher, which was next to the stove, but—although the gauge said it was charged and they had never used it—it would not discharge. Plaintiff handed the fire extinguisher to Alaina and told her to go to the front of the home, which she did.

Plaintiff then picked up the pot of burning oil and carried it through the laundry room toward an exit from the home, trying to get it outside. However, she dropped it and suffered severe burns. She reentered her home to rescue her daughters. She brought a negligence claim against the fire extinguisher's manufacturer and Alaina brought a negligence claim seeking damages for emotional distress. The defendant moved for summary judgment on Alaina's claim.]

A plaintiff must: (1) be located near the scene of the accident; (2) suffer a contemporaneous and sensory observance of the accident; and (3) be closely related to the victim. As such, the observance by the plaintiff does not have to be purely visual: one can witness the traumatic event by other sensory perceptions. In order to be contemporaneous, the observance must be an immediate and direct trigger for the emotional distress. *Bloom v. Dubois Reg'l Med. Ctr.,* 409 Pa.Super. 83 (Pa. Super. Ct. 1991) ("no buffer of time or space may exist to soften the blow").

In general, a plaintiff must prove physical injury to sustain a claim for NIED. Physical manifestations cannot be temporary, transitory, or fleeting, but rather severe or recurring. Moreover, medical evidence is not required in an action claiming NIED.

Defendants argue that Alaina did not witness her mother getting burned when Mrs. McDaniel dropped the flaming pot. In support of this position, Defendants rely primarily upon *Mazzagatti v. Everingham,* 512 Pa. 266 (Pa. 1986); *Bloom,* 409 Pa.Super. 83; *Armstrong,* 430 Pa.Super. 36; and *Yandrich v. Radic,* 495 Pa. 243 (Pa. 1981). This reliance is misplaced. In *Mazzagatti,* the Pennsylvania Supreme Court denied recovery to a mother who arrived to see her injured daughter *after* the traumatic accident had occurred. Similarly in *Bloom,* the court dismissed husband's claim where there was no infliction of injury by defendants when wife attempted to commit suicide, and in *Yandrich,* where plaintiff's decedent did not witness son's fatal accident. Finally, in *Armstrong,* the court denied recovery to a wife who was erroneously told by the hospital that her husband was the victim of a severe car accident, which the wife did not contemporaneously perceive.

Here, there is a genuine issue of material fact as to whether Alaina observed the traumatic events occurring contemporaneously with the alleged failure of the Fire Extinguisher. Alaina may have observed the traumatic event through a sense other than visual perception, like the auditory observances in *Krysmalski* or *Neff.* In *Neff,* the court permitted a plaintiff-wife to recover under NIED where she did not visually observe the actual accident, but saw a speeding vehicle heading for her husband's pickup truck, heard the collision, and immediately ran out of her home to view her husband unconscious on the lawn. Likewise, the court in *Krysmalski* held that a plaintiff-mother properly established a claim for NIED, since, even though the mother did not visually witness a negligent driver hit her children, she heard the collision and knew that her kin were outside in the parking lot. While it is true that Alaina did not *see* her mother getting burned, the parties disagree as to whether or not Alaina was "within earshot of the laundry room" when Mrs. McDaniel tried to remove the burning pot. (Accordingly, since Alaina "never left the house" during the incident that was caused by the alleged failure of the Fire Extinguisher, summary judgment for Plaintiffs' NIED claim cannot be granted.

Defendants also argue that the Plaintiffs' NIED claim is flawed, as Plaintiffs allege that "Alaina witnessed her mother's injuries only *after* they had already been sustained." Again, while it is true that Alaina did not see Mrs. McDaniel's severe burns to the face until after the fire hit her flesh, the parties disagree as to whether Alaina was "within earshot of the laundry room" when Mrs. McDaniel tried to remove the burning pot when she sustained burns, thereby contemporaneously taking in the traumatic event through auditory or olfactory cues. Therefore, it is recommended that Defendants' Motion for Summary Judgment be denied in this respect.

Finally, the Defendants claim that there is "no evidence that Alaina McDaniel suffers or suffered from any physical manifestations of emotional distress arising out of the fire." In doing so, Defendants primarily rely upon *Armstrong,* 633 A.2d at 609; *Toney v. Chester Cty. Hosp.,* 961 A.2d 192 (Pa. Super. Ct. 2008); and *Love,* 606 A.2d at 1175. Plaintiffs *have* adduced physical manifestations of the emotional distress, the extent of which must be assessed by the trier of fact. Plaintiffs contend that Alaina "has suffered from nightmares and continues to suffer from nightmares," that she is "anxious and very tense," that she is "afraid of seeing flames and is nervous when her mother is cooking dinner," and that she is "more cautious, nervous, and reactionary." Certainly, these are not conditions of "temporary fright, nervous shock, nausea, grief, rage and humiliation" that the court would deny in *Armstrong.* Instead, like in *Love,* where "symptoms of severe depression, nightmares, stress and anxiety" sufficiently stated physical manifestations of emotional suffering to sustain a cause of action for NIED when a daughter witnessed her mother's heart attack proximately caused by her physician, Plaintiffs have done just the same. And, despite the Defendants' contention that "Alaina has never received any medical treatment," Pennsylvania law has rejected the necessity of medical evidence as a requirement for a NIED claim. For these reasons, it is recommended that Defendants' Motion for Summary Judgment regarding NIED be denied.

Philibert v. Kluser

385 P.3d 1038 (Or. 2016) (Balmer, J.)

[Plaintiffs were brothers, ages 8 and 12, who saw their 7-year-old brother killed by a car while the three were in a crosswalk. The car narrowly missed them. They filed sued in negligence, seeking damages for the anguish caused by witnessing his death, but not for having feared being hit. Relying on the impact rule, the appellate court upheld the trial court's dismissal of the complaint. The plaintiffs appealed.]

The first element is that the bystander must witness a sudden, *serious physical injury* to a *third person* negligently *caused* by the defendant.

Second, the plaintiff must have suffered *serious* emotional distress. It is a truism that emotional distress is an unavoidable and essential part of life. For that reason, our cases allow compensation for only serious emotional distress. A bystander who experiences emotional harm that does not rise to the level of serious emotional distress, therefore, cannot recover for that harm.

Third, in order to recover, the plaintiff must have perceived the events that caused injury to the third person as they occurred. This contemporaneous perception is at the core of the bystander's action for damages. Observation of the scene of an accident after it has happened, or perceiving a recently injured person, does not meet this requirement. This bright line rule is justified in part by the fact that the distressing life experience of learning about the death or injury of a loved one is unavoidable. Its inevitability means that in a general way one is prepared for it. In comparison, the visceral experience of witnessing the sudden death or injury of a loved one by a negligent driver, as here, is *not* a certain part of life and therefore presents a stronger basis for allowing recovery against the tortfeasor.

The final element of the claim is that the physically injured person be a close family member of the plaintiff. Witnessing the injury of a stranger or acquaintance, while likely distressing, is not sufficient to recover. As we recognized three decades ago, however, formal legal relationships only imprecisely capture the reality of emotional connections in our society. The fraternal relationship of plaintiffs here to the person killed meets that requirement, but other cases may present closer questions as to the meaning of "close family member." *See Restatement* § 48 comment f ("A grandparent who lives in the household may have a different status from a cousin who does not.").

We recognize that the bystander recovery rule may give rise to the possibility of false or inflated claims and that aspects of the rule may seem arbitrary. For as long as courts have awarded damages for emotional injuries, there have been concerns about plaintiffs bringing false claims. Juries are charged with discerning truth from self-serving fiction when plaintiffs testify about their own injuries and are as competent to do this in claims for emotional injuries as they are in other cases. Laws also may be structured to deter false claims by sympathetic plaintiffs whose charisma may evoke inconsistent and unpredictable jury verdicts.

In this area of the law in particular, some arbitrariness cannot be avoided. The undesirable arbitrary aspect of rules must be balanced against the need to provide *ex ante* understanding of liability and assistance in the orderly administration of justice.

Notes and Questions

1. <u>Why Insist on Impact?</u> Arkansas strictly follows the impact rule, and Nevada and Georgia hold closely to it. Are those courts callous or does the impact rule serve to avoid complex policy choices best left to legislatures? In answering that, consider that while *Lee* abandoned the strict impact rule, what does it require? Would the

Grizzle plaintiff's spouse have compensable harm under *Lee*? Would it matter if the *Grizzle* plaintiff had been killed? What facts would allow for recovery of damages for distress to the spouse of the *Grizzle* plaintiff under *Lee*? Under a bystander or zone-of-danger negligence-based claim? A pre-*Lee* case states that under Georgia law, the "impact rule governs emotional distress claims in products liability cases." *Stewart v. C. of Georgia R. Co.*, 87 F. Supp. 2d 1333 (S.D. Ga. 2000). Does *Lee* change that or is the nature of strict liability such that a different definition of the required damage should apply?

2. <u>Comparing Approaches</u>. The *Lee* case relaxed the impact rule, but only slightly. *McDaniel* and *Philibert* are more typical. Does any rule seem effective to differentiate false claims but permit legitimate claims to proceed? And *Lee* allows damages, but for what distress? Did *McDaniel* or *Philibert* misapprehend the distinction between zone-of-danger and bystander claims? Does either court's analysis make sense? In addition, recall that the measure of damage for either harm is in the jury's enlightened conscience. *See also Sawyer Bros., Inc. v. Island Transporter, LLC,* 887 F.3d 23 (1st Cir. 2018) (affirming judge's award of $50,000 to zone-of-danger plaintiff). Consider how the type of harm matters for purposes of instructing the jury and admitting evidence.

3. <u>Limiting Remedies by Requiring Physical Presence and Perception</u>. In *Entergy Miss., Inc. v. Acey,* 153 So. 3d 670 (Miss. 2015), plaintiff's daughter was severely burned when she came in contact with a sagging power line. Someone called plaintiff and told her to rush to the scene, where she saw her daughter with "smoke coming from her daughter's skin, skin flaking and turning gray, fingers missing and bones exposed, and she could smell the odor of burning flesh." The majority held that because she witnessed "her daughter's injuries, not the accident itself" she was not a "bystander." The dissent viewed the requirements of bystander damages as "factors" and on balance concluded her mental anguish was foreseeable. In response, the majority asked whether a person owed a duty to prevent the mother from seeing her daughter's body. Despite the holding, other courts have relaxed the requirement, holding bystander damages available to a relative who witnessed an injury or death "or the gruesome aftermath of such an event minutes after it occurs." *Groves v. Taylor,* 729 N.E.2d 569 (Ind. 2000).

4. <u>Limiting Bystander Remedies by Requiring a Close Relationship</u>. The *Philibert* court explained that courts generally require a bystander plaintiff have a close legal relationship with the injured plaintiff. In one case, a pregnant woman invited her sister to be in the delivery room, but during birth the surgeon cut a large portion of the baby's scalp. The sister sued for bystander damages. The court held that, while the sister may have had a sufficiently close relationship with the woman, she did not have a sufficiently close relationship with the injured plaintiff, her nephew. *McDaniel v. St. Francis, Med. Center,* 2012 WL 2878202 (Ct. App. Cal. July 16, 2012). *See Coronel v. GEICO Ins. Agency, Inc.,* 2015 WL 5607643 (D. Ariz. Sept. 24, 2015)

[handwritten margin note: confused b/c there was close rel ₵ ct. dismissed complaint? wrong]

(fiancé of injured plaintiff not permitted to recover, and collecting cases stating that stepchildren have likewise been held outside the scope of the tort).

5. <u>Fraudulent Claim</u>? In *Jenson v. Arndt,* 2018 WL 1702408 (Ct. App. Minn. Apr. 9, 2018), plaintiff Misty Jensen was living with her fiancé, Charles McQuinn, and children from earlier relationships. They were returning from a short vacation, where they had agreed to marry, when McQuinn, who was driving, said they were going too slowly. He grabbed her hand, and suddenly accelerated, but the car left the road and rolled, killing him and injuring her. At deposition, Jensen testified in a deposition that, for a time after the accident, she experienced increased depression and insomnia and that she continued to experience anxiety attacks with difficulty breathing, uncontrollable crying, and a spike in body temperature that brings on headaches and sweating. She sued the estate of her deceased fiancé. She sought damages for the harm of witnessing him injured and for the anguish she experienced for her own safety. The court held both forms of damage were recoverable. However, in *Schack v. Schack,* 414 P.3d 639 (Alaska 2018), family members were at home and heard a car wreck. When they rushed to the scene, the saw their daughter being extracted from the car; she later died. Their daughter caused the wreck by failing to stop at a yield sign. Her family members filed a claim against her estate, which was denied. They then sued for bystander damages. The court held that because the daughter caused their harm, they could not recover. Can you explain these cases?

6. <u>Products Liability</u>. Restatement (Second) Torts § 402A(1) provides: "One who sells any product in a defective condition unreasonably dangerous to the user or consumer . . . is subject to liability for physical harm thereby caused to the ultimate user or consumer." The courts that have analyzed whether they should use, for a products liability claim, the same definition of "damage" for a negligence claim have generally done so. The court in *Schmidt v. Boardman Co.,* 11 A.3d 924 (Pa. 2011), explained that states that had abandoned the impact rule for products liability nonetheless at most permitted recovery only to the extent that a plaintiff-bystander or individual in the zone of danger could in a negligence case. A concurring opinion explained:

> Section 402A does not require a "physical impact" for recovery for injuries sustained from a defective product. Rather, the Restatement merely requires that one be "physically harmed." Indeed, the OISR notes that "physical impact and physical injury are not synonymous terms." In common usage, "to injure" relates specifically to the harm done to another: "to cause physical harm; to hurt." The American Heritage College Dictionary 714 (4th ed.). "To impact" someone or something, however, does not require harm; rather, it is "the striking of one body against another; collision." *Id.* 694. Further, Section 7 of the Restatement, which contains definitions of terms to be used throughout the Restatement, defines "physical harm" as "physical impairment of the human body. Where the harm is impairment of the body, it is called 'bodily harm,' as to which see § 15."

Restatement (Second) Torts § 7 cmt. e. Section 15 then defines "bodily harm" as "any physical impairment of the condition of another's body, or physical pain or illness." Restatement (Second) Torts § 15. Critically, comment b to Section 15 states that disturbances to nerve centers caused by fear or shock do not constitute bodily harm, but such fear and shock may "result in some appreciable illness or have some other effect upon the physical condition of the body which constitutes bodily harm." Restatement (Second) Torts § 15 cmt. b. Conspicuously absent from these definitional sections is any reference to the term "impact." Thus, Section 402A, by its plain language, and in accord with its accompanying sections and expansive commentary, does not require, or even infer, that one must be "physically impacted" by a defective product in order for a plaintiff to recover damages. Instead, the Restatement merely requires "physical harm," or, alternatively stated, "bodily harm" or "physical impairment." All these terms, used interchangeably in the Restatement (Second) of Torts and this Court's jurisprudence, are functionally identical and distinct from "physical impact."

7. <u>Zone of Danger Claims</u>. Most courts permit a person to recover damages for fear of suffering an impact if the person was in the "zone of danger" when another person suffered an impact. However, some courts limit recovery to persons who were not just in the zone of danger, but "closely related" to the person who suffered the impact, to impacts that caused death or severe bodily injury, or both. *See Engler v. Illinois Farmers Ins. Co.*, 706 N.W.2d 764 (Minn. 2005) (requiring both a close relationship to a person who was at least severely injured). They also disagree on the measure of damages, some permitting recovery only for the fear of being injured but others allowing recover for the anguish caused by witnessing negligent injury to another. *See id.*

8. <u>Consequential Damages</u>. If a plaintiff suffers the type of harm required by the state's approach to these claims, then in addition to damages for the distress, the plaintiff can recover consequential damages for things such as medical or psychiatric expenses and lost wages.

3. Battery

Battery requires that the defendant intended to cause a harmful or offensive contact with the plaintiff's person. *Swope v. Columbian Chems. Co.*, 281 F.3d 185 (5th Cir. 2002). The plaintiff does not need to have been aware the contact occurred, and indirect contact is sufficient: an object controlled by the defendant can cause the contact and, further, contact with something on the plaintiff is sufficient. *Id.* (contact "with an inanimate object controlled or precipitated by the actor, such as the surgeon's scalpel, a bullet or even a thrown hamburger"). Battery includes an intentional harmful *or* offensive contact. A harmful contact likely satisfies and overlaps with the impact requirement of negligence, but an "offensive" contact likely would not. Unlike negligence claims, for battery, merely an "unwanted touching itself constitutes the injury to the plaintiff." *Darnell v. Houston County Bd. of Ed.*, 234 Ga. App. 488 (1998).

Although "the harm inflicted is difficult or even impossible to quantify," an award of "general damages or presumed damages of a substantial amount can be recovered merely upon showing that the tort was committed at all." *Johnson v. Pankratz*, 2 P.3d 1266 (Ct. App. Ariz. 2000). *See Magma Copper Co. v. Shuster*, 118 Ariz. 151 (Ct. App. Ariz. 1977) (nominal damages proper because "plaintiff's rights were technically invaded even though he suffered, or could prove, no loss or damage."). The measure of damages for an offensive contact is an amount in the jury's enlightened conscience. *See Baccera v. Tucson Police Dept.*, 2009 WL 189067 (Ct. App. Ariz. June 12, 2009).

Johnson v. Jones
269 Or. App. 12 (Feb. 11, 2015) (Haselton, J.)

[Defendant, a 69-year-old-dentist who knew he had genital herpes, used an online dating site to meet the plaintiff, a 49-year-old woman. He did not tell her of his condition. After a few dates, they started kissing at her home. After it became clear they were going to have sex, she asked him to wear a condom, and he agreed. Instead, however, he surprised her by jumping on top of her as she lay naked on her bed and putting his penis in her mouth, and then they had intercourse. Immediately afterward, he became quiet. In response to her question as to whether they had "chemistry," he revealed he had genital herpes. She panicked and grew angry. He responded, "Don't worry, I'm not having any lesions," and told her he knew counselors she could talk to, and she should "see a doctor as soon as possible." She kicked him out of her house. She immediately saw a doctor and learned she had contracted genital herpes. It caused her severe pain and mental distress. She brought a battery claim. In addition to an award for her medical bills, the jury awarded $900,000 for the battery itself. The defendant appealed.]

A battery claim may derive from a contact that is either harmful or offensive in nature. That is so because "battery redresses injury both to an individual's physical integrity and to an individual's dignitary interests." *Doe v. Lake Oswego School District*, 353 Or. 321 (2013). Consequently, the actionable touching need not be physically harmful if it is offensive—that is, if it offends a reasonable sense of personal dignity—and the requisite scienter is the intent to engage in such offensive contact, and not the intent to cause physical harm from such contact. Thus, contrary to defendant's premise that plaintiff was required to prove that he acted with the intent to cause her physical harm (by infecting her), such an intent is inapposite with respect to the "offensive contact" variant of battery.

Here, as we will explain, the evidence was sufficient to permit the jury to determine that defendant intended to subject plaintiff to "offensive contact." We necessarily preface that discussion with a brief description of the meaning of the term "offensive contact" under Oregon law, because that is the referent of the requisite intent.

In *Doe*, the Oregon Supreme Court explained that a variety of circumstances, including the nature of the parties' relationship, are material to determining whether a defendant has engaged in actionable offensive contact:

> Familiarities not justified by the peculiar association of the parties must conform to the usages of the community and contacts not thus sanctioned may be actionable batteries. Although the state of mind of the actor may make offensive contact not otherwise so and, conversely, make inoffensive acts that, if done in anger, would be highly objectionable, nevertheless even well-intentioned acts, such as practical jokes or horseplay, may be actionable if they exceed the bounds of tolerable taste.

Consistent with those principles, the jury, in determining whether the contact was "offensive" and whether defendant acted with the necessary appreciation of that quality, demonstrating the requisite intent, could consider the relationship between the parties, the nature of the contact, and whether the contact conforms to the usages of the community.

Here, plaintiff presented evidence of defendant's knowledge and conduct that was sufficient to support a nonspeculative inference that defendant knew that he was subjecting plaintiff to a contact that would offend a reasonable sense of personal dignity. In particular, the jury could reasonably infer that defendant knew that plaintiff would not consent to unprotected sexual contact if she were aware of his condition — that is, such contact would be "offensive" — and that defendant, nevertheless, intentionally subjected plaintiff to such contact. To reiterate: Defendant — a medical professional who had lived with the social and health consequences of genital herpes for 20 years — knew that plaintiff was unaware of that condition; nevertheless, even when it became clear that he and plaintiff were going to engage in sexual contact, he did not disclose his condition. Further, even after plaintiff had expressly told defendant to use a condom and defendant had said that he would do so, he unilaterally proceeded to initiate unprotected sex. Given the parties' medical training and other circumstances, the jury could reasonably infer that defendant understood that plaintiff sought protection against exposure to STIs but proceeded in intentional disregard of her directive.

Given that evidence, the jury could find that defendant understood, in the totality of the circumstances, that subjecting plaintiff to sexual contact without disclosing his condition was offensive — that is, that it offended a reasonable sense of personal dignity — and that, notwithstanding that awareness, he nevertheless intentionally subjected plaintiff to such contact. Accordingly, the trial court correctly denied the directed verdict.

Myers v. Central Florida Inv. Inc.

592 F.3d 1201 (11th Cir. 2010) (Marcus, J).

[Plaintiff Myers sold timeshares for the defendant. The sole shareholder and CEO of defendant Central Florida Investments, Inc., was defendant David Siegel. Siegel was romantically interested in Myers, but she had a boyfriend. He tried to kiss her, offered to buy her lavish gifts, and even gave her a $10,000 check. She rebuffed him and said "Our friendship does not have a price tag on it. How many times do I have to tell you?"

He persisted and she resisted. He moved his office to be closer to hers. He would hug her at work and let his hand slip down and touch her behind in front of coworkers. He continued, at one point touching her breasts. When she began a new relationship, he touched her inappropriately, pinned her against the wall, and made lewd comments. Throughout this time, she reported Siegel to the company's HR department, but their response was: "What are you going to do, he's the president of the company?" Rumors began to spread, and she was humiliated. She was suspended in December 2000, earning $102,223.14 in her final year.

She filed an EEOC complaint, alleging sexual discrimination, but took no further action until three years later when CFI sued for $6,200 on an unpaid loan. She counterclaimed for battery and other claims. All claims but her battery claim were barred by limitations. The jury found that all the offensive touching occurred after May 21, 2000, the critical date for statute of limitations on battery. The jury awarded $102,223.14 in compensatory damages. Defendants appealed.]

Under Florida law, jury awards are evaluated under a five-factor test. Fla. Stat. § 768.74(5). Taking each factor in turn, we hold that the district court did not abuse its discretion in upholding the jury's award of compensatory damages.

The first factor asks whether the award evinces passion or prejudice. A jury instructed to consider compensatory damages for emotional harm is asked to place a dollar amount on one person's suffering. The inquiry is inherently subjective, as jurors bring their own experiences to bear on another person's humiliation, discomfort, and shame. The objective—to make a plaintiff whole—plainly is a difficult one, and the means employed are far from perfect. But we will not prohibit jurors from considering a legitimate measure as they go about their task.

A plaintiff's income is relevant insofar as it affords some indication, however imprecise, of the costs imposed on an employee whose time in the workplace is inundated and spoiled by a defendant's behavior. Many of the touchings described by Myers, particularly the two incidents during which Siegel pinned her against the wall in the spa, occurred in 2000, the year in which Myers earned $102,223.14 from CFI. She testified that Siegel's behavior during this period humiliated her in front of her coworkers and drained her of her desire to go to work. In attempting to set a dollar amount that would properly compensate her for emotional suffering, the jury was permitted to consider, among other things, her salary for the time in which she was subjected to the unlawful behavior. Her salary at the very least gives some indication to the jury as to how Myers valued her time at work, from which they may properly infer the amount of emotional suffering that flowed from those workplace batteries. To hold otherwise, and deprive juries of resort to income, would make the jury's difficult task that much more improbable.

The second statutory factor asks whether the jury ignored evidence or misconceived the merits of the case. As we have noted, the jury was permitted to conclude that several instances of battery occurred on or after May 21, 2000, the statutory cutoff. There is no reason to believe that a jury which has discounted the testimony of defense witnesses and the explanations of defense counsel has misapprehended a case. The standard of review for awards of compensatory damages for intangible, emotional harm is deferential to the fact finder because the harm is subjective and evaluating it depends considerably on the demeanor of the witnesses.

Florida's third statutory factor asks whether improper elements were considered, or if the verdict was based on conjecture. Defendants argue that emotional damages were never proven by medical testimony. But emotional damages need not be supported by medical testimony in Florida. Defendants also say that no reasonable jury could award $100,000 for a single battery, and that the award, therefore, took into account incidents unrelated to the battery, including time-barred material. Even if we were to assume that the jury did consider material external to the battery itself, we conclude that the award may still stand. Under Florida law, a tortfeasor is liable for the "entire unapportionable injuries" sustained by a plaintiff, even if those injuries were heightened by prior incidents for which the defendant cannot be held liable. *Cf. Gross v. Lyons,* 763 So.2d 276 (Fla. 2000) (noting that "subsequent tortfeasors have been liable for entire unapportionable injuries"); *C.F. Hamblen, Inc. v. Owens,* 127 Fla. 91 (Fla. 1937) ("It is settled law that where injuries aggravate an existing ailment or develop a latent one the person whose negligence caused the injury is required to respond in damages for the results of the disease as well as the original injury."). The jury was permitted to consider the role the sexual harassment and prior batteries played in heightening the damages flowing from this battery, even if that behavior was itself time-barred. *Cf. Stockett v. Tolin,* 791 F.Supp. 1536 (S.D. Fla. 1992) (stating that a plaintiff's "pre-existing" vulnerability, or "greater sensitivity, does not warrant any reduction in her recovery. The Defendants must take the plaintiff as they find her").

The fourth statutory factor asks whether the award is reasonably related to the damages suffered. This compensatory award of a little over $100,000 is not so great as to bear no reasonable relation to the damages she suffered. *See Baldwin v. McConnell,* 273 Va. 650 (Va. 2007) (approving a $100,000 compensatory award for assault and battery); *Nash v. Sue Har Equities, LLC,* 846 N.Y.S.2d 215 (N.Y. App. Div. 2007) (awarding $100,000 for assault). Furthermore, since this battery involved a boss plainly taking advantage of his employee over an extended time frame, we can tolerate damages which may be higher than normal. *Cf. Hughston v. New Home Media,* 552 F.Supp.2d 559 (E.D.Va. 2008) ("There can be few more insulting injuries than being subjected to unwelcome sexual touchings by a supervisor, accompanied by lewd solicitations for sex, in the workplace.").

The fifth and final statutory factor asks whether the award is supported by evidence and can be logically adduced by reasonable people. For all the reasons outlined above—the existence of the battery, the existence of prior harassment and touchings that might have heightened damage flowing from the battery, and the superior-subordinate relationship of Siegel and Myers—this award is supported by the evidence and appears to be the result of a logical process conducted by reasonable people.

Since the compensatory award falls within a range of damages reasonable under Florida law, it does not constitute a clear abuse of discretion for the district court to let it stand. Defendants are correct that a smaller award would have been reasonable, too, but this award is entitled to a presumption of validity, and they have failed to overcome that presumption.

Notes and Questions

1. Jury Awards. Juries are given broad discretion to determine the amount of damages for a harmful contact. E.g., Aldworth Co. v. England, 622 S.E.2d 367 (Ct. App. Ga. 2005) (affirming $750,000 award for punching plaintiff in the face, which had caused $10,000 in lost wages and medical expenses). In Stover v. Atchley, 374 S.E.2d 775 (Ct. App. Ga. 1989), the defendant choked his grandfather, spat on him, and threw him against a wall, while yelling "die old man, damn it, die!" A jury awarded $25,000. The defendant appealed, and the court affirmed:

> Generally, any unlawful touching is a physical injury to the person and is actionable. Moreover, the law infers bodily pain and suffering from personal injury and general damages are said to include the bodily suffering endured. The only guideline for awarding damages for pain and suffering is the enlightened conscience of an impartial jury. If the award is not so flagrant as to shock the conscience, it will not be disturbed.

> In the present case, the jury was authorized to find that the appellee had suffered physical injuries as the result of a violent, physical attack by the appellant. Thus, in the absence of any showing of actual bias, we cannot say that the verdict returned by the jury in this case, and approved by the trial judge, is so excessive as a matter of law as to justify the inference of bias.

Is it fair to compare the award in either principal case to these two to argue that the amount was either excessive or inadequate? In Myers, why was her salary relevant? Why was it proper for the Myers jury award to approximate the plaintiff's salary? If Ms. Myers had made $25,000 a year and the jury awarded $100,000, would that be reversed? In addition, what nuance on eggshell plaintiffs does Myers recognize? Consider also, if you compare verdicts to test their adequacy, does it matter how much the plaintiff in the case makes when making that comparison?

2. <u>A Sliding Scale</u>. As noted in the discussion of the "impact" earlier in this chapter, battery provides a remedy for a contact that is insufficient to be an "impact" for negligence. Has allowing damages for merely an offensive contact opened the floodgates of litigation and led to fake or exaggerated claims? What element of battery serves a purpose similar to the impact rule?

3. <u>Consequential Damages</u>. "It is a basic principle of law, known to first-year law students, that when an individual commits an intentional tort, such as battery, that person is liable for all harm proximately caused by the individual's intentionally wrongful action." *In re Shaw,* 2010 WL 3738028 (D. Nev. Sept. 20, 2010). So, for example, a plaintiff may recover past lost wages. *Lynch v. Fanning,* 859 N.E.2d 457 (Ct. App. Mass. 2006) (affirming award of lost wages to plaintiff who had been battered by condo owner at condo where plaintiff worked as a janitor, even though plaintiff did not return to work for 14 months after being medically cleared to return to work, given plaintiff's testimony that delay was because battery had made him afraid of returning to work, where plaintiff still lived). Consequential damages commonly arising from personal injury cases are fully discussed after all claims redressing harm to persons.

4. Assault

Olivero v. Lowe

995 P.2d 1023 (Nev. 2000) (Maupin, J.)

[Plaintiff, Montgomery Lowe, was in charge of a construction project to build a new home. Robert Louis Olivero was a construction worker at the site. Lowe confronted Olivero about construction being behind schedule. In response, Olivero pulled out a pistol, punched Lowe in the face, and threatened to kill Lowe unless he torn down part of the home. Lowe did so.

Lowe later sued Olivero, asserting claims for assault, battery, and intentional infliction of emotional distress (IIED). Lowe testified that the punch had caused pain and suffering, contusions, and emotional distress. Lowe testified the assault—both by being threatened with a gun and by having his life threatened unless he tore down part of the home—caused him severe emotional distress. He testified, however, that he had not sought medical or psychological treatment for any physical or emotional injury. After a bench trial, the trial court awarded Lowe compensatory damages of $5,000 for the battery, $5,000 for the assault, and no damages for IIED. The trial court reasoned that any recovery of distress caused by IIED was included in the damages from the assault and battery claims. Olivero appealed.]

Although Lowe required no medical or psychological treatment, we conclude that the district court properly awarded Lowe compensatory damages arising from both the assault and the battery.

First, there was a physical impact that provided the objective predicate for personal injury and emotional distress recovery in connection with the battery claim. Second, the nature of a claim of assault is such that the safeguards against illusory recoveries are not necessary. Third, claims for assault and battery provide the outer limits of extreme outrage. Thus, an assault, a tort that does not require a physical impact, is in and of itself a predicate for an award of nominal or compensatory damages without proof of "serious emotional distress." Thus, the standard of proof for emotional distress damages arising from assault and battery is not as stringent as the standard of proof requirement for bare claims of intentional or negligent infliction of emotional distress.

Lowe testified that he still experiences the terror of the incident through extreme nervousness, and that he has been forced to discontinue his independent contractor business out of fear of working in an unsecure environment.

It is the function of the trier of fact to award compensatory damages, and it is not the role of the appellate court to substitute its judgment for that of the trier of fact. There is no evidence to indicate that the damage awards to Lowe were excessive. Certainly the circumstances at issue were extreme enough to stimulate the extent of emotional distress described. Therefore, we conclude that the compensatory awards totaling $10,000 were not excessive.

Notes and Questions

1. <u>Less Concern for Fraud?</u> The *Olivero* court expressed what is implicit in many cases: with only negligently inflicted emotional distress, courts "worry" about false or exaggerated claims, concerns alleviated by requiring intent. The Restatement explains that "as the focus shifts from physical harm to other forms of harm, the intent to cause harm may be an important but not a sufficient condition of liability." Restatement (Third) of Torts: Liability for Physical Harm § 5 (Preliminary Final Draft No. 1 (2005). What else limits the reach of assault such that false or exaggerated claims will not be common?

2. <u>Is There a Remedy for Imminent Apprehension of an Offensive Contact?</u> Some courts recognize that the nature of the threat required and remedied by assault is distinct from battery: generally, "assault occurs when all the apparent circumstances, reasonably viewed, are such as to lead a person reasonably to apprehend a violent injury from the unlawful act of another." *Equal Empl. Opportunity Commn. v. Nunez, Inc.*, 2011 WL 13168394 (N.D. Ga. Feb. 28, 2011), *report and recommendation adopted*, 2011 WL 13175436 (Mar. 14, 2011). Put another way, some courts hold the apprehension of being imminently offensively touched is not an assault, but instead "an assault occurs when all the apparent circumstances, reasonably viewed, are such as to lead a person reasonably to apprehend a violent injury from the unlawful act of another." *Id.*

3. <u>Measure of Damage.</u> Assault provides a remedy for the distress caused by apprehending imminent violent injury, if intentionally caused. Where "the entire

injury is to the peace, happiness, or feelings of the plaintiff," the measure of damages is left to the "enlightened consciences of impartial jurors." *Dalton v. Vanheath, LLP,* 2013 WL 6858862 (M.D. Ga. Dec. 30, 2013). And, as noted above, if the plaintiff establishes assault, including the required damages, then consequential damages — psychiatric bills, lost wages, and the like — are recoverable.

5. Intentional Infliction of Emotional Distress or "Outrageous Conduct"

Many states follow Restatement (Second) Torts §46, which recognizes two claims, the first subsection for "direct" IIED claims and the second for "indirect" claims:

> (1) One who by extreme and outrageous conduct intentionally or recklessly causes severe emotional distress to another is subject to liability for such emotional distress, and if bodily harm to the other results from it, for such bodily harm.

> (2) Where such conduct is directed at a third person, the actor is subject to liability if he intentionally or recklessly causes severe emotional distress

> > a. To a member of such person's immediate family who is present at the time, whether or not such distress results in bodily harm, or

> > b. To any other person who is present at the time, if such distress results in bodily harm.

A defendant's conduct must "transcend all bounds of decency." The court in *Yarbrough v. SAS Systems*, 204 Ga. App. 428 (1992), provided a common definition of the required conduct:

> Liability for this tort has been found only where the conduct has been so outrageous in character, and so extreme in degree, as to go beyond all possible bounds of decency, and to be regarded as atrocious, and utterly intolerable in a civilized community. Generally, the case is one in which the recitation of the facts to an average member of the community would arouse his resentment against the actor, and lead him to exclaim, "Outrageous!"

This can include conduct that would not be actionable if done once, but had been repeated, or even once if the defendant had directed the conduct at a plaintiff the defendant knew was particularly vulnerable. In either circumstance, conduct that might not be "outrageous" may be so. Courts often determine, as a matter of law, whether the conduct is actionable. In doing so, they often reason that the less extreme the conduct, "the greater the need for evidence of physical injury or illness from the emotional distress." *Kelley v. City of Henderson*, 2017 WL 2802732 (D. Nev. June 27, 2017). In addition, as a historic relic, innkeepers and common carriers are liable for less serious misconduct, including a gross insult that causes severe distress.

A recent Kentucky case, *Hoover v. D.W. Wilburn, Inc.*, 2014 WL 5064459 (Ct. App. Ky. Jan. 9, 2015), listed collected cases holding this conduct as sufficient for a claim of IIED: (1) harassed the plaintiff by keeping her under surveillance at work and home, telling her over a CB radio that he would put her husband in jail and driving so as to force her vehicle into an opposing lane of traffic; (2) intentionally failed to warn plaintiff for five months that defendant's building, in which plaintiff was removing pipes and ducts, contained asbestos; (3) committed sexual harassment by frequent incidents of lewd name-calling coupled with multiple unsolicited and unwanted requests for homosexual sex; (4) a Catholic priest who used his relationship as marriage counselor for the plaintiff husband and his wife to have a sexual affair with the wife; (5) agreed to care for plaintiff's long-time companion animals, two registered Appaloosa horses, and then immediately sold them for slaughter; and (6) subjected plaintiff to nearly daily racial indignities for approximately seven years. *See Johnson v. Allen*, 613 S.E.2d 657 (Ct. App. Ga. 2005) (claim by female workers against employer who had hidden surveillance cameras in women's restroom); *Bakay v. Yarnes*, 2005 WL 1677966 (W.D. Wash. July 19, 2005) (maliciously killing plaintiff's pet cats).

That same case identified this conduct as insufficient: (1) refused to pay medical expenses arising out of an injured worker's compensation claim; (2) wrongfully converted the plaintiff's property in a manner that breached the peace; (3) negligently allowed his vehicle to leave the road and struck and killed a child; (4) committed reprehensible fraud during divorce proceedings by converting funds belonging to his spouse for the benefit of defendant and his adulterous partner; (5) wrongfully terminated the plaintiff; (6) displayed a lack of compassion, patience, and taste by ordering plaintiff, who was hysterical over the fact that she had just delivered a stillborn child in her hospital room, to "shut up" and then informing her that the stillborn child would be "disposed of" in the hospital; (7) erected a billboard referring to defendant's status as a convicted child molester; (8) wrongfully garnished plaintiff's wages using a forged agreement; (9) impregnated plaintiff's wife; (10) a Catholic priest sexually abused a 10-year-old boy; (11) chained a high school student to a tree by his ankle and neck; and (12) shot and killed a beloved family pet, which had been misidentified as a stray dog.

A plaintiff has a claim under subsection (2) of the Restatement against a defendant whose conduct was directed toward a third party only if the plaintiff suffered severe emotional distress and either: (a) was a family member then present or (b) the distress caused bodily harm. *See Waterhouse v. Hollingsworth*, 2010 WL 8250801 (Del. Super. Ct. May 3, 2010). The Restatement gives an example of a wife being present when her husband is murdered and states the requirement "may be justified by the practical necessity of drawing the line somewhere, since the number of persons who may suffer emotional distress at the news of an assassination of the President is virtually unlimited, and the distress of a woman who is informed of her husband's murder 10 years afterward may lack the guarantee of genuineness which her presence on the spot would afford. *The Caveat is intended, however, to leave open the possibility of situations in which presence at the time may not be required."* Restatement (Second) of Torts § 46 (1965) (emph. added). It goes on to state "there appears to be no essential reason why a stranger who is asked for a match on the street should not recover when the man who asks for it is shot down before his eyes, at least where his emotional distress results in bodily harm." *Id.* Can you think of reasons why recovery should be denied? Consider the following materials.

Turley v. ISG Lackawanna, Inc.

774 F.3d 140 (2d Cir. 2014) (Sack, J.)

[Plaintiff Elijah Turley long and happily had worked in the "pickler" department at a steel plant. After he filed a grievance against a co-worker, things changed. For several years afterward, racist slurs were hurled at him, he was threatened, referred to as a "boy," co-workers referred to him as "that f—n—-" over the company inter-com, and they had threatened him repeatedly. His complaints to management went unanswered. He brought a statutory claim based on race discrimination and an IIED claim, not against those co-workers, but against supervisors and plant managers. The jury awarded $1,320,000 in damages, finding liability against supervisor Sampsel and the corporate entity, Lackawanna, and separating out damages for IIED from that statutory claim. Defendants appealed.]

The IIED tort is problematic. It provides a remedy for the damages that arise out of a defendant engaging in extreme and outrageous conduct, which so transcends the bounds of decency as to be regarded as atrocious and intolerable in a civilized society. To prevail on such a claim, a plaintiff must establish that there was extreme and outrageous conduct, that the conduct was undertaken with intent to cause, or disregard of a substantial probability of causing, severe emotional distress, and that the conduct did in fact cause severe emotional distress.

The defendants principally contend the record contains insufficient evidence to hold Sampsell and Lackawanna liable in light of the high hurdles presented by New York's rendition of the tort. We conclude there is sufficient evidence.

Sampsell, the plant's head of security, was the only person the jury found liable on this claim, and his acts, the defendants contend, consisted largely of failing to respond appropriately to reports of harassment. Ordinarily, the failure to respond appropriately to complaints of harassment, on its own, will not be sufficiently egregious—"outrageous"—to amount to intentional infliction of emotional distress under New York law. General bureaucratic unresponsiveness, lethargy, or a failure to understand the gravity of a situation, although objectionable, is rarely if ever considered so beyond the pale as to reach the extreme threshold necessary for an IIED claim. But, under New York law, an IIED claim does not turn on a distinction between action and omission. The ultimate question remains whether the conduct proven at trial, in light of all the circumstances, was utterly intolerable in a civilized community.

Sampsell permitted the hate-ridden and menacing environment to persist for more than three years. On multiple occasions, he ignored, and failed to discipline employees responsible for, harassment of the plaintiff. He blocked the efforts of local police to investigate threats against Turley. Rather than address Turley's complaints, Sampsell set up a hidden camera that, whatever its intended purpose, in fact surveilled Turley while he worked. Although Sampsell was in charge of security for the plant, he did nothing when, in his presence, Turley was subjected to a vicious barrage of racial slurs. And when Turley and a witness went to Sampsell's office to report a particularly degrading verbal assault, they found Sampsell with the offending co-worker, laughing.

In these circumstances, Sampsell's behavior cannot be described as a simple failure to take timely action in response to a harassment complaint. Even a sluggish or incompetent response to two, three, or four complaints might not rise to clear the high bar set for this tort in this State. But Sampsell was a personal witness to the ongoing and severe indignity, humiliation, and torment to which the plaintiff was subjected over a substantial period of time—and he was in a position to do something about it. Instead, he continuously failed to respond for more than three years, blocking others' efforts to investigate serious threats, and, at times, seeming to encourage further harassment. On these facts, we see no error.

We also reject the defendants' claim that the compensatory damages award exceeded what is permissible. The calculation of damages is the province of the jury, and we will not vacate or reduce a jury award merely because we would have granted a lesser amount of damages.

The jury in the case at bar awarded Turley $1,320,000 for his past and future emotional distress, mental anguish, inconvenience, and loss of enjoyment of life. Most of the award was compensation attributed to the [statutory] harassment claim, with $260,000 awarded under the claim for IIED. The defendants argue that the compensatory award was disproportionately large relative to jury awards in similar cases. They are correct insofar as there are few recorded cases in which the plaintiff claimed exclusively intangible harms and received a compensatory damages award of quite this magnitude. For example, in a 2012 case involving a similarly protracted and vicious course of harassment, we upheld an award of $1 million, which the district court had reduced from $1.25 million. *See Zeno v. Pine Plains Cent. Sch. Dist.*, 702 F.3d 655 (2d Cir. 2012). But, as we noted at the outset of the opinion, the case before us appears to be unique, combining years of grotesque psychological abuse leading to a marked decline in Turley's mental health and well-being. He was hospitalized and diagnosed with, *inter alia*, post-traumatic stress disorder, depression, and panic disorder as a result of the harassment that he suffered. These injuries were extensive and well documented. The plaintiff in *Zeno*, by contrast, does not appear to have sought medical attention for his emotional injuries.

Moreover, a compensatory award of this magnitude is not entirely without precedent. The Sixth Circuit in *Pollard v. E.I. DuPont De Nemours, Inc.*, 412 F.3d 657 (6th Cir. 2005), affirmed a judgment granting, among other things, $1.25 million for IIED in a sexual harassment claim mirroring this one in terms of length and severity. Taking inflation into account, the $1.25 million award exceeds the $1.32 million compensatory damages award in this case. Smaller damages awards in cases dating back ten or more years and involving less severe conduct also support affirming a larger award in this case. *See, e.g., Phillips v. Bowen,* 278 F.3d 103 (2d Cir. 2002) (sustaining $400,000 award for distress after sheriff's deputy was "shunned" by colleagues and mistreated for supporting an opposing candidate for sheriff); *Chopra v. Gen. Elec. Co.,* 527 F.Supp.2d 230 (D. Conn. 2007) (sustaining award of $500,000 in non-economic damages where retaliatory actions by employer caused extreme stress and poor health); *Town of Hempstead v. State Div. Human Rights,* 233 A.D.2d 451 (2d Dep't 1996) (upholding $500,000 award for pattern of "extremely lewd and offensive conduct" over period of about nine months).

We thus acknowledge that the jury's compensatory award tests the boundaries of proportionality and predictability. But under the exceptional and egregious facts of this case, we conclude that the $1.32 million compensatory award was fair and reasonable. Recognizing also the deference that we owe to the district court, which was closer to the evidence, and therefore in a better position to determine whether a particular award is excessive, will not disturb that award.

Notes and Questions

1. <u>What Harm Is Required?</u> IIED is disfavored because it does not require fear of injury, as does assault; or contact, as does battery; or an impact or "physical manifestation" (to someone, even for derivative claims), as does negligence. What does it require?

2. <u>IIED as a Narrow Gap Filler.</u> The *Turley* defendants failed to argue in the trial court that IIED was unavailable because plaintiff had a statutory claim, yet courts hold IIED is "not intended to supplant or duplicate existing statutory or common-law remedies," *Creditwatch, Inc. v. Jackson,* 157 S.W.3d 814 (Tex. 2005), but solely allows "recovery in those rare instances in which a defendant intentionally inflicts severe emotional distress in a manner so unusual that the victim has no other theory of redress." *Conradt v. NBC Universal, Inc.,* 536 F. Supp. 2d 380 (S.D.N.Y. 2008). Another reason courts view IIED with disfavor is that recovery for IIED based upon words alone implicates the First Amendment. In *Gleason v. Smolinski,* 319 Conn. 394 (2015), a 31-year-old man, Bill, had gone missing in 2004, and was never heard from again. His mother and sister suspected his ex-girlfriend of foul play because of a bizarre love triangle. The mother and sister made disparaging remarks to her friends, put flyers up with Bill's picture near her home and the bus route she worked, and said they believed she had caused his disappearance. They confronted her, shouting, and calling her names. The ex-girlfriend sued the mother and sister, and the trial court held their conduct was sufficient, and her harm severe enough, to award $32,000 (along with $7,500 for defamation). The defendants appealed, asserting the award violated the First Amendment under *Snyder v. Phelps,* 562 U.S. 443 (2011), which held the First Amendment bars damages for claims based on

constitutionally protected speech. The appellate court remanded, ordering the trial court to consider whether, if protected speech were excluded, their conduct was sufficient to award damages for IIED.

3. <u>The Measure of IIED Damages and Recovery of Consequential Damages</u>. Although severe distress is required, the "eggshell" plaintiff rule applies. *See Offei v. Omar,* 2012 WL 2086294 (S.D.N.Y. May 18, 2012) (court awarded $250,000 in damages, on claims for battery and IIED, where defendant hotel guest had forcibly kissed plaintiff, a hotel maid, twice, fondled her breasts, and rubbed himself against her, noting that "perhaps because of cultural norms, the plaintiff appears to have been particularly vulnerable" and her "guilt and even shame" were exacerbated by publicity surrounding the event). In this regard, IIED can result in significant awards and is subject to deferential judicial review. As *Sabir v. Jowett,* 214 F. Supp. 2d 226 (D. Conn. 2002) (upholding $75,000 for IIED), explained, the "size of the verdict alone does not determine whether it is excessive," given the "necessarily uncertain limits of just damages," but can be set aside only if the size "so shocks the sense of justice as to compel the conclusion that the jury was influenced by partiality, prejudice, mistake or corruption." Courts scrutinize IIED awards because a successful plaintiff can recover consequential damages. *See Hughes v. Patrolmen's Benevolent Ass'n,* 850 F.2d 876 (2d Cir. 1988) (affirming lost wages where defendants' outrageous conduct ruined plaintiff's chance for promotion).

6. Harm to a Person That Harms Plaintiff's Relationship with That Injured Person

If a person is injured and could successfully assert a claim against a defendant, if that injury causes harm to a relationship between the injured person and the plaintiff, the plaintiff may also have a claim for damages for harm to that relationship. This claim is "loss of consortium." All states permit the spouse of an injured person to recover for loss of consortium. Some states allow someone other than a spouse to do so.

The loss of consortium plaintiff (the "LOC Plaintiff") need not have been a bystander, and loss of consortium damages are distinct from bystander damages: the "damage" required is harm to the relationship caused by the injury to the other person. So, for example, a husband whose wife was injured in a car wreck may have a loss of consortium claim against the other driver if the spouse's injuries harmed their marital relationship. The required harm is to "the interests of an injured party's spouse in the continuance of the marital relationship." *Johansen v. E.D. Restaurant Corp.,* 2001 N.Y. Slip Op. (N.Y. Supp. Ct. July 16, 2001). There are two aspects to the harm: (1) tangible (i.e., pecuniary) and (2) intangible.

Tangible harm includes expenses that the LOC Plaintiff incurred to replace services, such as for household chores, that the injured spouse is unable to do around the home. *Coho Resources, Inc. v. McCarthy*, 829 So. 2d 1 (Miss. 2002) ("Consortium does not consist alone of intangible mental and emotional elements, but may include services performed by the husband for the wife which have a monetary value."). Beyond that, as *Axen v. Am. Home Products Corp.*, 974 P.2d 224 (Ct. App. Or.), *mod.*, 981 P.2d 340 (1999), stated:

> The majority of courts have concluded that the only economic damages available to an uninjured spouse as part of a claim for loss of consortium are those damages incurred in replacing the material services and support previously provided by the injured spouse. A few jurisdictions have also included the reasonable cost of care provided to the injured spouse by the uninjured spouse, but the majority have followed the rule that those costs are more properly included in the injured spouse's claim.

Intangible losses include "the loss of support, love, companionship, affection, society, sexual relations, solace, and more." *Johansen.* Thus, a typical jury instruction on this aspect provides:

> On the claim brought by (spouse), you should award (spouse) an amount of money which the greater weight of the evidence shows will fairly and adequately compensate (spouse) for any loss by reason of [his wife's] [her husband's] injury, of [his] [her] services, comfort, society and attentions in the past [and in the future] caused by the incident in question.

The measure of damages for intangible harm is left to a jury's enlightened conscience. *Taylor v. Taylor*, 654 S.E.2d 146 (Ct. App. Ga. 2007). However, courts carefully instruct juries to not compensate the LOC Plaintiff for harm to the spouse and scrutinize verdicts to avoid that.

A claim can be brought with, before, after, or even without the injured spouse asserting a claim. However:

- A loss of consortium claim requires the injured person to have succeeded, or succeed, on a claim against the defendant, or the LOC Plaintiff must persuade the jury that the injured person could succeed on a hypothetical claim against the defendant. *Saranchuk v. Lello*, 2017 WL 4573742 (M.D. Pa. Oct. 13, 2017) (although it "remains a separate and distinct cause of action, a plaintiff still cannot recover for loss of consortium in the absence of the defendant's liability to his or her spouse."); *Erickson v. U-Haul Int'l.*, 767 N.W.2d 765 (Neb. 2009) ("Because George's right to recover for loss of consortium is derivative of his wife's claim, and she did not recover, he likewise cannot recover.")

- Defenses to the injured person that reduce or eliminate damages also apply to the LOC Plaintiff, including comparative fault of the injured person. *Thompson v. Brown & Williamson Tobacco Corp.*, 207 S.W.3d 76 (Mo. App. 2006) (LOC Plaintiff's damages reduced by fault of injured spouse).

A. Harm to a Marriage Caused by Defendant Injuring Plaintiff's Spouse

Generally, the LOC Plaintiff must have been married to the injured spouse at the time of the injury. In *Mueller v. Tepler*, 95 A.3d 1011 (Conn. 2014), a physician's medical malpractice allegedly injured a woman, Mueller. At that time, state law prohibited the LOC Plaintiff, Stacey, from marrying Mueller. After laws prohibiting same-sex marriage were found unconstitutional, Stacey and Mueller married and Stacey sought loss of consortium damages. The court applied the general rule that an LOC Plaintiff must have been married to the injured spouse at the time of the injury, but remanded.[1] Marriage at the time of injury is the majority rule. *Dionisio v. Buzi*, 7 Conn. L. Rpr. 43 (Sup. Ct. Conn. July 2, 1992).

Some states limit these claims by requiring the injured spouse to have suffered a physical injury, much like the impact rule, even if the states do not require the injured spouse to have suffered an impact in negligence. *Verschoor v. Mtn. W. Farm Bureau Mut. Ins. Co.*, 907 P.2d 1293 (Wyo. 1995) ("loss of consortium is derivative of actions sounding in tort and contemplates underlying liability to the spouse for tortious bodily harm."). *Compare Andress v. Nationstar Mortg.*, 2016 WL 75085 (E.D. Pa. Jan. 7, 2016) ("A claim for loss of consortium in the absence of physical injury is not cognizable under Pennsylvania law and plaintiffs' Second Amended Complaint includes no allegation of any physical injury to either spouse.") *with Pahle v. Colebrookdale Township*, 227 F. Supp. 2d 361 (E.D. Pa. 2002) (stating Pennsylvania law was unclear and permitting LOC Plaintiff to proceed because spouse had been "emotionally scarred" by an assault); *Dionisio v. Buzi,* 7 Conn. L. Rpr. 43 (Sup. Ct. Conn. July 2, 1992) (stating pecuniary loss to injured spouse is insufficient). As *Guerrera v. Cunningham*, 2008 WL 2068249 (Conn. Super. Ct. Apr. 30, 2008) explained:

> The court recognizes that causation and proof of damages may be more clearly ascertainable in a case of a physical injury than in a case of emotional harm, where there is no X-ray or MRI demonstrating the injury. However, these are factual determinations better left to the finder of fact than precluded by operation of law. The difficulty of assessing damages for

---

1. The court provided a narrow carve out:

   If Stacey amends the complaint on remand to allege that she and Mueller would have been married or in a civil union when the underlying tort occurred if they had not been barred from doing so under the laws of this state, the trial court must deny the defendants' motion to strike her loss of consortium claims. As this court did in Hopson, however, we emphasize that persons in Stacey's position, i.e., those who were barred from marrying when the underlying tortious conduct occurred, may not maintain a loss of consortium claim arising from such conduct when the injured person's claim for physical injuries has been concluded by judgment or settlement or the running of the statute of limitations before the date that this opinion is officially released.

   See Chirstiano v. Conn. Light & Power Co., 66 Conn. L. Rptr. 396 (Sup. Ct. Conn. Apr. 2, 2018) (striking complaint seeking to add claims).

loss of consortium is not a proper reason for denying the existence of such a cause of action inasmuch as the logic of that reasoning would also hold a jury incompetent to award damages for pain and suffering. The subjective states such as grief, fright, anxiety, apprehension, humiliation and embarrassment have long been viewed as genuine and deemed compensable under the concept of pain and suffering. The task of computing damages for a loss of consortium is no more difficult for a judge or jury than arriving at an award for pain and suffering. Although this language was applicable to the loss of consortium claim itself, it should be no less applicable to the predicate claim by the injured spouse.

There appears to be broad support in other state courts for including non-physical injuries as adequate predicate injuries to loss of consortium claims. Defendants present no persuasive reasons to justify their proposal to limit recovery for loss of consortium to cases in which the plaintiff's spouse suffers severe physical injury. Indeed, we perceive compelling grounds for not drawing this line. It is irrefutable that certain psychological injuries can be no less severe and debilitating than physical injuries. We could accept defendants' position only by rejecting the manifest truth that a marital relationship can be grievously injured when one spouse suffers a traumatically induced neurosis, psychosis, chronic depression, or phobia.

The use of the term "bodily harm" in the context of loss of consortium claims appears to have originated with the Restatement (Second) of Torts. Some states follow the Restatement requiring an "illness or other bodily harm" as a predicate to a loss of consortium claim, include Alabama, New York and Texas.

Since Connecticut appellate authority does not expressly prohibit emotional or psychological harm as predicate injuries for loss of consortium claims, and in the absence of any reasonable or logical basis for their exclusion, the court will [provide] parity between physical and psychological injuries underlying loss of consortium claims.

Steele v. Botticello

21 A.3d 1023 (Me. 2011) (Levy, J.)

[Mr. Botticello assaulted Mr. Steele who, at that time, was married to Mrs. Steele. Mr. Steele sued Mr. Botticello. During its pendency, Mrs. Steele separated from Mr. Steele. Mr. Steele settled his claim against Mr. Botticello. Although Mrs. Steele knew of that suit, she did not participate in it and it included no claim by her for loss of consortium. After it settled, she brought a loss of consortium claim against Mr. Botticello. Then she and Mr. Steele divorced. The trial court held the settlement and release of Mr. Steele's claim barred her claim and so granted Mr. Botticello's motion for summary judgment. Mrs. Steele appealed.]

In sum our prior decisions established that (1) although arising from the same underlying occurrence as the injured spouse's claim, a statutory loss of consortium claim can be asserted independently in *Dionne v. Libbey-Owens Ford Co.*, 621 A.2d 414 (Me. 1993); (2) an injured spouse's pre-injury release of liability does not bar the other spouse's independent loss of consortium claim in *Hardy v. St. Clair*, 739 A.2d 368 (Me. 1999); and (3) an injured spouse's settlement of a tort claim does not bar the other spouse's independent statutory loss of consortium claim because joinder in the underlying claim is not mandatory in *Parent v. E. Me. Med. Ctr.*, 884 A.2d 93 (Me. 2005).

In *Brown*, we considered how to apply a comparative negligence offset to wrongful death damages awarded for the surviving spouse and/or minor children's loss of consortium. Citing *Hardy* and *Parent*, we stated, "We have previously treated loss of consortium claims as independent claims," but

> after further consideration, we conclude that loss of consortium claims necessarily arise from the same negligent act as the underlying tort claims and are therefore subject to the same rules and limitations. Accordingly, we hold that a loss of consortium claim is a derivative claim, and to the extent our prior decisions have held otherwise, we overrule those decisions.

Brown thus concluded that loss of consortium damages awarded as part of a wrongful death claim are subject to reduction pursuant to the comparative negligence statute, 14 M.R.S. § 156 (2010), and that a jury may consider the deceased spouse or parent's comparative fault when determining loss of consortium damages.

As we acknowledged in *Hardy*, "the terms 'derivative' and 'independent' are imprecise, and may be misleading" as they are used to describe loss of consortium injuries and loss of consortium claims. *Hardy*, 1999 ME 142. A loss of consortium is an original injury that, on one hand, is independent because it is unique to one spouse, but on the other hand, is derivative of the injury to the other spouse. *See id.* Similarly, a loss of consortium claim is independent because it a statutorily-created right that may be asserted separately from the injured spouse's underlying claim, but at the same time, it is derivative because it arises from the same act that gave rise to the underlying claim and is therefore subject to the same rules and limitations. *See id.*

Notwithstanding the imprecision of these key terms, our decision in *Brown* clearly overruled *Hardy* and *Parent* to the extent that those decisions' characterization of a loss of consortium loss of consortium claim as wholly independent, and not derivative, meant that a loss of consortium claim is not subject to the same rules, limitations, and defenses as the underlying tort claim. In effect, *Brown* answered affirmatively the question left open in *Hardy* as to whether a loss of consortium claim may be subject to traditional common law or statutory defenses to the claims of the injured spouse. *Brown*, however, did not undermine or alter *Hardy* and *Parent's* shared premise that a loss of consortium claim may be brought separately from the claim and, in that respect, is more accurately described as capable of being asserted independently. Read together, *Brown, Hardy*, and *Parent* instruct that a loss of consortium claim and its underlying claim may be separately pursued even though the spouse's loss of consortium injury derives from the other spouse's bodily injury, both claims arise from the same set of facts, and both claims are subject to the same defenses. Because the two actions may be brought separately, they may also be settled separately, and the release of one claim does not necessarily preclude the other.

Eryn argues that her loss of consortium claim is still viable because she was not a party to Chris's release of claims, there is no danger of the Botticellos being exposed to double recovery, and the Botticellos failed to join her as a party to the case.[7]

Consistent with our clarification of *Brown*, section 302 establishes Eryn's independent right to recover damages for loss of consortium. Her claim is not directly barred by Chris's settlement and post-injury release of claims because she was not a party to that agreement. Nor is her claim barred by her failure to join or be joined in Chris's tort claim even though she was aware of his claim. Furthermore, Chris's settlement does not limit Eryn's damages because, in settling Chris's claim, the Botticellos' insurer did not consider any potential claims by Eryn and, therefore, Eryn's claim does not threaten the Botticellos or their insurer with a double recovery or inconsistent obligations.

Notes and Questions

1. <u>What Are the Derivative and Separate Aspects of the Claim</u>? The court at length tried to harmonize its case law on these concepts. Can you explain the overlapping but distinct nature of the LOC Plaintiff's and spouse's claims?

2. <u>Duration of Harm</u>. If harm to a marriage ends before trial, loss of consortium damages end. In addition, if an LOC Plaintiff divorces the injured spouse before trial, "damages are limited to the period during which the spouses were married, regardless of the reasons behind their divorce." *Bynum v. Magno*, 125 F. Supp. 2d 1249 (D. Haw. 2000); *see also Cmiech v. Electrolux Home Prods., Inc.*, 2009 WL 3103786 (M.D. Pa. Sept. 24, 2009) (separation ends damages period). If the LOC

---

7. Eryn also argues that the Botticellos had the burden to join her as a party. However, there is no statutory requirement that a party asserting a loss of consortium claim be joined in the underlying tort claim Nor is mandatory joinder required by rule in this instance. The Maine Rules of Civil Procedure provide, "A person who is subject to service of process shall be joined as a party in the action if (1) in the person's absence complete relief cannot be accorded among those already parties, or (2) the person claims an interest relating to the subject of the action." M.R. Civ. P. 19(a). In this case, complete relief could be accorded between Chris and the Botticellos without Eryn's participation, and Eryn was not a "person [who] claims an interest" until she asserted her loss of consortium claim. As a result, Eryn was not a party subject to mandatory joinder within the meaning of Rule 19(a).

Plaintiff dies before trial, courts split. On the one hand, the court in *Martin v. Ohio Cty. Hosp.*, 295 S.W.3d 104 (Ky. 2009) wrote:

> The courts have been exhorted that common sense must not be a stranger in the house of the law. It is apparent that the kinds of damage elements enumerated in the statute are those that describe the personal relationship, mental and physical, between spouses. It is equally apparent that the pain and deprivation coming from loss of such interactions does not magically disappear the day a spouse dies. It defies common sense to put a value on such losses while a spouse is lying incapacitated, but to say the loss is worthless after death. While grief and loss are borne in different ways by different people, it is nonetheless a common part of the human condition that a jury can properly evaluate based on the facts and circumstances of each case.

> Further full compensation cannot be had if the damages claimed are required to terminate at death. Indeed, in many cases death is so sudden or follows so quickly after the injury that to cut loss of consortium damages off at death is to essentially deny the cause of action to the spouse altogether. In creating the cause of action, the legislature did not indicate in the statute that it applied only when the victims survived. To read the statute that way would be to create a class of plaintiffs whose cause of action depended on the vagaries of fate, rather than an orderly operation of law. Can it reasonably be said that one whose spouse survives suffers more loss of consortium than one whose spouse dies?

> Moreover, allowing a loss of consortium claim only if the victim survives would appear to give perverse incentives to potential tortfeasors. Such a rule could create incentives to kill victims instead of leaving them disabled, as only by instantly killing the victim can the tortfeasor be guaranteed to owe no loss of consortium damages. While this logically follows the common law rule, it is obviously absurd.

In contrast, consider *T & M Investments, Inc. v. Jackson*, 425 S.E.2d 300 (Ct. App. Ga. 1992):

> The right of consortium exists only during the joint lives of the husband and wife, such evidence is essential to the jury's determination of this issue. The jury, without the date of death, could not calculate the duration of the "joint lives" for the purpose of fixing the award for loss of consortium. Therefore, the judgment entered on the jury's award of $18,250 to the estate of Marie Jackson must be reversed.

Finally, a jury that finds the harm will continue in the future should award damages for the length of the injury up to time it believes the first spouse will die — the "joint lives" of the spouses. *Beavers v. Davis*, 110 Ga. App. 248 (1964) (jury should award loss of consortium damages for the period it finds to likely be the shorter of spouses' lives).

3. <u>Distinct Harms</u>. Courts recognize a verdict awarding damages to the LOC Plaintiff but none to the injured spouse as inconsistent because "to prevail on a claim for loss of consortium, the claiming spouse must present competent testimony concerning the impact that the incident has had on the marital relationship." *Peterson v. Sun State Int'l Trucks., LLC,* 56 So. 3d 840 (Fla. Ct. App. 2011) (holding that without substantial, undisputed, and unrebutted testimony of an impact on the marriage, a zero award is proper). If there is such evidence, an award of nominal damages (e.g., $1) is required. *Id. See Conant v. Zerva,* 793 A.2d 1042 (R.I. 2002) (zero award proper because harm to marriage was disputed). On the other hand, why is an award of damages to the LOC Plaintiff but not the injured spouse inconsistent? *Ferraro v. Kelley,* 2011 WL 576074 (D. Mass. Feb. 8, 2011) (judge ordered jury to award at least $1 to injured spouse where original verdict awarded LOC Plaintiff $5,000 but $0 to injured spouse).

4. <u>Statutory Modification</u>. Some statutes require the LOC Plaintiff's spouse to have suffered even greater harm than an "impact." Utah requires proof that the injured spouse sustained "a significant permanent injury to a person that substantially changes that person's lifestyle" such as: "(i) a partial or complete paralysis of one or more of the extremities; (ii) significant disfigurement; or (iii) incapability of the person of performing the types of jobs the person performed before the injury." Utah Code Ann. 30-2-11. California requires the LOC Plaintiff to prove the spouse "suffered an injury that is sufficiently serious and disabling to raise the inference that the conjugal relationship is more than superficially or temporarily impaired. The injury may be physical or psychological, but psychological injury must rise to the level of a neurosis, psychosis, chronic depression, or phobia." *Fernandes v. TW Telecom Holdings Inc.,* 22013 WL 6583970 (E.D. Cal. Dec. 16, 2013). Why these different limitations? Think about the intangible aspect of the harm remedied by loss of consortium. Does that explain why a state that permits negligence claims merely with proof of a physical manifestation would deny relief to an LOC Plaintiff unless the spouse had, at least, suffered an impact? Does that approach serve a similar function to the impact rule? Does it have the same flaws?

B. Remedies for Harm to a Relationship Other Than Marriage

Courts and legislatures split on whether harm to a relationship other than between spouses is sufficient to constitute damage for loss of consortium and, if so, which relationships are sufficient. *See Campos v. Coleman,* 123 A.3d 854 (Conn. 2015) (collecting cases and statutes); *Owens v. Glob. Equip. Co., Inc.,* 2018 WL 3186980 (W.D. Ky. June 28, 2018) ("loss of parental consortium claims are only recoverable in conjunction with wrongful death actions."); *Gainer v. City of Troutdale,* 2016 WL 107957 (D. Or. Jan. 8, 2016) ("No Oregon appellate court has opined on whether this theory might be extended to encompass the benefits conferred by committed long-term unmarried partners."), *aff'd,* 715 F. App'x 649 (9th Cir. 2018).

If the claim is recognized, then the same principles in spousal loss of consortium claims apply, including the requirement that the LOC Plaintiff show the injured person has a compensable claim against the defendant, and defenses to the injured person's claim can defeat or reduce damages to the LOC Plaintiff. *Walsh v. Advanced Cardiac Specialists Chartered*, 273 P.3d 645 (Ariz. 2012) (jury award of zero damages to loss of parental consortium plaintiffs was not inconsistent even though defendant conceded liability for wrongful death of parent).

In determining whether to allow recovery for harm other than to a marriage, courts look to legal or blood relationships, not the actual warmth or closeness of the relationship (in other words, the quality of the relationship goes to the amount of damages, not the existence of a claim). This can leave "gaps" for relationships such as stepchildren or children of cohabitating couples. One court noted that some courts deny consortium claims to stepfathers of injured children or adult stepchildren in wrongful death cases, but permitted a child who was dependent on a stepparent to recover for loss of consortium in part because the state's wrongful death statute permitted such recoveries for wrongful death claims. *See Higgins v. Intex Recreation Corp.*, 99 P.3d 421 (Ct. App. Wash. 2004).

Consistent with that approach, courts often permit only those persons authorized under the state's wrongful death statute to bring a wrongful death claim to bring loss of consortium claim—even though the relationship is, and was, with a living but injured person. For example, *Benda v. Roman Catholic Bishop of Salt Lake City*, 384 P.3d 207 (Utah 2016) recognized loss of filial consortium by relying on its wrongful death statute:

> Utah law already recognizes a cause of action for loss of consortium due to tortious injury to one's spouse, and we see merit in extending the right to recovery for loss of consortium to the relationship between parents and a minor child. Like the relationship between spouses, the relationship between parents and a minor child is a legally recognized relationship involving legal obligations. Like the relationship between spouses, it also tends to be a particularly close relationship highly valued in society. *See, e.g., Ruden v. Parker, 462 N.W.2d 674* (Iowa 1990) ("Minor children, as a general rule, live with their parents, and during their early years the interaction between the parent and child is of great importance to the parents, the child and society as a whole."). Utah law already recognizes a right to recovery for loss of filial consortium in wrongful death cases. Boucher ex rel. *Boucher v. Dixie Med. Ctr., 850 P.2d 1179 (Utah 1992)* (Stewart, J., dissenting) ("a parent's cause of action for the loss of the companionship, society, and affection (i.e., consortium) of a child as a result of a wrongful death has been deemed so important in Utah that it is protected by our Constitution and by statute."). Just as the legislature saw merit in re-creating the cause of action for loss of spousal consortium, we see merit in extending

a cause of action for loss of consortium to parents of a tortiously injured minor child.

In adopting this cause of action, we provide some limited guidance. Like the claim for loss of spousal consortium, the claim for loss of filial consortium is "derivative from the cause of action existing in behalf of the injured person." Utah Code § 30-2-11(5). Additionally, we adopt the cause of action exclusively for cases where the injury meets the definition set forth in Utah Code section 30-2-11(1)(a). However, we do not at this time determine whether the minor child's injuries in this case satisfy the statutory definition; instead, we leave that determination, in the first instance, to the district court. Finally, we specifically hold that the claim is not cabined to the period of minority. That is, this cause of action allows parents to recover for the loss of filial consortium suffered from the time of the injury.Thus, we hold that parents may recover for loss of filial consortium due to tortious injury to a minor child in cases where the injury meets the definition set forth in Utah Code section 30-2-11(1)(a).

Notes and Questions

1. <u>Policy for Filial Loss of Consortium.</u> An author argued children should be able to recover for loss of parental consortium because of their greater emotional vulnerability and need for protection. Sean H. Williams, *Dead Children*, 67 Ala. L. Rev. 739 (2016). While true, why does a legal relationship determine whether a relationship was harmed by an injury to someone, rather than the quality of the relationship?

2. <u>Measure of Damages.</u> As with spousal loss of consortium, juries are given wide latitude in assessing damages for other forms of loss of consortium. In *Est. of Pearson ex rel. Latta v. Interstate Power and Light Co.*, 700 N.W.2d 333 (Iowa 2005), the 30-year-old LOC Plaintiffs' 60-year-old parents, Robert and Mary Pearson, burned to death in a house fire and they sought loss of parental consortium damages. The jury awarded about $500,000 to each plaintiff for each parent's loss, and the defendant appealed the trial court's denial of its motion to remit the amount of damages. In affirming, the appellate court stated:

> The loss of parental consortium includes the intangible benefits of companionship, comfort, guidance, affection, and aid of the parent in every parental relationship, and the tangible benefits of general usefulness, industry, and attention within the home and family, but does not include the value of tangible contribution or loss of monetary support from the injured parent. We have recognized a difference between proof of the fact a person sustained damages and proof of the amount of those damages. If the uncertainty lies only in the amount of damages, recovery may be had if there is proof of a reasonable basis from which the amount can be inferred

or approximated. Damages for loss of consortium are incapable of precise pecuniary measurement by the witnesses. Consequently, they are left to the sound discretion of the jury.

Our review of the record reveals Robert and Mary Pearson had a very close relationship with each of their children. All the Pearson children were in their thirties when their parents died. The Pearsons and their children spent almost every major holiday together. Rebecca and Neal lived in the town of Lone Tree with their parents. Rebecca's residence was a short distance from that of her parents. Over the years Rebecca was married, a week did not go by when Rebecca and her family did not have at least one meal at the Pearson home. Rebecca and her family usually spent their Sundays at the Pearson residence. Robert and Mary played a significant role in the development of Rebecca's children.

Neal saw his parents almost every day. Although Neal and Robert had separate trucking businesses, they both were in the same line of work. On weekends, Neal and his father would spend time washing their trucks, changing their oil, and getting their trucks ready for the next week's work. They were constant companions. When Neal's first wife died, Mary and Robert stepped in to help care for Neal and Neal's three small children. Mary cooked, cleaned, shopped, and watched the children. Mary took early retirement the summer before the explosion just so she could spend more time taking care of Neal's children. Neal's children often spent their evenings with the Pearsons and received advice and guidance from them. Neal has remarried but his second wife has been diagnosed with cancer. At the time of their death, Mary and Robert were providing some of the same guidance and child rearing help for Neal's three stepchildren.

Within several years of the explosion, Penny had been living in her parents' home. Although Penny lived in a different city from her parents at the time of the explosion, Penny talked to her parents almost every day. Robert and Mary provided invaluable guidance, advice, and counseling to Penny. Prior to the explosion, Penny recently married. She and her husband assumed custody of Penny's two stepdaughters. Penny and her family frequently returned to the Lone Tree area because that is where all of the stepdaughters' relatives lived. Robert and Mary would make trips to Council Bluffs two to three times a year to spend time with Penny and her family.

Although the awards for loss of parental consortium are sizeable, the awards are neither lacking in evidentiary support nor flagrantly excessive. The successor judge did not abuse his discretion by overruling IES's motion for a new trial or remittitur.

7. Wrongful Death and Survival Claims

At common law, there was no claim in favor of a person who had been killed by another: the claim died with the plaintiff. Statutes replaced that approach. Depending on the statute, if a defendant causes a person's death, two claims possibly arise: a survival claim and a wrongful death claim. In some states, both claims arise. The names are confusing. Summed up, a "survival claim" is usually a claim that, by statute, certain people (usually family members) can bring to recover damages as if the decedent had survived, and so the damages are typical personal injury damages, including pain and suffering prior to death, lost past and future (i.e., for the decedent's hypothetical lifetime) wages, and past medical expenses. The second type of claim, a "wrongful death claim," is in favor of the survivors and provides them damages similar to loss of consortium claims. Both claims require proof that the decedent would have prevailed on a claim upon which relief could have been granted—usually a negligence claim or a battery claim—but it caused death, not injury.

Hern v. Safeco Ins. Co of Ill.

125 P.3d 597 (Mont. 2005) (Cotter, J.)

[Becky Hern, daughter of Ardell and Robert Hern, was living with her parents in 1992 when she was a passenger on a motorcycle and was killed. At that time, it was being driven by her uninsured fiancée. Becky had car insurance with American Economy Insurance Company that included $300,000 in uninsured motorist (UM) coverage. Her parents also carried a multi-car automobile insurance policy with Safeco Insurance Company, which insured four of their vehicles, and that policy included a $500,000 UM limit per vehicle.

Ardell Hern, acting individually, as personal representative of Becky's estate and heirs, and Robert Hern and Becky's sister, Lisa Hern, sought to settle the UM claims with Safeco and American Economy. Safeco took the position that the Safeco policies did not "stack" and so the maximum was $500,000, not $2,000,000. The parties made a structured cash settlement with Safeco and American Economy worth $355,000.

A few years later, a class action was filed against Safeco and American Economy (the *Seltzer* class action) alleging Safeco charged multiple premiums for UM coverage on multiple vehicles but never intended to provide coverage beyond the amount for a single vehicle. Four years after that suit was filed, the *Seltzer* class action settled. As a result of the *Seltzer* Settlement, insureds who purchased UM coverage for multiple cars were able to have their claims reopened and readjusted. Safeco was required to notify its insureds of this opportunity. The Herns filed a claim based on this notice, but Safeco denied it, ostensibly because the damages could not exceed the first policy of $500,000.

The Herns then filed this suit, seeking the full $2 million. To do this, they had to prove the damages caused by Becky's death. In 2004, a jury found damages as follows:

Damages for the Estate of Becky Hern
1. Loss of earning capacity of Becky Hern $883,000.00
2. Pain and suffering experienced by Becky Hern   35,000.00
3. Value of household services performed by Becky Hern   140,000.00
4. Loss of established course of life for Becky Hern   1,500,000.00

Wrongful Death and Emotional Distress Damages for
Robert and Ardell Hern
1. Loss of society, comfort care, and companionship
    Robert $200,000.00
    Ardell   300,000.00
2. Grief, sorrow and mental anguish
    Robert   300,000.00
    Ardell   450,000.00
3. Funeral and Burial Expenses   2,034.10
Total $3,810,034.10

Although denying defendant a new trial, the trial court remitted damages to $2 million. Defendant appealed.]

Safeco argues that the District Court abused its discretion by giving a jury instruction that permitted the jury to award damages to the estate of Becky Hern for: 1) the loss of Becky Hern's ability to pursue an established course of life after the date of death and throughout the remainder of her life expectancy, and 2) the loss of Becky Hern's capacity to perform personal and household services after the date of death during the remainder of her life expectancy. Safeco asserts that Montana law does not allow these damages in a survival action because they are not damages suffered by Becky Hern. Safeco maintains that the court erroneously combined the elements of damage available in personal injury and wrongful death actions with those available in a survival action.

The Herns counter that damages recoverable in a survivorship action are identical to those available in a personal injury action and therefore it was not an abuse of the court's discretion to instruct the jury accordingly. They further note that they did not seek economic compensation for these particular losses in their wrongful death action, so there was no duplication of compensation.

We begin our analysis by briefly distinguishing the causes of action available in Montana to the survivors of a decedent whose death is caused by the negligence of another—*i.e.*, survival and wrongful death.

A "survival" action arises from § 27-1-501, MCA, which states in relevant part:

An action, cause of action, does not abate because of the death or disability of a party but whenever the cause of action or defense arose in favor of such party prior to his death or disability, it survives and may be maintained by his representatives or successors in interest.

A survival action raises claims that came into existence while the decedent was still alive. These claims survive his or her death, and the cause may be pursued against the responsible party by the decedent's personal representative. The damages that may be recovered in a survival action include lost earnings from the time of injury to death, the present value of reasonable earnings during the decedent's remaining life expectancy, medical and funeral expenses, reasonable compensation for pain and suffering, and other special damages. The source of the damages recoverable in the survival action are personal to the decedent and do not include damages suffered by the decedent's spouse, children or other heirs.

Section 27-1-513 creates a cause of action for wrongful death. Damages for wrongful death are non-specific and §27-1-323 provides that "damages may be given as under all the circumstances of the case may be just." Generally, damages under a wrongful death claim will include loss of consortium by a spouse, loss of comfort and society of the decedent suffered by the surviving heirs, and the reasonable value of the contributions in money that the decedent would reasonably have made for the support, education, training and care of the heirs had she lived. Otherwise stated, survival damages are personal to the decedent but are pursued by her personal representative, while wrongful death damages are personal to those who survive her.

Safeco alleges the jury was wrongly instructed on these damages. First, Safeco asserts that the jury instruction used by the District Court to permit a damage award to Becky's estate for Becky's lost ability to pursue an established course of life, Montana Pattern Jury Instruction (MPI) 25.07, is specifically a "personal injury" instruction addressing a "plaintiff" who has been permanently injured, as opposed to a "decedent." Safeco maintains that this instruction is inappropriate to a survivor claim.

The rationale for limiting this species of damages to personal injury claims was succinctly expressed in *Oberson v. U.S.* (D. Mont. 2004), 311 F.Supp.2d 917, "When the plaintiff has been permanently injured and where he will continue to suffer in the future from his injuries, reasonable compensation for the loss of an established course of life is a proper element of damage." In other words, loss of established course of life damages are intended to compensate for an injured person's loss of what she once had, and the accompanying realization that she will live the rest of her life without ever recovering her previous course of life. We therefore agree with Safeco, and conclude that damages of loss of established course of living are not recoverable in survivor actions. Therefore, we conclude the District Court incorrectly instructed the jury that it could award loss of established course of life damages in this survivor action.

Additionally, Safeco asserts that compensation for lost household services is a legitimate damage available in a personal injury claim under MPI 25.04, or a wrongful death action under MPI 25.20, but it is not appropriate for a survivor action. Technically, Safeco is correct. Nonetheless, we conclude for the reason set forth below that it was not an abuse of the District Court's discretion to include such a damage instruction in the survivor action.

In 1987, the Legislature amended § 27-1-501 to require that "actions brought under this section and 27-1-513 must be combined in one legal action, and any element of damages may be recovered only once." The primary purpose of this change was to prohibit double recovery in wrongful death and survivor actions. In the case before us, it is significant that the Herns, though entitled, did not seek to recover the value of household services performed by Becky as part of their wrongful death claim. As a result, there was no impermissible double recovery of these damages. Moreover, the damages awarded to the Herns are within the range of damages to which they were entitled. We conclude that the inclusion of the value of household services in the survivor action rather than the wrongful death action, while technically erroneous, does not constitute an abuse of discretion under these circumstances. We caution, however, that in the future, damages available in wrongful death actions should be included in the wrongful death portion of the verdict form.

The parties disagree as to which damage awards constitute the "loss of consortium" award. Safeco asserts that the jury's award of $750,000, ($300,000 to Robert and $450,000 to Ardell) designated on the verdict form as "grief, sorrow and mental anguish," constituted an erroneous "loss of consortium" award. The Herns argue that the $200,000 awarded to Robert and the $300,000 awarded to Ardell for "loss of society, comfort care, and companionship" represented the "loss of consortium" damages, and were correctly awarded.

Filial "consortium" is defined in *Black's Law Dictionary* 304 (7th ed.1999), as "a child's society, affection, and companionship given to a parent." Moreover, our cases have repeatedly utilized these same terms when describing loss of consortium damages. In *Pence v. Fox* (1991), 248 Mont. 521, we explained,

> While the term "loss of consortium" has been attached to the children's claim, the broader term, "loss of society and companionship," is equally appropriate. Use of the latter term avoids the narrower construction connoting this right derives primarily from the sexual relationship incident to marriage. While companionship may include sexual relations, courts have continued to regard loss of consortium to embrace all of those values — tangible and intangible — inherent in the family relationship. In his treatise, H. Clark, *Domestic Relations* § 10.1 (1968), Clark asserts that the term loss of consortium is equally appropriate in reference to the parent-child relationship to summarize "the multitude of rights and duties binding parents to their children and vice versa."

We therefore conclude that the $200,000 damages awarded to Robert and the $300,000 awarded to Ardell for "loss of society, comfort care, and companionship" constitute the "loss of consortium" damages awarded in this case.

Safeco maintains that Montana law does not recognize a parent's claim for loss of consortium for the death of an adult child. Furthermore, Safeco argues that Robert Hern, who was not Becky's personal representative, could not in any event lawfully assert a loss of consortium claim or a "grief, sorrow and mental anguish" claim, as only the personal representative may pursue such wrongful death damages.

As indicated above, under § 27-1-513 the personal representative of the decedent's estate is authorized to bring an action for wrongful death. This statute and its predecessor have been interpreted to mean that *only one* wrongful death action arising out of a wrongful death may be brought and the decedent's personal representative is the only person who may bring such an action. The personal representative holds the proceeds of any damage award for the heirs of the decedent and the award does not become part of the decedent's estate.

In the case before us, Robert was not the personal representative of Becky's estate and, therefore, it was error for the District Court to instruct the jury that it could award damages of any kind to Robert personally, in the wrongful death claim. Therefore, we vacate the $500,000 awarded to Robert as part of the wrongful death claim, $300,000 of which was for grief, sorrow, and mental anguish, and $200,000 for loss of consortium.

Notes and Questions

1. <u>Recovery for Pre-Death Pain and Suffering</u>. Post-impact pain and suffering are recoverable in survivor claims, as in any negligence case involving an impact or tort that caused physical harm, but where death is nearly immediate, the need for proof of pain and suffering and its duration arise. Hawaii, apparently alone, permits recovery without proof the decedent survived impact because "death never is simultaneous with the injury causing it—that there always is a faction of a moment, however immeasurable, before death results." *Excobar v. Airbus Helicopters SAS*, 2016 WL 5858636 (D. Haw. Oct. 4, 2016). In contrast, most courts hold a plaintiff must establish the decedent experienced "conscious" pain and suffering—"some cognitive awareness." *Fanning v. Sitton Motor Lines, Inc.*, 695 F. Supp. 2d 1156 (D. Kan. 2010) (analyzing recoverability where decedent had been "instantly" killed by a semi while walking on freeway); *Ditcharo v. State*, 2017 WL 4700823 (Ct. App. La. Oct. 18, 2017) ("a jury may award damage for pain and suffering in a survival action where there is the smallest amount of evidence of pain, however brief, on the part of the deceased, based on his actions or otherwise," and affirming award of $125,000 for post-impact pain and suffering where decedent's car hydroplaned, left highway, and caused him to be ejected, and he died at hospital, not at scene, and medical experts testified he bled out and did not have brain injuries); *Hengel v. Buffalo Wild Wings, Inc.*, 2013 WL 3970154 (E.D. Ky. July 31, 2013) (although no need

for "evidence showing the precise amount of time a decedent survived an injury-causing incident or how long the decedent was conscious, there must be some evidence of conscious survival.")

2. <u>Recovery for Pre-Impact Fear</u>. As noted above concerning negligence, courts split on whether pre-impact fear is recoverable. The same is true for survivor claims. In permitting them, the court in *Ward v. Stewart*, 286 F. Supp. 3d 321 (N.D.N.Y. 2017) explained:

> Damages for preimpact terror are designed to compensate the decedent's estate for the fear the decedent experienced during the interval between the moment the decedent appreciated the danger resulting in the decedent's death and the moment the decedent sustained a physical injury as a result of the danger. There must be some evidence that the decedent perceived the likelihood of grave injury or death before the impact, and suffered emotional distress as a result.

> In determining damages for conscious pain and suffering experienced in the interval between injury and death, when the interval is relatively short, the degree of consciousness, severity of pain, apprehension of impending death, along with duration, are all elements to be considered.

> Plaintiffs have the threshold burden of proving consciousness for at least some period of time following an accident in order to justify an award of damages for pain and suffering. The burden can be satisfied by direct or circumstantial evidence. However, mere conjecture, surmise or speculation is not enough to sustain a claim for pain and suffering damages. Without legally sufficient proof of consciousness following an accident, a claim for conscious pain and suffering must be dismissed.

In *Ward,* the trial court held that evidence showing the deceased race car driver had "raised his arms in a defensive posture" when struck while walking at a race was sufficient to avoid summary judgment on pre-impact damages. *Freed v. D.R.D. Pool Serv., Inc.,* 186 Md. App. 477 (2009) (fact issue on whether five-year-old who drowned in pool suffered pain and suffering while drowning and before death where medical expert testified it was reasonably certain boy had survived for two minutes).

In *Vargas v. Crown Container Co., Inc.,* 65 N.Y.S.3d 567 (N.Y. App. Div. 2d Dept. 2017), a jury awarded both forms of damage in a survivor case. The decedent had been pinned by a garbage truck as it backed into him, killing him. The defendants objected to jury awards of $1 million for pre-impact terror and $2 million for conscious pain and suffering, and the plaintiff consented to the trial court remitting to $250,000 and $750,000. Defendants appealed:

> Turning to the issue of damages, the plaintiffs correctly concede that the awards for pre-impact terror, conscious pain and suffering, past pecuniary loss, and future pecuniary loss were excessive. Pre-impact terror pertains to the emotional pain and suffering that the decedent may have endured

between the moment he was aware that the vehicle was about to hit him and the moment of impact. Ali testified that the decedent was facing the rear of the truck when Ali started the compactor. The plaintiffs' expert engineer testified that it would have taken less than a second for the truck to strike the decedent after it started moving in reverse. The plaintiff's medical expert testified that the decedent did not have any injuries that would have killed him instantly, nor did he lose consciousness immediately. The decedent would have experienced pain from multiple rib fractures and abrasions. In the medical expert's opinion, it took approximately one or two minutes for the decedent to die from his internal injuries. In view of the foregoing evidence, awards of $250,000 for pre-impact terror and $750,000 for conscious pain and suffering would constitute reasonable compensation.

3. <u>Wrongful Death Claims: Tangible and Intangible Harms</u>. The defendant in *Welch v. Haase*, 672 N.W.2d 689 (S.D. 2003), admitted liability for a car wreck that had caused the plaintiff's 18-year-old son, Caz, to die by suffocation. Yet the jury awarded nothing and the trial court denied plaintiff's motion for new trial. The appellate court reversed:

> "In every action for wrongful death the jury may give such damages as they may think proportionate to the pecuniary injury resulting from such death to the persons respectively for whose benefit such action will be brought." SDCL 21-5-7. With respect to pecuniary injury, Caz's mother and grandfather first identified what Caz would provide for them. The evidence reflected that Caz was especially close to his grandparents because he lived with them during high school after his mother moved to Aberdeen. The testimony also indicated that Caz planned to attend school. Caz's mother testified that Caz had been accepted to Mitchell Vo-Tech, where he planned to study computer programming. She testified that Caz "always told his grandpa and grandma he was going to college, and make a lot of money, and buy them a home." South Dakota law requires that the beneficiaries show that they could 'reasonably expect' to receive such benefits.

> In addition to the forgoing claim, in a wrongful death action, wherein the decedent was a minor, the loss of companionship and society, which may be expressed by, but is not limited to, the words 'advice,' 'assistance' and 'protection' are proper elements of damage for the jury to consider in reaching their verdict. This rule also applies in cases regarding the death of an adult child. Caz was eighteen years old at the time of the accident.

> With respect to a loss of companionship and society, Caz's mother testified that Caz was "a gentle guy" who "smiled all the time." She said that he was an avid hunter and fisherman, and he enjoyed bowling and playing football. Despite living in a different city, she maintained a close relationship with Caz, and they "talked every day on the computer at 10 o'clock." Caz's grandfather, Larry Welch, also testified that:

Caz Welch was my—he was a special grandson. We had him most of his life. And we loved him like a son. Me and him, we went fishing all the time. Hunting. Trapping. We went pheasant hunting. And just seemed like we was together all the time. And he would help me cut up deer, and I learned him to skin pheasants, and he would go down and he would work for Kucera's, skin peasants. We went camping together, took Darby with us. Went swimming. Went to the Keyapaha River thousands of times. And I think of him every day. He was just a special boy.

Larry Welch also testified about things that he and Caz were planning to do, but had not yet had a chance to do together. He stated that Caz "was like a son. And he was a buddy. And I ache for him every day."

Considering all of the foregoing, there was undisputed evidence of some pecuniary loss. Therefore, in light of Kleins' admission of liability for damages, we believe that the verdict on this cause of action was so disproportionate to the uncontested evidence as to defy common sense and logic. We therefore reverse and remand the wrongful death cause of action against Kleins for a new trial on damages.

The court also held the jury's no damages verdict for Caz's survival action—for his pain and suffering—was disproportionate and remanded for a new trial.

4. <u>Proprietor Decedents</u>. Economic damages can include lost profits of a business owned by the decedent. *Storer v. Crow Cork & Seal Co.*, 2017 WL 3632523 (W.D. La. Aug. 22, 2017) (finding a fact issue on whether decedent's death caused loss of franchise, which caused loss of profits to estate as lost earnings).

5. <u>Marrying into a Claim</u>? Courts reject the idea of a spouse "marrying into" a claim after injury but before death: the majority rule is the plaintiff must have been married at the time of death, not injury. *Domino's Pizza, LLC v. Wiederhold*, 248 So. 3d 212 (Ct. App. Fla. 2018). Should there be exceptions? Related to this, a seeming majority hold that a surviving spouse's remarriage is inadmissible, for reasons the court in *Katy v. Capriola*, 742 S.E.2d 247 (Ct. App. N.C. 2013) explained:

Both parties acknowledge that there is no North Carolina case which discusses the admissibility of remarriage of the surviving spouse in an action for wrongful death. However, North Carolina has long adhered to the collateral source rule, which provides a tort-feasor should not be permitted to reduce his own liability for damages by the amount of compensation the injured party receives from an independent source. We find this rule requires the exclusion of evidence of plaintiff's remarriage in the instant case. Defendants should not be permitted to reduce their liability for the damages caused by Mrs. Katy's death simply because plaintiff has remarried. Indeed, many jurisdictions have used the collateral source rule as a justification to exclude evidence of remarriage by the decedent's spouse in a wrongful death action. Thus, we conclude that the trial court properly excluded evidence of plaintiff's remarriage.

Some legislatures have abrogated this evidentiary exclusion, but courts limit the use of the evidence. For example, although the applicable statute stated "evidence of remarriage of the decedent's surviving spouse is admissible," the court in *Solis v. Virgin Islands Tel. Corp.*, 2016 WL 3552189 (D.V.I. June 23, 2016) explained:

> Under Florida's wrongful death statute, evidence of remarriage of the decedent's spouse is admissible. It has been held that this evidence is admissible for the sole reason of allowing the truth to be known and to keep the court from having to participate in a fraud upon the jury but not to mitigate damages recoverable by the surviving spouse. The Florida courts have reached this conclusion via an analysis that, like Plaintiffs' here, focused on the statutory placement of the "remarriage" phrase in relation to the phrase regarding recovery by the decedent's representative. *See Smyer v. Gaines*, 332 So.2d 655 (Fla. Ct. App. 1976). In *Dubil v. Labate*, 52 N.J. 255 (N.J. 1968), on which Plaintiffs rely, the court reached a conclusion similar to that of the Florida courts. In *Labate*, the court noted "the desirability of honestly presenting certain facts to a jury with instructions that it would be improper for them to consider these facts in their deliberations."
>
> In the case at bar, I endorse this approach. As a matter of policy, it strikes an appropriate balance between running counter to an atmosphere of truth, and running counter to the law of damages.[4] Therefore, I will deny the Motion, and will not exclude evidence of Diana Solis' remarriage. This ruling is qualified, however, in that Defendants shall not be permitted to argue that the remarriage should mitigate Plaintiffs' recovery. Additionally, the parties may address this issue through proposed jury instructions.

Which is the better view? What should a limiting jury instruction say?

6. <u>Judicial Review</u>. Wrongful death damages can include both economic and non-economic components. In *Finch v. Covil Corp.*, 2019 WL 1934523 (M.D.N.C. May 1, 2019), a jury awarded $32 million to the estate of man who at 70 years old developed cancer and then died as a result of exposure to defendant's products. The defendant argued that comparison to other cases showed $2 million was more appropriate. The court in rejected comparisons, stating:

> While the comparability approach gives the appearance of an objective counterweight to the jury's subjective analysis of intangible losses, that appearance is often illusory. As the briefing in this case shows, it is not easy

---

4. I note, too, that "remarriage of the spouse before the lawsuit is over should not result in a windfall for the person who negligently caused the death of the previous spouse. To so hold might well encourage a surviving spouse not to remarry until after the lawsuit for wrongful death is settled, not necessarily a socially desirable result." *Taylor v. So. Pac. Transp. Co.*, 130 Ariz. 516 (1981).

to define which cases are comparable and it is even harder to locate them for comparison. A comparison is only helpful if the cases are comparable, yet the information available in a reported decision is often incomplete or non-specific. Many verdicts are not reflected in reported decisions, and settlements amounts, which would also seem relevant in a comparability analysis, are opaque and even more difficult to obtain. But even if the Court had a comprehensive list of comparable cases, factual differences would still exist, and evaluating the significance of those differences would raise its own challenges.

Here, it is not clear that the North Carolina verdicts identified by Covil, were rendered in cases comparable to this one, as Covil provides no details for most cases, and for others, the period of pain and suffering was substantially shorter and the family relationships were different. Reviewing verdicts in mesothelioma cases from other states, would require the Court to evaluate whether the law on damages is different in a way that might have affected the verdict and to review scores of pages of materials from other trials to determine if the evidence was similar and the damages were "comparable." The Court declines this invitation and concludes in its discretion that a comparative approach would not be beneficial here.

The Court also declines Covil's implicit invitation to rely on its gut reaction to the size of the verdict based on its experience. Such subjective reactions by the presiding judge are no more reliable, accurate, or non-speculative than the jury's considered judgment. Here, the size of the verdict may have been a bit surprising, but, upon reflection, it was not shocking given the strength of the plaintiff's evidence and the weaknesses of Covil's defense.

Similarly, the court in *Dubuque v. Cumberland Farms, Inc.,* 101 N.E.3d 317 (Ct. App. Mass. 2018), rejected comparisons, observing: "One party may find an award that compares favorably; the other will find one that does not." But, without comparison, what is the basis for finding any award is excessive or inadequate?

8. When the Legal Remedy Is Inadequate: Enjoining Future Harm to Mind or Body

As stated in Chapter 1 and exemplified in Chapter 2, injunctive relief is the exception, not the rule. And as emphasized in Chapter 1, the type of harm threatened by the defendant is a critical factor in determining whether the remedy at law is adequate. Courts will enjoin a defendant who had or threatened to repeatedly and intentionally injure a plaintiff. In the context of threatened future physical harm, injunctions are available under the common law, and statutes allow entry of TROs and preliminary injunctions in specific circumstances, such as domestic violence.

The first case below involves a common law injunction, and the second discusses a common statutory scheme to enjoin likely future domestic violence.

Jennings Guest House v. Gibson

971 So. 2d 506 (Ct. App. La. 2007) (Thibodeaux, J.)

[Defendant Jayme Gibson was employed by the plaintiff retirement home, Jennings Guest House. It obtained a TRO and preliminary injunction to prevent her from entering the premises after learning she had stolen residents' medication and sold or used them, and had physically and verbally abused some residents. She appealed.]

Gibson contends that the trial court erred in issuing the TRO against her because Jennings Guest House: (1) failed to present specific facts by supporting affidavit that immediate and irreparable injury would occur before a hearing on the matter; (2) failed to meet the burden of proof on the face of the petition; (3) failed to give Gibson notice; [and] (4) failed to exhaust all legal remedies before seeking an injunction.

Irreparable harm or injury generally refers to a loss that cannot be adequately compensated in money damages or measured by a pecuniary standard. In the present case, the petition and the administrator's affidavit stated that Gibson was accused of taking the residents' drugs, that she had been violent, that she had been terminated, and that she continued to harass the residents and staff. While the petition and affidavit of plaintiff's representative do not use the terminology "irreparable injury," they allege facts showing past violence, past loss, and continuing harassment sufficient to show that irreparable injury, loss, or damage might result if the TRO were not issued. Therefore, the face of the petition and the affidavit of plaintiff's representative meet the burden of proof of irreparable harm, and Gibson's first two assertions are without merit.

In the present case, the attorney for Jennings Guest House, Mr. Millican, attached his affidavit to the petition specifically stating that Gibson had not been notified because "prior notice may cause irreparable harm to the plaintiff and/or his staff because of the defendant's known violent temper." Accordingly, Gibson's third assertion is without merit.

The party seeking injunctive relief must be without any other adequate legal remedy. Gibson asserts that Jennings Guest House did not avail itself of the other available legal remedies, such as having her arrested for trespass. She even suggests that having her arrested for simple battery or simple assault would have been remedies if she had truly been violent in the past. In the first place, we think that it is ludicrous to suggest a remedy more invasive and more inconvenient than a restraining order, which incarceration would surely be. This is not a case of restraining Gibson from making a living or selling her property. The restraining order in this case simply required her to stay away from a business where she no longer worked. Moreover, we note that under remedies requiring an arrest, once Gibson obtained her release while awaiting trial on such criminal charges, she would once again be available to harass elderly residents and employees at Jennings Guest House.

Gibson has suggested no other appropriate or adequate legal remedy, and we can think of none, that would compensate elderly residents who have been robbed of their medications or upset by violent behavior or outbursts, which could cause serious injury in the elderly. This assertion is equally without merit.

Ginsberg v. Blacker

852 N.E.2d 679 (Ct. App. Mass. 2006) (Laurence, J.)

[Defendant Jonathan Blacker was divorced from plaintiff Faye Ginsberg. Starting in January 2005, Blacker had become hostile and erratic toward her, blaming her for "ruining his life," telling her that her family "should be shot," calling at all hours and coming to her home without notice, finding her in the kitchen with her son. On February 3, 2005, he again entered the house unannounced and suddenly became enraged upon seeing his son with what he believed to be an unflattering haircut he mistakenly attributed to Ginsberg. He began yelling at her about the haircut, pulled at his own hair, paced back and forth, and acted aggressively. When she asked him to leave, he went "berserk" and, screaming and waving his hands very close to her face, came so close to her that she "could feel his spit on her face." She ran upstairs but he followed her, shouting obscenities and terrible names in front of their son.

Ginsburg sought an "abuse prevention order" from the trial court. She testified that Blacker had never hit her but that violence was "imminent." Blacker testified he had never raised his hand and denied all Ginsburg's allegations. The trial court issued the abuse prevention order after it found Blacker had placed Ginsberg "in fear of imminent serious physical harm" as required by a state statute. Blacker appealed.]

We note that [to find "abuse" sufficient to issue a "prevention order"] the conduct proscribed as abuse closely approximates the common-law description of assault. Under the common law, it is well established in this State that an act placing another in reasonable apprehension that force *may* be used is sufficient for the offense of criminal assault. In determining whether an apprehension of anticipated physical force is reasonable, a court will look to the actions and words of the defendant in light of the attendant circumstances. A central feature of "abuse" is that the victim's fear or apprehension caused by the defendant's words or conduct must be more than subjective and unspecified; viewed objectively the plaintiff's apprehension that force may be used must be reasonable.

We have no difficulty in upholding the judge's implicit findings that Blacker's conduct, by word and act, on February 3, 2005, was not only menacing by objective standards, but created an apprehension of imminent serious physical harm on the part of Ginsberg that was objectively reasonable, Blacker's intimidating behavior toward his ex-wife, as testified to by Ginsberg and credited by the judge, rationally could be interpreted by the judge as creating a picture of a volatile situation in which the possibility of physical abuse was present. Moreover, it readily could be inferred from Blacker's conduct on February 3, 2005, that Ginsberg, even if she had not expressly so testified, reasonably apprehended that force *might* be used against her at any moment, given his increasingly "erratic and unstable behavior" over the recent past that had "escalated" to the point that she felt "he's going to snap."

The requisite element, that the plaintiff must reasonably apprehend "imminent serious physical harm," is satisfied by the threat Blacker communicated through his hands flailing in Ginsberg's face, so close to her that his angry shouting caused his spittle to spray upon her face. While naked hands (and other body parts) are not, as matter of Massachusetts law, dangerous weapons, it has been acknowledged that they may be used to inflict "disabling or disfiguring injuries."

Blacker contends that Ginsberg could not have reasonably had an imminent fear of serious physical harm at the February 3, 2005, confrontation because he had never physically struck or harmed her during the course of their relationship (a fact Ginsberg conceded). The absence of physical harm prior to the abusive incident may be a factor to be considered in the totality of the circumstances but does not remove Blacker's conduct on February 3 from the category of abuse. The facts in *Commonwealth v. Gordon*, 407 Mass. at 343, are instructive on this issue. There, the court held that "abuse" as defined in G.L. c. 209A, § 1 (in the context of a prosecution for the defendant's violation of a c. 209A order to refrain from "abusing" his wife), could be found on the following facts that did not involve any past or contemporaneous physical abuse or violence:

In the present case, there was evidence of a verbal outburst between the defendant and his wife five days before the incident in question, during which the defendant called his wife a 'bitch' and a 'whore.' The wife testified that, at this time, she was 'upset,' and that she 'didn't know what the defendant was going to do next.' At the next meeting between the wife and the defendant, on November 15, 1988, the defendant arrived at the house unannounced, and when his wife refused to respond to the defendant's requests that she open the door, the defendant said that she was being 'immature and ridiculous.' Despite his wife's obvious unwillingness to speak with him, the defendant left his automobile when she appeared and prevented her from closing the front door by propping his back against it.

In these circumstances, we cannot say that a jury could not conclude beyond a reasonable doubt that the wife entertained a reasonable apprehension that her husband might physically abuse her. The fact that the defendant had violated an order to remain away from the house, the evidence of the tension between the parties, the previous verbal abuse by the defendant, and the defendant's physical actions in holding open the door when his wife clearly desired to avoid contact could reasonably be combined by the jury to create a picture of a volatile situation in which the possibility of physical abuse was present.

The facts in the instant case—Blacker's flying into a rage at an objectively trivial incident (his mistaken perception about his son's haircut), his pulling at his hair while pacing back and forth, his thrusting of his waving hands into Ginsberg's face while screaming at her so uncontrollably as to project his saliva into her face, his pursuing her upstairs and downstairs as she tried to avoid his presence, as well as his obscene verbal abuse, all done in the presence of his young son and against the background of his wishing that Ginsberg and her family "should be shot" for having "ruined his life"—are far more egregiously threatening and violent than those found sufficient to constitute abuse in *Gordon*.

The reasonableness of Ginsberg's apprehension here also contrasts sharply with those cases where the plaintiff's evidence has failed to establish abuse as defined in G.L. c. 209A, § 1. See, e.g., *Larkin v. Ayer Div. of the Dist. Ct. Dept.*, 425 Mass. 1020 (1997) (sending notices of a future lawsuit and court proceedings insufficient); *Wooldridge v. Hickey*, 45 Mass.App.Ct. 637 (1998) (conclusory assertions of ex-husband's having been "abusive" and "verbally abusive" without factual details, and with no explanation of why ex-wife felt apprehension of imminent physical harm, except unelaborated "because," insufficient); *Uttaro v. Uttaro*, 54 Mass. App.Ct. at 875 (complainant's fear of being arrested for violating an outstanding c. 209A order insufficient); *Carroll v. Kartell*, 56 Mass.App.Ct. at 87 (receiving frequent undesired telephone calls and mail from defendant desiring to "cultivate a friendship," without any menacing language or any menacing gestures by him on the few occasions they were together, insufficient); *Szymkowski v. Szymkowski*, 57 Mass.App.Ct. 284 (2003) (a divorced father's telling his seven year old daughter about peculiar and frightening dreams, tossing a milk container at her, cuffing her under the chin in irritation, kicking the back of her legs in irritation while both were in bed, and pinching her on the arm and leaving a mark, at various times, might be unacceptable parental behavior meriting modification of his custody and visitation rights under the divorce judgment, but were insufficient to establish c. 209A abuse); *Keene v. Gangi*, 60 Mass.App.Ct. 667 (2004) (placing of hidden video camera in girlfriend's bedroom by boyfriend who had a temper and occasionally said he could have someone "taken care of," insufficient).

Notes and Questions

1. <u>Repetition</u>. At common law or in statutory schemes, a single instance of violence or threat is likely insufficient to obtain an injunction because the remedy at law is adequate. What, practically speaking, does "adequate remedy at law" mean?

2. <u>Statutes</u>. The *Ginsberg* court's order was authorized by a state statute protecting victims of domestic violence, which are common. *See Caldwell v. Caldwell*, 257 So.

3d 1184 (Ct. App. Fla. 2018) (discussing statutes permitting injunctions upon proof of repeated sexual violence against a parent or minor child). These statutes make injunctive relief easier to obtain, but still are heavily tied to common law standards for injunctive relief and to substantive tort law, as *Ginsberg* itself shows. Other statutes have similar features. For example, anti-cyberstalking statutes permit enjoining electronic communications made "repeatedly" and "for the purpose of threatening, terrifying or harassing any person." *Head v. Robichaux,* 2018 WL 5733005 (Ct. App. La. Nov. 2, 2018). Likewise, statutes permit enjoining physical stalking—"intentional and repeated following or harassing of another person that would cause a reasonable person to feel alarmed or to suffer emotional distress." *Id.* Courts generally construe these statutes to require proof of harm in the form of a common law tort of assault or battery, as *Ginsberg* explains.

3. <u>Enjoining IIED</u>. As shown later, courts will not enjoin defamatory speech. Plaintiffs who have sought to enjoin defamatory speech through an IIED claim have, for that reason, also failed to obtain injunctive relief. *E.g., Kazal v. Price,* 2017 WL 6270086 (M.D. Fla. Sept. 8, 2017) (denying injunction against defamatory speech even though plaintiff also asserted IIED claim). However, in *Livingston v. Livingston,* 537 S.W.3d 578 (Ct. App. Tex. 2017), plaintiff Catherine Livingston brought IIED, assault, and false imprisonment claims against her stepson. The jury found for her only on the IIED claim, but awarded no damages. The trial court found it likely the stepson would repeat the conduct and—in addition to the evidence of aggressive behavior before trial, saw "a degree of visible aggressiveness" while the stepson was testifying at trial—permanently enjoined him and his agents from "directly or indirectly":

(i) Approaching within 1,000 feet (300 meters) of Catherine Livingston;

(ii) Knowingly entering upon any property where Catherine Livingston is located;

(iii) Contacting or attempting to contact Catherine Livingston by telephone, mail, delivery, email, in person or by any other means.

Problems

1. <u>Battery, Assault, or Both</u>? John Reynolds was using the microwave in a work break room while loosely holding a $10 bill. Reynolds was unaware that a co-worker, Bret MacFarlane, was behind him. When MacFarlane grabbed the bill from Reynolds' hand, Reynolds spun around and MacFarlane said, "That was too easy," and gave the bill back. A year later, Reynolds sued for IIED, assault, and battery. What result and award of damages?

2. <u>Pharmacy's Humiliating Disclosure</u>. A pharmacy employee disclosed to several people that plaintiff, a young engaged woman, was taking medicine for an embarrassing communicable disease. The information made its way to plaintiff's fiancé, causing plaintiff to seek medical and psychiatric treatment. The plaintiff sued the

pharmacy, asserting several claims, including IIED. Should the defendant move to dismiss, and if so, on what grounds?

3. <u>Battery and Assault</u>. Courts sometimes use "assault" to mean a battery. *E.g., Kipp v. Metz,* 2013 WL 2285980 (W.D. Pa. May 23, 2013) (awarding $3,000 in damages caused by a "physical assault"). Likewise, courts sometimes characterize a battery as a "completed assault" or that assault "is attempted battery, while battery is a completed assault." *Keum v. Virgin Am. Inc.,* 781 F. Supp. 2d 944 (N.D. Cal. 2011). In considering whether those statements are correct, ponder these hypotheticals: (a) While Lucy is blindfolded and unaware that Charlie is present, Charlie swings at her, trying to hit her, but misses. Charlie attempted a battery, but is that an assault? (b) Bob knows Susie does not want him to touch her, but he reaches across the table to caress her arm, and she pulls away and leaves. That's a battery; is it an assault?

4. <u>The Laughing Defendant</u>. Your clients were injured when, as a result of a road rage incident, a driver ran a red light and collided with their car. After the wreck, the defendant drove off, but shortly afterward returned and laughed at your clients while they were still pinned in the wreckage and in severe pain. A psychologist will testify that, to a reasonable degree of medical certainty, some of their distress was caused by the laughter, separate and in addition to the pain and suffering they experienced as a result of their physical injuries. How would you distinguish *Hendrix,* given that Mrs. Hendrix sought to testify that her distress had, likewise, been increased because of what she learned after the wreck as to its cause? Conversely, as the defendant, argue that Hendrix still denies recovery for this aspect of their distress, at least in negligence?

5. <u>Strict Impact Rule States and Bystander or Zone-of-Danger Claims</u>? Consider the point above that some courts deny pre-impact fear to plaintiffs who have suffered an impact, allowing only "pain and suffering." In a strict impact rule state that denies damages for pre-impact fear, should bystander or zone-of-danger claims ever be permitted? Or should bystander, but not zone-of-danger, claims be recognized? Be prepared to argue for different outcomes.

6. <u>Serving Our Country</u>. Suppose an LOC Plaintiff alleges that, but for her obligation to serve in the military, she would have married her current spouse before his injury. Sufficient?

7. <u>Sexual Abuse of Daughter by Therapist</u>. Your client is a therapist accused of sexually molesting the daughter of two parents. They have filed various claims, including an IIED claim for each parent's emotional distress. What questions will you ask your client to determine whether she might face liability for their distress?

8. <u>Injured Employee</u>. Your client is a sole proprietor whose best employee, Diego, was injured in a car wreck while on company business. As a result, he had to pay a part-time worker higher wages while Diego was unable to work, and the premiums for your client's workers' compensation insurance have doubled. In addition, at least one customer moved its business to a competitor during the time Diego was off

work. It is clear that the Diego was severely injured and the other driver was at fault. Does your client have a negligence claim against the driver who injured Diego? For what damages?

9. <u>Exposure During Surgery</u>. Your client is a former patient of a surgeon. She learned, reading the surgeon's obituary, that he died of AIDS and had been infected when he had performed major emergency surgery on your client after a car wreck. Upon learning of his condition, she was tested and was told she was HIV negative, and that — because the surgery had occurred more than a year ago, it was "extremely unlikely" she would ever become ill because of the surgeon's condition. For various reasons, the only claim available is negligence. Does recovery turn on whether the state is an impact state? What damages are recoverable?

10. <u>Talk Radio Loudmouth</u>. Your client, Karen Carpenter, wrote a letter to a local radio station complaining about a program it hosted. The radio station forwarded the letter to the host, who read it on the air. In doing so, he also made derogatory and sexually explicit comments about her, and he urged his listeners to call her and harass her at home. You are a judge deciding defendant's motion to dismiss plaintiff's claims: one claim is for defamation and you have concluded that it should be dismissed because the statements about Carpenter are protected by the First Amendment. The plaintiff asserts that the statements urging listeners to call and harass her — which some did — should not be dismissed because she alleges the other facts to support IIED and the First Amendment should not be a bar. How will you rule?

11. <u>When Did the Harm Occur</u>? A husband hired a lawyer to file a petition with the U.S. Immigration and Naturalization Service. In July 2009, the husband and wife learned the lawyer had not filed the petition on time and, as a result, the husband was deported in November 2009. The statute of limitations on the husband's potential legal malpractice claim had run in July 2004, and the wife filed a loss of consortium claim in late 2009, before the statute of limitations ran on that claim. Assuming the jurisdiction does not require an "impact" or injury, is the wife's claim for loss of consortium time-barred or not?

12. <u>Predeceased LOC</u>? Assume a state recognizes a claim for parental loss of consortium. Does a child whose father was killed in a car wreck before the child was born have a loss of consortium claim?

13. <u>Should an LOC Plaintiff Have to Show at Least an Impact or Intentional Tort on the Spouse</u>? As the chapter explained, some courts require the spouse of an LOC Plaintiff to have suffered physical harm — at least an "impact" and sometimes more. Imagine you represent a defendant whose fraud caused the plaintiff to become suicidal and withdrawn from a marriage, severely harming the marital relationship with the LOC Plaintiff. Why should loss of consortium damages not be available?

14. <u>Impact of a Release by the Injured Spouse</u>. The majority rule is that if the injured spouse releases the defendant from liability for the harm to that spouse, that

does not release the defendant from liability to the LOC Plaintiff. What arguments support the minority rule?

15. <u>What Is the Compensable Harm</u>? Given *Hendrix* and the notes following it, what is the compensable harm in a strict impact rule state? In a physical manifestation state? To avoid a jury awarding damages for noncompensable harms, how should it be instructed?

Chapter 4

Remedies Triggered by Harm to Plaintiff's Reputation, Dignity, or Privacy, and Remedies to Prevent Government Acts That Harm a Plaintiff's First Amendment Rights

The damage element of defamation requires harm to the plaintiff's reputation. Defamation includes written (libel) and oral (slander) statements. Some states distinguish between slander and libel by, for example, requiring proof of pecuniary loss for claims based upon an oral statement. *Teff v. Unity Health Plans Ins. Corp.*, 666 N.W.2d 38 (Ct. App. Wis. 2003). If the plaintiff is an entity, not a real person, some states permit it to assert defamation, while others have developed analogous claims called "trade libel" or "business disparagement." In contrast, reputational harm is ordinarily insufficient to constitute "damage" required for a breach of contract claim. This chapter first discusses monetary remedies for defamation and related claims before turning to the monetary remedies for invasion of privacy.

The chapter then examines when damages are inadequate to remedy those harms. Even though courts acknowledge that money often will be insufficient to remedy defamation, the general rule is that defamatory speech will not be enjoined because the First Amendment prohibits the government from regulating the content of speech. That principle allows the chapter to segue to claims by plaintiffs to enjoin government acts that have harmed, or threaten to harm, a plaintiff's First Amendment rights: consistent with the rule against enjoining defamatory speech, courts may enjoin government acts that inhibit free speech.

1. The Process to Determine Monetary Remedies for Defamation

Defamation requires proof that the defendant, with some fault (either negligence or "actual malice," depending on the "status" of the plaintiff), "published" a false statement and it either: (a) was defamatory per se and so the law presumes harm to the plaintiff's reputation and thus is presumed to have caused "general damages," or (b) was not per se defamatory (i.e., is per quod) and the plaintiff must prove publication caused economic harm, known as "special damages." If general damages are established, the plaintiff may, in addition to recovering harm to reputation, recover consequential damages such as lost income or mental anguish caused by the publication. Likewise, if the plaintiff proves the defendant's false statement was defamatory per quod and caused it specific economic losses, it, too, may recover consequential damages caused by the publication.

A. Whether a False Statement Was Defamatory Per Se or Per Quod

Defamatory statements are either per se or per quod. A statement is defamatory per se if, on its face, it falsely imputes: (1) criminal conduct punishable with prison and involving moral turpitude; (2) a communicable and loathsome disease; (3) misconduct in a person's trade, profession, office, or occupation; or (in some states) (4) serious sexual misconduct. *See Freer v. M&I Marshall & Ilsey Corp.,* 688 N.W.2d 756 (Ct. App. Wis. 2004). The second type of defamatory statements are per quod, or "not actionable per se." These include any false communication to a third party— someone other than the plaintiff—that tends to injure the plaintiff's reputation or to diminish esteem, respect, goodwill, or confidence in the plaintiff, or to excite derogatory feelings or opinions about the plaintiff. *See id.*

If a statement is defamatory per se, harm to reputation is presumed. The reason for the presumption is that no rational trier of fact could find that the statement did not harm the plaintiff's reputation. To obtain more than a nominal amount, a plaintiff must provide an evidentiary basis for a jury to award fair and just compensation. If the statement is only defamatory per quod, then a plaintiff must plead and prove that publication proximately caused an economic loss, and prove the amount of loss with reasonable certainty. Damages are not presumed because a rational trier of fact *could,* but need not, find a per quod false statement harmed the plaintiff's reputation. *See Am. Kitchen Delights, Inc. v. John Soules Foods, Inc.,* 2014 WL 4897506 (N.D. Ill. Sept. 29, 2014) (dismissing defamation claim because "special damages" must be pled in compliance with Fed. R. Civ. P. 9(g), and were not); *Collins v. BSI Fin. Serv.,* 2017 WL 1045062 (M.D. Ala. March 17, 2017) (same).

A plaintiff who establishes either: (a) defamation per se and so harm to reputation is presumed, or (b) defamation per quod, which caused the plaintiff to lose a specific economic loss in an amount proven with reasonable certainty, may, in addition, (c) recover consequential damages, including damages for mental anguish. Importantly, this means a plaintiff who proves defamation per se may recover consequential damages for specific economic losses caused by the publication in addition to, and not in lieu of, general damages for harm to reputation.

B. Whether Negligence or Actual Malice Is the Required Degree of Fault

The plaintiff must prove fault by the defendant. The minimum is negligence. Whether "actual malice" is required depends on both the status of the plaintiff and the context in which the statement was made. The first step is to identify whether, when the statement was made, the plaintiff was a public official, a general-purpose public figure, or a private figure. If the plaintiff was a private figure, the plaintiff may have been one of two kinds of "limited-purpose public figures." Depending on the status of the plaintiff at the time the statement was made, to establish "fault," the plaintiff may need to show the defendant made the false statement with "actual malice," not merely negligently.

1. <u>Public Officials</u>. Only public employees who had "substantial responsibility for or control over the conduct of governmental affairs" are deemed public officials for purposes of defamation law. *Rosenblatt v. Baer*, 383 U.S. 75 (1966). It is unsettled "how far down into the lower ranks of government employees" the designation extends. *New York Times v. Sullivan*, 376 U.S. 254, 283 (1964).

2. <u>General-Purpose Public Figures</u>. Only people who, at the time of publication, had such "persuasive power and influence that they may hold sway on any issue with which they choose to become involved" are general-purpose public figures. *United Inventory Serv., Inc. v. Tupperware Brands Corp.*, 2011 WL 13276821 (W.D. Tenn. Mar. 8, 2011). "General public figures are limited for the most part to those well-known 'celebrities' whose names have become a 'household word,' and who therefore can be regarded as having knowingly relinquished their anonymity in return for fame, fortune, or influence." *Id.* For business entities, the factors include: (1) the notoriety of the corporation to the average individual in the relevant geographic area; (2) the nature of the corporation's business; and (3) the frequency and intensity of media scrutiny that the corporation normally receives. *Id.* (holding Tupperware was a general-purpose public figure.)

3. <u>Limited-Purpose Public Figures</u>. There are two types of limited-purpose public figures: (a) "voluntary limited-purpose public figures," who had voluntarily thrust themselves to the forefront of a particular public controversy to influence its resolution; or (b) "involuntary limited-purpose public figures," who had become public figures through no purposeful action of their own, but instead had been drawn into a particular public controversy. *See id.* This latter category is extremely rare — requiring "actual malice" by "someone who by bad luck is an important figure in a public controversy, runs the risk of returning us to a conception of defamation law under which all defamation plaintiffs were required to prove actual malice when the allegedly defamatory statements occurred during discussion and communication involving matters of public or general concern, without regard to whether the persons involved are famous or anonymous." *Alharbi v. Beck*, 62 F. Supp. 3d 202 (D. Mass. 2014).

If the plaintiff at the time of publication was a limited-purpose public figure, then a final step is to determine whether the statement was about a matter of public or private concern. If the statement concerned a private matter, negligence is sufficient, but if it was about a matter of public concern, actual malice is required. The court in *Brady v. Klentzman*, 515 S.W.3d 878 (Tex. 2017), explained the meaning of "a matter of public concern" as follows:

> According to the Supreme Court, speech deals with matters of public concern when it can be fairly considered as relating to any matter of political, social, or other concern to the community. Public matters include a subject of legitimate news interest; that is, a subject of general interest and of value and concern to the public. Whether speech addresses a matter of public concern must be determined by the expression's content, form, and context as revealed by the whole record.
>
> Public matters include, among other things, commission of crime, prosecutions resulting from it, and judicial proceedings arising from the prosecutions. A report that a corporation and its principal stockholder had links to organized crime and used some of those links to influence the State's governmental process was a matter of public concern. Similarly, the disclosure of misbehavior by public officials is a matter of public interest, especially when it concerns the operation of a police department.

4. <u>Actual Malice Distinguished from Common Law Malice</u>. "Malice" is used in two contexts in which it has different, but overlapping, meanings. If actual malice is required because of the status of the plaintiff (e.g., the plaintiff was a general-purpose public figure), "actual malice" defines the level of "fault" the plaintiff must prove. To show actual malice, the plaintiff must prove the defendant had published the statement with knowledge that it was false or with reckless disregard as to whether it was false. As *Hearst Corp. v. Skeen*, 159 S.W.3d 633 (Tex. 2005) explained:

> A failure to investigate fully is not evidence of actual malice; a purposeful avoidance of the truth is. We analyzed evidence of purposeful avoidance when a talk show host was sued for libel after repeatedly accusing a judge of being corrupt. Although the host claimed that his accusations were based on his investigations, there was a complete absence of any evidence that a single soul ever concurred in the host's accusations of misconduct against the judge. All those who could have shown the host that his charges were wrong the host deliberately ignored. For example, the host made a false accusation that the judge had improperly delayed a criminal trial without even contacting any attorney involved in the case to inquire about the delay.

An understandable misinterpretation of ambiguous facts does not show actual malice, but inherently improbable assertions and statements made on information that is obviously dubious may show actual malice. In *Harte-Hanks Communics., Inc. v. Connaughton*, 491 U.S. 657 (1989), despite knowing the judicial candidate had turned the tape concerning bribery over to the police, the newspaper still published the improbable assertion that he intended to blackmail his opponent with the tape. Moreover, the sister's uncorroborated allegations were doubtful because every other witness the newspaper interviewed denied the sister's version of the events. Additionally, the sister's hesitant demeanor and inaudible responses in her taped interview with the newspaper raised "obvious doubts about her veracity." With the sister as the only source of the dubious allegations, the evidence showed the newspaper had recklessly disregarded the truth in publishing the article.

In the second context in which "malice" is used, it describes the level of culpability a plaintiff must show to in order overcome a defendant's common law qualified (or conditional) privilege. "Common law malice" in that context includes showing the defendant made a statement knowing it was false or with reckless disregard as to whether it was true, and a more subjective form of "malice" in the sense of "meanness" or spite. The inquiries are independent and distinct.

C. Did the Defendant "Publish" a False Defamatory Statement?

"Publication" requires that the defendant "publish" a false statement to someone besides the plaintiff. If only the plaintiff heard or read a false defamatory statement, it may anger or distress the plaintiff, but it cannot harm the plaintiff's reputation. In this regard, most states follow the "single publication rule." Under that approach, "any one edition of a book or newspaper, or any one radio or television broadcast is a single publication." *Life Designs Ranch, Inc. v. Sommer,* 364 P.3d 129 (Ct. App. Wash. 2015).

D. Was the Publication Protected by an "Absolute" or Conditional Privilege?

"Privilege" is a form of affirmative defense. Privileges fall into two categories: "absolute" and "qualified," but even "absolute" privileges are (in a sense) qualified.

"Cases in which absolute privilege applies are not numerous and they may be divided into three classes, namely: Proceedings of legislative bodies; judicial proceedings; and communications by military and naval officers." *Isle of Wight County v. Nogiec,* 704 S.E.2d 83 (Va. 2011). "Legislative bodies" generally includes subordinate governmental agencies, and both governmental actors and private citizens. *See Id.* "Judicial proceedings" includes court proceedings and adjudicatory administrative proceedings, and generally covers statements made by the judges, jurors, counsel, parties, or witnesses in open court, pretrial hearings, depositions, affidavits, and any of the pleadings or other papers in the case. *Yates v. Iowa West Racing Ass'n,* 707 N.W.2d 336 (Iowa 2005) ("judicial proceedings" included workers' compensation proceedings as well as statements made to a racing commission when acting in an adjudicatory capacity); *Gilmore v. L.D. Drilling, Inc.,* 2017 WL 5904034 (D. Kan. Nov. 29, 2017) (state department of labor proceeding deciding claim for wages was a "judicial proceeding"); *Clark Cnty. Sch. Dist. v. Virtual Ed. Software, Inc.*, 213 P.3d 496 (Nev. 2009) (extending privilege to legal assistant's statements so long as a proceeding "was contemplated in good faith and under serious consideration" and the statement was "related" to it). These privileges are "absolute" because even if made with malice, the statement cannot be the basis of defamation. However, the privilege does not cover statements made outside the proceeding or republication. *See Hearst Corp. v. Skeen*, 130 S.W.3d 910 (Tex. Ct. App. 2004), *rev'd on other grounds*, 159 S.W.3d 633 (Tex. 2005).

Conditional or qualified privileges include: (1) The public interest privilege, to publish materials to public officials on matters within their public responsibility; (2) the common interest privilege, to publish to someone who shares a common interest or, relatedly, to publish in defense of oneself or in the interest of others; (3) the fair comment privilege; and (4) the reporting privilege, to make a fair and accurate report of public proceedings. *Shirley v. Heckman*, 75 A.3d 421 (Md. Spec. App. 2013). A common example of a conditional privilege protects a statement by an employee, in the course and scope of employment, reporting to a supervisor the suspicious act of a co-worker. *See Nicholls v. Brookdale Univ. Hosp. Med. Center*, 2004 WL 1533831 (E.D.N.Y. July 9, 2004). Another accompanies statements to report criminal activity to authorities. *State Farm Mut. Cas. Co. v. Radcliff*, 987 N.E.2d 121 (Ct. App. Ind. 2013).

Conditional privileges can be overcome by showing "abuse." Typical examples of "abuse" include: (1) actual malice in the constitutional sense—i.e., the defendant knew the statement was false or made it with reckless disregard as to whether it was true; (2) the statement was not made to further the purpose for which the privilege exists; (3) the statement was made to someone who did not reasonably need to hear it (e.g., in addition to reporting a co-worker's suspicious act to a supervisor, an employee tells a co-worker); (4) the statement included false defamatory matter not reasonably related to the purpose for which the privilege exists; (5) the defendant was motivated by personal spite or ill will (often called "common law actual malice"); (6) the statement included strong or violent language disproportionate to the occasion; or (7) the defendant had acted in bad faith. *Goulmamine v. CVS Pharm., Inc.*, 138 F. Supp. 3d 652 (E.D. Va. 2015); *Carter v. Aramark Sports and Ent. Services, Inc.*, 835 A.2d 262 (Md. Spec. App. 2003).

2. Monetary Remedies for Defamation

A. The Demanding Requirements of Defamation Per Se

Hill v. Stubson

420 P.3d 732 (Wyo. 2018) (Davis, J.)

[Hill was superintendent of schools when she had led an effort to have the courts declare a statute, known as SF104, unconstitutional. She then retired. During the next election cycle, a state legislator, Stubson, made various statements while campaigning for office about Hill on his campaign's Facebook page, during debates, and in media interviews. Among other things, Stubson stated that while she had been superintendent, Hill had "committed many illegal acts" that the legislature knew of, but which it had not disclosed publicly. He also stated she had not fulfilled her obligations as superintendent. Hill sued Stubson for defamation. The trial court held the complaint alleged actual malice, but granted Stubson's motion to dismiss. Hill appealed.]

The First Amendment limits the circumstances under which a public official may maintain a defamation action for statements critical of her official conduct. *New York Times Co. v. Sullivan*, 376 U.S. 254 (1964). The constitutional guarantees of free speech and press prohibit a public official from recovering damages for defamatory statements unless it can be shown that the statements were made with actual malice. Acting on this premise, the district court dismissed Ms. Hill's complaint based on its dual conclusion that Ms. Hill was a public official for First Amendment purposes and that her complaint failed to allege facts sufficient to support a finding of actual malice. We agree that Ms. Hill's complaint alleges facts sufficient to establish her status as a public official for First Amendment purposes, but we disagree that her complaint failed to sufficiently allege actual malice.

Shortly after the Supreme Court decided *New York Times v. Sullivan*, it issued another decision in which it addressed who should be considered a public official for purposes of imposing the First Amendment actual malice requirement. *Rosenblatt v. Baer*, 383 U.S. 75 (1966). In *Rosenblatt*, the plaintiff was a former county recreation area supervisor who filed a libel action in response to a newspaper column that criticized his performance as area supervisor and implied he may have taken or misused the area's funds. In considering whether a recreation area supervisor was a public official the Court declined to draw any precise lines:

> In cases like the present, there is tension between this interest and the values nurtured by the First and Fourteenth Amendments. The thrust of *New York Times* is that when interests in public discussion are particularly strong, as they were in that case, the Constitution limits the protections afforded by the law of defamation. Where a position in government has such apparent importance that the public has an independent interest in the qualifications and performance of the person who holds it, beyond the general public interest in the qualifications and performance of all government employees, both elements we identified in New York Times are present and the New York Times malice standards apply.

In applying this framework to the case before it in *Rosenblatt*, the Court observed that based on the plaintiff's own assertions of his prominence in the community and the public interest in the recreation area, a strong argument could be made that plaintiff was a public official. In so remanding, however, the Court observed: "We remark only that, as is the case with questions of privilege generally it is for the trial judge in the first instance to determine whether the proofs show respondent to be a "public official." *Rosenblatt*, 383 U.S. at 88.

Importantly, the Court in *Rosenblatt* found the fact that the plaintiff no longer held the position of recreation supervisor to be of no significance to the public official inquiry.

> It is not seriously contended, and could not be, that the fact respondent no longer supervised the Area when the column appeared has decisional significance here. To be sure, there may be cases where a person is so far removed from a former position of authority that comment on the manner in which he performed his responsibilities no longer has the interest necessary to justify the *New York Times* rule. But here the management of the Area was still a matter of lively public interest; propositions for further change were abroad, and public interest in the way in which the prior administration had done its task continued strong. The comment, if it referred to respondent, referred to his performance of duty as a county employee.

Applying this framework, we conclude that Ms. Hill's complaint alleges facts sufficient to support a finding that she was a public official for First Amendment purposes when Mr. Stubson made his statements. The complaint alleges that Ms. Hill was sworn in as the Superintendent of Public Instruction in January 2011. That her position was one of five elected state officials is probably sufficient to establish that she held a position of "such apparent importance that the public has an independent interest in the qualifications and performance of the person who holds it, beyond the general public interest in the qualifications and performance of all government employees." *Rosenblatt*, 383 U.S. at 86. We need not, however, rely on that fact alone. The complaint goes on to allege the importance of Ms. Hill's work to the state and those who elected her, and it alleges the importance of her position as an office originally created by the first territorial legislature, as a member of the Wyoming Board of Land Commissioners, and as an ex officio member of the University of Wyoming Board of Trustees. We are thus satisfied that the complaint alleges facts sufficient to establish that the superintendent of public instruction is a public official for First Amendment purposes.

Because, however, Ms. Hill no longer held that position when the allegedly defamatory statements were made, we must also consider whether the complaint alleges facts sufficient to show continuing public interest in SF104 and Ms. Hill's performance in the office. We again conclude that it does. The complaint is replete with allegations of public interest in SF104 and allegations that Ms. Hill was very much a part of that public controversy. Paragraphs 39 and 40, in particular, allege:

> As soon as SF104 was signed by the governor, Mrs. Hill served the governor and the legislature (through the State of Wyoming) with a lawsuit challenging the constitutionality of SF104. The leadership of the legislature did not like being defied or challenged in court. Those who had sponsored and supported SF104 were not prepared for the public's response to what they had done.

The public reaction to SF104 was immediate. Members of the public became outraged and were condemning of legislators who had supported SF104. Legislators were flooded by thousands of emails, phone calls, and visits from members of the public who felt that those legislators had taken their vote in education.

The complaint also contains allegations sufficient to support a finding that the public interest in SF104 and Ms. Hill's tenure as superintendent had not waned when Mr. Stubson made his statements. The complaint alleges that the first statement, posted on Facebook, was made in response to a question from a journalist concerning SF104, and the second statement was made in response to an inquiry at a public debate. That these questions were being asked in 2016 indicates that the SF104 controversy was still a matter of public interest when Mr. Stubson made his statements. For these reasons we agree with the district court's finding that Ms. Hill was a public official for First Amendment purposes and was therefore required to allege facts sufficient to support a claim of actual malice. We turn then to the complaint's allegations relevant to Ms. Hill's required showing that Mr. Stubson made his statements with actual malice.

Ms. Hill's complaint seeks relief for the statements Mr. Stubson made on February 8, 2016 and June 24, 2016. As to those statements, the complaint asserts a claim only for defamation *per se*. It does not assert a claim for defamation with special damages. Because the claim was only defamation *per se*, our task is to determine whether the complaint alleges facts sufficient to state such a claim. We will first address the complaint's assertion of defamation *per se* based on the statements' alleged incompatibility with business, trade, profession, or office, and then its assertion based on the imputation of criminal conduct.

Ms. Hill's complaint alleges that Mr. Stubson's 2016 statements imputed matters incompatible with business, trade, profession, or office and were therefore actionable as defamation *per se*. Based on the requirements for this breed of defamation *per se*, we find that the complaint fails to allege facts sufficient to support the claim.

Under the Restatement, statements alleged to be incompatible with business, trade, profession, or office, to be actionable *per se* must affect the plaintiff in some way that is peculiarly harmful to one engaged in his trade or profession. The Restatement further specifies that "an imputation of misconduct of a public officer whose term has expired does not come within the rule stated in this Section." (Restatement (Second) of Torts § 573 at 194 cmt. c (1977)); *see also Cain v. Esthetique*, 182 F. Supp.3d 54 (S.D. N.Y. 2016) ("To establish slander *per se* under this category, the plaintiff must prove that she carried on the trade, business, or profession at the time the statement was made."); *Knelman v. Middlebury College*, 898 F.Supp.2d 697 (D. Vt. 2012) (recognizing claim may be actionable where plaintiff is not currently in position but is actively seeking same or similar position).

A federal court in New York explained the requirement that a defamation *per se* claimant be in the position at the time of the statements.

On the theory that defendant Geneen's description of him as a "communist" impugned his fitness for his two professions, journalism and international diplomacy, plaintiff contends that that description was slanderous *per se*. We disagree. Geneen's statement was allegedly made some six years after plaintiff left his last post in the foreign service and some two years after he stepped down as President of the United Nations Association. Because plaintiff was not pursuing a career in international relations at the time Geneen is said to have called him a communist, Geneen's statement cannot have impugned him in that career.

Korry v. Int'l Tel. & Tel. Corp., 444 F.Supp. 193 (S.D. N.Y. 1978).

Ms. Hill's complaint does not allege that she held the office of superintendent when Mr. Stubson made his statements in 2016, or that she was actively pursuing that office or a similar office. The complaint therefore fails to state a claim for defamation *per se* based on statements incompatible with business, trade, profession, or office.

Ms. Hill's complaint alleges that Mr. Stubson's statements that she was not following the law and had committed illegal acts imputed criminal offenses to her and were therefore actionable as defamation *per se*. At the outset, we note that our review of the complaint's allegations must focus on the statements the complaint attributes to Mr. Stubson. Our consideration looks to the words he used, not the characterization Ms. Hill gives the words. *See Dugan v. Mittal Steel USA Inc.*, 929 N.E.2d 184 (Ind. 2010) (rejecting plaintiff's attempts to equate "core exchange" with "theft" as a means to state claim for defamation *per se*); *Marcil v. Kells*, 936 A.2d 208 (R.I. 2007) (innuendo may not be used to enlarge meaning of language used).

To be actionable *per se*, a statement imputing a criminal offense must reference a crime that is (a) punishable by imprisonment in a state or federal institution, or (b) regarded by public opinion as involving moral turpitude. The Restatement describes crimes involving moral turpitude in the following terms:

> Moral turpitude has been defined as inherent baseness or vileness of principle in the human heart. It means, in general, shameful wickedness, so extreme a departure from ordinary standards of honesty, good morals, justice or ethics as to be shocking to the moral sense of the community. An analogy is found in the common rule that the conviction of a witness for a crime involving moral turpitude is admissible in evidence to impeach or discredit him.

> Regardless of the punishment to which the offender may be subjected by the terms of the particular penal code, the charge of a crime involving moral turpitude is actionable *per se*. Among these crimes are treason, espionage, murder, burglary, larceny, arson, rape, criminal assault, perjury, selling mortgaged chattels or diseased meat, kidnapping, wife beating, malicious mischief, indecent exposure, bootlegging, operating a bawdy house, and uttering a bad check. This is by no means a complete catalogue

of offenses. There are many other crimes, such as obtaining goods by false pretenses or making a fraudulent income tax return, that involve moral turpitude.

Given the Restatement requirements that a defamation *per se* claim of this type be based on imputation of a criminal offense, the complaint's factual allegations are insufficient. First, the statements in the complaint not only do not specify a criminal offense punishable by imprisonment or involving moral turpitude, they do not charge criminal conduct at all.

The term used was "illegal." Illegal means "not according to or authorized by law." *Merriam-Webster's Collegiate Dictionary* 618 (11th ed. 2012). The term criminal means "relating to, involving, or being a crime." *Id.* at 296. Accusing a person of illegal conduct is not the same as accusing her of criminal conduct. *See Fink v. Meadow Lake Estates Homeowners' Ass'n*, 384 Mont. 552 (2016) ("The published statements accused Fink of acting 'illegally,' but did not state she had committed a crime, upon which she premises her claim."); *McGee v. Gast*, 257 Ga.App. 882 (2002) (statement that scoutmaster committed "illegal activities" did not impute a criminal offense).

Even were we inclined to equate "illegal" and "criminal," the complaint contains no allegations that would elevate Mr. Stubson's statements to the level of defamation *per se*. The Restatement does not require technical precision in a statement accusing one of criminal conduct, but it must be apparent from the statement that the crime was one punishable by imprisonment or involving moral turpitude. *See* Restatement (Second) of Torts § 571 cmt. c ("It is not necessary that the defamer charge any particular criminal offense either by name or description, if the words used imply some crime of the type stated in Clauses (a) punishable by imprisonment and (b) involving moral turpitude."); *see also Lovings v. Thomas*, 805 N.E.2d 442 (Ind. Ct. App. 2004) (false imputation of a crime must bear some reasonably close relation to the legislative definition of a crime); *Graff v. O'Connell*, 2002 WL 450534 (Conn. Super. Ct. 2002) (statement that plaintiffs were operating illegal kennel not specific enough to be actionable as slander *per se*). The statements on which the complaint bases Ms. Hill's defamation *per se* claim contained no suggestion that Ms. Hill had engaged in conduct involving moral turpitude or conduct for which she could be imprisoned. The statements simply lacked the specificity required to be actionable as defamation *per se*. We uphold the district court's Rule 12(b)(6) dismissal.

Notes and Questions

1. <u>Uphill Battle</u>. What allegations showed Hill was a "public official" and that, though the statements were made after she quit, there was still a "public concern?" Could a rational jury find her reputation was not harmed by an accusation of "illegal" activity? What if the statements had so harmed her reputation that it was pointless to pursue her former career?

2. <u>Statements about Professions</u>. The Restatement limits this type of per se defamation to a statement that "ascribes to another conduct, characteristics or a

condition that would adversely affect his fitness for the proper conduct of his lawful business, trade or profession, or of his public or private office, whether honorary or for profit," and a comment states:

> When peculiar skill or ability is necessary, an imputation that attributes a lack of skill or ability tends to harm the other in his business or profession. Statements that a physician is a drunkard or a quack, or that he is incompetent or negligent in the practice of his profession, are actionable. So too, a charge that a physician is dishonest in his fees is actionable, although an imputation of dishonesty in other respects does not affect his character or reputation as a physician.
>
> Disparagement of a general character, equally discreditable to all persons, is not enough unless the particular quality disparaged is of such a character that it is peculiarly valuable in the plaintiff's business or profession. Thus, a statement that a physician consorts with harlots is not actionable per se, although a charge that he makes improper advances to his patients is actionable; the one statement does not affect his reputation as a physician whereas the other does so affect it.

Restatement (Second) of Torts § 573 (1977). *See Whitt v. Baldwin Cnty. Mental Health Cntr.*, 2013 WL 6511856 (S.D. Ala. Dec. 12, 2013) (statement executive had "dementia" not per se defamatory); *Manswell v. Heavenly Miracle Academy Serv., Inc.*, 2017 WL 948194 (E.D.N.Y. Aug. 23, 2017) (statement plaintiff daycare worker fired for hitting a child was per se defamatory). Can you see why a nexus is required?

B. The Measure of Damage for Harm to Reputation

Many courts hold that defamation per se creates a presumption of *some* reputational harm, and leave the jury to determine the amount. In such states, a plaintiff establishing defamation per se need not show any economic loss, but for a jury to award "more than nominal damages, the prevailing party must substantiate the amount requested as an award." *Robertson v. Doe*, 2009 WL 10676484 (S.D.N.Y. Dec. 17, 2009). While nominal damage is the minimum, the measure is left to "the enlightened consciences of an impartial jury." *Riddle v. Golden Isles Broadcasting, LLC*, 666 S.E.2d 75 (Ct. App. Ga. 2008). *See Teff v. Unity Health Plans Ins. Corp.*, 666 N.W.2d 38 (Ct. App. Wis. 2003) ("As the jury instruction, which the trial court looked to for guidance, provides: 'It is not required that plaintiff prove damages by any financial yardstick measuring dollars and cents. Injury to reputations, good name, and feelings are not subject to mathematical calculations or certainty.'"); *Halverson v. Spoor*, 381 P.3d 618 (Nev. 2012) ($50,000 proper general damage based on per se defamation "because of the impossibility of affixing an exact monetary amount for present and future injury to the plaintiff's reputation, wounded feelings and humiliation, loss of business, and any consequential physical illness or pain."); *Cluse v. H&E Equip. Serv., Inc.*, 34 So. 3d 959 (Ct. App. La. 2010) (reciting general damage verdicts of $25,000 for being accused over a Wal-Mart store intercom of stealing a bag of potting soil and $150,000 to an attorney defamed in a newspaper with a readership of 35,000).

A logical way to show reputational harm is to show publication caused a specific economic loss. But, as the following suggests, while economic loss can be evidence of reputational harm, it is not its measure, and, conversely, lack of proof of a specific economic loss does not mean publication caused no reputational harm.

State Farm Mut. Cas. Co. v. Radcliff

987 N.E.2d 121 (Ct. App. Ind. 2013) (Vladik, J.)

[After a massive storm, plaintiff Joseph Radcliff started a company to repair hail-damaged homes. He noticed that, unlike other insurers, State Farm was denying claims of many of his customers, and offered to help his customers with claims against State Farm. State Farm generated a flurry of publicity and conducted its own "insurance fraud" investigation into Radcliff and his company. Because of State Farm's complaints to authorities, Radcliff was arrested and charged with 14 felonies, which were later dismissed through a diversion agreement with the state. Then State Farm sued Radcliff for fraud and other claims. Radcliff and his company counterclaimed for, among other things, defamation. After a six-week trial, a jury awarded Radcliff and his company $14.5 million, one of the largest defamation judgments in history, a verdict that was not broken into general or special damages. State Farm appealed. On appeal, the court concluded that State Farm had committed defamation per se by publicizing and reporting to the authorities that Radcliff and his company had committed various crimes, held that Radcliff and his company had been limited-purpose public figures, and held the jury findings of actual malice were supported by the evidence. Finally, the court turned to the damage award.]

In an action for defamation *per se,* the plaintiff is entitled to presumed damages as a natural and probable consequence of the *per se* defamation. The jury may presume damages because the law presumes the plaintiff's reputation has been damaged, and the jury may award a substantial sum for this presumed harm, even without proof of actual harm. In addition, upon proper proof, the plaintiff is entitled to special damages, or financial damages arising as a consequence of the defamation.

In this case, Final Instruction No. 18 covered damages:

> If you find that Joseph Radcliff has proved that State Farm committed defamation, the law presumes that Joseph Radcliff has been damaged due to the nature of the statements made, and you may award such presumed damages. These may include reasonable compensation for harm to Joseph Radcliff's reputation.
>
> There is no definite standard or method of calculation to decide reasonable compensation for presumed damages. Joseph Radcliff is not required to present evidence of actual harm, or the opinion of any witness as to the

amount of reasonable compensation. Any award for presumed damages must be just and reasonable.

In addition to presumed damages, you must also award money that will fairly compensate Joseph Radcliff for other proven damages caused by State Farm's communication, including, but not limited to:

1. personal humiliation;

2. mental anguish and suffering;

3. physical harm; and

4. financial harm, if any, such as loss of business or income.

Joseph Radcliff must prove by the greater weight of the evidence that he suffered these other damages.

During closing arguments, Radcliff and CPM asked the jury for $30 million-$7.5 million in special damages and $22.5 million in presumed damages. The jury awarded them $14.5 million but did not break down its award into special damages or presumed damages.

State Farm first argues that Radcliff's "sole basis" for claiming special damages was that the defamation caused him financial harm, such as loss of business or income. We disagree with State Farm on this point as Final Instruction 18 defines special damages not only as financial harm caused by State Farm's actions but as personal humiliation, mental anguish, and suffering.

Nonetheless, continuing its argument, State Farm says the special damages were "solely premised" upon Radcliff's expert Dr. Jaffee's calculation of lost earnings for CPM. Dr. Jaffee, a respected professor at Indiana University Kelley School of Business and an economist, determined Radcliff's economic loss at $7.5 million. State Farm, however, asserts that the trial court erred in admitting Dr. Jaffee's testimony because his opinion lacked any indicia of reliability which misled the jury into artificially inflating Radcliff's damages.

On May 20, 2011 State Farm filed a Motion to Exclude Expert Testimony, arguing that Indiana Evidence Rule 702 required the exclusion of Dr. Jaffee as an expert witness because he was not qualified to testify as to damages. Following arguments made by the parties outside the presence of the jury, the trial court denied the motion. Because State Farm did not object when Dr. Jaffee testified, it acquiesced in the admission of his opinion and the issue is waived.

State Farm next argues that Radcliff and CPM failed to present evidence that State Farm proximately caused lost profits and earnings. A plaintiff pleading special damages due to defamation, whether per quod or *per se*, must plead and demonstrate that the special damages were incurred as a natural and proximate consequence of the wrongful act. State Farm asserts that Radcliff and CPM's other expert—Dr. Saxton—did not testify as to causation and Radcliff's testimony was not sufficient either because it established only "a short-term disruption in his relationships with suppliers, customers and employees following his arrest (a generous description of his testimony)."

Dr. Saxton was retained to testify as to the impact that Radcliff's arrest had on his business prospects for the future. Her theory was that the media attention did irreparable harm to Joe Radcliff. When she did her first "Google" search on Radcliff eighteen months after his arrest, her first thoughts were, "I don't see how this person can be in business anymore." Dr. Saxton said that the articles on the internet created "a very negative situation for him" because "the lead issues that get discussed are, first of all, his arrest, and then other things related to the idea of him ripping people off or there being complaints." Dr. Saxton emphasized that "the challenge with the internet is that once something is on the internet, it's virtually impossible to get rid of it." She concluded that his reputation was in a "virtually unrecoverable place now" and he could "do nothing to get out from under that." She testified in detail about Google's algorithm and how articles show up on the critical first page of results.

Despite this testimony, State Farm argues that Dr. Saxton's testimony does not establish causation because she said that she was not retained to testify whether Radcliff's difficulty would cause him monetary damages. But the reasonable inference from Dr. Saxton's testimony is that the internet articles on Radcliff, which were still accessible years later, will affect whom consumers choose to hire. But even assuming Dr. Saxton's testimony is not enough to establish causation, Radcliff's testimony is sufficient. Radcliff testified in detail that his arrest and the ensuing publicity — including the front page of The Indianapolis Star, local news media, and CNN — caused CPM to shut down.

Finally, State Farm argues that the verdict in this case is excessive. Citing other Indiana cases that had $1 million and less verdicts, State Farm claims that the $14.5 verdict in this case "exceeds all prior Indiana defamation verdicts by many multiples" and "can only be explained by passion, prejudice or the desire to punish an insurance company given the evidence presented." We will not engage in a comparative analysis in this case.

Here, the jury heard testimony of a man whose whole world — professionally and personally — was destroyed by State Farm's accusations and the accusations' role in his arrest, and it heard from Dr. Jaffee, who testified that Radcliff had $7.5 million in lost earnings, and Dr. Saxton, who explained that Radcliff's reputation was in a "virtually unrecoverable" place. The jury's damage award does not punish State Farm; rather, it attempts to compensate Radcliff for the longstanding consequences it caused on the only profession that Radcliff ever knew. Accordingly, the $14.5 million damage award is not excessive.

Longbehn v. Schoenrock

727 N.W.2d 153 (Ct. App. Minn. 2007) (Hudson, J.)

[Plaintiff Patrick Longbehn was a new police officer in a probationary period. He was also 34 years old and began dating an 18-year-old woman. The police chief told Longbehn he was being terminated after his probationary period because people in the community called him "Pat the Pedophile" because he was dating the 18-year-old, but, the chief said, no one actually believed he was a pedophile. Longbehn obtained another job with the department of corrections, but was fired for assaulting his girlfriend, a co-employee. She obtained a restraining order against him, and he checked himself into a psychiatric institute. He then brought a defamation claim against the defendant Schoenrock, who had—once—called plaintiff "Pat the Pedophile" in front of other people. Although the nickname had been commonly used in the community, its use did not start with Schoenrock. The jury awarded general, special, and even punitive damages. The trial court granted the defendant's motion for JMOL, holding "Pat the Pedophile" was not per se defamatory and plaintiff had not proven special damages. Plaintiff appealed.]

Here the jury awarded appellant special damages in the aggregate amount of $90,000 for past and future wage loss. But the district court concluded that the evidence was legally insufficient to prove that respondent's statement was the legal cause of any actual and special pecuniary loss. Even after reviewing the evidence in the light most favorable to appellant, we agree with the district court.

A plaintiff may recover special damages if he or she proves that the defamatory publication is the legal cause of any actual and special pecuniary loss. A defamatory publication actionable *per se* is the legal cause of special harm if it is a substantial factor in bringing about the harm.

Here, the record shows that respondent used the offensive nickname on one isolated occasion. There is no evidence that respondent originated the name or participated in its dissemination so as to justify imposing liability on him for any subsequent publication by others. In fact, the record shows that at the time of the incident, appellant was commonly known in the Moose Lake community by this derogatory nickname.

Next, the record indicates that the city's decision to terminate appellant was based on his conduct and that respondent's publication was not a substantial factor in bringing about appellant's termination. The chief of police never heard respondent make the defamatory publication. The chief testified that although the name was a reflection of appellant's loss of credibility in the community, the name was not the reason for the city's action. According to the chief, the factor playing the most significant role in the decision to terminate appellant as a police officer was the community's perception that appellant was overzealous and overbearing.

Finally, there is no evidence that respondent's publication caused appellant any loss of prospective employment. Appellant testified that after the city terminated his employment he did not actively seek employment as a police officer. But appellant presented no evidence at trial establishing that respondent's publication inhibited him from fulfilling his duty to mitigate damages or prevented him from realizing an expected gain. Furthermore, in light of appellant's termination from the department of corrections for assaulting his girlfriend and the related OFP, respondent's defamatory publication cannot reasonably be viewed as the legal cause of any future difficulty appellant may encounter in trying to obtain employment as a police officer. Based on the evidence submitted at trial, the district court did not err in concluding that respondent's publication was not the legal cause of any special harm appellant claims to have sustained.

The jury awarded appellant $230,000 for past and future harm to reputation, mental distress, humiliation, and embarrassment, as well as $3,000 for future health-care expenses. The district court concluded that the evidence was legally insufficient to establish a causal connection between respondent's statement and these general damages. But because respondent's statement is defamatory *per se*, general damages are presumed and appellant may recover without any proof of actual harm; accordingly, the district court erred with regard to this issue.

Appellant argues that the district court erred by concluding that the evidence did not support the amount the jury awarded for general damages. A reviewing court should not set aside a jury verdict on damages unless it is manifestly and palpably contrary to the evidence viewed as a whole and in the light most favorable to the verdict. But the district court has broad discretion in determining whether to set aside a verdict as being excessive and should not hesitate to do so where it feels the evidence does not justify the amount.

The presumption of general damages in cases of defamation *per se* affords little control by the court over the jury's assessment of the appropriate amount of damages. But in the absence of proof, general damages are limited to harm that would normally be assumed to flow from a defamatory publication of the nature involved. In *Gertz,* the Supreme Court stated:

> The common law of defamation is an oddity of tort law, for it allows recovery of damages without evidence of actual loss. Juries may award substantial sums as compensation for supposed damage to reputation without any proof that such harm actually occurred. The largely uncontrolled discretion of juries to award damages where there is no loss unnecessarily compounds the potential of any system of liability for defamatory falsehood to inhibit the vigorous exercise of First Amendment freedoms. The States have no substantial interest in securing for plaintiffs gratuitous awards of money damages far in excess of any actual injury.

Although the Minnesota Supreme Court has held that *Gertz*'s constitutional protections do not apply to a private plaintiff suing a private defendant on an issue not of public concern, we find *Gertz*'s proposition that states have no interest in securing gratuitous awards far exceeding actual injury to be persuasive. Based on the record in this case, including the context in which respondent made the defamatory statement, we conclude that $233,000 in general damages far exceeds the amount of past and future harm to appellant's reputation, mental distress, humiliation, and embarrassment that would normally flow from a publication of this kind. Accordingly, we remand for a new trial on general damages.

Notes and Questions

1. <u>What Amount for Pat</u>? Based upon the results in the other cases in this section, what is a reasonable award on remand? What would be a reasonable settlement? In answering, consider the costs both parties already incurred, the cost of retrial, that the jury will be instructed that the statement presumably caused damages—and then consider the amount this jury awarded.

2. <u>A Presumption</u>? In *Liberty Nat'l. Life Ins. Co. v. Daugherty*, 840 So. 2d 152 (Ala. 2002), the plaintiff testified his reputation had been excellent and remained so after the defendant's defamatory statement. The court rejected defendant's argument that testimony rebutted any presumption of damage: "[I]t would be anomalous conclusion for us to sanction the introduction of the evidence under review. To do so would have the effect of destroying, or at least seriously jeopardizing, the prevailing presumption of injury to reputation in the publication of a libelous statement." *See Cluse v. H&E Equip. Serv., Inc.*, 34 So. 3d 959 (Ct. App. La. 2010) (plaintiff's testimony he "did not know" whether the statements caused anyone "to think less of him" not an admission no harm occurred and did not rebut the presumption of harm).

In contrast, in *DeVito v. Schwartz*, 784 A.2d 376 (Conn. Ct. App. 2001), the statement was per se defamatory and the jury found the defendant had acted maliciously, but it awarded zero general damages. The court of appeals affirmed:

> Although the jury should have awarded Schwartz at least nominal damages, it set his damages at $0. Nonetheless, as a general rule an appellate court will not reverse and grant a new trial for a mere failure to award nominal damages. While nominal damages are awarded without proof of actual injury, they imply the smallest appreciable quantity with one dollar being the amount frequently awarded. The law, however, does not concern itself with trifles (*de minimis non curat lex*), and a judgment for plaintiff will not be reversed on appeal for a failure to award nominal damages, even though plaintiff is entitled to recover nominal damages as a matter of law. Because the facts of this case do not warrant an exception to that rule, we conclude that the court correctly refused to set aside the jury's verdict even though it awarded Schwartz zero damages.

3. <u>Consequential Damages</u>. A plaintiff who establishes defamation per se may recover consequential damages—including specific economic losses caused by the defamation. Put another way, a defamation per se plaintiff may, in addition to general damages, recover the same damages that a plaintiff asserting defamation per quod must establish to recover anything.

C. Special Damages Are Required for Defamation Per Quod and May Be Consequential Damages for Defamation Per Se

If a statement is not defamatory per se, courts do not presume any harm and even nominal damages are not allowed. *Hancock v. Variyam*, 400 S.W.3d 59 (Tex. 2013). Instead, the plaintiff must prove the defendant's publication was a substantial factor in causing some form of "special damage." "Special damage" generally requires proof of "loss of money or some other material temporal advantage capable of being assessed in monetary value." *Webster v. Wilkins*, 217 Ga. App. 194 (1995). "The loss of income, of profits, and even of gratuitous entertainment and hospitality will be special damage if the plaintiff can show that it was caused by the defendant's words." *Id.*; *see Whitt v. Baldwin Cnty. Mental Health Cntr.*, 2013 WL 6511856 (S.D. Ala. Dec. 12, 2013) ("Special damages include lost income" and so must meet Fed. R. Civ. P. 9(g).)

Special damages required for defamation per quod do not include the statement's impact on the plaintiff: "injury to the reputation must be alleged and proved as an essential link between the slanderous utterance and the special damage which constitutes the basis of recovery in actions per quod. The special damage, to which we now refer, must be of a *material* and, generally, of a *pecuniary* nature. *It must result from the conduct of a person other than the defamer or the defamed, and that conduct must be directly caused by the publication of the slander.*" *Accurso v. Gallo*, 2008 WL 5572954 (Conn. Supr. Dec. 29, 2008). If economic loss is proven, mental anguish damages may be recovered, but they "are not special damages unto themselves, but rather are parasitic damages, viable only when attached to normal (i.e., pecuniary) special damages." *Ducker v. Amin*, 2014 WL 1018050 (S.D. Ind. March 14, 2014).

Thus, a plaintiff must show a defamatory statement was a substantial factor—a cause—of "special damages" and establish the amount lost with reasonable certainty. Essentially, the plaintiff must show that it would have been better off had the statement not been made and, with reasonable certainty, the amount of damages to put it where it would have been but for the defendant's statement. Defendants regularly obtain summary judgment, or exclude evidence of lost profits, because plaintiffs cannot show a causal connection between the statement and economic loss.

Choctaw Town Square, LLC v. Kokh Licensee, LLC

2016 WL 443000 (W.D. Okla. March 16, 2016)

[The plaintiff, a business, alleged that defendant's television broadcast had defamed it. Relying on an Oklahoma statute limiting recovery against media defendants to special damages, the defendant moved for summary judgment of no causation. The court denied the motion: the plaintiff business offered the deposition testimony of Evans, who was the president of All-Star Electric, Inc., in which she testified that she had decided not to hire the plaintiff to perform a $250,000 contract (which would have netted the plaintiff $37,500) because she had been concerned that if she did so, then an All-Star customer might think poorly of All-Star. Evans was the sister of the CEO of the plaintiff. Later, the defendant filed a motion *in limine* to exclude this testimony to show causation of special damages. The court issued this order denying that motion.]

The question of *proximate cause* is generally one of fact for the jury. It becomes one of law *only* when there is *no evidence* from which a jury could reasonably find a causal nexus between the act and the injury. The *presence* of competent evidence to show this causal connection — i.e., whether there is *any* competent evidence that would support a jury finding of causation — is *in turn* a law question for the court.

Upon review, the court concludes that the "All-Star Electric" theory of damages is relevant and competent evidence. Although Ms. Evans testified that she did not believe the alleged defamatory statements, the decision not to employ plaintiff was based upon her perception that if any of All-Star Electric's customers had seen the broadcast and believed the alleged defamatory statements, it would have reflected against All-Star Electric. Consequently, Ms. Evans's employment decision was based upon her concern that All Star Electric's customers would believe the alleged defamatory statements concerning plaintiff. The court therefore concludes that Ms. Evans' testimony is relevant and competent evidence to demonstrate a causal connection between the alleged defamatory statements and the actual injury to plaintiff. The fact that Ms. Evans did not know whether any of her customers saw the subject broadcast does not make her testimony irrelevant or incompetent. The court concludes that Ms. Evans' testimony adequately establishes a causal nexus between the subject wrongful conduct and the injury.

Having concluded, for now, that Ms. Evans' testimony is admissible, the court will add one observation, an observation based on the fact that, in our system, one of the main reasons for permissive rules of evidence is that we tend quite strongly to give our juries credit for collectively having a modicum of common sense. As the court noted in its summary judgment order, there is ample reason for a jury to conclude that the proffered testimony from Ms. Evans is suspiciously convenient. The record now before the court detracts not one whit from that observation. The proffered testimony has, at this juncture, cleared the legal hurdles that have been thrown up, but, on a jury of eight, there may well be six or seven — if not eight — sets of eyeballs rolling when the plaintiff's CEO trots out his sister, in a fairly solitary role, to support a theory of damages that is noticeably attenuated, albeit admissible.

Notes and Questions

1. <u>Summary Judgment</u>. The "All-Star Electric Theory" was some evidence the defendant's publication caused economic loss, and so summary judgment was inappropriate. But, given that the judge did not believe it would persuade a jury, why deny summary judgment?

2. <u>Causation of Lost Prospective Employment</u>. In *Sadid v. Idaho St. Univ.,* 2013 WL 6490587 (D. Idaho Dec. 10, 2013), the plaintiff alleged that defendant's

defamatory statements that he was a security threat had caused prospective employers to not offer him jobs. The court granted the defendant's motion *in limine* to exclude evidence of a failed job search, writing:

> Courts have viewed with a jaundiced eye a plaintiff's claim for compensation based on lost job opportunities when the claim is based solely on their [*sic*] own testimony about their [*sic*] failed job search. In *Jones v. Western & Southern Life Ins. Co.*, 91 F.3d 1032 (7th Cir. 1996), for example, the Seventh Circuit upheld the district court's refusal to submit an item of special damages to the jury. The court explained that "with nothing but the plaintiff's own testimony, both with respect to the existence of the job opportunity itself and with respect to the amount of money it was worth, the district court correctly refused to submit this item of damages to the jury." *Id.* Earlier, the *Jones* Court explained that plaintiff was "under the misapprehension that he did not need to prove that the job either existed or was worth a particular amount of money in order for this question to be submitted to the jury." *Id. See also Tosti v. Ayik*, 476 N.E.2d 928 (Mass. 1985) (observing that in the case before it, "the record shows no comparable proof that the plaintiff's failure to obtain full-time employment from 1971 through 1982 was due to defendant's tortious acts").

Here, Dr. Sadid claims that potential employers were undoubtedly aware of Mr. Garner's comments, but the only proof he offers on this point tends to be sweeping statements such as this one: "In 2010 Defendant Garner's defamatory statements to the press went viral in cyberspace around the world." *Response*, Dkt. 183, at 3; *see also id.* at 5 ("there are statements in the press and circulated around the world by the Internet that Dr. Sadid is a security threat.") The fact that an article is available on the internet, however, does not necessarily mean employers would search for and find it. Additionally, even assuming potential employers or customers did find the article containing Garner's comments, the jury would have to further assume that these comments were, in fact, the reason Dr. Sadid was not hired. Then, Dr. Sadid would ask the jury to peg a specific dollar amount on the value of these lost job opportunities, based on his assessment of what the job opportunities were worth. *Cf. Jones* (in pointing out plaintiff's failure to prove specifics regarding his lost employment opportunity theory, the court asked "How do we know the potential employer was going to pay Jones only $125,000? Why not $150,000, or $500,000?").

3. <u>Salary and the Measure of Damage.</u> In *Yellow Book USA, Inc. v. Brandeberry*, 2011 WL 3240558 (S.D. Ohio July 28, 2011), Brandeberry alleged Yellow Book had defamed him. After the trial court found defamation per se, it granted Yellow Book's motion *in limine* to exclude evidence of special damages, stating:

> Ohio Jury Instructions on damages for defamation *per se* provide that the jury is to decide the amount of money that is reasonable and fair for Brandeberry's injuries directly caused by the alleged defamation. This

instruction will presumably be given to the Jury. Finally, the notes to this instruction provide that, in defamation *per se* cases, while no proof is necessary, the plaintiff may offer evidence about the amount of damages.

Brandeberry has not pled or identified any special damages. Thus, he is limited to seeking the amount of money that the jury decides is reasonable and fair for the alleged defamation *per se* and he may present evidence and argument regarding the amount of damages. The evidence will, of course, be subject to cross examination and rebuttal.

Yellow Book's Motion In Limine is granted in part and overruled in part. Brandeberry may not present evidence of special damages but he may discuss the amount of damages that is reasonable and fair for the alleged defamation *per se* in accordance with the jury instruction.

If special damages had been nonexistent or minimal, was defendant's motion wise?

4. <u>Why Not Always Require Actual Loss</u>? The Supreme Court has stated such proof is not required for defamation per se because a statement that had been defamatory per se "is all but certain" to have caused "serious harm," and that presuming damages "furthers the state interest in providing remedies for defamation by ensuring that those remedies are effective." *Dun & Bradstreet, Inc. v. Greenmoss Builders, Inc.,* 472 U.S. 749 (1985). Does it not also cause inexplicable awards? Why not require proof of actual economic loss in all defamation cases, as some states do by statute? *See* 42 Pa. C.S. 8343(a)(6) (statute requires "special harm resulting to the plaintiff from its publication" for all defamation claims).

3. Monetary Remedies for Reputational Harm Caused by Breach of Contract

As shown above, defamation is designed to remedy harm to reputation. Under tort law, if a statement was defamatory per se, damages to reputation are not speculative: they are, instead, *presumed* to have occurred and the jury is instructed to award them. In contrast, this section shows that harm to reputation for breach of contract is "speculative" and, except in extraordinary cases, cannot be recovered. The reasons for that are more fully examined in Chapter 8.

However, in the context of settling disputes, parties often include in settlement agreements a "nondisparagement clause," which generally prohibits either party from making disparaging statements about the other. Note that these clauses can prohibit true statements: they can prevent a former employer from stating, for example, the truthful reason why a former employee had been fired. The following cases show why, even in that context, tort law provides a greater remedy than contract law.

Klaymen v. Judicial Watch, Inc.

255 F. Supp. 3d 161 (D.D.C. 2017) (Kollar-Kotelly, J.)

[Plaintiff Larry Klaymen had worked for Judicial Watch, Inc., and in connection with his termination the parties entered into a settlement agreement that contained, among other things, an "antidisparagement" clause. Klaymen later sued Judicial Watch for breach of contract, including a claim that it had breached the antidisparagement clause. During suit, the court as a sanction limited the type of damages Klaymen could pursue. The parties asked the court for clarification on this issue, including what sort of damages could be pursued for breach of the antidisparagement clause. The court issued this order in response.]

As a general "rule," reputation damages are not recoverable for a breach of contract claim. *See, e.g., Redgrave v. Boston Symphony Orchestra*, 855 F.2d 888 (1st Cir. 1988) (explaining that Massachusetts is in agreement with "virtually all other jurisdictions" in holding that reputation damages are unavailable in contract actions); *Smith v. Positive Prods.*, 419 F.Supp.2d 437 (S.D.N.Y. 2005) ("Damages to reputation generally are not recoverable in a breach of contract."); *Stancil v. Mergenthaler Linotype Co., a Div. of Eltra Corp.*, 589 F.Supp. 78 (D. Haw. 1984) (adopting "the majority view that damages for injury to reputation are not properly awardable in a breach of contract suit."); *Herrera v. Union No. 39 School District*, 181 Vt. 198, 917 A.2d 923, 933 (2006) (holding that for breach of an employment contract, harm to reputation is considered to be "outside the range of foreseeable losses").

Although stated as a general rule, however, the unavailability of reputation damages actually stems from the application of two general requirements for recovering consequential damages in a breach of contract action. First, the consequential damages sought must have been "in the contemplation of both parties at the time they made the contract," *Redgrave*, 855 F.2d at 893 (stating the rule of *Hadley v. Baxendale*, 9 Exch. 341, 156 Eng. Rep. 145 (1854)). Second, consequential damages must be proved with reasonable certainty, beyond mere speculative loss. See *Redgrave*, 855 F.2d at 892.

1. Reasonable Contemplation of the Parties

In the District of Columbia, a plaintiff "is entitled to damages that were foreseeable at the time the contract was made. Damages are foreseeable if they are the sort that the parties would have reasonably envisioned, or are the sort that would flow naturally and obviously from the breach of the contract." Standardized Civil Jury Instr. for D.C. § 11.31. The question before the Court is whether the parties contemplated that reputation damages would be available for a breach of the nondisparagement provision in the Severance Agreement. The Agreement provides, in relevant part, that:

> Klayman expressly agrees that he will not directly or indirectly, disseminate or publish, or cause or encourage anyone else to disseminate or publish in any manner, disparaging, defamatory, or negative remarks or comments about Judicial Watch or its present or past directors, officers, or

employees. Judicial Watch expressly agrees that its present directors and officers namely Paul Orfanedes and Thomas Fitton, will not, directly or indirectly, disseminate or publish, or cause or encourage anyone else to disseminate or publish in any manner, disparaging, defamatory, or negative remarks or comments about Klayman. Nothing in this paragraph is intended to, nor shall be deemed to limit either party from making fair commentary on the positions or activities of the other following the Separation Date.

Plainly, a non-disparagement clause requires a different analysis than a contract provision which, for example, promises delivery of some component. It may be that if the deliverer breaches, and the buyer is unable to find an alternative supplier, he will be unable to produce his product, and will thereby suffer reputational harm among his customers and business peers. Nonetheless, absent some extenuating circumstances, reputation damages will not be recoverable because it is unlikely that the business parties contemplated that these damages would be compensable when they entered their run-of-the-mill sales contract. Here, however, the language of the Severance Agreement itself permits a reasonable inference that the parties contemplated that, if one made "disparaging, defamatory, or negative remarks or comments" about the other, he would suffer reputational harm, and that such harm would be compensable. Consequently, whether Plaintiff can recover for losses to his reputation rests on his ability to satisfy the second prong of the consequential damages analysis: proof of damages with reasonable certainty.

2. Reasonably Certain Loss

District of Columbia law requires that any consequential damages must be proved with reasonable certainty. In most cases, this general rule of the common law precludes a plaintiff from recovering reputation damages because such losses are "unduly speculative." *Redgrave*, 855 F.2d at 892. Nonetheless, some courts have reasoned that if a breach of contract causes the plaintiff to lose out on identifiable professional opportunities, the plaintiff may recover damages for such loss when the "monies for loss of the other employment" are "rationally calculable." *Redgrave*, 855 F.2d at 892.

In *Redgrave*, plaintiff argued that the Boston Symphony Orchestra's cancellation of her employment contract—due to her political affiliations—damaged her professional career because a "number of specific movie and theater performances" that would have been offered to her in the usual course of events were not offered to her as a result of the cancellation. The First Circuit distinguished Redgrave's claim for consequential damages based on the "loss of identifiable professional opportunities," from "nonspecific allegations of damage to reputation," allowing recovery of the former when the plaintiff presents "sufficient evidence" that the breach of contract proximately caused the loss of professional opportunities. Id.; *see also Rice*, 203 F.3d at 290 (reversing district court for permitting plaintiff to recover reputation damages absent sufficient proof of lost business opportunities); *Ainbinder v. Money Ctr. Fin. Grp., Inc.*, 2013 WL 1335997 (E.D.N.Y. Feb. 28, 2013) (finding that under New York law, "damages to reputation may be available where a plaintiff can prove specific business opportunities lost as a result of its diminished reputation"), report and recommendation adopted, 2013 WL 1335893 (E.D.N.Y. Mar. 25, 2013).

Plaintiff claims that Judicial Watch "orchestrated an effort to cause media outlets, including radio and television stations and broadcast and cable networks, to shun Plaintiff." Plaintiff further alleges that

> by threatening the media and directing media outlets that they could no longer refer to Klayman as Judicial Watch's founder and former Chairman, or ever discuss anything that concerned or related to Judicial Watch, Fitton and others breached the Severance Agreement and disparaged, defamed and portrayed Klayman in a false light.

Id. ¶ 44. As stated above, the disparagement claim has been described as "arising from the allegation that Judicial Watch actively misrepresented the reasons for Plaintiff's departure or otherwise created the allegedly false impression that he was forced to leave the organization." Though limited, the discovery record does contain facts that could support Plaintiff's recovery of damages for loss of identifiable professional opportunities, specifically a lost CNN appearance. Plaintiff made similar allegations regarding other media outlets.

The difficulty that Plaintiff faces, however, is that the materials furnished to the Court so far include no indication of the actual monetary damages that he sustained from these purported lost business opportunities. Plaintiff has not pointed the Court toward evidence tending to show what monetary benefits inured to him generally from such appearances, let alone from the specific appearances that were lost to him as a result of Defendants' allegedly disparaging conduct. Consequently, in order to finally resolve this question, the Court shall permit Plaintiff to identify such evidence, to the extent it exists, by filing a notice with the Court by June 30, 2017. This evidence must come solely from the current discovery record; no other materials shall be considered by the Court, as Plaintiff never produced evidence to support this claim during discovery. Absent such evidence, however, the Court shall not permit Plaintiff to testify as to the reputational harms that he allegedly sustained as a result of the claimed breach of the non-disparagement clause in the Severance Agreement.

Bakst v. Community Mem. Health Sys., Inc.

2011 WL 13214315 (C.D. Cal. Mar. 7, 2011) (Morrow, J.)

[Plaintiff Bakst had settled an earlier lawsuit by an agreement that included a "non-disparagement clause." He sued for breach of it in a second suit. Defendant Community Memorial Health System, Inc., moved *in limine* to exclude certain evidence.]

CMH also seeks to preclude Bakst from "presenting any argument or introducing any evidence purporting to establish that CMH caused Bakst emotional distress or mental suffering, or that it damaged his reputation or purported good name." CMH asserts that such evidence should be excluded as irrelevant and unfairly prejudicial because tort damages, such as damage to reputation or emotional distress, are not available on any of Bakst's remaining claims. Specifically, CMH contends that under California law, damages for breach of contract cannot include recovery for harm to reputation or for emotional distress. See *O'Neil v. Spillane*, 45 Cal.App.3d 147 (1975) ("the invariable rule pronounced by a legion of cases that damages are not recoverable for mental suffering or injury to reputation resulting from breach of contract"); 23 California Jurisprudence 3d Damages § 80 ("Ordinarily, a plaintiff cannot recover damages for mental suffering experienced as the result of a breach of contract").

Bakst concedes that he is not entitled to tort damages as he previously dismissed his claims for intentional and negligent infliction of emotional distress. He also represents that he does not intend to seek emotional distress damages at trial. As the parties are in agreement on this point, the court grants CMH's motion *in limine* to the extent that it seeks to preclude Bakst from proffering evidence of emotional distress.

Bakst asserts, however, that evidence of damage to his reputation is relevant to prove the essential elements of his claim for breach of the non-disparagement clause. To prevail on his breach of contract claim, Bakst must prove the existence of a valid contract, his performance of the contract or excuse for nonperformance, CMH's breach, and resulting damage. Implicit in the element of damage is that the defendant's breach caused the plaintiff's damage.

To prove that CMH breached the contract, plaintiff must demonstrate that the hospital made disparaging statements about him. Black's Law Dictionary defines disparagement as "a derogatory comparison of one thing with another"; "the act or an instance of castigating or detracting from the reputation of, esp. unfairly or untruthfully"; and "a false and injurious statement that discredits or detracts from the reputation of another's character, property, product, or business." Black's Law Dictionary (9th ed. 2009). Whether CMH's statements "detracted from Bakst's reputation" is thus inextricably intertwined with whether CMH breached the contract by making the statements. If a jury finds that a statement made by CMH "detracted from Bakst's reputation," he will have satisfied his burden of proving that CMH breached the contract. If a jury finds that CMH did not "castigate or detract from Bakst's reputation," then he will be unable to prevail on his first claim for relief. Thus, whether the statements were of a kind that would cause harm to Bakst's reputation is relevant to determine whether they constitute a breach of the contract.

It is also relevant to prove causation and damages. To establish these elements, Bakst must demonstrate that the allegedly disparaging statements caused him to lose employment opportunities. "The test for causation in a breach of contract action is whether the breach was *a substantial factor* in causing the damages." *U.S. Ecology, Inc. v. State*, 129 Cal.App.4th 887 (2005) (emphasis added). "The term 'substantial factor' has no precise definition, but it seems to be something which is more than a slight, trivial, negligible, or theoretical factor in producing a particular result." *Id.* Given that it is generally impossible to get inside the mind of a prospective employer to prove the exact reason it chose not to hire Bakst, Bakst will have to rely on circumstantial evidence to show causation and damages.

Bakst contends that CMH's disparaging statements impugned his reputation and caused prospective employers not to hire him, either because they did not want to work with him or because they were concerned that his poor reputation might be a liability to their organization. This is particularly evident in the declaration of Conrad Vernon, discussed in detail in the court's order on summary judgment. Vernon stated that he would have liked to hire Bakst, but was concerned that Vernon's consulting clients would not want to work with Bakst given his poor reputation. Evidence that CMH's statements harmed Bakst's reputation is thus directly relevant in assessing whether the statements were a substantial factor causing Bakst to lose employment opportunities. Cf. *Foley v. Interactive Data Corp.*, 47 Cal.3d 654 (1988) (Broussard, J., concurring and dissenting) ("breach of an employment contract by the employer can, in some situations, cause severe harm to an employee's reputation and ability to find new employment")

CMH contends that Bakst's theory of damages is legally flawed because he cannot adduce "specific facts" that "a specific job was lost due to CMH's statements." CMH appears to believe that Bakst is attempting to recover damages for generalized harm to his reputation. As discussed at length in the court's summary judgment order, however, Bakst has proffered direct evidence of specific jobs that he contends he lost as a result of CMH's breach. It does not appear that Bakst is seeking damages for the generalized harm to his reputation, but only for those employment opportunities lost because of CMH's allegedly disparaging conduct. Whether Bakst can adequately show the existence of a causal link between those lost opportunities and CMH's purportedly disparaging statements will be a question the jury will have to resolve.

In sum, while Bakst cannot proffer evidence that he has suffered emotional distress as a result of CMH's allegedly disparaging statements, he may offer evidence of harm to his reputation both to establish that CMH's breached the non-disparagement clause and that its alleged breach caused him to lose employment opportunities. He may not, however, proffer evidence of generalized reputational harm that is not directly tied to a particular lost employment opportunity.

Notes and Questions

1. <u>Contract and Tort</u>. One key principle, developed further in later chapters, is that contract remedies are more limited than tort remedies. The principal cases show, for example, that although both contract and tort law each require the amount of damages to be proven with "reasonable certainty," contract law requires "more" certainty. In that regard, is the recovery for breach of a nondisparagement clause akin to damages for defamation per se or per quod?

2. <u>What If Bakst Wins</u>? Suppose Bakst successfully shows a defendant's statement to Vernon caused Vernon not to hire him. What is the measure of damage?

3. <u>True Disparaging Statements</u>. While nondisparagement clauses typically would be breached by a false defamatory statement, depending on the wording they

can be reached by true statements. As *Eichelkraut v. Camp*, 513 S.E.2d 267 (Ct. App. Ga. 1999) explained:

> Appellants maintain that "the term 'disparagement' in the legal sense contemplates the making of a false statement in order to be actionable" and that because the statements made in the letters were true, they could not have been disparaging. We do not agree. It is true, as argued by appellants, that disparagement is identified as a form of slander or defamation under OCGA § 51-5-4(a)(4). But this statutory definition of a tort does not dispense with the cardinal rule of contract construction that in interpreting contracts, we must ascertain the intent of the parties. We conclude that the agreement clearly reflects the parties' intent that the non-disparagement clause applied to all derogatory communications, whether true or not.

4. <u>Privileges</u>. The few courts that have addressed it allow the same privileges that apply to defamation to be used against claims for breach of nondisparagement clauses. *E.g., Wexler v. Allegion (UK) Ltd.*, 374 F. Supp. 3d 302 (S.D.N.Y. 2019). They reason that, otherwise, a plaintiff is merely avoiding them by asserting a breach of contract claim instead of defamation, and "the privilege would be 'valueless' or 'meaningless' if the opposing party could bar application of the privilege just by drafting the claim with a non-tort label." *O'Brien & Gere Engineers, Inc. v. City of Salisbury*, 135 A.3d 473 (Md. 2016). Perhaps, but does it matter to that analysis whether the statement was true, or instead false and defamatory?

4. Monetary Remedies Triggered by Harm to a Business's Reputation

Corporations cannot suffer mental anguish, but have an interest in their reputations. Some states permit businesses to use defamation to remedy harm to a business reputation. *E.g., Energy Consumption Auditing Serv., LLC v. Brightergy, LLC*, 49 F. Supp. 3d 890 (D. Kan. 2014) (defendant referred to competitor's product as "junk" and "overpriced" and so imputed a lack of skill and integrity in the trade). Others do not permit businesses to use defamation, but recognize other claims. *R&R Int'l, Inc. v. Manzen, LLC*, 2010 WL 11504727 (S.D. Fla. Sept. 12, 2010) (applying defamation law but stating a business must show special damages); *Clark Cnty. Sch. Dist. v. Virtual Ed. Software, Inc.*, 213 P.3d 496 (Nev. 2009) (stating if a statement attacks a plaintiff's business reputation, plaintiff should assert defamation, but if it attacks quality of plaintiff's products or services, plaintiff must assert claim for business disparagement).

In this regard, the Restatement provides: "One who publishes a false statement harmful to the interests of another is subject to liability for pecuniary loss resulting to the other if (a) he intends for publication of the statement to result in harm to interests of the other having a pecuniary value, or either recognizes or should recognize that it is likely to do so, and (b) he knows that the statement is false or acts in reckless disregard of its truth or falsity." Restatement (Second) of Torts §623A (1977). Some states refer to the remedy created by §623A as "injurious false-hood," including New Mexico, Texas, and Delaware. *FLSmidth A/S v. Jeffco, LLC*, 2008 WL 4426992 (N.D. Okla. Sept. 25, 2008) (Oklahoma had not yet recognized this claim). The names and requirements vary, but some examples are:

- In Colorado, commercial disparagement requires the following elements: (1) a false statement; (2) published to a third party; (3) derogatory to the plaintiff's business in general, to the title to his property, or its quality; (4) through which the defendant intended to cause harm to the plaintiff's pecuniary interest, or either recognized or should have recognized that it was likely to do so; (5) with malice; (6) thus causing special damages. If a plaintiff cannot show special damages, there is no remedy. To establish special damages, the plaintiff must identify specific persons who refuse to deal with the plaintiff because of the disparagement, or causation of loss of a contract. *See ConcealFab Corp. v. Sabre Industries, Inc.*, 2017 WL 6297672 (D. Colo. Dec. 11, 2017);

- In Arizona, a plaintiff asserting injurious falsehood must show the publication of matter derogatory to plaintiff's business that is calculated to prevent others from dealing with him, causing pecuniary loss. *See eMove Inc. v. SMD Software Inc.*, 2012 WL 1379063 (D. Ariz. Apr. 20, 2012).

- In Texas, a plaintiff asserting business disparagement must establish: (1) defendant published false and disparaging information about it, (2) with malice, (3) without privilege, (4) resulting in special damages. While defamation chiefly remedies harm to personal reputation, business disparagement remedies economic harm. A defendant is liable "only if he knew of the falsity or acted with reckless disregard concerning it, or if he acted with ill will or intended to interfere in the economic interest of the plaintiff in an unprivileged fashion." *See In re Lipsky*, 411 S.W.3d 530 (Ct. App. Tex. 2013).

Federal Rule of Civil Procedure 9(g) applies. *Energy Consumption Auditing Serv., LLC v. Brightergy, LLC*, 49 F. Supp. 3d 890 (D. Kan. 2014) (collecting cases).

5. Monetary Remedies Triggered by Invasion of Privacy or Harm to Similar Interests

A. The Four Distinct Harms

Courts permit recovery for harm to privacy and other interests, but do not recognize the same claims and disagree on their precise elements. The court in *Felsher v. U. of Evansville*, 755 N.E.2d 589 (Ind. 2001) explained:

We begin our analysis by acknowledging the position taken in the Restatement (Second) of Torts, §652A(1) (1977): "One who invades the right of privacy of another is subject to liability for the resulting harm to the interests of the other."

This Court has previously observed that the term "invasion of privacy" is a label used to describe four distinct injuries: (1) intrusion upon seclusion, (2) appropriation of name or likeness, (3) public disclosure of private facts, and (4) false-light publicity. *Doe v. Methodist Hosp.*, 690 N.E.2d 681 (Ind.1997). In *Doe,* we examined the genesis of the privacy tort, apparently originating in an 1890 law review article written by Samuel Warren and future U.S. Supreme Court Justice Louis Brandeis. Professor William Prosser later characterized the authors as heralding "the emergence of a new, if ill-defined, right to privacy" signaled by several decisions granting relief "on the basis of defamation or invasion of some property right, or a breach of confidence or an implied contract." *Id.*

In *Doe,* we also noted the Second Restatement's view that the four injuries involved in the privacy tort are "only tenuously related." We explained that the four wrongs were separate and "united only in their common focus on some abstract notion of being left alone." *Id.*

Some states do not recognize any of the claims, while others only some. *See id.* (rejecting public disclosure of private facts); *Jews For Jesus, Inc. v. Rapp*, 997 So. 2d 1098 (Fla. 2008) (rejecting false light).

Graboff v. Colleran Firm

744 F.3d 128 (3d Cir. 2014) (Greenberg, J.)

[The American Association of Orthopaedic Surgeons and the American Academy of Orthopaedic Surgeons (collectively, "AAOS") were professional organizations of surgeons that adopt professional standards, including procedures for members to file grievances against each other. Dr. Meller was a member who filed a grievance against another member, Dr. Graboff, complaining that Dr. Graboff had written a report for a medical malpractice case in which he opined that Dr. Meller had committed malpractice. As a result of that grievance, Dr. Graboff was suspended from the AAOS, and it published an article describing the grievance proceeding.

Dr. Graboff asserted both defamation and false light claims against the AAOS. The jury found no defamation but found false light liability and awarded $196,000 in damages. The AAOS appealed, arguing that because it had not committed defamation, it could not be liable for false light.]

Pennsylvania has adopted the definition of false light invasion of privacy from the Restatement (Second) of Torts, which imposes liability on a person who publishes material that "is not true, is highly offensive to a reasonable person, and is publicized with knowledge or in reckless disregard of its falsity." *Larsen v. Phila. Newspapers, Inc.*, 375 Pa.Super. 66 (1988) (en banc). Although to the best of our knowledge the Pennsylvania Supreme Court has not addressed the contours of falsity in the false-light-invasion-of-privacy context, the Superior Court has defined falsity broadly in that context. A plaintiff can establish falsity by showing that a defendant selectively printed or broadcast true statements or pictures in a manner which created a false impression. Thus, even where a publication is literally true, discrete presentation of information in a fashion which renders the publication susceptible to inferences casting one in a false light entitles the grievant to recompense for the wrong committed. The Superior Court has drawn this broad definition from defamation law, which permits recovery where a publication was true, but implied falsehoods.

Applying this standard in *Larsen*, the Superior Court allowed the plaintiff's claim to survive a motion to dismiss where he alleged that a series of articles, although literally true, conveyed a false impression that he had lied under oath. *See also Krajewski v. Gusoff,* 53 A.3d 793 (Pa. Super. Ct. 2012) (reversing dismissal of false-light claim where factual statements in article "suggested a causal relationship" that could not be proven); *Santillo v. Reedel,* 430 Pa.Super. 290 (1993) ("A false light claim can be established where true information is released if the information tends to imply falsehoods.").

Falsity with respect to a defendant's statements thus carries the same meaning in the defamation and false-light-invasion-of-privacy contexts; indeed, the Superior Court drew its definition of falsity in the false-light-invasion-of-privacy context from its corresponding definition in the defamation context. And Pennsylvania inferior courts consistently apply the same analysis to both types of claims when the causes of action are based on the same set of underlying facts. Accordingly, publication of factually correct statements that convey a false impression can be actionable as defamation (if the statements had a grievous effect on one's reputation), or actionable as a false light invasion of privacy (if the statements would be highly offensive to a reasonable person). Clearly there is little difference between these claims in dealing with the consequences of a defendant's statements.

The District Court's instructions correctly told the jury that a defendant's statements in the defamation context could be false if the statements included untrue statements or if the statements implied something that was untrue. The Court, however, did not specifically charge the jury that a finding that the AAOS published a false statement was a prerequisite for Dr. Graboff to recover for false light invasion of privacy. Rather, the Court stated that the AAOS could be liable for false light invasion of privacy if it published statements that placed Dr. Graboff "before the public in a false light" and if the publication would be highly offensive to a reasonable person. This charge was correct as far as it went though it omitted an explanation that the AAOS could be liable in a false-light case if it made a factually untrue statement.

As we have explained, the District Court did not submit the case to the jury by asking for general verdicts on the two alleged torts. Instead, the Court submitted the case to the jury on interrogatories which, in addition to including a damages question that the jury needed to address only if it answered the liability questions in favor of Dr. Graboff, asked only three questions regarding liability on the tort claims involved on this appeal: (1) did Dr. Graboff show, by a preponderance of the evidence, that the AAOS made statements in the article that were either false, or (2) portrayed Dr. Graboff in a false light, and (3) did the AAOS act knowingly or with reckless disregard for the truth of its statement? JA 1262. The jury found that the article did not contain false statements but that it did contain statements that portrayed Dr. Graboff in a false light and that the AAOS acted knowingly or with reckless disregard for the truth. The completed interrogatories and answers read:

6. Do you find that Dr. Steven Graboff proved by a preponderance of the evidence that the American Academy of Orthopaedic Surgeons and American Association of Orthopaedic Surgeons ('AAOS') made statements in *AAOS Now* about Dr. Steven Graboff that:

(a) Were false?

___ YES _X_ NO

(b) Portrayed Dr. Steven Graboff in a false light?

_X_ YES ___ NO

If your answer to Question No. 6(a) or 6(b) is "YES", please proceed to Question No. 7. If your answers to Question No. 6(a) and 6(b) are "NO", please proceed to Question No. 9.

7. Do you find that the American Academy of Orthopaedic Surgeons and American Association of Orthopaedic Surgeons ('AAOS') knew or acted in reckless disregard for the truth or untruth of statements in *AAOS NOW* that were false or portrayed Dr. Steven Graboff in a false light?

_X_ YES ___ NO

We reiterate that the District Court treated these answers as making a finding in favor of Dr. Graboff for false light invasion of privacy and in favor of the AAOS on the defamation claim.

The AAOS challenges the jury's verdict as "incompatible (or at least inconsistent)." The AAOS argues that because the Court defined falsity as including "true statements that create a false impression," the jury's finding in interrogatory 6(a) that the AAOS had not published false statements precludes imposing liability on it either for defamation or false light invasion of privacy. In effect, the AAOS is arguing that, inasmuch as the jury found that it did not make false statements about Dr. Graboff, it could not have made statements portraying him in a false light.

We approach the incompatibility and inconsistency argument recognizing that inconsistent jury verdicts are an unfortunate fact of life in law, and should not, in and of themselves, be used to overturn otherwise valid verdicts. Rather, when faced with a seemingly inconsistent verdict, a court, to the extent possible, should read the verdict to resolve the inconsistencies.

We conclude that the answers to the interrogatories can be reconciled but that the District Court did not correctly treat the answers to resolve a possible inconsistency in them when it concluded that the jury found for the AAOS on the defamation claim and for Dr. Graboff on the false-light-invasion-of-privacy claim. The Court, applying Pennsylvania law, explained to the jury that Dr. Graboff could prove his defamation claim if the AAOS published either untrue statements or true statements that implied something untrue. The Court explained that the AAOS could be liable for false light invasion of privacy if it published statements that portrayed Dr. Graboff in a false light, but in so defining a false-light claim did not distinguish between untrue statements or statements that implied something untrue. Overall, when the entire charge is considered, it is clear that the Court split the bases for finding liability under the two causes of action at issue into two possibilities: i.e., factually false statements or statements whether or not true that implied something untrue.

The jury found that the AAOS had not published false statements, but had published statements that portrayed Dr. Graboff in a false light. Under the instructions, these responses support a finding of liability for both defamation and false light invasion of privacy; after all, as the District Court explained to the jury, it was not necessary for the jury to find a statement was untrue for there to be a recovery on a defamation claim. What the Court did, in effect, was to ask the false-light interrogatory twice, the first time as part of what the Court regarded to be the defamation claim interrogatory because falsity by implication was included in the definition of falsity and the second time in what the Court believed to be the false-light claim interrogatory. When we view the interrogatories in this way, the verdict was not inconsistent because the evidence supported a conclusion that the AAOS had made statements that were false inasmuch as they portrayed Dr. Graboff in a false light but that the statements were not factually false.

We cannot say that the jury did not follow the District Court's instructions in returning its verdict for, notwithstanding the Court's explanation that falsity includes statements false in themselves and statements false by implication, the Court separated the two categories of falsity and directed the jury to consider the categories in different answers, and the jury did exactly that. But we believe that the Court erred in its treatment of the verdict because the legal consequence of the jury's finding that the AAOS published statements portraying Dr. Graboff in a false light was that the AAOS was liable on both claims even though the jury found that the article did not make a false statement. Properly applied, the jury's determination trumps the AAOS's argument that its finding that the AAOS did not make false statements about Dr. Graboff precluded a finding of liability on either claim.

But even though the District Court did not read the verdict as it could have and, indeed, should have to resolve any seeming inconsistency in the verdict, the error was harmless because once we reconcile the liability aspects of the verdict, as we have done, the damages finding easily stands. The jury calculated damages for defamation and false light invasion of privacy together:

10. Please state the amount of damages, if any, that Dr. Steven Graboff suffered as a result of the liability you found against the American Academy of Orthopaedic Surgeons and American Association of Orthopaedic Surgeons ("AAOS")

For Intentional Interference with Prospective Contractual Relations, Defamation, and/or Publication in a False Light:

Past loss of earnings in a lump sum: $<u>140,000</u>

Future loss of earnings in a lump sum: $<u>0</u>

Noneconomic loss in a lump sum: $<u>56,000</u>

Because the jury assessed damages for both claims as a single unit, our reading of the verdict to provide that the AAOS was liable both for defamation and false light invasion of privacy allows the damages award to stand. In these circumstances, the District Court's error in treating the jury's answers to the interrogatories so as to exonerate the AAOS on the defamation claim was harmless because the error had no effect on the outcome of the case. Regardless of whether the jury found for Dr. Graboff only for false light invasion of privacy, as the District Court believed, or on both claims, its damage calculation would have been the same.

Notes and Questions

1. <u>What Harm Does Each Aspect of Invasion of Privacy Protect</u>? Which, if any, were implicated in *Graboff*? Consider whether an entity can establish the harm required by any of the four types of invasion of privacy claims. *Cf. Meyer Technology Solutions v. Kaegem Corp.*, 2017 WL 4512918 (N.D. Ill. 2017) ("corporations have no right to seclusion that is protected by tort law").

2. <u>Consent</u>. In *Herrera v. AllianceOne Receivable Mgmt., Inc.*, 2016 WL 7048318 (S.D. Cal. Dec. 5, 2016), a collection agency repeatedly called the plaintiff seeking collection of a debt he did not owe. He sued, asserting, among other claims, invasion of privacy. The debt collection agency asserted that a qualified privilege existed for debt collectors based upon the premise that debtors, as part of accepting credit, consent to reasonable steps to collect a debt even if that results in an intrusion upon seclusion. The argument failed. Why?

B. The Measure of Damages for Harm to Privacy Interests

Most states "have not precisely defined" the measure of damages for invasion of privacy. *Nguyen v. Taylor*, 723 S.E.2d 551 (N.C. Ct. App. 2012) (affirming $1 million for each plaintiff where defendant admitted it had made more than $10 million on sales of DVD that had put police officers in false light). Adopting invasion of privacy, the court in *Howard v. Aspen Way Enterprises, Inc.*, 406 P.3d 1271 (Wyo. 2017) stated damages were available for:

(a) the harm to his interest in privacy resulting from the invasion;

(b) his mental distress proved to have been suffered if it is of a kind that normally results from such an invasion; and

(c) special damage of which the invasion is a legal cause.

Not all courts take this approach. Some require proof of economic loss before other harms are compensable. For example, a California jury instruction states that a jury may award "economic losses which the plaintiff has sustained to date, or is reasonably certain to suffer in the future in respect to property, business, trade, profession or occupation which were caused by the defendant's invasion of plaintiff's privacy." Cal. Jury. Instruction 7.27. *If* economic losses are found, the California instruction requires the jury to award "damages that will reasonably compensate for (1) harm to plaintiff's reputation caused by the portrayal of the plaintiff in a false light, and (2) any mental or emotional distress caused by the invasion, if it is of a kind that normally results from such an invasion." *Id.* The following cases explore damages and illustrate how allowing remedies for invasion of privacy can, like defamation, implicate the First Amendment.

Roth v. Farner-Bocken Co.
667 N.W.2d 651 (S.D. 2003) (Caldwell, J.)

[Plaintiff Gregg Roth was a salesman with the defendant, Farner-Bocken Co. Roth had physical and mental health issues, and he had attended Alcoholics Anonymous. After defendant terminated Roth, Roth met with a lawyer to discuss suing the defendant for age discrimination. The lawyer declined Roth's case, but then mistakenly mailed sensitive materials that Roth had left with the lawyer to the defendant, not Roth. The defendant opened the package, photocopied its contents, put it in a new envelope with the lawyer's return address and mailed it to Roth.

Later, Roth, through another lawyer, did sue for age discrimination. After discovery showed that the defendant had opened the mail from his first lawyer, Roth added a claim for invasion of privacy. A jury found for defendant on the age discrimination claim but found for Roth on the invasion of privacy claim. Defendant appealed.]

In this case, there is sufficient evidence in the record indicating that reasonable minds could differ as to whether Farner had intruded upon Roth's seclusion, and the issue was properly submitted to the jury. Schmidt testified that after he opened the envelope addressed to Roth at Farner's business address, Schmidt realized it was from a law firm and meant for Roth, personally. Yet, Schmidt read the entire contents of the packet, made photocopies and disseminated them to his superior at Farner. Additionally, there was circumstantial evidence that a second letter from the same law firm addressed to Roth at Farner's business address was opened, read, photocopied and disseminated at Farner. Therefore, there was competent and substantial evidence upon which a jury could find Farner liable for invading Roth's privacy.

Farner contends that there was insufficient evidence to support an award of compensatory damages and that the award of $25,000 was excessive, arbitrary and a result of passion or prejudice and not supported by the evidence.

Generally, the amount of damages to be awarded is a factual issue to be determined by the trier of fact. However, an award of compensatory damages must not be the product of passion and prejudice and must be supported by the evidence. The test for determining if the jury verdict is the product of passion or prejudice is: "The damages, therefore, must be so excessive as to strike mankind, at first blush, as being, beyond all measure, unreasonable and outrageous, and such as manifestly show the jury to have been actuated by passion, partiality, prejudice or corruption." *Stormo v. Strong*, 469 N.W.2d 816 (S.D. 1991)

In *Kjerstad v. Ravallette Public., Inc.*, 517 N.W.2d 419 (S.D. 1994), we indicated there was competent evidence to support an award for compensatory damages on an invasion of privacy claim when the record reflected evidence that the plaintiffs had suffered both physical and emotional reactions to the invasion and had incurred medical expenses. We held the evidence supported compensatory damage awards of $500 and $200 in invasion of privacy claim when plaintiffs presented evidence that defendant had observed them using the restroom. However, we did not indicate that plaintiffs bringing invasion of privacy claims were required to demonstrate they had incurred medical expenses as a result of the invasion.

Other courts that have been asked to review awards for compensatory damages in invasion of privacy claims have struggled in their attempts to measure damages. *See Hill v. McKinley*, 311 F.3d 899 (8th Cir. 2002) (affirming jury's award of $2,500 in compensatory damages on invasion of privacy claim); *Mitchell v. Globe Int'l*, 817 F. Supp. 72 (W.D. Ark. 1993) (remitting compensatory damage award in invasion of privacy claim on remand from Eighth Circuit Court of Appeals with directions to substantially remit award); *Rohrbaugh v. Wal-Mart Stores, Inc.*, 212 W.Va. 358 (2002) (holding that if none of the Restatement damages are proven, nominal compensatory damages are to be awarded).

The *Mitchell* case involved an invasion of privacy claim based on publication of a picture of the 96-year-old plaintiff, a resident of Mountain Home, Arkansas, in a supermarket tabloid to illustrate a story about "'Paper Gal, Audrey Wiles' in Sterling, Australia, who had become pregnant by one of her customers, a 'reclusive millionaire' she met on her newspaper route.'" The Eighth Circuit Court of Appeals remanded that case for a substantial remittitur of compensatory damages after concluding that while the evidence supported a compensatory damage award, the amount awarded by the jury—$650,000—was shocking and exaggerated.

In its decision remitting the compensatory damage award the federal district court believed "the Harrison, Arkansas, jury, chosen from all walks of life, was better situated to make that decision than this court." It said, "This is an especially difficult task where the damages to be awarded are based on intangibles such as damage to reputation and mental suffering." *Id*. Ultimately, the court remitted the compensatory damage award to $150,000, because it believed the damages suffered by plaintiff due to the defendant's conduct were worth that much.

In addressing invasion of privacy claims, courts have recognized that damages in this area can be difficult to ascertain or measure by a pecuniary standard. Therefore, realizing the difficulty in determining damages, courts have found that a trier of fact is uniquely qualified to assess damages.

In this case, a South Dakota jury found Farner had committed an unreasonable, unwarranted, serious and offensive intrusion upon the seclusion of another. Furthermore, the jury found the invasion at issue—the opening, reading, photocopying and dissemination of Roth's mail—was one which would be offensive and objectionable to a reasonable man of ordinary sensibilities. Additionally, the jury heard testimony from Roth that he felt angry, betrayed and devastated upon learning of the invasion. Roth also testified that he sought help with his feelings over the intrusion from his sponsor and friends at Alcoholics Anonymous. Roth also testified that one of the documents in the intercepted package was a handwritten note, created upon the advice of his attorney, which documented Roth's experiences and feelings during his last few months of employment at Farner. Roth's wife testified that he was very hurt upon learning of the invasion, felt deceived and could not believe that somebody would open his mail and do that. She further testified that Roth could not sleep at night and drank a lot of coffee. Upon hearing the evidence and being instructed to fix the amount of damages based on findings of the harm to Roth's privacy interest and emotional distress suffered, the jury awarded the sum of $25,000 in compensatory damages.

Although the amount of the jury's award in this case gives us pause, we cannot say that there was no legal evidence upon which it could be based.

Patel v. Hussain

485 S.W.3d 153 (Ct. App. Tex. 2016) (McCally, J.)

[While defendant and plaintiff were in a romantic relationship, he secretly recorded them having sex, and her performing other intimate acts. He posted some of the videos on social media, and e-mailed others to friends. She brought several claims, including invasion of privacy. For that claim, the jury awarded her $107,500 for past mental anguish and $107,500 for future mental anguish. Defendant appealed the denial of his motion for a new trial based on excessive damages.]

To uphold a jury's award of mental anguish damages under a legal sufficiency review, there must be evidence of the existence of compensable mental anguish and evidence to justify the amount awarded. Mental anguish is only compensable if it causes a substantial disruption in daily routine or a high degree of mental pain and distress. Thus, mental anguish damages cannot be awarded without either (1) direct evidence of the nature, duration, or severity of the plaintiff's anguish, thus establishing a substantial disruption in the plaintiff's daily routine; or (2) other evidence of a high degree of mental pain and distress that is more than mere worry, anxiety, vexation, embarrassment, or anger.

Here, there is some evidence that Nadia's daily routine was substantially disrupted. Because of Patel's invasions of her privacy, she felt like a liability living at home with her family, and she wanted to remove herself from the situation. So she moved out of the house, and she chose an apartment with upgraded security features. Nadia's friend testified that Nadia was scared to go home and afraid that Patel was looking for her. Accordingly, Nadia would alter where she parked her car and asked friends to not share her whereabouts on social media or store her contact information in a phone. While she was living with her family, they had to take the phone off the hook to avoid Patel's calls. Nadia had to set up extra security with her cellular service provider to prevent Patel from hacking her accounts, and she changed her phone number several times in an attempt to avoid his calls and messages.

Nadia testified that she missed about five days of work because of Patel's conduct. Her family and friends similarly testified about how Nadia "changed a lot," looked like she was "nervous all the time," and suffered from a loss of confidence. Nadia had been active in the Muslim community, but she became less involved as a result of Patel uploading the secretly recorded video to the Internet. There was a "big difference" between Nadia's involvement in the community. She used to go out a lot with friends but now mostly only spends time with two friends. Nadia would avoid other friends because everyone knew about the video, they were talking about the video, and they had questions about it.

Even assuming, however, that all this evidence is actually no evidence of a substantial disruption of her routine, that lack of evidence did not negate the evidence that she did suffer compensable mental anguish. There is also evidence that Nadia suffered a high degree of mental pain and distress — more than mere worry, anxiety, vexation, embarrassment, or anger.

Of course, there is ample testimony that Nadia was embarrassed and worried. But Nadia was also frightened and scared all the time, and she suffered humiliation. Nadia's mother and close friends described the "horrible situation" Nadia had been living and how it had "just been hell" for her. Sakina testified how Nadia had been crying, screaming, shaking, and could only talk in between crying when discussing the issue about Patel. Nadia's friend had seen Nadia cry because of Patel's conduct, and Nadia was afraid that Patel was around. Another friend described how he had seen Nadia frightened and in pain. When Patel attempted to visit Nadia, she became distressed, flustered, panicked, scared, upset, and suffered a loss of focus. Nadia also testified that she did not know if she could trust anyone again and would not know if other people she met in the future had seen her video, or what they would think if they eventually knew about it. She feels like she "can't face anyone." The situation was so bad that she felt like she "just wanted to give up." She is nervous all the time now, and she had seen a licensed professional a few times before trial. Nadia was humiliated because all her friends were talking about the video.

Further, we note that the nature of the invasions of privacy here are particularly disturbing and shocking and should give rise to an inference of mental anguish resulting from the threats to Nadia's reputation. There is evidence that Patel secretly recorded Nadia masturbating. He then badgered Nadia and her mother for years by threatening to disclose the video to Nadia's friends, family members, and coworkers. On top of the other invasions of privacy, Patel ultimately uploaded the video to the Internet and then boasted about the 5,000 people who had viewed the video and 300 who had downloaded it. As shown by the text messages, Patel did this with the specific intent to ruin Nadia's reputation, ruin her life, and hurt her.

We hold that there is some evidence demonstrating a reasonable probability that Nadia will suffer compensable mental anguish in the future. Nadia testified about how her humiliation and fright were ongoing at the time of trial. Other witnesses testified about how Nadia had changed emotionally and altered her behavior by the time of trial. The jury could infer from the evidence of Nadia's mental anguish at the time of trial that Nadia would continue to suffer mental anguish in the future. And, Nadia expressed specific concerns about her future relationships and employment due to the distribution of the videos on the Internet.

Patel acknowledged in the text messages to Nadia, "The Internet is huge you will never find out where it's posted," and, "Can't stop SOCIAL MEDIA!!" Patel told Nadia to "accept that this is never going to go away" and that she would "never live this down." These messages conveyed the notion that pornography shared on the Internet can circulate indefinitely.

In sum, the evidence is legally sufficient to support the jury's award.

Notes and Questions

1. Any Comparison? $25,000 for reading mail, and $107,500 for revenge porn. Is there a way to explain to a client how much it could expect to pay, or receive, for invasion of privacy claims? Is any comparison to other cases helpful? Given the permanent nature of Internet harm, is $107,500 enough? As explained in Chapter 3, juries are given wide discretion in awarding the amount of damages that are purely for mental distress. There likely is no more certain means to award damages for distress, but why award money at all?

2. Internet. The Internet has changed many aspects of the law, and the principal case reflects that. Does the fact that anyone using Google to search for the defendant's name will find the case against him affect the analysis here at all?

3. First Amendment. The court in *Welling v. Weinfeld*, 866 N.E.2d 1051 (Ohio 2007), noted that the damage element of false light claims can implicate greater First Amendment concerns than defamation:

> The first involves cases where the defendant reveals intimate and personal, but false, details of plaintiff's private life, for example, portraying plaintiff as the victim of sexual harassment, or as being poverty-stricken, or as having a terminal illness or suffering from depression. These depictions are

not necessarily defamatory, but are potentially highly offensive. The second category encompasses portrayals of the plaintiff in a *more positive* light than he deserves.

What interest would a plaintiff have in preventing publication of *positive* information? How does the fact that defamation requires greater fault by public figures and the like affect that analysis?

6. When Monetary Remedies Are Inadequate

The principal case below states what is almost a universal rule: defamatory speech will not be preliminarily enjoined. *See Sindi v. El-Moslimany*, 896 F.3d 1 (1st Cir. 2018) (majority struck down injunction against words found by jury to be defamatory; dissenting judge would not have reached the issue but suggested the law may not be so clear); *Puruczky v. Corsi*, 2018 WL 1725614 (Ct. App. Ohio Apr. 9, 2018) (collecting cases holding preliminary injunctions against defamation are unconstitutional). A few states permit permanent injunctions of publishing words found by a jury to have been defamatory. *See Wagner Equip. Co. v. Wood*, 893 F. Supp. 2d 1157 (D.N.M. 2012) (citing a few cases permitting permanent injunctions as to words found defamatory by a jury). *See also Kramer v. Thompson*, 947 F.2d 666 (3d Cir. 1991) (Pennsylvania's constitution prohibits injunctions against defamation).

Kinney v. Barnes

443 S.W.3d 87 (Tex. 2014) (Lehrman, J.)

[Plaintiff Robert Kinney had been a legal recruiter with BCG Attorney Search, Inc., until 2004, when he left to start a competing firm. Several years later, BCG's President, Andrew Barnes, posted a statement on websites implicating Kinney in an unethical kickback scheme while he had been with BCG, and that was why BCG fired him. Kinney sued, but did not seek damages—only a mandatory injunction to delete the statements, and a prohibitory one from making the statements in the future. Defendants moved for summary judgment, asserting the relief sought was an impermissible prior restraint under the provision of the Texas Constitution equivalent to the First Amendment. The court of appeals affirmed, and Kinney appealed.]

Freedom of speech is not an absolute right, and the state may punish its abuse. To that end, the common law has long recognized a cause of action for damages to a person's reputation inflicted by the publication of false and defamatory statements. The U.S. Supreme Court and this Court have been firm in the conviction that a defamer cannot use her free-speech rights as an absolute shield from punishment.

In this case, Kinney's request for injunctive relief may be broken down into two categories. First, as reflected in the pleadings, Kinney would have the trial court order Barnes to remove the statements at issue from his websites (and request that third-party republishers of the statements do the same) upon a final adjudication that the statements are defamatory. Such an injunction does not prohibit future speech, but instead effectively requires the erasure of past speech that has already been found to be unprotected in the context in which it was made. As such, it is accurately characterized as a remedy for one's abuse of the liberty to speak and is not a prior restraint.

Kinney would also have the trial court permanently enjoin Barnes from making similar statements (in any form) in the future. That is the essence of prior restraint and conflates the issue of whether an injunction is a prior restraint with whether it is constitutional. As Professor Chemerinsky has aptly explained:

> Courts that have held that injunctions are not prior restraints if they follow a trial, or if they are directed to unprotected speech, are confusing the question of whether the injunction is a prior restraint with the issue of whether the injunction should be allowed. Injunctions are inherently prior restraints because they prevent future speech.

Erwin Chemerinsky, *Injunctions in Defamation Cases,* 57 Syracuse L.Rev. 157 (2007). Even in the few cases in which the Supreme Court has upheld a content-based injunction against speech, it has not been because the injunction was not a prior restraint, but because under the circumstances the restraint was deemed constitutionally permissible. Accordingly, we hold that an injunction against future speech based on an adjudication that the same or similar statements have been adjudicated defamatory is a prior restraint.

However, labeling respondents' action a prior restraint does not end the inquiry. Notably, the U.S. Supreme Court has never approved a prior restraint in a defamation case. However, the Court has not decided whether the First Amendment prohibits the type of injunction at issue in this case, leaving that question unsettled. Turning to the issue of whether the injunction against future speech sought by Kinney, though a prior restraint, is nevertheless permissible under the Texas Constitution, we hold that it is not.

Again, prior restraints bear a heavy presumption against their constitutionality. The proponent of such restraints thus carries a heavy burden of showing justification for the imposition of such a restraint. While prior restraints are plainly disfavored, however, the phrase itself is not a self-wielding sword, but a demand for individual analyses of how prior restraints will operate. In examining the propriety of injunctive relief, then, we bear in mind the category of speech sought to be enjoined and the effect of such relief on a person's liberty to speak freely.

"The traditional rule of Anglo-American law is that equity has no jurisdiction to enjoin defamation." Chemerinsky, 57 Syracuse L.Rev. at 167. Our decisions leave no doubt that Texas law is in accordance with this traditional rule with regard to future speech.

Injunctions against defamation are impermissible because they are necessarily ineffective, overbroad, or both. That is, "any effective injunction will be overbroad, and any limited injunction will be ineffective." Chemerinsky, 57 Syracuse L.Rev. at 171.

On the one hand, for any injunction to have meaning it must be effective in its purpose. The narrowest of injunctions in a defamation case would enjoin the defamer from repeating the exact statement adjudicated defamatory. Such an order would only invite the defamer to engage in wordplay, tampering with the statement just enough to deliver the offensive message while nonetheless adhering to the letter of the injunction. Kinney admitted as much at oral argument, agreeing that the injunction he is seeking would extend to speech that was "substantially the same" or made "non-substantive changes" to the statement that has been adjudicated defamatory.

But expanding the reach of an injunction in this way triggers the problem of overbreadth. Overbroad restrictions on speech are unconstitutional because of their potential to chill protected speech. In the defamation context, the concern is that in prohibiting speech found to be defamatory, the injunction unreasonably risks prohibiting nondefamatory speech as well.

The particular difficulty in crafting a proper injunction against defamatory speech is rooted in the contextual nature of the tort. In evaluating whether a statement is defamatory, the court construes it as a whole in light of surrounding circumstances based upon how a person of ordinary intelligence would perceive the entire statement. Given the inherently contextual nature of defamatory speech, even the most narrowly crafted of injunctions risks enjoining protected speech because the same statement made at a different time and in a different context may no longer be actionable. Untrue statements may later become true; unprivileged statements may later become privileged.

These concerns apply even more forcefully to an injunction that goes beyond restraining verbatim recitations of defamatory statements and encompasses statements that are "substantially similar." Subtle differences in speech will obscure the lines of such an injunction and make it exceedingly difficult to determine whether a statement falls within its parameters. For example, let us imagine a trial court enjoins a defendant from repeating the defamatory statement "John Smith sells handguns to minors," as well as similar statements. Can the defamer state more generally that Smith is engaged in the business of illegal gun sales or that Smith's business contributes to the nationwide problems with school shootings? Can the word "handgun" be changed to "shotgun."

By contrast, no such concerns arise when courts issue speech-related injunctions that are not prior restraints, such as ordering the deletion of defamatory statements posted on a website. There is a legally cogent division between mandatory injunctions calling for the removal of speech that has been adjudicated defamatory and prohibitive injunctions disallowing its repetition. The latter impermissibly chills protected speech; the former does not. The distinction thus arms trial courts with an additional tool to protect defamed parties while ensuring the State does not infringe upon the fundamental right to free speech.

Accordingly, we hold that the Texas Constitution does not permit injunctions against future speech following an adjudication of defamation. Trial courts are simply not equipped to comport with the constitutional requirement not to chill protected speech in an attempt to effectively enjoin defamation. Instead, as discussed below, damages serve as the constitutionally permitted deterrent in defamation actions.

Kinney raises the concern that a victim of defamatory speech by a judgment-proof, serial defamer can obtain no remedy in damages. Damages may not deter the serial defamer, either because she lacks the funds to pay the damages or because she has so much money that paying a series of fines is immaterial to her. It is also easy to imagine a scenario in which an award of damages, even if collectible, will not provide complete relief to the defamed plaintiff. Imagine a statement falsely accusing a person of pedophilia, for example. Presumably, an order prohibiting the statement from being repeated would be of paramount importance to the plaintiff. Yet, conditioning the allowance of prior restraints on a defendant's inability to pay a damage award would do just that.

Finally, we address Kinney's argument that the Internet is a game-changer with respect to the issue presented because it "enables someone to defame his target to a vast audience in a matter of seconds." The same characteristics that have cemented the Internet's status as the world's greatest platform for the free exchange of ideas,— the ease and speed by which any person can take on the role of the town crier or pamphleteer—have also ignited the calls for its receiving lesser protection.

However, the Supreme Court has steadfastly refused to make free speech protections a moving target, holding that "we must decline to draw, and then redraw, constitutional lines based on the particular media or technology used to disseminate political speech from a particular speaker." *Citizens United v. Fed. Election Comm'n*, 558 U.S. 310 (2010). And, with respect to the advent of the Internet, the Court has gone further in championing its role as an equalizer of speech and a gateway to amplified political discourse, holding there is no basis for qualifying the level of First Amendment scrutiny that should be applied to this medium.

We hold that, while a permanent injunction requiring the removal of posted speech that has been adjudicated defamatory is not a prior restraint, an injunction prohibiting future speech based on that adjudication impermissibly threatens to sweep protected speech into its prohibition and is an unconstitutional infringement on Texans' free-speech rights under Article I, Section 8 of the Texas Constitution. Because the trial court concluded that no injunction of any kind would be permissible, the court erred in granting summary judgment to the extent Kinney's requested injunction did not constitute a prior restraint.

Notes and Questions

1. <u>Is Deleting Effective</u>? What if a defendant, as ordered, deletes existing defamatory text and then reposts it? Recall that violation of an injunction results in contempt. But, now assume a person posts a false defamatory comment—"Hricik stole my money"—and is ordered to remove it. Then I steal money from that person. Now what? In addition, in light of *Kinney's* observation about wordplay, is a permanent injunction useful if it is narrowly drawn?

2. <u>Is Deletion Compelled Speech</u>? Kinney had abandoned a request for a mandatory injunction to order the defendants to post apologies for six months, and compelled speech is very likely unconstitutional. Is forcing a deletion any different? Consider that in the Trump case later in this chapter, the government's act of taking down comments in an online public forum was held to be content-based enforcement.

3. <u>Unintended Consequences</u>? Do you agree with the following from the dissent in *Sindi*?

> The majority's First Amendment ruling limits a defamation victim's right to secure protection from the harm that her obstinate defamers are likely to inflict. But, this ruling may have even broader implications, as I do not see why its logic applies only to remedies for defamation. *See, e.g., Aguilar v. Avis Rent A Car Sys., Inc.*, 21 Cal.4th 121 (1999) (holding that enjoining a defendant's use of racial epithets at the defendant's workplace was not an unconstitutional prior restraint because it was based "on his continuing course of repetitive conduct" that violated employment discrimination law).

4. <u>Contract Remedies</u>. As explained above, a plaintiff usually cannot recover for harm to reputation caused by breach of contract. In denying a preliminary injunction, a court held a breach of contract plaintiff "cannot convert monetary harm into irreparable harm simply by claiming that the breach of contract has prevented it from performing contracts with others and that this subsequent failure to perform will harm the plaintiff's reputation." *Healthcare Corp. of Am. v. Data RX Mgt., Inc.*, 2013 WL 1314736 (D.N.J. Mar. 28, 2013).

7. Enjoining Government Acts That Inhibit Free Speech

A government act can harm a plaintiff by chilling a plaintiff's First Amendment rights. The first step is to determine if the regulation is "content neutral." The government may not (with extremely narrow exceptions) regulate content of speech by favoring one viewpoint over the other. If the regulation is content neutral, the second step is to determine the type of "forum" being regulated. The extent to which the government may regulate the time, place, and manner of speech varies depending upon the "forum" the regulation impacts. This requires placing the property into one of three categories of "fora," all of which are *publicly owned* (in at least some sense, as shown) despite one category being denominated "nonpublic":

Type of Forum	Definition	Examples
Traditional Public Forum	Historically has been open for public expression and discourse.	Sidewalks, parks.
Designated Public Forum	Public property that, while not traditionally opened to speech without restriction, the state has intended to open for use, at times, by the public for expressive activity.	A sports stadium.
Nonpublic Forum	Publicly owned property where the government permits limited discourse.	A government worker's office.

A. Identifying the Type of Forum and Content-Based Regulation

Marilyn Manson, Inc. v. New Jersey Sports & Expo. Auth.
971 F. Supp. 875 (D.N.J. 1997) (Wolin, J.)

[New Jersey Sports & Exposition Authority operated Giants Stadium. NJSEA had agreed to permit OzzFest 97, a music festival consisting largely of "metal" bands, to be held there. However, it decided to cancel it because Marilyn Manson was to perform. Marilyn Manson, Inc., sought a preliminary injunction requiring NJSEA to let the band perform.]

The first element that this Court must consider in assessing whether a preliminary injunction is warranted is whether the plaintiffs likely will succeed on the merits. Crucially, the moving party need not demonstrate that it will undoubtedly win after a trial on the merits; to establish a *prima facie* case the moving party need only show a reasonable probability of prevailing on the merits. For the reasons discussed below, the Court finds that the plaintiffs have established a likelihood of success on the merits under various theories.

Plaintiffs argue that the NJSEA's prohibition of Marilyn Manson is an illegal "prior restraint" and content based restriction on plaintiffs' First Amendment Rights. To determine whether the NJSEA has acted in violation of the First Amendment to the United States Constitution, the Court must first examine the type of fora that exist under the pertinent constitutional jurisprudence and the constitutional requisites of these fora.[7]

---

7. Music and entertainment are undoubtedly protected speech for purposes of the First Amendment. *See, e.g., Ward v. Rock Against Racism*, 491 U.S. 781 (1989) ("Music, as a form of expression and communication, is protected under the First Amendment"); *Tacynec v. City of Philadelphia*, 687 F.2d 793 (3d Cir. 1982) ("[T]he Supreme Court has made it clear that entertainment, as well as political and ideological speech, is protected; motion pictures, programs broadcast by radio

The extent to which the government may limit activity protected by the First Amendment depends on the locale where the speech or conduct takes place. A government owned facility may be categorized as one of three types of fora: a traditional public forum, a designated or limited public forum, or a non-public forum. The primary factor in determining which category a given forum falls within is the manner in which the locale is used.

A "traditional public forum" is designated as such because it is a forum that has historically been used for public assembly, for discussion of public questions, and for communication of thoughts between citizens. A traditional public forum is a place that has as a principle purpose the free exchange of ideas. Streets, parks, municipal auditoriums and theaters are quintessential traditional public forums.

A given parcel of government property will not be considered a true public forum where the full exercise of First Amendment rights would be inconsistent with the special interests of a government in overseeing the use of its property. Nor is a public forum created merely because members of the public are permitted freely to visit a place owned or operated by the government. The decision to create a public forum must be made by intentionally opening a nontraditional forum for public discourse.

First Amendment activity in a public forum may be restricted by reasonable time, place, or manner regulations if the regulations are justified without reference to the content of the regulated speech, are narrowly tailored to serve a significant interest, and leave open ample alternative channels for communication of the information.

A "designated" public forum is created where the government intentionally opens public property that is not a traditional public forum for use by the public as a place for expressive activity. A designated public forum may be either of a limited or unlimited character. Although the state is not required to maintain the open status of the forum indefinitely, while the facility is open to the public, strict scrutiny analysis applies to any content-based regulation of protected speech. The Courts have recognized the creation of a designated public forum in disparate contexts. *See, e.g., Widmar v. Vincent*, 454 U.S. 263 (1981) (state university meeting facilities); *Madison Joint Sch. Dist. v. Wisc. Employment Relations Comm'n*, 429 U.S. 167 (1976) (school board meetings); *Southeastern Promotions, Ltd.*, (municipal auditorium and city leased theater).

A "non-public" forum is a publicly owned facility that "is not by tradition or designation a forum for public communication." The state may restrict speech in a non-public forum as long as the distinctions drawn are reasonable in light of the purpose served by the forum and are viewpoint neutral. A First Amendment violation occurs when the government denies access to a speaker solely to suppress the point of view he espouses on an otherwise includable subject. The government may prohibit all forms of communication as long as the ban is reasonable and content-neutral. The

---

and television, and live entertainment, such as musical and dramatic works, fall within the First Amendment Guarantee.").

challenged regulation need only be reasonable, as long as the regulation is not an effort to suppress the speaker's activity due to disagreement with the speaker's view.

The plaintiffs urge the Court to find that Giants Stadium is a public forum. The NJSEA argues that the Giants Stadium is a non-public forum, citing *International Soc'y for Krishna Consciousness, Inc. v. New Jersey Sports and Exposition Authority,* 691 F.2d 155 (3d Cir. 1982). The Court finds that at this stage it need not decide what type of forum Giants Stadium is because plaintiffs have sufficiently established a likelihood of success on the merits even under the standards applicable to a non-public forum.

In a non-public forum, as discussed above, the government may distinguish between speakers as long as the distinctions drawn are reasonable in light of the purpose served by the forum and are viewpoint neutral. The government cannot deny access to a speaker solely to suppress the point of view he espouses on an otherwise includable subject.

In this case, there is a substantial likelihood that plaintiffs will establish either that NJSEA's restrictions on the ability of Marilyn Manson to perform are unreasonable or content based. The NJSEA has indicated that it excluded Marilyn Manson from the concert because of the band's "antics." According to the NJSEA, these anticipated "antics" may have created security risks and may have tarnished the NJSEA's reputation and ability to remain a lucrative forum for concert events.

Thus, this does not appear to be a case when the government denies access to a forum because of the identity of the speaker; the NJSEA has not endeavored to make that claim. Nor does this appear to be a case in which the government denies access of an individual to a forum because of a subject matter limitation; indeed, the NJSEA would allow the remaining bands in the show and all of these bands are of the same musical genre-heavy metal. Rather, it appears that the NJSEA would deny Marilyn Manson access to Giants Stadium because of anticipated antics, *i.e.,* because of the anticipated content of Marilyn Manson's performance. The NJSEA's motivation, thus, appears to be content based rather than viewpoint neutral.

The clause on which the NJSEA relies for its authority to exclude Marilyn Manson from the show confirms the motivation of the NJSEA. Under the NJSEA's proposed contract, it may exclude a performer for: "grounds of character offensive to public morals, failure to uphold event advertising claims or violation of event content restrictions agreed to by both parties at the time of completion of this agreement." The only aspect of this clause that the NJSEA relies upon is that Marilyn Manson's performance is anticipated to be "offensive to public morals." This appears to be the quintessential essence of content based regulation.

The NJSEA has argued that safety concerns prompted its refusal to allow Marilyn Manson to play at Giants Stadium. But the NJSEA has put forth no evidence that its proffered safety concerns are legitimate rather than pretextual. To the contrary, no unlawful or violent activity has occurred on Marilyn Manson's current tour. And it appears that the plaintiffs have complied with NJSEA's requests for concessions intended to bolster security. Plaintiffs, for example, agreed to provide additional security and to address other safety measures. Thus, the proffered security concerns have been addressed and are no longer an impediment to the performance.

The NJSEA also argued that the inclusion of Marilyn Manson would tarnish NJSEA's reputation and ability to earn revenue. But, the NJSEA conceded at oral argument that the decision to exclude Marilyn Manson was not based on the economics of the show in question; the show was anticipated to earn substantial revenue. Rather, NJSEA argued that the inclusion of Marilyn Manson would somehow affect NJSEA's future ability to use the stadium. The NJSEA's argument is insufficiently concrete to be persuasive and there are no written guidelines defining what might endanger NJSEA's reputation. Consequently, the Court is not persuaded.

Additionally, it appears that the NJSEA's requirement that all performers sign a contract allowing the NJSEA to regulate the morality of concert programs may be an unreasonable restriction on access to even a non-public forum. Plaintiffs argue that the NJSEA's authority to reject any performer based on inadequately defined guidelines is an unconstitutional prior restraint on speech. The Court finds that there is a substantial likelihood that plaintiffs will prevail on this claim. Although the NJSEA may require that performers satisfy reasonable requirements in order to perform at Giants Stadium, it is not clear that all of the conditions that Giants Stadium imposes are reasonable-especially insofar as a required agreement that allows the NJSEA unfettered discretion in rejecting the content of a proposed performance on the basis of its morality. *See Sentinel Communications Co. v. Watts,* 936 F.2d 1189 (11th Cir. 1991) (recognizing as meritorious the argument that state system of permitting the placement of news racks at interstate rest area, a non-public forum, was a facially unconstitutional prior restraint because it subjected the constitutionally protected distribution of newspapers to the "standardless, unfettered discretion of Florida state officials").

The lack of any identifiable guidelines in restricting the content of programs appears clearly unreasonable. And the contractual provision allowing the NJSEA to reflect a performance because it does not comport with public morality appears equally problematic. Without proof of at least reasonable guidelines, the NJSEA system of choosing concert performances probably cannot pass constitutional muster.

Even if the plaintiffs were to fail to satisfy the burden of establishing a violation of their First Amendment rights under the non-public forum standard, plaintiffs likely could establish on a more fully developed record that Giants Stadium has become a limited public forum as a venue for artistic performances.

In *Krishna v. NJSEA,* the Third Circuit addressed the constitutionality of NJSEA's prohibition of monetary solicitations by Krishnas of patrons of the NJSEA's sporting facilities. The Third Circuit found that Giants Stadium was not a traditional public forum, because the complex did not resemble theaters and auditoriums created for the primary purpose of public communication and the exchange of views. According to the Third Circuit, the Meadowlands was a commercial venture designed to bring economic benefits to northern New Jersey through entertaining spectators with athletic events and horse races; thus, the Third Circuit found: "the complex is not intended to be a public forum, and it is not unreasonable for the Authority to prohibit outside groups from engaging in activities which are counterproductive to its objectives."

But, *Krishna v. NJSEA* is readily distinguishable and not determinative of the current public status of Giants Stadium in the context of the issues now before the Court. In *Krishna v. NJSEA*, although the Third Circuit termed Giants Stadium "non-public," the Court addressed the First Amendment rights of the patrons of the NJSEA's events and not the rights of performers to whom the NJSEA has opened its facilities to entertain audiences. Whereas in *Krishna v. NJSEA*, the NJSEA clearly did not open Giants Stadium to citizens to solicit charitable contributions, in this case it is undisputed that the NJSEA has opened Giants Stadium to performers in musical events. Where the government chooses to open a forum for a particular type of communicative activity, the government has created a limited public forum to that extent, and the government's restrictions on the content of speech are subject to strict scrutiny.

Indeed, plaintiffs have put forth substantial evidence to the effect that Giants Stadium is a limited public forum requiring strict scrutiny of the government's regulations on the content of speech in the forum. Plaintiffs point out that approximately thirty-eight public concerts, totaling more than seventy shows, have been held at Giants Stadium. Indeed, the NJSEA readily admits that over thirty different concerts have been held at Giants Stadium in recent years.

The Court would unhesitatingly reject, however, plaintiffs' argument that Giants Stadium is a public forum. As the NJSEA asserted, one may not perform at Giants Stadium at will.

Plaintiffs contend that if the injunctive relief is not granted, plaintiffs will have missed their only opportunity for "exposure to the national media and music industry representatives headquartered in New York City." Delsener/Slater charges that if the NJSEA is permitted to repudiate its agreement with Delsener/Slater, "NJSEA will have injured Delsener/Slater's business and reputation in the concert industry as a promoter that can be relied upon to provide a suitable New York area venue." Additionally, plaintiffs argue that a refusal to allow them to perform would be a deprivation of their First Amendment rights.

The NJSEA claims that there will be no irreparable harm for several reasons, including: (1) plaintiffs have no right to play at Giants Stadium because they did not sign a contract, (2) plaintiffs have waived their First Amendment rights, (3) plaintiffs' interest in the concert is merely financial, (4) Marilyn Manson could perform at other venues, and (5) OzzFest '97 could be held at another forum.

The Court disagrees with the NJSEA. The plaintiffs' potential First Amendment deprivation is undoubtedly an irreparable injury. And the plaintiffs will suffer other irreparable injuries, as well, including loss to reputation in the case of the promoters, and reduced public exposure in the case of the artists. Thus, the plaintiffs have established the prospect of irreparable injury sufficient to meet the requirement for a preliminary injunction.

According to the NJSEA, its goal is to advance the general welfare, health, and prosperity of the people of New Jersey by staging athletic contests, horse racing and other expositions; the NJSEA argues that by forcing it to permit Marilyn Manson to perform, the Court would erode the NJSEA's statutory authority to determine who may have access to its facilities. This alleged erosion of its power, according to the NJSEA, is the irreparable injury.

The Court again disagrees with the NJSEA. Of course, the NJSEA must have discretion to choose events fitting with its mandate under statute to earn revenue and entertain the public. And the NJSEA can impose reasonable restrictions comporting with its mandate. But the clause permitting moral censorship of any performance, does not appear reasonably calculated to fulfill the NJSEA's statutory responsibilities. Consequently, the NJSEA appears to have no legitimate state interest in enforcing the restrictive content clause of the contract. Moreover, on the facts of this case, it appears patently unreasonable that Giants Stadium would permit an entire concert of heavy metal bands, while excluding only one-Marilyn Manson-which has demonstrated no propensity for illegal activities on stage. Thus, the NJSEA will suffer no irreparable injury from allowing Marilyn Manson to perform at Giants Stadium. The Court will require plaintiffs to post a bond in the amount of $500,000 to cover any damage that might be caused by the preliminary injunction.

The NJSEA argues that the public interest will suffer if the preliminary injunction is granted because the NJSEA will no longer be able to act in a manner that will guarantee that the public interest will be promoted. The NJSEA has demonstrated no concrete need (in keeping with its public mandate) to exclude Marilyn Manson while allowing the other heavy metal bands to perform. And the NJSEA has indicated that the show will likely be a profitable economic endeavor, a strong indicator that a substantial number of community citizens would like to attend Marilyn Manson's performance. For these reasons, the Court finds that to promote the free expression of ideas, uncensored by a state actor who exercises unfettered discretion, warrants the grant of this preliminary injunction.

Notes and Questions

1. <u>Ban or Less?</u> *Marilyn Manson* shows that a ban on content need not be explicit. First Amendment rights can be impinged even by something less than a ban. In *Knight First Amend. Institute at Columbia Univ. v. Trump,* 928 F.3d 226 (2d. Cir. 2019), after President Trump had blocked certain people from replying to "tweets" on his official Twitter account, those blocked users sued, contending he blocked them from expressing speech in a government forum based upon their viewpoints, thus violating their First Amendment rights. The court's analysis of how traditional notions of "public *fora*" apply to virtual spaces was:

Whatever the challenges of applying the Constitution to ever-advancing technology, the basic principles of freedom of speech and the press, like the First Amendment's command, do not vary when a new and different medium for communication appears. A public forum, as the Supreme Court has also made clear, need not be spatial or geographic and the same principles are applicable to a metaphysical forum.

To determine whether a public forum has been created, courts look to the policy and practice of the government as well as the nature of the property and its compatibility with expressive activity to discern the government's intent. Opening an instrumentality of communication for indiscriminate use by the general public creates a public forum. The Account was intentionally opened for public discussion when the President, upon assuming office, repeatedly used the Account as an official vehicle for governance and made its interactive features accessible to the public without limitation. We hold that this conduct created a public forum.

The court also stated:

The fact that government control over property is temporary, or that the government does not "own" the property in the sense that it holds title to the property, is not determinative of whether the property is, in fact, sufficiently controlled by the government to make it a forum for First Amendment purposes. Temporary control by the government can still be control for First Amendment purposes.

After holding it was a public forum, the court then turned to whether Trump was engaging in viewpoint-based discrimination, and stated:

The government does not challenge the District Court's conclusion that the speech in which Individual Plaintiffs seek to engage is protected speech; instead, it argues that blocking did not ban or burden anyone's speech. Specifically, the government contends that the Individual Plaintiffs were not prevented from speaking because "the only material impact that blocking has on the individual plaintiffs' ability to express themselves on Twitter is that it prevents them from speaking directly to Donald Trump by replying to his tweets on the @realDonaldTrump web page."

That assertion is not well-grounded in the facts presented to us. The government is correct that the Individual Plaintiffs have no right to require the President to listen to their speech. However, the speech restrictions at issue burden the Individual Plaintiffs' ability to converse on Twitter with others who may be speaking to or about the President. President Trump is only one of thousands of recipients of the messages the Individual Plaintiffs seek to communicate. While he is certainly not required to listen, once he opens up the interactive features of his account to the public at large he is not entitled to censor selected users because they express views with which he disagrees.

The government's reply is that the Individual Plaintiffs are not censored because they can engage in various "workarounds" such as creating new If, for example, the President had merely prevented the Individual Plaintiffs from sending him direct messages, his argument would have more force. The government extends this argument to suggest that the Individual Plaintiffs are claiming a right to "amplify" their speech by being able to reply directly to the President's tweets. The government can choose to "amplify" the speech of certain individuals without violating the rights of others by choosing to listen or not listen. That is not what occurred here; the Individual Plaintiffs were not simply ignored by the President, their ability to speak to the rest of the public users of the Account was burdened. In any event, the government is not permitted to "amplify" favored speech by banning or burdening viewpoints with which it disagrees.

Tellingly, the government concedes that these "workarounds" burden the Individual Plaintiffs' speech. And burdens to speech as well as outright bans run afoul of the First Amendment. See United States v. Playboy Entm't Grp., Inc., 529 U.S. 803, 812 (2000) ("The distinction between laws burdening and laws banning speech is but a matter of degree. The Government's content-based burdens must satisfy the same rigorous scrutiny as its content-based bans."). When the government has discriminated against a speaker based on the speaker's viewpoint, the ability to engage in other speech does not cure that constitutional shortcoming. Similarly, the fact that the Individual Plaintiffs retain some ability to "work around" the blocking does not cure the constitutional violation. Neither does the fact that the Individual Plaintiffs can post messages elsewhere on Twitter.

2. <u>Ad Space in Public Transportation Facilities</u>. In *Am. Freedom Defense Initiative v. Wash. Metro. Area Transit Auth.*, 2018 WL 4000492 (Ct. App. D.C. Aug. 17, 2018), the court held that advertising space on buses and in bus stations was a nonpublic forum after it adopted a ban on issue-oriented advertising, but in *Northeastern Penn. Freethought Soc'y. v. County of Lackawanna Transit Sys.*, 2018 WL 3344910 (M.D. Pa. July 9, 2018), the court held that transit advertising space under a policy that prohibited "discussion of public issues," was a limited public forum. In both cases, however, the bans were upheld.

B. Time, Place, and Manner Restrictions

If a government act is content-neutral, it still may harm a plaintiff's constitutional right to speech. The line drawing in this area is, however, fact-intensive because often one person's right to speech interferes with another person's right to be left alone. As the Supreme Court stated, while the right to free speech "includes the right to attempt to persuade others to change their views and may not be curtailed simply because the speaker's message may be offensive to his audience," at the same time, "the protection afforded to offensive messages does not always embrace offensive speech that is so intrusive that the unwilling audience cannot avoid it." *Hill v. Colorado,* 530 U.S. 703 (2000). The court in *Clift v. City of Burlington, Vt.,* 925 F. Supp. 2d 614 (D. Vt. 2013), summarized recent Supreme Court decisions in this context:

> The Supreme Court has decided three cases involving buffer zones at medical facilities. In *Madsen v. Women's Health Center, Inc.,* 512 U.S. 753 (1994) and *Schenck v. Pro-Choice Network of Western New York,* 519 U.S. 357 (1997), the Supreme Court first confronted the issue in the context of court-issued injunctions prohibiting specific individuals or organizations from interfering with public access to clinics. In Madsen, a Florida state court initially enjoined a group of protesters from blocking or interfering with access to an abortion clinic in Melbourne, Florida. After that provision proved insufficient, the state court expanded its injunction to prohibit the protesters
>
>> (2) At all times on all days, from blocking, impeding, inhibiting, or in any other manner obstructing or interfering with access to, ingress into and egress from any building or parking lot of the Clinic.
>>
>>> (A) At all times on all days, from congregating, picketing, patrolling, demonstrating or entering that portion of the public right-of-way or private property within [36] feet of the property line of the Clinic. . . .
>>
>> (5) At all times on all days, in an area within [300] feet of the Clinic, from physically approaching any person seeking the services of the Clinic unless such person indicates a desire to communicate by approaching or by inquiring of the [petitioners]. . . .
>
> Reviewing the revised injunction, the Supreme Court determined that it was not content or viewpoint-based simply because it applied only to anti-abortion protesters; after all, they were the ones whose conduct gave rise to underlying lawsuit and justified the injunction. The Court also recognized that the injunction served a variety of legitimate government interests, including preserving a woman's freedom to seek lawful medical and counseling services, maintaining public safety and order, promoting the free flow of traffic on public streets and sidewalks, and protecting patients' privacy concerns.
>
> Whether each provision of the injunction was narrowly tailored to serve those interests presented a more difficult question. Explaining that court-issued injunctions generally pose a greater risk of "censorship and discriminatory application," the Court applied a more exacting standard than it would have for an identically-phrased legislative enactment. Instead of considering whether the injunction "promoted a substantial government interest that would be achieved less effectively absent the regulation," *Ward,* 491 U.S. at 799, the Court demanded that each provision "'be no more burdensome to the defendant than necessary to provide complete relief to the

plaintiffs.'" *Madsen*, 512 U.S. at 765 (*quoting Califano v. Yamasaki*, 442 U.S. 682 (1979). Using this heightened standard, the Court upheld the 36-foot fixed buffer zone (with respect to public but not private property) because it was necessary to protect access to the clinic; however, the Court struck down the prohibition on approaching patients or potential patients within 300 feet of the clinic because it burdened more speech than necessary.

Three years later, in *Schenck*, the Supreme Court revisited the issue when it considered the constitutionality of a preliminary injunction prohibiting abortion protesters from "demonstrating within fifteen feet from either side or edge of, or in front of, doorways or doorway entrances, parking lot entrances, driveways and driveway entrances of such facilities" (fixed buffer zones), or 'within fifteen feet of any person or vehicle seeking access to or leaving such facilities' (floating buffer zones)." 519 U.S. at 367. Once again, the Court determined that the governmental interests in "ensuring public safety and order, promoting the free flow of traffic on streets and sidewalks, protecting property rights, and protecting a woman's freedom to seek pregnancy-related services" were "significant enough to justify an appropriately tailored injunction," *id.*; however, the Court concluded that only the fixed buffer zone was in fact necessary to serve those interests. *Id.* In doing so, the Court acknowledged that the fixed buffer zone was a prophylactic measure, especially because an unchallenged portion of the injunction prohibited "blocking, impeding or obstructing access" to the clinic, but the Court deferred to the District Court's assessment that the fixed buffer zone was necessary to keep the clinic entrances clear. The Court in Schenck also swiftly rejected the suggestion that the term "demonstrating" was unconstitutionally vague, finding that when the injunction was read as a whole, "people 'of ordinary intelligence' (and certainly defendants whose demonstrations led to this litigation in the first place) have been given a reasonable opportunity to know what is prohibited.'" *Id.* (quoting *Grayned v. City of Rockford*, 408 U.S. 104 (1972)).

In *Hill v. Colorado*, the Supreme Court addressed the constitutionality of a legislatively-enacted buffer zone for the first time. 530 U.S. 703 (2000). In 1993, the Colorado General Assembly enacted a statute making it a misdemeanor to

> knowingly approach another person within eight feet of such person, unless such other person consents, for the purpose of passing a leaflet or handbill to, displaying a sign to, or engaging in oral protest, education, or counseling with such other person in the public way or sidewalk area within a radius of one hundred feet from any entrance door to a health care facility.

Colo.Rev.Stat. § 18-9-122(3). The General Assembly defined the term "health care facility" broadly to include "any entity that is licensed, certified, or otherwise authorized or permitted by law to administer medical treatment in Colorado]." And the General Assembly enacted a related provision making it a separate misdemeanor to "knowingly obstruct, detain, hinder, impede, or block another person's entry to or exit from a health care facility."

Despite having struck down similar provisions in *Madsen* and *Schenck*, the Court upheld the 8-foot floating buffer zone in *Hill*. Though the petitioners did not challenge the substantiality of the State's interest in enacting the statute, the Court reaffirmed the proposition that the state's general police powers "justified a special focus on unimpeded access to health care facilities and the avoidance of potential trauma to patients associated with confrontational protests." *Hill*, 530 U.S. at 715. The Court also clarified that the State could take into account "the interests of unwilling listeners in situations where 'the degree of captivity makes it impractical for the unwilling viewer or auditor to avoid exposure.'" *Id.* at 718 (quoting *Erznoznik v. City of Jacksonville*, 422 U.S. 205 (1975)).

Applying intermediate scrutiny, the Court found that the statute was also narrowly tailored and left open ample alternative channels for communication. *Hill*, 530 U.S. at 725. While the Court noted that the 8-foot separation would have little impact on demonstrators' ability to convey their message with signs, the Court conceded that the separation might make it more difficult for a speaker to be heard. *Hill*, 530 U.S. at 726. But because the statute placed no restriction on the use of amplification equipment, allowed a speaker to converse at a "normal conversational distance," and permitted protesters to remain stationary while individuals passed within 8 feet of them, there were sufficient alternative avenues of communication available to the protesters. *Id.* at 727.

Though the Court was also troubled by the burden placed on protesters' ability to distribute handbills, it noted that the statute did not "prevent a leafletter from standing near the path of oncoming pedestrians and proffering his or her material, which the pedestrians can easily accept." *Id.* The Court's discussion revealed that it would not insist on the least restrictive or least intrusive means of fulfilling the State's statutory goals, even when core forms of expression were burdened. Echoing *Schenck*, the Court explained that while the statute might "sometimes inhibit a demonstrator whose approach in fact would have proved harmless," this "aspect is justified by the great difficulty of protecting, say, a pregnant woman from physical harassment with legal rules that focus exclusively on the individual impact of each instance of behavior, demanding in each case an accurate characterization (as harassing or not harassing) of each individual movement within the 8-foot boundary." *Id.* "A bright-line prophylactic rule," the Court reasoned, "may be the best way to provide protection and, at the same time, by offering clear guidance and avoiding subjectivity, to protect speech itself." *Id.*

Finally, the Court rejected petitioners' contentions that the statute was unconstitutionally overbroad and vague in quick succession. The Court explained that it considered the statute's applicability to all persons and all health care facilities to be a constitutional "virtue, not a vice, because it was evidence against there being a discriminatory governmental motive." *Id.* As the statute simply amounted to a restriction on the places where certain communications could occur, rather than a complete ban, the Court insisted that the petitioners demonstrate that the overbreadth of the statute was both real and substantial-a threshold they could not meet. *Id.* When it addressed the vagueness challenge, the Court relied heavily on the presence of a scienter requirement, which in their view rendered quite remote the likelihood that a person of ordinary intelligence would not understand what conduct the statute prohibits. *Id.* Though the petitioners conjured up numerous hypothetical situations to test whether certain conduct would be proscribed by the statute, the Court, looking to the statute as a whole, thought that the statute was clear about what it prohibited and that its application was valid in the "vast majority of its intended applications." *Id.* (quoting *U.S. v. Raines*, 362 U.S. 17 (1960)).

With that background, consider the following case.

Central Park Sightseeing LLC v. New Yorkers For Clean, Livable & Safe Streets, Inc.

66 N.Y.S.3d 477 (N.Y. App. Div. 1st Dept. 2017) (Manzanet-Daniels, J.)

[Plaintiff Central Park Sightseeing LLC ("CPS") operated horse-drawn carriages around New York's Central Park. The Defendant New Yorkers for Clean, Livable & Safe Streets, Inc., was an animal rights organization that protested against the horse-and-carriage industry. Additional defendants were its members who had protested in the zones, alongside the curbs, where carriage operators and drivers picked up and dropped off customers who had been waiting in lines.

Plaintiff sued the defendants, asserting several claims and seeking a preliminary injunction. Evidence showed defendant's protesters harassing, yelling obscenities at, and threatening and intimidating drivers, customers, and potential customers, including those with young children; obstructing customers and potential customers from boarding horse carriages; blocking the passage of horse carriages; and engaging in loud and aggressive behavior in proximity to the horses, spooking them and endangering public safety.

The trial court granted a preliminary injunction to the extent of enjoining and restraining defendants "and/or anyone else who becomes aware of this Decision and Order" from:

1. physically blocking, impeding, or obstructing any persons from seeking or taking, or providing a lawful horse-carriage ride disembarking from Central Park South;

2. physically touching, pushing, shoving, or grabbing any such persons or horses;

3. yelling or shouting at, or aggressively accosting, any such persons, or any carriage horses, from a distance of less than nine feet;

4. physically blocking, impeding, or obstructing the progress of any such horse-carriage ride;

5. handing literature to persons situated within a horse carriage; and

6. counseling, facilitating, aiding, or abetting any other person from doing such things.

However, the order stated that the defendant's members could "protest, including picket, hold signs, hand out literature, bear witness, and raise their voices," noting that "the content of the speech is not at issue here; the manner of delivery is." The defendants appealed.]

Plaintiff established a likelihood of success on its cause of action for a public nuisance. The evidence, which includes videos, demonstrates that the protestors blocked paths and chased after moving horse-drawn carriages and that their loud and aggressive behavior frightened the horses, making them nervous and more likely to start, and creating a hazard to all involved; this evidence satisfies the public harm element of the cause of action. There is also ample evidence that plaintiff has sustained a "special injury" beyond that suffered by the community at large. Indeed, defendants have targeted plaintiff's business, encouraging seated passengers to leave their horse-drawn carriages and either not pay for their rides or ask for their money back, and telling one driver, "You might as well go back to the stables now. You're not going to do any business."

Plaintiff established a likelihood of success on the merits of its cause of action for tortious interference with contractual relations. The fact that a portion of plaintiff's horse-drawn carriage business is pre-purchased online and passengers approach carriages with vouchers in hand demonstrates both the existence of valid contracts and defendants' awareness of the contracts. As for passengers who book rides directly with carriage drivers, they surely have entered into contracts for services by the time their carriages have begun to move.

While, as defendants argue, the cancellation of pre-purchased tickets pursuant to the terms of the contract cannot support a cause of action for tortious interference with a contract, plaintiff's claims are not based solely on those contracts.

The tortious nature of defendants' conduct is demonstrated by, inter alia, their yelling at drivers and customers and potential customers while standing near horses, blocking access to carriages, and physically touching people—actions that appear on defendant Jill Carnegie's own list of "DON'T's" for her fellow protestors.

Plaintiff established irreparable harm by showing defendants' interference with its right to carry on a lawful business without obstruction and the danger that defendants' conduct poses to public safety and order.

The balance of the equities weighs in plaintiff's favor. Absent injunctive relief, plaintiff's business would continue to be harmed, and its drivers, customers, and potential customers, and members of the public would continue to be subjected to harassing and potentially dangerous conduct. Defendants will sustain no irreparable harm, since the injunction neither prevents them from exercising their First Amendment right to protest what they perceive to be a form of animal cruelty nor affects their message.

The injunction is content-neutral, and therefore we must ask "whether the challenged provisions of the injunction burden no more speech than necessary to serve a significant government interest" (*Madsen v. Women's Health Ctr., Inc.*, 512 U.S. 753 [1994]), here, the government's interest in public safety and order.

A "floating buffer zone" would, as defendant points out, make it "quite difficult for a protestor who wishes to engage in peaceful expressive activities to know how to remain in compliance with the injunction" and presents a "substantial risk" that much more speech will be burdened than necessary to protect public safety and order. We accordingly modify paragraph 3 of the injunction to prohibit any person from knowingly approaching within nine feet of another person in the loading/unloading zone, without that person's consent, for the purpose of handing a leaflet or bill or displaying a sign or engaging in oral protest or education of such other person.

Public sidewalks, streets, and ways are the "quintessential" public fora for free speech, and leafletting, signs, and displays are time-honored methods of communication enjoying First Amendment protection. Nonetheless, the Supreme Court has consistently recognized "the interests of unwilling listeners in situations where the degree of captivity makes it impractical for the unwilling viewer or auditor to avoid exposure" (*id.* at 718). We believe the instant injunction, as modified, respects the First Amendment rights of defendant protestors while recognizing the rights of carriage passengers to be free of unwanted intrusions.

The nine-foot zone represents a "conversational distance," allowing normal communication. The prohibition on "oral education and protest" ensures that casual conversation is not within the ambit of the injunction. Notably, the "knowingly approaches" requirement would allow a protestor to stand still while a passenger walks or rides past without running afoul of the injunction. A leafletter might stand in the path of pedestrians and proffer his or her literature, which the pedestrian can choose to accept or decline. Finally, it is to be noted that those standing in place with signs would remain unaffected by the injunction.

We draw a distinction between protestors in the loading and unloading zones, and those who follow the horses along the carriage roads and onto the surrounding streets. The First Amendment does not require that protestors be permitted to disrupt traffic, spook horses, and endanger public safety in order to convey their message. Courts have recognized a distinction between leafletting on public sidewalks and handing leaflets to the occupants of moving vehicles; the latter may be prohibited due to valid safety concerns posed by handing literature to persons on public roadways (*see e.g. Contributor v. City of Brentwood, Tenn.,* 726 F.3d 861 [6th Cir. 2013] [upholding portion of city ordinance that prohibited sale or distribution of literature to the occupant of any motor vehicle on a street in order to further "the goals of traffic safety and flow"]; *Gonzalez v. City of New York,* 2016 WL 5477774 [S.D.N.Y. Sept. 29, 2016] [rejecting First Amendment challenge to arrest for disorderly conduct for obstructing traffic]; *Cosac Found., Inc. v. City of Pembroke Pines,* 2013 WL 5345817 [S.D.Fla. Sept. 21, 2013] [upholding ordinance prohibiting solicitation or canvassing on roadways as exercise of significant government interest in regulating traffic flow and preventing injury to pedestrians and motorists]). Defendants have ample alternative channels of communication open to them through protest and leafletting in the pick-up/drop-off zones and on the surrounding public sidewalks.

As the United States Supreme Court has recognized, "When clear and present danger of interference with traffic upon the public streets, or other immediate threat to public safety, peace, or order, appears, the power of the state to prevent or punish is obvious" (*Cantwell v. State of Connecticut,* 310 U.S. 296). The government has "a strong interest in ensuring the public safety and order, in promoting the free flow of traffic on public streets and sidewalks, and in protecting the property rights of its citizens" (*Madsen,* 512 U.S. at 768).

Finally, the injunction is overbroad inasmuch as it purports to limit the free speech not only of defendants, but also of "anyone else who becomes aware of this decision and order." We accordingly modify to make it applicable to defendants and "those acting in concert with the named parties."

Accordingly, the order of the Supreme Court, New York County (Arthur F. Engoron, J.), entered February 22, 2017, which granted plaintiff's motion for a preliminary injunction to the extent of enjoining and restraining defendants "and/or anyone else who becomes aware of this Decision and Order" from (1) "physically blocking, impeding, or obstructing any persons from seeking or taking, or providing . . . a lawful horse-carriage ride disembarking from Central Park South"; (2) "physically touching, pushing, shoving, or grabbing any such persons or horses"; (3) "yelling or shouting at, or aggressively accosting, any such persons, or any carriage horses, from a distance of less than nine feet"; (4) "physically blocking, impeding, or obstructing the progress of any such horse-carriage ride"; (5) "handing literature to persons situated within a horse carriage"; and (6) "counseling, facilitating, aiding, or abetting any other person from doing such things [sic]," should be modified, on the law and the facts, to limit the applicability of the injunction to the named defendants and those acting in concert with the named defendants; to modify subsection (3) to prohibit defendants from knowingly approaching within nine feet of another person in the loading/unloading areas without that person's consent; to clarify that subsection (6) shall not apply to legal advice; and otherwise affirmed, without costs.

Notes and Questions

1. <u>Government Acts</u>. The government may restrict speech through statutes or ordinances as well as by granting an injunction in favor of a private citizen. The courts analyze their propriety under the First Amendment in the same way. Does that seem appropriate, or should an injunction receive more careful scrutiny, particularly if entered by a federal judge with life tenure?

2. <u>Line Drawing</u>. The principal case and the abortion cases all are forced to address the practical problems created by "floating buffers." Why is the "knowingly" requirement so important for that purpose?

Problems

1. <u>Cyberbullying</u>? The *Kinney* court emphasized that "cyber-bullying and online hate speech" were not involved in the case. The common law does not protect against mental anguish readily, and a threat made online likely would not constitute assault or IIED. Does your state have a statute applicable to "cyberbullying?" Hate speech?

2. <u>Public Forum or Not</u>? Several courts have addressed whether Facebook pages, Twitter feeds, and other social media of government officials are public fora or not. *E.g., Morgan v. Bevin*, 298 F. Supp. 3d 1003 (E.D. Ky. 2018) (governor's Facebook page); *Price v. City of New York*, 2018 WL 3117507 (June 25, 2018) (police Twitter feed). Find the social media page of a high-level state official and evaluate whether it is a public forum or not.

3. <u>Being at the Wrong Place at the Wrong Time</u>? At the Boston marathon bombing, a student from Saudi Arabia was injured. Police questioned him. Newspapers and other media reported pervasively around the world that he was an active participant in the bombing. His name, photograph, and description were broadcast widely for several days, and he agreed to be interviewed by news media to explain his innocence and that, in fact, he was merely watching the race. He filed suit, alleging defamation. Is he required to show actual malice?

4. <u>You So-and-So</u>. Your client owns a liquor store. After one of his employees checked prices at a competing store across the street, its owner came into your client's store and, with customers and suppliers present, called him an "asshole" and a "motherfucker." Your client is upset, more so because his mother died when he was a teenager, many years ago. Does your client have a claim for defamation per se? Same question, but are there circumstances where a reasonable listener would conclude that phrase was defamatory per se?

5. <u>Intra-Corporate Communications</u>. Courts split on whether a communication between employees of the same corporation is a publication covered by a qualified privilege, or not a "publication" at all. *See Newell v. JDS Holdings, L.L.C.,* 834 N.W.2d 463 (Ct. App. Iowa 2013). If a court holds it is not a "publication," is any remedy available? What if it is a "publication," but covered by a conditional privilege? From an employer's perspective, which is the better rule? From an employee's perspective? If it is treated as a "non-publication," is this license to defame fellow employees?

6. <u>Public Figure?</u> Your client told a reporter that, years ago, as a young woman she had been drugged and then raped by a famous comedian. After a magazine published a story including her allegations, the comedian had his lawyer write a letter to the magazine that denied her allegations and included statements challenging her credibility. Based on your investigation, the rape occurred as she stated and the other statements to the reporter are defamatory per se. Is your client required to establish malice?

7. <u>My Doctor's a Liar</u>. In one case, a court held that a statement that a nurse had forged doctors' signatures on patient records was defamatory per se under the "professions" prong, but in another case, the court held that a statement by a physician that the head of a surgery department, and physician, "lacked veracity" and "dealt in half-truths" was not. Are these reconcilable?

8. <u>My Husband's Not Addicted to Porn</u>. A husband and wife retained you because he was fired after it was falsely reported he was viewing pornography and visiting sites designed to acquire prostitutes using his work-issued computer. Does she have a defamation claim?

9. <u>Cops and the Neighbors</u>. Your client tells you the defendant told the police, and common neighbors, that he was a thief. Explain what is required to show defamation for the statements to police and statements to the neighbors, and why those standards differ.

10. <u>Consent to Intrusion Upon Seclusion</u>. In *Herrera v. AllianceOne Receivable Mgmt., Inc.,* 2016 WL 7048318 (S.D. Cal. Dec. 5, 2016), a collection agency repeatedly called plaintiff seeking collection of a debt he did not owe. He sued, asserting intrusion upon seclusion. The debt collection agency asserted a qualified privilege, recognized under California law, which permitted creditors to use reasonable steps to collect debts based upon premise that debtors, as part of accepting credit, consented to reasonable steps to collect a debt even if that results in an intrusion upon seclusion. The argument failed. Why?

11. <u>IIED</u>. Consider how permitting an IIED claim based solely upon words, rather than conduct, can punish speech that is protected by the First Amendment. Would allowing an IIED defendant to use defamation privileges solve the potential for IIED claims to run afoul of the First Amendment?

Chapter 5

Remedies Triggered by Harm to Freedom of Movement — Including Wrongful Criminal Prosecution and Similar Interests

This chapter begins with monetary remedies for false imprisonment and false arrest, which require harm to the plaintiff's freedom of movement. A shopkeeper who wrongfully detains a plaintiff for allegedly shoplifting, knowing the person was innocent, would be an example. Sometimes more than one person can cause detention, as, for example, when a shopkeeper gives false information to a police officer, and that causes the police officer to arrest the plaintiff. Depending on the facts, it may be only the shopkeeper who would be liable — for wrongfully procuring the arrest — or both the shopkeeper and the officer may be liable. This chapter then turns to claims triggered by the harm caused by a wrongfully instituted or continued criminal proceeding. Again, it may be that one person tells a prosecutor false information that causes the plaintiff to be prosecuted for a crime. In some states, one claim is used to determine liability whether or not a criminal proceeding occurs, while others use different claims depending on whether one occurred or even if a warrant had issued for the arrest. There is little uniformity and a fair amount of confusion as to the harms these claims remedy.

The chapter then turns to claims triggered by the harm caused by an abusive civil suit. While that may seem unrelated, those claims share much in common with criminal prosecutions. Finally, the chapter addresses when courts will enjoin criminal prosecutions or civil litigation, or the threats of them.

1. Monetary Remedies for False Imprisonment

Despite its name, most states do not require proof of either falsity or imprisonment. Instead, the claim of false imprisonment requires proving the defendant intended, or had substantial certainty, that it was unlawfully impinging a plaintiff's right to freedom of movement and the plaintiff was aware of the restraint. *See Rivera v. Double A Transp., Inc.*, 727 A.2d 204 (Conn. 1999). "Confinement" includes physical restraint as well as the use of authority or words to "restrain" the plaintiff.

Some courts hold a plaintiff must either have been aware of confinement *or* have been "harmed by it." *See Pope v. Rostraver Shop 'N Save*, 389 F. App'x 151 (3d Cir. 2010). With respect to awareness of confinement, that court explained that the required harm does not exist if the plaintiff knew of a "means of escape involving nothing more than slight inconvenience," and stated further that "in the absence of physical force or physical barriers, plaintiff must make some attempt to determine whether s/he is actually confined" because the harm does not rest on "a mere belief that one is confined."

While awareness or "harm" is required, mental anguish or economic loss are not, but they are recoverable as consequential damages. The court in *Kerman v. City of New York*, 374 F.3d 93 (2d Cir. 2004), distinguished between the required harm and consequential damages, and discussed the measure of damages:

> The damages recoverable for the period spent in a wrongful confinement are separable from damages recoverable for such injuries as physical harm, embarrassment, or emotional suffering; even absent such other injuries, an award of several thousand dollars may be appropriate simply for several hours' loss of liberty. *See, e.g., Hallenbeck v. City of Albany*, 99 A.D.2d 639 (3d Dep't 1984); *Woodard v. City of Albany*, 81 A.D.2d 947 (3d Dep't 1981). In *Woodard*, for example, the Appellate Division held that a plaintiff who provided "no indication that he incurred any substantial physical or mental injury as the result of his false imprisonment" could recover $7,500 for false arrest and false imprisonment. 81 A.D.2d at 947 (ordering a new trial on damages unless the plaintiff agreed to a remittitur of a $16,000 jury award to $7,500, the "plaintiff having only spent approximately five hours in jail."). Similarly, in *Hallenbeck*, where the plaintiff had provided "no indication that he incurred any substantial physical or mental suffering," the Appellate Division ruled that he could recover $10,000 for false arrest and confinement. 99 A.D.2d at 640 (ordering remittitur of a $25,000 jury award to $10,000 where the "plaintiff was detained three hours."). Thus, a verdict that a plaintiff should not receive more than nominal damages for physical injury, economic loss, or mental suffering does not foreclose a more substantial award.

Accordingly, the availability of compensatory damages for time lost as a result of an unlawful detention was recognized at common law. We disagree with the dissent's view that the common-law concept of loss of time encompasses only loss of economic opportunity. The only cases cited in support of that view are not false-imprisonment cases but rather are cases in which the plaintiffs sought compensation for earnings lost due to injuries suffered as a result of the defendants' negligence. We would agree that in such negligence cases, the "loss of time" concept focuses squarely on economic losses.

In the false-imprisonment context, however, the "loss of time" concept is not so narrow. A loss of time, in the sense of loss of freedom, is inherent in any unlawful detention and is compensable as "general damages" for unlawful imprisonment without the need for pleading or proof. The loss of time, an injury distinct from mental suffering or humiliation, may, but need not, have economic consequences; if recovery for an economic loss is sought, the common law treats that loss as an item of special damage that must be pleaded and proven.

The claim often arises in the context of falsely accused shoplifters, which raises the potential for a privilege known as the "shopkeeper's privilege."

Dillard Dept. Stores, Inc. v. Silva

106 S.W.3d 789 (Ct. App. Tex. 2003) (Ross, J.), *aff'd as mod.*,
148 S.W.3d 370 (Tex. 2004)

[Plaintiff Silva received a gift from a friend purchased at a store of Dillard's Department Stores, Inc. He went in to Dillard's to return it, but before he went to where he could do so, he did some additional shopping in Dillard's. He had a headache, and so to take an aspirin he went to a drinking fountain in the store. At that point, a Dillard security officer, with a gun holstered, accused him of theft, placed him on the floor, and handcuffed him. He was then taken up an escalator to an empty office. He was later led out in handcuffs to an awaiting police car.

He sued Dillard for false imprisonment and malicious prosecution. Dillard prevailed on the malicious prosecution claim, but on the false imprisonment claim, the jury awarded Silva past damages of $10,124.01 and future damages of $3,000. The jury awarded Silva past and future damages of $10,124.01 and $3,000.00, respectively. Dillard appealed.]

Dillard contends there was no evidence, or only factually insufficient evidence, to support the jury's finding of false imprisonment. To prevail under a false imprisonment claim, a plaintiff must prove (1) willful detention, (2) without consent, and (3) without authority of law.

Dillard contends the third element is missing in this case. Dillard bases this contention on the shopkeeper's privilege which expressly grants an employee the authority of law to detain a customer to investigate the ownership of property, so long as (1) the employee has a reasonable belief the customer has stolen or is attempting to steal store merchandise, (2) the detention was for a reasonable amount of time, and (3) the detention was in a reasonable manner. Dillard asserts there was no evidence Silva's detention was unreasonable.

The second component of the shopkeeper's privilege is whether the detention was for a reasonable amount of time. Here, both sides agree the detention was for at least an hour. Considering the totality of the circumstances, we cannot say Silva was detained for an unreasonable length of time.

The third component of the shopkeeper's privilege is whether the detention was in a reasonable manner. Again, Dillard contends there was no evidence the detention was not reasonable. Silva testified, however, that Rivera accused him of theft and placed him on the floor and handcuffed him. Silva said the officer emptied Silva's shopping bag onto the floor. Silva testified people were around him when he was taken upstairs in handcuffs and when he was later escorted to the police car. He further stated the officer and a woman made fun of him while he was being detained upstairs. Silva stated that, when the city police came to take him into custody, Rivera again placed him on the floor with his knee in his back and exchanged handcuffs with the city police. He further testified that he asked Rivera many times to check his car for the receipt, but these requests were ignored and that, during the entire time he was detained, no one asked him for any explanation. Dillard, on the other hand, points to Rivera's testimony, which "flatly contradicted Mr. Silva at every turn."

Silva's testimony provided the jury with evidence the detention was not conducted in a reasonable manner. Although the descriptions of the detention by Silva and Rivera were different, when parties introduce conflicting testimony in a jury trial, it is the duty of the jury to determine which witness is more credible. The verdict indicates the jury found Silva's story more credible than Rivera's. Generally, the reasonableness of a detention is a question of fact for the jury to decide. Silva's testimony was more than a scintilla of evidence to support the jury's finding. Dillard's first point of error is overruled.

In addressing damages, the jury was instructed to consider the following elements: physical pain and mental anguish, attorney's fees incurred in the original criminal proceeding, and attorney's fees in the expunction proceeding. Considering those four things, the jury was then asked to fill in a dollar amount for past damages and for future damages. The jury answered $10,124.01 for past damages and $3,000.00 for future damages. When a damages issue is submitted in broad-form, an appellate court cannot ascertain with certainty what amount is attributable to each element.

Dillard contests these awards because they are based, at least in part, on Silva's past and future legal expenses in connection with the criminal proceeding instituted against him for which Dillard was found not liable. Dillard also contends the record is totally devoid of any evidence to support an award for physical pain. We agree. However, because this was a broad-form question which allowed the jury to provide a single answer for Silva's physical pain and mental anguish, and his past legal fees, we still must address whether there was evidence of mental anguish.

In order to recover for mental anguish, a plaintiff must offer either direct evidence of the nature, duration, or severity of his or her anguish, thus establishing a substantial disruption in the plaintiff's daily routine, or other evidence of a high degree of mental pain and distress that is more than mere worry, anxiety, vexation, embarrassment, or anger. Mental anguish does include mental sensation of pain resulting from such painful emotions as grief, severe disappointment, indignation, wounded pride, shame, despair, and/or public humiliation. Recovery is warranted in such cases where the plaintiff's mental pain has risen to such a level that it has rendered him or her incapable of dealing with certain everyday activities. For instance, as a result of the mental pain, the plaintiff suffers from a myriad of negative emotions; some of these emotions may manifest themselves in such a way as to make it difficult for the plaintiff to eat, sleep, work, socially interact, or carry on any other activity which, until the time of the alleged injury, he or she could accomplish on a day-to-day basis without difficulty.

In this case, there was evidence that the incident had affected Silva in a greater way than mere worry, anxiety, vexation, embarrassment, or anger. Several witnesses testified that before the incident Silva was always happy, but after the incident his personality changed. Silva's roommate testified Silva experienced nightmares as a result of the incident. He testified Silva would cry about what had happened to him. There was testimony of activities that Silva enjoyed before this incident, such as shopping and dancing, that he no longer likes to do. Silva testified he suffered from depression because of this incident. He further testified this incident caused him to lose his pride, "his dignity as a citizen." This evidence is sufficient to support the jury's award of past and future damages for mental anguish. Because the damages question submitted to the jury was broad, evidence to support one of the elements is enough to support recovery of the award.

Notes and Questions

1. <u>Why Not More Money</u>? The introduction identifies the types of harm for which damages can be recovered. Did the *Silva* plaintiff seek all of them? Either way, how would a lawyer quantify each form of harm?

2. <u>Awareness</u>. A hospital had provided emergency care for two men who had been seriously injured while unlawfully in the United States. It then arranged transportation of the men to a hospital in their native country, Mexico, all while they were unconscious. *Cruz v. C. Iowa Hosp. Corp.*, 826 N.W.2d 516 (Iowa App. 2012). They later asserted a false imprisonment claim against the hospital, asserting that they were harmed because of the poor-quality healthcare they received in Mexico after transfer. The appellate court affirmed the trial court's grant of the hospital's motion for summary judgment, writing:

> a physical injury is not an element of false imprisonment. Indeed, the principal element of damages in an action for false imprisonment is frequently the disagreeable emotion experienced by the plaintiff. However, that type of damages appears to be available only where the plaintiff was aware of the confinement. The Restatement explains,
>
> > Where, however, no harm results from a confinement and the plaintiff is not even subjected to the mental disturbance of being made aware of it at the time, his mere dignitary interest in being free from an interference with his personal liberty which he has only discovered later is not of sufficient importance to justify the recovery of the nominal damages involved. Accordingly, no action for false imprisonment can be

maintained in such a case. There may, however, be situations in which actual harm may result from a confinement of which the plaintiff is unaware at the time. In such a case more than the mere dignitary interest, and more than nominal damages, are involved, and the invasion becomes sufficiently important for the law to afford redress.

Restatement (Second) of Torts §42 cmts. a, b. As an example of the latter situation, the Restatement sets forth the following scenario:

A, a diabetic, is suffering from shock brought on by an overdose of insulin. B believes A to be drunk, and without any legal authority to do so arrests A and locks him up over night in jail. In the morning A is released while still unconscious and unaware that he has been confined. On learning what has occurred A is greatly humiliated, and suffers emotional distress, with resulting serious illness. B is subject to liability to A for false imprisonment.

Id. cmt. b, illus. 5. Seizing on this scenario, Cruz and Saldana argue their poor recovery was a consequence of their confinement. While this argument is appealing at first blush, it cannot withstand closer scrutiny.

The serious illness suffered by the diabetic in the Restatement illustration was brought on by his discovery of the confinement and resulting emotional distress. Here, Cruz and Saldana's poor recovery resulted from the inadequate rehabilitative services they received in Mexico, not their supposed confinement by the hospital or resulting emotional distress from learning of the confinement.

Can you imagine a hypothetical where the plaintiff is harmed by — but not aware of — confinement?

3. <u>Pleadings</u>. Some courts hold humiliation — such the Silva plaintiff felt while taken from the store or "loss of time" in Kerman — are special damages that must be pled as required by Rule 9(g). Galicki v. N.J., 2016 WL 4950995 (D.N.J. Sept. 15, 2016).

2. Monetary Remedies for False Arrest

Several claims are triggered by harm to "the right to be free from deprivations of liberty interests caused by unjustifiable criminal charges and procedures." *Calero-Colon v. Betancourt-Lebron*, 68 F.3d 1 (1st Cir. 1995). Different claims have existed in the states for these claims and some states continue those distinctions while others "simplify" them into one claim. *See also Wallace v. Kato*, 549 U.S. 384 (2007) ("False arrest and false imprisonment overlap; the former is a species of the latter.").

While "false imprisonment consists of intentionally confining or restraining another person without his consent and with knowledge that he has no lawful authority to do so," false arrest typically is a claim only against a law enforcement officer who detained someone without "probable cause," which is "when the facts available to a detaining officer would not warrant a person of reasonable caution to believe detention appropriate." *Chavez v. County of Bernalillo*, 3 F. Supp. 3d 936 (D.N.M. 2014). And, again, it may be the officer had probably cause only because another person provided false information to that officer. That person, not the officer who acted in good faith, would be liable.

Wright v. Musanti

2017 WL 253486 (S.D.N.Y. Jan. 20, 2017) (Forrest, J.),
aff'd, 887 F.3d 577 (2d Cir. 2018)

[Defendant Jacqueline Musanti was walking to work in New York City when, she alleged plaintiff, Scott Wright, cut her off while he was also walking to work. She kicked him and "things went downhill from there. Plaintiff ended up under arrest and in a holding cell." Neither of them called the police, but they arrived and went to the building plaintiff had entered. Soon, defendant and a few of her co-workers also arrived there. Police asked those present about the altercation, but defendant did not ask anyone to speak to the police or hear their conversations. She told the police that plaintiff had cut her off to trip her and that she then kicked him because she felt attacked but did not tell police she had started the incident.

In the meantime, a minute after plaintiff arrived in his office, about nine officers came to his floor, approached his desk, told him he was under arrest, and handcuffed him—all in front of at least one co-worker. After 15 minutes, the police took him down the elevator and out of the crowded lobby to a patrol car, where he sat inside for about 45 minutes. During that time, several people saw him and a few took his picture.

During that time, the defendant asked police to press charges against the plaintiff. As a result, police took plaintiff to the nearest precinct where he spent 40 minutes in a cell and was then ordered to later appear in court. He then returned to work. He had a few minor scratches on his face, and the time from arrest to his return to work was about two hours.

He was charged with two counts of assault in the third degree, one count of attempt, and one count of harassment in the second degree. To address these charges, plaintiff appeared in criminal court five times throughout 2014, paid a flat fee of $5,000 for a criminal defense attorney, and paid $400 for a private investigator. The charges were dismissed in October 2014. Plaintiff then sued defendant for battery, assault, and false arrest. After a bench trial, the court issued these findings and conclusions.]

Under New York law, a private individual may be held liable for causing law enforcement to make a false arrest if the plaintiff establishes (1) the defendant intended to confine the plaintiff; (2) the plaintiff was aware of the confinement;

(3) the plaintiff did not consent to the confinement; and (4) the confinement was not otherwise privileged by virtue of, *inter alia*, a warrant, probable cause and/or immunity protection.

To prove intent, a plaintiff must establish the defendant affirmatively procured or instigated the plaintiff's arrest. Liability may attach only when the defendant has affirmatively induced the officer to act, such as by taking an active part in the arrest and procuring it to be made or showing active, officious and undue zeal to the point where the officer is not acting of his own volition. Merely seeking police assistance or furnishing information to law enforcement authorities who are then free to exercise their own judgment as to whether an arrest should be made and criminal charges filed cannot give rise to liability for false arrest, even if the information later proves to be false. *See also King v. Crossland Sav. Bank*, 111 F.3d 251 (2d Cir. 1997) ("When police independently act to arrest a suspect on information provided by a party, that party is not liable for false imprisonment—even if the information provided is later found to be erroneous.") However, a complainant can be held liable for false arrest if the complainant intentionally provided false information to instigate an arrest by law-enforcement officials, or had no reasonable basis for the report.

Further, under New York law, the existence of probable cause is an absolute defense to a false arrest claim. To establish probable cause, a defendant must prove that, at the time of the arrest and under the totality of the circumstances, a reasonable and prudent police officer would have thought that the plaintiff committed a crime.

On the present record, it is undisputed that plaintiff was aware of and did not consent to being confined. It is the other two elements—intent and probable cause—that require greater analysis. In that regard, the Court finds it helpful (for purposes of assessing damages *infra*) to consider plaintiff's arrest as comprising two separate instances of "confinement" by the police: (1) the police's decision to handcuff him and place him in the patrol car; and (2) the police's subsequent decision to take him to the precinct. The Court analyzes each of these instances of confinement separately. Based on the record, it appears that the arresting officers held open the possibility of releasing plaintiff from the patrol car until defendant indicated she wanted to press charges. Therefore, prior to that time, plaintiff is not liable for false arrest and is not responsible for any damages allegedly incurred. It is only after plaintiff indicated she wanted to press charges that she became liable for false arrest and any ensuing damages.

The Court turns first to plaintiff's initial confinement by the police—when, following the altercation outside, police officers came up to his floor, placed him in handcuffs and escorted him through the lobby and into the patrol car. Defendant is not liable for false arrest arising from this period of confinement because she did not affirmatively procure or instigate his arrest at this point. As a preliminary matter, neither defendant nor plaintiff called the police; the police responded to the scene independently. In the absence of any indication of what, if anything, defendant said to the police before they went up to plaintiff's floor, there is no basis upon which to hold defendant liable for falsely arresting plaintiff as he was handcuffed and escorted to the patrol car.

Defendant can be held liable, however, for falsely arresting plaintiff while the police detained him in the parked patrol car and transported him to and charged and booked him at the precinct. The record reveals two ways in which defendant affirmatively procured or instigated this portion of plaintiff's confinement. First, it appears to the Court that defendant intentionally provided false information to the police in order to bring about his arrest. Defendant told the police the same account to which she testified at trial, *i.e.*, that the altercation commenced when plaintiff purposefully cut her off on the street in order to trip her. Defendant at no point told the police that she was responsible for the encounter, or that the encounter resulted from a misunderstanding that spiraled out of control. To the contrary, she painted plaintiff as the sole and unmistaken aggressor, a characterization fundamentally at odds with what actually occurred. The intent behind these statements was to cause the police to arrest plaintiff.

Second, while plaintiff was waiting in the patrol car, defendant told the police — in response to their question — that she wanted to press charges. Had she said "no", it is at least likely that the police would have released plaintiff, thereby avoiding plaintiff's transport in the precinct, time spent in a jail cell and plaintiff's subsequent criminal prosecution. Thus, by deciding to press charges, defendant played an active part in the arrest alongside the police.

Defendant's liability for false arrest in the second portion of plaintiff's confinement is not vitiated by probable cause. The Court finds that defendant failed to establish — as it is her burden to do — that the police reasonably thought that plaintiff committed a crime. Defendant proffered no testimony from Officer Manetta, the arresting officer, or from other witnesses who spoke with the police. As a result, the sole proven bases for the arrest are the combination of defendant's fallacious witness statement, and defendant's decision to press charges. While the police may have, in fact, had probable cause to arrest plaintiff, defendant has not adduced sufficient evidence to prove that fact here.

Compensatory damages compensate the injured victim for injuries actually endured. Both pecuniary and nonpecuniary losses — such as emotional pain and suffering and loss of liberty — are compensable under New York law. To recover compensatory damages, a claimant must present evidence that provides the finder of fact with a reasonable basis upon which to calculate the amount of damages incurred. Damages for false arrest may be awarded only for the period from initial custody until arraignment, as subsequent damages resulting from continued incarceration are attributable only to the tort of malicious prosecution. *See also Palmquist v. City of Albany*, 492 N.Y.S.2d 487 (3d Dep't 1985) (declining to award legal fees for criminal defense where there was "insufficient proof in the record to establish that plaintiff's legal fees were limited to the defense of the arrest itself and not the criminal action.").

As for false arrest, the Court awards compensatory damages in the amount of $5,000. This award compensates plaintiff for non-pecuniary losses incurred during the portion of the arrest for which defendant is liable—*i.e.,* the period during which plaintiff was in the patrol car, held in a cell and booked at the precinct. Plaintiff suffered several distinct harms during this period: the embarrassment and humiliation of being held in a patrol car for 45 minutes as passers-by gawked and took photographs; the uncomfortable experience of spending forty minutes in a jail cell (and an hour at a precinct); and plaintiff's overall loss of liberty during these two hours. These damages are recoverable under the tort of false arrest.

Notes and Questions

1. The Harms in *Wright*. Like false imprisonment, false arrest does not require mental anguish or lost wages, but those may be consequential damages. In *Wright,* because the battery and assault had caused no actual damages, the court awarded $1 in nominal damages for those claims, yet $5,000 for wrongful detention.

2. The Measure of Damage. Mental distress caused by the fear of being imprisoned, the humiliation of being processed in jail, public scorn, and loss of friendship can lead to substantial awards in a jury's discretion. *See Brown v. City of Monroe,* 135 So. 3d 792 (Ct. App. La. 2014) (general damages of $20,000 to plaintiff arrested at her workplace, spent an hour in jail); *Family Dollar Trucking, Inc. v. Huff,* 474 S.W.3d 100 (Ct. App. Ark. 2015) (two employees awarded $3.25 million after being arrested because of employer's wrongful accusation of theft that caused them to spend a "short time" in jail, incur $2,500 in attorneys' fees, lose sleep, and suffer embarrassment and humiliation). In this regard, a defendant is responsible for mental distress caused even if the plaintiff is a person who, by culture or personality, is more sensitive than a reasonable person. *See Strader v. Ashley,* 877 N.Y.S.2d 747 (3d Dep't. 2009) (affirming $250,000 award where defendant had brought criminal charges against plaintiff that were reported in local newspaper, made plaintiff sick, and caused him to stop socializing for fear of public scorn). As a lawyer, how would you quantify this for a jury?

3. Monetary Remedies for Causing Wrongful Criminal or Civil Proceedings

Courts recognize that a person can be harmed when a proceeding that could result in confinement is instituted, even if the person is never confined. *Regency Motors of Metairie, L.L.C. v. Hibernia-Rosenthal Ins. Agency, LLC,* 868 So. 2d 905 (Ct. App. La. 2004) (recognizing a threat of doing so was insufficient). Courts also provide a remedy if the proceeding was civil. Further, some courts recognize that a proceeding might be instituted properly, but then process used for, or the suit continued for, an improper purpose.

Courts sometimes combine what once were separate claims into one, while others do not. For example, Pennsylvania distinguishes "between the common law torts of abuse of process and malicious use of process." *See generally, Villani v. Seibert*, 159 A.3d 478 (Pa. 2017) ("An abuse of process, either civil or criminal, arises where a party employs it for some unlawful object rather than for the purpose that the law intends it to effect; in other words, a perversion thereof, in distinction from malicious use of process, either civil or criminal, wherein the tortfeasor intends that the process have its proper effect and execution although it is wrongfully instituted."). On the other hand, the court in *Durham v. Guest*, 204 P.3d 19 (N.M. 2009), combined and reformulated the claims:

> We leave in place the combined tort of malicious abuse of process, but restate its elements as follows: (1) the use of process in a judicial proceeding that would be improper in the regular prosecution or defense of a claim or charge; (2) a primary motive in the use of process to accomplish an illegitimate end; and (3) damages. An improper use of process may be shown by (1) filing a complaint without probable cause, or (2) an irregularity or impropriety suggesting extortion, delay, or harassment, or other conduct formerly actionable under the tort of abuse of process. A use of process is deemed to be irregular or improper if it (1) involves a procedural irregularity or a misuse of procedural devices such as discovery, subpoenas, and attachments, or (2) indicates the wrongful use of proceedings, such as an extortion attempt. Finally, we emphasize that the tort of malicious abuse of process should be construed narrowly in order to protect the right of access to the courts.

Where the distinctions persist, abuse of process focuses on the time *after* a civil suit or criminal proceeding is instituted and not on the motive at the time of filing, and so abuse of process does not redress improper initiation of a civil proceeding. *EMC Outdoor, LLC v. Stuart*, 2018 WL 3208155 (E.D. Pa. June 28, 2018) ("the commencement or maintenance of a lawsuit, even for an improper purpose, does not constitute an abuse of process under Pennsylvania law"); *Laforge v. Richland Holdings, Inc.*, 2018 WL 525298 (D. Nev. Jan. 23, 2018) ("filing of a complaint with malicious intent is insufficient to state an abuse of process claim. Rather there must also be some act after filing that abuses the process."); *Stetter v. Blackpool*, 2010 WL 4117256 (D. Ariz. Oct. 19, 2010) ("Unlike the tort of malicious prosecution, which covers the initiation of civil proceedings with malice and without probable cause, abuse of process addresses misuse of process after proceedings have been initiated."); *Lehew v. Bd. of Comm'rs for Comanche Cnty. Okla.*, 2007 WL 9711067 (W.D. Okla. Jan. 11, 2007) (distinguishing malicious prosecution from abuse of process in that "the former lies for malicious initiation of process and the latter for a perversion of the process after it is issued."). For example, the court in *Turner v. Thomas*, 794 S.E.2d 439 (N.C. 2016) (Ervin, J., concurring in part), explained that if a proceeding had been instituted with probable cause, but the defendant had caused it to continue without probable cause, only a claim for malicious prosecution would lie:

The logic underlying that theory has been consistently recognized by leading encyclopedias and treatises addressing American tort law. *See* Restatement (Second) of Torts § 655 (stating that "a private person who takes an active part in continuing or procuring the continuation of criminal proceedings initiated by himself or by another is subject to the same liability for malicious prosecution as if he had then initiated the proceedings"); *id.* § 655 cmt. b (pointing out that "the rule stated in this Section applies when the defendant has himself initiated criminal proceedings against another or procured their institution, upon probable cause and for a proper purpose, and thereafter takes an active part in pressing the proceedings after he has discovered that there is no probable cause for them," and "applies also when the proceedings are initiated by a third person, and the defendant, knowing that there is no probable cause for them, thereafter takes an active part in procuring their continuation"); 52 Am. Jur. 2d *Malicious Prosecution* § 21, at 207-08 (2011) (stating that a malicious prosecution action can be maintained in the event that "the defendant instigated or encouraged, commenced or continued, initiated or procured, or caused or assisted in causing the prosecution complained of, or advised, aided, cooperated, or assisted in the prosecution of the case" and that "a person who had no part in the commencement of the action, but who participated in it at a later time, may be held liable for malicious prosecution"); W. Page Keeton et al., *Prosser and Keeton on the Law of Torts* § 119, at 872 (5th ed. 1984) (stating that "the defendant may be liable either for initiating or for continuing a criminal prosecution without probable cause").

An analysis of the reported decisions concerning this issue clearly indicates that the vast majority of American jurisdictions that have considered the viability of the "continuation" theory have recognized its existence.

These jurisdictions focus on whether process—such as a subpoena or writ of garnishment—issued after the proceeding was instituted was "abused." If a suit or criminal proceeding was filed without probable cause, there can be no malicious prosecution, but if a form of process after filing was used for an improper purpose, then a claim for abuse of process lies. Others require both a lack of probable cause and an improper purpose for any form of liability to attach. Consider which approach the following courts take and what these different approaches might mean.

Bhatia v. Debek

287 Conn. 397 (2008) (Schaller, J.)

[Plaintiff Ajai Bhatia met defendant Marlene Debek in Connecticut in 1990. In 1991, he moved to Florida for work. She followed in 1995, and bought a house where she and he lived and became engaged. Their daughter was born in August 1996, but in November she moved with her daughter, "T," without plaintiff, back to Connecticut. He visited a few times over the next two years.

In August 2000, his work brought him back to Connecticut. Upon return, he tried to visit his daughter, but defendant refused, and so plaintiff sued, seeking joint legal custody. In November 2000, a court ordered supervised visitation between the plaintiff and his daughter, but the defendant refused to permit it. Things escalated, with defendant placing an anonymous call to the state's Department of Children and Families ("department"), alleging that the defendant and her brother, Todd Debek, were abusing substances, neglecting the child, and had an unsafe home. The department investigated and found the claims unsubstantiated.

The plaintiff knew defendant's call had led to the investigation. In December she obtained an ex parte court order prohibiting the plaintiff from contacting her except during visitation exchanges, based on his alleged yelling. Things continued to worsen, and the defendant continued to refuse to let the plaintiff visit his daughter. In October 2001, the defendant reported to the department that the plaintiff had sexually abused T, and also reported this to the police. That same month, the court found the defendant in contempt of court for not permitting visitation. At the hearing, however, she stated she would not permit visits. The court ordered the defendant incarcerated for 96 hours, or until she allowed unsupervised visitation. The defendant remained incarcerated that entire time, during which T was in foster care.

The day after Christmas and as a result of defendant's reports, the plaintiff was arrested and charged with sexual assault in the first degree and risk of injury to a child. Those charges were tried. The jury acquitted the plaintiff on the first count, but deadlocked on second. The court dismissed the risk of injury charge after the state indicated it would not seek retrial.

The plaintiff sued for malicious prosecution. After a bench trial, the court found for the plaintiff and awarded damages. The defendant appealed denial of her post-trial motions.]

We have summarized the required showing for both causes of action as follows: To establish either cause of action, it is necessary to prove want of probable cause, malice and a termination of suit in the plaintiff's favor. In a cause of action for malicious prosecution, the plaintiff additionally must establish that the defendant caused the proceeding to be instituted. This requirement is due to the fact that, unlike a vexatious litigation claim, in which the underlying civil action was filed either by the defendant herself, acting pro se, or by an attorney acting on behalf of the defendant, in a malicious prosecution action, a public official, acting on behalf of the state, institutes the criminal action against the malicious prosecution plaintiff. It is, therefore, more problematic in a malicious prosecution action, as opposed to an action for vexatious litigation, for the plaintiff to connect the defendant with the actual institution of the underlying action. In accordance with the indirect connection between the underlying action and the defendant in a malicious prosecution action, we have specified the initiation of the underlying action as a separate element in malicious prosecution cases, as opposed to vexatious litigation cases, in which the plaintiff is not required to establish that the defendant initiated the underlying action.

Another reason that malicious prosecution, but not vexatious litigation, requires the showing that the defendant initiated or procured the institution of criminal proceedings against the plaintiff is because the first element of the tort allows for a limited immunity to a private citizen accused of malicious prosecution. The purpose of this immunity is to further the policy of encouraging private citizens to assist in law enforcement. A private person can be said to have initiated a criminal proceeding if he has insisted that the plaintiff should be prosecuted, that is, if he has brought pressure of any kind to bear upon the public officer's decision to commence the prosecution. But a private person has not initiated a criminal proceeding if he has undertaken no more than to provide potentially incriminating information to a public officer. In such a case, *if the defendant has made a full and truthful disclosure* and has left the decision to prosecute entirely in the hands of the public officer, he cannot be held liable for malicious prosecution. This limited immunity attempts to strike a careful balance between the need to encourage private citizens to assist in law enforcement with the need to protect individuals against false and malicious accusations. This careful balancing, not necessary for the tort of vexatious litigation, reflects a significant difference between the nature of the underlying actions in the two torts.

Turning to the nature of the initiation element, we emphasize that a defendant is entitled to the limited immunity provided by this element only if the defendant has made a full and truthful disclosure. A private person cannot escape liability if he knowingly presents information that is false. In other words, a private citizen who knowingly provides false information to a public officer is not entitled to the limited immunity provided under the initiation element, even if that person brought no pressure to bear on the public officer and left the decision to prosecute entirely in the hands of that public officer. Not extending immunity from liability to such persons is consistent with the public policy underlying the immunity, to encourage private citizens to *assist* in law enforcement, a policy that is not furthered by immunizing from liability persons who knowingly provide false information.

There is ample support in the record to support a finding that, during the course of the underlying criminal action, the defendant knowingly presented information she knew to be false. The trial court cited to some of this evidence in support of its express finding that the defendant had acted with malice. For example, the trial court cited to the finding of the trial court in the custody action (custody court) that the defendant's claims that T told her that the plaintiff had sexually abused her were not credible. The court further relied on the fact that the defendant waited two days after T allegedly told her about the inappropriate touching before she reported the abuse. That delay, contrasted with the defendant's swift consultation with a pediatrician the day after T's first unsupervised visitation with the plaintiff—because, she claimed, T was experiencing vaginal discomfort—persuaded the court that the defendant was not telling the truth about the incident that gave rise to the allegations of sexual abuse.

We now turn to the second element of malicious prosecution, termination of the criminal proceedings in favor of the plaintiff. In the plaintiff's criminal trial, the jury acquitted him of the charge of sexual assault in the first degree, but was deadlocked on the charge of risk of injury to a child. The trial court subsequently dismissed the risk of injury charge, after the prosecution informed the court that T would not testify in the event of a retrial.

We have never required a plaintiff in a vexatious suit action to prove a favorable termination either by pointing to an adjudication on the merits in his favor or by showing affirmatively that the circumstances of the termination indicated his innocence or nonliability, so long as the proceeding has terminated without consideration. Instead, we have always viewed the issue of whether the prior outcome was 'favorable' to the plaintiff as relevant to the issue of probable cause. We set forth two concerns that guide us in our consideration of whether the underlying proceedings terminated in the plaintiff's favor. The first is the danger of inconsistent judgments if defendants use a vexatious suit or malicious prosecution action as a means of making a collateral attack on the judgment against them or as a counterattack to an ongoing proceeding. The second is the unspoken distaste for rewarding a convicted felon or otherwise 'guilty' party with damages in the event that the party who instituted the proceeding did not at that time have probable cause to do so. The question we must resolve, then, is whether the dismissal of the risk of injury charge implicates either of these concerns. The first concern, the danger of inconsistent judgments, clearly is not implicated, because the risk of injury charge was dismissed and there are no ongoing criminal proceedings for the plaintiff to attack collaterally through the present action for malicious prosecution. The second concern, the distaste for rewarding a guilty party with damages, also is not implicated, because the trial court had ample evidence to support its conclusion that the defendant lied when she reported to the department and the police that her daughter had told her that the plaintiff had sexually abused her. Under the circumstances of the present case, therefore, the fact that the jury was deadlocked on the risk of injury charge does not signify that the proceedings did not terminate in the plaintiff's favor.

The third element of malicious prosecution is lack of probable cause. "Probable cause" has been defined as the knowledge of facts sufficient to justify a reasonable person in the belief that he has reasonable grounds for prosecuting an action. Mere conjecture or suspicion is insufficient. Moreover, belief alone, no matter how sincere it may be, is not enough, since it must be based on circumstances which make it reasonable. Although want of probable cause is negative in character, the burden is upon the plaintiff to prove affirmatively, by circumstances or otherwise, that the defendant had no reasonable ground for instituting the criminal proceeding. The existence of probable cause is an absolute protection against an action for malicious prosecution, and what facts, and whether particular facts, constitute probable cause is always a question of law.

The very same facts that support a finding that the defendant initiated the underlying criminal prosecution also support a finding that the defendant lacked probable cause to institute that action. That is, the only evidence that would support a conclusion that the defendant had probable cause to institute the action—her claims that T told her that the plaintiff had touched her inappropriately—is undermined by all of the evidence in the record that persuaded the trial court that T made no such statement, including evidence that the defendant coached T to testify, the delay in reporting the alleged abuse, and T's lack of any symptoms of abuse.

The last element of malicious prosecution requires that the defendant acted with malice, primarily for a purpose other than that of bringing an offender to justice. There is ample support in the record for the trial court's finding that the defendant acted with malice. The record reveals that the defendant repeatedly attempted to prevent the plaintiff from exercising his visitation rights with T, and the trial court found that the defendant's report of the alleged sexual abuse was one of many attempts to keep the plaintiff from being with T.

Finally, we address the defendant's claim that the trial court's damages award was unsupported by the evidence. We disagree. The compensatory damages awarded consisted of $500,000 for loss of income and diminution of future income due to the defendant's conduct, $130,000 for attorney's fees incurred to defend the criminal prosecution, $4500 for the plaintiff's bail bond premium and $2.5 million for emotional distress, loss of reputation and humiliation.

In reviewing a trial court's award of compensatory damages the trial court has broad discretion in determining damages. The determination of damages involves a question of fact that will not be overturned unless it is clearly erroneous. To authorize a recovery of more than nominal damages, facts must exist and be shown by the evidence which affords a reasonable basis for measuring the plaintiff's loss. The plaintiff has the burden of proving the nature and extent of the loss. Mathematical exactitude in the proof of damages is often impossible, but the plaintiff must nevertheless provide sufficient evidence for the trier to make a fair and reasonable estimate.

We conclude that there is sufficient evidence in the record to support the trial court's award of compensatory damages. The plaintiff testified at trial that he paid the $4500 for the bail bond premium, and that his total bill for attorney's fees for his criminal defense amounted to at least $130,000. The trial court was entitled to credit that testimony. As for the award for loss of income and diminution of future income, the court based its award on evidence that established that, prior to the criminal prosecution, the plaintiff had earned $100,000 a year. He was terminated from his employment following his arrest, and thereafter had difficulty obtaining and keeping any employment other than menial jobs.

The defendant claims that the award of $2.5 million is unreasonable. We acknowledge that it is an uncommonly large award. We are mindful, however, that, although it is difficult to measure emotional distress in terms of money, an award of damages for pain and suffering is peculiarly within the province of the trier of fact. The court, in explaining the liberal award, emphasized the "staggering" nature of the plaintiff's emotional distress, loss of reputation and humiliation, stating: "It is difficult to imagine anything worse than being falsely accused of sexually assaulting your own child and having the accuser brainwash the child into believing the false allegations." With this background, we cannot say that the trial court's award was clearly erroneous.

Adams v. Aidoo

2012 WL 1408878 (Del. Super. Mar. 29, 2012) (Brady, J.),
aff'd, 58 A.3d 410 (Jan. 3, 2013)

[Ninette and Yaw Aidoo were married. In October 2006 they were building a home in a new neighborhood at the same time as Ashley Adams, who lived two doors down. The three were friendly, and invited each other in to look at furnishings, décor, and the like. However, in February 2007, Adams stopped allowing this, and in April the Aidoos' daughters told the Aidoos that Adams had moved a sprinkler to spray them as they walked by her home on the way from school. Adams accused the Aidoos of various misconduct, and she said to them that her property had dropped $100,000 because African Americans were in the neighborhood; the Aidoos were African American. She also stated she was going to buy a pit bull and set it on their family, and complained to the homeowners' association that their back deck blocked her view.

On the night of October 1, 2007, Yaw's cell phone received a text message stating: "After Ninette goes to sleep, you can sneak over and give me what I really need. It has been a long time. Ashlee." The Aidoos did not recognize the phone number or name. They called, and eventually someone answered and was angry. Worried that they were being watched, Ninette called the police. Officer Selhorst arrived and learned the phone number belonged to Ashley Adams, who lived two doors down. The next night, Selhorst visited Adams, who said she had received three phone calls the night before but did not text Yaw. Selhorst obtained a warrant, based on harassment, and handcuffed Adams. After a few minutes, Selhorst uncuffed her.

Adams filed suit against the Yaws, seeking $3.1 million in damages, alleging various claims including malicious prosecution. They counterclaimed, asserting abuse of process. The trial court dismissed Adams' claims before trial, and that was affirmed on appeal. At trial, the jury awarded the Aidoos $250,000 in damages. Adams then moved for a new trial.]

As to the tort of abuse of process, at the trial for this matter, the Court instructed the jury as follows:

One who willfully uses the legal system whether through a criminal or civil action in the courts or in a regulatory agency, against another, primarily to accomplish a purpose for which the system is not designed, is responsible to the person against whom the legal process was used for any harm caused by such a use.

I have determined as a matter of law that Ashley Adams caused legal process to issue against Yaw and Ninette Aidoo in the nature of a civil lawsuit. The purpose of a civil lawsuit is to seek compensation for injury resulting from someone else's wrongful conduct.

The elements that Yaw and Ninette Aidoo must prove are: An improper or wrongful purpose in using the legal process, that is, an ulterior purpose; and two, a willful act in the use of the system not proper in the regular conduct of legal proceedings.

Adams argues the Aidoos failed to allege facts that Adams engaged in a perversion of process after she filed her Complaint and before the Aidoos filed their Counterclaims.

Actions leading up to a defendant's initiation of legal proceedings against a plaintiff suing or countersuing the defendant for abuse of process in a separate legal action are relevant to an abuse of process analysis. Therefore, the jury's consideration of any evidence presented at the hearing as to Adams' purpose in suing the Aidoos was proper.

The Aidoos presented sufficient evidence to the jury for a reasonable jury to conclude Adams abused process in using the legal system to accomplish a purpose for which the system is not designed. Based on the evidence, the jury could easily have concluded Adams used process to pursue her claims against the Aidoos for several reasons other than redress, which will be detailed in the following paragraphs.

When Adams testified at trial, she confirmed many aspects of her use of process in this case which the Aidoos claim were abusive. The jury was able to review Adams' initial thirty-one-count Complaint and her twenty-count Amended Complaint. She testified that she asserted multiple causes of action against the Aidoos, including lewdness, stalking, misuse of a computer system, trespass and peeping into Adams' windows or intending to peep into Adams' windows, menacing, criminal nuisance, terroristic threatening, and causing Adams to suffer physical pain and suffering. In relation to those claims, Adams testified she never called the police or sought medical treatment. Adams confirmed that she sought $21 million in her amended complaint against the Aidoos. She also confirmed that she sent four sets of interrogatories to the Aidoos, with over 100 questions, many of which included sub-parts, and over 50 document requests. Yaw testified that the copies of motions and documents that his attorney sent to him in relation to this case would easily create a four-foot stack of paper. By the time of Yaw's testimony, the Aidoos' legal bills amounted to $79,206.07, with only $21,819.44 of that balance having been paid by that point. The trial for this matter spanned six days, with a seventh day for the return of the jury's verdict.

At trial, the Aidoos presented abundant evidence of Adams' lack of proper purpose or alternative purposes in carrying out this litigation against them. Adams confirmed that in her Complaint for this action, she alleged the Aidoos caused ten written police complaints to be written against her from September, 2007 to November, 2007. When the Aidoos' counsel asked if she had proof of that, she responded she did not have ten, she had six that she was able to obtain, and they were produced in this case. When counsel asked if she would go get those complaints from the materials she brought to Court, Adams returned to the witness stand with two reports— one relating to the driveway incident from September 11, 2007, and the other from the text message incident from October 1, 2007. What is perhaps most notable is the evidence that Officer Selhorst decided independently and without input or request from the Aidoos to attain a warrant for Adams' arrest after he spoke to Adams about the text message incident. Ninette testified on cross-examination, "We did not want you arrested. We did not ask Officer Selhorst to arrest you. I just wanted you to stop harassing us. I just wanted someone else to come over and talk to you because I had pleaded, pleaded with you to leave us alone; leave us alone."

That the jury could reasonably have concluded Adams sued the Aidoos for a purpose other than to seek redress for her damages is bolstered by the fact that the jury could reasonably have concluded that Adams actually sent the text message that was the initial cause of action of this litigation and therefore had no damages for which to seek redress.

The Court need not ascertain what the jury believed to be Adams' precise purpose in carrying out this litigation. It is sufficient only that the jury believed, by a preponderance of the evidence, that Adams used the legal system to carry out her lawsuit against the Aidoos for a purpose other than to seek compensation for some injury resulting from wrongful conduct. Since the Aidoos presented evidence of several conceivable improper purposes which might underlie Adams' intentions, the Court finds the jury's verdict that Adams abused process is not against the great weight of the evidence, and therefore it shall not be disturbed.

Adams contends that the jury was required to determine the difference between the torts of abuse of process and malicious prosecution, and that failure to so instruct the jury was clear error. Adams did not object to the jury instructions on this basis at trial, and she raises the issue for the first time in her Motion. Therefore, the Court must review the issue under a clear error standard.

The tort of abuse of process derives from the tort of malicious prosecution. At common law, malicious prosecution was a remedy for unjustifiable criminal proceedings, and the action evolved into a cause of action for wrongful civil proceedings, initially called "malicious use of civil process." The two actions are often confused, and overlap where an abusive litigant uses the legal system to oppress others. Once either tort is proven, damages are generally the same. The distinction between the malicious prosecution and abuse of process is at best, unclear, to both laypersons and legal scholars.

The elements a plaintiff must prove in an abuse of process claim in Delaware are: (1) an improper or wrongful purpose in using legal process; and (2) a willful act in the use of the system not proper in the regular conduct of legal proceedings. The mere carrying out of process to an authorized conclusion does not result in liability, even if the process is carried out with bad intentions. A party alleging abuse of process must show some definite act or threat not authorized by the process, or aimed at an objective not legitimate in the use of the process.

In comparison, the requirements for malicious prosecution are: (1) the institution of civil or criminal proceedings; (2) without probable cause; (3) with malice; (4) termination of the proceedings in the aggrieved party's favor; and (5) damages were inflicted upon the aggrieved party by seizure of property or other special injury. Delaware courts disfavor malicious prosecution claims and approach them with careful scrutiny.

Despite the similarity of the two, malicious prosecution and abuse of process are separate torts that a party may assert hand-in-hand. Abuse of process is concerned with perversion of the process after it has been issued, in comparison to malicious prosecution which focuses on the initiation of that process. It only makes sense that malicious prosecution addresses a litigant's intent in initiating a legal action against an individual, while abuse of process addresses a litigant's use of the legal system to perpetuate an improper purpose to sue by using, or abusing, the imposition of proceedings that accompany litigation upon an individual.

In this case, the Aidoos asserted a malicious prosecution claim against Adams, but that claim was dismissed before trial. The standard of guilt for a civil case is that a jury must find by a preponderance of the evidence that a defendant committed all the necessary elements of a tort. The standard is not that a jury must find a plaintiff has demonstrated that a defendant has committed a tort by a preponderance of the evidence, and not some other tort. Providing instructions as to both malicious prosecution and abuse of process, while only abuse of process was in issue, in this case would likely have misled or confused the jury as to both the issues it was to decide and the applicable standards of law. Contrary to Adams' contention, to provide instructions as to both torts would have jeopardized the fairness and integrity of the trial process. Therefore, the Court did not err in not instructing the jury to determine the difference between malicious prosecution and abuse of process.

Notes and Questions

1. The Remedies. The principal cases take distinct approaches to the harm of improper litigation. One is more tolerant of abusive tactics; or, put another way, one is less willing to impose liability for instituting a civil or criminal proceeding.

What are the differences and when would they matter? The *Aidoo* court laid out in detail (much is omitted) the evidence the Aidoos' lawyer introduced to establish the claim. What evidence showed each element, including that the Aidoos had prevailed on Adams' claim? *Cf. Dinkins v. Calhoun*, 2018 WL 2248572 (Ct. App. Tex. May 17, 2018) (plaintiff filed suit while prior case was on appeal).

2. <u>What Is the Trigger Harm</u>? "Generally, special damages mean that the prior action interfered with a plaintiff's person or property or proof of concrete harm that is considerably more cumbersome than the physical, psychological or financial demands of defending a lawsuit," *Brown v. Cty. of N.Y.*, 65 N.Y.S.3d 490 (N.Y. Sup. Ct. 2017), and must be an "injury which would not necessarily result in all suits prosecuted to recover for a like cause of action." *Winter v. Pinkins*, 2017 WL 5496278 (S.D.N.Y. Feb. 17, 2017). Damage is special if it is "some concrete harm that is considerably more cumbersome than the physical, psychological or financial demands of defending a lawsuit." *Sankin v. Abeshouse*, 545 F. Supp. 2d 324 (S.D.N.Y. 2008); *Shea v. Winnebago Cnty. Sheriff's Dept.*, 2018 WL 3949219 (7th Cir. Aug. 16, 2018) (malicious prosecution action based on civil proceedings must have resulted in "special damage beyond the usual expense, time or annoyance in defending a lawsuit"); *Chappelle v. Baybridge Capital Advisors, LLC*, 2017 WL 1096783 (Ct. App. Mich. March 21, 2017) ("A succession of lawsuits may constitute a special injury under some circumstances."); *Harmon v. Gordon*, 712 F.3d 1044 (7th Cir. 2013) (excessive suits can suffice); *Maytown Sand & Gravel, LLC v. Thurston Cnty.*, 2018 WL 3765517 (Wash. Aug. 9, 2018) (attorneys' fees may suffice).

Sufficient harm has been held to include seizure in the earlier proceeding of the plaintiff's property and the plaintiff's arrest. *Winter v. Pinkins*, 2017 WL 5496278 (S.D.N.Y. Feb. 17, 2017). In *dicta, Chappelle, supra*, stated "injury to one's fame (as by a scandalous allegation), injury to one's person or liberty, and injury to one's property" would suffice. However, other courts have held that "reputational damages" are insufficient. *Batchelor v. Alexis Properties, LLC*, 2018 WL 1611662 (Del. Super. Apr. 3, 2018). If the harm is beyond the normal hassle of litigation, damages for mental anguish may be recoverable. *See LeBlanc v. Pynes*, 69 So. 3d 1273 (La. Ct. App. 2011) (awarding two plaintiffs $45,000 in total general damages for defendant falsely reporting them for having made improper loans); *Burkhead v. Davis*, 505 S.W.3d 784 (Ct. App. Ky. 2016) ($50 award affirmed).

3. <u>Are Defense Costs Recoverable</u>? Courts that do not count attorneys' fees as sufficient to be "damages" hold that if there was the required damage, then the defense costs of the earlier proceeding are recoverable consequential damages. *See Wilburn v. Nash*, 382 Wis. 2d 833 (Ct. App. Wis. May 22, 2018) ("while counsel fees and costs [incurred in the earlier action] may be an element of damages in a successful malicious prosecution action, they do not by themselves constitute the special grievance necessary to make out the cause of action.").

4. <u>Porn Troll</u>. The plaintiff in *Metro Media Enter. Inc. v. Steinruck*, 912 F. Supp. 2d 344 (D. Md. 2012), sued defendant for illegally downloading copyrighted

pornography. The defendant counterclaimed for "malicious use of process." The trial court granted plaintiff's motion to dismiss that counterclaim:

> The only facts set forth by Defendant that could potentially support an abuse of process claim relate to the issuance of the subpoena to Defendant's ISP and the ensuing settlement letter transmitted by Plaintiff. The lawful purpose of the subpoena was to compel the ISP to divulge Defendant's name and address, which, in turn, would enable Plaintiff to file an amended complaint naming the proper defendants and requesting the issuance of summonses. While the fact that Plaintiff also used that information to convey a settlement offer is clearly outside the scope of the subpoena, the purpose of the settlement letter was not to attain some collateral objective. Indeed, it proposed to resolve the suit. The only threat contained in Plaintiff's "extortive shakedown letter," as Defendant calls it, is that Plaintiff would formally name Mr. Steinruck as a defendant if he declined to settle. Insofar as this constitutes a "threat," it is no different from those routinely presented in demand letters to potential defendants prior to the filing of law suits in court. While it is likely true, given the salacious nature of the film, that Plaintiff had substantial leverage in settlement discussions, there is nothing wrong with presenting a defendant with a settlement offer prior to proceeding with litigation, and the fact that Plaintiff may have had an ulterior motive is inconsequential in the abuse of process analysis. *See Wallace v. Mercantile County Bank,* 514 F.Supp.2d 776 (D.Md. 2007) ("no liability is incurred where the defendant has done nothing more than pursue the lawsuit to its authorized conclusion regardless of how evil his motive may be."). Moreover, Defendant has not suffered an "arrest or a seizure of property," as required to establish a claim of abuse of civil process under Maryland law. To the extent that he has suffered reputational harm from the association of his name with the unauthorized downloading and/or uploading of pornography, his injury was self-inflicted. A procedure was put in place by which Defendant could have vindicated his vehement denials of liability without publicly revealing his identity. He elected to reveal his name, however, and he cannot now reasonably assert that damages attributable to this revelation were caused by Plaintiff.

> In sum, the facts presented in the counterclaim do not support a cause of action for abuse of process. Accordingly, Plaintiff's motion to dismiss will be granted.

5. <u>Termination</u>. For malicious prosecution based upon instituting a proceeding, as opposed to abuse of a process issued afterward, no remedy is available unless the proceeding terminated in plaintiff's favor. The court in *J&G Realty, LLC v. Bongiorno,* 2016 WL 8468092 (Conn. Super. Dec. 20, 2016) described the three approaches to that element:

The first and most rigid, requires that the action have gone to judgment resulting in a verdict of acquittal, in the criminal context, or no liability, in the civil context. The second permits a vexatious suit action even if the underlying action was merely withdrawn so long as the plaintiff can demonstrate that the withdrawal took place under circumstances creating an inference that the plaintiff was innocent, in the criminal context, or not liable, in the civil context. The third approach, while nominally adhering to the "favorable termination" requirement, in the sense that any outcome other than a finding of guilt or liability is favorable to the accused party, permits a malicious prosecution or vexatious suit action whenever the underlying proceeding was abandoned or withdrawn without consideration, that is, withdrawn without either a plea bargain or a settlement favoring the party originating the action.

Can you see why courts would disagree on this? And why, in courts that recognize abuse of process for post-institution conduct, termination in plaintiff's favor is usually not required?

6. Privileges. Courts sometimes give even greater protection to a defendant because of the role it played in the prior proceeding. *See McKinney v. Okoye*, 282 Neb. 880 (2011) (extending defamation cases to create a qualified privilege against malicious prosecution for statements by a pathologist to a prosecutor that an infant had died of child abuse while at plaintiff's daycare center); *Simms v. Seaman*, 308 Conn. 523 (2013) (no need for privilege for attorneys in prior proceeding because of malice requirement); *MacDermid v. Leonetti*, 310 Conn. 616 (2013) (employee's statements to workers' compensation board absolutely privileged).

4. When Monetary Remedies Are Inadequate

The filing of a single civil lawsuit or wrongfully instituting a single criminal process will not permit an award of an injunction against further filings because the remedy at law is adequate. Where a person has repeatedly abused process, courts will consider injunctive relief but recognize that it will limit that person's right to petition government or potentially interfere with criminal justice.

A. Enjoining a Pending Criminal Prosecution

Courts will rarely enjoin ongoing criminal prosecutions pending in state or federal court. Among other things, a civil suit to enjoin a criminal charge involves a different burden of proof. An injunction against a state proceeding implicates the Anti-Injunction Act, which provides that "a court of the United States may not grant an injunction to stay proceedings in a State court except as expressly authorized by Act of Congress, or where necessary in aid of its jurisdiction, or to protect or effectuate its judgments." 28 U.S.C. § 2283. That statute "does not qualify in any way the principles of equity, comity, and federalism that must restrain a federal court when asked to enjoin a state court proceeding." *Gates v. Strain*, 885 F.3d 874 (5th Cir. 2018).

Those principles—called "*Younger* abstention" after *Younger v. Harris*, 401 U.S. 37 (1971)—require denying injunctive relief if three criteria are met (unless narrow exceptions exist). Specifically, a federal court should not enjoin a state court proceeding under the Anti-Injunction Act if: "(1) the federal proceeding would interfere with an ongoing state judicial proceeding; (2) the state has an important interest in regulating the subject matter of the claim; and (3) the plaintiff has an adequate opportunity in the state proceeding to raise constitutional challenges." *Id.* Exceptions permit injunctions only if: "(1) the state-court proceeding was brought in bad faith or to harass the federal plaintiff; (2) the federal plaintiff seeks to challenge a state statute that is flagrantly and patently violative of express constitutional prohibitions in every clause, sentence, and paragraph, and in whatever manner and against whomever an effort might be made to apply it, or (3) where other extraordinary circumstances threaten "irreparable loss that is both great and immediate." *Id.*

Boyajian v. City of Atlanta

2009 WL 4797206 (N.D. Ga. Dec. 9, 2009) (Story, J.)

[Plaintiff had the hobby of raising and breeding "tame" wild cats in Atlanta since 1977 as part of wild cat conservation. In 2007, residents complained and the City cited him for violating two city ordinances: § 16-04.004, for commercial use of an accessory structure in R-2 zoning and § 30-65, for operating a business without a business license. Instead of defending those charges, the plaintiff sought a declaratory judgment and an injunction against the City from enforcing those code provisions. The plaintiff then moved for a preliminary injunction.]

Plaintiff seeks a preliminary injunction barring Defendant from enforcing City of Atlanta Ordinance § 30-65 and its exception, § 30-72, as well as § 16-04.4004. A preliminary injunction is an extraordinary and drastic remedy.

Following a hearing, the Court finds that Plaintiff has met its burden of demonstrating the criterion required under the preliminary injunction analysis. Plaintiff has shown a substantial likelihood of success on the merits primarily because the Court has serious reservations as to whether the Ordinances that the City seeks to enforce are even applicable to Plaintiff. Enforcement of City of Atlanta Ordinance § 30-65 and its exception, § 30-72, as well as § 16-04.4004 will cause irreparable harm to Plaintiff, forcing him to relocate or be subject to criminal prosecution. While the Court recognizes that the nature of Plaintiff's activities may be causing complaints from the public, those concerns do not warrant the "reinterpretation" of the Ordinance asserted by the City. The public at large would not be served by altering the interpretation of this Ordinance to try to address this isolated circumstance. Accordingly, Plaintiff's Emergency Motion for Preliminary Injunction is GRANTED. The Defendant is ORDERED to refrain from enforcing City of Atlanta Ordinance § 30-65 and its exception, § 30-72, as well as § 16-04.4004 to Plaintiff's detriment until such time as this Court has ruled on the merits of Plaintiff's suit.

Notes and Questions

1. Ripeness. In *Boyajian* the city had cited Mr. Boyajian. What if, instead, in 2007 he noticed the statute on his own and had become worried the city might enforce it against him? "The general rule is that equity will not interfere to prevent the enforcement of a criminal statute even though unconstitutional. The mere existence of a criminal statute is not such a threat as to present a justiciable controversy." *Walker v. State*, 2018 WL 3414224 (Md. Spec. App. July 13, 2018). Exceptions to this rule are discussed below.

2. Permanent Relief. Later proceedings in *Boyajian* showed citations had been issued after neighbors had complained about "numerous wild cat escapes," which led the city to learn Boyajian was operating a business without a license. After being cited, he applied for a business license, but was denied because his business was not a permitted use for the zoning in his neighborhood. After two years of litigation, the trial court held on summary judgment that the ordinances were void for vagueness and entered a permanent injunction against their enforcement. *Boyajian v. City of Atlanta*, 2011 WL 1262162 (N.D. Ga. March 31, 2011).

3. Federal Injunctions Against Federal Criminal Prosecution. Just as federal courts generally abstain from enjoining ongoing state criminal prosecutions, so too, federal courts generally abstain from enjoining ongoing federal criminal proceedings: the criminal-defendant/civil-plaintiff can raise any challenges in the ongoing criminal case. *See Huntress v. U.S. Dept. of Justice*, 2013 WL 2297076 (W.D.N.Y. May 24, 2013).

B. Enjoining Threatened Criminal Prosecution

Ordinarily, the mere existence of a criminal statute is insufficient to permit a civil litigant to challenge its enforceability. Further, and as a general rule, it is insufficient even if the plaintiff has been threatened with prosecution. There are exceptions, however, as *Stolt-Nielsen, S.A. v. U.S.*, 442 F.3d 177 (3d Cir. 2006), explained:

> There is an exception to this general rule, however, in order to avoid a chilling effect on constitutional rights. *See Dombrowski v. Pfister*, 380 U.S. 479 (1965) (recognizing that the threat of criminal prosecution creates the potential for a serious chill upon First Amendment rights); *Hynes v. Grimes Packing Co.*, 337 U.S. 86 (1949) (recognizing that the threat of prosecution may deny fishermen the right to earn a livelihood). The Supreme Court has typically applied the exception in the First Amendment context, and in such cases has recognized,

a criminal prosecution under a statute regulating expression usually involves imponderables and contingencies that themselves may inhibit the full exercise of First Amendment freedoms. The assumption that defense of a criminal prosecution will generally assure ample vindication of constitutional rights is unfounded in such cases. We have not thought that the improbability of successful prosecution makes the case different. The chilling effect upon the exercise of First Amendment rights may derive from the fact of the prosecution, unaffected by the prospects of its success or failure.

Dombrowski, 380 U.S. at 486; *see Ashcroft v. ACLU*, 542 U.S. 656 (2004) (upholding preliminary injunction against criminal enforcement of Child Online Protection Act because "where a prosecution is a likely possibility, yet only an affirmative defense is available, speakers may self-censor rather than risk the perils of trial").

C. Enjoining Threatened Civil Litigation

The First Amendment protects the right to petition the government, which includes the right to sue. However, a narrowly tailored injunction against an abusive litigant can be constitutional.

Camastro v. W. Va. Alcohol Bev. Control Commn.

2015 WL 729665 (N.D. W. Va. Feb. 19, 2015) (Stamp, J.)

[Plaintiff Camastro filed 13 separate suits against defendant, the West Virginia Alcohol Beverage Control Commission. Each suit challenged its decision concerning his businesses. Each suit raised substantially the same issues. The defendant moved for sanctions, but the court instead required Camastro to show cause as to why he should not be enjoined from filing related suits. This is its decision.]

The All Writs Act, 28 U.S.C. § 1651(a), provides federal courts with the power to limit access to the courts by "vexatious and repetitive litigants." *Cromer v. Kraft Foods N. Am., Inc.*, 390 F.3d 812 (4th Cir.2004). This statutory power is tempered by a party's constitutional guarantees of due process of law and access to the courts. U.S. Const. amend. XIV, § 1.

A pre-filing injunction is a drastic remedy, which must be used sparingly. The United States Court of Appeals for the Fourth Circuit has prescribed a four-pronged evaluation for considering whether a pre-filing injunction is substantively warranted:

A court must weigh all the relevant circumstances, including (1) the party's history of litigation, in particular whether he has filed vexatious, harassing, or duplicative lawsuits; (2) whether the party had a good faith basis for pursuing the litigation, or simply intended to harass; (3) the extent of the burden on the courts and other parties resulting from the party's filings; and (4) the adequacy of alternative sanctions. *Id.*

Before a court issues such an injunction, a litigant should receive notice and an opportunity to be heard. As mentioned above, this Court heard from the plaintiff and counsel for The City of Wheeling defendants regarding the issuance of a pre-filing injunction at the February 18, 2015 hearing. Before examining each prong, this Court notes that, because the plaintiff is proceeding pro se, this Court is approaching this issue with particular caution, understanding that a pre-filing injunction against a pro se plaintiff should remain very much the exception to the general rule of free access to the courts. Furthermore, this Court has liberally construed the plaintiff's pleadings throughout the proceeding.

This Court finds that all four of the factors weigh heavily in favor of issuing a pre-filing injunction. A court "should not in any way limit a litigant's access to the courts absent exigent circumstances, such as a litigant's continuous abuse of the judicial process by filing meritless and repetitive actions." *Id.* This Court is aware of at least thirteen suits in state court and two in this federal court, all arising from the same or essentially the same transactions or occurrences. After analyzing those civil actions, this Court finds that the plaintiff has engaged in vexatious and harassing conduct and that his lawsuits are duplicative. Accordingly, the first prong is satisfied as the plaintiff's series of civil actions demonstrates.

Regarding the second prong, the facts demonstrate that the plaintiff lacked a good faith basis for pursuing the litigation. In his argument against Rule 11 sanctions, the plaintiff states that, regarding the alleged denial of his applications, he "used the court system because that's what you're supposed to do." He further claims that he is "asking the Court to protect" him. In addition to that claim, he reiterates on multiple occasions that The City of Wheeling defendants sent this Court "misleading information," which resulted in the dismissal of his civil actions, including his most recent one in this Court. After reviewing the pleadings, this Court finds that the plaintiff is not pursuing the litigation in good faith, but intends on harassing The City of Wheeling defendants. This Court acknowledges that the plaintiff, like any other plaintiff, has a right to seek redress through the judicial system. However, the plaintiff, and any other plaintiff, does not have the right to continually file actions based upon the same grievances. The doctrines of res judicata, collateral estoppel, the *Rooker-Feldman* doctrine, and other preclusive doctrines demonstrate such a limitation upon litigants. Therefore, the plaintiff has failed to demonstrate any good faith basis for pursuing the litigation.

As to the third requirement under *Cromer*, concerning the burden on the courts and the parties from the plaintiff's actions, this Court does not consider at this point the burden on the Court. This Court does note, however, the burden placed upon The City of Wheeling defendants. The City of Wheeling defendants rightfully point out that the plaintiff's most recent civil action names as a defendant not only a deceased individual, but also a former mayor who has not held that position for several years. The City of Wheeling defendants also demonstrated the costs associated with spending their time responding to the plaintiff's actions, costs incurred in consulting with insurance counsel, and other time and money spent by The City of Wheeling defendants. This Court finds that those were all undue burdens caused by the litigant's filings, and are to be considered under *Cromer*.

Lastly, this Court has considered alternative sanctions and finds no appropriate alternative sanction. The City of Wheeling defendants point to two sanctions that the plaintiff received from state court. In particular, The City of Wheeling defendants claim that the plaintiff received monetary sanctions in 2001, and later a narrowly tailored pre-filing injunction. Since those sanctions, however, the plaintiff has still continued to file actions in both state court and this federal court. Although this Court could impose monetary sanctions, the most appropriate sanction appears to be a pre-filing injunction.

This Court orders that a pre-filing injunction be issued. This Court "must ensure that the injunction is narrowly tailored to fit the specific circumstances at issue." *Id*. The plaintiff may not file an action in this United States District Court related to the claims brought in this civil action without first obtaining leave by the undersigned judge or another judge in the United States District Court for the Norther District of West Virginia. Those claims include, but are not limited to, the following: (1) a continuous conspiracy to violate his civil rights through the denial of his applications for certain licenses regarding his attempt to build a car wash, the installation of certain billboards, his application for a video lottery café license with a liquor permit, and the removal of his signs stating that the public officials of The City of Wheeling are "corrupt;" (2) a violation of his civil rights through the denial of his application for a video lottery license with a liquor permit and enacting overly stringent zoning laws; (3) intentional interference with the plaintiff's business relations by denying his applications for installing certain billboards, opening a car wash, denying his application for a video lottery license with a liquor permit, and failing to respond to the plaintiff's inquiries about building a hotel; (4) violating his First Amendment rights by removing his billboards that stated certain public officials were "corrupt"; and (5) that The City of Wheeling defendants took no action in preventing individuals from parking near and trespassing on the plaintiff's business property. Furthermore, the plaintiff is enjoined from filing in this United States District Court any civil action alleging matters that are similar to, substantially similar to, or identical to the matters raised in this civil action.

This Court believes that this pre-filing injunction is narrowly tailored to fit the particular circumstances of this case. This injunction shall not apply to the filing of timely notices of appeal to the Court of Appeals and papers filed solely in furtherance of such appeals.

Notes and Questions

1. <u>Which Elements</u>? Recall that a party seeking a preliminary injunction must show irreparable harm, that the harm of denying the injunction exceeds the harm it will cause, and the public interest favors an injunction. Which of those elements are in issue in such cases, and why is the harm to the movant irreparable given its remedy of malicious prosecution? Although a single frivolous suit can cost a party thousands of dollars in attorney fees alone, a single suit—or even a handful of failed suits—ordinarily will not result in an injunction. The remedy at law is adequate. Further, any injunction, even if warranted, must be narrow.

2. <u>A Narrow Remedy</u>. Unlike the decision in the principal case, in *Cromer* the district court had imposed a prefiling injunction against "any and all filings in this case" and "any filing in any other, unrelated case" in that court without first obtaining permission to do so from a magistrate. The court held the injunction was "not narrowly tailored to fit the particular circumstances of the case" because "nothing in the record justified infringing upon his right to bring suit in unrelated cases." Instead, state and federal courts hold that "a categorical ban on future filings" is improper because it "leaves no room for potentially meritorious filings." *Fatta v. M&M Properties Mgt.*, 735 S.E.2d 836 (Ct. App. N.C. 2012).

3. <u>Enjoining Filings in Another State's Courts</u>. Often these injunctions are sought where, in response to being named as a defendant in a suit in one state, the defendant as plaintiff files suit in another state. In such circumstances, the court may enjoin the defendant from prosecuting the other "to prevent vexatious harassment, oppression, or fraud, unconscionable or inequitable advantage, irreparable injury, evasion of domiciliary laws, etc. However, each case must be determined by its own facts." *In re Harrier Tr.*, 259 So. 3d 402 (Ct. App. La. 2018). A court enjoining a litigant from filing a suit must have personal jurisdiction over the defendant, because the order does not enjoin the foreign court, but the litigant.

4. <u>State Courts Enjoining Federal Filings</u>. State courts lack power to order a party to dismiss a federal court action. *Przybysz v. B2K Systems, LLC*, 249 So. 3d 1096 (Ala. 2017) ("court does not have the authority to order Przybysz, Byker, and GAM to dismiss their federal action against Smith"); *BancInsure, Inc. v. Jacobs*, 2015 WL 5092845 (D. Nev. Aug. 26, 2015) ("the Oklahoma state court's order was itself impotent to enjoin even that State's own residents from initiating or maintaining an *in personam* federal action").

5. <u>Federal Courts Enjoining State Filings</u>. The "necessary in aid of its jurisdiction" exceptions are narrow but include where: "(1) the district court has exclusive jurisdiction over the action because it had been removed from state court; or, (2) the state court entertains an in rem action involving a *res* over which the district court has been exercising jurisdiction in an *in rem* action." *Upper Chattahoochee Riverkeeper Fund, Inc. v. City of Atlanta*, 701 F.3d 669 (11th Cir. 2012). As to the last exception, a court assuming jurisdiction over property may exclude another court

"to prevent unseemly conflicts between the federal and state courts and to prevent the impasse which would arise if the federal court were unable to maintain its possession and control of the property, which are indispensable to the exercise of the jurisdiction it has assumed." *United States v. Sid-Mars Rest. & Lounge, Inc.,* 644 F.3d 270 (5th Cir. 2011).

Problems

1. Civil or Criminal? A client reported you to the state bar association, falsely asserting that you stole funds from her. You have prevailed in that proceeding, which could have resulted in you losing your license. You are examining whether, for purposes of a malicious prosecution claim, a bar grievance is civil or criminal. What is the rule in your jurisdiction? Why? If there is no clear answer, what facts would you argue to persuade a court to characterize a bar disciplinary proceeding as "criminal" or "civil"?

2. The Repeat Plaintiff. Your client is the city of Chicago. Two years ago, a police officer sued your client for having been unlawfully suspended for a month without pay. You lost at trial but won on appeal two months ago. Your client called today and explained that the same person has filed another suit, claiming that the city was retaliating against him for having brought the first suit. Among the claims are one that the city had maliciously prosecuted the first case. What are the good arguments against any relief?

3. Prior Arbitration. You are in a jurisdiction that has not decided whether a prior arbitral award can serve as the predicate for a malicious prosecution or abuse of process claim. Why should invocation of an arbitral proceeding be sufficient, or not, for civil malicious prosecution or abuse of process?

4. Shopkeeper: Element or Defense? Courts split on whether a plaintiff must show a merchant acted unreasonably or the defendant must show it acted reasonably. Assume you are at trial representing the defendant in a jurisdiction where it is an open question as to who bears the burden. There are reasonable arguments on both sides. You, however, believe that, either way, this jury will rule for your client. Your client, however, wants you to assert that plaintiff must prove unreasonableness in order to establish precedent for other shoplifting cases. What should you explain to your client about the risks, in this case, of doing so if that is wrong?

5. Restraint? The plaintiff in *Wallace v. Stringer,* 553 S.E.2d 166 (Ct. App. Ga. 2001) was emerging from a store pushing a baby carriage when a store clerk accused her of stealing a baby blanket. He took it and told her to return into the store to "deal" with it, and plaintiff went back into the store. The appellate court held there was a jury question as to whether plaintiff had been restrained. In contrast, summary judgment was proper on a false imprisonment claim by an employee who was told to remain at work to be questioned about possible misconduct, because that

was "voluntary consent." *Carter v. Aramark Sports & Enter. Serv., Inc.,* 153 Md. App. 210 (2003). Why the difference?

6. <u>The Sleeping Client</u>. Suppose your client explains to you that he went to a friend's home, and as agreed stayed in a guest bedroom. In the middle of the night, the friend locked the door to plaintiff's room. In the morning, your client awoke after the friend unlocked the door. This disturbed your client. Is there a claim for false imprisonment and, if so, what are the likely damages?

7. <u>Injury But No Awareness</u>. Your client was in a store when he passed out. To avoid injury, the shop owner took your client to a side room and immediately called 911. Your client was unconscious the entire time, but fell from the chair, where the store owner had set him, onto the floor. Your client suffered severe injuries as a result of that fall. Your research shows that some courts permit recovery of false imprisonment if either the plaintiff was aware of confinement or if confinement caused injury. Is there any harm you can think of that would not be covered by a negligence claim?

8. <u>Duty to Release</u>? Imagine three scenarios: in one, a store owner mistakenly locks a customer in a store; in a second, the store owner intentionally locks a customer in the store; in a third, the store owner mistakenly locks the customer in, but when the owner was leaving the parking lot, the owner saw the person locked in the store and drove off, leaving the person locked in. Which of these scenarios leads to a likely verdict of false imprisonment, and what is the time frame for the damages and what are they?

9. <u>Stuck on the Tarmac</u>. Your client was one of more than 100 passengers confined inside an airplane while it sat on the tarmac during a severe snowstorm. The airline was negligent in that, although the storm was forecast, it should not have let the passengers board and then did not have on hand enough ground crew to get passengers off airplanes. Your client was stuck on board for nearly eight hours, and toilets overflowed and some passengers became verbally abusive toward the crew. Is this false imprisonment? If so, what damages?

10. <u>Consent</u>? Courts split on whether consent is an affirmative defense to false imprisonment or an element of the claim. Does your jurisdiction have an approach?

11. <u>Procurement</u>? Your client, a nurse, has been sued for malicious prosecution. He had told police that he had believed the doctor he worked for was overcharging insurance companies. The police conducted a full investigation and, based solely on the results obtained, prosecute the doctor. Your client explains to you that he in fact had made up the story he told police. Did your client procure the proceeding?

12. <u>Misidentification</u>. Your client, a store owner, has been sued because he mistakenly identified the plaintiff as the person who had written a bad check. The complaint alleges the misidentification was a result of negligence. Can you move to dismiss and, if so, on what basis?

13. <u>Misidentification Identified</u>. Alex, the brother of your client, was caught stealing headphones from a store, but identified himself as his twin brother, Houston, who is your client. The store let Alex go, then called police and swore out a complaint for Houston's arrest. He was arrested and hired a lawyer. Later, Alex felt guilty and returned to the store and explained what he had done. The store told Alex never to return but did nothing to notify the police or district attorney, and shortly afterward Houston was arraigned, incurring attorneys' fees and expenses. Does Houston have a claim for malicious prosecution against Alex? Against the store? For what damages for each claim?

14. <u>Botched Medical Malpractice</u>. Your client is a surgeon. You recently successfully defended a medical malpractice case against her brought by Julian. Your client had operated on Julian and after the surgery he had unexpected complications. You had obtained summary judgment for your client after depositions of the plaintiff's experts revealed that there was insufficient evidence that your client had caused the complications. Your client wants to sue for abusive litigation, since she incurred $150,000 in attorneys' fees and costs in defending the suit. She has asked you to take the case on a contingent fee basis. Will you ?

Chapter 6

Remedies Triggered by Harm to, or Interference with Rights in, Personal Property

The most common claim used to remedy harm to personal property (a "chattel") is negligence. However, it requires *physical harm* to a chattel and the other elements of negligence. Physical harm can be a consequential damage of battery, assault, or IIED; for example, if defendant hit plaintiff with plaintiff's own vase, which shattered.

Two claims are triggered by physical harm to a chattel, but they do not *require* it. Instead, conversion and trespass to chattels are also triggered by harm to the plaintiff's right to use and enjoy personalty. Given the growing value of intangible property, such as webpages and e-mail, the remedies allowed only by these once-obscure claims are increasingly important given the general rule that negligence requires physical harm to personalty.

Ordinarily, money is sufficient to remedy harm to a chattel. However, an equitable claim called "replevin" is available where damages are inadequate, and this chapter discusses it.

1. Monetary Remedies for Physical Harm to Personal Property

A. The General Measures of Damage

The plaintiffs in the cases in this chapter asserted different claims to recover damages for physical damage to a chattel. With narrow exceptions, the measure of damages for physical harm is the same, regardless of the claim. The goal is to put the plaintiff in the position it was in immediately prior to the harm. Generally, that is done by awarding the lesser of: (a) the pre-tort fair market value of the item or (b) the cost to repair it. *See Braum v. Kinderdine,* 27 N.E.3d 602 (Ct. App. Ohio 2015). There are exceptions, however.

In addition, a plaintiff may be able to recover consequential damages, such as expenses for renting a car while one was repaired, loss-of-use damages (when the plaintiff was unable to rent out an item while it was being repaired, or lost wages because she was unable to work without the chattel), and impaired value (i.e., the loss "caused by market perceptions that a vehicle involved in an accident, though fully repaired is worth less than the same vehicle that has never been damaged." *Am. Mfrs. Mutual Ins. Co. v. Schaefer*, 124 S.W.3d 154 (Tex. 2003)).

Applying these rules requires proof of: (a) pre-tort fair market value; (b) post-tort fair market value; and (c) reasonable costs to repair. If a plaintiff seeks (d) permanent impairment or (e) the expense of loss of use or lost income, additional evidence is required. The following cases explore these issues.

Price v. High Pointe Oil Co.

828 N.W.2d 660 (Mich. 2013) (Markman, J.)

The common-law rule with respect to the damages recoverable in an action alleging the negligent destruction of property was set forth in *O'Donnell v. Oliver Iron Mining Co.*, 262 Mich. 470 (1933). *O'Donnell* provides:

> If injury to property caused by negligence is permanent or irreparable, the measure of damages is the difference in its market value before and after said injury, but if the injury is reparable, and the expense of making repairs is less than the value of the property, the measure of damages is the cost of making repairs.

Michigan common law has continually followed the *O'Donnell* rule. Accordingly, the long-held common-law rule in Michigan is that the measure of damages for the negligent destruction of property is the cost of replacement or repair. Because replacement and repair costs reflect *economic* damages, the logical implication of this rule is that the measure of damages excludes *noneconomic* damages and the latter are not recoverable for the negligent destruction of property. *See also* Restatement Torts, 2d, § 911 comment e ("Even when the subject matter has its chief value in its value for use by the injured person, if the thing is replaceable, the damages for its loss are limited to replacement value, less an amount for depreciation.").

With the foregoing principles in mind, we respectfully decline to alter the common-law rule that the appropriate measure of damages for negligently damaged property is the cost of replacement or repair. We are not oblivious to the reality that destruction of property or property damage will often engender considerable mental distress, and we are quite prepared to believe that the particular circumstances of the instant case were sufficient to have caused exactly such distress. However, we are persuaded that the present rule is a rational one and justifiable as a matter of reasonable public policy.

First, one of the most fundamental principles of our economic system is that the market sets the price of property. This is so even though every individual values property differently as a function of his or her own particular preferences. Inherent in this principle is that any property an individual owns is presumably *valued by that individual* at or above its market rate. Otherwise, he or she presumably would not have purchased the property or continue to own it. Just as an individual typically does not pay for this surplus value, the law does not necessarily compensate that individual where that surplus value has been lost.

Second, economic damages, unlike noneconomic damages, are easily verifiable, quantifiable, and measurable. Thus, when measured only in terms of economic damages, the value of property is easily ascertainable. Employing market prices in calculating compensation for property damage eliminates the need to engage in subjective determinations of property value and enables the legal system to undertake commonplace and precise determinations of value. This explains why, at least where the plaintiff has not sustained physical injury, the cost of the property's replacement or repair has been the traditional standard for making a plaintiff "whole" under the law. This is so despite the fact that nearly every case involves *some* measure of emotional harm—if only from the stress of litigation—to victimized parties.

Third, limiting damages to the economic value of the damaged or destroyed property limits disparities in damage awards from case to case. Disparities in recovery are inherent in legal matters in which the value of what is in dispute is neither tangible nor objectively determined, but rather intangible and subjectively determined. Indeed, both objective and subjective disparities would result. Objective disparities would arise because, even if noneconomic harms were precisely quantifiable, identical injuries to identical properties could lead to severe mental distress for one person, while causing only minor annoyance for another. Subjective disparities would arise because noneconomic harms *cannot* be precisely quantified, so we must normally rely on juries to determine (1) whether noneconomic harms were caused, (2) the extent of such harms, and (3) the monetary value of such harms. The disparity in assessing damages by different fact-finders would presumably compound with each step in this chain of conjecture.

Fourth, the present rule affords some reasonable level of certainty to businesses regarding the potential scope of their liability for accidents caused to property resulting from their negligent conduct. As explained earlier in this opinion, under the Court of Appeals' rule, those businesses that come into regular contact with real property—contractors, repairmen, and fuel suppliers, for example—would be exposed to the uncertainty of not knowing whether their exposure to tort liability will be defined by a plaintiff who has an unusual emotional attachment to the property or by a jury that has an unusually sympathetic opinion toward those emotional attachments. Insurers would have a similarly difficult time calculating the extent of the risks against which they are insuring.

Sykes v. Sin

(Ct. App. Ga. 1997) (Eldridge, J)

[Plaintiff Sykes sued defendants for damage to his car as a result of a wreck. The trial court granted a partial directed verdict to defendants, reasoning that because plaintiff had failed to prove the value of the car before the wreck, he could not prove damages based upon the difference between that value and its value after the wreck. The jury found for the plaintiff but awarded no damages. Plaintiff appealed the trial court's denial of his motion for new trial.]

When a plaintiff seeks recovery for damages to an automobile, he may claim the reasonable value of repairs made necessary by the collision, together with hire on the vehicle while rendered incapable of use, and the value of any permanent impairment, provided the aggregate amount of these items does not exceed the fair market value of the automobile before the injury. In the alternative, plaintiff may prove the difference in fair market value of the property before the injury and afterwards.

In proving damage to an automobile, the owner of property is considered to be qualified to state his opinion as to the fair market value. Lay opinion evidence as to the value of an item, in order to have probative value, must be based upon a foundation that the witness has some knowledge, experience or familiarity with the value of the property or similar property and he must give reasons for the value assessed and also must have had an opportunity for forming a correct opinion. The testimony of the owner of property as to his opinion of the value of the property, without giving his reasons therefor, is inadmissible in evidence as it has no probative value, because the jury has no way to judge the weight and credibility of the lay opinion without the foundation.

In this case, the sole testimony as to the value of the plaintiff's automobile immediately after the accident was given by the plaintiff. The plaintiff described the damage to the automobile; when asked what he felt the value of the automobile was after the collision, the plaintiff testified, "well, that would be a difficult question to answer because I didn't really have any estimates because I give no thought to selling it like it was. Of course, I'm sure at the time if I would have just called some junk yard to come out and get it, it wouldn't have been worth very much, maybe a thousand dollars, probably, would have been all I'd get for it." However, the plaintiff did not testify that he had priced the vehicle at various salvage yards to determine what the salvage value of the automobile was. In fact, the plaintiff gave no explanation whatsoever as to how he had arrived at the $1,000 figure. Therefore, the plaintiff failed to give a basis or foundation to show he had an opportunity to form an accurate opinion, and, as such, there was no probative evidence as to the fair market value of his automobile immediately after the collision.

In any event, even if the plaintiff had presented probative evidence as to the fair market value of the automobile immediately after the collision, the plaintiff had not proven the fair market value of his automobile immediately prior to the collision in order for the jury to make a determination as to the difference between the two figures. Testimony regarding the damage to an automobile alone is not sufficient to establish a foundation for an owner to base his opinion of the value of the automobile immediately before and immediately after the collision. In order for a proper foundation to be laid to show that a lay witness had an opportunity to form a correct opinion of the difference between the value of the automobile immediately prior to the collision and immediately afterwards, in addition to testimony describing the damage to the automobile, a lay witness would have to show other reasons to support his opinion, such as the purchase price, the manner in which he had maintained the automobile, and the overall condition of the automobile immediately before the collision, the actual cost of repairs or actual salvage value, or other relevant evidence to provide the jury with some guidance as to the value and the extent of the loss. The sole testimony as to the fair market value of the automobile immediately prior to the collision was given by the plaintiff.

In establishing the fair market value of his automobile prior to the collision, the plaintiff initially attempted to establish the purchase price. The plaintiff stated that his son located the automobile in 1990 or 1991. The plaintiff went on to testify that his son did not pay any money for the car, but that the plaintiff traded a 1974 Cadillac Fleetwood and a 1979 BMW 735 plus $3000 cash for the automobile. However, he tendered no evidence as to the value of either the 1974 Cadillac or the 1979 BMW at the time they were traded. Plaintiff also testified that after the automobile was purchased, he had it repainted. However, while the plaintiff stated he thought the paint job was worth about $1000, he never paid any money for the paint job or gave any explanation as to how he arrived at this figure. Therefore, the plaintiff's attempt at establishing that he initially paid $15,000 for the automobile failed.

The plaintiff, also, attempted to establish the fair market value of the automobile immediately prior to the collision by testifying that prior to the accident he checked the want ads in the newspaper on a monthly basis and talked with other "people who had another car in that area" to determine for what price cars of the same model and type were selling. The plaintiff opined that, based on the information he received, his automobile had a fair market value of $9,000 to $10,000 immediately prior to the collision. However, he did not testify that the condition of his automobile, i.e., the way it was maintained, the mileage, the condition of the interior and exterior, accessories, and the general mechanical condition, was comparable to the automobiles other people had or the automobiles he found in the newspaper want ads on which he had based his opinion. Therefore, the plaintiff failed to lay a proper foundation to show that he had an opportunity to form a correct opinion, and such testimony was not probative evidence to prove the fair market value of his automobile immediately prior to the collision.

Therefore, under the evidence presented, the trial court did not err in granting the partial directed verdict. In fact, the trial court erred in letting the issue of special damages go to the jury at all, because such damages, in aggregate, cannot exceed the fair market value of the automobile prior to the collision and place the plaintiff in a position superior to that which he previously held. Thus, absent proof of the fair market value immediately prior to the collision, any other special damages can not be calculated as coming within the maximum limit on recovery.

Notes and Questions

1. <u>Sentimental Value and Distress</u>. The *Price* case states the majority rule. *See In re Air Crash at Belle Harbor, New York on Nov. 12, 2001,* 450 F. Supp. 2d 432 (S.D.N.Y. 2006) (belongings destroyed when plane crashed into home); *Broadfoot v. Aaron Rents, Inc.,* 409 S.E.2d 870 (Ga. 1991) (damage to antiques).

2. <u>What Is Missing</u>? In *Canal Ins. Co v. Tullis,* 515 S.E.2d 649 (Ct. App. Ga. 1999), the defendant's truck collided with Helton Trucking Company's dump truck, which was insured by Canal Insurance Company. To satisfy Helton's insurance claim, Canal paid $19,389.59 for repairs. As subrogee to Helton, Canal sued Tullis, seeking those costs less the $1,000 deductible Helton had paid. The trial court granted defendant's motion for directed verdict because Canal had failed to prove repair costs had not exceeded the truck's pre-tort fair market value. Plaintiff appealed, and the appellate court affirmed:

> In this case, the appellant opted to prove the damages to its insured's dump truck by showing the reasonable and necessary cost of repairs. While Canal presented evidence at trial showing the cost of repairs, it failed to put up any evidence of the fair market value of its insured's dump truck immediately before the collision. In fact, Canal concedes on appeal that it did not present any evidence of the fair market value of its insured's dump truck at trial. Absent proof of the fair market value immediately prior to the collision, any other special damages cannot be calculated as coming within the maximum limit on recovery. This is true even when a plaintiff is only seeking recovery for the reasonable value of repairs made necessary by the collision, and is not also seeking recovery for hire on the vehicle while rendered incapable of use or the value of any permanent impairment. The total amount of property damages recovered by a plaintiff for damages caused to his vehicle as the result of a collision cannot exceed the fair market value of the vehicle prior to the collision and place the plaintiff in a position superior to that which he previously held.

> In view of the absence of any evidence showing the market value of plaintiff's vehicle immediately before the collision in the case *sub judice,* plaintiff has failed to carry its burden under either of the above formulas.

Since the dump truck had *some* value, especially since Canal paid a lot to repair it, why not let a jury award a reasonable amount? Why not let the jury infer that it was more than $19,389.59? In that regard, consider the observations of *Smith v. White,* 712 S.E.2d 717 (Ct. App. N.C. 2011):

> The authorities are in conflict upon whether the cost of repairing injured property is competent evidence of the difference between the market value before and after the injury. The authorities which have been brought to our attention are cases in which the repairs have been actually made and the amount paid therefor was sought to be shown in order to establish the

difference in market value, and in these cases we find the weight of authority in favor of the admissibility of such evidence. However, in the case at bar the evidence offered was not of the actual cost paid for repairing, but of an estimate of the cost thereof. The estimate sought to be shown was that of the foreman of the repair shop of the City Chevrolet Company, who examined the automobile which was damaged and made an estimate of the cost of repairing that car. While evidence of such an estimate of the cost of repairs might not be as convincing as evidence of the cost of the actual repairs, we think this difference relates to the weight thereof rather than to its competency—and the weight of evidence is for the jury, while the admissibility of evidence is for the court. The correct and safe rule is the difference between the value of the machine before and after its injury, and in estimating this difference it is proper for the jury to consider the cost and expenses of repairs.

Why should, or would, a jury give less weight to an estimate than a paid bill? Why not, if as in *Canal*, payment was actually made, let the jury infer that repair costs had to be less than that amount?

3. <u>Market Value at Different Times</u>? Generally, the time of the injury controls value. Where an item's value fluctuates wildly, courts sometimes permit plaintiffs to pick the highest value at the time of the tort, the time of trial, or, in some states, at other times in-between. The court in *Farmer v. Farmer*, 259 P.3d 256 (Wash. 2011) described the "New York Rule," which "measures damages using the highest value of the [chattel] between the time the victim learns of the conversion and a reasonable time thereafter," but excludes the time between the act of conversion and the victim's notice of the conversion on the theory that, "if the victim had wanted to sell the [chattel] during that interval, he would have learned of the conversion." The *Farmer* court reasoned that because courts used at least seven measures of damages for conversion of stock, stock options and other assets of fluctuating value, that counseled "against our adopting a single, universal approach for all cases." Georgia permits a plaintiff to recover the highest market value between the date of conversion and trial, unless the defendant returned the property before trial, in which case damages are limited to diminution in value. *Lamb v. Salvage Disposal Co. of Ga.*, 535 S.E.2d 258 (Ct. App. Ga. 2000). Plaintiffs must be sure to adduce proof of value on the pertinent date.

4. <u>Which Market(s) and Proper Proof</u>? Generally, fair market value is the price that "would result from fair negotiations between an owner willing to sell and a buyer desiring to buy." *Withers v. Wilson*, 989 A.2d 1117 (Ct. App. D.C. 2010). There are exceptions to, and limitations on, the general rules explored in this section. What market value governs for clothing, furniture, and household items? Markets for used goods exist online or in thrift stores. Yet courts do not require plaintiffs to use these markets. In *Yazdani-Beioky v. Tremont Tower Condo. Ass'n.*, 2011 WL 1434837 (Ct. App. Tex. Apr. 14, 2011), the defendant, in a rampage, had broken

furniture and other items in a condo's common area. The jury awarded damages and the defendant appealed. The appellate court affirmed:

Generally, the measure of damages to personal property is the difference in its market value immediately before and immediately after the injury, at the place where the damage occurred. Market value is defined as the amount that a willing buyer who desires to buy but is under no obligation to buy, would pay to a willing seller who desires to sell but is under no obligation to sell. This definition presupposed an existing, established market. However, not all property has a "market value." For example, the Texas Supreme Court has recognized, as a matter of common knowledge, that used household goods, clothing and personal effects have no market value in the ordinary meaning of that term.

Generally, when market value does not exist, replacement value is the means of assessing damages. However, in some situations, replacement value does not properly measure damages because it may represent an economic gain to the plaintiff. Under this second measure of damages, a plaintiff would receive an economic gain if, for example, he were awarded the replacement cost for used household goods, clothing, or personal effects.

When the replacement cost would represent an economic gain to a plaintiff whose property has been destroyed, the measure of damages is the actual worth or value of the articles to the owner for use in the condition in which they were at the time of the incident excluding any fanciful or sentimental considerations. Nevertheless, in determining actual value, a factfinder may consider original cost and cost of replacement, the opinions upon value given by qualified witnesses, the gainful uses to which the property has been put as well as any other facts reasonably tending to shed light upon the subject. In determining damages, the factfinder has discretion to award damages within the range of evidence presented at trial.

Generally, a property owner is qualified to testify to the value of her property even if she is not an expert and would not be qualified to testify to the value of other property. An entity's agent may testify to the value of the entity's property if the agent's position within and duties to the entity warrant applying a presumption that they are familiar with the entity's property and its value.

The trial court awarded $3,380.59 in damages. On appeal, Yazdani challenges only the remaining $1,799.28, which represents the damage to property that was not successfully repaired.

The Association's manager testified that following the incident, she "went shopping and looked at items similar to" the remaining items. The remaining items had the following replacement costs at essentially the time of loss:

Property	Replacement Cost
Credenza	$800
Chair	$600
End Table	$250
Lamp	$150
Vase	$400
TOTAL	$2,200

The manager testified that she had no knowledge of the items' original costs and that she was not working for the Association when the items were purchased. She testified that the credenza, chair, and end table were purchased in 2004, but she did not mention when the lamp or vase was purchased.

In announcing its judgment, the trial court explained that it was discounting the replacement costs of the items. The trial court explained that it was, however, awarding the Association the full value for the vase because "vases don't depreciate." Excluding the vase, the items had a total replacement cost of $1,800, for which the court awarded $1,399.28, reflecting a discount of $400.72 or 22.26%.

The Texas Supreme Court has held that a factfinder may consider replacement cost to determine actual value. The manager's testimony regarding the replacement costs for similar items determined shortly after the incident is some evidence of the actual value of the items to the Association.

Yazdani also contends that the evidence is factually insufficient because there was no evidence of the amounts of depreciation or the proposition that the vase did not depreciate. As noted above, and contrary to Yazdani's suggestions, replacement cost is meaningful evidence of actual value, and the evidence established a total replacement cost of $2,200. The trial court as factfinder was within its discretion.

Why shouldn't market value—as reflected in secondhand stores—control? Conversely, consider which market value is relevant if the defendant destroys a new car for sale at a dealer. A used car?

B. Damages for Loss of Use and Impaired Value

J&D Towing, LLC v. Am. Alt. Ins. Corp.

478 S.W.3d 649 (Tex. 2016) (Willet, J.)

[J&D Towing, LLC bought a 2002 Dodge 3500 tow truck in April 2011 for $18,500. In December 2011, as the driver was headed to repossess a car, Cassandra Brueland sideswiped the tow truck. She admitted fault. J&D promptly began to negotiate with

Brueland's insurer, and in February 2012, Brueland's insurer settled by paying J&D $25,000, the policy limit for property damage. In March 2012, J&D bought another truck and resumed its business.

J&D then sued its insurer, American Alternative Insurance Corporation, under an underinsured-motorist provision, seeking damages for the loss of use of the truck. At trial, J&D showed various ways to measure the loss of use between the accident and the date it had replaced the truck. It sought either $27,866.25 or $29,416.25, with the difference being whether the jury awarded damages for nine or ten weeks. AAIC presented no evidence at trial. The trial court held Texas law permitted loss-of-use damages in total-destruction cases, and the jury awarded J&D $28,000. After verdict, the trial court held a hearing to determine the credit to which AAIC was entitled because of Brueland's insurer's payment. It found J&D's truck had been worth $19,500 at the time of the wreck, and so AAIC was entitled to a credit of $5,500—the amount that the settlement with Brueland's insurer exceeded the truck's pre-tort fair market value and that, as a result, already partially compensated J&D for its loss of use.

The trial court entered judgment for J&D for $22,500. AAIC appealed, asserting Texas law did not permit loss-of-use damages in total-destruction cases. The court of appeals agreed and so reversed and rendered for AAIC. J&D appealed.]

We begin with first principles. Compensation is the chief purpose of damages awards in tort cases. Indeed, we have long held that the basic reason underlying rules for the ascertainment of damages for any tortious act is a fair, reasonable, and proper compensation for the injury inflicted as a proximate result of the wrongful act complained of. Reasonable and proper compensation must be neither meager nor excessive, but must be sufficient to place the plaintiff in the position in which he would have been absent the defendant's tortious act. In this way, compensation through actual-damages awards functions as an instrument of corrective justice, an effort to put the plaintiff in his or her rightful position.

Where personal property has been only *partially* destroyed, Texas law is clear as to direct and loss-of-use damages. The default rule for measuring direct damages is the difference in the market value immediately before and immediately after the injury to such property at the place where the damage was occasioned. But this rule is not absolute. For example, where it would be economical and reasonable to repair the property, the owner of the injured property may instead recover the reasonable costs of such replacements and repairs as are necessary to restore the damaged article to its condition immediately prior to the accident. Additionally, whether the owner recovers direct damages under the default rule or otherwise, the owner may recover loss-of-use damages, such as the pecuniary loss of the use of an automobile damaged in a collision.

Where personal property has been *totally* destroyed, however, Texas law is less clear. As an initial matter, the measure of direct damages is the fair market value of the property immediately before the injury at the place where the injury occurred.

But we have not yet directly spoken on loss-of-use damages in total-destruction cases.

A majority of jurisdictions permitted loss-of-use damages in partial-destruction cases, but prohibited loss-of-use damages in total-destruction cases. *Why* that prohibition existed is not as obvious. But regardless of the theoretical underpinnings of the prohibition, recent caselaw and treatises have shifted away from the prohibition. And the reasons for the shift appear to coalesce around one simple point: The owner of totally destroyed personal property may suffer loss-of-use damages to the same extent that the owner of partially destroyed personal property may suffer loss-of-use damages—permitting the damages in the latter case and not the former is, therefore, illogical.

But even beyond the impressive number of courts that have endorsed the availability of loss-of-use damages in total-destruction cases, the near uniformity in the reasoning underlying these decisions is particularly persuasive. The reasoning may be properly viewed in terms of two interrelated arguments.

The first argument is that any distinction between partially destroyed and totally destroyed personal property for purposes of loss-of-use damages is unpersuasive. The second argument flows from the first and emphasizes that loss-of-use damages *must* be available in total-destruction cases pursuant to the principle of full and fair compensation.

But it is perhaps the *Restatement (Second) of Torts* that best captures this change in the law. Section 927 in the *Restatement (First) of Torts* permits a plaintiff whose personal property was totally destroyed to recover the value of the property at the time and place of destruction, but it requires the plaintiff to choose between interest on that value and loss-of-use damages. The *Restatement (Second) of Torts* fundamentally changed that recovery scheme. Section 927 now provides, in relevant part:

(1) When one is entitled to a judgment for the conversion of a chattel or the destruction or impairment of any legally protected interest in land or other thing, he may recover . . .

(a) the value of the subject matter or of his interest in it at the time and place of the conversion, destruction or impairment;. . . .

(2) His damages also include:

(a) the additional value of a chattel due to additions or improvements made by a converter not in good faith;

(b) the amount of any further pecuniary loss of which the deprivation has been a legal cause;

(c) *interest from the time at which the value is fixed; and*

(d) *compensation for the loss of use not otherwise compensated. . . .*

We agree with this modern trend, and we now hold that the owner of personal property that has been totally destroyed may recover loss-of-use damages in addition to the fair market value of the property immediately before the injury.

Permitting loss-of-use damages in total-destruction cases, however, is not a license for unrestrained raids on defendants' coffers. As with all consequential damages, the availability of loss-of-use damages is necessarily circumscribed by commonsense rules. To begin with, the damages claimed may not be too remote. This is not to say they must be the usual result of the wrong, but they must be foreseeable and directly traceable to the tortious act. The damages also must not be speculative. Although mathematical exactness is not required, the evidence offered must rise above the level of pure conjecture. Moreover, the damages may not be awarded for an unreasonably long period of lost use. Whether framed as a duty of mitigation or a doctrine of avoidable consequences, the principle is the same: A plaintiff may not recover loss-of-use damages for a period longer than that reasonably needed to replace the personal property. That principle compels a plaintiff's diligence in remedying his loss and deters an opportunistic plaintiff from dilly-dallying at the expense of the defendant. After all, the role of actual damages is to place the plaintiff in his *rightful* position, not the position he *wishes* to acquire.

Applying those principles to the facts of this case, we find that the trial court did not abuse its discretion in submitting the loss-of-use-damages question to the jury and did not err in denying AAIC's JNOV motion. We therefore reverse and render judgment for J&D.

Level 3 Commun., LLC v. TNT Constr., Inc.

220 F. Supp. 3d 812 (W.D. Ky. 2016) (Stivers, J.)

[Defendant TNT Construction Inc., accidentally severed a cable owned by plaintiff Level 3 Communications, LLC. Plaintiff sought $61,288.98 in repair costs and $3,369,894.42 in loss-of-use damages. Defendant moved for summary judgment on loss of use.]

Level 3 has provided evidence showing that it was unable to use the Cable for 6.3 hours because TNT severed it. Thus, at first glance, it appears that Level 3 could be entitled to loss-of-use damages. The question, however, is whether the particulars of Level 3's fiber-optic cable system change this conclusion for purposes of summary judgment.

Numerous courts from other jurisdictions have addressed whether a telecommunications company can recover loss-of-use damages under circumstances similar to those here. Some courts have allowed damages for loss of use, and others have not. In spite of the split, however, there are common threads running through the cases. A majority of decisions hold that a telecommunications company is not entitled to loss-of-use damages for a damaged fiber-optic cable when there is no resultant interruption of service because all traffic on the cable is quickly rerouted to redundant capacity in the company's network. For example, in *MCI Worldcom Network Services v. Lind*, 2002 U.S. Dist. LEXIS 26467 (S.D. Fla. Dec. 17, 2002), the court held that MCI was not entitled to loss-of-use damages where there was "no evidence that MCI was unable to provide uninterrupted service to its customers as a result of the damage to the cable by the defendant." Other courts, however, have held that a telecommunications company is entitled to loss-of-use damages in cases where service is lost.

Application of the "spare boat" doctrine may shed light on whether using redundant capacity instead of renting a replacement prohibits recovery for loss-of-use damages. Two leading cases considering this doctrine are *The Cayuga*, 5 F.Cas. 329 (C.C.E.D.N.Y. 1870), *aff'd*, 81 U.S. 270 (1871), and *Brooklyn Eastern District Terminal v. United States*, 287 U.S. 170 (1932). In *The Cayuga*, a ferry and another boat collided. The owners of the ferry had a spare boat that they used while the ferry was being repaired. As a result, the ferry owners did not suffer a pecuniary loss while the ferry was inoperable. Nonetheless, the circuit court concluded and the Supreme Court affirmed that the ferry owners were entitled to loss-of-use damages, even though the owner did not actually have to rent a replacement boat.

In *Brooklyn Terminal*, a tugboat was damaged in a collision. The tugboat's owner did not obtain a substitute boat while the tug was being repaired, but instead worked its other boats overtime. Under those circumstances, the Supreme Court refused recovery of loss-of-use damages, distinguishing *The Cayuga* as follows:

> The doctrine of the "spare boat" cases is invoked by the petitioner as decisive in its favor, but we think without avail. Shipowners at times maintain an extra or spare boat which is kept in reserve for the purpose of being utilized as a substitute in the contingency of damage to other vessels of the fleet. There are decisions to the effect that in such conditions the value of the use of a boat thus specially reserved may be part of the demurrage. If no such boat had been maintained, another might have been hired, and the hire charged as an expense. The result is all one whether the substitute is acquired before the event or after. However, there has been a refusal to extend the doctrine to boats acquired and maintained for the general uses of the business.

> So here. The petitioner was engaged in an established business using tugs for a single purpose. It had no thought to turn that business into one of a different kind while this tug was out of service. Mindful of the need to minimize the damages, it used to the full its available resources, and was able by special effort to make them do the work. We are unable to accept the argument that the expenses which it saved are to be charged to the respondent as if they had not been saved at all.

Many recent cases involving damaged fiber-optic cables rely on the distinction articulated in *Brooklyn Terminal* in determining whether a telecommunications company's redundant capacity prevents recovery of loss-of-use damages. For example, in *MCI WorldCom Network Serv. v. Atlas Excavating, Inc.*, 2006 WL 3542332 (N.D. Ill. Dec. 6, 2006), the court allowed loss-of-use damages because the plaintiff used its redundant capacity for emergencies only, and not in its general business. On the other hand, in cases such as *MCI WorldCom Network Serv., Inc. v.*

OSP Consultants, Inc., 266 Va. 389 (2003), courts have refused to allow recovery for loss-of-use damages where the plaintiff used its redundant capacity in the ordinary course of business and did not reserve it expressly for emergencies.

TNT argues that Level 3 cannot recover loss-of-use damages because Level 3 has redundant capacity in its network. TNT claims that Level 3 was able to instantly reroute all of the traffic on the Cable so that no service was interrupted. Level 3, however, has produced evidence showing that service was interrupted, which distinguishes the present case from cases like *Lind*. Moreover, Level 3 has produced evidence that shows it uses its redundant system solely for emergencies. As a result, for purposes of summary judgment, this case is more like *The Cayuga* than *Brooklyn Terminal*, which indicates loss-of-use damages are available as a general matter.

Likewise, the fact that Level 3 failed to rent replacement capacity and suffered no pecuniary loss as result of the Cable's severance is not dispositive. Kentucky's highest court has not clearly held that loss-of-use damages are unavailable when the aggrieved party fails to rent a replacement. *Pope's Adm'r v. Terrill*, 308 Ky. 263 (1948) ("It does not appear that this court has made a definite declaration on the precise abstract point one way or the other. And it is not necessary to explicitly do so here."). In *Pope*, the court stated that "it is generally held that such failure does not preclude recovery, although the good faith intention of actually using, or the character of such intended use, may affect the amount of recovery." *Id.*

While no Kentucky court has held that proof of actual pecuniary loss is a prerequisite to recovery of loss-of-use damages, the Restatement (Second) of Torts recognizes that loss-of-use damages are available to compensate for injury to land or chattels regardless of whether the injured party suffers pecuniary loss. Moreover, commentators have noted that adherence to the rule that the party requesting loss-of-use damages be required to prove actual pecuniary loss to recover is misplaced because it "fails to recognize that ownership of a chattel carries with it the right to use or control the use of that chattel." James M. Lee, *Loss of Use Damage for Injuries to Interests in Commercial Chattels*, 15 Fordham Urb. L.J. 235 (1983).

For purpose of summary judgment and based on general Kentucky common law principles and various opinions from sister courts throughout the country addressing the specific issue at hand, the Court concludes Level 3 is entitled to seek loss-of-use damages for the 6.3 hours it was deprived of using the Cable.

But how to measure Level 3's loss of use? Ah, there's the rub. Indeed, while not delineated as such, many—if not all—of TNT's arguments go to Level 3's use of rental value to calculate its damages, which it contends is inappropriate under Kentucky law.

Kentucky courts have recognized that the value of the use of property is not susceptible of precise measurement, but that rental value is a relevant factor. In some cases, the market rental value is the most accurate measure of loss-of-use damages possible. *Pope*, 214 S.W.2d 276 ("Where a commercial automobile is involved, the market rental value of such a machine is probably as accurate a measurement as may be produced."). That market rental value, however, must be reasonable and capable of accurate estimation.

In determining whether market rental value is a reasonable, accurate measure of Level 3's loss-of-use damages, the first question is whether a rental market exists. In *Kentucky Utilities Co. v. Consolidated Tel. Co.*, 252 S.W.2d 437 (Ky. 1952), Kentucky's highest court refused to use market value to measure damages to a telephone line because "in ordinary circumstances a portion of a telephone system would not be marketable as such" and thus "any estimate of the market value of a portion of a telephone system would be conjectural." *Id*. Likewise, in *The Cayuga*, the court explained that the general rule of measuring the value of loss of use by rental value "can only be intended to be applied in cases where there is such a market to refer to." *The Cayuga*, 5 F.Cas. 326.

Turning to the circumstances at hand, Level 3 proposes its loss-of-use damages be measured by the cost of renting 18,816 DS-3s for 6.3 hours. As other courts have recognized, there is no market for renting DS-3 cables on an hourly or even weekly basis. This same circumstance is supported by the record in this case. It appears that no telecommunications company would ever actually rent replacement capacity for such a short term.

This case is not comparable to other Kentucky cases that measure the loss of use by rental value. The lion's share of those decisions dealing with rental value in the context of damaged automobiles. In such cases, accurately measuring the rental value of the damaged property is not an issue because there is a well-defined market for renting vehicles. Moreover, it is apparent that the courts in those cases assumed that the injured party could have actually rented a reasonable substitute. Here, however, there is no market and thus no like assumption can be made—as the court in *Lind* observed under similar circumstances, "no party in the company's position would have reasonably considered renting a replacement transmission system."

Rental value may be appropriate in cases involving automobiles and other property where such value is capable of easy and accurate estimation, but it is not appropriate here. In fact, the majority of courts from other jurisdictions addressing this issue in nearly identical lawsuits brought by telecommunications companies against contractors have held that measuring loss-of-use damages by a theoretical rental value is inappropriate.

In light of these circumstances, Level 3's proposed measure of damages offends general principles of damages law. Under Kentucky law, the object of compensatory damages is to make the injured party whole to the extent that is possible to measure his injury in terms of money. The object is not to place the plaintiff in a better position than he would have been had the wrong not been done. Moreover, an injured party may not make a profit out of an injury to his property.

Allowing Level 3 to measure its damages by the costs associated with an imaginary rental of 18,816 DS-3s for 6.3 hours would result in a windfall for Level 3 and put it in a position better than before the Cable was cut. Level 3 seeks over $3.3

million—more than 50 times repair costs—even though it is not aware of any profits lost, refunds paid to customers, or even one lost customer related to the cut cable. Any such measure of damages would go far beyond compensating Level 3 for that of which it was wrongfully deprived and would clearly operate as a windfall profit.

Level 3 argues that the determination of its damages is up to a jury. That may be true, as far as it goes. The measure of damages, however, is a legal matter. It is improper to authorize the jury to fix damages without confining it to the applicable measure of damages. That being said, within reasonable bounds, the ultimate determination of Level 3's loss-of-use damages will be left to the jury. What Level 3 seeks at this point is far from reasonable.

Notes and Questions

1. <u>Should Loss of Use Be Banned</u>? The widely recognized common law prohibition against loss-of-use damages made little sense if the goal was compensation, but made ample sense when viewed in the light of history. The last few paragraphs of the *J&D Towing* case reveal concerns about excessive loss-of-use damages. Should they be banned even in damaged personalty cases?

2. <u>Loss of One Car of a Fleet</u>. In *PurCo Fleet Serv., Inc. v. Koenig*, 240 P.3d 435 (Ct. App. Colo. 2010), the defendant, Koenig, rented a car from National Car Rental and agreed to pay National "for all damage to or loss of the vehicle, based on repair cost or estimated repair cost, at National's option, diminished value of the vehicle as determined by National, plus National's loss of use (regardless of fleet utilization) and administrative charges, regardless of who is at fault." She damaged the car by hitting a deer. After she returned it, National assigned its claim for damages to PurCo, which handled all of National's claims under an agreement that entitled it to retain 50% of loss-of-use damages and the administrative charge. After Koenig agreed to pay all but the loss-of-use damages and the administrative charge, PurCo sued for breach of contract. The trial court granted Koenig's motion for summary judgment, and PurCo appealed. The court wrote in part:

> Under traditional damages theory, a party may not recover special or consequential damages unless it proves that it has sustained or will sustain a loss resulting from the other party's conduct. This theory has been applied in an unusual manner in the context of loss of use of personal automobiles. Toward the beginning of the Twentieth Century, as the family auto became less of a luxurious rarity and more of a staple item, needed for transport to the owner's job, courts began to award loss of use damages to automobile owners on the theory that there was intrinsic value in the ability to have a car available for use. Alan E. Brownstein, *What's the Use? A Doctrinal and Policy Critique of the Measurement of Loss of Use Damages*, 37 Rutgers L.Rev. 433 (1985).
>
> Under this intrinsic theory of loss, the existence of a loss of some (unspecified) magnitude is presumed once the vehicle is unavailable because it is

being repaired. Courts latched onto the cost of renting a replacement vehicle (lease-in rental value) as a readily quantifiable damages measure. Thus, in numerous cases, including in Colorado, the owner of a family auto was awarded lease-in rental value as loss of use damages, even if no replacement vehicle was actually rented. The theory for awarding such damages rested on the so-called "egalitarian view," a concept that a car owner who might not be able to afford to rent a substitute should not be penalized for that inability by being denied damages for the rental amount, where a more wealthy owner who was able to rent a substitute might be awarded that element of damages.

Over time, the intrinsic loss of use theory gained traction among American courts and commentators. This view is reflected in the comments to Restatement (Second) of Torts sections 928 and 931 (1979), particularly comment b to section 931(a), which states:

> The owner of the subject matter is entitled to recover as damages for the loss of the value of the use, *at least the rental value of the chattel* or land *during the period of deprivation*. This is true *even though the owner in fact has suffered no harm* through the deprivation, as when he was not using the subject matter at the time or had a substitute that he used without additional expense to him.

Restatement (Second) of Torts § 931 cmt. b (emph. added).

While the theory of intrinsic loss permeated decisions concerning family cars, many courts declined to presume a loss when the damaged item was a commercial chattel leased out to others to produce income. Instead, they required that the plaintiff demonstrate an actual, economic loss, rather than just a presumed, intrinsic loss. Thus, there is significant disagreement among case authorities and commentators as to whether any economic loss, other than a presumed intrinsic loss, needs to be shown to recover for loss of use of commercial chattels.

We are persuaded by those authorities holding that, in the context of commercial chattels, a plaintiff must demonstrate an actual, economic loss rather than just an assumed intrinsic loss. It could be questioned why the measure of damages should be different in a commercial context rather than a private one. In our view, the purpose of awarding loss of use damages in a commercial setting is to compensate the plaintiff for the *lost opportunity to earn income* from the chattel. Thus, we conclude that in order to recover damages for loss of use of a commercial chattel that is normally rented out for profit, its owner must demonstrate that it lost the opportunity to earn income from the chattel.

3. <u>Lost Income as Loss of Use</u>. In *French v. Dilleshaw*, 723 S.E.2d 64 (Ct. App. Ga. 2012), the plaintiff was an independent truck driver. Defendant damaged plaintiff's truck in a wreck, and plaintiff sought lost wages for the time during which

the truck was being repaired, about three months. The court held he could recover lost earnings only "for the reasonable period of time which it would take him to make other arrangements for carrying on his profession" and that the amount had to be shown with "reasonable certainty." The three-month period was reasonable, but as to the amount, the plaintiff earned a living by hauling loads each week, and earnings and costs varied among the seasons and needs. The court held the verdict was supported by earning statements for two months before, and one month after, the accident. The court emphasized that reasonable certainty "does not mean absolute certainty, and if absolute certainty were required, lost earnings could seldom, if ever, be proven with the requisite certainty, at least in cases in which the earnings are not invariable and fixed definitively."

4. Diminished Value. The "vast majority of states allow, as a component of damages for injury short of destruction to personal property, recovery of a decrease in value if repair has not restored the property to its pre-injury value or condition." *Gov't Employees Ins. Co. v. Bloodworth*, 2007 WL 1966022 (Ct. App. Tenn. 2007). However, a North Dakota statute limits damages to either the cost to repair or diminution in value (and so, at most, the item's pre-tort fair market value). Ohio, the District of Columbia, and Maryland permit recovery of impaired value and repair costs, but the total cannot exceed the "diminution in value prior to the repairs." *Id.* Under that approach, consider a car worth $40,000 before and $25,000 immediately after a wreck, and so a $15,000 gross diminution in value. If, after $10,000 worth of repairs, the car is worth $30,000, the plaintiff may recover a total of $15,000. In jurisdictions where there is no cap, the plaintiff could recover $20,000; in North Dakota, $10,000. Which better makes the plaintiff whole? Which increases the risk of over- or under-compensation?

C. Harm to Sentimental or Similar Interests in Property

Barking Hound Village, LLC v. Monyak

787 S.E.2d 191 (Ga. 2016) (Thompson, J.)

[Plaintiffs boarded two dogs with a kennel operated by defendants, Barking Hound Village, LLC, and Furman: Lola, an eight-year-old "mixed-breed dachshund" and Callie, a 13-year-old mixed breed Labrador Retriever. The defendant knew that Callie needed pain medication. The defendant instead mistakenly gave the drug to Lola. Given the dosage and difference in the dogs' sizes, this caused Lola to experience kidney failure three days after they picked their dogs up. Despite nine months and $67,000 of extensive veterinary care, Lola died. Plaintiffs prevailed on summary judgment, and on appeal the only issue was the measure of damages.]

Generally, in a suit to recover damages to personal property it is a well-established principle that a plaintiff cannot recover an amount of damages against a tortfeasor greater than the fair market value of the property prior to impairment. However, over 120 years ago this Court decided that such a limitation was not appropriate in negligence cases involving the injury or death of an animal. Instead, this Court determined that where an animal is negligently injured and subsequently dies as a result of those injuries, the proper measure of damages recoverable by the animal's owner includes not only the full market value of the animal at the time of the loss plus interest, but also expenses incurred by the owner in an effort to cure the animal.

By ensuring that property owners whose animals are negligently injured by another are able to recoup reasonable expenses incurred in attempting to save the animal, this Court's decisions are consistent with the position taken by courts in a majority of states, including those which have adopted an actual value to the owner measure of damages to determine a pet dog's worth, *see Strickland v. Medlen*, 397 S.W.3d 184 (Tex. 2013) (recognizing that "while actual value cannot include the owner's 'feelings,' it can include a range of other factors such as purchase price, reasonable replacement costs breeding potential special training veterinary expenses related to the negligent injury, and so on"), as well as those which have declined to do so, *see Shera v. N.C. St. Univ. Veterinary Teaching Hosp.*, 219 N.C.App. 117 (2012) (awarding plaintiffs damages for the death of their 12-year-old dog due to veterinary malpractice in the amount of $3,105.72, which amount included reimbursement for the cost of the dog's medical treatment plus the replacement cost for a similar dog).

At the time this lawsuit was filed, the Monyaks' injured dog was still alive and the veterinary fees incurred were in the neighborhood of $10,000. The fact that the dog's treatment ultimately proved unsuccessful and the animal died nine months later should not prevent the Monyaks from seeking compensatory damages for the reasonable veterinary fees incurred in their attempt to save their pet. Rather, we conclude, pursuant to long-established Georgia precedent, that the proper measure of damages recoverable by the Monyaks for the negligent injury and death of their dog includes both the dog's fair market value plus interest *and* any reasonable medical costs and other expenses they incurred in treating the animal for its injuries.

While we are sympathetic to the concerns expressed by the parties and others regarding the difficulties in establishing the fair market value of a family pet, this Court long ago stated that, the value of a dog may be proved as that of any other property, by evidence that he was of a particular breed, and had certain qualities, and by witnesses who knew the market value of such animal, if any market value be shown.

Although we find the Court of Appeals erred in applying an actual value to owner measure of damages in this case, we find no error in that court's determination that Georgia precedent does not allow for the recovery of damages based on the sentimental value of personal property to its owner. Instead, we agree with those courts which have held that the unique human-animal bond, while cherished, is beyond legal measure.

This does not mean, however, that all qualitative evidence regarding the plaintiffs' dog is inadmissible. As in *Chalker*, we see no reason why opinion evidence, both qualitative and quantitative, of an animal's particular attributes—e.g., breed, age, training, temperament, and use—should be any less admissible than similar evidence offered in describing the value of other types of personal property. The key is ensuring that such evidence relates to the value of the dog in a fair market, not the value of the dog solely to its owner.

Of course, determining the reasonableness of medical treatment and the reasonableness of its cost is a function for the factfinder and well within the capability of jurors who routinely are asked to ascertain the appropriate value of professional services in other types of cases. The burden of establishing the reasonableness of any medical treatment provided in light of the animal's injuries, condition and prognosis, as well as the reasonableness of the cost of that treatment considering factors such as the nature of the services rendered, the time required to perform them, and all attending circumstances rests with the animal's owner.

Notes and Questions

1. <u>The Key?</u> The *Barking Hound* court stated the "key" was to identify "the value of the dog in a fair market, not the value of the dog solely to its owner." Imagine on remand you're representing one party: what arguments will you make about value and reasonable care? Does "temperament" open the door to evidence of sentimental value, or value to the owner?

2. <u>Special Value.</u> Some courts permit awards of "special value" of sentimental items. *Ladeas v. Carter,* 845 S.W.2d 45 (Ct. App. Colo. 2000) (destroyed videotape of deceased father's last words). In *Countrywide Home Loans, Inc. v. Thitchener,* 124 Nev. 725 (2008), the defendant "trashed out" the contents of the condo owned by the plaintiffs, mistaking it for a unit that it had foreclosed upon. The plaintiffs sued for conversion and the jury awarded $321,690. The court wrote:

> Countrywide argues that the jury's award of special damages was excessive, based on the district court's failure to give its proposed jury instruction on special value. Because of this, Countrywide asserts that the amount of special damages awarded for the Thitcheners' irreplaceable but nonmarketable property was not supported by the record. We disagree. The district court has broad discretion to settle jury instructions, and its decision to give or decline a particular instruction will not be overturned absent an abuse of discretion or judicial error.
>
> According to the Restatement (Second) of Torts § 911, when converted property's value to the owner exceeds its market value, the owner may be compensated for its special value, which is measured by "factors apart from those entering into exchange value that cause the article to be more desirable to the owner than to others." With respect to irreplaceable property, these factors include, among other rational measures of value, the property's original cost, the quality and condition of the property at the time of the loss, and the cost of reproduction, but exclude subjective considerations

of sentimental value.[17] Because it ensures that the amount of special damages will be objectively assessed, and thereby accords with a plaintiffs burden to present competent evidence to support a reasonably accurate amount of damages, we adopt the Restatement's valuation method for irreplaceable property.

Here, the district court gave the following jury instruction on special value: "Where there is the destruction of personal property without a market value, it does not mean the property is valueless and that damages cannot be recovered by the plaintiff, rather, plaintiff is entitled to damages based upon the property's special value to the plaintiff." By contrast, Countrywide's jury instruction would have prohibited the jury from considering the property's sentimental value, and would have directed it to consider only "the value of the lost or damaged personal property to the Thitcheners."

While Countrywide's proposed instruction on special value was correct as far as it went, it was incomplete because it failed to explicitly differentiate between special value and ordinary market value. As such, it approximated an instruction on actual damages, which could have inappropriately constrained the jury to awarding the Thitcheners the mere exchange value of their irreplaceable possessions.[19] Moreover, while the district court's jury instruction properly distinguished between special value and market value, it failed to restrict the jury from attempting to monetize the Thitcheners' sentimental attachment to their property. Both the district court's instruction and Countrywide's proposed instruction, therefore, were incomplete in their own regard. However, neither of the instructions necessarily misstated the law. Thus, we do not perceive any abuse of discretion in the district court's decision to refuse Countrywide's proposed jury instruction in favor of the instruction that was ultimately submitted to the jury.

Alternatively, Countrywide argues that there was insufficient evidence that the Thitcheners' irreplaceable possessions had enough special value to support the $321,690 award of special damages. We disagree. Since special damages are a species of compensatory damages, a jury has wide latitude in awarding them. So long as there is an evidentiary basis for determining an

---

17. *See Landers v. Municipality of Anchorage*, 915 P.2d 614, 618 (Alaska 1996) (explaining that an irreplaceable item's special value under § 911 may be based on such things as original cost or cost to reproduce). As the illustrations in § 911, comment e, demonstrate, special value is a measure of compensatory damages designed to allow a plaintiff to recover for the personal time and effort invested in acquiring or producing an item "or necessary to spend to reproduce it," even if the market would not normally reward that investment.

19. *See* Restatement (Second) of Torts § 911 cmt. e (1979) (noting that where irreplaceable but nonmarketable articles have special value "it would be unjust to limit the damages for destroying or harming the articles to the exchange value").

amount that is reasonably accurate, the amount of special damages need not be mathematically exact.

At trial, the Thitcheners testified that they would not sell certain irreplaceable possessions that were lost in the "trash-out" regardless of the amount offered. While this testimony alone is legally insufficient as a measure of special value,[22] the Thitcheners introduced a list of their irreplaceable possessions. Among other things, the list included Gerald Thitchener's military medals, certificates, and commendations, as well as other tangible markers of Gerald and Katrina's personal achievements, a portrait of a deceased parent, autographed memorabilia, various heirlooms, and family photos and video footage, which cannot be reproduced. Although the jury was not given an exact measure for determining the special value of these possessions, we cannot conclude that the award of $321,690 in special damages was based on improper considerations of sentimental value.

Viewing the evidence in the light most favorable to the verdict, the jury was presented with facts allowing it to dispassionately evaluate the time and resources that the Thitcheners invested in acquiring their irreplaceable possessions. Thus, a sufficient evidentiary basis supports the $321,690 award of special damages.

Does $321,690 sound reasonable to you? Is there any reasonable way to debate that? Consider the rule that "for unique, designer items such as a mink coat, the owner's testimony alone will not suffice to prove the fair market value" but instead an expert must be used. *Parham v. CIH Properties, Inc.,* 208 F. Supp. 3d 116 (D.D.C. 2016).

3. <u>Graves, Corpses, and Related Exceptions</u>. Grave desecration has permitted an award of mental distress damages. *Hairston v. Gen'l Pipeline Constr., Inc.,* 704 S.E.2d 663 (W. Va. 2010). Likewise, they can be recovered for negligently interfering with the right to possess a human corpse. *Cochran v. Securitas Security Serv., USA, Inc.,* 2017 IL 121200 (Sept. 21, 2017).

Some courts permit awards above fair market value if the defendant maliciously destroyed personalty. *Plotnik v. Meihaus,* 208 Cal. App. 4th 1590 (Ct. App. Cal. 2012) (setting a cat on fire, killing a dog by hurling a large can at it, and shooting a horse were sufficient). In this regard, note that a tort can be intentional but not malicious or willful. *See Bace v. Babitt,* 2012 WL 2567153 (S.D.N.Y.), *report adopted,* 2012 WL 2574750 (S.D.N.Y. July 3, 2012) ("a plaintiff cannot recover for his mental suffering caused by an injury to his property, at least if the defendant has not maliciously intended to cause such mental suffering. Because there was no evidence that the City seized appellant's 1992 Subaru with the specific intent of causing injury to appellant, appellant was not entitled to any damages for mental

---

22. *See Campins v. Capels,* 461 N.E.2d 712 (Ind. Ct. App. 1984) (speculative responses to hypothetical offers to sell generally are not enough to support a determination of special value).

anguish."). In *Plotnik,* the court held that the defendant had *not* committed IIED but awarded mental anguish damages for trespass to chattels because the defendant had hit a small dog with a bat, injuring its leg. The plaintiff did not see the defendant hit its dog. The court affirmed the jury award — $2,600 in veterinary bills, $210 for a small stroller for the dog to use during recovery and $20,000 for emotional distress.

Even if mental anguish is not recoverable, the sentimental value of destroyed property can indicate the amount of mental anguish caused by a defendant. In *Chryar v. Wolf,* 21 P.3d 428 (Ct. App. Colo. 2000), the defendant landlord wrongfully entered plaintiff's apartment and put plaintiff's belongings on the sidewalk with a sign saying, "Take Free." The plaintiff sued for intentional infliction of emotional distress, seeking anguish damages caused by the loss of a family bible, photographs, a chessboard, a military uniform, personal journals and certificates, and short novels the plaintiff was writing. The appellate court affirmed even though it recognized that "the evidence supporting the $3850 portion of the award" for loss of that property "was supported only by incompetent evidence of the property's sentimental value to Chryar." The court stated:

> We now hold that sentimental and emotional value of property may be considered in awarding damages in connection with claims for intentional or reckless infliction of emotional distress. Only a reasonable, and not unusual, sentimental and emotional value may be considered in such actions. We acknowledge the difficulty in dealing with the computation of a virtually unmeasurable mental process, sentiment. But this presents no greater challenge than what is normally occasioned in assessing damages for emotional distress. It will, in the end, be for the trier of fact to make this determination.

> Here, Chryar asserted a claim for outrageous conduct against Wolf. Such tort involves intentionally or recklessly causing emotional distress to another through conduct which goes so far beyond the bounds of decency as to be regarded as atrocious and utterly intolerable in a civilized community. The trial court found that Wolf's conduct did rise to such a level. Wolf does not contest this finding, other than to suggest that her conduct did not cause Chryar severe emotional distress. However, the record reflects that Wolf's conduct was "the straw that broke the camel's back" and triggered two suicide attempts on his part.

> The trial court awarded Chryar $3850 for items whose value to Chryar was largely sentimental or emotional in nature. The court's award in this respect was, however, significantly lower than what Chryar requested. The trial court's award was not, under the circumstances, unreasonable, and we will not set it aside simply because the court may have erroneously categorized this amount as property, rather than emotional distress, damages.

2. Monetary Remedies for the Harm of Interfering with Rights in Personalty

As stated in the introduction, trespass to chattels and conversion do not require physical damage to a chattel. They also provide a remedy for interfering with a plaintiff's right to use and control its personalty.

The distinction between trespass to chattels and conversion is that "trespass to chattels involves relatively minor damages or deprivation, while conversion involves consequences which justify the right of the plaintiff to recover the full value of the personal property affected." *Madison Capital Co. v. S&S Salvage, LLC*, 507 F. App'x 528 (6th Cir. 2012). Otherwise, trespass to chattels is the proper claim. "In an action for conversion, title to the chattel passes to the defendant, so that he is in effect required to buy it at a forced judicial sale." *EDI Precast, LLC v. Carnahan*, 982 F. Supp. 2d 616 (D. Md. 2013).

More specifically, the elements of conversion are: (1) the plaintiff had legal title to the converted property; (2) the plaintiff had possession of the property or the right to possess it at the time of the conversion; (3) the defendant exercised dominion over the property in a manner that denied the plaintiff's rights to use and enjoy the property; (4) the defendant intended to interfere with the plaintiff's possession; (5) the defendant refused plaintiff's demand for its return, or demand was excused (for example, because it clearly would have been futile to ask for return); (6) the defendant's act caused; (7) damage. The damage can be either physical harm or substantial interference with use, but it must be sufficient to require the defendant to pay the full value of the chattel.

Trespass to chattels requires: (1) intent, (2) physical interference with (3) possession, (4) resulting in harm. Typically, the harm can be: (a) to the possessor's materially valuable interest in the physical condition, quality, or value of the chattel, (b) if the possessor is deprived of the use of the chattel for a substantial time, or (c) to some other legally protected interest of the possessor. *See Engle v. Unified Life. Ins. Co.*, 2014 WL 12508347 (S.D. Cal. Oct. 27, 2014).

While they are usually intentional torts, "it is not necessary that the actor intended to commit what he knows to be a trespass or a conversion. It is, however, necessary that his act be one which he knows to be destructive of any outstanding possessory right, if such there be." *Mathis v. County of Lyon*, 2014 WL 1413608 (D. Nev. Apr. 11, 2014), *aff'd*, 591 F. App'x 635 (9th Cir. 2015). The "intent" element of conversion is particularly counterintuitive: "neither good nor bad faith, neither care nor negligence, neither knowledge nor ignorance, are of the gist of the action of conversion." *Diamond St. Ins. Co. v. Deardorff*, 2011 WL 1459018 (E.D. Cal. Apr. 15, 2011). Instead, although the defendant need not have used the property, the defendant must have "an intention or purpose to convert the goods and to exercise ownership over them, or to prevent the owner from taking possession of his property." *Id.* Thus, no conversion occurs if a defendant lawfully possesses plaintiff's chattels, but through negligence they are destroyed because that "is not an act of dominion over them." *Id.*

A case illustrating a key limit of the harm protected by these claims is *Wilkinson v. United States,* 564 F.3d 927 (8th Cir. 2009). The Wilkinsons had owned 750 acres of "allotted" Indian land held in trust by the Bureau of Indian Affairs. They had mortgaged their "allotments" to the Farm Service Administration, a government agency, in the 1980s, but had defaulted on the mortgages. The FSA later asked the BIA to assist it in collecting on the plaintiff's debt by leasing out 315 acres of their land to a third party to farm. Over plaintiffs' objections, the BIA did so. With half their land leased out, they abandoned their remaining land and farm equipment, but appealed the decision to lease out their land. A year later, they prevailed because the BIA lacked authority to lease their land. Nonetheless, BIA local officials ignored the ruling and leased their land again, even as late as 2002. In this suit, plaintiffs claimed conversion of their farm equipment. The trial court awarded damages, and the government appealed. This court reversed the holding of conversion:

> The Wilkinsons cite no case where a court found conversion based solely on an indirect interference with a specific use of property and without interference with physical possession of that property. While there may be instances where interference with an owner's right to use his property may completely deprive the owner of the possibility of any enjoyment thereof or benefit therefrom even without interference with possession, conversion is primarily an offense against *possession* of property that consists of an act in derogation of the plaintiff's *possessory* rights. Thus, few interferences will amount to conversion if they do not interfere with the possessory interest, and it remains the case that where there is no denial of plaintiff's property, and no claim of property in the defendant, there can be no conversion.

At common law, there is a separate claim for "trespass to chattel" that is generally regarded as differing from conversion only in degree, and where interference is not complete, trespass to chattel may be a more appropriate claim. *See Pearson v. Dodd,* 410 F.2d 701 (D.C. Cir. 1969) ("Where the intermeddling falls short of the complete or very substantial deprivation of possessory rights in the property, the tort committed is not conversion, but the lesser wrong of trespass to chattels."); Restatement (Second) of Torts § 222A cmt. a (explaining that "the present rule regards conversion as an exercise of the defendant's dominion or control of the chattel, as distinguished from a mere interference with the chattel itself, or with possession of it").

Because a conversion must be the equivalent of a forced sale to the defendant, the tort of conversion is more severe than the tort of trespass to chattel, which generally is something less than a forced sale justifying payment of full value of the chattel. The "forced sale" nature of conversion emphasizes the essential distinction between conversion and trespass to chattel; namely, in a conversion, the interference is so severe as to justify the serious remedy of payment of the *full value* of the chattel. It follows, then, that a claim of conversion cannot stand where the interference is too incomplete to totally deprive the plaintiff of the chattel.

Our conclusion that no conversion occurred is further supported by the fact that the district court did not appear to consider ownership of the equipment to pass to the BIA (as it would if converted for full value), because, under North Dakota law, a plaintiff may be awarded *either* the value of the property *or* the return of the property. Allowing the Wilkinsons to both retain the farm equipment and receive the full value of the farm equipment would be contrary to the notion of a "forced sale" and inconsistent with North Dakota law.

In considering the district court's holding that the BIA's trespass had the secondary effect of converting the farm equipment, we are left with a definite and firm conviction a mistake has been made.

The usual measure of damages for conversion is the fair market value of the chattel at the time and place of conversion. *U.S. Bank Tr. Nat. Ass'n v. Venice Md LLC*, 92 F. App'x 948 (4th Cir. 2004). The usual measure of damages for trespass to chattels is less because trespass to chattels does not require interference sufficient to compel the defendant to pay the chattel's full value, so a plaintiff generally may recover only the actual damage suffered by reason of the impairment of the property, along with damages for the loss of its use. *See In re Apple & ATTM Antitrust Litig.*, 2010 WL 3521965 (N.D. Cal. July 8, 2010) ("loss of use of a personal phone for a few days before receiving a free replacement phone" was not a "substantial" time and so not a trespass to chattels), *vacated in part on other grounds*, 826 F. Supp. 2d 1168 (N.D. Cal. 2011).

A. Monetary Damages for Interference with Rights in Tangible Personalty

Mahana v. Onyx Acceptance Corp.

96 P.3d 893 (Utah 2004) (Parrish, J.)

[A 1994 Mazda pickup was purchased in California. The purchaser then defaulted on the loan that he had taken from Onyx Acceptance Corp. The truck was later purchased by 19-year-old Mahana from a car dealer in Arizona for $9,000, who began paying on his loan. (The title appeared clean because Onyx failed to properly perfect its lien.) Three years later, and while current on his loan, Mahana was living in Utah when Onyx had the truck, with Mahana's personal property in it, towed from his work while he was working. Mahana sued Onyx for conversion, and kept making payments on the truck. The parties first had the court decide liability, and 18 months after Onyx had taken the truck, the trial court held that Mahana was its lawful owner. Onyx returned it, and then the trial court awarded $11,880 in damages. Onyx appealed.]

The district court arrived at the value of Mahana's lost use by relying on the retail rental value of small vehicles such as those that Rick Warner Toyota provided to Mahana as a courtesy. Onyx asserts that the award based on the rental value of these vehicles was excessive because it was greater than the amount Mahana originally paid for the truck.

Onyx's challenge to the particular amount of the compensatory award is a question of fact that we will reverse only if clearly erroneous. For the reasons explained herein, we find no clear error in the district court's use of the retail rental cost of replacement vehicles as the measure of the value of Mahana's lost use, even though it resulted in an award that exceeded the purchase price of the truck.

In setting the compensatory award, the district court considered a number of factors. These included the purchase price of the truck, the retail rental value of comparable trucks, and the retail rental value of small cars such as those Rick Warner Toyota provided to Mahana. The court settled on the retail rental value of small cars, despite the fact that such cars were not comparable to the converted property. The court observed:

> Mahana couldn't tow jet skis, haul items for personal use or go camping with the replacement cars. There was also sentimental value to Mr. Mahana from having a pickup truck as opposed to a car. Frankly the court is cognizant that this 19 year old single male went from a pickup truck equipped with a CD player, amplifier and additional speakers to a Dodge Neon. The ride, for him, was just not the same.

The district court determined that using the retail rental value of small pickups would result in an "inequitable windfall for the plaintiff," because the resulting figure of $21,600 so greatly exceeded the $9,000 purchase price of the truck. Recognizing that some measures of the value of lost use would result in an inappropriately large award, the district court moderated the lost use calculations by basing them on the retail rental value of small cars such as those that Rick Warner Toyota provided to Mahana during the period he was without his truck.

Onyx argues that it was clearly erroneous for the district court to award damages in excess of the amount Mahana originally paid for the truck. We disagree. When property is wrongfully taken by another, it is possible for the resulting consequential damages to exceed the amount paid for the property. Lost use, a form of consequential damages, may appropriately be used to measure the damages resulting from a conversion in circumstances such as these. Because such consequential damages bear no necessary relationship to purchase price, we find no clear error in the fact that the compensatory award exceeds the purchase price of the truck.

Lysenko v. Sawaya

7 P.3d 783 (Utah 2000) (Russon, J.)

[Burger King Corporation leased land from defendants, the Sawayas, to build a restaurant. The 15-year lease provided that any additions or improvements made by Burger King would become the property of the Sawayas if not removed within 15 days of termination of the lease. Burger King built a building and sublet it to plaintiff, Peter Lysenko. That sublease provided that any personal property he installed would remain his personal property after the sublease ended. He purchased and installed equipment necessary to run a Burger King, financing it through a bank that took a security interest in the property.

Burger King and Lysenko disputed certain amounts claimed by Burger King, and Lysenko closed the restaurant in April 1993, but the lease did not expire until February 1994. As that time approached, the Sawayas informed Lysenko, Burger King, and the bank that any equipment left in the building 15 days after termination of the lease would belong to them. Burger King and the bank stated that because of their interests, Lysenko could not remove the equipment. The Sawayas refused Lysenko's request to remove the equipment.

Meanwhile, Lysenko arranged for one of his former employees, Curtis Loosli, to purchase the bank's security interest in the equipment. On February 8, 1994, Central Bank sold its security interest in the equipment to Loosli, who then conveyed his interest to Lysenko. However, Lysenko did not remove the equipment after the lease terminated. Instead, the Sawayas leased the building to HB Properties, which opened a restaurant there in September 1994. HB Properties discarded some of Lysenko's remaining equipment but retained and used most of it.

Lysenko sued the Sawayas, arguing that they had converted the equipment by unlawfully preventing him from removing it. Lysenko sought either possession of the equipment or its value. At trial, Lysenko's expert witness gave two ways to value the equipment: (1) "in-place" value, measuring its value in a going concern ($35,185); and (2) "salvage" value, measuring the value of the equipment removed from the restaurant and sold ($10,980).[2] The Sawayas argued that Lysenko was entitled to either no damages or salvage value.

The court granted judgment to Lysenko, holding Lysenko's perfected security interest entitled him to possess the equipment and the Sawayas had converted the

---

2. According to traditional usage, "salvage" value (also referred to as "scrap" value) describes "the value of an asset after it has become useless to the owner" or "the amount expected to be obtained when a fixed asset is disposed of at the end of its useful life." *Black's Law Dictionary* 1550 (7th ed.1999). The term "salvage" value is a misnomer in the instant case because Lysenko's expert employed the term to describe the fair market value that Lysenko's undamaged, usable equipment would have if removed from the premises. Nonetheless, to avoid confusion, we will use the term "salvage" value in this opinion for the limited purpose of describing the valuation measure offered by Lysenko and ultimately adopted by the trial court.

equipment by interfering with that right. The court awarded the salvage value and an additional $2,000 for the equipment that HB Properties had discarded. The court below affirmed and Lysenko appealed.]

As a general rule, the measure of damages for conversion is the value of the property at the time of the conversion, plus interest. In *McKeon v. Williams*, 312 Or. 322 (1991), which, like the case before us, dealt with a landlord's conversion of a tenant's personal property that remained on the premises, it was held that the appropriate method for determining the value of property at the time of conversion depended upon whether the tenant had a right to possess the premises when the conversion occurred. In that case, tenants leased a building for the purpose of operating a restaurant. Before their lease terminated, the tenants closed the restaurant and eventually stopped paying rent to the landlord, who then filed an action for restitution of the building. The court determined that the tenants' right to possess the premises had ended and ordered them to turn over the building to the landlord. Thereafter, the tenants requested permission from the landlord to remove their restaurant equipment, but the landlord denied their request. The landlord then leased the building to a new tenant who operated a restaurant on the premises using the same equipment.

In an action that followed, the jury found that the landlord converted the tenants' equipment, and awarded damages to the tenants for the value of the converted equipment. The court instructed the jury that the proper measure of damages for conversion was the "fair market value of the property *after removal* from the landlord's premises." *Id.* (emph. added). On appeal, the tenants argued that they were instead entitled to the in-place value of the equipment because the landlord leased the building to a new tenant who continued to use the equipment.

The *McKeon* court affirmed, noting that the important factual distinction to be made is *when* the conversion occurred. Examining rulings from other state courts, the *McKeon* court concluded in this regard:

1. If a landlord converts a tenant's on-premises personal property while a tenant has the right to possess the premises, the measure of damages is the "in-place" fair market value of the converted property.

2. If a landlord converts a tenant's personal property left on the premises after the tenant's right to possession has ended, the measure of damages is the fair market value that the property would have, if removed from the premises.

This rule serves the fundamental purpose of compensatory damages, which is to place the plaintiff in the same position as if the tort had not been committed. *See* Restatement (Second) of Torts § 903 cmt. a. If, on the one hand, the conversion occurs while the plaintiff is still entitled to possess the premises and use the personal property in place (or if the plaintiff is entitled to assign or sublet the premises, to sell the property in place to the assignee or sublessee), then the plaintiff is entitled to the value of the property in place. If, on the other hand, the plaintiff's right to occupy the premises has ended, such as after the termination of a lease, the plaintiff no longer possesses the right to use the personal property in place, but is entitled only to remove the property and sell it.

U.S. Bank Tr. Nat'l. Ass'n. v. Venice Md LLC

92 F. App'x 948 (4th Cir. 2004) (Per Curiam)

[Landlord took possession of equipment in a restaurant and hotel over the objection of Metropolitan Bank and Trust, which notified the landlord that it had a security interest in the equipment because its owner had defaulted on the loan used to purchase it. The landlord continued to operate the restaurant. The bank asserted trespass to chattels seeking damages of the restaurant's gross revenues during the landlord's operation, which lasted several months. The district court decided that the appropriate measure for trespass to chattels was the fair rental value of the items, which it determined was $25,000 each month. The landlord appealed.]

The Landlord argues that the appropriate measure of damages for trespass to chattel is diminution in value. Because the district court found that any diminution in value of the Inn personal property was nominal, the Landlord contends that Metropolitan should have been awarded only nominal damages.

Under Maryland law, the measure of damages for trespass to a chattel is the diminished value of the chattel which results from the damage actually sustained from the time of the taking until the return of the goods. However, additional damages adequate to compensate an owner for other injurious consequences which result in a loss greater than the diminished or market value may be allowed.

The district court was under no obligation to limit its damage award to the diminished value of the chattel as a result of the trespass. Rather, it was authorized to apply an additional measure of damages to compensate Metropolitan for the forced rental of its property. Had the district court applied only a diminution in value measure, the Landlord would have enjoyed a windfall, paying only nominal damages for wrongfully possessing items that would have cost between $20,000 and $62,000 in monthly rental fees. Therefore, as an additional remedial measure, the district court apparently considered the measure of damages for conversion in determining the damage award for trespass. Although the district court should have first used diminution in value as the measure of damages and then, finding that inadequate, should have granted Metropolitan the fair rental value of its property, we find no error in the ultimate result reached. We therefore affirm the district court's damage award of $25,000 per month.

Notes and Questions

1. Why Conversion in *Burger King* but Trespass to Chattels in *Venice?* Why would the defendant's damage theory in each case be inadequate? In *Venice,* what other measures of damages could the defendant have pointed to that would have resulted

in a lower, and potentially more reasonable, recovery? If the *Venice* equipment had a value of $20,000, would trespass to chattels have been appropriate?

2. <u>Loss of Use</u>. Much like physical damage arising from negligence, courts split on whether and when an award of full fair market value precludes loss-of-use damages. *Mahana* permitted them, but another Utah court held that awarding "both market value and damages for loss of use would be tantamount to an award of double damages inasmuch as it would equate to charging the defendant for the property and then continuing to charge rent for its continued possession." *Firkins v. Ruegner,* 213 P.3d 895 (Ct. App. Utah 2009).

3. <u>Harm of Interference</u>. In *G.M. Sign Inc. v. Stealth Security Sys., Inc.,* 2015 WL 9268416 (N.D. Ill. 2015), the defendant sent junk faxes to the plaintiff who sued for conversion and asserted the fax had exercised complete control over, not the fax machine, but the paper and ink used to print the fax. The court emphasized that it is not the value of the chattel, but the degree of interference with its use that governs, and so nominal damages were permitted.

B. Damages for Interference with Rights in Intangible Personalty

Porters Bldg. Centers, Inc. v. Sprint Lumber
2017 WL 4413288 (W.D. Mo. Oct. 2, 2017) (Smith, J.)

[Plaintiff Porters Building Center was a family-owned lumber supply business selling to commercial builders. The defendants were at-will employees of Porters when they began to communicate with defendant Sprint Lumber about switching to work for Sprint. While still employed with Porters, the employees, including Jerry Downey, sought to persuade Porter customers to switch to Sprint, and sent some Sprint credit applications. Porter sued the former employees and Sprint. Downey filed a counterclaim for trespass to chattels, asserting Porter employees had been able to access his personal Gmail account by using one of Porter's computers because he had saved his username and password on that computer. Porter moved for summary judgment on Downey's counterclaim.]

Downey contends he held a possessory interest in his email communications, the intrinsic value of which was based "in part on the private and confidential nature of the communications," and Plaintiff "intermeddled" with his possessory interest. Downey also alleges Plaintiff used information in his emails for personal and professional gain, which impaired the condition, quality, and value of his property. Plaintiff argues it is entitled to summary judgment on this counterclaim because it is based upon an intangible privacy right, Plaintiff did not dispossess Downey of anything, and Plaintiff did not cause actual damage to the property.

A trespass to chattel may be committed by intentionally intermeddling with a chattel in the possession of another. There must be a disturbance of plaintiff's possession, which may be done by an actual taking, a physical seizing, removal from their owner, or by exercising a control or authority over them inconsistent with their owner's possession. The required intent is present when an act is done for the purpose of using or otherwise intermeddling with a chattel or with knowledge that such an intermeddling will, to a substantial certainty, result from the act.

The Court must first decide whether an email communication is chattel. Chattel is defined as "movable or transferable property; esp. personal property," and "personal chattel is defined as a tangible good or an intangible right." *Weicht v. Suburban Newspapers of Greater St. Louis, Inc., 32 S.W.3d 592 (Mo. Ct. App. 2000).* Neither party cites a case deciding whether email communications are chattel in Missouri. This is not surprising given the sparse Missouri case law on trespass to chattel.

Trespass to chattel is an archaic common law claim. The Tenth Circuit recently discussed this claim when faced with deciding whether the opening and examining of emails constituted a Fourth Amendment. *U.S. v. Ackerman*, 831 F.3d 1292 (10th Cir. 2016). The Tenth Circuit noted "the warrantless opening and examination of (presumptively) private email correspondence seems pretty clear to qualify as exactly the type of trespass to chattels that the framers sought to prevent when they adopted the Fourth Amendment." *Id.* Of course, as the Tenth Circuit stated, "the framers were concerned with the protection of physical rather than virtual correspondence. But a more obvious analogy from principle to new technology is hard to imagine" *Id.*

As referenced in *Ackerman*, many courts have applied trespass to chattels to actions taken in cyberspace. But there is no consensus among the courts. Some courts found personal intangible property is chattel. Other courts concluded trespass to chattel, including a claim related to intangible property, must have a connection to tangible property.

While the parties disagree on whether email communications are chattel, the parties failed to address whether Downey's email communications were connected to something tangible. Fortunately, several district courts recently shed light on this issue as it relates to Google's network, the same network utilized by Downey. These cases establish Google stores its customers' e-mail content on servers located in the United States and abroad. On its website, Google states that "rather than storing each user's data on a single machine or set of machines, we distribute all data across many computers in different locations." Accordingly, Downey's email communications are connected to something tangible—*i.e.,* Google's servers.

This Court can only speculate as to what Missouri courts would do in this particular instance. While the Missouri Supreme Court has held personal property can be tangible or intangible, it is unknown if it would extend a claim for trespass to chattel to email communications. If this case pertained to tangible letters written by Downey, he could bring a trespass to chattel claim. If Downey printed the subject email communications, this Court believes he could bring a trespass to chattel claim.

The Court is persuaded by the Tenth Circuit's statements in *Ackerman* and the other courts that have determined "chattel" extends to intangible property when the intangible property is connected to a tangible object. The Court concludes Missouri courts would find a trespass to chattel claim includes an email communication when the email communication is connected to a tangible object, such as a server.[15] As such, Downey may maintain such an action against Plaintiff, and Plaintiff's summary judgment motion on this counterclaim is denied.

Notes and Questions

1. <u>What Harm and What Measure of Damages</u>? The value of the *Porters* email was in the information, not the server space. Accessing the email did not interfere with the plaintiff's use of the information. Downey did not own Google's server, or pay for using it. What is the harm remedied by trespass to an intangible chattel? What measure of damages is proper?

Rarely, a court reviews a verdict on just trespass to an intangible chattel (because the value is in the information used, not the trespass itself). In *Eysoldt v. Proscan Imaging*, 957 N.E.2d 780 (Ct. App. Ohio 2011), the plaintiff, Jeff Eysoldt, registered domain names and email accounts with GoDaddy.com. One of those domains was myrejuvenate.com, which he used for a business webpage for Rejuvenate Aesthetic Laser Centers. A dispute developed between Eysoldt and his partners in that business, and one of the partners called GoDaddy and asked it to transfer the myrejuvenate.com domain name to her. GoDaddy instead transferred all domain names and emails associated with Eysoldt's password and username to her, and resulted in Eyesoldt being locked out of his accounts. When Eysoldt received an email from GoDaddy informing him of the transfers, he submitted a required form to cancel it. Further, he emailed the GoDaddy employee who had done the transfer and asked him to transfer all but myrejuvenate.com back, but the employee refused to do so. The jury awarded compensatory damages for this, which the court held was a trespass to chattels. Neither the opinion nor briefing reveals the amount of damages, however. What should it be?

2. <u>Intangible Card</u>? In *Gallardo v. FedEx Kinko's Office & Print Serv., Inc.*, 2008 WL 2143011 (D. Md. May 12, 2008), the plaintiff left her "green card"—a federal registration document that indicated she was a lawful permanent resident of the United States—on the counter of defendant's store. She noticed soon after she left and called: an employee promised to keep it in a locker at the store. Instead, it was discarded. She sued because the loss caused her several months' delay in travels and

---

15. Even if it did not take judicial notice of Google's servers storing customers' email data, the Court, in light of the dicta in *Ackerman* and the cases finding intangible property can form the basis of a trespass to chattels claim (regardless of whether the intangible property was connected to something tangible), would find Downey could bring a counterclaim for trespass to chattels as it relates to his email communications.

attorneys' fees and government fees to obtain a replacement. The court held that a green card was not tangible property under Maryland law:

> In general, with respect to intangible property rights like those alleged here, Maryland only recognizes conversion claims that involve the type of intangible property rights that are merged or incorporated into a transferable document.

> Defendant contends that because a Green Card is not a document into which intangible property rights are merged, it is not a proper subject of a trespass or conversion action. A Green Card, according to defendant, "serves only to symbolize immigration status," "has no intrinsic value," and cannot be sold or transferred; in other words, "the fact that the Green Card was itself destroyed did not destroy Plaintiff's rights as a legal resident alien." In support of its argument that a Green Card does not incorporate the type of intangible property rights contemplated in a tort for conversion or trespass, defendant cites *Robinson v. St. Clair County,* 144 Ill.App.3d 118 (App.Ct. of Ill. 1986).

> In *Robinson,* the plaintiff premised her bailment and conversion claims on the confiscation of "a medical card for aid to families with dependent children," without which her infant son was unable to obtain medical care and ultimately died of pneumonia. The court dismissed the plaintiff's action, holding that

>> the Medical Eligibility Card, or green card, is not property and does not entitle its holder or the persons named thereon to property. It is symbolic of a status; it reflects the entitlement to medical assistance. The green card has no intrinsic value and it does not represent anything of intrinsic value. It cannot be sold, exchanged, assigned, or otherwise transferred, and it cannot be pledged or given as security.

> FedEx Kinko's argues that the "facts of this case are indistinguishable" from the facts in *Robinson,* and that, because Gallardo's "Green Card is not a transferable document, it cannot be the subject of a claim for bailment, trespass, trover or conversion."

> Plaintiff, in turn, argues that whether a Green Card is properly the subject of a trespass or conversion suit is an issue of first impression in Maryland, and attempts to distinguish it from the underlying document and holding in *Robinson.* She cites *Liddle v. Salem Sch. Dist.,* 249 Ill.App.3d 768 (App. Ct.Ill.1993), where the court found a letter, withheld from a high school student for seven months, that informed the student he was being recruited for a basketball scholarship, properly the subject of a conversion claim. In distinguishing the scholarship letter, the *Liddle* court stated that "while the medical eligibility card in *Robinson* contained information necessary to

process an application for medical benefits, the wrongful retention, loss, or destruction of the card could not deprive the holder of access to those benefits." The plaintiff in *Liddle,* on the other hand, "did not know of his status as a person being considered for a scholarship. Thus, it is this *information* that is claimed to constitute the property that was the subject of the bailment." *Id.* (emph. in original).

Plaintiff makes a series of arguments for why her Green Card is more similar to the scholarship letter in *Liddle* than the Medical Eligibility Card in *Robinson*. First, she argues that the Green Card, which "is expected to be used by the holder in nearly all transactions of daily life where proof of lawful presence and identity are necessary," embodies a broader spectrum of rights than the medical eligibility card, which only connotes eligibility for medical services. Where a medical card is misplaced, a medical provider can make a telephone call to confirm an individual's entitlement; plaintiff points out that "there is no phone number the employer can call to verify an alien's legal status in the United States." Plaintiff also points to the Green Card's photo-identification feature as "inextricably linking it to its holder like a driver's license or passport." Finally, plaintiff details the privileges and benefits that accompany permanent legal residency status, arguing that "the multitude of intangible property interests that flow from lawful permanent residency coalesce to make the green card more than just a symbol of status because it imbues the holder with, among other things, the right to work and lawfully receive compensation."

Contrary to plaintiff's arguments, a Green Card is more akin to the medical eligibility card in *Robinson* than the scholarship letter in *Liddle*. The individual rights that are symbolized by a Green Card are not extinguished if the Green Card is destroyed any more than an individual's status as a licensed driver is destroyed with his driver's license. In either case, the document's renewal may inconvenience the holder, but it does not destroy the status, and it cannot be transferred to confer rights or status on another. In addition, unlike the scholarship letter in *Liddle,* the loss or destruction of Gallardo's Green Card did not deprive her of any information or knowledge. Gallardo was aware of her status as a permanent resident and could obtain a new Green Card confirming that status through administrative channels. Accordingly, her claim for trespass or conversion cannot lie and will be dismissed.

Courts continue to struggle with whether to recognize harm to intangible property and, if so, what measure of damages to award. *See J&J Sports Prods. Inc. v. Jaschkowitz,* 2016 WL 2727015 (E.D. Ky. May 6, 2016) (noting that a minority of courts had extended conversion to intangible property in a case where defendant had intercepted satellite TV signals).

3. When Monetary Remedies Are Inadequate

Common law replevin is "a possessory action in which a claimant seeks to recover both possession of personal property that has been wrongfully taken or detained and damages for its unlawful detention." *Mason v. Farm Credit of So. Colo.,* 419 P.3d 975 (Colo. 2018). The plaintiff must show not only title, but also the exclusive right of immediate possession of the property "as against the defendant but is not required to set up such title or right as against the whole world." *Fenton v. Balick,* 821 F. Supp. 2d 755 (E.D. Pa. 2011).

Much like common law replevin, section 716(3) of the UCC permits a buyer to seek replevin for goods, but only "if after reasonable effort he or she is unable to effect cover for such goods or the circumstances reasonably indicate that such effort will be unavailing" or certain more limited circumstances exist. Often, buyers rely upon specific performance, not replevin, when sellers breach.

Roy Bayer Tr. v. Red Husky, LLC
13 N.E.3d 415 (Ct. App. Ind. 2014) (Robb, J.)

[In August 2008, Plaintiff Red Husky, LLC leased a 1998 Kenworth semi-tractor to Daniel Bowne. In August 2010, Bowne leased a building owned by defendant Roy Bayer Trust to store the Kenworth. Ms. Harris was the trustee for that trust. Bowne stopped paying rent and also defaulted on the lease with Red Husky. In September 2011, Harris refused to permit Red Husky to retrieve the Kenworth from the building, and in November 2011, Red Husky sued Harris, the trust, and Bowne, seeking replevin and damages. Bowne defaulted and Red Husky obtained summary judgment of replevin against Harris the trust in September 2012 (and so Red Husky obtained the Kenworth). Later, after a hearing on damages, it was awarded $10,000 in damages against the trust and Harris for deterioration to the Kenworth during the time they had refused to release it to Red Husky They appealed.]

In replevin actions, the usual measure of damages would be the value of the loss of use, measured by the fair rental value, if possible. Apart from loss of use, the trial court may also award damages for any deterioration in the value of the property while in the hands of the defendant.

In determining damages, the trial court concluded Red Husky was entitled to recover $10,000 as a result of deterioration. This figure was supported by evidence that the fair market value of the Kenworth was $16,000, and it was sold for only $6,000 due to deterioration that occurred while Harris held the Kenworth between September 2011 and September 2012.

The trial court did not, however, determine whether it was appropriate to award damages for loss of use during the same time period. Red Husky presented evidence at the damages hearing as to the fair rental value of the Kenworth and that the Kenworth may have been leased to another lessee had Harris not detained it.

It is entirely possible the trial court did not believe the Kenworth would have been leased even if Red Husky had possession or that the trial court believed nominal damages as to loss of use were appropriate. That said, it is clear from the trial court's order on damages that loss of use was not considered at all in the amount awarded. Therefore, we believe it is appropriate to remand to the trial court for a determination of damages for loss of use of the Kenworth during the September 2011 through September 2012 period.

We take notice of *McCready v. Harrison,* 2009 WL 62260 (S.D. Ind. 2009). In *McCready,* the court held, in a replevin action, loss of use damages must be reasonable in relation to the fair market value of the property: "Damages for the detention of certain property may conceivably under some circumstances amount to more than the value of the property itself, but on the other hand, the damages for such detention should not be permitted to become so far out of line with the value of the property as to be clearly disproportionate and oppressive." *Id.*

We recognize that *McCready* is not binding precedent, but we believe the rule it espouses is a prudent one and should be considered in determining damages in a replevin action. The amount of damages in a replevin action must be limited to a reasonable amount—both as a general matter and in relation to the fair market value of the property. And although deterioration and loss of use are separate theories of recovery, we believe the *total* damages award is subject to a requirement of reasonableness.

As a final point, we do not agree with Harris's assertion that the trial court's damage award with respect to deterioration was an abuse of discretion. Harris maintains the Lease to Purchase Agreement gave Bowne a right to possession of the Kenworth until June 5, 2012, and thus Harris should not be liable for damages for wrongful detention prior to that date. However, Bowne was in default of the lease agreement with Red Husky long before that date, and as a result, Red Husky was entitled to retake possession of the Kenworth.

We conclude the trial court did not err by awarding summary judgment in favor of Red Husky. Further, we conclude the trial court's award of damages based on deterioration of the Kenworth is supported by the evidence but remand for a determination of whether Red Husky is entitled to additional damages for loss of use.

Havens Steel Co. v. Commerce Bank, N.A.

317 B.R. 75 (Bankr. W.D. Mo. 2004) (Venters, J.)

[Havens Steel Company ("Havens" or "Debtor") is a steel construction company that provided design-build services to contractors and subcontractors, including procuring materials and designing, making, and erecting steel structures. It agreed to design steel structures for The Austin Company and to procure the necessary steel, and then make, construct, and erect the finished steel at the project site as required by a contract Austin had with a third party.

To do so, Austin obtained a loan from Commerce Bank. As part of the loan agreement, Austin gave Commerce a security interest in inventory purchased for the Austin project. During performance of the project, Havens filed for bankruptcy. At that time, some structures had been erected into the project, and of the steel that had been fabricated into structures, some remained at Havens' Ottawa, Kansas, plant while others were at the project site but stored and not yet erected into the project.

Austin sought a declaratory judgment that it was a buyer in ordinary course of all of the steel. There was no evidence that Austin knew of Commerce's security interest and so was a buyer in the ordinary course of business. However — given the different locations and status of the steel — the issue was *which* steel had been "bought" by it and "sold" by Havens. After a bench trial, the judge issued this opinion.]

There are at least five potential points at which the ascendancy to the honored role of BIOC can be fixed — upon contracting, upon identification of the goods, upon transfer of title, upon delivery, or upon acceptance of the goods — but only transfer of title and identification have received serious consideration. And, not surprisingly, the parties do not agree on which event controls. To the extent that Commerce recognizes that BIOC status is an issue here, it advocates using title as the watershed, and as mentioned above, Commerce contends that title did not pass until the steel was incorporated into the project. (Austin maintains that it took title to the steel when it paid for the steel.) Austin, on the other hand, argues that a buyer attains BIOC status when goods are identified to a contract, and the parties have stipulated that all of the steel at issue had been identified.

Commerce's position — as well as the position of the cases favoring title as the determining factor — is that a sale must have taken place in order for a purchaser to be a BIOC, and "sale" is defined in UCC Article 2 (§ 2-106) as the passing of title from the seller to the buyer for a price. Therefore, Commerce reasons, a purchaser cannot be a BIOC until it obtains title to goods. The Court declines to adopt this position for four reasons.

First, the Court believes that it misconstrues the statute. The statute does not specifically require that a sale has taken place (interposing "contract for sale" would be equally sensible), and to the extent that § 1-201 implicitly requires a sale, the reference to Article 2's definition of sale is unwarranted in light of Article 2's express de-emphasis of the importance of title, and perhaps more importantly, the existence of a specific cross-reference to Article 2 in another part of the statute. Rules of statutory construction dictate that the cross-reference to Article 2 in one section militates against a reference to Article 2 where it is not mentioned.

Second, identification makes more sense in the context of the statute. One of the requirements of § 1-201 (discussed in greater detail below) is that a BIOC either has possession of the goods or has "the right to recover the goods from the seller under Article 2." The quoted section of the statute is understood to refer to a buyer's remedy to recover goods from an insolvent seller under § 2-502 or a buyer's right to replevin or specific performance under § 2-716. A review of these provisions reveals that identification, rather than title, is key to the buyer's right to recover goods. See UCC §§ 2-502, 2-716.

Third, there is an apparent trend in the case law away from transfer of title as the point at which BIOC status is attained.

Finally, from a policy standpoint we note that using identification rather than passage of title advances Article 9's policy of protecting innocent buyers and places the risk of loss on the secured party who has the ability to protect itself by requiring various inventory controls and reports12 and who may be in a better position to absorb the loss.

Therefore, the Court concludes that a buyer attains BIOC status at the time goods are identified to a contract, and in this case, the parties stipulated that all of the steel had been identified to the Subcontract.

Having determined that Austin had reached the point in the transaction when it could qualify for BIOC status, whether Austin actually attained BIOC status with regard to particular steel turns on the final test set forth in § 1-201, which limits BIOC status to buyers who "take possession of the goods or have a right to recover the goods from the seller under Article 2." Because Austin had physical possession of the 402,305 pounds of steel (worth $154,485.12) located at the Project site, no further discussion is necessary; Austin was a BIOC with regard to that steel. Austin was also a BIOC of most of the steel at the Ottawa Plant as of the petition date, but the application of the statute with regard to that steel is not as straightforward.

At first blush, the statute appears to preclude Austin from being a BIOC of the steel in the Debtor's possession on the petition date because Austin did not have physical possession of that steel and Austin did not have the right to recover it under Article 2, inasmuch as the Subcontract was not covered by Article 2.14 However, upon comparison of the revised § 1-201 to its predecessor statute and a consideration of cases applying the predecessor statute and of the official comment to revised § 1-201, we find that a party that can establish a common law (versus an Article 2-based) "right to recover" may qualify as a BIOC, assuming the other requirements of the statute are met.

The former UCC § 1-201 did not contain the requirement that a BIOC have possession of or the right to recover the good from the seller under Article 2.15 Nor did the cases applying former § 1-201. Based on a review of the cases applying former § 1-201, the incorporation of the "right to recover" requirement into revised § 1-201 is most likely a function of the fact that BIOC litigation most often arises in the context of a replevin action brought by or against the buyer of goods in which the seller's lender has a security interest, and establishing a right to possession is a fundamental element of a replevin action. In light of the origins of the "right to recover" requirement, the Court does not believe that the embodiment of that requirement into

§ 1-201 was intended to limit recourse under the statute to only Article 2 buyers. Official Comment 9 to Revised § 1-201 further supports this interpretation, stating:

> The penultimate sentence of § 1-201(9) prevents a buyer that does not have the right to possession as against the seller from being a buyer in ordinary course of business. Concerning when a buyer obtains possessory rights, see Sections 2-502 and 2-716. However, the penultimate sentence is not intended to affect a buyer's status as a buyer in ordinary course of business in cases (such as a "drop shipment") involving delivery by the seller to a person buying from the buyer or a donee from the buyer. The requirement relates to whether as against the seller the buyer or one taking through the buyer has possessory rights.

This Comment suggests that the inclusion of the Article 2 "requirement" was for referential value rather than for purposes of restricting the statute to Article 2 contracts. Therefore, the Court believes that a party that establishes its possessory rights over goods as against the seller, without reference to Article 2, also qualifies as a BIOC under this portion of the statute. The Court finds that Austin had such a right with respect to the steel located at the Ottawa Plant and which had been identified for the Project.

There are at least two common law causes of action which would give rise to Austin's right to recover. And it is no surprise that these parallel similar rights were granted by Article 2 to purchasers of goods. Under a replevin theory (UCC § 2-716(3)), Austin had a right to recover the goods for which it had paid, and Austin had an equitable right to specific performance (UCC § 2-716(1) and (2)) for delivery of all of the steel in the Debtor's possession, although Austin would have to pay for any steel for which payment was owing.

To prevail on a replevin claim under Missouri common law, a party must establish that it is entitled to possession of the property, that the defendant has exercised unauthorized control over the property, and that the defendant deprived plaintiff of its right to possession. In the context of the hypothetical posed by § 1-201, and the artificial circumstances in which this issue has arisen, the second two requirements are inapplicable. For in the absence of the Debtor's bankruptcy filing and the Court's order creating the segregated account, Commerce likely would have exercised its right as a secured creditor and taken possession or control of the inventory. The effect of that conduct, which must be implied here, would be that Commerce would have been in possession or control of the steel to the exclusion of Austin. Therefore, all that is required here to establish a right to replevin is Austin's superior possessory right to the steel, and the Court finds that Austin has that right because it paid for the steel and, therefore (as discussed below), held title to the steel.

Based on the Stipulation and the evidence submitted by Austin, the Court found (above) that Austin paid for $447,260.08 of the steel located at the Ottawa Plant. The parties did not agree, however, as to the effect of Austin's payment for that steel. As detailed earlier, Austin contends that under the Subcontract title to the steel passed "no later than payment," whereas Commerce argues that title did not pass upon payment, but, rather, title to the steel passed upon incorporation of the steel into the final project. Although the parties spent considerable time debating this point, the Court dispatches it easily.

Under a non-Article 2 contract, title passes at the time agreed upon by the parties, and a contract is the best evidence of the parties' intent. In this case, the Subcontract provides a clear indication of the parties' intent regarding the passage of title. Paragraph 8.2.1 states: "the Subcontractor (the Debtor) warrants that title to all Work covered by an Application for Payment will pass to the Owner no later than the time of payment."

Under Missouri law, a plaintiff is entitled to specific performance as a matter of right if there is no adequate remedy at law and the contract is fair and plain. Although specific performance relating to the sale of personal property is less common than for real estate, specific performance is appropriate when the goods are unique or difficult to obtain elsewhere.

In this case, specific performance is warranted because there is no adequate remedy at law, inasmuch as the steel at issue had either been custom-ordered or fabricated to Austin's specifications, and the Court finds that the contract was fair and plain, as evidenced by the parties' stipulation to the values of the steel at issue. That some of the steel at the Ottawa Plant may not have been ready for delivery as of the petition date is not a barrier to Austin's recovery here because the values to which the parties stipulated account for the lesser value of the undelivered, partially fabricated, and fabricated steel.

In short, the Court reiterates its findings in this section that § 1-201's requirement that a BIOC have a right to recover the goods under UCC Article 2 encompasses the right to recover goods under non-Article 2 law, and Austin had a right to recover the undelivered steel for which Austin paid under either a common law replevin or specific performance theory.

Austin also fulfills § 1-201's requirement that Austin "take possession of the goods or have a right to recover the goods from the seller under Article 2," because Austin had "constructive possession" of the paid-for, undelivered steel, and the Court interprets "possession" as used in the statute to include "constructive possession."

Constructive possession is a concept, used in a variety of contexts, which recognizes that there are circumstances under which the right or ability to possess an object is strong enough to give rise to the legal effect of "possession" in the absence of actual physical possession. Accordingly, the Court finds that Austin's possessory rights, arising from Austin's payment for and title to the steel, were sufficiently strong to imbue Austin with constructive possession of the steel, in the context of § 1-201.

The Court interpretation of "possession," as used in § 1-201, to encompass constructive possession is supported by the fact that the UCC does not define possession and the suggestion in the Official Comment to § 9-313 that "possession" in the code does not require actual possession. Official Comment 3 states that agency principles should be applied to determine whether a party not in actual possession of collateral should be considered to have constructive possession of it, although the comment does not use that specific term. So, for example, a secured creditor may have a perfected security interest in certain collateral, e.g., a certificated security, for which possession is necessary to perfect, if the secured creditor's agent is in possession of the collateral. The Comment goes on to say that a court could find that the debtor may have possession of the collateral (thereby defeating perfection), if the collateral is possessed by a person in control of the debtor, even if that person holds the collateral for the ostensible benefit of the secured creditor. Thus, in light of the flexible definition of possession contemplated by the Official Comment, the Court finds it appropriate to apply that term to the situation where a seller of goods retains the goods after full payment for those goods and the transfer of title to the buyer.

Further, the decision to apply constructive possession principles here also advances the apparent goal of § 1-201 (and § 9-320), which is to provide BIOC protection to innocent buyers.

Thus, the Court finds that with regard to the steel located at the Debtor's Ottawa Plant and for which Austin had paid, Austin had constructive possession of that steel and such possession satisfies § 1-201's requirement that a BIOC have possession of the goods.

In sum, for the reasons stated above, the Court finds that Commerce's security interest in the steel identified to the Austin project as of the petition date terminated to the extent Austin qualifies as a buyer in ordinary course of business under UCC § 9-320. The Court further finds that Austin qualifies as a buyer in ordinary course of business with regard to the $154,485.12 worth of steel in Austin's possession and the $384,017.08 worth of steel for which Austin had paid, and which was located at the Debtor's Ottawa Plant. Thus, in total, Austin has an interest superior to Commerce in $538,502.20 of the $732,283.56 of steel at issue. In light of the Court's March 25, 2004, ruling, as incorporated in the May 10, 2004 Final Order, this finding translates to a requirement that Commerce turn over to Austin $538,502.20 of the money Commerce now holds in the segregated account.

Notes and Questions

1. <u>Why Was the *Red Husky* Truck Unique?</u> Ordinarily, replevin is available only if the item is in some ways unique: "Thus a 'Ford truck' is not unique, but an antique Ferrari is 'sufficiently unique' to be" subject to replevin. *John Paul Mitchell Sys. v. Quality King Distributors, Inc.,* 106 F. Supp. 2d 462 (S.D.N.Y. 2000). Consider for a moment whether the truck in *Red Husky* was "unique enough." What about a "run-of-the-mill" Ferrari?

2. <u>Juries</u>. Replevin is a legal claim and so a jury decides factual disputes. As a result, it is a legal remedy that results in specific relief, and so is unusual in American jurisprudence.

Problems

1. <u>Card Counting Plaintiff</u>. You are a judge presiding over a trial. Neal Gorsuch, the plaintiff, asserted conversion because the defendant, a casino, would not exchange $925 worth of chips he had won for cash. The jury awarded $925 in damages. Now, the casino has moved for JMOL. How should you rule and why?

2. <u>"It's Not Dead Yet."</u> Your office buys toner cartridges for its laser printers. You've noticed that the printer indicates a cartridge is out of toner, but, in fact, there's plenty of toner left. Your office spends $15,000 per year on these cartridges. Do you have a claim for conversion or trespass to chattels against the cartridge maker? Apart from fraud, any other claim?

3. <u>Billboard</u>. Your client runs an outdoor advertising company. It had an agreement with a landowner giving it an easement to place a billboard on landowner's land. Landowner sold the land to defendants, who informed the restaurant—which had an ad on the billboard—to pay them, not your client, because they owned the billboard. Litigation has been protracted but, after six years, you have obtained summary judgment that the plaintiffs converted the billboard. You are preparing for the damages hearing, and have received defendants' brief, which asserts damages should be measured by the value of the billboard at the time and place of conversion, which is almost nothing. The rents received by the plaintiffs total more than $8,000. What is your argument to use a different measure?

4. <u>Practical Problems</u>. Identify who would want to ensure the evidence is introduced and what the proper measure of damages would be if each lawyer does her job: (a) Plaintiff's dump truck has been damaged. The pre-tort fair market value was $10,000; its value after the harm was $9,000, and repair costs were $1,250. There was no loss of use as plaintiff had another dump truck available. (b) Plaintiff's car, which he used as an Uber driver, was damaged. The pre-tort fair market value was $10,000, its value after the harm was $9,000, the cost to repair was $1,250, and he had to rent a car while his was in this shop at a cost of $420 for one week. (c) While taking a test drive of a car owned by plaintiff (a new car dealer), defendant wrecked it. The wholesale cost was $27,500; the retail price was $32,500; its value after the wreck was $25,000; and repair costs were $2,000 (the dealer had to use a body shop for repairs; it did only maintenance), and after repairs its market value is $25,000.

5. <u>What Burning Smell</u>? Defendant was driving a horse trailer while transporting, per agreement, plaintiffs' valuable horses. Defendant smelled smoke but continued onward. After several cars passed with their occupants waving animatedly at him, he pulled to the side of the road and found the horse trailer engulfed in flames.

The horses died as a result. Why does the "intent" aspect required for each claim result in trespass to chattels and conversion fail? What is the additional reason why trespass to chattels fails?

6. <u>The Black Market</u>? Your client is a pharmacy, and someone broke in and stole a significant quantity of drugs. The security system used by the pharmacy and operated by the defendant failed to immediately detect the break-in, and the defendant's employees ignored the alarms that eventually did go off. The thieves sold the drugs to addicts for about $1 million, your client would have made $100,000 in net profits in ordinary sales to consumers, and the wholesale cost of the drugs was $50,000. The defendant security company has admitted liability and offered $50,000 to settle the matter prior to trial. The thieves still have the money and argue $50,000 is the measure of damages. Explain your pre-suit negotiating strategy, including arguments that $1 million is the proper measure of damages. Consider the arguments the security company's and thieves' lawyers will likely make and your responses.

7. <u>Red Card</u>? Imagine a state requires its citizens to carry a red card. Failure to carry a card can subject a citizen to criminal prosecution. Further, the state requires its citizens to show a red card to be eligible for employment and participate in certain state-funded programs. If in *Gallardo* a "red card" had been taken, and not a green card, would the plaintiff have had a claim? If you answered yes, consider that those facts describe a green card — they were not discussed in the *Gallardo* case. *See Farm Lab. Organizing Comm. v. Ohio State Hwy. Patrol,* 308 F.3d 523, 546 (6th Cir. 2002). If you answered no, why not? Can *Gallardo* be explained as just a bad decision, the failure to produce needed evidence, or even had those facts been of record, was there a sufficient basis to deny recovery in *Gallardo*?

8. <u>Unusual Enough</u>? The *Red Husky* case and the other materials show that some things are "sufficiently unique" to warrant specific relief. Suppose your client agreed to buy a car, but now the defendant refuses to sell it. It was only one of 6,000 made, and it was manufactured six years ago. What more would you want to know to bolster your argument that the car is "sufficiently unique" to warrant specific relief? What would you ask your client or seek to understand by factual research?

Chapter 7

Remedies Triggered by Harm to, or Interference with Rights in, Real Property

As with personal property and as explained in Chapter 6, if physical harm to real property occurs, its owner likely has an ordinary negligence claim. In addition, the claim of trespass to land remedies physical harm, as does the claim of nuisance. But, much like conversion and trespass to chattels do with personal property, trespass to land and nuisance permit recovery of damages for physical harm to land, but do not require it. Physical injury is sufficient to be "damage" for trespass to land and nuisance, but those claims are triggered also by harm to "the interest in the exclusive possession of land" and "the interest in the private use and enjoyment of the land." Restatement (Second) of Torts § 821D. This chapter begins with those two claims and the measure of damages for the interests each protects, then turns to the measure of damages for physical harm to real property. Next it covers when those remedies at law are inadequate. As mentioned previously, when enjoyment of land or a plaintiff's health or safety are the harm being remedied, money is less likely to be adequate than an injunction.

1. Monetary Remedies for Physical Harm to Real Property

Generally, tort damages are designed "to put an injured person in a position as nearly as possible equivalent to his position prior to the tort." *A-W Land Co., LLC v. Anadarko E&P Co. LP*, 2017 WL 4161278 (D. Colo. Sept. 20, 2017). To determine the measure of damages for physical harm to real property, the threshold issue is whether the harm is permanent or temporary. Determining whether a trespass is permanent or temporary turns on whether the costs to abate are reasonable. For example, if the defendant builds a structure on plaintiff's land, whether it is permanent or temporary turns on whether it can be removed or altered at reasonable expense. *Rosquist v. Clark*, 2018 WL 4847080 (Ct. App. Ky. Oct. 5, 2018).

If the harm is temporary—it has been or can be abated reasonably—a "plaintiff usually recovers the depreciation in the rental or use value of his property during the period in which the nuisance exists, plus any special damages. Rental value and use value are not necessarily the same thing, and some courts allow a plaintiff who actually occupies the premises to recover the 'use value,' or special value to him, but limit the recovery of the owner who does not occupy the premises to the more objective measure of rental value." *Kores v. Calo,* 15 A.3d 152 (Ct. App. Conn. 2011).

If a harm is permanent, the *A-W Land* court explained that courts generally award diminution in value unless "diminution of market value cannot be calculated or it is otherwise not appropriate," in which case "loss [is] measured by the cost of restoring the property to its original, pre-trespass condition." "The choice between these two primary measures is dictated by several factors, such as whether the owners' intended use of the property requires its restoration, and whether the injury to the land is repairable." *Id.* As that court explained, however, the temporary and permanent distinction also indicates the duration of loss-of-use damages:

> Diminution in value or cost of repair are concerned with providing relief based on the state of the property once the trespass has *concluded*. To address losses that occur *during* the trespass, Colorado law also authorizes an award of damages to reflect the landowner's loss of use of the land. Loss of use reflects a loss of the owner's ability to receive rent or the loss of an ability to carry on an economic enterprise on the property, measured in terms of a hypothetical loss of rental value.

Likewise, an award of future diminished value for temporary harm is improper, as the *Orange Cnty. Water Dist. v. Unocal Corp.,* 2016 WL 11201024 (C.D. Cal. Nov. 3, 2016) court explained:

> If a nuisance can be abated, once it is removed, there will no longer be a nuisance to depreciate the value of the property. For example, airport noise, once removed, will no longer deflate the value of affected property. Therefore, the paradigmatic judicial resolution of continuing nuisance is ordering defendants to abate the nuisance and compensating plaintiffs for loss of use of their property. Obviously, recovering both a judicial order for abatement of the nuisance (or the necessary funds to remediate) *and* prospective damages for decreased property value in continuing nuisance cases would constitute double recovery, an impermissible windfall.

Courts take different approaches as to whether, and at what point, the cost to restore land due to permanent harm becomes unreasonable and so constitutes waste. Generally, restoration costs can exceed the diminution in value caused by a permanent harm, but must not be "disproportionate to the diminution in value." *Ga. Northeastern Railroad, Inc. v. Lusk,* 277 Ga. 245 (2003). If so, the plaintiff will be awarded only diminution damage, which—if the plaintiff sells the land—makes it whole. However, if the plaintiff wants to keep but restore the property to its former condition and restoration costs exceed diminution in value, the plaintiff will be "forced to partially pay out of pocket to effect such repairs and therefore are not truly made whole." *Brooks v. City of Huntington,* 768 S.E.2d 97 (W. Va. 2014).

Forcing a plaintiff to sell land to be made whole led to the "reason personal" exception that permits an award of cost to repair that exceeds diminution in value. *Id.*

Martin v. Bank of America

2018 WL 3614171 (N.J. Super. App. Div. July 30, 2018) (Per Curiam)

[Plaintiffs sued defendant Bank of America alleging its negligence in grading its land to a higher level caused flooding to plaintiffs' land and a one-time water infiltration of their basement. After a six-week trial, the jury found that defendant's trespass had diminished the value of plaintiffs' home. The parties had agreed the judge would determine the measure of damages, and he awarded $25,000 as diminution in value, not the costs to restore the property, which would have been about $750,000. Plaintiffs appealed.]

Pertinent to the judge's determination, plaintiffs presented evidence that restoration costs, including raising the grade of the house, pool, deck, patio and grounds three feet to the level of the abutting section III properties, totaled approximately $750,000. They presented no evidence as to the diminution in value or the cost of waterproofing the basement.

Conversely, BOA adduced proof that the diminution in value of the property totaled $25,000, representing $475,000 for the value of house without water infiltration, less $450,000 for the value of house as adjusted by what appeared to be a one-time water infiltration. BOA also presented evidence that it would cost $28,000 to completely waterproof the basement.

At the close of all evidence the judge issued a lengthy oral opinion, observing:

> the restoration costs put forth by plaintiffs are not reasonable. This is not a unique bit of property. Plaintiffs have said that they simply want to live in Howell Township because of the school system. They have not identified anything unique about this particular property such that it would not constitute unreasonable economic waste to invest $750,000 into a house that is apparently worth $450,000.

> Considering as I must the overall limitation of reasonableness, the court finds that diminution in value better reflects the plaintiffs' actual loss, rather than the restoration costs.

In so ruling, the judge found that plaintiffs were seeking more than restoration costs, i.e., "a change in the topography of their property. They're asking that soil be added to the property that wasn't there. They're asking that the house be put in a position it never was in before. They're asking for new vegetation" Further, "They are asking for a very different house than the one that they purchased."

We review de novo the trial court's legal determination as to the appropriate measure of damages for plaintiffs' common law claims. The appropriate measure of damages for injury done to land is a complex subject and courts have responded to such claims in a great variety of ways depending upon the evidence in the particular case.

In almost every case concerning damages to real property, one of two measures is employed. Both measures have a wide sphere of application, and the court's selection of one test or the other is basically an assessment of which is more likely to afford full and *reasonable* compensation.

The first measure, described as the most commonly mentioned in the opinions, is diminution of value. Under this measure the plaintiff is entitled to recover the difference in the value of his property immediately before and immediately after the injury to it, that is, the amount his property has diminished in value as a result of the injury. The diminution-of-market-value measure of damages is generally applicable in cases in which the harm to land is permanent. This measure has been applied in similar cases involving damage caused by excessive excavation on an adjoining lot, *McGuire v. Grant*, 25 N.J.L. 356 (1856) (measure of damages "is not what it will cost to restore the lot to its former situation, or to build a wall to support it, but what is the lot diminished in value by reason of the acts of the defendant"), and involving damage caused by the overflow of water resulting from the negligent maintenance of drainage pipes and ditches, *Kita v. Borough of Lindenwold*, 305 N.J. Super. 43 (App. Div. 1997).

The second measure, the replacement-cost or restoration-cost measure, awards the plaintiff the reasonable cost of restoring or repairing the damage. This measure is generally applied where the damage is temporary. For example, restoration-cost was applied in a faulty construction case involving damage from the defective installation of glass panels.

Further, the Restatement (Second) of Torts section 929 affords a plaintiff the option to elect the measure of damages as follows:

> (1) If one is entitled to a judgment for harm to land resulting from a past invasion and not amounting to a total destruction of value, the damages include compensation for
>
> (a) the difference between the value of the land before the harm and the value after the harm, *or at his election in an appropriate case,* the cost of restoration that has been or may be reasonably incurred. . . .

Although the Restatement does not explicitly define "appropriate case," comment b to subsection 1(a) of section 929 of the Restatement (emph. added) explains:

> Restoration: Even in the absence of value arising from personal use, the reasonable cost of replacing the land in its original position is ordinarily allowable as the measure of recovery. Thus if a ditch is wrongfully dug upon the land of another, the other normally is entitled to damages measured by the expense of filling the ditch, if he wishes it filled. *If, however, the cost of replacing the land in its original condition is disproportionate to the diminution in the value of the land caused by the trespass, unless there is a reason personal to the owner for restoring the original condition, damages are measured only by the difference between the value of the land before and after the harm.* This

7 · REMEDIES FOR HARM TO OR INTERFERENCE WITH RIGHTS IN LAND 243

would be true, for example, if in trying the effect of explosives, a person were to create large pits upon the comparatively worthless land of another.

> On the other hand, if a building *such as a homestead is used for a purpose personal to the owner, the damages ordinarily include an amount for repairs, even though this might be greater than the entire value of the building.* So, when a garden has been maintained in a city in connection with a dwelling house, the owner is entitled to recover the expense of putting the garden in its original condition even though the market value of the premises has not been decreased by the defendant's invasion.

In selecting between these two measures of quantifying property damages, our courts have recognized that "it can be unfair to use the restoration-cost method when 'the cost of repairs vastly exceeds the probable market value of the property. *See also* Model Jury Charge (Civil), 8.40, "Trespass to Real Property" (2018) ("The measure of damages to be awarded to a plaintiff entitled to a verdict is the difference between the fair market value of his/her property before and after the trespass by the defendant.").

For example, in *Correa*, 196 N.J. Super. at 277, the plaintiffs, who purchased a home from the defendant for $25,000, brought an action to recover damages allegedly caused by defendant's deliberate concealment of latent defects. The jury awarded the plaintiffs $33,000 in compensatory damages, reflecting the cost to raise and straighten the house. We reversed the damage award, finding that "the cost of repairs approach should not be employed where it would result in unreasonable economic waste." *Id*. We reasoned as follows:

> By virtue of the age of the building and its present condition, the cost of reconstruction is not an appropriate measure of plaintiff's loss. This is so because the cost of repairs vastly exceeds the contract price and the probable market value of the property. It would be anomalous to compel defendant to provide plaintiff with what essentially amounts to a totally refurbished home, which would be a result far exceeding what is necessary to make plaintiff whole. Rather, the diminution in value caused by defendant's deceit better reflects plaintiff's actual loss and satisfies the reasonable expectations of the parties.

Nonetheless, in some circumstances, reasonable repair costs that exceed the diminution of the property's value are appropriate such as where the property owner wishes to use the property rather than sell it. As plaintiffs argue, restoration costs may be appropriate in instances where the land is used as a residence, or where the property had a peculiar value to the owner.

However, contrary to plaintiffs' argument, restoration costs are not a mandatory measure of damages in "homestead" cases. The cardinal principles are flexibility of approach and full compensation to the owner, within the overall limitation of reasonableness.

Here, although plaintiffs had a "reason personal" for seeking to restore the property, as the trial judge properly found, completion of the repairs would result in unreasonable economic waste. As the trial judge aptly recognized, plaintiffs' restoration costs of $750,000 to regrade the property and raise the house, would exceed what is necessary to make plaintiffs whole. Indeed, restoration would completely change the condition of the property. Additionally, the cost of restoration greatly exceeds the $25,000 diminution in the market value of the property especially where, as here, there was evidence in the record that plaintiffs could completely waterproof their basement for $28,000.

Moreover, the property flooded years before plaintiffs purchased it in 2005. Thus, awarding plaintiffs full restoration costs of $750,000 would be unreasonable and would not represent their actual loss. Accordingly, diminution in value was the appropriate measure of damages because it was more likely to afford full and *reasonable* compensation.

Notes and Questions

1. <u>Personal Reason</u>? Why would a court recognize a personal reason exception? Why didn't the plaintiffs in the principal case fit within it? Does the holding of *Wiesrum v. Harder,* 316 P.3d 557 (Alaska 2013) — holding that restoration costs that exceed diminution in value "may be awarded only to the extent that restoration costs are objectively reasonable in light of the property owner's reason personal and the diminution in value of the property" — explain it? *See Brooks v. City of Huntington,* 234 W. Va. 607 (2014) ("most courts which have permitted recovery of cost of repair in excess of pre-injury market value still require the award to be objectively reasonable in light of the diminution in value and/or pre-injury market value.").

2. <u>Bright-Line Personal Reason</u>? In *Brooks v. City of Huntington,* 768 S.E.2d 97 (W. Va. 2014), the court stated "it will seldom be the case that [a homeowner] will not be able to pay lip service to the 'reason personal' exception, thereby entitling him to cost of repair even if he had no intention of repairing the property." But if a homeowner cannot predict whether he will recover more than diminution in value, what leverage does the defendant gain in settling disputes? Consider whether the *Brooks* court's approach is better:

> We therefore hold that when residential real property is damaged, the owner may recover the reasonable cost of repairing it even if the costs exceed its fair market value before the damage. The owner may also recover the related expenses stemming from the injury, annoyance, inconvenience, and aggravation, and loss of use during the repair period. If the damage cannot be repaired, then the owner may recover the fair market value of the property before it was damaged, plus the related expenses stemming from the injury, annoyance, inconvenience, and aggravation, and loss of use during the time he has been deprived of his property.
>
> That is not to say, however, that there are no limitations on such an award. Damages must be assessed in the manner most appropriate to

compensate the injured party for the loss sustained in the particular case. Like all compensatory damages awards, an award of cost of repair for injury to residential real property is still subject to review for reasonableness and excessiveness. Citing need for practical good sense, most courts which have permitted recovery of cost of repair in excess of pre-injury market value, still require the award to be objectively reasonable in light of the diminution in value and/or pre-injury market value.

Recognizing that damages grossly in excess of a property's pre-damage market value smacks uncomfortably of economic waste, to accommodate our policy concerns of full compensation, any such award must be subject to reasonable limitations. Therefore, to the extent that damages for cost of repair to residential real property exceed the fair market value of the property before it was damaged, damages awarded for cost of repair must be reasonable in relation to its fair market value before it was damaged. The measure of reasonable cost of repair damages is an issue for the trier of fact, but may be found to be unreasonable as a matter of law if unreasonably disproportionate to the fair market value of the property prior to the damage.

3. <u>Proving Values</u>. The owner may, with proper foundation, provide an opinion, as *Nat. Gas Pipeline Co. of Am. v. Justiss*, 397 S.W.3d 150 (Tex. 2012) explained:

Many federal courts recognize that, notwithstanding the Property Owner Rule, an owner's conclusory or speculative testimony will not support a judgment. The United States Court of Appeals for the Fifth Circuit has held that although "in general, an owner is competent to give his opinion on the value of his property such testimony cannot be based on naked conjecture or solely speculative factors." *King v. Ames*, 179 F.3d 370 (5th Cir. 1999). If an owner's estimate is speculative, the owner's testimony may be of such minimal probative force to warrant a judge's refusal even to submit the issue to the jury. The Tenth Circuit has stated "the owner's qualification to testify does not change the 'market value' concept and permit him to substitute a 'value to me' standard for the accepted rule, or to establish a value based entirely upon speculation." *United States v. Sowards*, 370 F.2d 87 (10th Cir. 1966). Thus, a landowner's testimony as to the value of his property is not always sufficient testimony on which a verdict can be based. Instead, there must be a basis for the landowner's valuation, and when the landowner's own testimony shows that his valuation has no probative value, the district court may determine that the landowner's testimony alone is insufficient to support a jury verdict.

4. <u>Stigma</u>. Courts use "stigma damage" to refer to different concepts. What if Parcel A is contaminated with cancer-causing chemicals and Parcel B is not, but its fair market value is reduced because it is adjacent to Parcel A? Can Parcel B's owner sue the polluter because of this "stigma?" Some courts use "stigma" to refer to the diminution in value that will affect Parcel A after it is "restored"—the cancer-causing agent can be removed or reduced below harmful levels, but even afterward

a "stigma" reduces Parcel A's value. This is diminution in value of a parcel that had been harmed by defendant. The following explores this concept.

Muncie v. Wiesemann

548 S.W.3d 877 (Ky. 2018) (Cunningham, J.)

[The Muncies' land had been damaged by heating oil leaking from a storage tank on adjoining land owned by Wiesemann. Wiesemann had partially settled the Muncies' trespass claim for $60,000, the cost to remediate the damage, but the Muncies demanded "stigma" damages. The courts below held that the Muncies had been made whole, and they appealed.]

Wiesemann argues that, because the $60,000 remediation was accepted by the Muncies in the partial settlement agreement for their actual damages, the Muncies cannot separately seek stigma damages for the diminution in value of their property. She argues that awarding the Muncies stigma damages after the remediation damages were settled would result in a "double recovery" for the Muncies. For support, Wiesemann cites *Ellison v. R & B Contracting, Inc.*, 32 S.W.3d 66 (Ky. 2000), for the proposition that when property is damaged, the injured party may seek either the cost of repair of the loss of value of the property, but not both.

In order to recover stigma damages, our case law requires that plaintiffs must have suffered actual property damage. Further, if injured parties receive repair costs that make them whole, then they cannot recover stigma damages that would compensate them above the diminution in their property's value. *Id.* ("the amount by which the injury to the property diminishes its total value operates as an upper limit on any damage recovery.") But, if remediation damages for repair costs is insufficient to make the injured party whole, then a recovery for stigma damages up to the monetary value of the diminution may be proper.

Stated differently, the damages recoverable for an actual injury to real property are equal to the sum of the costs of repair *and* the difference in fair market value of the property before the injury and after it has been repaired. If there is a difference in fair market value after the physical injury has been repaired, then that is the appropriate measure of stigma damages.

For instance, the Court of Appeals has recognized that the *Ellison* rule assumes a claimant has the ability to repair the property damage. *Mountain Water Dist. v. Smith,* 314 S.W.3d 312 (Ky. App. 2010). "The effect of *Ellison* is to prevent a claimant from seeking cost of repair damages that exceed the diminution in fair market value the claimants are seeking diminution in value damages, in part, because they claim they were unable to repair the damage, and may present evidence to that effect in the form of an appraisal." *Id.*

Correspondingly, the dissenting judge on the court in the case at bar cited to persuasive authority from Utah's highest court for an accurate description of stigma damages:

Stigma damages compensate for loss to the property's market value resulting from the long-term negative perception of the property in excess of any
recovery obtained for the temporary injury itself. Were this residual loss
due to stigma not compensated, the plaintiff's property would be permanently deprived of significant value without compensation.

Walker Drug Co. v. La Sal Oil Co., 972 P.2d 1238 (Utah 1998).

We concur with that definition of stigma damages and adopt the reasoning in
Smith. Physical injury to property is often repairable, but stigma damages are meant
to assess the value of and redress injury which is not able to be repaired. Stigma
damages measure the amount by which a real property's value is diminished in
excess of repair costs. Once the oil is removed and the environmental response team
departs, stigma is what remains—by its nature, it cannot be repaired.

The courts below were correct that stigma damages are a measure of damages
stemming from the actual injury to property. However, if remediation damages
are settled but a claim on the stigma damages resulting from the actual injury is
reserved, then the injured party may be awarded stigma damages regardless of the
partial settlement on remediation.

Unquestionably, the devil is in the details for these types of cases. We can only
provide broad principles of law. The method for the computation of damages is easily stated but can be difficult to understand. They can also be difficult to prove.
Hopefully, the following will clarify the matter.

When property is damaged by trespass, the degree of the damage is determined
at the moment such injury is completed. The recovery shall be the difference in
value of the property before the injury occurred, and the value immediately after it
is completed. The after-value shall take into account stigma damages, if any. Damages will also include the cost of any repair or remediation.

Here, there was no factual discovery, as the case was dismissed as a matter of
law on a motion for summary judgment. The question whether stigma damages
exist is entirely a matter of proof. An appraisal or other acceptable evidence may
demonstrate stigma damages as a measurable diminution in the fair market value of
the Muncies' property resulting from the stigma of the oil contamination and subsequent environmental response. Those damages may be recovered in addition to
the settled repair costs. Therefore, this case should be remanded for a factual determination as to whether the Muncies were fully compensated for the diminution in
fair market value of their property by the $60,000 partial settlement for repair costs.

Notes and Questions

1. <u>Remand</u>? On remand in *Wiesemann,* what will the jury decide? Imagine you
are the plaintiffs' lawyer seeking to show that a "stigma" has reduced the value of
their land. What evidence will you look for? Can you think of scientific evidence
that might matter? Comparative real estate sales? What sort of evidence will the
defense look for? In sum, how do you prove property carries a "stigma" despite

being fully "restored"? Can you think of an analogy to personal property—something that, though repaired, is worth less than something that has never been damaged? Is this "real" damage or caused by perception? If perception, should someone who owns a lot next to the Wiesemanns' be able to recover stigma damages because his land has been polluted? What about the owner of a lot a block away?

2. <u>Diminished Value with Temporary Harm</u>? Is it consistent with *Brooks v. City of Huntington*, 768 S.E.2d 97 (W. Va. 2014), that a homeowner can recover the cost to repair, even if it is disproportionate to the pre-injury fair market value of the property and residual diminished value? That court stated:

> The rationale behind permitting this variation from the general rule is that "residual" diminution in value is not duplicative of the cost of repair, *i.e.* the property still has lost value even after it is repaired.

> In *Wade v. S.J. Groves & Sons Co.*, 283 Pa.Super. 464 (1981), the court permitted recovery for both cost of repairs and residual diminution in value where a permanent change in a drainage field above the plaintiffs' property created a depreciation in the subject property despite the fact that repairs had corrected "most of the problem" caused by negligent filling of an adjacent gully. The court noted that plaintiffs' expert testified that "a prospective buyer who was informed of the history of the property would pay less for the property than he would otherwise have been willing to pay, due to the possibility, albeit remote, of another slide and because of the necessity of regularly maintaining the drainage pipes, ditches and catch basins in repair over the years." *Id.* The court found no error in the "allowance of damages for the cost of repairs in addition to the reduction in the fair market value of the property where the injury to such property is partially reparable and partially permanent." *Id.*

> Moreover, in *Hartzell v. Justus Co., Inc.*, 693 F.2d 770 (8th Cir. 1982), the court permitted recovery of both cost of repair as well as alleged residual depreciation in market value: "There was no double recovery here: the verdict was not for the cost of repair plus the *entire* decrease in market value, but rather for cost of repair plus the decrease in market value that still existed after all the repairs had been completed." *See John Thurmond & Assoc., Inc. v. Kennedy*, 284 Ga. 469 (2008) ("Although unusual, it may sometimes be appropriate, in order to make the injured party whole, to award a combination of both measures of damages. In such cases, notwithstanding remedial measures undertaken by the injured party, there remains a diminution in value of the property, and an award of only the costs of remedying the defects will not fully compensate the injured party."); *Morris v. Ciborowski*, 113 N.H. 563 (1973) (upholding award of diminution in value where such award "did not include but was in addition thereto" cost of repair).

Certainly a scenario where damaged residential real property maintains a residual loss of value after repairs are effected is conceivable. In the instant case, there was expert testimony that the neighborhood had "died" and that even if no further flooding occurred, the market in the neighborhood would not recover. Such residual loss of value is closely akin to so-called "stigma damages" which are common in environmental contamination cases. The Court can perceive of no reason why such damages, to the extent they are not duplicative of any other element of damage, should not be recoverable by an injured plaintiff. Therefore, where the owner of residential real property which is damaged can establish that the pre-damage fair market value of the residential real property cannot be fully restored by repairs and that a permanent, appreciable residual diminution in value will exist even after such repairs are made, then the owner may recover both the cost of repair and for such remaining diminution in value.

However, we admonish the lower courts to assess a claim for this newly-recognized element of residential property damage with guarded scrutiny before submitting it to the jury. It is only in the extraordinary case that repair of damaged residential real property will not fully restore its prior market value. Mere cosmetic damage, speculative decreased future market value, or damage which can be readily and fully remediated are an insufficient foundation for a claim of residual diminution in value. The trial court must ensure that, particularly where cost of repair exceeds the property's fair market value before the damage, any claim for residual diminution in value is truly and reasonably necessary to achieve the cardinal objective of making the plaintiff whole.

3. <u>Diminished Value of Properties Adjacent to the Physically Damaged Property</u>. As shown above, a landowner whose property has been physically harmed by, for example, a defendant's contaminants can recover damages, and those damages can include the cost of repair and the difference in value of the property before the harm and after repair (the "diminished value" or "stigma damages"). Consider the owner of land next door, one who cannot show contamination has yet crossed onto her land but whose property is worth less because of the "stigma" of the adjoining contaminated parcel. Can that landowner recover?

Courts have generally rejected negligence claims based on contamination to an adjoining landowner. *Donavan v. Saint-Gobain Performance Plastics Corp.*, 2017 WL 3887904 (N.D. N.Y. Sept. 5, 2017) (landowner could recover diminution in value only by alleging actual contamination of his groundwater, not just nearby wells); *cf. Chestnut v. AVX Corp.*, 776 S.E.2d 82 (S.C. 2015) (leaving undecided whether a negligence claim based on contamination requires actual intrusion onto land, merely stigma damages, or a modified approach).

In *Smith,* plaintiffs' land adjoined a uranium enrichment facility, from which an underground plume of chemicals was seeping onto plaintiffs' land. The levels were not a health threat, but they alleged the chemicals' presence diminished the value of their land. The court stated that if there is "actual injury to the real estate," then damages for diminution in value were potentially recoverable. The court explained the line between mere "stigma" damages—or "harm to the reputation of the realty"—and "an actual injury or harm":

> We know that mere damage to the reputation of realty does not entitle one to recovery, as that injury is more imaginary than real. Likewise, the mere presence of contaminants may only damage the property's reputation and not its use. The Court of Appeals set the bar for a compensable harm in negligent trespass cases to fall at the point where the contaminants cause a health hazard. Relying on our rationale in a products liability case with a question as to "harm to the person," the court reasoned that the mere presence of PCBs itself was not an injury, that some physical harm needed to be shown.

> This Court is not as forgiving in identifying actual injury to real property, whether by intentional or negligent trespass. When the intrusion is through imperceptible particles not visible to the naked eye, there may still be an actual injury. In *Commonwealth ex rel. Dep't of Natural Res. v. Stephens,* 539 S.W.2d 303 (Ky. 1976), a takings case, the Court recognized damages for interfering with a property's use where no physical injury existed to the property (the owner was prohibited from certain uses of his property). And in nuisance cases, the court allowed damages for interfering with the use and enjoyment of property without a physical intrusion. Property owners are not required to prove contamination that is an actual or verifiable *health* risk, nor are they required to wait until government action is taken. An intrusion (or encroachment) which is an unreasonable interference with the property owner's possessory *use* of his/her property is sufficient evidence of an actual injury (or damage to the property) to award actual damages.

> When the parcel's groundwater is contaminated, whether by imperceptible particles or visible particles, to the extent that it cannot be used for consumption by humans, animals, or crops, there is an actual injury. When ponds and streams have to have signs posted to prevent swimming, fishing, drinking, or other otherwise normal uses, there is an unreasonable interference with one's use and enjoyment. The amount of harm, if any, to the individual parcels, and the corresponding measure of actual or compensatory damages will depend upon the proof introduced at trial—an issue of fact. To the extent that the property owners prove actual or compensatory damages for the harm (the cost of restoring the property to the pre-trespass condition), the amount by which the injury to the property diminishes its total value operates as an upper limit on any damage recovery. Thus, the diminution in the property's value due to an intentional trespass is a recognized measure of damages after, or if, an actual injury has been found.

The two dissenting judges dissented for very different reasons. Judge Cunningham wrote:

> Once an intentional trespass is shown, the diminution in the property value should, in and of itself, be sufficient to award damages. I do not believe that actual harm — as the majority defines such harm — is required for damages to be awarded in intentional trespass.
>
> In fact liability is imposed for intentional trespass when there is an intrusion, even when it is harmless. Liability is imposed for negligent trespass only when there has been harm to the property. This suggests that no harm is required in intentional trespass, and that once that is established damages are computed. If nominal damages are authorized for intentional trespass, then certainly actual damages should be.
>
> Here, the totally innocent and complaining property owners have had their property invaded by unseen particles to the extent that the trespassing party has provided an independent water source. If the presence of this intrusion reduces the value of the property, then those landowners should be compensated.
>
> The past Kentucky cases would indicate that a person subject to intentional trespass is entitled to nominal damages only when other damages cannot be proven. They certainly infer that when other damages are proven they should be recoverable. I do not agree with the majority opinion that in order to have a right of recovery of compensatory damages under Kentucky law, the property owner must show proof of actual harm or injury. It doesn't seem logical to allow someone to receive nominal damages — which are unspecific and nonexistent — and not afford compensatory damages which are real and discernible.
>
> It seems critical to this writer not to become bogged down in semantics in debating the terms "harm" and "damages." When this case is distilled to its simplest form, a clear and cogent need for judicial redress surfaces. There exists an innocent property owner. There is a willful and intentional trespasser upon that property. The trespass causes a change in the property. Because of that change, a free and willing buyer is reluctant to pay the same money as he or she would have paid without the change. There is harm. There is damage.
>
> Neither should we be moved by the law's aversion to compensating for a mere "stigma" upon real estate. The trespass here is real. It is not a stigma. It is neither imagined by the owner or the general public. The decrease in market value to that trespass is not irrational, fantastical, or rooted in emotion. The PCB's may be unseen, but they are not without manifest results. Property buyers are as reasonable in their reluctance to purchase a potential need for future litigation as they would be of accepting a cloud upon the title.

I do not accept the prediction that such a holding would have the potential of opening the proverbial floodgates of litigation. Common experience of the industrial age has taught us that those entities capable of perpetuating such trespasses are also more than capable of taking care of themselves. Unless the diminution of the value of their property is recoverable in our courts upon a mere showing of intentional trespass, individual homeowners cannot.

Judge Minton dissented for the opposite reason:

Kentucky should join other states in requiring proof of actual harm to sustain a viable action for the intentional trespass of imperceptible particles. As stated by the Supreme Court of Washington, "no useful purpose would be served by sanctioning actions in trespass by every landowner within a hundred miles of a manufacturing plant. Manufacturers would be harassed and the litigious few would cause the escalation of costs to the detriment of the many." *Bradley v. American Smelting and Refining Co.*, 104 Wash.2d 677 (1985).

I would require proof that the contaminants constitute a scientifically demonstrable health or safety hazard at the levels shown to be present on the property. Basing a determination of actual harm on demonstrable scientific evidence instead of on a subjective fear would better preserve our longstanding rule that denies recovery for a diminution in property values based solely on a stigma.

When parcels adjoin each other, one set of issues arises. Where the pollution or contaminant is airborne, or if there are multiple potential sources, similar issues and causes-in-fact arise. *See In re Tennessee Valley Authority Ash Spill Litig.*, 805 F. Supp. 2d at 483 (concluding that "a trespass claim under Tennessee law may be premised upon the entry onto property of intangible particles and that there is no requirement of actual and substantial harm," but "plaintiffs must show causation, that particles from the ash spill, either tangible or intangible, entered plaintiffs' properties and would not have done so" but for the defendant's acts).

2. Monetary Remedies for Entering, or Interfering with Interests in, Land

Trespass and nuisance share common ground. First, because of the harm required for each claim, the plaintiff must own, or have a lawful right to occupy, the property at the time of injury. *See Conn. Comm. Bank v. Massey Bros. Excavating, LLC,* 2016 WL 8468069 (Conn. Sup. Ct. Dec. 15, 2016) (no trespass because defendant dumped soil on property before plaintiff bought it). Second, all states permit recovery for intentional trespass or nuisance. *In re Resource Tech. Corp.*, 2010 WL 5158113 (N.D. Ill. Dec. 10, 2010), *aff'd,* 662 F.3d 472 (7th Cir. 2011).

But then divisions begin. First, most states adhere to the traditional dividing line between trespass and nuisance, which limits trespass to physical (tangible) invasion of plaintiff's property and allows nuisance to remedy substantially interference with the use and enjoyment of plaintiff's property not caused by a physical entry. Second, while all states recognize intentional trespass or nuisance, some states permit claims based upon negligence.

A. Monetary Remedies for Entering Another's Land

I. The Elements of Trespass — Including the Required Harm

"The essential elements of a modern common law trespass claim are: (1) an intentional entry or holdover (2) by the defendant or a thing; (3) without consent or legal right." *Davis v. Westphal, 405 P.3d* 73 (Mont. 2017) (citing Restatement (Second) of Torts §§ 158 and 163 (1965)). The presence can be of a person or a thing, and it can take the form of an unauthorized entry, exceeding the scope of permitted use or access, placing something on the plaintiff's land, or failing to remove something from the plaintiff's land as required. *Id.*

All states recognize intentional trespass. However, and like its counterparts in the context of personal property — conversion and trespass to chattels — intentional trespass does not require proof the defendant had "intended to enter or remain upon property owned or controlled by another," but instead "only requires proof that the tortfeasor intentionally entered or remained, or caused a third party or thing to enter or remain, upon the property of another regardless of the tortfeasor's knowledge, lack of knowledge, or good faith mistake as to actual property ownership or right." *Id.* As *Anduze v. Leader,* 2015 WL 5158942 (V.I. Super. Aug. 31, 2015) explained:

> Across all jurisdictions, there is no deviation from the principle that a defendant will be liable for trespass if the defendant intentionally enters the plaintiff's land while the plaintiff was in possession of that land. A defendant also commits a trespass by removing something from the plaintiff's land that the defendant was not entitled to remove, or by placing something on the plaintiff's land that the defendant was not entitled to place. While the plaintiff's consent provides a defendant with a defense to a trespass claim, a defendant's mistaken belief that he or she owned the property upon which the trespass was committed provides no such defense. Some jurisdictions have expanded upon the common-law definition of trespass by, for example, defining the distance above and below the surface of a plaintiff's property in which a trespass can occur, by distinguishing between an innocent trespasser and an intentional trespasser, or by explaining the difference between claims for intentional trespass and negligent trespass.

Some states recognize "negligent trespass" as a distinct claim, while others, as explained below, take into account the defendant's culpability in assessing whether mental anguish damages are recoverable. Section 165 of the Restatement defines negligent trespass as follows:

> One who recklessly or negligently, or as a result of an abnormally danger-ous activity, enters land in the possession of another or causes a thing or third person so to enter is subject to liability to the possessor if, but only if, his presence or the presence of the thing or the third person upon the land causes harm to the land, to the possessor, or to a thing or a third person in whose security the possessor has a legally protected interest.

The court in *Alleyne v. Diageo USVI, Inc.,* 63 V.I. 384 (2015), applied Section 165 to a motion to dismiss a claim by landowners against a rum distillery for causing "rum fungus" to develop on their land because of the distillery's airborne emissions:

> Plaintiffs allege in their Complaint that "as a direct and proximate result of the Defendants' reckless or negligent conduct as alleged herein, rum fun-gus and ethanol from Defendants' St. Croix alcoholic beverage production operations entered upon, accumulated upon, and physically invaded Plain-tiffs' real and personal property causing harm." Plaintiffs likewise reallege several of the allegations from their negligence claim in their negligent tres-pass section. As previously explained, Plaintiffs have alleged that a "thing" under the definition of trespass has invaded their land. Therefore, Plaintiffs have alleged facts and allegations plausible enough to sufficiently state a claim and to survive Defendants' motion to dismiss under Federal Rule of Procedure 12(b)(6).

To consider if there is much difference between "intent" and "negligence" in this context, consider *Merrick v. Diageao Ams. Supply Co.,* 5 F. Supp. 3d 865 (W.D. Ky. 2014). *Merrick* was a Kentucky case brought against the same defendant in *Alleyne,* but for causing particles to land on plaintiffs' property that had created "whisky fungus." Kentucky law required physical harm for negligent, but not intentional, trespass. However, the court stated that intentional trespass "need not be accompa-nied by actual knowledge of wrongdoing" and that plaintiffs' allegation that defen-dant's ethanol emissions were causing fungus was sufficient.

Democracy Partners, LLC v. Project Veritas Action Fund

285 F. Supp. 3d 109 (D.D.C. 2018) (Huvelle, J.)

[Democracy Partners, LLC ("Plaintiff") provided political consulting services to Democratic party candidates. It had private offices with 24-hour security and electronic pass cards were required for access. Several individuals and a conserva-tive political entity, Project Veritas Action Fund ("the PV defendants") allegedly arranged it so Plaintiff would hire one of the individual defendants, Allison Maass, as an intern by creating a fake biography for her and helping her to hide her iden-tity and references. Defendants' real alleged goal was to have Ms. Maass gain access to Plaintiff's offices and learn confidential information by attending meetings, receiving email, and having personal conversations with Plaintiff's employees and clients and then share that information with conservative groups. Plaintiff learned of this by seeing social media postings by Ms. Maass and sued for trespass and other claims. Defendants moved to dismiss the trespass claim.]

The elements of a claim for trespass are "(i) an unauthorized entry (ii) onto the plaintiff's property (iii) that interferes with the plaintiff's possessory interest." *Council on American-Islamic Relations Action Network, Inc. v. Gaubatz*, 793 F. Supp.2d 311 (D.D.C. 2011) ("*CAIR 2011*").

The PV defendants argue that the complaint fails to adequate allege an unauthorized entry because Maass "had consent to be physically present in the office," and "consent to enter land, even if procured through a misrepresentation, bars a later trespass claim." To support their argument, defendants rely entirely on case law from other jurisdictions, indicating in a footnote that "based upon the undersigned counsel's research, neither the D.C. Court of Appeals nor the D.C. Circuit has ruled on this question of trespass law."

Although the PV defendants are correct that there is no *controlling* precedent, the Court agrees with Judge Kollar-Kotelly's decision in *CAIR 2011*, which concluded that under District of Columbia law, "consent given upon fraudulent misrepresentations will not always defeat a claim for trespass." *CAIR 2011*, 793 F.Supp.2d at 345. For example, "consent *may* be ineffective if induced by a substantial mistake concerning the nature of the invasion of the owner's interest or the extent of the harm to be expected from it and the mistake is known to the other or induced by the other's misrepresentation." *Id.* In addition, although defendants are correct that there are cases in other jurisdictions where courts have rejected trespass claims against defendants who misrepresented their identities in order to conduct surreptitious filming on business properties, a key factor in those cases is that the recordings took place in publicly accessible places.

The complaint also alleges that Maass exceeded the scope of any consent by secretly recording conversations in Democracy Partners' office to turn over to the PV defendants. As a general matter, a condition or restricted consent to enter land creates a privilege to do so only in so far as the condition or restriction is complied with. Therefore, on-site employees may exceed the scope of their invitation to access, and so not be rightfully on, the employer's property at a place or time forbidden by their employer. As plaintiffs' "consent" to Maass' entry does not vitiate the allegation of unauthorized entry, the Court will not dismiss the trespass claim on that basis.

The PV defendants next argue that the complaint fails to adequately allege "interference with the plaintiff's possessory interest," because Maass "did not disrupt the Plaintiffs' "exclusive possession" of the property or damage the physical property in any way. However, under District of Columbia law all that is required to satisfy the third element of trespass is an allegation that the defendant "intentionally entered the plaintiff's residence and thereby interfered with the plaintiff's possessory interest." *See, e.g., Robinson v. Farley*, 264 F.Supp.3d 154 (D.D.C. 2017). As the court in *Robinson* observed in refusing to dismiss a trespass claim against the District of

Columbia, "the District makes no attempt to explain how the degree of the alleged intrusion into the plaintiff's possessory interest has any bearing on the validity of a trespass claim, and well-settled authority indicates that it has none." *Id.*; *see also* Restatement (Second) of Torts § 158 cmt. h (1965) ("A trespass by way of an entry by the actor in person may be a mere momentary invasion."). The complaint adequately alleges this element of a trespass claim.

The PV defendants' final argument is that the complaint fails to allege facts to support any actual damages proximately caused by Maass' alleged trespass. However, even if that were true, it would not be a reason to dismiss the trespass claim, because a claim of trespass can proceed even if there are no actual damages.

Notes and Questions

1. Why a Remedy? Why award damages to plaintiffs such as in the principal case, who suffer no real "damage" and other claims likely redress any misuse of information or harm? What interest is protected by trespass that is not protected by those claims? What if the defendant pours a cup of water onto plaintiff's Arizona land in summer, and it quickly evaporates? If the defendant's crop-dusting permits pesticide to float onto plaintiff's land? If defendant's smokestacks emit cancer-causing chemicals that land on plaintiff's property, but are invisible and may never cause any harm at all?

2. Negligent Trespass. Is this claim necessary? If a defendant negligently causes physical injury by entering plaintiff's land, why wouldn't a negligence claim ordinarily suffice?

II. The Measure of Damages for Trespass

"Because the legal harm is the interference with another's right to exclusive possession of property, an unauthorized tangible presence on the property of another constitutes a trespass regardless of whether the intrusion caused any other harm." *Davis v. Westphal*, 405 P.3d 73 (Mont. 2017). Nominal damages can be recovered "without regard for the shortness of the period of the interference or the absence of pecuniary harm." *Smith v. Carbide & Chems. Corp.*, 226 S.W.3d 52 (Ky. 2007).

Boring v. Google Inc.

362 F. App'x 273 (3d Cir. Jan. 28, 2010) (Jordan, J.)

[Plaintiffs sued Google, alleging trespass and other claims based upon Google's car driving on their private road while taking pictures for "Street View" on Google Maps. The district court granted Google's motion to dismiss the trespass claim for failing to state a claim upon which relief could be granted. Plaintiffs appealed.]

The District Court dismissed the Borings' trespass claim, holding that trespass was not the proximate cause of any compensatory damages sought in the complaint and that, while nominal damages are generally available in a trespass claim, the Borings did not seek nominal damages in their complaint. While the District Court's evident skepticism about the claim may be understandable, its decision to dismiss it under Rule 12(b)(6) was erroneous. *no, it's an intentional tort*

Trespass is a strict liability tort, both exceptionally simple and exceptionally rigorous. Under Pennsylvania law, it is defined as an unprivileged, intentional intrusion upon land in possession of another. Though claiming not to have done so, it appears that the District Court effectively made damages an element of the claim, and that is problematic, since "one who intentionally enters land in the possession of another is subject to liability to the possessor for a trespass, although his presence on the land causes no harm to the land, its possessor, or to any thing or person in whose security the possessor has a legally protected interest." Restatement (Second) Torts § 163.

Here, the Borings have alleged that Google entered upon their property without permission. If proven, that is a trespass, pure and simple. There is no requirement in Pennsylvania law that damages be pled.[7] It was thus improper to dismiss for failure to state a claim. Of course, it may well be that, when it comes to proving damages from the alleged trespass, the Borings are left to collect one dollar and whatever sense of vindication that may bring, but that is for another day. For now, it is enough to note that they bear the burden of proving that the trespass was the legal cause, *i.e.*, a substantial factor in bringing about actual harm or damage, if they want more than a dollar.

Brown v. Smith

920 A.2d 18 (Md. Ct. App. 2007) (Adkins, J.)

[Every day for 1,670 days, to get to and from his property, the defendant trespassed by driving on the plaintiff's private road across plaintiff's land. The trial court awarded $5 per day as nominal damages. The court of appeals reversed in this opinion.]

Although each trespass is a separate legal injury that could theoretically merit a "per trespass" measure of damages, we have not been directed to any Maryland case that permitted such an award as nominal damages. Nor have we found a reported Maryland case of nominal damages that significantly exceed the one cent to one dollar amounts commonly awarded as "nominal" damages.

Thus, recovery of nominal damages is important not for the amount of the award, but for the fact of the award. Nominal damages are not compensation for loss or injury, but rather recognition of a violation of rights. In the absence of authority limiting an award of nominal damages, the prevailing view appears to be that, although the amount of nominal damages is not limited to one dollar, the nature of the award compels that the amount be minimal.

---

7. While it may be true that for some claims, the failure to seek nominal damages waives a claim for nominal damages, that is not the case with trespass claims.

Thus, even though the sum awarded as nominal damages may vary somewhat according to circumstances, nevertheless, the award may be deemed excessive if it cannot reasonably be considered "minimal" in the circumstances of the case. *See, e.g., Chesapeake & Potomac Tel. Co. v. Clay,* 194 F.2d 888 (D.C. Cir. 1952) (reducing award of $500 to $1); *Pierson v. Brooks,* 115 Idaho 529 (Ct. App. 1989) ("the sum of $2,500 is more than nominal"); *Keesling v. City of Seattle,* 52 Wash.2d 247 (1958) ($1 per day damage award for trespass of power transmission line six inches onto plaintiff's property was substantial and unsupported compensatory award, not nominal damages).

To affirm a substantial damage award that is categorized by the trial court as "nominal damages" would invite uncertainty for trial judges and juries regarding what are "nominal damages" and how they differ from compensatory damages. When a court or jury makes an actual damages award, it must focus on the nature and extent of the injury to the plaintiff, applying well defined legal principles about how that injury may translate into a dollar amount. When a court or jury makes a nominal damages award, however, it need not focus on the injury to the plaintiff, but merely on recognition of the right. If we were to allow a judge or jury to award a substantial sum as so-called "nominal damages," which are neither based on the injury nor subject to the legal principles governing damage awards, we would be creating a new class of damages that are neither compensatory nor punitive. With such an uncertain foundation, any award of this nature poses an intolerable risk of an arbitrary result.

Although a plaintiff in a trespass case, unlike in most cases, need not prove the exact amount of injury in order to secure compensatory damages, a nominal damages award should not substitute for or be confused with a compensatory damage award. A court or jury well might give a different award when focusing on the injury (compensatory damages) than when focusing on the violation (nominal damages). We believe it necessary that the two categories of awards remain separate and distinct, even in a trespass case. The $8,350 damage award in this case simply cannot be justified as nominal.

Notes and Questions

1. Is "Harmless Trespass" a Misnomer? What harm *does* trespass require and remedy? Along those lines, the *Smith* court applied the majority rule governing "nominal damages" for trespass. Do you believe it is adequate? Conversely, why permit a claim where the remedy is so small?

2. Nominal Damages Isn't the Goal. Plaintiffs' lawyers assert trespass claims for nominal damages for rational reasons. For example, if two adjoining landowners dispute a boundary, one may sue for trespass and the other may seek a declaratory judgment that it has acquired title to the disputed parcel through adverse possession. In that circumstance, if the trespass claim succeeds, the party asserting it will obtain a judgment establishing that it has the right to prevent the party from entering the land, in addition to nominal damages. Trespass can also provide a basis to

award damages for statutory claims: some state law claims permit recovery of damages if, for example, a party commits an unlawful act. Trespass can be that unlawful act. In addition, some states permit an award of attorneys' fees for a successful trespass claim. Of course, plaintiffs asserting trespass typically seek damages for other harms caused by trespass. Two forms of harm often caused directly by a trespass are annoyance and inconvenience to the landowner and harm to the real property (including buildings and structures, as well as crops, trees, and the like).

3. Culpability as a Factor? The court in *Coinmach Corp. v. Aspenwood Apt. Corp.*, 417 S.W.3d 909 (Tex. 2013), addressed the measure of damages where a landlord ejected a trespassing tenant. It noted "we have rarely addressed trespass damages in detail," and explained:

> Thus, one who invades or trespasses upon the property rights of another, while acting in the good faith and honest belief that he had the lawful and legal right to do so is regarded as an innocent trespasser and liable only for the actual damages sustained. In calculating the actual damages sustained, the measure of damages in a trespass case is the sum necessary to make the victim whole, no more, no less. When the trespass causes a temporary injury, the amount necessary to place the plaintiff in the position it would have been in but for the trespass generally includes the cost to repair any damage to the property, loss of use of the property, and loss of any expected profits from the use of the property.

> By contrast, tenants who knowingly and intentionally trespass, or who do so maliciously, may be liable for additional forms of damages. For example, Texas courts have required a showing of deliberate and willful trespass and actual property damage before awarding damages for emotional distress or mental anguish, thereby limiting the potential for such "excessive liability." *Pargas of Longview, Inc. v. Jones*, 573 S.W.2d 571 (Ct. App. Tex. 1978) ("Actual damages resulting from mental distress may be recovered, as a separate and independent element, *when caused by a deliberate and willful trespass* in which *actual damage* to plaintiff's property is sustained."

Given this, and the discussion in the introduction to trespass, what differences exist between intentional and negligent trespass? Finally, why does the defendant's intent make mental anguish a more likely consequence of trespass, or why does physical harm, if done negligently, do so?

B. Monetary Remedies for Nuisance

I. The Elements of Nuisance — Including the Required Harm

Expressing a sentiment that many courts have, one court recently began a case by stating: "This is a nuisance case, but that does not tell you much." *Crosstex N. Tex. Pipeline, L.P. v. Gardiner*, 505 S.W.2d 580 (Tex. 2016). A nuisance is "a substantial, unreasonable, interference with another's interest in the private use and enjoyment of their property." *Alleyne v. Diageo USVI, Inc.,* 63 V.I. 384 (V.I. 2015).

Pestey v. Cushman

788 A.2d 496 (Conn. 2002) (Vertefeuille, J.)

[Plaintiffs' home was across a rural highway from defendants, who in 1991 expanded their dairy operations to include a 42,000-square-foot structure and manure pit. While at first plaintiffs noticed only odors typical with a livestock operation, over time they grew more pungent and the smell changed to a sharp, burnt smell. In 1997, defendants installed a system intended to convert manure into energy, and the smell become even more acrid, smelling of sulfur and sewage. This was caused by defendant's system being undersized and overloaded. At times, the smell awoke the plaintiffs from their sleep and forced them to keep their windows closed.

Plaintiffs asserted a negligence-based nuisance claim. The jury returned a verdict for the plaintiffs for $100,000, finding defendants were negligent, which was required by a state statute protecting farming operations from nuisance claims without proof of negligence. The court awarded both diminution in value and damages for interfering with use and enjoyment of property. Defendants appealed, asserting error in the jury instructions.]

In order to analyze properly the defendants' claim, we must reexamine and clarify the elements that a plaintiff must prove to prevail on a claim for damages in a common-law private nuisance cause of action. Specifically, we must clarify two sources of confusion. First, we must distinguish the concept of unreasonable interference with the use and enjoyment of property from the concept of an unreasonable use of property. Second, we must reaffirm the distinction between private and public nuisance actions.

A private nuisance is a nontrespassory invasion of another's interest in the private use and enjoyment of land. The law of private nuisance springs from the general principle that it is the duty of every person to make a reasonable use of his own property so as to occasion no unnecessary damage or annoyance to his neighbor. The essence of a private nuisance is an interference with the use and enjoyment of land.

The defendants' claim is based on the principle of private nuisance law that, in determining unreasonableness, "consideration must be given not only to the interests of the person harmed but also to the interests of the actor and to the interests of the community as a whole." 4 Restatement (Second) § 826, comment (c). "Determining unreasonableness is essentially a weighing process, involving a comparative evaluation of conflicting interests." *Id.* Unreasonableness cannot be determined in the abstract, but, rather, must be judged under the circumstances of the particular case.

In the present case, the trial court instructed the jury with respect to the unreasonableness element of the nuisance claim in the following manner: "You must also ask yourselves whether the defendants' use of their property was reasonable.

A use which is permitted or even required by law and which does not violate local land use restrictions may nonetheless be unreasonable and create a common-law nuisance. You must consider and weigh the location of the defendants' dairy farm, the size of the farm, the manner in which they operate the farm, including their handling and maintenance of the manure, the free stall barn, the milking parlors and the anaerobic manure digester and associated equipment and any other circumstance which you find proven which indicates whether the defendants were making a reasonable use of their property." The court stated further: "The question is not whether the plaintiffs or the defendants would regard the condition as unreasonable, but whether reasonable persons generally looking at the whole situation impartially and objectively would consider it to be reasonable."

As the charge indicates, the trial court instructed the jury to consider a multiplicity of factors in determining the unreasonableness element. The defendants' argument that the instruction did not adequately instruct the jury to consider the defendants' interests assumes that the factors set forth by the trial court only regard the plaintiffs' interests. Such an assumption is unwarranted.

Although the trial court's jury charge was proper this area of the law has been prone to confusion, and our case law has been no exception. Our nuisance jurisprudence has become muddled and is in need of clarification. Only after we clarify this area of the law can we determine fully whether the jury charge in this case was proper.

"There is perhaps no more impenetrable jungle in the entire law than that which surrounds the word 'nuisance.'" W. Prosser & W. Keeton, § 86, p. 616. This court has stated often that a plaintiff must prove four elements to succeed in a nuisance cause of action: (1) the condition complained of had a natural tendency to create danger and inflict injury upon person or property; (2) the danger created was a continuing one; (3) the use of the land was unreasonable or unlawful; and (4) the existence of the nuisance was the proximate cause of the plaintiffs' injuries and damages. These elements developed through a long line of cases that can be described best as public nuisance cases.

Despite its grounding in public nuisance law, this four factor analysis has since been applied without distinction to both public and private nuisance causes of action. Although there are some similarities between a public and a private nuisance, the two causes of action are distinct. Indeed, Professors Prosser and Keeton in their treatise on the law of torts have stated: "The two have almost nothing in common, except that each causes inconvenience to someone, and it would have been fortunate if they had been called from the beginning by different names." W. Prosser & W. Keeton § 86. Public nuisance law is concerned with the interference with a public right, and cases in this realm typically involve conduct that allegedly interferes with the public health and safety. See, e.g., Beckwith v. Stratford, 129 Conn. 506 (1942) (plaintiff brought nuisance action against defendant municipality for injuries sustained in fall allegedly caused by defectively constructed sidewalk).

Private nuisance law, on the other hand, is concerned with conduct that interferes with an individual's private right to the use and enjoyment of his or her land. Showing the existence of a condition detrimental to the public safety, or, as the first two elements of the four factor analysis discussed previously require, showing that the condition complained of had a natural tendency to create a continuing danger, is often irrelevant to a private nuisance claim. In light of the fundamental differences between these two distinct causes of action, we conclude that further attempts to employ the four part test discussed previously herein in the assessment of private nuisance causes of action would be imprudent; private nuisance claims simply do not fit comfortably within the same analytical rubric as public nuisance claims. We must restate, therefore, the elements that a plaintiff must prove to prevail on a claim for damages in a common-law private nuisance action.

In prescribing these specific elements, we look to the leading authorities in the field of common-law private nuisance for guidance. According to the Restatement (Second) of Torts, a plaintiff must prove that: (1) there was an invasion of the plaintiff's use and enjoyment of his or her property; (2) the defendant's conduct was the proximate cause of the invasion; and (3) the invasion was either intentional and unreasonable, or unintentional and the defendant's conduct was negligent or reckless. 4 Restatement (Second) §822. Although the language used in this third element does not make the point clearly, under this test, showing unreasonableness is an essential element of a private nuisance cause of action based on negligence or recklessness. Professors Prosser and Keeton define the plaintiff's burden in a similar manner. According to their view, a plaintiff in a private nuisance action must demonstrate that: (1) the defendant acted with the intent of interfering with the plaintiff's use and enjoyment of his or her property; (2) the interference with the use and enjoyment of the land was of the kind intended; (3) the interference was substantial; and (4) the interference was unreasonable. W. Prosser & W. Keeton, §87. In the context of a private nuisance, they define a defendant's intent as meaning merely that "the defendant has created or continued the condition causing the interference with full knowledge that the harm to the plaintiff's interests are occurring or are substantially certain to follow." Id.

This requirement of unreasonableness, a part of the third element in the test set forth in the Restatement (Second) and the fourth element in the test enunciated by Professors Prosser and Keeton, often has been stated, not in terms of whether the interference was unreasonable, but, rather, in terms of whether the defendant's conduct was unreasonable. In its charge to the jury, the trial court in the present case framed the inquiry in such a manner.

Although similar, "the two concepts-unreasonable interference and unreasonable conduct—are not at all identical." W. Prosser & W. Keeton, §87. "Confusion has resulted from the fact that the interference with the plaintiff's use of his property can be unreasonable even when the defendant's conduct is reasonable. Courts have often found the existence of a nuisance on the basis of unreasonable use when what was meant is that the interference was unreasonable, i.e., it was unreasonable for the defendant to act as he did without paying for the harm that was knowingly inflicted on the plaintiff. Thus, an industrial enterprise who properly locates a cement plant or a coal-burning electric generator, who exercises utmost care in the utilization of known scientific techniques for minimizing the harm from the emission of noxious smoke, dust and gas and who is serving society well by engaging in the activity may yet be required to pay for the inevitable harm caused to neighbors." *Id.*, §88. As this example amply demonstrates, while an unreasonable use and an unreasonable interference often coexist, the two concepts are not equivalent, and it is possible to prove that a defendant's use of his property, while reasonable, nonetheless constitutes a common-law private nuisance because it unreasonably interferes with the use of property by another person.

On the basis of our reexamination of our case law and upon our review of private nuisance law as described by the leading authorities, we adopt the basic principles of §822 of the Restatement (Second) of Torts and conclude that in order to recover damages in a common-law private nuisance cause of action, a plaintiff must show that the defendant's conduct was the proximate cause of an unreasonable interference with the plaintiff's use and enjoyment of his or her property. The interference may be either intentional or the result of the defendant's negligence. Whether the interference is unreasonable depends upon a balancing of the interests involved under the circumstances of each individual case. In balancing the interests, the fact finder must take into consideration all relevant factors, including the nature of both the interfering use and the use and enjoyment invaded, the nature, extent and duration of the interference, the suitability for the locality of both the interfering conduct and the particular use and enjoyment invaded, whether the defendant is taking all feasible precautions to avoid any unnecessary interference with the plaintiff's use and enjoyment of his or her property, and any other factors that the fact finder deems relevant to the question of whether the interference is unreasonable. No one factor should dominate this balancing of interests; all relevant factors must be considered in determining whether the interference is unreasonable.

The determination of whether the interference is unreasonable should be made in light of the fact that some level of interference is inherent in modern society. There are few, if any, places remaining where an individual may rest assured that he will be able to use and enjoy his property free from all interference. Accordingly, the interference must be substantial to be unreasonable.

Ultimately, the question of reasonableness is whether the interference is beyond that which the plaintiff should bear, under all of the circumstances of the particular case, without being compensated. With these standards in mind, we turn to the present case.

In reaching its verdict, the jury completed a set of interrogatories provided by the trial court. Each interrogatory asked the jury whether the plaintiffs had proven a specific element of the private nuisance claim, and the jury answered each interrogatory affirmatively. The first interrogatory asked: "Did the plaintiffs prove that the defendants' dairy farm produced odors which unreasonably interfered with the plaintiffs' enjoyment of their property?" This interrogatory correctly captured the crux of a common-law private nuisance cause of action for damages, i.e., whether the defendants' conduct unreasonably interfered with the plaintiffs' use and enjoyment of their property. It correctly stated that the focus in such a cause of action is on the reasonableness of the interference and not on the use that is causing the interference. In light of this conclusion, the fourth interrogatory, which involved the unreasonable use element that is at issue in this case, was superfluous. The fourth interrogatory asked: "Did the plaintiffs prove the defendants' use of their property is either unreasonable or unlawful?" As our previous discussion herein demonstrates, a plaintiff seeking damages in a common-law private nuisance cause of action is not required to prove that the defendant's conduct was unreasonable. Rather, the plaintiff must show that the interference with his or her property was unreasonable. The fourth interrogatory, therefore, in effect, required the plaintiffs to prove an additional, nonessential element to prevail on their claim. We conclude that the jury interrogatories and the jury charge, considered together, properly informed the jury of the necessary elements of a common-law private nuisance cause of action for damages and provided the jury with adequate guidance with which to reach its verdict. Accordingly, the trial court's jury charge was proper under the law as clarified herein.

Notes and Questions

1. <u>Nuisance Per Se.</u> In *Nottke v Norfolk So. Ry. Co.,* 264 F. Supp. 3d 859 (N.D. Ohio 2017), the court explained "absolute nuisance," called "nuisance per se" in many states. It arises when a defendant intended conduct that causes substantial interference with the plaintiff's land regardless of the precautions used by the defendant:

> Absolute nuisance, on the other hand, does not require proof of negligence. Where the harm and resulting damage are the necessary consequences of just what the defendant is doing, or is incident to the activity itself or the manner in which it is conducted, the law of negligence has no application and the rule of absolute liability applies. The primary meaning of nuisance does not involve the element of negligence as one of its essential factors. One who emits noxious fumes or gases day by day in the running of his factory may be liable to his neighbor though he has taken all available precautions.

2. <u>Public Nuisance.</u> As a general rule, only the government has standing to enjoin a "public nuisance" and no individual can obtain damages. A public nuisance affects each citizen more or less equally. For example, contamination of a city's groundwater is a public nuisance. However, "even a public nuisance can permit a private suit for damages when an individual or smaller group 'sustains a special loss' that is different in kind from the harm suffered by the rest of the community. In this way, a private wrong may be distinguished from a common injury to the public, and a private right of action is restored." *Benoit v. St.-Gobain Performance Plastics Corp.,* 2017 WL 4331032 (N.D.N.Y. Aug. 16, 2017).

3. <u>Interference with Use and Enjoyment</u>. An easement holder cannot sue for trespass but can assert nuisance. *E.g., Simonson v. Ropp*, 2016 WL 551214 (Sup. Ct. Conn. Jan. 15, 2016) (holding defendant could assert trespass against neighbor for damage done by trucks leaving an easement on a shared driveway, but plaintiff could only state nuisance claim against plaintiff for placing objects in driveway to make construction more difficult). *See Boyne v. Town of Glastonbury*, 110 Conn. App. 591 (2008) (future interest holder could assert nuisance claim). Similarly, a plaintiff whose use and enjoyment of property is unaffected by a defendant's activities cannot assert nuisance even if the plaintiff establishes diminution in value. *Myrick v. Peck Elec.*, 204 Vt. 128 (2017).

II. *The Measure of Damages for Nuisance*

McGinnis v. Northland Ready Mix, Inc.

344 S.W.3d 804 (Ct. App. Mo. 2011) (Smart, J.)

[Plaintiff, Rhonda McGinnis, owned two pieces of property that adjoined the family-run cement plant owned by defendant Northland Ready Mix, Inc.. One property included a home that she rented to tenants, and the other was her small repair shop. Plaintiff alleged that water containing sand, gravel, and cement overflowed from NRM's plant, depositing sediment onto the properties and causing her to be unable to mow the lawn, preventing her and her tenants from driving onto the property. She sued for nuisance. The jury awarded $50,000 for temporary nuisance due to the water and dust and noise. The trial court directed a verdict on the trespass claim. Defendant appealed.]

The measure of damages for temporary nuisance is the decrease in the property's rental or useful value while the nuisance exists and incidents of damage, including, for example, loss of comfort and health. The recovery is limited to the damage actually sustained to the commencement of the suit, but not for prospective injury. Compensatory damages can also be granted for inconvenience and discomfort caused by the nuisance. In computing compensatory damages, there is no precise formula or bright line test to determine non-economic losses. Each case must be considered on its own facts, with the ultimate test being whether the award fairly and reasonably compensates the plaintiff for the injuries sustained.

NRM contends the court erred in allowing McGinnis's expert appraiser, Robin Marx, to testify regarding the reduction in the "market value" of rent obtainable for each of McGinnis's properties during the period of the nuisance because market value is the proper measure of damages for permanent nuisance, not temporary.

Here, Marx's testimony to the jury was limited to the amount of market value reduction in *rental value* of McGinnis's properties through the time of trial, consistent with the standard for temporary nuisance damages. He testified that because of the nuisance created by NRM, the rental value of McGinnis's Schell Road property suffered a total lost rental value of $42,720, and the 69 Highway property had a total lost rental value of $50,033, based on the "market's perception" of what fair rental value would have been. Marx did not take into account any future losses and based his calculations off of comparable properties, and, to accommodate for rent fluctuations, Marx averaged rent figures based on the averages for the past fifteen years of what the rent would have been. Because Marx's valuations only took into account the nuisance's effect on the *decrease in rental or useable value* of McGinnis's properties, and not a permanent market devaluation in the property as a whole.

NRM also argues McGinnis failed to show actual damage because Marx testified only as to market-based damages and did not take into account McGinnis's lack of demonstrable rental losses suffered during the 178-month duration of the nuisance. While damage is one element required for a claim of nuisance, NRM cites no authority that in order to determine damage for a temporary nuisance, the market-based rental loss must be offset by the actual rental loss shown to have been suffered by the owner claiming nuisance; and we find none. In fact, to prove damage from a temporary nuisance requires only a showing of the depreciation of the rental or usable value of the property during the continuance of the injury. To hold otherwise would prevent an owner who was occupying his own property encumbered by a temporary nuisance from ever proving damage because there is technically no rental loss, an absurd result. The jury could reasonably have believed Marx's testimony that McGinnis's property suffered a market-based rental loss, even though she had tenants during a majority of the 178 months of the nuisance, demonstrating damage to McGinnis.

In any event, in a temporary nuisance case, not all damages need be financial in character. McGinnis could be awarded compensatory damages for discomfort and inconvenience caused by the nuisance. McGinnis testified that she had to deal with a constantly saturated and muddy backyard and was forced to clean up the sand, sediment, and other debris washed onto her property from NRM's concrete plant. It was within the province of the jury to consider McGinnis's testimony and award any appropriate damages.

The jury awarded McGinnis a $50,000 verdict. The jury was not required to explain its calculation of damages in this case, and we cannot determine how the jury decided on its verdict. Nor can we or anyone else decide how much, if any, was to compensate McGinnis for inconvenience and discomfort or decrease in rental value. This court gives great deference to a jury's decision regarding the appropriate amount of damages. Here, McGinnis presented evidence suggesting damages of more than $178,000. Sufficient evidence was presented to support an award of $50,000.

Notes and Questions

1. Why Not Trespass? In *McGinnis*, why did the trial court direct a verdict to the defendant on plaintiff's trespass claim? If it had succeeded, would the damages be the same?

2. <u>Public or Private</u>? Why was the nuisance in *McGinnis* not public? Or was it, but the plaintiff had standing because of the nature of her injury? Consider this passage from *Walker v. Williams,* 2016 WL 6555886 (Del. Ch. Nov. 4, 2016), *aff'd sub nom. Kane v. Willliams,* 166 A.3d 943 (Del. 2017), addressing whether a plaintiff, trying to close an auto repair shop, could rely on code and zoning violations:

> Consistent with Plaintiffs' view of the law, the owner of a beach house on Slaughter Beach would have standing to sue to enforce the adequacy of the circuit breakers in a barn in Delmar, or a deficiency in the scantlings of the roof rafters of a corn crib in Woodenhawk. Such a reading would allow precisely the kind of officious intermeddling, nuisance and strike suits that the standing requirement is intended to prevent. While the examples above are reductios ad absurdum, they are not so far off the mark here. I am sure that Plaintiffs' complaints about traffic, noise and odor caused by Williams' hobby are sincere (despite the fact that I found these intrusions fail to constitute a nuisance-in-fact). Just as clearly, however, the Plaintiffs have no interest in the structural integrity of Williams' Pole Building; their arguments with respect to Williams' compliance with the Building Code — discovered, presumably, during the pendency of this action — are simply a cudgel with which to beat the Defendant unrelated to any injury-in-fact the Plaintiffs might have suffered.

Some statutes limit nuisance. *E.g., Toftoy v. Rosenwinkel,* 983 N.E.2d 463 (Ill. 2013) (Farm Nuisance Suit Act precluded homeowner's suit).

3. <u>Objective Market Value</u>? Even though nuisance protects an owner's use and enjoyment, courts require proof of market value loss through competent evidence "to impose an objective criteria upon an otherwise rather subjective tort." *Brockman v. Barton Brands, Ltd.,* 2009 WL 4252914 (W.D. Ky. Nov. 25, 2009). Do you agree?

C. Annoyance and Inconvenience Damages for Trespass or Nuisance

Under the Restatement, both trespass and nuisance each permit recovery of damages for the harm of annoyance and inconvenience. "As an example, damages can be awarded for the time and effort spent cleaning up a flooded basement, for the lingering smell, and for the loss of hobby activities that would otherwise have been conducted in that basement." *A-W Land Co., LLC v. Anadarko E&P Co. LP,* 2017 WL 4161278 (D. Colo. Sept. 20, 2017).

Most courts recognize this form of harm as distinct from "mental anguish" associated with claims such as infliction of emotional distress. *See id.* ("'Pure' emotional distress damages, however, that are not tied to any physical injury or intrusion on the land are not recoverable."). The court in *Babb v. Lee County Landfill SC, LLC,* 747 S.E.2d 468 (S.C. 2013), emphasized its nature and distinguished it from mental distress:

"Interest in use and enjoyment" also comprehends the pleasure, comfort and enjoyment that a person normally derives from the occupancy of land. Freedom from discomfort and annoyance while using lands is often as important to a person as freedom from physical interruption with his use or freedom from detrimental change in the physical condition of the land itself. This interest in freedom from annoyance and discomfort in the use of land is to be distinguished from the interest in freedom from emotional distress. The latter is purely an interest of personality and receives limited legal protection, whereas the former is essentially an interest in the usability of land.

If recoverable, the amount is left to a jury's enlightened conscience. *Bord v. Hillman*, 780 S.E.2d 725 (Ct. App. Ga. 2015).

Babb v. Lee County Landfill SC, LLC

747 S.E.2d 468 (S.C. 2013) (Hearn, J.)

[A federal court certified the question of whether South Carolina law permits recovery of damages for loss of enjoyment or use apart from economic losses caused by a temporary trespass or nuisance. The following is part of the South Carolina Supreme Court's response.]

To the extent South Carolina's trespass and nuisance case law discusses annoyance, discomfort, interference with the enjoyment of property, loss of enjoyment of life, or interference with mental tranquility, those cases speak in terms of injury to one's property interest in the use and enjoyment of property.

Thus, from their inception through to today, trespass and nuisance have been actions limited to the protection of one's property interests. They have never served to protect against harms to one's person. To permit plaintiffs to recover for annoyance and discomfort to their person as a component of trespass or nuisance damages, as opposed to as related to their property interests, would be to unhinge trespass and nuisance from the traditional property locus and transform them into personal injury causes of action. Not only would it represent a drastic expansion of trespass and nuisance beyond the realm of property, it would also represent a fundamental change in our tort law jurisprudence which does not permit recovery for sheer annoyance and discomfort. *See Dooley v. Richland Mem'l Hosp.*, 283 S.C. 372 (1984) (declining to recognize a negligent infliction of emotional distress cause of action and holding that damages for emotional distress are generally not recoverable in a negligence action absent some physical manifestation). In short, allowing recovery for personal annoyance and discomfort under the guise of trespass and nuisance would be the stealth recognition of an entirely new tort.

The damages recoverable for trespass and nuisance being strictly limited to damages to one's property interests, the only proper measure of them is the value of the property. A well-known principle of property law is that property consists of a bundle of rights. The value of a piece of property is the value of all of the rights one obtains through ownership of the property. Thus, included in the value of property are the rights of exclusive possession and use and enjoyment protected by the trespass and nuisance causes of action respectively. To the extent those interests are harmed by a temporary trespass or nuisance, the harm would be reflected in the lost rental value of the property.

In other words, lost rental value includes the annoyance and discomfort experienced as the result of a temporary trespass or nuisance. The lost rental value of the property is the difference between the rental value absent the trespass or nuisance and the rental value with the trespass or nuisance. The rental value with the trespass or nuisance present would be less, in part, because a hypothetical renter would have to suffer the annoyance and discomfort of the nuisance or trespass. Thus, the lost rental value measures the monetary value of the harm to the property interest. Furthermore, because lost rental value includes damages caused by annoyance or discomfort, to permit a plaintiff to recover both the lost rental value plus an additional sum for annoyance and discomfort would be to permit a double recovery.

We have already recognized the lost rental value of property as the measure of and limit on damages for a temporary harm to property in our decision in *Gray v. So. Facilities, Inc.,* 256 S.C. 558 (1971). There, the plaintiff asserted a negligence claim against the defendant for pumping gasoline into a creek behind the plaintiff's home which later ignited, setting the creek ablaze. At trial, the defendant was granted an involuntary nonsuit on the ground the plaintiff had not sustained any actual or physical damages. Reviewing the grant of involuntary nonsuit, the Court stated:

> The general rule is that in case of an injury of a permanent nature to real property, by the pollution of a stream, the proper measure of damages is the diminution of the market value by reason of that injury, or in other words, the difference between the value of the land before the injury and its value after the injury. Where the pollution of a stream results in a temporary or nonpermanent injury to real property, the injured landowner can recover the depreciation in the rental or usable value of the property caused by the pollution.

Id. at 569. Thus, while not explicitly using the terms trespass or nuisance, the Court held that lost rental value is the proper measure of damages for a temporary harm to real property, which would include a temporary trespass or nuisance.

We extend the holding in *Gray* to cover trespass and nuisance claims for the reasons previously stated. Accordingly the lost rental value of property is the sole measure of temporary trespass and nuisance damages.

Notes and Questions

1. A New Tort? The *Babb* court stated that allowing recovery "would be the stealth recognition of an entirely new tort." Some courts take a similar view. One stated: "We have not been pointed to any case that explains that 'inconvenience and discomfort' damages are entirely separate and distinct from damages assessed

for the loss of 'use and enjoyment' of real property or for loss of quality of life, or that there is some dramatic difference between these claims that turns on entirely separate jury instructions." *Ely v. Cabot Oil & Gas Corp.*, 2015 WL 6406391 (M.D. Pa. Oct. 21, 2015).

Other courts disagree. For example, the plaintiffs in *Johnson v. Paynesville Farmers Union Coop. Oil Co.*, 817 N.W.2d 693 (Minn. 2012), were organic farmers who alleged pesticides drifting from defendants' operations were a nuisance. The court held that because they alleged it caused additional weed growth (and cost to control them), record-keeping burdens, and physical ailments, damages for inconvenience and discomfort were recoverable. Other courts allow damages for this type of harm as a separate component or do so only upon proof of some greater degree of fault or misconduct. *See Kass v. Cooley Dickinson Hosp., Inc.*, 2006 WL 1555942 (Mass. Land Ct. June 8, 2006) ("trespass damages can be measured by the property owner's loss of use and enjoyment of his/her property when (1) the fair rental value is not calculable or appropriate, or (2) when there is evidence of emotional distress that is not reflected in the loss of fair rental value."), *aff'd*, 875 N.E.2d 548 (Ct. App. Mass. 2007); *Vieira Enterp., Inc. v. McCoy*, 8 Cal. App. 5th 1057 (Ct. App. Cal. 2017) (discomfort and annoyance damages available for trespass plaintiff who arrived home to see defendant had physically obstructed plaintiff's driveway and then threatened him); *Land Baron Inv. v. Bonnie Springs Family, LP*, 356 P.3d 511 (Nev. 2015) ("damages for nuisance include personal inconvenience, discomfort, annoyance, anguish, or sickness" and awarding them where defendants had in the middle of the night caused anxiety, lost sleep, and upset).

2. <u>Entities and Vacant Landowners</u>. Courts split on whether only an occupant can recover damages for this form of harm. The Restatement precludes a landowner who does not occupy the land from recovering annoyance damages "except as they may have affected the rental value of his land." Restatement (Second) of Torts §929 (1979). Adopting this view, one court explained why a landlord who owned but rented out a home destroyed by a mudslide caused by the defendant could not recover these damages:

> Annoyance and discomfort damages are intended to compensate a plaintiff for the loss of his or her peaceful occupation and enjoyment of the property. As the court explained in *Webster v. Boone*, 992 P.2d 1183 (Colo. App. 1999), We recognize that annoyance and discomfort by their very nature include a mental or emotional component, and that some dictionary definitions of these terms include the concept of distress. Nevertheless, the 'annoyance and discomfort' for which damages may be recovered on nuisance and trespass claims generally refers to distress arising out of physical discomfort, irritation, or inconvenience caused by odors, pests, noise, and the like. *See Burt v. Beautiful Savior Lutheran Church*, 809 P.2d 1064 (Colo. App. 1990) (damages on trespass claim included loss of use of basement and annoyance and discomfort caused by smell in the home following water damage); *Miller v. Carnation Co.*, 39 Colo. App. 1 (1977)

(damages for annoyance and discomfort caused by flies and rodents from neighboring poultry ranch). Our cases have permitted recovery for annoyance and discomfort damages on nuisance and trespass claims while at the same time precluding recovery for 'pure' emotional distress. *See Slovek v. Bd. of Cnty. Comm'rs.*, 697 P.2d 781 (Ct. App. Colo. 1984) (holding that damages for annoyance and discomfort were available on trespass claim, but that recovery for emotional distress was not available where there was no allegation of negligent infliction of emotional distress or outrageous conduct); *Calvaresi v. Nat'l Dev. Co.*, 772 P.2d 640 (Ct. App. Colo. 1988) (in action for tortious injury to land, plaintiffs were entitled to put on evidence to establish discomfort, annoyance, physical illness, and loss of use and enjoyment of property, but were not entitled to recover damages for emotional distress).

Kelly v. CB&I Constructors, Inc., 102 Cal. Rptr. 3d 32 (Ct. App. Colo. 2009). *See Nichols v. City of Evansdale, Iowa*, 687 N.W.2d 562 (Iowa 2004) (discomfort and annoyance damages not recoverable because plaintiffs were not occupying land at time of trespass). But other courts permit recovery for annoyance and inconvenience without harm to the property and even if the plaintiff was not present when the trespass occurred. *E.g., Hensley v. San Diego Gas & Elec. Co.*, 7 Cal. App. 5th 1337 (2017) (asserting *Kelly* was incorrect *dicta*). Is there a correct answer to the lines being drawn, or is this fact-dependent?

As for entities, in *Oglethorpe Power Co. v. Estate of Forrister*, 332 Ga. App. 693 (2015), the court stated that "a limited liability company may have a cause of action for 'discomfort and annoyance' affecting the use of its property for the purposes intended by its members and those they permit to join them" and that "'discomfort and annoyance' damages are separate from emotional distress." Does this mean that in South Carolina entities should get *lower* loss-of-use damages? Or is the nature of an LLC behind the result?

3. <u>Mental Anguish?</u> Some courts permit recovery of mental anguish damages—as distinct from "annoyance and inconvenience" damages—but usually only against a defendant who trespassed repeatedly and either intentionally or maliciously. *E.g., Akers v. D.L. White Constr., Inc.*, 320 P.3d 428 (Idaho 2014) ($10,000 in mental anguish damages proper where defendant while trespassing purposefully ran dump truck within two feet of plaintiff and was otherwise bullying and confrontational); *Minihan v. Stiglich*, 311 P.3d 922 (Ct. App. Or. 2013) ($10,000 in mental anguish damages proper where defendant had threatened and physically intimidated plaintiff and his wife while trespassing). Consider the difference between distress from knowing a trespass is occurring and distress caused by being threatened by a trespassing defendant. The court in *Land Baron Inv. v. Bonnie Springs Family, LP*, 356 P.3d 511 (Nev. 2015), explained the overlap and distinctions:

> Courts differ on whether a plaintiff must prove physical harm to recover for emotional distress arising under a nuisance claim. *Compare Bailey v.*

Shriberg, 31 Mass. App. Ct. 277 (1991) (concluding that evidence of physical injury is necessary in an emotional distress claim based on nuisance), *with Herzog v. Grosso*, 41 Cal.2d 219 (1953) (determining that occupants could recover for mere annoyance and discomfort, such as lack of sleep, for a cause of action for nuisance). However, it seems to be the prevailing view in most jurisdictions that, in a nuisance action, an owner or occupant of real estate is entitled to recover damages for personal inconvenience, discomfort, annoyance, anguish, or sickness, distinct from, or in addition to, damages for depreciation in value of property or its use. *See, e.g., Kornoff v. Kingsburg Cotton Oil Co.*, 45 Cal.2d 265 (1955) (reiterating that "once a cause of action for trespass or nuisance is established, an occupant of land may recover damages for annoyance and discomfort that would naturally ensue"); *Webster v. Boone*, 992 P.2d 1183 (Colo. App. 1999) (damages for nuisance claim can include discomfort and annoyance); *Reichenbach v. Kraska Enters., LLC*, 105 Conn. App. 461 (2008) (trier of fact can consider discomfort and annoyance in nuisance damages claim). Further, Restatement (Second) of Torts §929 provides that the damages for nuisance include "discomfort and annoyance" to the occupants.

This court has not previously addressed emotional distress damages arising under a nuisance claim. We conclude that California, Colorado, Connecticut, and the Restatement offer the better-reasoned approach for recovering damages based on a nuisance claim. Because damages for nuisance include personal inconvenience, discomfort, annoyance, anguish, or sickness, an occupant need not show physical harm to recover.

3. When the Remedy at Law Is Inadequate

As explained above, if the harm is "abated," then damages will be sufficient. However, if it is "continuing" or threatened to repeat, then injunctive relief may be available. The court in *Orange County Water Dist. v. Unocal Corp.*, 2016 WL 11201024 (C.D. Cal. Nov. 3, 2016), explained why the remedy at law is inadequate and expanded upon the measure of damages:

> The California Supreme Court codified continuing nuisance doctrine in the case *Williams v. S. Pac. R. Co.*, 150 Cal. 624 (1907). The *Williams* Court, examining a railroad's trespassing construction of track on the plaintiff's property, distinguished between permanent and continuing injury. Continuing injury cases are characterized by transient injury; "it is not presumed that the wrongful conduct will be continued" and therefore "a new cause of action arises at each moment." *Id.* at 626. In contrast, permanent injury cases arise when injury has occurred and by definition will continue forever.

The permanent/continuing nuisance distinction determines the remedies available to injured parties. In continuing injury cases, each moment gives rise to a claim, so plaintiffs can recover only the damages which have accrued up to the institution of the action. If a nuisance is a use which may be discontinued at any time, it is considered continuing in character and persons harmed by it may bring successive actions for damages until the nuisance is abated. Recovery is limited, however, to actual injury suffered prior to commencement of each action. Prospective damages are unavailable. Victims of a continuing nuisance can, however, bring successive claims for subsequent damage. The remedy for a continuing nuisance was either a suit for injunctive relief or successive actions for damages as new injuries occurred. In permanent injury cases, where injury is irrevocable, all damages, past and prospective, are recoverable in one action, and the entire cause of action accrues when the injury is inflicted or the trespass committed.

The rationale for the limitation on damages in continuing injury cases is tied to the fact that the injury is capable of being abated. The paradigmatic measure of damages for permanent nuisance is diminution in property value. However, if a nuisance can be abated, once it is removed, there will no longer be a nuisance to depreciate the value of the property. For example, airport noise, once removed, will no longer deflate the value of affected property. Therefore, the paradigmatic judicial resolution of continuing nuisance is ordering defendants to abate the nuisance and compensating plaintiffs for loss of use of their property.

Obviously, recovering both a judicial order for abatement of the nuisance (or the necessary funds to remediate) *and* prospective damages for decreased property value in continuing nuisance cases would constitute double recovery, an impermissible windfall. Because they can be abated, however, parties alleging the existence of a continuing nuisance may not recover diminution in value damages.

California law on continuing nuisance damages is nuanced and varied. In addition to *Williams*, the California Supreme Court's decision in *Baker v. Burbank-Glendale-Pasadena Airport Auth.*, 39 Cal. 3d 862 (1985), is instructive. *Baker* involved homeowners adjacent to Burbank Airport who sued alleging that the "noise, smoke, and vibrations from flights over their homes" constituted a nuisance. *Id.* The lower court had held that since the flights were operated in accordance with federal law, they could not be abated and therefore constituted a permanent nuisance (the statute of limitations barred plaintiffs from seeking relief from permanent nuisances). *Id.* After a lengthy exposition on the development of continuing nuisance doctrine, the California Supreme Court held that "airport operations are the quintessential continuing nuisance," and accordingly remanded to the lower court for further proceedings. As relevant here, *Baker*'s exposition of continuing nuisance doctrine contained the following three sentences: "On the other hand, if a nuisance is a use which may be discontinued at any time, it is considered continuing in character and persons harmed by it may bring successive actions for damages until the nuisance is abated. Recovery is limited, however, to actual injury suffered prior to commencement of each action. Prospective damages are unavailable." *Id.*

Many cases, often parroting *Baker*, state the rule that damages accrued after the filing of a complaint cannot be recovered for continuing nuisance. However, Defendants overstate California law when they indicate it is unanimous regarding preclusion of post-filing damages. A number of cases diverge from *Williams*, *Baker*, and their progeny. Particularly relevant here, courts have distinguished between prospective injury and post-filing damages. Specifically, they indicate that the time-of-filing limit in continuing nuisance requires *the injury* to occur before the complaint is filed but *damages* caused by that injury, even if incurred after the complaint's filing, are recoverable. Implicitly, these cases understand *Williams'* and *Baker*'s prohibition on prospective damages to preclude post-judgment, damages, not post-filing, pre-judgment, damages. Cases also occasionally diverge from loss of use damages and instead award loss of rental value damages.

There are two ways courts have applied continuing nuisance damages relevant to this case. First, courts have awarded plaintiffs claiming nuisance the cost of abatement in lieu of equitable injunctive relief ordering defendants' abatement of the nuisance. Second, courts have applied the continuing nuisance damages limitation.

1. Cost of Abatement. The typical paradigm for continuing nuisance damages is abatement and loss of use. Abatement is rooted in equitable, injunctive relief. One who suffers damage from a continuing nuisance has two causes of action and two remedies; the one, a suit for damages which is an action at law, and the other, a suit to enjoin or abate the nuisance, which is in equity. Such equitable relief remains common in continuing nuisance cases.

Sometimes, courts award plaintiffs the cost of abatement, rather than issue an injunction ordering defendants' abatement of a nuisance. This occurs even when abatement has not yet occurred and therefore the damages accrued by bearing future remediation costs are necessarily prospective. Some cases, additionally, limit the types of costs that count as abatement costs. Cases have, however, denied abatement costs incurred more than three years *before* the filing of a complaint for continuing nuisance.

2. Limiting Damage Awards. While many cases state *Baker*'s rule or variations thereof, only a handful *apply* its limit on prospective damages in continuing nuisance cases. Of that handful of cases, most deal with prospective damages for diminution in value, which are more closely akin to permanent nuisance damages. Turning to cases directly relevant to the issue before the Court, only a handful have considered damages incurred *between* complaint-filing and judgment. Some cases deny recovery of such damages. Others, consistent with the injury/damages distinction, expressly countenance recovery of damages that accrue during the lawsuit arising from pre-complaint injuries. Similarly, courts that have used loss of rental value to determine continuing nuisance damages have awarded loss of rental value extending past the time of filing of a complaint.

As previously discussed, continuing nuisance damages do not include prospective damages because, in conjunction with abatement, they would constitute a windfall double remedy. Formulations of continuing nuisance's damages limitation vary, and they include versions that countenance post-filing pre-judgment damages. Courts have awarded plaintiffs claiming nuisance the cost of abatement in lieu of equitable injunctive relief ordering defendants' abatement of the nuisance. Applications of continuing nuisance's damages limitation mostly deal with precluding post-abatement damages for continued injury, such as stigmatic depreciation in property value.

The Court finds that Plaintiff may recover post-filing, pre-judgment abatement expenses. There are no precedential cases with facts on point that preclude post-filing, pre-judgment damages to compensate plaintiffs for abatement activities.

A. Removing Encroachments

Rose Nulman Park Found. v. Four Twenty Corp.

93 A.3d 25 (R.I. 2014) (Indeglia, J.)

[Rose Nulman owned land described as "a diamond on the necklace that is Rhode Island's beautiful coastline." In 1984, real estate developers Robert C. Lamoureux and Four Twenty Corporation acquired a parcel of land and divided it into two lots. One parcel abutted Rose Nulman's land and was known as the Four Twenty property. Ms. Nulman died some years later.

In 2006, her family created the Rose Nulman Park Foundation (the "Foundation") to preserve and maintain her property as a free public park. A 2008 settlement agreement among Nulman family members provided that if the Foundation's trustees allowed the park to be used other than as a free park, each trustee was jointly and severally obligated to pay $1.5 million to a charity.

In 2009, Lamoreaux and Four Twenty hired Carrigan Engineering to assist with obtaining all permits needed to construct a single-family home on the Four Twenty property. Carrigan Engineering prepared a plan showing its location. After obtaining all permits, construction began in November 2009 and was completed in January 2011. At that time, Four Twenty agreed to sell the Four Twenty property for $1.9 million, but the buyer's survey showed the entire home was in the park. Lamoureux immediately contacted the Foundation, which said the land could not be sold and the house would have be destroyed or moved. Negotiations failed.

The Foundation sued, alleging a continuing trespass and seeking a mandatory injunction ordering the house removed and the park restored to its original condition. At the bench trial, Ms. Carol Nulman testified the $1.5 million payment in the settlement agreement was to ensure the property was never sold or built on. She further testified the Nulmans paid liability insurance, lawn care maintenance, and property taxes on the park. The only structure in the park was a gazebo, which was a memorial to Rose Nulman. Lamoureux testified he had spent $619,000 to build the 13,000-square-foot home. Thirteen thousand square feet was 6.6% of the 4.5-acre park. Lamoreaux testified the house could not be moved without obtaining permits and, if they could be obtained, moving would cost $300,000 to $400,000. The trial court granted mandatory injunctive relief requiring removal of the property within 180 days. Defendants appealed.]

In *Santilli v. Morelli*, 102 R.I. 333 (1967), this Court explicitly adopted the general rule that "a continuing trespass wrongfully interferes with the legal rights of the owner, and in the usual case those rights cannot be adequately protected except by an injunction which will eliminate the trespass." Since then, this Court has adhered to that principle.

We have also acknowledged, however, that this general rule is not absolute and that, accordingly, in exceptional cases, a court may, in its discretion, decline to follow it where the injunctive relief would operate oppressively and inequitably. *See Adams v. Toro*, 508 A.2d 399 (R.I. 1986) ("The general rule will not apply in those exceptional cases where the rights of the landowner can be adequately protected without resort to injunctive relief that would operate oppressively and inequitably against the encroaching party."). We have held that these exceptional circumstances include, but are not limited to, acquiescence, laches, or a *de minimis* trespass.

In addition to these discrete situations, we have also held that courts may withhold injunctive relief after balancing the equities or, put another way, considering the relative hardships to the parties. However, this Court has never stated — nor do we now hold — that a trial court is required to balance the equities before granting injunctive relief in a continuing trespass case. Moreover, as this Court has emphasized, the issuance and measure of injunctive relief rest in the sound discretion of the trial justice.

This Court has repeatedly made clear that a departure from the general rule that a continuing trespass should be remedied by injunctive relief is justified only in exceptional circumstances. We are satisfied that the case at bar does not involve such exceptional circumstances which would render such coercive relief inequitable or oppressive. Indeed, we are of the opinion that a fair balancing of the equities supports the trial justice's decision to grant injunctive relief.

The defendants emphasize that this case does not involve knowing or deliberate conduct, that this Court has concluded justifies the imposition of injunctive relief without balancing the equities. They further insist that Lamoureux's reliance on hired experts was "utterly reasonable," and that, accordingly, he had the "clean hands" which would make balancing appropriate. The trial justice, in fact, agreed that Lamoureux's reliance on Carrigan's site development plan was justified, but stated that it did not suffice to exempt defendants from liability. We agree with the trial justice's conclusion.[7]

The defendants urge us to follow the example of courts in other jurisdictions, which have relied on the balancing of the equities or the relative hardships to the parties, in denying injunctive relief in cases where the encroachment was innocently done and the hardship to the defendants would greatly outweigh any harm to the plaintiffs. *See, e.g., Proctor v. Huntington,* 169 Wash.2d 491 (2010) (denying injunctive relief in a case where the encroachment by the defendants of their house, garage, and well onto the plaintiff's land was the result of a "good-faith surveying mistake," and where any benefit to the plaintiff from the removal would be minimal); *Szymczak v. LaFerrara,* 280 N.J.Super. 223 (App. Div. 1995) (stating that an injunction was not warranted when the injunction required the destruction of the defendant's home where the encroachment was due to an innocent mistake and where the encroachment was on an undeveloped lot belonging to the plaintiff). We find these cases to be inapposite to the case at bar. The defendants averred at oral argument that the encroachment here has not caused plaintiff any substantial injury because the portion of the Nulman property on which the house was built was overgrown with brush.

We deem defendants' arguments to be without merit and conclude that the harm to plaintiff more than outweighs the hardships to defendants in having to remove the house. We begin by emphasizing, as did the trial justice, that an encroachment of some 13,000 square feet is not a minimal one. The encroachment here is not small enough that a balancing of the equities makes the hardship to defendants outweigh the harm to plaintiff. Moreover, we note that Carol and Joel Nulman, as the Trustees of the Foundation, would potentially be personally liable for paying the $1.5 million penalty in the event that the house is permitted to remain on the Nulman property. While the defendants insist that the trial justice erred in considering

---

7. We do, however, find it curious that Lamoureux, as someone who, according to his own testimony, has been developing real estate for approximately forty years, was entirely unaware of the different classes of surveys and, moreover, in spite of the money he planned to expend based on Carrigan's plan, failed to make any inquiry as to the significance of the caveat on Carrigan's site development plan that it was a Class III survey.

the potential hardship that would be inflicted on the individual trustees, as non-parties to the suit, it is accepted that in balancing the equities, a court may consider the interests of third parties and of the public in general.

Finally we must consider the interests of the public. Ms. Nulman testified that the intent in starting the Foundation was to ensure that the land was never developed as "it's a historic spot surrounded by the ocean and we should maintain this for the public use. The sentimental value to the public is enormous." This clear commitment of the land's use as community space satisfies us that any attempt to build on even a portion of the property would constitute an irreparable injury, not only to plaintiff but to the public.

In conclusion, we are not unsympathetic to the defendants' plight and agree that this is, as the trial justice acknowledged, an "unfortunate situation." We are, however, convinced that it would be an unjust result to order the transfer of title to a portion of the Nulman property to the defendants or award only money damages. While the defendants may well have clean hands, the plaintiff is certainly an innocent party as well. Indeed, we note that the plaintiff has been put to the inconvenience of protecting its right to its property in court as a consequence of wanting to ensure that the public would always be able to enjoy the property in its natural state.

The case is remanded with directions that the defendants be given a reasonable period of time to comply.

Notes and Questions

1. <u>Insufficient Harm</u>? In *DiMarzo v. Fast Trak Structures*, 747 N.Y.S.2d 637 (N.Y. Sup. Ct. 2002), the defendant purchased a lot next to plaintiff and built a building and improvements, including a water drainage system that discharged water onto plaintiff's land. The trial court ordered the system changed, but the appellate court reversed, stating that the area where the water entered plaintiff's land had been wet prior to installation of the pipe because water had been carried there by a 15-inch drainage ditch on defendant's land. Is that *de minimis*? Why wasn't the *Nulman* trespass *de minimis*?

2. <u>Malice</u>. Some state statutes permit issuance of mandatory injunctions to prevent ongoing malicious trespass or nuisance. By decision or statute, some courts may order destruction of structures erected out of spite, which are not a nuisance or trespass. The court in *Geiger v. Carey*, 170 Conn. App. 459 (2017) explained:

> General Statutes § 52-480 provides in relevant part: "An injunction may be granted against the malicious erection, by or with the consent of an owner, lessee or person entitled to the possession of land, of any structure upon it, intended to annoy and injure any owner or lessee of adjacent land in respect to his use or disposition of the same."
>
> General Statutes § 52-570 provides: "An action may be maintained by the proprietor of any land against the owner or lessee of land adjacent, who

maliciously erects any structure thereon, with intent to annoy or injure the plaintiff in his use or disposition of his land."

These statutory sections set forth what are commonly referred to as "spite fence" actions; one, § 52-480, for injunctive relief that may be brought by an owner or lessee of adjacent land and the other, § 52-570, for legal damages that may be brought by the proprietor of land. The word "proprietor" means an owner. The elements essential to prove each statutory section are the same. Each statute requires the following: (1) the defendant to have built a structure on said defendant's land; (2) the erection of the structure must have been malicious; (3) the defendant must have intended to injure the enjoyment of the adjacent landowner's land by the erection of the structure; (4) the structure must impair the value of the plaintiff's land; (5) the structure must be useless to the defendant; and (6) the enjoyment of the plaintiff's land must be, in fact, impaired. Our Supreme Court has ruled that all or only a portion of a fence may be maliciously erected.

Deciding whether a structure has been erected maliciously does not involve a journey deep into the defendant's heart. Whether a structure was maliciously erected is to be determined rather by its character, location and use than by an inquiry into the actual motive in the mind of the party erecting it.

Where a statute or clear evidence of repetition is not present, courts balance factors more closely. In *Am. Condo Ass'n. Inc. v. Mardo,* 140 A.3d 106 (R.I. 2016), a statute mandated removal of an intentionally erected unlawful structure absent "exceptional circumstances" such as when doing so would "operate oppressively and inequitably" including "acquiescence, laches, or a *de minimis* trespass." In *Mardo,* a defendant expanded his condo while he and the owners' association had a dispute over whether he could do so. The court found "exceptional circumstances" because plaintiffs had not pursued injunctive relief at that time. *See Bauman v. Turpen,* 138 Wash. App. 1012 (2007) (affirming order requiring destruction of improvement that violated covenant even though defendants had believed it complied because defendants "knew their neighbors disputed their interpretation of the covenant but continued to work even though" the plaintiffs had sued).

B. Preventing Future Harm to Health or Safety

Where the defendant has been found to have committed a nuisance but threatens to continue the activity, injunctive relief may be available. Further, some courts permit injunctive relief where a defendant appears likely to engage in conduct that will be a nuisance:

Jurisdictions that recognize anticipatory nuisance as a cause of action define it as an act, occupation, or structure which is not a nuisance per se, but which may become a nuisance by reason of circumstances, location or surroundings. Parties alleging anticipatory nuisance must meet a high burden to show that a nuisance will inevitably or necessarily result from the act or thing which it is sought to enjoin. Courts have considered the burden for anticipatory-nuisance claims to be closely related to the clear and convincing evidence standard, as courts will deny relief until a nuisance has been committed where the thing sought to be enjoined may or may not become such, depending on its use or other circumstances.

Steffensen-WC, LLC v. Volunteers of Am. of Utah, Inc., 369 P.3d 483 (Ct. App. Utah 2016). *See Simpson v. Kollasch*, 749 N.W.2d 671 (Iowa 2008) (declining to enjoin proposed "hog confinement facilities" because, "while the neighbors raised legitimate concerns, our role in this case is not akin to a zoning board.").

Bowling v. Nicholson
51 N.E.3d 439 (Ct. App. Ind. 2016) (Altice, J.)

[The Bowlings moved into their home on 2.6 acres in rural Indiana in 1995. In 2004, the Nicholsons bought an adjacent four-acre parcel adjacent to and south of the Bowlings' property. In 2010, the Nicholsons installed an outdoor hydronic heater, or outdoor wood boiler (OWB), to heat their home, saving them $300 dollars per month on utility bills.

The OWB emitted plumes of thick, acrid smoke, noxious odors, and air particulates onto the Bowlings' property that significantly interfered with use and enjoyment. It was so bad some of the Bowlings' friends and family refused to visit them because of the air conditions in and around their home. The smoke aggravated Ms. Bowlings' asthma condition and caused repeated bronchitis, coughing, wheezing and shortness of breath, scratchy throat, fatigue, hoarseness, sinus pressure, and nasal congestion. She had to go the hospital for treatments and take medication. They called the police to the Nicholson's home 197 times and the fire department 60 times. The Bowlings also called other agencies, but repeated observations and unannounced inspections revealed only one violation—which occurred when the Nicholsons by mistake burned cardboard in the OWB.

In October 2013, the Bowlings sued, asserting nuisance, trespass, negligence, and gross negligence. They promptly moved for a preliminary injunction. A year later, the court held a hearing and then denied their motion for preliminary injunction. The Bowlings appealed.]

To establish irreparable harm, the Bowlings were required to show that the harm they suffered cannot be compensated for through damages upon resolution of the underlying action.

Throughout their pleadings, the Bowlings consistently alleged that the Nicholsons' operation of their OWB constitutes a nuisance. Indeed, in objecting to the discovery request for their medical records, the Bowlings specifically asserted that they were not seeking damages for medical harm or personal injury, but rather, their action was for property-related nuisance claims. Nuisance is defined by Ind. Code § 32-30-6-6, which provides: "Whatever is (1) injurious to health; (2) indecent; (3) offensive to the senses; or (4) an obstruction to the free use of property so as essentially to interfere with the comfortable enjoyment of life or property, is a nuisance, and the subject of an action." The Bowlings presented evidence to establish that operation of the OWB was offensive to the senses and/or an obstruction to their free use of their property. The harm they allege relates in large part to the loss of use and enjoyment of their property.

[handwritten margin note: nuisance elements.]

The trial court, in concluding that the Bowlings had not established irreparable harm, indicated that it considered harm only as it related to a property loss in the form of loss of property value or physical damage to the Bowlings' property. The trial court's findings and conclusions, however, do not address the elements of the Bowlings' underlying nuisance claim. Specifically, the trial court did not address the Bowlings' evidence or claims as they related to operation of the OWB as offensive to the senses or as an obstruction to the free use of their property such that its continued use interferes with the Bowlings' enjoyment of their property. The Bowlings' nuisance claim was not based on a loss of property value or physical damage. We agree with the Bowlings that the trial court's findings and conclusions fail to address the element of irreparable harm in light of the Bowlings' underlying nuisance claims.

Next, the Bowlings argue that the trial court failed to assess their likelihood of success on the merits of their nuisance claim. To obtain a preliminary injunction, the party seeking the injunction must have a reasonable likelihood of prevailing on the merits. To demonstrate this element, the moving party is not required to show that he is entitled to relief as a matter of law, but only that success on the merits is probable. Thus, for purposes of seeking a preliminary injunction, the Bowlings need only have shown that the Nicholsons' use of their OWB is likely to be deemed a nuisance under I.C. § 32-30-6-6.

Here, the trial court's conclusion of law that comes closest to making a determination regarding the Bowlings' likelihood of success provides:

> A review of the case law regarding Preliminary Injunctions finds that most of them relate to covenants not to compete, contract law, or breaches of trade secrets. None of the available cases refers to a neighbor seeking to stop another from using his/her property to its full advantage based upon a perceived but unproven irreparable harm to property.

First, as noted above, the trial court did not apply the proper standard in considering the issue of irreparable harm in light of the Bowlings' nuisance claim. Second, the trial court's statement that "most" of the cases it reviewed did not concern a nuisance claim is not dispositive of whether a preliminary injunction is warranted in this case. The trial court's conclusion in this regard falls short of assessing the likelihood of success of the Bowlings' nuisance claim.

As to the third element, we agree with the Bowlings that the trial court did not properly apply the "balance of harms" factor. The court concluded that the Bowlings "admitted they had no photographs of any alleged damages to the property nor any analysis or other form of documentation which would provide the Court with sufficient information with which to formulate an assessment of any property harm." However, as discussed above, the harm alleged by the Bowlings as part of their nuisance claim is the loss of use and enjoyment of their property, which is based upon an environmental condition alleged to have been created by the Nicholsons' operation of their OWB. It is this harm that must be balanced against the harm to the Nicholsons, which is in the nature of higher electric heating bills. In its findings and conclusions, the trial court did not summarize or even acknowledge the Bowlings' evidence in this regard. In fact, on the Bowlings' side of the balancing analysis, the trial court relied upon its mistaken determination that the harm to be considered is actual harm to the property. On remand, the trial court must balance the proper harms so as to protect the property and rights of the parties.

Finally, the Bowlings assert that the trial court applied the wrong standard with respect to the public interest element of a preliminary injunction. The trial court concluded:

> The Court is hard pressed to find how granting an injunction based upon the facts as presented serves the greater public. If a homeowner follows the law and regulations and despite constant contact with governing bodies no error is found, an injunction under those circumstances would cause a negative effect on the public's right to quiet enjoyment of their own property.

Whether the public interest is disserved is a question of law for the court to determine from all the circumstances.

Here, there are competing interests — the Bowlings' right to quietly enjoy their own property and the Nicholsons' right to operate their OWB on their property. The competing interests identified give rise to a private nuisance claim, which arises when it has been demonstrated that one party has used his property to the detriment of the use and enjoyment of another's property. Contrary to the trial court's conclusion, however, the fact that the Nicholsons' operation of their OWB does not violate the law or regulations is not dispositive of whether a preliminary injunction would disserve the public interest. To hold such would bar injunctive relief in all cases of nuisance *per accidens, i.e.,* where an otherwise lawful use may become a nuisance by virtue of the circumstances surrounding the use. Thus, the trial court's conclusion with respect to the public interest element is clearly erroneous in that it is based solely on the fact that the Nicholsons' operation of the OWB has not violated any laws or regulations. We therefore reverse and remand.

Walker v. Kingfisher Wind, LLC

2016 WL 5947307 (W.D. Okla. Oct. 13, 2016) (DeGiusti, J.)

[When defendant Kingfisher Wind, LLC announced plans to construct a number of wind turbines near plaintiffs' homes, they promptly sued for anticipatory nuisance. After discovery, defendant moved for summary judgment on plaintiffs' claim for a permanent injunction. This is the court's order granting that motion.]

Oklahoma law further recognizes a claim for "anticipatory nuisance," i.e., a plaintiff can seek injunctive relief without having to wait for the actual infliction of a loss. However, the harm suffered must be irreparable — not compensable in money damages — and the evidence must be clear and convincing that there is a reasonable probability of injury, not just a mere apprehension. Further, the complained-of injury "must not be nominal, theoretical or speculative. Here, Plaintiffs advance solely a cause of action for anticipatory nuisance, and seek only permanent injunctive relief.

The Court must consider whether Kingfisher has identified a lack of evidence on an essential element of Plaintiffs' anticipatory nuisance claim, and whether Plaintiffs have come forward with sufficient evidence to present a triable issue. If Plaintiffs' evidence is insufficient, it cannot, as a matter of law, achieve actual success on the merits, i.e., that the KWP is, or will constitute a nuisance. Further, to be entitled to its requested relief — a permanent injunction — Plaintiffs must not only show actual success on the merits, but must also make out a clear and unequivocal showing of the remaining elements of the equitable remedy.

For their anticipatory nuisance claim, Plaintiffs rely almost entirely on asserted adverse health effects and annoyance caused by the turbines. Kingfisher asserts that Plaintiffs have failed to present more than merely speculative proof of harm from the operation of the turbines.

On the record before it, the Court concludes that Plaintiffs have failed to make the required showing of likely harm. Specifically, Plaintiffs have failed to show a triable issue that there exists a reasonable probability an injury will occur as a result of the wind farm's operation. The harm alleged by Plaintiffs and their experts, at this juncture, is speculative at best, and in the Court's view, a reasonable trier of fact could not conclude, based on the evidence presented to date, that the shadow flicker or sound/infrasound from the turbines has caused or will cause adverse health effects to Plaintiffs. Moreover, the Court finds that the aesthetic concerns voiced by certain plaintiffs, based on the current record and absent any significant evidence of adverse health effects, are insufficient alone to constitute an actionable nuisance. At this late stage of the litigation, after a full opportunity to conduct discovery and marshal evidence, the injuries cited by Plaintiffs are simply too speculative to constitute harm sufficient under their anticipatory nuisance theory and, as discussed *infra*, to support the mandatory injunctive relief requested.

For a party to obtain a permanent injunction, it must prove: (1) actual success on the merits; (2) irreparable harm unless the injunction is issued; (3) the threatened injury outweighs the harm that the injunction may cause the opposing party; and (4) the injunction, if issued, will not adversely affect the public interest. A permanent injunction is an extraordinary remedy, thus, the right to relief must be clear and unequivocal. As noted above, a mere fear or apprehension of injury is insufficient. Moreover, the Court recognizes that mandatory permanent injunctions are looked upon disfavorably and are generally only granted in compelling circumstances.

In addition to the failure of proof regarding the harm required to establish a claim for anticipatory nuisance, the balance of hardships as between the parties cannot reasonably be viewed as tipping in favor of Plaintiffs. Defendant correctly points out that, because Plaintiffs elected not to pursue preliminary injunctive relief, there was no legal impediment to its continued construction—and completion—of the wind farm during the pendency of this case. Thus, the KWP is now operational, at a cost of approximately $450,000,000. Plaintiffs' stated reason for eschewing the pursuit of preliminary injunctive relief early on in this case—that they would not likely have been able to afford an injunction bond—is unavailing (the Court has wide discretion in determining the amount of a bond. In the face of Plaintiffs' speculative evidence of injury from the KWP, the enormous cost and delay associated with the relief sought by Plaintiffs strongly militates against an injunction here, and compels the clear conclusion that the balance of hardships here does not tip in Plaintiffs' favor.

Because Plaintiffs have failed to make an adequate showing of success on the merits, irreparable harm, or that the threatened injury outweighs the harm that the injunction would cause Kingfisher, the Court need not consider the remaining factor regarding the issuance of an injunction. Thus, Plaintiffs have not established the existence of a triable issue regarding likely harm sufficient to support their claims of anticipatory nuisance, and have failed to demonstrate that a rational trier of fact could find in their favor regarding an entitlement to permanent injunctive relief.

The Court's ruling is confined to the particular facts and circumstances of this case, and the singular claim advanced by Plaintiffs. Based on the record before it, the Court only concludes that Plaintiffs, under their present theory of *anticipatory* nuisance, have failed to meet their burden of showing injury will likely occur from the turbines' operation, and that they would be entitled to the remedy they seek.

Notes and Questions

1. <u>What Result on Remand in *Bowling*</u>? Ordinarily, health or safety is a strong factor indicating injunctive relief is appropriate, as cases below further illustrate. However, does that cut one, or both, ways in *Bowling*? Further, in considering how

the *Bowling* trial court could balance the scope of the injunction and whether to grant it at all, consider *Biglane v. Under The Hill Corp.*, 949 So. 2d 9 (Miss. 2007):

> In the case at hand, the trial court exercised its power to permit continued operation of the Saloon while setting conditions to its future operation. Namely, it found that the Saloon could not "operate its business with its doors and windows opened during any time that amplified music is being played inside the saloon." The chancery court found "that such a limitation is reasonable in that it should help contain the noise within the saloon, and should discourage the bar patrons from congregating or loitering in the streets outside of the saloon."

> From a review of the record it is clear that the chancery court balanced the interests between the Biglanes and the Saloon in a quest for an equitable remedy that allowed the couple to enjoy their private apartment and while protecting a popular business and tourist attraction from over-regulation. Accordingly, we agree that the Saloon was a private nuisance to the Biglanes and affirm the trial court's equitable conditions placed upon its continued operation.

2. <u>Statistics Show the Harm Won't Recur</u>. In *Heidkamper v. Odom,* 880 So. 2d 362 (Ct. App. Miss. 2004), defendant Heidkamper built a pond that, sometimes when it rained, caused water damage to plaintiff's adjoining property. Plaintiff sought damages for past harm and a mandatory injunction requiring defendant to install drainage pipes and lower the level of the pond. While suit was pending, defendant took some steps to stop the problem and that stopped damage during the previous three years. Even so, the trial court granted mandatory permanent injunctive relief. The defendant appealed and the court affirmed:

> The party requesting an injunction must show a threat of imminent harm, rather than mere fear or apprehension alone. To obtain a permanent injunction, a party must show an imminent threat of irreparable harm for which there is no adequate remedy at law. It is likewise true, however, that the remedy by injunction is preventive in its nature, and that it is not necessary to wait for the actual occurrence of the injury, since, if this were required, the purpose for which the relief is sought would, in most cases, be defeated.

> Heidkamper argues there is no evidence to support an injunction as there is an absence of imminent, irreparable harm to the adjacent property owners. Heidkamper contends he has already taken remedial measures with the installation of the drainage pipe, and since its installation the Odoms and LeBlanc have not experienced any flooding on their properties. He notes that the Odoms and LeBlanc have admitted that their land is currently dry, but that they feared an overflow in the future.

Heidkamper's expert witness, Ulmer, testified that it would take a ten, twenty-five, or fifty year rain to produce enough rainfall for the pond to overflow again. These are storms that statistically, rather than chronologically, occur every ten, twenty-five, and fifty years, and are so delineated by the amount of rainfall. Ulmer stated, that while it is statistically unlikely, that there is no way to predict when these rains will actually occur, and that is it possible to have closely recurring twenty-five and fifty year storms.

As previously mentioned, it is not necessary to wait for the actual occurrence of the injury as an injunction is preventative in nature. It was not an abuse of discretion for the chancellor to find an injunction necessary based on the likelihood that the pond, in its present condition, would overflow causing further damage to the adjacent properties.

If future harm is statistically unlikely to occur, how can it be likely to repeat itself? In that regard, however, notice the standard of review: if the trial court had denied injunctive relief, would this court have reversed?

3. <u>Criminal Laws</u>. The *Leider v. Lewis*, 394 P.3d 1055 (Cal. 2017), court explained the limited role of criminal statutes and ordinances in civil nuisance law:

> Conduct against which injunctions are sought in behalf of the public is frequently criminal in nature. While this alone will not prevent the intervention of equity where a clear case justifying equitable relief is present, it is apparent that the equitable remedy has the collateral effect of depriving a defendant of the jury trial to which he would be entitled in a criminal prosecution for violating exactly the same standards of public policy. The defendant also loses the protection of the higher burden of proof required in criminal prosecutions and, after imprisonment and fine for violation of the equity injunction, may be subjected under the criminal law to similar punishment for the same acts. For these reasons equity is loath to interfere where the standards of public policy can be enforced by resort to the criminal law, and in the absence of a legislative declaration to that effect, the courts should not broaden the field in which injunctions against criminal activity will be granted. Thus, the basis for an action such as this must be found in our statutes rather than by reference to the common law definitions of public nuisance.

However, a violation of a criminal law can evidence a private nuisance. For example, in *Szuch v. FirstEnergy Nuclear Operating Company*, 60 N.E.2d 494 (Ct. App. Ohio 2016), the defendant allowed its employees to train for defending a nuclear power plant by using a shooting range on the premises that violated noise ordinances. The court below denied injunctive relief and the court affirmed, explaining:

> Here, the court found that there is no reliable evidence demonstrating that the shooting range affects any public interest, but that the range does

serve a critical public interest by complying with the mandatory training requirements for nuclear plant safety personnel.

In arguing that the court abused its discretion, appellants cite the diminution of property value as the irreparable harm sufficient to grant an injunction. Appellants next argue that an injunction will not harm third parties because FENOC could use, and has used in the past, other shooting ranges to qualify its security personnel. Further, appellants contend that an injunction would serve the public interest because it would ensure that shooting ranges abide by NRA guidelines, which have as their goal the development of good relationships between range operators and the neighboring property owners and community at large.

Notwithstanding appellants' arguments, we hold that the trial court did not abuse its discretion in denying the injunction. First, we note that the diminution of property value is remediable in law through damages that may be proven and compensated for in money. Thus, that injury is not irreparable. Furthermore, the harm is mitigated by the fact that appellants do not reside on the property, only using it for recreation (and the occasional storage of fishing equipment) instead, and FENOC only fires once or twice during the week, and never on the weekends. Finally, we cannot disagree with the trial court that the continued operation of the shooting range is in the public's interest as it provides the required training for security officers at a nuclear power plant.

4. <u>Balancing and the Scope of Injunctive Relief and "Coming to the Nuisance."</u> As explained in Chapter 2, if a court decides injunctive relief is proper, it will balance the interests in determining the scope of any injunctive relief. For example, in *Eaton v. Cormier,* 748 A.2d 1006 (Me. 2000), the plaintiffs obtained an injunction against a rock quarry that was found to have been a nuisance, but it was permitted to operate from 10:00 a.m. to 2:00 p.m. daily. *See Daugherty v. Ashton Feed & Grain Co., Inc.,* 208 Neb. 159 (1981) (enjoining operation of equipment at grain storage facility to certain hours during weekdays); *De Nucci v. Pezza,* 114 R.I. 123 (1974) (limiting freight terminal's operations to daylight hours).

In this regard, the *Eaton* court noted that courts consider whether the plaintiff "came to the nuisance" in determining the scope of relief. In this regard, in *Holubec v. Brandenberger,* 214 S.W.3d 650 (Ct. App. Tex. 2006), the defendants built a home near a large tract of land owned by the plaintiff at a time when the area was vacant pasture. Then the defendant placed a massive sheep feedlot 135 feet from the plaintiffs' home. The trial court permanently enjoined its operation anywhere on the defendant's land. The appellate court reversed because the evidence was undisputed that, if the sheep were kept more than 1,000 feet away, it would not be a nuisance.

4. Other Remedies for Harm to Interests in Real Property

A. Ejectment of an Unlawful Occupier of Plaintiff's Real Property

Davis v. Westphal

405 P.3d 73 (Mont. 2017) (Sandefur, J.)

[The parties owned adjoining 10-acre wooded lots in Montana. The Davises' tract was undeveloped and they lived in California. The Westphals mistakenly assumed a line of pink survey flags marked the boundary between the lots and cut down trees that were, in fact, on the Davises' property. Later they began to build a large workshop and a septic system in that area. When the Davises visited and saw the work in progress, they obtained a survey that showed the structures were on their land and informed the Westphals of that fact in November 2015. The Westphals finished construction and then asked to resolve the mistake.

In June 2016, the Davises sued, seeking, among other relief, an order to have the encroachments removed and the land restored. That month, at the hearing on the Davises' motion for a preliminary injunction, the parties agreed the Davises would drop the request for a preliminary injunction and the Westphals would remove the encroachments and restore the property. However, when by September 2016 the Westphals had not begun to remove the encroachments, the Davises moved for summary judgment and sought a declaratory judgment of trespass, an order ejecting the encroachments and restoring the property, and a permanent injunction against construction of improvements that did not comply with zoning laws. The Westphals opposed and asked for an additional year to remove the encroachments, noting the Davises did not live on their lot and had not improved it, and that winter was coming.

The trial court granted summary judgment and declared the shop, septic system, and tree-fellings to be trespasses, but denied ejectment, immediate removal of the encroachments, and the request for permanent injunctive relief. The Davises appealed.]

Though related tort claims of common origin for enforcement of an owner's right to exclusive possession of real property, common law trespass and common law ejectment are technically distinct causes of actions providing distinct remedies. In contrast to a common law trespass claim for damages and a modern statutory claim for judgment declaring a trespass as a predicate for supplemental legal or equitable relief, common law "ejectment" is an independent cause of action of ancient origin and greatly evolved purpose and scope. In modern form, common law ejectment is an action at law brought against a trespasser in possession of all or a portion of real property for immediate possession of the property based on proof of superior title and the right to immediate possession.

Long predating modern declaratory judgment Acts, the primary relief available on an ejectment claim is a judgment declaring that the plaintiff has the *right* to immediate possession of the property. A successful plaintiff may also recover damages in ejectment as compensation for the loss of use of the property during the duration of the trespass. Equitable defenses were not available to counter ejectment claims at common law. However, with the modern merger of law and equity, equitable defenses, and even affirmative relief, may be available, as equitable, to counter or ameliorate a common law ejectment claim.

Due to its limited nature as a mere declaration of right to possession, a judgment of ejectment is not self-executing. The remedy available at law to effect a judgment of ejectment is execution under a special writ known at common law as a writ of possession or ejectment, commanding the sheriff or levying officer to deliver possession of the property to the plaintiff by removing the defendant and personalty from the property. Though ejectment technically lies to remedy a real property encroachment, a writ of possession commanding the sheriff to remove the defendant and personalty will generally not abate a substantial physical encroachment affixed to land. While a writ of possession could conceivably command a sheriff or levying officer to enter onto real property and affirmatively remove a trespassing encroachment, our general execution statutes govern writs of possession under Montana law. Davises did not raise the question of whether §§ 25-13-201, -301(1) (d), and -307, MCA, would permit issuance of such an extraordinary writ of execution before the District Court and the issue is not properly before us at this time.

Independent of common law trespass and ejectment claims, a modern declaratory judgment action is also available to determine the "rights, status, and other legal relations" of the parties on any matter in dispute. Sections 27-8-201 and -301. Statutory declaratory judgment claims merely supplement other claims and remedies independently available at law or in equity. Prohibitive and mandatory injunctive relief are forms of supplemental relief available where "necessary or proper" to effect or enforce a declaratory judgment. As an alternative or supplemental remedy to pre-existing common law trespass and ejectment claims, a party may seek redress of a trespassing real property encroachment by seeking a declaratory judgment of trespass, supplemental damages as otherwise provided by law, and supplemental injunctive relief for abatement of the encroachment as otherwise authorized in equity.

Here, Davises obtained summary judgment declaring that Westphals' tree-felling and encroaching building and drain field constituted civil trespasses. As far as it goes, that declaratory judgment was the substantive equivalent of a judgment of ejectment declaring Davises' right to exclusive possession of their property to the exclusion of the subject encroachments. Thus, Davises successfully obtained an interlocutory judgment, prevailing on their alternatively pled declaratory judgment and common law ejection claims. Except for as yet undetermined damages not at issue on appeal, and in contrast to any supplemental injunctive relief otherwise appropriate in equity, no other relief at law is currently available to Davises on their common law ejectment claim prior to final judgment.

To the extent that Davises assert that the District Court erred by failing to further order ejectment of the subject encroachments, their "immediate removal," and restoration of the property, they seek forms of relief that are either premature or beyond the scope of relief available on a common law ejectment claim. Except as supplemental equitable relief, an order compelling a trespasser to remove an encroachment and to restore the property to its prior condition is not a cognizable form of relief available at law on a common law ejectment claim. We hold that the District Court did not err in declining to grant relief at law other than a declaration of trespass on Davises' common law ejectment claim.

As to injunctive relief, it is unclear whether Davises assert that the District Court erred by failing to grant injunctive relief pursuant to §27-8-31 (relief supplemental to declaratory judgment), or as equitable relief supplemental to their common law ejectment claim. More significantly, it is further unclear from their briefing whether Davises assert that the court erroneously denied preliminary injunctive relief, permanent injunctive relief, or both. Regardless temporary and permanent injunctive relief are equitable remedies governed by general principles of equity. The grant or denial of permanent or preliminary injunctive relief is highly discretionary and critically dependent on the particular facts, circumstances, and equities of each case.

District courts have broad discretion to grant preliminary injunctive relief. On evidence or competent affidavit considered *upon hearing*, a court may issue a preliminary injunction at any time before final judgment. In considering whether to issue a preliminary injunction, the court must exercise its discretion only in furtherance of the limited purpose of preliminary injunctions to preserve the status quo and minimize the harm to all parties *pending final resolution on the merits*. The "status quo" is generally "the last actual, peaceable, uncontested condition" preceding the controversy at issue. If a preliminary injunction will not accomplish its limited purposes, then it should not issue. Thus a preliminary injunction should not issue absent an accompanying prima facie showing, or showing that it is at least uncertain, that the applicant will suffer irreparable injury *prior to final resolution on the merits*.

Inter alia, Davises assert that, upon granting summary judgment declaring the encroachments as trespasses, the District Court erred by failing to go further and issue a preliminary injunction for their removal pursuant to §27-19-201(3) (preliminary enjoinder of wrongful conduct "tending to render judgment ineffectual"). However, preliminary injunctions may not issue except upon evidence or affidavit considered at a duly noticed hearing. Davises abandoned their initial motion for a preliminary injunction by stipulation long before they moved for summary judgment, did not clearly articulate a renewed request for a preliminary injunction in their summary judgment motion, and in any event failed to request a preliminary injunction hearing on or incident to their motion for summary judgment. Moreover, though they requested that the court "order ejectment" of the encroachments, compel Westphals to remove the encroachments, provide for "forcible" removal if necessary, and conditionally authorize them to remove them if Westphals failed to act, nowhere in Davises' conflated summary judgment motion and briefing was a factual *showing* that the failure to grant a preliminary mandatory injunction would render ineffectual any subsequent final judgment that might include, as appropriate, final injunctive relief. We will not hold a district court in error for failing to address an issue that parties did not timely raise.

Permanent injunctive relief, also known as final injunctive relief, is available only where necessary to prevent irreparable injury in the absence of a plain, speedy, and adequate statutory or common law remedy. Irreparable injury is a harm or wrong: (1) not fully or effectively remedied by compensatory damages; (2) in regard to which adequate, non-speculative compensation is difficult to determine; or (3) of a recurring or continuous nature such that full and effective redress would otherwise require a multiplicity of successive actions at law. A statutory or common law remedy may be inadequate to fully or effectively remedy a harm or wrong either due to the nature of the cause of action or the form of relief ordinarily available thereon.

Injunctive relief is generally not available to remedy a trespass where an action at law for damages or ejectment will provide complete relief. However, compensatory damages are generally inadequate to fully remedy a continuous or recurring encroachment on real property.

Regardless of a determination of a trespass, the grant or denial of mandatory injunctive relief remains highly discretionary dependent on the unique facts and circumstances of each case. Though legal title must generally prevail if the equities are equally balanced or balance against the trespasser, the court must carefully weigh and balance the equities in each case when exercising its broad discretion to grant or deny injunctive relief. Thus, though often appropriate on a balance of the equities in particular cases, mandatory injunctive relief is not available to remedy a trespassing real property encroachment as a matter of right in every case.

Here the District Court has yet to grant or deny permanent injunctive relief upon entry of final judgment following full consideration of the equities. The court's grant of summary judgment declaring the subject encroachments as trespasses was merely an interlocutory order. Permanent injunctions are available only upon entry of a final judgment. In its summary judgment order, the District Court did not make a final determination precluding mandatory injunctive relief upon further proceedings prior to entry of final judgment. The court merely concluded that Davises presented "insufficient information" in support of their motion for summary judgment "to determine whether coercive supplemental relief" is "necessary or appropriate" in addition to money damages "at this point in time." In narrowly concluding that Davises "have provided no evidence upon which" to conclude, "*as a matter of law* that money damages" will be "insufficient to remedy the harm," the District Court merely concluded that Davises failed to satisfy their initial burden under M. R. Civ. P. 56 of showing a complete absence of any genuine issue of fact material to their requested equitable relief.

The summary judgment record was devoid of any evidence sufficient for the District Court to assess the urgency of removal and restoration, the burden and cost of removal and restoration, Westphals' means and ability to effect removal and restoration on the timeline requested, or any other relevant equitable consideration. Under these circumstances, we hold the District Court's *interlocutory* denial of preliminary or final mandatory injunctive relief was neither irreconcilable with its summary judgment declaring a trespass nor a manifest abuse of discretion.

Notes and Questions

1. <u>Judgment of the Right to Possess</u>. *Davis* makes clear that ejectment is proper when a plaintiff shows a defendant wrongfully possesses a portion of plaintiff's property. *See Enbridge Energy Ltd. P'shp. v. Engelking,* 830 N.W.2d 723 (Wis. App. 2013) (ejectment supported by allegation defendant used portion of land plaintiff had right to possess). Yet why was ejectment denied in *Davis?*

2. <u>Stretching Ejectment?</u> In *Lillien v. Hancock,* 2011 WL 3276722 (Conn. Sup. Ct. June 29, 2011), neighbors each owned a one-seventh undivided interest in a right-of-way, and so were co-owners of that right-of-way. The Hancocks constructed a $120,000, two-foot-wide and five- to eight-foot-high stone wall on the right-of-way, and a driveway and curb. The Lilliens sued for ejectment, contending that the structures deprived them of use of their undivided interest in the right-of-way. The court held that the wall "effectively dispossesses the Lilliens of their interest in the portion of the right-of-way on which the wall is situated as well as the portion of the right-of-way within the confines of the wall" and so ordered ejectment and issued an injunction requiring the Hancocks to remove the wall from the right-of-way, stating:

> The Hancocks also argue that the Lilliens have not made the necessary showing to justify the injunctive relief of ordering the removal of any or all of the improvements. Essentially, they contend there will be no irreparable injury if the improvements are not removed. The court agrees that the plaintiffs have not proved any irreparable injury caused by the driveway or asphalt curbing; in fact, the claim of ejectment has not been proven as to either improvement. The driveway, along with other driveways along Northside Lane, necessarily occupies a portion of the right-of-way. The encroachment, if any, of the curbing is minimal at best, and does not support a claim of ejectment. However, the stone wall presents a different story. For two reasons, set forth below, the plaintiffs' arguments are not persuasive.

There is convincing evidence that a substantial portion of the wall along Northside Lane is improperly located on the commonly owned right-of-way. The court determines that the existence of irreparable harm is not the sole basis for granting an injunction, and that the plaintiffs' success on their claim of ejectment itself provides the basis for an order removing, or ejecting, the Hancock wall. As noted earlier, the wall effectively denies the plaintiffs the use and enjoyment of their one-seventh interest in that part of the right-of-way underneath and behind the wall. The action of ejectment has been authoritatively defined as seeking the "specific restitution" of land. An appropriate remedy in an ejectment case is a judgment of possession. The result of a successful ejectment claim is to put the plaintiff in possession of the subject land. There is no other way known to this court to place the plaintiffs in effective joint possession of the whole of the right-of-way than to give actual meaning to the word "ejectment" and order removal of the Hancock wall from the right-of-way.

In addition, the law in Connecticut (and elsewhere) recognizes that interests in real property are more often susceptible to the protections of equitable remedies such as an injunction than other interests. For instance, Connecticut courts have found specific performance an appropriate remedy for breach of contract claims involving the purchase or sale of real property. Indeed, the Appellate Court has likened the remedy of specific performance to a form of injunctive decree. The Connecticut Supreme Court has held that in cases regarding restrictive covenants on real property, there is an exception to the general rule that substantial irreparable harm must threaten before an injunction will issue. "A restrictive covenant may be enforced by injunction without a showing that violation of the covenant will cause harm to the plaintiff, so long as such relief is not inequitable." *Hartford Electric Light Co. v. Levitz*, 173 Conn. 15 (1977). The court determines, while a considerable undertaking, that it is not inequitable to order the Hancocks to remove the wall from the right-of-way. This determination rests in part on the analysis set forth above in dismissing the Hancocks' comparative hardship defense, and also in recognition that while reasonable people may differ as to the extent of the Lilliens' injury, the responsibility for the unfortunate placement of the wall lies with the Hancocks.

Doesn't the court's order bar the Hancocks from using the right-of-way?

3. <u>Damages for Loss of Use and Harm to the Property Prior to Ejectment</u>. The general rule is that the plaintiff, upon succeeding in ejectment, is entitled to damages to compensate for the unauthorized use of its land and damages for any harm done. Generally, the measure of damages for loss of use are the same as for trespass and nuisance, and include:

- A defendant who wrongfully occupies an apartment is liable for the reasonable rental value as well as for any physical damages the defendant caused;[3]
- Where the defendant wrongfully planted crops on plaintiff's land, the measure of damages is not the value of the crops but the fair market rental value of the land for the period of wrongful possession;[4]

4. <u>Duty to Mitigate</u>. After obtaining ejectment, or after the defendant voluntarily vacates the premises, the plaintiff must take reasonable steps to reduce or eliminate damages. For example, if a landlord ejects a tenant from a rental home, the landlord has an obligation to use reasonable efforts to lease the home. As shown in this book, failure to do so means the defendant is not responsible for damages that could have been avoided had the plaintiff used reasonable care, but it also means the defendant is responsible for expenses the landlord incurred in exercising reasonable care to mitigate damages.

B. Wrongful Ejectment or Forcible Detainer, and Constructive Eviction

Marina Food Associates, Inc. v. Marina Restaurant, Inc.
394 S.E.2d 824 (Ct. App. N.C. 1990) (Wells, J.)

[Plaintiff ran a restaurant in a building leased from defendants. The defendants failed to maintain the building properly, and plaintiff closed its restaurant. Because of a leaking roof and other defects the defendants had failed to repair, the county denied a license to reopen. Plaintiff sued for constructive eviction. The jury found for the plaintiff and defendants appealed.]

An act of a landlord which deprives his tenant of that beneficial enjoyment of the premises to which he is entitled under his lease, causing the tenant to abandon them, amounts to a constructive eviction. Put another way, when a landlord breaches a duty under the lease which renders the premises untenable, such conduct constitutes constructive eviction. Furthermore, a lease includes the implied covenant of quiet enjoyment. Where a lessee has been constructively evicted, the covenant of quiet enjoyment has also been breached.

Based on our conclusion that the evidence of breach of the lease was sufficient to support the jury's verdict, we must reject defendants' contentions with regard to

---

3. *Waldman v. Waldman*, 2010 WL 4137159 (Ky. Ct. App. Oct. 22, 2010) (awarding amount of rent expert testified was reasonable, but affirming denial of claim for damages to apartment because, among other things, property that defendant allegedly took from apartment appeared in both "before" and "after" photographs submitted by landlord).

4. *Watson v. Mense*, 298 S.W.3d 521 (Mo. 2009) (holding award of value of soybeans grown on plaintiff's land because it failed to consider the defendant's expenses, the value of their labor, or any value for the risk they undertook in farming the soybeans, and remanding to determine the fair market rental value).

these claims as well. The landlord's breach of the lease rendered the premise unfit for plaintiff's purposes. Such action constituted constructive eviction which automatically operated as a breach of the implied covenant of quiet enjoyment.

Defendants' final contention with regard to their motions for directed verdict and judgment notwithstanding the verdict is that the evidence was insufficient to show that plaintiff suffered damages as a result of defendant's conduct. We disagree. A breach of a lease agreement by the lessor may give rise to a claim for damages by the lessee. In this case the lessor's breach resulted in constructive eviction of the tenant. It is well settled that a tenant may recover damages that proximately result from a wrongful eviction. A tenant's general damages in such a case are the value, at the time of the eviction, of the unexpired term, less any rent reserved. However, a tenant's recovery is not limited to the value of the leasehold interest only, but may also include compensatory damages for pecuniary losses proximately resulting from the eviction, including conversion of personal property and, in the case of a business, loss of profits when such loss is ascertainable to a reasonable degree of certainty. Therefore, plaintiff's evidence as to the value of its lease was sufficient to support the jury's verdict for damages.

Notes and Questions

1. <u>Damages for Wrongful or Constructive Eviction</u>. Depending on the statute, wrongful eviction damages can include the value of the lost rent (e.g., if the plaintiff must rent a similar apartment at a higher rent), lost profits, and any deposit. *Bianchi v. Hood*, 513 N.Y.S.2d 541 (N.Y. Sup. Ct. 1987). Where constructive eviction constitutes a breach of contract or an implied covenant of quiet enjoyment, contract damages are available. *See Katz Deli of Aventura, Inc. v. Waterways Plaza, LLC,* 183 So. 3d 374 (Ct. App. Fla. 2013) (constructive eviction breached covenant of quiet enjoyment and so contract damages, including lost profits of business, were recoverable).

2. <u>Alternative Measures of Damage</u>. The court in *WSG W. Palm Beach Dev., LLC v. Blank*, 990 So. 2d 708 (Ct. App. Fla. 2008), analyzed damages to a constructively evicted dentist:

> There are two measures of damages for wrongful eviction resulting from the breach of a lease agreement. In a claim for wrongful eviction, a tenant may recover general damages consisting of the difference between the market value of the leasehold and the rent payable, as well as lost profits that can be determined with a reasonable degree of certainty. In addition, a tenant may be able to recover damages for losses that are the natural, direct, and necessary consequences of the breach when they are capable of being estimated by reliable data, and are such as should reasonably have been contemplated by the parties.

> Here, the tenant chose not to close down his successful dental practice because of the eviction, but worked diligently to continue it. That practice reaped an annual profit in excess of $375,000. As the trial court noted, had

the tenant suffered lost profits for the remaining period of the lease, he would have incurred damages in excess of $1,000,000. The tenant, however, chose to avert the loss of profits by recreating a location to continue his practice.

The only way the tenant could have been compensated for the damages caused by the landlord's admitted breach—the use of an improved premises for the remaining period of the lease—was for the trial court to consider the evidence as to improvements, the use of which was lost for the unexpired term. And, because the property was leased for a special purpose—a dental practice—the tenant was entitled to his actual and necessary expenses incurred in preparing to continue his dental practice.

The tenant produced evidence that it could not move the improvements from the existing location to the new property thereby incurring expenses in replicating his dental practice. The trial court found these losses supported by reliable evidence. Those findings were supported by competent, substantial evidence, which we will not disturb.

We are fully cognizant that, more often than not, the measure of damages for wrongful eviction will be the difference between the fair market value of the lease and the tenant's rent expense plus lost profits. We are also fully aware that the alternative measure of damages employed in this case is supported by Florida law.

The question of whether the cost to improve the new property was reasonably within the contemplation of the landlord before it breached the lease is answered by the principle applied in *Natural Kitchen, Inc. v. American Transworld Corp.*, 449 So.2d 855 (Fla. 2nd DCA 1984): The parties need not have contemplated the precise injuries which occurred, as long as they could have reasonably been expected to flow from the breach. *Id.*

> All that is necessary, in order to charge the defendant with a particular loss, is that it is one that ordinarily follows the breach of such a contract in the usual course of events, or that reasonable men in the position of the parties would have foreseen as a probable result of breach. It is not necessary that the parties should have given the matter a moment's thought or should have expressed themselves on the subject.

The evidence also supports that the loss was reasonably contemplated by the parties. The tenant is a dentist operating a practice in a prime medical location, appropriately outfitted for decades. It is reasonable for the landlord to expect that the tenant would need to either move his existing equipment or outfit a new location with new equipment.

3. Market Values. In *Daftary v. Prestonwood Market Square, Ltd.*, 399 S.W.3d 708 (Ct. App. Tex. 2013), a landlord brought a forcible detainer action against a commercial tenant. The lease rate was $12 per square foot and expired on June 30,

2008. The tenant continued to occupy the space and paid rent at that rate until September 2009, when the landlord stated either the tenant could enter a new lease or pay holdover rent. The tenant refused, and the landlord gave the required 30 days' notice on December 21, 2009, and then brought a forcible detainer action. The court awarded possession to the landlord, but the tenant sought trial *de novo*, as the statute permitted. Then, the day before trial in January 2011, the tenant vacated the premises and admitted the landlord was entitled to possession. The trial court awarded damages from December 21, 2009, to the date of trial, calculated at $26,000. The appellate court reversed: there was no evidence of the fair market value of the space between December 2009 and the date of trial, only the value as of June 2008.

4. <u>Mental Anguish</u>. Broadly worded statutes have been interpreted to permit recovery of all damages proximately caused, including lost profits and mental anguish. *Harding v. Savoy*, 323 Mont. 261 (2004); *see Harding v. Savoy*, 323 Mont. 261 (2004) (forcible detainer statute permitted recovery for mental anguish); *Graci v. Palazzo*, 119 So. 3d 741 (Ct. App. La. 2013) (affirming $20,000 for emotional distress, court stated "tenant is entitled to damages for uninhabitable premises; these damages include mental anguish").

C. Quieting Title

Relief in a quiet title action may include an order removing any "clouds" from the record title. "A 'cloud' on a title may be an encumbrance or a recorded document that has any tendency to impair the fee owner's ability to exercise the rights of ownership. Even a contract, or other document that does not actually encumber a party's title, may be a cloud if it would create an unnecessary complication that would have to be explained to a buyer or title insurer." *Inglewood Holdings, LLC v. Jones Engineers, Inc.*, 197 Wash. App. 1055 (Ct. App. Wash. 2017). State statutes regulate quiet title claims; the following cases are typical.

Kobza v. Tripp

18 P.3d 621 (Ct. App. Wash. 2001) (Sweeney, J.)

[The Tripps, the Kobzas' parents, and a third family jointly owned several parcels. In the early 1970s, they divided the parcels and created an easement in favor of the Kobzas' parents. In 1972, the Kobzas' parents permitted the Tripps to build a fence that blocked the easement. In 1994, the Kobzas' parents divorced and quitclaimed their interests to the Kobzas. In turn, they agreed to sell the land for $35,000, assuring the prospective buyer that an easement existed. However, the Tripps objected and the buyer backed out. The Kobzas then sued to quiet title in the easement, an injunction against interfering with the easement, and $35,000 in damages. The trial court awarded all relief. The Tripps appealed.]

An action to quiet title is equitable and designed to resolve competing claims of ownership. In Washington, such actions are governed by RCW 7.28.010.[2] An action to quiet title allows a person in peaceable possession or claiming the right to possession of real property to compel others who assert a hostile right or claim to come forward and assert their right or claim and submit it to judicial determination. Even if the claim asserted (here the absence of an easement) is absolutely invalid, the parties are still entitled to a decree saying so. Another and more colorful way of stating the same proposition is that the object of the statute is to authorize proceedings for the purpose of stopping the mouth of a person who has asserted or who is asserting a claim to the plaintiff's property. It is not aimed at a particular piece of evidence, but at the pretensions of the individual.

Because a quiet title action is a claim for equitable relief, damages are ordinarily not allowed. The relief is spelled out in the statute. The plaintiff "may have judgment in such action quieting or removing a cloud from plaintiff's title." RCW 7.28.010. And for that reason, quiet title actions are frequently coupled with other *legal* causes of action such as ejectment, unlawful detainer, or (and probably most appropriately here) slander of title.

The complaint here sets out the elements for a quiet title action but then requests damages for the lost sale simply because "Defendants have refused to allow Plaintiffs the use of said easement and are claiming that said easement has reverted to the Defendants by abandonment and adverse possession." The Tripps have the right to contest the easement by resisting an *equitable* quiet title action without being subject to a damage award, at least in the absence of some pleading, or proof, of some other *legal* cause of action.

In sum, before we can consider the propriety of the court's damage award, we must know the cause of action on which it is based. Here, there is no cause of action stated nor is there any identified in the court's findings. We have then neither the authority nor the inclination to try to force this square peg (the facts here) into some round hole (a viable legal cause of action for damages).

The Kobzas prayed for equitable relief, quiet title, and injunction. And the court granted that relief. We therefore reverse only that portion of the trial court's judgment awarding special damages.

Notes and Questions

1. <u>Slander of Title</u>. Quieting title does not result in damages and so a plaintiff must assert a claim permitting their recovery. No damages are presumed from slander of

---

2. "Any person having a valid subsisting interest in real property, and a right to the possession thereof, may recover the same by action in the superior court of the proper county, to be brought against the tenant in possession; if there is no such tenant, then against the person claiming the title or some interest therein, and may have judgment in such action quieting or removing a cloud from plaintiff's title." RCW 7.28.010.

title, but they are recoverable if "the plaintiff can show the loss of a specific, pending sale that was frustrated by the slander." *Allen-Pieroni v. Pieroni*, 535 S.W.3d 887 (Tex. 2017). While that corresponds to the $35,000 awarded in the principal case, "the seller's lost profit from the sale is not the relevant measure of those damages." *Id.* Instead, the usual measure is "the difference between the contract price (the amount the plaintiff would have received but for the defendant's title disparagement) and the property's market value at the time of trial with the cloud removed." *Id.* In this regard, Restatement of Torts § 633, cmt. d provides:

> The extent of the pecuniary loss caused by the prevention of a sale is determined by the difference between the price which would have been realized by it and the salable value of the thing in question after there has been a sufficient time following the frustration of the sale to permit its marketing. The depreciation of the thing from any cause after such time has elapsed is immaterial.

2. *Quia Timet*. In many states, actions to quiet title evolved from the equitable claim "*quia timet.*" In a few states, distinctions remain. *E.g., Mancuso v. TDGA, LLC*, 301 Ga. 671 (2017) (explaining distinctions, including right to jury trial for *quia timet*—which clears title "against the world"—but not to quiet title, which removes only "particular" clouds).

3. <u>Title to Out-of-State Property</u>. As a general rule, courts lack power to adjudicate title to real property located in another state, but a court with personal jurisdiction over the parties may compel specific performance of a contract that requires transfer of such an interest. "Some courts have described the distinction as whether the case involves a 'naked question of title.'" *Devon Energy Prod. Co., L.P. v. KCS Resources, LLC*, 450 S.W.3d 203 (Ct. App. Tex. 2014).

Problems

1. <u>Prepare a Chart</u>. The law gives special treatment to protect against harm to land or interests in it. To review, prepare a chart that identifies the elements of the claims that relate to real property, including the required type of harm, the typical types of harm, and the measures of damages for each. Use this as a template:

Claim	Elements	Required Harm and Measure of Damage	Other Common Harms and Measure of Damages
Trespass			
Nuisance			
Quiet Title			
Ejectment			
Wrongful Ejectment			

2. <u>Consider the Interests of Parties to a Lease to an Apartment</u>. In light of the discussion of ejectment and the ability of landlords and tenants to agree to available remedies, what would a landlord want to include and exclude as available remedies? Conversely, what would a tenant want to include and exclude?

3. <u>A Mitigation Problem</u>. The Smiths owned 40 acres of land with a small home. They sold the property to their daughter, reserving a life estate in the home. The daughter sold the land to the Seamsters, subject to her parents' retaining the life estate in the home. The Smiths moved off the property to another home, but they left behind, scattered over five acres of the land (in storage buildings and outside), cars, pickup trucks, cabs from pickup trucks, a tractor, various other farming equipment, scrap metal, and other machines. The Smiths refused the Seamsters' request to remove this personal property from the five acres. The Seamsters sued and succeeded on their claim of ejectment of the plaintiff's personal property (from other than the home) and, in addition, the trial court awarded $1,200 as loss-of-use damages for the five acres ($100 a month for 12 months). The trial court rejected the Smiths' argument that the Seamsters should have been required to mitigate damages by attempting to lease the five acres. The Smiths appeal. How should the court rule?

4. <u>Ejectment or What</u>? You represent Nelson, the owner of a condominium in a townhouse-style development. Another owner, Russo, recently enclosed an area behind his unit, both on the ground floor and above it. It now blocks the view of your client. You have reviewed the condominium documents and it is clear that the enclosed area is part of the common area owned by the condominium association, and is not the separate property of Nelson, who has no interest in it whatsoever. What claim should you bring and what relief should you seek?

5. <u>What Value</u>? Your client operated a bagel shop in a store leased from Bob Dunkin. Dunkin failed to maintain the building, allowing water to leak through the roof, which forced your client to close the store and re-open in a nearby space. During the period between closure and opening, Bob Dunkin's employees entered the space without your client's permission and certain equipment was damaged, and some is missing. Your client cannot afford experts, but wants to recover the value of that equipment. How will you prepare your client to do so and what evidence will you gather?

6. <u>Drones on Defendant's Land Filming Plaintiff on Her Land</u>. Some state statutes provide a claim for money damages in favor of a plaintiff filmed by a defendant operating a drone even if the drone does not enter the airspace over the plaintiff's land. You are an attorney for a committee at a state legislature that has been assigned this task. What should the elements of this claim be? What measure of damages? When, if ever, should injunctive relief be available?

7. <u>Missing Evidence</u>? Defendants owned land uphill from plaintiffs. Defendants' negligence caused water to flood plaintiffs' land and home, damaging a retaining

wall and their backyard. Plaintiffs sought to recover the cost to repair the damage as well as the diminished value of the land and home after repairs. The cost to repair was established at $43,000, but no repairs had, at the time of trial, been made. The plaintiffs' real estate expert testified that, just before the flood, the plaintiff's property appraised between $155,000 and $160,000, and, had the flood never happened, at the time of trial would have appraised at $140,000. One plaintiff testified that, at the time of trial and had the property not been damaged at all, the property would only have sold for $81,500. The jury awarded $43,000 for repair costs, and $25,000 for damages for diminution in value. The appellate court affirmed the award of cost to repair, but held there was no evidence to support *any* award of diminution in value and so rendered judgment for plaintiff in the amount of $43,000. What evidence was missing? Why would awarding diminution in value overcompensate plaintiffs?

8. Contiguous Parcel. You represent the defendant, who has been sued for nuisance because he contaminated two of three contiguous parcels of land owned by the plaintiff. The third parcel has not been contaminated, but publicity surrounding the spill has, plaintiff's evidence shows, been widespread. The plaintiff had intended to sell the three parcels to a developer and contends that the parcels have their highest value as a unit. The plaintiff introduces evidence that the cost to restore the two contaminated parcels is $100,000 and, as restored, the value to the buyer is $1 million, but had the contamination never occurred, the value would have been $1.5 million. Thus, the plaintiff seeks $600,000 in damages. Explain the basis for arguing there is no evidence to award the plaintiff any damages.

9. Annoying Trespasser. Assume you represent the defendant in a jurisdiction where mental anguish damages are recoverable for intentional, malicious trespasses. Your client purchased a 60-acre parcel with no access to a road. The plaintiffs, a husband and wife, refused your client's request for permission to build a roadway over their land so he could access the road. After that, your client bulldozed a roadway over their lot, destroying trees and damaging the plaintiffs' land. While doing so and while the wife was at work, he threatened the husband with a beating and otherwise bullied him. Both plaintiffs seek damages for harm to their land, annoyance and inconvenience, and mental distress. With respect to the wife's claim, how would you distinguish the cases that permit recovery for mental anguish?

10. Who Gets What? Assume two parcels of land are adjacent to defendant's property, and that defendant has been found liable for creating a private nuisance, through loud operation of a smoky factory, one that is "permanent." One parcel is owned and occupied by Plaintiff A, and the other is owned by Plaintiff B, but rented as a home to Plaintiff C. Explain which, if any, types of harm each plaintiff has suffered and what the measure of damages is.

11. Slipping Jimmy. Your client owns a store in a mall, and recently a person slipped and fell outside of the store, in an area not under your client's control, and fell into the storefront window, damaging it ($10,000) and ruining some clothing

and items that were on display ($4,000). The store had to be closed for two days, causing lost profits of about $12,000 based upon historical sales averages, and your client suffered aggravation in having to deal with cleaning up, and was cut while doing so, but did not require medical care. Your client wishes to sue for trespass damages. The potential defendant clearly accidentally fell into the storefront. What claims will you suggest and what damages might likely be recovered?

12. <u>Noise</u>. Your clients want to sue the owner of a cement plant that opened next to a cemetery where their beloved grandfather is buried in a plot he bought before his death. The graveyard is covered, regularly, with dust and ash and the noise makes visitation difficult. Are there any barriers to recovery for trespass or nuisance? Can you think of a way to overcome any?

13. <u>Blocking the Easement</u>. Your client is a neighbor of the Donaldsons. They share a driveway. You have examined the property records and the driveway is on the Donaldsons' land, but your clients have an easement for ingress and egress over it. The Donaldsons have been blocking the driveway with various toys, bikes, and other obstacles to annoy your clients. Your clients want this to stop. What claim would you suggest and what damages are available?

14. <u>Which Law</u>? Why is an Ohio plaintiff's suit against an Indiana factory for emitting smoke causing odors on plaintiff's land governed by Indiana law? *Alleyne v. Diageo USVI, Inc.*, 63 V.I. 384 (2015).

15. <u>Mental Anguish and Annoyance in the Context of Injunctions</u>. If a plaintiff is unable to obtain either mental anguish or annoyance damages, or neither, how does that factor in to whether the remedy at law is inadequate if the defendant's actions are bothering the plaintiff's peaceful enjoyment of her land?

Chapter 8

Remedies Triggered by Economic Loss

Economic loss is required to satisfy the damage element for a claim of breach of contract. In contrast, only a few tort claims are available to a plaintiff who suffers only economic harm. This chapter first discusses monetary remedies for breach of contract, and then turns to when those damages are inadequate and so injunctive relief, including relief in the form of "specific performance," is available. It then analyzes the few tort claims where economic loss is sufficient to constitute damage, the measure of damages for those claims, and when those monetary remedies are inadequate and thus injunctive relief is available.

Finally, this chapter turns to certain "equitable" gap-filling claims or remedies that allow plaintiffs to obtain relief, not necessarily for economic losses they suffered, but that prevent the defendant from retaining an "unjust" economic benefit that otherwise could not be remedied by a tort or contract claim.

1. Breach of Contract

A. The Three Types of Common Law Contract Damages and *Hadley's* Limitation on Two of Them

The typical elements of a claim for breach of contract are: "(1) a contract, (2) performance by the party seeking recovery, (3) breach of the contract by the other party, and (4) damages." *L-3 Communics. Corp. v. E.R. Lewis Transp., Inc.*, 2005 WL 3591987 (D. Utah. Dec. 30, 2005). The three common forms of contract damages are expectancy, reliance, and restitution.

Restitution is perhaps the simplest: "the injured party is entitled to restitution for any benefit that he has conferred on the other party by way of part performance or reliance." Restatement (Second) of Contracts § 373(1) (1981). "The idea behind restitution is to restore—that is, to restore the non-breaching party to the position he would have been in had there never been a contract to breach." *Republic Sav. Bank, F.S.B. v. United States*, 584 F.3d 1369 (Fed. Cir. 2009). Thus, restitution returns benefits a plaintiff conferred on defendant, such as a down payment.

Expectancy is designed to put a plaintiff in the economic position that, but for the breach, it would have occupied. It requires determining how much money the plaintiff would have *netted* (as profit or loss) had the defendant performed, and is usually measured by: (a) the loss in the value to him of the other party's performance caused by its failure or deficiency, plus (b) any other loss, including incidental or consequential loss, caused by the breach, less (c) any cost or other loss that he has avoided by not having to perform. *CR-RSC Tower I, LLC v. RSC Tower I, LLC*, 56 A.3d 170 (Md. 2012). The court in *Coppola Const. Co., Inc. v. Hoffman Enterprises Ltd. Partn.*, 117 A.3d 876 (Ct. App. Conn. 2015) explained the rationale behind this formula:

> The sum of damages awarded as compensation in a breach of contract action should place the injured party in the same position as he would have been in had the contract been performed. The injured party, however, is entitled to retain nothing in excess of that sum which compensates him for the loss of his bargain. Guarding against excessive compensation, the law of contract damages limits the injured party to damages based on his actual loss caused by the breach. The concept of actual loss accounts for the possibility that the breach itself may result in a saving of some cost that the injured party would have incurred if he had had to perform. In such circumstances, the amount of the cost saved will be credited in favor of the wrongdoer that is, subtracted from the loss caused by the breach in calculating the injured party's damages.

A threshold requirement for recovery of expectancy and reliance damages — but not restitution — is that the plaintiff had been ready, willing, and able to perform the contract. The court in *In re Asia Glob. Crossing, Ltd.*, 404 B.R. 335 (S.D.N.Y. 2009) explained why:

> The general rule is that following repudiation of a contract, the nonbreaching party may seek expectation damages *or* restitution for the benefits she conferred on the other party. Restatement (Second) of Contracts § 373(1) ("On a breach by non-performance that gives rise to a claim for damages for total breach or on a repudiation, the injured party is entitled to restitution for any benefit that he has conferred on the other party by way of part performance or reliance.").

> These alternative remedies protect different interests that a party to a contract holds. Expectation damages, the traditional measure of a nonbreaching party's damages, aim to put the nonbreaching party in as good a position as she would have occupied had there been full performance. Restitution, by contrast, aims to restore the nonbreaching party to as good a position as the one she occupied before the contract was made, without attempting to compensate her for consequential harms.

> Where the nonbreaching party seeks damages (used here in the general sense of a monetary remedy for breach of contract) measured by her restitutionary interest, the ready, willing, and able requirement is inapt. That requirement prevents a nonbreaching plaintiff from claiming *profits* she

would not otherwise have been entitled to but for the defendant's breach. This risk of unjust enrichment, however, is nonexistent when a plaintiff seeks damages measured by her restitutionary interest. Since the plaintiff is only seeking to recover the benefit she conferred on the defendant, there is, logically, no possibility that an award of damages will confer benefits on the plaintiff to which she is not entitled.

A simple hypothetical illustrates the point. Suppose that *B* pays *S* $1,000 for an option to buy *S's* house for $100,000 at any point within the next five years. Three years into the option term, *S* repudiates the option. *B* sues, seeking damages of $50,000, which is equal to the current market price of the house ($150,000) less *B's* purchase price ($100,000). To recover, *B* must show she was ready, willing, and able to exercise the option when *B* repudiated. Otherwise, *B* would be awarded profits that she was not certain to earn. If *B* was not ready, willing, and able to exercise the option, she would have earned nothing notwithstanding *S's* repudiation.

Suppose, however, that instead of purchasing an option to buy the house, *B* makes a $20,000 down payment on the $100,000 purchase price, and the parties agree that *S* will turn over title when *B* pays the balance of the purchase price, which must occur within five years. Before *B* does so, *S* repudiates the contract by selling the house to *B2* for $200,000. *B* sues to recover her down payment. Here the law does not require *B* to show she was ready, willing, and able to perform. As the Corbin treatise explains:

> If the plaintiff has made money payments to the defendant and there is later a failure of consideration therefore, involving a repudiation by the defendant or any other breach going to the essence of the contract, the plaintiff can maintain an action for restitution of the money so paid to the defendant, with interest. It makes no difference what was the performance promised by the defendant but not rendered by him; in various cases it has been failure to transfer land or goods or to render some agreed service. The cases so holding are so numerous as to make their citation both impossible and unnecessary.

Reliance damages require measuring the expenses the plaintiff paid to third parties that would have been avoided but for the particular contract. An award puts the plaintiff in as good a position as it "would have been in had the contract not been made." *Designer Direct, Inc. v. DeForest Redevelopment Auth.*, 313 F.3d 1036 (7th Cir. 2002). Overhead expenses are generally not recoverable unless plaintiff shows: (a) they were allocated to the breached contract and (b) it likely would have recouped them on other projects. *Id.*

Under *Hadley v. Baxendale*, 9 Ex. 341 (1854), expectancy and reliance damages are largely limited to "those damages in contemplation at the time of the formation of the contract." *Vanderbeek v. Vernon Corp.*, 25 P.3d 1242, 1245 (Colo. App. 2000), *aff'd*, 50 P.3d 866 (Colo. 2002). For those measures of damage, the harm for which reliance or expectancy damages are sought must have been of the type, and the loss must have been in an amount, that either: (a) a reasonable defendant in the circumstances at the time of contracting would have known breach would cause; or (b) at the time of contracting the defendant actually knew breaching the particular contract would cause. In contract parlance, (a) "general damages" are an amount and type that ordinarily flow from breach of the type of contract in the circumstances involved, but (b) "special damages" do not do so. While general damages thus satisfy the damage element and are recoverable if the amount is proven with reasonable certainty, special damages satisfy the damage element and are recoverable only if at the time of contracting the defendant had known, or at least had "contemplated," that a breach of the particular contract would likely cause the type of harm and the amount of damage.

For example, a contract that expressly identifies a particular type of harm renders losses for that type of harm recoverable. So, a lease that states "Landlord acknowledges lost profits are likely to result upon breach" makes at least *some* amount of lost profits recoverable "special damages." While such an explicit identification is sufficient, it is not required.

The courts disagree on the precise test, and so the precise jury instructions. For example, in *Linc Equip. Serv., Inc. v. Signal Med. Serv., Inc.,* 319 F.3d 288 (7th Cir. 2003), the defendant had agreed to transport an MRI machine knowing the plaintiff intended to rent it to third parties. The machine was damaged during shipment and that caused plaintiff to lose rental income. In analyzing whether that lost rental income was "general damage," the court wrote:

> We doubt that Illinois requires "express contemplation" of consequential damages—or that, if it does, this phrase implies a subjective as opposed to an objective inquiry. Although the district judge and the parties did not mention it, *Hadley v. Baxendale,* 9 Ex. 341 (1854), remains the dominant source of law on the recovery of consequential damages for breach of contract, and we have held that Illinois follows *Hadley*'s approach. What *Hadley* holds is that a consequential loss is compensable only if "reasonably foreseeable," not that it must be "expressly contemplated." Although the phrase "expressly contemplated" crops up in some Illinois cases, that state's judiciary has explained that it is used as a synonym for foreseeability.

As a comparison, California appears to be closer to a "should have known" standard than Illinois appears to take. The court in *DIYA TV, Inc. v. KAXT, LLC,* 2018 WL 1312448 (Ct. App. Cal. Mar. 14, 2018) explained California's approach this way:

> General damages are often characterized as those that flow directly and necessarily from a breach of contract, or that are a natural result of a breach. Because the occurrence of general damages is sufficiently predictable, the parties are deemed to have contemplated them at the time of contracting.

Special damages, which are required to be pleaded with particularity are losses that do not arise directly and inevitably from any similar breach of any similar agreement, but are secondary or derivative losses arising from circumstances that are particular to the contract or to the parties. A party assumes the risk for special damages liability for unusual losses arising from special circumstances only if it was advised of the facts concerning special harm which might result from breach. If, however, the surrounding circumstances are special and unusual, such as would not themselves have been foreseen by an ordinary person, damages resulting from that injury are not recoverable unless the defendant was clearly warned of the probable existence of those unusual circumstances or if, because of the defendant's own education, training and information, there was reason to foresee the probable existence of such circumstances.

Further, courts disagree on whether the inquiry includes subjective knowledge, or is purely objective. *See Sunnyland Farms, Inc. v. C. N.M. Elec. Co-op., Inc.*, 301 P.3d 387 (N.M. 2013) (switching from requiring "an explicit or tacit agreement by the defendant that he or she will assume particular damages if he or she breaches," to what it determined was the less stringent approach of holding "a defendant is liable only for those consequential damages that were objectively foreseeable as a probable result of his or her breach when the contract was made."). Further still, some courts hold that *Hadley* applies only to "the kind, not the amount, of damage." *Fla. Power & Light Co. v. Westinghouse Elec. Corp.*, 597 F. Supp. 1456 (E.D. Va. 1984), *aff'd in part, rev'd in part*, 826 F.2d 239 (4th Cir. 1987).

As a further illustration of the complexities behind, but the significance of, the meaning of "general damages," the court in *Core-Mark Midcontinent, Inc. v. Sonitrol Corp.*, 370 P.3d 353 (Ct. App. Colo. 2016), analyzed several aspects of *Hadley* and took these positions:

- Losses that are a "natural" result of the breach are those an ordinary person of common experience would expect; such a person would assume the circumstances to be those that have usually existed in similar cases within that person's experience.

- Actual foresight is not required; the losses need only be reasonably foreseeable as a probable consequence of the breach by an ordinary person of common experience.

- The injury actually suffered must be of a kind a prudent person had reason to foresee and of an amount that is not beyond the bounds of reasonable prediction.

- There is no requirement that the breach itself, or the particular way that the loss came about, be foreseeable.

- The loss must have been a foreseeable, though not necessary or certain, result of the breach.

- The mere circumstance that some loss was foreseeable, or even that some loss of the same general kind was foreseeable, will not suffice if the actual loss was not foreseeable.
- Foreseeability is judged by what was foreseeable when the contract was entered into.

In addition to *Hadley's* limitation on expectancy damages, a plaintiff cannot recover expectancy in two common circumstances: (a) when the amount cannot be proven with reasonable certainty, or (b) if the plaintiff cannot show it had been ready, willing, and able to perform the contract. Further, a plaintiff may elect not to seek expectancy if, for example, performance by the defendant would have netted a loss to the plaintiff. *P.C. Data Centers of Pa., Inc. v Fed. Express Corp.,* 113 F. Supp. 2d 709 (M.D. Pa. 2000).

Because *Hadley* applies to reliance, the expenses must have been foreseeable to the defendant "at the time of contract formation" and so include only those expenses flowing "from the breach (a) in the ordinary course of events, or (b) as a result of special circumstances, beyond the ordinary course of events, that the party in breach had reason to know." *Stovall v. United States,* 94 Fed. Cl. 336 (Fed. Cl. 2010).

The *Hadley* limitation ordinarily means that damages for mental anguish "are available in breach of contract actions only in extraordinary contractual circumstances." *Brossia v. Rick Const., L.T.D. Liability Co.,* 81 P.3d 1126 (Ct. App. Colo. 2003). *See Lookshin v. Union Planters Bank,* 2006 WL 3147330 (S.D. Tex. Oct. 30, 2006) (no award for bank's breach of lease of safety deposit box by permitting theft of $500,000, which had caused plaintiff severe distress).

Finally, confusion arises further because courts sometimes also refer to "special damages" as "consequential damages" or "indirect damages." Likewise, they sometimes refer to "general damages" as "direct damages." Further, the question of recoverability of damages often arises in the context of interpreting whether the parties' agreement excluded, or included, certain types of damages, and an agreement that excludes "consequential damages" begs the question of what that means. The following shows that, although fuzzy, the distinction remains critical to analyzing contracts, litigating cases, and advising clients.

Freeman v. Duhamel

1997 WL 524119 (Del. Super. Ct. May 29, 1997) (Herlihy, J.)

[The Freemans had hired Duhamel to inspect a home they were considering buying. They noticed the kitchen floor was not level, but Duhamel failed to recognize that the cause was a makeshift support structure under the kitchen. The Freemans purchased the home, discovered the problem, then sued Duhamel, seeking the cost to install supports to level the floor. The trial court found Duhamel had breached the contract and awarded damages. Both sides appealed.]

The proper measure of damages, in an action brought under either contract or tort, for defects in the design or construction of a home, is the cost of repairs, unless the cost of repairs is clearly disproportionate to the probable loss in value of the home. That is the normal measure of damages if an action were brought against a seller or builder. However, this is an action against a home inspector. While the question of the appropriate measure of damages in an action against a negligent home inspector appears to be one of first impression in Delaware, courts of several other states have used the measure of damages in actions against home and termite inspectors similar to the measure of damages used in Delaware in actions against builders or owners.

The court in *Krol v. Goldring*, 38 Conn.Supp. 610, 458 A.2d 15 (1982) justified this measure of damages in an action against inspectors:

> If the defendant had performed the contract in a competent and work-manlike manner, then one of two things would presumably have occurred. Either the plaintiffs would not have purchased the house or they would have received an adjustment in the purchase price reflecting the amount required to correct the structural damage. In either event, the plaintiffs would not have had to expend their own money to make the necessary repairs. We conclude, therefore, that the measure of damages applied by the trial court was correct.

Like the court in *Krol*, the trial court said "if the purchasers had been informed of the makeshift support system beneath the kitchen floor, they would have undoubtedly either attempted to rescind the Sales Agreement or negotiated a reduction in the purchase price." However, unlike *Krol*, the trial court did not award damages based on the cost to repair. Because the trial court found that the sagging in the kitchen floor was observable at the time of the sale and the problem had not worsened since the sale, the cost to repair is the cost of repairing the makeshift columns to prevent further sagging to the kitchen floor.

The record, both from testimony and exhibits before the trial court, shows a range of cost of repair. The dispute is which one in that range is the legally appropriate cost. There is no factual dispute involved in this determination.

An estimate by Michael Paul to make permanent columns or a permanent wall below the kitchen was $500. This estimate was made by a structural engineer. This repair would prevent further sagging, but would not level the floor.

John Heyn, another structural engineer, estimated in a written report that a repair to the floor would cost approximately $5,000. Mr. Heyn did not testify at the trial. This evidence was his estimate in a report prepared prior to trial. The estimate included the cost of leveling the kitchen floor. As discussed above, because the sagging in the floor was observable at the time of purchase, the Freemans are not entitled to the cost to level the floor.

Mark Fenimore, a contractor, prepared a written estimate of repairs and also testified at trial. He estimated repairs at $18,320. This included the cost of replacing the kitchen cabinets. The defendants argue that replacing the kitchen cabinets is excessive. If the floor is repaired and made level, the kitchen cabinets will likely have to be replaced. Fenimore testified as such. Also, Larry Hughes, the Freemans' structural engineer stated that, although he could not render an opinion of whether the cabinets would definitely need replacing, he said, "it's very likely that the cabinets would not go back into their original position."

The problem with the testimony of Fenimore and Hughes is that the Freemans are not entitled to a level floor or new cabinets. The floor was not level at the time of purchase and the other cosmetic problems were either visible or were not caused by the sagging floor. The Freemans are only entitled to an amount necessary to prevent further sagging which is probably as much as would have been escrowed at closing had the Freemans known in a timely fashion of the floor underpinning. The only evidence on this point is the estimate by Michael Paul. The Court finds that the cost of repairing the makeshift columns is $500.

While the cost of repair is generally the only measure of damages, the Court, where necessary to effect complete justice, can award the party not in default other expenses incident to the contract. In this case, the Freemans' paid $190 for the home inspection. Because the failure to report the makeshift columns was a breach in the duty of care which went to the heart of the agreement between the parties, this Court finds that in order to effect complete justice, the Freemans are entitled to that cost. Therefore, in addition to the $500, the Freemans are entitled to the $190 for the home inspection.

Maine Rubber Int'l v. Environmental Mgmt. Group, Inc.

324 F.Supp.2d 32 (D. Me. 2004) (Hornby, J.)

[Plaintiff Maine Rubber International was planning to relocate its tire manufacturing business and had hired the defendant Environmental Management Group, Inc., to conduct a "Phase I Assessment"—an environmental study—of a possible new location, called the DuraStone property. EMG inspected the property and advised Maine Rubber it was "clean." As a result, Maine Rubber waived a clause in its contract to purchase the DuraStone site as to its environmental condition. Six months later, the EPA found the DuraStone property had environmental hazards. As a result, Maine Rubber terminated the contract to buy that property and, instead of its planned orderly relocation of its business to the DuraStone property, relocated its business on an expedited basis and at higher costs to another location. As a result, Maine Rubber lost profits and lost the benefit of expenditures it had made preparing for the move to the DuraStone property.

Maine Rubber sued EMG for breach of contract. The jury found EMG in breach and awarded Maine Rubber $1,900 as the price paid to EMG, $211,625.51 for expenditures Maine Rubber paid to third parties in anticipation of the DuraStone move, and $486,600 in lost profits. In the following opinion, the trial court addressed EMG's renewed JMOL motion and motion for new trial.]

Special or consequential damages, like lost profits or reliance expenditures, are generally not recoverable. Under Maine law such damages are recoverable, however, if at the time the contract was formed they were or should have been reasonably foreseeable or contemplated by both parties as a probable result of a breach.

Thus, under Fed R. Civ. P. 50, judgment as a matter of law depends upon whether there was a "legally sufficient evidentiary basis" for a jury to determine that these damages were reasonably foreseeable at the time the contract was made. The only evidence as to the expectations of Maine Rubber and EMG at the time the contract was formed came from the testimony of Stuart Brown ("Brown"), former president and chief operating officer of Maine Rubber. Everything EMG might reasonably have contemplated as a result of the breach specific to Maine Rubber it would have learned from Brown. According to Brown's testimony, he told EMG who Maine Rubber was and what it did for business. (There was no testimony by any EMG employee who recalled speaking with Brown or knowing anything about Maine Rubber's potential plans for moving to the DuraStone property.) Brown explained to EMG that Maine Rubber had a loan with Fleet Financial and that Fleet referred Maine Rubber to EMG because Maine Rubber was contemplating purchasing the DuraStone property.

There was no testimony that Brown discussed with EMG the benefits or advantages of the DuraStone property compared to Maine Rubber's existing facility or any other potential site; no testimony that he told EMG about Maine Rubber's profit expectations at the new location; and no testimony that he told EMG that Maine Rubber had a phased move plan designed to prevent production and profit losses as a result of the move. Additionally, the low contract price for performing the site assessment, $1,900, suggests that the parties never contemplated the risk of liability for lost profits, here $486,600.

EMG is in the business of performing environmental site assessments with corporate entities. A jury could reasonably conclude that EMG should be generally aware that its customers have financial stakes in the properties to be assessed. But lost profits are not the type of damages that the contracting parties would ordinarily expect as a result of a Phase I Environmental Assessment that failed to discover hazardous substances. Instead, as a result of an inadequate site assessment, the parties would reasonably expect expenses resulting from hazardous substances being on the property, *i.e.*, future cleanup costs on the site, fines for having toxins located on the property, best resale value if the property was unusable, etc.

In the absence of any evidence that the parties contemplated Maine Rubber's lost profits as a consequence of breach at the time the contract was made or any evidence that lost profits would be generally expected for this type of breach, I conclude as a matter of law that Maine Rubber's lost profits were not reasonably foreseeable as a result of breach at the time contract was made. They are therefore not recoverable.

EMG argues that the jury's damages award for out-of-pocket expenses is speculative, disproportionate to the contract price, and against the weight of the evidence. Under Maine law, speculative damages may not be awarded. The out-of-pocket expenses are certainly not speculative in the sense of being based upon conjecture;

Maine Rubber presented at trial actual expenses it incurred in preparing for the DuraStone move, EMG argues that the amount is nevertheless speculative because Maine Rubber produced insufficient evidence at trial to show that in fact it would have terminated the DuraStone contract but for the EMG breach.

Proof that Maine Rubber would have terminated the contract earlier if it learned of environmental problems sooner certainly would be sufficient to establish causation for the claim for lost reliance expenditures. But that was not Maine Rubber's case. Instead, Maine Rubber presented evidence at trial that it learned of the environmental problems so late in the process that there was insufficient time to assess or cure them before the DuraStone closing date and therefore that it had little choice but to rescind the DuraStone contract and move elsewhere under time pressure, thereby losing the value of the amounts it had spent on the DuraStone acquisition. In other words, Maine Rubber's premise was not that earlier knowledge would necessarily have led to contract termination, but that it would have provided Maine Rubber with time to assess the problems and cure them rather than be forced into an expedited move to a different location, forfeiting the value of what it had spent on the DuraStone site. Thus, Maine Rubber did provide sufficient evidence from which the jury could find that EMG's breach forced Maine Rubber to terminate the DuraStone contract and caused Maine Rubber to lose the benefits of its out-of-pocket expenses. This conclusion also disposes of EMG's weight of the evidence argument.

A contract price's lack of proportionality to the loss may indicate whether such damages were foreseeable. But here the out-of-pocket expenses paid by Maine Rubber to third parties on the aborted DuraStone move are exactly the type of reliance costs one would expect a prospective purchaser to spend in preparing to move to a new property. A defective Phase I assessment would obviously render many of these expenditures valueless when, like here, environmental hazards later were found on the property prior to closing and the land sale contract was terminated. Their value was lost to Maine Rubber when it cancelled the DuraStone move. EMG has performed hundreds of site assessments for commercial and industrial companies for the purpose of evaluating the environmental condition of prospective manufacturing sites. The evidence established that EMG knew that its reports were relied upon in real estate decisions and transactions and that the accuracy of these reports was important and that it knew Maine Rubber was obtaining this assessment with a view to acquiring the DuraStone property. EMG should reasonably have foreseen that its clean bill of health would lead to Maine Rubber making expenditures for engineering costs, legal fees, site plan consulting, site studies, public relations, geotechnical investigations and design work, and that those would be valueless if Maine Rubber later had to abort the move because of undiscovered environmental hazards.

I therefore conclude that the jury's award of out-of-pocket reliance expenditures to Maine Rubber was not speculative, not against the weight of evidence, and not disproportionate to the contract price in a way that would make such damages unforeseeable when the contract was made.

Notes and Questions

1. <u>The Cases</u>. Which type of damages were in issue in each case? In *Freeman*, if at the time of purchase the floor had been level, but immediately afterward it sagged because of the undisclosed defect, what other facts would be needed for a court to award either $18,320 or $5,000? In *Maine Rubber*, why were reliance damages, but not lost profits, foreseeable?

2. <u>Events after Contracting</u>. In *CR-RSC Tower I, LLC v. RSC Tower I, LLC*, 56 A.3d 170 (Md. 2012), defendant Landlords in 2004 leased two tracts of land to plaintiffs, Tenants, who intended to construct two towers, each with 350 apartments. Construction was delayed because of various factors, disputes, and litigation. Then, in 2008, the real estate market crashed and so, instead of performing, the Tenants sued for damages. They relied upon *Hadley* and persuaded the trial court to exclude evidence of the crash, asserting that anticipated profits at the time of contracting were the proper measure. The jury's $36 million verdict was affirmed on appeal. The Landlords appealed to the state supreme court, which affirmed in a split decision. The majority reasoned that post-contracting evidence was irrelevant, stating:

> Measuring contract damages by the value of the item at the time of breach is eminently sensible and actually takes expected lost profits into account. The value of assets for which there is a market is the discounted value of the stream of future income that the assets are expected to produce. New York courts have thus explicitly upheld damage awards based on what knowledgeable investors anticipated the future condition and performance would be at the time of breach and have rejected awards based on what the actual economic conditions and performance were in light of hindsight.

> Appellants are unclear about the time at which damages are to be determined under the rule they espouse. Certainly they are not entitled to select the precise date on which the vessels had their highest value or a period of time that was profitable but that excludes periods where losses occurred. If the time of trial governed, the rule would be a two-edged sword. New York courts have expressly refused to adopt this "wait and see" theory of damages.

Id. The majority saw no evidence of strategic behavior by the tenants. The dissent argued that "post-breach evidence of actual performance must be admitted to avoid providing a financial windfall based on inaccurate prediction" and the majority had made the Landlords "guarantors of future profits."

The Restatement states that "the expectation interest is not based on the injured party's hopes when it made the contract but on the actual value that the contract would have had to it had it been performed." Restatement (Second) of Contracts Section 344, comment b, at 104. The Restatement provides this example:

> A makes a contract with B under which A is to pay B for drilling an oil well on B's land, adjacent to that of A, for development and exploration purposes. Both A and B believe that the well will be productive and will

substantially enhance the value of A's land in an amount that they estimate to be $1,000,000. Before A has paid anything, B breaks the contract by refusing to drill the well. Other exploration then proves that there is no oil in the region. A's expectation interest is zero.

Finally consider this observation from *Leaf Invenergy Co. v. Invenergy Wind LLC*, 2018 WL 1882746 (Del. Ch. Apr. 19, 2018):

> Contract damages are ordinarily based on the injured party's expectation interest, but that concept is a term of art that does not depend on what the parties subjectively expected. Instead, the court determines an amount that will give the injured party the benefit of its bargain by putting that party in the position it would have been but for the breach. Parties can contract for a specified remedy, such as in a liquidated damages clause, but unless they memorialize their subjective beliefs in such a way, those beliefs do not establish the measure of damages. Expectancy damages must be tied to and limited by the express promises made to the plaintiff in the Agreement.

If the goal is an objective determination at the time of contracting, is subjective belief relevant?

MVP Health Plan, Inc. v. OptumInsight, Inc.

2017 WL 3669558 (N.D.N.Y. Aug. 24, 2017) (Sannes, J.)

[Defendant OptumInsight, Inc., agreed to provide actuarial analyses to MVP Health Plan, Inc., to allow MVP to determine how to price health plans for its commercial customers, who in turn would offer them to their employees. Optum and MVP had a long relationship and Optum knew why MVP needed the analyses. Optum provided inaccurate calculations that caused MVP to set the premiums for its health plans too low, and as a result it suffered $12 million in lost profits. The trial court found that MVP's breach caused those losses, but then examined whether those lost profits were general, or consequential, damages.]

Courts applying New York law typically find that lost income from third-party arrangements are consequential damages on grounds that they are one step removed from the naked performance promised by the defendant. *See also Tractebel Energy Mktg. v. AEP Power Mktg.*, 487 F.3d 89 (2d Cir. 2007) ("Lost profits are consequential damages when, as a result of the breach, the non-breaching party suffers loss of profits on collateral business arrangements."); *First Niagara Bank N.A. v. Mortgage Builder Software, Inc.*, 2016 WL 2962817 (W.D.N.Y. May 23, 2016) ("Although there is no bright-line rule stating that fees flowing from a third party cannot constitute general or compensatory damages, such cases are rare.").

Here, the lost income MVP suffered as a result of its mispriced health plans is closely tied to Optum's breach, because MVP relied on Optum's complex actuarial calculations and projections to set plan premiums. Nevertheless, MVP's lost income was a step removed from Optum's promised performance. The asset that Optum contracted to provide MVP was accurate actuarial calculations and analysis, submission to CMS, and certification of the bids' accuracy—not final pricing determinations or insurance for the plans' financial well-being. Thus, this is not one of the rare exceptions to the trend in this circuit; rather, this is a typical case where the ability of the non-breaching party to operate his business, and thereby generate profits on collateral transactions, is contingent on the performance of the primary contract" and the breach hinders the non-breaching party's business. That the potential damages—surmounting $12 million—far surpass the contract price also weighs in favor of a finding that such a disproportionate risk was not assumed. For these reasons, the Court finds that MVP's lost income on third-party health plan contracts constitutes consequential damages.

Having determined that these damages are consequential, the Court next considers whether Plaintiff is entitled to them. In New York,

> Loss of future profits as damages for breach of contract have been permitted under long-established and precise rules of law. First, it must be demonstrated with certainty that such damages have been caused by the breach and, second, the alleged loss must be capable of proof with reasonable certainty. In addition, there must be a showing that the particular damages were fairly within the contemplation of the parties to the contract at the time it was made.

Kenford Co. v. County of Erie, 67 N.Y.2d 257 (1986). The *Kenford* court did not mean that the parties must have contemplated the *injury* at the time of contracting, but rather the liability for loss of profits over the length of the contract. *See also* Dobbs Law of Remedies § 12.4(6) ("If foreseeability of damages is to be the test at all, it must not be understood as a simple factual term but as a term of art, a kind of shorthand for the more complex idea that damages should be limited as the parties intended.").

Here, there is no evidence that the parties contemplated Optum's liability for MVP's health plan losses. As MVP argues, it may be that "the losses incurred by MVP as a result of Optum's breach were certain;" however, it is the parties' contemplation of liability—not just injury—that is at issue. Optum did not agree to act as an insurer for MVP's health plans or to otherwise accept liability for losses on third-party contracts. As a result, MVP is not entitled to recover lost income under the parties' contract.

Unlike the lost income injury, the contract price for Optum's services constitutes general damages. General contract damages are compensation calculated by the value of the very thing to which the plaintiff was entitled. Here, as noted above, MVP contracted for reasonable actuarial work that abided by the ASOPs. In consideration for this service, MVP tendered $332,981.44. The actuarial work that Optum provided MVP was worthless and MVP is entitled to recover the value of Optum's services, or $332,981.44.

Bonanza Rest. Co. v. Wink

2012 WL 1415512 (Del. Super. Apr. 17, 2012) (Stokes, J),
aff'd, 65 A.3d 616 (Del. 2013)

[Plaintiff Bonanza Restaurant Company had four franchise agreements with defendant Robert Wink, under which Wink agreed to set up four restaurants and then assign them to four others, who would operate the restaurants and pay royalties, based on sales, to Bonanza. Wink agreed that he would guarantee those payments if any assignee defaulted. All four defaulted, Wink refused to pay, and Bonanza sued for breach of contract, seeking $1.3 million in lost royalties. Wink moved for summary judgment that those lost royalties were not recoverable because the parties' agreement excluded recovery of "consequential" damages and instead limited damages to "recovery of actual damages sustained." This is the court's opinion denying Wink's motion.]

Because the Franchise Agreements and the Guaranties do not define the terms "actual damages" or "consequential damages," the Court presumes the parties intended their ordinary meaning. The term "actual damages" encompasses both "direct" and "consequential" damages. Direct damages are those inherent in the breach, which in this case is the closing of the restaurants by New Franchisees. Direct damages are the necessary and usual result of the defendant's wrongful act; they flow naturally and necessarily from the wrong. Direct damages compensate the plaintiff for the loss that is conclusively presumed to have been foreseen by the defendant from his wrongful act. The measure of damages for breach of contract may include reasonably certain lost profits, which are defined as damages for the loss of net income to a business.

Profits lost on other contracts or relationships resulting from the breach may be classified as consequential damages. That is, if the party's expectation of profit is incidental to the performance of the contract, the loss of that expectancy is consequential. Consequential damages, also known as special damages, are those that result naturally but not necessarily from the wrongful act, because they require the existence of some other contract or relationship. Consequential damages are not recoverable unless they are foreseeable and are traceable to the wrongful act and result from it. The distinction between direct and consequential damages is the degree to which the damages are a foreseeable and highly probable consequence of a breach.

A contractual restriction on consequential damages, standing alone, does not preclude recovery of lost profits; that is, lost profits cannot mechanically be classified as consequential damages. Historically, courts have had difficulty establishing a workable distinction between direct and consequential damages, and the results vary with the facts.

In this case, it was not only probable but inevitable that if the restaurants closed, royalty payments would cease. Such is the nature of royalties. Each Franchise Agreement requires payment weekly royalty fees in the amount of 4 percent of gross weekly sales, sent weekly by electronic funds transfer. These fees are payable for the duration of each Franchise Agreement, one of which was due to expire in 2014 and three of which were to expire in 2011. But if there are no gross weekly sales, there are no royalty fees to pay. Loss of such royalties is inherent to the breach of Franchise Agreements and is not related to other contracts or relationships. As amounts due directly under the Franchise Agreements, these losses are direct damages, not consequential damages stemming from other contracts or relationships.

Thus, the waiver of consequential damages in the Franchise Agreements does not preclude recovery of the claimed damages. The losses were inevitable and flowed necessarily from the closings. The royalty fees, as set forth in the Franchise Agreements, were inherent to the nature of the contracts, and the Court finds that they are actual and direct damages guaranteed by Wink.

Notes and Questions

1. <u>Distinctions</u>? Why were lost profits in *Bonanza* general damages but special damages in *Optum*? Does this explanation from *SOLIDFX, LLC v. Jeppesen Sanderson, Inc.*, 841 F.3d 827 (10th Cir. 2016), help?

> Direct damages refer to those which the party lost from the contract itself—in other words, the benefit of the bargain—while consequential damages refer to economic harm beyond the immediate scope of the contract. Lost profits, under appropriate circumstances, can be recoverable as a component of either (and both) direct and consequential damages. Thus, for example, if a services contract is breached and the plaintiff anticipated a profit under the contract, those profits would be recoverable as a component of direct, benefit of the bargain damages. If the same breach had the knock-on effect of causing the plaintiff to close its doors, precluding it from performing other work for which it had contracted and from which it expected to make a profit, those lost profits might be recovered as "consequential" to the breach.
>
> Thus, while it is true that lost profits often fall within the larger category of consequential damages, lost profits that flow directly from the breach of the contract itself are properly characterized as direct damages.

2. <u>Pleading Special Damages</u>. In *DeRosier v. Util. Sys. of Am., Inc.*, 780 N.W.2d 1 (Ct. App. Minn. 2010), DeRosier had bought undeveloped hillside property, intending to build a house. The builder told DeRosier he needed substantial fill to level the lot to build the home. DeRosier noticed Utility Systems of America, Inc., was excavating a nearby lot. He proposed to a USA foreman that, instead of trucking the dirt far away, that USA dump the fill on his lot. In July 2004, USA agreed. In late August 2004, DeRosier gave the city a permit he had obtained, allowing deposit of 1,500 cubic yards of fill to the USA foreman, and then left on a 10-day vacation. When DeRosier returned, his property was covered with 6,500 cubic yards of fill. DeRosier's builder told him a house could not be built unless the fill was removed

and the builder withdrew from the project. When DeRosier complained to USA, at first it denied responsibility but, after DeRosier threatened suit, it agreed to remove the excess fill for $9,500. DeRosier refused and instead hired G&T Construction to remove the excess fill, and then sued for $46,629 as the cost to remove the excess fill and for added expenses to construct a foundation. The trial court found breach and entered judgment against USA of general damages of $22,829 (the cost to remove the fill), and consequential damages of $8,000, consisting of additional construction costs caused by the delay. USA appealed, and the court wrote:

> Minnesota pleading rules generally require only "a short and plain statement of the claim" and "a demand for judgment for the relief sought." Minn. R. Civ. P. 8.01. The rules, however, specify that "special damage shall be specifically stated." Minn. R. Civ. P. 9.07. Although remedies are to be liberally administered, the burden of pleading and proving consequential loss still remains on the buyer alleging the damage. understand the phrase "consequential loss" or "consequential damages" and the issue before us, we must recognize the difference between *general* and *special* damages. Special damages require specific pleading but general damages do not.
>
> General damages, as opposed to special damages, naturally and necessarily result from the act complained of. Minnesota courts have stated, the term 'consequential damages' usually refers to those items of damages which, because of particular circumstances, are to be distinguished from 'general' damages. Consequential damages are commonly called special damages. Special damages are the natural, but not the necessary, result of a breach. Although special or consequential damages flow naturally from the breach, they are not recoverable unless they are reasonably foreseeable to the parties at the time of the breach. Because consequential (or delay) damages were not pleaded, we conclude that the district court erred in awarding DeRosier $8,000 as consequential damages.

Consider that Rule 9(g) merely requires mentioning the type of special damage, not any great amount of detail. What would it have taken for the lawyer to recover that $8,000 for his client? What did the other lawyer do to save her client $8,000?

3. <u>Distress and Pleading</u>. Although the majority rule is that distress damages are not recoverable for breach of ordinary contracts, when they are recoverable, some courts hold mental anguish damages are "general damages" while others hold they are "special damages." *Compare Baldwin v. Panetta*, 4 So. 3d 555 (Ct. App. Ala. 2008) (if recoverable, mental anguish damages are general damages) *with Derkevorkian v. Lionbridge Tech., Inc.*, 2006 WL 197320 (D. Colo. Jan. 26, 2006) (plaintiff could not recover mental anguish damages that would have been recoverable if pled as special damages). Why does it make sense to say that if mental anguish damages are recoverable, they are general damages in terms of *Hadley*? Consider how important this may be. *See Woodkrest Custom Homes, Inc. v. Cooper*, 108 So. 3d 460 (Ct. App. Miss. Jan. 22, 2013) (in affirming jury award of $30,000 in mental anguish damages, court noted plaintiff had not pled them as special damages, as the court

believed was required, but that defense counsel had not raised that pleading defect nor whether they were recoverable for breach of this contract).

B. The UCC Measures of Damage

Many provisions of the UCC are implicated when a contract between merchants for the sale of goods is breached. The principal sections are these, and in many respects they reflect the common law categories of expectancy, reliance, and restitution:

§ 2.708 Seller's Damages for Non-Acceptance or Repudiation.

(a) Subject to Subsection (b) and to the provisions of this chapter with respect to proof of market price (Section 2.723), the measure of damages for non-acceptance or repudiation by the buyer is the difference between the market price at the time and place for tender and the unpaid contract price together with any incidental damages provided in this chapter (Section 2.710), but less expenses saved in consequence of the buyer's breach.

(b) If the measure of damages provided in Subsection (a) is inadequate to put the seller in as good a position as performance would have done then the measure of damages is the profit (including reasonable overhead) which the seller would have made from full performance by the buyer, together with any incidental damages provided in this chapter (Section 2.710), due allowance for costs reasonably incurred and due credit for payments or proceeds of resale.

§ 2.709. Action for the Price

(a) When the buyer fails to pay the price as it becomes due the seller may recover, together with any incidental damages under the next section, the price

(1) of goods accepted or of conforming goods lost or damaged within a commercially reasonable time after risk of their loss has passed to the buyer; and

(2) of goods identified to the contract if the seller is unable after reasonable effort to resell them at a reasonable price or the circumstances reasonably indicate that such effort will be unavailing.

(b) Where the seller sues for the price he must hold for the buyer any goods which have been identified to the contract and are still in his control except that if resale becomes possible he may resell them at any time prior to the collection of the judgment. The net proceeds of any such resale must be credited to the buyer and payment of the judgment entitles him to any goods not resold.

(c) After the buyer has wrongfully rejected or revoked acceptance of the goods or has failed to make a payment due or has repudiated (Section 2.610), a seller who is held not entitled to the price under this section shall nevertheless be awarded damages for nonacceptance under the preceding section.

§ 2.710. Seller's Incidental Damages

Incidental damages to an aggrieved seller include any commercially reasonable charges, expenses or commissions incurred in stopping delivery, in the transportation, care and custody of goods after the buyer's breach, in connection with return or resale of the goods or otherwise resulting from the breach.

§ 2.711: Buyer's Remedies in General; Buyer's Security Interest in Rejected Goods.

(a) Where the seller fails to make delivery or repudiates or the buyer rightfully rejects or justifiably revokes acceptance then with respect to any goods involved, and with respect to the whole if the breach goes to the whole contract (Section 2.612), the buyer may cancel and whether or not he has done so may in addition to recovering so much of the price as has been paid

(1) "cover" and have damages under the next section as to all the goods affected whether or not they have been identified to the contract; or

(2) recover damages for non-delivery as provided in this chapter (Section 2.713).

(b) Where the seller fails to deliver or repudiates the buyer may also

(1) if the goods have been identified recover them as provided in this chapter (Section 2.502); or

(2) in a proper case obtain specific performance or replevy the goods as provided in this chapter (Section 2.716).

(c) On rightful rejection or justifiable revocation of acceptance a buyer has a security interest in goods in his possession or control for any payments made on their price and any expenses reasonably incurred in their inspection, receipt, transportation, care and custody and may hold such goods and resell them in like manner as an aggrieved seller (Section 2.706).

§ 2.712: "Cover;" Buyer's Procurement of Substitute Goods.

(a) After a breach within the preceding section the buyer may "cover" by making in good faith and without unreasonable delay any reasonable purchase of or contract to purchase goods in substitution for those due from the seller.

(b) The buyer may recover from the seller as damages the difference between the cost of cover and the contract price together with any incidental or consequential damages as hereinafter defined (Section 2.715), but less expenses saved in consequence of the seller's breach.

(c) Failure of the buyer to effect cover within this section does not bar him from any other remedy.

§ 2.713: Buyer's Damages for Non-Delivery or Repudiation.

(a) Subject to the provisions of this chapter with respect to proof of market price (Section 2.723), the measure of damages for non-delivery or repudiation by the seller is the difference between the market price at the time when the buyer learned of the breach and the contract price together with any incidental and consequential damages provided in this chapter (Section 2.715), but less expenses saved in consequence of the seller's breach.

(b) Market price is to be determined as of the place for tender or, in cases of rejection after arrival or revocation of acceptance, as of the place of arrival.

§ 2.714: Buyer's Damages for Non-Delivery or Repudiation

(a) Where the buyer has accepted goods and given notification (Subsection (c) of Section 2.607) he may recover as damages for any non-conformity of tender the loss resulting in the ordinary course of events from the seller's breach as determined in any manner which is reasonable.

(b) The measure of damages for breach of warranty is the difference at the time and place of acceptance between the value of the goods accepted and the value they would have had if they had been as warranted, unless special circumstances show proximate damages of a different amount.

(c) In a proper case any incidental and consequential damages under the next section may also be recovered.

§ 2.715: Buyer's Incidental and Consequential Damages.

(a) Incidental damages resulting from the seller's breach include expenses reasonably incurred in inspection, receipt, transportation and care and custody of goods rightfully rejected, any commercially reasonable charges, expenses or commissions in connection with effecting cover and any other reasonable expense incident to the delay or other breach.

(b) Consequential damages resulting from the seller's breach include

(1) any loss resulting from general or particular requirements and needs of which the seller at the time of contracting had reason to know and which could not reasonably be prevented by cover or otherwise; and

(2) injury to person or property proximately resulting from any breach of warranty.

The following case focuses on the buyer's breach and Section 2.714, and cases in Chapter 6, Remedies Triggered by Harm to, or Interference with Rights in, Personal Property, address other provisions.

Rexnord Indus., LLC v. Bigge Power Constructors, LLC

947 F. Supp. 2d 951 (E.D. Wis. 2013) (Adelman, J.)

[Shaw Constructors, Inc., had a contract to construct a nuclear power plant, and entered into a contract with Bigge Power Constructors to build derricks that it would need as part of that project. Bigge, in turn, contracted with Rexnord Industries, LLC, to provide 20 steel castings, at a price of $4.5 million, to be used in constructing the derricks for Shaw. Bigge refused to pay the final $1 million, and Rexnord filed suit.

Bigge counterclaimed, asserting Rexnord had failed to deliver the castings on time in accordance with a schedule in their agreement and that it its failure to perform a "root cause analysis" had caused the castings to not perform properly. The damages caused by these failures were additional costs and time delays.

Rexnord moved for summary judgment that none of those damages were recoverable because the agreement excluded liability for "special, consequential or incidental damages of any kind, and regardless of whether such liability arises in contract, in tort, or by operation of law." The trial court issued this opinion addressing that motion.]

Initially, I note that Bigge eventually "accepted" all the castings, and so the starting point for an analysis of the remedies available to Bigge is UCC § 2-714, which in California is codified as Cal. Com.Code § 2714. That provision provides that where the buyer has accepted goods "he or she may recover, as damages for any nonconformity of tender, the loss resulting in the ordinary course of events from the seller's breach as determined in any manner that is reasonable." Id. § 2714(1). Comment 2 to 2-714 states that the "non-conformity" referred to in 2-714(1) includes "any failure of the seller to perform according to his obligations under the contract." In the present case, Bigge alleges that Rexnord failed to perform two of its obligations under the contract—the obligation to deliver the castings in accordance with the schedule, and the obligation to perform a root cause analysis. Assuming that Bigge proves that Rexnord failed to perform these obligations, Bigge may recover "the loss resulting in the ordinary course of events from" each failure. Damages that flow in the ordinary course from the breach are usually referred to as "direct" or "general" damages. These damages may be contrasted with incidental and consequential damages, which are available under 2-714(3) unless they have been excluded, as they have been here.

In the present case, it is relatively easy to dispose of the argument that Bigge's damages are incidental. The text of 2-715(1) enumerates a list of damages that a buyer may recover as incidental damages, but the actual definition of incidental damage appears in Comment 1 to 2-715. The comment states that the damages listed in the text "are merely illustrative of the typical kinds of incidental damage" and that incidental damages fall into one of three categories: (1) reasonable expenses incurred in connection with the handling of rightfully rejected goods; (2) reasonable expenses incurred in connection with the handling of goods whose acceptance may justifiably be revoked; and (3) reasonable expenses incurred in connection with effecting cover. Bigge's damages do not fall into any of these categories. Bigge did not reject the castings, revoke acceptance of the castings, or effect cover by purchasing substitute castings,1 and thus none of its expenses could be deemed to have been incurred in connection with those acts.

Rexnord points out that the text of 2-715(1) lists "any other reasonable expense incident to the delay" as an example of incidental damage and contends that any damages caused by its failure to deliver the castings in accordance with the schedule falls within this language. However, delay damages of this sort do not fit within any of the categories identified in Comment 1, and thus they do not appear to be among the kinds of damages the drafters of the UCC had in mind when drafting 2-715(1). Moreover, the phrase "any other reasonable expense incident to the delay" is vague. Use of the definite article "the" before "delay" suggests that the reader is being referred to some exact delay that is identified earlier in 2-715(1), yet no such delay is identified there or anywhere else. Thus, it is not clear what "the delay" refers to.

However, given that the preceding forms of incidental damage identified in 2-715(1) and the kinds of incidental damage identified in Comment 1 relate to expenses associated with rejecting goods and effecting cover, the most reasonable interpretation is that "the delay" refers to some delay associated with those acts. Again, in the present case, Bigge did not reject the castings or effect cover by purchasing substitute castings, and so Bigge's delay-related damages do not constitute incidental damages. I thus proceed to the question of whether Bigge's damages are consequential rather than direct.

As noted, the UCC provides that a buyer's remedy includes direct damages, which are those that flow in the ordinary course from the breach. The UCC does not define consequential damages, which are sometimes referred to as "special" damages. Instead, the Code relies on the principles relating to consequential damages that have been developed in contract law generally. In contract law generally, the leading case concerning consequential damages is the famous *Hadley v. Baxendale, 9 Ex. 341*, 156 Eng. Rep. 145 (1854). In that case, the plaintiffs owned a mill and experienced a broken crank shaft. They needed to send the broken shaft to the manufacturer so that the manufacturer could use it as a model for a new one. The plaintiffs contracted with the defendants, who were common carriers, to transport the shaft to the manufacturer. The plaintiffs informed the defendants that they were in a hurry, and the defendants promised that the shaft could be delivered to the manufacturer in a day's time. However, due to the carrier's neglect, delivery of the shaft was delayed, with the result that the mill's replacement shaft arrived several days later than expected. The plaintiffs did not have a spare shaft on hand, and so the plaintiffs could not operate their mill during the period of delay caused by the carrier's neglect. The plaintiffs thus sought to recover, as damages for the carrier's breach of contract, the lost profits for the period of delay. The court held that the plaintiffs could not recover lost profits, and this holding was based on the distinction between direct and consequential damages (although the court did not use those terms). In making this distinction, the court first identified the general rule governing damages:

> Where two parties have made a contract which one of them has broken, the damages which the other party ought to receive in respect of such breach of contract should be such as may fairly and reasonably be considered either

arising naturally, i.e., according to the usual course of things, from such breach of contract itself, or such as may reasonably be supposed to have been in the contemplation of both parties, at the time they made the contract, as the probable result of the breach of it.

The court then identified a subset of these damages—now known as consequential damages—as those that would ordinarily follow from a breach of contract under "special circumstances." The court reasoned that if the defendant knew about the plaintiff's special circumstances at the time of entering the contract, then the defendant should be liable for the damages ordinarily following a breach of contract under those circumstances; however, if the defendant did not know about the plaintiff's special circumstances, then the defendant should not be liable for those damages. With respect to the mill's lost profits, the court observed that the carrier had no reason to know that the mill would not be able to operate and generate profits while the shaft was in transit, since one would ordinarily expect a mill to have a spare shaft on hand so that it could continue operations in the event that the shaft in use broke. Because the carrier did not know about the mill's "special circumstances"—i.e., that it did not keep a spare shaft on hand—the carrier could not be held liable for the damages attributable to those special circumstances.

Like most courts, those in California follow *Hadley v. Baxendale*. Thus, for purposes of the present case, the distinction between direct and consequential damages can be stated as follows: Direct damages are those that Rexnord, at the time of contracting, would reasonably have expected to follow from its breaches, assuming that it did not have knowledge of any circumstances peculiar to Bigge—circumstances analogous to the mill's not having a spare shaft on hand. Thus, Bigge's direct damages are those that Rexnord would reasonably have expected an ordinary purchaser of metal castings to incur in the event that Rexnord delivered the castings late or failed to carry out its obligation to perform a root cause analysis. In contrast, Bigge's consequential damages are those that Rexnord, at the time of contracting, would reasonably have expected to follow from its breaches under any circumstances that are peculiar to Bigge. Under the rule of Hadley, Rexnord would be liable for such consequential damages if Bigge had communicated its special circumstances to Rexnord at the time of contracting. However, because in this case the parties have agreed to exclude all consequential damages, Rexnord is not liable for consequential damages even if Bigge is able to prove that Rexnord knew about its special circumstances. Thus, the key question is whether the damages Bigge claims are those that Rexnord would reasonably have expected an ordinary purchaser of metal castings to incur as a result of its breaches.

With respect to Rexnord's alleged failure to perform an adequate root cause analysis, it is clear that the expenses Bigge reasonably incurred in hiring separate consultants to perform the analysis, as well as any of its own, internal resources reasonably incurred in performing the analysis, would be direct damages. This is so because, at the time of contracting, Rexnord would have known that if it did not properly perform a needed root cause analysis, an ordinary purchaser of metal castings would have to incur expenses in connection with either performing that analysis itself or hiring someone else to perform the analysis. In other words, there was nothing special about Bigge's circumstances that caused it to incur such expenses. Thus, any expenses Bigge reasonably incurred to obtain the root cause analysis called for by the contract are recoverable, assuming of course that Bigge is able to establish that Rexnord breached the root cause analysis provision of the contract in the first place.

However, whether Rexnord is liable for the expenses Bigge incurred because of Rexnord's breach of its scheduling obligations cannot be decided now. To decide whether such expenses are direct or consequential, I would need to know whether Rexnord should have expected an ordinary purchaser of metal castings to incur them or whether they were the result of Bigge's special circumstances. For example, Bigge claims that it incurred "personnel" and "equipment" expenses as a result of the delay. Should Rexnord have expected an ordinary purchaser of metal castings to incur these expenses, or would Rexnord have been justified in assuming that the purchaser would have arranged its affairs such that it could have used its personnel and equipment on other projects while it waited for Rexnord to deliver the castings, thereby avoiding any wasted expense? The record does not shed any light on that question. Similarly, the record does not enable me to determine whether an ordinary purchaser of castings would have incurred the additional expenses that Bigge paid to Schuff Steel. Accordingly, given the present state of the record, I cannot grant summary judgment to either party on the question of whether Bigge's delay-related expenses constitute consequential damages.

Notes and Questions

1. Subjective? Does the principal case focus primarily on a subjective or objective view of *Hadley's* role in determining damages? In the commercial context, does either approach make more sense?

2. Incidental Damages. This phrase occurs in the UCC but is not common in common law damages. The trial court in *Crescent U. City Venture, LLC v. APA., Inc.*, 2019 WL 3765313 (N.C. Super. Aug. 8, 2019), examined its meaning at length:

> Courts in many jurisdictions have grappled with distinguishing incidental and consequential damages, often under Article 2 of the Uniform Commercial Code (the "UCC"). The prevailing and often-cited articulation of the difference between the two comes from Judge Neaher in *Petroleo Brasileiro, S.A. Petrobras v. Ameropan Oil Corp.*, 372 F. Supp. 503 (E.D.N.Y. 1974):
>
>> While the distinction between the two is not an obvious one, the Code makes plain that incidental damages are normally incurred when a buyer (or seller) repudiates the contract or wrongfully rejects the goods, causing the other to incur such expenses as transporting, storing, or reselling the goods. On the other hand, consequential damages do not arise

within the scope of the immediate buyer-seller transaction, but rather stem from losses incurred by the non-breaching party in its dealings, often with third parties, which were a proximate result of the breach, and which were reasonably foreseeable by the breaching party at the time of contracting.

Id. This distinction led Judge Neaher to conclude that expenses the plaintiff paid in penalties were not incidental damages because they stemmed from the plaintiff's dealings with other parties who were not a party to the breached contract. Numerous courts have cited *Petroleo Brasileiro, S.A. Petrobras* for this rule. *See, e.g., Sprague v. Sumitomo Forestry Co.,* 104 Wash.2d 751 (Wash. 1985) (ruling that loss incurred due to nonbreaching party's delay in performing a contract for a third party was not properly characterized as incidental damage and stating "the fact that defendant's conduct proximately caused plaintiff's loss is irrelevant to this analysis" and that "the focus is upon losses arising within the scope of the immediate contract").

While these cases concern contracts for the sale of goods, the standard they provide for identifying and distinguishing incidental and consequential damages is reasonable and appears consistent with North Carolina common law. See N.C.P.I.-Civil 503.70 (defining incidental damages by reference to costs associated with performance under the contract or minimizing the loss resulting from the defendant's breach of the contract). There is thus significant persuasive authority to support defining incidental damages as expenses incurred in mitigating and dealing with losses arising within the scope of the immediate contract and consequential damages as "losses incurred by the non-breaching party in its dealings, often with third parties, which were a proximate result of the breach, and which were reasonably foreseeable by the breaching party at the time of contracting." *Petroleo Brasileiro,* 372 F. Supp. at 508.

3. No Market? In *JRM Hauling & Recycling Serv., Inc. v. Newark Group, Inc.,* 95 Mass. App. Ct. 1106 (2019), plaintiff had contracted with cities to collect curbside recycling and had in 2004 agreed to deliver the loose paper that it collected to the defendant, which used the paper to make products. At first defendant used all of the paper it received, but demand for its products dropped and by 2014 it was only using 10% of the loose paper it received, selling the rest at a loss, and repudiated the agreement. At trial, plaintiff introduced evidence of the market price of baled paper, not loose paper. The trial court awarded damages because the UCC permits use of a market price of comparable goods if "there is no evidence available of the current market price at the time and place of tender." The court reversed, stating this provision was only available "when a good is so rare that sales are infrequent," and because the absence of any market for an "abundant commodity" showed that "the market price was zero dollars." It remanded to award nominal damages.

C. Who Can Recover Damages for Breach of Contract?

Tort law limits who can recover damages for harm to another through various ways, including limitations on who can sue for loss of consortium. As shown below, the only common negligence-based claim that allows recovery for purely economic harms expressly limits who can sue for losses.

Contract law likewise limits the scope of who can sue. Generally, only a party to a contract can sue for its breach. An exception exists for any "intended third-party beneficiary" of the breached contract. To determine whether a plaintiff was an intended third-party beneficiary, courts apply Restatement of the Law 2d, Contracts, Section 302 (1981):

(1) Unless otherwise agreed between promisor and promisee, a beneficiary of a promise is an intended beneficiary if recognition of a right to performance in the beneficiary is appropriate to effectuate the intention of the parties and either:

(a) the performance of the promise will satisfy an obligation of the promisee to pay money to the beneficiary; or

(b) the circumstances indicate that the promisee intends to give the beneficiary the benefit of the promised performance.

(2) An incidental beneficiary is a beneficiary who is not an intended beneficiary.

The first step is to read the contract because it may expressly define who is, or is not, an intended or incidental third-party beneficiary. If an agreement expressly includes or excludes a plaintiff, ordinarily that is dispositive. *Bariteau v. PNC Fin. Serv. Group,* 285 F. App'x 218 (6th Cir. 2008). If the agreement is silent or ambiguous, courts examine the circumstances.

United Parcel Serv. Co. v. DNJ Logistic Group, Inc.
2017 WL 3097531 (W.D. Ky. July 20, 2017) (Strivers, J.)

[Plaintiff United Parcel Service Co. agreed with defendant DNJ Logistics Group, Inc., that DNJ would take certain UPS packages that UPS delivered to certain airports and take them to the proper airline for further transit. DNJ was required to send weekly invoices to UPS based upon the weight and destination of each package handled for UPS by DNJ. UPS did not pay the invoices. Instead, plaintiff UPS Worldwide Forwarding paid them. Plaintiffs became concerned DNJ had overbilled them by inflating the weight of packages and sued DNJ and its owner, who moved to dismiss.]

Defendants also argue that Worldwide Forwarding's breach of contract claim should be dismissed because Worldwide Forwarding was neither a party to nor an intended third party beneficiary of the Agreement. It is undisputed that Worldwide Forwarding did not sign the Agreement, but it is well established that a third person may, in his own right and name enforce a promise made for his benefit even though he is a stranger both to the contract and the consideration. That said, only a third-party who was intended by the parties to benefit from the contact has standing to sue on a contract; an incidental beneficiary does not acquire such right. A third party is an intended beneficiary if the promisee's expressed intent is that the third party is to receive the performance of the contract in satisfaction of any actual or supposed duty or liability of the promisee to the beneficiary. In short, all that is necessary is that there be consideration for the agreement flowing to the promisor and that the promisee intends to extract a promise directly benefiting the third party. The central issue to determining whether the contract is intended to benefit a third party is the relevant intent of the promisee who purchases the promise from the promisor.

In this case, DNJ is the promisor, UPS is the promisee, and Worldwide Forwarding is the third party. Plaintiffs have alleged that DNJ received consideration under the Agreement in the form of payments. Plaintiffs have also alleged that "Worldwide Forwarding contracted with UPS for UPS to perform—or arrange to have performed—air transportation services that would enable Worldwide Forwarding to fulfill its obligation to transport packages and cargo by air," that "UPS contracted with DNJ in order to provide certain of those services for Worldwide Forwarding," and that "Worldwide Forwarding paid DNJ for the invoices submitted to Plaintiffs pursuant to the Agreement."

What more needs to be alleged to survive a motion to dismiss? Well, according to Defendants, Plaintiffs' allegations, even if taken as true, do not show that Worldwide Forwarding is an intended third-party beneficiary of the Agreement because "there is nothing in the Agreement that shows the parties intended DNJ to assume a direct obligation to Worldwide Forwarding or that the Agreement was made and entered into directly and primarily for Worldwide Forwarding's benefit." Actually, Defendants contend that the "express terms of the Agreement prove that Worldwide Forwarding cannot be an intended beneficiary of the Agreement." Defendants maintain that the terms of the Agreement are so antithetical to Worldwide Forwarding's claimed third-party beneficiary status that the Court cannot look outside the Agreement's four corners.

Defendants posit that Worldwide Forwarding cannot be considered an intended third-party beneficiary of the Agreement solely because it is not mentioned in the Agreement. Defendants are correct that Worldwide Forwarding is not named in the Agreement, but that does not preclude Worldwide Forwarding from being an intended third-party beneficiary.

Moreover, Defendants' reliance on the Agreement's express terms and canons of contract construction is misplaced because the analysis of UPS' intent for Worldwide Forwarding to be a third-party beneficiary is not confined to the terms of the Agreement. The inquiry into third-party beneficiary status is different from ordinary contract interpretation, and Kentucky law directs courts to consider surrounding circumstances in the third-party beneficiary context. It is appropriate to consider the surrounding circumstances when determining whether a party is an intended beneficiary of the contract. As a result, "the intent to benefit a third party 'need not be expressed in the agreement itself; it may be evidenced by the terms of the agreement, the surrounding circumstances, or both.

Defendants rely on *Bariteau v. PNC Financial Services Group Inc.*, 285 Fed.Appx. 218, 220-21 (6th Cir. 2008), and *King v. National Industries, Inc.*, 512 F.2d 29 (6th Cir. 1975), in support of their position, but those cases are not dispositive. In *King*, the trustee for a company in bankruptcy argued that the company was a third-party beneficiary of a purchase agreement between its parent and another entity in which a large percent of the company's shares were sold. The case was appealed after the district court granted summary judgment against the bankruptcy trustee. On appeal, the court did start its third-party beneficiary analysis with an examination of the agreement at issue, consistent with the principles articulated above. In examining the agreement, the court found that it "revealed no indication of an intent on the part of the promisee to benefit" the company claiming third-party beneficiary status. In fact, the agreement indicated otherwise in providing that "the terms, provisions and conditions of this agreement shall bind and benefit the parties hereto and their respective successors, legal representatives and assigns." As a result, the court concluded that the company was only an incidental beneficiary. Notably, however, the agreement was the only evidence the Court considered because the plaintiff submitted no other probative evidence in support of the third-party beneficiary claim.

Meanwhile, in *Bariteau*, the plaintiff did submit an affidavit to support his claim that he was an intended beneficiary of an "agreement" between a bank and a corporation, which agreement required two or more board members to sign before sums exceeding $1,000 could be withdrawn from the corporation's bank account. The court, however, found the affidavit unhelpful for two reasons. First, and most importantly to Defendants here, it stated that "when an agreement itself establishes that an individual is not a third-party beneficiary of it, extrinsic evidence generally has little role to play." *Id*. The court found the agreement before it established that the plaintiff was not an intended third-party beneficiary at least in part because the agreement made no mention of the plaintiff, who "was not even an investor in the corporation at the time the agreement was executed and did not learn of the agreement until after the corporation's bankruptcy." *Id*. Second, "even on its own terms, the affidavit confirmed that the plaintiff was at most an incidental beneficiary of the agreement." *Id*.

This case is different. Unlike *King*, this matter is before the court on Defendants' 12(b)(6) motion to dismiss, and Plaintiffs have not relied solely on the Agreement in pleading Worldwide Forwarding's third-party beneficiary status. Instead, Plaintiffs have alleged circumstances surrounding the Agreement that, taken as true, suggest that Worldwide Forwarding was an intended third-party beneficiary. Specifically, Plaintiffs have alleged that Worldwide Forwarding paid DNJ directly for services performed under a contract that UPS entered into to satisfy its obligations to Worldwide Forwarding. These facts are certainly more suggestive of third-party beneficiary status than those involved in *King* or *Bariteau*. Moreover, contrary to Defendants' position, not even the *Bariteau* court focused solely on the terms of the agreement at issue. It noted in determining that the "agreement itself offered no indication that it was designed to benefit the plaintiff," that the plaintiff was not an investor when the agreement was made and did not learn of the agreement until months later—all circumstances extrinsic to the contract. More fundamentally, the court *did* consider extrinsic evidence (the affidavit) in rendering its decision; the extrinsic evidence was simply insufficient to carry the day. Indeed, the Sixth Circuit recently clarified *Bariteau*, explaining that it "is best understood as simply explaining that extrinsic evidence should not be used to contradict an agreement that unambiguously establishes that a party is *not* a third party beneficiary."

While the Agreement, when considered in a vacuum, may not alone establish that Worldwide Forwarding was an intended third-party beneficiary, it does not unambiguously establish that Worldwide Forwarding is *not* a third party beneficiary. The reference to "affiliates" in some sections but not others is far from an unambiguous disclaimer of third-party beneficiary claims. Overall, the Court finds that Plaintiffs have alleged sufficient facts (again, taken as true for the present motion) for the Court to infer that there is consideration for the agreement flowing to DNJ and that UPS intended to extract a promise from DNJ directly benefiting Worldwide Forwarding. Therefore, DNJ's motion will be denied on this point.

Harris Moran Seed Co. v. Phillips

949 So. 2d 916 (Ct. App. Ala. 2006) (Thompson, J.)

[This suit was between merchants under the UCC. A wholesaler, Harris Moran Seed Company, had sold tomato seeds to a retailer, Clifton, with an express warranty of their quality. Clifton then sold the seeds to farmers, who sued HMSC for breach of that warranty. The jury found the warranty was intended to benefit the ultimate purchasers, the farmers. HMSC appealed.]

A warranty, whether express or implied, is made by a *seller* to its *buyer*. HMSC was not the farmers' immediate seller and the farmers were, therefore, not in vertical privity with HMSC. However, in an appropriate case, straightforward traditional third-party beneficiary analysis can be successfully used to impose liability on a warrantor not in privity with a purchaser. There are many recurring situations where representations made only to an immediate buyer are made for the benefit of a downstream buyer. At this point, there is space for the importation of third-party beneficiary law. Section 7-2-313, Ala.Code 1975, a part of Alabama's version of the Uniform Commercial Code, deals with express warranties. Part 2 of the Official Comment to that section explains:

> Although this section is limited in its scope and direct purpose to warranties made by the seller to the buyer as part of a contract for sale, the warranty sections of this Article are not designed in any way to disturb those lines of case law growth which have recognized that warranties need not

be confined either to sales contracts or to the direct parties to such a contract. The matter is left to the case law with the intention that the policies of this Act may offer useful guidance in dealing with further cases as they arise. Although third-party-beneficiary analysis may allow a vertical non-privity plaintiff to recover based on a remote seller's warranty, some courts have held that the obligations of a warrantor are not conceived of as third party obligations, but rather as direct obligations running from the warranting seller to the complainant downstream. In these cases, common law third party beneficiary theory has played no role extending the coverage of Section 2-313.

In Alabama, a vertical nonprivity purchaser who has suffered only direct or consequential economic loss cannot recover from a remote manufacturer under an *implied* warranty theory. However, privity rules have been applied less restrictively to express as opposed to implied warranties.

Alabama courts have not had the opportunity to decide whether a vertical nonprivity purchaser who has suffered only economic loss can recover from a remote seller or manufacturer under a theory that the purchaser is a third-party beneficiary of a contract containing the manufacturer's *express* warranty to a dealer or an intermediate seller. In a recent case, however, the Alabama Supreme Court indicated that a vertical nonprivity purchaser might be able to recover against a manufacturer under just such a theory. *See Bay Lines, Inc. v. Stoughton Trailers, Inc.,* 838 So.2d 1013 (Ala. 2002).

In *Bay Lines,* Crane, a manufacturer of fiberglass-reinforced side panels for use on truck trailers, warranted to Stoughton, a manufacturer of truck trailers, that the fiberglass reinforcement on the panels would not "delaminate" during a period of 10 years of normal use. The warranty was "limited to the original equipment purchaser." Bay Lines, a trucking company that bought trailers from a dealer who sold trailers built by Stoughton, sued Stoughton and Crane when the fiberglass panels on the trailers it purchased delaminated. Bay Lines alleged an AEMLD claim; claims of negligence and wantonness in manufacturing and assembling the trailers; breach of an express warranty; and breach of contract, contending that it was a third-party beneficiary of the contract containing the warranty given by Crane to Stoughton. The trial court entered a judgment on the pleadings in favor of Stoughton and dismissed the claims against Crane. Bay Lines appealed.

The Alabama Supreme Court affirmed, holding that Bay Lines could not assert a claim on the warranty because the warranty was clearly limited to Stoughton as the first purchaser from Crane. With respect to the third-party-beneficiary claim, the court held: "Bay Lines presented no evidence indicating that Crane knew, when it sold the panels to Stoughton, that Bay Lines was a purchaser of Stoughton's products, *or that Crane intended to protect future customers of Stoughton, such as Bay Lines, when it warranted its products to Stoughton.* Bay Lines, therefore, cannot rely on the warranty to support its third-party-beneficiary claim against Crane." 838 So.2d at 1018 (emph. added).

In the present case, there was substantial evidence indicating that HMSC did intend to protect future customers of Clifton Seed Company and other users when it warranted its products to Clifton Seed Company. The farmers elicited testimony from HMSC senior sales representative Michael Hannah that HMSC was aware that, if the seeds it produced and sold to Clifton Seed Company were defective, then end users like the farmers in this case would suffer significant financial losses. "Foreseeability [alone], however, does not confer third-party beneficiary status." *See In re Masonite Corp. Hardboard Siding Prods. Liab. Litig.,* 21 F.Supp.2d 593 (E.D.La. 1998) (rejecting homeowners' argument — that they were third-party beneficiaries of a contract between exterior-hardboard-siding manufacturer and suppliers from whom builder purchased siding — "because it was foreseeable — indeed, inevitable — that the siding would be in the homeowners' possession after it was installed"). Nevertheless, foreseeability of harm to end users is a factor bearing on the question whether the contracting parties intended to benefit third parties like the farmers when they executed their dealer agreement. That agreement employed the terms "end user," "customer," and "buyer or user" at several places. For example:

- Seeds at times carry seed-borne diseases which may not be apparent to the Seller, Buyer or User. All risks of nonperformance, reduced performance and/or crop damage due to these factors shall be assumed by the buyer and user.

- Buyer and user agree that if HMSC refunds an amount equal to the price Buyer or User paid for HMSC seeds, this limitation of liability will not have failed in its essential purpose.

- This Limitation of Warranty and Liability is the entire agreement between Harris Moran Seed Company and Buyer or User. Buyer and User agree that. . . .

Other sections of the agreement required Clifton Seed Company to "resell the Products in compliance with all applicable labeling laws" and to "give buyers and other transferees explicit and specific notice, prior to the sale or transfer, of the HMSC Limitation of Warranty and Liability."

In the present case, we conclude that HMSC and Clifton Seed Company, the contracting parties, not only had end users like the farmers in mind when they reached their agreement, but also specifically provided for those end users to be notified of HMSC's "exclusive express warranty" that the seeds were "true to type."

We conclude that there was substantial evidence indicating that when HMSC sold and warranted the seeds to Clifton Seed Company it intended to benefit future customers of Clifton Seed Company and other end users like the farmers in this case. The trial court did not err in submitting to the jury the breach-of-contract claim premised on the "true to type" express warranty based on a third-party-beneficiary theory.

Notes and Questions

1. Express Identification. For an effective use of third-party beneficiary designation, *see Gator Apple, LLC v. Apple Texas Restaurants, Inc.,* 442 S.W.3d 521 (Ct.

App. Tex. 2014) (clause in franchise agreement prohibited franchisee from "poach-ing" employees of fellow franchisees and stated each franchisee "shall be deemed to be a third-party beneficiary of this provision and may sue and recover against the offending party the liquidated damages herein set forth; provided however, the failure by Franchisee to enforce this Section shall not be deemed to be a violation of this Section."). Should UPS consider adopting this clause?

2. <u>Beneficiaries of Wills</u>. Courts split on whether a beneficiary, harmed by an attorney's failure to draft a will as its testator intended, can sue the attorney as an intended third-party beneficiary. The split ranges from absolute prohibition to the approach in the UPS case. Why such disagreement over attorneys?

3. <u>Third-Party Beneficiaries Are Bound by the Contract</u>. If the agreement that makes the plaintiff a third-party beneficiary has enforceable limitations on dam-ages (e.g., a liquidated damages clause), they bind the third-party beneficiary. *Harris Moran Seed Co. v. Phillips*, 949 So. 2d 916 (Ct. App. Ala. 2006) (farmers were bound by clause in contract between distributor and wholesaler that limited damages).

D. When Monetary Remedies Are Inadequate

I. *General Requirements for Specific Performance*

As explained in Chapter 2, specific performance is a form of injunctive relief available to a party to a contract to obtain an order compelling performance. Spe-cific performance is "an equitable remedy for a breach of contract, rather than a separate cause of action." *Swimwear Sol., Inc. v. Orlando Bathing Suit, LLC*, 309 F. Supp. 3d 1022 (D. Kan. 2018).

A party seeking specific performance must generally show: (a) the terms of the contract are reasonably certain, (b) either that it has performed or that it is "ready, willing and able to perform," (c) the remedy at law is inadequate, and (d) both parties *could* seek specific performance (i.e., there is "mutuality of remedies). *See Eichenblatt v. Kugel*, 2018 WL 3202079 (E.D.N.Y. May 15, 2018). In addition, because an order of specific performance is an injunction, the requirements of Rule 65 apply, and so for preliminary injunctive relief a showing of "irreparable harm" is required. In addition, the opposing party can show the contract is invalid or unenforceable or raise other defenses that justify denial of this remedy, not all relief: those defenses are discussed later.

a. A Reasonably Certain Contract

i. *The General Rule*

Because an order of specific performance is an injunction, it must provide notice as to what is required so that the parties covered by the injunction can avoid violat-ing it and being held in contempt. The court in *Juergensen Def. Corp. v. Carleton Techs., Inc.*, 2009 WL 2163181 (W.D.N.Y. July 20, 2009), explained this common rea-son to deny relief:

It would be impossible for any order of this Court to articulate with any specificity what is meant by an injunction requiring the parties to re-establish their working relationship. Further, any injunction that vaguely enjoined defendants from "breaching its contractual obligations" would fail to put defendant on notice as to the specific conduct required or prohibited and would run afoul of the requirement that "[e]very order granting an injunction and every restraining order must: (A) state the reasons why it issued; (B) state its terms specifically; and (C) describe in reasonable detail—and not by referring to the complaint or other document—the act or acts restrained or required." Fed. R. Civ. P. 65(d)(1); *see also Diapulse Corp. of Am. v. Carba, Ltd.*, 626 F.2d 1108 (2d Cir. 1980) ("A court is required to frame its orders so that those who must obey them will know what the court intends to forbid. Basic fairness requires that those enjoined receive explicit notice of precisely what conduct is outlawed. An order which does not satisfy the requirement of specificity and definiteness will not withstand appellate scrutiny.").

This procedural requirement often leads courts to deny specific performance. *E.g., TAS Distrib. Co. v. Cummins Engine Co.*, 491 F.3d 625 (7th Cir. 2007) (affirming denial of specific performance of contract requiring "all reasonable efforts"); *Baron Financial Corp. v. Natanzon,* 509 F. Supp. 2d 501 (D. Md. 2007) (denying specific performance of contract requiring "best efforts"). In *In re Visitation of K.M.*, 2017 WL 657641 (Ill. Cir. Ct. Feb. 17, 2017), plaintiffs were the biological family of a child they gave up for adoption to the defendants. They sought specific performance of an alleged oral agreement to permit post-adoption visitation. The trial court dismissed the complaint, stating:

> An agreement that calls for services over a period of time, especially where special skill knowledge, judgment, or discretion is involved, is characterized as a contract for personal service. Such contracts require a relationship of cooperation and trust between the parties to the contract. If a contract requiring X to paint one's house requires a relationship of cooperation and trust between the parties to the contract, certainly a contract that requires X to allow his child to visit with someone on a regular basis likewise does. Now try to imagine a contract between X and Y requiring X's minor child to mow Y's grass. Such a contract is not that far removed from a contract between X and Y requiring X's minor child (a legal stranger to Y) to spend time, and implicitly entertain or be entertained by Y.

> So, for all the reasons that a court cannot grant specific performance of a personal service contract, specific performance of the alleged postadoption visitation contract is unavailable.

Keatley v. Bruner

194 Wash. App. 1010 (Ct. App. Wash. 2016) (Becker, J.)

[Duane Bruner and Sandra Keatley were involved in an "intimate, familial" relationship from 1982 to 2002. During that time, Bruner bought the "Chapman Road property"—10 acres of land on Chapman Road that had for many years been in Keatley's family. Together, they developed the Chapman Road property with a home and a shop, and Bruner built a barn to run a cattle operation on it and on some land Keatley owned separately.

On March 22, 2005, without using attorneys, they drafted and executed a contract for Bruner to sell the Chapman Road property to Keatley. The contract was titled "Earnest Money Receipt and Agreement." Bruner as "seller" and Keatley as "purchaser" signed the agreement, which stated that Keatley agreed to buy the described property and Bruner agreed to sell it. The contract recited Bruner's acknowledgement of receipt of a check for $1,000 as earnest money, and identified the "Parcel# WK2713005 located at 1176 Chapman Road and adjacent Parcel # WK2713007, being about 10 acres," and a price of $295,000. It also stated, "Title of Seller is to be free of encumbrances or defects" and that earnest money of $1,000 had been paid.

They continued to use the property. During this time, Keatley asked Bruner at least every three months whether he wanted her to close on the contract, and Bruner repeatedly assured Keatley there was no hurry. She had the financial ability to close on the property. In October 2010, the value of the property reached $500,000 and Keatley demanded closing, but Bruner refused, stating the contract had expired.

Keatley filed suit, seeking specific performance of the property sale for $295,000. The trial court found Keatley and Bruner intended to create an open-ended purchase option contract. The trial court based that finding on the fact that they testified the date was left open to allow Keatley time to find financing and on the parties' conduct after the agreement had been signed. The trial court ordered specific performance and Bruner appealed. After agreeing with the trial court that Keatley had given Bruner $1,000 despite his denial, the appellate court stated the judgment for $295,000, not $294,000, was a "scrivener's error." It then turned to Bruner's challenge to the trial court's "finding of fact M."]

Bruner also assigns error to finding of fact M, that the contract implicitly required Keatley to demand closing within a reasonable time: "Given the lack of a closing date, the Court will infer a 'reasonable amount of time' for closing and, under the circumstances of this case, Keatley's demand for closing in October 2010 was within a reasonable amount of time."

Bruner claims that by inferring the parties intended to impose a "reasonable time" limit on closing, the court inserted a term not agreed upon by the parties. He argues this finding is inconsistent with the finding that the parties intentionally left the closing date open to allow Keatley time to obtain financing.

A court is not at liberty to write a contract for the parties they did not write themselves. But the lack of a definite closing date does not render an agreement fatally defective. An open ended option is enforceable so long as closing occurs within a reasonable time after acceptance. What is a reasonable time is to be determined by the circumstances of a case and the purpose of the parties that entered into an agreement. The trial court correctly considered the longstanding intimate familial relationship that existed between Keatley and Bruner before they entered into the contract as well as the purpose of their agreement. We find no error in finding of fact M.

Bruner contends that the contract is unenforceable because material terms are missing. Preliminary agreements must be definite enough on material terms to allow enforcement without the court supplying those terms. Specific performance cannot be decreed unless the terms are complete and free from doubt, making the precise act which is to be done clearly ascertainable. *Hubbell v. Ward,* 40 Wn.2d 779 (1952). In *Hubbell,* the purchaser agreed to pay $9,000 down and sign a contract for the balance. The seller refused to go forward with the transaction. The purchaser sued and obtained a decree of specific performance directing the seller to enter into a real estate contract according to the terms of the earnest money agreement. The decree was reversed on appeal because the agreement failed to reflect any understanding of what the terms of the future contract for the balance would be; it only "contemplated that a real estate purchase contract which would contain new and additional terms might be executed in the future."

The *Hubbell* court identified 13 material terms that must be specified in an option contract to enter into a future real estate contract. Bruner sets forth 7 of the *Hubbell* terms that are missing from his agreement with Keatley, and he argues that their absence makes the agreement unenforceable: (1) time and manner for transferring title; (2) procedure for declaring forfeiture of earnest money; (3) allocation of risk with respect to damage or destruction; (4) insurance provisions; (5) responsibility for taxes, repairs, and water and utilities; (6) restrictions, if any, on capital improvements, liens, removal or replacement of personal property, and (7) a closing date.

In applying *Hubbell,* the problem is not one of determining how many more terms are included in one agreement or another, but whether a particular agreement includes sufficient material terms. We do not enumerate those items which constitute material terms which must be agreed upon in the earnest money agreement. The general principle must be applied factually in each case. Bruner does not attempt to demonstrate that the seven *Hubbell* terms he lists were necessary to make this particular contract enforceable.

The contract is not a preliminary agreement to enter into a future contract, as was true in *Hubbell.* Keatley and Bruner did not contemplate entering into a future real estate contract with new and additional terms. Their contract identifies the seller, the buyer, the property to be sold, and the price; and it states that the title is to be free of encumbrances or defects upon transfer. The omission of a closing date is not a fatal defect, because as discussed above, it was proper under the circumstances for the trial court to enforce the agreement upon finding that Keatley demanded closing within a reasonable amount of time. We conclude the contract specified sufficient material terms to make it enforceable.

McKinney/Pearl Rest. Partners, L.P. v. Metro. Life Ins. Co.

241 F. Supp. 3d 737 (N.D. Tex. 2017) (Boyle, J.)

[Plaintiff leased space for a restaurant from the defendants. Section 7(b)(ii) of the lease required defendants to "keep and maintain in good condition and repair: (A) the roof and structural system of the Restaurant Building." Plaintiff sued, requesting specific performance of that obligation. Defendants moved for summary judgment on that request.]

First, specific performance is an equitable remedy that is normally available only when the complaining party cannot be fully compensated through the legal remedy of damages. And generally speaking, the measure of damages for a landlord's breach of covenant to repair or keep in repair the demised premises is the difference between the contract rental of the premises and the rental value of the premises in their unrepaired condition. Plaintiff argues this general rule does not address the present situation, where the tenant wishes to remain in possession of the premises going forward; however, in such cases, courts have held that where the injury to the property has not resulted in its total loss and the repair of the damaged property is economically feasible, the plaintiff may elect to recover the reasonable cost of repairs.

And though Plaintiff repeatedly argues that specific performance is the preferred remedy to compensate for an injury related to real property because real property is unique, the typical case illustrating this principle involves the sale of real property, not a landlord's duty to repair leased property. Plaintiff also provides no authority for its assertion that the recovery of damages for past injuries does not establish an adequate remedy at law. Thus, the Court finds that Plaintiff has an adequate remedy at law for Defendants' alleged breach of the Lease Agreement in the form of the monetary damages it agreed to.

Furthermore, a court has no power to decree specific performance in any manner except in keeping with the terms of the agreement made by the parties. Here, the disagreement is over the landlord's obligation to "keep and maintain in good condition and repair: (A) the roof and structural system of the Restaurant Building." Lease Agreement § 7(b)(ii). It is beyond dispute that the parties do not agree what constitutes a structural system in "good condition and repair," or what actions would need to be taken to bring the premises up to this standard should a jury find Defendants breached this provision. This is the very basis of Plaintiff's breach of contract claims. The Lease does not prescribe specific repairs the landlord must undertake and which the Court could specifically order; rather, it outlines a continuing obligation—as discussed above—that the landlord "keep and maintain" the structural system in a certain condition, to wit, "good condition and repair."

A court generally will not decree a party to perform a continuous series of acts which extend through a long period of time and require constant supervision by the court. Although Plaintiff argues the Court need only decree specific performance in accordance with the Lease and that it is up to Defendants to figure out the details, the Court does not find § 7(b)(ii), requiring the landlord to "keep and maintain in good condition and repair" the structural system of the building, susceptible to an order of specific performance in this case. It is a familiar doctrine that a court of equity will not exercise its jurisdiction to grant the remedy of specific performance, however inadequate may be the remedy of damages, whenever the contract is of such a nature that the decree for specific performance cannot be enforced and its obedience compelled by the ordinary processes of the court. For these reasons, summary judgment is granted for Defendants on Plaintiff's request for specific performance.

Notes and Questions

1. <u>Parol Evidence to Provide the Missing Details</u>? The general rule is that "if the contract is incomplete and it is necessary to resort to parol evidence to ascertain what was agreed to, the remedy of specific performance is not available." *929 Flushing LLC v. 33 Dev. Inc.*, 28 N.Y.S.3d 267 (N.Y. Sup. 2016).

2. <u>Which Portion</u>? The contract in *T&G Enterp., LLC v. White*, 298 Ga. App. 355 (2009), stated the "portion of property to be sold is portion containing house." The court denied specific performance and the appellate court affirmed:

> A court of equity will not decree the specific performance of a contract for the sale of land unless there is a definite and specific statement of the terms of the contract. The contract must identify the land to be sold with reasonable definiteness by describing the particular tract or furnishing a key by which it may be located with the aid of extrinsic evidence. Because a decree for specific performance operates as a deed, the description in the decree should be as definite as that required for a deed. Where land is so vaguely described that the writing provides no key to its identification, specific performance will not be decreed.

3. <u>Lawyering Strategy</u>. In *Dover Shopping Ctr., Inc. v. Cushman's Sons, Inc.*, 164 A.2d 785 (N.J. Super. App. Div. 1960), the owner of a shopping center sought a mandatory injunction to keep a Cushman's bakery open. The injunction "does nothing more than require defendant to reopen and resume its retail bakery business, to display the name of 'Cushman's' on the outside of the premises, to keep the store open as required by paragraph Third of the lease, and to maintain a manager or salesperson in charge." Can you explain why the landlord might have sought that narrow injunction, and why, in light of the modern trend, a lawyer seeking to force an anchor tenant to remain open might seek one like it? Did the order in *Dover Shopping* improperly involve the court in an ongoing relationship? Was the landlord relying on the baker's self-interest?

4. <u>Personal Service Contracts</u>. In *Rettig v. TUV Rheinland Rail Scvs., Inc.*, 2012 WL 13014025 (N.D. Ga. Mar. 14, 2012), the plaintiff Thomas Rettig was a German citizen working for TUV Rheinland Rail Sciences, Inc. Rettig was an at-will employee but alleged TUV/RSI promised to sponsor him and his family through

the process to obtain a green card. Rettig alleged that TUV/RSI breached that agreement by eliminating his position. He and his family sued for breach of contract and then moved for a preliminary injunction to prevent TUV/RSI from terminating him until completion of suit. The court held that Rettig had established a likelihood of success on the merits because a jury could conclude the parties had made an agreement to employ him through the process of obtaining a green card, and that was a sufficiently definite contract to support specific performance. It then turned to whether he was likely to succeed at obtaining specific performance:

> The ultimate, preferred remedy the plaintiffs seek, specific performance, is generally not available in a case where an employee claims a breach of an employment contract. If an employer wrongfully terminates an employee, the employee's only recourse is the recovery of damages; he has no right to recover the position and title of his employment. The court notes that in other contexts, reinstatement — arguably a form of "specific performance" of an employment contract — may be available.

> Although most remedial labor statutes specifically authorize courts to order reinstatement of employees fired in violation of the statute, reinstatement is not normally ordered in common law cases. Historically, the rationale derives from the rule in equity that personal service contracts may not be specifically enforced. This rule was based on the doctrine of mutuality; an employee cannot be ordered to work for an employer, and therefore an employer should not be ordered to employ someone against its wishes. As a practical matter, reinstatement carries with it the potential for unhappiness and retaliation down the line. For all of these reasons, few employees seek reinstatement in common law actions.

Mark A. Rothstein et al., *Employment Law* § 9.23 (4th ed. 2009).

> Thus, the court concludes that under Georgia law, Rettig cannot ultimately prevail in his request for specific performance of the contract under Georgia law. If he cannot win specific performance of his personal services contract upon the conclusion of this action, then it would be inappropriate to order an injunction to effectively give him the same remedy now.

ii. Exceptions: Blue Penciling Non-competition Clauses

Employment agreements often contain provisions designed to prevent employees, after the employment relationship ends, from disclosing the employer's confidential information (by a "nondisclosure agreement" or "NDA"), from soliciting the employer's customers (through "nonsolicitation agreement"), or by otherwise unfairly competing (through a "noncompetition agreement"). Although breach of such provisions often supports an award of specific performance, courts require these clauses to be reasonable in order to be enforced.

Courts require agreements to be clear, and often state they will not rewrite the parties' agreement. *Midwest Sign & Screen Printing Supply Co. v. Dalpe*, 386 F. Supp.

3d 1037 (D. Minn. 2019). However, by statute or by common law, courts frequently "blue pencil" overly broad clauses in employment agreements and enjoin violations (i.e., order specific performance by the former employee). An article recently summarized the approaches to this issue:

> In some states, a court may not rewrite a noncompete agreement to make it enforceable. This is the first type of enforcement approach known as the no-modification approach. In no-modification jurisdictions, a state will not enforce an agreement that is unreasonable in any part. This is essentially an all-or-nothing approach to enforceability, in which a court may not rewrite an overly broad noncompete agreement. Therefore, if the agreement is unreasonable as written, then a court will not enforce it at all.

> A second approach is known as the blue-pencil rule, in which a court modifies the noncompete agreement and enforces the agreement as modified, rather than taking the all-or-nothing approach. Depending on the jurisdiction, the blue-pencil rule varies in application and is either strictly or liberally applied. A strict application of the blue-pencil rule limits what courts may do to alter the noncompete agreement. For example, in North Carolina, a court may choose not to enforce a distinctly separable part of a covenant in order to render the provision reasonable, but it may not otherwise revise or rewrite the covenant.

> In other blue-pencil jurisdictions, states adopt a liberal application of the blue-pencil rule, which allows courts to rewrite an overbroad noncompete agreement to reasonably limit the restrictions found in the agreement. For example, in Florida, a court may not refuse to enforce a noncompete agreement solely because the geographical area is unreasonable, but rather must modify an unreasonable restriction and enforce the agreement as modified. While the Florida statute requires courts to use the blue-pencil approach in all circumstances of unreasonable noncompetes, other liberal blue-pencil states direct their courts to use this re-writing approach, unless the court should find that the agreement was drafted in bad faith.

Jessica Weltge, *Blue Penciling Noncompete Agreements in Arkansas and the Need for A Public Policy Exception*, 2017 Ark. L. Notes 1954 (2017).

Motion Control Sys., Inc. v. East

546 S.E.2d 424 (Va. 2001) (Lacy, J.)

[Motion Control Systems, Inc., designed and made custom motors, and so protected its proprietary information regarding those products through keeping customer lists confidential, removing identifying marks from components, and requiring its employees agree to certain terms. In 1997, MCS asked defendant Gregory East to sign a "Confidentiality and Noncompetition Agreement" that, as proposed, included Paragraph 3(b):

> Employee agrees that for a period of two years after termination of their employment with the Company in any manner whether with or without cause, the Employee will not within a one hundred (100) mile radius of the Company's principal office in Dublin, Virginia, directly or indirectly, own, manage, operate, control, be employed by, participate in, or be associated in any manner with the ownership, management, operation or control of any business similar to the type of business conducted by the Company at the time of the termination of this Agreement. The term "business similar to the type of business conducted by the Company" includes, but is not limited to any business that designs, manufactures, sells or distributes motors, motor drives or motor controls.

However, East was concerned that the final sentence would prohibit work in areas outside the scope of MCS's business. He consulted a lawyer, and suggested MCS delete the phrase "but is not limited to." MCS agreed and added the word "currently," changing the final sentence to: "The term 'business similar to the type of business conducted by the Company' currently includes any business that designs, manufactures, sells or distributes motors, motor drives or motor controls." The parties signed the agreement.

East resigned from MCS in December 1998, and was hired by Litton Systems, Inc., in August 1999 as a supervisor at its manufacturing plant that made certain motors.

MCS sued to enforce the agreement and to prevent East from revealing its proprietary information. The trial court found that MCS and Litton made some of the same products and that MCS reasonably believed Litton was going to move into more of the same products and put MCS out of business.

However, the trial court concluded that the covenant not to compete was unenforceable because the final sentence of paragraph 3(b) "imposed additional restraints which are far greater than reasonably necessary to protect MCS in its legitimate business enterprise." However, it did enjoin East from "disclosing to anyone any confidential, proprietary or trade secret information of Motion Control," even though the trial court found that Litton had not attempted to gain any trade secrets and East had not "made any disclosure of any trade secret or any other like fact." East appealed.]

Covenants not to compete are restraints on trade and accordingly are not favored. The validity of a covenant not to compete is determined by applying not only the general principles of contract construction, but also legal principles specifically applicable to such covenants. The employer bears the burden to show that the restraint is reasonable and no greater than necessary to protect the employer's legitimate business interests. The restraint may not be unduly harsh or oppressive in curtailing the employee's legitimate efforts to earn a livelihood and must be reasonable in light of sound public policy. As a restraint of trade, the covenant must be strictly construed and, if ambiguous, it must be construed in favor of the employee. On appeal, our examination of the covenant not to compete presents a question of law which we review de novo.

In this appeal, the two-year time period and geographic area covered by MCS' covenant not to compete are not at issue. Rather, the sole issue is whether the language of Paragraph 3(b) is overbroad. Relying on our cases that have approved language similar to that contained in Paragraph 3(b), MCS argues that the present restraint is no greater than necessary to protect its interests because the language is "narrowly tailored" to protect MCS from former employees disclosing its proprietary or confidential information to competitors. We disagree.

The covenants not to compete in the cases upon which MCS relies contained some, but not all, of the language used in Paragraph 3(b). These covenants stated that the former employee could not be involved in "any business similar to the type of business conducted by" the employer, *Roanoke Eng'g Sales Co. v. Rosenbaum*, 223 Va. 548 (1982), or that the employee would not work for a competitor who "renders the same or similar services as Employer," *Blue Ridge Anesthesia & Critical Care v. Gidick*, 239 Va. 369 (1990), thus limiting prohibited employment to other business "similar" to the employer's business. The prohibition in this case goes further, however. By defining a "similar business" as " any business that designs, manufactures, sells or distributes motors, motor drives or motor controls," MCS's covenant also prohibits employment in any business, for example, that sells motors, regardless of whether the motors are the specialized types of brushless motors sold by MCS. As the trial court concluded, under this provision, the restricted activities "could include a wide range of enterprises unrelated to" the business of MCS. Although the change in language suggested by East may have narrowed the range of prohibited employment, neither before nor after the alteration was the prohibited employment restricted to businesses which engage in activities similar to those in which MCS engaged.

Accordingly, we conclude that the trial court did not err in holding that the covenant not to compete in this case imposed restraints that exceeded those necessary to protect the legitimate business interests of MCS and, therefore, was unenforceable.

The trial court, finding that East had knowledge of MCS's trade secrets, enjoined East from disclosing MCS's confidential, trade secret, or proprietary information to anyone, pursuant to Code § 59.1-337. That section provides in pertinent part:

> Actual or threatened misappropriation may be enjoined. Upon application to the court, an injunction shall be terminated when the trade secret has ceased to exist, but the injunction may be continued for an additional reasonable period of time in order to eliminate commercial advantage that otherwise would be derived from the misappropriation.

By its terms, this section requires actual or threatened disclosure of trade secrets. The only basis cited by the trial court for issuing the injunction was that East had knowledge of the trade secrets of MCS. The trial court made no findings that East had actually disclosed or threatened to disclose such information. To the contrary, the trial court specifically found that East had not disclosed "any trade secret or any other like fact." Mere knowledge of trade secrets is insufficient to support an injunction under the terms of Code § 59.1-337.

Deutsche Post Glob. Mail, Ltd v. Conrad

292 F. Supp. 2d 748 (D. Md. 2003), *aff'd*, 116 F. App'x 435
(4th Cir. 2004) (Motz, J.)

[Deutsche Post Global Mail, Ltd., required Gerard Conrad and Guy Gemmill to agree to an employment agreement that provided in section 5, titled "Restriction and Covenant Not to Compete:"

(a) Sales Representative covenants and agrees that during the term of his/her employment with the Company, and in the event of and for a period of two (2) years following the termination of his employment with the Company for any reason, he/she shall not, without the prior written consent of the Company, directly or indirectly:

. . . (ii) Engage in any activity which may affect adversely the interests of the Company or any Related Corporation and the businesses conducted by either of them, including, without limitation, directly or indirectly soliciting or diverting customers and/or employees of the Company or any Related Corporation or attempting to so solicit or divert such customers and/or employees, or

(iii) Engage in any capacity whatsoever (whether as stockholder, officer, director, employee, agent, consultant, advisory or investor) in any form of business entity seeking to engage or engaging in any activity which is then in competition with the company or any Related Corporation in such geographical or territorial markets as the Company or any Related Corporation then is doing or seeking to do business. It is intended that this prohibition of competitive activity be proscribed only in such geographical area in which the Company then is engaged. Sales Representative agrees that the term, scope, and geographic area of the covenants contained herein are reasonable and necessary; however, if any court of competent jurisdiction shall determine this covenant to be unenforceable as to either the term, scope, or geographic area imposed above, then this covenant nevertheless shall be enforceable by such court as to such shorter term, such lesser scope or within such lesser geographic area as may be determined by the court to be reasonable and enforceable. If such court shall refuse to enforce this covenant as to a particular geographic area, then, in such event, the parties hereto declare and agree that for a period of two (2) years from the date on which employment of Sales Representative terminates for any reason, Sales Representative shall be prohibited from soliciting all persons to whom the Company has sold products or rendered services during the three (3) year period immediately preceding the termination of the Sales Representative.

Conrad and Gemmill left DPGM to form a competing business, Postal Logistics International. DPGM asserted Conrad and Gemmill violated restrictive covenants in their employment contracts by forming PLI and by soliciting DPGM's customers. Conrad and Gemmill admitted they had breached by soliciting customers of

DPGM, but argued the covenants were unenforceable. Below is the court's opinion on summary judgment.]

Under Maryland law, a restrictive covenant will be upheld if the restraint is confined within limits which are no wider as to area and duration than are reasonably necessary for the protection of the business of the employer and do not impose undue hardship on the employee or disregard the interests of the public.

DPGM is now only seeking to enforce a very narrow portion of the restrictive covenants — specifically, that part of section 5(a)(ii) prohibiting the direct or indirect solicitation or diversion of DPGM customers, as well as attempted solicitation or diversion. Defendants argue that even this single restriction is unreasonable in scope (as to activities, duration, and geography), that it is unnecessary to protect DPGM's business, that it imposes an undue hardship on Conrad and Gemmill, and that it is contrary to the public interest. DPGM claims that the covenants are not unreasonable as written, but that even if they are, the court can edit them to make them reasonable.

Before determining if the restriction on solicitation of customers is reasonable, I must address the preliminary question of a court's ability to limit a covenant to only one of its sections. Maryland law does permit courts to "blue pencil," or excise language from restrictive covenants that is unnecessarily broad. Traditionally, such editing has been limited to removing the offending language without supplementing or rearranging the remaining language.

Here, in order to enforce the non-solicitation of customers provision in Conrad and Gemmill's restrictive covenants, I would only have to make two modifications: strike out section 5(a)(iii) completely and strike out a substantial portion of section 5(a)(ii). The latter section, which prohibits engaging in any activity that may adversely affect DPGM, would be eliminated, as well as the references in that section to "any Related Corporation." It currently reads:

> Engage in any activity which may affect adversely the interests of the Company or any Related Corporation and the businesses conducted by either of them, including, without limitation, directly or indirectly soliciting or diverting customers and/or employees of the Company or any Related Corporation or attempting to so solicit or divert such customers and/or employees.

Were I to blue pencil this language, the edited version of section 5(a)(ii) would simply read, "Engage in soliciting or diverting customers of the Company or attempting to so solicit or divert such customers."

Although I have substantial doubts about the wisdom of any blue pencil rule,[3] removing section 5(a)(iii) and the offending language from 5(a)(ii) would not involve any rewriting or reorganizing of the remaining language. Therefore, it would be in line with what Maryland courts have traditionally done under the blue pencil rule.

Notes and Questions

1. <u>Blue Pencil or Not?</u> Given the difficulties of knowing if a covenant is "reasonable," does denying blue penciling make sense? If so, which approach gives the best incentives for employers, employees, and prospective employees and employers to draft concise and lawful clauses and so avoid litigation and reduce costs? Outside this context, courts state they will not "rewrite contracts" for parties. Given the chilling effect of an overly broad covenant, why salvage them? After all, a typical employee is not likely to seek a declaratory judgment of overbreadth, and a prospective employer may be unwilling to risk a suit by the former employer. In addition, consider whether an employer in a state where blue penciling is permitted will have an incentive to write a narrow clause. Was the judge in *Deutsche Post* right that "blue penciling encourages an employer to impose an overly broad restrictive covenant, knowing that if the covenant is challenged by an employee the only consequence suffered by the employer will be to have a court write a narrower restriction for it"?

2. <u>No Mutuality Needed</u>. The common law rule is that an employer will not order an employer to rehire an employee in part because doing so almost invariably involves a court in an ongoing relationship; yet courts will enforce covenants not to compete against former employees. There is no "mutuality" of remedies: a court will enforce a covenant not to compete but will not compel rehiring of a former employee.

3. <u>Public Policy</u>. In *Mufreesboro Med. Clinic, P.A. v. Udom,* 166 S.W.3d 674 (Tenn. 2005), the court analyzed a covenant not to compete that restricted the practice of physicians, and applied a more stringent standard in light of the American Medical Association's view that such clauses were unethical. The legislature overruled that decision shortly thereafter, and most states apply the same test to covenants not to compete involving medical care. *See id.* Should they?

4. "<u>Competition</u>." In *Midwest Sign & Screen Printing Supply Co. v. Dalpe,* 386 F. Supp. 3d 1037 (D. Minn. 2019), the former employer was a supplier of paints, inks, frames, and similar materials. It sued its former employee, Dalpe, to enforce a covenant not to compete, which provided that Dalpe would not, for 12 months, "own, work for or assist any entity that offers products or services that compete with products or services that Midwest offers." The court held the 12-month period was reasonable, but noted it lacked any geographic limitation and that it would preclude Dalpe from working at an office supply store that sold similar products. In response to Midwest's argument that this was ludicrous, the court wrote:

> Though it characterizes Laird's position on this issue as "ludicrous," Midwest has neither argued nor explained why it does not compete with office-supply or similar businesses. There is no evidence, for example, showing that Midwest customers do not also obtain products and services Midwest sells from these types of businesses. In addition to prohibiting Dalpe from working for a seemingly vast array of employers, the Agreement seems unreasonably overbroad because it would prohibit Dalpe from

working in roles with these employers that are entirely dissimilar from his Northwest Sales Manager position. Hypothetically, for example, he would be prohibited from managing inventory, directing human resources, or even working as a delivery driver because each of these roles would entail "working for an entity that offers products or services that compete with Midwest's."

The only source of a limitation that might resolve these problems (or perhaps provide a starting point for blue-penciling the Agreement to resolve them) is the term "compete." There may be a reasonable definition of this term that might have the effect of narrowing the reach of the Agreement's non-compete covenants, but Midwest does not identify it. Its submissions do not address its intended or preferred interpretation of this word. When asked at the hearing what "products or services that compete with products or services that [Midwest] offers" means, Midwest responded initially by implying that the phrase's meaning is self-evident: "That means products or services that compete with products or services that Midwest offers." Midwest also suggested that the "common, everyday reading" of "compete" should be limited by how it is understood within the industry, but there is no evidence in the record suggesting an industry understanding of the term, much less one that reasonably would narrow the breadth of the restriction. Perhaps businesses like Midwest share an understanding that they do not compete with businesses—for example, retail office-supply stores—though they may sell some of the same products. But the record contains no evidence of that. Midwest does not contend that the non-compete provisions should (or may) be blue-penciled to address this issue, and the breadth of these provisions, the inability to clearly define the scope of "products or services that compete with Midwest's," and the absence of evidence showing the Parties' intent with respect to this issue seem to make that task impracticable and unwise. *Cf. Southland Metals, Inc. v. Am. Castings, LLC,* 800 F.3d 452 (8th Cir. 2015) (addressing a noncompete in a business-to-business agreement that did not define "compete," which made the contract ambiguous and required looking to "extrinsic evidence to determine the intent and meaning of the parties").

In some cases, by contrast, employment agreements have defined what it meant to "compete." *See, e.g., Prime Therapeutics v. Beatty,* 354 F. Supp. 3d 957 (D. Minn. 2018) (defining "Competitive Product" based on products "marketed, sold or under development during the twelve months preceding Employee's termination," as well as being "of the same general type" and "used for the same or similar purposes," among other things); *Life Time, Inc. v. Glory Gains Gym LLC,* 2018 WL 2539095 (D. Minn. June 4, 2018) (finding non-compete that defined "Competing Business" as an organization "engaged in the business of providing fitness club-related services" was reasonable); *Bos. Sci. Corp. v. Duberg,* 754 F. Supp. 2d 1033

(D. Minn. 2010) (defining "Competitive Product" and providing examples: "such products include, but are not limited to, cardiac pacemakers, implantable defibrillators resynchronization devices, and leads"). In other cases, non-competes have contained explicit exceptions or "carve-outs" that clearly identify non-competing roles. *See, e.g., Prime Therapeutics*, 354 F. Supp. 3d at 963 (leaving employee "free to work for or provide services to a competitor" provided the employee "has not assumed a position with a competitor that would lead to the inevitable disclosure of Confidential Information"); *Vascular Sols., Inc. v. Pedregon*, 2009 WL 2743022 (D. Minn. Aug. 26, 2009) (providing that "nothing in this agreement shall prohibit the employee's employment by any entity which engages in a business with a product or service competitive with any product or service of employer so long as" the new employer "takes reasonable measures to insure that the employee is not involved with or consulted in any aspect of the design, development, production, marketing, or servicing of such competitive product or service"); *Medtronic, Inc. v. Advanced Bionics Corp.*, 630 N.W.2d 438, 453 (Minn. Ct. App. 2001) ("It is expressly understood that the employee is free to work for a competitor of Medtronic provided that such employment does not include any responsibilities for, or in connection with, a Competitive Product as defined in this Agreement."). The Agreement does not include these features, making these cases distinguishable. Because the non-compete covenants are likely overbroad and unenforceable, Midwest is not likely to prevail on the merits of its claim that Dalpe breached these terms.

How would you define "compete" in the *Midwest* case?

5. <u>Affiliated Corporations</u>. As explained above, courts generally limit claims for breach of contract to parties to the agreement and intended third-party beneficiaries. In *CDW LLC v. NETech Corp.*, 2012 WL 527449 (S.D. Ind. Feb. 16, 2012), the court noted that under Wisconsin law a corporation could not sue to enforce restrictive covenants owed by a former employee of an affiliated corporation, even if "their businesses are intertwined and the success of one is dependent on that of the other."

b. Plaintiff Must Have Performed, or Have Been Ready, Willing, and Able to Perform

As discussed more fully in the *Bisbee* and *Fazzio* cases below, a party seeking specific performance must have "substantially performed its contractual obligations and was willing and able to perform its remaining obligations." *Liberty Affordable Hous., Inc. v. Maple Ct. Apartments*, 998 N.Y.S.2d 543 (Ct. App. N.Y. 2015). Thus, for example, before a court will compel the sale of land, a buyer "must demonstrate that he was ready, willing, and able to perform on the original day or, if time is not of the essence, on a subsequent date fixed by the parties or within a reasonable time thereafter." *Id.* If a contract does not state time is of the essence, courts generally allow parties a reasonable time after the date set for closing to complete performance. *Dishner Developers, Inc. v. Brown*, 145 N.C. App. 375, *aff'd*, 354 N.C. 569 (2001).

c. Plaintiff's Remedy at Law Must Be Inadequate, and for Interlocutory Relief, Denial Must Cause Irreparable Harm

When permanent injunctive relief in the form of specific performance is sought, courts require proof of "an inadequate remedy at law, not irreparable harm." *JPMorgan Chase Bank, N.A. v. Winget*, 510 F.3d 577 (6th Cir. 2007). In this context, specific performance is awarded because of the "incompleteness or inadequacy of the remedy at law as applied to the contract sought to be specifically enforced under the facts shown." *Id.*

Courts split on whether the adequacy of legal remedy includes whether any money judgment will be collectible. In some states, even if the party opposing specific performance has but "may dissipate bank assets, a judgment for money damages is adequate and injunctive relief is improper, notwithstanding the possibility that a money judgment will be uncollectible." *Absolute Activist Value Master Fund Ltd. v. Devine*, 2017 WL 3188502 (M.D. Fla. July 25, 2017) (inadequacy turns on "whether a judgment can be obtained, not whether, once obtained, it will be collectible.") However, in other states, the legal remedy is inadequate if the defendant "may become insolvent before a final judgment can be entered and collected." *IPS Steel LLC v. Hennepin Indus. Dev., LLC*, 2018 WL 3093959 (C.D. Ill. Feb. 23, 2018).

Courts distinguish between "irreparable harm" and "inadequate remedy at law" if a party seeks preliminary injunctive relief in the form of specific performance. Where a party doing so equated "inadequate remedy at law" with "irreparable harm," the court in *Travelers Cas. and Sur. Co. of Am. v. Padron*, 2017 WL 9360906 (W.D. Tex. Aug. 2, 2017) wrote:

> Such a conflation of the specific performance's inadequate remedy at law requirement and the preliminary injunction's irreparable injury requirement is improper. The Southern District of New York has addressed the issue, and the Court finds its reasoning persuasive:

> No case cited by plaintiff, nor any uncovered by independent research, makes the automatic connection urged by plaintiff between the ordinary remedy of specific performance and the extraordinary remedy of a preliminary injunction. Indeed, to do so would be to create a *per se* rule that would eliminate the crucial "irreparable harm" branch of the test for preliminary injunctions, in such cases where specifically enforceable contractual provisions are at issue. Moreover, to create such a linkage would be to misconceive the differing requirements for a grant of specific performance under New York law, and for the issuance of a preliminary injunction as established by the Second Circuit. Under New York law there exists a broad range of situations in which the remedy at

law will be considered to be 'inadequate' in the context of an action for specific performance.

This liberal standard standards in sharp contrast to the Second Circuit's narrow definition of irreparable harm as an injury requiring a remedy of more than mere monetary damages.

Correctly viewed, then, a showing of an inadequate remedy at law is a *sine qua non* of granting injunctive relief, but it is not synonymous with a showing of irreparable harm, and does not, without such a showing, support the granting of a preliminary injunction.

See Allied World Specialty Ins. Co. v. Abat Lerew Constr., LLC, 2017 WL 1476131 (D. Neb. Apr. 24, 2017) ("The fact that Allied may be ultimately be entitled, under Nebraska law, to the equitable remedy of specific performance after proving its case, does not mean that an order granting specific performance is appropriate or necessary at this time."); *Int'l Fidelity Ins. Co. v. Talbot Constr., Inc.,* 2016 WL 8814367 (N.D. Ga. Apr. 13, 2016) ("The absence of an adequate remedy at law is a precondition to any form of equitable relief. The requirement of irreparable harm is needed to take care of the case where although the ultimate relief that the plaintiff is seeking is equitable, implying that he has no remedy at law, he can easily wait till the end of trial to get that relief. Only if he will suffer irreparable harm — that is, harm that cannot be prevented or fully rectified by the final judgment after trial — can he get a preliminary injunction.").

An inadequate remedy at law is often found for transfer of interests in real property, but rarely for transfer of interests in a chattel, unless it is a rare car or plane, stock in a closely held corporation, art, a family heirloom, or chattels with uncertain market value. *See Peterson v. HVM L.L.C.,* 2015 WL 3648839 (D.N.J. June 11, 2015) (specific performance proper "when an agreement concerns possession of property such as heirlooms, family treasures and works of art that induce a strong sentimental attachment."). The following examines these paradigms.

i. Agreements to Transfer an Interest in Real Property

The common law rule that a damage award is inadequate for breach of contract to transfer an interest in real property "arose in medieval England where land ownership was a primary indicator of the owner's social status and voting rights. Specific performance was necessary because courts of law simply could not value expectations such as social status or the right to vote for a representative in Parliament, and substitute performance was virtually impossible because of the unavailability of land for sale." *Real Est. Analytics, LLC v. Vallas,* 72 Cal. Rptr. 3d 835 (Cal. App. 4th 2008). Although those reasons no longer exist, the rule remains: "(1) each parcel of land is unique and therefore there can be no adequate replacement after a breach; and (2) monetary damages are difficult to calculate after a party refuses to complete a land sales contract, particularly expectation damages," and this is true even if the buyer had a contract to "flip" the property and so there is an exact amount of damage. *Id.*

EMF Gen. Contracting Corp. v. Bisbee

774 N.Y.S.2d 39 (N.Y. App. Div. 1st Dept. 2004) (Saxe, J.)

[In March 1998, Plaintiff EMF General Contracting Corp., a construction company, agreed to buy two vacant lots from Michael Bisbee for $7,500 per lot, paying $1,500 for each lot, which Bisbee put in escrow. Bisbee had been a registered mortgage broker for 17 years and was familiar with valuing property. The closing was scheduled for April 1998, but a survey and title search brought problems to light. Lawyers for EMF and Bisbee periodically communicated about the issues, and in June 1999 Bisbee's lawyer faxed a letter to one landowner to settle a boundary issue, but never received a response. Nothing more happened until early 2000, when EMF informed Bisbee it would accept the lots with existing boundary problems. In March 2000, EMF demanded and set a closing in April. Bisbee did not show up. By early 2003, the lots appraised for $85,000 each. EMF performed its obligations or showed it had been ready and able to do so despite the title issues.]

Generally, the equitable remedy of specific performance is routinely awarded in contract actions involving real property, on the premise that each parcel of real property is unique. The court has discretion to deny such relief as equity and justice seem to demand in the light of the circumstances of each case, and the available equitable defenses include serious unfairness, undue hardship, and laches, or unreasonable prejudicial delay. But, the court's discretion to grant or deny specific performance of a contract for the sale of realty is not unlimited; unless the court finds that granting a decree of specific performance would be a drastic or harsh remedy, or work injustice, the court must direct specific performance.

At the outset, it bears emphasis that there was no unfairness in the deal itself; the contract was fair when entered into. Yet, the passage of time before this action was commenced and the property's increase in value require consideration of a number of rules and cases.

A common fact pattern in which specific performance is denied is discussed in Dobbs's treatise on the law of remedies:

The speculating land buyer. One of the most common patterns in denying specific performance is the case in which the buyer has contracted in a way that permits him to postpone purchase for a long period for which he has paid no option price. For instance, the buyer may find title defects which give him the right to seek a cure and delay performance accordingly. Or he may obtain extensions for various reasons. If the seller concludes that the buyer has abandoned the contract or breached it and refuses to perform, the buyer may wait for long period before suing for specific performance in order to determine whether the land will increase in value. Any of these devices may be used by buyers as means of getting what in effect is a free

option; if the price rises, the buyer will eventually sue for specific performance. If it does not, the buyer drops the deal. Many of the doctrines—
unfairness, hardship, laches—are invoked in just such cases to defeat the
buyer's attempt to get a free ride by denying specific performance." 3 Dobbs,
Remedies at 303.

In other words, where it is established that the buyer has made excuses in order
to delay closing on the contract, with an actual purpose of waiting to see whether
to enforce the contract depending upon whether the market value of the subject
property increases or decreases, the courts will not grant specific performance.

However, in the present case, although the value of the property increased, the
trial court did not find that EMF was behaving in any sort of disingenuous or
manipulative fashion, or using insignificant title defects for the purpose of delaying
the purchase in order to see whether the market value of the property went up or
down. Rather, plaintiff was legitimately attempting to resolve the real defects in title
so as to effectuate the purchase. Furthermore, while the 2003 valuation of the property is undisputed, there was no evidence showing what the property's value was at
the time plaintiff commenced the action, and so there is no basis to conclude that
plaintiff's decision in March 2000 to take action to enforce the contract was based
upon an increase in value.

Accordingly, the judgment of the Supreme Court which, after a nonjury trial,
dismissed plaintiff's cause of action for specific performance, awarded plaintiff
$25,000 in damages with interest from April 22, 2000, and directed defendant to
return plaintiff's $1,500 down payment check, should be reversed, with costs, the
award of damages vacated, judgment granted on plaintiff's cause of action for specific performance, and the matter remanded.

Notes and Questions

1. Should the Rule Be History? Some argue that the rule that land is unique, given
how it is marketed and sold now, is antiquated and should not apply, particularly
to commercial properties. *See* Tanya D. Marsh, *Sometimes Blackacre Is a Widget:
Rethinking Commercial Real Estate Contract Remedies*, 88 Neb. L. Rev. 635 (2010).
Do you agree? Consider this California statute: "It is to be presumed that the breach
of an agreement to transfer real property cannot be adequately relieved by pecuniary compensation. In the case of a single-family dwelling which the party seeking
performance intends to occupy, this presumption is conclusive. In all other cases,
this presumption is a presumption affecting the burden of proof." Consider also
that leases or transfers of interests in units of cooperative apartments are generally
not "real property" in terms of specific performance. *Lezell v. Forde*, 891 N.Y.S.2d
606 (Sup. Ct. N.Y. 2009) (contract to transfer interest in a cooperative apartment
governed by UCC Article 2).

2. Specific Performance for Sellers. Specific performance is available to sellers, as
the court in *Ash Park, LLC v. Alexander & Bishop, Ltd.*, 783 N.W.2d 294 (Wis. 2010)
explained:

Courts have traditionally awarded specific performance of a contract for the sale of land without a prerequisite that the non-breaching party demonstrate that legal damages would be inadequate. Restatement (Second) of Contracts § 360 cmt. e (1981) ("Contracts for the sale of land have traditionally been accorded a special place in the law of specific performance. The seller who has not yet conveyed is generally granted specific performance on breach by the buyer."); Edward Yorio, *Contract Enforcement: Specific Performance and Injunctions* 281 (1989) ("Traditionally, when a buyer reneged on a promise to purchase realty, specific performance was almost universally available to remedy the breach.").

We conclude that the circuit court did not erroneously exercise its discretion by ordering specific performance without requiring Ash Park to demonstrate that a remedy at law would be inadequate.

3. <u>Acreage Shortfalls</u>. A seller who agrees to sell more than he owns can seek specific performance. In *Wooten v. Lightburn*, 579 F. Supp. 2d 769 (W.D. Va. 2008), *aff'd*, 350 F. App'x 812 (4th Cir. 2009), the trial court denied specific performance at a reduced price:

Virginia law recognizes an equitable right of abatement of the purchase price in situations where there is a deficiency in quantity when the property in question was sold by the acre or by estimation, where the quantity was material in assessing the price. This equitable remedy of abatement is generally enforced by a request for specific performance. Falling in line with other equitable remedies, the right to abatement of the purchase price should be imposed only when it is equitable to do so under the facts and circumstances of each particular case. However, where the evidence shows that the parties expressly agreed that the purchaser should bear the risk of a deficiency, no equitable relief should be granted.

In that case, the seller had agreed to sell 1,977 acres at $2,150 per acre, but a survey showed he owned 182 fewer acres than that. The court found the buyer had not agreed to take the risk of a deficiency and so ordered specific performance at the abated price.

ii. Agreements to Transfer a Rare Opportunity or Chattel

The general rule is that the remedy at law is adequate where the contract is to transfer commodities. *GLL Air, LLC v. Mid-S. Services, Inc.*, 2014 WL 12623246 (M.D. Fla. Oct. 10, 2014) ("generally the injunctive remedy of specific performance is not available for contracts involving personal property where the good is commonly manufactured," such as an airplane). Related to this, a remedy at law is adequate if the contract relates to a chattel with a readily ascertainable market value, such as shares of publicly traded stock. *LG Capital Funding, LLC v. PositiveID Corp.*, 2017 WL 2556991 (E.D.N.Y. June 12, 2017) ("courts routinely refuse to order specific performance" when a "defendant breaches its obligation to deliver public stock.").

However, if the contract is for a "unique" chattel, courts consider "whether an item is custom built, whether the item has historical or sentimental significance, and whether the item was designed to particular specifications." *Slidell, Inc. v. Millennium Inorganic Chemicals, Inc.*, 2004 WL 1447921 (D. Minn. June 28, 2004), *aff'd*, 460 F.3d 1047 (8th Cir. 2006). Specific performance may also be available where the source of the product is unique, as well as "other proper circumstances," such as "where (a) a breaching seller is the only available source or (b) a breaching buyer is the only available customer." *Hemlock Semiconductor Corp. v. Kyocera Corp.*, 2018 WL 3949110 (6th Cir. Aug. 16, 2018). Under the UCC, a court may order specific performance of a contract for the sale of goods where "the goods are unique or in other proper circumstances," and output and requirements contracts typically satisfy this requirement.

Mirion Techs. (Canberra), Inc. v. Sunpower, Inc.

2017 WL 5090436 (S.D. Ohio Nov. 6, 2017) (Graham, J.)

[Mirion Technologies (Canberra), Inc., had a Supply Agreement with Sunpower, Inc., under which Sunpower was to supply Mirion with cryocoolers, a device used in nuclear radiation detectors. The agreement did not specify any quantity Sunpower was required to provide. When Sunpower stopped supplying cryocoolers, Mirion sued for specific performance under the UCC.]

The Sixth Circuit has described requirements contracts under Ohio law as a contract which calls for one party to furnish materials or goods to another party to the extent of the latter's requirements in business. In the absence of a definite quantity term, the parties are obligated to deal in good faith regarding quantity requests.

Some jurisdictions recognize the validity of a nonexclusive requirements contracts-one in in which the buyer is not required to purchase the goods solely from the seller to the contract. . . .

Even if recognized as viable, a nonexclusive requirements contract must provide a basis for determining a reasonable quantity term, such as a stated estimate in the contract of the amount of goods required. Mirion has submitted evidence that its procurement officer discussed a purchase forecast (the ramp-up schedule) with a counterpart at Sunpower before the Supply Agreement was executed. But the schedule was not incorporated into or referenced in the Supply Agreement, and the Agreement does not otherwise state an estimate of Mirion's requirements. Sixth Circuit case law is clear that if nonexclusive requirements contracts are to be recognized at all, the contract itself must provide a sufficient basis for determining a reasonable quantity term. *See Orchard Grp.*, 135 F.3d at 428 (finding no basis where purported agreement indicated a range between 0 and 1 million units of film); *Cyril Bath*, 892 F.2d at 466 (applying Ohio law and finding that contract which listed annual production estimates was sufficient); *City of Louisville v. Rockwell Mfg. Co.*, 482 F.2d 159 (6th Cir. 1973) (applying Kentucky law and finding that a quantity estimate of "approximately 7650 parking meters" in the contract was sufficient).

The Supply Agreement does not contain a quantity estimate; thus, the court finds that Mirion has not demonstrated a likelihood of success in showing that the Agreement is a nonexclusive requirements contract.

Nor has Mirion demonstrated a likelihood of success of showing that the Supply Agreement is an exclusive requirements contract. The Ohio Supreme Court has defined a requirements contract as a contract in writing whereby one agrees to buy, for sufficient consideration, all the merchandise of a designated type which the buyer may require for use in his own established business. In other words, a requirements contract exists when "one party promises to buy exclusively, and the other party agrees to deliver specific goods or services which the buyer may need, for a certain period of time."

Mirion does not dispute that the Supply Agreement contains no language requiring it to buy all of its cryocooler requirements for the Cryo-Cycle II from Sunpower. The Agreement does not require Mirion to buy any cryocoolers at all from Sunpower, nor does it prohibit Mirion from purchasing cryocoolers from another supplier.

Mirion correctly notes that a promise to purchase exclusively from one supplier may be either implicit or explicit. Mirion contends that the parties implicitly understood that Sunpower would be supplying Mirion's entire need for cryocoolers. According to Mirion, the ramp-up schedule supports this implicit understanding, as does the testimony of Jeffrey Hatfield, former site manager for Sunpower.

The court finds that Sunpower has failed to demonstrate a likelihood of success of showing an implicit obligation that Mirion would obtain cryocoolers exclusively from Sunpower.

"Output and requirements contracts involving a particular or peculiarly available source or market present today the typical commercial specific performance situation." O.R.C. § 1302.90, Off. Cmt. 2. Although the statute does not exclude non-requirements contracts from its scope, practically speaking, a buyer to a non-requirements sales contract may well face difficulties of proof in seeking specific performance. Output and requirements contracts, explicitly cited as examples of situations in which specific performance may be appropriate, by their nature call for a series of continuing acts and an ongoing relationship. And it is where a contract calls for continuing sale of unique or 'noncoverable' goods that the Official Comment "contemplates that at least in some circumstances specific performance will issue contrary to the historical reluctance to grant such relief in these situations."

Sunpower argues that because the Supply Agreement is not a requirements contract, Mirion can prevail only if the goods are unique. That is, Sunpower would remove the "other proper circumstances" prong of the statute as a way in which Mirion could show it is entitled to specific performance. If Mirion did not obligate itself to refrain from obtaining cryocoolers from another supplier, so the argument goes, then Mirion has the contractual ability to obtain cover. The court, however, has not found any authority to support Sunpower's categorical proposition that a buyer to a non-requirements contract cannot avail itself of the "other proper circumstances" prong of the statute. A buyer might have the contractual freedom to obtain cover, but the statute and case law look to the commercial feasibility of finding cover and whether the buyer has the ability to go to the marketplace and actually obtain a replacement.

The focus of the court's inquiry, therefore, is twofold: whether Sunpower's cryocoolers are unique and, even if they are not unique, whether Mirion is able to obtain cover. Courts have said that a good is unique if it is rare, one of a kind, or nearly impossible to replace. Other courts look to the uncertainty of valuing the good, in keeping with the precept that specific performance is available only when there is no adequate remedy at law. The U.C.C. provides that "test of uniqueness must be made in terms of the total situation which characterizes the contract." O.R.C. § 1302.90, Off. Cmt. 2.

The court finds no support for Mirion's claim that Sunpower's CryoTel GT cryocooler is unique. It may be that high-purity germanium detectors are one of a kind, in comparison to other radiation detectors, in their sensitivity to radioactivity. It may be that hybrid cryostats are the best option available for cooling germanium crystals. And it may be that cryocoolers, which make the detectors and cryostats operational, are devices which reflect sophisticated design and technology. But within the nuclear energy industry in which the parties operate, cryocoolers are not unique or rare goods, nor are they incapable of being valued. Mirion's own witness, James Colaresi, testified that when Sunpower terminated the prior supply agreement with Canberra in 2013, Canberra "came up with a fairly long list of potential companies" with whom it could approach about supplying a cryocooler for Canberra's Cryo-Cycle II. Canberra "pared down that list to about five and then ultimately selected two Twinbird and Thales out of the five." He further testified that cost was the consideration that drove Canberra's selection of Twinbird. During the hearing, the court heard of no material changes in the marketplace from 2013 to present day. Sunpower remains one of many potential suppliers of cryocoolers. The value of these goods-as expressed by their cost-is ascertainable to Mirion. Indeed, the reason Mirion pursued Sunpower over Thales in early 2017 was not the uniqueness of Sunpower's product but the higher costs associated with Thales.

Mirion argues that cryocoolers have a number of important features and that reliability is one of them. The court agrees that in evaluating uniqueness, it should view the totality of the situation and consider the characteristics or attributes of a good which are important to the parties and to others in the relevant marketplace or industry. *See Sedmak v. Charlie's Chevrolet, Inc.*, 622 S.W.2d 694 (Mo. Ct. App. 1981) (examining the "mileage, condition, ownership and appearance" of a collectible automobile). Sunpower does not dispute, and common sense dictates, that reliability is an important feature of a machine or a scientific instrument.

According to Mirion, Sunpower is uniquely able to produce a cryocooler that drops into the Cryo-Cycle II and performs reliably. This claim has slim factual support. Though Webb and Colaresi testified that Lihan's product is generally less reliable than Sunpower's, Mirion failed to produce documents or data regarding the respective reliability of Lihan's and Sunpower's cryocoolers. This leaves the court without specific information from which it could determine, for instance, the comparative failure rates of the two makes of cryocoolers, the average lifespan of a Lihan cryocooler before it fails and whether the failure rate or lifespan of Lihan devices has improved over time.

The court finds that Mirion has shown only that the Sunpower cryocooler perhaps is better than Lihan's on the reliability front, not that the Sunpower device is unique. Lihan's device is not so unreliable that Mirion is unable to sell its Cryo-Cycle II, as was the case when Canberra attempted to work with Twinbird. Mirion/Canberra has sold its product with the Lihan cryocooler since December 2014 and has addressed the reliability issues with Lihan's product through a warranty return program. As Webb and Colaresi testified, Mirion has a "fairly large" service team that is equipped to "immediately" replace defective cryocoolers with new ones.

For the same reasons that Mirion has not shown that Sunpower's product is unique, Mirion has not established that it is unable to obtain cover. *See Kaiser Trading Co. v. Associated Metals & Minerals Corp.,* 321 F. Supp. 923 (N.D. Cal. 1970) (noting that cover can refer to the "scarcity of goods" or to "when the goods contracted for cannot be purchased on the open market"). Mirion's experience with Lihan proves that it is commercially feasible for Mirion to obtain an alternative supply of cryocoolers. Mirion has access to enough of a supply from Lihan to produce the Cryo-Cycle II and fill warranty returns.

Again, numerous potential suppliers exist for Mirion. Now that the relationship with Sunpower has indeed failed, Mirion remains able to obtain cryocoolers from Lihan, including during any interim period in which Mirion would seek to work with Thales or another potential supplier on research and development.

Accordingly, the court finds that Mirion has not established a strong likelihood of success on its claim for specific performance.

Reed Found., Inc. v. Franklin D. Roosevelt Four Freedoms Park, LLC

964 N.Y.S.2d 62 (N.Y. Sup. Ct. 2012) (Ramos, J),
aff'd, 964 N.Y.S.2d 152 (N.Y. App. Div. 1st Dept. 2013)

[The Reed Foundation, Inc. (the "Foundation"), in a series of agreements, donated $2.5 million to Franklin D. Roosevelt Four Freedoms Park LLC (the "LLC") a donation that, along with others, enabled it to construct the FDR Four Freedoms Park (the "Park") in New York City. As part of the agreements, the LLC agreed to construct a "Threshold" that would include "Threshold Recognition Text" at a specific location in specified font and size. The LLC stated that its architects and other donors had "aesthetic concerns" about the agreed placement, but the Foundation insisted on specific performance: the agreement specified that preliminary injunctive relief was appropriate for any material breach.

Two weeks before dedication of the park was to occur, the Foundation filed suit for specific performance. By that time, all other aspects of construction had been completed except for placement of the Threshold Recognition Text. It waived its request to enjoin the dedication until after the text was engraved. In opposition, the LLC asserted that complying with the agreement would constitute "defacing a work of art." After concluding the Foundation had breached, the court turned to the remedy of specific performance.]

By its very nature, such a unique and precise honorary recognition is not subject to monetary valuation. This Court understands that this lasting recognition of the Foundation's role in erecting the Park has significance to the Foundation and its principals. New York courts have granted specific performance in analogous situations involving unique projects and momentous events, with clear uncertainty in valuation (*see Robins v Zwirner*, 713 F.Supp.2d 367 (S.D.N.Y. 2010) (seller's refusal to convey "unique works of art" by an artist constitutes irreparable harm to the purchaser); *David Tunick, Inc. v Kornfeld*, 838 F.Supp. 848 (S.D.N.Y. 1993) (art collector who contracted to buy a specific Picasso print was not obligated under the UCC to accept a substitute print of the same Picasso painting because, as art prints are "by definition, unique," an art purchaser is entitled to receive the print that "he viewed as uniquely beautiful"); *Chabert v Robert & Co.*, 273 AD 237 (1st Dept 1948) (specific performance appropriate to require promisor to sell a rare oil of "special and unascertainable value to the plaintiff" that could not be calculated for a damage award); *see also Barry v Dandy, LLC*, 2007 WL 2917248 (NY Sup Ct, New York County 2007) (ordering event planner to specifically perform obligation to provide promisee a suitable wedding hall).

This Court is disturbed by the actions of the LLC. No potential donor in this State should be made to fear that its generosity will be diminished by strategically delayed artistic whims of a charity's managers. Public policy and the public's interest in charitable giving require that philanthropy trump fashion.

Notes and Questions

1. <u>$2.5 Million?</u> Why doesn't the purchase price/donation amount show certain value and thus an adequate remedy at law? What consequences would flow from adopting that approach?

2. <u>Output Contracts.</u> The *Mirion* case held the plaintiff did not have a requirements contract, but an exclusive requirements contract is generally sufficient to obtain specific performance under the UCC. The same is true for specific performance of output contracts. For example, in *Int'l Casings Group, Inc. v. Premium Standard Farms, Inc.*, 358 F. Supp. 2d 863 (W.D. Mo. 2005), the plaintiff ICG moved for a preliminary injunction seeking to force the defendant PSF to honor its agreement to provide hog casings to ICG. PSF argued ICG could not establish irreparable harm because a spot market was available to buy hog casings. The court noted that under the UCC goods are "unique" if a "particular or peculiarly available source or market" exists or where there is an inability to obtain cover goods." *Id.* Thus,

to determine whether ICG had an alternative remedy available that would support denying an injunction, "the alternative remedy must be as certain, prompt, complete, and efficient to attain the ends of justice as a decree of specific performance." *Id.* In holding the spot market was insufficient, the court wrote:

> Processing companies purchase hog casings from one of two sources in the industry: (1) long-term supply contracts with a slaughterhouse like those at issue in this dispute, or (2) the spot market where buyers may purchase casings that are not subject to long-term contracts. PSF asserts that ICG can obtain adequate cover goods from the spot market to supplement its supply. The parties do not generally dispute that ICG can obtain additional hog casings from the spot market; however, the parties vigorously dispute whether those casings are satisfactory for ICG's particular purposes.
>
> Under its contracts with PSF, ICG controls the initial processing and cleaning mechanisms that it uses to prepare the casings. These methods are proprietary and specific to ICG and the casings that it sells to its customers. If ICG is forced to seek casings from suppliers on the spot market, then it will not have control over the processing and cleaning of the casings and it will not be able to implement its proprietary methods. Moreover, to produce the casings that it sells to its customers, ICG needs casings from its suppliers that have certain characteristics including, but not limited to, consistent color and slip and certain length percentages. All of these characteristics that ICG needs bear on the quality of the casings and the credible evidence does not suggest that the spot market can produce casings of the same quality as PSF.
>
> At the hearing PSF demonstrated that ICG can obtain other hog casings from the American spot market and from foreign casings markets. However, PSF did not demonstrate that these replacement casings are of the same quality and specification as ICG obtains from PSF. ICG has demonstrated that the casings produced by PSF are not fungible and not readily available on the spot market; thus, the Court concludes on the current record that ICG cannot find cover goods to replace PSF's casings.
>
> In addition to being unable to find comparable cover casings, ICG also established that it will suffer harm to its good will and reputation in the casings industry if an injunction is not issued. Without PSF's casings, ICG will be unable to satisfy its obligations to its customers, thereby causing those customers to look to other suppliers. The loss of customers is further exacerbated by the limited pool of potential new customers. This loss of good will can be a basis for irreparable harm and the Court finds that ICG will suffer irreparable harm unless it grants ICG's pending Motion.

3. <u>Land</u> <u>*and*</u> <u>Personalty</u>. In *Curran v. Barefoot*, 645 S.E.2d 187 (Ct. App. N.C. 2007), defendant agreed to sell a lake house along with all personal property on the land

(with a few specific exceptions), including three boats. After the defendant refused to perform, the buyer sued for specific performance. The court granted that relief, explaining that power to grant "specific performance rests, not on the distinction between real and personal property, but on the ground that damages at law will not afford a complete remedy." The seller appealed and the court of appeals affirmed:

> Other state jurisdictions have held specific performance may be granted for breach of a contract to sell real property that includes personal property. "Where part of an entire contract relates to ordinary personal property and the rest to a subject matter, such as land, over which equity jurisdiction is commonly exercised, specific performance may be had of the whole contract, including the part that relates to personal property." *Taylor v. Highland Park Corp.*, 210 S.C. 254 (S.C. 1947); *see Henderson v. Fisher*, 236 Cal. App.2d 468 (1965) ("Where only part of the subject matter of the contract consists of land, specific performance of the whole of the contract may be decreed even though compensation in money would be an adequate remedy for the promisor's failure to perform that part of the contract calling for the transfer of ordinary chattels.")

The Supreme Court of Georgia considered a case concerning specific performance of a contract involving both real and personal property in *Gabrell v. Byers*, 178 Ga. 16 (Ga. 1933). A property owner had contracted to sell her farmland, along with all personal property located thereon, for a lump sum. The contract specifically listed all the personal property including livestock, six mules, farm equipment, and vehicles. When the purchaser failed to make the first payment, the seller sued and sought specific performance. The court stated:

> As a general rule, the remedy of a decree for specific performance relates only to real estate, and is not applicable to personalty. So the cardinal rules which apply to the remedy of specific performance are applied with greater strictness where personalty is concerned than where realty is involved. In the case at bar the contract, including both real estate and various species of personal property, is entire and indivisible, so far as the remedy by decree for specific performance is concerned.

The Supreme Court of Georgia in *Gabrell* relied heavily on *Carolee v. Handelis*, 103 Ga. 299 (Ga. 1898), which also concerned specific performance of a contract involving personal property: the sale of real property containing a fruit stand. The court noted that the merchandise was perishable and to not order specific performance would have allowed for destruction of the merchandise.

The value of a unitary vacation home to a buyer is the furnished lake house and accessories. This value is similar to the value to a buyer of a working farm including the farmland, livestock, and implements. Just as the farmland in the case above would be much less desirable if the items of livestock and implements were not conveyed, a barren lake house without the personal property listed in the contract would not provide plaintiffs a "complete remedy."

The trial court did not err as a matter of law by awarding plaintiffs specific performance of a contract involving real property and incidental personal property to be conveyed part and parcel therewith as a unit. This assignment of error is overruled.

iii. Uncertain Damages and Other Bases

Pepsi-Cola Bottling Co. of Pittsburg, Inc. v. Bottling Group, LLC

2009 WL 873020 (D. Kan. Mar. 30, 2009) (O'Hara, J.)

[Pepsi-Cola Bottling Co. had, prior to this suit, sued Bottling Group, LLC. Pepsi brought this suit alleging that BGL was violating the settlement agreement in that case, which prohibited BGL from using pallets and "shells" (another way to transport large volumes of bottled soda) with the word "Pepsi" on them. Pepsi moved for a preliminary injunction to order specific performance of the settlement agreement.]

Defendant argues that plaintiff cannot show it suffers irreparable harm from defendant's use of the Pepsi-labeled shells and pallets, which defendant alleges plaintiff is required to do to obtain specific performance. Although plaintiff argues it is not required to show irreparable harm to obtain specific performance, it argues that it is suffering irreparable harm from defendant's conduct now and will continue to do so in the future.

Relying on cases interpreting federal law, defendant asserts plaintiff must show irreparable harm to obtain specific performance. In determining whether a preliminary injunction was appropriate, one court stated that:

> While irreparable harm is frequently found upon the breach of an exclusivity provision, that finding does not rest solely on the breach of the agreement and the resulting loss of exclusivity rights. Rather, the irreparable harm findings are based on such factors as the difficulty in calculating damages, the loss of a unique product, and existence of intangible harms, such as loss of goodwill or competitive market position.

Defendant acknowledges that irreparable harm can be shown when damages at law cannot adequately compensate the injury or cannot be reasonably measured. The case on which defendant relies also states that irreparable injury may be found where the subject matter of the contract is of such a special nature or peculiar value that damages would be inadequate. Although plaintiff encourages the court not to condition relief solely on whether plaintiff can demonstrate irreparable harm, it argues that money damages are inadequate. The court therefore need not decide whether plaintiff must show irreparable harm, as argued by defendant, but will require plaintiff to show money damages would be inadequate.

Plaintiff relies on the Restatement (Second) of Contracts' factors for determining whether damages are inadequate, including: (a) the difficulty of proving damages with reasonable certainty, (b) the difficulty of procuring a suitable substitute performance by means of money awarded as damages, and (c) the likelihood that an award of damages could not be collected. Plaintiff argues that it cannot obtain the substantial equivalent of defendant's promise not to use the Pepsi name to sell competing product. Plaintiff argues monetary damages are inadequate because it has no means to show a loss of actual sales from defendant's conduct and that the agreement also constrains future conduct. Plaintiff states that since the conduct has continued for a long period of time, it has no baseline for comparison of sales without the practice.

The court finds that defendant's conduct has damaged, and continues to damage, plaintiff's goodwill, ability to control its brand name, and its franchise integrity. Monetary damages for these intangible harms would be difficult to ascertain with reasonable certainty and would not be a suitable substitute for specific performance. The court notes that defendant's conduct has continued for years, making it even more difficult for plaintiff to attempt to calculate damages. The court finds that a remedy at law is inadequate, because it is not as plain, complete, and efficient as the remedy of specific performance.

Notes and Questions

1. <u>Harm to Trade Secrets, Goodwill, and Similar Interests</u>. The principal case involved trademark infringement, but misappropriation of trade secrets, injury to goodwill, and other less tangible harms often serve to establish irreparable harm or an inadequate remedy at law. *E.g., HCC Specialty Underwriters, Inc. v. Woodbury,* 289 F. Supp. 3d 303 (D.N.H. 2018); *Stuhlbarg Int'l Sales Co. v. John D. Brush & Co.,* 240 F.3d 832 (9th Cir. 2001) (loss of goodwill resulting from inability to fill customer orders constituted irreparable harm). Further, as noted above, some courts will "blue pencil" certain restrictive covenants in employment agreements, and those often serve to protect confidential information from being misused.

2 <u>Specific Performance to Pay Money</u>? Specific performance "to compel the payment of money *past due* under a contract, or specific performance of a *past due* monetary obligation, was not typically available." *Cent. States ex rel. McDougall v. Health Spec. Risk, Inc.,* 2012 WL 5006054 (N.D. Tex. Oct. 18, 2012), *aff'd,* 756 F.3d 356 (5th Cir. 2014). As to specific performance of future payments, though rare, it can be ordered "to prevent future losses that either were incalculable or would be greater than the sum awarded. For example, specific performance might be available to enforce an agreement to lend money when the unavailability of alternative financing would leave the plaintiff with injuries that are difficult to value; or to enforce an obligor's duty to make future monthly payments, after the obligor had consistently refused to make past payments concededly due, and thus threatened the obligee with the burden of bringing multiple damages actions." *Great-West Life & Annuity Ins. Co. v. Knudson,* 534 U.S. 204 (2002).

d. Mutuality of Remedy, Unless Excepted

Mutuality of remedy is an "archaic contract principle with so many exceptions that its validity today is questionable." *Fid. and Dep. Co. of Md. v. Big Town Mech., LLC*, 2017 WL 5165044 (D. Nev. Nov. 7, 2017). Historically, it "required, as a condition of seeking specific performance, that both parties be susceptible to specific performance." *Id.* And so, "a contract for personal services would lack mutuality of remedy because a court cannot compel specific performance of personal services even though it can compel specific performance of payment for those services." *Id.* This is why courts enforce covenants not to compete even though at common law a court will not order reinstatement by a former employer.

When it is required, it is sufficient if mutuality of remedy exists when specific performance is sought. Thus, a party who performs an agreement is entitled to specific performance. "Mutuality of remedy may be subsequently supplied by performance of the party who seeks specific performance." *Longfellow v. Racetrac Petroleum, Inc.*, 2008 WL 2404233 (Tex. Ct. App. June 12, 2008). So, for example, a contract by a parent with a minor child in which the child agreed to care for the parent until death in exchange for ownership of a home becomes specifically enforceable upon death of the parent even though mutuality of remedies was lacking until then. *Sayres v. Wheatland Group, LLC*, 79 Va. Cir. 504 (Va. Cir. 2009) ("at the time of the institution of the suit, appellee (the infant) having fully performed the contract on his part, there was no want of mutuality of obligation and remedy, and specific performance was rightly decreed."). In these circumstances, the party seeking specific performance *has performed*.

When required, the lack of mutuality of remedy does not affect the validity of a contract or its terms; it affects specifically, whether specific performance is available.

II. Contracting Around the Requirements for Specific Performance

Courts split on whether to give no, some, or controlling weight to clauses that purport to bind courts to award specific performance or stipulate to some or all of its requirements. *Compare United BioSource LLC v. Bracket Holding Corp.*, 2017 WL 2256618 (Del. Ch. May 23, 2017) ("It is a cardinal principle of the law that jurisdiction of a court over the subject matter cannot be conferred by consent or agreement.") *with TP Group-Ci, Inc. v. Smith*, 2016 WL 6647947 (N.D. Ill. Nov. 10, 2016) ("contractual stipulations as to irreparable harm alone suffice to establish that element for the purpose of issuing injunctive relief."). Perhaps at one end of the spectrum consider *Swarovski Retail Ventures Ltd. v. JGB Vegas Retail Lessee, LLC*, 416 P.3d 208 (Nev. 2018), where the owner of the Grand Bazaar mall sought to compel a jewelry store, Swarovski, to remain open and pointed to the lease. The court emphasized the importance of the lease in determining whether specific relief was proper:

> In order for injunctive relief to issue in the context of a commercial lease, there must be evidence within the agreement that the tenant's importance to the project and the potential for irreparable harm upon early termination

were reasonably contemplated by both parties at the time they made the contract.

This court need look no further for an example of such a provision than to the licenses issued by JGB to Wahlburgers and Giordano's, two other tenants of the Grand Bazaar Shops. The continuous operations clauses in the licenses issued to Wahlburgers and Giordano's read:

> Subtenant acknowledges that its continued operation of the Subleased Premises is of the utmost importance to the Project and to the other occupants thereof and to Sublandlord in the licensing and renting of space in the Project, the renewal of other subleases and license agreements in the Project, the maintenance of Percentage Rent and the character and quality of the other occupants [of] the Project.

In these continuous operations clauses, the landlord sets forth in clear language that the tenant's early termination would result in noneconomic and unquantifiable damage, such as the lessened "character and quality of the other occupants." Thus, the tenant is put on notice that its uniqueness sets it apart from the other tenants and that economic damages may not sufficiently render the landlord whole upon the tenant's breach.

Here, in contrast, Swarovski's license contained a standard continuous operations clause with none of the particularized language demonstrated above. Moreover, under the terms of the license, Swarovski was allowed to terminate the lease early under certain conditions, and was thereby mandated to leave *with* the allegedly irreplaceable Swarovski Starburst Crystal. Even where the license outlined Swarovski and JGB's sponsorship relationship—which the district court found was the basis for injunctive relief— there is no indication that JGB would suffer irreparable harm without Swarovski as a sponsor. Rather, the license states, permissively, "Swarovski has requested the right to be a sponsor" and "JGB is amenable to granting such sponsorship right to Swarovski."

Would it have mattered if every lease stated irreparable harm would occur? Conversely, why do some courts give no weight to such clauses, but this court found them dispositive?

2. Tort Remedies Triggered by Economic Loss

A few tort claims require economic harm to the plaintiff as "damage," and economic harm, alone, is sufficient to constitute the required "damage." Recall that economic losses may be recoverable as *consequential damages,* but that does not mean the "damage" element of that claim is satisfied by economic harm: "the mere fact that one who has received an injury to his person suffers as a result thereof a monetary loss such as expenditures for doctor's bills does not make the injury any less an injury to a person," but instead they are "damages resulting from an injury to the person." *Brent v. Hin*, 254 Ga. App. 77 (2002).

These tort claims include fraud, intentional interference with contract, intentional interference with prospective business relationships, and negligent misrepresentation. All except the last are intentional torts. While tort claims discussed in other chapters may permit recovery of economic losses as consequential damages, each requires another form of harm — an impact, a harmful or offensive contact, detention, fear of arrest, or harm to reputation, for example — before recovery for consequential damages is permitted.

This chapter raises what should be clear from the foregoing discussion of contract claims: a plaintiff with a breach of contract claim who also asserts a tort claim might recover greater damages than *Hadley* might allow. For example, the court in *Harden v. Vertex Assocs., Inc.* 487 S.E.2d 12 (Ct. App. Ga. 1997), upheld verdicts of $50,000 in fraud and $27,000 for breach of contract, stating tort law "authorizes a broader range of damages than those generally authorized for breach of contract; thus, the general damages award under the fraud claim is not 'excessive' simply because it does not mirror the amount awarded under the breach of contract claim." *See also Stephen A. Wheat Trust v. Sparks*, 325 Ga. App. 673 (2014) ("general damages awarded on a fraud claim may cover a broader range of damages than those awarded on contract claims" and the "broader range is not necessarily limited to pecuniary losses and includes inconvenience.")

A. Monetary Remedies for Fraud and Fraudulent Inducement of Contract

Fraud and fraudulent inducement share much in common, but fraudulent inducement is narrower and creates an election of remedies issue that fraud does not. Fraudulent inducement caused a plaintiff to enter into an agreement, and so creates the need for the plaintiff to "elect" whether to sue for breach of contract or, instead, to seek rescission of the contract because of the fraud and seek damages. A fraudulent inducement claim can include fraud *and* contract damages. Finally, in addition to being claims for damages, fraud or fraudulent inducement can be an affirmative defense. For example, a party sued for breach can assert the contract was induced by fraud and avoid suit on the contract.

I. Fraud

The elements of fraud are "(1) a material misrepresentation of a presently existing or past fact; (2) knowledge or belief by the defendant of its falsity; (3) an intention that the other person rely on it; (4) reasonable reliance thereon by the other person; and (5) resulting damages." *McConkey v. AON Corp.*, 804 A.2d 572 (N.J. Super. App. Div. 2002). Some courts treat fraud based upon concealment as "fraudulent concealment," while others instead state "in nondisclosure cases, a party's silence amounts to a representation where the law imposes a duty to speak. In other words, failing to speak when the law imposes a duty to do so replaces the essential element of a 'false, material representation' in a fraudulent misrepresentation case." *Doe v. Ratigan*, 481 S.W.3d 36 (Ct. App. Mo. 2015). In either event, unless the defendant had a duty to speak, fraud must be based upon an affirmative misrepresentation of a material fact.

The general goal of fraud damages is similar to contract expectancy damages and is to "restore the injured party to the position it would have been in had the wrong not been committed." *Nordyne, Inc. v. Fla. Mobile Home Supply, Inc.,* 625 So. 2d 1283 (Ct. App. Fla. 1993). That goal requires that fraud damages be flexible. However, two measures of fraud damages are common: (1) the "benefit of the bargain," which is measured by the difference between the actual value of the property and its value had the representations about it been true; and (2) the "out-of-pocket" loss, which is the difference between the purchase price and the real or actual value of the property. *Totale, Inc. v. Smith*, 877 So. 2d 813 (Ct. App. Fla. 2004). Just as courts sometimes deny contract plaintiffs their expectancy, so too do they sometimes deny fraud plaintiffs the benefit of the bargain even if the amounts are proven with reasonable certainty. On the other hand, courts sometimes preclude fraud plaintiffs from recovering benefit of the bargain damages.

Brown v. Bennett

136 S.W.3d 552 (Ct. App. Mo. 2004) (Lowenstein, J.)

Brent and Angela Bennett appeal a judgment in a court-tried case awarding Wanda Brown $17,825 in compensatory and $10,000 in punitive damages in her fraud action against the Bennetts. The judgment is affirmed.

The Bennetts, who were in the home construction business, sold Brown their house in Columbia, Missouri. Brown had no expertise about real estate or the home construction business. The closing took place on April 20, 2001. In the sales contract, the Bennetts stated, "SELLER has no knowledge of the existence of past uncorrected defects or problems with the property" and were asked to disclose any "settling, flooding, drainage, grading, or soil problems," to which they answered, "No." Brown read the contract before signing it.

Both statements were false, and the Bennetts knew they were false. The house's backyard was prone to flooding when it rained, because of flawed yard grading by the subdivision developer. The flawed grading caused runoff from fourteen lots to drain into the Bennetts' backyard. The developer was supposed to install three swales to handle the runoff, but had only installed one.

The Bennetts had previously complained to the City of Columbia about the flooding. At one point, Mrs. Bennett told the City that her "backyard [was] completely flooded, almost got into house." Mrs. Bennett demanded that the City do something soon. The City said the pooling was normal, that it would take at least a year just to develop a plan to deal with it, and that doing so was not a priority.

In their dealings with Brown and her real estate agent, the Bennetts said nothing about the flooding. Before and after signing the contract, Brown inspected the property several times. Her experienced real estate broker also inspected the property, as did a professional inspector Brown hired. None of them saw any pooling in the backyard. Brown learned of the pooling problem a few weeks after closing. As a result of the pooling, Brown was unable to plant a flower garden in the affected area, it was difficult to mow the lawn, and the yard was useless as a playground for her young relatives.

Brown filed this fraud action against the Bennetts. After a bench trial, it was established that Brown's house in its current condition is worth $140,000, but with a normal backyard, $163,000. The cost to fix the flooding problem was disputed. Mr. Bennett testified that regrading the existing swale, at a cost of $220, would solve the problem. When the Bennetts owned the property, Columbia's storm water manager recommended a different kind of repair. An engineer Brown hired recommended the same repair suggested by the City and estimated that it would cost $17,825. The trial court entered judgment in favor of Brown, awarding her $17,825 in compensatory and $10,000 in punitive damages.

In their final point, the Bennetts submit that the trial court conferred a windfall on Brown, because Mr. Bennett had testified that the flooding problem could be fixed for $200, whereas the trial court awarded Brown $17,825 in compensatory damages. In addition, the Bennetts claim, the repair technique Brown's expert recommended would redound to the benefit of other homeowner's in the neighborhood.

Compensatory damages in a fraud action where the defrauded party retains the property are limited to the benefit of the bargain from the sales transaction. To make Brown whole, it was unnecessary to award damages measured by the diminution in value of her property; awarding the cost of repair would make give her the benefit of the bargain. *See Wasson v. Schubert*, 964 S.W.2d 520, 525 (Mo. App. 1998).[3]

Notes and Questions

1. Why Not Expectancy? The court in footnote 3 explains when damages are capped at repair costs. Why did plaintiffs did not receive the largest recovery?

2. Lost Millions. In *Totale, Inc. v. Smith*, 877 So. 2d 813 (Ct. App. Fla. 2004), the plaintiff invested $100,000 in a corporation, expecting a huge return. The only evidence of what that value would have been were the plaintiff's vague recollections that the company was expected to be worth more than $130 million. Instead, it was worthless. The court held the benefit of the bargain could not be determined with reasonable certainty and limited recovery to out-of-pocket losses, rejecting the jury award of $350,000. Does the verdict itself indicate uncertainty?

---

3. *Wasson* and other cases say that the cost-of-repair test is "clearly limited to situations where repairs are only a small percentage of the diminution in value." 964 S.W.2d at 525. However, Brown has not cross appealed, and so whether the court was correct in deciding whether to award cost-of-repair instead of diminution-in-value compensatory damages is not before this court.

3. <u>Mental Anguish</u>. Courts split on whether mental anguish damages are recoverable for fraud, with some prohibiting them, some allowing them in all cases, and others limiting them to malicious fraud or that which causes physical injury. Surveying this split, one court adopted "a fair balance that permits recovery of damages for emotional injury which, by reason of either an accompanying or consequential 'physical' injury, is objectively ascertainable." *Hoffman v. Stamper*, 867 A.2d 276 (Md. 2005). *See Zeigler v. Fisher-Price, Inc.*, 261 F. Supp. 2d 1047 (N.D. Iowa 2003) (denying distress damages where fraud caused plaintiff to buy a toy that caught fire and destroyed plaintiff's home and personal property); *St. Paul Fire & Marine Ins. Co. v. Clark,* 566 S.E.2d 2 (Ct. App. Ga. 2002) (permitting award of mental anguish damages).

II. Fraudulent Inducement

Fraudulent inducement exists when the defendant's fraud caused a plaintiff to make a contract with the defendant. Ordinarily, a party asserting fraudulent inducement may not assert the contract is void because of the defendant's fraud *and* seek damages for breach of contract. Instead, generally a plaintiff must "elect" a remedy: seek contract damages or avoid the contract because of fraudulent inducement. However, if the remedies for fraud and for breach of contract are not inconsistent, then no election is required.

Caruthers v. Underhill

326 P.3d 268 (Ct. App. Ariz. 2014) (Swann, J.)

[Defendant James Underhill and his son Clinton Underhill were officers and shareholders of Underhill Transfer Company, which managed commercial real estate. James allegedly assisted Clinton in buying shares in UTC from other shareholders at prices based upon false appraisals. Four shareholders later filed suit against both Clinton and James: Caruthers, Tanouye ("Plaintiffs"), Allen, and Macbeth. They asserted fraud against Clinton, and conspiracy and aiding and abetting against James.

On the sixth day of a 10-day trial, the judge asked the shareholders' counsel asked if plaintiffs had elected a remedy. Shareholders' counsel stated that Plaintiffs elected rescission, and Allen and Macbeth would seek damages. The next day, the trial court granted James's motion for JMOL on Plaintiffs' claim for rescission against him, reasoning rescission was unavailable against him since he had not received any shares—only Clinton had. The trial court permitted the jury to render an advisory verdict on rescission. It found for Allen and Macbeth and awarded them damages, and found for the Plaintiffs, holding they were entitled to rescission. The jury also found plaintiffs had not unreasonably delayed in seeking rescission. The trial court thus awarded judgment for damages to Allen and Macbeth but denied Plaintiffs' motion for new trial. They appealed.]

Plaintiffs prevailed on the liability portion of their claims but received no relief because the court held after trial that the remedy they elected was unavailable to them as a matter of law. We hold that the election-of-remedies doctrine cannot be applied to compel a high-stakes choice between a real remedy and an illusory remedy—a successful plaintiff is entitled to an available remedy.

The election-of-remedies doctrine provides that a party who has been fraudulently induced to enter into a contract must choose to either disavow the contract and seek a return to the *status quo ante,* or affirm the contract and sue for damages for breach. A claimant may not both repudiate the contract and then sue on it to gain the benefit of the bargain. As Professor Dobbs explains, "the two remedial approaches, one based on affirmance, the other on avoidance, are inconsistent in the sense that they point in different directions. In some cases and with some claims they are inconsistent in the added sense that the plaintiff who recovered both kinds of remedies might be getting more remedial desert than he should." 3 Dan B. Dobbs, *Law of Remedies* § 12.7(6), at 186 (2d ed. 1993) [hereinafter 3 Dobbs].

The doctrine therefore prevents aggrieved parties from prevailing on logically inconsistent theories of the case, and serves to guard against overcompensation. But if alternative theories of recovery are factually consistent, an inconsistency does not arise until one of the remedies is satisfied, and therefore consistent remedies may be pursued concurrently even to final adjudication, but the satisfaction of one claim bars the other one. And "if the award of both types of remedies can be justified as providing full compensation, or as providing full restitution, then the remedies are not truly inconsistent." 3 Dobbs § 12.7(6), at 187.

Accordingly, the election of remedies doctrine merely prevents a plaintiff from both repudiating a contract and then suing on it to gain the benefit of the bargain. The doctrine does not bar a party seeking rescission from receiving damages. A plaintiff electing rescission is entitled to those damages that are necessary to make him whole. A defrauded party may not only receive back the consideration he gave, but also may recover any sums that are necessary to restore him to his position prior to the making of the contract. Where there is no danger of allowing recovery more than once for a single item of loss, there is therefore no reason for the application of the election-of-remedies rule.

In this case, election of remedies was never necessary. Plaintiffs did not seek to recover on inconsistent theories of liability. They had only one theory of the case: fraud. They did not sue for breach of contract, and their case did not depend on affirmance of the contract. To be eligible for either tort damages or rescission, Plaintiffs were required to prove a single set of facts. Because the remedies of damages and rescission were not based on inconsistent theories, Plaintiffs should not have been compelled to choose one remedy to the exclusion of the other. They established liability and were therefore entitled to be made whole—whether by rescission, damages, or a combination of the two.

We cannot reverse on the ground that the court applied the election-of-remedies doctrine, however, because Plaintiffs invited the error. They never objected to the notion that they were required to choose between remedies, and in fact affirmatively set the error in motion by arguing in their February 2009 motion to amend that they would make an election. By the rule of invited error, one who deliberately leads the court to take certain action may not upon appeal assign that action as error. In other words, "one who misconceives the law governing his rights in a trial, and succeeds in convicting the court thereof, ought to be estopped to take any advantage of it upon appeal. This rule applies even where, as here, there is no evidence that the error was invited for the improper purpose of profiting on appeal. In considering Plaintiffs' appeal, we therefore assume that the election-of-remedies doctrine had application and decide whether relief was properly denied under it.

The election-of-remedies doctrine requires an election between two or more inconsistent remedies that actually exist at the time of the election. If in fact or in law only one remedy exists, there can be no election by the pursuit of another and mistaken remedy. The concept of election is meaningless if only one remedy exists.

To help avoid mistaken elections and allow plaintiffs to take advantage of any possible development in the evidence which would show them entitled to recovery and thus prevent them being forced to elect in advance and at their peril which theory they will proceed upon, our rules of civil procedure allow inconsistent pleadings until the conclusion of trial. But an election must be made at the conclusion of the case and once an election has been made with due knowledge of the facts, a party cannot complain if the remedy selected is inadequate.

In denying Plaintiffs' motion for new trial, the superior court held that they were bound by their election of rescission because they made that election with full knowledge that the remedy might be unavailable. The court explained that "as early as 2009, over a year and a half before the trial, Plaintiffs knew there was considerable uncertainty as to whether they would prevail on their rescission remedy," and "Plaintiffs could not have relied on the court's Rule 50(a) Order denying Clinton's motion for judgment as a matter of law in making their election" because "Plaintiffs made their election of rescission on October 29, 2010, during their case-in-chief, and the court did not issue its Rule 50(a) Order until November 9, 2010."

It is true that when Plaintiffs informed the court on October 29 that they would be electing rescission, they had reason to know that the defendants debated that remedy's availability. But that fact did not bind Plaintiffs to the election of a nonexistent remedy. Plaintiffs did not acquiesce to dismissal of their damages claim until after the court ruled on November 9 that the evidence did not support the defendants' objections to rescission, and Plaintiffs reasonably expected that they were not legally barred from obtaining rescission. This is not a case in which the remedy Plaintiffs elected proved merely to be "inadequate," as it would have been had they elected damages and received a smaller award than they sought. This is a case in which Plaintiffs prevailed, yet received *no* remedy. In these circumstances, there was no reason that the damages remedy should not have been revived when the court reversed its earlier ruling and found that rescission was unavailable. To hold otherwise would be to extend the scope of the election-of-remedies doctrine beyond its just purposes and permit a doctrine of equitable origin to be used to accomplish an inequitable result.

We reverse the judgment against Plaintiffs and remand for new trial. The new trial shall address the merits of the claims against James and the relief that may be recovered on the jury verdicts against Clinton. On remand, the election-of-remedies doctrine shall not bar Plaintiffs from seeking rescission, damages, or a combination thereof on their verdicts against Clinton.

Notes and Questions

1. Election of Remedies. Generally a party may *plead* that a contract exists but was breached or, in the alternative, the contract was induced by fraud and should be rescinded and fraud damages made available. Modern "liberal pleading standards, combined with a relaxed election-of-remedies approach, allowed plaintiffs to pursue both a contract action seeking contract remedies, including a remedy of rescission, and a tort action based on fraud within the same case." *Stabler v. First Bank of Roscoe,* 865 N.W.2d 466 (S.D. 2015) (explaining also that emotional distress damages are recoverable for fraudulent inducement claims). Even so, some states require election before suing—and so pre-suit client conduct can waive one claim or the other. *See Pentagon Properties, Inc. v. Wheat,* 740 S.E.2d 374 (Ct. App. Ga. 2013).

2. Fraudulent Oral Promises. A party may enforce an oral promise that violates the statute of frauds if the defendant made the promise intending not to perform. As *Irish Oil and Gas, Inc. v. Riemer,* 794 N.W.2d 715 (N.D. 2011) explained:

> The statute of frauds cannot be used as a defense in a tort action for deceit, even when the statute serves as a valid defense to a breach of contract action:
>
>> Since a promise necessarily carries with it the implied assertion of an intention to perform it follows that a promise made without such an intention is fraudulent and actionable in deceit. This is true whether or not the promise is enforceable as a contract. If the agreement is not enforceable as a contract, as when it is without consideration, the recipient still has, as his only remedy, the action in deceit. The same is true when the agreement is oral and made unenforceable by the statute of frauds.
>
> *Restatement (Second) of Torts* §530, cmt. (c). The *Restatement Second of Contracts* further supports the position that the statute of frauds does not prevent a plaintiff from pursuing a deceit claim based on an otherwise unenforceable oral agreement. Section 143 states that "the Statute of Frauds does not make an unenforceable contract inadmissible in evidence for any purpose other than its enforcement in violation of the Statute."

B. Tortious Interference with Contract or a Business Relationship

I. Tortious Interference with Contract

Tortious interference remedies the economic harm caused when a defendant causes a third party to breach a contract with the plaintiff, or causes a third party to discontinue an existing business relationship with the plaintiff, or causes a third party to not do business with the plaintiff in the first place. Liability does not attach, however, to a party who provides disinterested advice that causes the person to breach a contract if the advice is offered without the intent to obtain the benefits of the contract or relationship or to injure the plaintiff. Put another way, it requires "some active persuasion, encouragement, or inciting that goes beyond merely providing information in a passive way." *KW Plastics v. U.S. Can Co.*, 2001 WL 135722 (M.D. Ala. Feb. 2, 2001). Some states characterize intentional interference with an existing contract and interfering with a business relationship as a single claim. Others maintain distinct claims, while still others permit recovery only if a defendant harms an existing contractual relationship, not a prospective relationship.

Harris Group, Inc. v. Robinson

209 P.3d 1188 (Ct. App. Colo. 2009) (Bernard, J.)

[Several employees of the Plaintiff, Harris Group Inc. ("the company"), coordinated leaving the company to form a competing business. While still employed with the company, they copied files, deleted information, and when they left for their new company ("the new business") they immediately sent form letters to the company's customers by which they could terminate their relationship and transfer business to them. The company filed suit against its former employees and the new business, asserting various claims, including intentional interference with contract. The jury awarded the company $1.9 million in compensatory damages and $650,000 in punitive damages. The company and former employees appealed.]

The tort of interference with existing or prospective contractual relations is an intentional tort. Restatement (Second) of Torts ch. 37 introductory note. According to Restatement section 767 comment a, this tort has three forms. Only one of these forms is at issue here, but we must discuss another form to provide an appropriate context for our analysis.

The first form occurs when a defendant causes a third party not to perform the terms of an existing contract with a plaintiff. It is defined by Restatement section 766:

> One who intentionally and improperly interferes with the performance of a contract (except a contract to marry) between another and a third person by inducing or otherwise causing the third person not to perform the contract, is subject to liability to the other for the pecuniary loss resulting to the other from the failure of the third person to perform the contract.

The second form occurs when a defendant interferes with a prospective business relation between a plaintiff and a third party. Its elements are listed in Restatement section 766B:

> One who intentionally and improperly interferes with another's prospective contractual relation (except a contract to marry) is subject to liability to the other for the pecuniary harm resulting from loss of the benefits of the relation, whether the interference consists of
>
> (a) inducing or otherwise causing a third person not to enter into or continue the prospective relation or
>
> (b) preventing the other from acquiring or continuing the prospective relation.

In order to prove this form of the tort, it is not necessary to show that an underlying contract exists, but, rather, the plaintiff must show that intentional and improper interference prevented a contract from being formed.

The goal to be achieved by these forms of the tort is to protect the integrity of contracts. However, that interest is not absolute, and must be balanced against the interests of the parties and society. These personal and social interests, which are described by the Restatement as "privileges," include the ability to engage in business and compete with others.

Thus, to achieve the balance between protecting contracts and preserving privileges, a plaintiff must show more than that a defendant intentionally interfered with an existing contract or with prospective contractual relations. There must also be proof that such interference was "improper." Restatement § 767.

Generally, the factors to be considered when deciding whether interference was improper are listed in section 767. These factors require a fact finder to evaluate the interests of the parties and the interests of society as part of the process of deciding whether interference with a contract should result in a finding of liability. Section 767 states:

> In determining whether an actor's conduct in intentionally interfering with a contract or a prospective contractual relation of another is improper or not, consideration is given to the following factors:
>
> (a) the nature of the actor's conduct,
>
> (b) the actor's motive,
>
> (c) the interests of the other with which the actor's conduct interferes,
>
> (d) the interests sought to be advanced by the actor,
>
> (e) the social interests in protecting the freedom of action of the actor and the contractual interests of the other,
>
> (f) the proximity or remoteness of the actor's conduct to the interference, and
>
> (g) the relations between the parties.

[handwritten marginal note: What is improper?]

However, when the parties are business competitors, and the conduct in question involves intentional interference with prospective contractual relations or contracts terminable at will, the general factors outlined by section 767 do not apply. This is because

> one's privilege to engage in business and to compete with others implies a privilege to induce third persons to do their business with him rather than with his competitors. In order not to hamper competition unduly, the rule stated in [section 768] entitles one not only to seek to divert business from his competitors generally but also from a particular competitor. And he may seek to do so directly by express inducement as well as indirectly by attractive offers of his own goods or services.

Section 768 cmt. b. This privilege to engage in business and to compete" rests on the belief that competition is a necessary or desirable incident of free enterprise. Superiority of power in the matters relating to competition is believed to flow from superiority in efficiency and service. If the actor succeeds in diverting business from his competitor by virtue of superiority in matters relating to their competition, he serves the purposes for which competition is encouraged." Section 768 cmt. e.

Section 768 is specifically constructed to balance society's interest in free competition and a competitor's interest in free business activity against the relationship of parties to a prospective contract. This balance means that "greater protection is given to the interest in an existing contract than to the interest in acquiring prospective contractual relations, and as a result permissible interference is given a broader scope in the latter instance." Section 767 cmt. j.

This same analysis applies to contracts terminable at will. A contract terminable at will is one that may be terminated at any time without legal consequence; that is, there is no breach if the contract is terminated. The Restatement provides less protection for contracts terminable at will because interference with such contracts affects a future expectancy, not a legal right. However, some interference is not permissible.

> If the actor diverts the competitor's business by exerting a superior power in affairs unrelated to their competition there is no reason to suppose that his success is either due to or will result in superior efficiency or service and thus promote the interest that is the reason for encouraging competition. For this reason economic pressure on the third person in matters unrelated to the business in which the actor and the other compete is treated as an improper interference.

Section 768 cmt. e.

Thus, section 768 sets forth specific factors to be applied when analyzing whether a business competitor's intentional interference with prospective contractual relations or with contracts terminable at will is privileged or a tort.

> (1) One who intentionally causes a third person not to enter into a prospective contractual relation with another who is his competitor or not to

continue an existing contract terminable at will does not interfere improperly with the other's relation if

> (a) the relation concerns a matter involved in the competition between the actor and the other and

> (b) the actor does not employ wrongful means and

> (c) his action does not create or continue an unlawful restraint of trade and

> (d) his purpose is at least in part to advance his interest in competing with the other.

(2) The fact that one is a competitor of another for the business of a third person does not prevent his causing a breach of an existing contract with the other from being an improper interference if the contract is not terminable at will.

"Wrongful means" constitute impermissible interference with prospective contracts or contracts terminable at will:

> If the actor employs wrongful means, he is not justified under the rule stated in this Section 768. The predatory means discussed in § 767, Comment c, physical violence, fraud, civil suits and criminal prosecutions, are all wrongful in the situation covered by this Section. On the other hand, the actor may use persuasion and he may exert limited economic pressure.

Section 768 cmt. e.

Our supreme court has recognized that the definition of "wrongful means" is not open-ended. Indeed, in footnote 6 of *Amoco Oil Co.*, the supreme court cited cases from other jurisdictions that recognize the limited nature of the description in section 768 comment e. For example, "wrongful means" are those that are intrinsically wrongful—that is, conduct which is itself capable of forming the basis for liability of the actor, illegal, or "wrongful by reason of a statute or other regulation, a recognized rule of common law, an established standard of a trade or profession, violence, threats or other intimidation, deceit or misrepresentation, bribery, unfounded litigation, defamation or disparaging falsehood. *See also Occusafe, Inc. v. EG & G Rocky Flats, Inc.*, 54 F.3d 618 (10th Cir. 1995) ("in the context of a claim for tortious interference with prospective economic advantage, 'wrongful means' refers to conduct such as 'physical violence, fraud, civil suits, and criminal prosecutions.")

When analyzing Kansas law, the Tenth Circuit indicated that it viewed "wrongful means" similarly to the descriptions contained in *Amoco Oil Co.* The federal court predicted that the Kansas Supreme Court would interpret the phrase "wrongful means" to require "independently actionable conduct." *DP-Tek, Inc. v. AT&T Global Info. Solutions Co.*, 100 F.3d 828 (10th Cir. 1996). Such conduct is, of itself, capable of establishing the basis of a defendant's liability.

The argument of the former employees and the new business focuses on the instructions that addressed contracts that were terminable at will. The company claims that the former employees were at-will employees, and that they and the new business used wrongful means to interfere with the company's contracts and prospective business relationships with the other employees and clients.

Thus, the business competition privilege would apply to protect the former employees, after they left the company, and the new business from liability for intentional interference with those contracts, unless the factors listed in section 768 were established. Specifically, the issue before the jury was whether the former employees and the new business used wrongful means when they intentionally interfered with the contracts terminable at will.

Here, the jury was instructed that the former employees and the new business may lose the business competition privilege if they use "wrongful means" of inducement, for example: fraud, intentional interference with contract, intentional interference with prospective business relations, physical violence, threats of criminal prosecution, or threats of civil suit.

The jury found that the former employees and the new business had committed other torts that would qualify as wrongful means of inducement.

- The jury found the former employees and the new business liable for conversion.
- The jury found the former employees liable for the tort of breach of fiduciary duty.
- The jury awarded the company punitive damages for the torts of conversion and breach of fiduciary duty, after being instructed that to award such damages it was required to "find beyond a reasonable doubt that the new business or the former employees acted in a fraudulent or malicious manner in causing the company's damages."

The torts of conversion and breach of fiduciary duty constitute wrongful means of inducement. They are independently actionable; capable of forming the basis of liability for the actor; or wrongful by reason of a recognized rule of common law or deceit or misrepresentation. Indeed, breach of a fiduciary duty constitutes wrongful means, thus rendering the business competition privilege unavailable. Further, here, in its award of punitive damages, the jury found that these torts were committed in a fraudulent and malicious manner.

Therefore, we conclude that the error in the instruction concerning wrongful means was harmless. The error did not prejudice the substantial rights of the former employees and the new business because the jury's findings concerning the torts of conversion and breach of fiduciary duty constituted wrongful means. Because the wrongful means listed in the instruction were clearly meant as illustrations of wrongful means, and not an exhaustive list, the jury was free to consider conversion and breach of fiduciary duty as the wrongful means necessary to find that the former employees and the new business had improperly interfered with the company's contractual relations.

Put another way, even if the jury had been given a correct instruction, which (1) excluded the wrongful means unsupported by evidence—physical violence, threats of criminal prosecution, or threats of civil suit; (2) excluded the tort—intentional interference with contract—to which the business competition privilege applied; and (3) added the torts—conversion and breach of fiduciary duty—that qualified as wrongful means, we conclude that the jury would probably have reached the same verdicts.

Notes and Questions

1. Variations. Some states do not require the same degree of improper conduct. *E.g., Oakley, Inc. v. Nike, Inc.*, 988 F. Supp. 2d 1130 (C.D. Cal. 2013) ("intentional interference with contractual relations does not require that a defendant's conduct be independently wrongful" let alone "require that the actor's primary purpose be disruption of the contract").

2. The Stranger to the Contract Rule and Related Concepts. A defendant who breaches a contract cannot be sued for tortiously interfering with that contract: any claim is for breach. As a corollary, a corporation's agent cannot interfere with that corporation's contract if "interference is undertaken in good faith and for a bona fide organizational purpose." *Hawk Enterprises, Inc. v. Cash Am. Intern., Inc.*, 282 P.3d 786 (Ct. App. Okla. 2012). Likewise, a parent corporation generally cannot tortiously interfere with the contract of a subsidiary, but a claim will lie if the conduct was not privileged, as that court explained:

> We find that the determination of whether a parent corporation can be liable for tortious interference with the contracts of a subsidiary is a question that must be determined on a case by case basis, analyzing the factors provided in the Restatement:

>> In determining whether an actor's conduct in intentionally interfering with a contract or a prospective contractual relation of another is improper or not, consideration is given to the following factors:

>> (a) the nature of the actor's conduct,

>> (b) the actor's motive,

>> (c) the interests of the other with which the actor's conduct interferes,

>> (d) the interests sought to be advanced by the actor,

>> (e) the social interests in protecting the freedom of action of the actor and the contractual interests of the other,

>> (f) the proximity or remoteness of the actor's conduct to the interference and

>> (g) the relations between the parties.

3. Privileges. Privileges are often asserted against tortious interference claims. *See Anderson Dev. Co. v. Tobias*, 116 P.3d 323 (Utah 2005) (petitioning government is a privilege against liability for tortious interference based upon defendant's effort to stop competitor from opening a business by opposing needed zoning changes).

In *Mantia v. Hanson*, 79 P.3d 404 (Ct. App. Or. 2003), the defendant counterclaimed against plaintiff and his lawyers, asserting the pending suit against it was, itself, tortious interference. The court noted that although Oregon had long recognized an "absolute" privilege against claims for defamation based upon statements made in litigation with some relation to it, it had also held lawyers liable for malicious prosecution for instituting a claim without probable cause or abusing process, and in those cases the courts "did not refer to any possible application of absolute privilege as a bar to a 'wrongful initiation' or 'malicious prosecution' claim." It then noted that Oregon courts had disagreed on whether an absolute privilege applied to tortious interference claims. Because one element of a tortious interference claim based upon litigation was that the tortious-interference plaintiff prevailed in the underlying suit, but the claim against the defendant was still pending, the claim was not ripe. But it held that "improper means" could be a baseless suit brought to interfere with a contract. Given the elements of malicious prosecution, did this effectively recognize a conditional privilege for litigation?

4. <u>A Few States Recognize Negligent Interference.</u> In California, for example, a jury instruction exists for negligent interference with prospective business opportunities, but not negligent interference with contract—although some California courts permit the claim. *E.g., Orthotec, LLC v. Eurosurgical, S.A.*, 2007 WL 1830810 (Ct. App. Cal. June 27, 2007); *see Motwani v. Wet Willies Mgmt. Corp.*, 2017 WL 3311256 (E.D. La. Aug. 3, 2017) (Louisiana law uncertain).

II. Tortious Interference with a Prospective Business Relationship

Some states permit recovery of damages for harm to a preexisting business relationship, and others, to specific prospective business opportunities. The court in *Com. Ventures, Inc. v. Rex M. & Lynn Lea Fam. Tr.*, 177 P.3d 955 (Idaho 2008), set out typical requirements:

> (1) The existence of a valid economic expectancy; (2) knowledge of the expectancy on the part of the interferer; (3) intentional interference inducing termination of the expectancy; (4) the interference was wrongful by some measure beyond the fact of the interference itself (*i.e.*, that the defendant interfered for an improper purpose or improper means); and (5) resulting damage to the plaintiff whose expectancy has been disrupted.

Courts require the plaintiff to plead "with particularity the relationships or opportunities with which defendant is alleged to have interfered." *UMG Recordings, Inc. v. Global Eagle Enter., Inc.*, 117 F. Supp. 3d 1092 (C.D. Cal. 2015). In addition, "the defendant's knowledge must be similarly specific." *Muir v. Navy Fed. Credit Union*, 744 F. Supp. 2d 145 (D.D.C. 2010) (allegation defendant knew plaintiff "wished to develop apartments" not sufficient when interference was with plaintiff's acquisition of financing). For some courts, "a purpose on the defendant's part to financially injure or destroy the plaintiff is essential." *In re Anderson*, 2018 WL 3726156 (Bankr. E.D. Wis. Aug. 2, 2018).

Further, the defendant's improper conduct must cause the loss. The jury instruction in *Russo v. Thornton*, 2018 WL 1786888 (Conn. Super. Mar. 22, 2018), emphasized causation:

> If you find that the defendants tortiously interfered with the plaintiffs' contracts and/or business expectancies, then you must decide if the plaintiffs have proven that they suffered an actual loss as a result of that interference. The plaintiffs must prove that but for the tortious interference, there was a reasonable probability that the plaintiffs would have continued or entered into a contract and/or business relationship with or made a profit from the sale of its products to its existing customers. The mere possibility of entering into a contract or making a profit is not enough.

Where the harm is not loss of an actual contract, courts require proof of much more than a generalized assertion that, but for the defendant's wrongful conduct, the plaintiff lost money. The court in *Wash. Consulting Group. v. Raytheon Technical Serv. Co., LLC,* 2013 WL 1562128 (Wash. March 7, 2013), emphasized the required "damage:"

> A valid business expectancy requires a probability of a future contractual or economic relationship and not a mere possibility. In effect, the purported expectancy must be commercially reasonable to anticipate, and that there is a reasonable likelihood that the plaintiff would have secured it. In effect, a plaintiff seeking to prosecute a claim sounding in tortious interference with prospective business advantage must demonstrate that there was a reasonable probability of future economic benefit in order to survive a motion for summary judgment. Accordingly, plaintiff must demonstrate that, under an objective test, there is a reasonable certainty that without the defendant's misconduct, plaintiff would have realized the expectancy.

The measure of damage is "the loss suffered by the plaintiff, including the opportunities for profits on business diverted from it." *In re Gormally*, 550 B.R. 27 (Bankr. S.D.N.Y. 2016); *see In re Shields*, 2010 WL 4813585 (E.D. Cal. Nov. 19, 2010) ("the measure of damages for interference with prospective economic advantage may include (a) the pecuniary loss of the benefits of the contract; and (b) consequential losses for which the interference is a legal cause."). However, the measure of such tort damages is "different from tortious interference with contract as the damages are not strictly based upon contract rules." *Hill v. Heritage Resources, Inc.*, 964 S.W.2d 89 (Ct. App. Tex. 1997).

Havilah Real Property Servs. LLC. v. VLK, LLC

108 A.3d 334 (Ct. App. D.C. 2015) (Blackburne-Rigsby, J.)

[In 2004, Vicky Lynn Karen formed VLK, LLC with LaMar Carlson, with whom she had previously been in a romantic relationship. VLK flipped distressed properties in Southeast Washington, D.C. Karen believed Carlson had wrongfully transferred $10,000 from VLK to use to assist his new romantic interest, Joan Alderman, and her company, Havilah Real Property Services, LLC, to buy properties in competition with VLK. VLK sued Carlson, Alderman, and Havilah in Maryland state court. In connection with that suit, VLK filed *lis pendens* on 51 Havilah properties located in D.C. (A *lis pendens* gives notice on real property records that litigation concerning the property is pending.) The jury found that Carlson had breached fiduciary duties to VLK, but otherwise found for Alderman and Carlson. VLK released the *lis pendens* a few days after judgment.

Havilah then filed this suit, alleging that the *lis pendens* had been filed because Karen had romantic feelings for Carlson and was jealous of Alderman's relationship with him and had tortiously interfered with prospective sales of 31 of the 51 properties. The evidence was undisputed that Alderman had successfully flipped all of her properties until the *lis pendens* were filed and made the properties unmarketable. After a two-week trial, the jury found for plaintiff and awarded $602,942. Defendant appealed.]

The District of Columbia has not conclusively resolved the question of whether the filing of a notice of *lis pendens* ancillary to litigation over real property interests is protected by an absolute or a conditional privilege against a claim of tortious interference with contract and/or prospective advantage; thus, in deciding this issue, our review is *de novo*. Appellate courts across the country are divided.

The majority of jurisdictions have concluded that the filing of *lis pendens* is protected by an absolute privilege, so that any subsequent lawsuit for tortious interference based on such filings is barred as a matter of law, even if the lawsuit underlying the *lis pendens* filings was asserted in bad faith or with malice. Consequently, neither the plaintiff's motive nor evidence tending to show motive is relevant" in jurisdictions that adopt the absolute privilege rule; rather, the only relevant inquiry is whether the *lis pendens* notices bore a *reasonable relation* to the action filed. On the other hand, a few states have concluded that the filing of *lis pendens* is only conditionally or "qualifiedly" privileged, meaning that an action for tortious interference arising from such filings are generally barred, but can be maintained if the underlying litigation was brought in bad faith or with malice.

We disagree and conclude that our adoption of the Restatement's formulation of the claim of tortious interference compels us to hold that the filing of a notice of *lis pendens* is only protected by a conditional privilege in the District of Columbia. If the litigation underlying the *lis pendens* filing was pursued in good faith, then both it and any notice of *lis pendens* filed in connection with that action are privileged and thus cannot form the basis for any valid claim of tortious interference. If the underlying litigation is found not to have been pursued in good faith, then no privilege attaches to the underlying litigation, and a defendant can be liable for all damages proximately caused by that litigation, including damages occasioned by the filing of *lis pendens* related to that litigation. Our acceptance of the conditional privilege rule comports with other courts that have similarly adopted the Restatement. We also believe that it is the fairer rule because it provides an adequate remedy to parties that have suffered harm as a result of litigation over real property interests filed in bad faith.

Consistent with our case law and the Restatement's construction of the legal justification and privilege defense, we hold that the recordation of *lis pendens* ancillary to litigation over real property interests is only protected by a conditional privilege against a claim of tortious interference with contract and/or prospective advantage in the District of Columbia. This means that a defendant may avoid liability if he or she can establish that the notice of *lis pendens* was filed pursuant to litigation that was initiated in good faith. Whether the underlying litigation was undertaken in good faith is a question of fact for the jury to decide.

Jurisdictions that have extended the absolute privilege rule have adopted or accepted one or more of the following rationales in doing so:

> (1) with few exceptions, any publication made in judicial proceedings enjoys an absolute privilege from subsequent claims of defamation; (2) the only purpose of recording a notice of *lis pendens* is to put prospective buyers on constructive notice of the pendency of the litigation; (3) the notice of *lis pendens* is purely incidental to the action in which it is filed, refers specifically to that action, and has no existence apart from that action; and (4) the recording of a notice of *lis pendens* is in effect a republication of the proceedings in the action and is, therefore, accorded the same absolute privilege as any other publication in that action.

Admittedly, the logic for concluding that *lis pendens* filings are absolutely privileged is not unpersuasive.

While we reject the "absolute privilege" analytical framework that is set forth in this line of cases, our ruling today—which makes the privilege status of a *lis pendens* filing dependent on the good faith basis of the underlying litigation—vindicates many of the same concerns that provide the rationale for those decisions. *Lis pendens* filings do serve a socially beneficial function in safeguarding the rights of third parties. As a general rule, litigants should be incentivized to make such filings without fear of reprisal. However, for the reasons set forth above, we see no reason to extend such protection, as many of the "absolute privilege" jurisdictions appear to have done, to litigants who have initiated the underlying litigation in bad faith. In fact, this court has similarly concluded that publications made during the course of judicial proceedings are absolutely privileged from subsequent claims of defamation. This recognition of an absolute privilege for judicial publications in the context of a defamation suit is based on the public policy of securing to attorneys as officers of the court the utmost freedom in their efforts to secure justice for their clients.

Consequently, the question of whether VLK was entitled to the privilege defense for the thirty-one notices of *lis pendens* depended on whether VLK initiated the underlying Maryland lawsuit in good faith, which was a factual question for the jury to decide at trial.

We next turn to VLK's alternative argument that Havilah failed to present evidence at trial that it had specific business relationships that it lost as a result of VLK's pursuit of the underlying litigation, or that VLK knew about a particular relationship and intentionally interfered with it.

A trial court may grant a motion for judgment as a matter of law only if no reasonable juror, viewing the evidence in the light most favorable to the prevailing party, could have reached the verdict in that party's favor. VLK's argument that Havilah failed to identify specific business relationships can be disposed of by reference to our decision in *Carr v. Brown*, 395 A.2d 79 (D.C. 1978). In *Carr*, we stated that under the tort of interference with prospective advantage, "business expectancies, not grounded on present contractual relationships but *which are commercially reasonable to anticipate,* are considered to be property and therefore protected from unjustified interference." *Id.* (emph. added). We further observed that these expectancies are considered reasonable in cases where "there is a background of business experience on the basis of which it is possible to estimate with some fair amount of success both the value of what has been lost and the likelihood that the plaintiff would have received it if the defendant had not interfered." *Id.*

Here there was sufficient evidence for the jury to conclude that it was commercially reasonable for Havilah to anticipate selling its thirty-one properties at issue, sales which were thwarted by VLK's initiation of litigation and ancillary filing of *lis pendens.* For example, the voluminous amount of documentation that Havilah proffered into evidence showed that it actively marketed the properties, and that it had generated genuine interest in the properties prior to the filings of *lis pendens.* In addition, Alderman testified that Havilah purchased the properties in the first half of 2007, a time when people were buying "properties at an 'alarming rate,'" and that it was successful in marketing and selling at least some of the properties until the *lis pendens* were filed. Robinson, Havilah's real estate agent, corroborated Alderman's testimony, stating that he assisted Alderman in entering sales contracts for some of the properties at issue, but that deals fell through after the *lis pendens* were filed. As attested by Konopka, Havilah's expert witness on *lis pendens,* a *lis pendens* filing makes it practically impossible for a property to be sold because of the potential risks involved for buyers. Accordingly, the jury could reasonably conclude that Havilah had realistic expectancies in the sale of the thirty-one properties, which were damaged by the initiation of the litigation and the resulting filing of *lis pendens,* and that VLK was conscious of Havilah's expectancies.

With respect to the issue of damages, VLK essentially argues that the diminished fair market value method of calculating Havilah's damages relied on by the trial court to instruct the jury was too uncertain and speculative because it was premised on the "unfounded" assumption that Havilah could have sold all of its properties during the intervening time that the *lis pendens* were in place. We disagree. Damages may not be based on mere speculation or guesswork. The evidence offered must form an adequate basis for a reasoned judgment. However, damages need not be calculated with mathematical precision so long as they are based on a reasonable estimate of relevant data.

Under the Restatement, a party is specifically entitled to any consequential damages, which, in the context of *lis pendens* filings made in connection with bad faith litigation, include the diminishment in fair market value. We recognize that, based on the specific facts of this case, the fair market value method of calculating damages may appear overly generous to Havilah, given that the value of property generally fell across the country between 2007 and 2009 due to the subprime mortgage crisis. However, as the *Askari* court explained:

> This rule is not intended to penalize a buyer who files a *lis pendens*. Changing conditions in the real estate market may work to the buyer's benefit or to his disadvantage. For example, if the property has increased in value when the *lis pendens* is lifted, the damages the buyer must pay are accordingly reduced. In some cases the buyer may pay no damages. The buyer's damages are subject to change because the filing of a *lis pendens* does not place valuation of the property in a state of suspended animation.

225 Cal.Rptr. at 292. Based on the foregoing, we conclude the diminished fair market value method was not an improper method for calculating damages stemming from *lis pendens* filings made in connection with bad faith litigation. Accordingly, the trial court did not err in instructing the jury to apply the fair market method in calculating Havilah's damages.

Notes and Questions

1. <u>Causation</u>. The defendant's conduct must have been a substantial factor causing the loss of the potential income. *Bally Tech. Inc. v. Bus. Intell. Sys.*, 2012 WL 3656498 (D. Nev. Aug. 23, 2012) (no causation where prospective buyer had reduced its offer to buy plaintiff's business for reasons unrelated to defendant's acts).

2. <u>Negligence</u>? Some courts hold negligence is sufficient but otherwise apply the elements of intentional interference. *Orthotec, LLC v. Eurosurgical, S.A.*, 2007 WL 1830810 (Ct. App. Cal. June 27, 2007). Other courts require intent. *E.g., Ragsdale v. Mount Sinai Med. Tr. of Miami*, 770 So. 2d 17 (Ct. App. Fla. 2000); *R.M. Bacon, LLC v. Saint-Gobain Perf. Plastics Corp.*, 2018 WL 1010210 (N.D.N.Y. Feb. 20, 2018).

III. The Measure of Tortious Interference Damages: Contract Damages for a Tort?

A tortious interference plaintiff must show that, but for the defendant's conduct, it would have obtained the contract or opportunity and, with reasonable certainty, the amount of damages. Courts often state that the measure of damages is the net profits that plaintiff lost because defendant caused it to be "unable to finalize contracts with X, Y, and Z and consequently lost commissions that it had anticipated earning on those contracts." *LDCircuit, LLC v. Sprint Commun. Co., L.P.*, 364 F.

Supp. 2d 1246 (D. Kan. 2005). The court in *Hylant Group, Inc. v. Cummings*, 2011 WL 767399 (N.D. Ohio Feb. 28, 2011), gave this instruction:

> Lost profits are calculated by deciding what the plaintiff was entitled to receive had the plaintiff and (insert name of third party) (continued their) (entered into a) business relationship. You should then add other damages, if any, suffered by the plaintiff as a result of the defendant's improper interference. From this sum you should subtract the amount, if any, that the plaintiff saved by not having to fully perform in the business relationship. You may only award damages the existence and amount of which are reasonably certain and have been proved to you by the greater weight of the evidence. You may not award damages that are remote or speculative.

However, other courts state that contract measures of damages — expectancy, reliance, and restitution — do not necessarily limit tortious interference claims. One court explained:

> The basic measure of actual damages for tortious interference with contract is the same as the measure of damages for breach of the contract interfered with, to put the plaintiff in the same economic position he would have been in had the contract interfered with been actually performed.

> The general rule, however, is not without exception. Although breach of the interfered-with contract is probably the most common measure of damage, tortious interference does not limit the damage for the tort to that alone. Damages for tortious interference with contract are necessarily limited to damages proximately caused by the act of interference and do not extend to any other breach of the contract that the contracting party happened to commit.

> A plaintiff must adduce substantial, competent evidence of a character that can permit reasonable men and women to determine that damage was caused by the breach of contract or tortious interference, and to assess with reasonable certainty the amount of damage and degree of causation of the damage by the breach of contract or tortious interference relative to other factors. *See also* Restatement (Second) of Torts §774A cmt. e (1979) ("The party who tortiously interfered and the contract breaker are both wrongdoers, and each is liable for the entire loss that he has caused.").

Palla v. Bio-One, Inc., 424 S.W.3d 722 (Ct. App. Tex. 2014) *See Jones v. Wells Fargo Bank*, N.A., 2014 WL 3906297 (D. Colo. Aug. 7, 2014) ("the measure of damages may depart from contractual damages when necessary to make the innocent party whole.").

For these reasons, courts have affirmed verdicts for less than contract damages against a tortious interference defendant while awarding full contract damages against the breaching defendant. *See Palla v. Bio-One, Inc.*, 424 S.W.3d 722 (Ct. App. Tex. 2014) ("the damages related to tortious interference could, and apparently did, differ from the total damages for Bio-One's breach of the Agreement"); *see also Koehler v. Packer Group, Inc.,* 53 N.E.3d 218 (Ill. Ct. App. 2016) (affirming verdict against one defendant for $205,000 and another for $720,000 for interfering with same contract because "the two defendants engaged in different conduct and played different roles in the series of events leading to plaintiff's termination" from his job).

Fraidin v. Weitzman

93 Md. App. 168 (1992) (Bishop, J.)

[The Dormans hired Sheldon Braiterman and Andre Weitzman, of the firm Braiterman & Johnson, to represent them in a suit against Fraidin, agreeing to pay a 50% contingency fee. Weitzman left the firm and started his own firm. At some point, the Dormans executed a fee agreement giving Weitzman a 50% contingency interest. Weitzman won verdict of $366,949.86 for the Dormans. However, Fraidin then met secretly with the Dormans and they agreed to settle for $50,000. Just before signing the settlement, the Dormans wrote a letter "firing" both Weitzman and the Braiterman & Johnson firm.

Weitzman and the Braiterman & Johnson firm then sued Fraidin and his corporation for tortiously interfering with their fee arrangement with the Dormans, and the Dormans for breach of contract. After a 29-day trial the jury awarded plaintiffs $183,474.94 against Fraidin and $25,000 against the Dormans. Fraidin and his corporation appealed.]

Appellants contend that the fee agreement violated public policy, and was, therefore, "unenforceable" and incapable of forming the basis of a suit for tortious interference with contract. Specifically appellants claim: 1) Weitzman's fee was excessive; 2) Weitzman had a greater stake in the litigation than the Dormans; 3) Weitzman obtained the Dormans' consent to the fee agreement in an improper and unethical manner; and 4) the power of attorney provision contained in the fee agreement gave Weitzman unlimited discretion to control the litigation.

A suit for tortious interference with contract does not depend upon whether the underlying agreement was "enforceable;" it depends upon whether the agreement was "valid." Only a valid agreement can support a claim for tortious interference with contract; an invalid agreement cannot. Thus, appellants' argument is that, because the fee provision was excessive, the contract between the Dormans and their attorneys was invalid and, consequently, not capable of serving as the basis of a suit for tortious interference with contract.

We disagree. Under the circumstances, the Contract was not excessive, rather, it was a valid contract capable of serving as the basis of a suit for tortious interference with contract. We explain.

The elements of tortious interference with contract are: 1) existence of a contract between plaintiff and a third party; 2) defendant's knowledge of that contract; 3) defendant's intentional interference with that contract; 4) breach of that contract by the third party; 5) resulting damages to the plaintiff. Appellants' argument is directed at the first element of the tort. A valuable discussion of the type of contract that will support a claim for tortious interference is included in R. Gilbert, P. Gilbert & R. Gilbert, Maryland Tort Law Handbook, § 7.3 (1986):

> Obviously if there is no valid contract, one cannot be said to have interfered with its existence. Thus, if D interferes with an invalid agreement between P and O by inducing O to abandon pursuit of the invalid agreement, D is not liable to P.

A similar statement is contained in W. Page Keeton, Prosser and Keeton on Torts § 129 at 994-95 (5th ed. 1984):

> Virtually any type of contract is sufficient as the foundation of an action for procuring its breach. It must of course be valid, in force and effect, and not illegal as in restraint of trade, or otherwise opposed to public policy, so that the law will not aid in upholding it.

Thus, the general rule is that for there to be a right of action against one for contractual interference, there must be in existence a valid contract subject to that interference. *See also, Annotation, Interference with Invalid Contract,* 96 A.L.R.3d 1294 (1980) ("All of the cases in this annotation involving invalid contracts support the view that, regardless of the particular ground for invalidity there is no liability for interfering with an invalid contract.)

Although a 50 percent contingency fee is high, the fee agreement was not excessive, or invalid, based on the facts of this case.

The jury awarded a total of $183,474.94 in compensatory damages on the count of tortious interference with contract: $91,737.47, plus interest, each to Braiterman, P.A. and Weitzman. This amount is precisely one-half the amount of the judgment in Dorman v. Fraidin. Appellants make two arguments with respect to the compensatory award: 1) the award should be limited to $25,000 — one-half the amount the Dormans received to settle the claim; 2) because the Dormans are jointly and severally liable with appellants for damages caused by the Dormans' breach of contract, the compensatory award against appellants must be modified.

In *Rite Aid Corp. v. Lake Shore Investors,* 298 Md. 611 (1984), the Court of Appeals considered how damages for interference with a contract are to be measured. The damages include such damages as would reasonably flow from a tortious contractual interference, and may include pecuniary loss of the benefits of the contract, consequential losses, emotional distress, actual harm to reputation, and, in the appropriate circumstances, punitive damages. Under the facts of this case, we hold that the compensatory damages are not limited to $25,000 (one-half the amount of the settlement).

This precise point was addressed in *State Farm Ins. Co. v. Gregory,* 184 F.2d 447 (4th Cir. 1950), and we find its reasoning persuasive:

It is argued that the recovery should have been limited by the percentage provided for in the contingent fee as applied to the amount of the compromise and not as applied to the face of the policy; but it is clear that the damages recoverable as the result of the wrongful interference with contract should not be limited to the proceeds of the settlement which resulted from the wrongful interference. The jury might well have concluded that, but for the interference, plaintiff would have recovered the full amount of the policy for his client and would have been entitled to the percentage thereof provided for in his contract for contingent fee. The settlement at less than the face of the policy was based upon the elimination of the plaintiff's fee by the wrongful interference with his contract; and damages for the wrongful interference with his contract; and damages for the wrong should embrace all elements reasonably flowing therefrom and not be limited by the amount of the settlement made in its perpetration. To permit this would be to permit the wrongdoer to profit to that extent from the wrong that he has perpetrated.

Financial statements showed appellants' net worth to be well in excess of that needed to satisfy the *Dorman v. Fraidin* judgment. The jury could have concluded from these statements that, but for Fraidin's interference, Braiterman, P.A. and Weitzman would have recovered the full amount of their contingent fee.

Appellants argue the $183,474.94 compensatory award entered against them for tortious interference with contract should be reduced by $25,000 to account for the $25,000 compensatory award entered against the Dormans for breach of contract. Appellants' argument that Braiterman, P.A. and Weitzman are being compensated twice for the value of the contract has some merit, but a reduction in the judgment against appellants is not required at this time.

In *Lake Shore*, the Court of Appeals specifically adopted as the law of Maryland the provisions of § 774A of Restatement (Second) Torts. Section 774A(2) provides:

> In an action for interference with a contract by inducing or causing a third person to break the contract with the other, the fact that the third person is liable for the breach does not affect the amount of damages awardable against the actor; but any damages in fact paid by the third person will reduce the damages actually recoverable on the judgment.

The comment to this section explains:

> The fact that the plaintiff may have a cause of action against the person who has broken his contract does not prevent recovery against the defendant who has induced or otherwise caused the breach, or reduce the damages recoverable against him. The defendant and the contract breaker are both wrongdoers and each is liable for the entire loss that he has caused. Even a judgment obtained for breach of the contract if it is not satisfied does not bar or reduce recovery from the one who has caused the breach. But since the damages recoverable for breach of the contract are common to the

actions against both, any payments made by the one who breaks the contract or partial satisfaction of the judgment against him must be credited in favor of the defendant who has caused the breach.

Accordingly, appellants are not entitled to a reduction in the amount of the judgment against them for tortious interference with contact. Should the Dormans satisfy the judgment against them appellants would be entitled to a credit.

Notes and Questions

1. <u>Above Expectation</u>? The *Fraidin* court refused to offset the damages against Fraidin by the $25,000 verdict against Fraidin. Why? More fundamentally, given that clients like the Dormans have the right to settle claims for any amount, and over a lawyer's objection, what were the "improper means" and how did they *cause* damage? In answering, consider that interfering with an at-will contract "is actionable, because, until one of the contracting parties terminates the contract, the parties are in a subsisting relation that presumably will continue and is of value to the plaintiff." *Topper v. Midwest Div., Inc.*, 306 S.W.3d 117 (Ct. App. Mo. 2010).

2. <u>Defendant's Profit as Plaintiff's Damages</u>? Courts split on whether, if a defendant causes a third party to break a contract with the plaintiff, the defendant's profit is an appropriate measure of damages. The *Developers Three v. Nationwide Ins. Co.*, 582 N.E.2d 1130 (Ct. App. Ohio 1990), court rejected that approach:

> We find the arguments against recovery of a defendant's profits more persuasive than the arguments in favor. We are reluctant to abandon a purely compensatory damage formula unless policy and precedent clearly support an unjust enrichment theory of recovery. We conclude that neither supports such a recovery in this instance. First, an award of defendant's profits is not the only means of discouraging a tortfeasor from interfering with a business relationship while calculating that his profits will exceed the injured party's losses. In some cases, a defendant's conduct will make him susceptible to an award of punitive damages. In fact, punitive damages may serve well to counterbalance the unavailability of an unjust enrichment theory in tortious interference cases.

However, "several jurisdictions have allowed this measure of damages largely on the theory that an intending tortfeasor should not be prompted to speculate that his profits might exceed the injured party's losses, thus encouraging commission of the tort." *Great Am. Opportunities, Inc. v. Cherrydale Fundraising, LLC*, 2010 WL 338219 (Del. Ch. Jan. 29, 2010) ("such a measure of damages may be used to compensate a plaintiff in cases, such as this one, where actual loss is not readily ascertainable."). The *TruGreen Companies, L.L.C. v. Mower Brothers, Inc.*, 199 P.3d 929 (Utah 2008), court adopted a middle ground:

> We find especially instructive the analysis in *Am. Air Filter Co. v. McNichol*, 527 F.2d 1297 (3d Cir. 1975). The Third Circuit held that where "there are no injuries alleged other than pecuniary losses the measure of

damages for interference with contractual relations will be identical to that for breach of contract." In that case, Michael McNichol left American Air Filter to work for John F. Scanlan, Inc., a direct competitor of American. Because McNichol had signed a non-compete contract with American, American sued Scanlan for tortious interference. The court refused to adopt American's argument that its damages should be measured by "an accounting for profits earned by Scanlan from sales by McNichol." *Id.* The court stated that "an accounting is an essentially equitable remedy and has not served as a substitute for legal damages." *Id.* The court then went on to say,

> The basic failing of the plaintiff's theory is that the defendant's profits are not necessarily equivalent to the plaintiff's losses. The defendant's profit margin may be higher than plaintiff's for any number of reasons—e.g., product more efficiently made or distributed. To compel defendant to disgorge these profits could give plaintiff a windfall and penalize the defendant, neither of which serves the purpose of contract damages.

By holding that purely pecuniary losses from tortious interference are measured by the same standard as breach of contract, we need only look to the *Trilogy* standard that we adopted above for contract damages. The measure of damages, therefore, is the plaintiff's lost profits. Because proving lost profits can be difficult, there may be times, as we discussed above, when it is appropriate to look to the defendant's gains if such gains can be shown to correspond with the loss of plaintiff.

We therefore reject TruGreen's argument for unjust enrichment damages in tortious interference with contract cases. Thus, we also reject TruGreen's reliance on *Nat'l Merch. Corp. v. Leyden*, 370 Mass. 425 (1976). In *Leyden*, the court held that unjust enrichment might be a proper remedy for tortious interference cases. It justified this position in part

> because an intending tortfeasor should not be prompted to speculate that his profits might exceed the injured party's losses, thus encouraging commission of the tort. Nor should such a defendant be heard to say that the unjust enrichment remedy is unfairly "punitive" because the plaintiff may recover more than his exact loss, when use of a tort measure might allow the defendant to retain some part of his ill gotten gains.

We are persuaded by the efficient breach arguments discussed above. When an efficient breach occurs, a breaching party may retain its profits in excess of a plaintiff's losses as long as the plaintiff is made whole. As was stated in *Lake River Corp. v. Carborundum Co.*, 769 F.2d 1284 (7th Cir. 1985), such a standard is beneficial to both parties because the nonbreaching party receives what it bargained for and the breaching party is able to retain its profits made through its more efficient business practices. In the realm of tortious interference with contract or economic relations, it would be inconsistent to require the party inducing the breach to disgorge its excess profits while permitting the breaching party to retain its excess profits.

In sum, we hold that the plaintiff's lost profits is the appropriate measure of damages for tortious interference with a competitor's contractual and economic relations. We recognize, however, that lost profits may be difficult to ascertain and therefore allow for the examination of a defendant's gains when there is a sufficient correspondence between them. We explicitly state, however, that we are ruling on pecuniary losses and not injury to reputation or mental suffering.

3. <u>Mental Anguish</u>. Some courts allow recovery if distress had been "reasonably to be expected to result from the interference," *Minton v. Quintal,* 369 P.3d 853 (Ct. App. Haw. 2016), but others disallow it, *Soukup v. Sedgwick Claims Mgmt. Serv., Inc.,* 2012 WL 3134223 (Ct. App. Tex. Aug. 2, 2012), and others require proof that outrageous acts caused severe distress. *Di Loreto v. Shumake,* 38 Cal. App. 4th 35 (1995). For example, in *Musa v. Jefferson County Bank,* 620 N.W.2d 797 (Wis. 2001), the defendant bank held a mortgage that gave it the right to approve the sale of a hotel operated by the plaintiff, Musa. Musa sued, alleging the bank had intentionally interfered with potential sale of the hotel. The jury awarded him no damages other than $4,000 for mental health expenses. In a split decision, the majority affirmed, writing:

> In order to recover mental health care expenses, or any health care expenses for that matter, a plaintiff must bring forth evidence that the charges were reasonably and necessarily incurred for treatment of injuries or conditions arising from the occurrence which is the subject of the action. Thus, while the defendant contends that there is a qualitative difference between mental health treatment and other forms of medical care, we find no legally significant differences in the context of recovery of medical expenses.

> Moreover, mental health treatment expenses do not implicate the policy concerns that have caused courts to exercise reserve in the context of emotional distress damages and which justify the substantial other damages requirement. The difficulty in establishing the authenticity of a claim of emotional distress and the fear of unlimited liability on the part of the tortfeasor have historically led courts to place impediments in the way of a plaintiff's access to emotional distress damages.

> We have no reason to believe that the authenticity of mental health treatment expenses poses a problem given the likely existence of documentation of those expenses. Likewise, we note that a tortfeasor's liability for mental health treatment expenses is not without limits. Such expenses are submitted in a specific dollar amount and must be established to be both reasonable in amount and necessary.

Defendant's other challenge to the compensatory damage award is that the award of mental health treatment expenses is subject to a foreseeability requirement, which cannot be satisfied in this case. Defendant directs us to the Restatement (Second) of Torts § 774A, which imposes a foreseeability requirement on damages for "emotional distress or actual harm to reputation." For the same reasons that he offers in support of the substantial other damages requirement, he argues that we should apply principles of emotional distress damages to mental health treatment costs.

As we explained above, however, we refuse to treat the requirements for emotional distress damages as necessarily applicable to mental health treatment expenses. Therefore, even if we were to adopt and follow lockstep the Restatement section, we would reject the notion that the foreseeability provision is necessarily applicable to mental health treatment expenses. Accordingly, we do not subject the award of mental health treatment expenses to a foreseeability requirement grounded in the authority offered by the defendant.

The dissent wrote:

The important prerequisite here is before any damages for emotional injury can be recovered in an intentional tort that does not have the infliction of emotional distress as its gravamen, there must be substantial other damage, proof of some significant harm stemming from the tort that is separate and apart from any claimed emotional injury. If there is such harm, then the law will recognize a collateral, causal emotional injury, assuming it is severe, as legitimate and compensable. If there is not, then the law will not allow recovery of damages related to emotional distress, on the theory that if the tortious conduct has caused no (or insubstantial) damage, then any emotional reaction to it does not deserve to be compensated.

4. <u>A Contract, No Breach, Yet Damages</u>? Some courts hold that causing breach of contract is not required, but it is sufficient if a defendant causes "performance to be more expensive or burdensome." Restatement (Torts) 766A; *but see Italverde Trading, Inc. v. Four Bills Lading Numbered LRNNN 120950*, 485 F. Supp. 2d 187 (E.D.N.Y. 2007) (requiring breach).

C. Negligent Misrepresentation

I. The Elements — Including the Required Harm

"The harm sought to be remedied for negligent misrepresentation is the reliance on a negligently made false representation." *Ridgeway v. Royal Bank of Scotland Group*, 2013 WL 1985016 (D. Conn. May 13, 2013). Most states limit "negligent misrepresentation" to Restatement (Second) of Torts § 552:

(1) One who, in the course of his business, profession or employment, or in any other transaction in which he has a pecuniary interest, supplies false

information for the guidance of others in their business transactions, is subject to liability for pecuniary loss caused to them by their justifiable reliance upon the information, if he fails to exercise reasonable care or competence in obtaining or communicating the information.

(2) Except as stated in Subsection (3), [which describes the liability of a person under a public duty to provide information] the liability stated in Subsection (1) is limited to loss suffered

(a) by the person or one of a limited group of persons for whose benefit and guidance he intends to supply the information or knows that the recipient intends to supply it; and

(b) through reliance upon it in a transaction that he intends the information to influence or knows that the recipient so intends or in a substantially similar transaction. . . .

Ordinarily, silence cannot be the basis of misrepresentation, unless the defendant: (1) owed the plaintiff a fiduciary duty; (2) voluntarily disclosed information, but not the whole truth or its partial disclosure conveyed a false impression; or (3) made a statement that it later learned was misleading or untrue. *Brown & Brown of Tex., Inc. v. Omni Metals, Inc.*, 317 S.W.3d 361 (Ct. App. Tex. 2010).

Courts disagree on the breadth of "limited group of persons." In *Petrillo v. Bachenberg*, 139 N.J. 472 (1995), the court held an attorney who wrote a misleading real property report for a broker was liable to the buyer because a buyer was merely "foreseeable." Other states require the plaintiff to have been "either the intended recipient of the information or a *known* indirect recipient." *EKCO Int'l Trade Corp. v. Zihni Holding, AS,* 1995 WL 406124 (S.D.N.Y. July 7, 1995) (rejecting extension to "any reasonably foreseeable recipient of the information"). The following examines this narrow negligence-based claim.

Hernandez v. Coldwell Banker Sea Coast Realty
735 S.E.2d 605 (Ct. App. N.C. 2012) (Stroud, J.)

[In 2007, Plaintiff agreed to buy a multiunit residential property in North Carolina for $205,000, subject to obtaining an appraisal and with an option to terminate if the property did not appraise at or above that price. Defendant Avent Appraisals, Inc., performed the appraisal. Plaintiff never read or saw the appraisal. It described the property as a "triplex" although it was a duplex, and comparisons in the appraisal were to triplexes. A few years later, she fell in default on the mortgage and the lender foreclosed on the property. She then sued several defendants, including asserting a claim under Section 552 against Avent. The trial court granted its motion for summary judgment, and plaintiff appealed.]

In *Raritan River Steel Co. v. Cherry, Bekaert & Holland,* 322 N.C. 200 (1988), our Supreme Court addressed the issue of the scope of an accountant's liability for negligent misrepresentation in the context of financial audits. The Court noted four different approaches but adopted § 552, including the limitations in section (2)(a) & (b). The Court explained its understanding of the Restatement in determining an accountant's liability:

> As we understand it, under the Restatement approach an accountant who audits or prepares financial information for a client owes a duty of care not only to the client but to any other person, or one of a group of persons, whom the accountant or his client intends the information to benefit; and that person reasonably relies on the information in a transaction, or one substantially similar to it, that the accountant or his client intends the information to influence. If the requisite intent is that of the client and not the accountant, then the accountant must know of his client's intent at the time the accountant audits or prepares the information.

Id. The Court further explained the reasoning behind its adoption of the Restatement:

> the standard set forth in § 552 represents the soundest approach to accountants' liability for negligent misrepresentation. It recognizes that liability should extend not only to those with whom the accountant is in privity or near privity, but also to those persons, or classes of persons, whom he knows and intends will rely on his opinion, or whom he knows his client intends will so rely. On the other hand, as the commentary makes clear, it prevents extension of liability in situations where the accountant "merely knows of the ever-present possibility of repetition to anyone, and the possibility of action in reliance upon the audited financial statements, on the part of anyone to whom it may be repeated." *Restatement (Second) of Torts* § 552, Comment h. As such it balances, more so than the other standards, the need to hold accountants to a standard that accounts for their contemporary role in the financial world with the need to protect them from liability that unreasonably exceeds the bounds of their real undertaking.

Id. The Supreme Court specifically rejected the application of the reasonable foreseeability test as adopted by *Alva*, "because it would result in liability more expansive than an accountant should be expected to bear," explaining that

> An accountant performs an audit pursuant to a contract with an individual client. The client may or may not intend to use the report for other than internal purposes. It does not benefit the accountant if his client distributes the audit opinion to others. Instead, it merely exposes his work to many whom he may have had no idea would scrutinize his efforts. We believe that in fairness accountants should not be liable in circumstances where they are unaware of the use to which their opinions will be put. Instead, their liability should be commensurate with those persons or classes of persons whom they know will rely on their work. With such knowledge the auditor can, through purchase of liability insurance,

setting fees, and adopting other protective measures appropriate to the risk, prepare accordingly.

It is instructive that Judge Cardozo, the architect of reasonable foreseeability as the touchstone for products liability, *MacPherson v. Buick Motor Co.*, 217 N.Y. 282 (1916), declined to adopt the same standard for accountants' liability in *Ultramares Corp. v. Touche, Niven & Co.*, 255 N.Y. 170 (1931). Judge Cardozo distinguished accountants from manufacturers because of the potential for excessive accountants' liability. He wrote that if accountants could be held liable for negligence by those who were not in privity, or nearly in privity, accountants would face "liability in an indeterminate amount for an indeterminate time to an indeterminate class." Because of this potential for inordinate liability Judge Cardozo concluded, as do we, that accountants should be held liable to a narrower class of plaintiffs than the class embraced by the reasonable foreseeability test.

Id. The Court also held that the plaintiff Raritan's claim for negligent misrepresentation was properly dismissed, as this claim required actual reliance on the defendant's audit statements. The Court held that "a party cannot show justifiable reliance on information contained in audited financial statements without showing that he relied upon the actual financial statements themselves to obtain this information" and there was no justifiable reliance, as the plaintiff Raritan "alleged that it got the financial information upon which it relied, essentially IMC's net worth, not from the audited statements produced by defendants, but from information contained in Dun & Bradstreet." *Id.*

Application of § 552, and its limitations to liability in section (2)(a) & (b) require the plaintiff to allege and put forth evidence showing that (1) she was a person or one of a limited group of persons for whose benefit and guidance the appraiser intended to supply the information or that the appraiser knew that the recipient intended to supply the information to the plaintiff, and (2) justifiable reliance on that information. Justifiable reliance requires that the plaintiff actually relied on the information.

In addressing the first requirement there are no allegations that she was one of a limited group of persons for whose benefit and guidance defendant Avent intended to supply the appraisal report or that defendant Avent knew that the lender intended to supply it to plaintiff. In fact, plaintiff alleges that "Defendant Avent prepared the appraisal report for the lender and the intended use of the appraisal report was for the lender to evaluate the property appraised for a mortgage finance transaction." The appraisal report itself defines the "lender/client" as Southeast Mortgage Services and specifically states, "the intended user of this appraisal report is the lender/client" and "this appraisal is for the intended use of the assigned lender/client and/or their assigns for mortgage lending purposes and is not intended for any other use."

As to justifiable reliance, plaintiff did allege that she "relied on Defendant Avent's appraisal in deciding to proceed with the purchase of the appraised property and in obtaining a mortgage to finance said purchase." Even so the forecast of evidence by the parties shows that plaintiff did not actually rely on defendant Avent's appraisal. Plaintiff admitted in her deposition that she never viewed a copy of the appraisal prior to closing. She also never talked to defendant Avent prior to purchasing the property. In fact, the purchase contract contained an appraisal contingency provision allowing plaintiff the option of terminating the purchase if the property did not appraise at a value which equaled or exceeded the sale price. However, this contingency expired on or before 30 April 2007 and defendant Avent performed the appraisal on 16 May 2007; plaintiff still closed on the purchase of the property without reviewing the appraisal. Additionally, plaintiff admits in her brief on appeal that she "did not scrutinize the appraisal at any time, as generally buyers are not familiar enough with the forms to easily interpret them." Plaintiff further argues that the lender relied on defendant Avent's appraisal in approving the loan and she relied on the bank's reliance. However the justifiable reliance required by the Restatement is the plaintiff's actual reliance on the information in the report, not reliance via a third party such as the lender. We hold that the trial court's grant of summary judgment was proper.

Notes and Questions

1. <u>Who Can Sue</u>? Does the limitation in Section 552 serve the same purpose as the limitation on contract claims to intended third-party beneficiaries? Don't the elements of duty or proximate cause functionally already limit negligence claims? Why additional limits?

2. <u>Guiding Others</u>? *United Parcel Serv. Co. v. DNJ Logistic Group, Inc.,* 2017 WL 3097531 (W.D. Ky. July 20, 2017), is discussed above. UPS's subsidiary, Worldwide Forwarding, hired the defendant to provide logistical support by moving packages from incoming airlines to other airlines at certain airports. UPS alleged the defendant was overcharging it and included a Section 552 claim. The defendant moved to dismiss, asserting it was not in the business of providing information to guide UPS in business decisions:

> While the scope of this recently adopted tort is not yet well-defined, the Kentucky Supreme Court in *Giddings & Lewis, Inc. v. Industrial Risk Insurers,* 348 S.W.3d 729 (Ky. 2011), indicated that a negligent misrepresentation claim premised on Section 552 is available only when the defendant is in the business of supplying information. In *Giddings & Lewis,* the court considered whether Section 552 applied to product manufacturers and reviewed cases where negligent misrepresentation claims were found to be viable. The court first looked to the facts of *Presnell,* noting that it involved a contractor suing a construction consulting firm for negligent misrepresentation. Synthesizing Kentucky cases dealing with this type of claim, the court explained:

These cases are instructive because they all involve a party who "supplies false information for guidance of others in their business transactions" and is liable to the recipient for failing to "exercise reasonable care or competence in obtaining or communicating the information." A construction consulting firm and an attorney providing a title opinion, as well as an auctioneer, offer services which consist of information upon which others will rely. A manufacturer of a product is not in the business of supplying information but rather the product itself and, only incidentally, information about the product.

Worldwide Forwarding's negligent misrepresentation claim does not align with the Kentucky Supreme Court's present conception of that tort. DNJ is not in the business of supplying information for the guidance of others, and it did not do so in this case. Instead, it transported packages and sent bills for services rendered. In this respect, DNJ is more like a product manufacturer than a consulting firm, an attorney, or an auctioneer. As a result, Plaintiffs cannot credibly allege that the invoices DNJ sent to UPS constituted information supplied for the guidance of Worldwide Forwarding in its business transactions.

II. The Measures of Damage

Burke v. Harman

(Ct. App. Neb. 1998) (Sievers, J.)

[John Burke lived in Nebraska and made his living making and selling carvings of Native Americans, early Americans, civil war figures, and the like. To give them authenticity, he would collect historically relevant artifacts, study them, and then sell them. As part of that effort, in 1993 he bought a blanket for $115 from an antiques dealer who advised Burke that it was not a true Navajo chief's blanket from the 1850s, but one made in the 1930s in the Southwest. An actual Navajo chief's blanket would have cost hundreds of thousands of dollars.

Burke took the blanket home and put it on the floor in front of his fireplace. A month later, Burke's friend, Mr. Hackett, was visiting and noticed the rug and suggested that Burke investigate it. Burke recalled that he had sold some other items to a man, Mr. Harman, and so called him and arranged to meet him at his home with the blanket.

Harman was also a collector of historic artifacts, including Native American weavings. He had bought and sold several and had learned the first step in determining a blanket's value was to determine if it was a Mexican knock-off. Harman had a substantial home library of reference books, including two on the specific type of Navajo chief blanket that Burke had purchased.

The trial court held the plaintiff had not sought the proper measure of damages, and so dismissed the claim under Section 552, but allowed the jury to decide Burke's fraud claim. It found for the defendant. Plaintiff appealed.]

Burke's version of the meeting is that after Harman rolled out the blanket for examination, Harman told Burke that it was Mexican and that in Santa Fe it was worth $1,500 to $2,000. Harman offered Burke $500 plus two Indian Skookum dolls for the weaving. When Burke refused that offer, Harman offered $1,000 cash, which Burke accepted. Burke had also brought an Indian basket along, which Burke sold to Harman for $250. Harman admits in his testimony that he was asked by Burke, "What do you think it is?" But he relates that he told Burke that it could be Mexican or Indian and that he gave no opinion as to its value except in reference to its condition in relation to the rug he had acquired from Deeds, Harman saying that Burke's weaving was in poorer condition. Harman testified that he liked the weaving and that he asked what Burke wanted for it, to which Burke responded with, "What will you give me?" Harman responded by offering Burke $500 in cash plus the two Indian Skookum dolls which he had lying on the table, preparing to pack them to take to Santa Fe. Harman related that Burke did not think the dolls were worth the $500 asserted by Harman. Harman testified that he then said, "I'll give you a thousand dollars for your blanket." According to Harman, Burke's response was, "Hell, yes. I'll sell it for $1,000." Harman paid Burke $1,250 in cash for the blanket and the basket, and Burke and Hackett left.

The blanket was identified as a Navajo chief's blanket, first phase, Ute style. Howard Grimmer, the former owner of Morning Star Gallery in Santa Fe, which handles valuable Indian artifacts, put the matter in perspective when he testified that even if a person had $500,000 in a checking account and wanted to buy a first phase blanket on a particular day, he did not think that anyone could do it, because the blankets are very rare, and there are only a handful of them in public hands and those only move occasionally. Harman sold the blanket a year after he got it from Burke to an individual in New York for $290,000. The parties have stipulated that on August 1, 1993, the blanket Burke sold to Harman had a fair market value of $290,000.

The matter of damages takes a bit of a tortured path through the Restatement. Section 552 outlines the basic requirements of the theory of recovery for negligent misrepresentation, and we have no doubt that §552 encompasses Burke's claim against Harman. Harman clearly had a pecuniary interest in the transaction. Section 552B(1) sets forth the damages for negligent misrepresentation and provides:

> (1) The damages recoverable for a negligent misrepresentation are those necessary to compensate the plaintiff for the pecuniary loss to him of which the misrepresentation is a legal cause, including
>
> > (a) the difference between the value of what he has received in the transaction and its purchase price or other value given for it; and
> >
> > (b) pecuniary loss suffered otherwise as a consequence of the plaintiff's reliance upon the misrepresentation.

Section 552B(2) excludes damages for "the benefit of the plaintiff's contract with the defendant." In § 552B, comment *a*, we are referred to the Restatement (Second) of Torts § 549(1) (1977), as the comment states:

> The rule stated in this Section applies, as the measure of damages for negligent misrepresentation, the rule of out-of-pocket loss that is stated as to fraudulent misrepresentations in Subsection (1) of § 549. Comments *a* to *f* under § 549 are therefore applicable to this Section so far as they are pertinent.

Section 549, entitled "Measure of Damages for Fraudulent Misrepresentation," states:

> (1) The recipient of a fraudulent misrepresentation is entitled to recover his damages in an action of deceit against the maker the pecuniary loss to him of which the misrepresentation is a legal cause, including
>
> (a) the difference between the value of what he has received in the transaction and its purchase price or other value given for it; and
>
> (b) pecuniary loss suffered otherwise as a consequence of the recipient's reliance upon the misrepresentation.

It is, of course, important to remember that although this section defines recoverable damages for fraudulent misrepresentation, § 552B "borrows" § 549(1) for the measure of damages for negligent misrepresentation.

Section 549(1), comment *a*. at 109, states that the most usual loss "is when the falsity of the representation causes the article bought, sold or exchanged to be regarded as of greater or less value than that which it would be regarded as having if the truth were known." In the context of negligent misrepresentation, it is not whether the truth is known, but, rather, whether reasonable care or competence was exercised in obtaining or communicating the information which forms the alleged misrepresentation. In this case, under Burke's evidence, the alleged misrepresentation is what Harman said the blanket was and what it was worth.

Burke seeks $289,000, which is the difference between the value parted with at the time of the misrepresentation (it is crucial here to recall the parties' stipulation that on August 1, 1993, the blanket had a "fair market value of $290,000") and the value of what he received in return, $1,000 in cash. In fact, in this connection, we again observe that on the fraudulent misrepresentation claim, the court instructed the jury that if it found for Burke, it must return a verdict of $289,000. In short, the trial court directed what the amount of a verdict would be—a finding as a matter of law as to Burke's out-of-pocket damages—should liability be found.

Notes and Questions

1. <u>Mental Anguish</u>? Even though Section 552(B) limits damages to "pecuniary" losses, a few courts have awarded, in addition to those losses, damages for mental distress. *E.g., Ridgeway v. Royal Bank of Scotland,* 2013 WL 1985016 (D. Conn. May 13, 2013). The court in *Pearson v. Simmonds Precision Products, Inc.,* 624 A.2d

1134 (Vt. 1993), explained why a majority deny recovery of mental distress damages as consequential damages:

> The damages recoverable are those necessary to compensate the plaintiff for the pecuniary loss suffered, and not emotional distress. *Federal Land Bank Ass'n v. Sloane*, 825 S.W.2d 439 (Tex. 1991) (in an action for negligent misrepresentation under the Restatement, plaintiff may not recover damages for mental anguish). In *Branch v. Homefed Bank*, 6 Cal.App.4th 793 (Ct.App.1992), a recovery for emotional distress was denied in an action for negligent misrepresentation. With facts similar to those presented here, the court stated:
>
> > In sum, this was a case in which plaintiff's direct loss resulting from the negligent conduct of the defendant was economic. The consequential injury resulting from economic loss in terms of emotional distress is not compensable. Recovery for worry, distress and unhappiness as the result of loss of a job is not permitted when the defendant's conduct is merely negligent.

Why is mental distress caused by economic loss not recoverable in negligence but mental anguish caused by seeing a loved one injured, for example, is? Does this limitation sound like a contract principle influencing tort damage?

3. Key Differences between Contract and Tort Damages

This chapter has shown that only a few tort claims remedy purely economic harm and that the measure of damages for that harm is generally narrower, looking at the contemplation of the parties, not the general notion that a plaintiff in tort is liable under the "thin skulled plaintiff" rule. However, at times contract and tort remedies can overlap. Further, at times a harm that is protected by contract might have a measure of damages in tort, and a court may, as Judge Gorsuch did in the principal case below, use that measure. This section examines the problems that arise when contract and tort remedies overlap. Consider the following:

- Fewer injured plaintiffs can sue for breach of contract: only a party to the contract or an intended third-party beneficiary may do so.

- If more than one defendant causes a single harm, the requirement that a breach be a "substantial factor" in causing damages requires "more culpability than in tort before a defendant would be liable. Phrased differently, an injury in contract would have fewer 'substantial factors' than would the same injury in tort." *Zetter v. Griffith Aviation, Inc.*, 2006 WL 1117678 (E.D. Ky. Apr. 25, 2006).

- Some courts "have required greater certainty in the proof of damages for breach of contract than in tort." *Ohio Envtl. Dev. Ltd. Partn. v. Envirotest Sys. Corp.*, 478 F. Supp. 2d 963, 973 (N.D. Ohio 2007).

- Apportionment of fault under statutory comparative fault schemes normally does not apply to breach of contract claims;
- Ordinarily, the "eggshell" plaintiff rule does not apply to contract claims; further, specific harms can be excluded or limited by contract including in the form of liquidated damages clauses.

Kearl v. Rausser

293 F. App'x 592 (10th Cir. 2008) (Gorsuch, J.)

[Plaintiff, Dr. Rausser, made an oral agreement in late 2000 with three other professional economists under which he agreed to share proceeds of the sale of several hundred thousand shares of stock, to the extent its price exceeded $11.08 per share, based on the amount of work each performed over a period of a few years, ending on November 29, 2003. On that date, however, he refused to split the proceeds. Instead, over the next three years, he sold the stock at various times, with its price ranging from $31.15 to $54.88 per share. The value of shares of stock fluctuated over time, however, and the trial court permitted the jury to hear evidence of the value of the shares from the date of breach until trial. The jury awarded more than $5 million. The trial court denied the defendant's motion for a new trial, and it appealed.]

The district court rightly instructed the jury that if it found a plaintiff entitled to damages, it should award damages that would fairly compensate that plaintiff by putting him in the same position he would have been in had the defendant fully performed. The court further and again quite correctly instructed the jury that the award must be based on the evidence and must be reasonably certain and not speculative. However, as he did before the district court, Dr. Rausser complains before us that the jury received no instruction about the need for determining a date on which the contract was breached, and no instructions on the date(s) on which the stock was to be valued for purposes of calculating damages. Indeed, he stresses, plaintiffs were permitted to seek, and the jury was allowed to find, damages completely without reference to the date of breach. Dr. Rausser argues, and we agree, that this was legal error.

We review the jury instructions as a whole *de novo,* with an eye toward whether they adequately informed the jury of the governing law. Under Utah law, the general rule is that the date the defendant breaches his contractual obligation to deliver stock is the date on which damages are measured. *Coombs & Co. of Ogden v. Reed,* 303 P.2d 1097 (Utah 1956). Under this rule and in a case such as this one in which the market price of the goods in question is easily ascertainable, the date of breach is not only central to the calculation of damages, but is often the only real issue for the jury to decide on damages. After the date of breach has been determined, calculating damages frequently becomes a simple math problem. The importance of the date of breach in a contract action is highlighted by the distinction between damages in tort versus contract. The goal of damages in the tort context is to compensate a plaintiff for actual loss. In contract, on the other hand, the goal is not to compensate for the actual loss that may have occurred, but instead to compensate the party for its expected gain, measured at the time of contracting, from anticipated full performance. Admittedly, in cases of lost profits the practical distinction between these two concepts may be limited. *See Huffman v. Saul Holdings Ltd. P'ship,* 194 F.3d 1072 (10th Cir. 1999) (noting that lost profits in a breach of contract action "frequently represents fulfillment of the non-breaching party's expectation interest"). But the analytic distinction between measuring damages based on an *ex ante* expectation versus an *ex post* actual loss counsels hesitation in allowing a jury to consider evidence and award damages without any guidance as to temporal limitations on the defendant's liability.

The district court's instructions erroneously permitted plaintiffs to pursue a damages theory at trial that had no connection whatsoever to the date of breach. Instead of seeking to measure their losses as of the date of Dr. Rausser's breach, plaintiffs were free under the jury instructions given to argue for damages months and even years after any possible breach date. Indeed, plaintiffs' damages theory valued the stock as of the dates of Dr. Rausser's sales and, for the stock he retained, the date of trial. As the Utah Supreme Court has explained, the difficulty with this approach is that it "allows a plaintiff to ride the stock market at the defendant's risk and expense until trial or until the defendant sold, which might not take place until years later," in effect transforming defendant into a surety against any intervening loss of value unrelated to the transactions at issue in the case at hand. *Broadwater v. Old Republic Sur.,* 854 P.2d 527 (Utah 1993). While such a measure of damages was once regularly utilized in the tort context, even in that context Utah no longer adopts this free-form approach to damages. *Id.*

Though the date of breach is an essential starting point for assessing contract damages under Utah law, we acknowledge it may not be the end point for two related reasons. First, drawing on Utah's then-existing version of the Uniform Sales Act, the *Coombs* court acknowledged that the rule it set down was not a hard and fast rule, but applied only "in the absence of special circumstances showing proximate damages of a greater amount." *Coombs,* 303 P.2d at 1097. Second, such special circumstances may exist here; both parties note that a number of jurisdictions have applied the so-called "New York" rule of damages to actions involving, as this case does, a breach of contract to deliver stock, and it is at least possible Utah would do the same.

Under the New York rule, damages are based on the highest intermediate value of the stock between the time of breach and a reasonable time after the owner receives notice of breach. This rule gives an aggrieved buyer an opportunity to consult counsel, find and employ a new broker, and assess the market to determine whether covering in the market—buying the product in question from a different broker—is advisable at prevailing market prices. Further, the New York rule allows for the possibility that a buyer may not have the funds available to purchase stock at a market price significantly higher than the contract price, and so may need time to raise funds if he does elect to cover. This last concern may have particular relevance where, as here, a court is confronted with a contract exchanging services for a good that fluctuates significantly in value—such as stock.

It is not clear, however, that Utah would go so far as adopting the New York rule in contract cases. On the one hand, a case such as this one—in which services are exchanged for stock of substantial value—exposes a discontinuity between the standard notion of expectation damages, with its goal of making a plaintiff whole, and damages measured on the date of breach. On the other hand, to date Utah has only adopted the New York rule in tort cases, most notably the conversion context for which that rule was originally conceived. And at least some courts have suggested that its introduction into the contract realm would be inappropriate, risking the possibility of rewarding a plaintiff for actions taken with the benefit of hindsight, rather than simply replacing his or her expectation at the time of contracting. The New York rule also injects a certain amount of uncertainty by requiring speculation as to the meaning of a "reasonable period" to cover.

However much play in the joints Utah may allow in the date on which stock is valued in a breach of contract action—whether it would require a straightforward date of breach theory or adopt the New York rule—one thing is clear. Under either approach, determining the date of breach is the essential starting point. Under the general rule set out in *Coombs,* of course, the date of breach is also the ending point. But even under the New York rule, the date of breach is crucial because it is from that day that the reasonable period to cover is measured. Without a date of breach, in other words, the jury has no way to think about how much time a plaintiff may reasonably take before being expected to enter the market, and thus no way of determining the "highest intermediate price" between the date of breach and the end of that period.

In light of our holding with respect to the correct measure of damages, we are also compelled to agree with Dr. Rausser that the district court abused its discretion in admitting into evidence share prices on the date on which Dr. Rausser actually sold stock. Under any cognizable theory of contract damages, these dates are legally irrelevant. Plaintiffs' only argument in defense of these dates is that a jury could reasonably have found a breach each time Dr. Rausser sold shares, but such a theory finds support neither in the general rule set out in *Coombs* nor the New York rule Utah has adopted in the conversion context. Dr. Rausser breached his contractual obligation on whatever date delivery of the stock to plaintiffs was due, and plaintiffs have made no showing that delivery was due, purely coincidentally, on the dates Dr. Rausser elected to sell his shares; neither have they shown that the prices on those dates correspond to a reasonable period in which plaintiffs could cover. Simply put, the admission of these dates rested on a legally erroneous concept of permissible contract damages.

On remand, there are two possibilities. The first is a new trial on damages. Any such new trial would, consistent with our holding above, require damages to be measured by reference to the date of breach. Whether that would be the end point of the analysis (per *Coombs*), or only the starting point (per the New York rule), remains an open question. We leave that question open in significant measure because the choice between these two rules has not been sufficiently briefed on appeal to allow us to predict which rule Utah would adopt. The district court, accordingly, would either need briefing on which of these two damages remedies is proper under Utah law, or it would need to certify the question to the Utah Supreme Court. . . .

Alternatively, plaintiffs may, at their option, choose to accept a remittitur of damages based on the price of CRA stock on November 29, 2003 under a straightforward date-of-breach damages analysis. There was evidence adduced at trial to support a finding that breach occurred on November 29 (which is not to say that as a matter of law breach occurred on that date). It was on that date that the parties' venture was complete; they knew whether the CRA loans needed to be repaid, and on that date the period for measuring each party's contribution to the billables was concluded. Moreover, Dr. Rausser has maintained throughout this litigation that as a matter of law the date of breach is November 29. On remand, he therefore is estopped from asserting a different date of breach. If the plaintiffs do accept a remittitur to damages based on the share price on November 29, such a damages award would use the proportions of stock the jury awarded to each plaintiff, and merely multiply that number by $31.69.

Notes and Questions

1. <u>What Measure?</u> Was the plaintiff seeking restitution, reliance, or expectancy? If the latter, why does the date of breach matter?

2. <u>Different Measures.</u> Some courts have applied the "New York Rule" to breach of contract claims, including *Burns v. Prudential Securities, Inc.*, 857 N.E.2d 621 (Ct. App. Ohio 2006), which involved damages for breach of contract to sell stock:

> The trial court instructed the jury on the measure of damages as follows:

>> The measure of damages for breach of contract is the difference between the value of the investments at the time of the unauthorized reallocations on or about October 7, 8, and/or 9, 1998, and the highest intermediate value those investments reached between October 7, 1998 and a reasonable period of time after the plaintiffs received notice of the unauthorized reallocations.

> This language follows the "conversion theory" measure of damages also known as the "New York rule." In general, New York courts have applied this theory in calculating damages when an item of fluctuating value is wrongfully sold, converted, or not purchased when it should have been. Pursuant to this theory, a plaintiff can receive either the value of the stock at the time of the wrongful act or the highest intermediate stock price between the date of the act and a reasonable time thereafter during which the stock could have been replaced by the plaintiff, whichever is greater. However, contrary to Pickett's and PSI's assertions that the calculation is

only for conversion, the New York rule can also be used to measure damages for a breach-of-contract action.

> In *In re Dickinson* (1916), 171 A.D. 486, the New York Appellate Division explained that an unauthorized sale, not having been made pursuant to a client's instructions, may give rise to several causes of action. The court held that whether a client proceeds against a broker for conversion or asserts a right to recover damages for a breach of contract for an unauthorized sale of stock, the measure of damages is the same. In an action, based on contract, for damages for a broker's unauthorized sale of stock, the damages would be determined by the highest market price of the stock within a reasonable time after the customer's discovery of the unauthorized sale. Although the New York rule is often cited in connection with conversion actions, it is not limited to conversion alone. Rather, the rule is likewise applicable in cases where stock "was not delivered according to contractual or other legal obligation, or was *otherwise improperly manipulated.*" *Schultz*, 716 F.2d at 141. Accordingly, we find that the trial court properly instructed the jury on the applicability of the New York rule to the plaintiffs' breach-of-contract action.

Was then-judge Gorsuch wrong? *See also Kinsey v. Cendant Corp.*, 588 F. Supp. 2d 516 (S.D.N.Y. 2008) (stating *Lucente* rejected the New York Rule for contract claims, but it applied to conversion claims and rejected argument that damages should be based on average price between date of wrong and trial). Why isn't the average price a more reasonable measure?

3. *CR-RSC Towers*? Recall that the *CR-RSC Towers* case held evidence that, after contracting, the real estate market crashed, was inadmissible. Doesn't it raise the same concerns as *Kearl?* Why not always let the fact-finder consider post-contracting, or post-breach, evidence?

4. Why More Money in Tort? Most jurisdictions would allow juries to award more than the value on the date of the conversion. As explained in Chapter 6, Remedies Triggered by Harm to, or Interference with Rights in, Personal Property, states commonly permit the plaintiff to elect the higher value on dates that typically include the date of conversion, the date the plaintiff discovered conversion, and trial. Why is the measure different in contract? Why is tort law more generous?

5. Liquidated Damages as a Cap on Tort Damages? The court in *Sulzer Carbomedics, Inc. v. Oregon Cardio-Devices, Inc.*, 257 F.3d 449 (5th Cir. 2001), explained why an enforceable liquidated damages clause did not limit damages for tortious interference:

> To allow [the tortiously interfering defendant] to enforce the limitation would undermine the aim of awarding damages for tortious interference, which is to place the injured party in the same economic position it would have been in had the contract not been breached. The district court

correctly noted that Texas law holds that although such damages are not recoverable for breach of contract, a party found liable for tortious interference with a contract may be liable for, among other things, emotional distress or actual harm to reputation, if those injuries are reasonably to be expected to result from the interference. Thus, the measure of damages for breach of contract and tortious interference with a contract are not necessarily the same. In fact a claim for interference with contract is one in tort and damages are not based on contract rules; therefore, it is not required that the loss incurred be one within the contemplation of the parties to the contract itself at the time the contract was made. The district court therefore did not err in determining that the limitation of liability provision in Carbomedics's contract with Clark did not preclude St. Jude's liability for tortious interference.

Similarly, the court in *Fowler Homes, Inc. v. Welch Assocs., Inc.*, 793 S.W.2d 660 (Tex. 1990), held it was no defense to tortious interference that the defendant had caused the other party to the plaintiff's contract to terminate it in compliance with its notice provision.

A. The Economic Loss Doctrine's Impact on Tort Remedies

If a plaintiff has a breach of contract claim to recover economic losses caused by the defendant, allowing the plaintiff to assert, in addition, a tort claim that permits recovery for economic loss, could avoid the limitations on contract damages from *Hadley*, and potentially those limitations in the contract itself (for example, in the form of a liquidated damages clause or an exclusion of consequential damages). The Supreme Court recognized that allowing tort claims could let contract law "drown in a sea of tort." *East River S.S. Corp. v. Transamerica Delaval, Inc.*, 476 U.S. 858 (1986).

While originally rooted in the understandable effort to police against erosion of *Hadley* and related principles, its reach is expansive and has resulted in inexplicable and irreconcilable holdings. Some courts, for example, hold that fraud claims are barred if the losses are only economic. Some have held it bars all negligent misrepresentation claims, while others hold it bars such claims if the plaintiff and defendant have a contract; still others hold the opposite: privity of contract is required to support negligent misrepresentation.

Suppose plaintiff buys a car and it is defective and doesn't work, but no one is injured: the car just won't run. The plaintiff presumably has a breach of contract claim, but does the plaintiff have a negligence claim? Probably not. But what if the car explodes, and by good luck no one or nothing (other than the car itself) is damaged? What if the explosion damages other property, like the garage where the car was parked when it exploded?

For example, in *Chrysler Corp. v. Taylor*, 234 S.E.2d 123 (Ct. App. Ga. 1977), the court held the trial court had erred in failing to direct a verdict for a manufacturer where a consumer had sued in negligence for loss of the benefit of his bargain. "The history of the doctrine of strict liability in tort indicates that it was designed to govern the distinct problem of physical injuries." *Id.* Recovery for a loss of bargain because of the purchase of allegedly defective goods, in other words, is properly pursued only under warranty law—contract. *Id.*

There are exceptions, however. Most courts recognize three exceptions to the economic loss doctrine: (1) where the plaintiff sustains personal injury or property damage from a sudden or dangerous occurrence caused by the defendant's product; (2) where the plaintiff's economic harm was caused by a defendant's fraud; or (3) for negligent misrepresentation under Section 552.

Fabbis Enterp., Inc. v. Sherwin-Williams Co.

40 Misc. 3d 1203(A) (N.Y. City Ct. 2013) (Panebianco, J.)

[A Fabbis Enterprises, Inc., employee went to a Sherwin-Williams Co. store and explained that he was repainting the exterior of a 32-foot cabin cruiser and wanted durable, high-gloss exterior paint. He bought the paint the manager recommended and followed the instructions. But the finish was dull, not glossy. He went back to the store and was told to apply a clear top coat. He did so, but it was not glossy and turned yellow when exposed to soft drinks, gasoline, and other products common to boating. In total, he spent $750 at the store, but it cost $14,000 to have the top coat and paint removed and the boat repainted to a glossy finish. Fabbis asserted a negligent misrepresentation claim against Sherwin-Williams which moved to dismiss based upon New York's economic loss doctrine. This is the court's opinion on that motion.]

The economic loss rule stands for the proposition that an end-purchaser of a product is limited to contract remedies and may not seek damages in tort for economic loss against a manufacturer. Thus, economic losses, such as damage to the product itself and consequential damages, may not be recovered in an action predicated on strict products liability or negligence, unless personal injury or injury to property other than the product is alleged.

The economic loss doctrine reflects the principle that defects related to the quality of the product are relevant to the parties' expectancies, such as loss of bargain, and are not recoverable in tort, relegating such claims to the law of contracts and warranty which governs the economic relations between suppliers and consumers of goods. The rule bars recovery by both remote downstream purchasers, and those who purchased the product directly from the manufacturer or supplier.

To determine whether the rule applies to a given case, a court should consider factors such as "the nature of the defect, the injury, the manner in which the injury occurred, and the damages sought" (*Hodgson, Russ, Andrews, Woods & Goodyear v. Isolatek Intl. Corp.*, 300 A.D.2d 1051, 1052 [4th Dept 2002]). Critical to a determination of whether a tort claim is barred by the economic loss doctrine is whether damages are sought for the failure of the product to perform its intended purpose, in which case recovery is barred by the economic loss doctrine, or for direct and consequential damages caused by a defective and unsafe product.

Several cases illustrate the *Hodgson, Russ* approach for determining whether the rule applies. In *Hodgson, Russ,* the Appellate Division concluded that the rule was inapplicable where "the damages sought were not the result of the failure of the product to perform its intended purpose of fireproofing," but were instead caused by mold and fungus on the product, which, after remedial measures proved unsuccessful, resulted in plaintiff's decision to demolish two entire floors.

In *Praxair, Inc.,* the plaintiff brought negligence and strict liability claims against the manufacturer of an insulation coating product used as a joint sealant for its cryogenic testing facility in Tonawanda, New York. The central claim was that the damages (extensive corrosion to the piping system employed throughout the facility) were caused by the inclusion of chlorides as an ingredient of the product. Applying the Fourth Department's *Hodgson, Russ* approach, the federal court noted the absence of any allegations in the pleadings that the claimed damages resulted from the product's failure to perform its intended purpose as an insulation joint sealant. Accordingly, the court denied the manufacturer's motion to dismiss the tort claims as barred by the economic loss doctrine.

Reaching the opposite conclusion—that the plaintiff's negligence cause of action is barred, and therefore must be dismissed—is the more recent case of *Bristol Village, Inc. v. Louisiana-Pacific Corporation,* 2013 WL 55698 (WDNY, Jan. 3, 2013). In that case, an assisted living facility located in Clarence Center, New York, brought suit against a product manufacturer alleging that, as a result of defective trim board, plaintiff's structure sustained significant water damage. Applying *Hodgson, Russ,* the court granted the motion to dismiss, concluding "that the damage claimed relates to the expectations of the parties regarding the performance of [the product], thus relegating these plaintiffs to contractual remedies such as warranty."

Not relying upon *Hodgson, Russ,* but illustrating a similar, economic loss rule analysis is *Weiss v. Polymer Plastics Corp.,* 21 AD3d 1095 (2d Dept 2005). In that case, homeowners brought suit alleging that the synthetic stucco' manufactured by the defendant allowed water to infiltrate the stucco causing direct loss to the stucco itself as well as consequential damages to the plywood substrate. Reasoning that the stucco "did not perform properly to protect their home," the Second Department affirmed the order of Supreme Court, Nassau County which dismissed all tort-based claims as barred by the economic loss rule. As the *Praxair* court noted, "not only did the Second Department in *Weiss* not discuss whether the damage to the plywood substrate constituted other property' sufficient to avoid the economic loss doctrine, but the initial determination that the damages were attributed to the failure of the defective stucco to properly perform rendered it unnecessary for the court to consider whether the other property' exception to the economic loss doctrine applied."

Also consistent with the *Hodgson, Russ* approach is *Hemming v. Certainteed Corp.,* 97 A.D.2d 976,. There, "the essence of plaintiffs' claims was that the siding systems did not perform properly to protect their homes and, as a consequence, they suffered direct loss to the siding itself and consequential damages to their homes. Accordingly, the Fourth Department held that the tort claims were barred by the doctrine.

Here, the product was intended to serve as a durable, high gloss marine finish. Plaintiff alleges that the product is neither durable nor high gloss nor suitable for marine use. In other words, the essence of the claim is that the product failed to perform its intended purpose. Furthermore, unlike the water damage to the underlying structure in *Weiss, Hemming* and *Bristol Village,* or the corrosive damage to the piping system in *Praxair,* in the instant case, there is no alleged damage to the boat itself, except for the consequential damages inherent in having to remove the paint, which are properly characterized as "economic loss." That the siding in *Hemming,* the trim board in *Bristol Village* or the stucco in *Weiss* had to be removed in order to ultimately repair each structure was not sufficient to avoid application of the economic loss rule in each of those cases. Similarly, the removal of the alleged inadequate paint does not preclude the application of the economic loss doctrine.

Fabbis seeks to distinguish the economic loss rule cases, arguing that, here, a customer was simply sold the wrong type of paint. But, that is a bootstrapping argument. It was the wrong type of paint because it allegedly failed to properly perform its intended purpose. The language on the paint cans themselves describe the product as "durable" and "glossy or semi-glossy". It is clear that the Plaintiff's actual complaint is with the performance of the product. Therefore the economic loss doctrine does apply.

Although this Court is sensitive to the *ad hominem* argument that a strict application of the economic loss doctrine may relegate plaintiff to arguably insufficient, contract law damages, this Court is bound to apply the law as it presently stands. While some states recognize an exception to the economic loss doctrine for negligent misrepresentation claims, this Court can find no cases to support such an exception under New York law.

In re Takata Airbag Prods. Liab. Litig.
193 F. Supp. 3d 1324 (S.D. Fla. 2016) (Moreno, J.)

[Plaintiffs asserted Mazda fraudulently concealed that its cars' airbags had defects. Mazda moved to dismiss.]

Pennsylvania's Supreme Court has expressly reserved the question of whether the economic loss rule bars claims for fraudulent misrepresentation. *See David Pflumm Paving & Excavating, Inc. v. Found. Servs. Co.,* 816 A.2d 1164 (Pa.2003) (holding that the economic loss rule barred claims of negligence and that claim for fraudulent misrepresentation failed for other reasons, stating "there are no Pennsylvania

Supreme Court or Superior Court cases that indicate that the economic loss doctrine bars a claim for fraudulent misrepresentation. However, for the reasons stated in the text, we need not address that issue in this case.")

While noting a split of authority on the matter, the Third Circuit has predicted that Pennsylvania's Supreme Court would apply the economic loss rule to claims of intentional fraud relating to the quality or character of the goods sold. *See Werwinski v. Ford Motor Co.*, 286 F.3d 661 (3d Cir.2002). As Plaintiffs observe, some Pennsylvania lower courts continue to apply an exception to the economic loss rule for claims of intentional torts. *See, e.g., Teledyne Techs. Inc. v. Freedom Forge Corp.*, 2002 WL 748898 (Pa.Com.Pl. Apr. 19, 2002) (noting an absence of Pennsylvania case law on the subject and conflicting decision in Pennsylvania's federal courts). Yet, other Pennsylvania lower courts have approved the Third Circuit's logic in *Werwinski's* regarding the economic loss rule, as it pertains to claims brought under Pennsylvania's Unfair Trade Practices Act and Consumer Protection Law ("UTPCPL").

Notwithstanding some lower state court opinions to the contrary, the Court agrees with the reasoning of the Third Circuit in *Werwinski* and its conclusion that Pennsylvania's Supreme Court would apply the economic loss rule to bar claims of intentional fraud relating to the quality of the goods at issue, as opposed to fraud that had nothing to do with the quality of the good sold.

In an opinion largely adopted by Pennsylvania's Supreme Court, the United States Supreme Court adopted the economic loss doctrine, stating "a manufacturer has no duty under either negligence or strict-liability theory to prevent a product from injuring itself." *E. River S.S. Corp. v. Transamerica Delaval, Inc.*, 476 U.S. 858 (1986). The Court stated that "contract remedies would drown in a sea of tort" if products liability remedies progressed too far. *Id.* at 866. The Court also explained that "the need for a remedy in tort is reduced when the only injury is to the product itself and the product has not met the customer's expectations, or, in other words, that the customer has received insufficient product value." *Werwinski*, 286 F.3d at 671. The Court further stated, "The maintenance of product value and quality is precisely the purpose of express and implied warranties" and "warranty law sufficiently protects the purchaser by allowing it to obtain the benefit of its bargain." *E. River*, 476 U.S. at 874.

In *REM Coal Co. v. Clark Equip. Co.*, 386 Pa. Super. 401(1989), Pennsylvania's Supreme Court adopted *East River*. There, the court phrased the issue as:

> the appropriateness of permitting recovery in tort where a product malfunctions because of an alleged defect in the product but the malfunction causes no personal injury and no injury to any other property of the plaintiff. The question is whether a cause of action in tort, as opposed to one sounding solely in contract, is an appropriate vehicle for obtaining such a recovery.

The court explained that "contract theories such as breach of warranty are specifically aimed at and perfectly suited to providing complete redress in cases involving economic losses." The court elaborated, "All of such losses are based upon and flow from the purchaser's loss of the benefit of his bargain and his disappointed expectations as to the product he purchased. Thus, the harm sought to be redressed is precisely that which a warranty action does redress." Additionally, the court added that the proper focus of the economic loss rule is not on the type of risk associated with the defect, rather, it is "on the actual harm for which plaintiff seeks recovery." *Id.* Accordingly, the court held that the economic loss rule barred claims based on strict products liability and negligence. The court found that to hold otherwise "would certainly erode the important distinctions between tort and contractual theories." *Id.*

The logic expressed by *REM Coal* need not stretch far, if at all, to apply to claims of fraudulent concealment where a plaintiff alleges harm only to the product. The Court would vitiate the economic loss rule if it were to hold that the economic loss rule did not bar claims for intentional fraud, when that fraud directly relates to the quality of the product, and the only harm alleged is to the product itself. Essentially, any plaintiff could bypass the economic loss rule by adding a claim of fraudulent concealment to their complaint. Such a holding would erode the distinctions between tort and contract theories that Pennsylvania's Supreme Court has sought to preserve.

The Court finds, as did the Third Circuit in *Werwinski*, that Pennsylvania courts' use of the "gist of the action doctrine" in the fraud context lends support to application of the economic loss rule in the fraud context. *See eToll v. Elias/Savion Adver., Inc.*, 811 A.2d 10 (Pa. Super. Ct. 2002). The gist of the action doctrine "bars plaintiffs from bringing a tort claim that merely replicates a claim for breach of an underlying contract." *Werwinski*, 286 F.3d at 680. In *eToll*, the court elaborated upon the gist of the action doctrine, stating that "courts have not carved out a categorical exception to avoid fraud, and have not held that the duty to avoid fraud is always a qualitatively different duty imposed by society rather than by the contract itself." *eToll*, 811 A.2d at 19. "Rather, the cases seem to turn on the question of whether the fraud concerned the performance of contractual duties. If so, then the alleged fraud is generally held to be merely collateral to a contract claim for breach of those duties. If not, then the gist of the action would be the fraud." *Id.*

This distinction in the gist of the action doctrine—whether the fraud concerns the performance of contractual duties or whether the fraud is merely collateral to the contract claim—is essentially the same type of distinction the Third Circuit, in *Werwinski*, predicted the Pennsylvania Supreme Court would make regarding the economic loss rule.

In the case at hand, Plaintiffs claim Mazda fraudulently concealed information regarding the alleged Inflator Defect. Plaintiffs on the economic loss track have alleged only economic harm arising from this alleged fraudulent concealment. The alleged fraud pertains only to the quality of Mazda's product, i.e. the vehicle is not as safe (and may at times be lethally dangerous) as advertised. Accordingly, in the fraudulent concealment claims, Plaintiffs allege the same facts that would support breach of warranty claims. Accordingly, the Court holds the economic loss doctrine bars Birdsall's claim for fraudulent concealment.

Notes and Questions

1. <u>Using Contract Law to Swamp Tort Law?</u> Given that some narrow torts are recognized to remedy economic losses, does it make sense to deny recovery if a plaintiff has both claims? Doesn't that defeat the purpose underlying fraud, for example?

2. <u>Calamities and Dead Chickens</u>. Some courts hold that even if the injury is only to the product itself, a negligence claim is permitted but only if there is certain kind of event. "There is a general duty under tort law, independent of any contract, to avoid causing a sudden and calamitous event which, although it may only cause damage to the defective product itself, poses an unreasonable risk of injury to other persons or property." *Argonaut Midwest Ins. Co. v. McNeilus Truck and Mfg., Inc.*, 2013 WL 489141 (N.D. Ga. Feb. 8, 2013). Where the exception is recognized, fire and explosions and the like satisfy the accident exception. *E.g., Lumbermen's Underwriting Alliance v. Blout Int'l, Inc.*, 207 WL 7603709 (N.D. Ga. Feb. 5, 2007) (machine caught fire). But less traumatic events that cause damage to something other than the product can suffice. For example, in *WTI, Inc. v. Jarchem Indus.*, 2012 WL 3101656 (N.D. Ga. July 30, 2012), the defendant sold the plaintiff an ingredient used in processing chicken meat. The defendant sold the ingredient to Tyson. When Tyson used the ingredient, it injured the chickens. As a result, the plaintiff gave Tyson a credit and sued the defendant in negligence. The court held that because the ingredient had hurt something — Tyson's chickens — the economic loss rule was no bar to the negligence claim against the defendant.

3. <u>Damage to Other Property</u>. Other courts hold that a calamitous event is not enough — what is required is that the product damage something other than itself; otherwise, the economic loss doctrine bars all tort claims. As *Smith v. Nissan N.A., Inc.*, 2018 WL 4691612 (W.D. Tenn. Sept. 27, 2018), explained:

> Although certain products-liability cases addressing the economic-loss doctrine involve particularly calamitous occurrences, such as fires or crashes, the owner of a defective product that malfunctions and simply does not work is in the same position with respect to his or her ability to use the product. In the context of more calamitous events, the United States Supreme Court chose a bright-line rule that precludes recovery in tort when a product damages itself without causing personal injury or damage to other property. Thus, it follows that the remedies available to these similarly situated product owners in less calamitous cases of product defects should derive from the parties' agreements, not from the law of torts, lest we disrupt the parties' allocation of risk. To hold otherwise would make it more difficult for parties to predict the consequences of their business transactions. However existing law continues to permit tort recovery for personal injury and damage to property other than the product itself.

In *Indiana Farm Bureau v. CNH Indus., Am., LLC,* 130 N.E.3d 604 (Ct. App. Ind. 2019), the plaintiff purchased two products, months apart—a combine and a corn head—from the same seller, intending to use them together to harvest corn. The two parts had to be combined to do so. One part injured the other, and the court held that the economic loss doctrine prevented a tort claim, limiting the plaintiff to contract remedies, which were narrower. If the plaintiff had bought the parts from two sellers, would that matter? Would it matter if a combine could be combined, not only with a corn head, but other parts?

In *TreeHouse Foods, Inc. v. Sunopta Grains and Foods Inc.,* 2019 WL 1429337 (N.D. Ill. Mar. 29, 2019), the defendant was a commercial supplier of sunflower kernels who had sold kernels contaminated with listeria to the plaintiff, which in turn sold them to its customers. Among others, the plaintiff asserted a negligence claim and asserted it was within the Illinois approach that negligence claims were permitted if a "dangerous event" caused harm to "other property." The defendant moved to dismiss that claim, and the court, although skeptical, assumed that contamination was a "dangerous event," and reasoned that if the contaminated products had been mixed with other products, then the "other property" provision would be satisfied, but allegations that the plaintiff's equipment had been contaminated and it had resold the kernels were insufficient.

4. <u>Fraud</u>. Despite the fact that fraud requires economic harm as "damage," some courts apply the economic loss rule to bar them. For example:

- Michigan and New Jersey appear to bar fraud claims even where there is no privity of contract between plaintiff and defendant, if the misrepresentation relates to the quality or characteristics of the goods subject to the contract. Thus, under this approach, a defendant who intentionally misrepresents the quality of goods sold will, at most, be subject to contract remedies. *See Cyberco Holdings, Inc. v. Am. Express Travel Related Serv. Corp.,* 2002 WL 31324028 (S.D.N.Y. Oct. 16, 2002); *Murphy v. Procter & Gamble Co.,* 695 F. Supp. 2d 600 (E.D. Mich. 2000). The "is the fraud separate from the contract" approach appears to be the dominant view of the impact of the economic loss rule on fraud claims. *E.g., Schreiber Foods, Inc. v. Lei Wang,* 651 F.3d 678 (7th Cir. 2011) (Wisconsin law); *Ares Funding, LLC v. Ma Maricopa, LLC,* 602 F. Supp. 2d 1144 (D. Ariz. 2009).

- In Maine, the economic loss rule does not preclude fraudulent inducement claims, but does bar fraud claims if the "misrepresentation only goes to the quality or quantity of the goods promised in the contract." *Am. Aerial Serv., Inc. v. Terex USA, LLC,* 39 F. Supp. 3d 95 (D. Me. 2014). *See Strathmore Web Graphics v. Sanden Machine, Ltd.,* 200 WL 33975406 (W.D. Ky. May 16, 2000) (similar Kentucky rule).

- Minnesota's legislature has twice attempted to block application of the rule to fraud claims. *See Marvin Lumber & Cedar Co. v. PPG Indus., Inc.,* 223 F.3d 873 (8th Cir. 2000).

• Some courts—oddly—hold that this judicially developed doctrine can eviscerate a *statutory* fraud claim. *See G&F Graphic Serv., Inc. v. Graphic Innovators, Inc.,* 18 F. Supp. 3d 583 (D.N.J. 2014) (collecting cases that discuss this issue).

Consider some implications. Normally, a plaintiff can rescind a contract induced by fraud and elect to pursue fraud claims. Apparently, in states where no fraud claim is permitted, this is not possible. *See Ashland Hosp. Corp. v. Provation Med. Inc.,* 2014 WL 5486217 (E.D. Ky. Oct. 29, 2014). Does barring fraud mean fraud is the kind of harm expected in contracting? In other states, a plaintiff may plead breach of contract and fraud, but must make an election of remedies upon verdict. *Enhance-it LLC v. Am. Access Techn., Inc.,* 413 F. Supp. 2d 626 (D.S.C. 2006).

5. <u>Section 552 Negligent Misrepresentation</u>. Perhaps the most confusing application of the economic loss rule occurs when a plaintiff brings a Section 552 negligent misrepresentation claim. Some courts hold that a plaintiff with a contract cannot assert a claim under Section 552 against a party to the contract, while others hold that unless the plaintiff has a contract with the defendant, it cannot assert a Section 552 claim. *See* Garrett W. Hunkins, *The Current State of the Economic Loss Doctrine as Applied to Intentional and Negligent Misrepresentation Claims: A Comparative Analysis,* 87 U. Mo. K.C. L. Rev. 1085 (2016).

Problems

1. <u>Arbitration Clause</u>. Your client has asked you to draft an arbitration clause that requires the other party to arbitrate, but permits your client to seek specific performance and damages. What will you advise your client?

2. <u>Partnership Selling Land</u>. You are an appellate court judge on a three-judge panel, about to confer with your fellow judges on the propriety of the trial court's grant of a preliminary injunction. You believe the injunction was wrongly granted on the single ground of inadequacy of remedy at law, or irreparable harm. The plaintiff and defendants had a partnership agreement. The defendants had intended to sell the only asset of the partnership, and the plaintiff sued, asserting that selling the land would be a breach of contract and breach of fiduciary duty. Plaintiff seeks a preliminary injunction to prevent the depletion of the partnership's assets and to preserve sufficient funds in the partnership with which to satisfy any future money judgment in favor of the plaintiff. The trial court held the plaintiff had demonstrated an inadequate remedy at law because the unsold real estate was the partnership's only asset, and so if the defendants were not enjoined from selling it, the plaintiff faced the possibility of an uncollectible judgment. What arguments will you make to persuade your colleagues to reverse?

3. <u>Fired Employee</u>. You represent a client who, you believe, was fired from his job because the manager of the store where he worked held a grudge against him. In addition to a breach of contract claim against the employer, would a claim for intentional interference with contract likely succeed against the manager personally?

4. <u>Liquidated Damages Clause</u>. Your client has been sued for intentionally caus-ing the breach of a contract between the plaintiff and a third party. The actual dam-ages caused by the breach appear to be well over $500,000. However, the contract contains a liquidated damages clause stating that the exclusive remedy in the event of a material breach is $25,000. Assuming that it is enforceable, does that limit your client's damages, given that damages for intentional interference with contract are identical to breach of contract damages? What if, instead, actual damages were zero but a valid liquidated damages clause stated damages in the event of breach were $250,000. Could the plaintiff use that clause to recover damages?

5. <u>Excluding Consequential Damages</u>. Suppose the clause in the foregoing hypo-thetical stated:

> *Damages.* In no event will either party be liable to the other for incidental, special or consequential damages, including but not limited to loss of antic-ipated revenues or profits or good will, for the termination or cancellation of this Agreement for any reason whatsoever.

Is a party who tortiously interferes with that contract able to avoid liability for dam-ages excluded by the agreement? If not, why doesn't that place the plaintiff in a bet-ter position than performance?

6. <u>Losing Traction</u>. Your client, John Deere Company, entered into a four-year contract with Don Daring Company. Daring, through two stores, sells sporting goods, golf equipment, and residential yard equipment made by Deere. For what-ever reason, Daring was never able to meet the sales quotas sought by Deere. In fact, Daring operated at a loss for its business over the three years of the agreement (losses of $139,865 in 2018; $150,720 in 2017; and $172,783 in 2016). At the start of the final year of the contract, Deere had demanded that Daring buy an additional 44 "Turf Tater" lawn machines made by Deere, and that Daring hire an additional salesperson to "push the product out the door ASAP." Daring refused, and Deere terminated the contract. Daring has sued Deere for breach of contract, asserting that the demand to purchase the 44 Turf Tater machines and hire an additional salesperson breached the agreement. What form of damages are these? How will you argue they are not recoverable, and procedurally how will you make that argu-ment: (a) after discovery closes; (b) in pretrial motions; and (c) at trial?

7. <u>Catch Me Outside the CVS</u>? Imagine a plaintiff had, before an accident, taken guitar lessons and formed a band. The band was gaining an audience and had signif-icant YouTube views. A record producer, Rich Rubin—who had produced albums for the Arctic Monkeys and Hank Williams IX—had emailed the band about pos-sibly auditioning for a record contract. As a result of the accident, however, plaintiff can no longer perform. If Rubin testifies that he likely would have produced a rec-ord for the band, and if there is evidence that records produced by Rubin more often than not bring in more than $500,000 to each band member, how would a court likely rule on whether those lost profits are recoverable?

8. <u>A Damaged Boat</u>. Your client had agreed to buy a ship, the *Brazilian Friend-ship*, but the owner sold it to a third party, Pappas. The ship's former owner has no assets, and Pappas is the only likely defendant, and a claim for intentional interference with contract can be stated against him. Your client has proposed giving you a 35% contingent fee. You have investigated, and discovered letters showing that your client, had it been able to buy the *Brazilian Friendship*, intended to "flip it" six months later. During the six months they would have had ownership, they would have chartered the ship out to others (i.e., rented it like a car) to use for shipping. You have determined that the six months' of chartering revenue would have netted $3 million ($500,000 each month), and that the ship could have been resold for an additional net profit of $18 million. You know that Pappas resold the ship at about the same time your client had intended to, and netted $1.2 million. Your client had no intention of purchasing a different ship to use to generate revenue during the six months. Given those facts, what is the likely recovery? What if, instead, your client acquired a replacement vessel, but it took one full month after learning of the breach to find a replacement vessel? What if, in addition to that, they had to pay a higher fee to the replacement boat's owner, and so the net profit for each of the five months was $400,000? Would mental anguish damages likely be recoverable?

9. <u>Damaged or Not?</u> Your client came to you several months ago and asked how it could go about trying to get a customer, who had a contract with a competitor of your client, to breach that contract and instead make an agreement with your client. You advised your client of the scope of the claims that could be asserted. A few months after that, your client sent you an email and admitted offering a bribe of $10,000 to the president of the customer if he would switch to your client and breach the contract with the competitor. You advised your client to withdraw that offer and to not repeat it. Your client did so. Yesterday, your client called and said that the customer gave notice of termination to the competitor and had lawfully terminated the agreement. Your client then asked you to draft a contract between your client's business and the customer. However, you then received a complaint filed against your client asserting tortious interference. Liability?

10. <u>False Promise of Solvency</u>. Your client is a construction contractor. Defendants agreed to pay $325,000 for your client to build them a home. Defendants obtained a loan to fund construction. Six months into construction, they fell behind on payments.They assured your client they were able to fund the construction. Once construction was completed, they still owed $245,000 and they declared bankruptcy. The result was a foreclosure sale to a third party, and your client's business was destroyed, causing $2.4 million in damages above the $245,000 remaining on the contract. Your client has advised you whether it is limited to the $245,000 breach of contract damages or may, instead or in addition, seek fraud damages that would include potentially punitive damages, mental anguish, and, of course, the lost profits. Your client has been in business for many years with a successful history of profit.

11. <u>Lawyering Lesson</u>. You are representing Mr. Gao, who was an officer of Corporation A. On his behalf, you sued other corporate officers over mismanagement of that business. Those defendants counterclaimed, alleging he had mismanaged Corporation A. You have been ordered to mediation. At 11:00 p.m., the parties appeareed to have reached an agreement on key terms. The mediator has prepared a handwritten MOU, which states in full:

> The parties agree to negotiate in good faith to reach a definitive agreement embodying payment up to $7.3 million to Gao as follows:
>
> 1. $2,000,000 upon execution of this agreement and entry of dismissal with prejudice by the court (guaranteed)
>
> 2. $500,000 in 1/2020 (guarantee [sic])
>
> 3. Balance on non-guaranteed basis over 10 years from 2 based on Corporation A's profit.
>
> Gao returns shares
>
> Global resolution (including dismissals w [sic] prejudice of all litigation world [sic])
>
> Mutual covenant not to compete or impair mutual obligations
>
> Mutual releases

Is this enforceable? If not, before you leave a mediation where you believe settlement has been reached, what will you do? More importantly, before leaving to attend your first mediation session, what will you have in draft form on your laptop?

12. <u>Expelled</u>. Your client, McGaha University, was sued for wrongfully suspending a student, Mr. Morehouse, for one semester and for wrongfully removing 32 credits (about two semesters) from his transcript in retaliation for his complaints about the removal process. The evidence shows that your client breached its agreement with the plaintiff to follow written procedures before suspending him for one semester and removing two semesters' worth of credits. Morehouse's expert, a respected economist, has prepared a report quantifying his damages based upon lost income as if he had timely graduated from school. His expert offers two theories: (a) assuming a best-case scenario where Morehouse returned to school to complete his degree, his loss would be $103,377, which included an estimate of lost income based on an estimate of what he would be earning if he already had a degree, and additional tuition; and (b) assuming Mr. Morehouse did not finish college—which was statistically likely for someone his age out of school for more than six months, which he was as he was working at a local store—he would lose a million dollars in earnings over the course of his lifetime. Morehouse's expert opined the present value of a million dollars was $524,000. You are preparing your client's damages expert and helping her prepare a report. What flaws are in Morehouse's report, and what theory of damages will you use?

13. <u>Break-In</u>? Your client is a pharmacy, and someone broke in and stole a significant amount of drugs. The security system used by the pharmacy and operated by the defendant failed to immediately detect the break-in, and the defendant's employees ignored the alarms that eventually did go off. The thieves sold the drugs to addicts for about $1 million; your client would have made $100,000 in net profits in ordinary sales to consumers, and the wholesale cost of the drugs was $50,000. The defendant security company has admitted liability and offered $50,000 to settle. The thieves still have the $1 million, but assert that $50,000 is the proper measure of damages. Explain your pre-suit negotiating strategy, including arguments that $1 million is the proper measure of damages. Consider the arguments the security company's and thieves' lawyers will likely make and your responses to them.

14. <u>Billing Consultant</u>. One of your firm's long-time clients recently decided to retain an outside billing consultant to audit your firm's bills. Each year for the past 10 your firm had billed the client about $3 million, resulting in a profit of $2.3 million to the firm each year. The client advised you that the consultant advised it that more than $500,000 in recent billings were excessive and, as a result, it was not paying them; further, it was terminating its relationship with your firm. (Clients have the right to terminate lawyers at-will.) Does your firm have a claim against the consultant? What damages would be recoverable if its advice was negligent?

15. <u>Approaches to the Economic Loss Doctrine</u>. In Garrett W. Hunkins, *The Current State of the Economic Loss Doctrine as Applied to Intentional and Negligent Misrepresentation Claims: A Comparative Analysis,* 84 U.M.K.C. L. Rev. 1085 (2016), the author wrote:

> Commercial parties' claims should be limited to the law of contract with a few specific exceptions. Contracts generally leave contracting parties exposed to far more predictable liabilities than do tort actions; contract remedies reflect more the contract at issue rather than a jury's view of every scrap of evidence of harm a plaintiff can muster. Exemplary and punitive damages should be strongly limited to situations involving fraud and misrepresentations; instead the parties should bargain for and allocate the risks of negligence, misrepresentation, and liability for such conduct within the contract itself.

Do you agree? What is your state's approach to the economic loss doctrine?

Chapter 9

Remedies Triggered by Unjust Enrichment of the Defendant

The claims, or remedies, in this chapter are best thought of as narrow, gap-filling efforts by courts to avoid unjust results. Many are available only if a remedy in contract or tort is unavailable, but where leaving the parties as they are would result in the defendant retaining an unjust benefit. They are not commonly asserted, the law varies among the states, and often a state's law is not well developed. This chapter reviews common approaches to these doctrines in fact patterns where they do arise.

1. Promissory Estoppel

The elements of promissory estoppel are: "A promise which the promisor should reasonably expect to induce action or forbearance on the part of the promisee or a third person and which does induce such action or forbearance is binding if injustice can be avoided only by enforcement of the promise." Restatement (Second) of Contracts § 90(1) (1981). A plaintiff's detrimental reliance upon the promise must be "of a sufficiently definite and substantial nature so that injustice will result if the 'promise' is not enforced." *Miller v. Lindsay-Green, Inc.*, 2005-Ohio-6366 (Ct. App. 2005). Promissory estoppel is generally not available when the parties have an enforceable contract. *Univ. of Miami v. Intuitive Surgical, Inc.*, 166 F. App'x 450 (11th Cir. 2006). As a result, it is often asserted if the parties' contract is unenforceable, and courts often permit plaintiffs to plead both breach of contract and promissory estoppel. *Donald Marshall Berlin v. Bank of Am., N.A.*, 101 F. Supp. 3d 1 (D.D.C. 2015) ("Because it is not yet clear which side will prevail on the issue of whether the later agreement was a valid contract, Plaintiffs must be allowed to proceed with both claims.").

The remedies for promissory estoppel are flexible but based upon contract damage concepts. *See* Restatement § 90 cmt. d ("A promise binding under this section is a contract, and full-scale enforcement by normal remedies is often appropriate. But the same factors which bear on whether any relief should be granted also bear on the character and extent of the remedy. In particular, relief may sometimes be limited to restitution or to damages or specific relief measured by the extent of the promisee's reliance rather than by the terms of the promise."); *Walser v. Toyota Motor Sales, U.S.A. Inc.*, 43 F.3d 396 (8th Cir. 1994) (reliance damages awarded under promissory estoppel where lost profits were "far from a certainty"); *Merex A.G. v. Fairchild Weston Sys., Inc.,* 29 F.3d 821 (2d Cir. 1994) ("If successful on a promissory estoppel claim, the plaintiff is not entitled, as of right, to expectation damages; the court retains the discretion to award relief to avoid injustice, and can mold that relief as justice requires.); *Chedd-Angier Prod. v. Omni Publications Int.,* 756 F.2d 930 (1st Cir. 1985) (in permitting expectancy measure, court stated "whether to charge full contract damages, or something less, is a matter of discretion delegated to the district court"); *Hunter v. Hayes,* 533 P.2d 952 (Colo. Ct. App. 1975) ("When a plaintiff's recovery is predicated on findings of a promise and detrimental reliance thereon, there is no fixed measure of damages to be applied in every case. Rather, the amount of damages should be tailored to fit the facts of each case and should be only that amount which justice requires.").

Toscano v. Greene Music

21 Cal. Rptr. 3d 732 (Cal. App. 4th Dist. 2004) (O'Rourke, J.)

[Plaintiff Joseph Toscano was unhappy with his job as an at-will employee working as general manager of Fields Piano. He began to search for another job, and Greene Music offered him one in July 2001, to start on September 1, 2001, also as an at-will employee. He accepted and on August 1, 2001, resigned from Fields Piano. Two weeks later, Greene withdrew its offer. Toscano found lower wage jobs elsewhere.

Toscano sued Greene. Only his claim for promissory estoppel went to bench trial. The trial court rejected Greene's effort to exclude evidence of Toscano's expectancy damages in the form of wages from September 1, 2001, until his then-planned future retirement in 2017, including expert testimony putting lost wages at $417,772. The court awarded $536,833, reasoning that since Toscano had moved to higher-paying jobs in the past, he likely would have left Greene later for a better job. The court denied Greene's motion for new trial, and it appealed.]

As we explain, we hold a plaintiff's lost future wages from the former at-will employer are recoverable under a promissory estoppel theory as long as they are not speculative or remote, and are supported by substantial evidence.

Under the doctrine of promissory estoppel, a promise which the promisor should reasonably expect to induce action or forbearance on the part of the promisee or a third person and which does induce such action or forbearance is binding if injustice can be avoided only by enforcement of the promise. The remedy granted for breach may be limited as justice requires. Promissory estoppel is a doctrine which employs equitable principles to satisfy the requirement that consideration must be given in exchange for the promise sought to be enforced. The elements of promissory estoppel are (1) a clear promise, (2) reliance, (3) substantial detriment, and (4) damages measured by the extent of the obligation assumed and not performed.

Unless there is unjust enrichment of the promisor, promissory estoppel damages should not put the promisee in a better position than performance of the promise would have put him. However, such a limitation does not preclude recovery of some measure of future income relinquished as a result of a plaintiff's detrimental reliance. Conceptually, promissory estoppel is distinct from contract in that the promisee's justifiable and detrimental reliance on the promise is regarded as a substitute for consideration required as an element of an enforceable contract. There appears to be no rational basis for distinguishing the two situations in terms of the *damages* that may be recovered; both may involve the problem of ascertaining a future loss of profits, actually a problem of presenting adequate proof. Complete contractual recovery may include, under some circumstances, loss of profits when the loss is definite rather than speculative. Because the doctrine is equitable in nature, the court should have broad judicial discretion to fashion remedies in the interests of justice.

Given the equitable underpinnings of promissory estoppel a plaintiff who relinquished his job in reliance on an unfulfilled promise of employment, may on an appropriate showing recover the lost wages he would have expected to earn from his former employer but for the defendant's promise. Under these circumstances, such a damage measure is in keeping with the equitable nature of promissory estoppel. The object of equity is to do right and justice. It does not wait upon precedent which exactly squares with the facts in controversy, but will assert itself in those situations where right and justice would be defeated but for its intervention. It has always been the pride of courts of equity that they will so mold and adjust their decrees as to award substantial justice according to the requirements of the varying complications that may be presented to them for adjudication. The powers of a court of equity, dealing with the subject-matters within its jurisdiction, are not cribbed or confined by the rigid rules of law. From the very nature of equity, a wide play is left to the conscience of the chancellor in formulating his decrees. It is of the very essence of equity that its powers should be so broad as to be capable of dealing with novel conditions. Equity acts in order to meet the requirements of every case, and to satisfy the needs of a progressive social condition, in which new primary rights and duties are constantly arising, and new kinds of wrongs are constantly committed.

We apply the settled rule, however, that the court's damage award in these circumstances must not be speculative, remote, contingent or merely possible. Analogizing to a claim for lost profits, we conclude that damages for the loss of future earnings in this context are recoverable where the evidence makes reasonably certain their occurrence and extent.

Our holding necessarily rejects the notion that the at-will nature of Toscano's former employment with Fields is a strict impediment to recovery of future wages that Toscano would have earned at Fields had he not relied on Greene's promise. It is well settled that at-will contractual relations can be the subject of claims for intentional interference with contract, based on the principle that a third party's interference with an at-will contract is actionable interference with the contractual relationship because the contractual relationship is at the will of the parties, not at the will of outsiders. We see no reason why this principle should not extend to permit recovery of damages under the equitable theory of promissory estoppel here, where there is no dispute Greene induced Toscano to terminate his at-will employment relationship in reliance on an unfulfilled job offer. The trial court correctly concluded that under these circumstances, Toscano suffered a compensable loss at the hands of a third party. The only limitation on Toscano's recovery is that the fact and extent of his lost future earnings must be proven with reasonable certainty.

We conclude that even giving deference to the trial court's ruling and drawing all inferences in Toscano's favor, the evidence was too speculative to lend support to the trial court's award of Toscano's lost future earnings from September 1, 2001, to his retirement.

Roberta Spoon, Toscano's damages expert, testified that in calculating Toscano's lost wages for the remainder of his career, "all I have done is arithmetic. I have simply analyzed the numbers." She testified she was not aware that Toscano's employment with Fields called for any specific tenure. Indeed, Spoon admitted Toscano could have quit or been fired from that job from the time he resigned to the present. She simply assumed Toscano would have continued employment with Fields or another employer at a comparable salary, observing that he had never in the past changed employers for anything other than a pay increase.

Spoon's testimony does not establish Toscano had a definite expectation of continued employment with Fields for any particular period of time. Even drawing all inferences in Toscano's favor, it is evident her supposition was based only on Toscano's history of remaining with his employers until offered new employment. However, *Toscano's* intentions or practices are not relevant to whether he could expect to remain with Fields until his retirement, where his employment with Fields was at will. Even taking that evidence as true, evidence of Toscano's intentions does not establish with any reasonable certainty that Fields, an at-will employer who had the right to terminate Toscano at any time for any reason, had some different understanding of the terms of Toscano's employment, or that it would have continued to employ him until the end of his career. Neither party presented testimony from Jerry Goldman, Toscano's boss at Fields. An expert's opinion must not be based upon speculative or conjectural data. If the expert's opinion is not based upon facts otherwise proved or assumes facts contrary to the only proof, it cannot rise to the dignity of substantial evidence. Although the *fact* of Toscano's damage was established, Spoon's conclusions as to the *extent* of Toscano's lost employment were wholly conjectural. We cannot ascertain with any certainty how Spoon reached her assumption as to Toscano's continued employment, particularly in view of her admission that Fields could have fired Toscano for any reason.

The trial court further based its damages award on the fact there was "no evidence that indicates Toscano would have left Fields for a job which pays substantially less than he was earning there." But as we have stated, such evidence is insufficient to support a claim of lost future income from Fields to Toscano's retirement. As a consequence, we vacate the award of Toscano's lost wages from Fields calculated from September 1, 2001, to the date of his retirement in 2017 and remand the matter for a new trial on the matter.

The award of future earnings calculated from September 1, 2001 to the date of Toscano's retirement in 2017 is vacated and the matter remanded for a new trial on the issue of damages only. The judgment is otherwise affirmed.

Dynalectric Co. of Nev. Inc. v. Clark & Sullivan Constructors, Inc.
255 P.3d 286 (Nev. 2011) (Per Curiam)

[Clark and Sullivan Constructors, Inc. (C&S), was interested in serving as a general contractor of a project to expand a medical facility ("the Project"). To do so, it solicited bids from subcontractors to do parts of the work. Dynalectric Company submitted a bid to C&S to perform the Project's electrical work and assured C&S its bid was accurate. C&S incorporated Dynalectric's bid into its bid for the general contract. C&S was the low bidder, and it was awarded the contract. But, when Dynalectric repudiated its obligations, C&S had to pay other subcontractors to do the electrical work and paid more than Dynalectric's bid.

C&S sued Dynalectric, asserting promissory estoppel. The court awarded $2.5 million, the difference between the contract price with Dynalectric and what C&S paid replacement subcontractors. Dynalectric appealed.]

Following the Restatement, we hold that the district court may award expectation, reliance, or restitutionary damages for promissory estoppel claims. Although promissory estoppel is conceptually distinct from traditional contract principles, there is no rational reason for distinguishing the two situations in terms of the damages that may be recovered. In sum, no single measure of damages will apply to each and every promissory estoppel claim; instead, to determine the appropriate measure of damages for promissory estoppel claims, the district court should consider the measure of damages that justice requires and that comports with the Restatement's general requirements that damages be foreseeable and reasonably certain.

We now consider whether the district court used the appropriate measure of damages when it awarded C & S promissory estoppel damages representing the difference between Dynalectric's bid and the amount that the three replacement contractors charged C&S to complete the same work.

Drennan v. Star Paving Co., 51 Cal.2d 409 (1958), the seminal promissory estoppel case in the subcontract bidding context, illustrates how damages should typically be computed in this situation. In *Drennan,* a general contractor was preparing a bid for a construction project. Before the general contractor submitted its bid, a subcontractor submitted a bid of $7,131.60 to the general contractor to perform the paving portion of the project. The general contractor then incorporated the subcontractor's bid into its own bid for the project. Shortly thereafter, the subcontractor informed the general contractor that it would not perform the work for the price it had originally quoted in its bid. Ultimately, the general contractor obtained a replacement pavement subcontractor to complete the work at a cost of $10,948.60. The *Drennan* court affirmed the trial court's determination that the general contractor was entitled to $3,817, the difference between the subcontractor's bid and the amount that the general contractor had to pay the replacement subcontractor to complete the work.

In the decades since *Drennan*, courts have consistently and uniformly applied the same measure of damages for promissory estoppel claims arising from a subcontractor's repudiation of its obligations to a general contractor. *See, e.g., John Price Assocs., Inc. v. Warner Elec., Inc.*, 723 F.2d 755 (10th Cir. 1983) (appropriate measure of damages for general contractor's promissory estoppel claim was the difference between nonperforming electrical subcontractor's bid and the bid of the substituted subcontractor that completed the work); *Preload Tech. v. A.B. & J. Const. Co.*, 696 F.2d 1080 (5th Cir. 1983) (damages were properly calculated as the difference between the original subcontractor's bid and the replacement subcontractor's bid). We see no reason to depart from the well-established measure of damages used in *Drennan*.

As previously noted, Dynalectric's bid was for $7,808,983. C&S was forced to pay $10,310,598 to three replacement subcontractors to complete the work that Dynalectric refused to perform. Thus, the district court awarded C&S $2,501,615, the difference between Dynalectric's bid and the amount C&S paid to the replacement subcontractors. This measure of damages placed C&S in the same position that it would have occupied if Dynalectric had performed as it promised, and thus, it constitutes expectation damages.

It is plain that justice required this measure of damages and that the damages the district court awarded were foreseeable and reasonably certain. As the district court found, Dynalectric made an unequivocal promise by submitting a bid to C&S for the electrical subcontracting of the Project. Dynalectric thereafter repeatedly assured C&S of the accuracy of the bid that it had submitted. The record demonstrates that Dynalectric fully anticipated that C&S would rely on its bid by incorporating it into its own bid for the Prime Contract. The record also shows that Dynalectric is an experienced and sophisticated subcontractor that could readily anticipate that C&S would be forced to use replacement electrical subcontractors at a higher cost to complete the work that it refused to perform. Finally, the damages that the district court awarded were reasonably certain because C&S presented detailed evidence showing that $2,501,615 represented the difference between Dynalectric's original bid and the amount that the three replacement subcontractors charged.

Notes and Questions

1. <u>Reliance or Expectancy?</u> The court in *Dynalectric* essentially gave the plaintiff its benefit of the bargain damages (whatever profit it would have made on Dynaletric's bid, C&S made after being paid the difference in costs for the electrical work). What damages could Toscano recover on remand? A concurring opinion in *Devon Med., Inc. v. Ryvmed Med., Inc.*, 60 So. 3d 1125 (Fla. 4th Dist. App. 2011), examined

courts' approaches to promissory estoppel damages and indicated the result in *Dynalectric* may fall into an exception:

> The first approach is the plurality view, and it does not allow the party to recover his lost profits. According to this view, under promissory estoppel a plaintiff may recover only reliance damages, the amount necessary to restore the injured party to the position it would have occupied had the promise not been made.

> This state appears to follow the first approach. Three Florida cases have approved reliance damages for promissory estoppel in commercial law cases. In *Young v. Johnston*, 475 So.2d 1309 (Fla. 1st DCA 1985), the first district allowed a plaintiff whose putative contract with a homebuilder had fallen apart after the plaintiff failed to receive construction financing the damages he incurred in relying on the putative contract, *i.e.,* the money he spent in securing a loan commitment from the bank. The first district reversed the verdict for benefit-of-the-bargain damages, however, because there was no actual contract. *Id.* at 1314. Next, in *Revlon Group Inc. v. LJS Realty, Inc.,* 579 So.2d 365 (Fla. 4th DCA 1991), this court approved recovery of $144,000 for leasehold improvements made by the assignee of a lease, holding that the assignor was responsible under the "doctrine of promissory estoppel." Finally, in *Sunshine Bottling Co. v. Tropicana Prods., Inc.,* 757 So.2d 1232 (Fla. 3d DCA 2000), on a promissory estoppel claim, the third district allowed recovery of $592,000 that a bottling company "expended in restructuring its plant."

> Even those jurisdictions that allow the recovery of lost profits through promissory estoppel, however, require that the party prove them with reasonable certainty, something not done in this case. *E.g., Walters v. Marathon Oil Co.,* 642 F.2d 1098 (7th Cir. 1981) (holding that promissory estoppel, as an equitable doctrine, allowed the recovery of lost profits where the party had proven "the amount of the lost profits with reasonable certainty").

The court in *Heritage Constructors, Inc. v. Chrietzberg Elec., Inc.,* 2015 WL 3378377 (Ct. App. Tex. March 4, 2015), reached the opposite result from *Dynalectric* on the same facts. Heritage had been general contractor and had relied upon a bid from Chrietzberg to do electrical work, but Chrietzberg repudiated. Heritage obtained a verdict for the difference between Chrietzberg's bid and what it paid replacement contractors, but the court of appeals reversed:

> In this case, there was no evidence that distinguished any of the damages Heritage sought for promissory estoppel from the damages it sought for breach of contract, i.e., for the benefit of its unenforceable contract. Therefore, we sustain Electric's point of error that there is no evidence of damages recoverable under promissory estoppel. Since we have found that Heritage's breach of contract claim is barred by the statute of frauds and there is no evidence of damages recoverable under its promissory estoppel claim, we

hold that Heritage is not entitled to judgment on these claims. Having sustained Electric's error on these points, we need not address its other points related to the breach of contract and promissory estoppel claims, or the damages related to those claims. In addition, we need not address the points of error of Heritage related to the damages awarded under these theories.

What damages are recoverable to general contractors in Texas if the contract is unenforceable?

2. <u>Reliance</u>. In *Savage v. Shannon Const. Co.,* LLC, 2003 WL 22133728 (Conn. Super. Aug. 28, 2003), the plaintiff committed to buy a home, being constructed by the defendant, if the plaintiff could sell his current home and if he could get a mortgage sufficient to buy the new home. He never sold his home and could not obtain a mortgage, and so the builder, before the date it was to sell the home to the plaintiff, sold it to a third party. The court ordered the builder to refund, with interest, deposits the plaintiff had paid to the builder, but held that expenses the plaintiff had incurred were not recoverable under promissory estoppel:

> Reliance damages may be the measure of damages in a claim based on a theory of promissory estoppel, loss incurred by the plaintiff in reasonable reliance on the promise. A fundamental element of promissory estoppel, is the existence of a clear and definite promise which a promisor could reasonably have expected to induce reliance. Thus, a promisor is not liable to a promisee who has relied on a promise, if judged by an objective standard, he had no reason to expect any reliance at all. With no assurance to the defendant that he was a ready, willing, and able buyer at the time of the breach, the plaintiff is not entitled to reliance damages.

2. Restitutionary Remedies and Claims

Courts sometimes order a defendant to compensate a plaintiff for a benefit the plaintiff bestowed on the defendant to the extent it is unjust for the defendant to retain it. As the court in *Davenport v. Litton Loan Servicing, LP,* 725 F. Supp. 2d 862 (N.D. Cal. 2010) explained:

> A plaintiff advances a basis for obtaining restitution if he or she demonstrates defendant's receipt and unjust retention of a benefit. The fact that one person benefits another is not, by itself, sufficient to require restitution. Instead, the person receiving the benefit is required to make restitution only if the circumstances are such that, as between the two individuals, it is unjust for the person to retain it.
>
> The benefit of the narrower view is that it effectively delineates precisely what unjust enrichment means and how it works. There are several factual scenarios where a theory of unjust enrichment has historically supported restitution as a remedy. A plaintiff may, for example, advance a claim as

an alternative to breach of contract when the parties have a contract that was procured by fraud or is for some reason unenforceable. Or, where the plaintiff cannot assert title or right to possession of particular property, but nevertheless can show just grounds for recovering money to pay for some benefit the defendant received from him, the plaintiff has a right to restitution at law through an action derived from the common-law writ of assumpsit (this method implies a contract at law, or a quasi-contract). Finally, a plaintiff may seek restitution in equity, ordinarily in the form of a constructive trust or an equitable lien, where money or property identified as belonging in good conscience to the plaintiff could clearly be traced to particular funds or property in the defendant's possession.

While they agree on the concept that a defendant should not be unjustly enriched, courts disagree on the details. The court in *Rich v. Simoni*, 2014 WL 4978442 (N.D. W. Va. Sept. 30, 2014), noted that some courts treat these claims or remedies "as essentially the same" while others recognize "legally significant" distinctions between them. Some typical approaches are summarized below, but they are merely typical. Significantly, the remedy for the last two is, not merely an award of damages, but an award, on specific property, of a lien or of title.

Claim	Basis	Remedy
Quantum Meruit	If plaintiff had performed services for or conferred benefits on the defendant, the court implies a contract for defendant to compensate plaintiff.	Courts disagree on whether the remedy is the benefit to defendant, the cost to plaintiff, or either of the two.
Unjust Enrichment (or quasi-contract)	If plaintiff had performed services or conferred benefits pursuant to an illegal or unenforceable agreement, the court implies an obligation to compensate plaintiff.	An amount to prevent unjust enrichment to defendant.
Restitution	If defendant had obtained plaintiff's property through fraud or embezzlement, the court implies an obligation to compensate plaintiff.	An amount to prevent unjust enrichment to defendant.
Disgorgement	If defendant had obtained a benefit by breaching a fiduciary duty to plaintiff, court implies an obligation to compensate plaintiff.	An amount to disgorge ill-gotten gains from defendant, whether obtained from plaintiff or third parties.
Constructive Trust	If defendant would otherwise be unjustly enriched, court implies an obligation to transfer title to specific property or its proceeds to plaintiff.	An order establishing plaintiff holds legal title to specific property.
Equitable Lien	If defendant otherwise would be unjustly enriched, court imposes a lien on specific property or its proceeds to satisfy a debt related to that property.	An order establishing a lien in favor of plaintiff on specific property.

A. *Quantum Meruit* or Unjust Enrichment?

Some courts hold that if unjust enrichment is proven, then "*quantum meruit* is the measure of damages." *Johnson Utilities, LLC v. Swing First Golf, LLC,* 2015 WL 5084101 (Ct. App. Az. Aug. 27, 2015). Another court held that only *quantum meruit* is proper to recover the reasonable value of services rendered. *Learning Annex Holdings, LLC v. Rich Global, LLC,* 860 F. Supp. 2d 237 (S.D.N.Y. 2012) (dismissing unjust enrichment claim after jury verdict on both, which awarded one recovery of $14.6 million). And still another held that either *quantum meruit* or unjust enrichment was proper, but the measure of damages for each would be the value of services, not the benefit conferred. *C.A.F. & Assocs., LLC v. Portage, Inc.,* 2012 WL 5077677 (W.D. Ky. Oct. 18, 2012).

Further, courts disagree on whether unjust enrichment is a claim or a remedy that must be tethered to a claim. *Compare Ghirardo v. Antonioli,* 14 Cal. 4th 39 (1996) (standalone claim) *with Melchior v. New Line Prod., Inc.,* 106 Cal. App. 4th 779 (2003) ("unjust enrichment does not describe a theory of recovery, but an effect: the result of a failure to make restitution under circumstances where it is equitable to do so."). Either way, if a defendant has been unjustly enriched, the remedy may be a form of restitution. *See, e.g., Doe I v. Wal-Mart Stores, Inc.,* 572 F.3d 677 (9th Cir. 2009) ("Unjust enrichment is commonly understood as a theory upon which the remedy of restitution may be granted."); Restatement of Restitution § 1 (1936) ("A person who has been unjustly enriched at the expense of another is required to make restitution to the other."). As a remedy, it takes from the defendant and awards to the plaintiff a benefit the plaintiff bestowed on the defendant if it is unjust for defendant to retain that benefit.

Unjust enrichment is often used when the parties in fact had a contract and one party performed but the contract was illegal or unenforceable. *Martz v. PNC Bank, N.A.,* 2006 WL 3840354 (W.D. Pa. Nov. 30, 2006). If both parties performed, there can be no unjust enrichment, in part because there was no reliance on the invalid contract. *Id.*

The following cases are typical of fact patterns leading to *quantum meruit* or unjust enrichment claims, and each carries important lessons about introducing evidence of different measures of damages for these claims, given the uncertainty around the proper measure. As an example, in *Jaamsheed v. Johnson,* 2018 WL 3096601 (Conn. Sup. Ct. Feb. 26, 2018), the court stated the general measure of damages is "not loss to the plaintiff but the benefit to the defendant; although where the contract is unenforceable, the contract price may be evidence of value." Does the contract price reflect the value received, or given? In this regard, are courts drawing bright lines about which measure is correct—cost to defendant or value to plaintiff—when in fact the degree of enrichment might ordinarily best be fairly measured by the benefit received, but "can be measured by the reasonable value of the plaintiff's services in certain instances"? *Jones v. Mackey Price Thompson & Ostler,* 355 P.3d 1000 (Utah 2015).

Young v. Young

191 P.3d 1258 (Wash. 2008) (Sanders, J.)

[Plaintiff Judith Young wanted to move her otter sanctuary from rural Georgia. Judith's nephew, Jim Young, and his wife, Shannon Young, lived in Washington state and knew of property that might work for Judith, but it was run down and needed work. The three agreed that Jim and Shannon would do the work to make the property ready for Judith and her otters. Judith then bought the property in 1998 for $1,050,000 and included Jim's name on the title to allow him to obtain permits and approvals needed for the improvements. Based on their conversations, Jim believed Judith would compensate him for his work and expenses.

While working and living rent-free on the property, Jim and Shannon extensively remodeled the house, demolished an older farmhouse, repaired a number of outbuildings, replaced well equipment, cleared land, and replaced the fencing. Their work was of workmanlike quality or better. In 2001, they recognized Judith was not going to move, and the three agreed that the land would become a cattle ranch.

By the end of 2002, their relationship had soured. In early 2003, Judith sued Jim and Shannon to quiet title in Judith's name. They counterclaimed for unjust enrichment. Expert testimony established the improvements, if made by a contractor, would have cost Judith $760,382. The value of the property increased between $1,150,000 to $1,450,000, but only $750,000 to $1,050,000 of the increased value was attributable to Jim and Shannon's work. The trial court's approach to damages was reversed by the appellate court and Judith appealed.]

Jim and Shannon argue the measure of recovery is either the market value of the services provided or the increase in value attributable to their work. Judith argues the circumstances of the claimant affect the measure of recovery.

Jim and Shannon characterize the measure of recovery as "unjust enrichment" whilst Judith characterizes the measure of recovery as "*quantum meruit.*" As an initial matter we take this opportunity to conceptually clarify the distinction between "unjust enrichment" and "*quantum meruit.*" Washington courts have historically used these terms synonymously, but the distinction between them is legally significant. Our purpose is to standardize the nomenclature and eliminate unnecessary multiplicity of terms.

Three elements must be established in order to sustain a claim based on unjust enrichment: a benefit conferred upon the defendant by the plaintiff; an appreciation or knowledge by the defendant of the benefit; and the acceptance or retention by the defendant of the benefit under such circumstances as to make it inequitable for the defendant to retain the benefit without the payment of its value. In other words the elements of a contract implied in law are: (1) the defendant receives a benefit, (2) the received benefit is at the plaintiff's expense, and (3) the circumstances make it unjust for the defendant to retain the benefit without payment.

"*Quantum meruit*," on the other hand, is the method of recovering the reasonable value of services provided under a contract implied in fact. A contract implied in fact is an agreement depending for its existence on some act or conduct of the party sought to be charged and arising by implication from circumstances which, according to common understanding, show a mutual intention on the part of the parties to contract with each other. The services must be rendered under such circumstances as to indicate that the person rendering them expected to be paid therefor, and that the recipient expected, or should have expected, to pay for them. In other words the elements of a contract implied in fact are: (1) the defendant requests work, (2) the plaintiff expects payment for the work, and (3) the defendant knows or should know the plaintiff expects payment for the work.

In sum, "unjust enrichment" is founded on notions of justice and equity whereas "*quantum meruit*" is founded in the law of contracts, a legally significant distinction. After reviewing the trial court's findings of fact and conclusions of law, we find it is unclear whether there was a contract implied in fact or a contract implied in law. Clearly Judith received a benefit at the plaintiff's expense and the circumstances make it unjust for her to retain that benefit without payment. Equally clear, however, is Judith's request for the work, Jim's reasonable expectation of payment for the work, and Judith's knowledge that Jim expected compensation.

Under a contract implied in fact, Jim and Shannon's recovery would be limited to the value of services rendered. Nevertheless, Jim and Shannon do not to argue for an implied-in-fact contract. Therefore, we must determine Judith's obligation under an implied-in-law contract and the equitable theory of unjust enrichment.

In the abstract the issue is whether the proper measure of recovery under unjust enrichment is the market value of the services rendered or the claimant's actual cost to render those services. In real terms the issue is whether the trial judge properly deducted $258,516 from the cost Judith would have paid a normal contractor to perform the work performed by Jim and Shannon, or whether Jim and Shannon are entitled to the full amount despite not incurring certain costs normally incurred in a business relationship.

Washington law states the measure of recovery for unjust enrichment to a faultless claimant for the claimant's improvement to land is measured in one of two ways. It may be measured by the amount which the benefit conferred would have cost the defendant had it obtained the benefit from some other person in the plaintiff's position. Alternatively, it may be measured by "the extent to which the other party's property has been increased in value or his other interests advanced." Restatement (Second) Of Contracts § 371(b).

Here, the value of the first measure is $760,382 while the value of the second measure is between $750,000 and $1,050,000. Therefore, under Washington law Jim and Shannon are entitled to an award between $750,000 and $1,050,000. Within this range the trial court, reviewing the complex factual matters involved in the case, has tremendous discretion to fashion a remedy to do substantial justice to the parties and put an end to the litigation. Yet here the trial court awarded $501,866, supposing the circumstances of the claimant affected the quantum of recovery. We find no support for this proposition.

Certainly, when a court calculates the recovery for unjust enrichment not all cost is recoverable. As stated in the Restatement (Second) Of Contracts, "a party's expenditures in preparation for performance that do not confer a benefit on the other party do not give rise to a restitution interest." Restatement (Second) Of Contracts § 370 cmt. a; *see also Davenport*, 725 F. Supp. 2d 862 cmt. b (stating, "expenditures are excluded to the extent that they conferred no benefit."). Here, however, the trial court deducted "mobilization/demobilization costs; the cost of providing supervision, tools and general equipment; the cost for debris disposal; a markup for overhead and profit; and construction contingency; the cost of bonds; insurance and business taxes; and the cost of Washington State sales tax." Undoubtedly some of these costs conferred a benefit to Judith.

Contrary to the dissent's assertion, the benefits derived from some of these costs are independent of the formality of the relationship. For example, Judith benefited by having Jim and Shannon dispose of the debris generated by the improvements she requested. Moreover, Judith benefited by having Jim and Shannon provide tools and equipment. In short, justice requires Judith to pay for the benefit she received from these services. The trial court erred in totally deducting all of these costs without an examination of whether these costs had some consequential relationship to the value of the benefit conferred. Such a *blanket* exclusion of a plaintiff's overhead, costs, and profits is improper unless the court determines that they have *no* meaningful relationship to the value of the benefit conferred and the extent to which a defendant has been enriched.

Judith argues the court should not be constrained when calculating the unjust enrichment award based on improvements to real property. Instead, Judith argues, the trial court should have broad discretion to fashion a remedy based on the unique facts and circumstances of the parties. Judith's argument overlooks the focus of an unjust enrichment calculation.

The obligation to repay the debt or disgorge the value of the received benefit focuses on the *receiver* of the benefit, not on the *provider* of the benefit. *See* Restatement of Restitution: Quasi Contracts and Constructive Trusts § 155(1) (stating "the measure of recovery for the benefit thus received is the value of what was received"). Where money is awarded to protect a claimant's restitution interest, it may, depending on what "justice requires, be measured either by the reasonable value of what the other party has received, *as viewed through the eyes of the recipient,* by looking to what the recipient would have had to pay someone in the claimant's position to obtain the goods or services, or by the extent to which the other party's property has been increased in value.

Judith understands the phrase "in the claimant's position" to mean the court considers the claimant's circumstances when calculating his recovery. The claimant's position, however, refers to similar providers of like services, not the actual claimant; otherwise, the quantum of recovery would always be limited by the claimant's actual cost. Unjust enrichment recovery is limited only by the claimant's actual cost when the claimant is at fault. Here, neither Jim nor Shannon was at fault, so they are entitled to full restitution of Judith unjust enrichment. Phrased alternatively, Judith must disgorge the entire value of the benefit she received as determined by either the fair market value of the services rendered or the amount the improvements enhanced the value of the property.

Notably, Judith requested the work. Under circumstances where a person asks for and receives valuable improvements to property the person is required to pay the market value of what was received. *See* Restatement Of Restitution § 155, cmt. d (stating "the fact that she asked for them shows that they are of value to her and normally she would be required to pay the market price of such services.").

Judith's theory of recovery is based on preventing a supposedly unconscionable gain to the claimant. Yet, her theory of recovery permits a defendant to retain some benefit. Under circumstances where the claimant is at fault and/or the defendant did not consent to the benefit such a theory of recovery may be sound. But where the claimant is not at fault and the defendant agreed to the improvements, fairness and justice dictate the defendant should be held to pay the entire amount as measured by how much it would have cost the defendant to purchase the improvements or by how much the improvement enhanced the value of the property. Restatement Of Restitution, § 158, cmt. d (stating "where it is clear that the owner did desire improvements, it is fair that she should pay for them.").

We hold when calculating an unjust enrichment award in a quasi-contract action for improvements to real property the award may not be reduced by the claimant's actual cost absent fault by the claimant or inconsequential relationship to the benefit conferred to the defendant. We remand to the trial court for recalculation of Jim and Shannon's award.

Mogavero v. Silverstein

790 A.2d 43 (Md. Spec. App. 2002) (Salmon, J.)

[Plaintiff Samuel Mogavero had been a successful general contractor, retiring at 48 in 1985. He was friends with defendant Larry Silverstein, who resided in one of the warehouses Mogavero had converted into luxury lofts. In 1997, Silverstein allegedly orally agreed to pay Mogavero 5% of the costs to convert a warehouse into similar lofts. Silverstein fired Mogavero a year into the planning stages of the work, which resulted in successful new lofts.

Mogavero asserted breach of contract and *quantum meruit*. Silverstein obtained summary judgment on the contract claim, the court finding their oral contract was too indefinite as to the scope of Mogavero's work. The court also granted summary judgment on Mogavero's *quantum meruit* claim, holding that Mogavero was required to prove the value of the benefit of Mogavero's services to Silverstein, not the reasonable value of those services. Because Mogavero had only introduced evidence of the value of the services, not the benefit conferred on Silverstein, no evidence to support *quantum meruit*. Mogavero appealed.]

No Maryland case *explicitly* sets forth the elements that must be proven to establish a contract implied in fact. But cases from other jurisdictions have done so. For example, in *Eaton v. Engelcke Mfg., Inc.*, 37 Wash.App. 677 (1984), the court said:

> A contract implied in fact is an agreement depending for its existence on some act or conduct of the party sought to be charged and arising by implication from circumstances which, according to common understanding, show a mutual intention on the part of the parties to contract with each other. The services must be rendered under such circumstances as to indicate that the person rendering them expected to be paid therefor, and that the recipient expected, or should have expected, to pay for them. A true implied contract, or contract implied in fact, does not describe a legal relationship which differs from an express contract: only the mode of proof is different.

The Maryland cases seem to abide generally by the rule that if specific services are requested by the defendant, the contract is treated as one implied in fact and recovery is allowed for the reasonable value of the plaintiff's services; but if there is no meeting of the minds as to what services are to be rendered, the contract is treated as one implied in law, where the measure of damages is the amount, if any, of the defendant's gain-not the reasonable value of plaintiff's services.

As to the case at bar, it cannot be said that the parties entered into a contract implied in fact. The facts in this case are distinguishable from any of the cases where the Maryland courts have awarded implied-in-fact damages. In cases where implied-in-fact damages were found to be due, there was in every case a meeting of the minds as to the nature and extent of the duties undertaken by the plaintiff on behalf of the defendant. Here, as already demonstrated, there was no such meeting of the minds. To reiterate, for an implied-in-fact contract to exist, the obligation must arise from mutual agreement and intent to promise, when the agreement and promise have simply not been expressed in words, and there must be a meeting of the minds. Thus, no contract can be inferred; and if a contract cannot be inferred, no implied-in-fact contract can be said to exist.

Notes and Questions

1. <u>Result</u>? The *Mogavero* court held that Mogavero had been required to establish the value of the benefit of Mogavero's services to Silverstein and, without that evidence, there was no basis to award damages under *quantum meruit*. Why? Assuming Mogavero had proven the reasonable value of the services, how could the value of the benefit to Silverstein differ? Could it be more than the reasonable value? Less?

The *Mogavero* court held the plaintiff had established an "implied in law" contract, but required proof of the gain to Silverstein, and so affirmed summary judgment on that claim:

> On the other hand, appellant did prove an implied-in-law contract with appellees. While no assent between the parties and no meeting of the minds was proven, the law nevertheless implies a promise on the part of the defendants to pay. In such situations, the law requires restitution to the plaintiff of something that came into defendants' hands but belongs to the plaintiff in some sense. Mr. Mogavero failed to prove the value to the defendants of the services he rendered. Because restitution damages are the same as damages recoverable for unjust enrichment, and because the measure of damages for unjust enrichment is the gain to the defendant, not the loss by the plaintiff, the motions judge did not err when she granted summary judgment.

2. <u>No Benefit</u>. Some courts allow *quantum meruit* even if *no benefit* accrued to the defendant but services were "merely performed with knowledge and consent" of the defendant. *C.A.F. & Assocs., LLC v. Portage, Inc.*, 2012 WL 5077677 (W.D. Ky. Oct. 18, 2012). In *Isaacs v. Lawson*, 2012 WL 5274431 (Ct. App. Ky. Oct. 26, 2012), the defendant, Isaacs, owned land and was constructing a home. In a two-paragraph email, the Lawsons agreed to buy it, once completed, for $292,000, with $20,000 down, which they paid. As construction progressed, the Lawsons were permitted to have upgraded appliances installed, at their cost. The parties could not close, and the Lawsons sued, seeking specific performance or a $46,406, representing their down payment and the cost of the upgrades. The court held the real estate contract itself was unenforceable under the statute of frauds, but the defendant had known the plaintiffs were installing the upgrades. The trial court found plaintiffs entitled to all damages to avoid unjust enrichment, and the appellate court affirmed:

> Isaacs next argues that the circuit court erred in basing the award for the cost of the appliances and improvements on the Lawson's retail receipts rather than the increase in value of the home. He maintains that though the Lawsons paid retail prices for all of the items they purchased, as a builder, Isaacs and Cornett would have been able to purchase these items at a lower cost. Isaacs contends that the measure of damages under *quantum meruit* is not the amount that the Lawsons paid for the items, but rather the value received by Isaacs. The focus of his claim of error on this issue is that the measure of the remedy under the theory of *quantum meruit* is the value conferred upon Isaacs rather than the amount paid by the Lawsons.

> It is helpful to examine the distinction between *quantum meruit*, which requires no proof of the defendant's retained benefit, and the theory of unjust enrichment, which does require such proof:

>> *Quantum meruit* literally means as much as he has deserved. In like manner, the damages thereunder are based upon a legal fiction implying an obligation to pay reasonable compensation for services rendered.

Although never specifically enunciated in this Commonwealth, it has been recognized that recovery under *quantum meruit* does not depend upon the conferment or retention of a benefit, as such is not absolutely necessary for recovery. We are convinced that this is a correct statement of law.[3]

By contrast, unjust enrichment is a distinct theory of restitutionary relief wherein damages are based directly upon the benefit conferred and retained. To prevail upon an unjust enrichment claim, it must be demonstrated: (1) benefit conferred upon defendant at plaintiff's expense; (2) a resulting appreciation of benefit by defendant; and (3) inequitable retention of benefit without payment for its value. Unlike *quantum meruit,* a benefit must be conferred and retained before one may recover under unjust enrichment.

Thus, once the elements of *quantum meruit* have been proven, damages are awarded based on the value of the services rendered rather than the benefit received. We conclude that this rule is applicable to both goods and services rendered, as the elements of *quantum meruit* apply equally to both. Additionally, damages arising under the theory of *quantum valebat,* or the apparent 19th century analog to *quantum meruit* meaning "as much as it was worth," were overturned only upon a showing that they were flagrantly excessive.

The Lawsons offered proof of damages based on their cost of purchasing the appliances and improvements. Isaacs did not rebut this evidence before the circuit court nor offer countervailing proof of damages. The presumption is that a trial court conducts its proceedings according to law, and renders the correct judgment under the facts developed before it. Isaacs has not overcome this presumption, and based on the totality of the record and the case law, we find no error in the circuit court's determination of damages arising under the Lawsons' claim of *quantum meruit.*

In contrast, in *Martin v. Comcast Cablevision Corp.,* 338 P.3d 107 (Ct. App. N.M. 2014), the defendant cable company strung its cable on a line over plaintiff's land where two other lines had an easement. Plaintiff wrote to its owner and demanded compensation. Eventually, he sued for an order burying the cable and for past damages, asserting unjust enrichment. The court awarded $200 per month for diminished use of his land from their installation until they were buried. The trial court awarded rent but denied unjust enrichment. Plaintiff appealed, but the appellate court affirmed, reasoning nothing was taken by Comcast and so there was no "benefit" other than "the savings it realized by using Appellant's property without

---

3. Particularly, under the third element of quantum meruit, services must have been either: (1) accepted, (2) received, or (3) rendered with knowledge and consent. Thus, the services may have resulted in a "benefit" when accepted or received but may not have resulted in a benefit when merely performed with knowledge and consent. Simply put, a benefit may be conferred and retained under *quantum meruit*; however, same is not necessary to recover under *quantum meruit.*

paying for the privilege, *i.e.,* the rental value of the land." Do you agree? *See also Terrell v. Pippart,* 724 S.E.2d 802 (Ct. App. Ga. 2012) (former fiancé obtained *quantum meruit* for time and money spent improving home that he and ex fiancée had intended to live in).

3. <u>Contract a Bar</u>? Courts often permit plaintiffs to plead both a valid contract and, in the alternative, *quantum meruit,* relying on it only if the contract is held invalid or unenforceable. *Hercules, Inc. v. Tomaszewski,* 2011 WL 6951839 (Del. Ct. Comm. Pleas Dec. 29, 2011). *But cf. Duke Energy Indiana, Inc. v. Comcast of Indianapolis, LP,* 2015 WL 5554050 (S.D. Ind. Sept. 21, 2015) (requiring plaintiff plead why contract might be invalid, and if parties stipulate its validity, equitable claim was improper). Some courts hold unjust enrichment is unavailable if a contract exists, but others allow it; and still others hold a valid contract is "simply one of the factors considered" in equity. *S. Cnty. Post & Beam, Inc. v. McMahon,* 116 A.3d 204 (R.I. 2015); *see Delta Elec. v. Biggs,* 63 V.I. 876 (2011) (unjust enrichment "triggered only where there is no contract or under an unconsummated or void contract").

B. Restitution or Disgorgement?

McBride v. Boughton, 20 Cal. Rptr. 3d 115 (Ct. App. Cal. 2004), elaborated on the bases for restitution:

> There are several potential bases for a cause of action seeking restitution. For example, restitution may be awarded in lieu of breach of contract damages when the parties had an express contract, but it was procured by fraud or is unenforceable or ineffective for some reason. Alternatively, restitution may be awarded where the defendant obtained a benefit from the plaintiff by fraud, duress, conversion, or similar conduct. In such cases, the plaintiff may choose not to sue in tort, but instead to seek restitution on a quasi-contract theory (an election referred to at common law as "waiving the tort and suing in assumpsit"). *See, e.g., Murrish v. Industrial Indemnity Co.* (1986) 178 Cal.App.3d 1206 (election to waive tort and sue in assumpsit is a fiction that broadens remedies available to plaintiff, but does not create a contract where none existed). In such cases, where appropriate, the law will imply a contract (or rather, a quasi-contract),[6] without regard to the parties' intent, in order to avoid unjust enrichment.

In *Dunkin v. Boskey,* 82 Cal. App. 4th 171 (Ct. App. Cal. 2000), an infertile man (Dunkin) and a woman (Boskey), both unmarried, agreed in writing that Dunkin

---

6. "Quasi-contract" is simply another way of describing the basis for the equitable remedy of restitution when an unjust enrichment has occurred. Often called *quantum meruit,* it applies where one obtains a benefit which he may not justly retain. The quasi-contract, or contract 'implied in law,' is an obligation created by the law without regard to the intention of the parties, and is designed to restore the aggrieved party to his former position by return of the thing or its equivalent in money. The so-called 'contract implied in law' in reality is not a contract Quasi-contracts,

had parental rights to a child that Boskey planned to conceive through artificial insemination from an anonymous donor. The pair became estranged when the child was about two years old and Boskey moved and refused to allow Dunkin to visit. Dunkin sued for damages, but the court held the agreement was against public policy, but it was awarded damages in the form of restitution. In remanding to determine the amount, the court wrote:

> We add that the measure of damages to which appellant is entitled for unjust enrichment is synonymous with restitution. Restitution is defined as restoration of the status quo by the awarding of an amount which would put plaintiff in as good a position as he would have been if no contract had been made and restores to plaintiff value of what he parted with in performing the contract. In modern legal usage, its meaning has frequently been extended to include not only the restoration or giving back of something to its rightful owner, but also compensation, reimbursement, indemnification, or reparation for benefits derived from, or for loss or injury caused to, another. Ordinarily the benefit to the one and the loss to the other are co-extensive, and the result is to compel the one to surrender the benefit which he has received and thereby to make restitution to the other for the loss which he has suffered. Equitable considerations govern the award of unjust enrichment, however. Thus, a party seeking restitution must generally return any benefit that it has received. Respondent may therefore be entitled to an offset to the extent her conduct has conferred an incidental benefit on the economic interest of appellant that was harmed, but not for the benefit appellant received from his relationship with the child.

What might this measure of damages consist of?

Cross v. Berg Lumber Co.

7 P.3d 922 (Wyo. 2000) (Lehman, J.)

[Plaintiff Berg Lumber Co. in 1991 bought a road grader for $19,700. Without its knowledge, a contractor took it in late 1991 to grade a road for lumbering. In doing so, the contractor damaged trees and gates, buried irrigation ditches, and marred roads on a ranch owned by defendant, Cross. When Berg found out, the grader was on Cross ranch. Cross told Berg he wanted to use the grader to repair the damage that had been done. Berg agreed this was fair. Several months later, Berg sent a truck to get the grader, but Cross said he had not repaired all the damage. Again in 1992 and 1993, Cross would not let Berg get the grader. In 1996, when Berg called Cross,

---

unlike true contracts, are not based on the apparent intention of the parties to undertake the performances in question, nor are they promises. They are obligations created by law for reasons of justice.

Cross said the grader had been stolen, and Berg reported the theft to the police. In late 1996, Berg hired a plane and flew it over Cross's ranch and saw the grader.

Berg sued, seeking replevin of the grader and loss-of-use damages. At trial, the evidence showed the rental value of the grader was $2,500 a month. The trial court awarded plaintiff $67,500 for loss of use, based on $2,500 per month for 27 months between the date of conversion (October 1996) and the date of trial (January 1999) and ordered replevin. Defendant appealed.]

Although actions in replevin are restitutionary in character, they are classified as tort actions. Restitutionary damages may be an appropriate remedy for the tort of conversion where other methods of computing damages are inadequate. For some types of tort actions and for certain kinds of breaches of contract, the injured party has an option of seeking restitutionary recovery. In these cases, damages are measured by the benefits received by the defendant rather than the losses sustained by the plaintiff.

> The plaintiff may waive the tort and sue in assumpsit, meaning that the plaintiff can have a restitutionary recovery for the gains the defendant made by converting the chattel. For example, if the chattel was worth $10 when it was converted by the defendant, and he later sells it for $20, the plaintiff would choose this option.

Dobbs, *The Law of Torts* § 67 (2000).

Unjust enrichment is an indefinable idea in the same way that justice is indefinable. But many of the meanings of justice are derived from a sense of injustice, and this is true of restitution since attention is centered on the prevention of injustice. Not all injustice but rather one special variety: the unjust enrichment of one person at the expense of another. This wide and imprecise idea has played a creative role in the development of an important branch of modern law.

In modern terms, an action of assumpsit is not technically a waiver of tort, but rather it is the choice of one of two alternative remedies. "One whose money or property is taken by fraud or embezzlement, or by conversion, is entitled to restitution measured by the defendant's gain if the victim prefers that remedy to the damages remedy." Dobbs, *Law of Remedies* § 4.1(1)

Wyoming has recognized that restitutionary damages are historically related to, yet distinct from, the equitable cause of action termed "unjust enrichment:" The plaintiff's claim, as set out in his complaint, is for the benefit gained by the joint tortfeasors' action. If a benefit is derived by the wrongdoers, recovery may be had on the basis of a promise implied in law and the benefit recovered. The touchstone of the rule is the moral obligation arising out of unjust enrichment to the tortfeasor. The principle is of ancient origin. It has lost its early common law fictions and is firmly entrenched as a cause of action with only its "historical echoes" remaining.

Thus, restitution is an appropriate remedy for some tortious conduct. Despite the historic limitation on the assertion of equity jurisdiction, the availability of the legal restitution remedy is not dependent upon inadequacy of alternative remedies.

The phrase "unjust enrichment" is used in law to characterize the result or effect of a failure to make restitution of, or for, property or benefits received under such circumstances as to give rise to a legal or equitable obligation to account therefor. It is a general principle, underlying various legal doctrines and remedies, that one person should not be permitted unjustly to enrich himself at the expense of another, but should be required to make restitution of or for property or benefits received, retained, or appropriated, where it is just and equitable that such restitution be made, and where such action involves no violation or frustration of law or opposition to public policy, either directly or indirectly. Where wrongfully detained property has a value for use, the measure of damages is the value of such use during the detention period.

The district court in this case found that Cross' conduct was "certainly egregious," but did not rise to "the level of misconduct necessary to support attorney's fees or punitive damages." Although there are some overlapping policies underlying the doctrines supporting punitive damages and the unjust enrichment remedy, they are not the same. One purpose of tort damages is to compensate the plaintiff for his loss, but the measurement of such loss is not always an exact science. Since restitution may exceed mere compensation to the plaintiff without exceeding the defendant's unjust gain, it is not punitive. In the context of conversion, courts have recognized the legitimacy of restitutionary damages:

> However plausible, the appellant cannot be heard to say that his wrongful invasion of the respondent's property right to exclusive use is not a loss compensable in law. To hold otherwise would be subversive of all property rights since his use was admittedly wrongful and without claim of right. The theory of unjust enrichment is applicable in such a case.

Developers Three v. Nationwide Ins. Co., 64 Ohio App.3d 794 (1990). Thus, the unjust enrichment remedy is not punitive but is one method of compensating the plaintiff's loss. This remedy is particularly appropriate where the plaintiff's loss is more difficult to measure than the defendant's unjustly saved avoidance costs. Thus, "while inadequacy of the damage remedy is not a prerequisite to restitution, the fact of inadequacy strengthens the case for restitution." G. Palmer, § 1.6 at 39. Certainly, an award of restitution can be harsh and is not appropriate in all cases, but where a tortfeasor consciously and wrongfully misappropriates another's property, he should expect to be dealt with harshly:

> The remedy in restitution rests on the ancient principle of disgorgement. Beneath the cloak of restitution lies the dagger that compels the conscious wrongdoer to "disgorge" his gains. Disgorgement is designed to deprive the wrongdoer of *all gains flowing from the wrong rather than to compensate*

the victim of the fraud. In modern legal usage the term has frequently been extended to include a dimension of deterrence. Disgorgement is said to occur when a "defendant is made to 'cough up' what he got, neither more nor less." From centuries back equity has compelled a disloyal fiduciary to "disgorge" his profits. He is held chargeable as a constructive trustee of the ill-gotten gains in his possession. A constructive trustee who consciously misappropriates the property of another is often refused allowance even of his actual expenses. Where a wrongdoer is shown to have been a conscious, deliberate misappropriator of another's commercial values, gross profits are recoverable through a restitutionary remedy.

Warren v. Century Bankcorporation, Inc., 741 P.2d 846 (Okl. 1987) (emph. in original).

In the case at bar, it would be difficult to calculate Berg's loss in terms of opportunity costs. Also, by converting and concealing the grader and then lying about its whereabouts, Cross engaged in willfully deceptive misconduct that should be discouraged. For these reasons, application of the unjust enrichment remedy is appropriate. The question remains, how does one measure the amount to be disgorged? There are five factors that assist in measuring restitution:

1. the increased assets in the hands of the defendant from the receipt of property;

2. the market value of services or intangibles provided to the defendant, without regard to whether the defendant's assets were actually increased; that is, the amount which it would cost to obtain similar services, whether those services prove to be useful or not;

3. the use value of any benefits received, as measured by (i) market indicators such as rental value or interest or (ii) actual gains to the defendant from using the benefits, such as the gains identified in item (5) below;

4. the gains realized by the defendant upon sale or transfer of an asset received from the plaintiff;

5. collateral or secondary profits earned by the defendant by use of an asset received from the plaintiff, or, what is much the same thing, the savings effected by the use of the asset.

Dobbs, *Law of Remedies* § 4.5(1).

The damages awarded in this case are supported by the second factor, the market or rental value of the grader (even if the grader did not prove to be useful); the third factor, the use value of the grader; and the fifth factor, the savings effected by using the grader.

This measure of damages can be termed negative unjust enrichment, *i.e.,* the defendant was unjustly enriched by not having to rent a road grader. A benefit is conferred upon the defendant where, by tortiously using the plaintiff's property, he saves expense or loss that might otherwise be incurred—benefit is any form of advantage. Thus, to measure negative unjust enrichment or recoverable profit, courts may consider saving of expense. Unjust enrichment can occur when a defendant uses something belonging to the Plaintiff in such a way as to effectuate some kind of savings which results in or amounts to a business profit.

Historically, tort and contract have been the primary fonts of civil liability at common law; yet restitution based on unjust enrichment is also a vital legal theory. Not every circumstance demands application of the disgorgement principal; but in certain cases, where justice so requires, the law empowers judges and juries with this important tool to remedy wrongdoing. This is such a case.

Notes and Questions

1. <u>Home Run</u>? Had the grader owner sued for conversion, it would have obtained the grader's value at the time and place of conversion and loss-of-use damages. Why not sue for conversion, unless loss-of-use damages for conversion cannot exceed pre-tort fair market value?

2. <u>Attorneys</u>. In *Sheppard, Mullin, Richter & Hampton, LLP v. J-M Mfg. Co.*, 425 P.3d 1 (Cal. 2018), a law firm charged a client $3 million in fees. The client refused to pay the last $1 million and instead asserted that because the firm had an undisclosed conflict of interest, it had to disgorge some of the $2 million it had been paid. The court agreed:

> When a law firm seeks compensation in *quantum meruit* for legal services performed under the cloud of an unwaived (or improperly waived) conflict, the firm may, in some circumstances, be able to show that the conduct was not willful, and its departure from ethical rules was not so severe or harmful as to render its legal services of little or no value to the client. Where some value remains, the attorney or law firm may attempt to show what that value is in light of the harm done to the client and to the relationship of trust between attorney and client. Apprised of these facts, the trial court must then exercise its discretion to fashion a remedy that awards the attorney as much, or as little, as equity warrants, while preserving incentives to scrupulously adhere to the Rules of Professional Conduct.

3. <u>Disgorgement</u>. As noted in the introduction, "restitution" and "disgorgement" both permit awards exceeding the benefit conferred. In a case involving defendant's aiding and abetting another defendant's breach of fiduciary duty to the plaintiff, *Am. Master Lease LLC v. Idanta Partners, Ltd.*, 171 Cal. Rptr. 3d 548 (Ct. App. Cal. 2014), the court explained why:

> We begin with the law of restitution. An individual is required to make restitution if he or she is unjustly enriched at the expense of another. A person is enriched if the person receives a benefit at another's expense. Benefit

means any type of advantage. The fact that one person benefits another is not, by itself, sufficient to require restitution. The person receiving the benefit is required to make restitution only if the circumstances are such that, as between the two individuals, it is *unjust* for the person to retain it.

Disgorgement as a remedy is broader than restitution or restoration of what the plaintiff lost. There are two types of disgorgement: restitutionary disgorgement, which focuses on the plaintiff's loss, and nonrestitutionary disgorgement, which focuses on the defendant's unjust enrichment. Typically, the defendant's benefit and the plaintiff's loss are the same, and restitution requires the defendant to restore the plaintiff to his or her original position. However, many instances of liability based on unjust enrichment do not involve the restoration of anything the claimant previously possessed including cases involving the disgorgement of profits wrongfully obtained. The public policy of this state does not permit one to take advantage of his own wrong regardless of whether the other party suffers actual damage. Where a benefit has been received by the defendant but the plaintiff has not suffered a corresponding loss or, in some cases, any loss, but nevertheless the enrichment of the defendant would be unjust the defendant may be under a duty to give to the plaintiff the amount by which the defendant has been enriched.

Moreover, it is not essential that money be paid directly to the recipient by the party seeking restitution. The emphasis is on the wrongdoer's enrichment, not the victim's loss. In particular, a person acting in conscious disregard of the rights of another should be required to disgorge all profit because disgorgement both benefits the injured parties and deters the perpetrator from committing the same unlawful actions again. Disgorgement may include a restitutionary element, but it may compel a defendant to surrender all money obtained through an unfair business practice regardless of whether those profits represent money taken directly from persons who were victims of the unfair practice. Without this result, there would be an insufficient deterrent to improper conduct that is more profitable than lawful conduct.

Disgorgement based on unjust enrichment is an appropriate remedy for aiding and abetting a breach of fiduciary duty. For example, in *County of San Bernardino v. Walsh, supra,* 158 Cal.App.4th 533, the defendant, the vice-president of a waste management company, was negotiating a new contract with the county. He and the former county administrative officer (CAO) agreed to bribe the current CAO to award the contract to the waste management company, along with an additional consulting agreement that would benefit the former CAO and the defendant. When the county discovered the bribery scheme, the county sued the current CAO, the former CAO, and the defendant. Affirming the trial court's decision finding them liable for breaching or inducing a breach of the current CAO's fiduciary duty, fraud, unfair competition, and unjust enrichment, the Court of Appeal held: "Disgorgement of profits is particularly applicable in cases dealing with breach of a fiduciary duty, and is a logical extension of the principle that public officials and other fiduciaries cannot profit by a breach of their duty. Where a person profits from transactions conducted by him as a fiduciary, the proper measure of damages is full disgorgement of any secret profit made by the fiduciary regardless of whether the principal suffers any damage." *Id*. Even though the defendant was not in a fiduciary relationship with the county, the court held that his "active participation in the breach of fiduciary duty by another rendered him accountable for all advantages he gained thereby." *Id*.

Note that "disgorging" the benefit from the defendant is deemed insufficient to prevent intentional harmful conduct. Does that also explain the grader case? If a person could take a chattel and never pay more than its value, but its use exceeds that, is conversion—if capped by loss-of-use damages—sufficient, or is the equitable remedy of restitution needed?

C. Constructive Trust or Equitable Lien?

While the elements of these two claims are similar, the remedies are radically different: "while both may serve to remedy unjust enrichment, the difference is that restitution is measured differently—where the constructive trust gives a complete title to the plaintiff, the equitable lien only gives him a security interest in the property." *Rawlings v. Rawlings*, 358 P.3d 1103 (Utah 2015). Although not awarding title to plaintiff, a plaintiff with an equitable lien has much more leverage than a money judgment—particularly if the defendant has one, or few, assets. Constructive trusts or equitable liens also may be imposed upon specific proceeds of specific property:

> Under the Restatement, constructive trust is not confined to a buyer-seller relationship and it "permits the claimant to assert ownership of (i) specifically identifiable property for which the defendant is liable in restitution or (ii) its traceable product by the rules of §§ 58-59." Restatement § 55 cmt. g. The first scenario arises when the property on which a claimant seeks to impose a constructive trust is the same property in dispute in the underlying litigation. See Restatement § 55 cmt. g. The second scenario arises when the property in dispute in the original litigation or the proceeds from its disposal has been commingled with defendant's other property. See Restatement § 55 cmt. g. Section 59, to which comment g to section 55 refers, provides that, "If property of the claimant is deposited in a common account or otherwise commingled with other property so that it is no longer separately identifiable, the traceable product of the claimant's property may be identified in property acquired with withdrawals from the commingled

fund, or a portion thereof." Restatement § 59. In this scenario, even if direct identification of a claimant's asset is impossible, section 59 creates "tracing fictions," giving claimant "the ability to trace the claimant's assets" when "there have been intermediate withdrawals from a commingled fund." Restatement § 59 cmt. d. These are also known as the "tracing rules."

Yokozeki v. Carr-Locke, 2017 WL 1160569 (D. Mass. March 28, 2017). Courts use different approaches to "tracing" but it "simply allows a plaintiff to trace the specific property or a particular fund when the defendant has either commingled it with the defendant's other assets or exchanged it for other property. *See* 53 C.J.S. *Liens* § 29 (2012) ("[W]here the owner of property subject to a lien commingles it with other property alike in quality and value, the lien is not extinguished so long as there is on hand sufficient property alike in quality and value to satisfy the lien."); id. § 49 ("If the property on which an equitable lien is held has been sold before foreclosure, the court can trace the funds from the sale and impress a lien upon any property acquired with the proceeds.")."

Lawry v. Palm

192 P.3d 550 (Ct. App. Colo. 2008) (Graham, J.)

[Defendant Roy Palm owned Frying Pan Anglers, Inc., a fly-fishing retailer and licensed outfitter—meaning it could provide commercial guide services on Colorado rivers. Palm personally owned a forest service permit, SOP89, that gave FPA that right. Plaintiff Robyn Lawry had worked for FPA for several years. In 2003, Palm agreed to sell Lawry his shares of FPA for $150,000, to be paid over 18 months. He also agreed to work for a salary for FPA for 10 years as a consultant. Palm told Lawry that SOP89 could not be in FPA's name, but had to be in his own, but their agreement provided he would hold the permits solely for FPA's benefit.

The parties proceeded, and FPA bought another permit—the "Grizzly Permit." However, a year later, Palm resigned. He also told the Forest Service that FPA was no longer authorized under either SOP89 or the Grizzly Permit. As a result, FPA could not guide anglers and its employees quit. Lawry sued, asserting a constructive trust over SOP89. The trial court granted that relief, ordered Lawry to pay the remaining amount owed on the $150,000, and ordered Palm to transfer the Grizzly permit. Palm appealed the award of a constructive trust over SOP89.]

A constructive trust is a flexible equitable remedy that may be imposed to prevent unjust enrichment. It enables the restitution of property that in equity and good conscience does not belong to the defendant. By imposing a constructive trust, a court awards the successful plaintiff a personal order requiring the defendant to transfer specific property to the plaintiff. The doctrine of constructive trusts is extremely flexible.

Here, the Forest Service permits are the principal means by which FPA earns revenue. The parties' agreement contemplated that Permit SOP89 would be held in trust and used exclusively in FPA's name and for its benefit. Specifically, the agreement acknowledges that the permits held by defendant "are necessary for and relevant to the operation and running of the Business by FPA"; that defendant will hold the permits "absolutely for the benefit of the business"; and that the "continued holding and availability of these licenses is integral to the ongoing viability of the business." One could hardly posit a clearer example of a business asset upon which a constructive trust can be imposed.

Defendant also argues that, because the trial court rejected the breach of fiduciary duty claim, concluding that no confidential relationship existed between the parties, no constructive trust could be imposed. However, a confidential relationship is not a requirement for imposing a constructive trust. A constructive trust can attach to property obtained by fraud, duress, *or* the abuse of a confidential relationship, *or* to any other property that 'in equity and good conscience' does not belong to the constructive trustee.

In its decision to impose a constructive trust, the trial court found that the parties were in a "continuing business relationship" and that defendant abused that relationship by misadvising Lawry "into believing that only defendant could hold the permit," and by failing properly to disclose "his knowledge of the permitting system to wrongfully deprive FPA of the permit which was part and parcel of the sale of FPA." The court also found that plaintiffs "relaxed their vigilance due to defendant's representations that he would hold the permits and work for FPA for 10 years"; that defendant's misrepresentations concerning the permit "induced Lawry to allow defendant to retain the permit upon the transfer of the business"; and that "Lawry was justified in her trust of defendant, and defendant abused Lawry's trust by retaining the assorted permits." Finally, the court determined defendant would be unjustly enriched if he were allowed to "retain a primary asset of the business."

In its order denying defendant's motion for C.R.C.P. 59 relief, the trial court affirmed its decision to impose a constructive trust on Permit SOP89, but did so without making a specific finding that a confidential or other business relationship existed between the parties:

> The Court determined that the agreement between the parties ("Agreement") set forth terms indicating that Plaintiffs were to retain Defendant's services as an employee or independent contractor for a period of ten years. As noted by the Court, the primary purpose of the Agreement was to effectuate the sale of Frying Pan Anglers, Inc. to Lawry. Importantly, under the terms of the Agreement, the Permit was to be held by Defendant for the exclusive use and benefit of FPA, which created value in the Permit. At the suggestion of Defendant, as seller, and the uninformed agreement by Lawry, as buyer, the Permit was to be held for the exclusive benefit of Frying Pan Anglers, Inc., as the Permit plays an integral role in the successful operation of the business. The Agreement thus contemplated that

upon cessation of Defendant's service to FPA, Defendant was required to facilitate the transfer of the Permit by executing and submitting the United States Forest Service *Holder Initiated Revocation of Existing Authorization Form,* FS-2700-3a ("Form"). The Court opines that it would be manifestly unjust to permit Defendant to retain the Permit if he is no longer serving Frying Pan Anglers, Inc. in any capacity. The Court serves as a mechanism, through its imposition of a constructive trust, to compel Defendant to initiate in good faith the submission of the Form, while the United States Forest Service determines whether transfer will ultimately be effectuated.

We are not persuaded by defendant's argument that his representation to Lawry—that only he could hold Permit SOP89—was a representation of law, and therefore, not actionable. In support of this argument, defendant relies on *Two, Inc. v. Gilmore,* 679 P.2d 116 (Colo. App. 1984), which states: "A representation of law is only an expression of opinion and is impotent to void a contract or support an action for damages. A representation of what the law will or will not permit to be done is one upon which the party to whom it is made has no right to rely. If he does so it is at his own risk. The truth or falsehood of such a representation can be tested by ordinary vigilance and attention." *Id.*

Even if defendant's representation was one of law, plaintiffs have not sought to void the contract or enforce defendant's representation concerning the transferability of the permit. Rather, plaintiffs sought to enforce defendant's express promise under the contract to hold the permit for the absolute benefit of FPA. Thus, defendant's reliance on *Gilmore* is misplaced.

For the same reasons, we also reject defendant's contention that the trial court's imposition of a constructive trust was in error because plaintiffs unjustifiably relied upon defendant's misrepresentations concerning the permitting process and had a duty to inquire as to the transferability of the permit.

In re Courson

409 B.R. 516 (Bankr. E.D. Wash. 2009) (Rossmeissl, J.)

[Courson had an ownership interest in Randalls Auto Sales, Inc. He took a loan from First Security Bank to buy a boat and trailer for $37,874. As part of the loan, Courson was required to keep the boat and trailer insured. Wells Fargo Bank acquired the loan from First Security Bank.

Randalls sold the same boat and trailer at about the same time for $34,000 to Jeff Buxton, who used a loan from Gesa Credit Union to do so. It also required him to insure the property. Buxton insured the boat through Safeco Insurance Company. A year later, the boat and trailer were destroyed in an accident. Safeco paid Gesa $29,200 for the loss. Neither Gesa nor Safeco knew of Wells Fargo's loan.

Courson declared bankruptcy. Wells Fargo obtained a nondischargeable judgment against Courson for $37,874. It then sought to assert an equitable lien on the proceeds that Safeco had paid to Gesa. Gesa moved to dismiss that claim.]

The Washington Supreme Court has recently restated the principles upon which an equitable lien can be declared.

> An equitable lien will be enforced in equity against specific property, though there is no valid lien at law; equity imposes liens either to carry out the intention of the parties to give a security or to prevent injustice, regardless of the intent. Equitable liens fall into two categories: (1) "those created to give effect to an intention of the parties to secure payment of an obligation by subjecting to the payment of an obligation specified property, such as equitable mortgages and equitable pledges, and (2) those created by the court to protect a party against inequitable loss, regardless of intent.

Sorenson v. Pyeatt, 158 Wash.2d 523 (2006).

The first category of equitable liens secures the intentions of the parties. Wells Fargo and Gesa did not intend to deal with each other; therefore, they had no mutual intentions to be enforced. An equitable lien can not be declared based on this category of equitable liens.

The second category of equitable liens protects against an inequitable loss. It is under this category that Wells Fargo seeks a lien.

The seminal Washington case on the issue of equitable liens is *Falconer v. Stevenson,* 184 Wash. 438 (1935). It speaks of the limits of the remedy: "But the doctrine of equitable lien has its prescribed boundaries as well as that of subrogation; it is not a limitless remedy to be applied according to the measure of the conscience of the particular chancellor any more than, as an illustrious law writer said, to the measure of his foot." 184 Wash. at 442.

The appellants in *Sorenson* urged the court to adopt a more expansive interpretation. The court declined this invitation saying in part: "It is a well established rule that an equitable remedy is an extraordinary, not ordinary form of relief. A court will grant equitable relief only when there is a showing that a party is entitled to a remedy and the remedy at law is inadequate."

The *Sorenson* decision refers to a number of circumstances where equitable liens can be imposed including securing property settlement, alimony payments, the award of community property, and imposing an equitable lien where defendant purchased a property with money embezzled from the plaintiff. *Sorenson* stands for the proposition that the equitable lien remedy is a narrow one to be applied only in certain limited and recognized circumstances.

One of the areas where Washington courts have recognized equitable liens as an appropriate remedy deals with insurance proceeds where the first party has covenanted to insure property against loss for the benefit of a second party but has taken insurance only in his own name. In such cases the courts will impose an equitable lien on the insurance proceeds for the benefit of the second party. A number of other Washington cases recognize the propriety of imposing an equitable lien in this limited circumstance.

Here Wells Fargo seeks to expand the concept of equitable liens beyond the limited scope of the facts in the cases above cited. It is not seeking to establish an equitable lien against Courson its debtor, who had covenanted to keep the collateral insured for the benefit of First Security Bank. Nor does it seek to establish an equitable lien against Buxton, Courson's successor in interest, who might arguably be bound by the covenant to insure for the benefit of Wells Fargo. It did not sue Buxton, rather it seeks to impose and enforce an equitable lien against Gesa, a party with which it did not deal.

The attempt to extend the doctrine of equitable lien beyond the narrow confines of existing law was explicitly rejected in the case of *Sorenson*. There the court in rejecting a plea to "step outside the parameters" of the existing case law said: "It must be kept in mind that an equitable lien is a remedy for debt determined to be owed in law. In each equitable lien case brought to our attention, an equitable lien was imposed only upon the property or interest owned by the person incurring the debt." 158 Wash.2d at 537. The court then continued:

> In sum, the Lenders have not provided this court with authority which establishes that a Washington court may impose an equitable lien upon the property of a third party in order to satisfy a judgment entered against another person who has been determined to legally owe the debt. What is more, applying general equity principles, we do not see how we would be preventing an injustice by allowing the legal rights of Sorenson in this case to be cut down in order to provide the Lenders a "meaningful" remedy for Barbara Pyeatt's fraudulent conduct.

Courson is the person that owes the debt to Wells Fargo. Wells Fargo is seeking to impose and enforce an equitable lien against Gesa, a party not liable for Courson's debt. Applying *Sorenson*, Wells Fargo is not entitled to an equitable lien against Gesa, unless some general equity principle should be invoked to prevent an injustice.

Security Bank/Wells Fargo financed Courson's purchase of a boat and trailer from Randall's and perfected its security interest. Courson had some interest in, or position with, Randall's. Randall's sold the Courson boat and trailer to Buxton, who financed the purchase through Gesa, which took a security interest in the collateral although that security interest was not perfected. Neither Buxton nor Gesa were aware at the time that the boat and trailer were First Securities/Wells Fargo's collateral. Buxton, and then Gesa, learned about the title problem on the collateral about a year after the purchase. Buxton insured the boat and trailer with Safeco and made Gesa the loss payee on the policy. The boat was destroyed and Safeco paid

Gesa for the loss pursuant to the policy. Only after the loss was paid did Safeco learn of Wells Fargo's interest.

Wells Fargo, Buxton and Gesa are all innocent victims of Courson's misdeeds. It is not clear why equity would intervene to benefit one innocent party against another. Wells Fargo argues that Gesa was somehow negligent in the transaction and, therefore, the loss should fall on it. On facts much more egregious, in *Sorenson*, the court refused to impose an equitable lien on Sorenson's property despite the fact that she had participated in activity that amounted to a fraudulent transfer of the property to avoid creditors and possibly even drug enforcement officials. If such conduct did not justify imposition of an equitable remedy, the relatively innocent action of Gesa in this case does not support an equitable remedy.

The *Sorenson* court discusses this requirement of balancing equities as follows:

> It is a fundamental maxim that equity will not intervene where there is an adequate remedy at law. In determining whether to exercise equitable powers, Washington courts follow the general rule that equitable relief will not be accorded when there is a clear, adequate, complete remedy at law. Furthermore, we think it a good equity policy that the person against whom the legal remedy is sought and authorized should be the same person against whom the equitable remedy is sought.

The respondents in *Sorenson* had argued that their remedy at law against Pyeatt was inadequate because Pyeatt did not have enough funds and property to pay the judgment. The court dismissed this argument observing that the remedy at law was valid, even if the likelihood of payment was small.

In this case, Wells Fargo has a valid remedy at law against Courson in this court's non-dischargeable judgment against him. Its questionable collectibility does not alter that fact. In any event, Wells Fargo seeks an equitable remedy against Gesa, who is not liable at law, and such equitable relief is not available under *Sorenson*.

Estate of Cowling v. Estate of Cowling

847 N.E.2d 405 (Ohio 2006) (Pfeifer, J.)

[Grace and Garnard Cowling married in 1967, each having been married before and each with children from a prior marriage. By the mid-1990s, each had various brokerage accounts with joint rights of survivorship. In 1996, Grace transferred exclusive control to Garnard, who put them into an account he designated as transfer-on-death ("TOD") to his children by a prior marriage. Garnard died in 1998, and $325,538.69 in stocks transferred on his death to his three children, the Cowlings.

Grace filed an equitable claim against the Cowlings, asserting a constructive trust over the funds, fraud, and other claims. At trial, Grace's expert testified that 74% of the funds were attributable to contributions she had made, basing that opinion on her investments, the sale of stocks, and tax returns and other evidence. The jury found Grace had proven $255,354 in damages.

The Cowlings still possessed the stocks at trial, but then sold them to make cash deposits as security for appeal, and those funds were held by the Lorain County Clerk. The Cowlings appealed and the court of appeals reversed the holding of an equitable trust. Grace appealed. After holding the jury had properly been instructed to determine Grace's net contributions, the court addressed the imposition of a constructive trust based upon tracing.]

The parties agree that tracing is a necessary predicate to the imposition of a constructive trust in Ohio. See *Ashley S. Hohimer, Constructive Trusts in Bankruptcy: Is an Equitable Interest in Property More Than Just a "Claim"?* (2003), 19 Bankr. Dev.J. 499, 510–511 ("Tracing is a process where the claimant basically must be able to point to the identifiable property or fund and say, 'This is mine.' If the funds or property are untraceable—meaning the claimant cannot determine where they were deposited or what the debtor has done with them—the equitable remedy is not available").

A claimant seeking the imposition of a constructive trust must specify the particular property over which the constructive trust is to be placed. If the form or possessor of the property over which the constructive trust should be placed changes during a lawsuit, the claimant should be given an opportunity to conduct discovery, if necessary, and present evidence of the new location or form of the property over which the trust should be placed.

A constructive trust is an equitable remedy that must be imposed on particular assets, not on a value. For example, if a party is inequitably deprived of 100 shares of stock that are valued at $10,000, a constructive trust should be imposed over 100 shares of stock, not $10,000. The value of the stock may decrease to $9,000 through no fault of the present possessor. In that instance, it would be inequitable to impose a constructive trust for a higher dollar amount than the stock's new value. Similarly, should the stock rise, the beneficiary of a constructive trust should not be deprived of that increase in value.

Constructive trusts should be placed over the property of the party who wrongfully obtained the property. When, as in this case, the property was subsequently transferred to third parties, a constructive trust can be imposed.

We must consider whether Grace's estate presented sufficient evidence regarding her claim for the imposition of a constructive trust to defeat a motion for directed verdict and a motion for judgment notwithstanding the verdict. We must consider whether Grace's estate presented clear and convincing evidence of the inequitable situation or unjust enrichment that would result if the Cowlings retain the assets and whether Grace's estate provided clear and convincing evidence tracing the assets from the joint and survivorship accounts in the name of Grace and Garnard to property held by the Cowlings.

Garnard withdrew all of the assets that he subsequently transferred to his children from joint and survivorship accounts that were in his and Grace's names. Grace's estate presented evidence indicating that these withdrawals exceeded Garnard's contributions. Garnard transferred all of the assets that he had withdrawn from the joint and survivorship accounts to his children. Construing this evidence most strongly in Grace's estate's favor, reasonable minds could only conclude that inequity had been proven by clear and convincing evidence. We conclude that Grace's estate presented sufficient evidence with respect to this element of a constructive-trust claim to survive motions for a directed verdict and judgment notwithstanding the verdict.

As to the tracing requirement, the parties stipulated that at the time of the trial, the assets that Garnard had transferred to his children were in the same form in which Garnard had received them. According to the stipulation, the Cowlings retained the assets throughout the trial and (with the exception of Reddington, who paid her share of the assets to Grace's estate) then sold the assets to post cash deposits for an appeal. We conclude that the evidence and stipulations on the record are sufficient to satisfy the tracing requirement.

This case is in equity. Despite the imprecision of some of the standards we apply in equity, we can only conclude, under any standard, that the Cowlings would unjustly benefit in the absence of a constructive trust. Accordingly, we reverse the decision of the court of appeals. The trial court's order for a constructive trust, however, cannot stand unmodified.

The trial court did not specify the particular assets over which the constructive trust was to be imposed. That was error, and we hereby order that the constructive trust be specifically imposed over the assets currently held by the Lorain County Clerk of Courts. The trial court ordered that the constructive trust be placed over a specific dollar amount, which now, given the conversion of assets into cash, is appropriate. At the time, however, the trust should have been placed over the proportion of the specific assets held by the Cowlings that equaled Grace's net contributions, as determined by the jury.

The total value of the assets on February 8, 1998, the day of Garnard's death, was $325,358.69. The jury determined damages of $255,354.00. The trial court order should be modified to place a constructive trust over 78.5 percent ($255,354.00 divided by $325,358.69) of the assets held by each appellee in their current form.

We hereby order the reinstatement of the trial court's order for the imposition of a constructive trust and modify the order to place the constructive trust over the assets currently held by the Lorain County Clerk of Courts.

Notes and Questions

1. <u>What If Wells Fargo Had Succeeded</u>? Would it have obtained what it lent Courson, or what Safeco paid Gesa? Why does the fact that Courson is unlikely to pay a judgment to Wells Fargo insufficient to show an inadequate remedy at law?

2. <u>Comparison to Constructive Trust</u>. If a court awards a plaintiff a money judgment, the plaintiff becomes a judgment creditor of the defendant with no right to specific property. An equitable lien is on specific property and permits the plaintiff to seek to foreclose on the lien or allows the court to order its sale. *See Jones v. Bourassa*, 383 S.W.3d 888 (Ct. App. Ark. 2011) (court awarded daughter an equitable lien on home in father's name to extent she had made improvements to it, noting trial court had "ordered the clerk of the court to sell the property at public auction if judgment was unsatisfied thirty days after order entered"). How does that differ from the remedy of constructive trusts?

3. <u>Commingling</u>. The *Cowling* case involved tracing stocks to cash. Where cash is intermingled with other funds, tracing becomes more complex. The significance of tracing cannot be understated if the defendant lacks assets to pay the plaintiff (and other creditors): "'Equitable' restitution requires tracing the money or property the plaintiff seeks to recover to identifiable assets in the defendant's possession (thus permitting imposition of a constructive trust or equitable lien), whereas 'legal' restitution seeks imposition of a merely personal liability upon the defendant to pay a sum of money." *F.T.C. v. Com. Planet, Inc.*, 815 F.3d 593 (9th Cir. 2016). Courts use four different approaches to trace funds in comingled accounts:

> Courts have adopted several approaches to tracing exempt funds in a commingled account, including: (1) the lowest intermediate balance approach ("LIBA"); (2) the pro-rata approach; (3) the last-in, first-out approach ("LIFO"); and (4) the first-in, first-out approach ("FIFO"). LIBA operates on a common-sense view that dollars are fungible and cannot practically be earmarked in an account. Under LIBA, proceeds are presumed to remain in the account as long as the account balance is equal to or greater than the amount of the proceeds deposited. Under the pro-rata approach, withdrawals from a commingled account are attributed to the several funds in proportion to their respective sizes at the time of the withdrawals. Under LIFO, withdrawals against the account reduce the most recent deposits first, while under FIFO they reduce the oldest first.

In re Wiltsie, 463 B.R. 223, 227–28 (Bankr. N.D.N.Y. 2011). The Restatement (Third) of Restitution and Unjust Enrichment § 59 (2011) emphasizes flexibility:

> (1) If property of the claimant is deposited in a common account or otherwise commingled with other property so that it is no longer separately identifiable, the traceable product of the claimant's property may be identified in
>
> > (a) the balance of the commingled fund or a portion thereof, or
> >
> > (b) property acquired with withdrawals from the commingled fund, or a portion thereof, or
> >
> > (c) a combination of the foregoing,
>
> in accordance with the further rules stated in this section.

(2) If property of the claimant has been commingled by a recipient who is a conscious wrongdoer or a defaulting fiduciary (§ 51) or equally at fault in dealing with the claimant's property (§ 52):

(a) Withdrawals that yield a traceable product and withdrawals that are dissipated are marshaled so far as possible in favor of the claimant.

(b) Subsequent contributions by the recipient do not restore property previously misappropriated from the claimant, unless the recipient affirmatively intends such application.

(c) After one or more withdrawals from a commingled fund, the portion of the remainder that may be identified as the traceable product of the claimant's property may not exceed the fund's lowest intermediate balance.

(3) If property of the claimant has been commingled by an innocent recipient (§ 50), the claimant's property may be traced into the remaining balance of the commingled fund and any product thereof in the manner permitted by § 59(2), but restitution from property so identified may not exceed the amount for which the recipient is liable by the rules of §§ 50 and 53.

(4) If a fund contains the property of multiple restitution claimants (such as the victims of successive fraud by the recipient):

(a) Each claimant's interest in the fund and any product thereof is determined by the proportion that such claimant's contributions bear to the balance of the fund upon each contribution and withdrawal, but only if the accounting necessary to this calculation can be established without using the presumptions or marshaling rules of § 59(2).

(b) If the evidence does not permit the court to distinguish the interests of multiple restitution claimants by reference to actual transactions, such claimants recover ratably from the fund and any product thereof in proportion to their respective losses.

(5) The balance from time to time of a commingled fund may be determined by whatever method of accounting is practicable and appropriate to the circumstances of a particular case.

3. Resulting Trust

Patterson v. Patterson

2017 WL 1433310 (Ct. App. Tenn. Apr. 20, 2017) (Stafford, J.)

[In 2003, Plaintiff Peggy Patterson ("Stepmother") and her husband ("Father"), collectively ("Homeowners") bought a home. Shane Patterson ("Stepson") did not contribute to the purchase but lived there. Stepson alleged they had agreed he would pay the mortgage and other costs, and eventually they would convey the home to him. He made improvements and payments on the property. Father passed away in 2015 and Stepmother sued to eject Stepson from the property.

Trial testimony was in sharp conflict as to any agreement. Stepson testified he had made improvements including repairing a chicken coop ($7,000), wrapping a barn in tin ($8,000), and building a horse barn ($22,000), for a total of $37,000. He argued for a resulting trust and sought unjust enrichment in the alternative. The trial court awarded possession to Stepmother and ordered her to pay $37,000 as unjust enrichment damages to Stepson but denied his claim for a resulting trust. Both parties appealed.]

> The imposition of a resulting trust is an equitable remedy; the doctrine of resulting trust is invoked to prevent unjust enrichment. Such a trust is implied by law from the acts and conduct of the parties and the facts and circumstances which at the time exist and surround the transaction out of which it arises. Broadly speaking, a resulting trust arises from the nature or circumstances of consideration involved in a transaction whereby one person becomes invested with a legal title but is obligated in equity to hold his legal title for the benefit of another, the intention of the former to hold in trust for the latter being implied or presumed as a matter of law, although no intention to create or hold in trust has been manifested, expressly or by inference, and there ordinarily being no fraud or constructive fraud involved.
>
> While resulting trusts generally arise (1) on a failure of an express trust or the purpose of such a trust, or (2) on a conveyance to one person on a consideration from another—sometimes referred to as a "purchase-money resulting trust"—they may also be imposed in other circumstances, such that a court of equity, shaping its judgment in the most efficient form, will decree a resulting trust—on an inquiry into the consideration of a transaction—in order to prevent a failure of justice. However, the particular circumstances under which a resulting trust may arise varies from jurisdiction to jurisdiction.

In re Estate of Nichols, 856 S.W.2d 397 (Tenn. 1993). However, the overriding principle pertaining to resulting trusts is that the trust must arise at the time of the purchase, attach to the title at that time and not arise out of any subsequent contract or transaction.

Resulting trusts can be proven by parol evidence, with the following caveat: A trust may rest upon parol agreement where the declaration of trust is made prior to or contemporaneous with the transfer of the interest in realty. Ordinarily, the testimony of a single, interested witness would not be sufficient to establish a trust by clear, cogent and convincing evidence. The parol testimony may be admitted, not to show an agreement to purchase for another, but to show that the purchase money was paid by the party claiming, notwithstanding the deed was taken in the name of another person.

At the outset, we note that Stepson's testimony that an agreement had taken place prior to the purchase of the property may not be used to establish a resulting trust. Rather, his testimony that he actually incurred an obligation to pay at the time of the purchase of the property would be relevant to support his claim. Stepson does not dispute that he did not contribute to the down payment, did not participate in closing, and did not sign any agreement obligating him to pay for the property. Thus, the issue becomes whether Stepson met his burden of proving a resulting trust based only on his testimony, and Brother's testimony, that he incurred an obligation to pay based on a purported agreement with Homeowners prior to the purchase of the property.

Here, in its written order, the trial court found that Stepmother and Father "used their own money to make the $50,000.00 down payment to purchase the property" and that Stepson "did not participate in the purchase or closing of the property and did not furnish consideration for the purchase of the property." As a result, the trial court concluded that "a resulting trust has not been proven by the evidence."

Accordingly, where the facts are disputed as to the purpose of the purchase of the property, it seems clear that Tennessee law requires one of the following to be shown by clear and convincing evidence in order to establish a resulting trust: (1) that the party claiming the trust contribute to the initial payment of the purchase price; or (2) that the party claiming the trust incurred an absolute legal obligation to pay at the time of the purchase of the property, typically by signing a promissory note allowing the record owner to purchase the property. Neither scenario has been shown by clear and convincing evidence in this case. Based on the foregoing, we cannot conclude that the trial court erred in finding that Stepson failed to establish the necessary elements of a resulting trust by clear and convincing evidence.

4. Equitable Indemnity or Equitable Subrogation

Frymire Engr. Co. v. Jomar Int'l., Ltd.

259 S.W.3d 140 (Tex. 2008) (Willet, J.)

[Renaissance Hotel hired Price Woods, Inc., as general contractor for renovations to a hotel. Price Woods retained Frymire Engineering, Inc., as a subcontractor to do HVAC work. In its contract with Price Woods, Frymire agreed to indemnify Price Woods or the hotel for any damage it caused and to have insurance, which it obtained from Liberty Mutual Insurance Company. Frymire in its work used a valve made by Jomar International, Ltd. The valve failed and flooded the hotel, causing $460,000 in damages. The hotel demanded payment, and Liberty Mutual paid.

Liberty Mutual and Frymire then sued Jomar for equitable subrogation for Liberty Mutual's payment to the hotel (and Frymire's payment of the deductible). The hotel did not sue Jomar. Jomar moved for summary judgment, but there was evidence that Jomar's valve in fact had been defective. The trial court granted the motion, the court of appeals affirmed, and Frymire and Liberty Mutual appealed.]

The doctrine of equitable subrogation allows a party who would otherwise lack standing to step into the shoes of and pursue the claims belonging to a party with standing. Texas courts interpret this doctrine liberally. Although the doctrine most often arises in the insurance context, equitable subrogation applies in every instance in which one person, not acting voluntarily, has paid a debt for which another was primarily liable and which in equity should have been paid by the latter. Thus, a party seeking equitable subrogation must show it involuntarily paid a debt primarily owed by another in a situation that favors equitable relief.

The court of appeals held that Frymire failed to satisfy any of these requirements, determining that Frymire paid the hotel owner "to satisfy its own contractual obligation" and that the payment was voluntary and did not unjustly enrich Jomar. Frymire contends that the court of appeals misapplied the subrogation requirements. According to Frymire, the indemnity payment extinguished the tort debt primarily owed by Jomar; the indemnity payment was an involuntary payment made pursuant to a binding contractual obligation; and Jomar will be unjustly enriched if it escapes liability for its defective product because of Frymire's contractual payment. We address each of these issues in turn, considering the evidence in the light most favorable to Frymire, the nonmovant.

A right to subrogation is often asserted by one who pays a debt owed by another, but we have yet to directly address what constitutes a debt owed by another. Frymire contends that it satisfied Jomar's debt by paying for the damages incurred by the hotel and is thus entitled to recoup that payment through equitable subrogation. Jomar counters that the debt in question is the contractual debt owed by Frymire to the hotel. Jomar claims that Frymire covered the damage according to the terms of a contract to which Jomar was not a party and of which Jomar did not have notice, thus satisfying a debt owed by Frymire. Furthermore, Jomar argues that Frymire should be prevented from asserting the rights of a party, the hotel, to which Frymire was directly indebted.

Jomar correctly argues that Frymire's contractual payment fulfilled a debt owed by Frymire to the hotel; however, the satisfaction of this contractual debt does not foreclose the existence and satisfaction of another debt owed by Jomar to the hotel. We have previously permitted subrogation-based claims to proceed under similar circumstances.

In *Keck, Mahin & Cate v. Nat'l Union Fire Ins. Co. of Pittsburgh, PA*, 20 S.W.3d 692 (Tex. 2000) an excess insurer, acting on behalf of its insured, settled a lawsuit against the insured according to the terms of the policy. The excess insurer then sued the primary insurer for negligence and the defending law firm for legal malpractice, asserting claims on behalf of the insured under the doctrine of equitable subrogation. The underlying facts in *Keck* are strikingly similar to the facts highlighted by Jomar in this case. The insured relied on the excess insurer for payment and never sought to recover damages from the law firm or the primary insurer. Furthermore, the excess insurer's settlement payment fulfilled a contractual obligation owed to the insured and was made according to a policy to which the law firm and the primary insurer were not parties and of which they did not have prior notice. Nevertheless, we permitted the excess insurer's claims to proceed.

Jomar attempts to distinguish *Keck* on the basis of its context and the identity of the party receiving payment. Unlike *Keck,* this case does not arise in the context of excess liability insurance. Additionally, the excess insurer in *Keck* satisfied its contractual debt with the insured through payment to a third party whereas Frymire paid a contractual debt directly to the hotel owner. These differences do not persuade us to reach a different result here. Equitable subrogation applies in *every* instance in which one person has paid a debt for which another was primarily liable.

In response to Jomar's summary judgment motion, Frymire presented a report on the water leak from its expert, Johnie Spruiell. Spruiell determined that a properly designed valve would not have failed under these circumstances. We conclude that Frymire satisfied its summary judgment burden to provide evidence that a design defect primarily caused the rupture, and therefore, that Jomar is primarily responsible for the resulting damage.

Having determined that Frymire showed some evidence that it paid a debt primarily owed by Jomar, we turn to the next, and most frequently disputed, element of equitable subrogation — an involuntary payment. A payment is voluntary when the payor acts without any assignment or agreement for subrogation, without being under any legal obligation to make payment, and without being compelled to do so for the preservation of any rights or property. Texas courts are liberal in their determinations that payments were made involuntarily. According to Jomar, Frymire voluntarily entered the contract and voluntarily satisfied the hotel owner's demands for payment, so it is not entitled to equitable subrogation.

Our equitable subrogation holdings describe involuntary payments as legal obligations and payments that are made for the protection of some interest of the party making the payment; these descriptions easily encompass a contractual obligation. Frymire would lack standing to seek equitable subrogation if Frymire had contracted with Jomar, rather than with Price Woods, to pay the hotel's damages caused by Jomar. This common-sense reading reflects the equitable nature of equitable subrogation.

Jomar's argument that Frymire cannot assert equitable subrogation because its indemnity payment was under a voluntary contract would, if accepted and applied to other contracts, be a radical departure from long-settled Texas subrogation law. For instance, insurance policies are contracts, too, and if the hotel's property insurer had paid the hotel for the cost of repairs pursuant to a policy agreement, it would certainly be able to assert an equitable subrogation claim against Jomar.

The situation here is not much different. Frymire agreed to "indemnify and hold Price Woods, Inc. and [the hotel owner] harmless from any and all liability which may be incurred by reason of Frymire's performance of the work." When the water line ruptured, the hotel owner made a claim on Frymire for indemnification under the contract. In this case, no legal duty obligated Frymire to confer a benefit on Jomar—Frymire paid the hotel owner to satisfy contractual indemnity obligations owed to Price Woods. Frymire's decision to contract with Price Woods was voluntary; its duty to honor that contract was not. Having acted to satisfy a legal obligation and to protect its interests under the contract (and its reputation in the marketplace), Frymire involuntarily extinguished a debt primarily owed by Jomar to the hotel owner.

Even though Frymire has shown evidence that its indemnity payment satisfies the first two elements of equitable subrogation, it must still show that the circumstances of the case favor equitable relief. According to Jomar, the hotel owner could have pursued tort claims against Jomar but chose not to; therefore, any hypothetical tort claims against Jomar should not be relied upon for determining unjust enrichment. Given the evidentiary presumption that Jomar's faulty product primarily caused the water damage, we have no trouble concluding that Jomar would be unjustly enriched were Frymire not permitted to pursue its claims.

We hold that Frymire has standing to pursue its claims against Jomar under the doctrine of equitable subrogation because the evidence supports Frymire's contentions that it (1) paid a debt primarily owed by Jomar, (2) did so involuntarily, and (3) seeks subrogation in a situation where Jomar would be unjustly enriched if Frymire were precluded from pursuing its claims.

Notes and Questions

1. Equitable Fiction. Equitable subrogation has been called "a legal fiction whereby one party stands in the shoes of a creditor to pursue a claim belonging to that creditor." *Holley v. Holley and Taylor, Inc.,* 2017 WL 549010 (Ct. App Tex. Feb. 10, 2017). Was the payment by Frymire "involuntary?" What does "involuntary" mean? Further, which element of equitable subrogation was satisfied by the fact that Jomar's product had caused the damage?

2. Equitable Indemnity and Contractual Indemnity. Common law indemnity is generally unavailable if a contractual right exists. In *Liberty Mut. Ins. Co. v. Milender White Constr. Co.,* 2017 WL 6361418 (D. Colo. Dec. 13, 2017), Milender White Construction Company had a subcontract for Double H Masonry to perform masonry work. The property owner required MWCC to obtain a payment bond—guaranteeing every subcontractor would be paid—and MWCC obtained a bond from Liberty Mutual Insurance Company. As part of the agreement with Liberty Mutual, MWCC agreed to indemnify Liberty Mutual for any claims it had to pay under the

bond. Double H Masonry sued Liberty Mutual under the bond. Liberty Mutual then brought in MWCC as a third-party defendant, asserting MWCC owed Liberty Mutual indemnity under their agreement and at common law. MWCC then moved for summary judgment on the common law indemnity claim, asserting that it was precluded because of their agreement. The trial court denied the motion:

> The surety's right to indemnity is well established at common law. A surety may maintain an action for pure common law indemnity where there is no contract between it and the indemnitor; although the recognized modern practice is for sureties to condition their issuance of bonds upon the execution by the contractor and other designated indemnitors of written agreements of indemnity. However, the law does not suggest that a surety loses its common law rights the moment it enters into an indemnity agreement, and rather, the court must consider the terms of that indemnity agreement in determining what common law rights the surety may assert. A survey of the relevant law demonstrates that reliance on contractual indemnity does not preclude the surety from also relying on common law indemnity. *See Hawkins Const. Co. v. First Federal Savings and Loan Ass'n*, 416 F. Supp. 388 (S.D. Iowa 1976) ("First Federal is relying upon contractual indemnity and common law or implied indemnity reliance on one theory does not foreclose reliance on the other"). *But see Charlotte Motor Speedway, Inc. v. Tindall Corp.*, 195 N.C. App. 296 (2009) (holding there "can be no implied contract where there is an express contract between the parties in reference to the same subject matter," in case where the parties executed an express indemnification provision that, by its terms, did not cover the losses for which plaintiff sought indemnification).
>
> MWCC has cited the court to no case law indicating that a surety cannot rely on common law indemnity where the court finds that an indemnity agreement does not address the nature of the indemnity sought, and I find that the law suggests common law indemnity may serve to protect the interest of the surety where the Parties' contractual agreement is silent as to the question. Indeed, this is a result congruent with the long history of equitable remedies available to sureties. Thus, the court construes this claim as Liberty asserting a right to indemnity in the absence of a written agreement. As explained below, a surety seeking such relief is limited only by whether the surety shares in any of the wrongdoing.
>
> The law of indemnity is well settled in South Dakota law: indemnification arises when a party discharges a liability that equitably should have been discharged by another. The Eighth Circuit has described South Dakota common law as follows: "the law does not preclude indemnity between joint tortfeasors but the situations in which indemnity is allowed are exceptional and limited." *Henningson, Durham & Richardson, Inc. v. Swift Bros. Const. Co.*, 739 F.2d 1341 (8th Cir. 1984). In affirming that an architecture firm

was not entitled to indemnity from a general contractor due to the firm's own negligence, the Eighth Circuit relied on South Dakota law in explaining, "if a person seeking indemnity personally participates in an affirmative act of negligence, or is physically connected with an act of omission by knowledge or acquiescence in it on his part, or fails to perform some duty in connection with the omission which he has undertaken, he is deprived of the right of indemnity." *Id.* Specifically, before a joint tortfeasor can shift one hundred percent of the recovery upon another joint tortfeasor, he must show a proportionate absence of contributory negligence on his part. *See Massey Ferguson Credit Corp. v. Bice*, 450 N.W.2d 435 (S.D. 1990) ("If a person seeking indemnity personally participates in an affirmative act of negligence, or is physically connected with an act of omission by knowledge or acquiescence in it on his part, or fails to perform some duty in connection with the omission which he has undertaken, he is deprived of the right of indemnity.").

This principle is supported by the Restatement (Second) of Torts § 886B, which provides that where no written agreement exists, indemnity may lie as follows: "if two persons are liable in tort to a third person for the same harm and one of them discharges the liability of both, he is entitled to indemnity from the other if the other would be unjustly enriched at his expense by the discharge of the liability." The Restatement sets forth several instances in which indemnity is granted under this principle, including in relevant part: (1) where "the indemnitee acted pursuant to directions of the indemnitor and reasonably believed the directions to be lawful; (2) "the indemnitee was induced to act by a misrepresentation on the part of the indemnitor, upon which [the indemnitee] justifiably relied"; (3) "the indemnitor performed defective work upon land or buildings as a result of which both were liable to the third person, and the indemnitee innocently or negligently failed to discover the defects"; and (4) "the indemnitor was under a duty to the indemnitee to protect him against the liability to the third person." *Id.* The underlying basis for indemnity is the presupposition that the indemnitee is not *in pari delicto* with the indemnitor. *Id.* at comments a, c ("the unexpressed premise has been that indemnity should be granted in any factual situation in which, as between the parties themselves, it is just and fair that the indemnitor should bear the total responsibility, rather than to leave it on the indemnitee or to divide it proportionately between the parties by contribution"). Thus, pure common law indemnity is an equitable remedy available to one who is exposed to liability because of the active fault or negligence of another, but is without negligence or fault on his own part.

MWCC argues that it is entitled to summary judgment on this claim because Liberty essentially forsook its common law right to indemnity when it entered into the Indemnity Agreement. I disagree, and find, albeit narrowly, that where an indemnity agreement is silent as to an issue of indemnification, and the court, in giving due consideration to prevailing policy concerns, construes the silence in the principal's favor that the principal is not liable for the indemnity sought, the surety may resort to its common law rights to pursue indemnity from the principal. The salient question, then, is whether Liberty was passively or actively involved in the negligence that gave rise to the bad faith claim.

I find that MWCC has not carried its burden of proof as to whether the bad faith claim arose as a result of Liberty's active negligence. For instance, MWCC asserts that Double H. Masonry alleged "Liberty breached the duty of good faith and fair dealing in a number of respects, including its alleged conscious 'failure to comply with its duties under the Bond,' failure to provide Double H with a copy of its investigative file, failure to independently and reasonably investigate Double H's claims and its denial of Double H's claims without a reasonable basis." Liberty responds in part that "Milender was steadfast in its insistence that Liberty deny the claim," and Liberty's representative, Mr. Medeiros, attests that on December 5, 2014, he wrote to Double H. Masonry to confirm receipt of the notice of claim and to request that Double H. Masonry "provide additional documents to Liberty to allow Liberty to complete its investigation." Double H. Masonry initiated the South Dakota Action one month later, on January 9, 2015. Notably, the South Dakota Action did not resolve the question of Liberty's liability. For these reasons, I must DENY MWCC's Cross Motion for Summary Judgment as to Liberty's second claim.

Problems

1. <u>Medical Bills</u>. Your client is a hospital that provided medical care to the defendants. The agreement with them provided they would be responsible for "charges not covered" by insurance. Defendants refused to pay. You filed suit, seeking payment under the signed agreement between your client and the defendants. The trial court has held that the contract is invalid because "charges" is indefinite and its meaning could only be determined by examining other documents beyond the contract that were not mentioned in it. What theory is best to use to recover some amount of money from the defendants?

2. <u>Tear It Down and Start Rebuilding</u>. Your client, Lori, was married to Antone when they purchased a home in 2004 for $200,000. They purchased it from Antone's parents with a second mortgage of $50,000. When a balloon payment was due, they could not pay it, and so they sold the property to Antone's parents for $160,000. Title was in Antone's parents' name, but they agreed to permit the couple to live in the house if they paid the mortgage, which they did irregularly. In early 2011, they decided to add a second floor and asked her parents for a loan to do so. They provided $73,000 toward the project. Antone's parents did not know of this project. Antone decided to tear down and rebuild the home on his own and

completed the outside. Antone decided to sell the home, and Lori's parents learned that the title was in Antone's parents' name. Antone's parents learned of the work Antone had done, and said not to worry and they would reimburse them. The house sold for $400,000 and Antone's parents paid Lori's parents nothing. What is the best theory of recovery against Antone's parents, and what is the likely measure of recovery? If the house increased in value to $177,000 as a result of his work, does that impact the analysis and, if so, how?

3. <u>Be Sure He Gets Nothing</u>. Your clients' daughter, Loretta, recently died after a brief bout with cancer. Loretta had begun dating Howard in Miami, Florida, in 2010. He moved in with Loretta and your clients shortly afterward in a house she owned in Miami. In 2012, Loretta and Howard moved with his parents to north Florida and her parents moved out of the Miami home. Loretta began to rent that house to third parties. Loretta purchased 10 acres of land and a mobile home, all titled in her name. They had one checking account into which all funds were deposited, including $70,000 Howard inherited in 2015. He purchased equipment for his landscaping business from the account, and deposited income in it, and she deposited rent from the Miami home, and paid expenses for it, and general bills, from the account, as did he. She did not work outside the home. In 2017, Loretta was diagnosed with late stage cancer, and she died in mid-2017. During that time, Howard cared for her, including driving her to the doctor and hospital, and paying $21,000 in medical bills from the joint account.

Howard has sued, seeking the money he spent on medical bills, $50 per day for each day (120) he drove Loretta to the hospital or doctor, and he seeks an equitable lien on the property based upon improvements he made to it using his work equipment. You have deposed Howard. You asked him if he had expected to be reimbursed for the medical care when he paid it, and he said "I would have taken her to the hospital and paid those bills no matter what. I loved her." Asked how much he valued the improvements, he stated that it was between $28,000 and $43,000. He testified that she had told him that she would make a will giving him the property, but had not done so. The complaint alleges Loretta had fraudulently induced him to make the improvements by promising to will it to him, but she had refused to do so. The property is worth about $210,000 and there are no liens on it.

Your clients need the property, free of the lien, because they want to go on a round-the-world cruise to overcome the grief of losing Loretta. What is the argument against recovery of the medical bills? Against the equitable lien?

4. <u>The Father</u>. Your client was told by a woman he was living with in his home that he was the father of her child. He believed her, and as a result quit his job so he could stay at his home to care for the girl, who was born in 2007. A year later, the woman moved out of the home and told him she would stop paying the bills and he would have to return to work. Because he did not believe the girl was ready for daycare, he continued to act as her full-time care giver for another six months. In 2009, he went back to work, and your client and the woman agreed he would have custody

of the girl 10 days each month. However, a few months later, she announced she was moving about 500 miles away. Your client filed suit, and learned that the girl was not his daughter and, although he had also sought custody, he abandoned that. Now, he has asked you if he has any viable claim to recover damages of any kind.

5. <u>Promised a Job, Too.</u> Your client, MaryLou, is a lawyer. She had been working with the Solomon firm doing personal injury work when she saw an advertisement from a firm, the Wright firm, seeking a criminal defense lawyer. Marylou had always wanted to practice criminal law. On February 20, 2017, she interviewed with the Wright firm, and was called back for a second interview a few days later, and a third interview a few days after that. The two firms were only a block away from each other. During those interviews, your client explained that she had wanted to change practice areas, and that if she were given an offer, she would quit the Solomon firm, giving two weeks' notice. The Wright firm offered Marylou a job, but without identifying a start date or length of employment. Salary, parking, and other terms were arranged. The next day, Marylou informed the Solomon firm she was quitting to change practice areas, and gave her two weeks' notice. The day after that, the Wright firm withdrew the offer, explaining that it had become concerned it would be unable to properly train her, since she had no criminal experience. Marylou explained to her supervising partner at the Solomon firm what had happened, and asked what the chances she could get her old job back were, and was told, "none." Does she have a claim against the Wright firm? If so, what are the damages and remedies?

6. <u>Preemptive Strike</u>. A city sued a manufacturing company with a facility in the city, alleging it had created a nuisance, in part by causing toxic chemicals to enter a river flowing through the city. In its answer, the defendant asserted that the city was partially responsible for the harm since it, too, had used the toxic chemicals. As a result, the defendant contended that any damage award to the city would result in unjust enrichment to the city. The court called this claim "absurd." Do you agree?

Chapter 10

Vicarious and Derivative Liability

Liability for harm caused by a tort can be imposed on a person other than the one who actually caused the harm. For example, *respondeat superior* makes an employer vicariously liable—i.e., strictly liable without proof of fault by the employer—for certain tortious harm of an employee. On the other hand, some doctrines impose liability on a party other than the person who directly caused the harm, but not vicariously, and not completely. For example, a car owner who lets a friend drive the car is not, without more, liable for damages the friend causes in a car wreck, but is liable if the owner had "negligently entrusted" the car to the friend—not for all of the harm caused, but only the portion of harm attributable to her own negligence, not that caused by the friend.

These doctrines implicate the growing number and scope of state apportionment statutes. Among other things, those statutes permit defendants to request that juries apportion fault to parties and, as well, to non-parties. If the jury apportions some fault to a non-party, that party is not bound by the judgment, but a defendant's liability is reduced by that amount. Thus, if a jury apportions fault 75% to a defendant and 25% to a non-party, the defendant's liability to the plaintiff is reduced by 25%, but plaintiff cannot use that verdict to obtain relief against the non-party. Indeed, some states permit liability to be assigned to non-parties who are immune from liability to the plaintiff. For example, some states hold that a jury can consider "the 'fault' of a tortfeasor, notwithstanding that he may have a meritorious affirmative defense or claim of immunity against any liability to the plaintiff." *Walker v. Tensor Mach. Ltd.*, 779 S.E.2d 651 (Ga. 2015); *but see Machin v. Carus Corp.*, 799 S.E.2d 468 (S.C. 2017) ("a nonparty may be included in the allocation of fault only where such person or entity is a 'potential tortfeasor,' which, under our law, excludes the plaintiff's employer who is immune from suit.")

Liability for harm caused by breach of contract, in contrast, ordinarily is imposed only upon the party who breached the contract—and limited by *Hadley*—or on a stranger to the contract whose tortious interference caused the breach. As noted below, however, some state apportionment statutes may permit the party who breached a contract to apportion liability to others, though in narrow circumstances.

1. Vicarious Liability for the Harm Caused by Another Person

A. An Employer Is Generally Vicariously Liable for Harm Caused by an Employee, not a General Contractor

Vicarious liability is an exception to the general rule that an injured person must seek any remedy from the person who caused the injury. The key distinction in the law is that generally an employer is vicariously liable for the acts of an employee, but not an independent contractor.

Under traditional *respondeat superior* analysis, a principal is vicariously liable for the harm caused by the tort of its agent if the act that caused the harm had been committed within the scope of the agency. The reason an employer is liable for all of the harm caused by a negligent employee that occurred in the course and scope of employment is because the employer had the right to control the employee. Vicarious liability is not a cause of action, but is instead imputed liability based upon the legal relationship between the principal and the agent who caused the harm. As a result, the plaintiff must have a claim for relief against the agent. *Moorhouse v. Stand., New York,* 997 N.Y.S.2d 127 (N.Y. App. Div. 1st Dept. 2014) ("claim of vicarious liability cannot stand when there is no primary liability upon which such a claim of vicarious liability might rest"). If the plaintiff can establish liability, then the principal is vicariously liable.

In cases where the issue is whether the employee was acting in course and scope, the Restatement (Second) provides the following test:

(1) Conduct of the servant is within the scope of employment if, but only if:

(a) it is of the kind he is employed to perform;

(b) it occurs substantially within the authorized time and space limits;

(c) it is actuated, at least in part, by a purpose to serve the master; and

(d) if force is intentionally used by the servant against another, the use of force is not unexpectable by the master.

(2) Conduct of the servant is not within the scope of employment if it is different in kind from that authorized, far beyond the authorized time and space limits, or too little actuated by a purpose to serve the master.

Restatement (Second) of Agency §228. Section 229(2) suggests applying these factors when the conduct, though not authorized, nonetheless is deemed to be within course and scope:

(a) whether or not the act is one commonly done by such servants;

(b) the time, place and purpose of the act;

(c) the previous relations between the master and the servant;

(d) the extent to which the business of the master is apportioned between different servants;

(e) whether or not the act is outside the enterprise of the master or, if within the enterprise, has not been entrusted to any servant;

(f) whether or not the master has reason to expect such an act will be done;

(g) the similarity in quality of the act done to the act authorized;

(h) whether or not the instrumentality by which the harm is done has been furnished by the master to the servant;

(i) the extent of departure from the normal method of accomplishing an authorized result; and

(j) whether or not the act is seriously criminal. . . .

In applying these factors, courts have as a general rule concluded that an employer is not vicariously liable for the harm caused by an accident of an employee while driving an employer's car commuting to, or from, home and work. *Feltner v. PJ Operations, LLC*, 2018 WL 3312127 (Ky. App. July 6, 2018). However, if the employer requires an employee to drive from her home to a customer's location, or from wherever the employee is to a location for the business, this is within course and scope. *Id.* Nonetheless, if the employee "deviates" during a commute "for however short of a time period, to do acts which are not connected with the employer's business, the relationship is suspended and the employee is not acting within the scope of his employment." *Id. See Hicks v. Heard,* 678 S.E.2d 145 (Ct. App. Ga. 2009) (daughter driving home from school in father's company's car not in course and scope).

Conversely, a principal is generally not vicariously liable for harm caused by an *independent* contractor, which is defined as a person (or entity) that renders a service in the course of an occupation, and is controlled by the principal only with respect to the result, not the means by which it is accomplished. Because the principal lacks control, the principal ordinarily is not liable for harm caused by an independent contractor. However, the right to control can be explicit or implied. In addition, a principal or employer is vicariously liable for injuries caused by an independent contractor or employee: (1) carrying on an abnormally dangerous activity, or (2) engaging in an activity that is inherently dangerous or poses a peculiar risk of physical harm. The exceptions for activities that pose a peculiar risk or are inherently dangerous are functionally identical.

The rule that a principal is liable for harm of an employee but not an independent contractor means that principals have incentives to characterize every relationship as being with an independent contractor, not an employee. The label "independent contractor" does not control, but instead the ability to control can exist despite an agreement denying it. Even so, parties must carefully consider the impact of how they characterize the relationship, for reasons the court in *Kerl v. Rasmussen*, 672 N.W.2d 71 (Wis. App. 2003), *aff'd*, 682 N.W.2d 328 (Wis. 2004) explained:

> The majority of other jurisdictions that have considered franchisor liability for the negligence of a franchisee. Courts require franchisors to exercise more than the right to control uniformity of appearance, products and administration in order to find a duty owed to a party injured by a franchisee's negligence. Indeed, such standards enable a franchisor to protect its franchise and trade name. Thus courts have declined to find a franchisor vicariously liable where the franchise agreement retained the right to inspect and enforce standards. Nor is a general right to terminate the franchise agreement for noncompliance sufficient to create liability. *See Pizza K, Inc. v. Santagata*, 249 Ga.App. 36 (2001) (franchise agreement retaining right to inspect franchisee's establishment and to terminate for noncompliance with franchise standards not sufficient control of day-to-day activities to create agency relationship); *Viches v. MLT, Inc.*, 127 F.Supp.2d 828 (E.D. Mich. 2000) (imposition of uniform practices, right to inspect franchisee's premises and right to terminate the agreement does not render franchisor liable for franchisee's negligence).

> The prevailing standard focuses on whether the franchisor controls the specific 'instrumentality' which allegedly caused the harm. This is illustrated by a number of cases where a franchisee's employee has been injured by third parties and has claimed the franchisor was responsible for inadequate security; courts have declined to impose liability when there was no showing of the franchisor's control over security measures.

> Under the prevailing view the most significant factor to consider is the degree of control that the franchisor maintains over the daily operations of the franchisee or more specifically, the manner of performing the very work in the course of which the accident occurred.

Nathans v. Offerman

922 F. Supp. 2d 271 (D. Conn. 2013) (Eginton, J.)

[Defendant Offerman was up to bat for his team, the Ducks, when he charged the pitcher and hit him. The pitcher sued Offerman and the Ducks, asserting battery. The Ducks moved for summary judgment, asserting the battery occurred outside of Offerman's scope of employment.]

In determining whether an employee has acted within the scope of employment, courts look to whether the employee's conduct: (1) occurs primarily within the employer's authorized time and space limits; (2) is of the type that the employee is employed to perform; and (3) is motivated, at least in part, by a purpose to serve the employer. Here, there is no dispute that Offerman's conduct occurred within the time and space limits of the employer. Whether his conduct was of the type that the

Ducks employed him to perform and was motivated in part by a purpose to serve the Ducks is disputed.

In *Mullen v. Horton,* the Appellate Court of Connecticut examined the line between mere misguided efforts and abandonment of an employer's business:

> Here the trier of fact could reasonably have found that Horton's sexual relations with the plaintiff during their pastoral-psychological counseling sessions, were a "misguided effort" at psychologically and spiritually counseling the plaintiff, rather than an abandonment of the counseling. Just as the YMCA employee's assault on the basketball court in *Glucksman,* and the employee's assault on the customer who had littered in *Pelletier* represented extreme and clearly unauthorized methods of maintaining order and thereby furthering their employers' business, Horton's engaging in sexual contact with the plaintiff during counseling sessions also could represent an extreme and clearly unauthorized method of spiritually and emotionally counseling the plaintiff and thereby furthering the church's business.

Mullen, 46 Conn.App. at 767. The court distinguished the above cases from *Brown v. Housing Auth.,* 23 Conn.App. 624 (1990), where a mechanic left his job route, followed the plaintiff's car, and attacked the plaintiff with a hammer, finding that the mechanic necessarily abandoned his employer's business to pursue and attack the plaintiff. Street brawling with random members of the public has nothing to do with maintaining machines, even when travel is part of the job. There, the mechanic's violence was not foreseeable because it was "in no way connected to the defendant's business." Similarly, in *Gutierrez v. Thorne,* 13 Conn.App. 493 (1988), repeated sexual assaults by an employee were held to have no connection to the defendant employer's business of training mentally retarded persons regarding daily living skills. Finally *Nutt v. Norwich Roman Catholic Diocese,* 921 F.Supp. 66 (D. Conn. 1995) held that a priest's showing pornographic films to young boys and then criminally sexually molesting them in out-of-town motel rooms could not reasonably be viewed as a mere misguided effort at pastoral counseling. The priest had wholly abandoned his pastoral duties.

The location of the dividing line between the cases is significantly based on the foreseeability of the unauthorized conduct in question. Inappropriate sexual relations between a psychological counselor and a client are somewhat predictable, as are physical altercations during a basketball game, or even in a retail store, where employees are instructed to prevent mischief on the premises. Furthermore, a master does not escape liability merely because his servant loses his temper while he is conducting the master's business. This is especially true where the conduct is foreseeable or expected. Indeed, the Restatement (Second) of Agency § 245 provides:

> A master is subject to liability for the intended tortious harm by a servant to the person or things of another by an act done in connection with the

servant's employment, although the act was unauthorized, if the act was not unexpectable in view of the duties of the servant.

a. Types of situations. *Whether or not an employment involves, or is likely to lead to, the use of force against the person or property of another is a matter of fact to be decided by the trier of fact.* Since opportunities and provocations arise in a great variety of ways, no attempt is made to make an exhaustive category of situations in which the master may be found liable. However, certain situations recur with sufficient frequency to call for mention. These occur when the servant: (a) acts in the protection of or recaption of his master's property, or (b) *in excess of zeal in competition, or (c) engages in a fight arising out of a dispute connected with his work for his employer.* In all of these situations the liability of the principal depends fundamentally upon the likelihood of a battery or other tort in view of the kind of result to be accomplished, the customs of the enterprise and the nature of the persons normally employed for doing the work.

The Restatement lists three situations that recur with sufficient frequency to be mentioned. Two of the three, action in excess of zeal in competition and fighting arising out of a dispute connected with work for one's employer, apply here. In professional baseball, it is not unexpected for a batter to charge the mound after being hit by a pitch. While it may be unusual for the batter to bring his bat to the fight, Offerman's alleged digression from duty was not so clear-cut that the disposition of the case becomes a matter of law. Resolving all ambiguities and drawing all permissible factual inferences in favor of plaintiff, the Court will allow the trier of fact to determine whether a wilful tort of the servant has occurred within the scope of the servant's employment and was done to further his master's business. Therefore, defendant's motion for summary judgment on the issue of *respondeat superior* will be denied.

Hughes v. Metro. Gov't of Nashville and Davidson Cnty.

340 S.W.3d 352 (Tenn. 2011) (Wade, J.)

[The plaintiff, a firefighter, had been injured while jumping out of the way of a front-end loader being driven by a county employee. The plaintiff sued the county, which raised the defense of sovereign immunity. However, under Tennessee law, the county's immunity had been waived for liability for negligent acts of county employees acting within course and scope of employment, but not for liability for their intentional torts. At the time of the injury, the employee had been authorized to drive the front-end loader, but the injury was caused by a prank: the driver had slammed the loader down, which had caused the plaintiff to jump and injure himself. The jury found the county liable. The court of appeals affirmed the finding that the driver was in course and scope and the tort was not intentional. The county appealed.]

Turning to the factors used in determining whether the acts of an employee, although not authorized, are so similar or so incidental to authorized conduct as to fall within the scope of employment, we would initially observe that there was no evidence that driving a vehicle in an intimidating manner was reasonably expected by Metro. That suggests the Defendant may not have been acting within the scope of his employment. What was common, however, was that the Defendant was required to return his equipment to the Metro facility at the end of each work day. Other factors lend support to the finding by the trial court that the Defendant acted within the scope of his employment: the incident occurred during working hours along the access road that led to the Public Works facility, and took place while the Defendant was operating a vehicle furnished by Metro, a task he was specially trained and directed to do. Arguably, the Defendant's manner of driving did not *extensively* depart from the normal method of returning the front-end loader to the Public Works facility at the end of the work day. Finally, the Defendant's misuse of the front-end loader did not qualify as "seriously criminal," as even if his operation of the equipment constituted criminal assault, such an offense would qualify as a misdemeanor rather than a felony. Thus, while no proof suggests that any "horseplay" by the Defendant was authorized by Metro, the offensive manner in which he operated Metro's vehicle could be properly described as incidental to his authorized duties.

While his operation of the equipment so as to cause fear in others could be characterized as "a personal project," there is no evidence that the Defendant made such a departure from his duties as a Metro employee that his acts, as a whole, could be considered a venture of a "purely personal" nature. In summary, the evidence does not preponderate against the finding that the Defendant acted within the scope of his employment.

Bruntjen v. Bethalto Pizza, LLC

18 N.E.3d 215 (Ct. App. Ill. 2014) (Chapman, J.)

[Bethalto Pizza LLC operated a pizza restaurant under the name "Imo's Pizza" as a franchisee of Imo's Franchising, Inc. A delivery driver for Bethalto's had, while delivering a pizza, caused an accident, severely injuring plaintiff, Bruntjen. Bethalto admitted its employee had crossed the center line while speeding, and that he had been acting within the course and scope of employment at that time. Bruntjen contended Imo's was vicariously liable for the negligence of Bethalto's employee. The jury found Imo's vicariously liable and awarded $2.3 million. Imo's appealed.]

A written contract is not conclusive of the nature of the relationship between the parties. Despite an agreement labeling the relationship as that of an independent contractor, the facts of the case can demonstrate an agency status. The nature of the relationship depends on the actual practice between the parties and, as a general rule, is a mixed question of law and fact to be submitted to the jury. In determining whether a person is an agent or an independent contractor, the court's cardinal consideration is the right to control the manner of work performance, regardless of whether that right was actually exercised.

After a careful review of the record, we find that the agreement, the confidential operating manual, and the driver contract provided ample evidence along with trial testimony that Imo's had the right to control many aspects of Bethalto's daily operations. These documents allowed Imo's to control employment decisions, training, safety, daily maintenance, wage and hour requirements, record-keeping, supervision and discipline of employees, and hiring and firing, as well as the right to terminate the franchise relationship with Bethalto. The agreement required the franchisee "to operate the Store and provide delivery service in accordance with the operational standards as may be established by Franchisor from time to time." While Imo's characterizes many of these directives as suggestions or recommendations that were left up to the franchisee's discretion, the frequent use of terminology such as "must," "require," and "mandatory" belies that characterization. The manual expressly indicated that its numerous italicized provisions were mandatory. In addition, some of the provisions that were not italicized expressly mandated compliance. One such nonitalicized provision in the manual stated: "You must be open on New Year's Eve. We suggest you stay open until 2:00 a.m." The jury could have reasonably inferred that the use of compulsory language evidenced Imo's right to operational control and that provisions like "You must be open on New Year's Eve" were not mere suggestions or recommendations.

There was evidence that Imo's control extended specifically to the pizza delivery drivers. Pizza delivery was required under the agreement. Imo's prescribed the minimum delivery area. Imo's required Bethalto to name Imo's Franchising, Inc., as an additional insured on all general liability and nonowned auto insurance policies. Imo's required the stores to pay a fee equal to 4% of their sales. The manual required Bethalto to adhere to guidelines in hiring, supervising, and terminating the drivers. The manual included eight pages of detailed requirements entitled "Hiring and Supervising Drivers." Imo's required that drivers "*have a Good Driving Record as established by a motor vehicle report (MVR).*" (Emph. in original.) The manual further provided:

> *This means the MVR must be checked before someone is hired <u>and at least every 6 months while an individual who is working for you has any driving responsibilities</u>. If a driver's MVR changes so they no longer have a Good Driving Record, they must be prohibited from performing further driving for you.*"
> (Emph. in original.)

Bethalto was required to keep every MVR it obtained in the employee's file. A full page was devoted to what defined a good driving record. One requirement was that a driver have fewer than three moving violations in the preceding three years.

The manual contained an appendix A with forms. The following forms were mandatory as indicated: "Procedure for New Driver's MVR Report — This form is mandatory"; "Driver Eligibility Guidelines — These guidelines are mandatory"; "Driver Contract — This form is mandatory"; and "Safe Work Practices for Drivers — These practices are mandatory." The procedure for new driver's MVR report and driver eligibility guidelines contained numerous specific requirements for hiring. Imo's required that Bethalto calculate the hourly rate of drivers to ensure that they receive minimum wage; if they did not, Bethalto was required to make up the difference. The driver contract stated that a driver could be terminated for not "performing the work with safety and expedition."

Under the agreement, Imo's reserved the right to terminate the franchise if Bethalto did not perform the mandatory obligations under the confidential operating manual.

Imo's contends that Bethalto conducted business without interference from Imo's in its operations or procedures. Assuming this to be true, it is not determinative of the agency status. It is the *right* to control rather than the *fact* of control that is determinative of agency. Likewise, the fact that the agreement expressly stated that Bethalto was an independent contractor is also not determinative of the relationship.

Applying these rules of law and factors to this case, we find that the evidence adduced at trial was sufficient to support the jury's finding on agency. The existence of an agency relationship was genuinely disputed and properly a question to be decided by the jury and not prior to trial.

Notes and Questions

1. Exception for Intentional Torts. Normally, a plaintiff with a battery claim can assert the intentional tort, but there are often practical reasons not to do so, particularly if the person who committed the battery has few or no financial resources: insurance generally does not cover intentional tort claims, employers are generally not vicariously liable for the intentional torts of their employees, and sovereign immunity generally does not permit liability for intentional torts of government employees. This encourages pleading "negligent" intentional torts, which is what *Hughes* plaintiff did even though: "the concept of a negligent battery or a negligent assault is an anomalous one in a vast majority of American jurisdictions. It seems almost unquestioned that a formed intention is an essential element of assault and battery and that mere negligence is insufficient." *Higgins v. TJX Cos.,* 331 F. Supp. 2d 3 (D. Me. 2004).

2. Pleading and Presenting to the Jury Alternative Claims. The Federal Rules of Civil Procedure and most state rules permit plaintiffs to plead alternative theories because the evidence available at the time of filing a complaint may not clearly show what happened. So, a plaintiff could plead that a police officer had acted *either* negligently *or* intentionally, and if the evidence supports one inference or the other, the jury may be instructed on both theories. Is doing so inconsistent with battery?

3. Vicarious Liability for Intentional Torts Through Ratification. An employer can be liable for intentional torts if it ratifies the agent's acts, an issue often raised when a supervisor sexually harasses an employee. Ratification requires a plaintiff show the employer: (1) had actual knowledge of the tortious conduct of the offending employee and that the tortious conduct was directed at and visited upon the

complaining employee; (2) that based on this knowledge, the employer knew, or should have known, that such conduct constituted sexual harassment; and (3) that the employer failed to take steps reasonably calculated to halt the harassment. *Kurtts v. Chiropractic Strategies Group, Inc.,* 481 F. App'x 462 (11th Cir. 2012).

4. Other Bases for Imposing Vicarious Liability for Harms by Independent Contractors. In *Stout v. Warren,* 290 P.3d 972 (Wash. 2012), a bail bonding company hired an independent contractor, Mr. Golden (a bounty hunter), to capture Stout, who had jumped bail on a bond issued by the company. Golden rammed Stout's car at 70 mph, severely injuring Stout. Stout asserted the bonding company was vicariously liable. The court held that one exception—liability for conduct in "abnormally dangerous activities" did not apply—but the bonding company was liable because it had employed Golden "to do work involving a special danger to others which the employer knows or has reason to know to be inherent in or normal to the work, or which he contemplates or has reason to contemplate when making the contract" and so was "subject to liability for physical harm caused to such others by the contractor's failure to take reasonable precautions against such danger." The court explained:

> In order for vicarious liability to apply under these sections, (1) the activity itself must pose a risk of physical harm absent special or reasonable precautions (i.e., the risk must be inherent to the activity), (2) the risk must "differ from the common risks to which persons in general are commonly subjected," (i.e., the risk must be "peculiar" or "special"), (3) the principal must know or have reason to know of the risk, and (4) the harm must arise from the contractor's negligence with respect to the risk that is inherent in the activity. Elements (1) and (2) are properly treated as questions of law.

> In the context of fugitive defendant apprehension, there is a peculiar risk of harm absent special precautions (i.e., elements (1) and (2) of the peculiar risk exception are satisfied). *See Hayes v. Goldstein,* 120 Ohio App.3d 116 (1997) ("We are convinced that there is an indisputable danger inherent in the apprehension of one who has failed to answer to a charge levelled in a court of law."). This risk is twofold. First, there is a risk that the force that the bail bond recovery agent is authorized to employ will be exercised in a negligent or reckless manner causing physical harm. Second, there is a risk that the bail bond recovery agent's negligent actions will cause the fugitive defendant to respond in a manner that causes physical harm to others. For example, if a bail bond recovery agent enters a fugitive defendant's home without identifying himself and fails to secure the fugitive defendant, the fugitive defendant might exercise deadly force in self-defense that causes physical harm to a third party.

> The risks peculiar to and inherent in fugitive defendant apprehension differ from common risks to which members of the public are generally subjected. Members of the public are, in general, not subject to the risk of others mistakenly breaking into their homes or mistakenly apprehending

them, nor are members of the public generally subject to the risk of being caught in the cross fire between fugitive defendants and those who would recapture them.

Are the "abnormally dangerous activity" and "peculiar risk" forms of vicarious liability distinct from the general test under Section 228? Wouldn't a court applying those factors reach the same result?

B. Vicarious Liability under the Family Purpose Doctrine

Griffith v. Kuester

780 F. Supp. 2d 536 (E.D. Ky. 2011) (Bunning, J.)

[While water skiing, the plaintiff's decedent was killed by a MasterCraft boat owned by a husband and wife. The wife was driving it at the time and was negligent; the husband had not been present. The plaintiff sued both wife and husband, asserting he was vicariously liable under the family purpose doctrine. The court issued this order on the husband's motion for summary judgment.]

The rationale for the doctrine was when the owner of an automobile furnishes it for the use and enjoyment of the members of his family, the members of the family so using the automobile with the consent of the owner become his agent in carrying out his purpose. In addition to agency principles, Kentucky courts have found that the doctrine is also premised on justice or supposed necessity or humanitarian principles designed to protect the public. As a matter of public policy, the parent, who not only made the vehicle available for use but is also the only financially responsible party, should bear the liability for the plaintiff's injuries. Pursuant to K.R.S. § 235.300, the family purpose doctrine is also applicable to the use and operation of vessels or motorboats.

In order to recover under the doctrine, the plaintiff must prove: (1) that the vehicle was owned or controlled by the defendant; (2) that the vehicle was maintained by the defendant for the use and benefit of members of his family; (3) that the vehicle was being used at the time of the incident by a person whom the defendant was under a legal obligation to support; and (4) that the person using the vehicle was doing so pursuant to a family purpose. The basic premise of the doctrine is that the head of the family will be responsible for an accident while the vehicle is being driven within the scope of the family purpose. Therefore, this requires that the vehicle be used with consent, express or implied, and for the purposes intended. The "family purpose" has been defined as including the convenience, pleasure, or benefit of the family.

The Kentucky Supreme Court has never ruled on whether a co-owner of a vehicle can be held liable for the other co-owner's negligent operation pursuant to the family purpose doctrine. In fact, few jurisdictions have even addressed the issue, and a split of authority exists in the very few cases that have addressed it. *See Sheppard v. Weekly*, 72 Or.App. 86 (1985) (holding that when husband and wife are co-owners and enjoy equal rights to use and control a vehicle, the husband cannot be held liable pursuant to the family purpose doctrine for the wife's negligent operation of the vehicle); *Rushing v. Polk*, 258 N.C. 256 (1962) (holding that the family purpose doctrine does not apply to husband and wife joint owners, without proof of actual agency between them). *But see Marcus v. Everett*, 195 Neb. 518 (1976) (holding that the family purpose doctrine did apply to husband and wife joint owners, because husband contributed the use of his half of the vehicle and therefore furnished the vehicle to his wife, a member of his family).

During oral argument, Plaintiff's counsel asserted that the only element that must be satisfied in order to apply the family purpose doctrine is that the vehicle, or boat in this instance, was being operated pursuant to a family purpose at the time of the accident. However, if that were indeed the case, injured parties would seek to invoke the doctrine far more often than the case law reveals. More importantly, applying the doctrine in the manner espoused by Plaintiff would ignore the other elements which have been required to apply the doctrine. Furthermore, a review of the case law finds that Kentucky courts have limited the application of the doctrine. For instance, a parent and owner of a vehicle provided for family purposes is not liable for the negligent operation of an adult child whom the parent is under no legal obligation to support.

While Kentucky courts have been silent on the specific issue before the Court, they have repeatedly applied the family purpose doctrine based on principles of agency and equity, a point seemingly lost on Plaintiff's counsel. Additionally, the courts have emphasized that the defendant must exercise some degree of control over the vehicle. Therefore, the Court finds that the doctrine is inapplicable to the instant case. Co-ownership, in and of itself, refutes an agency theory. As co-owners of the MasterCraft, neither spouse had greater rights to the boat to the exclusion of the other. Therefore, Mr. Kuester could not have either given permission to or denied use of the boat that Mrs. Kuester legally owned. As such, Mr. Kuester did not furnish the boat to Mrs. Kuester to bring the incident within the recognized scope of the family purpose doctrine.

Notes and Questions

1. <u>Joint and Several or Apportioned</u>? About 25 states have either a common law or statutory family purpose doctrine, but by statute or caselaw they split on whether liability is apportioned or vicarious. *See Young v. Beck*, 251 P.3d 380 (Ariz. 2011) (holding common law approach of joint and several liability survived enactment of apportionment statute because there was no "fault to apportion" under family purpose doctrine).

2. <u>What Policies Does It Further</u>? Consider the incentives the family purpose doctrine creates for parents to adequately insure children who drive. The principal case offers that as the primary rationale for this doctrine. What other policies does it serve?

2. Claims That Partially Shift Damages

A. Negligent Hiring, Negligent Retention, and Negligent Supervision

Unlike vicarious liability, negligent retention is a claim that requires negligence. For example, these claims under Ohio law have five elements: "(1) the existence of an employment relationship; (2) the employee's incompetence; (3) the employer's actual or constructive knowledge of such incompetence; (4) the employee's act or omission causing the plaintiff's injuries; and (5) the employer's negligence in hiring or retaining the employee as the proximate cause of plaintiff's injuries." *Southerland v. Sycamore Community Sch. Dist. Bd. of Educ.*, 125 F. App'x 14 (6th Cir. 2004). Sometimes it is easy to impose liability on the employee, but not the employer.

Breach for a negligent hiring claim requires showing that "the employer knew or should have known that the employee was unfit" for the job, focusing on "the adequacy of the employer's pre-employment investigation into the employee's background." *Malicki v. Doe*, 814 So. 3d 347 (Fla. 2002). Breach of duty for a negligent supervision or negligent retention claim focuses on conduct after hiring and requires showing the employer should have known of the employee's unfitness but failed to act reasonably, such as by investigating, firing, or re-assigning the employee.

G4S Secure Sols. USA, Inc. v. Golzar
208 So. 3d 204 (Ct. App. Fla. 2016) (Scales, J.)

[Defendant G4S Secure Solutions, USA ("Wackenhut"), had been considering hiring Eric Owens as a security guard. On the employment application, he checked a box indicating he had no prior criminal convictions, but a background check found he had been convicted for disorderly conduct. The background check did not reveal the details and, despite the inconsistency, Wackenhut did not ask what happened and it hired him. In fact, he had been convicted of peeking into an inhabited building.

Plaintiff, Golzar, was a female high school student in her room undressed when she saw someone filming her. It turned out to be Owen. Golzar testified she had experienced some generalized illnesses and physical problems including weight gain, nightmares, and feelings of anxiety. However, after the incident she excelled in her senior year of high school and in her freshman year of college. She obtained a verdict of $1.3 million against Golzar for invasion of privacy and against Wackenhut for negligent retention. Wackenhut appealed the denial of its motion for directed verdict.]

The Florida Supreme Court has crafted limited exceptions to Florida's impact rule, recognizing that certain torts are necessarily devoid of physical harm and are of such a nature that the only foreseeable damages resulting from those torts are emotional damages that are non-economic in nature. For example, in *Abril,* the Court recognized that "the only reasonable damages arising from a breach of Florida's HIV confidentiality statute are emotional distress." 969 So.2d at 207. Similarly, our Supreme Court has noted that Florida's impact rule does not apply to any intentional tort such as defamation, invasion of privacy and intentional infliction of emotional distress.

Against this backdrop, we analyze the torts of negligent hiring, negligent retention, and negligent supervision, *i.e.,* the three causes of action alleged against Wackenhut by Golzar. Specifically, we must determine, as a matter of first impression, whether to include these torts as limited exceptions to Florida's impact rule. At the outset, we note that we have been provided no Florida case in which a court has not applied the impact rule to claims of negligent hiring, negligent retention, and negligent supervision.

In fact, several federal courts have applied Florida's impact rule to preclude a plaintiff's recovery of purely non-economic damages for these torts. Additionally, in addressing whether Florida's impact rule applies to the tort of negligent training, this Court has expressly held that the impact rule precludes recovery for such purely non-economic damages. Nevertheless, Golzar argues that the Florida Supreme Court's decision in *Abril,* which post-dates our decision in *Cardoso,* expands by implication the exceptions to Florida's impact rule. We do not read *Abril* so broadly.

In *Abril,* a medical lab, contracted by Florida's Department of Corrections, faxed false HIV test results of a Department of Corrections employee in violation of Florida's HIV confidentiality statute. The trial court dismissed Abril's actions seeking compensatory damages for mental anguish and emotional distress based upon Florida's impact rule. Abril's lawsuit was reinstated after Florida's Supreme Court determined that violation of Florida's HIV confidentiality statute is the type of tort for which the *only* reasonably foreseeable damages are emotional distress damages.

While Golzar's damages stemming from Wackenhut's failure to properly investigate Owens's prior California conviction are, like Abril's damages, emotional distress damages, it can hardly be said that the *only* reasonably foreseeable damages from any negligent hiring, negligent retention, and negligent supervision tort are emotional distress damages. Indeed, Florida jurisprudence is replete with examples of an employer being held liable for personal injury damages and economic damages for its negligent hiring, negligent retention, or negligent supervision. *See, e.g., Tallahassee Furn. Co., Inc. v. Harrison,* 583 So.2d 744 (Fla. 1st DCA 1991) (affirming a jury verdict for negligent retention where furniture deliveryman brutally attacked plaintiff in her home).

Plainly, unlike in *Abril,* economic damages, as well as emotional distress damages, are reasonably foreseeable when an employer fails to screen and vet an employee properly. We do not view the torts of negligent hiring, negligent retention, and negligent supervision as torts in which the only foreseeable damages are non-economic damages; therefore, we conclude that *Abril* is distinguishable.

Understandably, but without citing any precedent, Golzar urges us essentially to *merge* Owens's intentional conduct (that is, his invasion of Golzar's privacy) with Wackenhut's negligent conduct, without differentiating between the two parties' distinct actions. Golzar argues that when the only foreseeable damages stemming from an employee's intentional conduct are non-economic, then Florida's impact rule should have no applicability to the employer's negligent conduct that facilitated the employee's intentional conduct.

Almost by definition, however, the torts of negligent hiring, negligent retention, and negligent supervision are fundamentally distinct from the employee's underlying, intentional wrong. Florida's impact rule applies only to the torts of negligent hiring, negligent retention, and negligent supervision. In our view, blurring the distinction would be the functional equivalent of imposing vicarious liability on an employer for the intentional tortious conduct of its employee. Florida courts have consistently rejected this notion. We do not read *Abril* so as to require such a "merger."

Finally, Golzar suggests that *Abril* can be read to impose vicarious liability on an employer when it is foreseeable that the damages resulting from both (i) the employee's intentional tort, and (ii) the employer's negligent hiring, are purely non-economic.

We do not read *Abril* as standing for the proposition that an employer is somehow *vicariously liable* for the intentional tort of its employee. Importantly, in *Abril,* the Department of Corrections was vicariously responsible pursuant to statute for the negligence of the laboratory. No such statutory undertaking is implicated in this case. There is no indication in *Abril,* or in any other case cited to us, that an employer should be vicariously liable for an intentional tort of its employee committed outside the scope of employment.

While we are indeed sympathetic with Golzar in this case, and find Owens's behavior to be reprehensible, in our view, these considerations are not sufficient to waive the applicability of Florida's impact rule to the torts of negligent hiring, negligent retention, and negligent supervision.

We reverse the judgment on appeal and remand with instructions to enter final judgment in favor of Wackenhut.

Shephard, J., dissenting,

The Florida Supreme Court has long acknowledged that the impact rule generally is inapplicable to recognized torts in which damages are often predominantly emotional. Included early on among those exceptions were "emotional distress damages for torts such as invasion of privacy. Taliya suffered an invasion of her privacy in this case. G4S had a "special professional duty" to each resident of the gated community which it was engaged to protect. *See Rowell v. Holt,* 850 So.2d 474 (Fla. 2003) (holding that a public defender owed a special professional duty to a client who had been unlawfully detained to obtain his immediate release). It was foreseeable that a security guard who had once been a Peeping Tom would engage in such conduct again. None of the legal or historically advanced policy reasons for the application of the impact rule are served by denying Taliya recovery from G4S in this case.

Notes and Questions

1. <u>Who Was Right</u>? The majority's approach to employer liability — requiring the employee cause an impact — nullifies a significant proportion of claims that likely will be made against employers. Does the limitation seem sound?

2. <u>The Impact of Admitting *Respondeat Superior*</u>. If a plaintiff asserts liability based upon *respondeat superior* and a negligence-based claim such as negligent retention, and the employer admits the employee was within course and scope, then of what relevance is the employer's knowledge of the propensity of the employee to drive poorly or otherwise cause harm? Courts split. Some follow the "*McHaffie* Rule," and so "when an employer acknowledges vicarious liability for its employee's negligence, a plaintiff's direct claims against the employer are barred." *Greene v. Grams*, 384 F. Supp. 3d 100 (D.D.C. 2019). Instead of "preempting" negligence-based claims, other courts hold "an employer may be liable for injuries caused both by its own independent negligence in hiring, training, retaining, or supervising an employee and, at the same time, under the doctrine of *respondeat superior* for the injuries caused by its employees' negligent behavior." *MV Transp., Inc. v. Allgeier*, 433 S.W.3d 324 (Ky. 2014).

B. Negligent Entrustment

Negligent entrustment is based upon the defendant entrusting the person who injured the plaintiff with the item that caused the harm. Thus, a plaintiff injured by a car driven by defendant may assert a negligent entrustment claim against the car owner, who permitted defendant to drive it knowing the defendant was drunk.

Snell v. Norwalk Yellow Cab, Inc.

52 Conn. L. Rptr. 43 (Conn. Super. May 24, 2011) (Jennings, J.)

[A cab driver left his cab running in a parking lot when Bowden and Johnson stole it. Johnson drove the cab from the parking lot, but later Bowden took over driving and he was driving when he ran over the plaintiff and injured her. She brought a negligence claim against the cab driver for negligence and asserted his employer was liable under *respondeat superior*. The cab driver and his employer, the only defendants, sought to have the jury apportion liability to Johnson and Bowden by filing an "apportionment complaint." Plaintiffs moved to strike a claim in the apportionment complaint that asserted a negligent entrustment claim against Johnson for permitting Bowden to drive the stolen cab.]

While this is an issue of first impression in Connecticut, the defendants urge this court to adopt the decision of the Massachusetts Appeals Court in *Salamone v.*

Riczker, 32 Mass.App.Ct. 429 (1992), premising negligent entrustment liability on "physical dominion" rather than a defendant's ownership of the car. The defendants also argue that a ruling in the plaintiff's favor would result in a car thief being held to a lesser standard of care than an individual authorized to possess the vehicle, a result the defendants deem absurd.

Superior Court decisions have consistently held that ownership is not a necessary element of the tort of negligent entrustment. This court has not found any Superior Court cases where a thief was held liable in tort for negligently entrusting the stolen motor vehicle. In Massachusetts, however, the Appeals Court had opportunity to consider whether liability could attach against a teenaged boy who was accused of "through an act of usurpation, filching the keys" of his father's car and negligently entrusting the car to a friend who proceeded to strike a jogger with the car. *Salamone,* at 429. The question upon review, as framed by the Appeals Court, was "what constitutes *control* of property sufficient to make a negligent entrustment." *Id.* The Court answered as follows: "The better view is to think of control for purposes of negligent entrustment in terms of the ability to determine whether another may use the potentially dangerous instrumentality. To hold otherwise would produce the paradox that a person who comes into unauthorized physical control of a car, such as a car thief, would be less subject to civil liability for negligent entrustment than someone authorized to have physical control, such as an owner." *Id.*

The Indiana Court of Appeals considered a similar question where two defendants, who were friends of the owner of the car, were accused of negligently entrusting the car keys to the owner after they obtained the keys without the owner's permission. *Lather v. Berg,* 519 N.E.2d 755 (Ind.App. 2 Dist. 1988). The issue as framed by the court was "can either defendant be liable for negligent entrustment of a motor vehicle that they neither owned nor had a right to control?" *Id.* After quoting and discussing Section 308 of the Restatement (Second) of Torts the Indiana court held that, "the defendants had no legal right to deny the owner control of his car because they neither owned it nor had a right to control it. Therefore, the trial court properly entered summary judgment for the defendants on the theory of negligent entrustment." *Id.*

The Supreme Court of Illinois reached a similar result in *Zedella v. Gibson,* 165 Ill.2d 181 (1995), where a father was accused of negligently entrusting a car to his son. The father argued that he could not be liable for negligent entrustment because he and the son were co-owners of the car and accordingly, the father did "not have a superior right to the possession or control of the vehicle." *Id.* The Illinois court concluded that "entrustment must be defined with reference to the right of control of the subject property. In essence, if the actor does not have an exclusive or superior right of control, no entrustment of the property can occur." *Id. See also Snodgrass v. Baumgart,* 25 Kan.App.2d 812 (1999) (pursuant to Section 308 of Restatement (Second) of Torts, a husband is not liable for negligently entrusting a car to his wife when the wife "shared an equal right to use and to possess the car with her husband" and the husband "lacked a superior or exclusive right of control over the car").

Accordingly, this court decides that the result reached by the Massachusetts Appeals Court is inconsistent with the Restatement which has guided Connecticut's trial courts in determining the scope of the negligent entrustment doctrine. Connecticut courts have held that the defendant's ownership of the car is not an element of the tort but they have not gone so far as to rule that mere physical dominion over the car without the lawful right of possession can lead to liability. Accordingly, the court grants the motion to strike count two of the apportionment complaint.

Ali v. Fisher

145 S.W.3d 557 (Tenn. 2004) (Anderson, J.)

[After being injured in a car wreck, plaintiff asserted a negligence claim against the defendant, Fisher, who had been driving the other car, and a claim of negligent entrustment against that car's owner, Scheve. The trial court concluded that negligent entrustment did not result in the car owner's vicarious liability, but required apportionment of damages. The jury awarded $500,000 and found the owner 20% at fault and the other driver 80% at fault. The trial court initially entered judgment against the driver for $400,000 and $100,000 against the owner, but then held the owner vicariously liable and entered judgment jointly and severally against both for $500,000. The court of appeals reversed. Plaintiff appealed.]

We begin our analysis by reviewing the familiar principles of comparative fault established in *McIntyre v. Balentine*, 833 S.W.2d 52 (Tenn. 1992). In *McIntyre*, we adopted a system of modified comparative fault by which a plaintiff who is less than fifty percent (50%) at fault may recover damages in an amount reduced by the percentage of fault assigned to the plaintiff. At the same time, we abandoned the concept of joint and several liability of tortfeasors and replaced it with a fault-based system of liability whereby a tortfeasor would be liable only to the extent of the percentage of fault assigned by the jury.

Despite these settled principles requiring the allocation of fault among the parties, Ali contends that Scheve was vicariously liable for Fisher's negligence based on his negligent entrustment. Although negligent entrustment requires proof that a chattel was entrusted to one incompetent to use it with knowledge of the incompetence, and that its use was the proximate cause of injury or damage to another, this Court has never specifically addressed the issue of whether a claim of negligent entrustment results in the entrustor's vicarious liability for the negligent acts of the entrustee.

Because Tennessee courts have not addressed the specific issue presented in this case, we examine decisions in other jurisdictions. For example, the Kansas Supreme Court has addressed this precise issue and has held that fault in a negligent entrustment case must be apportioned between the entrustor and an entrustee. In *McCart v. Muir*, 230 Kan. 618 (1982), the jury found that the father of the negligent driver was liable to the plaintiffs for negligently entrusting his son with the car used in the accident. In concluding that the trial court erred in failing to instruct the jury on comparative fault, the Kansas Supreme Court said:

> Liability in a negligent entrustment case is not founded upon the negligence of the driver of the automobile but upon the primary negligence of the entruster in supplying the chattel, an automobile, to an incompetent and reckless driver. The nature and extent of negligence of the entruster and of the entrustee are separate and distinct. The percentages of fault may be different in amount and should be determined separately.

The Kansas Supreme Court therefore held that the liability of a negligent entrustor should be determined according to the principles of comparative fault and that the negligent entrustor's fault must be compared to the entrustee's level of fault.

The Kansas Supreme Court's conclusion is consistent with numerous later decisions holding that negligent entrustment does not necessarily create vicarious liability.

In contrast, the plaintiff relies on *Loom Craft Carpet Mills, Inc. v. Gorrell*, 823 S.W.2d 431 (Ct. App. Tex. 1992), in which the Court of Appeals of Texas concluded that negligent entrustment liability is derivative in nature and that the entrustor may be held liable for the entrustee's negligence. The court reasoned:

> If the owner is negligent, his liability for the acts of the driver is established, and the degree of negligence of the owner would be of no consequence. When the driver's wrong is established, then by negligent entrustment, liability for such wrong is passed on to the owner. We believe the better rule is to apportion fault only among those directly involved in the accident, and to hold the entrustor liable for the percentage of fault apportioned to the driver.

In our view, the plaintiff's arguments, and the analysis in *Gorrell*, are not persuasive and are at odds with the numerous authorities recognizing that the tort of negligent entrustment does not create vicarious liability. In addition, we believe comparative fault principles as illustrated in *McCart* reflects the better-reasoned approach for several reasons.

First, the allocation of fault by the jury between the entrustor and the entrustee is entirely consistent with the principal goal of comparative fault, i.e., to link one's liability to one's degree of fault in causing harm. Moreover, the allocation of fault among the parties promotes the fairness that underlies the system of comparative fault.

Second, the analysis in *McCart* is consistent with decisions that have explicitly or implicitly recognized that negligent entrustment does not necessarily create vicarious liability. The act of negligent entrustment and the act of negligent operation of a vehicle are separate and distinct. The tort of negligent entrustment is committed when control of the entrusted chattel is relinquished by the entrustor to a person the entrustor knows to be incompetent to use it. Accordingly, the argument that a negligent entrustment claim does not arise until the entrustee's negligence causes harm does not alone make negligent entrustment derivative of the entrustee's negligence.

Third, the *McCart* analysis is consistent with the fact that we have only rarely departed from the allocation of fault required under the system of comparative fault we adopted in *McIntyre*.

Accordingly the jury must allocate the fault between the defendants.

Notes and Questions

1. <u>What Were the Defendants Trying to Do</u>? Had the *Snell* defendants succeeded, the jury would have been asked whether Johnson had negligently entrusted the vehicle to Bowden and, if so, to apportion fault to the extent that negligence caused the harm. Why would defendants do this when the plaintiff did not sue Bowden (or Johnson)? As to the approaches to whether negligent entrustment results in apportionment or vicarious liability, what incentives does each approach create?

2. <u>Underage Car Rental</u>. Car rental companies generally do not rent to drivers under 25 because of their high accident rates. Yet courts have held that, by itself, renting to drivers under age 25 is insufficient to constitute negligent entrustment. *Amparan v. Lake Powell Car Rental Companies*, 882 F.3d 943 (10th Cir. 2018) (collecting cases). Why? What if it rented to someone over 25 with an expired license?

3. <u>Entrusting Chattels Besides Cars, or Even Land</u>? Courts have permitted plaintiffs to recover for negligently entrusting various chattels, including guns and boats. *E.g., Herland v. Izatt*, 345 P.3d 661 (Utah 2015) ("Utah public policy supports imposing a duty on gun owners to exercise reasonable care in supplying their guns to others whom they know, or should know, are likely to use the gun in a manner that creates a foreseeable risk of injury to themselves or third parties."); *Morris v. Giant Four Courners, Inc.*, 294 F. Supp. 3d 1207 (2018) (store sold gasoline to intoxicated person who then crashed while driving drunk). *See* Jefferson W. Fisher, *Negligent Entrustment of a Firearm: Provoking Thought on a Claim Rejected*, Tex. B.J. 790 (Nov. 2018).

So far Texas courts have rejected applying negligent entrustment to guns. In addition, plaintiffs have been unsuccessful in using negligent entrustment when injured on real property. *Bjerk v. Anderson*, 911 N.W.2d 343 (N.D. 2018) (holding plaintiff, whose son had died from an overdose in a "drug house," could not state negligent entrustment against landowner); *Euell v. Madeira, LLC*, 2012 WL 386494 (Conn. Super. Jan. 12, 2012) (stating court had found no authority permitting the claim). Why would it matter whether the plaintiff had been harmed by a chattel or use of land?

4. <u>Vicarious Liability or Apportionment</u>? Some courts agree with the principal case that negligent entrustment requires apportionment, *e.g., Martell v. Driscoll*, 302 P.3d 375 (Kan. 2013), but others reason that "once negligent hiring or

entrustment is established, liability for the employee's negligent operation of the vehicle is passed on to the employer, and the employer's acts are of no consequence in determining its degree of responsibility." *Williams v. McCollister*, 671 F. Supp. 2d 884, 891 (S.D. Tex. 2009). Is that reasoning sound? On the other hand, why is an employer vicariously liable for an employee's negligence but only proportionally at fault if the harm results from negligent retention? Imagine a judgment-proof employer and wealthy employee and weigh the different approaches.

5. <u>First-Party Negligent Entrustment Claims</u>. Can a party who receives a chattel from a defendant sue if injured because the defendant should have known better? Courts approach so-called "first party negligent entrustment" claims differently. In *Herland v. Izatt*, 345 P.3d 661 (Utah 2015), a woman had killed herself with a gun given to her by the defendant when she was intoxicated. The court explained the approaches to first-party negligent entrustment claims by intoxicated plaintiffs:

> Intoxicated individuals will likely find it difficult to recover for injuries that are caused, at least in part, by their own intoxication. Utah's comparative fault rule bars recovery where the plaintiff is fifty percent or more at fault. Indeed, some states have concluded that the comparative fault rule completely bars first-party recovery as a matter of law because in their reasoning an intoxicated plaintiff will never be less than fifty percent at fault for injuries he or she causes. But we do not agree with this reasoning, since it is not our prerogative to carve out exceptions to the comparative negligence regime established by the Utah Legislature.

The court in *Gozleveli v. Kohnke*, 2015 WL 3917089 (S.D. Fla. June 25, 2015), elaborated on that point:

> At first blush, comparative negligence in a negligent entrustment case seems counter-intuitive—had [the defendant] not negligently entrusted the [vehicle to the plaintiff], there would have been no accident, end of story. Restatement (Second) of Torts § 390 states that someone who supplies a chattel to another whom the supplier knows, or has reason to know, to be likely to use it in a manner involving unreasonable risk of physical harm to himself and others is subject to liability. Comment c of § 390 notes that one who accepts and uses a chattel knowing that he is incompetent to use it safely will usually be in such contributory fault as to bar recovery. But where a jurisdiction employs a comparative fault theory rather than contributory fault, the fact finder is tasked with apportioning percentage of fault of liability rather than holding that the entrustee is completely barred from recovery.

> First-party negligent entrustment comparative fault cases often arise where a car is loaned to a driver that the entrustor knows is incompetent but where the entrustee also knows, or should know, that they are incompetent to drive. For example a first-party negligent entrustment theory may be pursued in conjunction with comparative negligence where the evidence established negligence on the part of the plaintiff in consciously deciding to

take control of the vehicle, even though he knew he was in no condition to drive. It was appropriate to weigh and consider that evidence under comparative negligence principles, in relation to the evidence which tended to establish negligence on the part of the defendant who turned the car over to one whose faculties he either knew or should have known were impaired by drinking.

C. Negligence Claims Against Parents for Harm Caused by Their Child

K.H. v. J.R.

826 A.2d 863 (Pa. 2003) (Saylor, J.)

[A 14-year-old boy shot another boy in the stomach with a BB gun. The parents of the injured boy sued the 14-year-old and his father, J.R., who had joint legal custody but was the noncustodial parent, asserting negligence against the 14-year-old and parental liability against the father. The trial court granted summary judgment to the father, and the jury awarded $4,625 against the 14-year-old. The trial court then reconsidered its grant of summary judgment and held the father jointly and severally liable. The father appealed that ruling.]

Although a parent/child relationship by itself is insufficient to render the parents liable for the tortious acts of their children, liability may attach where the negligence of the parents makes the injury possible. Section 316 of the Restatement reflects this principle by limiting the duty of a parent to control the conduct of a child to those instances in which a parent has the ability to control the child, knows of its necessity, and has the opportunity to do so. While the extension of liability is further conditioned upon a finding that the failure to control created an unreasonable risk of harm, resolution of the present issue involves consideration of the ability and opportunity requisites. In this regard, the terms are further defined in the commentary following Section 316, which indicates that:

> The duty of a parent is only to exercise such ability to control his child as he in fact has at the time when he has the opportunity to exercise it and knows the necessity of so doing. Indeed, the very youth of the child is likely to give the parent more effective ability to control its actions and to make it more often necessary to exercise it.

A.H.'s parents maintain that ability and opportunity under Section 316 of the Restatement are satisfied through J.R.'s rights and obligations as a legal custodian with shared custody. The effect of a shared custody arrangement upon a parent's liability for a failure to control a child is an issue of first impression before this Court; however, as noted, the Superior Court addressed this circumstance in *J.H. v. Pellak*, 764 A.2d at 68. In *Pellak*, the parents of the minor defendant had a shared custody arrangement, during the course of which the father had purchased an air pistol and an air rifle for his son that were stored, used and maintained solely at the father's home. Although the mother was aware of the air rifle, she did not know of the existence of the air pistol. While in the physical custody of the father, the minor, who was twelve years of age, used the air pistol to shoot a friend. The parents of the victim initiated an action for negligent supervision against, *inter alia,* the minor defendant's mother. In affirming the entry of summary judgment in favor of the mother, the Superior Court concluded that, as the mother did not know of the existence of the air pistol, she was unaware of the need to supervise, and, as she did not have physical custody at the time of the incident, she was not in a position to exercise control. Concerning the effect of the shared custody arrangement, the court in *Pellak* reasoned that:

> In conclusion, we make clear that the duty to exercise reasonable care to control a child must be limited. It arises when a parent at the relevant time knows or should know of the need to exercise parental control and has the ability and opportunity to do so. Neither shared physical custody nor *shared legal custody* for a child changes that standard. . . .

> Legal custody is defined by statute as the legal right to make major decisions affecting the best interest of a minor child, including, but not limited to, medical, religious and educational decisions. Shared legal custody is specifically designed to invite input from both parents on such *major* decisions. Shared legal custody was never intended to govern the myriad of daily domestic decisions that a parent with physical custody makes. Nor was it intended to be the basis for imputing negligence to a parent who did not know of the need to exercise control and did not have the ability or opportunity to do so.

Courts in other jurisdictions have similarly considered the ability and opportunity requirements under Section 316 of the Restatement in declining to subject parents to liability absent such proof of presence and proximity. Although defining ability and opportunity as physical presence at the exact instant of the tort would be unduly restrictive and would undermine the duty to supervise recognized in Section 316 of the Restatement, supervision and control assume a measure of present ability to discipline.

We therefore agree with the reasoning of the Superior Court in *Pellak* that one's status as a legal custodian is not, in and of itself, dispositive in establishing the ability and the opportunity to control. In this case, the fact that J.R. was aware of the BB gun and agreed to allow N.R. to take it to his mother's home does not alter the absence of evidence demonstrating ability and opportunity to control or provide a meaningful basis for distinguishing *Pellak.* Moreover, considering the difficulty and emotion that often attend custody arrangements, imposing a duty to supervise upon a non-custodial parent would unnecessarily interject additional tension into the domestic relations arena. Thus, we conclude that the trial court properly awarded summary judgment to J.R., and that the Superior Court erred in reversing the order.

Notes and Questions

1. <u>Not in Texas</u>. In *Danielle A. v. Christopher P.*, 776 N.Y.S.2d 446 (N.Y. Sup. Ct. Feb. 13, 2004), a boy shot another boy with a paintball gun powered by carbon dioxide canisters. The court held that possessing such a gun violated New York penal laws against possessing "air guns," and found the parents had purchased the gun and 500 paintballs. Thus, they were liable under Section 316 because they not only knew of and allowed the dangerous activity, they consented and approved of it.

2. <u>Statutory Modifications</u>. In addition to ordinary negligence-based claims, some state statutes impose vicarious liability on parents for their children's malicious or willful torts. *See, e.g.*, Cal. Civ. Code § 1714.1 (capping damages at $25,000); *Beddingfield v. Linam*, 127 So. 3d 1178 (Ala. 2013) (discussing Alabama's statute). An Ohio statute imposes joint and several liability on a parent of a minor child who "willfully damages property" or "commits acts cognizable as a 'theft offense'" under an Ohio criminal statute. *Gurry v. C.P.*, 972 N.E.2d 154 (Ct. App. Ohio 2012) (parent vicariously liable for minor's theft and destruction of a car). Why would a legislature make a parent vicariously liable for a child's intentional tortious conduct, but not for negligence?

3. Conspiracy and Aiding and Abetting

The effect of conspiracy is to "allow a plaintiff to spread liability to those involved in causing the underlying tort." *Lorillard Tobacco Co. v. Alexander*, 123 So. 3d 67 (Ct. App. Fla. 2013) (conspiracy creates vicarious liability; *see Dunn v. Rockwell*, 689 S.E.2d 255 (W. Va. 2009) (same). Similarly, aiding and abetting is a "legal doctrine that imposes liability on persons who, although not actually committing a tort themselves, share with the immediate tortfeasors a common plan or design in its perpetration." *Hip Hop Bev. Corp. v. Michaux*, 2016 WL 8578912 (C.D. Cal. Nov. 30, 2016), *aff'd*, 729 F. App'x 599 (9th Cir. 2018). To impose liability under conspiracy or aiding and abetting, a plaintiff must prove the defendant was more than passively involved or knew of planned wrongful conduct. Conspiracies can be based upon physical harm or pecuniary damage. *See Karachi Bakery India v. Deccan Foods LLC*, 2017 WL 4922013 (D.N.J. Oct. 31, 2017) (dismissing conspiracy claim for failing to plead special damages in compliance with Rule 9(g)).

A majority of states hold that conspiracy and aiding and abetting are not tort claims for damages but instead doctrines to impose vicarious liability. Conspiracy generally requires: (1) a combination between two or more persons, (2) to do a criminal or an unlawful act (or a lawful act by criminal or unlawful means), (3) an act done by one or more of those persons pursuant to the scheme or agreement to further its objective, (4) that causes damage to the plaintiff. *See Fischer v. Ulysses Partners, LLC*, 2016 WL 8669889 (Conn. Super. Nov. 8, 2016). One conspirator may act, and the other may merely have agreed to participate. *Id.*

Aiding and abetting generally requires: (1) the party whom the defendant aided must have performed a wrongful act that caused injury to plaintiff; (2) the defendant must have generally been aware of his role as part of an overall illegal or tortious activity when he provided that aid; and (3) the defendant must have knowingly and substantially assisted the wrongful act. *See id.* Thus, a key distinction between civil conspiracy and aiding and abetting is that an aider and abettor defendant need not have agreed but must have given substantial assistance to the defendant who injured the plaintiff while having been aware that the assistance would aid in injuring the plaintiff.

A minority view recognizes conspiracy as a claim. For example, under South Carolina law, "the tort of civil conspiracy has three elements: (1) a combination of two or more persons, (2) for the purpose of injuring the plaintiff, and (3) causing plaintiff special damage." *Glass v. Rockwell Collins, Inc.,* 2018 WL 2149313 (D.S.C. May 10, 2018). The first element requires direct or circumstantial evidence from which a jury may reasonably "infer the joint assent of the minds of two or more parties to the prosecution of the unlawful enterprise." *Id.* "The gravamen of the tort of civil conspiracy is the damage resulting to the plaintiff from an overt act done pursuant to the combination, not the agreement or combination *per se.*" *Id.* As a result, a complaint should be dismissed if the "plaintiff merely repeats the damages from another claim instead of specifically listing special damages as part of their civil conspiracy claim."

Similarly, a minority views aiding and abetting to be a claim, as the court in *Grant v. John Hancock Mut. Life Ins. Co.,* 183 F. Supp. 2d 344 (D. Mass. 2002) explained:

> Under Massachusetts law, two types of civil conspiracies exist. There is precedent supporting a very limited cause of action in Massachusetts' for 'civil conspiracy' of a coercive type. In order to state a claim plaintiff must allege that defendants, acting in unison, had some peculiar power of coercion over plaintiff that they would not have had if they had been acting independently. The second type of civil conspiracy is akin to a theory of common law joint liability in tort.
>
> The first type, the "true conspiracy," has most frequently been applied to combinations of employers or employees working together in concerted refusals to deal. Outside of this context, a claim of civil conspiracy is rare and a very limited cause of action. he plaintiff must allege and prove that by mere force of numbers acting in unison the defendants exercised some peculiar power of coercion of the plaintiff which any individual standing in a like relation to the plaintiff would not have had. Evidence of joint activity, even tortious activity, is insufficient to prove a coercive conspiracy.
>
> The second type of conspiracy is not an independent action, but rather involves "concerted action," whereby liability is imposed on one individual for the tort of another. Under this theory, a defendant may be held liable for actions done by others pursuant to a common design or with the defendant's

substantial assistance or encouragement. Key to this cause of action is a defendant's substantial assistance, with the knowledge that such assistance is contributing to a common tortious plan. Thus, plaintiff must establish a common plan to commit a tortious act where the participants know of the plan and its purpose and take affirmative steps to encourage the achievement of the result. *Grant v. John Hancock Mut. Life Ins. Co.*, 183 F. Supp. 2d 344 (D. Mass. 2002)

In re Dicamba Herbicides Litig.

359 F. Supp. 3d 711 (E.D. Mo. 2019) (Limbaugh, J.)

[Plaintiffs were farmers. Neighboring farmers planted crops that were genetically modified to be resistant to a herbicide called dicamba. Plaintiffs' crops were damaged when the neighboring farms used dicamba on their crops. The plaintiffs sued Monsanto for manufacturing the dicamba, under the theory that by selling dicamba-resistant seeds, Monsanto was negligent because dicamba would fall onto neighboring crops and damage them. The plaintiffs sued other defendants for assisting with the marketing of the dicamba and genetically modified seeds as part of a product and system called "Xtend Crop System." Defendants moved for summary judgment on claims that they had conspired or aided and abetted each other.]

Plaintiffs bring conspiracy claims against the defendants in Arkansas, Illinois, Kansas, Mississippi, Missouri, Nebraska, South Dakota, and Tennessee. To prove a civil conspiracy, plaintiffs must show that: (1) two or more persons (2) have combined to accomplish a purpose (3) that is unlawful, oppressive, or accomplishes some purpose not in itself unlawful or oppressive by unlawful, oppressive, or immoral means, (4) to the injury of another. Three relevant states require plaintiffs to prove a fifth element: that there was a meeting of the minds on the object or course of action to be taken. A conspiracy claim cannot stand alone—rather, the function of a conspiracy claim is to extend liability in tort beyond the active wrongdoer to those who have merely planned, assisted or encouraged the wrongdoer's acts.

Defendants insist that this Court should dismiss the conspiracy claims because conspiracy requires an underlying intentional tort. With the dismissal of plaintiffs' trespass claims, defendants say, plaintiffs have no underlying intentional tort to support a conspiracy.

Plaintiffs insist that the relevant jurisdictions all allow civil conspiracy cases to proceed without an underlying intentional tort, relying heavily on the Illinois Supreme Court's language in *Adcock v. Brakegate Ltd.*, 645 N.E.2d 888 (Ill. 1994), and the Restatement (Second) of Torts § 876. The Illinois Supreme Court held that although "a civil conspiracy is based upon intentional activity, the element of intent is satisfied when a defendant knowingly and voluntarily participates in a common scheme to commit an unlawful act or a lawful act in an unlawful manner." *Id.* The court then added, "we reject defendant's claim that a cause of action for civil conspiracy does not arise unless one of the conspirators commits an intentional tort in furtherance of the conspiracy." *Id.* Similarly, the Iowa Supreme Court, relying on *Adcock*, held that "so long as the underlying actionable conduct is of the type that one can plan ahead to do, it should not matter that the legal system allows recovery upon a mere showing of unreasonableness (negligence) rather than requiring an intent to harm." *Wright v. Brooke Group Ltd.*, 652 N.W.2d 159, 173 (Iowa 2002).

The Restatement appears to require only a underlying tortious or otherwise unlawful act. Restatement (Second) of Torts § 876(a). The Restatement—which, inexplicably, is not quoted in the briefing—states in pertinent part:

> For harm resulting to a third person from the tortious conduct of another, one is subject to liability if he
>
> (a) does a tortious act in concert with the other or pursuant to a common design with him, or
>
> (b) knows that the other's conduct constitutes a breach of duty and gives substantial assistance or encouragement to the other so to conduct himself, ...

Restatement (Second) of Torts § 876 (1979). Under these provisions, it appears that liability attaches whether the underlying tort is intentional or negligent.

To be sure, there is ample caselaw from relevant jurisdictions recognizing conspiracy claims based on non-intentional torts. Those cases notwithstanding, defendants press the point (which the plaintiffs concede) that parties cannot conspire to commit negligence, which, of course, is the rationale behind the conventional requirement for an underlying intentional tort. Soon after the adoption of § 876 in 1979, the United States Court of Appeals for the D.C. Circuit in *Halberstam v. Welch*, 705 F.2d 472 (1983) explored in detail the legal framework regarding vicarious liability for concerted action. The court observed that the two subsections of Restatement § 876 correspond generally to two variations of vicarious liability: subsection (a) of the Restatement corresponds to conventional conspiracy, or concerted action by agreement; subsection (b) corresponds to aiding-abetting liability, concerted action by substantial assistance. As the *Halberstam* court explained it,

> The prime distinction between civil conspiracies and aiding-abetting is that a conspiracy involves an agreement to participate in a wrongful activity. Aiding-abetting focuses on whether a defendant knowingly gave "substantial assistance" to someone who performed wrongful conduct, not on whether the defendant agreed to join the wrongful conduct.

The court lamented that "courts and commentators have frequently blurred the distinction between the two theories of concerted liability." *Id.* Although *dicta*, the *Halberstam* court also observed that "it is difficult to conceive of how a conspiracy could establish vicarious liability where the primary wrong is negligence, but a secondary defendant could substantially aid negligent action." *Id.* This appears to be a tacit recognition of the truism that parties cannot conspire or intend to commit negligence under subsection (a). In contrast, aiding-abetting liability under subsection (b) does not depend on an agreement to commit an underlying tort, whether intentional or negligent. Notably, cases relied upon by plaintiff, in which the courts approve of a conspiracy to commit negligence, do not address this dichotomy.

In this case, plaintiffs allege a scheme to market, sell, and expand sales and profits from the Xtend Crop system, and they describe the defendants' intertwined activities at length. However, plaintiffs are not entirely clear which tort claims may serve as the underlying tortious conduct to the conspiracy count, much less do they identify which prong of the Restatement they are proceeding under. It appears that they have alleged intentional tortious conduct on the parts of both defendants to sustain a conspiracy claim for, at least, false advertising and fraudulent misrepresentation under the Lanham Act. As for counts going to negligence, it unclear whether plaintiffs are grounding their claims under the Restatement's subsection (a), the conventional conspiracy theory, or under subsection (b), the aiding-abetting theory. If brought under subsection (b), it is irrelevant, as noted, whether the underlying tortious act is intentional or negligent. On the other hand, if the negligence claims are brought under subsection (a), this Court would be faced with the difficult task of reconciling the claims with the truism that parties cannot conspire to commit negligence. In any event, this Court need not decide the propriety of the underlying negligence claims until plaintiffs have clarified whether those claims are grounded in subsections (a) or (b), and the parties have fully briefed these additional issues. And if indeed plaintiffs make clear that the underlying negligence claims are being brought under subsection (b), the conundrum posed under subsection (a) need not be addressed. As such, the Court denies the motion to dismiss as it pertains to the remaining underlying intentional torts and withhold ruling on the propriety of underlying negligence claims.

Notes and Questions

1. <u>Negligent Conspiracy?</u> Courts have held that parties cannot conspire to be negligent, but reason that it is because they must have the specific intent to agree. *E.g., N. Am. Van Lines, Inc. v. Emmons,* 50 S.W.3d 103 (Ct. App. Tex. 2001). If a party decides to drive carelessly, does that mean they were not negligent?

2. <u>Scope of Liability for Conspiracy or Aiding and Abetting</u>. The common law majority rule is that a party who aids and abets, or who conspires, is jointly and severally liable for all of the harm. Whether an applicable apportionment statute changes that turns on the statute and whether conspiracy or aiding and abetting are themselves claims. *Compare Waldman v. Stone,* 599 F. App'x 569, 574 (6th Cir. 2015) ("At one time, Kentucky indeed had a common-law rule that co-conspirators are each liable for all of the damages that result from the conspiracy. But the Kentucky legislature was free to abrogate that rule, which it did by enacting K.R.S. 411.182. That statute provides that a court must apportion liability in "*all* tort actions." (Emphasis added.) And a claim for civil conspiracy to defraud is a tort action.) *with Fid. & Guar. Ins. Underwriters Inc. v. Wells Fargo Bank, Nat. Ass'n,*

2006 WL 870683 (S.D. Tex. Mar. 31, 2006) (holding that, at least when liability is derivative and not vicarious, "joint and several liability as between the derivatively liable party and the primary actor still applies, but the apportionment accounts for recovery by the hiring or entrusting employer from the driver, based on the percentages of responsibility assessed by the jury."). *See* Restatement (Third) of Torts: Apportionment of Liability § 13 ("a person whose liability is imputed based on the tortious acts of another is liable for the entire share of comparative responsibility assigned to the other."). In this regard, it can be difficult to apply the plain language of some state apportionment statutes to conspiracy and aiding and abetting, perhaps because the issue likely was not even considered. *See generally* William D. Underwood & Michael D. Morrison, *Apportioning Responsibility in Cases Involving Claims of Vicarious Derivative, or Statutory Liability for Harm Directly Caused by the Conduct of Another*, 55 Baylor L. Rev. 617 (2003) (noting the Texas legislature likely did not consider derivative or vicarious liability concepts when adopting the state's statute).

3. Partnerships, Joint Ventures, and Joint Participation. States recognize other means to impose vicarious liability. For example, a partner is generally vicariously liable for harm caused by a partner. *Firestone v. VanHolt,* 186 S.W.3d 319 (Ct. App. Mo. 2006). A partnership requires an express or implied agreement: (1) "to place their money, effects, labor and skill, or some or all of them, in lawful commerce or business;" (2) "divide the profits of that commerce or business in a specified proportion;" and (3) "bear the loss of that commerce or business in a specified proportion." *Id.*

There is less uniformity on the names and contours of other doctrines, but they share some common themes and concepts. States commonly impose vicarious liability on those involved in a "joint participation," "joint enterprise," or a "joint venture" that causes harm. But the terms have very different meanings.

For example, in California, vicarious liability based upon a "joint venture" requires that the defendant and the party that caused the harm "have joint control over the venture (even though they may delegate it), they must share the profits of the undertaking, and the members must each have an ownership interest in the enterprise." *Myrick v. Mastagni,* 185 Cal. App. 4th 1082 (2010). Much less is required in Georgia: in *Holman v. Ferrell,* 550 S.E.2d 470 (Ct. App. Ga. 2001), while racing with another car, the defendant crossed the center line and injured the plaintiff. The plaintiff sued the driver and his passengers. Because there was no evidence the passengers had "attempted to exercise control over the operation of the vehicles or encouraged the drivers to engage in illegal activity," the court granted them summary judgment.

Somewhere in the middle is Missouri. In *Firestone v. VanHolt,* 186 S.W.3d 319 (Ct. App. Mo. 2006), the plaintiff brought a wrongful death action after a car wreck. The other driver was a roofer with his own business. The accident occurred while he was driving to work a roofing job that had been successfully bid on by another business, Akers Home Improvement. The plaintiff asserted Akers was vicariously liable for the harm because the driver and Akers were in a "joint venture." The appellate court reversed summary judgment for Akers, stating that there was some evidence of: (1) an express or implied agreement; (2) a common purpose; (3) a community of pecuniary interest in that common purpose and (4) equal voice, giving an equal right of control in the direction of the enterprise. The appellate court reversed summary judgment for Akers because both Akers and the driver "exercised some degree of control over various aspects of" the roofing job.

If one party has a superior right of control, then a joint enterprise does not exist. Thus, for example, an employer cannot be liable under a joint venture theory for the harm caused by its employee because of the employer's control. *N. Am. Van Lines, supra.*

4. <u>Intra-Corporate Liability or Liability of Shareholders, Officers, or Directors</u>. Ordinarily, one corporation is not liable for harm caused by another, even if the harm was caused by a wholly owned subsidiary. Likewise, ordinarily a shareholder, officer, or director is not liable for harm caused by the corporation, even if the person had general managerial or supervisory powers. However, liability may be imposed against both affiliated corporations or corporate constituents under certain circumstances.

Vicarious liability can be imposed if the corporation that caused the harm was the "alter ego" of another corporation. Each corporation is presumed to be a distinct legal entity, separate from its shareholders, officers, directors, and affiliated corporations. *See Hatfield v. Allenbrooke Nursing & Rehab Cntr., LLC,* 2018 WL 3740565 (Ct. App. Tenn. Jan. 17, 2019). To "pierce the corporate veil" a party must show: (1) one corporation is a "sham or dummy" of the other; (2) the two corporations are in fact identical or indistinguishable; or (3) one corporation is merely an instrumentality or agent of the other. *Id.* Some courts require proof of "fraud"—that one corporation was "organized and operated as merely a tool" of another corporation. *Id.*

Finally, direct (as opposed to vicarious) liability for harm can be imposed on a person or entity in control of the particular operation by the corporation that caused the harm. *Id.* (explaining the degree of involvement must consist of more than monitoring performance, supervising budgets, and articulating general policies and procedures). Complete control over management and general operations does not create liability, however, but "direct control or extensive involvement" over the specific cause of the harm is sufficient. *Id.*

5. <u>Joint Ventures by Corporations or Their Constituents</u>. Courts generally hold that liability under a "joint venture" approach cannot be used to impose liability on a corporation for the acts of its affiliate, or a constituent based upon the acts of the corporation in which the person is an officer or director. This is because the corporation acts through its agents. *See Hatfield* (collecting cases holding plaintiffs may not use "theories of joint venture or joint enterprise to attribute a corporation's liability to its shareholders or its parent corporations").

Problems

1. <u>Motorcycle Dealer</u>. Your client is a motorcycle dealer. Under state law, to operate a motorcycle on the streets, the driver must have a special endorsement on their license. Brandon Freeman purchased a motorcycle from your client and died in an accident on the streets three days later. He had told your client's saleswoman that he had never owned a motorcycle but had driven one. After Brandon selected a motorcycle, the saleswoman asked to see Brandon's license and saw he did not have the special endorsement. She told him he could not operate the motorcycle on the streets without it. Brandon said he understood. The saleswoman has told you that, as Brandon left the store riding the motorcycle, he appeared to be driving competently. However, the police concluded that the cause of death was incompetence caused by inexperience and lack of a helmet, though one was located at the scene of the accident, attached to the motorcycle. Should you move to dismiss the parents' claim of negligent entrustment?

2. <u>Uninsured Motorist</u>. Courts have held that, without more, letting an uninsured motorist use a car is not negligent entrustment. Why?

3. <u>The Wrong Thief Has Deep Pockets</u>. A client has come to you. She was run over by a stolen cab. Thief A drove the cab initially, but then let Thief B drive, and she was driving when the accident occurred. Your pre-suit investigation has shown that the cab company is insolvent, the cab company employee has left the country, and Thief B has no assets, but Thief A recently came into a significant inheritance of more than $1 million. Your client's likely damages are around $500,000. Distinguish *Snell* or argue it was incorrectly decided.

4. <u>Bite 'Em Barry!</u> A police officer was driving late at night when an oncoming car swerved into the officer's lane, and he swerved to avoid collision. The officer made a U-turn and gave chase. The car kept driving. The officer called ahead and other officers set out spikes in the road and had their lights activated. The chasing officer pulled alongside the driver, whose window was down, and through loudspeakers ordered him to stop. The driver proceeded, but then pulled to the side and stopped. He did not exit the car, despite the officer's order to do so. Then he drove off again, toward the spikes and other cars, but stopped, got out of the car, and walked around it. Another officer had a police dog named Barry, and warned the driver if he did not put his hands on the car he would release the dog and the driver would be bitten. The driver stood near the passenger side door but did not put his hands on the car. Just as he began to do so, the officer released the dog, and it severely bit the driver. It turned out the driver was suffering from a severe hypoglycemic event and lacked cognitive function to understand what was happening. Plaintiff sued for negligence, asserting claims against the officer and employer, the police department. The state's law permits recovery only for battery, not negligence. A jury awarded the driver $675,000 and the defendants have asked you to explain the arguments on appeal.

5. <u>Employee Not Negligent, but Employer Liable</u>. A jury has returned a verdict in a simple case against employer and employee that turned on whether the employee

ran a red light: the plaintiffs' evidence was that he did; the defendants' was that he did not. The plaintiffs, injured in the wreck, sued the driver for negligence and her employer for negligent entrustment. The jury's verdict found that the driver had not run the red light, but found the plaintiff had proven all elements of negligent entrustment. Can the verdict stand?

6. <u>Trespassing Workers</u>. Chloe and Dirk are neighbors who share a common driveway. Chloe decided to expand her home in a way that Dirk found objectionable. In response, Dirk placed objects in the driveway (trash cans and other things). Chloe's general contractor and its subcontractors often drove deliberately off the driveway and into Dirk's yard to get to and from Chloe's home. This was a trespass that caused damage to Dirk's yard, despite their best efforts. Dirk has sued Chloe for trespass. What strategy would you recommend for her?

7. <u>Bad Evidence; Good Strategy</u>? Imagine you represent an employer sued for horrific injuries caused by an employee in a car wreck. The case has been filed and the plaintiff has asserted vicarious liability and negligent hiring and retention. Your initial investigation revealed that the employee had been in several prior accidents that your client had ignored and paid settlements "off the books" to avoid insurance payments. You believe the jury will find negligent hiring and supervision. Can you see an advantage to be gained by admitting course and scope in your answer?

8. <u>Vicarious or Apportionment</u>? Assume your state has not yet decided whether negligent entrustment results in apportionment or vicarious liability. Likewise, assume your state has not decided whether a defendant who intentionally harmed the plaintiff can apportion fault to a negligent non-party. Be prepared to argue both sides.

Chapter 11

Punitive Damages

1. Whether Punitive Damages Are Permitted

Whether punitive damages are permitted turns on the claim and state law. This section shows that an intentional tort does not automatically result in punitive damages. On the other hand, at common law, preponderant evidence of gross negligence is sufficient to sustain an award of punitive damages. *See Booth v. Robertson*, 374 S.E.2d 1 (Va. 1988) (noting a "general reluctance to allow punitive damages in run-of-the-mill personal injury cases"). Whether by common law or statute, many courts require greater culpability. *See McReynolds v. Matthews*, 2018 WL 279991 (S.D. Miss. Jan. 3, 2018) (common law requires clear and convincing evidence of gross negligence); Utah Code Ann. §78B-8-201(1)(a) (punitive damages permissible only "if compensatory or general damages are awarded and it is established by clear and convincing evidence that the acts or omissions of the tortfeasor are the result of willful and malicious or intentionally fraudulent conduct, or conduct that manifests a knowing and reckless indifference toward, and a disregard of, the rights of others."). Some statutes require greater culpability, but only for certain claims. *E.g.*, Pa. Stat. Ann. tit. 40, §1303.505 (barring punitive damages against health care providers for gross negligence but allowing them for "willful or wanton conduct or reckless indifference to the rights of others").

Significantly, when an entity is sued, the analysis changes. The court in *Merrimack College v. KPMG LLP*, 108 N.E.3d 430, 443 (Mass. 2018), explained that imputed knowledge and conduct do not apply in this analysis:

> Where an employee has engaged in misconduct, and where a person harmed by that misconduct seeks punitive damages against the employer, that misconduct will not necessarily be imputed to the employer. Rather, in awarding punitive damages, it is the actions of the employer, not the actions of that employee, that are the appropriate focus, and it is the employer's conduct that must be found to be outrageous or egregious. And, in determining whether the employer engaged in outrageous or egregious conduct, we look to whether members of senior management participated in the misconduct, or acquiesced in it by knowing of the misconduct and failing to remedy it. The misconduct of lower-level employees—even those at the supervisory level—is insufficient to warrant punitive damages. In this context, we depart from the usual rules of imputation because an award of punitive damages requires a moral judgment that the defendant's conduct

is so blameworthy that it justifies punishment rather than merely compensation. Accordingly, conduct by an employee that is sufficient to hold an employer vicariously liable for compensatory damages does not necessarily suffice to justify punitive damages against the employer. To support an award of punitive damages, a jury must find the employer itself to be morally blameworthy, and that requires a finding that a member of the employer's senior management was morally blameworthy.

A Kentucky statute makes an employer liable for punitive damages only if the employer authorized the conduct, anticipated it, or ratified it. *See St. Joseph Healthcare, Inc. v. Thomas,* 487 S.W.3d 864 (Ky. 2016).

Fenwick v. Oberman

847 A.2d 852 (R.I. 2004) (Per Curiam)

[A jury awarded Plaintiff David Fenwick $1 for a battery claim he brought against his former supervisor, Claire Oberman. Plaintiff appealed, asserting the trial court had erred in excluding evidence of past animosity between the two, and that it had erred in charging the jury and in failing to give instructions he requested.]

The Providence office of the United States Department of Housing and Urban Development (HUD) provided the forum for this confrontation. The plaintiff had been working at HUD under the supervision of defendant since December 1988. Presumably, June 3, 1994, was to be a day like no other. At some point during that day, defendant entered the room where plaintiff's desk was and asked to borrow a book with fax cover sheets. When plaintiff left his desk to assist her, he noticed that his books no longer were on the bookshelf where he usually kept them. What happened next is a source of contention.

The plaintiff testified that he asked about his books, and defendant told him that they were moved so that copy paper could be placed on the bookshelf. This prompted a heated argument between plaintiff and defendant. The plaintiff testified that at some point during this exchange, defendant grabbed him by the throat and began choking him. He said that he grabbed her arm and eventually removed it from his throat. According to plaintiff, defendant then grabbed his face, with her palm on his chin, her fingers on one cheek and her thumb on the other, and started squeezing it. He said that he had to use a great deal of force to remove her hand at that point. He testified that she touched his face a third time, tapping the underside of his chin and saying, "Tsk, tsk, tsk, tsk."

The defendant relayed a very different version. She testified that when she entered the room, plaintiff "started throwing a temper tantrum" and yelling that she had no right to move his things. According to defendant, she responded that she had not moved the office materials and suggested that defendant ask a third party about his books. The defendant testified that plaintiff began throwing reams of paper on the floor, and that she kept picking them up. At that point, defendant testified, she attempted to calm plaintiff down by placing her finger under his chin, but that plaintiff grabbed her arm and twisted it away. She said that the contact lasted for "a split second" and that she did not touch him again after that.

The jury also heard two other HUD employees' descriptions of the fight. Elaine Carpentier (Carpentier) testified that she was in the room when the incident occurred, but she did not recall any of the words that plaintiff or defendant uttered at the time. Carpentier testified that she saw defendant grab plaintiff somewhere between the jaw and the neck area, but that it did not appear that she was attempting to choke or otherwise harm plaintiff. Carpentier also indicated that there was only one incident of contact and that defendant did not touch plaintiff again.

Another HUD employee, Gertrude Hall (Hall), testified that, although she could not see the combatants' hands during the incident, it appeared that plaintiff grabbed defendant's arm and pushed it down. Hall said that plaintiff began yelling "sexual harassment" and his face went gray. Hall did not see any swelling on plaintiff's throat, but said that there was a reddish mark on one of his cheeks and that defendant had red marks on her wrist.

At the close of all evidence, plaintiff requested that the trial justice consider an award of punitive damages. The trial justice determined that there was nothing in the testimony "that would justify a hint of punitive damages," denied his request, and instructed the jury on assault and battery. So doing, the trial justice rejected several of the plaintiff's requested instructions dealing with criminal battery and punitive damages. The jury found that defendant did commit a battery, but that plaintiff was neither assaulted nor injured. Accordingly, the jury awarded plaintiff $1 in nominal damages. The plaintiff timely appealed.

We begin by addressing plaintiff's challenge to the trial justice's refusal to issue an instruction on punitive damages. A party is entitled to a jury instruction in accordance with the law relevant to the issues raised by the parties and the evidence presented. The evidence presented in this case reveals that punitive damages were inappropriate and, therefore, the trial justice did not err in refusing to charge the jury on that issue.

This Court consistently has looked askance at punitive damages except in egregious circumstances. Punitive damages are appropriate only in the rare circumstances when a defendant's conduct requires deterrence and punishment over and above that provided in an award of compensatory damages. A party seeking punitive damages must produce evidence of such willfulness, recklessness or wickedness, on the part of the party at fault, as amounts to criminality that should be punished.

Whether a party has met this rigorous standard is a question of law. The trial justice makes the preliminary legal determination of whether there are adequate facts to support an award of punitive damages. If the trial justice determines that the evidence justifies a punitive damages award, the trier of fact makes the ultimate determination of whether and to what extent such damages should be awarded.

The plaintiff argues that because defendant's conduct constituted criminal battery, punitive damages were justified. This Court has defined battery as an act that was intended to cause, and does cause, an offensive contact with or unconsented touching of or trauma upon the body of another, thereby generally resulting in the consummation of the assault. Aside from the obvious higher standard of proof required to establish criminal battery, the law recognizes no distinction between criminal and civil battery.

The fact that a battery may also be criminal in nature does not automatically require an instruction on punitive damages. For example, in *Picard v. Barry Pontiac-Buick, Inc.*, 654 A.2d 690 (R.I. 1995), we held that punitive damages were inappropriate because, although a battery had occurred, there was no evidence of malice or bad faith on the part of the defendant. The plaintiff in *Picard* alleged that the defendant lunged at her while she attempted to photograph him. She testified that the defendant grabbed her around the shoulders, spun her around and then released her when someone said, "let her go." The defendant denied touching the plaintiff, although he admitted that he attempted to touch her camera. Against that factual backdrop, we held that punitive damages were inappropriate because there was no evidence of malice or bad faith on the part of the defendant. On the other hand, we held in *Sherman v. McDermott*, 114 R.I. 107 (1974), that punitive damages were appropriate when the defendant-police officer arrested the plaintiff and beat him with a club on the head and legs while two other police officers held the plaintiff down. These facts, the Court concluded, were sufficiently malicious, wanton and willful to support an award of punitive damages.

The battery that defendant committed against plaintiff did not rise to the level of malice requiring a punitive damages award. Here, the trial justice found only that "defendant placed her hand over plaintiff's mouth during an office dispute." The melee between plaintiff and defendant was more akin to the exchange in *Picard* than the brutal, mob-like beating in *Sherman*. Thus, the trial justice made the correct preliminary legal determination that the facts did not justify an award of punitive damages.

Notes and Questions

1. <u>Intentional Torts</u>. If a jury could find an intentional tort, should a judge deny a request to instruct the jury on punitive damages? Consider the explanation from *Braun v. Medtronic Sofamor Danek, Inc.*, 719 F. App'x 782 (10th Cir. 2017), that a finding of fraud did not establish the culpability for punitive damages:

> There is a distinction between recklessness with respect to the truth or falsity of a representation while knowing that there is insufficient knowledge to support the representation and reckless disregard of the known harm that could come to another because of such a misrepresentation. The former relates to a fraudster's knowledge of her lack of knowledge upon which to base a representation or, in other words, the knowledge of a serious risk that her representation will be false—this recklessness turns on the risk of falsity. The latter relates to the fraudster's knowledge of the risk of harm that may come about by a fraudulent representation—this recklessness turns,

not on the risk of falsity, but the risk of harm to others and their rights. In other words, knowing that one lacks a basis for a representation is distinct from the knowledge of the risk of harm that may result from that misrepresentation. Fraud requires the former; punitive damages requires the latter.

Because these are distinct forms of recklessness, an award of punitive damages is not automatic upon the establishment of the recklessness required—as a minimum threshold—for liability for fraudulent inducement; accordingly, the basis for the application of the ostensible aggravating circumstances standard is not present. In other words, Medtronic is mistaken in asserting that absent an additional aggravating circumstance requirement, "punitive damages would be available in *every* fraudulent inducement case" because the minimum scienter requirement for fraudulent inducement actually would not overlap with a scienter that is sufficient for an award of punitive damages.

Similarly, in *Beall v. Holloway-Johnson*, 446 Md. 48 (2016), the trial plaintiff obtained a verdict for compensatory damages for negligence, but the trial court had not submitted her battery claim to the jury. On appeal, the court stated that "civil battery may be committed without actual malice" and reasoned that because a judge cannot allow a jury to consider actual malice, for purposes of punitive damages without any evidence, "it would be improper for a trial court to imply routinely in [a civil battery claim] based purely on a determination that a *prima facie* case of each claim was established by a preponderance of the evidence." The court then examined the record and found no evidence of malice, and so no harm in not submitting the battery claim.

Finally, consider the observation that IIED itself "touches upon an intriguing question: the nexus between the requisite findings undergirding an intentional infliction claim and the findings necessary to allow an award of punitive damages under such a claim." *Borden v. Paul Revere Life Ins. Co.*, 935 F.2d 370 (1st Cir. 1991). In *Barnett v. Baker*, 2017 IL App 152443 (Il. Ct. App. March 8, 2017), the court held that Illinois law did not permit recovery for IIED of punitive damages if the jury awarded compensatory damages because, in that circumstance, "compensatory damages serve as punishment." Do you agree?

2. <u>Federal Pleading</u>. Because punitive damages are not compensatory damages, some courts hold that a request for punitive damages need not comply with Fed. R. Civ. P. 9(g). *Dowdy v. Coleman Co.*, 2011 WL 6151432 (D. Utah Dec. 12, 2011). However, a split exists, as *Holick v. Burkhart*, 2018 WL 4052154 (D. Kan. Aug. 24, 2018), explained:

Generally speaking, special damages are defined as "*compensatory damages* for a harm other than one for which general damages are given." Restatement (Second) of Torts §904 (1979) (emphasis added). By contrast, the Restatement defines "punitive damages" as damages "other than compensatory or nominal damages." *Id.* §908(1). Similarly, Black's Law

Dictionary equates "actual damages" with "compensatory damages," and then goes on to define "punitive damages" as damages "awarded in addition to actual damages." DAMAGES, Black's Law Dictionary (10th ed. 2014). These sources collectively define "special damages" as a form of actual or compensatory damages, while "punitive damages" are expressly excluded from the category of actual or compensatory damages.

Based on the foregoing, the undersigned judge respectfully disagrees with prior decisions in this district that punitive damages are special damages for purposes of Rule 9(g). Accordingly, Defendant's argument on this point is rejected. And, in any event, even in this district the cases recognize that under Rule 9(g), the pleading party need only allege the circumstances upon which the punitive damages claim is made. As noted, *supra*, the amended complaint on file in this case makes allegations that would help support a request for punitive damages, even though the words "punitive damages" were not included in the pleading.

The court includes the above discussion to avoid any misunderstanding as to the scope of the magistrate judge's ruling: it does not eliminate the possibility that Plaintiff might be able to pursue relief that includes punitive damages. *To the extent Plaintiff plans to seek punitive damages at trial, Plaintiff is nevertheless admonished to include that among his requested relief in the pretrial order.* Whether a jury may ultimately consider an award of punitive damages in this case is a decision that will have to wait for another day.

3. <u>State Pleading</u>. Some states require pleadings to allege facts supporting malice or gross negligence. For example, Florida requires pleading a "reasonable basis" that a party acted with "intentional misconduct or gross negligence." Fla. Stat. § 768.72(1), (2). Conclusory allegations are insufficient and instead "a plaintiff must plead specific acts committed by a defendant." *Douse v. Boston Scientific Corp.*, 314 F. Supp. 3d 1251 (M.D. Fla. 2018). "'Intentional misconduct' means that the defendant had actual knowledge of the wrongfulness of the conduct and the high probability that injury or damage to the claimant would result and, despite that knowledge, intentionally pursued that course of conduct, resulting in injury or damage." *Id*. Requiring greater detail reduces availability of punitive damages.

2. State and Federal Constitutional Limits on the Amount of Punitive Damages

A. Constitutional and Statutory Limitations

State laws, procedural rules, and federal constitutional principles regulate the amount of punitive damage awards. Unlike compensatory damages, punitive damages are not intended to make the plaintiff whole. Instead, their purpose is to punish the defendant and to deter others from engaging in similar conduct. The amount of punitive damages is carefully limited.

Myers v. Central Florida Inv. Inc.

592 F.3d 1201 (11th Cir. 2010) (Marcus, J.)

[This case is also discussed in Chapter 3: Plaintiff Myers sold timeshares for the defendant. The sole shareholder and CEO of defendant Central Florida Investments, Inc., was defendant David Siegel. Siegel was romantically interested in Myers, but she had a boyfriend. He tried to kiss her, offered to buy her lavish gifts, and even gave her a $10,000 check. She rebuffed him and said "Our friendship does not have a price tag on it. How many times do I have to tell you?" He persisted, and she resisted. He moved his office to be closer to hers. He would hug her at work and let his hand slip down and touch her behind in front of co-workers. He continued, at one point touching her breasts. When she began a new relationship, he touched her inappropriately, pinned her against the wall, and made lewd comments. Throughout this time, she reported Siegel to the company's HR department, but their response was: "What are you going to do? He's the president of the company." Rumors began to spread, and she was humiliated.

She was suspended in December 2000, earning $102,223.14 in her final year. She filed an EEOC complaint, alleging sexual discrimination, but three years passed. Then CFI sued her, asserting she owed $6,200 on an unpaid loan. She counter-claimed, including a claim for battery, and other claims. All of her other claims, however, were barred by statutes of limitation, but the jury found that all of the touching occurred after May 21, 2000, the critical date for statute of limitations on battery. The jury awarded her $102,223.14 in compensatory damages and $5.3 million in punitive damages, which were reduced ("remitted") by the district court to $500,000, the statutory cap put in place by Florida's legislature. Defendants appealed, asserting no punitive damages were recoverable and Myers asserted defendants had waived any remittitur.]

Florida law provides that:

> A defendant may be held liable for punitive damages only if the trier of *outline* fact, based on clear and convincing evidence, finds that the defendant was personally guilty of intentional misconduct or gross negligence. As used in this section, the term:
>
> > (a) "Intentional misconduct" means that the defendant had actual knowledge of the wrongfulness of the conduct and the high probability that injury or damage to the claimant would result and, despite that knowledge, intentionally pursued that course of conduct, resulting in injury or damage.

Fla. Stat. § 768.72(2). Decades of Florida case law have made it clear that a finding of battery is sufficient to trigger punitive damages. Inasmuch as the Florida courts have on this issue been unequivocal, the district court did not err by allowing punitive damages here.

The district court was empowered, however, to remit the award if it determined that it was unreasonable. *See id.* § 768.73(1)(d). The factors the trial court is obliged to consider when assessing the excessiveness of a punitive award are the same factors it must consider when assessing the amount of a compensatory award. In Florida, the courts must conduct this review in order to make certain that the manifest weight of the evidence does not render the amount of punitive damages assessed out of all reasonable proportion to the malice, outrage, or wantonness of the tortious conduct.

Under Florida law, the purpose of punitive damages is not to further compensate the plaintiff, but to punish the defendant for its wrongful conduct and to deter similar misconduct by it and other actors in the future. Supreme Court of Florida, therefore, has determined that the wealth of the defendant is a factor for consideration in determining the reasonableness of a punitive award: an award must be reviewed to ensure that it bears some relationship to the defendant's ability to pay and does not result in economic castigation or bankruptcy of the defendant. While it is not an accurate rule of law that the greater a defendant's wealth, the greater must be punitive damages, a jury may properly punish each wrongdoer by exacting from his pocketbook a sum of money which, according to his financial ability, will hurt, but not bankrupt.

This punitive award of $500,000 does not offend Florida Statute § 768.74(5). Given the many years during which Siegel touched and harassed Myers in the workplace, his repeated and public humiliations of her, and his refusal to desist despite her repeated requests, the award can hardly be said to evince passion, prejudice, or corruption. The award does not reveal that the court ignored evidence or considered improper elements, nor is the award otherwise illogical. Simply stated, the trial court could find that the $500,000 punitive award bore a reasonable relation to the damage that would flow from a battery preceded by so much sexual misconduct in the workplace.

Furthermore, the punitive damage award would not result in the economic castigation or bankruptcy of the defendants. The district court heard testimony that CFI's net worth exceeded $471,000,000 and Siegel's $324,000,000. Since defendants' ability to pay the original $5,378,863.14 judgment is, by their own post-trial admission, plain, the amended $500,000 punitive award cannot be said to bear an unreasonable relationship to their ability to pay.

Under Florida law, punitive damages also are subject to a statutory cap, and Myers asserts that it was improperly applied here. Section 768.73(1)(a) of the Florida Statutes provides that "an award of punitive damages may not exceed the greater of: 1. Three times the amount of compensatory damages awarded to each claimant entitled thereto, consistent with the remaining provisions of this section; or 2. The sum of $500,000." But there are statutory exceptions to this general rule, one of which provides that, "[w]here the fact finder determines that at the time of injury the defendant had a specific intent to harm the claimant and determines that the defendant's conduct did in fact harm the claimant, there shall be no cap on punitive damages." *Id.* § 768.73(1)(c). In other words, in order for a punitive award greater than $500,000 to stand, a Florida jury must have found *both* specific intent to harm and actual harm.

There is no question that the jury did not make any such overt findings. The jury answered eight questions on the verdict form, none of which addressed specific intent to harm or actual harm. However, the inquiry does not end there. The jury verdict is considered alongside the jury instructions, and if the two can be read together to show that the jury made the required findings, then a heightened award may still stand.

The district court's instructions to the jury regarding battery read this way:

> A battery is an intentional infliction of harmful or offensive contact upon the person of another. To prevail on her battery claim, the Plaintiff must prove each of the following facts by a preponderance of the evidence:
>
> *First:* That David Siegel intended to touch the Plaintiff's person;
>
> *Second:* That David Siegel actually touched the Plaintiff against her will; and
>
> *Third:* That the contact was harmful or offensive to the Plaintiff.

There is no natural reading of the verdict alongside the instructions that yields the conclusion that the jury made the requisite findings. As the instructions make clear, a civil battery might be supported where a defendant had specific intent to offend, not harm, and where the defendant effected an offensive, but not harmful, contact. Therefore, it can hardly be said that the findings of specific intent to harm and actual harm inhere in a jury verdict of civil battery.

The district court did make passing reference to the twin requirements when issuing instructions on punitive damages, encouraging the jury to "consider whether, at the time of the injury or damage, David Siegel had a specific intent to harm the Plaintiff and the conduct of David Siegel did in fact harm the Plaintiff." Yet the court never instructed the jury that it *must* find specific intent to harm or actual harm.

Furthermore, the district court was entitled to apply the statutory cap of its own volition: where a portion of a verdict is for an identifiable amount that is not permitted by law, the court may simply modify the jury's verdict to that extent and enter judgment for the correct amount. Because the Florida statute does not require a motion by the aggrieved party, we need not consider whether the defendants properly moved for application of the statutory cap.

The defendants also challenge the constitutionality of the $500,000 punitive award, asserting that they did not have fair notice that they might be liable to pay a punitive award so much greater than the compensatory award.

The foundation of the due process inquiry is found in *B.M.W. of N. Am., Inc. v. Gore*, 517 U.S. 559 (1996). "Elementary notions of fairness enshrined in our constitutional jurisprudence dictate that a person receive fair notice not only of the conduct that will subject him to punishment, but also of the severity of the penalty that a State may impose." *Id*. While "punitive damages may properly be imposed to further a State's legitimate interests in punishing unlawful conduct and deterring its repetition," and states "have considerable flexibility in determining the level of punitive damages that they will allow," an award runs afoul of the due process clause when it "can fairly be categorized as 'grossly excessive' in relation to these interests." *Id*. To help determine when an award is grossly excessive, the Supreme Court has adopted three guideposts for a court's consideration: "the degree of reprehensibility" of the defendant's actions; "the disparity between the harm or potential harm suffered by the plaintiff and his punitive damages award; and the difference between this remedy and the civil penalties authorized or imposed in comparable cases." *Id*.

Proper due process analysis of a punitive award in the Eleventh Circuit requires first that we identify the state's interest in deterring the relevant conduct and the strength of that interest. Next, we review the district court's findings regarding the three *BMW* guideposts. While we are mindful of the difficulty of our task, we are guided by the understanding that the constitutional question ultimately hinges on whether a defendant had adequate notice that its conduct might subject it to this punitive damage award.

The state's interest in deterring defendants' conduct is strong. As the Supreme Court of Florida has stated:

> There can be no doubt at this point in time that both the state of Florida and the federal government have committed themselves strongly to outlawing and eliminating sexual discrimination in the workplace, including the related evil of sexual harassment. The statutes, case law, and administrative regulations uniformly and without exception condemn sexual harassment in the strongest possible terms.

Byrd v. Richardson-Greenshields Secs., Inc., 552 So.2d 1099 (Fla. 1989). Furthermore, the state's interest in protecting workers from sexual discrimination extends to both statutory and common law claims: "Public policy now requires that employers be held accountable in tort for the sexually harassing environments they permit to exist, whether the tort claim is premised on a remedial statute or on the common law." *Id*.

There is no question that Florida has a considerable interest in protecting workers from the kind of sexual misconduct to which Myers was subjected for so many years. The jury found a battery by a superior on an employee in the workplace. This battery followed a long period during which Siegel and CFI subjected Myers to sexual harassment, but for which recovery was barred by the statute of limitations. Furthermore, Myers' repeated complaints, both to Siegel and other CFI executives, were ignored and rebuffed. This unchecked pattern of antisocial behavior from Siegel and CFI underscores the need for punitive damages as a means to correct evildoing in areas not covered by the criminal law.

With awareness of the powerful state interests in play, we turn next to the *Gore* guideposts. The first is the degree of reprehensibility, and it is "the most important indicium." *State Farm Mut. Auto. Ins. Co. v. Campbell*, 538 U.S. 408 (2003). The Supreme Court, in *State Farm*, identified five specific factors for consideration:

> We have instructed courts to determine the reprehensibility of a defendant by considering whether: the harm caused was physical as opposed to economic; the tortious conduct evinced an indifference to or a reckless disregard of the health or safety of others; the target of the conduct had financial vulnerability; the conduct involved repeated actions or was an isolated incident; and the harm was the result of intentional malice, trickery, or deceit, or mere accident.

538 U.S. at 419. While there is no requirement that a certain number of the five *State Farm* factors be present in order to support a finding of reprehensibility, reprehensibility grows more likely as more factors are present.

The district court took each *State Farm* factor in turn. On the first factor, the court noted that "the harm here was emotional rather than economic." As the jury heard evidence that Myers felt upset, embarrassed, humiliated, and degraded by Siegel's actions at CFI, this finding of fact does not constitute clear error.

On the second factor, the district court noted that "there is some disregard of health at play insofar as Plaintiff's emotional health was involved." Since there was plenty of evidence here, concerning both the battery and the sexual harassment, suggesting an indifference or reckless disregard towards Myers' health, whether physical or emotional, it was not clear error for the district court to so find.

On the third factor, the district court found that the employment relationship mattered: "financial vulnerability is implicated somewhat because, although this battery claim did not involve financial consequences for Plaintiff *per se,* the events did occur in the workplace and Plaintiff's boss—who controlled Plaintiff's earnings—was the one who committed the acts." Myers presented evidence that she feared making too big a deal of the touchings and harassment because Siegel was her boss and she did not want to lose her job. She testified that she stayed at CFI in part because she needed the money, and because she knew that her chosen industry would not be as kind to a person without a college degree as had been CFI. The district court's determination, therefore, that the superior-subordinate relationship between Siegel and Myers injected a sense of financial vulnerability into their interactions cannot constitute clear error.

On the fourth factor, the district court wrote, "there is some evidence of repeated actions, though only a six-month time period is at issue." We note, however, that a jury may consider material external to the charge in determining the reprehensibility of the charge itself. *See Gore,* 517 U.S. at 577 ("Certainly, evidence that a defendant has repeatedly engaged in prohibited conduct while knowing or suspecting that it was unlawful would provide relevant support for an argument that strong medicine is required to cure the defendant's disrespect for the law."). Moreover, "evidence of other acts need not be identical to have relevance in the calculation of punitive damages." *Id.*

In this case, there was voluminous evidence of repetition presented to the jury. Myers described a pattern of sexual touching from Siegel beginning in 1995 and ending in 2000. He touched her in the office, in the restaurant, in the spa, in the treatment room, and on the dance floor. He touched her legs, her behind, and her shoulders. The district court's only error was the suggestion that the similar prior transgressions that are time-barred are in no way relevant to the reprehensibility inquiry; such a conclusion does not flow from our precedents.

On the fifth and final factor, the district court noted that "battery is an intentional tort, although malice is not required for its commission." Inasmuch as battery in Florida can be sustained by an intent to do mere offense, the district court's determination that intentional malice was not present is not clearly erroneous.

After the analysis of the *State Farm* factors, the district court turned to *Gore* and concluded that "Mr. Siegel's conduct is at the low to middle range of the reprehensibility scale." This is a factual finding, for which the district court is allowed in its discretion to weigh the severity of each factor. In light of the ample evidence that Myers suffered emotional distress, that she decided to stomach the objectionable conduct for fear of losing her job and her income, that the behavior persisted for years and over her frequent objections, and that no one at CFI seemed to care, we cannot say that the district court's conclusion regarding reprehensibility is clearly erroneous.

The second *Gore* guidepost is the ratio of punitive damages to actual harm inflicted on the plaintiff. The "proper inquiry is whether there is a reasonable relationship between the punitive damages award and *the harm likely to result* from the defendant's conduct as well as the harm that actually has occurred." *Gore,* 517 U.S. at 581. On this issue, "comparison between the compensatory award and the punitive award is significant." *Id.* In particular, the ratio of punitive to compensatory damages is instructive. Nevertheless, the Supreme Court has consistently rejected the notion that the constitutional line is marked by a simple mathematical formula, even one that compares actual *and potential* damages to the punitive award.

In this case, the amended judgment set punitive damages at $506,847.78 and compensatory damages at $103,622.09. Since this yields a ratio of punitive to compensatory damages of approximately 4.89:1, the district court's finding that the ratio was "less than 5 to 1," is not clearly erroneous. The district court then concluded that "this ratio does not suggest an excessive award." Notably, this Court has approved of a number of punitive awards where the ratio of punitive to compensatory damages exceeded 4.89:1. *See Johansen,* 170 F.3d at 1327 (ratio of 100:1); *Goldsmith,* 513 F.3d at 1283 (ratio of 9.2:1); *U.S. EEOC v. W&O, Inc.,* 213 F.3d 600 (11th Cir. 2000) (ratio of 8.3:1); *Action Marine, Inc. v. Cont'l Carbon, Inc.,* 481 F.3d 1302 (11th Cir. 2007) (ratio of 5.5:1); *see also Bogle v. McClure,* 332 F.3d 1347 (11th Cir. 2003) (ratio of 3.8:1). Furthermore, on the one occasion where this Court has struck down a punitive award for constitutional excess, it reduced an award with a ratio of 8,692:1 to an award with a ratio of 2,173:1. *See Kemp v. Am. Tel. & Tel. Co.,* 393 F.3d 1354 (11th Cir. 2004) (reducing the punitive award from $1,000,000 to $250,000 when compensatory damages amounted to $115.05). Those cases, like this one, implicated powerful state interests, from protection of the environment, to the elimination of workplace discrimination, to the protection of consumers.

Again, the state interest in protecting employees from repeated offensive sexual touchings by the boss in the workplace is strong. Furthermore, the $506,847.75 punitive award bears a reasonable relationship both to the harm Myers has suffered and to the harm likely to result should CFI not be penalized now. The district court, therefore, did not err in determining that the punitive ratio of 4.89:1 does not offend constitutional due process.

The third and final *Gore* guidepost is a comparison between "the punitive damages award and the civil or criminal penalties that could be imposed for comparable misconduct." 517 U.S. at 583. When considering criminal penalties, a reviewing court considers *both* fines and imprisonment. These peripheral sanctions are significant because they can serve to give fair notice to potential tortfeasors of the magnitude of sanctions they might face for their actions.

The district court determined that Florida's statutory cap on punitive damages was the most appropriate comparison point. This was error. The fact that some torts can be punished up to $500,000 does not put people on notice that battery might be punished up to $500,000. Rather, the district court should have compared the punitive award to the sanctions available for a criminal battery.

However, even after determining that the district court applied the wrong comparison point, we still ultimately affirm its conclusion. We do so because the proper comparison point did provide unambiguous notice to the defendants of the seriousness of their tort. Battery is a crime in Florida punishable by up to a year in prison, which is a serious criminal sanction. The due process clause is violated when defendants do not have fair notice of the magnitude of the punitive sanctions they might face. Because battery can carry a prison term of a year, residents of Florida have fair notice that battery is an offense with formidable consequences. A $500,000 punitive award fits comfortably within this array of potential sanctions.

As a final matter the courts are empowered to consider the financial resources of the defendant when determining the constitutionality of an award. Undeniably, the $500,000 punitive award is a serious sanction and may not be taken lightly.

It will not, however, bankrupt or cripple these wealthy defendants. Moreover, the trial judge could readily find that a lesser award would not provide the same level of deterrence.

Notes and Questions

1. A More "Valuable" Plaintiff the More the Punitives? If Ms. Myers had made $25,000 a year, would the punitive damage award have withstood scrutiny? What does that indicate about the underlying analysis?

2. Why Conduct Toward Others Is Suspect. Assume a defendant was malicious and through this conduct harmed multiple persons, and each sues for punitive damages. If courts do not reduce awards for that possibility, it creates the risk "of multiple punitive damage awards for the same conduct." *State Farm*, 538 U.S. at 423.

3. Defendant's Profits as a Basis. The Supreme Court has focused the constitutional analysis of punitive damages on the harm to the plaintiff, not the profit to the defendant. At least one court has considered that testing the propriety of a punitive damages award to an individual plaintiff may be constitutionally infirm. *Johnson v. Ford Motor Co.*, 113 P.3d 82 (Cal. 2005).

4. Per-Defendant? *Horizon Health Corp. v. Acadia Healthcare Co., Inc.*, 520 S.W.3d 848 (Tex. 2017), emphasized the required analysis in multi-defendant cases:

> Courts that have examined this question generally agree that the constitutional inquiry into the amount of exemplary damages turns on their effect on the individual defendant. For example *Huynh v. Phung*, No. 2007 WL 495023 (Tex. Ct. App. 2007) rejected the argument "that damages should be assessed based on a ratio of combined exemplary damages to compensatory damages, rather than based on a ratio of individual exemplary damages to compensatory damages." As that court explained, "because exemplary damages are awarded on an individual basis and require separate jury findings as to each defendant, the proper method for reviewing the constitutionality of exemplary damages is to compare the exemplary damages awarded against each individual with the compensatory damages awarded against that individual."

> Moreover, calculating the constitutionally permissible ratio by comparing the total compensatory damages recoverable to the total exemplary damages awarded fails to contemplate the scenarios in which defendants act with varying degrees of reprehensibility—as is the case here. It also runs counter to the court's task of determining whether any of the defendants' due-process rights were violated and shifts the court's focus away from a particular defendant's conduct to the defendants' conduct collectively. Because exemplary damages are assessed by the jury on a per-defendant basis according to each defendant's culpability, the alleged excessiveness of those damages must also be evaluated on a per-defendant basis.

Consequently, we hold that the court of appeals did not err by analyzing the constitutionality of the exemplary damages awards on a per-defendant basis on rehearing.

Our determination that the ratio must be calculated on a per-defendant basis answers only half of the question. We still must determine whether the joint-and-several compensatory award or the compensable harm caused by each defendant is the proper denominator for calculating the ratio of compensatory to exemplary damages. That is, we must determine whether courts must calculate the ratio based on the harm each individual defendant caused rather than the harm for which each individual defendant is jointly and severally liable. Acadia argues that if exemplary damages are not to be assessed using the per-judgment approach, then they should be assessed by comparing the exemplary damages per individual defendant to the actual damages per individual defendant:

<u>Exemplary damages per individual defendant</u>
Actual damages per individual defendant

In other words, Acadia argues that comparing the individual awards of exemplary damages to the aggregate amount of actual damages awarded against all defendants yields an unconstitutionally excessive exemplary damages award under the facts of this case. We agree.

Given that the purpose of exemplary damages is to punish defendants for civil wrongs and to deter future misconduct, the punishment should fit the misconduct rather than a state's joint and several liability regime. Compensatory and exemplary damages undoubtedly serve different purposes, and the joint and several liability regime is intended to further the purpose of compensatory damages—redressing concrete losses caused by the defendant's wrongful conduct. Stated differently, we do not believe that a person should be punished by the assessment of exemplary damages simply because of his or her ability to pay, which is the case when a defendant is held jointly and severally liable for an entire compensatory damages award even though that defendant only caused a small portion of the plaintiff's injury. We note that while Texas law allows defendants faced with joint-and-several compensatory awards to seek contribution from the other wrongdoers if required to pay the entire award, this is not the case with exemplary damages given that Texas law does not allow joint-and-several exemplary damages awards. Thus, we hold that in determining the basis for a constitutionally permissible amount of exemplary damages, courts must consider the harm each defendant actually caused and assess the punishment based on that harm because this approach most closely matches the punishment to each defendant's misconduct.

5. <u>Determining the Amount in Controversy</u>. A defendant seeking to establish the minimum amount in controversy may rely on punitive damage requests. However, three separate analyses are required.

First, to count toward the amount in controversy, more is required than mere conclusory allegations in a complaint:

> While it is true that punitive damages may be a factor in determining whether the jurisdictional requirement has been met, a defendant's reliance purely on the inclusion of a request for punitive damages in the petition's plea for relief, unsupported by other facts, is insufficient to satisfy the jurisdictional requirement. *See Treat v. Thermoguard Equipment Inc.,* 2008 WL 4453104 (N.D. Okla. Sept. 29, 2008) ("Conclusory statements regarding punitive damages are insufficient to meet the burden of showing underlying facts supporting the requisite jurisdictional amount."). Here, defendant has alleged no jurisdictional facts beyond referring to plaintiff's very spare statement of her claim (itself insufficient to support an inference of jurisdiction), noting that plaintiff requested punitive damages and noting that Oklahoma has a statute limiting those damages. Such allegations are not, without more, a basis for jurisdictional facts which support an inference that more than $75,000 is in play.

Burton v. Celtic Ins. Co., 2009 WL 10671292 (W.D. Okla. Aug. 26, 2009). The court in *Tolliver v. Delmarva Found. for Med. Care,* 2018 WL 3629590 (D. Del. July 31, 2018) explained the second step:

> A court may include them in the amount in controversy unless the demand is patently frivolous and without foundation. Punitive damage claims are *per se* patently frivolous and without foundation if they are unavailable as a matter of state substantive law. If appropriately made a request for punitive damages will generally satisfy the amount in controversy requirement because it cannot be stated to a legal certainty that the value of the plaintiff's claim is below the statutory minimum.

The third step assumes a plaintiff pleads facts showing punitive damages are not precluded as a matter of law and might be awarded. How great a ratio should a court assume? The court in *Campbell v. Hartford Life Ins. Co.,* 825 F. Supp. 2d 1005 (E.D. Cal. 2011), wrote:

> When assessing the probable amount of unspecified punitive damages for jurisdictional purposes, courts may look to verdicts in analogous cases as a reasonable approximation. To this end, Defendant attempts to highlight jury verdicts with substantial punitive damage awards. *See, e.g.,* Notice of Removal, ¶ 16 (*citing Filippo Industries, Inc. v. Sun Insurance Co.,* 74 Cal.App.4th 1429 (1999) (jury awarded $850,000 in contract damages

along with $4,125,000 in tort damages for bad faith and $750,000 in punitive damages)).

6. <u>Ratios</u>. In other contexts, courts have abjured relying on the amount of damages awarded in another case as indicating the reasonableness of a jury award. Is looking at ratios from other cases any more reliable? Consider Utah's approach: an award of $100,000 is excessive if it exceeds actual damages by more than 3:1, but an award greater than $100,000 is excessive unless the ratio is lower. *Biesele v. Mattena*, 2019 UT 30 (2019). Does that make more sense?

7. <u>Reductions for Past Awards</u>. Some states require that any award of punitive damages be reduced by prior awards, permitting an exception if any prior awards, were insufficient. *Philip Morris USA Inc. v. Martin,* 262 So. 3d 769 (Ct. App. Fla. 2018).

B. When a Punitive Damage Award Is Too High or Too Low: Remittitur and Additur

If a court concludes a verdict of punitive damages exceeds a statutory or constitutional limit, it may award a new trial or "remit" (reduce) the amount to the statutory maximum or to what it perceives to be the proper constitutional amount. A plaintiff can appeal any remittitur. An appellate court may, regardless of the district court's action, also remit the amount or remand for a new trial. State courts, but not federal courts, may use "additur" where, in the alternative to a new trial, the court increases the punitive damages award: "Additur is not an option as it is barred by the Seventh Amendment in federal court." *Ebrahem v. Coach Leasing Inc.,* 2013 WL 5664990 (S.D.N.Y. Oct. 17, 2013).

Hollis v. Stonington Dev. LLC

394 S.C. 383 (Ct. App. S.C. 2011) (Few, J.)

[Stonington was a real estate development corporation. The Hollis family owned 19 acres that had been in their family for generations. Stonington bought land nearby and began development, which caused flooding to the Hollises' home. Stonington violated various statutes and made false statements to the Hollises, and flooding continued. They finally filed suit and a jury awarded $400,000 to restore their property, and $3.5 million in punitive damages. The trial court reduced the compensatory damages to $315,000 to account for prior payments by settling defendants. Stonington appealed the award of punitive damages. After finding some evidence that Stonington had been "reckless, willful, or wanton" and its conduct had been "reprehensible," the court reviewed the amount of punitive damages.]

In order to evaluate the reasonableness of the amount of the award, however, we must determine the degree of reprehensibility. In doing so, we must consider whether

(i) the harm caused was physical as opposed to economic; (ii) the tortious conduct evinced an indifference to or a reckless disregard for the health or safety of others; (iii) the target of the conduct had financial vulnerability; (iv) the conduct involved repeated actions or was an isolated incident; and (v) the harm was the result of intentional malice, trickery, or deceit, rather than mere accident.

Our analysis of the first two of these considerations indicates Stonington's misconduct involved a lesser degree of reprehensibility. First, although the Hollises and Robinsons incurred significant monetary damages, they did not suffer any physical harm. Finding only economic harm would typically weigh against reprehensibility.

Second, while Stonington's conduct did demonstrate an indifference to the property rights of others, it did not evince an indifference to or reckless disregard for the health or safety of people. Reckless disregard for the property rights of others can be sufficient misconduct to support an award of punitive damages. However, when evaluating the degree of a defendant's reprehensibility in a post-trial review of the award, the defendant's reprehensibility is not enhanced pursuant to this second consideration unless it involves the reckless disregard for the health or safety of people.

As to the third consideration, the record does not indicate, and neither of the parties argues, whether the Hollises and Robinsons were financially vulnerable. Thus, the third consideration does not favor a lesser or a higher degree of reprehensibility.

The fourth and fifth considerations, however, indicate a higher degree of reprehensibility. As to the fourth consideration, no evidence was presented as to whether Stonington or its members had engaged in similar conduct on other development projects. However, Stonington's conduct involved repeated actions towards the Hollises and Robinsons, and thus was not an isolated incident. In the face of repeated requests from the Hollises and Robinsons to fix the ongoing problems, and despite repeated official notices of regulatory violations, Stonington continued for over four years6 to engage in conduct the jury determined to be reckless. Finally, as to the fifth consideration, the Hollises and Robinsons' harm was to some extent the result of intentional deceit, rather than mere accident. Stonington made repeated promises to the Hollises and Robinsons that it would fix the problems caused by its development, but failed to take any meaningful steps to fulfill those promises. As a particular example of its deceitful conduct, Stonington told them it would provide a conservation easement so that they would have a fifty-foot buffer of trees to protect their property from runoff. Stonington then clearcut the trees, leaving itself with a tax deduction of $1 million and the Hollises and Robinsons with no protection from stormwater runoff.

Considering the entire record in this case in light of the five factors discussed above, we find that Stonington's misconduct was moderately reprehensible.

The ratio of punitive damages awarded by the jury in this case to actual damages is 8.75 to 1.7 We find this to be an excessive disparity between the punitive damages awarded and the harm actually suffered by the Hollises and Robinsons. In making this determination, and in setting the amount to which punitive damages must be reduced, we have considered the likelihood that the award will deter the defendant from like conduct; whether the award is reasonably related to the harm likely to result from such conduct; and the defendant's ability to pay.

We note initially that the parties have given us little information to use in evaluating the first and third considerations. As to the first consideration, deterrence, the record does not clearly indicate whether Stonington is an ongoing entity in the development business or whether it was created solely for this one project. Therefore, it is difficult to analyze the deterrent effect the punitive damages award will have on Stonington. The record indicates that Stonington still owns large tracts of undeveloped land in the subdivision and is developing the subdivision in phases. Thus, the jury's award will likely have a deterrent effect as to Stonington's future work on this development.

In upholding the award, the trial court relied on the deterrent effect this award may have on others in the development business. In its post-trial order the court stated: "The jury's punitive damages award will send a strong message to developers that such a way of doing business is not acceptable to the people of Richland County." We significantly discount the importance of this consideration in evaluating the constitutionality of the award. The deterrent effect the imposition of punitive damages may have on others cannot be used as a significant basis for upholding an award of punitive damages.

Deterrence has long been an important consideration in the imposition of punitive damages. In *Mitchell*, the supreme court began its discussion of the history of due process limitations on punitive damages awards by stating "the practice of awarding punitive damages originated in principles of common law to deter the wrongdoer and others from committing like offenses in the future." 385 S.C. at 584. Summarizing its decision reducing the award of punitive damages in *Mitchell*, the supreme court stated: "We are also certain that a $10 million award will adequately vindicate the twin purposes of punishment and deterrence that support the imposition of punitive damages." *Id.*

The concept of deterrence includes the specific effect on the party against whom the award is imposed and the general effect the award will have on others similarly situated. In *Gamble v. Stevenson*, the supreme court listed as one of the factors a trial court may consider in its post-trial review of punitive damages the "likelihood the award will deter the defendant or others from like conduct." 305 S.C. 104 (1991). In *Mitchell*, the supreme court stated, "Gamble remains relevant to the post-judgment due process analysis," and repeated the "or others" language in its discussion of Gamble. 385 S.C. at 586. However, listing deterrence as a specific consideration in the analysis of the "ratio" guidepost under *Gore*, the *Mitchell* court omitted the "or others" language. *Id.*

Because of the trial court's consideration of the deterrent effect on other developers to justify this punitive damages award, the omission of the "or others" language is significant in our review of the trial court's decision. The *Mitchell* court noted that "much of the [United States] Supreme Court's punitive damages jurisprudence has focused on the type of evidence that may be used to support a punitive damages award." *Id.* In support of the point that "the Supreme Court has continued to delineate the contours of punitive damages awards that 'run wild,'" the court cited *Campbell*, 538 U.S. at 422, for the proposition that "punitive damages awards may not be based on out-of-state conduct," and *Philip Morris USA v. Williams*, 549 U.S. 346 (2007), for the proposition that "a punitive damages award that is based on evidence of harm to persons other than the plaintiff will violate due process." *Mitchell*, 385 S.C. at 586. Just as these decisions have limited the use of harm "to others" as a basis of a punitive damages award, we believe there are significant concerns associated with using a punitive damages award's deterrent effect "on others" to justify the amount of an award. Thus, although the deterrent effect on the specific defendant must be considered, the general deterrent effect on others who are not connected to the case is not a significant factor in analyzing the constitutionality of an award.

This case, however, presents a "deterrence" consideration somewhere in the middle. Stonington's only representative to testify at trial described the members of Stonington Development, LLC. In particular, the witness's testimony indicates that the managing member of Stonington is heavily involved in the development business, not only with Stonington, but with several other corporate entities doing development work in the area. In considering the deterrent effect the punitive damages award will have on Stonington, we find it appropriate to consider the fact that its managing member is independently involved in the development business, and the punitive damages award is highly likely to deter him from similar misconduct in the future.

The second consideration is whether the award is reasonably related to the harm likely to result from such conduct. In making this comparison, we note that the award of actual damages was substantial. Both our supreme court and the United States Supreme Court have stated that when the actual damages awarded are substantial, a lesser ratio, perhaps only equal to compensatory damages, can reach the outer limits of the due process guarantee. The fact that the actual damages award in this case is substantial helps us to evaluate whether the punitive damages award is reasonably related to the harm likely to result from similar conduct. We find the award of $3.5 million is not reasonably related to the likely harm.

We must also consider whether the amount to which we reduce the award is reasonably related to the likely harm. While a $2 million award results in a ratio of 5 to 1, considerably higher than the actual damages, such an award is reasonably related to the harm likely to result from ignoring stormwater management regulations on large residential development projects such as the subdivision created by Stonington.

As to the third consideration, other than evidence that Stonington still owns large portions of the original development, the record contains no direct evidence of Stonington's ability to pay a punitive damages award.

The third guidepost is the difference between the punitive damages awarded by the jury and the civil penalties authorized or imposed in comparable cases. There are two civil penalties that could be applied to Stonington's misconduct. First, the South Carolina Department of Health and Environmental Control, other State agencies regulating stormwater, and even local governments may impose a civil penalty of $1,000.00 a day against any person violating the "Standards for Storm-water Management and Sediment Reduction" contained in Chapter 72 of the South Carolina Code of Regulations. The regulation provides the penalty may be imposed for any violation of a stormwater management or sediment control ordinance or regulation, and it specifically allows a separate penalty for each day the violation continues. Viewing the evidence in the light most favorable to the Hollises and Robinsons the maximum daily fine that could have been imposed on Stonington ranged from $857,000.00 to $1.612 million.

Under federal law, the Administrator of the Environmental Protection Agency may seek a civil penalty of up to $25,000.00 per day for misconduct similar to that engaged in by Stonington. Stonington's violations of these regulations could have resulted in a total penalty that far exceeds the punitive damages figures we are considering in this case.

Because we find the award of $3.5 million in punitive damages is excessive and violates due process, we must reduce the award [or remand for a new trial]. In reducing the amount of the punitive damages, we are not permitted to make the determination independent of the jury of what we think the appropriate amount of punitive damages should be in this case. Rather, in deference to the jury, we may do no more than determine the upper limit of the range of punitive damages awards consistent with due process on the facts of this case, and set the amount of punitive damages accordingly.

Therefore, reviewing *de novo* the trial court's determination of constitutionality, but deferring to the jury's constitutional role as factfinder, we find the upper limit of the range of punitive damages awards consistent with due process on the facts of this case to be $2 million, and we reduce the award accordingly.

Notes and Questions

1. <u>Standards of Review</u>? The court in *Borne v. Celadon Trucking Serv., Inc.*, 532 S.W.3d 274 (Tenn. 2017), analyzed the appropriate standards of review of a trial court's remittitur and an appellate court's decision to do the same. It explained that "over time trial courts have acquired broader authority to suggest a remittitur," and were no longer required to find the verdict was excessive "as to indicate passion, prejudice, corruption, or caprice," but instead could suggest it when the verdict

"even is within the range of reasonableness, i.e., is supported by material evidence in the record." The appellate court reviews that decision under a preponderant evidence standard, applying a three-step process:

> First, we examine the reasons for the trial court's action since adjustments are proper only when the court disagrees with the amount of the verdict. Second, we examine the amount of the suggested adjustment since adjustments that totally destroy the jury's verdict are impermissible. Third, we review the proof of damages to determine whether the evidence preponderates against the trial court's adjustment.

> The primary purpose of the first prong, looking at the trial court's stated reasons for the adjustment, is to determine whether the trial court disagreed with other than the amount of the verdict. While the trial court's denial of the motion for new trial is some indication that the trial judge agreed with the jury as to the defendant's liability, we look at the trial court's actions overall to determine whether the trial judge disagreed with the facts as found by the jury.

> The second prong requires the appellate court to determine whether the trial court's suggested additur or remittitur totally destroys the jury's verdict. In making this determination, there is no set mathematical formula or percentage to use. Appellate courts have at times looked at whether the additur or remittitur "would result in an award not only proportionally different from the jury verdict but also substantially different in absolute terms.

> For the third prong of the three-step review, we look at the proof to ascertain whether the evidence preponderates against the trial court's additur or remittitur. As noted above, this prong requires us to defer to the jury's decision on the credibility of the witnesses and also to that of the trial judge in his capacity as thirteenth juror.

Does this sound like judges supplanting juries? If the plaintiff refuses remittitur, it must re-try the case (ordinarily), and then appeal the grant of the first remittitur. Does this usurp too much power?

2. <u>Remit or New Trial</u>? If the trial court holds the award is too great, it may offer the plaintiff a choice of accepting a lower ("remitted") amount or a new trial. On appeal, the court may do the same—but not all the time. In *Southern Union Co. v. Irvin*, 563 F.3d 788 (9th Cir. 2009), the court of appeals in an earlier decision vacated a punitive damage award of 153 times actual damages and remanded for the trial court to remit the award. The trial court offered and the plaintiff accepted four times the actual damages, and the defendant appealed. The appellate court held three times actual damages was the constitutional limit and stated that there was no reason to remand for the trial court to try again and so remanded with instructions to award three times the actual damages unless the plaintiff opted for a new trial.

Problems

1. <u>Removal, Remand, and Punitives</u>. You represent a plaintiff who sued defendants in state court. Defendants timely removed to federal court. You have been assigned a judge who is perceived to be hostile to plaintiffs, and so you hope to remand. Your client has asserted a claim for battery based upon a single punch thrown in a bar fight. You have pled damages of $15,000, of which $3,000 represents your client's lost wages and $12,000 are general damages for battery, and a statement that plaintiff seeks "punitive damages as appropriate under the law." What arguments do you have in favor of remand, based on failure to show plaintiff will not (to a legal certainty) recover more than $75,000?

2. <u>No Punitive Damages</u>? Michigan prohibits punitive damages in order to foster the stability of corporations doing business there. Consider whether that approach is any more sensible than the process required to assess, measure, and review them as discussed in this chapter. On the other hand, should Michigan law apply to a harm that occurs in Colorado, even if caused by a Michigan corporation?

3. <u>The Impact of Comparisons</u>. The general trend over the last few decades is clearly toward capping punitive damages, reducing their availability (by eliminating them or capping them), and reducing the permissible ratio of punitive to compensatory damages. Consider what that means for the deterrent effect of punitive damages. On the other hand, should a defendant arguing that a ratio is high emphasize that only more recent cases should be considered? What argument does a plaintiff have in response to that?

4. <u>Comparisons and Reality</u>? Although courts state that they are comparing similar cases, consider the subjectivity of awards of noneconomic damages, such as pain and suffering. Imagine two cases, the first with an "eggshell plaintiff," where a jury awarded $10,000 in mental anguish damages and found that $30,000 was proper to deter that defendant. If in the second case the exact same facts occur, but the jury awards a particularly stoic plaintiff only $5,000 in damages, does that mean $30,000 is too much? Flip the order of the cases, and consider the issue. If you think that, over time, things will average out, consider which way they will average out (given the note above); and, even then, is that necessarily true given how infrequently civil cases are tried and, in those few cases, how rarely punitive damages are awarded?

5. <u>Negligence Plus What and So What</u>? Some courts hold that a negligence claim may serve as the basis for an award of punitive damages, but only if the defendant's conduct "goes beyond mere negligence and into the realm of behavior which is willful, malicious or so careless as to indicate wanton disregard for the rights of the parties injured." *Ditzler v. Wesolowski,* 2006 WL 2546857 (W.D. Pa. Sept. 1, 2006). Should punitive damages awarded under this "lesser" standard also be subject to lower ratios than, for example, punitive damages awarded for an intentional tort?

Chapter 12

The Impact of the Single Action Rule and *Res Judicata*: Plaintiff Must Assert Claims and Seek All Damages

Preceding chapters explored the "trigger" harms and explained that if the plaintiff succeeds on a claim, including establishing the type of harm required by the claim, the plaintiff can recover for that harm and, in tort, for consequential damages. As has hopefully become clear, sometimes a plaintiff may have one claim and it will allow recovery of all damages, but at other times multiple claims must be asserted.

This chapter explains why, if a plaintiff has a claim for relief, it must seek all damages that were caused, or will be caused in the future, by the conduct, and it must assert every claim it has that arose out of the same set of facts. The requirement that a plaintiff assert all claims, and seek all damages, is caused by *res judicata* and a particular form of it known as the "single action rule." This chapter first addresses that principle.

The chapter then examines common forms of past and future damages. Some cases in this chapter analyze these as general damages—the harm required by the claim—while others as consequential damages. Be sure to consider whether the damages in the case are the required harm for the claims we have addressed, consequential damages for one or more claims, or neither.

Chapter 13 deals with the other consequence of the single action rule: because a plaintiff must assert all claims, it may be that more than one claim permits recovery of damages for the same harm. If so, there is the potential for duplication of awards. This chapter discusses that issue and the related problem of inconsistent remedies: a plaintiff who asserts it was induced by fraud to enter an agreement cannot both seek contract damages and fraud damages. It must "elect" remedies.

Chapter 14 then addresses the question of what to do about the fact that the plaintiff is recovering at trial, in the judgment, an award of *past* damages and, potentially, *future* damages. An award at trial for expenses incurred years earlier undercompensates a plaintiff, but an award at trial for future damages overcompensates it. Courts use interest to address that problem.

Collectively, these chapters show the types of harm and measures of damage commonly available, how courts ensure there is no duplication, and how they adjust for the time value of money. The need to seek all potential past and future dam-ages – and so identify which claim or claims must be asserted and what direct and consequential damages must be sought—is caused by the single action rule and *res judicata*.

1. The Single Action Rule Requires a Plaintiff to Assert All Claims and Seek Damages for All Past and Future Direct and Consequential Damages

If a plaintiff has suffered the type of harm that is "damage" for a claim, that starts the running of the statute of limitations. A statute of limitations precludes recovery of monetary damages if a plaintiff waits "too long" to file a claim. Determining whether the statute of limitations has run requires analyzing two issues: when the claim "accrued" and how long the statute gave the plaintiff to file that claim.

A typical personal injury negligence claim accrues on the date the injury occurred. So long as a plaintiff sues within the time provided by the applicable stat-ute of limitations, the claim is not barred. But complexities arise quickly: what if a surgeon completes an appendectomy and leaves a sponge in the plaintiff's body. She has no symptoms for three years, but then she experiences stomach pain and sees her regular doctor, who identifies the sponge as the problem and informs the plaintiff she has slowly developed a serious injury. Did plaintiff's claim accrue on the date of the operation, or only when she discovered the injury? What if she had, for two years before going to her regular doctor, ignored symptoms that would have led a reasonable person to go to see a doctor?

Generally, courts hold a claim "accrues" when a plaintiff knows or should know of an injury. "Accrual" starts the statute of limitations. Importantly, a plaintiff who knows, or should know, of an injury must sue even if the plaintiff does not know the full extent of the harm: "A cause of action accrues when the plaintiff knows or reasonably should know that he had been legally injured by the alleged wrong, how-ever slightly. The fact that the plaintiff's actual damages may not be fully known until much later does not affect the determination of the accrual date." *Pustejovsky v. Rapid-Am. Corp.*, 35 S.W.3d 643 (Tex. 2000). Once the date of accrual of a claim against a defendant is known, the second step is to identify which statute of limita-tions applies to the claim, and determine whether, given that date, the claim can be, or was, filed within the specified number of years. A typical state might bar a tort claim two years after it accrued, and bar a contract claim four years after accrual.

Thus, to return to the botched appendectomy, if the plaintiff, knowing she had experienced unusual discomfort right after the appendectomy, had been told by her regular physician about the sponge, even if she first experienced serious pain two years later, the claim would be time-barred. A claim exists because the plain-tiff knew of *some* harm, and the plaintiff cannot "wait" to see if other harms arise because a plaintiff "does not have a discrete cause of action for each harm." *Gideon v. Johns-Manville Sales Corp.*, 761 F.2d 1129 (5th Cir. 1985).

Res judicata or the single action rule requires a plaintiff who knows, or should know, of wrongful conduct that has caused some injury to seek all damages caused by, or to be caused by, the harm. *See Stephens v. Dixon*, 536 N.W.2d 755 (Mich. 1995) (plaintiff's claim for later-emerging neck disorder accrued when plaintiff sustained injuries in car wreck, not when she learned of the disorder); *Jones v. Trs. of Bethany Coll.*, 351 S.E.2d 183 (W. Va. 1986) (claim accrued when plaintiff sustained noticeable injury from traumatic event, not when latent injury later manifested itself).

This may require filing suit long before the plaintiff has reasonable medical evidence of the long-term impact: "a plaintiff may not split this cause of action by seeking damages for some of his injuries in one suit and for later-developing injuries in another. The cause of action inheres in the causative aspects of a breach of a legal duty, the wrongful act itself, and not in the various forms of harm which result therefrom. He does not have a discrete cause of action for each harm." *Gideon v. Johns-Manville Sales Corp.*, 761 F.2d 1129 (5th Cir. 1985). As a result, a plaintiff must seek damages based upon showing that, at the time of trial, it is more likely than not the plaintiff will in the future have that illness. If not, the claim is barred by *res judicata* or claim preclusion. Some courts have recognized a few narrow exceptions.

Hindmarsh v. Mock

57 P.3d 803 (Idaho 2002) (Trout, J.)

This is a case about two people, one automobile collision and two lawsuits. *Res judicata* prevents the same plaintiff from bringing multiple lawsuits against the same defendant for actions arising from the same event. There is no principled justification for ignoring *res judicata* simply because small claims court is involved.

Res judicata is comprised of claim preclusion (true *res judicata*) and issue preclusion (collateral estoppel). Under principles of claim preclusion, a valid final judgment rendered on the merits by a court of competent jurisdiction is an absolute bar to a subsequent action between the same parties upon the same claim. The three fundamental purposes served by *res judicata* are: First, it preserves the acceptability of judicial dispute resolution against the corrosive disrespect that would follow if the same matter were twice litigated to inconsistent results. Second, it serves the public interest in protecting the courts against the burdens of repetitious litigation; and third, it advances the private interest in repose from the harassment of repetitive claims.

The doctrine of claim preclusion bars not only subsequent relitigation of a claim previously asserted, but also subsequent relitigation of any claims relating to the same cause of action which were actually made or which might have been made. Moreover, other courts have held that the doctrine applies even where the prior litigation was a small claims action. The present case presents a matter of first impression for this Court regarding the *res judicata* effect of a judgment in small claims court.

The law is settled on the applicability of *res judicata* to splitting claims. The more compelling question presented is whether Hindmarsh has the better view when it comes to small claims court: justice is best served by shielding small claims court judgments from the preclusive effect of *res judicata*. We must also decide if the present case falls within one of the unique situations where *res judicata* does not apply.

The Court of Appeals has already applied *res judicata* to small claims court judgments. The fact that Hindmarsh is seeking a different remedy and broaching new issues in the district court action does not matter — *res judicata* bars subsequent relitigation of any claims relating to the same cause of action which were actually made or which might have been made. Hindmarsh contends that if plaintiffs have their other remedies cut off because they first sought remedy in small claims court, such plaintiffs will be dissuaded from going to small claims court at the outset.

There is no compelling reason for this Court to create an exception to *res judicata* for small claims court. No such exception exists for other courts of limited jurisdiction. Moreover, a plaintiff who voluntarily commences suit in small claims court cannot then complain of alleged procedural due process violations as a result of the truncated proceedings. The informal nature of small claims court should have no bearing on the post-judgment effects of suing in small claims court. *Res judicata* is dependent, not upon the form of the proceeding, but rather on whether the judgment is final, valid, and rendered by a court of competent jurisdiction. The plaintiff chose her venue, she should not only be able to take advantage of the benefits of that choice, but should also be bound by the consequences.

Hindmarsh argues that the application of *res judicata* under these circumstances would work a hardship on her and other small claims plaintiffs because they do not have an attorney to advise them of the necessity of bringing all claims at one time. This argument overlooks the provisions of Idaho R. Civ. P. 81(i), which permits a magistrate judge in a small claims case to "vacate, reconsider, or correct clerical errors in the judgment, at any time" upon good cause. No Rule 81 motion was filed. Had she obtained relief from the small claims judgment, there would have been no bar to her assertion of all relevant claims in the district court action.

Furthermore, Hindmarsh's case does not fit into any of the unique situations where courts have held that *res judicata* does not apply. First, Hindmarsh's claim for physical injuries was ripe at the commencement of the small claims court litigation, which occurred almost six months after the auto collision. Next, the small claims court had jurisdiction to award damages for personal injuries, and it was Hindmarsh's choice to bring suit in a court where her damages were capped by a jurisdictional amount.

Notes and Questions

1. <u>Claim or Remedy</u>? The *Hindmarsh* court uses each term. Which is it? Consider in your response that under Fed. R. Civ. P. 8, *res judicata* is an affirmative defense.

2. <u>A Different Result If Hindmarsh Had Not Known of Her Injuries</u>? Assume that she had been injured in a wreck on February 25, 1999, and in small claims court in July 1999 sought only property damages. Although she was then experiencing back and neck pain, she was treating herself with over-the-counter pain relievers, and had not seen a physician. In April 2000, she saw an orthopedic surgeon when the pain relievers stopped working. The surgeon opined that the wreck had substantially and materially worsened her pre-existing orthopedic condition. In September 2000, she sued for personal injury damages. Think about the result under *Hindmarsh*. Then consider the analysis from *Isaac v. Truck Serv., Inc.*, 752 A.2d 509 (Conn. 2000), and be prepared to argue it reaches the better answer:

> Automobile accidents are one of the most common occurrences in our society. Most of those accidents that ultimately result in litigation involve, at one stage or another, claims for both property damage to the vehicle involved and personal injuries to the people involved. Thus, in focusing on those cases that involve those two types of claims, we focus on one of the paradigmatic examples of civil litigation in the judicial system. We also know that typically the amount of the property damage claim will be ascertained much sooner than the ultimate value, whether by settlement or by litigation, of the personal injury claim. Moreover, we know that, if the claimant has collision insurance, typically she will use that source of funds to repair her car, and leave to her insurer the collection of that expense, including the amount of the deductible, from the alleged tortfeasor; and, if there is no collision insurance, the claimant typically will be required to repair her car out of her own funds and will want to collect that expense from the alleged tortfeasor as soon as possible. This leads us to conclude that claimants, alleged tortfeasors and the judicial system will be better served by encouraging the prompt adjudication of contested property damage claims through the small claims process, without the inhibiting opportunity costs that the imposition of the claim preclusion doctrine would impose.

> Our small claims system is statutorily designed to achieve the inexpensive, prompt, informal and final adjudication of contested monetary claims involving limited amounts of money. Our rules of practice are designed with the same aims in mind. Furthermore, the plaintiff has the right to forgo the small claims process; and the defendant in a small claims action has the right to opt out of that process by moving to transfer the action to the regular docket.

> Thus, where the parties have litigated to final judgment a small claims action for property damage arising out of an automobile accident, it fairly

may be assumed that they have chosen to do so because the goals of inexpensive, prompt, informal and final adjudication were consistent with their goals in resolving their particular dispute. Just as our law, as a matter of policy, encourages the voluntary settlement of civil disputes; it also, as a matter of policy, should encourage the inexpensive, prompt, informal and final adjudication of civil disputes that fall within the jurisdictional limits that the law makes available for such adjudication. By permitting the parties to bring motor vehicle property damage claims to final, prompt and inexpensive resolution we would be furthering that policy. Furthermore, we would be furthering the policy of freeing the regular civil docket from the burden of such claims.

Finally, applying the doctrine of claim preclusion to [such] a small claims judgment would give a prudent claimant the incentive to delay litigation of that claim until such time as his or her personal injury claim resulting from the accident could be filed on the regular docket. This would, in turn, mean that the regular docket, designed mainly for the more substantial personal injury claim, would be further encumbered by an accompanying claim for property damage, despite the availability of a prompt, informal and final adjudication of the property damage claim on the small claims docket.

Furthermore, as the defendants in this case have brought to our attention, when the claimant's collision insurer, rather than the claimant personally, has litigated the property damage claim on a subrogation basis, some courts have held that the doctrine of claim preclusion does not bar the later assertion of the claimant's personal injury claim. Our conclusion that the doctrine does not apply in this case simply renders both instances-where the property damage claim has, and has not, been paid by the collision insurer-consistent with each other.

In this analysis, however, we must also take into account the interest of the alleged tortfeasor, and the incentives and disincentives afforded him. If we were to hold that claim preclusion does not bar the later assertion of her personal injury claim, we also should hold that issue preclusion should not apply to that claim as well. Otherwise, a small claims judgment in favor of or against the plaintiff might later be used by or against her in her personal injury action to assert, on the basis of issue preclusion, that liability already had been fully and finally litigated. In any event, unless the doctrine of issue preclusion were not applied to such a small claims judgment, there would be an incentive on the part of the defendant to remove the small claims action to the regular docket, and an accompanying disincentive to litigate the issue on the small claims docket.

Therefore, for the same policy reasons that underlie our conclusion that the doctrine of claim preclusion does not apply to a small claims motor vehicle property damage judgment, we conclude that the doctrine of issue preclusion also does not apply to such a judgment. With these twin conclusions in place, the parties, although free to litigate the property damage aspect of their motor vehicle dispute on the regular docket if they so choose, will at least be free of unnecessary disincentives to do so on the small claims docket instead.

3. <u>Once Triggered, the Single Action Rule Is Largely Unforgiving</u>. The *Hindmarsh* plaintiff knew she had been injured, and after the *Isaac* plaintiff saw her doctor, she also knew of *an* injury. Under the single action rule, once knowing of *an* injury, a plaintiff must sue within the statute of limitations and seek damages for all future harms. Imagine Ms. Hindmarsh had been severely injured and faced years of medication, physical therapy, and a lifetime of diminished earning capacity as a result of permanent brain injuries. Then imagine she was 21 years old when this happened, and still in college. The single action rule forces plaintiffs to seek all future harms in a single suit. Now, imagine you were her lawyer, and had not filed the Rule 81 motion after she came to you.

4. <u>Exceptions to the Single Action Rule</u>. First, some courts recognize "in limited circumstances an exception to *res judicata* where the plaintiff's current complaint alleges a separate and distinct disease or condition from that asserted in an earlier action. The exception has primarily been recognized in asbestos cases." *See Morin v. United States,* 2016 WL 4385840 (D. Nev. Aug. 15, 2016). The court in *Daley v. A.W. Chesterton, Inc.,* 37 A.3d 1175 (Pa. 2012), explained this "separate disease rule":

> While the separate disease rule initially developed from, and has since been applied in, cases involving a cause of action for a nonmalignant disease, followed by a cause of action for a malignant disease, the concerns the rule was designed to address are not limited to situations where a plaintiff suffers one nonmalignant asbestos-related disease and one malignant asbestos-related disease. Indeed, the same difficulties that led the *Marinari* court to conclude that the single cause of action rule was unworkable in situations where an asbestos plaintiff is first diagnosed with a nonmalignant disease, and subsequently diagnosed with a malignant disease, are equally present in situations where an asbestos plaintiff is diagnosed with a malignant disease, and later diagnosed with a separate and distinct malignant disease caused by the same asbestos exposure.

> For example, with regard to mesothelioma, the estimated latency period for mesothelioma is 30 to 50 years, whereas the estimated latency period for asbestosis and most lung cancers is 10 to 20 years. Thus, it is unlikely a plaintiff would be diagnosed with mesothelioma until long after he had been diagnosed with, and the statute of limitations had expired for, lung cancer. In addition, mesothelioma is often difficult to diagnose, due to nonspecific early symptoms and the lengthy latency period. As the California Supreme Court recognized in *Hamilton v. Asbestos Corp., Ltd.,* 22

Cal.4th 1127 (2000), "malignant mesothelioma is a very rare cancer, even among persons exposed to asbestos; no one can predict whether or when such a person will develop mesothelioma." Requiring a plaintiff to seek damages for a potential future diagnosis of mesothelioma at the time he is diagnosed with lung cancer not only imposes nearly insurmountable evidentiary hurdles on the plaintiff, but also may subject a defendant to payment of damages for a serious disease which a vast majority of plaintiffs will not actually develop.

In view of these circumstances, we conclude that a plaintiff who is diagnosed with a malignant disease, and later diagnosed with a separate and distinct malignant disease caused by the same asbestos exposure, may benefit from the separate disease rule.

The burden of establishing that a particular asbestos-related malignant disease is "separate and distinct" from another must be borne by the plaintiff. In this regard, we note that relevant factors may include evidence that the diseases: developed by different mechanisms; originated in different tissue or organs; affected different tissue or organs; manifested themselves at different times and by different symptoms; progressed at different rates; and carried different outcomes.

To the extent Appellants assert that allowing more than one lawsuit for separate and distinct asbestos-related malignancies will overburden the courts and promote overcompensation or duplicate damages, we do not agree. As discussed above, mesothelioma is an extremely rare disease; it is estimated that between 1000 and 2000 cases are diagnosed in the United States each year. As also noted above, studies have not shown a strong or consistent link between asbestos exposure and non-respiratory cancers. Thus, the likelihood of a plaintiff contracting two separate and distinct asbestos-related malignancies appears to be remote.

Finally, we reject Appellants' argument that the Superior Court's holding below violates the doctrine of *res judicata*. The doctrine of *res judicata* will preclude an action where the former and latter suits possess the following common elements: (1) identity of issues; (2) identity in the cause of action; (3) identity of persons and parties to the action; and (4) identity of the capacity of the parties suing or being sued. Because we have concluded that Appellees' cause of action for mesothelioma is distinct from his prior cause of action for lung cancer, the doctrine of *res judicata* does not apply.

Accordingly, for all of the reasons discussed above, we hold that the separate disease rule, as adopted in Pennsylvania, allows a plaintiff to file an action for a malignant asbestos-related disease, even if he previously filed an action for a different malignant asbestos-related disease, provided the second or subsequent action is based on a separate and distinct disease which was not known to plaintiff at the time of his first action, and is filed within the applicable statute of limitations period. Accordingly, we affirm the Superior Court's order reversing the trial court's grant of summary judgment in favor of Appellants, and we remand the matter for further proceedings.

Second, some courts permit—in the initial action—recovery of distress damages for fear of future disease, as the court did in *ExxonMobil Corp. v. Ford*, 71 A.3d 105 (Md. 2013), *mod.*, 71 A.3d 144 (Md. 2013):

> To recover emotional distress damages for fear of contracting a latent disease, a plaintiff must show that (1) he or she was exposed actually to a toxic substance due to the defendant's tortious conduct; (2) which led him or her to fear objectively and reasonably that he or she would contract a latent disease; and, (3) as a result of the objective and reasonable fear, he or she manifested a physical injury capable of objective determination.

Finally, a few courts permit, again in the initial action, "medical monitoring" damages, which are future medical expenses for tests as necessary to detect the likely future illness. The court in *Brown v. St.-Gobain Performance Plastics Corp.*, 2017 WL 6043956 (D.N.H. Dec. 6, 2017), explained the split:

> Some states allow recovery for the costs of such medical monitoring. The plaintiffs rely heavily, for example, on the Supreme Court of Appeals of West Virginia's decision that, even absent present, physical injury, "a cause of action exists under West Virginia law for the recovery of medical monitoring costs, where it can be proven that such expenses are necessary and reasonably certain to be incurred as a proximate result of a defendant's tortious conduct." *Bower v. Westinghouse Elec. Corp.*, 206 W.Va. 133 (W.Va. 1999). To sustain such a claim,
>
> > the plaintiff must prove that (1) he or she has, relative to the general population, been significantly exposed; (2) to a proven hazardous substance; (3) through the tortious conduct of the defendant; (4) as a proximate result of the exposure, plaintiff has suffered an increased risk of contracting a serious latent disease; (5) the increased risk of disease makes it reasonably necessary for the plaintiff to undergo periodic diagnostic medical examinations different from what would be prescribed in the absence of the exposure; and (6) monitoring procedures exist that make the early detection of a disease possible.
>
> *Id.* Other states have likewise recognized a right to similar recovery against exposure to toxic chemicals. *See, e.g., Potter v. Firestone Tire & Rubber Co.*, 863 P.2d 795 (Cal. 1993) ("a reasonably certain need for medical monitoring is an item of damage for which compensation should be allowed"); *Ayers v. Jackson Twp.*, 525 A.2d 287 (N.J. 1987) (recognizing "the cost of medical surveillance as a compensable item of damages" in toxic tort litigation). *See also Baker v. Saint-Gobain Performance Plastics Corp.*, 232 F.Supp.3d

233 (N.D.N.Y. 2017) (denying motion to dismiss tort claims against Saint-Gobain seeking medical-monitoring costs as damages) In doing so, several courts have relied, at least in part, on the conclusion of the Court of Appeals for the District of Columbia that a plaintiff "ought to be able to recover the cost for the various diagnostic examinations proximately caused by the defendant's negligent action." *Friends for All Children, Inc. v. Lockheed Aircraft Corp.*, 746 F.2d 816 (D.C. Cir. 1984) (addressing claims for compensation for medical evaluations of passengers following an airplane crash).

Still other states have rejected an expansion of negligence doctrine to encompass potential, not present, physical injury. *See, e.g., Henry v. Dow Chem. Co.*, 701 N.W.2d 684 (Mich. 2005) (economic losses incurred by paying for medical monitoring "are wholly derivative of a *possible, future* injury rather than an *actual, present* injury. A financial 'injury' is simply not a present physical injury, and thus not cognizable under our tort system."); *Lowe v. Philip Morris USA, Inc.*, 183 P.3d 181 (Or. 2008) ("the present economic harm that defendants' actions allegedly have caused—the cost of medical monitoring—is not sufficient to give rise to a negligence claim").

But to illustrate how narrow those few exceptions are, consider *Schlumberger Tech. Corp. v. Pasko*, 544 S.W.3d 830 (Tex. 2018). In that case, the plaintiff, Pasko, was burned by a caustic chemical. He timely sued several defendants, but more than two years after the accident he was diagnosed with skin cancer that, doctors said, was attributable to the chemical exposure. He sued Schlumberger—for not warning him of the presence of the carcinogen—more than two years after the incident, but less than two years after being diagnosed with cancer. The trial court granted the defendant summary judgment and the Texas Supreme Court ultimately affirmed, writing:

> Ordinarily, the legal injury rule dictates that accrual occurs when a wrongful act causes a legal injury, even if the fact of injury is not discovered until later, and even if all resulting damages have not yet occurred. Absent some exception, such as the discovery rule, injuries that arise or develop after the legal injury are still deemed to have accrued on the same date as the legal injury that caused them. However, to avoid the sometimes shocking results caused by application of the legal injury rule, an exception is recognized: the discovery rule. The discovery rule delays accrual until the plaintiff knew or in the exercise of reasonable diligence should have known of the wrongful act and resulting injury. A related doctrine, the latent occupational disease rule, defers accrual until a plaintiff's symptoms manifest themselves to a degree or for a duration that would put a reasonable person on notice that he or she suffers from some injury and he or she knows, or in the exercise of reasonable diligence should have known, that the injury is likely work-related. Courts applying either the discovery rule or the latent occupational disease rule must determine when a plaintiff knew or, in the exercise of reasonable diligence, should have known she has been injured.

Here, the summary judgment evidence and the pleadings establish that (1) Pasko sustained severe burn injuries to his body when he came into contact with backflow liquids on May 6, 2013; (2) he knew immediately that he had been burned by the liquids and sought medical treatment; and (3) he knew that Schlumberger's employees assigned him to the cleanup job without providing protective equipment. Schlumberger established conclusively that pursuant to the legal injury rule, Pasko's cause of action accrued that day.

The court of appeals based its holding, in part, on Schlumberger's failure to offer evidence suggesting that Pasko was aware of Schlumberger's alleged wrongful conduct before he was diagnosed. But whether the discovery rule applies turns on whether the injured person is aware that she has an injury and that it was likely caused by the wrongful acts of another. It does not turn on whether the injured person knows the exact identity of the tortfeasor or all of the ways in which the tortfeasor was at fault in causing the injury. Nor does it turn on when the full effects of the injury became known or developed. In this case, Pasko knew he was injured by the fluids and that he had not been provided safety equipment to protect him from coming into contact with them. It does not matter, for purposes of when his cause of action accrued, that he did not develop, or learn that he had developed, cancer until four months later.

Notice that for the "separate disease rule," a plaintiff can bring a separate lawsuit if the "separate" disease manifests itself later. Medical monitoring and "fear of" damages focus on the time of filing the first lawsuit, and require proof, *then,* of each doctrine's requirements to obtain recovery. Given the Pennsylvania court's statements, how would you expect courts to rule on requests by a person with asbestosis of medical monitoring, or "fear of," damages for mesothelioma?

These doctrines do not afford wide latitude for plaintiffs to assert subjective bases for recovery. As noted for "fear of" damages, the plaintiff typically must have a physical manifestation that was caused by the exposure, and that is the basis for then showing medical testimony of a reasonable fear of the latent disease. As *In re Paulsboro Derailment Cases*, 2015 WL 5028301 (D.N.J. Aug. 18, 2015), wrote:

> While the Court agrees with Plaintiffs that they need not demonstrate that they are likely to develop cancer to a "reasonable medical probability," they still cannot defeat summary judgment without showing a genuine dispute of fact as to the reasonableness of their fears. *See Mauro v. Raymark Indus., Inc.,* 116 N.J. 126 (1989) (differentiating between a claim for the enhanced risk of developing a disease, which requires a degree of "reasonable medical probability," and a claim for emotional distress stemming from fear of disease, and recognizing "the right of a plaintiff who has sustained physical injury because of exposure to toxic chemicals to recover damages for emotional distress based on a reasonable concern that he or she has an

enhanced risk of further disease"). Where, as here, a reasonable jury could not find that Plaintiffs' fears are reasonable, a genuine dispute of material fact does not exist.

2. Common Forms of Past and Future Damages

As stated in the introduction to this chapter, some of the cases in this chapter award the damages as general damages for the claim, while others are consequential damages. That does not affect the measure of damages, but be sure to consider whether the damages awarded in each case are in the form required by the claim or are, instead, consequential damages.

A. Lost Earnings, Diminished Earning Capacity, and Medical Expenses

Lost income takes different forms, depending upon whether the plaintiff is a human being or an entity. For human plaintiffs, it takes the form of lost wages, salary, commissions, tips, and the like, or lost profits if the plaintiff was a sole proprietor of a business. For entities, economic loss takes the form of lost profits.

Diminished earning capacity and lost income are distinct. A plaintiff about to graduate medical school may have no lost wages, being a full-time student, but if severely injured will have diminished earning capacity. A judge explained the distinction in *Rossi v. Groft*, 2013 WL 2403655 (N.D. Ill. May 31, 2013):

> The parties' use of the term "past and present lost income" blurs the distinction between a lost earnings claim and a diminished earning capacity claim. In general, a lost earnings claim compensates the plaintiff for the amount time that he or she was incapacitated and unable to work at the job that the plaintiff had at the time of injury. *See, e.g., Turner v. Chicago Transit Auth.*, 122 Ill.App.3d 419 (Ill. Ct. App. 1984). A diminished earning capacity claim, on the other hand, is calculated by deducting the amount plaintiff is capable of earning after his injury from the amount he was capable of earning prior to his injury, and awarding plaintiff the difference. Past income is relevant for a diminished earning capacity claim but is not dispositive. Damages for diminished earning capacity can be awarded even for parties who have never worked, such as children.
>
> The *Turner* case describes the differences between a lost earnings claim and a diminished earning capacity claim. There, the plaintiff Turner was unemployed at the time of the accident, which incapacitated him for 18 months. Prior to his unemployment, plaintiff had worked as a heavy machine operator. After the accident, plaintiff alleged that due to his injuries, he was limited to working as a light machine operator. The court

found that plaintiff's unemployment at the time of the accident precluded him from making a lost earnings claim for his 18 month incapacitation. His unemployment, however, did not preclude him from claiming an amount for diminished earning capacity as he was unable to work in his prior position as a heavy machine operator. '

It not clear from the materials before the court on the motion that Rossi intends to present a lost income claim, that is, a contention that, because of the injury he was unable to work at his position as a loan officer for any period of time. At his deposition, he testified that he was not working at the time of the accident, the offices were closing, and that he did not know the date he last worked. The *Turner* case would preclude a lost income claim based on such a record, but Rossi's response does not really argue for such a claim.

Rather, it appears that Rossi will be making a diminished earning capacity claim, and he has retained vocational economist David Gibson to opine on such a claim. The absence of tax returns, 1099 income statements or other proof of income does not preclude Rossi from presenting evidence related as to his diminished earning capacity as prior income is not the measure of damages for that claim, although the absence of such records may be relevant to the jury's evaluation of Rossi's diminished earning capacity claim.

Past lost wages thus "are the actual loss of income due to an inability to perform a specific job a party held from the time of injury to the date of trial. It generally requires evidence of the plaintiff's actual earnings prior to and after injury." *Strauss v. Contl. Airlines, Inc.,* 67 S.W.3d 428 (Tex. Ct. App. 2002). With past diminished earning capacity, usually, the amount of time between injury and trial is reasonably short and a plaintiff's injuries did not preclude her from returning to her old job after an accident, and so plaintiff seeks past lost wages, not past diminished earning capacity. However, where a significant amount of time has passed and plaintiff's injuries precluded her from returning to her former job or profession, diminished earning capacity damages can become significant. Indeed, past diminished earning capacity damages may exist without past lost wages.

If a jury finds the plaintiff will be unable to work at all for some time in the future, the measure of damages is what the plaintiff would have made but for the injury. A jury may also award future lost wages if future medical care will require missing work. *See Smith v. Smith's Food & Drug Centers, Inc.,* 2014 WL 3734363 (D. Nev. July 29, 2014) (including such lost wages in determining whether a case had been properly removed to federal court). In contrast, diminished earning capacity requires imagining two futures: the one that plaintiff, but for defendant's harm, "should have" lived, and the one that it "will" live. Diminished earning capacity is an award for the overall decline in earning potential caused by the defendant. For example, but for the defendant's harm, the plaintiff high school student would have become a brain surgeon, but because of it, plaintiff will only be able to work at a fast-food restaurant.

Albert v. Hampton

2003 WL 24054824 (Iowa Dist. Ct. Jan. 14, 2003) (Dillard, J.)

[Before the wreck in this case, Plaintiff Robin Albert, on April 1, 1997, had previously been in a car accident that injured her back, causing her back and hip pain. She had a series of treatments with a chiropractor, ending April 1999. Her chiropractor testified that pain caused by the that accident had been alleviated by then. On July 15, 1999, she was in the accident that led to this suit: Plaintiff was driving when the defendant sideswiped her car. From then until trial she experienced headaches, sometimes severe, lower and mid-back pain and weakness, some hip pain, and tingling and numbness in her arms. However, apart from tingling and numbness in her arms, Plaintiff had experienced those symptoms before the wreck. Plaintiff and her husband testified that as a result of her injuries she could no longer do various activities without substantial discomfort, including gardening, exotic bird raising, boating, hunting, wallpapering and painting, and washing dishes. She testified that she suffered "stabbing sharp pain" that affected other activities, including sleeping, sexual relations, driving, walking, and ordinary bending and twisting. She testified that the pain had not gotten better.

She saw her chiropractor, Dr. Nolz, 102 times between the accident and trial, December 6, 2002. She and Dr. Nolz testified that each visit eliminated or reduced her pain, but it returned two weeks later. Dr. Nolz testified that the accident had caused her to suffer a 10 percent permanent partial disability. However, his opinion was based solely his review of x-rays taken in October 2002. Dr. Nolz testified her condition would not change and she would need twice-monthly treatments to alleviate pain, and two chiropractic visits each month. By the time of trial, she was taking only "a substantial amount of Tylenol Extra Strength."

One other health professional's opinions were received: two letters—dated April 2, 2001, and February 7, 2002, from Dr. Delbridge. The earliest stated that "her current difficulties, including headaches and her current treatment requirements are as a result of her accident of July 15, 1999," but that "she does not have permanent impairment based upon *Guides to Evaluation of Permanent Impairment* 5th edition, however, she does have difficulties doing recreational activities." He further stated that "as long as she continues in her same job, she may not have difficulty working, but if she changed jobs or had to change vocations for one reason or another," it was likely "she would have trouble doing heavy work or work that required a good deal of bouncing or head turning." In his second letter, he stated "difficulties with her neck and back and discomfort" would continue "indefinitely" and he did not "anticipate that she is going to improve in the foreseeable future. She is not able to do as many jobs now as she was before." Finally, Plaintiff and her husband Ronald that they had less frequent sex, which was sometimes painful for her, and they were having marital problems, those were related to numerous factors totally unrelated to the accident or injuries. She had not mentioned this to Dr. Nolz.

At the time of trial, she testified that her medical expenses were $5,560.60, including $4,061 paid to Dr. Nolz for chiropractic treatment and $130 to Dr. Delbridge. However, the judge noted that "several billings which appear not to be treatment related. Five entries are described as "copying/sec. costs." Two entries are described as "attorney copies," and one entry is described as "narrative report." The total sum of those entries equals $470, and the judge concluded they were litigation expenses, not medical expenses. Of "medical expenses," she claimed $1,369.60 for 4,280 miles of transportation to and from the doctor's office. However, the judge noted that 102 round trips to Dr. Nolz actually would be 40 miles per round trip, and 60 were to visit her other doctor, which was further away. She claimed lost wages for 42 days which she claimed having to leave work an hour early to keep chiropractor appointments and sought $624 for lost wages. The judge noted, however, that some trips were for other purposes. The total for "non-legitimate" lost wages was $33.50. The judge found her remaining life expectancy was 33 years.]

In this civil case the Plaintiff must prove every measure of damages by a preponderance of the evidence. Iowa Civil Jury Instruction 100.3. There is a distinction between proof of the fact that damages have been sustained and proof of the amount of those damages. Damages are denied where the evidence is speculative and uncertain whether damages have been sustained. But if the uncertainly lies only in the amount of damages, recovery may be had if there is proof of a reasonable basis for which the amount can be inferred or approximated. On the other hand, overly speculative damages cannot be recovered.

Past medical expenses include the reasonable value of necessary hospital charges, doctor's charges, prescriptions and other medical services from the date of injury to the present time. *Id.* 200.6. Future medical expenses includes the present value of reasonable and necessary hospital charges, doctor's charges, prescriptions, and other medical services which will be incurred in the future. *Id.* 200.7

An injured party may recover for loss of earnings which includes the reasonable value of lost wages from the date of injury to the present time. *Id.* 200.8. A party is also entitled to an award of damages for loss of future earning capacity. Loss of future earning capacity is the present value loss of future earning capacity. Loss of future earning capacity is the reduction in the ability to work and earn money generally rather than in a particular job. *Id.* 200.9.

A party is entitled to damages for loss of full mind and body in the past and future. Loss of function of the mind or body in the past is from the date of the injury to the present time and includes the loss of mind or body which is the inability of a particular part of the mind or body to function in a normal manner. Future loss of mind or body must be reduced to present value. *Id.* 200.10 and 200.11B.

The element of loss of function of the body is broadly inclusive of various physical injuries. We are convinced, however, that this element of damage relates to functional impairment as opposed to structural impairment of the body. It is the inability of a particular body part to function in a normal manner. Loss of full mind and body is separate and apart from impairment of earning capacity. Overlapping of damages is not permitted.

Also distinct from other measures of damage is physical and mental pain and suffering, past and future. Physical and mental pain and suffering may include, but not limited to, bodily suffering, discomfort, mental anguish or loss of enjoyment of life. Future pain and suffering must be adjusted to present value. *Id.* 200.12 and 200.13B. Injuries to the person, pain and suffering and total disability are incapable of pecuniary measurement by witnesses and must be left to the sound judgment of the fact finder based on the evidence. The pain and suffering which the law allows is not confined to mere physical aches. It includes as well the mental anguish, the sense of loss and burden and the inconvenience and embarrassment which a person who is materially crippled or disabled in body or limb can never escape.

The Plaintiff is entitled to recover for injuries even if she had a pre-existing condition as long as that pre-existing condition was aggravated or made active by the injury in the instant case. The Plaintiff is not entitled to recover for any physical ailment or disability which existed before the accident nor is she entitled to recover for any injuries or damages which she has now which were not caused by Defendant's actions. *Id.* 200.32. Similarly, if the Plaintiff had a previous infirmed condition which made her more susceptible to injury than a person in normal health, the Defendant is responsible for all injuries and damages which are experienced by Plaintiff proximately caused by defendant's actions, even though the injuries claimed produce a greater injury than those which might have been experienced by a normal person under the same circumstances. *Id.* 200.34.

The Plaintiff showed by a preponderance of the evidence that the Defendant's negligence was the proximate cause of injuries which she suffered to her back and neck. The injuries resulted in no direct loss of earnings by the Plaintiff but earnings were lost during part of her employment only to accommodate her scheduled chiropractic treatments. Termination from her job at Pool Tech eliminated any further record of lost earnings. The credible evidence adduced at trial showed that the injuries produced a painful condition which will affect the Plaintiff for the remainder of her life. No medical treatment will eliminate the effects of Plaintiff's injuries . . . and the only effect of any type of treatment will be to temporarily reduce or eliminate the painful condition. The evidence shows that the Plaintiff will live with a cycle of pain and freedom from pain for the remainder of her life. The evidence does not support the conclusion that the Plaintiff's earning capacity will be affected in any respect.

Plaintiff is entitled to past chiropractic and medical expenses which the Court calculates at $3,721. The mileage claimed by Plaintiff does not qualify as a medical expense in the Court's view.

Plaintiff is entitled to lost wages to the extent that she actually missed work to attend chiropractic treatments. After the adjustment for the days which were not legitimately claimed for that purpose, the Plaintiff's lost wages were $590.50. In light of the evidence presented, this Court finds no basis for any award for future lost earnings or earning capacity. Based upon Plaintiff's record of readily finding employment at comparable wages and the long hours which Plaintiff has worked in the period between the accident and trial, there is no reason to believe that there has been any loss in earning capacity. Any conclusion to the contrary would be based upon speculation.

The most consistent evidence presented at trial was that the Plaintiff has experienced chronic pain as a result of this accident and will continue to suffer in the future. It is also clear from the only medical evidence presented at trial that the Plaintiff has suffered some, albeit minor, partial disability. The more compelling evidence was the opinion of Dr. Delbridge in reaching the conclusion that there was a disability but without assigning a percentage. In this particular case the Plaintiff's pain, loss of full mind and body and chiropractic expenses are all part of a single unit or concept. The injury suffered by the Plaintiff is a combination of the factors normally attributable to loss of full mind and body and pain and suffering.

Concomitantly, those measures of damage are replaced by chiropractic expenses because those procedures tend to alleviate or eliminate the effects of Plaintiff's pain and disability. To award damages separately would be extremely difficult to do without inadvertently awarding duplicate damages. This is true for future damages as well as for assessing a fair figure for past pain and past full loss of mind and body. The dilemma is that Plaintiff's pain and disability would have been and will be continuous if Plaintiff receives no treatment. On the other hand, if Plaintiff obtains frequent treatment, her pain and disability become *de minimis*. The Undersigned finds the rendition of awards suggested by each party unpersuasive. In short, Plaintiff wants too much and Defendant wants too little.

In light of the dilemma created by the nature of the Plaintiff's injuries, this fact finder believes that the Plaintiff's past pain combined with her past loss of full mind and body to be separate from her chiropractic expense which was devoted to her reduction or elimination of those damages for only a brief period of time. Her condition appears to have stabilized by mid-November, 1999. Consequently, using her chiropractic treatment bills as a measure, Plaintiff is entitled to $1,040 for her past loss of full mind and body and pain.

Plaintiff's future medical expense, pain and loss of full mind and body is much more difficult to calculate. The problem is exacerbated by the requirement that future damages be reduced to present value in light of the record made by the parties. Because the Defendant failed to present evidence to show a reduction to present value and the Plaintiff concedes that 55 percent is a fair reduction, this Court adopts .55 as the fair multiplier.

A calculation of future chiropractic expense can best be done based upon past history and an application of common sense. During the 1,225 days between the accident and the trial, the Plaintiff visited her chiropractor 102 times. Dr. Nolz testified that the visits were reasonable and necessary but that two visits per month would be reasonable and necessary in the future. Over the 33 years of Plaintiff's life expectancy, $33 per visit would yield $26,136 in chiropractic costs which would have a present value of $14,378.

There is a basic problem with Dr. Nolz's opinion. First, it is self-serving and perhaps a conflict of interest for the beneficiary receiving the $33 per visit to express the opinion that each visit is necessary and that the patient can do absolutely nothing on her own to deal with the problem. Second, the type of treatment being provided could simplistically be described as a back rub. Other reasonable options are available to the Plaintiff which would cost less than the chiropractic treatments. That puts into direct question whether the chiropractic treatments are reasonable and necessary expenses. There is every reason to believe that Ronald, for instance, could learn to provide the same treatment in a safe and beneficial manner at no or very little cost. In addition, Ronald providing massage therapy could have a beneficial effect on the marriage relationship of the Plaintiffs. Further, it is quite difficult to accept as credible evidence the concept that the Plaintiff can do absolutely nothing on her own to reduce her pain. The Court finds that opinion as credible as the outdated concept that pregnant women should avoid activity during pregnancy. The Court notes that there is a tendency in the medical community to wean patients from continual treatment while there is a tendency among chiropractors to encourage continual treatment. This conclusion is supported by a comparison of the two letters from Dr. Delbridge with the opinion letter of Dr. Nolz.

Plaintiff's future pain and loss of full mind and body in the future is problematic because only part of Plaintiff's future includes employment. This is a factor because of the evidence adduced at trial showing long work hours and substantial driving to and from work by the Plaintiff. It is reasonable to infer that Plaintiff's work and driving habits exacerbate, to some extent, her physical ailments. Plaintiff claims, and it is reasonable to infer from a preponderance of the evidence, that Plaintiff will have a 19 year future work expectancy as part of her 33 year life expectancy. The Undersigned concludes that the 14 years of life expectancy following retirement will not include pain and loss of full mind and body or chiropractic expense attributed to this accident which can be calculated. This is particularly true because it is reasonable to infer that aches, pains and discomfort tend to naturally grow or increase as a person ages. That conclusion was supported by the testimony of Dr. Nolz who alluded to aches and pains associated with the aging process.

This Court finds that a fair award for future chiropractic expense, pain and loss of mind and body must be one figure. The primary reason is the inter-relationship previously discussed in this ruling. A fair figure, adjusted for present value, would be $8,276.

Judgment is entered in the total sum of $13,627.50, plus interest.

Pilgrim's Pride Corp. v. Cernat

205 S.W.3d 110 (Ct. App. Tex. 2006) (Morris, J.)

[A truck driven by an employee of defendant Pilgrim's Pride Corporation rear-ended a smaller truck, injuring Cernat. The jury awarded Cernat damages for various harms, including diminished earning capacity. Pilgrim's Pride appealed.]

The evidence of Cernat's past lost earning capacity is shown by his prior activities as compared with his activities after the accident. Cernat was a self-employed immigrant from Romania, who was naturalized in 1991. He had purchased and remodeled a home in Hot Springs, had purchased some land there, cleared it, and built on the property a four-car shop and garage in which he was planning to work as a mechanic. The record shows that he personally did all of the labor involved in these projects and also shows that he had worked on cars for acquaintances. Marin Tomulet, the owner of an automobile repair business, stated he had attempted to hire Cernat, but Cernat would not move to Dallas.

Pilgrim's Pride argues that the award is unsupported because there was no evidence of Cernat's actual earnings before and after the injury. Loss of earning capacity, however, is not measured by what a person actually earned before injury, but what the worker's capacity to earn a livelihood actually was, even if he or she had never worked in that capacity in the past. *See McIver v. Gloria*, 140 Tex. 566 (1943) (jury must determine value of minor's loss of earning capacity from common knowledge and sense of justice). To recover for diminished earning capacity in a particular occupation, it is not always necessary for the plaintiff to have been working in and deriving earnings from that occupation before injury, as long as earnings from that occupation would provide a true measure of that plaintiff's earning capacity.

Pilgrim's Pride points to Cernat's lack of income-producing activity, coupled with his wife's testimony that the income reflected on their federal income tax returns was from her job as a nurse, to show that Cernat had no earning capacity. Lack of income does not necessarily prove lack of earning capacity. Cernat was not employed as a mechanic, though there was substantial evidence he had done such work regularly and been paid for it. It is beyond question Cernat was working on their residence and had built a garage and office building on land that he cleared of trees. This is not a situation where a "couch potato" was injured and then claimed lost income.

This is similar — though with genders switched — to cases where the plaintiff is a housewife. In such a situation, the actual money value of her services need not be proved. When a plaintiff is employed at a fixed wage or salary, the amount of his or her previous earnings ordinarily must be shown. To recover diminished earning capacity in a particular occupation, it is not always necessary for the plaintiff to have been working in and deriving earnings from that occupation before injury, as long as earnings from that occupation would provide a true measure of that plaintiff's earning capacity.

Certainly, evidence exists that Cernat's physical limitations would prevent him from doing the type of physical labor he had been performing in the past; that these limitations would extend into the future; that he would suffer a permanent disability and a fifteen percent total body impairment; and that there were some things, such as climbing a ladder and driving a truck, he could no longer do. It is clear that Cernat's earning capacity was well in excess of the amount awarded by the jury, even if limited to the $30.00 per hour he earned in automobile repair, without recourse to the testimony about his expected income from the purchase, repair, and resale of wrecked automobiles.

Under these facts, based on the evidence of the type of work performed by Cernat that he was no longer capable of performing, and on the available evidence of his abilities and the income he had actually earned, we cannot conclude that the jury's award was without support in the record. The evidence is legally and factually sufficient to support the jury's award on lost earning capacity in the past.

Lee v. Smith

816 S.E.2d 784 (Ct. App. Ga. 2018) (Rickman, J.)

[The complaint in this case was filed in 2014 based upon a car wreck in which defendant Lee injured plaintiff Smith. At that time, Smith was a college student. Smith's initial discovery responses in 2016 stated he was not seeking lost earnings. In May 2017, on the last day to do so, Smith provided this supplemental interrogatory answer:

> In addition to past, current and future lost earnings, Smith has further suffered special and/or general damages in the form of, inter alia, diminished earning capacity, diminished ability to work, labor or earn wages. Since the date of the accident giving rise to this lawsuit, Smith's occupation changed upon graduation from Auburn University in May 2016 from collegiate high jumper to professional high jumper. As a result of the injuries suffered during the collision and the reasonable and necessary medical treatment resulting therefrom (including surgery in January 2017), Smith has lost earnings (including contract, sponsorship, incentive, appearance and various other forms of earnings associated with his profession) in an amount to be more fully shown at trial.

At trial, Lee admitted fault but contested damages. The jury awarded $2 million. Defendant appealed the denial of his motion for directed verdict on damages.]

The sole issue for the jury was the amount of damages. Smith's agent testified that professional high jumpers make money through sponsorship contracts, appearance fees, and prize money for competing in different track meets. He further testified that the length of a professional career for a high jumper was approximately ten years and that, if not for the surgery he had to undergo as a result of the accident, Smith would have earned "conservatively about a million dollars" over the course of his career. Additionally, the agent testified that, if not for the surgery, he would have been able to negotiate a contract for Smith in 2017 that he was "reasonably certain" would have included incentive bonuses if Smith was able to reach certain jump heights. When discussing incentive bonuses, the agent explained that, hypothetically, if Smith had an incentive bonus and was to break a world record he might earn $100,000 solely due to the jump height.

Smith's agent opined that while it was "reasonably certain" that Smith would make $1,000,000 during his career, he could have made $2.5 million under the potential 2017 contract. Additionally, Smith's agent testified that in May 2016 Smith was ranked fifth in the world. In Smith's agent's opinion, a high jumper ranked in the top ten in the world would make approximately $4,000,000 over his career and a top five high jumper would make around $6,000,000. The jury returned a verdict in favor of Smith in the amount of $2,000,000.

Lee contends that the trial court erred by denying his motion for directed verdict regarding Smith's claim for lost future earnings. Specifically, Lee argues that Smith's lost earnings claim was speculative and should have been dismissed.

Lee asserted special damages claims for both loss of future earnings and diminished earning capacity. A loss of future earnings claim requires proof of loss of definite earnings that would have been received in the future but for an injury even though the injury is not permanent. However, a claim for diminished earning capacity requires a physical injury resulting in permanent or total physical disability and, involves numerous considerations, among which are, first, the earnings before the injury, earnings after the injury, probability of increased or decreased earnings in the future, considering the capacity of the injured party, effects of sickness and old age, etc. While proof of the plaintiff's actual earnings, either before or after the injury, is not essential to the establishment of the value of the plaintiff's decreased earning capacity, there must nevertheless appear some evidence, either direct or circumstantial, tending to show what the plaintiff was capable of earning both before and after the injury.

Smith presented evidence, through his doctor, that the accident caused Smith's injuries "to a reasonable degree of medical certainty." After the accident, the injury worsened until surgery was medically necessary. The doctor opined that the injury negatively impacted Smith's high-jumping performance, including his performance at the Olympics. The doctor also testified that because of the injury and the resulting surgery, Smith had sustained a permanent injury, and would be unable to achieve the high-jumping status he reached prior to the injury and unable to return to the Olympics.

Smith's agent testified that prior to the surgery Smith was ranked fifth in the world and that a high jumper ranked in the top ten in the world would make approximately $4,000,000 over his career and a top five high jumper would make around $6,000,000. Smith's agent opined that if not for the surgery he had to undergo as a result of the accident, Smith would have earned "conservatively about a million dollars" over the course of his career. Smith's agent also testified that, if not for the surgery, he would have been able to negotiate a contract for Smith in 2017, and under that contract he would have had the potential to make 2.5 million dollars.

We find that Smith presented some evidence tending to show what he was capable of earning both before and after the injury and, therefore, some evidence of diminished earning capacity. Accordingly, the trial court did not err in denying Lee's motion for directed verdict. See *Alto Park Super Mart, Inc. v. White*, 216 Ga. App. 285 (1995) (trial court did not err in charging the jury on future earnings where there was evidence that the plaintiff was injured, the injury was worsening, eventually he may be unable to work at his current job, and he was unable to work as many hours a day as he could before he was injured); *see also Michaels v. Kroger Co.*, 172 Ga. App. 280 (1984) ("The general rule that the amount of damages must be proved with a reasonable degree of certainty and cannot be based on guesswork does not mean that only a plaintiff who works on an everyday basis and on the date of the injury can prove a diminished earning capacity. Nor does the rule mean that one who works intermittently cannot recover for diminished earning capacity, i.e. an artist, sculptor, professional athlete, author, actor, dancer, singer, musician, or even a lawyer.").

Volusia County v. Joynt

179 So. 3d 448 (Ct. App. Fla. 2015) (Berger, J.)

[Plaintiff was a young woman sunbathing on a beach when she was run over by defendant's truck and severely injured. The jury awarded $500,000 in lost future earning capacity. The defendant appealed.]

The County convincingly argues that Joynt failed to meet her burden. Although she put on evidence sufficient to establish reasonable injury, Joynt failed to demonstrate any diminished ability to earn money in the future and failed to present evidence that would allow the jury to quantify the amount of an award.

Prior to May 2010, Joynt was employed as a paraeducator, which is a teaching-related position within a school, where she was generally responsible for specialized or concentrated assistance for students in elementary and secondary schools.

However, at the time of the accident, she was voluntarily unemployed, earning no income.[2]

Just over a year after the accident, Joynt resumed her employment as a reading intervention paraeducator working full-time for $18,000 per year with benefits. Although she faced some physical challenges, the record reflects those challenges did not affect her ability to do her job. Joynt testified that she loved her job as a paraeducator and intended to continue her employment the following school year. Joynt's principal, Brandi Flisram, confirmed that she planned on having Joynt return to her position for the following school year, opining that students like her, she is an effective teacher, and her evaluation was above satisfactory. In fact, Ms. Flisram noted that many of Joynt's students actually tested out of the reading intervention program due to her teaching ability. Ms. Flisram had no concerns about Joynt's progression as an educator, and she further testified that none of Joynt's physical limitations would affect Joynt's ability to be promoted, although she would be reevaluated if her health ever declined.

Joynt relies on the latter part of Ms. Flisram's testimony to support the damage award, arguing that a simple review of the trial transcript by Ms. Flisram, which contained the testimony of various doctors describing her injuries, would likely cost Joynt her career. She claims the jury could have surmised that, although optimistic about her future, she is reasonably certain to lose her job as a paraeducator due to her injuries. To that end, she asserts the $500,000 award is equivalent to earning $17,241.38 per year, assuming she would have worked until the social security retirement age of sixty-five. This argument is purely speculative. As the trial court acknowledged:

> Now, you know, the problem with that is [the jury] may be out for hours anguishing over this because there's not really any evidence as to how they could come up with a number and upon which they could base a number, so what does a full time teacher make. And it's, based on this evidence, I think sheer speculation to say she's likely to get fired when she gets back. I mean, I guess you can argue it, but I'm not sure there's really any evidence that she's going to be.
>
> What other evidence is there other than, I guess, you could just kind of speculate that someone with these injuries—and I don't diminish her injuries. I'm not trying to denigrate that at all, but I just don't know how you can say, well—what age would they pick out, 50, 55, 45, 60? It just would be pure, abject speculation, wouldn't it?

Yes, which is why it was error to submit this claim to the jury. We find there was absolutely no testimony presented to indicate Joynt was completely disabled from

---

2. In May 2010, Joynt and her husband agreed that she would take a break from work until their youngest child started kindergarten. During this break, Joynt was injured in the accident.

further gainful employment as the result of her injuries or was unable to work to the same age she would have otherwise. Indeed, the opposite is true. As the County highlights, the evidence demonstrates that Joynt's earning capacity did not diminish, but rather increased after the accident. And, while this fact alone does not necessarily preclude recovery, it certainly makes it more difficult for Joynt to show an economic loss. Inasmuch as the record fails to establish Joynt's diminished earning capacity as a paraeducator, we conclude the jury's award of $500,000 in damages for loss of future earning capacity is not supported by competent, substantial evidence.

Notes and Questions

1. <u>Money for Pain</u>. The *Albert* court's opinion applying jury instructions provides a rare insight into pain and suffering damages. The court equated medical expenses as compensating plaintiff, fully, for the pain and suffering. Why is that analysis both logical and absurd? Is there an alternative? More specifically, given advances in medicine and the increasing pace of those advances, is relying on past awards any indication of whether future pain and suffering, beyond a short time, is likely?

2. <u>Life Expectancy</u>. If a defendant caused an injury that will permanently cause pain and suffering, a jury must determine the plaintiff's life expectancy. *McKeown v. Woods Hole*, 9 F. Supp. 2d 32 (D. Mass. 1998) (court "troubled by the absence" of actuarial tables because "a plaintiff who is 25 years old and experiences the same injuries as a plaintiff who is 65 years old will likely incur a greater duration of pain and suffering in the future due to the 25 year old plaintiff's greater life expectancy.") Consider the impact on awards of the fact that life expectancy tables show certain races have shorter life expectancies than others.

3. <u>Comparing Awards to Other Verdicts</u>. Consider the validity of comparing a verdict amount in today's dollars with one from decades ago. Shouldn't inflation be considered? On the other hand, if pain management medication is better today, shouldn't that matter?

4. <u>Traumatic Permanent Injuries to Young Plaintiffs</u>. Future damage awards require lawyers to prepare imaginary worlds for juries. Lawyers for each side, but particularly the defense, must carefully consider how specifically each wants the jury to categorize damages. *See Jones v. MetroHealth Med. Center*, 89 N.E.3d 633 (Ct. App. Ohio 2017) (analyzing statutory scheme requiring offset of awards of future lost income). Further, large awards can implicate a young plaintiff's ability to qualify for Medicaid or Social Security—but a jury might be instructed to offset future damages for those benefits. *See id.*

5. <u>The Two Speculative Worlds of Future Lost Earnings</u>. Are the principal cases irreconcilable or are they the result of the inherently speculative nature of future damages? Don't all future awards require imagining two worlds that never existed—and never will? Consider what the court in *Strauss v. Cont'l. Airlines, Inc.*, 67 S.W.3d 428 (Ct. App. Tex. 2002) stated:

In determining what evidence is sufficient to support a claim of loss of earning capacity, no general rule can be laid down, except that each case must be judged upon its peculiar facts, and the damages proved with that degree of certainty of which the case is susceptible. Consequently, the required certainty will necessarily vary. Where the plaintiff is a child, who has never earned any money, the jury must determine the value of the child's lost earning capacity from their common knowledge and sense of justice. Likewise, when the plaintiff is a housewife, the actual monetary value of her services need not be proved. However, where the plaintiff is employed at a fixed wage or salary, the amount of his previous earnings ordinarily must be shown. Where the plaintiff seeks special damages for loss of earning capacity in a particular business, the amount of his earnings or the value of his services in that business must be shown with reasonable certainty. The certainty of the proof required is also affected by the nature of the plaintiff's injuries. Thus, if the plaintiff's earning capacity is not totally destroyed, but only impaired, the extent of his loss can best be shown by comparing his actual earnings before and after his injury.

6. <u>Increasing Income Does Not Bar Diminished Earning Capacity</u>. That is because "a plaintiff need not show a loss of income as compared to his pre-accident income," *Branan v. Allstate Ins. Co.*, 761 So. 2d 612 (Ct. App. La. 2000). As the principal cases show, a plaintiff need not show any pre-accident income.

7. <u>Experts</u>? Consider court's explanation from *Burger v. Galey*, 2014 WL 3778972 (D. Nev. July 31, 2014), as to why it denied defendants' motion for summary judgment as to plaintiff's damages for future diminished earning capacity arising out of a car wreck:

Future lost income and diminished earning capacity are economic damages in Nevada. The plaintiff bears the burden of proving both the fact and the amount of damage. However, so long as the plaintiff introduces evidence enabling a jury to find the plaintiff was damaged, some uncertainty as to the actual amount of damage is allowed. Thus, like any other category of damages, a jury may award damages for prospective loss of wages or diminished earning capacity if the plaintiff introduces evidence from which the jury can reasonably ascertain the losses. This evidence need not be conclusive; it is sufficient to present evidence upon which reasonable minds might disagree.

When an injury or disability is subjective and not demonstrable to others (such as headaches), expert medical testimony is necessary before a jury may award future damages. Nevada law allows nonmedical expert witnesses to assist in determining damages. The credibility of witnesses and the weight to be given their testimony is within the sole province of the trier of fact.

Viewing the evidence in the light most favorable to Burger, there are genuine disputes of material fact regarding Burger's future earning capacity. Burger has introduced expert testimony from two medical doctors regarding the injury in his lumbar spine and the need for surgery to correct this injury. This testimony would allow a reasonable jury to find that Burger will require surgery. Burger's rehabilitation expert and one of his doctors testified that he will not be able to handle heavy duty work for some period of time after [a successful] surgery. Burger currently works in a job that requires him to handle heavy equipment. A reasonable jury could find that Burger is entitled to damages because he will not be able to perform the job he is qualified to do for some period after surgery. If the jury finds Burger is entitled to damages for lost wages, Burger can introduce expert testimony as to the amount of damages in several different scenarios, from which a reasonable jury could ascertain the amount of damages. Burger thus has met his burden of presenting evidence demonstrating genuine issues of material fact. It is up to the jury to decide whether he is entitled to recover for loss of future earnings or diminished earning capacity, and in what amounts.

Defendants emphasize that no doctor has definitively stated that Burger will have to miss work or change careers after surgery. While medical testimony is necessary to establish an injury or disability, Burger has met this requirement through the testimony of Dr. Cash and Dr. Selznick. Dr. Cash testified that Burger will not be able to perform his current job for six months after surgery. Kostelac, Burger's rehabilitation expert, opines Burger will not be able to continue in his current job, regardless of surgery. Kostelac bases her opinion on prior experience and the reports of Burger's doctors. It is up to the jury whether such testimony is believable. Burger has submitted sufficient evidence for a reasonable jury to find he is entitled to damages for loss of future income or diminished earning capacity. For these reasons, I deny Defendants' Motion.

B. Lost Profits

Some courts state that a business that never made a profit cannot suffer "loss profits." *E.g., Midwest Coal, LLC v. Cabanas,* 378 S.W.3d 367 (Ct. App. Mo. 2012) ("the uncontroverted evidence established that Plaintiff was not generating a profit prior to Defendant's alleged fraudulent misrepresentation and Plaintiff's consequent decision not to purchase AFI's slurry. In the absence of evidence of past profitability, as required by Missouri law, Plaintiff cannot prove damages."). If a defendant caused a business to lose even more money (say, for example, going from losing $10,000 a year to losing $20,000), is that different from causing a business to go from earning a profit of $20,000 to making only $10,000? *See DIYA TV, Inc. v. KAXT, LLC,* 2018 WL 1312448 (Ct. App. Cal. March 14, 2018) ("A plaintiff is not required to show a profitable business in order to recover damages for lost revenue. If that were the rule, a breaching party would never be accountable for harm to a business operating at a loss.")

Beyond that, courts struggle with a plaintiff that is a "new business." In this regard, it may be helpful to think of a "new business" as being like a severely injured young plaintiff seeking diminished earning capacity. If a defendant injures a child or a young adult, there is nothing, or very little, evidence in the form of lost wages to know how much the plaintiff "would have" earned. While all courts permit juries to imagine an injured child's diminished earning capacity—because of the "wrongdoer rule" (which bars a defendant from using its wrongdoing to argue the jury must speculate about the damage it caused)—some states preclude recovery of profits for a "new business" without a "sufficient" history of profits.

I. The Different Approaches to Lost Profits

Juice Ent., LLC v. Live Nation Ent., Inc.

2018 WL 2357748 (D.N.J. May 23, 2018) (Walls, J.)

[Juice Entertainment, LLC was formed in 2009 and had produced concerts and similar events for fewer than 5,000 attendees. In 2011, it made an agreement with State Fair Event Management to stage an electronic dance music event at the 2011 New Jersey State Fair. The agreement had a deadline for Juice Entertainment to book the performers and identify them to SFEM. Juice Entertainment was in negotiations that would have led to signing certain performers, but those negotiations failed, and SFEM then canceled the agreement. Juice Entertainment sued several defendants, including Live Nation Entertainment, Inc., and asserted various claims. Live Nation moved for summary judgment on, among other things, the claim for lost profits.]

The new-business rule operates here to bar Plaintiffs from recovering lost profits. New Jersey courts have applied the new-business rule in analogous cases. In *Seaman v. U.S. Steel Corp.*, 166 N.J. Super. 467 (App. Div. 1979), the plaintiffs operated a marine-salvage business and sought to construct a 100-ton-capacity floating crane. The plaintiff found that the steel plates it purchased from the defendant to build the crane were faulty, and sued for lost profits, including lost profits under a contract that required the use of the crane, and loss of the crane's monthly rental value. Because the plaintiff had "never operated a crane of this size in their business, nor had they ever rented such a crane to others," the court found that those claimed lost profits were too speculative to recover. *Id.* Similarly, in *Weiss v. Revenue Building & Loan Assoc.*, 116 N.J.L. 208 (E&A 1936), the new-business rule precluded lost-profits recovery for a plaintiff who sought to transition from operating a rooming house to a fifty-six unit residential property. *See also Sea Crest Enterp., LLC v. City of Elizabeth*, 2006 WL 2590327 (N.J. App. Div. Aug. 8, 2006) (affirming denial of lost-profits recovery under new-business rule where plaintiff, an "experienced builder," had never worked on "a major redevelopment project" like the one at issue, and where "the numerous contingencies that had to be satisfied made the completion of the project with the anticipated profits too uncertain to form the basis for an award of damages").

While Plaintiffs may have successfully promoted and produced smaller shows, the Event was of a much larger scale, and Plaintiffs' sole foray into large-scale outdoor-event production resulted in losses, not profits. Lost-profits damages are thus "too remote and speculative to meet the legal standard of reasonable certainty."

BMK Corp. v. Clayton Corp.

226 S.W.3d 179 (Ct. App. Mo. 2007) (Cohen, J.)

[Jay-Max Sales supplied foam to coal mines in the Colorado region. Miners used the foam to block off passages, other than the one being mined, to help fresh air flow. Miners asked Jay-Max for a better foam, and it found a better foam from BMK Corporation. BMK did a market study and estimated its revenues during the first three years of a proposed four-year deal would exceed $4 million. BMK agreed to supply Jay-Max with foam, and Jay-Max would distribute it in the Colorado region. BMK, in turn, made an agreement with Clayton Corporation under which for four years Clayton agreed to make foam for BMK and, further, that Clayton would not sell its foam to mines in the Colorado region. BMK learned that Clayton was selling its foams directly to mines in the Colorado region, in breach of the agreement. BMK sued Clayton, asserting breach of contract and other claims. BMK sought the profits it would have made had Clayton performed. The jury found for BMK and awarded $1 million. Clayton appealed.]

At trial Boehm, BMK's CFO and a licensed C.P.A., testified about BMK's lost profits, explaining in detail exactly how he calculated the amount of BMK's damages. Boehm relied not only on the testimony of [the vice-president of Jay-Max, the Director of Sales with Clayton (who negotiated the agreement) and the President of another mine foam company], but also on information obtained by him while preparing BMK's 2000 marketing study and matters discussed and contemplated by the parties during the negotiation and execution of the Agreement. Boehm explained in detail the basis and assumptions for his calculations. Clayton, moreover, dissected and challenged these assumptions during cross-examination and through the testimony of its own expert witness, Thomas Hoops, C.P.A. Boehm calculated BMK's lost profit damages through a straightforward application of revenue and cost numbers, gross and net profit margins, and quantities of product bought and sold.

As the Supreme Court held in *Coonis v. Rogers*:

> The general rule as to the recovery of anticipated profits of a commercial business is that they are too remote, speculative, and too dependent upon changing circumstances to warrant a judgment for their recovery. They may be recovered only when they are made *reasonably certain* by proof of actual facts, with *present data* for a *rational estimate* of their amount when this is made to appear, they may be recoverable.

429 S.W.2d 709 (Mo. 1968) (emph. added). When seeking damages for loss of profits from the interruption of an established business "proof of the income and expenses of the business for a reasonable time anterior to its interruption, with a consequent establishing of the net profits during the previous period, is indispensable." *Id.*

Clayton argues that, under *Coonis,* BMK's lost-profit evidence lacked sufficient certainty to warrant a judgment in its favor. However, the *Coonis* standard of proof only applies in cases where the loss of expected profits flows from the destruction of or injury to a business. *Harvey v. Timber Resources, Inc.,* 37 S.W.3d 814 (Mo. App. E.D. 2001). When a plaintiff sues for damages arising directly out of a breach of contract, he or she need not prove past profits or expenses. Thus, where the breach alleged consists of prevention of performance, the party not in default may generally recover the profits which would have resulted to him from performance. Moreover, where "loss is ascertainable with reasonable certainty from the breach and the profits claimed are not speculative or conjectural and were within the contemplation of the parties when the contract was made" *any* plaintiff—even a new business—may seek lost profits arising from a breach of contract. *Id.*

Clayton attempts to distinguish *Harvey* by asserting that BMK's lost-profit damages did not flow from a breach of contract, but rather from "a contractual right to engage in the business of selling mine foam." Clayton's distinction is not persuasive. As the record establishes, the jury awarded BMK $1 million in lost profits under BMK's breach of contract claim for damages arising from Clayton's breach of the contract. *Harvey's* logic controls the present matter.

In *Harvey,* this Court further held that a plaintiff may recover for lost profits that he or she establishes with reasonable—not absolute—certainty. "Certainty," however, "means that damages have been suffered and not exact proof of the amount." *Id.* "Where the fact of damage is clear, it is reasonable to require a lesser degree of certainty as to the amount of loss, leaving a greater degree of discretion to the jury, subject to the usual supervisory power of the court." *Id.* Once the plaintiff has established the *fact* of lost profits, to establish the *amount* of lost profit with reasonable certainty, all that is required by Missouri courts" is that it be supported by the best evidence available. Moreover, a business owner's testimonial evidence is sufficient to provide the trier of fact with a rational basis for estimating damages to the plaintiff, including lost profits. Thus, once the plaintiff has put forth the best evidence available, the amount of damages is a question for the jury.

BMK proved the fact of damage with reasonable certainty and provided a rational basis for the jury to estimate the amount. Clayton does not dispute that it had a four-year exclusive Agreement with BMK and that, at the time the parties entered the Agreement, they contemplated substantial profits resulting from sales of mine foam. As discussed above, BMK presented sufficient evidence that Clayton breached its contract with BMK, causing BMK to lose four years of profits arising out of the Agreement. BMK has, therefore, proved the fact of damage with reasonable certainty.

BMK also presented sufficient evidence to provide the jury with a rational basis for determining the amount of BMK's damages. At trial, Boehm testified to BMK's damages flowing from the breach of the Agreement and explained in detail exactly how he calculated them. Boehm outlined the basis for his calculations, the assumptions underlying them and walked the jury through each step of calculating the net profits lost by BMK as a result of Clayton's breach. Point denied.

Notes and Questions

1. <u>New at What</u>? The *Juice Entertainment* plaintiff had promoted concerts for two years. What was "new"? If a New Jersey Wal-Mart started a sushi bar, would Wal-Mart be a "new business"? Whether a business is "new" or not can critical. In that regard, consider the *RSB Labs* case, discussed below, which distinguished *Weiss* and *Seamans* and held the business was not a "new" one.

2. <u>Not Quite Barred</u>. "The general rule under Illinois law is that a new business has no right to recover lost profits" because a new business has "no history of profits, so any lost profits damages would be speculative," but lost profits may be recovered if the new business "offers expert testimony featuring convincing and non-speculative evidence sufficient to prove lost profits." *Antrim Pharm. LLC v. Bio-Pharm, Inc.*, 310 F. Supp. 3d 934 (N.D. Ill. 2018).

3. <u>Lost Profits or General Damages</u>? As *BMK* illustrates, particularly in states with strict rules against new businesses, it is important to determine whether the contract falls outside the scope of the rule. The *Tractebel Energy Mktg., Inc. v. AEP Power Mktg., Inc.*, 487 F.3d 89 (2d Cir. 2007), court explained:

> Lost profits are consequential damages when, as a result of the breach, the non-breaching party suffers loss of profits on collateral business arrangements. In the typical case, the ability of the non-breaching party to operate his business, and thereby generate profits on collateral transactions, is contingent on the performance of the primary contract. When the breaching party does not perform, the non-breaching party's business is in some way hindered, and the profits from potential collateral exchanges are "lost." Every lawyer will recall from his or her first-year contracts class the paradigmatic example of *Hadley v. Baxendale*, where Baxendale's failure to deliver a crank shaft on time caused Hadley to lose profits from the operation of his mill. 156 Eng. Rep. 145 (1854). In New York, a party is entitled to recover this form of lost profits only if (1) it is demonstrated with certainty that the damages have been caused by the breach, (2) the extent of the loss is capable of proof with reasonable certainty, and (3) it is established that the damages were fairly within the contemplation of the parties.
>
> By contrast, when the non-breaching party seeks only to recover money that the breaching party agreed to pay under the contract, the damages sought are general damages. The damages may still be characterized as lost profits since, had the contract been performed, the non-breaching party

would have profited to the extent that his cost of performance was less than the total value of the breaching party's promised payments. But, in this case, the lost profits are the direct and probable consequence of the breach.[20] The profits are precisely what the non-breaching party bargained for, and only an award of damages equal to lost profits will put the non-breaching party in the same position he would have occupied had the contract been performed.

See also Hansen Co., Inc. v. RedNet Envtl. Serv., 909 N.W.2d 228 (Iowa App. 2017) ("RedNet only sought lost profits on a single contract not future contracts or future business lost due to the breach. In other words, RedNet did not seek damages because it was forced to close its doors and could have made future profits had it continued in business. The only anticipated profit sought was the contract with Hansen, and RedNet's bid had been carefully prepared based upon past projects and profit margins."). If New Jersey law recognizes this approach, did the *Juice Entertainment* plaintiffs fit within it? Does this explain the difference between *Juice* and *BMK?*

4. <u>Uncertainty Over What</u>? One court stated that "the rule that lost profits cannot be speculative or uncertain relates more especially to the uncertainty as to cause, rather than uncertainty as to the measure or extent of the damages." *P.A. Lines, Inc. v. Jah*, 2011 WL 13176018 (N.D. Ga. Sept. 27, 2011). Can't the new business rule be justified on both aspects?

Consider *Katz Deli of Aventura, Inc. v. Waterways Plaza, LLC*, 183 So. 3d 374 (Ct. App. Fla. 2013), where the plaintiff restaurant owner sued its landlord for constructive eviction, which the court treated as breach of the implied covenant of quiet enjoyment. The landlord failed to keep the roof in repair and it leaked. The leaking grew worse, slowly causing a loss of business and its eventual closure due to open flows of water, mold, and a musty smell. The leaking had begun sometime in 2002, and the plaintiff closed the store and sued in July 2003. After refurbishing the store, the landlord relet it in October 2003 at a much higher rent. The plaintiff sought lost profits, but the defendant asserted the value of the restaurant was the proper measure because it had been destroyed, and the only evidence of value was a $1.5 million estimate in an insurance policy. The trial court held future lost profits for the

---

20. New York long ago clarified the distinction between profits as general or consequential damages in *Masterton & Smith v. Mayor of Brooklyn*, 7 Hill 61, 68–69 (N.Y. Sup. Ct. 1845):

> When the books and cases speak of the profits anticipated from a good bargain as matters too remote and uncertain to be taken into account in ascertaining the true measure of damages, they usually have reference to dependent and collateral engagements entered into on the faith and in expectation of the performance of the principal contract. But profits or advantages which are the direct and immediate fruits of the contract entered into between the parties stand upon a different footing. It is difficult to comprehend why, in case one party has deprived the other of the gains or profits of the contract by refusing to perform it, this loss should not constitute a proper item in estimating the damages.

remainder of the initial lease was the proper measure and awarded $800,000. Both parties appealed:

A trial court's determination as to the *method* of calculating damages is reviewed de novo, while findings of fact regarding the *amount* of damages sufficiently proven are subject to review for clear error. Some cases have held that when a business is totally destroyed, the proper measure of damages is the market value of the business at the date of the loss. However, where, as here, a business continues after suffering from an act of negligence the business is entitled to recover the lost profits attributable to defendant's negligent act, but cannot recover both lost profits, and the market value of the business.

This case presents us with a unique set of facts where the record does not disclose when exactly the negligent act and the breach of the lease occurred. The leaks began sometime in 2002, but the building did not become untenable until May 2003. It is similarly unclear what the "date of loss" would be under the market value theory of recovery, or what Katz's market value would be because its market value steadily declined due to the leaks caused by Waterways' grossly negligent behavior. To compound matters, Katz was not "completely destroyed" when the leaks started, when Waterways breached the lease, or even when Katz turned in its keys and moved out. The record reflects that Katz attempted to reopen but was unable to do so largely because its cash flow was tied up in the Katz Aventura location. Although Katz had ceased doing business, the company itself remained. The company still had inventory on hand and at least some goodwill in the community. There is no bright line for when the business was "completely destroyed," we simply know that the business never reopened. Awarding market value for a business that has been slowly reduced to nothing due to a defendant's breach, thereby leaving the plaintiff without an adequate recovery, would be completely inequitable, and is not the law in Florida.

Waterways reached a new lease agreement with the subsequent tenants a mere twenty-six days after Katz moved out, before the roof repairs had even been completed. Waterways reached this new lease agreement very quickly and for substantially higher monthly rental payments. Thus, Katz could not have reopened its business at that location even if it had wanted to do so. Instead, Katz was forced to try to find another suitable location with insufficient capital and with a vastly decreased reputation. The record reflects that most of the company's (and the family's) money had been invested in the Aventura business and Katz had suffered substantial losses in its business reputation due to the leaky and moldy interior for the last year it was in business in the Plaza. Due to these factors, and others, Katz was not able to reopen at another location.

Under these unique circumstances, we hold that lost profits is a proper measure of damages because Waterways' long-term continuing breach of the contract allowed Katz to stay in business for a year, but slowly depreciated the market value of that business, thus rendering an award of market value damages insufficient to make Katz whole. As noted above, the primary goal in a breach of contract case is to restore the plaintiff to the position it would have been in had the contract been properly performed. The only remedy that sufficiently restores Katz on these facts is an award of lost profits that have been proven with reasonable certainty.

A business can recover lost prospective profits regardless of whether it is established or has any track record. The party must prove that 1) the defendant's action caused the damage and 2) there is some standard by which the amount of damages may be adequately determined.

Any 'yardstick' used to show the amount of profits must be reasonable, and the loss of the profits as a result of the defendant's conduct must be reasonably certain. Lost profits must be established with a reasonable degree of certainty and must be a natural consequence of the wrong. The projected profits cannot be mere speculation or conjecture, but the inability to prove a precise damages amount will not prevent a plaintiff from recovering so long as it is clear that some loss resulting from the defendant's actions is certain.

Katz's history of success at the Pembroke Pines location, at its former smaller location within the Plaza, and during its short tenure in the larger location prior to the leaks, demonstrate that this was a moderately successful deli that would have continued to yield profits if not for the leaks. The history of sales from these locations, along with the sales projections and unrebutted expert testimony calculating likely prospective profits, provided a sufficient yardstick by which to measure Katz Deli's prospective profits. As such, the use of lost profits as a measure of damages was proper in this case.

Lost profits must be established with a reasonable degree of certainty and must be a natural consequence of the wrong. The fact that a party has not yet exercised an automatic renewal provision in a contract does not necessarily preclude it from recovering damages that extend to that portion of a lease. Rather, the question is whether the renewal of the lease and any profits that would have been realized through the renewal of that lease were reasonably certain.

Here, Katz argues it would have renewed its lease through the end of 2022 with reasonable certainty because the deli was operating successfully prior to the water leaks, and because its rent payment was well below market value. Indeed, Katz points to the subsequent tenants that were still operating in its former space in the Plaza at the time of trial in 2012 as evidence that it would have renewed its lease. Those successor tenants were paying substantially higher rent payments, but nonetheless continued to renew their leases with Waterways and operate their businesses through the end of the trial period below. Katz also correctly points out that even if its deli and market were struggling, it could have subleased the premises at a substantially higher rent rate and reaped a similar profit that Waterways is now making on the market rental rates.

While this argument has merit, whether the lease renewal and the lost profits stemming from that renewal were reasonably certain is a question of fact to be determined by the finder of fact. The trial court, who is the finder of fact in a bench trial, made a specific finding that an award of lost profits extending past the initial lease term was too speculative. We cannot say the trial court's conclusion was clearly erroneous, and therefore we affirm the denial of lost profits past the initial lease term.

II. Causation and Amount of Lost Profits

To recover lost profits, a plaintiff must prove by preponderant evidence that the defendant caused *some* lower income, and the amount with "reasonable certainty." Even in jurisdictions that do not bar, or require greater proof for new businesses, the standard is still high: courts often dismiss complaints by new businesses for lost profits, or grant summary judgment on those claims, or exclude expert reports as speculative. *See Pot Luck, LLC v. Freeman*, 2010 WL 908475 (S.D.N.Y. March 8, 2010) (dismissing complaint stating that "claims for lost profits in unsuccessful entertainment ventures have received a chilly reception"); *Madowitz v. Woods at Killington Owners' Ass'n.*, 196 Vt. 47 (2014) (granting summary judgment to lost profits claim based upon real estate development).

The courts permit new businesses to rely upon any reasonable manner to quantify lost profits for new businesses, but two are common: (1) the before-and-after method, and (2) the yardstick method. Each generally requires expert testimony from qualified experts.

The before-and-after method compares plaintiff's profits before and after the wrongful conduct, and the argument is that, but for the defendant's conduct, plaintiff would have continued to make what it had made before then. This is available only to established businesses because there must be a sufficient "track record" of past performance. *See Spring Window Fashions Div., Inc. v. Blind Maker, Inc.*, 184 S.W.3d 840 (Ct. App. Tex. 2006) (eight years' past performance sufficient). The inference the plaintiff makes is that, but for the defendant's act, its profits would have continued as they had in the past. The problem generally faced is causation: was it the defendant, or something else — the economy, changes in consumer demand, bad business decisions, or something besides the defendant's conduct — that caused the change in profits?

The yardstick method compares the plaintiff's profits to comparable businesses, and the argument is that, but for the defendant's conduct, the plaintiff's business would have made what they had previously made. "The yardstick test is generally used when a business has not been established long enough to compile an earnings record that would sufficiently demonstrate lost profits. This test compares the profits of businesses that are closely comparable to the plaintiff's. The Restatement illustrates it thus:

> A employs B as master of a whaling ship on a five-year voyage, the compensation to be a share of the net proceeds of oil taken on the voyage. After two years B is wrongfully discharged and at once brings action. Although the earnings of the ship after B's discharge are contingent and uncertain, B may be able to lay a sufficient basis for their estimation by giving evidence of the conditions and experience in the whaling industry.

Restatement (First) of Contracts § 331 illus. 10 (1932). The "yardstick method requires that the businesses used as a standard for plaintiff's business be 'as nearly identical to the plaintiff's business as possible.'" *Thermotek, Inc. v. Orthoflex, Inc.*, 2016 WL 4678888 (N.D. Tex. Sept. 7, 2016), *aff'd*, 875 F.3d 765 (5th Cir. 2017). "Among the factors to consider are: similarity of products sold; respective markets of the two companies; the capital and organizational structures of the two firms; and whether the plaintiff and its yardstick conducted business, administratively and operationally, in the same way." *Harris Wayside Furniture Co., Inc. v. Idearc Media Corp.*, 2008 WL 7109357 (D.N.H. Dec. 22, 2008). "Evidence of the similarities between the businesses enables reasonable conclusions to be drawn about how plaintiff may have performed based on the yardstick company's performance, but for the alleged intervening cause." *Id.*

Both methods require detailed evidence. In *Lump v. Larson*, 2015 WL 509674 (Ohio Ct. App. Feb. 9, 2015), Larson was an attorney who sued for several hundred thousand dollars for intentional interference with prospective business relations. After a bench trial, the court awarded $1,731.75. Plaintiff appealed but the appellate court affirmed, writing:

> While Larson may have proven the gross amounts of the contracts with documents and corroborating information, he merely asserted that he would have made a particular amount of profits. Indeed, Larson simply stated his lost-profit amounts without any itemization or explanation of how he calculated them. Moreover, Larson failed to "prove lost profits with calculations based on facts. For example, Larson failed to offer any documents or information related to his cost basis in the equipment he was to sell under the agreements. Nor did Larson offer any documents or information related to his costs of providing the services under the purported agreements, such as transportation, labor, and installation costs. For these reasons, the trial court's conclusion that Larson failed to

prove the "resulting damages" element of the tortious-interference-with-business-relationships cause of action is not against the manifest weight of the evidence.

Larson's briefing on appeal reflects that he fails to grasp that "resulting damages" is one of the elements of the tortious-interference-with-business-relationships cause of action that he needed to prove to prevail on the cause of action.

The following cases apply the two common—but not exclusive—methods and the quality and nature of the evidentiary support required.

RSB Lab. Serv., Inc. v. BSI Corp.

847 A.2d 599 (N.J. Super. Ct. 2004) (Fuentes, J.)

[After 25 years as registered nurses, in 1996 Ruth Yao and her sister formed a corporation to operate a "bleeding station," which is an office to which doctors refer patients to have blood or other fluids drawn and analyzed. In late 1998, the sisters decided to transform the business to a full-service laboratory. As part of this, they changed the name of their company to RSB Laboratory Services, Inc., and set out to buy the additional lab equipment they would need. Ruth was qualified to operate the new equipment the company would need to expand, but had no actual experience operating it. Ruth spoke to and ordered refurbished equipment from BSI Corporation. BSI failed to deliver working equipment and the training it had agreed to provide along with it. For months, RSB sought BSI's assistance and reported problems, but to no avail. RSB eventually sued BSI. The jury awarded $254,763.55, which included lost profits. BSI appealed.]

With regard to lost profits, plaintiff called certified public accountant Bruce Jonas as an expert witness. In preparation to offer an opinion on the subject, Jonas: (1) reviewed documents listing revenues collected by laboratories from referrals made by plaintiff; (2) interviewed the Vice President of Client Services, a billing company performing work for laboratories and other medical facilities; (3) ascertained the quantities of reagent necessary for operation of a laboratory; and (4) reviewed profiles of large publicly-traded medical laboratories to determine whether revenue in the industry was rising.

Jonas admitted, however, that he had not reviewed plaintiff's business records or tax returns, although he had lengthy discussions with Yao. He explained that those documents were not relevant to plaintiff's potential success as a laboratory because they had been prepared when plaintiff was operating as a "bleeding station." Nonetheless, Jonas opined that, rather than being an entirely new business, a laboratory was a "natural follow up" to a bleeding station.

In determining lost profits, Jonas chose to use the revenue reports. He selected the reports generated by Alex, a lab used by plaintiff, as the "best available data to simulate what plaintiff would look like as an operating laboratory." He reviewed seven months of Alex's revenue reports, from August 1997 to February 1998, listing revenues totaling $113,320 for work submitted to Alex by plaintiff. He did not, however, simply utilize Alex's entire revenue stream as a measure of plaintiff's potential profits. He limited his inquiry to the forty-two physicians who had referred patients to plaintiff as a bleeding station. He then chose only nine of those physicians as a prospective referring base. These nine physicians were considered because they (a) had placed an order in at least three of the seven months; (b) their referrals had averaged more than $100; and (c) had generated a payment in either of the last two months. He thus concluded that these nine physicians would continue to refer business to plaintiff when it became an operational laboratory.

Jonas next added the average of the monthly collections reported by Alex from the nine chosen physicians ($14,238) and deducted 5% from that amount, to account for any tests or procedures that plaintiff would not have been able to perform, and derived a projected gross monthly revenue of $13,526. Jonas cross-checked that amount by using a collection rate of 40% to 45%, thereby calculating that plaintiff's yearly gross billings would total $382,000.

Jonas then reduced the gross revenues of the nine physicians by plaintiff's projected monthly expenses, or $8,004.75, which included salaries, the cost of chemicals, and waste removal, and which resulted in a net monthly projected revenue of $5,521.25. Jonas ultimately calculated projected lost profits for plaintiff operating as a laboratory of $77,000 (one year), $140,000 (two years), $194,000 (three years), $242,000 (four years), and $284,000 (five years). The four-year period selected corresponded to the length of the lease. Jonas admitted, however, that he did not know what the failure rate was for new laboratories.

According to Jonas, this methodology conformed to standard accounting practices. The information he relied upon was of the type generally relied upon by accountants in performing this type of revenue projection. His opinion as to lost profits was within a reasonable degree of accounting certainty, conservative and "probably the bottom end of the range." Defendant presented no expert testimony regarding lost profits.

Defendant argues that the Law Division erred in denying its motions for summary judgment, and for judgment, because plaintiff's lost profits claim was barred by the new business rule. Although believed bound by the new business rule, both judges who heard defendant's motions expressed doubt that plaintiff was in fact a new business. The judge who heard the summary judgment motion stated: "I don't know that what plaintiff is projecting here is totally innovative. I think that there is a distinction. They have a business, or [sic] rather routine, straightforward kind of business. There are other businesses that one can look to. One might be able to provide a reasonable basis for jurors to make a determination. Which isn't to say, that we at the trial level, are not bound by the existence of a new business rule."

In denying defendant's motion the trial judge specifically found that plaintiff was not a new business, explaining that, "plaintiff was an extension of an existing business albeit a bleeding business. It was an ongoing operation, although different in kind. The future business, or the new business, rationale had appeal, because the success of that enterprise is ordinarily uncertain. In this case we had a certain business that was making money in this context. It was an expansion. This enterprise was not a new business starting as much."

The court also found credible Jonas's testimony that plaintiff had a base of referring physicians who "had confidence" in Yao and would continue to refer business to plaintiff once it expanded into providing laboratory work. Thus, the judge found that Yao on behalf of plaintiff "had the goods, she had the machine, and she was licensed. By August of 1999 she was set up to go at that point. But for the water bath not filling we may have had a viable concern at that point and this would have been 95% of her business. She had the name, she had people that worked with her, and they were referring business to plaintiff as she had a track record that I think was amply demonstrated either in Brookdale or Alex or CDS, where she was a conduit. She had been in the community and has been represented for a while at this point."

Here, defendant argues that the court erred in denying its motions because plaintiff's claim for lost profits was barred by the new business rule.

Perhaps the time has come for our State to join the majority of jurisdictions that have abandoned this anachronistic rule for the more flexible approach of the Restatement. Until the Supreme Court says otherwise, the new business rule remains the law in this State. Therefore, the question remains whether plaintiff is a new business subject to the rule.

Here plaintiff had been operating as a bleeding station since 1996, drawing blood and other bodily fluids and sending those fluids to other laboratories for analysis and testing. The laboratories paid plaintiff a commission on those referrals and sent plaintiff written records verifying those amounts. In late 1998, plaintiff sought to expand its business to include the laboratory work, using its same employees, facilities, and customer base. It needed only new equipment and a license to accomplish the expansion.

Here plaintiff had operated a bleeding station and sought to expand that business using existing clients and referring physicians, thereby resulting in readily ascertainable profits. We thus agree with the trial court. The new business rule is inapplicable in this case. The record here provides a rational basis in which to calculate profits with a reasonable degree of certainty.

Notes and Questions

1. <u>New Business?</u> The *RSB* court concluded the rule did not apply because the plaintiff was not a new business. It distinguished *Weiss* and *Seaman*. Can you? Consider *Slip-n-Slide Records, Inc. v. TVT Records, LLC*, 2007 WL 3232274 (S.D. Fla. Oct. 31, 2007), where the plaintiff sued defendants for tortiously interfering with its

agreement to distribute the second album by Pitbull the Rapper (Armando Perez), *Welcome to the 305*. The jury awarded $2.3 million in lost profits, and the appellate court affirmed, stating:

> The case before this Court is distinguishable from those cases involving new businesses or undeveloped products. The evidence of record here is that SNS is a well-established and successful recording company. The 305 Album was in the pipeline for pressing and imminent distribution by a known distribution company. The album was slated for distribution in April or May of 2005, less than one year after the release in August 2004 of Pitbull's debut album, M.I.A.M.I.," which had enjoyed success in the marketplace. As discussed in more detail below, SNS's expert witness, Gregory McBowman, compared the 305 Album to the "M.I.A.M.I." and remix "M.I.A.M.I." albums, and to albums by artists in the same genre (Dirty South) that SNS previously had successfully marketed and released. Given that the 305 Album would have been released in close temporal proximity to the release of Pitbull's successful earlier albums, and given that the 305 Album was in the same genre as other successful SNS albums, there was a track record upon which an expert could base projections of sales of the 305 Album. That the sales history for Pitbull albums was not lengthy, or that there may have been differences in the music of Pitbull and comparable artists, goes to the weight, not reliability, of McBowman's methodology. The jury found, and this Court agrees, that there was a reasonable basis upon which to project future profits for the 305 Album as McBowman testified.

> TVT challenges the factual basis for McBowman's methodology and argues that his sales projections for the 305 Album, which ranged from 500,000 units ("worst case" scenario) to 700,000 units ("most likely" scenario) to 1,100,000 units ("best case" scenario), were clearly outside the scope of any reasonable degree of certainty. TVT claims these ranges were merely theoretical ranges and no methodology was given to the jury to select between them. TVT challenges McBowman's comparison with the sales of other supposedly-comparable albums; his failure to consider certain marketing expenses incurred and marketing techniques utilized with respect to the comparable albums; his failure to consider the estimates of Boothe and the ADA representative, both of whom projected lower unit sales for the 305 Album than McBowman did; and his calculation of profits which failed to include numerous line items for expenses including marketing and promotion expenses, advertising, and royalties.

> Again, the Court concludes that these are issues that go to the weight of McBowman's testimony, not to its legal admissibility or reliability. TVT identifies what it perceives as deficiencies in McBowman's testimony, but those were matters for the jury to consider. To estimate SNS's lost profits, McBowman compared sales of eight other albums marketed and released by SNS of similar genre artist, as well as the sales by TVT of two other

Pitbull records, to arrive at an estimate of the likely sales of the 305 Album that SNS would have generated, taking into account both the business experience of SNS and the sales ability of Pitbull. McBowman then calculated estimated sales of the 305 Album for "worst case," "most likely," and "best case" scenarios. He then calculated the net profits that SNS would generate under each scenario. Though obviously not experts, both Julian Boothe and Ted Lucas found McBowman's opinions as to projected sales plausible. Testimony by the ADA representative suggesting that album sales would have been lower created at best a conflict in the testimony, but did not render McBowman's methodology unreliable.

McBowman testified that since the ultimate issue was the lost profits to be earned by SNS, sales generated from albums by SNS's other artists were more germane to his analysis than sales of albums by TVT or any other record label. Despite TVT's arguments that certain marketing techniques (videos, songs, and radio spins) were more relevant, McBowman provided reasoned testimony why his opinion of SNS's track record of marketing was more relevant to his analysis. TVT could have presented rebutting evidence directly challenging the methodology underlying McBowman's opinions, but it did not. Instead, TVT's expert provided an alternative methodology for calculating damages in this case. This undermines TVT's post-trial challenge to McBowman's methodology as to either admissibility or reliability. The fact that the jury also rejected in part McBowman's profits calculations, either because it found his analysis exaggerated and/or because it agreed in part with TVT's profits expert, shows that the jury gave McBowman's testimony the weight that it reasonably deemed appropriate given the facts of the case. This all points against TVT's position here that a new trial is required on the compensatory damage issue.

The strengths and weaknesses in his opinions were for the jury to evaluate. McBowman was subjected to rigorous cross-examination. TVT did not present evidence that specifically contradicted his methodology. TVT's music industry economist, Barry Massarsky, presented an alternative estimate of lost profits based on his comparison of sales of "old" and "new" albums, in an amount of $29,000.00, but his opinion did not specifically rebut McBowman's methodology. TVT is, in essence, asking the Court to reweigh the evidence on lost profits that was presented to the jury through the two sides' experts. It is the province of the jury to weigh the evidence, assess credibility, and consider conflicting expert testimony.

The jury had before it the two experts' methodologies for calculating lost profits. The jury was properly instructed, without objection from TVT, as to SNS's burden on proving lost profits and the manner in which lost profits are calculated under the law. It is fair to say that the jury conducted its own analysis of the evidence on damages. Exhibit P13A is a schedule that was made a part of the record at trial and contains in table form McBowman's estimate of the damages SNS sustained as a result of the 305 Album not being released and sold. McBowman predicted damages in the amount of $8,183,003 (best case scenario); $5,162,396 (most likely scenario), and $3,597,577 (worst case scenario). The jury's compensatory damages award of $2,227,200 was less than that projected by McBowman under the worst case scenario. Obviously the Court cannot say which costs the jury deducted, but it is clear from the amount of the damages award that this jury did not blindly accept McBowman's (or Massarsky's) testimony. Rather, the jury carefully weighed the evidence and reached an independent conclusion as to damages based on all the evidence before it. Based on this record, and absent evidence to the contrary, the Court presumes the jury followed the Court's instructions. The Court finds the weight of the evidence supports the jury's compensatory damages award. There is no basis here on which to grant TVT's request for a new trial.

2. <u>What Methods</u>? Did Jonas use the yardstick or before-and-after method? Why wasn't the other an option? Why did he make the various adjustments he did? Why are the requirements for yardstick so stringent? What method was used in *Murtha*? Why was it much more relaxed?

C. Mitigation Costs as Consequential Damages

Chapter 16 shows that failure to mitigate damages can serve to cut off liability for damages that, by using reasonable care, could have been avoided. As a corollary, reasonable expenses to mitigate are recoverable damages. So, for example, reasonable expenses a landlord incurs in reletting commercial space are recoverable. In that context, the court in *New Mkt. Acquisitions, Ltd. v. Powerhouse Gym*, 212 F. Supp. 2d 763 (S.D. Ohio 2002), explained, expenses by the landlord for "major structural changes are not recoverable as mitigation expenses." *See In re Andover Togs, Inc.*, 231 B.R. 521 (Bankr. S.D.N.Y. 1999) (long-term capital improvements that "yield a betterment to the leasehold," such as construction of common corridor, may not be included in a computation of damages for breach of lease).

DeRosier v. Util. Sys. of Am., Inc.
780 N.W.2d 1 (Ct. App. Minn. 2010) (Minge, J.)

[DeRosier had bought undeveloped hillside property, intending to build a house. The builder told DeRosier he needed substantial fill to level the lot to build the home. DeRosier noticed Utility Systems of America, Inc., was excavating a nearby lot. He proposed to a USA foreman that, instead of trucking the dirt far away, that USA dump the fill on his lot. In July 2004, USA agreed. In late August 2004, DeRosier gave the city permit he had obtained allowing deposit 1,500 of cubic yards of fill to the USA foreman, and then left on a 10-day vacation. When DeRosier returned, his property was covered with 6,500 cubic yards of fill. DeRosier's builder told him a house could not be built unless the fill was removed and the builder withdrew from the project. When DeRosier complained to USA, at first it denied responsibility but, after DeRosier threatened suit, it agreed to remove excess fill for $9,500. DeRosier refused and instead hired G & T Construction to remove the excess fill, which charged him $22,829. DeRosier sued defendant USA for breach of contract. The court found breach and awarded $22,829. Defendant appealed.]

We first note that if USA had merely offered to cure, DeRosier would have been obliged to accept to mitigate damages. An implied right to cure exists in situations where cure is possible. Upon receiving proper notice, a party that defectively performs may cure if done within a reasonable time and there is adequate assurance of performance. *See* Restatement (Second) of Contracts § 237 cmt. 6 (1979) (noting that nonbreaching party is not relieved of duty to perform until defect can no longer be cured); *id.* § 350 cmt. g ("It is reasonable for the injured party to rely on performance by the other party even after breach when the breach is accompanied by assurances that performance will be forthcoming.").

Here, DeRosier notified USA of the defective performance, requesting that the excess fill be removed under threat of lawsuit. USA, however, only offered to fix the fill problem on condition that DeRosier make further payments. A breaching party may not insist that the damaged party pay additional compensation to correct work for which the breacher had already been fully paid to perform. Although USA had not received monetary payment for its work, it had benefited from its agreement with DeRosier and the absence of a monetary payment is not a material distinction. We conclude that because USA did not attempt to cure, but rather proposed a new contract with new consideration, USA waived its right to cure.

Nevertheless, DeRosier may still have had an obligation to enter into that new contract if such a step was a reasonable way to mitigate damages. Acceptance of USA's offer would have saved DeRosier over $13,000. The issue, then, is whether rejection of that offer was unreasonable.

Outside of employment situations, one reported Minnesota court decision has considered whether it is unreasonable to reject a breaching party's subsequent offer that would mitigate damages. *Coxe v. Anoka Waterworks Elec. Light & Power Co.,* 87 Minn. 56 (1902). In *Coxe,* the supreme court held that a buyer who contracted to purchase goods on credit did not have to accept an offer of the same goods for a cheaper cash price. The court reasoned that imposing the new contract as a mitigation requirement would entirely abrogate the contract as made by the parties, and force upon them another and wholly different one, made by the court. The rationale of *Coxe* would not require such agreements to mitigate, especially where the new contract would supplant the old one without preserving a right to enforce the original agreement.

Other states have faced the issue and have held that the nonbreaching party can recover its full damages despite refusing the breacher's new offer that would have minimized the loss. *See Zanker Dev. Co. v. Cogito Sys., Inc.,* 215 Cal.App.3d 1377

(1989) (holding landlord need not mitigate damages by reletting to tenant that repudiated lease); *Stanley Manly Boys' Clothes, Inc. v. Hickey*, 113 Tex. 482 (1925) (no one "should be required to contract a second time with one who has without cause breached a prior contract with him"); *City Nat'l Bank v. Wells*, 181 W.Va. 763 (1989) ("The plaintiff here justifiably revoked his acceptance of the defective truck and had no obligation to afford the defendant yet another opportunity to repair it.").

We conclude that when one party to the contract defectively performs and subsequently offers to correct the breach through a new contract, the nonbreaching party may generally decline the offer and still recover its full damages. Special circumstances may rebut the reasonableness of the rejection and call for exceptions to this rule. The facts before us support DeRosier's decision: (1) the $9,500 payment demanded was substantial; (2) DeRosier was not unreasonable in believing that acceptance could constitute an accord and satisfaction; (3) other hauling services were readily available; and (4) DeRosier's relationship with USA was strained as USA was blaming DeRosier.

On this record, we conclude that DeRosier did not have an obligation to accept USA's $9,500 offer and that DeRosier is entitled to the costs he incurred in using others to remove the excess fill.

Notes and Questions

1. Factors to Consider? The article the *DeRosier* court cited as providing factors to consider when a breaching party offers to cure, but at additional cost, states:

> The service contract cases have the following common characteristics which override judicial reluctance to "reward" the breacher by imposing a mitigation requirement on the injured party.
>
> 1. The additional demand by the breacher which constitutes the material breach is not onerous.
>
> 2. The acceptance of the additional demand does not constitute an accord and satisfaction. Although there is usually no specific discussion of this point, the cases apparently assume that an action for damages has not been waived by the injured party.
>
> 3. There is no uncertainty as to whether the breacher will perform the second offer.
>
> 4. The alternative to accepting the demand is "great" damage. Of course, by definition this means that the injured party has no equivalent available substitute transaction.

Robert A. Hillman, *Keeping the Deal Together after Material Breach—Common Law Mitigation Rules, the UCC, and the Restatement (Second) of Contracts*, 47 U. Colo. L. Rev. 553 (1976).

2. <u>Employment Cases</u>. Defendants in wrongful termination cases often assert that the plaintiff's lost wages should be reduced because of failure to mitigate. "It is a well-established rule that where one is under contract for personal service, and is discharged, it becomes his duty to dispose of his time in a reasonable way, so as to obtain as large compensation as possible, and to use honest, earnest and intelligent efforts to this end. He cannot voluntarily remain idle and expect to recover the compensation stipulated in the contract from the other party." *Sheriff of Suffolk County v. Jail Officers and Employees of Suffolk County*, 990 N.E.2d 1042 (Mass. 2013). In that case, a sheriff was found to have wrongfully terminated a jail officer. The court explained the burden that an employer in that circumstance faces to show failure to mitigate:

> An employer meets this burden of proof by proving the following: (a) one or more discoverable opportunities for comparable employment were available in a location as convenient as, or more convenient than, the place of former employment, (b) the improperly discharged employee unreasonably made no attempt to apply for any such job, and (c) it was reasonably likely that the former employee would obtain one of those comparable jobs.
>
> Additionally, the employer must show what the employee could have earned in other similar work. An unemployed or underemployed claimant need not go into another line of work, accept a demotion, or take a demeaning position. [Instead, comparable work is] employment that offers similar long-term benefits and opportunities for promotion as compared to the original position. See Greenway v. Buffalo Hilton Hotel, 951 F.Supp. 1039 (W.D.N.Y. 1997), *aff'd as modified*, 143 F.3d 47 (2d Cir. 1998) ("In order for the work to be comparable or substantially similar, the new position must afford a plaintiff virtually identical promotional opportunities, compensation, job responsibilities, working condition, and status as the former position").
>
> It is beyond dispute that an employer must demonstrate the availability of "comparable employment," not just any employment. Given Upton's occupation as a correction officer, it is simply irrelevant to the issue of mitigation that he may have been able to further offset his lost earnings by working on a more permanent basis as a restaurant employee, carpenter, or bouncer. It is quite clear that the three positions identified by the sheriff are not comparable or remotely similar to Upton's employment as a correction officer. Further, employment as a restaurant employee, carpenter, or bouncer does not offer the same stability, benefits, or potential for promotion. Accordingly, the judge correctly concluded that the sheriff had failed to demonstrate the availability of comparable employment opportunities, or what Upton could have earned in an available comparable position elsewhere.

3. <u>Moving Expenses</u>. In *Georgia Dermatologic Surgery Centers, P.C. v. Pharis*, 792 S.E.2d 747 (Ct. App. Ga. 2016), a doctor was wrongfully terminated from the

defendant, GDSC, a dermatology center. To mitigate, his professional corporation opened a dermatology center. The jury awarded start-up expenses as mitigation costs. Defendant appealed and the court reversed:

> Pharis sought to recover as damages the expenses incurred in opening up his new medical practice on the theory that, but for GDSC's breach of his employment contract, he would not have incurred the expenses, and because the expenses were reasonably incurred in order to mitigate and lessen his damages. *See* Restatement (Second) of Contracts § 347, comment (c) ("Incidental losses," which, like any other loss actually suffered, are recoverable, "include costs incurred in a reasonable effort, whether successful or not, to avoid loss."). At the close of Pharis's case, GDSC moved for a directed verdict on Pharis's claim for start-up expenses on the ground that the evidence showed that those costs were paid by the PC, which was not a party to the case. The trial court denied the motion, commenting that Pharis and the PC are "one and the same as a matter of liability law." As part of its special verdict, the jury awarded Pharis $283,321 in damages "for start-up expenses."

> The evidence showed that the $283,321 at issue were costs incurred by the PC in the course of opening the business where Pharis resumed his medical practice after GDSC breached the employment contract. Specifically, the evidence showed that of the $283,321 in costs, $273,321 was attributable to the PC's purchase of depreciable assets, primarily medical equipment, and the remaining $10,000 was attributable to the legal costs of organizing the PC. A cardinal precept of corporate law is that corporations are separate legal entities from their shareholders, officers, directors, and employees even in the situation in which a corporation is owned solely by one person. Thus, funds expended by the PC to establish the medical practice were not expended by Pharis. Rather, they were funds paid by a non-party with no standing to complain of the breach of contract at issue.

> Pharis suggests that, at the least, he could have recovered as damages $110,000 in his personal savings that he contributed to the PC. But even if the PC used those funds to pay for start-up costs, Pharis made a capital contribution to the corporation; he did not pay the start-up costs. Rather, the costs were paid by the PC and inured to the PC's benefit, largely in the form of equipment. Accordingly, we find that the trial court erred in allowing the jury, over GDSC's motion for directed verdict, to award Pharis costs incurred by the PC in establishing its business. The judgment is reversed in part, and the trial court is instructed to deduct the amount awarded on Pharis's claim for start-up expenses ($283,321, as set forth in the jury's special verdict), but the judgment is otherwise affirmed.

Problems

1. <u>Deposition Preparation</u>. While a college student, 20-year-old Susie Jones suffered a permanent brain injury. She can work at low-wage jobs that do not require concentration or stress. How will you prepare her for deposition? What questions would you ask if you were defense counsel?

2. <u>Life Expectancy Shortened</u>. You represent a defendant in a suit where your client is accused of severely and permanently injuring the plaintiff in an unprovoked fight. You have a damages expert preparing a Rule 26 report on future lost income. Another expert, a physician, has concluded that the injuries have reduced plaintiff's life expectancy. Consider whether, and how, you would rely on that fact in closing arguments. If you were the plaintiff, what would you expect and how would you respond to those arguments?

3. <u>Increased Earnings and Diminished Earning Capacity</u>. Courts state that it is difficult for a plaintiff whose earnings increased after an injury to prove diminished earning capacity. Why does that not preclude them, and why would that make it more difficult?

4. <u>Freelance Model</u>. You are a judge deciding a slip-and-fall case. The plaintiff was 19 years old when he slipped and fell in a store. Prior to the fall, he had worked as a file clerk for a law firm. He had, in addition, started work as a "freelance model," and his photographs had been used in a local magazine. He wants to testify about future diminished earning capacity caused because of disfigurement to his face caused by the fall. The defendant has moved *in limine* to exclude any evidence of economic losses, beyond medical expenses and lost past wages from his clerk position (he has returned to that position). There is no evidence of any diminished earning capacity other than as a future model. How will you rule?

5. <u>One Blank for the Amount of Damages</u>? Can you explain why a plaintiff with multiple claims would want a "general verdict" (a single question that asks whether the plaintiff proved its claim or claims by preponderant evidence and, if so, the amount of damages) while a defendant would prefer a special verdict, asking the jury whether the plaintiff proved each element of each claim by preponderant evidence and the measure of damages for each claim?

6. <u>Gunshot Wound</u>. Your client is a 13-year-old boy who accidentally shot himself in the leg, necessitating its amputation. After three years, you are finally at trial in federal court in Louisiana. The jury just returned its verdict, finding the gunmaker liable under negligence theory. The jury awarded damages for past and future medical expenses, but no damages were awarded for physical impairment, mental anguish, or pain and suffering. What will you do and how do you believe the trial court will rule? What arguments should you anticipate defense counsel will make?

7. <u>Third Time Will Be an Unlucky Charm</u>? A plaintiff filed suit, asserting a negligence claim alleging her exposure years earlier to defendant's beryllium had reduced

her lung capacity, and seeking compensatory damages. At that time, the medical testimony was that, while her lung capacity had diminished—which was consistent with beryllium exposure—it was also consistent with many other causes, such as cigarette smoking. In addition, her lung capacity was within normal ranges and so was not a compensable physical injury for purposes of negligence. Thus, she had no "injury" required for a negligence claim and had no claim. She filed this suit which permitted "medical monitoring," but not "fear of" damages. Years later, she joined a class action suit asserting negligence and seeking an order requiring "medical monitoring." The defendant moved to dismiss her negligence claim as violating the single action rule and *res judicata*, and the court granted the motion and the appellate court affirmed. Can you explain why it did so but held that other plaintiffs, who had never sued before, could obtain medical monitoring?

8. <u>Lack of Clear Triggers</u>. The Kentucky Supreme Court—a strict impact rule state—rejected medical monitoring damages, identifying several problems including "inconsistent 'triggers,' or prerequisites to a claim, from jurisdiction to jurisdiction." *Wood v. Wyeth-Ayerst Laboratories, Div. of Am. Home Products*, 82 S.W.3d 849 (Ky. 2002). Would you expect states that permit negligence claims without an impact to also be more likely to award medical monitoring damages?

9. <u>Futures</u>. The single action rule requires juries to award damages for not only what might have been, but what might be—but they cannot speculate. Consider my own life: if I had been injured when I was a high school senior, the evidence would have showed that I had been a good student, but not great, and that I had hoped to go to law school but, before then, was headed to the local university which was a good, but not great, school. If I had been seriously injured, wouldn't it seem absurd if my lawyer had argued that I would have, but for the injury, gone on to college to graduate near the top of my class, and then attend a top-15 law school and graduate with honors before then becoming an associate at a major international law firm, and making in the top few percentiles of national income? Or, would they have believed the defense lawyer, who would have pointed out that my jobs until then had included a very brief (six-week) stint at McDonald's, a year-long job as a phone solicitor, and prior to that, working for my parents at their restaurant, and so, given my lackluster high school performance, I would have, if anything, been lucky to manage a fast-food restaurant? Consider the alternatives to letting a jury "speculate" in this way.

Chapter 13

The One Recovery Rule and Election of Remedies

The single action rule and *res judicata* require a plaintiff to assert every claim it has that arises out of the same "common nucleus of operative facts," as Chapter 12 showed. This creates two problems.

The first is that two claims may permit recovery of damages for the same harm. The "one recovery rule," or "one satisfaction rule," seeks to ensure that juries do not award damages for the same harm for each claim. At the same time, as has been seen, some claims do not permit an award of the same damages. Mental anguish damages, for example, are generally not available for breach of contract.

The second problem is that some remedies are inconsistent. As shown previously, for example, a plaintiff cannot obtain an injunction against future damage for nuisance and also seek damages for future harm. Similarly, as also shown, a plaintiff asserting fraudulent inducement of contract cannot seek both to rely on the contract but also seek fraud damages: asserting that the contract is rescinded due to fraud is inconsistent with relying upon it.

The one recovery rule and election of remedies are thus created by the single action rule, but are distinct problems. "The election-of-remedies doctrine applies when a party is pursuing inconsistent yet coexistent remedies for the same wrong. Remedies requiring an election would be, for example, seeking an injunction for specific performance of a contract and rescission of that same contract. It is an affirmative defense that must be affirmatively pled and proved by a defendant." *Diep Tuyet Vo v. Vu*, 2016 WL 2841286 (Ct. App. Tex. 2016). In contrast, if a "jury verdict contains more than one acceptable measure of damages, a plaintiff may be forced to elect prior to judgment the recovery he wants by waiving the surplus findings with respect to the damages." *Id.*

1. The One Recovery Rule

The one recovery rule is implicated if a plaintiff asserts two claims that permit recovery of damages for the same harm. Not all claims do. However, some do, whether as consequential or direct damages. When this is the case, a plaintiff may not recover twice for the same harm. For example, in *Thompson v. R.J. Reynolds Tobacco Co.*, 760 F.3d 913 (8th Cir. 2014), the plaintiff, while alive, sued for damages for cancer caused by tobacco and obtained a $1 million judgment and then settled that case and released the defendant. After he died, his survivors brought a wrongful death claim. The court held it barred by the one recovery rule.

Thus, with both aspects in place, the one recovery rule ensures that a plaintiff will be fully compensated for a single injury, but not receive duplicative compensation. As *X-It Products, LLC v. Walter Kidde Portable Equip., Inc.*, 227 F. Supp. 2d 494 (E.D. Va. 2002), explained:

> The doctrine is remedial in nature and does no more than prevent double recovery. Although the doctrine has been interpreted many ways, what it means in this case is that a plaintiff is entitled to the greatest amount recoverable under any single theory pled that is supported by the evidence. Where a plaintiff seeks recovery for the same damages under different legal theories, only a single recovery is allowed. *Transamerica Occidental Life Ins. Co. v. Sanders*, 91 F.3d 134 (4th Cir. 1996) (vacating judgment and remanding for plaintiff's election of remedies because plaintiff "is not entitled to damages for both causes of action on the same conduct"); *Winant v. Bostic*, 5 F.3d 767 (4th Cir. 1993) ("although a party may assert claims for money damages based on fraud, breach of contract, and unfair and deceptive trade practices, he may succeed on only one basis").

While the one recovery rule applies even if the plaintiff "asserts multiple, consistent theories of recovery," *Kenney v. Palmer-Stuart Oil Co., Inc.*, 2017 WL 4581800 (W.D. Va. Oct. 13, 2017), it is critical to assess whether the claims in fact seek damages for the same harm.

Further, the one recovery rule is implicated by settlements from other defendants for the same harm: ordinarily, a defendant is entitled to a credit for payments made by settling defendants. *Chuttke v. Fresen*, 86 N.E.2d 1263 (Ct. App. Ill. 2017). A "setoff" generally is a defendant's request to reduce damages because a third party (including a settling defendant) has already paid the plaintiff for the same injury. *Chuttke v. Fresen*, 86 N.E.2d 1263 (Ct. App. Ill. 2017). To avoid more than one recovery, a defendant is entitled to "set off" any judgment by those amounts. *K.S. v. Detroit Public Schools*, 153 F. Supp. 3d 970 (E.D. Mich. 2015).

Arcangel v. Huntington A. Hotels, LLC

2018 WL 5885517 (D. Md. Nov. 9, 2018) (Xinis, J.)

[Plaintiffs Gilbert and Marygrace Arcangel stayed in room 807 at a Marriott Hotel and allegedly were bitten by bedbugs. They told the hotel, which had a pest control company come, but it allegedly failed to properly inspect for and exterminate bedbugs. They filed suit in state court against the hotel operator asserting in Count I a state law negligence claim for placing them in an infested room, and in Count II a state law statutory claim asserting a violation of Maryland Consumer Protection Act by impliedly representing the room was fit for occupancy. For each count, they sought $75,000. They also asserted a negligence claim in Count III against the pest control company, seeking $75,000.

The defendants removed the case to federal court, asserting that the plaintiffs effectively sought $150,000 in damages against the hotel operator and so the case was removable. The plaintiffs moved to remand. This opinion denied that motion.]

The Complaint pleads both common law negligence and violations of the MCPA. Each are separate causes of action designed to address different harms. In Maryland, to succeed on a negligence claim, a plaintiff must prove four well-established elements: (1) that the defendant was under a duty to protect the plaintiff from injury, (2) that the defendant breached that duty, (3) that the plaintiff suffered actual injury or loss, and (4) that the loss or injury proximately resulted from the defendant's breach of the duty. To state a claim under the MCPA, Plaintiffs must allege: (1) an unfair or deceptive practice or misrepresentation that (2) is relied upon, and (3) causes them actual injury. Accordingly, where negligence claims seek to compensate Plaintiffs for damages proximately caused by a breach of a duty owed to them, an MCPA claim seeks redress for Plaintiffs' injuries caused by reliance on Defendants' misleading or deceptive statements or omissions.

Consequently, the "one harm, one recovery" rule is not applicable here. The one harm one recovery rule prohibits recovering twice for the same misconduct and where the damages claimed are related and duplicative. But Plaintiffs have pled at least three distinct offenses; the first, sounding in negligence, alleges breach of duty of care by placing Plaintiffs in a room with a preexisting bed bug infestation. The second, the MCPA violation, stems from Defendants impliedly representing that Room 807 was free from infestation when Defendants knew or should have known it was not. The third, also sounding in negligence, alleges a breach of duty by the pest control company in detecting and eradicating bed bugs. Because the three claims are based on different conduct causing different harms, each of the ad damnum clauses must be added to capture the total damages sought. *See, e.g., Baron v. Directv, LLC*, 2016 WL 6078263 (D. Md. Oct. 17, 2016) (aggregating ad damnum clauses to find a substantial amount in controversy when Plaintiff had alleged conversion, violation of the Maryland Consumer Debt Collection Act, violation of the MCPA, fraud, and restitution—unjust enrichment). Put differently, if Plaintiffs prevailed on both negligence claims and the MCPA claim, they could recover full damages on each count precisely because the three counts offer different theories of recovery. When aggregated, the ad damnum clauses for these three counts exceed the $75,000 threshold.

K.S. v. Detroit Public Schools

153 F. Supp. 3d 970 (E.D. Mich. 2015) (Lawson, J.)

[Plaintiff Khody Sanford was a student when he was sexually harassed by one defendant, Pugh, and the other defendants (the "DPS defendants") failed to take proper action. He brought assault, battery, and IIED claims against Pugh, and various statutory claims against the DPS defendants. The DPS defendants settled at trial, agreeing to pay $350,000 to plaintiff. The jury returned a verdict against Pugh for $250,000 for battery and IIED.

Pugh then asserted that he was entitled to a setoff of the jury's award because of the DPS defendants' agreement to pay $350,000. The court issued this order in response.]

When determining whether the DPS defendants' settlement payment will compensate the plaintiff for the "identical injury" for which the jury returned its verdict, the nature of the conduct causing the injury and the label attached to the plaintiff's claims are of little relevance. In assessing whether a double recovery would occur, it is necessary to go beyond the theoretical damages and look at the actual damages sought and proved by plaintiff in the case at bar to determine the extent of the overlap of damages, if any. The Court begins by looking at the damages alleged and sought in the complaint. When assessing the nature and extent of the injury for which the jury awarded the plaintiff damages, the court should consider the verdict form in combination with the jury instructions.

One illustration of the application of the one recovery rule can be found in *Chicilo v. Marshall*, where the plaintiff recovered compensatory damages in an action under 42 U.S.C. § 1983 for illegal arrest and detention, and later also secured a jury verdict in state court on claims of false arrest and imprisonment. The court of appeals held that emotional trauma that the plaintiff suffered as a result of the deprivation of her civil rights was inseparable from the emotional distress that was caused by the same arrest and imprisonment for which the jury returned a verdict in the state court case. Because "the damage awards received in both the federal court action and the state court action compensate the same injuries, those being injuries to plaintiff's emotional and psychological well-being," the court ordered that the judgment be adjusted to reflect an offset for the federal court damages. 185 Mich. App. at 71 (1990).

Another example is *Grace v. Grace*, where a woman recovered damages from her ex-husband for fraudulently concealing marital assets. She previously had recovered a settlement in a legal malpractice case against her divorce attorney, whom she accused of failing to uncover those same marital assets in the divorce proceeding. The court of appeals held that the settlement amount properly was set off against the jury verdict in the fraud case, because the "plaintiff has sought to recover damages for an injury identical in nature, time, and place against both defendant and her divorce attorney." 253 Mich. App. at 369.

According to the amended complaint in this case, the plaintiff sought recovery from both Pugh and the DPS defendants on the ELCRA claim for "emotional, psychological, and physical injuries, and the permanent and serious impairment of plaintiff's academic and social development." On the Title IX claim against the DPS only, the plaintiff's damages claim was based on "physical injuries, mental and emotional distress, pain, grief and anguish, medical expenses and the loss of earning capacity, all past, present, and future." He also sought damages against Pugh alone on the battery claim for "emotional, psychological, and physical injuries, and the permanent and serious impairment of plaintiff's academic and social development" and on the IIED claim for "severe emotional distress to plaintiff." There is considerable overlap in the nature of the damages requested against the DPS defendants and against Pugh in the amended complaint. However, those damages are not identical.

The settlement with the DPS defendants, as described on the record, was meant to cover the plaintiff's claim for damages—which included loss of earning capacity—plus attorney's fees, for which the DPS defendants could be liable under Title IX, see 42 U.S.C. §1998(b), and ELCRA, see Mich. Comp. Laws §37.2802. The jury verdict addressed only the plaintiff's damages for emotional distress or emotional suffering, which was limited by the jury instructions to "mental anguish and embarrassment, humiliation, or mortification." Because the jury returned a verdict in Pugh's favor on the ELCRA claim, the plaintiff cannot recover attorney's fees against him. There was no economic component in the verdict, such as the loss of earning capacity, which was included in the settlement with the DPS defendants. It can fairly be said that the DPS defendants' settlement was meant to compensate the plaintiff for a certain measure of emotional suffering. But despite some overlap, there is a distinct identity in the damages awarded by the jury and the amount to be paid by the school district. Therefore, requiring defendant Pugh to pay the full judgment would not offend the one recovery rule.

On another level, allowing Pugh a *pro tanto* reduction of his liability to the plaintiff based on the DPS defendants' settlement would not do substantial justice. It has been observed that the one recovery rule was intended to prevent unjust enrichment to a plaintiff by preventing overcompensation, although those "financial and judicial economy policies appear to convey more solicitude towards fairness to the nonsettling tortfeasor than to the injured party." *Banks ex rel. Banks v. Yokemick*, 177 F.Supp.2d 239, 260 (S.D.N.Y. 2001). But "the law contains no rigid rule against overcompensation." *McDermott, Inc. v. AmClyde*, 511 U.S. 202 (1994). And "several doctrines recognize that making tortfeasors pay for the damage they cause can be more important than preventing overcompensation." As one court noted:

> The one-compensation rule, grounded in unjust enrichment, is not to be applied in such a way as to generate unjust enrichment to the only litigating defendant. It would be unjust enrichment to give the only defendant who was eventually found liable a full *pro tanto* credit for the full amount paid by the others.

Rose v. Associated Anesthesiologists, 501 F.2d 806, 809 (D.C. Cir. 1974). This is particularly true where the conduct by defendant Pugh amounted to intentional torts that caused the damages that the jury found, and set in motion the chain of events that prompted the settlement—funded by the taxpayers—by the other defendants.

Defendant Pugh is not entitled to any setoff or credit against his liability to the plaintiff based on the settlement by the DPS defendants.

Notes and Questions

1. <u>Who Was Arguing for Higher Damages and Same Harms</u>? In the first case, which party was asserting the plaintiff was not barred by the one recovery rule from obtaining more than $75,000? Assume that the MCPA permitted fraud damages: in what way did they differ from those available for negligence? In the second, who was arguing the harm was the same? Do the cases make sense?

2. <u>Illustrations</u>. Particularly where easily measured economic losses are involved, courts apply the one recovery rule to prevent duplicative awards. *E.g., Imgarten v. Bellboy Corp.,* 383 F. Supp. 2d 825 (D. Md. 2005) (applying one recovery rule to identical awards of $808,927 for breach of contract and for a statutory violation); *Kenney v. Palmer-Stuart Oil Co., Inc.,* 2017 WL 4581800 (W.D. Va. Oct. 13, 2017) (worker seeking lost wages under three claims subject to one recovery rule).

3. <u>Exceptions</u>. The collateral source rule, discussed below, permits recovery of damages from a defendant despite receipt of payments from a third party, and is viewed by some courts as an exception to the one recovery rule. *See Chuttke v. Fresen,* 86 N.E.2d 1263 (Ct. App. Ill. 2017).

2. Election of Remedies

Election of remedies is intended to prevent a party from obtaining not overlapping damages, but inconsistent remedies. For it to apply: "(1) the remedies available to a party must be coexisting and inconsistent; (2) the party must actually bring an action seeking one of the remedies available to [it]; and (3) [the party] must pursue the action to final judgment. Thus, the doctrine applies only where the remedies are inconsistent, not merely concurrent or cumulative."*Berkley Trace, LLC v. Food Lion, LLC,* 2013 WL 3777040 (D. Md. July 18, 2013).

Help v. Chevron U.S.A., Inc.
361 P.3d 63 (Utah 2015) (Durham, J.)

[Plaintiff Jenna Helf was employed by defendant Chevron U.S.A. Inc. at an oil refinery when her supervisor instructed her to add sulfuric acid to a pit, and the resulting chemical reaction created a poisonous gas that injured her. She obtained workers' compensation benefits, but then sued Chevron, alleging it was liable for an intentional tort because she had followed her supervisor's instructions. The trial court denied Chevron's motion for summary judgment that her claim was barred by election of remedies, and it appealed.]

In its most basic terms, the election of remedies doctrine prevents double redress for a single wrong. If a defendant wrongfully retains possession of a plaintiff's cow, for example, the plaintiff may not recover both the cow *and* the reasonable value of the cow. The plaintiff must elect one of these two remedies.

The election of remedies doctrine also refers to a plaintiff's choice between legally or factually inconsistent theories of recovery for a single wrong. One common example of the application of this rule occurs when a plaintiff is not paid for services rendered to a defendant. The plaintiff may either recover damages for breach of contract or, if no valid contract governs the services provided, the plaintiff may recover the reasonable value of the services under a quantum meruit claim. Because a breach of contract remedy requires a valid, enforceable contract, while a quantum meruit remedy presupposes that no contract governs the services provided, a plaintiff may recover only one of these two inconsistent remedies.

Thus, at its core, the election of remedies stands for the rather straight-forward principle that a plaintiff may not obtain either (1) a double recovery or (2) legally or factually inconsistent recoveries for the same wrong. The more difficult question is when a plaintiff should be deemed to have made an irrevocable election between available remedies or theories of recovery.

Where a plaintiff must choose between alternative remedies for a single theory of liability, an election is not final until a judgment is fully satisfied. Courts treat this type of election as a choice between consistent remedies because the remedies do not rest upon irreconcilable factual or legal theories. Thus if a plaintiff obtains a judgment authorizing a writ of replevin for the return of a cow wrongfully obtained by a defendant, the election is not final until the cow is returned. If the plaintiff later discovers that the cow had died while in the defendant's possession, the plaintiff may still pursue a claim for payment of the reasonable value of the cow. *See Largilliere Co., Bankers, v. Kunz,* 41 Idaho 767 (1925) (permitting a plaintiff to simultaneously pursue both a claim for damages for the conversion of a flock of sheep and a writ of replevin for the return of the sheep "until a satisfaction of its demand is obtained" because these two remedies are consistent).

If a plaintiff must choose between inconsistent theories of liability, on the other hand, older cases held that a plaintiff makes a binding election between these theories of liability upon filing a complaint based upon one of these conflicting theories. Commentators and courts alike have long criticized this antiquated version of the election of remedies doctrine, however, noting that this rule is unduly harsh to plaintiffs "and frequently results in injustice." Charles P. Hine, *Election of Remedies, A Criticism,* 26 Harv. L.Rev. 707 (1913)

The harshness of this branch of the election of remedies doctrine in the nineteenth century and early twentieth century rested upon the strict pleading requirements of the time. During this period, several jurisdictions still followed the common law rule prohibiting pleadings in the alternative, although the trend was toward permitting alternative pleadings. Other jurisdictions did not permit plaintiffs to amend their complaint to plead an alternative theory of recovery. These pleading rules, combined with a strict application of the election of remedies doctrine, required plaintiffs to choose at their peril between inconsistent theories of recovery when initiating a lawsuit.

The advent of liberal pleading rules, however, has eliminated this harsh interpretation of the election of remedies doctrine. Utah's modern pleading rules permit litigants to plead inconsistent theories of recovery in the alternative. Utah R. Civ. P. 8(e) ("A party may state a claim or defense alternately or hypothetically.").

In the 1957 case, *Parrish v. Tahtaras,* we recognized that these liberal pleading rules obviated the former rule that a plaintiff's election among inconsistent remedies in a complaint is irrevocable. 7 Utah 2d 87 (1957). In that case, an architect sued the defendants under a breach of contract theory to recover for services rendered. At a bench trial, however, the court awarded damages under a quantum meruit theory after granting a motion to amend the complaint to conform to the proof. We held that "the alternate remedies of breach of contract or in quantum meruit, although formerly limited by a strict election doctrine, may be pleaded in alternative form and may even be inserted by amendment late in the proceedings." Therefore, "it was not error for the trial judge to allow amendment late in the proceedings to show this alternative plea, the defendants not being in any way prejudiced by the ruling."

In a later case, we confirmed that modern pleading rules dictate that a court may not require a plaintiff to elect between inconsistent claims prior to trial:

> Rule 8(e) of our Rules of Civil Procedure permits either party to plead in the alternative, either in one count or defense, or in separate counts or defenses. To require a party to make an election between the alternative counts or defenses, particularly at the pretrial stage of the proceedings, would be to emasculate the rule and render it meaningless.

Rosander v. Larsen, 14 Utah 2d 1 (1962). This is in line with the modern view that a plaintiff may present inconsistent theories of liability at trial. *Rule v. Brine, Inc.,* 85 F.3d 1002 (2d Cir. 1996); 28A C.J.S. *Election of Remedies* § 6 (2008) ("Many cases hold that a party is not required to elect between remedies before the trial or during the course of the trial or before the conclusion of trial, or at the pleading stage; he or she may plead and litigate inconsistent remedies and submit different theories of recovery to the jury, and is not required to elect a remedy prior to the submission of the case to the jury or prior to the jury's verdict." (footnotes omitted)). Once the fact-finder and the judge have resolved all factual and legal disputes related to the inconsistent theories of liability, the plaintiff is then entitled to the one remedy (if any) that is supported by the final determination of the law and the facts. *Genetti v. Caterpillar, Inc.,* 261 Neb. 98 (2001) ("Although initially a buyer may present both theories and need not elect between them, the finding of either final acceptance or revocation of acceptance of nonconforming goods ultimately determines the available remedy.")

Thus unless another doctrine, such as estoppel, dictates that a plaintiff's election among inconsistent remedies is final at an earlier stage of the litigation, an election is not binding until one remedy is pursued to a determinative conclusion.

In applying these general principles to this case, we must examine the remedies available to an injured worker. A worker injured on the job may potentially recover either worker's compensation benefits or intentional tort damages. These two remedies are inconsistent. Workers' compensation benefits are paid to workers injured by an "accident arising out of and in the course of the employee's employment." Utah Code § 34A-2-401(1). These benefits are the exclusive remedy for work-related accidents. In order to recover tort damages for an injury, on the other hand, a worker must prove that an injury was caused by an intentional tort rather than an accident. The question before this court, therefore, is when does an injured worker make a binding election between these two inconsistent remedies?

If these two remedies could be pursued in a single forum, the answer would be simple. The worker could plead in the alternative that the injury was caused by either an accident or an intentional tort, and after the fact-finder made a final determination regarding the nature of the injury, the worker would elect the remedy available under the facts found by the jury or administrative body. The problem, of course, is that a worker may not pursue these two remedies in a single forum. The labor commission has exclusive jurisdiction to award workers' compensation benefits for accidents, while the district court has exclusive jurisdiction to award damages for an intentional tort.

Because these remedies must be adjudicated in separate forums, a strict application of the election of remedies doctrine presents injured workers with a cruel dilemma. If a worker choses to apply for and receives workers' compensation benefits, the worker may be deemed to have made a binding election of this remedy because the worker pursued it to a determinative conclusion. By accepting workers' compensation benefits for urgent financial needs, such as medical expenses or living expenses if the worker becomes disabled, a worker who may have been injured by an intentional tort would be barred from asserting a tort claim. If the worker instead elects to forego workers compensation benefits and gambles on an intentional tort claim, the worker would have to survive without any benefits, and the burden of sustaining potentially protracted litigation, until the completion of the trial and inevitable appeal or appeals. This hardship would in most cases be extreme because any worker contemplating a lawsuit would likely be severely injured in order to justify the expense and stress of a lawsuit against a well-funded employer.

Moreover, if the lawsuit lasts longer than the statute of limitations for a workers' compensation claim, then the worker (or the worker's family if the worker was killed) will be denied *any* recovery for the injury if the lawsuit is unsuccessful. Because of the one-year statute of limitations for the recovery of most medical expenses and death benefits under workers' compensation, at minimum, a worker or heir who chooses to pursue a tort remedy will almost certainly lose the ability to claim these benefits if the lawsuit is unsuccessful. Ms. Helf's lawsuit, for example, has lasted twelve years so far and she has not been able to bring her case to trial yet, much less the likely posttrial appeal. The duration of this litigation has already greatly surpassed the current statute of limitations for any type of workers' compensation benefit. Thus, under a strict application of the election of remedies doctrine, workers would risk losing both remedies if they make a bad guess as to which remedy was appropriate.

This interpretation of the election of remedies doctrine, similar to the much-criticized application of the doctrine in the early twentieth century, effectively requires an injured worker to choose at peril between inconsistent remedies at an unreasonably early stage in the litigation. Forcing this choice is especially harsh because of the difficulty of predicting the outcome of an intentional tort suit. Because the line between an accident and an intentional tort is based upon the subjective knowledge and intent of the worker's supervisors, which most often must be inferred from the surrounding circumstances, the worker is in a poor position to evaluate the odds of success before a jury resolves this factual dispute.

There is a fairly even split of authority among state supreme courts as to whether the election of remedies doctrine requires workers to make this choice between workers compensation benefits and a tort lawsuit. By our count, eight state supreme courts have held that a final adjudication of a right to receive workers' compensation benefits constitutes a binding election that bars an intentional tort lawsuit. But nearly as many state supreme courts (we found seven) have held that a worker may pursue both remedies and that the receipt of workers' compensation benefits does not act as a bar to the pursuit of a tort remedy.

Many of the courts that have rejected a strict application of the election of remedies doctrine have reasoned that it would require the worker to make a "gambler's choice":

> Workmen's compensation is above all a security system; a strict election doctrine transforms it into a grandiose sort of double-or-nothing gamble. Such gambles are appealing to those who still think of the judicial process as a glorious game in which formal moves and choices are made at peril, and in which the ultimate result is spectacular victory for one side and utter defeat for the other. The stricken workman is in no mood for this kind of play, and should not be maneuvered into the necessity for gambling with his rights, under the guise of enforcing a supposed penalty against the employer.

Suarez v. Dickmont Plastics Corp., 229 Conn. 99 (1994). Because most injured workers and their families are in no position to gamble on a tort remedy or wait out a lengthy and expensive litigation, the strict application of the election of remedies doctrine would effectively insulate employers from tort liability for intentionally caused injuries or death. Thus employers would not be discouraged from engaging in intentional misconduct and would escape any meaningful responsibility for its abuses.

We agree with the courts that have rejected a strict application of the election of remedies doctrine to injured workers.

As an equitable judicial principle, the election of remedies doctrine should be applied to produce fair outcomes for litigants. It certainly applies to prevent the worker from obtaining a double recovery or recovering two inconsistent remedies. But it should not be applied to force the worker to make a binding election before knowing how a jury will resolve an intentional tort claim.

The district court, therefore, correctly ruled that the election of remedies doctrine does not bar Ms. Helf's lawsuit against Chevron. To avoid a double recovery, however, if Ms. Helf eventually prevails, she may not retain the inconsistent remedies of workers' compensation benefits and an award for tort damages. In order to prevent an inconsistent recovery, a worker who recovers civilly against his employer may no longer receive workers' compensation benefits and must reimburse the workers' compensation carrier to the extent the carrier paid workers' compensation benefits, or by permitting the carrier to become subrogated to the claimant's civil claim to the extent of benefits paid.

Notes and Questions

1. <u>Post-Trial Tort Over Contract</u>. In *Bushnell Landscape Indus. v. Grover Landscape Serv., Inc.*, 2013 WL 3214398 (Ct. App. Cal. June 26, 2013), the plaintiff purchased rice hulls that it mixed into its soil mix to use as potting soil for its plant nursery inventory. The rice hulls were contaminated with toxic levels of copper and killed many plants. Plaintiff filed suit, asserting claims of both negligent misrepresentation and breach of an oral contract. The jury found for plaintiff on both claims and awarded $1.33 million and found the plaintiff 25% at fault. The plaintiff then elected the contract claim, since it was not subject to the comparative fault statute. On appeal, defendant argued that the award had to be reduced by 25%. The court disagreed, affirming the trial court, and writing:

> In its 'conventional form,' the doctrine of election remedies 'is stated as follows: Where a person has two concurrent remedies to obtain relief on the same state of facts, and these remedies are inconsistent, he must choose or elect between them; and if he has clearly elected to proceed on one, he is bound by this election and cannot thereafter pursue the other. Election of remedies has been defined to be the right to choose or the act of choosing between different actions or remedies where plaintiff has suffered one species of wrong from the act complained of. Broadly speaking, an election of remedies is the choice by a plaintiff to an action of one of two or more coexisting remedial rights, where several such rights arise out of the same facts, but the term has been generally limited to a choice by a party between

inconsistent remedial rights, the assertion of one being necessarily repugnant to or a repudiation of the other.

Defendant claims that the election of remedies doctrine should not apply because the jury was never asked to consider inconsistent remedies. However, defendant fails to cite any authority in support of his contention. We are unaware of any authority stating that the election of remedies doctrine is predicated on the *jury* being asked to consider inconsistent remedies. To the contrary, if the remedies are inconsistent, then it is the *plaintiff* who must choose between them.

The election of the contract remedy over the tort remedy was appropriate under the facts of this case. The monetary award plaintiff would receive under the negligence claim and the breach of contract claim provided for two different amounts. Under the negligence claim, the $1.33 million award would be reduced by 25 percent under the comparative fault doctrine. Under the breach of contract claim, the award amount would not be reduced. These remedies were inconsistent while based on the same set of facts. Therefore it was not error for the trial court to allow plaintiff to choose the remedy based on the breach of contract and warranty claims.

Problems

1. <u>Jury Instruction</u>? You represent the defendant in a case where the plaintiff is set to try two claims—one for assault and another for battery. The evidence likely establishes liability: your client threatened the plaintiff with a tire iron when she found the plaintiff with your client's boyfriend. Your client then hit the plaintiff with the tire iron, causing broken bones in plaintiff's hand. Although liability is clear, the plaintiff's demands to settle the case have been, in your view, too high. You need to write a jury instruction that avoids allowing the jury to award duplicative damages. Write a jury instruction for the harm and measure of damages for the assault claim and for the battery claim, and also write an instruction that informs the jury how to avoid duplication of awards. The plaintiff seeks $6,000 in medical bills (presumably entirely from the battery), $2,500 in psychiatric bills (it is unclear whether those were caused solely by one, or instead by the combined effect of defendant's acts), and $20,000 in mental anguish damages (again, it is unclear whether one, or both, acts caused this harm).

2. <u>Verdict Form</u>. Based upon the same set of facts, how will you draft a verdict form?

3. <u>Review Your Work as Plaintiff's Counsel</u>. Look at your work for the first two problems and consider them as opposing counsel. What objections would you make, or what alternative verdict form would you propose? Would it affect your approach if you are concerned that the assault claim is weak?

4. <u>Shoplifter</u>. You are presiding judge in a jury case where evidence showed the plaintiff had been shopping and had just left the defendant's store when a store employee ordered him back into the store, falsely accused him of shoplifting, and then made the plaintiff disrobe in a men's room stall to check for stolen merchandise. He found none. The jury found for the plaintiff. It returned verdicts of (a) $25,000 actual damages and $50,000 punitive damages on the claim for false imprisonment and (b) $25,000 actual damages and $50,000 punitive damages on the claim for assault and battery. The defendant has moved the trial court to reform the verdict to one award of $75,000. How will you rule and why?

5. <u>Defamed Shoplifter</u>. You represent a defendant retailer who has been sued by the plaintiff. The plaintiff alleges that, as he was leaving a store, a cashier falsely used the store's intercom to yell that the plaintiff was trying to shoplift, and that caused store's security officer to negligently injure the plaintiff while tackling him. Plaintiff seeks damages of $50,000 for a negligence claim (consisting of medical bills and lost wages, as well as pain and suffering) and $30,000 for defamation per se. Is this case removable? That is, do these damages overlap? Will the plaintiff be required to elect remedies?

6. <u>IIED</u>. As stated in Chapter 3, IIED is "disfavored" and courts often dismiss IIED claims as "duplicative" of other claims. In that regard, some courts state, seemingly as a universal rule, that IIED damages will be duplicative of damages caused by assault or battery, and even malicious prosecution. Even assuming that is true, if a plaintiff moved to dismiss a complaint you had filed that alleged both IIED and battery, can you articulate arguments why dismissal on the pleadings would be improper? Imagine that you are able to try two claims, including one for IIED. Some courts hold that, even if a jury awards different amounts of damages, IIED damages likely duplicate other claims. Does that make sense?

7. <u>Defamatory Letter and IIED</u>. Consider a plaintiff who alleges that the defendant mailed a letter to police, copying the defendant on it, that defamed the plaintiff. Months later, the police arrived at plaintiff's door and arrested him. How would you plead IIED and defamation to avoid duplication?

8. <u>Fraud and Contract and Electing Remedies</u>. Punitive damages are unavailable for breach of contract, but can be awarded for fraud claims. On the other hand, some states by statute permit parties prevailing in breach of contract claims to obtain attorney fees incurred to sue for, or defend, the breach of contract claim. In addition, insurance generally does not cover fraud damages or punitive damages. Consider a plaintiff who prevails at trial on both theories. What facts will drive the decision as to which award to accept? Consider also how lawyers should record time in cases where one claim, but not others, permit awards of attorney fees.

Chapter 14

Pre- and Post-Judgment Interest

"Past" in remedies refers to damages incurred before trial; "future" refers to those that will be incurred afterward. For many cases, of course, all damages are in the past. For serious personal injuries, damages may extend beyond trial. The jury must award all past and future damages at once. This requires adjusting the amounts to reflect the fact that the verdict gives past damages "too late" and future ones "too soon." In addition, entry of judgment does not mean the plaintiff receives compensation.

Three procedures are used to take these facts into account. First, prejudgment interest may be awarded to compensate for past damages only being awarded at judgment. Second, future damages may be reduced to present value, since the judgment awards the plaintiff for damages not yet incurred. Finally, the amount in the judgment receives post-judgment interest, from entry of judgment until the plaintiff is paid. This chapter analyzes those issues.

1. Prejudgment Interest on Certain Past Damages

To the extent a judgment includes past damages, prejudgment interest serves to avoid under-compensation for the plaintiff's lost use of money from the time it incurred losses in the past until the time of judgment. Because it compensates for past lost use of money, prejudgment interest "may not be awarded on lost *future* wages and benefits because they are not due and owing prior to the entry of judgment. Simply put, since future wages are not due, there is no delay in the receipt of the money, and therefore, a plaintiff does not experience a loss on such earnings." *Harris Group, Inc. v. Robinson*, 209 P.3d 1188 (Ct. App. Colo. 2009). *See Jackson v. United States*, 2015 WL 5174238 (S.D. W. Va. Sept. 2, 2015) ("Plaintiffs are only entitled to recover prejudgment interest on special or liquidated damages incurred *up until the date judgment is rendered*. Hence, this Court will not award prejudgment interest on special damages—lost wages and income, medical expenses, and out of pocket expenses—that accrues after the judgment.").

Although its purpose is clear, courts differ on which awards are subject to prejudgment interest and, like all remedies, determining its availability requires a claim-by-claim analysis. The following explains common approaches to determining whether prejudgment is available and, if it is, when it begins to accrue and at what rate. Under the *Erie* Doctrine, state law governs an award of prejudgment interest on damages for a state law claim, and federal law governs awards for federal claims. *Romag Fasteners, Inc. v. Fossil, Inc.,* 2018 WL 3918185 (D. Conn. Aug. 16, 2018); *Jack Henry & Assocs., Inc. v. BSC, Inc.,* 753 F. Supp. 2d 665 (E.D. Ky. 2010) (holding state law applied to state claims before the court, not to federal claims).

Despite its goal, prejudgment interest is only available for *certain past* damages. Trial courts generally have discretion as to whether to award prejudgment interest, but it must be sought. Some states hold prejudgment interest is "special damages" that must be pled, and the federal courts seem split. *United States v. All Meat and Poultry Prods. Stored at Lagrou Cold Storage,* 470 F. Supp. 2d 823 (N.D. Ill. 2007). A plaintiff also must request the judgment include the award of prejudgment interest so that it is subject to post-judgment interest. *See Chicago Import, Inc. v. Am. States Ins. Co.,* 2016 WL 4366494 (N.D. Ill. Aug. 16, 2016) (allowing plaintiff to seek prejudgment interest in motion to amend judgment, in which it had not sought it, because it had pled request and included it in its pretrial order).

Generally, prejudgment interest is available only on "liquidated" past damage awards. "Prejudgment interest is allowable where the amount of damages is definitely ascertainable by mathematical computation, or if the evidence furnishes data that makes it possible to compute the amount without reliance on opinion or discretion." *Harris Group, Inc. v. Robinson,* 209 P.3d 1188 (Ct. App. Colo. 2009). Thus, a dispute over the amount is not determinative, but instead the inquiry is whether "the evidence furnishes data which, if believed, makes it possible to compute the amount with exactness, without reliance upon opinion or discretion." *Port United Inc. v. Sestus LLC,* 2014 WL 12521331 (D. Ariz. Sept. 29, 2014) (amount was "liquidated" even though jury's award differed from the amount plaintiff had sought).

If an award is liquidated, courts have discretion to find when prejudgment interest begins to accrue. For example, a plaintiff who proved he had been wrongfully underpaid for years argued that prejudgment interest on lost wages should run from the date of each past paycheck, but the trial court awarded it only running from the date the employee was fired. *Rodriguez v. Consolidation Coal Co.,* 524 S.E.2d 672 (W. Va. 1999) ("prejudgment interest is calculated from the date the cause of action accrued," and the trial court's conclusion "that the date the action accrued was the date the Appellee was discharged from employment" was not an abuse of discretion). As another example, while most courts' prejudgment interest begins to run on a contract action "ordinarily the date of the breach," *Touch-N-Buy, LP v. Giro-Check Fin., Inc.,* 2018 WL 2093949 (E.D. Mich. May 7, 2018), courts have discretion to hold otherwise. *Port United Inc. v. Sestus LLC,* 2014 WL 12521331 (Sept. 29, 2014) (although plaintiff's letter demanded defendant perform contract, its first claim for damages was only in filing of complaint, and so they began to accrue only then). Thus, ordinarily when a series of payments are due from the defendant, or paid as expenses by the plaintiff, prejudgment interest becomes available "from the date each payment was due and remained unpaid." *Pursley v. Pursley,* 144 S.W.3d 820 (Ky. 2004).

Federal courts hold that, if prejudgment interest is proper and an award is requested, it is "an abuse of discretion not to award it unless there are exceptional circumstances, such as "(1) whether the claimant has been less than diligent in prosecuting the action; (2) whether the defendant has been unjustly enriched; (3) whether an award would be compensatory; and (4) whether countervailing equitable considerations militate against a surcharge." *Tryg Ins. v. C.H. Robinson Worldwide, Inc.,* 2018 WL 4146601 (D.N.J. Aug. 30, 2018). *See Sensonics, Inc. v. Aerosonic Corp.,* 81 F.3d 1566 (Fed. Cir. 1996) (trial court erred by denying prejudgment interest simply because it was difficult to calculate).

As for the amount of prejudgment interest, absent an agreement or controlling statute, the "rate of prejudgment interest and whether it should be compounded or uncompounded are matters left to the discretion of the district court." *See Takeda Pharma., U.S.A., Inc. v. West-Ward Pharma. Corp.,* 2018 WL 6529289 (D. Del. Nov. 12, 2018). Even when not bound by statute, courts often rely on statutes setting post-judgment interest. *See Tryg Ins. v. C.H. Robinson Worldwide, Inc.,* 2018 WL 4146601 (D. N.J. Aug. 30, 2018). The amount of prejudgment interest can exceed the amount of the damages or be a significant component of them. *Milwaukee v. Cement Div., Nat'l Gypsum Co.,* 515 U.S. 189 (1995) ($5.3 million prejudgment interest on $1.7 million damages); *U.S. Fidelity & Guaranty Co. v. Old Orchard Plaza LP,* 776 N.E.2d 812 (Ill. Ct. App. 2002) ($650,000 prejudgment interest on $2 million).

Precision Heavy Haul, Inc. v. Trail King Indus., Inc.

228 P.3d 895 (Ct. App. Ariz. 2010) (Weisberg, J.)

[Plaintiff Precision Heavy Haul, Inc., bought a trailer to transport heavy loads from Trail King Industries, Inc. After it was in an accident, Precision sued Trail King, asserting a defect with the trailer caused the accident, damaging both it and a transformer it was hauling. Trail King asserted Precision had been comparatively at fault. At trial, Precision's owner testified it had incurred $694,550.87 in damages, and the jury found Trail King 100% at fault and awarded that amount to Precision. Precision appealed the denial of prejudgment interest.]

An exhibit summarizing Precision's damages was admitted at trial. The listed damages were: rigging and crew expenses in the amount of $28,590.00; crane and salvage crew expenses in the amount of $14,768.02; payment to Precision's customer for damages to the energy transformer in the amount of $495,000.00; and funds owed to Precision but set off by its customer in the amount of $156,192.85. These requested damages totaled $694,550.87. At trial, Trail King ultimately did not challenge the accuracy of the total damages. Instead, it denied any negligence but asked, if found negligent, that the jury attribute a percentage of comparative fault to Precision, thereby reducing its own liability.

Rejecting any attribution of fault to Precision, the jury returned a verdict finding Trail King 100% at fault and awarding Precision damages in the exact amount requested. Precision then moved for a determination of its right to prejudgment interest. It argued that a claim is liquidated if the evidence furnishes data which, if believed, makes it possible to compute the amount with exactness, without reliance upon opinion or discretion. Because its damages could be precisely calculated by simple computation Precision sought prejudgment interest from the date of the accident, i.e., when it became obligated to pay its customer for the damaged transformer. Precision also asserted that although the expenses for crews, hotels, meals, and equipment rental occurred over time, the final expenses had been incurred by January 22, 2001 and thus that these damages, which totaled $43,358.02, should accrue interest as of that date. It requested a total of $365,936.97 in prejudgment interest.

Trail King objected, arguing that when a jury must exercise its discretion to apportion fault, the claim is not liquidated. Without Arizona precedent on point, it cited a South Dakota case in which the supreme court there upheld the denial of prejudgment interest in a construction defect case in which the plaintiff was found to be thirty percent at fault. *S. Dakota Bldg. Auth. v. Geiger-Berger Assoc.*, 414 N.W.2d 15 (S.D. 1987). That court held that although the plaintiff's loss became liquidated upon receiving the billing for the repairs, and upon paying for such repairs, prejudgment interest could not accrue because the defendants could not know what portion of the damages they would have to pay until the jury had allocated fault among the parties.

Trail King also relied upon *Wisper Corp. N.V. v. California Commerce Bank,* 49 Cal.App.4th 948 (1996), which interpreted a statute identical to that of South Dakota. Because the jury had found the plaintiff to be seventy-five percent at fault and therefore had awarded "a mere 25 percent of its claimed damages," the court reasoned that the "large discrepancy" between the amount sought and the amount awarded militated against finding that the plaintiff's damages were sufficiently "certain" for purposes of prejudgment interest.

Trail King also argued that because Precision's damages included a number of "estimated and indefinite" items subject to jury scrutiny for reasonableness and causation, the damages were unliquidated. Precision, of course, disagreed and replied that any uncertainty over *liability* for the accident should not bar prejudgment interest if the amount of damages was certain. It argued that at the very least its damages were liquidated on the day it paid the transformer's owner for the damages to the transformer.

The trial court acknowledged differing approaches taken by our sister states in cases involving comparative fault but found *Wisper* persuasive and concluded that because "the jury was charged with deciding comparative fault in a manner that made Plaintiff's damages wholly dependent upon that sliding scale the award was unliquidated. Thus, because of the comparative negligence defense, the court awarded interest on Precision's damages only from the date of the verdict.

Although the impact of comparative negligence upon liquidated damages is a novel issue in Arizona, our case law has established that uncertainty about a defendant's liability, even when a trial is necessary to establish the extent of liability for the plaintiff's damages, does not preclude such a plaintiff from receiving prejudgment interest. For example, in a legal malpractice action, we upheld an award of prejudgment interest to a successful plaintiff that had suffered an adverse judgment in underlying litigation. *Hyatt Regency Phoenix Hotel Co. v. Winston & Strawn,* 184 Ariz. 120 (App. 1995). The defendant law firm argued that the malpractice claim was not liquidated because the jury had the option to find the firm not liable for all of the damages. We held that even if the extent of liability was in dispute, "the *amount* of those damages was not." *Id.* The verdict comprised the exact amounts of the plaintiff's attorneys' fees and the underlying adverse judgment, and once the jury found that the defendant had caused those losses, the amount of its liability was deemed to have been certain.

We reached a similar result in *Alta Vista Plaza,* There the plaintiffs demanded $918,000.00 from the defendants' insurer for fire damage to several stores in a shopping center and later filed suit for negligence. The jury awarded $835,927.00 in damages. By stipulation, the court increased the award by $51,696.55 (as well as prejudgment interest on this additional amount). When the plaintiffs sought prejudgment interest on the jury's award from the date of the loss, the defendants claimed that interest could not accrue before the date of demand for the losses suffered and that the claim was unliquidated on the date of demand because the amount demanded was greater than the amount awarded by the jury. The trial court, however, concluded that each component of demanded damages became liquidated as the plaintiffs notified the defendants of the specific repair cost for each store.

On appeal, we held that because the "repair costs and architect's fees were readily ascertainable by accepted standards of valuation," the tort claim was liquidated for purposes of prejudgment interest even though "the case had to be tried." We noted that although a jury may have to make factual findings in a plaintiff's favor in order to determine the *amount* of damages, as long as "the evidence furnish data which, *if believed,* makes it possible to compute the amount with exactness," the claim is liquidated. *See also Fleming v. Pima County,* 141 Ariz. 149 (1984) (wrongfully discharged employee was entitled to prejudgment interest on each paycheck as it came due, even if employer disputed its liability).

In the instant case, although Trail King hotly disputed the extent of its liability for Precision's damages, the amount of damages Precision had suffered easily could be calculated from the uncontested evidence. The various amounts paid to its client and crew were known, provided to Trail King, and not challenged. The primary issue was not whether Precision had been damaged or in what amount, but what percentage of the damages Trail King would have to pay. Given that the jury awarded Precision the entire amount of damages sought, only an award of prejudgment interest on those damages will make Precision whole.

We also note that a defendant's general attack on the reasonableness of a plaintiff's claimed damages does not necessarily thereby render those damages unliquidated. Here, Trail King focused its reasonableness challenge on the $156,192.87

which Precision said was set off by its customer. When the superior court ruled that, because the jury had to apportion fault, Precision's entire claim was unliquidated, the court did not address whether Trail King's challenge of the reasonableness of the customer setoff portion of the damages rendered that portion unliquidated. Thus, we also remand to the superior court the resolution of that question.

For the foregoing reasons, we reverse the superior court's denial of prejudgment interest to Precision on the amounts awarded for damages to the transformer as well as for crew, rigging, and salvage expenses. We also remand the issue of whether Trail King's challenge of the reasonableness of the customer setoff portion of the judgment rendered that portion unliquidated.

Exmark Mfg. Co. v. Briggs & Stratton Corp.

2019 WL 1596822 (D. Neb. Apr. 15, 2019) (Baitailon, J.)

[Plaintiff prevailed in a patent infringement suit and the court awarded prejudgment interest on royalty payments that would have been due quarterly. The damages period began in 2004, plaintiff sued in 2010 (damages are recoverable in patent suits for a six-year period before suit and until judgment), and judgment was entered in December 2018. During this time, the U.S. Treasury rate was near zero percent, but the cost to borrow—even at prime rate—was much higher. Defendant argued the U.S. Treasury rate was appropriate for the entire period, but plaintiff sought what it called an "equitable" approach: the T-bill rate for the period before suit had been filed, and prime rate afterward.]

The court agrees that application of the U.S. Treasury rate when the rate was at historic lows is a severe penalty and is not sufficient to adequately compensate Exmark. Exmark has shown that its cost of borrowing was significantly higher than the U.S. Treasury rate during the applicable period and also exceeded the prime rate. Also, the court previously rejected Briggs's arguments relating to Exmark's delay in bringing suit in the court's ruling on the defense of laches in the earlier trial. Accordingly, the Court finds Exmark's motion should be granted and the Court will amend the judgment to reflect an award of prejudgment interest in the amount of $5,964,111.

Notes and Questions

1. <u>Extent of Damage versus Amount</u>? Is the distinction between the proportion of fault and damages meaningful? Are the courts that reject *Trail King* wrong in determining amounts are "unliquidated" where liability is disputed? Why was the *Trail King* case remanded?

2. <u>Huge Ranges</u>. Of course, plaintiffs argue for compounding and at high rates, and defendants push for simple interest at low rates. Courts seek to compensate the party for lost use of funds. Did the court in *Exmark* correctly balance the interests? Why do you suppose Exmark's lawyers chose not to seek more than prime, or prime for the entire period?

3. <u>A Verdict Liquidates Unliquidated Damages</u>. For purposes of prejudgment interest, a verdict "liquidates" unliquidated damages. *Bosem v. Musa Holdings, Inc.*, 46 So. 3d 42 (Fla. 2010). Thus, a plaintiff should seek prejudgment interest for the period between verdict and judgment, which can be a significant period of time.

4. <u>Liquidated Damages Evaporate</u>. A plaintiff, Faigin, asserted a claim for breach of an employment contract against his employer, FRC. The jury awarded $1.3 million, mostly in past damages. The appellate court in *Faigin v. Signature Group Holdings, Inc.*, 150 Cal. Rptr. 3d 123 (Cal. Ct. App. 2012), affirmed denial of prejudgment interest, stating:

> Faigin consistently sought damages of three times his annual salary until the trial court excluded his written employment contract with Fremont General on FRC's motion *in limine*. The amount of damages sought was uncertain from that date forward. Faigin acknowledges that the claim on which he prevailed at trial was unliquidated. He does not challenge either the exclusion of his written employment contract or the denial of relief on his count for breach of the written contract. Yet he seeks to invoke the certainty of the involuntary termination payment provision in the written employment contract in arguing that the amount of damages was known throughout the litigation.
>
> FRC defended against Faigin's count for breach of the written employment contract until the middle of trial when the trial court rejected the claim and granted leave to amend the complaint to allege the claim on which Faigin prevailed at trial. We conclude that the court reasonably concluded that the claim on which Faigin prevailed at trial was unliquidated and uncertain, that in these circumstances the denial of prejudgment interest would not result in a windfall to FRC and that an award of prejudgment interest in these circumstances would result in a windfall to Faigin. Faigin has shown no abuse of discretion in the denial of prejudgment interest.

5. <u>Awards on Unliquidated Amounts</u>. In narrow circumstances courts award prejudgment interest on unliquidated amounts. In the admiralty case of *Borges v. Our Lady of the Sea Corp.*, 935 F.2d 436 (1st Cir. 1991), the court explained this exception to the general rule:

> It has been held that prejudgment interest may be awarded on damages for past intangible loss, such as pain and suffering. At common law, prejudgment interest traditionally was not allowed on unliquidated tort claims. In *Rivera v. Rederi A/B Nordstjernan*, 456 F.2d 970 (1st Cir. 1972), we noted that "a plaintiff's immediate loss and the usual delay in payment may warrant the granting of prejudgment interest" on unliquidated tort claims, including claims for pain and suffering. Other circuits have also ruled that prejudgment interest on past pain and suffering is allowable. *See Deakle v. John E. Graham & Sons*, 756 F.2d 821 (11th Cir. 1985) (award of prejudgment interest on portion of verdict which represented recovery for pain

and suffering, mental anguish, and maintenance and cure not an abuse of discretion); *Hillier v. Southern Towing Co.,* 740 F.2d 583 (7th Cir. 1984) (in admiralty cases, prejudgment interest may be awarded for past pain and suffering and for past loss of society).

6. <u>Legislation</u>. A West Virginia statute provides that "if the judgment or decree, or any part thereof, is for special damages the amount of the special damages shall bear interest at the rate in effect for the calendar year in which the right to bring the same shall have accrued. Special damages includes lost wages and income, medical expenses, damages to tangible personal property and similar out-of-pocket expenditures, as determined by the court." *See Tri-State Petroleum Corp. v. Coyne,* 814 S.E.2d 205 (W. Va. 2018). Does this simplify the analysis? Other states codify the common law approach. *E.g., Hayne v. Green Ford Sales, Inc.,* 2010 WL 2653410 (D. Kan. June 29, 2010) ("prejudgment interest is governed by Kan. Stat. Ann. § 16-201 and may be awarded only on liquidated claims, i.e., when both (a) the amount due and (b) the date on which the amount is due are fixed and certain or definitely ascertainable. Whether to award prejudgment interest is a matter within the discretion of the trial court."). Finally, other state statutes allow a plaintiff to make a written demand on a defendant that, if rejected, allows for recovery of prejudgment interest, usually if the plaintiff obtains a judgment exceeding the rejected offer. *E.g., Arellano v. Primerica Life Ins. Co.,* 332 P.3d 597 (Ct. App. Az. Aug. 12, 2014). Can you explain the incentives this creates?

2. Future Damages May Be Reduced to Present Value

Because of the single action rule, a judgment will award damages that the plaintiff has not then incurred. To avoid overcompensation, *some,* but not all, future damages are subject to reduction to present value. The following explores two distinct issues on which courts disagree: (a) how to reduce future economic losses reduced to present value, and (b) are damages for future pain and suffering or mental anguish reduced to present value, and if so, how?

A. Reducing Future Economic Losses to Present Value

Awards of damages for future economic losses should be reduced to present value. An award, today, of a cost that will not be incurred until 10 years from now may overcompensate the plaintiff. Experts are *required* in most circumstances to assist the court, or jury, in determining how to reduce those projected future damages to present value. Doing so requires determining the likely future rate of inflation, returns on investment, life expectancy, and then applying those variables to the harms experienced by the plaintiff. Courts apply different approaches to accomplish this, and typically expert witnesses are used to explain to juries how to do so. The Florida Supreme Court, in adopting jury instructions in *In re Stand. Jury*

Instructions in Civ. Cases-Rpt. No. 15-01, 192 So. 3d 1183 (Fla. 2016), provided typical instructions and explained their use and limitations:

501.7 REDUCTION OF DAMAGES TO PRESENT VALUE

Any amount of damages which you allow for [future medical expenses], [loss of ability to earn money in the future], or [(describe any other future economic loss which is subject to reduction to present value)] should be reduced to its present money value and only the present money value of these future economic damages should be included in your verdict.

The present money value of future economic damages is the sum of money needed now which, together with what that sum will earn in the future, will compensate (claimant) for these losses as they are actually experienced in future years.

NOTES ON USE FOR 501.7

1. Designing a standard instruction for reduction of damages to present value is complicated by the fact that there are several different methods used by economists and courts to arrive at a present-value determination. See, for example, *Delta Air Lines, Inc. v. Ageloff*, 552 So.2d 1089 (Fla. 1989)(using approach similar to calculation of cost of annuity); *Loftin v. Wilson*, 67 So.2d 185 (Fla. 1953) (lost stream of income approach); *Beaulieu v. Elliott*, 434 P.2d 665 (Alaska 1967) (total offset method); *Culver v. Slater Boat Co.*, 688 F.2d 280 (5th Cir. 1982) (discussing real interest rate discount method and inflation/market rate discount methods); and *Bould v. Touchette*, 349 So.2d 1181 (Fla. 1977) (even without evidence, juries may consider the effects of inflation).

2. Until the Florida Supreme Court or the legislature adopts one approach to the exclusion of other methods of calculating present money value, the committee assumes that the present value of future economic damages is a finding to be made by the jury on the evidence; or, if the parties offer no evidence to control that finding, that the jury properly resorts to its own common knowledge as guided by instruction 501.7 and by argument.

If a jury finds the plaintiff has proven by preponderant evidence that it will reasonably likely experience future economic losses, it must also determine what amount the plaintiff has established with reasonable certainty. Expert testimony *may* be required to show *whether* future economic losses will occur and, if they do, how long the losses will persist. Does the jury, or court, reduce that to present value? If so, how?

Wright v. Maersk Line, Ltd.

2003 WL 470335 (S.D.N.Y. Feb. 24, 2003) (McKenna, J.)

[Plaintiff was injured and sued his employer. The jury found the plaintiff and defendant each 50% at fault and awarded plaintiff (a) $50,000 in past lost earnings; (b) future lost earnings of $235,000; (c) past pain and suffering of $200,000; and (d) future pain and suffering of $510,000. The parties had agreed during trial to permit the court to reduce future damages to present value. This opinion resolves the parties' disputes on how to do so. (The court's analysis of reducing the pain and suffering damages is provided in the next section).]

Because of the apportionment of fault, the damages awarded in those respective categories must be, and hereby are, reduced to the following amounts: (a) $25,000, (b) $117,500, (c) $100,000, and (d) $255,000.

After conferring with the parties, the Court instructed the jury that, on January 16, 2002 (the day prior to the verdict), the work life expectancy of a person of the age of plaintiff was 14.9 years, and the life expectancy of such a person was 30.6 years. (Tr. 934–940.)

It is not disputed that the award for future lost earnings must be reduced to present value. In the Second Circuit, reduction to present value must take into account both inflation and the opportunity to invest money:

> because a dollar received in the future will almost surely have less purchasing power than a dollar has today, we have required estimates of lost future earnings to reflect the effect of inflation. In addition, because a dollar received today may be invested and produce a larger sum of money in the future (even though that sum will have less purchasing power than an equivalent sum has today), we have required that damages for loss of earnings that would have been received in the future must be discounted to reflect the fact that, even if there were no inflation, a dollar received today is worth more than the right to receive a dollar in the future.

Oliveri v. Delta S.S. Lines Inc., 849 F.2d 742, 746 (2d Cir. 1988).

The first step in reducing an award for future lost earnings to present value is to establish a discount rate that combines the inflation and interest rates.

> One way is to increase the estimated future earnings by the estimated inflation rate. The other way is to decrease the interest rate that will be used to discount the sums awarded by subtracting the estimated inflation rate from the estimated interest rate to arrive at an inflation-adjusted discount rate. Obviously, it would be incorrect to use both methods.

Oliveri, 849 F.2d at 746.

Here, defendant submits the declaration of an economist, Patrick A. Gaughan, who concludes that a 3% net discount rate is appropriate. He arrives at that rate by subtracting an inflation rate of 3% from an interest rate of 6%. The 6% interest rate, he states "is consistent with, indeed lower than, the historical rate of return on long-term Treasury securities, as set forth in the publication *Stocks, Bonds, Bills, and Inflation: 2002 Yearbook,* by Ibbotson Associates."

Applying a 3% net discount rate here, Prof. Gaughan reduces the $117,500 award for future lost earnings to $96,444, and the $255,000 award for future pain and suffering to $170,297.

Plaintiff submits the declaration of an economist, A.E. Rodriguez, who concludes that a 2% net discount rate is appropriate. He arrives at that rate by utilizing what he regards as a more accurate equation, and reference to the three-month treasury bill yield, rather than to a long term government security yield. Applying a 2% net discount rate here, Mr. Rodriguez reduces the $117,500 award for future lost earnings to $102,758.

The Supreme Court, in an analogous case (under the Federal Employer's Liability Act), has noted that "the average accident trial should not be converted into a graduate seminar on economic forecasting." *Monessen S.W. R. Co. v. Morgan,* 486 U.S. 330 (1988). The discount rate should be based on the rate of interest that would be earned on the best and safest investments.

The Court—without finding fault with either expert's analysis—finds that the 2% rate suggested on behalf of plaintiff is better founded, because it is based on more conservative investments. The mistakes, if such they be, in Mr. Rodriguez' approach that Prof. Gaughan points out in reply do not affect this basic conclusion. Accordingly, the award for future lost wages will be reduced to $102,758.

Notes and Questions

1. <u>Do the Math</u>. How much, per year, did the jury conclude the plaintiff would lose in income? How much for experiencing pain?

2. <u>Why Did the Lawyers Not Let the Jury Reduce to Present Value</u>? The court stated that reduction to present value should not require a graduate course in economics. Would it have? Consider that the judge instructed the jury as to how long it should assume the plaintiff would work, and how long plaintiff would live. What trial testimony would that have required? Given that the experts' opinions did not diverge much, was it more efficient for both parties to simply let the judge decide? Won't that often be the case?

B. Future Pain and Suffering and Mental Anguish May Be Reduced to Present Value

Some courts use the same approach for reducing damages awards for future pain and suffering, or mental anguish, as they do to reduce future awards of economic losses. In *Wright v. Maersk Line, Ltd.,* above, after verdict the parties asked the trial court to determine how to reduce the jury's award of future pain and suffering damages to present value:

> In *Oliveri*, the Second Circuit addressed, in addition to questions regarding the discounting of an award for future lost earnings, issues regarding the discounting of an award for future pain and suffering. After a survey of its case law on the subject of discounting awards for future non-pecuniary losses, it concluded that the appropriate course is to accept the concept of discounting awards for non-pecuniary losses, but to forgo the precision

appropriate for discounting future earnings. All that is required for awards of non-pecuniary future damages is that the time value of money be taken into account.

That should be done by the same fact-finder that determines the amount of the award, without any precise mathematical adjustments. The time value of such an award is sufficiently recognized by permitting defendant's counsel to argue that awards for future non-pecuniary losses are being received now, rather than in the future, and may be somewhat reduced to reflect the opportunity to invest such awards, and to permit the plaintiff's counsel to point out that any such reduction may be tempered by the likelihood that inflation will reduce the purchasing power of any sum awarded. If requested to do so, the trial judge can bring these general considerations to the jury's attention but should make it clear that the precise method appropriate for discounting awards for pecuniary losses need not be followed.

In the present case, however, the matter is not that simple. Here, neither side (as far as the Court's recollection goes and the parties' citations to the record show) asked the Court to give any instructions at all to the jury regarding the discount of an award for future pain and suffering, and none was given. Neither side made any relevant argument to the jury on the issue, and there is nothing in the record to suggest that the jury considered it. Yet Second Circuit law seems clearly to require some sort of discount.

In *Oliveri*, there was also a difficulty with respect to the discount of an award for future pain and suffering: the district court had told the jury that "future figures" would be reduced by 2%, the jury awarded $50,000 for future pain and suffering, and the district court, after verdict, reduced the award by 2%. The Second Circuit, since the matter was resolved incorrectly by the district court, and not considered by the jury (as requested by the plaintiff), found it faced several choices, none of which is ideal.

> [1] We could order a new trial on damages, but that would be unfair to the plaintiff, who should not lose the award he obtained just because the discounting task was taken from the jury over his objection. [2] We could use the remittitur device, just as we have for future wages and determine a remittitur amount by using the correct discount method and a 2% inflation-adjusted discount rate. That solution, however, would apply to an award for a non-pecuniary loss the "delusive exactness," that we have rejected for such awards. [3] We could leave undisturbed the District Judge's 2% subtraction, amounting the $1,000, but that would reflect approval of an incorrect discounting method. [4] Finally, we could permit the plaintiff to recover in full the $50,000 the jury awarded.

In *Oliveri*, the Court of Appeals chose the fourth option, letting the $50,000 award stand because it "suspected that had this jury been given the generalized advice concerning discounting that we conclude is appropriate for non-pecuniary future losses, it would most likely still have awarded $50,000."

Here, *Oliveri*'s option [1], a new trial on damages, would also be unfair to plaintiff (even though he did not seek to have the issue put to the jury), because, here, the jury did consider its award, and plaintiff should not have to surrender a fully considered damage award merely on the discounting issue. As to option [2], a remittitur, that would unfairly give plaintiff the benefit because he did not seek to have the matter put to the jury (unlike the plaintiff in *Oliveri*). Option [3] is not relevant, since, here, no discounting method has been applied so far. Option [4] is not fair to defendant, which seeks to have to the law requiring the discount of the award applied, since this Court is unable to say that the jury would likely have come to the same award, as in *Oliveri*.

In the circumstances of the present case, the Court concludes that the fairest way to apply the law is for the Court to discount the award by a correct method (which is what defendant seeks) and to apply the 2% discount rate, which plaintiff argues is appropriate for future lost earnings and which Oliveri has recommended as a figure to which parties are encouraged to agree. The Court reduces the award to $194,177.

What should the parties have done under *Oliveri*? Assuming it was not oversight, what incentive did each side have for not doing this? The court explained how it arrived at $194,177:

This amount was calculated in much the same manner as that used by Mr. Rodriguez in computing the net present value of the award for future lost income. Th jury award was divided by 30 years ($255,000/30 = $8,500) and, for each year, this amount was multiplied by the percentage set forth in Appendix C of the New York Pattern Jury Instructions. The present value factor for Year 1 was set, as Rodriguez did. Thus, for Year 2, $8500 was multiplied by 0.980392 for a present value of $8,333.33. After calculating each of the thirty years, the total present value of the award is approximately $194,177.

Does that explain why the parties wanted the judge to decide? To avoid angering a judge, does that help you consider why—if the parties' experts are not far apart on what discount rate applies—lawyers should agree to have the court decide the issue and alert the court to their agreement? Consider the following alternative approach.

CSX Transp., Inc. v. Begley

313 S.W.3d 52 (Ky. 2010) (Per Curiam)

CSX complains that the trial court refused to instruct the jury on present value as follows:

If you find in favor of the Plaintiff and decide to make an award for pain and suffering in the future, you must take into account the fact that the money awarded by you is being received all at one time instead of over a period of time extending into the future and that the Plaintiff will have the use of this money in a lump sum. You must, therefore, determine the present value or present worth of the money which you award for future pain and suffering.

The Supreme Court determined in *Chesapeake & Ohio Ry. Co. v. Kelly* that "when future payments or other pecuniary benefits are to be anticipated, the verdict should be made up on the basis of their present value only." Thus, a FELA defendant is entitled to an instruction that the lump sum awarded for future economic damages must be based on the present value of the stream of income the plaintiff expects to lose due to the injury or the stream of medical and other expenses that the plaintiff expects to incur. CSX asserts that the rule applies to future pain and suffering as well as to economic damages and that the trial court committed reversible error in this case by refusing the instruction. We disagree.

Kelly and the subsequent Supreme Court cases addressing present value concerned future economic damages. The court has yet to decide squarely whether damages for future pain and suffering must also be reduced to present value. Our research reveals no uniform rule among the lower federal courts that have addressed the matter in a case controlled by federal law. Most federal circuits, most states, and the Restatement (Second) of Torts favor exempting future noneconomic damages from the present value rule. Absent a decision by the Sixth Circuit, we find the majority view to be more persuasive and note its conformity with Kentucky law. . . .

Damages for pain and suffering are exempt from the present value rule because they differ in kind from damages for future wages and expenses. Damages for future wages involve the loss of an anticipated stream of income, the amount of which can be calculated from market-based factors such as past wages, fringe benefits, and unreimbursed employee expenses; anticipated wage increases due to raises and promotions; remaining work life; and inflation. Damages from an injury also include expenses, such as for future medical care, which can likewise be calculated from relevant market-based factors. Predicting the total anticipated loss for each future year involves some degree of speculation, but an annual figure can be calculated with reasonable certainty and reduced to present value. Such is not the case with pain and suffering.

No objective standard exists to measure degrees of physical and emotional pain and suffering and no market exists to determine their economic value. Thus, awards for future pain and suffering involve a greater degree of speculation than those for economic losses. The factual bases for such damages include the nature and extent of the injury and its likely effect on the plaintiff. Although argument based on a *per diem* figure may assist a jury in reaching a fair and reasonable dollar amount as compensation for pain and suffering, experience teaches us that plaintiffs may or may not experience pain and suffering in a predictable pattern each day or each year. Thus, use of the method should not be construed to imply an undue degree of precision in anticipating the probable degree of pain and suffering that a plaintiff will experience at a given time. Jurors determine what fairly and adequately compensates a plaintiff under the evidence "guided by their observation, experience and sense of fairness and right.

We conclude that the trial court did not err by refusing CSX's present value instruction. Instruction 9 directed the jury, if it found CSX to be negligent, to "find from the evidence and award Begley such damages, if any, you believe he has sustained as a result of mounting and dismounting moving equipment. Verdict Form B indicates that the jury awarded Begley $250,000 in damages for pain and suffering "to fairly and adequately compensate him for his injuries." Such damages need not be reduced to present value.

Notes and Questions

1. Lump Sum Approach. The principal case explains that most courts leave the jury to its own devices about how to determine the amount of damages for future pain and suffering. Consider how an expert would do so. In lump sum jurisdictions, plaintiffs' lawyers of course use strategies to maximize recovery of general damages for pain and suffering, and defense lawyers seek the opposite.

3. Post-Judgment Interest on the Judgment

Whether post-judgment interest is available, and at what rate, turns on the law of the forum issuing the judgment. As a result, federal law controls whether, and at what rate, to award post-judgment interest in federal court; otherwise the law of the state court issuing the judgment controls. FELA claims—which Congress permitted plaintiffs to bring in either state or federal court—create an exception, as *Alby v. BNSF Ry. Co.*, 2018 WL 3716257 (Minn. App. Aug. 6, 2018) explained:

> We conclude that postjudgment interest constitutes a part of a FELA plaintiff's "proper measure of damages," and that postjudgment interest therefore is an issue of substance that is governed by federal law. Our conclusion that postjudgment interest is substantive is consistent with the principles of national uniformity intended by Congress when it enacted FELA A plaintiff who brings a FELA action in state court should be subject to the same rule regarding prejudgment interest regardless of the state in which the action is commenced." Because the state interest rate is nearly 20 times the federal interest rate, the application of Minnesota's postjudgment interest rate in FELA cases could create a disparity in FELA cases based solely on whether the plaintiff's claim is brought in federal or state court. Because we conclude that the district court did not err in determining that postjudgment interest is a substantive matter in a FELA case, we affirm the application of the federal rate.

The general rule is that only in unusual cases should courts use their discretion to deny post-judgment interest, and it runs from the date of entry of the judgment.

As to the amount, ordinarily it is set by statute, but if not, trial courts have discretion to determine the rate and compounding. If an award is reversed on appeal and remanded for a new trial on all aspects, then post-judgment interest is available only after entry of any judgment after the second trial.

Hadley v. Maxwell

84 P.3d 286 (Wash. Ct. App. 2004) (Brown, J.)

[In 1994, Mrs. Hadley was injured when she was a passenger in a car driven by her husband in a collision with a car driven by Helen Maxwell. She and her husband sued Maxwell in 1996. In 1998, the case was tried, and the jury was instructed that any negligence by Mr. Hadley would not reduce Mrs. Hadley's recovery. The jury found Maxwell 100% at fault and awarded Mrs. Hadley $125,000 and her husband $11,000. The judgment stated it bore interest at 12% from the date of the judgment, June 8, 1998. Maxwell did not appeal damages, only liability. In 2000, the Washington Supreme Court reversed on a procedural issue, and remanded for a new trial. The case was retried on liability, and a second jury on January 9, 2003, found the same as the first jury, finding Maxwell 100% at fault. The Hadleys' lawyer submitted a form of judgment that provided that either pre- or post-judgment interest ran from the date of the 1998 judgment. The trial court held pre-judgment interest did not apply and awarded post-judgment interest only as of the 2003 judgment. The Hadleys appealed the denial of interest before 2003.]

Generally, a prevailing party in a civil trial is entitled to postjudgment interest. With exceptions not relevant here, interest ordinarily accrues from the date judgment is entered. However, if the judgment is challenged on appeal, the statute partly states:

> That in any case where a court is directed on review to enter judgment on a verdict or *in any case where a judgment entered on a verdict is wholly or partly affirmed on review, interest on the judgment or on that portion of the judgment affirmed shall date back to and shall accrue from the date the verdict is rendered.*

RCW 4.56.110(3) (emph. added).

This issue revolves around the italicized portion of the statute. The Maxwells contend the Supreme Court reversed the entire judgment, thus rendering RCW 4.56.110(3) inapplicable. The Hadleys contend the Supreme Court impliedly affirmed the damages judgment because it reversed solely on the issue of liability.

Awards reversed on review do not bear interest. *Fisher Props., Inc. v. Arden-Mayfair, Inc.,* 115 Wash.2d 364 (1990). The Maxwells incorrectly contend *Fisher* requires interest to run from the date of the second judgment. The *Fisher* court was concerned with a narrow exception to the rule that interest on a *reversed* award does not run back to the date of the original partially affirmed judgment.

In a previous opinion, the Supreme Court *partially* reversed an award and directed the trial court to consider alternative measures of damages on the *reversed* issues. Recognizing an exception exists where an award is modified, the Supreme Court reasoned its remand required the trial court to determine the *reversed* damages anew. "The mandate necessitated new findings and a new judgment, not a simple mathematical computation." *Id.* Accordingly, the Supreme Court held interest could not run "on the portions of the judgment reversed by this court from the date of the original judgment." *Id.* Implicitly, the Supreme Court did not disturb interest on the *affirmed* claims accruing from the date of the original judgment.

Here, this court affirmed the judgment in its entirety. But the Maxwells petitioned solely the liability issue of collateral estoppel. The Supreme Court agreed and therefore reversed on that issue alone. The Supreme Court specifically noted the Hadleys' damages had been fully and vigorously litigated and the Maxwells did not petition for review of that award; therefore, the Supreme Court did not require relitigation of that issue. Thus, the Supreme Court impliedly affirmed the damages award. On remand, the trial court merely had to do the simple arithmetic of apportioning the damages for Mr. Hadley per the jury's liability verdict. *See id.* (interest calculation per remand order is a simple mathematical task). For Mrs. Hadley, no apportionment was even necessary because she was a non-negligent party.

Given all, we hold the Hadleys are entitled to interest from the 1998 judgment. Because this court affirmed the 1998 damages award without challenge, the interest accrues from the date of the 1998 verdict. The Supreme Court's opinion is consistent with this view. Since the trial court misinterpreted the effect of the Supreme Court's partial reversal of this court, it misapplied the statute, and therefore erred.

Notes and Questions

1. <u>Change the Facts</u>. What if retrial included Mrs. Hadley's proportion of fault? What if the jury in 2003 had found Mr. Hadley 20% at fault instead of again finding Maxwell 100% at fault? That would suggest the amounts are not liquidated, but the court held nonetheless post-judgment interest applies. What does that say about one distinction between post- and pre-judgment interest?

2. <u>Post-Judgment Interest on Prejudgment Interest</u>. Some states may require the judgment to specify that post-judgment interest applies to prejudgment interest. *See* William Herring, *No Postjudgment Interest on Prejudgment Interest?*, 76 Aug. Fla. B.J. 30 (2002) (judge had been trying "over the past six years, with mixed results, to get plaintiffs' attorneys to draft their final judgments to provide for an award of post-judgment interest on prejudgment interest").

Problems

1. <u>Statute</u>. You're litigating a case in Michigan. As noted above, under its approach, prejudgment interest is not available on future damages, which are defined as damages found by the jury as that will accrue after the finding is made. Otherwise, however, it is calculated "from the date of filing the complaint" and is based "on the entire amount of the money judgment, including attorney fees and other costs." Assume you represent one party in a case involving a car wreck that had caused the

plaintiff serious injuries. The accident happened in 2015, and suit was filed within a few weeks of the accident. Due to various delays, none of them caused by the parties in any bad faith or as a result of misconduct, the case finally went to judgment in 2019. During the last six months of the case, the medical bills for various reasons increased from $100,000 to more than $1,000,000. Michigan courts split on whether, despite the language of the statute, post-filing damages accrue interest from the filing of the complaint. Consider the purposes of prejudgment interest, and also this statutory approach. What purposes of prejudgment interest are furthered by applying the statute in its "plain text"? What purposes are undermined? Can you think of alternatives to this approach that further some purposes without undermining others?

2. <u>Statutory Claims</u>. Congress does not always specify whether prejudgment interest is available for a statutory claim. For example, claims for copyright infringement do not expressly provide for prejudgment interest, and courts split on whether it is permitted or, indeed, required. In that regard, the Copyright Act entitles the copyright owner "to recover the actual damages suffered by him or her as a result of the infringement, and any profits of the infringer that are attributable to the infringement and are not taken into account in computing the actual damages." That makes it sound like prejudgment interest should be available, yet courts split. What is the contrary argument?

3. <u>Future Damages</u>. Because prejudgment interest is not available on future damages, how would you, if representing a defendant, structure a verdict form in a case where future damages are sought? Why would a plaintiff have less incentive to do so?

4. <u>*Quantum Meruit* and Prejudgment Interest</u>. In some states, an award of prejudgment interest is mandatory for awards based on *quantum meruit,* while in others it is discretionary and in still others it is impermissible. Given the nature of *quantum meruit,* can you explain why courts would split?

Chapter 15

Post-Verdict Procedures to Control Damages

Although the precise procedures vary among jurisdictions, if a jury returns a verdict that is facially flawed, each party's lawyer must consider whether it must act before the jury is discharged or may raise the issue in a post-trial motion. *See Small v. Sayre*, 384 P.3d 785 (Alaska 2016) (plaintiff waived objection to inconsistent verdict by not clearly identifying it for trial judge before jury was discharged).

Motions or objections typically take three forms. First, a party may assert that the verdict is improper. Typically, these objections must be made before the jury is discharged. Second, a defendant can assert the jury's awards are too high and move for remittitur. Third, in many state courts, plaintiffs can assert an award was too low and move for additur. (Not all states permit additur, and in federal court it is generally unconstitutional.) Lawyers moving for a new trial often, in the alternative, request additur or remittitur, as shown below. The latter two objections may be, and typically are, made only in post-trial motions where the party that lost the verdict may, in addition, assert that judgment should be entered in its favor.

1. Setting Aside Inconsistent Verdicts

Wiltz v. Welch

651 F. App'x 270 (5th Cir. 2016) (Per Curiam)

[Plaintiff Joseph Wiltz was rear-ended in slow-moving traffic, and filed a complaint in state court, asserting a negligence claim and seeking damages for pain and suffering, lost wages, past and future medical expenses, and loss of enjoyment of life. Defendants—Welch and her insurer—removed the case to federal court. Defendants admitted liability and trial focused on damages.]

During trial, it was revealed that Wiltz was a serial plaintiff with pre-existing injuries who had failed to disclose his full medical history to the doctors treating him. His medical history included an accident in 2011 where he injured his neck, back, and shoulders; a 2005 accident where he injured his neck; a work related incident in 1997 where he hurt his lower back; and an accident in 1991 where he injured his back. Wiltz failed to disclose any of these previous accidents to one of his treating doctors and even told him that he had never before experienced back or neck pain.

Wiltz also answered discovery untruthfully and incompletely, and could not recall a great deal of the information unfavorable to his case, needing to be reminded of such information on cross-examination. Nevertheless, the jury returned a verdict in Wiltz's favor. The jury compensated Wiltz for his past medical expenses, but denied any general damages for pain and suffering, as well as any other special damages for lost income or future medical expenses.

Wiltz filed a motion for new trial or, in the alternative, amendment of judgment, contending that the jury's verdict—awarding special damages for past medical expenses, but refusing to award any general damages—was inconsistent under Louisiana law, thus amounting to an abuse of discretion on the jury's part. The district court denied Wiltz's motion. It found that the jury could have reasonably concluded that Wiltz proved that he was entitled to recover past medical costs, but that he did not prove that he endured any compensable pain and suffering. Wiltz appealed.

Wiltz argues that the district court erred in denying his motion for a new trial because the jury's verdict awarding him past medical expenses but no general damages is contrary to Louisiana law.

A motion for a new trial based on an inadequate or inconsistent jury award is governed by Louisiana state law in this diversity action. A party is entitled to a new trial when the verdict or judgment appears clearly contrary to the law and the evidence. When granting a new trial, the court can evaluate the evidence, draw its sic own inferences and conclusions, and determine whether the jury erred in giving too much credence to an unreliable witness. Yet, Louisiana courts still accord jury verdicts great deference. The assessment of 'quantum' or the appropriate amount of damages, by a jury is a determination of fact, and is entitled to great deference on review. The jury's verdict should not be set aside if it is supportable by any fair interpretation of the evidence.

The Louisiana Supreme Court has recognized that "a jury verdict awarding medical expenses but simultaneously denying damages for pain and suffering will most often be inconsistent in light of the record." *Wainwright*, 774 So.2d at 75. But "a verdict awarding medical expenses yet denying general damages is not *per se* invalid." *Id.* (noting that courts of many states "generally have rejected the factfinder's determination as to damages only where the failure to award general damages is factually inconsistent with a reasonable reading of the record, giving due deference to the jury's findings of fact."). "Under certain circumstances the evidence of record supports both an award of medical expenses and a concurrent denial of general damages. Effectively, then, the ultimate question has been whether the factfinder made inconsistent awards and thus abused its discretion." *Id.*

Numerous Louisiana court decisions have held that a jury's award of medical expenses and denial of general damages for pain and suffering were inconsistent in light of the record. *See e.g., Robinson v. Gen. Motors Corp.*, 328 So.2d 751 (La. Ct. App. 1976) (finding award of medical expenses but no damages for pain and suffering improper where plaintiffs' objective physical injuries included a broken nose, bruised chest, bruised leg, a visible bump, and rib separation). But Louisiana courts have also found a jury's award of medical expenses and denial of general damages consistent in light of certain records. *See e.g., Coleman v. U.S. Fire Ins. Co.*, 571 So.2d 213 (La. Ct. App. 1990) (affirming jury's award of special damages without general damages because the jury could have reasonably found that plaintiff did not suffer any injuries from the fender bender but was justified in getting a medical checkup after the accident).

In our view, the demarcation line for these cases is whether the plaintiff has proven objective injuries that require medical care. If a plaintiff establishes objective injuries, then a jury's failure to award damages for pain and suffering is an abuse of discretion. But if a plaintiff fails to prove objective injuries and instead incurs medical expenses for evaluative or precautionary purposes, then a jury's award of special damages but no general damages is not an abuse of discretion. Wiltz's case falls into the latter category.

We find that the jury did not abuse its discretion by failing to award Wiltz general damages because there was insufficient evidence to conclude that his collision with Welch resulted in compensable pain and suffering and that his medical care was something more than evaluative or precautionary in nature. Considering the testimony and exhibits introduced at trial, particularly Wiltz's own testimony and the testimony of the doctors, Wiltz did not prove that he suffered from objective physical injuries as a result of the accident. Wiltz saw several doctors following the accident. But merely seeking medical care, without more, does not establish that he suffered from objective injuries warranting an award of damages for pain and suffering. Accordingly, the jury's award of past medical expenses without an award for pain and suffering is not inconsistent or illogical.

Wiltz argues, in the alternative, that the district court erred by failing to grant his motion to amend the judgment to award additional damages. This argument is meritless. It is well established that a federal court cannot unilaterally increase the damages awarded by a jury.

McBeath v. Bustos

2014 WL 1088000 (Ct. App. Cal. Mar. 18, 2014) (Epstein, J.)

[Plaintiff Graham McBeath sued defendant Evan Bustos for negligence arising out of a car wreck. The jury found Bustos negligent but apportioned a majority of fault to McBeath. It awarded $36,513.50 in special damages, but no general damages. The trial court denied McBeath's motion for new trial, and he appealed.]

Code of Civil Procedure § 657 states: "A new trial shall not be granted upon the ground of insufficiency of the evidence to justify the verdict or other decision, nor upon the ground of excessive or inadequate damages, unless after weighing the evidence the court is convinced from the entire record, including reasonable inferences therefrom, that the court or jury clearly should have reached a different verdict or decision." A trial court has broad discretion in ruling on a new trial motion, and the court's exercise of discretion is accorded great deference on appeal. An abuse of discretion occurs if, in light of the applicable law and considering all of the relevant circumstances, the court's decision exceeds the bounds of reason and results in a miscarriage of justice. Accordingly, we can reverse the denial of a new trial motion based on insufficiency of the evidence or inadequate or excessive damages only if there is no substantial conflict in the evidence and the evidence compels the conclusion that the motion should have been granted.

Also, when a verdict has been returned for the exact amount of special damages in a case where substantial general damages were obviously incurred, and where a strong case of negligence has been made, a denial of a new trial by the trial court *must* be held an abuse of discretion and a judgment on a verdict in an insufficient amount may not be affirmed. In other words, a judgment for no more than the actual medical expenses occasioned by the tort would be inadequate. It cannot be said, however, that because a verdict is rendered for the amount of medical expenses or for a less amount the verdict is inadequate as a matter of law. Every case depends upon the facts involved. Courts may uphold verdicts awarding special but not general damages where contradictory evidence raises doubts about whether such damages were actually incurred, or there is insufficient or conflicting evidence on the elements of damage.

Here, the jury's verdict of special damages, with no general damages, cannot be justified by the evidence. In awarding special damages of $36,513.50 to McBeath, the jury compensated him for his requested amount of medical costs resulting from the accident. His medical complications were uncontested and supported by expert testimony. Dr. Wilson verified that the force of the accident was sufficient to cause a fatality. He also corroborated McBeath's testimony about his C-1 condyle fracture, extended pain, and ongoing medical challenges due to the accident. By finding Bustos to be negligent, and failing to award McBeath any general damages, the jury issued a verdict similar to that in *Haskins,* where the court ordered a new trial to determine the issue of general damages after the jury awarded in effect nothing for the pain, suffering and inconvenience which inevitably accompany the type of injuries involved. The evidence here was neither insufficient nor conflicting. It showed that McBeath suffered from the injuries of the accident. As a result, the court erred in denying McBeath's motion for a new trial.

Also, the jury was not entitled to disregard the court's instructions on noneconomic damages. It appears that the court instructed jurors that they "must decide how much money will reasonably compensate McBeath for the harm. This compensation is called 'damages.' The amount of damages must include an award for each item of harm that was caused by Bustos's wrongful conduct." The instructions listed McBeath's request for $36,513.60 in economic medical damages and $250,000 in noneconomic damages for pain and suffering. During closing arguments, McBeath's counsel expressly requested that the jury "reimburse my client for the pain and suffering that he incurred in this horrific accident." Even Bustos's counsel conceded that "there is some pain and suffering" involved in McBeath's recovery from the accident. When the evidence at trial was uncontested that McBeath suffered pain as a result of the accident, and jurors were on notice as to the instructions on general damages, they were required to apply the law as given by the trial court. Thus, in failing to award any amount for general damages, the jury improperly disregarded its instructions to compensate McBeath for his pain and suffering caused by Bustos.

Bustos argues we should not disturb the jury's verdict because of an alleged evidentiary conflict at trial regarding the nature and extent of McBeath's suffering. He emphasizes that Dr. Wilson described McBeath's recovery as "good," and testified that many patients with C-1 condyle fractures do not seek treatment. As a result, Bustos contends the jury could have reasonably concluded that McBeath suffered no pain and suffering. He cites the trial court's statement of decision on the motion for a new trial, which described how McBeath was "knocked unconscious in the accident, was able to pull himself out of the wreck, required no invasive surgery and was required to wear a chest and neck brace in order to prevent further injury to his back. While such a restraint would be uncomfortable, a jury could certainly conclude that McBeath's discomfort would not be sufficiently serious to warrant an award for pain and suffering."

In *Miller,* the appellate court affirmed a jury award of plaintiff's exact amount of requested medical damages with no award of noneconomic damages. It found the evidence of plaintiff's injuries was contested where defendant had demonstrated that plaintiff falsified her injuries and physicians had indicated she was not harmed by defendant's conduct. In short, "the evidence would amply support a finding that plaintiff received no injury whatever. Similarly, the court in *Rayii,* dismissed plaintiff's challenge to the inadequacy of noneconomic damages. Concluding that the evidence was in substantial conflict, the court highlighted how defendants showed that plaintiff's injuries were preexisting or caused by subsequent other actions, and had healed by the time of trial.

Unlike those two cases, the undisputed evidence here shows that McBeath suffered at least some pain due to defendant's conduct. He testified to being prescribed painkillers and spending more than two days in the hospital. There was no evidence to contradict McBeath's testimony regarding the pain he suffered and the impact of the resulting injuries on his life. Bustos's counsel presented no competing expert witnesses, or evidence that McBeath suffered no general damages. Accordingly, unlike the cases on which Bustos relies, the evidence at trial did not raise doubts about whether McBeath incurred some general damages. As a result, the court abused its discretion in denying McBeath's motion for a new trial.

Notes and Questions

1. Does the Exact Amount of Medicals Mean Something? Is each award arbitrary?

2. Get It Right Next Time? If Mr. Wiltz came to you after another car wreck and explains his litigious past, what will you recommend he do to avoid this same

outcome? Does the answer to that question explain why plaintiffs' personal injury lawyers often refer clients to the same physicians?

3. <u>Federal Court Additur</u>. In rare instances, federal courts can award additur. It applies only if "the jury has properly determined liability and there is no valid dispute as to the amount of damages." *Roman v. Western Mfg., Inc.*, 691 F.3d 686 (5th Cir. 2012).

4. <u>Federal Rule for New Trials</u>. While the principal cases were decided by state courts, federal courts apply similar standards to whether to grant a new trial:

> A court may grant a motion for a new trial if the court finds the verdict is against the weight of the evidence, the damages awarded are excessive or inadequate, the trial was unfair, or prejudicial error was committed. The grounds for granting a new trial must be that the verdict is against the *weight* of the evidence, not merely the preponderance of the evidence. Courts do not grant new trials unless it is reasonably clear that prejudicial error has crept into the record or that substantial justice has not been done, and the burden of showing harmful error rests on the party seeking a new trial. A district court should not grant a new trial if the jury's verdict is clearly within the universe of possible awards which are supported by the evidence.

Starks v. Advantage Staffing, LLC, 217 F. Supp. 3d 917 (E.D. La. 2016). Would the outcome in *Wiltz* have been different under this standard?

5. <u>Courts Regularly Permit Similar Awards to Stand</u>. Many juries award the plaintiff's medical bills, but no or very little general damages, and the trial court's denial of a new trial is upheld. *Getson v. Scott*, 116 Wash. App. 1012 (2003) (affirming denial of new trial in car wreck case where jury awarded the cost of plaintiff's ER visit ($455), but no general damages and none of $48,661 in additional medical expenses because it could have concluded plaintiff failed to show car wreck was cause of injury that required additional medical care).

2. Setting Aside Quotient or Compromise Verdicts

Agiz v. Heller Indus. Parks, Inc.

2018 WL 2089978 (N.J. Super. App. Div. May 7, 2018) (Per Curiam)

[As a result of a racing accident, Plaintiff Hussein Agiz suffered amputation of his right arm and leg, a brain contusion, and other injuries. He sued Heller Industrial Parks, which had permitted drag racing to occur inside of its massive warehouse. The jury found the driver who had hit Agiz 40% at fault, and Heller 60% at fault. The foreperson announced the damages at $4,355,515 for future medical care and $2,301,313 for future pain and suffering.]

At that point, plaintiff's counsel requested the judge poll the jury to confirm the pain and suffering award; before that occurred, defense counsel requested a sidebar.

The judge then temporarily excused the jury. The fact that the pain and suffering award ended in an uneven number prompted discussion the jury may have returned a "quotient verdict."[4] After a brief discussion of *Shankman*, the judge and the attorneys agreed the judge would poll the jury and ask if each juror agreed with the verdict, but not inquire further unless "something comes up."

The judge then polled the jury on the liability percentages and both damage awards. Each of the seven jurors confirmed the accuracy of the verdicts but stated nothing further. The judge made no inquiry regarding the unusual circumstance of the jury's award for pain and suffering ending in an uneven number.

Plaintiff then filed the post-judgment motion under review. The trial judge heard extensive oral argument. Plaintiff's counsel argued the significance of the pain and suffering verdict ending in an odd number:

> In over a hundred jury verdicts, I've never had in the pain and suffering line item any verdict other than with zeros at the end. It does not exist. For medicals, yes. For life care plans, yes. But you don't have a pain and suffering award that ends with an odd number as we had. You just don't have it.

Heller's counsel did not dispute this assertion nor did the court.

The judge issued an order denying additur and granting plaintiff a new trial for pain and suffering damages only, on the basis the jury violated its charge in the calculation of the damages. The judge stated,

> The court is of the opinion, based upon the verdict and a review of the evidence presented at trial by plaintiff's expert witness on economic losses, that the jury improperly utilized the economic analysis of the expert on economic losses to apply to non—economic losses. This court is further of the opinion that the non-economic loss verdict is neither a quotient verdict nor a compromised verdict. The court finds that the verdict does not comport with the court's instructions. Such a verdict results in a manifest injustice to the plaintiff. The court is of the opinion that a clearly unjust result has occurred.

The judge then granted plaintiff a new trial on non-economic damages only and further provided, "The prior award for economic damages stands and shall not be re-tried."

Although neither party argues the pain and suffering verdict represented a quotient verdict or compromise verdict, we review the case law concerning these types of errant verdicts for completeness and as background information relevant to the issues under review.

---

4. A quotient verdict occurs when deliberating jurors commit to accept, as their final decision, the average of their respective personal assessments of monetary damages prior to calculating that average. *Shankman v. State*, 184 N.J. 187 (2005). Quotient verdicts are illegal.

As noted, a quotient verdict occurs when deliberating jurors commit to accept, as their final decision, the average of their respective personal assessments of monetary damages prior to calculating that average. Quotient verdicts are illegal in New Jersey because they are at odds with the essential jury function because such agreements have the capacity to foreclose all subsequent discussion, deliberation, or dissent among jurors. Generally, proof of such averaging is, alone, insufficient to have unearthed an illegal quotient verdict.

In *Shankman*, the Court instructed trial judges—when confronted with circumstances suggesting that a damages award may represent an improper quotient verdict—to not rest solely upon the jury polling process to vitiate concerns of impropriety. The Court held that it was insufficient for the trial judge in that case to poll each juror about whether he or she "agreed with" the damages verdict. Instead, the Court held the trial judge should have asked the jurors whether the jurors had made an advance agreement to accept an averaged figure, at least when the judge "had been asked to do so by counsel." *Id.* In *Cavallo v. Hughes*, 235 N.J. Super. 393 (App. Div. 1989), we declined to vacate a potential quotient verdict where counsel failed to request any follow-up questions. However, we recommended in future cases when similar issues arise that the trial judge specifically inquire whether there was a prior agreement.

Compromise verdicts result from the improper mix of issues involving liability with those involving damages. An improper compromise verdict usually occurs when a close call on liability in favor of the plaintiff results in a low verdict on damages. That is, the jury is unsure on liability, so finds the defendant liable, but compromises by issuing a low amount of damages.

Based upon *Shankman* and *Cavallo*, the trial judge here should have specifically asked the jurors whether they had made an advance agreement to accept an averaged figure. At the same time, the judge should have inquired whether the jurors discounted their pain and suffering award to present value. This would have allowed the court to determine with certainty whether the jury had returned a quotient verdict.

3. Setting Aside Excessive or Inadequate Verdicts

Additur or remittitur may be directed toward some, or all, aspects of damages: a defendant might not contest a jury's award of the plaintiff's past medical bills, but contend its award of pain and suffering damages is too high. Similarly, a plaintiff could challenge only an award of pain and suffering as too low but leave the other amounts unchallenged. And, of course, each party may challenge aspects of an award that the other believes is perfectly proper. The cases below illustrate all angles of post-trial practice.

Typically, state procedure requires that if the trial court grants a motion for remittitur or additur, its order must give the party that it adversely affects the option to accept the court's amount, or face a new trial on, at least, damages. *Nieves v. St. Farm Mut. Auto. Ins. Co.,* 248 So. 3d 240 (Ct. App. Fla. 2018). "Only when the parties agree with the trial court's amount of remittitur or additur will remittitur or additur be enforced" instead of awarding a new trial. *Id.* (Because party did not accept amount, court instead ordered a new trial limited to only amount of lost future medical expenses.) So, for example, a trial court could order remittitur of pain and suffering damages from $100,000 to $25,000, and its order would specify that the plaintiff and defendant could accept the $25,000 or a new trial would be held—someday—on some or all issues. Thus, in a sense the trial court's award is conditional: if both parties do not accept it, there will be a new trial.

The net effect is to force the parties to weigh the costs and risks of a new trial— on some or all issues—against the amount specified by the trial court. *See Baudanza v. Comcast of Mass., Inc.,* 912 N.E.2d 458 (Mass. Sup. Ct. 2009). Of course, often they examine those alternatives and negotiate a different number and settle the case. (The party that believed the first verdict was correct can, after any second trial if it comes out worse for it, appeal the grant of the new trial. In addition, some states permit trial courts to certify an award for interlocutory appeal.) However, a party may not accept the additur or remittitur and also appeal it, unless the state permits acceptance under "protest," as some do. The following cases, thus, also provide a framework for the incentives behind those choices.

A. Controlling Excessive Verdicts through Motions for New Trial or Defendants Moving for Remittitur or Plaintiffs Moving for Additur

Most courts give juries wide latitude to determine damages such as pain and suffering and mental anguish. Judicial review is highly deferential as well. *See id.* Nonetheless, courts do reverse such awards, usually when the defendant contends the award is too high, but (as discussed here but analyzed more fully in the next section), often when they are too low or when the jury awards medical expenses, lost wages, or both—but no general damages.

Three procedures are available to trial courts, and in some states appellate courts, if a verdict is found shockingly high or low. The most common form of relief is for a trial court to award a new trial, either on all issues, damages, or part of damages. The second two procedures are mirror images of each other: additur is used by a plaintiff to move the court to enter judgment for more than the jury found, and remittitur is used by a defendant to move for a judgment with a lower amount.

When an award is too high, federal courts and most state courts may use "remittitur." *See Antilles School, Inc. v. Lembach,* 2016 WL 948969 (V.I. 2016) (noting a majority of states have adopted remittitur). When an award is too low, federal courts may not use "additur" (it is unconstitutional, *see id.*), but some legislatures have authorized their courts to do so. State statutes that permit remittitur where a jury award "deviates materially" from reasonable compensation have been upheld despite attacks under state and federal constitutional rights to trial by juries. *See Soto v. Sacco*, 398 P.3d 90 (Ariz. 2017) (collecting cases).

Even when either procedure is authorized, courts are reluctant to displace jury findings, particularly where damages are "general" in the sense of being subject to the discretion of the jury to determine: "a court is not at liberty to simply substitute its own judgment as to the amount of damages for the findings of a jury." *Elsevier, Inc v. Comprehensive Microfilm & Scanning Serv., Inc.*, 113 U.S.P.Q.2d 1739 (M.D. Pa. 2014). This section analyzes how additur and remittitur impact monetary damages and describe the procedures and lawyering strategies involved. The issues raised here arise in cases elsewhere in this chapter.

If a jury awards no general damages, doesn't that mean the impact did not cause an injury that caused the need for medical care? The existence of the type of harm required by a tort is critical because, as shown in prior chapters, without proof of the type of harm required, no "special" damages are recoverable. The court in *Kanahele v. Han*, 263 P.3d 726 (Haw. 2011), succinctly stated the key role of harm in a negligence case:

> It is well established that a personal injury plaintiff is generally entitled to recover damages for all the natural and proximate consequences of the defendant's wrongful act or omission; where a defendant's liability to a personal injury plaintiff is established, a jury verdict which awards the plaintiff special damages but no general damages for pain and suffering is generally regarded as improper, inasmuch as the inescapable conclusion is that the jury awarded medical expenses which the plaintiff had incurred and failed to award any damages for pain and suffering. Thus, Petitioner is correct that when an award of special damages indicating physical injury is rendered, a zero award of general damages is improper and generally results in a new trial on general damages when liability is not disputed.

Without an award of *some* amount for the harm required by the tort, nothing was proximately caused by any tortious conduct, to put it another way.

Averette v. Phillips

185 So. 3d 16 (Ct. App. La. 2015) (McDonald, J.)

[Plaintiff Lana Averette was rear-ended by a truck driven by defendant Adam Phillips while employed by Entergy, also a defendant. She suffered spinal injuries. The jury found for the plaintiff and awarded her exactly what she had sought in damages: $42,373 for past lost wages, $58,378 for past medical expenses, $75,000 for past mental anguish and emotional distress, $75,000 for past lost enjoyment of life, $75,000 for past pain and suffering, and $500,000 for future medical expenses, for a total award of $825,751 in damages. Defendant asserted, among other things, the award was inconsistent and moved for a new trial. Plaintiff asserted they were not inconsistent but, if they were, she should be awarded lost future general damages. The district court denied all motions. All parties appealed, but the plaintiff's argument that it was erroneous to not award future general damages was conditioned on the court holding that the verdict was inconsistent.]

At trial, Ms. Averette's attorney argued she would need future spinal rhizotomies and epidural steroid injections to prevent future pain and impairment to her future enjoyment of life and gainful employment. Ms. Averette's attorney asked the jury not to award her future general damages, but to award her the cost of the future medical treatments. The jury gave Ms. Averette the exact amount she asked for in every category of damages.

Entergy and Mr. Phillips maintain that because Ms. Averette waived her claim for future pain and suffering, which was the reason she would need future medical procedures and medication, she waived her claim for future medical expenses. Entergy and Mr. Phillips argue that the law is clear that a plaintiff cannot have future medical expenses without future pain and suffering.

A jury verdict awarding medical expenses, but simultaneously denying damages for pain and suffering will most often be found inconsistent in light of the record. The courts have acknowledged, however, that under certain circumstances the evidence of record supports both an award of medical expenses and a concurrent denial of general damages. Effectively, then, the ultimate question has been whether the factfinder made inconsistent awards and thus abused its discretion. A reviewing court must ask whether the jury's determination that plaintiff is entitled to certain medical expenses but not to general damages is so inconsistent as to constitute an abuse of discretion. Only after the reviewing court determines that the factfinder has abused its much discretion can that court conduct a *de novo* review of the record.

Generally, when a party complains about an inconsistent verdict because future special damages were awarded and future general damages were not awarded, it is the *plaintiff* asking to be awarded future general damages *in addition to* the future special damages that were awarded. This appeal presents the issue in a different posture, wherein the *defendants* are maintaining that because future special damages were awarded without an award of future general damages, the future special damages award *should be vacated* because without future pain and suffering, there is no need for future medical treatment. Entergy and Mr. Phillips have cited no cases wherein an award of special damages for medical expenses has been vacated because there was no award of general damages.

Ms. Averette asked for future medical treatments to minimize and prevent pain, and that was what the jury awarded. Ms. Averette did not ask for future general damages because she would have minimal pain and suffering between medical procedures. Ms. Averette's attorney revealed his trial strategy in his closing argument as follows:

> We're going to put all our eggs in that radiofrequency ablation, the nerve burning. We're going to put all our eggs in the epidural basket and ask you to give an award only for that, only for that, and give her twenty years of that. By my math if she gets twenty years of the epidurals, that's three

610 · 15 · POST-VERDICT PROCEDURES TO CONTROL DAMAGES

610   15 · POST-VERDICT PROCEDURES TO CONTROL DAMAGES

hundred thousand dollars ($300,000). If she gets twenty years of the nerve burning, that's two hundred and twenty thousand ($220,000). Let's round up and just keep it at five hundred thousand dollars ($500,000).

It's a lot of money, but it's a lot of medical. She's going to have to have that. There is no evidence, whatsoever, that she's not going to have to have that. There's nothing, zero, zip, de nada. Every doctor said the same thing. And if she doesn't get those, then she's going to have to have a surgery which is going to bump up that number. We're saying let's be conservative, but make sure that when she leaves here that you've given her the tools that she needs to do her job. She's not asking you to pay for her to sit at home and watch Jerry Springer. She's not asking you to do anything but give her what she needs, not what she wants because you've already heard this is uncomfortable. It's what she needs.

Before I get to the past pain and suffering and the past issues, I want to talk about the future. Again, we're going to put our money where our mouth is. If this stuff is working, why would she have pain? Why would she have suffering? Why would she have mental anguish? Now, let's be honest. She's going to have some because she's going to have to miss work. She's going to have to do all of this, but I'm going to put my money where my mouth is, zero. Future mental anguish, zero; future loss of enjoyment of life, zero. We're asking you put the eggs in that basket. We're taking a chance. Lawyers do not usually come in and say this is where we want to go. They don't put in on the line like this. You've heard the evidence. I'm asking you to put it on the line, and what kind of guy would I be if I didn't. Even if she's going to have it, even if she's going to have risks, even if she's going to have pain, even if she's going to have bad days, I'm asking you to make some leaps. I have to as well.

Clearly, Ms. Averette's attorney made a strategic decision to ask for twenty years of conservative medical treatment and no future general damages, effectively waiving future general damages. Obviously, the jury agreed with Ms. Averette's treatment plan and agreed with her counsel's closing argument that she was foregoing future general damages and asking for twenty years of conservative future medical treatment. Thus, the jury's verdict was not inconsistent in light of Ms. Averette's request.

Under the particular facts of this case, we cannot say that the district court abused its discretion in giving Ms. Averette future special damages and no future general damages award.

Theriot, J., dissenting,

I agree with the majority that Ms. Averette made a strategic decision during closing argument to ask for twenty years of conservative medical treatment and no future general damages. I disagree with the majority that Ms. Averette effectively waived future general damages.

Opening and closing statements of counsel are not evidence. The trial court in the instant case correctly instructed the jury as such.

The trial court showed the blank verdict form to the jury. The trial court further explained the section of the verdict form regarding damages and instructed the jury to consider the damages they feel were proved and what that award amount should be. At no time during the instruction phase did the trial court state Ms. Averette waived any of the listed damages found on the verdict form. I cannot find that Ms. Averette waived her rights to any of the damages enumerated on the verdict form.

I further find an award of $500,000 for future medical expense while at the same time awarding $0 for future general damages constitutes legal error. The jury failed to follow the instructions of the trial court. The failure to award future general damages while awarding $500,000 for future medical expense is so inconsistent as to constitute an abuse of discretion.

Having determined the fact finder abused its discretion, I would proceed with a *de novo* review to determine what amount of damages is reasonable on the record before us. Noting Ms. Averette has answered the appeal and preserved her rights on appeal, this court's *de novo* review may increase or decrease the amount awarded for future medical expenses, future pain and suffering, future mental anguish and emotional distress, and future loss of enjoyment of life. Therefore, rather than affirm, I would amend the jury award to reflect the amount of damages proved and render judgment accordingly.

Notes and Questions

1. Specials Without Generals? Does the jury's finding of liability, coupled with an award of special damages, mean the defendant established harm but the amount was not established with reasonable certainty? Or is it sign of a compromise verdict?

2. Post-Trial Procedure. In *Balderas v. Starks*, 138 P.3d 75 (Ct. App. Utah 2006), the defendant collided with plaintiff's car. The jury found the defendant liable, and awarded $3,237 for plaintiff's past chiropractor bills, but nothing for pain and suffering. Upon hearing the verdict, the plaintiff's lawyer argued to the judge that the jury had to award *some* amount of special damages, and the judge instructed the jury that there was a "small error" and that the jury "must award something for general damages. Any amount is sufficient." Plaintiff's counsel did not object, and the jury returned a verdict of $1. On appeal, plaintiff argued the verdict was insufficient. The appellate court agreed that as a general rule an award of special damages without general damages was improper, but that it did not need to decide if that rule applied when a nominal amount was awarded, stating:

> In this case, we acknowledge that Balderas's counsel asked to have the jury sent back out after it awarded no general damages. However, if counsel continued to believe the revised damage award of $1.00 was contrary to law, as claimed on appeal, counsel should have objected again when the new verdict was read. Counsel did not object to the nominal damage award after

it was read or at any other time before the jury was discharged. Nor did counsel object when the court instructed the jury that it could award "*any amount*" of general damages to make the verdict consistent. (Emph. added.) Understandably, the jury likely believed that it was acting consistently with the instruction when it awarded a nominal sum. For these reasons, we hold that Balderas has waived his right to argue on appeal that the jury verdict, as once revisited, was impermissibly inconsistent.

Compare *Balderas* to *Morton Roofing, Inc. v. Prather*, 864 So. 2d 64 (Fla. 5th Dist. App. 2003). In this car wreck case, the plaintiff Jody Prather sued the defendants in negligence after a car wreck. The jury awarded Prather $43,177.65 in past medical expenses, $430,526 for future medical expenses, zero damages for past loss of wages, $963,590 for loss of earning capacity, zero damages for past noneconomic (pain and suffering) damages and $250,000 for future noneconomic (pain and suffering) damages, for a total of $1,687,293.65 in damages. Plaintiff's counsel argued the verdict was inconsistent, asserting the award of future pain and suffering required the jury to enter some amount for past pain and suffering. The defendant agreed, and the trial judge instructed the jury:

> There is an inconsistency in your verdict. You found that there was damages for future pain and suffering and disability, etcetera; but you didn't find any in the past. To find that she'll have it in the future but have none in the past is inconsistent, so I'm going to send you back in with the verdict and have you consider that a little more. And if you can reach a determination of any past pain and suffering, disability, etcetera, write that figure in and correct the totals, and then we'll be finished.

Back deliberating, the jury wrote and asked whether it had to keep future noneconomic damages the same. In response, the trial judge told the jury to reconsider the inconsistency of $250,000 for the future and nothing in the past, but stated the jury could not change future damages. The defendant objected to that aspect of the court's instruction.

Later, the jury modified the award for past pain and suffering by drawing a line through the zero and writing in $25,000. The verdict form reflects that at some point the $250,000 award for future pain and suffering had been struck through and the figure $225,000 inserted, but it was then returned to $250,000. Defendant appealed, but the appellate court affirmed:

> The parties conceded below that the verdict for non-economic damages was legally inconsistent and needed to be reconsidered. This concession implicates the general principle set out in *Stevens Markets, Inc. v. Markantonatos*, 189 So.2d 624 (Fla.1966). Until a verdict in a civil action is accepted by the trial court, the entire case remains in the hands of the jury:
>
>> The validity of a verdict is a question for the Court and until it is received and recorded by the Court, it is still within the control of the jurors. It is clearly the right and duty of the Court before discharging

the jurors to call their attention to a defective verdict and give them an opportunity to return a proper verdict. When they are sent back to further reconsider the matter, the case is still in their hands. They are not bound by their former action. They are at liberty to review the case and to bring in an entirely new verdict.

Stevens Markets involved an action for damages for false imprisonment, unlawful detention, unauthorized search and battery arising out of the detention and search of the minor plaintiff on suspicion of shoplifting. The jury verdicts as initially returned were for zero compensatory damages and $5,000 punitive damages for the minor plaintiff and $1,500 compensatory damages for the plaintiff's father. The trial court announced that the jury had obviously misunderstood the instructions and directed the jury to reconsider the compensatory award to the minor plaintiff without further considering the punitive damages awarded to her or the compensatory award to her father. The supreme court reversed the district court of appeal's affirmance of this ruling, finding it was legal error.

Stevens Markets reflects that under Florida law, where a defective verdict is returned and the defect discovered before the jury is discharged, resubmission by the court is a legal duty, not simply a discretionary call.

What do these cases teach about handling inconsistent verdicts in the trial court? *See also Jones Lang Lasalle Midwest, LLC v. Lanzatech, Inc.,* 2017 Il. App. 162600 (Nov. 1, 2017) (by failing to object at time of verdict defendant waived objection to award of $205,000 as "nominal damages").

B. Using Additur to Increase Jury Awards

Nelson v. Erickson

190 Wash. App. 1003 (Ct. App. Wash. 2015) (Lau, J.),
aff'd, 377 P.3d 196 (Wash. 2016)

[In December 2010, defendant Michael Erickson "totaled" his Jeep when he rear-ended a car driven by plaintiff Jess Nelson. Nelson sued Erickson in October 2012. Under Washington law, the parties were required to enter a nonbinding arbitration. The arbitrator awarded Nelson $11,167 in special medical damages, $234.59 in out-of-pocket expenses, and $32,000 in general damages for pain and suffering.

In May 2013, Erickson requested a trial *de novo*, as allowed by Washington law. Before trial, in September 2013, Nelson offered to settle for $26,000, but Erickson rejected the offer. For trial, the parties stipulated that Nelson had been injured in the wreck and incurred $9,361 in medical expenses for the eight months immediately following the accident, but Erickson contested the remaining $1,806 in medical bills, denied future medical expenses were needed, and asserted Nelson should not recover any past or future damages for pain and suffering.

At the three-day trial, Nelson and his family and friends described how he had limited his activities after the wreck, foregoing fly fishing and boating, and his wife testified she had considered moving out because his pain made living with him unbearable. Nelson had received eight months of chiropractic treatments.

Plaintiff's expert, Dr. Harper, and his physical therapist, Mr. Washeck, testified Nelson had neck and back injuries that, if the pain continued, would require cervical epidural injections at $3,000 each, and these were needed to alleviate pain. The expert testified Nelson had degenerative disk disease that had been aggravated by the wreck. Defendant's medical expert, Dr. Jackson, agreed with Nelson and his family's testimony as to the likely pain and its impact, agreed that six to eight months of chiropractic treatment may have been appropriate, as was the medication he had taken, but testified that Nelson had suffered a soft tissue injury to his neck and lower back that would return to normal within three weeks to four months. He testified he could find no objective evidence that correlated with causing his ongoing subjective symptoms of pain.

In closing arguments, defendant's lawyer conceded liability and that Nelson had ongoing pain, but asserted there was no evidence that the accident had caused pain extending beyond six to eight months after the wreck. After being instructed that Nelson bore the burden to prove damages and causation, the jury returned the following verdict, totaling $24,167:

(1) Stipulated medical expenses: $9,361.00

(2) Past medical expenses: $1,806.00

(3) Future medical expenses: $10,000.00

(4) Past noneconomic damages: $3,000.00

(5) Future noneconomic damages: $0.00

The trial court denied Nelson's motion for a new trial but granted the motion for additur, replacing the $0 award of future noneconomic damages with $3,000. The court held the jury's verdict of future medical expenses was inconsistent with its denial of future pain and suffering because the injections were to alleviate pain. Erickson appealed.]

Erickson argues that the trial court erred by granting additur.

Determination of the amount of damages is within the jury's province, and courts are reluctant to overturn a verdict when fairly made. *Palmer v. Jensen*, 132 Wash.2d 193 (1997). This court begins with the presumption that the jury's verdict was correct. A decision to increase a jury's award is reviewed de novo.

A trial court may grant additur where the jury's verdict on its face is so inadequate as to indicate it must have resulted from passion or prejudice. The question of whether a plaintiff is entitled to general damages turns on the evidence. Although there is no per se rule that general damages must be awarded to every plaintiff who sustains an injury, a plaintiff who substantiates her pain and suffering with evidence is entitled to general damages. Where the record shows categorically an award for special damages but not for proved general damages, additur and a new trial may lie.

Appellate courts look to the record in determining whether sufficient evidence supports a verdict. If the verdict is within the range of credible evidence, the trial court lacks discretion to find passion or prejudice affected the verdict for the purpose of awarding additur.

Erickson relies on *Lopez v. Salgado-Guadarama,* 130 Wash.App. 87 (2005). In *Lopez,* plaintiff sued the defendant after a low impact, no property damage car accident. At trial, the defendant's expert witness claimed a quick recovery and no objective findings supported the plaintiff's pain. The jury awarded special damages for medical expenses, but no general damages for pain and suffering. The trial court denied the plaintiff's motion for a new trial or additur. Division Three of this court affirmed, concluding that unlike in *Palmer,* the defendant disputed every aspect of the plaintiff's damages, and the plaintiff's credibility was in question. The court held that "given the evidence, the jury was entitled to conclude that the plaintiff incurred reasonable medical expenses as a result of the accident, while at the same time concluding he failed to carry his burden of proving general damages." *Lopez* at 93.

Nelson analogizes to *Palmer.* There, the plaintiff presented uncontested medical evidence that she experienced pain after she was rear-ended by the defendant. The jury returned a verdict for $8,414.89 in special damages claimed at trial. The jury declined to award general damages for pain and suffering. The trial court denied the plaintiff's motion for a new trial. The Supreme Court reversed, concluding that the jury's failure to award general damages was contrary to the evidence because she presented uncontroverted evidence of ongoing, serious pain. The court reasoned, "a plaintiff who substantiates her pain and suffering with evidence is entitled to general damages." *Palmer* at 201. The court concluded that the jury's failure to provide for such an award was contrary to the evidence.

This case is more like *Palmer.* Nelson presented undisputed evidence that three years postaccident, he continued to suffer chronic pain from the accident. Nelson, his friends, and family testified to Nelson's ongoing pain and its effect on his daily and recreational activities. Both Dr. Jackson and Dr. Harper agreed that Nelson was pain-free before the accident. Dr. Jackson, Dr. Harper and physical therapist Washeck all agreed that existence of chronic, ongoing pain three years postaccident is a permanent injury. Dr. Jackson and Dr. Harper suggested treatment modalities for a person suffering chronic pain-referral to a pain management specialist, treatment by rheumatologist, additional physical therapy, medication, and treatment with injections. Dr. Jackson acknowledged his medical review indicated no other cause for Nelson's present pain complaints. Erickson agreed in closing remarks that Nelson was truthful when he testified that three years postaccident he continued to experience pain. He referred to Nelson as "an honest guy." Counsel disputed a discrete issue—whether Nelson's symptoms after eight months of treatment were proximately caused by the accident. The jury awarded $10,000 for future medical expenses, the exact amount Nelson requested in his closing argument. But it declined to award any amount for future pain and suffering. This award of future medical treatment expenses necessarily establishes that the accident proximately caused Nelson's injuries and need for future medical treatment.

Our review of the record shows the jury's omission of future general damages for pain and suffering is contrary to the evidence discussed above. Here the jury awarded $10,000 for future medical expenses. The trial evidence established Nelson's need for future medical treatment due to his ongoing chronic pain. In awarding damages for future medical expenses, the jury necessarily determined that such future expenses were reasonable, necessary, and causally related to the accident and for treatment of Nelson's ongoing chronic pain. Unlike in *Lopez* and *Herriman,* here there was no evidence of preexisting neck-back pain, exaggeration, malingering, emotional component or lack of credibility. As Erickson candidly acknowledged, Nelson is "an honest guy."

In sum, the medical and lay witness evidence substantiates Nelson's claim that he experienced past and future special and general damages. We conclude the jury's verdict providing no damages for future general pain and suffering contradicts the evidence. Accordingly, we affirm the court's grant of additur in the amount of $3,000.

Gunno v. McNair

2016 WL 6805006 (W. Va. Nov. 17, 2016) (Per Curiam)

[Plaintiff Ashley Gunno was injured in a car wreck with defendant Kevin C. McNair. Plaintiff was treated at the scene by emergency responders and transported to the hospital for evaluation. She told the treating physicians of pain in her neck and stated that if the doctor moved her legs, she experienced intense back and neck pain. She was released from the emergency room but continued to experience pain and soreness, which kept her from sleeping. She testified that the pain was miserable and that she could not move without experiencing more pain.

Plaintiff saw Dr. Matthew Walker, an orthopedic specialist, to address persistent pain in her neck, which she described as radiating down her arms when she moved her neck, back pain, and intermittent burning sensations. Dr. Walker examined her and recommended one month off work for recovery. Dr. Walker also recommended physical therapy, which she received, and use of a TENS unit for pain. Plaintiff testified that this only gave temporary relief. Dr. Walker discharged her from his care because there was nothing more he could do to treat her symptoms.

Plaintiff then saw Dr. Jay McClanahan, a chiropractor, because, she testified, her neck pain grew more severe than her back pain. Dr. McClanahan ordered her to remain off work for three to four more weeks. From October 2011 through the spring of 2012, he gave her a total of 30 treatments. He opined that she had decreased range of motion and muscle spasms. While she was not completely pain free following her treatments, she returned to work with restrictions and eventually was released to her normal work as a nurse.

Plaintiff testified that she continued to feel pain while at work and at home despite maintaining a home therapy program, including use of a TENS unit. She later was treated by the Holzer Clinic, receiving trigger point injections that initially relieved the pain, but it eventually returned. She also received another 10 to 15 treatments from Dr. McClanahan concentrating on pain relief and increasing her range of motion, but discontinued them for lack of funds. She testified her pain continued and it interfered with caring for her son, born after the accident in 2014.

In June 2012, plaintiff sued defendant for damages arising from the accident. At trial, Dr. McClanahan testified that she had a permanent injury and will never fully recover. In addition, Dr. McClanahan suggested that she will continue to suffer flare-ups and nothing could be done. Petitioner's husband, Rick Comer, testified about his wife's pain and suffering.

Defendant called Dr. Bruce Guberman, who had reviewed plaintiff's medical records and examined her on May 29, 2013. At that time, she was still experiencing pain, but he testified that her injuries were subjective and not supported by the objective diagnostic tests he administered, which resulted in normal findings. However, Dr. Guberman acknowledged her past medical records contained objective evidence of her pain and injury. Finally, Dr. Guberman testified that plaintiff told him that a month after the wreck, she had fallen, which increased her neck pain.

As a result of a strategic trial decision, plaintiff's lawyer chose not to offer her medical bills into evidence or to seek recovery of the amount of the medical bills or lost wages. The defendant moved for JMOL after plaintiff rested as to damages for past medical expenses, past lost wages, past vocational loss, future medical expenses, future lost wages, and future vocational loss. The jury found plaintiff was injured as a proximate result of the accident, but as to the amount of damages for harms and losses, including, but not limited to past and/or future physical and mental pain and suffering and reduced ability to enjoy life, the jury awarded $0 in damages. Plaintiff appealed from the trial court's denial of plaintiff's motion for new trial.]

While both Petitioner and Respondent present arguments on the inadequacy or adequacy of the jury's award of damages for Petitioner's losses, we need not address this issue. Instead, the core issue presented in this appeal is whether the jury verdict was inherently inconsistent. While the lower court's order denying a new trial does not directly discuss any inconsistencies in the verdict, Petitioner did allege in her motion for a new trial that the verdict was inconsistent. Instead of addressing these *inconsistencies*, the circuit court's order instead focused on the *adequacy* of the jury's award of zero dollars for Petitioner's losses. When jury verdicts answering several questions have no logical internal consistence and do not comport with instructions, they will be reversed and the cause remanded for a new trial. Petitioner argues that the jury's finding that Petitioner was injured as a result of the accident—an accident that Respondent admits was his fault—is inconsistent with an award of zero damages for her losses.

In determining whether jury verdicts are inconsistent, such inconsistency must appear after excluding every reasonable conclusion that would authorize the verdict. While this Court has previously addressed alleged inconsistencies in jury verdicts, this is an instance where the Court has been asked to examine the issue in the context of an automobile accident, where a jury finds liability on the part of the defendant but awards no damages. The Alabama Court of Civil Appeals recently examined an almost factually identical scenario in *Daniel v. Passmore*, 998 So.2d 1079 (Ala. Civ. App. 2008). In *Daniel*, the plaintiffs, a wife and husband, were involved in an automobile accident with the defendant. The jury returned a verdict in which it determined that the defendant was liable for the automobile accident. The jury awarded $600 to the wife and $0 to the husband. On appeal, the Alabama court found that a jury verdict awarding $0 to the husband was inconsistent with the jury's decision regarding the defendant's liability. The court reiterated that "where a jury in a negligence action returns a verdict for the plaintiff but awards *no* damages such a verdict is inconsistent as a matter of law." *Id.* 989. The jury verdict in the case at bar is similarly inconsistent.

In the present appeal, the jury resolved any questions of injuries by making a finding that Petitioner was injured as a proximate result of the automobile accident. The award of zero dollars in damages is inherently inconsistent with the finding that Petitioner was injured as a proximate result of the accident. Petitioner's past pain and suffering is amply supported by her own testimony, her husband's testimony and the testimony of her treating chiropractor. We therefore conclude that Petitioner is entitled to a new trial to determine her damages as a result of Respondent's negligence.

Chief Justice Ketchum, concurring:

After the inconsistent interrogatories were returned, the plaintiff's lawyers did not request that the court return the jury for further consideration of its answers and award damages based on its finding that the plaintiff was injured in the car wreck. If the plaintiff's lawyers had requested the jury be required to further deliberate, the court, in its discretion, could have returned the jury for further deliberation on damages.

Even if the plaintiff's lawyers waived any defect in the verdict form, I still would grant a new trial on damages. The defendant did not assert that the plaintiff failed to object to the inconsistent interrogatory answers and that the plaintiff waived the right to a new trial. Waiver was not argued before the trial court or before this Court in the present appeal.

Loughry, J., dissenting:

I suspect the jury may have found the absence of any evidence concerning the petitioner's medical bills or lost wages was a reflection on the credibility of her injury. This lack of evidence, along with the respondent's vigorous challenge to the petitioner's personal credibility, pre-existing conditions, and subsequent injury that occurred one month after the vehicle accident, easily explains the jury's conspicuous conclusion that the petitioner was not injured to an extent that warranted a monetary recover.

More importantly, unlike special damages, which are capable of calculation, pain and suffering can never be an "uncontroverted amount." Indeed, the "amounts" awarded for such damages lie solely within the discretion and judgment of the jury.

This Court has wisely stated that it is true that there is no market price or monetary equivalent for pain and suffering or for injuries of a nonpermanent nature, and a jury award for these will generally not be disturbed because of the small amount awarded. "The sole measure of damages for pain and suffering is the enlightened conscience of fair and impartial jurors." *Atlanta Transit System v. Robinson*, 213 S.E.2d 547 (Ga. App. 1975). The majority's continued refusal to respect the sanctity and considerable discretion of the jury is very troubling. However, the majority's attempt to twist the petitioner's argument into something which it (mistakenly) believes provides a more direct route to relief is simply inexplicable.

Ortega v. Belony

185 So. 3d 538 (Ct. App. Fla. 2015) (Shepherd, J.)

[Plaintiff Blanchard Belony suffered a broken neck from a car wreck and spent eight days in the hospital as a result. He was given the choice of surgery or wearing a "halo"[1] for three months while the break mended. He chose the halo and for those three months lived with his brother, who assisted him with his bathing and other needs. He experienced difficulty sleeping, and, on one occasion, had to return to the hospital briefly to have the screws in his halo tightened. At the end of three months Belony's injuries had substantially healed, and the halo was removed.

He still had mild neck pain, however, but his doctors did not recommend any further treatment. Less than a year after the accident, and at the time he filed suit, he sought treatment from an orthopedic spinal surgeon, Dr. Mark Eskenazi, who noted that Belony's neck fracture had almost completely healed. Dr. Eskenazi recommended surgery, which Belony again refused, instead opting for three injections to his neck. Dr. Eskenazi administered the injections and told Belony to return if he felt any worse. After the injections, Belony felt almost normal. By the time of trial, Belony had no difficulty performing the activities of daily living, had not returned to seek treatment from Dr. Eskenazi in over a year, and did not intend on seeking any future surgical procedures.

---

1. A halo is "an orthopedic device used to immobilize the head and neck (as to treat fracture of neck vertebrae) that consists of a metal band placed around the head and fastened to the skull usually with metal pins and that is attached by extensions to an inflexible vest." Merriam-Webster Medical Dictionary, *http://www.merriam-webster.com/medical/halo.*

The jury found Belony 70% comparatively fault and awarded him his full $32,971.86 in past and future medical expenses, but zero damages for past and future pain and suffering. The trial court believed the verdict was inconsistent and ordered the jury to reconsider the pain and suffering award. After additional deliberations, it awarded Belony $5,000 in past and future pain and suffering. Belony moved for additur. At the hearing on that motion, the trial judge expressed "shock" at the pain and suffering award and stated that the jury must have been "coldblooded" to return such a low verdict. The trial court entered judgment for pain and suffering of $250,000 because the pain and suffering award shocked the conscience of the trial court. Defendant appealed.]

Damages for pain and suffering are difficult to calculate, have no set standard of measurement, and for this reason are uniquely reserved to a jury for their decision. When attempting to quantify a damage award for pain and suffering in a personal injury case, the trier of fact deals with the most intangible element of the award. One court has described it as "an attempt to measure that which is immeasurable." *Food Fair Stores, Inc. v. Morgan*, 338 So.2d 89 (Fla. 2d DCA 1976). For this reason, a pain and suffering verdict is "clothed with a presumption of regularity and is not to be disturbed if supported by the evidence.

The well-established test for determining the adequacy of a jury verdict is simply whether a jury of reasonable persons could have returned that verdict. The familiar refrain that the trial court cannot sit as a seventh juror applies.

In this case, there is no basis on which to conclude that a jury of reasonable persons could not have reached a $5,000 award for pain and suffering on the evidence presented. The record in this case does not establish the jury was improperly influenced by prejudice, passion, or corruption. Belony was a stoic plaintiff whose injuries healed quickly and, after a three month recovery, had no need of future medical treatment. Although Belony suffered a severe, permanent injury in the car accident, he has proven to be resilient in his recovery and by the time of trial, felt "almost normal." Therefore, the jury did not act unreasonably in concluding, as it did, that $5,000 was a reasonable award for Belony's past and future pain and suffering.

Notes and Questions

1. <u>Do the Cases Create Predictability</u>? Most cases settle. Do these cases facilitate that by rendering the amount of damages more predictable? In rendering trial preparation simpler? Consider those same issues when reading the next group of cases, which present not just low verdicts, but zero general damage awards and yet significant special damage awards.

2. <u>After Verdict</u>. Each side's lawyers must assess the verdict in light of the evidence and decide whether to file post-judgment motions. How do they know if they're likely to win at trial and have that withstand appeal? What determines "excessiveness"—particularly in zero general damage cases—but in all cases? What guides a trial court in making that assessment? The *Gunno* concurring judge explained what

plaintiffs' lawyers should do, but which this one did not do. Why did the majority and concurrence save the plaintiff from her lawyer's error? Given the result in *Belony*, how much difference would it likely have made in terms of the amount of award? Conversely, should the plaintiff's lawyer in *Belony* have sought a new trial after the award of $5,000, rather than ask for enhancement? Further, would the *Belony* court have affirmed if the award had been $50,000? How much is too much when — one assumes — the *Belony* court would have found the original zero damages award shockingly low?

3. <u>Do Rich People Hurt More</u>? The *Gunno* case points out the strategy of not seeking medical bills or lost wages when those are minimal. But minimal compared to what? What, further, does it say about the social judgment behind the amount of damages for pain and suffering if it is tied to medical expenses or lost wages? What incentive does it create for plaintiffs, plaintiffs' lawyers, and doctors?

4. <u>What Incentives</u>? The jury, and dissent, in *Gunno* obviously thought the plaintiff was exaggerating her injuries, and the testifying doctor had a financial incentive to assist in that effort. In contrast, Belony took an (apparently) safer route, but one that objectively involved a lot of pain and suffering. If you were advising a plaintiff today, what do these cases teach you about strategy to maximize damages? Is that socially beneficial?

5. <u>Deterrent Effect of Tort Law</u>? Many theorists state tort compensation is designed to force people to act reasonably. Does *Belony* undermine that approach, or does it suggest the goal of compensation overrides deterrence?

6. <u>Which Case Is More Deferential to Juries</u>? Ordinarily, the issue on review of damage awards for pain and suffering is that the award is shockingly high, but these cases present the opposite issue. When examining verdicts for shockingly high results, the prior section shows that some courts compare similar awards in the jurisdiction: should they not compare *low* results to the *high-end* awards? If not, does the net effect of this process of judicial review in both trial and appellate courts press tort damages downward over time?

7. <u>Zero General Damage Awards with Specials</u>. What does this reflect? *See Kanahele v. Han*, 263 P.3d 726 (Haw. 2011) (jury awarded $1 in nominal compensatory damages but $12,000 for past medical treatments); *Micalizzi v. Stewart*, 181 Conn. App. 671 (2018) (awarding $7,325 in past medicals but no general damages). A desire by juries to compensate plaintiffs for out-of-pocket expenses? Isn't that misdirected, since doing so encourages treating physicians to freeload off defendants?

8. <u>Negligence versus Intentional Torts</u>. In *Right v. Breen*, 890 A.2d 1287 (Conn. 2006), the court concluded that a zero general damages award in a personal injury case where the defendant admitted liability, but denied causing the injuries plaintiff complained of, did not require an award of even nominal damages. The jury awarded no damages, but post-trial the judge awarded $1 as nominal damages that, under state law, permitted an award of costs (of $467). The court held that "actual damages must be sustained" in negligence, and so the jury's verdict meant the

defendant had not established causation of damages and held that only for intentional torts did liability alone justify an award of nominal damages.

C. The Scope of Any New Trial

Lawyers for each side must consider whether to seek, in the alternative to additur or remittitur or in addition to it, the scope of any new trial. Should it be as to all issues, all damages, or merely the damage award that caused the need for a new trial?

Smedberg v. Detlef's Custodial Serv. Inc.

940 A.2d 674 (Vt. 2007) (Reiber, J.)

[Plaintiff Jean Smedberg slipped and fell, injuring her spine, which required fusion surgery. She sued Detlef's Custodial Services ("DCS" or "Detlef's") in negligence. The jury found DCS liable, but also found that plaintiff was 50% at fault. The jury awarded plaintiff $27,015.25 in medical damages and $45,500.00 in lost wages, but awarded no damages for past or future pain and suffering or loss of enjoyment of life. The medical and lost-wages awards were reduced by 50% for plaintiff's negligence, and judgment was entered for $36,257.63. The trial court denied plaintiff's motion for a new trial or, in the alternative, additur. She appealed.]

Rulings on motions for new trial are within the discretion of the trial court. When reviewing a trial court's decision on a motion for new trial, we afford the decision all possible presumptive support, similar to the support the trial court owes to a jury verdict. We view the evidence in the light most favorable to the non-moving party. However, a jury's verdict should not be upheld if there is evidence that the jury compromised its verdict.

The superior court denied plaintiff's motion for a partial new trial or additur on the basis that the court could not "conclude with certainty on the record that the jury was without a basis to find plaintiff's evidence on pain and suffering unpersuasive." Plaintiff contends that the jury had no basis to find that she did not endure any pain or suffering as a result of the slip and fall and ensuing spinal surgery, and that the superior court therefore erred in denying her motion for a partial new trial or additur.

As noted, plaintiff's motion clearly sought a new trial solely on the issue of damages; plaintiff could have, but did not, request a new trial on all issues. As a general matter, a new trial may properly be limited to a single issue only where the issue sought to be retried is clearly separable from the other issues. See *Gasoline Prods. Co. v. Champlin Refining Co.*, 283 U.S. 494 (1931) ("Where the practice permits a partial new trial, it may not properly be resorted to unless it clearly appears that the issue to be retried is so distinct and separable from the others that a trial of it alone may be had without injustice."). Our review of plaintiff's Rule 59 motion thus has two parts: first, whether the trial court erred in denying the motion; and second, whether a new trial should be on all issues or on damages alone.[2]

The evidence is undisputed that plaintiff slipped, hit her head on a concrete wall, and fell to the floor. At trial, defendant did not claim that plaintiff's later cervical fusion surgery was not reasonable and necessary treatment for her accident-related injuries. Indeed, the jury explicitly found as much when it determined that plaintiff incurred the full amount of her claimed medical expenses as a result of the accident, reduced by 50% for her own negligence. The jury also awarded plaintiff approximately 60% of her claimed lost wages. The question, then, is whether the $0 pain-and-suffering award was consistent with the rest of the verdict and was supported by the evidence, or reflected an improper compromise or decision based on prejudice or confusion. If the jury has disregarded the reasonable and substantial evidence, or found against it, through passion, prejudice, or some misconstruction of the matter, that judgment requires that the court's discretion be exercised to set aside the verdict.

In addition to plaintiff's own testimony about her pain, the record reflects the testimony of two medical witnesses. One, a pain-management specialist, testified that he "heavily suggested" that plaintiff undergo cervical decompression and fusion surgery when her ongoing physical-therapy regimen failed to abate her pain. He noted that, prior to surgery, "she could barely tolerate simple sitting and standing." He testified that the surgery is intended both immediately to take the pressure off the nerves in the spine to relieve pain and permanently to immobilize a portion of the spine so that the nerves will not be impinged upon and cause pain again. The first objective is accomplished by "cutting away some of the disk material that's putting direct pressure on the nerve." The second requires attaching a piece of metal or bone to the spine to "restrict the motion so that the vertebrae don't bend up and down and don't create a pinching effect on the nerve." Plaintiff underwent the surgery, and the doctor testified that afterwards "there was still spasm and guarding in the muscles surrounding the neck, which were quite painful to her." Finally, the

---

2. Although plaintiff's motion requested only a partial new trial, we have no doubt that the trial court had the power to order a complete new trial. See *Hamasaki v. Flotho*, 39 Cal.2d 602 (1952) (where question of liability is close, damages are inadequate, and compromise is apparent, "most reasonable response" to motion for new trial on damages alone is a new trial on all issues). For the same reason, we do not believe that the dissent's reading of Rule 59 is the correct one: an additur is not an appropriate remedy where the verdict is internally inconsistent or suggests compromise. See *Chenell v. Westbrook College*, 324 A.2d 735 (Me. 1974) (holding—under Maine's Rule 59, from which our rule is derived—that a new trial without an opportunity for additur "is legally proper only when there is a sustainable finding not only that the damages are inadequate but also that such inadequacy reflects a compromise"); *Shere v. Davis*, 95 Nev. 491 (1979) ("Due to the interrelationship of the liability and damage issues, the case was not a proper one for a new trial limited to damages. Thus, additur was also inappropriate. Although the motion requested only additur or a new trial limited to the issue of damages, the trial court had the power to grant a new trial on all issues.").

pain-management specialist testified he expected her pain would last for the rest of her life.

The second doctor to testify, a neurosurgeon, described the decompression and fusion surgery. The surgery, which the doctor agreed was "very invasive," was intended to address "neck and right arm pain" caused by a disk protrusion. The surgery involved inserting a small titanium "cage" between two vertebrae in her neck to immobilize them until they eventually fused together. The surgeon further testified that plaintiff had "probably more post-surgery arm pain than most people" due to the "settling" of her bones around the titanium cage.

Although our review of the jury's award—and the trial court's decision on the motion for new trial—is deferential, we will not endorse a verdict that fails to compensate a plaintiff for damages proven, or one that is internally inconsistent or evidences compromise. Where, as here, the jury has evidently disregarded the reasonable and substantial evidence, or found against it, through passion, prejudice, or some misconstruction of the matter, that judgment requires that the court's discretion be exercised to set aside the verdict. Viewing the evidence in the light most favorable to the verdict does not cure it of its internal inconsistency. We conclude that the denial of the motion for new trial must be reversed, and turn to the question of the proper scope of the new trial on remand.

We have not closely considered the question of what the scope of a new trial should be under circumstances like these. In *Nourse*, the plaintiffs—a husband and wife who were injured in a car accident—moved for a new trial on damages alone after a jury verdict awarded no more than $110 for their general damages despite finding liability and awarding special damages. In a brief opinion, we remanded for a new trial on all issues: "Since it appears that the verdict itself was the result of compromise justice and fairness require that the cause be remanded for a new trial on all issues, including liability." 140 Vt. at 186. We take this opportunity to elaborate on the *Nourse* rationale.

Two California cases, *Leipert v. Honold*, 39 Cal.2d 462 (1952), and *Hamasaki v. Flotho*, 39 Cal.2d 602 (1952), suggest the same result. In *Leipert*, a personal-injury plaintiff moved for a partial new trial (on damages only) after a jury verdict of $2,200 for severe head injuries, a broken pelvis, ruptured bladder, and abdominal operation. The motion was granted, and the defendant appealed. The California Supreme Court concluded that the trial court had abused its discretion in granting the motion for partial new trial because: (1) the damages were inadequate, (2) the issue of liability was close, and (3) the circumstances indicated that the verdict was probably the result of prejudice, sympathy, or compromise. Both the defendant and the plaintiff in *Leipert* stated that, if the order granting the new trial were reversed, they wished the underlying judgment to stand rather than conduct a new trial on all issues. Therefore, the California Supreme Court affirmed the judgment, but did not foreclose the possibility of a complete new trial under similar circumstances if a party requested one.

In *Hamasaki,* a little boy darted into the street and sustained serious injuries when he was hit by a car. The jury returned a verdict for the boy for $1,000, including a stipulated $817 for medical expenses. That left $183 to cover his general damages (pain and suffering) for a brain concussion, broken clavicle, skull fractures, and other injuries. The defendants moved for a new trial on all issues, and the motion was denied. The plaintiffs moved for a partial new trial on damages only, and the motion was granted after defendants refused an additur of $7,500. The defendants appealed, and the California Supreme Court reversed. Citing *Leipert,* the court concluded that a new trial on damages only was inappropriate because: (1) the damages were inadequate, (2) the issue of liability was close, and (3) the inadequacy of the damages suggested compromise. The controlling question on appeal in *Hamasaki* therefore was "whether or not the trial court, on plaintiffs' motion for a new trial on the issue of damages only, had power to grant a new trial on all issues." The California statute governing new trials, similar to V.R.C.P. 59, provided that a verdict "may be vacated in whole or in part, and a new or further trial granted on all or part of the issues, on the application of the party aggrieved." The court held that "if the limited new trial sought would be prejudicial to the opposing party, the granting of a complete new trial is the most reasonable response to the motion.

We conclude that the standards announced in these cases are consistent with our prior cases and our rules, and so adopt the following standards today. As noted above, a new trial on damages alone will not generally be proper unless the issue to be retried is clearly distinct from the others and may be tried alone without injustice. In particular, a new trial on damages alone is not appropriate when: first, the issue of liability is close; second, the damages awarded are grossly inadequate; and third, the circumstances indicate that the verdict was the result of prejudice or an improper compromise. Here, all three of these circumstances were present, and it is not at all clear that the damages issue is "distinct and separable" from the hotly contested issue of liability.

First, the issue of liability was very close. Under Vermont law, defendants are not liable for harms caused when the plaintiff's negligence exceeds the defendant's. Here, the evidence introduced by both sides focused principally on liability, and the jury concluded that plaintiff and defendant were each 50% negligent. As reflected by the 50-50 verdict, the liability issue could not have been closer.

Second, the damages awarded—$0 for past and future pain and suffering and loss of enjoyment of life—were grossly inadequate given the evidence adduced at trial. This is not a case where plaintiff's injuries are de minimis or speculative, or where medical expenses were incurred only to rule out the possibility of injury. *Cf. Hunter v. Sorensen,* 201 Neb. 153 (1978) (affirming $0 pain-and-suffering verdict because "jury could have reasonably concluded that plaintiff suffered only a bruise to his knee as a result of the accident"); *Whitney v. Akers,* 247 F.Supp. 763 (W.D.Okla.1965) (upholding $0 pain-and-suffering verdict because physical injuries were minor and only medical expenses incurred were for examination to verify that no serious injuries were caused). Rather, plaintiff underwent invasive surgery involving "cutting her throat open" to reach the cervical discs that were herniated when she slipped in the hallway.

There was no dispute at trial over whether the surgery was reasonable and necessary, nor meant to remedy anything other than injuries sustained in the hallway slip and fall. Under these facts, a $0 pain-and-suffering award was grossly inadequate.

Finally, although there is no evidence of compromise apart from the verdict itself, we conclude that the inconsistencies in the verdict itself strongly suggest that it was a compromise. See *Stanton v. Astra Pharm. Prods., Inc.*, 718 F.2d 553 (3d Cir.1983) ("Inconsistent answers to the other special interrogatories further suggest that the verdict was a compromise."); *Hatfield v. Seaboard Air Line R.R.*, 396 F.2d 721 (5th Cir.1968) (jury responses to special interrogatories finding defendant liable for plaintiff's serious injuries but awarding nominal damages "can be seen only as the result of either a compromise on one of the liability issues or as an attempt to render a verdict for defendant with defendant paying the costs."). Because we cannot say on this record that the jury finally determined liability, the new trial must be on all issues.

Allen, J., dissenting in part.

In her original motion before the trial court, plaintiff moved, in the alternative, for an additur, and the plain language of V.R.C.P. 59(a) requires the court to offer one to defendant before a new trial is granted. This would be a fair result for both parties. If plaintiff elected not to seek a new trial and accepted the original jury verdict, she would be in the same position as if she had not appealed the verdict. Defendant would not be prejudiced by such a result in the sense that, notwithstanding its cross-appeal, it has not challenged the jury's finding of liability or the amount of damages awarded to plaintiff. On the other hand, if plaintiff elected to seek a new trial, defendant would have the opportunity to accept a reasonable additur imposed by the trial court in lieu of a new trial. For her part, plaintiff could appeal if she were not satisfied with the additur imposed by the court. This way, both parties could avoid the unwanted and unnecessary expense of going through another trial.

Notes and Questions

1. <u>What Happened</u>? First, how could the jury rationally reach the verdict it did? Second, what was the dissent's disagreement, and who should have done what to avoid it? Does the dissent's approach make sense? If so, on remand, what amount would you, as trial judge, believe was appropriate? As a lawyer for the plaintiff? As a lawyer for the defendant?

2. <u>Juries Minimize Damages to Compromise Liability</u>. Consider this from *Silva v. Mateo*, 2008 WL 2058711(Cal. Ct. App. May 15, 2008):

> When the jury fails to compensate plaintiff for the special damages indicated by the evidence, and despite the fact that his injuries have been painful, makes no award or allows only a trifling sum for his general damages,

the only reasonable conclusion is that the jurors compromised the issue of liability, and a new trial limited to the damages issue is improper. A contrary conclusion is justified only when the evidence of defendant's negligence is overwhelming. *See also Malcomson v. Pool*, 276 Cal.App.2d 378 (1969), (limited new trial order reversed; verdict was about $20 more than "medical specials" but included nothing for lost wages shown to exceed $5,000); *Lauren H. v. Kannappan* 96 Cal.App.4th 834 (2002) (order of a complete new trial affirmed; a compromise verdict was indicated by excessive special damages and zero general damages in case of severe injuries and conflicting evidence of liability).

Chapter 16

Contract-Specific Defenses

1. Reformation or Rescission

Fraudulent inducement can lead to rescission, as can mistake. Unlike fraudulent inducement, mistake does not lead to recovery of damages and fraudulent inducement does not permit reformation: reformation for mistake involves *affirming* the contract but asserting its terms should be changed because of a mistake, and so is inconsistent with fraudulent inducement, which seeks to avoid the contract.

A party fraudulently induced into a contract may seek to rescind it. Rescission is also available to a party who enters a contract by "mistake." Rescission seeks to put the parties in the position they were prior to the agreement. Reformation, in contrast, is sought where a party wants to affirm a contract but believes the contract does not accurately reflect their agreement because of a mistake. Thus, a plaintiff seeks to reform the agreement to express the parties' true intent. That effort runs into the parol evidence rule.

Faivre v. DEX Corp. N.E.
913 N.E.2d 1029 (Ct. App. Ohio 2009) (Klatt, J.)

[Plaintiff Patrick Faivre started as an executive with defendant DEX Corporation Northeast in April 2005. In September 2006, in a meeting with DEX executives and HR personnel, he was informed he was being terminated. As he left that meeting, DEX gave him a severance letter that DEX had already signed, stating it gave him three months' severance pay, through November 30, 2006. In fact, the letter stated he would receive his salary through November 30, 2007. Faivre noticed this later, and signed the agreement and mailed it to DEX's general counsel, who had signed it, Alan Kheel. When Kheel reviewed it, he realized the typographical error and immediately advised Faivre in writing that DEX did not accept the agreement and sent a replacement page with a 2006 date. Instead of accepting, Faivre filed suit, seeking a declaration, breach of contract damages, and asserting promissory estoppel. The trial court reformed the agreement to reflect a 2006 date. Faivre appealed.]

By his assignments of error, Faivre first argues that the parol-evidence rule bars the consideration of any evidence extrinsic to the severance agreement. The trial court relied upon such extrinsic evidence to determine that a unilateral mistake occurred. Faivre contends that the trial court erred in doing so. We disagree.

The parol-evidence rule is a substantive rule of law developed centuries ago to protect the integrity of written contracts. According to this rule, a writing intended by the parties to be a final embodiment of their agreement cannot be modified by evidence of earlier or contemporaneous agreements that might add to, vary, or contradict the writing. By prohibiting the introduction of extrinsic evidence to alter or supplement the parties' final, complete expression of their agreement, the parol-evidence rule ensures the stability, predictability, and enforceability of written contracts and effectuates a presumption that a subsequent written contract is of a higher nature than earlier statements, negotiations, or oral agreements.

Ohio courts have recognized certain exceptions to the parol-evidence rule. Among these exceptions is the allowance of extrinsic evidence to prove mistake. *Gen. Tire, Inc. v. Mehlfeldt* (1997), 118 Ohio App.3d 109 (holding that parol evidence "may be used to prove the existence of a mistake" and finding a unilateral mistake) ("*Mehlfeldt I*"). Because courts may consider parol evidence of a mistake, the trial court did not err in reviewing the extrinsic evidence that DEX offered to prove that it had made a unilateral mistake.

Moreover, Faivre cannot rely upon the integration clause in the severance agreement to bar parol-evidence of a mistake. The rule of contract integration is a corollary principle to the parol-evidence rule, as the degree of integration determines whether the parol-evidence rule applies to a contract. *Miller v. Lindsay-Green, Inc.*, 2005-Ohio-6366 ("A corollary principle to the parol evidence rule is the rule of contract integration, whereby the degree of finality and completeness of a contract determines whether the parol evidence rule is applicable"). Logically, then, when the parol-evidence rule does not apply, neither does the rule of contract integration. Therefore, the presence of an integration clause does not vitiate an established exception to the parol-evidence rule.

Next, Faivre argues that the trial court erred in finding that DEX made a unilateral mistake. We disagree.

A unilateral mistake occurs when only one party has an erroneous belief as to the facts. An erroneous belief as to the contents of a writing that expresses the parties' agreement is a mistake. Here, DEX primarily relied upon Kheel's affidavit testimony to establish that it had made a unilateral mistake. Kheel testified that, on behalf of DEX, he had offered Faivre three months of severance and gave Faivre a written severance agreement that he believed was consistent with the verbal offer. When Kheel later reviewed the severance agreement, he found a typographical error that in effect provided Faivre with 15 months — not three months — of severance. Like the trial court, we find that this evidence establishes that DEX had an erroneous belief as to the contents of the severance agreement. Because DEX was the only party to hold this erroneous belief, it committed a unilateral mistake.

Faivre, however, contends that Cuff, who he alleges drafted the severance agreement, meant to give him 15 months of severance. Based on this contention, Faivre argues that the severance agreement accurately reflects the terms that DEX wanted in the parties' contract. We find this argument unavailing. Nothing in the record reveals Cuff's true intent, much less establishes that she—as DEX's agent—purposefully offered Faivre 15 months of severance. Kheel, the only person to testify on DEX's behalf, unequivocally stated that the inclusion of "November 30, 2007" instead of "November 30, 2006" constituted a typographical error. Given Kheel's testimony, a trier of fact could only conclude that DEX mistakenly believed that the severance agreement actually stated "November 30, 2006." As it did not, DEX made a unilateral mistake.

Finally, Faivre argues that the trial court erred in granting DEX relief for its unilateral mistake. Although we agree with Faivre that the trial court erred in reforming the severance agreement, we ultimately conclude that the trial court properly granted DEX summary judgment on the basis of unilateral mistake.

Courts may use reformation to modify a written instrument so that the face of the writing reflects the actual intent of the parties. Generally, courts do not reform contracts when a party makes a unilateral mistake. However, where the mistake occurred due to a drafting error by one party and the other party knew of the error and took advantage of it, the trial court may reform the contract. Reformation is appropriate if one party believes that a contract correctly integrates the agreement and the other party is aware that it does not, even though the mistake was not mutual.

In the case at bar, the trial court found that DEX made a unilateral drafting error that Faivre discovered and used to his advantage. The trial court invoked its equitable power of reformation to modify the "Termination Date" stated in the severance agreement to November 30, 2006. In doing so, the trial court improperly employed reformation to create a new contract that included a term to which Faivre never agreed.

An action for reformation is not to create an obligation but to establish the content of the instrument as intended by the parties. *See also Amsbary v. Brumfield,* 177 Ohio App.3d 121 ("The purpose of reformation is not to make a new agreement but to give effect to the one actually made by the parties, which is not accurately reflected in the written agreement"). Thus, in order to reform a written contract, an underlying agreement between the parties must exist. The court then can reform the written contract so that it matches the terms of that underlying agreement. For example, in *L.B. Trucking,* an alleged oral agreement between the parties set the price of shot rock at $3.00 per ton, but the party that drafted the written contract mistakenly listed the price at $3.50 per ton. In that case, the trial court could reform the contract because the parties had reached an agreement (for $3.00 per ton) and reformation would allow the court to modify the written contract to mirror that underlying agreement.

Here, Faivre never agreed to three months of severance. Although DEX orally offered Faivre three months of severance during the September 6, 2006 meeting, Faivre left the meeting without accepting or rejecting that offer. Thus, the trial court's reformation of the severance agreement bound Faivre to a contractual term that he never accepted. In essence, the trial court created a new contract that reflected only DEX's intent. Because a court cannot use reformation to create new contractual obligations, we conclude that the trial court erred in reforming the severance agreement.

This conclusion, however, does not end our analysis. In its motion for summary judgment, DEX also argued that rescission was an appropriate remedy for its unilateral mistake. We agree.

A court may grant a rescission of a contract on the basis of a unilateral mistake. Ohio courts apply Section 153 of the Second Restatement of Contracts to determine whether to rescind a contract due to one party's mistake. According to that section,

> Where a mistake of one party at the time a contract was made as to a basic assumption on which he made the contract has a material effect on the agreed exchange of performances that is adverse to him, the contract is voidable by him if he does not bear the risk of the mistake under the rule stated in § 154, and
>
> > (a) the effect of the mistake is such that enforcement of the contract would be unconscionable, or
> >
> > (b) the other party had reason to know of the mistake or his fault caused the mistake.

Restatement (Second) of Contracts (1981). Thus, unless the mistaken party bears the risk of a mistake, a court may rescind a contract if (1) one party made a mistake at the time the parties executed the contract, (2) the mistake had a material effect on the agreed exchange of performances that was adverse to the mistaken party, and (3) the other party had reason to know of the mistake.

As we concluded above, DEX presented evidence establishing that it made a mistake when it drafted and executed the severance agreement. Moreover, no one disputes that DEX's mistake had a material effect on the scope and extent of the performance required of DEX. Instead of necessitating the payment of only three months of severance, the severance agreement, as drafted, mandated the payment of 15 months of severance.

Faivre, however, argues that DEX cannot avoid the severance agreement, because (1) he did not have reason to know of the mistake and (2) DEX bore the risk of the mistake. We find both arguments unavailing.

First, we conclude that Faivre's deposition testimony establishes that he had reason to know that the severance agreement contained a mistake. "A person has reason to know a fact if he has information from which a person of ordinary intelligence would infer that the fact in question does or will exist." Restatement (Second) of Contracts (1981), Section 19, Comment *b*. Faivre testified that, at the September 6, 2006 meeting, Kheel presented him with the severance agreement and reviewed the severance agreement with him. In the course of reviewing the severance agreement,

Kheel stated that DEX was offering Faivre only three months of severance. Kheel also said that Faivre's severance would continue through November. During his later, more thorough review of the severance agreement, Faivre realized that it indeed extended his severance through November, but November *2007*, not November *2006*. Faivre understood that a three-month period of severance would end on November 30, 2006, and that the severance agreement, as written, would entitle him to severance payments for 15 months. Given the discrepancy between the verbal offer and the severance agreement, as well as the character of the error (the difference between a "6" and "7"), Faivre had reason to know that a mistake had occurred.

Second, we conclude that DEX did not bear the risk of the mistake. Pursuant to Section 154 of the Second Restatement of Contracts:

A party bears the risk of a mistake when

(a) the risk is allocated to him by agreement of the parties, or

(b) he is aware, at the time the contract is made, that he has only limited knowledge with respect to the facts to which the mistake relates but treats his limited knowledge as sufficient, or

(c) the risk is allocated to him by the court on the ground that it is reasonable in the circumstances to do so.

Restatement (Second) of Contracts (1981).

Faivre does not advance any argument under subsection (b), and we do not believe that that subsection has any applicability to this case. Faivre, however, argues that DEX must bear the risk of the mistake because (1) it agreed to bear the risk in the integration clause and (2) DEX's negligence in drafting the severance agreement makes assigning the risk of the mistake to DEX reasonable.

Under subsection (a), a party accepts the risk of a mistake if it agrees "to perform in spite of mistake that would otherwise justify its avoidance." Here, nothing in the severance agreement provides that DEX will perform even if a mistake would warrant rescission. Faivre argues that DEX agreed to perform despite the mistake in the integration clause. However, the integration clause (if it applied) would only preclude evidence of a mistake; it does not indicate which party bears the risk of a mistake once a party proves that a mistake occurred.

Subsection (c) is a "catchall provision" that permits a court to allocate the risk of a mistake to the mistaken party if, under the totality of the circumstances, it would be more equitable or reasonable to do so. Here, Faivre contends that DEX should bear the risk of the mistake because its own negligence caused the typographical error. Again, we find Faivre's argument unpersuasive. A party's negligence is immaterial where the mistake is in the expression of the contract and the other party knew of the mistake and took advantage of it. As we concluded above, Faivre had reason to know that the severance agreement contained a typographical error. Instead of seeking clarification regarding the length of the severance period, Faivre attempted to take advantage of DEX's error. Therefore, equity and reasonableness do not require us to place the risk of the mistake on DEX due to its negligence.

Because DEX satisfied the requirements of Section 153 of the Second Restatement of Contracts, it is entitled to rescission of the severance agreement. Accordingly, we conclude that the trial court did not err in denying Faivre summary judgment or in granting DEX summary judgment. We, therefore, overrule Faivre's assignments of error.

For the foregoing reasons, we overrule Faivre's first and second assignments of error. However, because the trial court failed to grant DEX the appropriate relief, we reverse the judgment of the Franklin County Court of Common Pleas, and we remand this cause to that court. On remand, the trial court must grant DEX a rescission of the severance agreement and enter judgment in favor of DEX.

SCI Minn. Fun. Serv., Inc. v. Washburn-McReavy Fun. Corp.

795 N.W.2d 855 (Minn. 2011) (Gildea, J.)

[SCI owned many funeral businesses, including Crystal Lake Cemetery Association, which SCI wholly owned. In the late 1990s, Crystal Lake had acquired two vacant lots, one in Colorado and the other in Burnsville, Minnesota, which could be used as future cemeteries. In 2005, SCI placed several funeral homes and cemeteries on the market. One such business was Crystal Lake. Because Minnesota law prohibited sales of cemeteries for profit, the sale was made as one of Crystal Lake's stock, and under the parties' agreement SCI agreed to sell all of its shares of Crystal Lake to Corinthian Enterprises, LLC, who eventually sold the stock to Washburn-McReavy. None of the sales documents mentioned the two vacant lots, and no individual involved in negotiating any of the sales knew Crystal Lake owned the two lots. In 2007, SCI learned that Crystal Lake owned the Colorado lot, and SCI and Corinthian sued Washburn seeking equitable relief. During that suit, Washburn learned of the Minnesota lot. The trial court refused to reform or rescind any of the agreements to exclude from the sale the two lots, and SCI and Washburn appealed.]

We turn next to consideration of the district court's conclusion that rescission was not available to appellants in this case. Rescission is an equitable remedy. In general, a court may order an agreement rescinded if both parties were mistaken with respect to facts material to the agreement. Appellants argue that rescission is allowed on two grounds—mutual mistake and the absence of mutual assent. We address each argument in turn.

Appellants first argue that they are entitled to rescission based on mutual mistake. The district court relied on *Costello v. Sykes*, 143 Minn. 109 (1919), and held that appellants were not entitled to rescission. Appellants contend that *Costello* does not apply to this case because the subject matter of the agreements was the three cemeteries and not shares of Crystal Lake stock. Specifically, appellants argue that because the parties agreed to treat the stock sale as an asset transaction for tax purposes, this treatment provides evidence that the subject matter of the sale was the cemeteries and not the stock. Appellants also contend that because of the vast difference between what the parties actually transferred—three cemeteries and two vacant lots (valued at $3 million)—and what the parties intended to transfer—three cemeteries (valued at $1 million)—we should not apply *Costello*. Alternatively, appellants contend that we should overturn *Costello*.

In *Costello*, the plaintiff purchased 10 shares of stock in the Calhoun State Bank from the defendant shareholders. *Id.* At the time of the purchase, the parties to the transaction believed that the bank was capitalized, that its assets and liabilities were known, and that "the surplus and profits" stated in the books were accurate. *Id.* The parties were mistaken in all respects. Specifically, the parties to the sale were "mutually mistaken as to the assets of the bank, the actual value and the book value of its stock, and the amount of its surplus and undivided profits." *Id.* The parties were mistaken because employees of the bank, who had misappropriated bank funds, altered the bank's records to conceal their actions. Based on the mistakes, the plaintiff sued for rescission of the contract.

The question presented in the case was whether the mistake alleged is of such a character as to give rise to a right to rescind. We held that it was not. Specifically, we concluded that a sale of corporate stock may not be "rescinded merely because both parties were mistaken about the nature or extent of the assets or liabilities of the corporation" as long as the "means of information are open alike to both and there is no concealment of facts or imposition." *Id.* We reached this conclusion because the subject matter of the contract was the stock of the bank, and the purchaser received the shares of stock that he intended to buy. Under these circumstances, where the purchaser's complaint was only about the value of the shares, and "in the absence of fraud or inequitable conduct," rescission was not an available remedy. *Id.*

Costello bars rescission in this case. *Costello*, like this case, involved the sale of stock. The parties' intent, as reflected in their written agreement, was to transfer all of SCI's stock in Crystal Lake to Corinthian and then to Washburn. Even if there was a mistake as to the value of the transaction, as appellants contend, under *Costello* we do not look behind the form of the transaction when the mistake is one of value. As we said in *Costello*, "a mistake relating merely to the attributes, quality, or value of the subject of a sale does not warrant rescission." *Id.* We hold that under the rule of *Costello*, appellants are not entitled to rescission.

If we conclude, as we have, that *Costello* bars the rescission claim, appellants urge us to overrule *Costello*. Based on the principle of stare decisis, we are extremely reluctant to overrule our precedent and require a compelling reason to do so. Appellants contend that we should overrule *Costello* because under *Costello*, there could never be rescission in a stock sale transaction. We do not read *Costello* so broadly.

Contrary to appellants' argument, in *Costello* itself, we suggested situations where rescission might be possible even in a stock sale. We noted that rescission might be possible when the parties are mistaken about the actual existence or identity of the stock. For example, rescission might be available if the parties believe they are selling and purchasing shares of stock in Company X and instead, they are selling and purchasing shares of Company Y. We also noted that courts might grant rescission in the context of the sale of stock when there has been dishonesty by one of the parties. *Costello* therefore should not be read to bar rescission in all stock sale transactions, even though it operates to bar rescission in this case. . . .

In sum, appellants have not presented any compelling reason for us to depart from our established precedent. Under that precedent, we hold that rescission does not apply in this case.[6]

As an alternative to their mutual mistake argument, appellants argue that they are entitled to rescission due to a lack of mutual assent. Specifically, appellants contend there was no mutual assent between the parties when forming the stock sale agreement because there was only a "meeting of the minds" to sell, purchase, and transfer the cemeteries and not the vacant lots. The formation of sales contracts requires mutual assent among the parties involved in the transaction. Mutual assent entails a meeting of the minds concerning a contract's essential elements. Whether mutual assent exists is tested under an objective standard.

When viewed under an objective standard, there was mutual assent to sell the Crystal Lake stock. The stock sale agreement clearly stated that "SCI does hereby agree to sell, transfer, assign and deliver all of the issued and outstanding shares of capital stock of Crystal Lake which are owned by SCI." In the context of a stock sale agreement, the law presumes that all assets and liabilities transfer with the stock. When the undisputed evidence is examined under an objective standard, it establishes that mutual assent existed to sell the Crystal Lake stock, which included the vacant lots as part of the assets. We therefore hold that appellants are not entitled to rescission for lack of mutual assent.

We turn next to consideration of appellants' claim for reformation. Reformation is an equitable remedy that is available when a party seeks to alter or amend

---

6. Rather than rely on *Costello*, appellants urge that we apply the analysis from the Restatement (Second) of Contracts § 152 to assess the rescission claim. *See* Restatement (Second) of Contracts § 152 (1981) (explaining that "where a mistake of both parties at the time a contract was made as to a basic assumption on which the contract was made has a material effect on the agreed exchange of performances, the contract is voidable by the adversely affected party unless he bears the risk of the mistake under the rule stated in § 154"). Outside the stock sale context, we have relied on the Restatement's basic-assumption test in section 152 to examine claims for rescission based on mutual mistake. Even if we were to apply the basic-assumption test of section 152, the rescission claim would still fail. Under section 152, rescission is not available if the party "bears the risk of the mistake." Restatement (Second) of Contracts § 152. As discussed more fully below, because SCI had the opportunity to exclude property that was not utilized in the operation of Crystal Lakes' cemetery business, SCI bore the risk of any mistake here, and rescission is therefore not appropriate even assuming there had been a mutual mistake for purposes of assessing rescission under section 152. *See* Restatement (Second) Contracts § 154 cmt. B (1981) (stating that a party may "agree, by appropriate language or other manifestations, to perform in spite of mistake that would otherwise justify his avoidance").

language in a contract so that the contract reflects the parties' true intent when they entered into the contract. The court of appeals applied the rule from *Costello* to bar the reformation claim. Appellants contend that *Costello* was about rescission and that the case has no application to the reformation claim. Further, appellants argue that even if *Costello* applies, it does not control this case because the subject matter of the stock sale agreement was the cemeteries and not the stock itself. For its part, Washburn contends that *Costello* applies to the reformation claim because "the foundation for both reformation and rescission in this case is the alleged 'mutual mistake.'" Washburn therefore contends that, given our holding in *Costello*, appellants are not entitled to reformation because the subject matter of the stock sale agreement was all of the shares of Crystal Lake stock.

We agree with appellants that *Costello* is not determinative of the reformation claim. While it is true, as Washburn argues, that appellants' reformation and rescission claims are both grounded in mutual mistake, reformation and rescission are different forms of equitable relief. In reformation, a contract is modified to reflect the parties' true intent, whereas in rescission, the entire contract is voidable. When the relief seeks to void the entire contract, the additional analysis from *Costello*, which focuses on the form or subject matter of the transaction that the part seeks to undo (i.e., a stock sale), applies. But we have never used that additional analysis in the reformation context, where the relief does not seek to unwind the transaction but simply to modify it to reflect the parties' actual intention. We likewise decline to do so here.

Instead, we apply our precedent setting forth the elements a plaintiff must prove to establish a prima facie case of reformation. A party seeking reformation must prove that: (1) there was a valid agreement between the parties expressing their real intentions; (2) the written instrument failed to express the real intentions of the parties; and (3) this failure was due to a mutual mistake of the parties, or a unilateral mistake accompanied by fraud or inequitable conduct by the other party. The plaintiff must establish these elements through evidence which is clear and consistent, unequivocal and convincing. This is the quantum of proof appellants must demonstrate, and we have characterized this level of proof as a "high" burden.

We conclude that appellants have not met the requirements for reformation as a matter of law. Even if appellants had satisfied the first element, appellants did not demonstrate that the agreements failed to express the parties' true intentions, the second element, or that any such failure was due to a mutual mistake, the third element.

With respect to the second element, appellants contend that while the parties intended to transfer all of Crystal Lake's assets through the stock sale, the parties made a mutual mistake because the stock sale agreement did not exclude the vacant lots from the transactions, and therefore the agreement did not reflect the parties' true intentions. But the stock sale agreement gave SCI the right to exclude the vacant lots because these lots were not used in the cemetery business. Specifically, the language of the agreement provided that SCI "shall and may cause to be removed" from the Crystal Lake sale all assets owned by Crystal Lake that are "not utilized in or related to the operation of the Business in its present form." Under this provision, SCI removed certain assets, including computers and computer software, from the transaction. But SCI took no action to remove the vacant lots.

Appellants acknowledge that SCI could have excluded the vacant lots under this provision, but contend the provision is not dispositive because none of the parties was aware of the existence of the vacant lots. But under Minnesota law, when a business sells and transfers all of its stock, it is selling *all* of its assets and liabilities unless the business has expressed otherwise. *Cf. Specialized Tours, Inc. v. Hagen*, 392 N.W.2d 520 (Minn. 1986) ("When a business is sold through the transfer of assets, the assets alone pass to the buyer. When a business is sold through a stock transfer, the buyer assumes not only the assets of the corporation, but also the liabilities. This greater risk justifies greater protection for the stock purchaser."). Because SCI had the right to exclude the vacant lots under the plain terms of the stock sale agreement, as a matter of law appellants cannot prove that the agreement did not reflect the parties' true intention.

With respect to the third element necessary for reformation, appellants' claim also fails as a matter of law. The undisputed facts establish that appellants have not proven that the stock sale agreement failed to express the parties' true intentions because of a mutual mistake. Any mistake here regarding the vacant lots was SCI's mistake alone because it was SCI that failed to remove the lots from the transaction.

Appellants argue that SCI could not remove the lots because it was unaware of their existence. But under general corporate law principles, a corporation is charged with constructive knowledge of all material facts of which its officer or agent acquires knowledge while acting in the course of employment within the scope of his or her authority. Consequently, even though those who negotiated the deal for SCI may not have known about the vacant lots, those employees at SCI who purchased the vacant lots and paid the property taxes on them were aware of SCI's ownership (through its ownership of the Crystal Lake stock) of the vacant lots. There is no evidence in the record or any contention that the employees who purchased the vacant lots and paid the property taxes on the land were acting outside the scope of their employment when engaging in these activities. Accordingly, their knowledge is imputed to SCI generally.

Because someone at SCI was aware of the existence of the vacant lots, and Minnesota law imputes this knowledge to the entire company, SCI could have removed the vacant lots from the sale. SCI failed to do so, and therefore, any mistake was a unilateral mistake. A court cannot reform a contract based on a unilateral mistake unless there was some evidence of fraud or inequitable conduct. The district court did not find either type of conduct, and the parties do not challenge that conclusion. On this record, we hold that appellants have not met the third element necessary for reformation.

In sum, the undisputed evidence establishes that appellants cannot prove that the stock sale agreement failed to express the true intentions of the parties because of a mutual mistake. We therefore hold that appellants are not entitled to reformation.

2. Liquidated Damages Clauses

A party suing for the amount specified in a valid liquidated damages clause ("LDC") recovers that amount as its exclusive remedy instead of its actual damages. *East Brunswick Bd. of Ed. v. GCA Serv. Group, Inc.*, 2014 WL 438541 (D.N.J. Sep. 4, 2014). Although it is far more common for a party who breached a contract to contend the amount is too high, an aggrieved party can assert the amount is too low. The test for whether the clause is valid or an invalid "penalty" is the same.

A. Identifying Liquidated Damages Clauses

VICI Racing, LLC v. T-Mobile USA, Inc.

763 F.3d 273 (3[d] Cir. 2014) (Baylson, J.)

[VICI Racing LLC owned a sports car racing team, and T-Mobile USA, Inc., was its corporate sponsor. Their Sponsorship Agreement required VICI to field racing teams, and for the cars, uniforms, and other materials to show T-Mobile's logos. T-Mobile was required to pay the following to VICI: (a) 2009 Race Season: $1,000,000.00 payable by April 1, 2009; (b) 2010 Race Season: $7,000,000.00 payable by January 1, 2010; and (c) 2011 Race Season: $7,000,000.00 payable by January 1, 2011. A heading "Limitation of Liabilities" contained section 11.2, which stated in all capital letters: "[t]he maximum aggregate liability of either party and any of its affiliates to the other party, and the exclusive remedy available in connection with this agreement for any and all damages, injury, losses arising from any and all claims and/or causes of action, shall be limited to $20,000 or the aggregate payments payable under this agreement, whichever is higher."

T-Mobile did not pay the 2010 payment, and VICI sued. The trial court ordered T-Mobile to pay $7 million on summary judgment, and T-Mobile appealed. VICI filed a cross-appeal, seeking an additional $7 million pursuant to what it contends is a liquidated damages clause in the contract.]

T-Mobile claims that the District Court erred when it awarded $7 million to VICI based on T-Mobile's failure to make the 2010 payment. It argues that by awarding the full 2010 payment amount the District Court failed to properly apply the principles of expectation damages. VICI, in its cross-appeal, claims that the District Court erred when it declined to award $7 million for T-Mobile's failure to make the 2011 payment. VICI argues that section 11.2 of the Agreement is a liquidated damages clause that precludes the District Court from awarding anything other than

$14 million to VICI—that is, the total amount that T-Mobile failed to pay under the Agreement.

We first address VICI's contention that section 11.2 of the Sponsorship Agreement was a liquidated damages clause, for a finding in VICI's favor on this point would moot any further discussion of damages.

In Delaware, "contract law allows parties to establish only a good faith estimation of actual damages sustained as a result of a contract's termination." *Del. Bay Surgical Servs., P.C. v. Swier,* 900 A.2d 646 (Del. 2006). This good faith estimation is known as liquidated damages.

> Liquidated damages are a sum to which the parties to a contract have agreed, at the time of entering into the contract, as being payable to satisfy any loss or injury flowing from a breach of their contract. It is, in effect, the parties' best guess of the amount of injury that would be sustained in a contractual breach, a way of rendering certain and definite damages which would otherwise be uncertain or not easily susceptible of proof.

Id. To determine whether a contractual provision is one for liquidated damages, Delaware courts ask whether the provision unambiguously demonstrates the parties' intention to set a fixed amount to be paid in the event of breach. A term is ambiguous when the provision is reasonably or fairly susceptible of different interpretations or may have two or more different meanings.

Section 11 of the Agreement, entitled "Limitation of Liabilities," provides:

> 11.1 Even if either party has been advised of the possibility of damages, they will not be liable to the other party for any damages including without limitation: special, indirect, incidental, punitive, consequential, or treble damages; loss of privacy damages, personal injury or property damages; or *any damages whatsoever* resulting from the transactions contemplated under this agreement.
>
> 11.2 The *maximum* aggregate liability of either party and the *exclusive* remedy available in connection with this agreement for any and all damages, injury, losses arising from any and all claims and/or causes of action, shall be limited to *$50,000 or the aggregate payments payable under this agreement* [$14 million], whichever is *higher.*

We are not persuaded that section 11.2 is a liquidated damages clause. First, section 11's heading reads "Limitation of Liabilities," not "Liquidated Damages." Although a provision's heading is not dispositive to the analysis, the remainder of section 11.2 is replete with language that establishes that this clause is indeed a liability limitation provision. First, section 11.2 sets the "maximum aggregate liability" under the contract. Limiting the maximum liability does not set a fixed sum, as required under Delaware liquidated damages law; it merely erects a damages ceiling. Second, the provision states that any and all damages "shall be limited"—words that communicate an unmistakable intention to limit liability, not set a fixed sum. Finally, the payments contemplated by the provision also fail to set a fixed sum. Instead, it calls for a payment of $50,000 or the "aggregate payments payable under the agreement, whichever is higher."

The structure of the rest of the Agreement also supports the conclusion that section 11.2 was not intended to provide liquidated damages. A liquidated damages provision is permitted when the damages from a breach would otherwise be difficult to predict or calculate. The payment schedule set forth in section 4 of the Agreement, however, makes it clear what damages VICI could expect to incur in the event of a breach. Section 11's limitation-of-liability language, when read together with section 4, clearly sets the maximum possible damages available to VICI. Accordingly, it makes little sense to construe a clause to be a liquidated damages provision when damages are relatively easy to calculate by reference to the Agreement.

As VICI recognizes, section 11.2 does use the phrase "exclusive remedy," which could suggest that the provision contemplates a liquidated remedy. The better reading of those words, however, is that T-Mobile's liability is limited to paying $50,000 or the remainder owed under the contract, whichever is higher. As we have discussed, these payment possibilities essentially reiterate the expectations of the parties under the contract and thus do not provide for liquidated damages. Moreover, even if the words "exclusive remedy" would support a liquidated damages reading, the remainder of section 11.2 would be ambiguous at best. Under Delaware law, a liquidated damages clause must be unambiguous. We therefore affirm the District Court's judgment not to construe the Agreement to provide a liquidated damages remedy.

B. The Impact of Liquidated Damages Clauses on Monetary Remedies

Entergy Serv., Inc. v. Union Pacific Railroad Co.
35 F. Supp. 2d 746 (D. Neb. 1999) (Strom, J.)

[Union Pacific Railroad agreed in an "Interim Agreement" to regularly transport coal to power plants owned by Entergy Services, Inc., during specific time-cycles (i.e., to deliver the coal in large amounts during short windows of time, not small deliveries scattered about). The parties agreed that each month ESI would inform UP how much coal it needed, and UP would provide that amount of coal, but that any shortfalls could be made up within three months. The agreement contained a liquidated damages clause. UP failed to deliver coal as required by the contract. ESI filed suit, seeking, in addition to the amount stated in the liquidated damages clause, additional damages; UP asserted that the liquidated damages clause was the sole amount of actual damages available. Both parties moved for summary judgment, and and in this opinion, the district court agreed with ESI.]

UP had a duty to deliver coal and for each month in which deficits were not made-up, UP breached its duties under the contract. Accordingly, to that extent, the first part of plaintiff's motion for summary judgment will be granted.

UP seeks a determination that the liquidated damages clause in the Interim Agreement provides Entergy's sole remedy for UP's breach. Entergy seeks a ruling that its remedies for UP's breaches are not limited to recovery of liquidated damages.

A liquidated damages provision is generally not a limit on *remedies,* but instead provides an agreed-upon measure of *damages.* For example, it has been held that a "liquidated damages clause does not preclude other remedies available at law or equity, absent the clear intention of the parties to the contrary. There is no language in the Interim Agreement §8.B.5 indicating that liquidated damages are to be the sole remedy in the event of a breach. The liquidated damages clause of the Interim Agreement provides as follows:

> if, at the end of the succeeding calendar quarter Railroads have failed to make up all Deficit Tonnage to a Destination for reasons solely attributable to Railroad, *Railroads shall pay to Shipper,* in accordance with Section 15, *not as a penalty but as compensation for obtaining alternate fuel supply in the form of liquidated damages,* agreed upon as reasonable, a Deficit Service Payment for all remaining Deficit Tonnage to Newark, Arkansas and/or White Bluff, Arkansas, equal to 20% of the weighted average Agreement Rate.

(Emph. added). The liquidated damages provision contains no words of exclusivity indicating that it was intended to be the exclusive remedy for breach. In fact, §8.2.5 can be compared with the liquidated damages provision in the 1991 Interim Agreement implicated when Entergy fails to perform. This liquidated damages provision states that in the event the Shipper (i.e., Entergy) fails to perform, the Shipper shall pay "as compensation for lost traffic volumes or added service expenses in the form of liquidated damages, agreed upon as reasonable, *and intended by the parties to be in full settlement for Shipper's failure* to meet its Minimum Annual Volume Requirement." It is apparent from this provision that the parties clearly knew how to draft a liquidated damages provision which was intended to be in full settlement for a breach. In interpreting a contract, the whole context is to be considered even though the immediate object of inquiry is the meaning of an isolated clause. Thus, this liquidated damages clause does not preclude all other remedies available at law or equity to Entergy.

Although the liquidated damages provision is not Entergy's exclusive remedy, the provision precludes Entergy from seeking its actual monetary damages to a certain extent. The language of the liquidated damages clause in §8.B.5 provides that UP "shall" pay to Entergy liquidated damages. "A 'shall' provision for liquidated damages gives the party who does not breach the contract only one option: he can sue for specific performance, but he cannot sue for actual damages; the stipulated figure is the only option he has for damages." *McMaster v. McIlroy Bank,* 9 Ark.App. 124 (1983). The court in *McMaster* found that the word "shall" is contrary to using the word "may" which would give the non-breaching party the added option of suing for actual damages or for the liquidated damages amount. In another case, the court found that where the contract language used the word "shall," the non-breaching party was entitled only to the liquidated sum and not the actual amount of damages. *Hearrell v. Rogers*, 7 Ark.App. 230 (1983). *See also In re ATG Electronics, Inc.*, 1997 WL 563609 (Bankr. W.D. Tenn. 1997) (because the contract contained a provision for liquidated damages which used the word "shall" in the event of a breach, the non-breaching party was limited to that contractual term and was precluded from seeking actual damages). Thus, the liquidated damages provision prevents Entergy from arguing that it has the option of electing either the liquidated amount or the actual damages.

However, it is possible that a liquidated damages clause is exclusive as to one kind of harm, but that it does not cover other harms at all, as to which normal damages would be recoverable. In other words, a stipulated damages clause may address only one of several possible breaches. The liquidated damages provision at issue in this case provides that if UP fails to make up its Deficit Tonnage, UP shall pay liquidated damages to Entergy "not as a penalty but *as compensation for obtaining alternate fuel supply.*" (Interim Agreement § 8.B.5) (emp. added). The express language of this provision states that UP will pay the stipulated amount of liquidated damages for Entergy's cost of obtaining alternate fuel. Thus, Entergy cannot claim as actual damages the amount it spent to obtain alternate fuel supplies because this amount is covered by the liquidated damages provision.

The liquidated damages provision does not preclude Entergy from seeking any other damages which it may have sustained as a result of UP's failure to deliver coal. If Entergy can show that it incurred consequential damages which were not part of the cost of obtaining alternate fuel supplies, Entergy may be able to seek actual damages for these amounts.

Having determined that the liquidated damages clause does not provide Entergy's exclusive remedy, UP's motion for summary judgment is denied to the extent that it seeks to dismiss the case. However, as discussed above, Entergy is precluded from seeking actual damages directly relating to the cost of obtaining alternate fuel supplies.

Notes and Questions

1. <u>LDC?</u> Was the clause a liquidated damages clause or, instead, a limitation on liability for certain types of harm? Why does that matter for the analysis?

2. <u>Impact on Other Mitigation</u>. A party seeking damages in a liquidated damages clause has no duty to mitigate damages. *See Days Inn Worldwide, Inc. v. Hazard Mgmt. Group, Inc.*, 2012 WL 5519356 (S.D.N.Y. Nov. 13, 2012) (collecting cases). But, at the time of breach, the aggrieved party will have the incentive to reduce damages since it may not succeed in litigation and won't know for certain if the liquidated damages clause is enforceable. Does the rule discourage reasonable conduct? If the rule assumes the parties negotiated an amount that reflects mitigation, does a reasonable incentive still exist?

3. <u>Impact on Specific Performance</u>. If a clause expressly excludes specific performance, it is not available. On the other hand, a clause "that allows for liquidated

damages or specific performance, which are both equitable remedies, is valid." *E.g.,*
In re Polo Builders, Inc., 388 B.R. 338 (Bankr. N.D. Ill. 2008). If the clause is silent
or ambiguous, then whether specific performance is available instead of, or in addition to, the amount in the clause, turns on contract interpretation. *Dean V. Kruse*
Found., Inc. v. Gates, 973 N.E.2d 583 (Ct. App. Ind. 2012).

4. <u>Impact on Tortious Interference Damages</u>. The court in *Sulzer Carbomedics,*
Inc. v. Oregon Cardio-Devices, Inc., 257 F.3d 449 (5th Cir. 2001), explained why an
enforceable liquidated damages clause did not limit a contracting party's damages
for tortious interference:

> To allow [the tortiously interfering defendant] to enforce the limitation
> would undermine the aim of awarding damages for tortious interference,
> which is to place the injured party in the same economic position it would
> have been in had the contract not been breached. The district court cor-
> rectly noted that Texas law holds that although such damages are not recov-
> erable for breach of contract, a party found liable for tortious interference
> with a contract may be liable for, among other things, emotional distress or
> actual harm to reputation, if those injuries are reasonably to be expected
> to result from the interference. Thus, the measure of damages for breach
> of contract and tortious interference with a contract are not necessarily the
> same. In fact a claim for interference with contract is one in tort and dam-
> ages are not based on contract rules; therefore, it is not required that the
> loss incurred be one within the contemplation of the parties to the contract
> itself at the time the contract was made. The district court therefore did
> not err in determining that the limitation of liability provision in Carbo-
> medics's contract with Clark did not preclude St. Jude's liability for tortious
> interference.

C. Invalidating Liquidated Damages Clauses as Penalties

Barrie School v. Patch

933 A.2d 382 (Ct. App. Md. 2007) (Raker, J.)

[Andrew and Pamela Patch enrolled their daughter, Christiana, in The Barrie
School—a private, nonprofit Montessori school—for the 2004–2005 academic year.
The enrollment agreement they signed while paying a $1,000.00 non-refundable
deposit provided that if the Patches withdrew their daughter from enrollment after
May 31, 2004, they would pay the remaining tuition for the entire academic year
($13,490.00) as liquidated damages. They withdrew their daughter on July 14, 2004,
but refused to pay the remaining tuition. The Barrie School filed suit for breach of
contract, seeking the $13,490. The parents sought return of their $1,000 deposit.
The trial court held the LDC was valid, but that The Barrie School had no duty to
mitigate and, solely because it had failed to do so, denied The Barrie School any
recovery. The Barrie School appealed.]

Because respondents seek to set aside the bargained for contractual provision in the Agreement stipulating damages in the event of breach, respondents have the burden of proving that the clause should not be enforced. Placing the burden of proof on the challenger is consistent with giving the non-breaching party the advantage inherent in stipulated damages clauses, that of eliminating the need to prove damages, and with the general principle of Maryland law that assumes that bargains are enforceable and that the party asking the court to invalidate a bargain should demonstrate the justice of his or her view.

Despite their general propriety, a clause purporting to provide liquidated damages will be deemed invalid as a penalty where the amount agreed upon is grossly excessive and out of all proportion to the damages that might reasonably have been expected to result from such breach of the contract. As Professor Williston has noted, "a liquidated damages provision will be held to violate public policy, and hence will not be enforced, when it is intended to punish, or has the effect of punishing, a party for breaching the contract, or when there is a large disparity between the amount payable under the provision and the actual damages likely to be caused by a breach, so that it in effect seeks to coerce performance of the underlying agreement by penalizing non-performance and making a breach prohibitively and unreasonably costly." 24 RICHARD A. LORD, WILLISTON ON CONTRACTS § 65:1, at 216–23 (4th ed. 2002).

We have long recognized that one of the most difficult and perplexing inquiries encountered in the construction of written agreements is determining whether a contractual clause should be regarded as a valid and enforceable liquidated damages provision or as a penalty. Thus, if there is doubt whether a contract provides for liquidated damages or a penalty, the provision will be construed as a penalty.

Maryland courts will uphold a liquidated damages clause as valid, and not a penalty, if it satisfies two primary requirements. First, the clause must provide a fair estimate of potential damages at the time the parties entered into the contract. Second, the damages must have been incapable of estimation, or very difficult to estimate, at the time of contracting.

As we have indicated, in the absence of a statute providing otherwise, Maryland courts determine the validity of a liquidated damages clause by looking to the stipulated loss at the time of the contract's formation, and not actual losses resulting from breach.

In the case *sub judice,* the lower courts found correctly that § 3 of the Agreement was a valid liquidated damages clause and not a penalty. The sum in § 3 was a reasonable forecast of just compensation for potential harm caused by a breach of the Agreement. The damages contemplated in the Agreement were neither grossly excessive nor out of all proportion to those which might have been expected at the time of contracting. *See Lake Ridge Academy v. Carney,* 66 Ohio St.3d 376 (1993) (finding that a year's tuition constitutes a reasonable liquidated sum for breach of a school enrollment contract).

The actual damages resulting from breach would have been very difficult to estimate at the time of contracting as well. The Barrie School's Chief Financial Officer testified to this effect before the District Court, stating as follows:

> The budget's developed in November and December of the preceding year, and reviewed and approved in January of the preceding year. We determine the total number of expenses, faculty and otherwise, to instruct our students, and we then, because we're a non-profit and we try to have a balanced budget, we then determine what tuition level needs to be set, and the number of students to meet the revenue goal. So to parse out of that the effect of one student is very difficult.

As the Circuit Court noted, "it would be next to impossible to assign an exact amount as to the impact of losing one child for the school year." Section 3 of the Agreement constitutes a valid liquidated damages clause.

Respondents argue that there exists a duty to mitigate damages even in the face of a valid liquidated damages clause. Respondents would have us hold that there is such a duty because parties to a contract are required usually to minimize loss in the event of breach. In *Circuit City v. Rockville Pike*, 376 Md. 331 (2003), we addressed the concept of mitigation of damages, stating as follows:

> We have recognized generally that, when one party breaches a contract, the other party is required by the 'avoidable consequences' rule of damages to make all reasonable efforts to minimize the loss sustained from the breach and can charge the defending party only with such damages as, with reasonable endeavors and expense and without risk of additional substantial loss or injury, he could not prevent.

As we made clear mitigation of damages helps to determine the proper amount of damages resulting from a breach of contract. In other words, it is part of the law of court-assessed damages.

Liquidated damages differ fundamentally from mitigation of damages. While mitigation is part of a court's determination of actual damages that have resulted from a breach of contract, liquidated damages clauses are the remedy the parties to a contract have determined to be proper in the event of breach. Where the parties to a contract have included a reasonable sum that stipulates damages in the event of breach, that sum replaces any determination of actual loss. Professor Williston has explained this principle as follows:

> One purpose of a liquidated damages provision is to obviate the need for the nonbreaching party to prove actual damages. Thus, where the liquidated damages clause represents a reasonable attempt by the parties to agree in advance upon a sum that will compensate the nonbreacher for any harm caused by the breach, in lieu of the compensatory contract damage to which the nonbreacher would otherwise be entitled, the clause will be upheld.

LORD, *supra* § 65:1, at 230. It follows naturally that once a court has determined that a liquidated damages clause is valid, it need not make further inquiries as to actual damages. This includes a determination of whether the parties attempted to mitigate damages resulting from breach.

Judge Richard Posner of the United States Court of Appeals for the Seventh Circuit noted the distinction between liquidated damages and the duty to mitigate in *Lake River Corp. v. Carborundum Co.*, 769 F.2d 1284 (7th Cir. 1985). That case involved a shipping contract in which one party to the contract failed to fulfill the terms of the agreement after market prices shifted. Although the court found that the contractual clause at issue was invalid as a penalty, the court nonetheless explained the distinction between mitigation of damages and liquidated damages, stating as follows:

> Mitigation of damages is a doctrine of the law of court-assessed damages, while the point of a liquidated-damages clause is to substitute party assessment; and that point is blunted, and the certainty that liquidated-damages clauses are designed to give the process of assessing damages impaired, if a defendant can force the plaintiff to take less than the damages specified in the clause, on the ground that the plaintiff could have avoided some of them.

As Judge Posner noted in *Lake River*, the purpose of § 3 of the Agreement would be "blunted" if The Barrie School were required to mitigate damages. The parties to the Agreement determined that a certain sum would be paid in order to avoid the necessity of determining actual damages that might have resulted from breach. As a necessary conclusion, § 3 of the Agreement was a comprehensive sum that eliminated the need to calculate actual losses, including any mitigation of damages that might have occurred. Maryland's approach to liquidated damages supports this conclusion, as we view such clauses as "binding agreements *before the fact* which may not be altered to correspond to actual damages determined after the fact." *Heister*, 392 Md. at 156. Because mitigation of damages is part of a post-breach calculation of actual damages, in the absence of a statute mandating mitigation of damages, there exists no duty to mitigate damages where a valid liquidated damages clause exists.

Section 3 of the Agreement is a valid liquidated damages clause and not a penalty. Therefore, The Barrie School had no duty to mitigate damages and was entitled to the sum enumerated in § 3 of the Agreement.

Finally, in addition to arguing the duty to mitigate, respondents claim the defense of no-actual-harm. Respondents contend that because The Barrie School filled their daughter's space and actually enrolled more students than anticipated originally, the school suffered no harm from its breach of the Agreement. We reject this defense in this context. The same rationale we rely on in rejecting the duty to mitigate in the face of a valid liquidated damages provision applies to the no-actual-harm defense. Such a defense negates the benefit of an agreed-upon or stipulated damages clause and deviates from our acceptance of the principle that the time of contract formation is the appropriate point from which to judge the reasonableness of a stipulated amount of damages. It would also breed uncertainty in the calculation of damages, because if we were to accept the no-actual-harm defense, why would courts not then give greater damages than contemplated when the damages actually exceeded the stipulated amount?

Reversed and remanded.

Bell, C.J., dissenting.

Integral to the inquiry into the validity of a liquidated damages clause is determining whether the clause is fair and reasonable. The vantage point from which that determination is made is critical to, and may be dispositive of, that inquiry. The Majority maintains that "the time of the contract formation is the appropriate point from which to judge the reasonableness of a liquidated damages provision." Focusing exclusively on this "prospective view" leads the Majority to the conclusion it reaches.

There is another view, however. Because the validity of a liquidated damages does not become an issue until one of the parties breaches the contract to which it relates, it follows, logically, that the review of a liquidated damages clause to determine whether it is a penalty should include the effect of the breach, at the least, whether actual damage have been incurred. Commenting on this "retrospective view," the first Restatement of Contracts noted:

> If the parties to an agreement honestly but mistakenly suppose that a breach will cause harm that will be incapable or very difficult of accurate estimation, *when in fact the breach causes no harm at all or none that is incapable of accurate estimation without difficulty, their advance agreement fixing the amount to be paid as damages for the breach . . . is not enforceable.*

§ 339 at comment e (emphasis added). The second Restatement is to like effect, stating:

> Two factors combine in determining whether an amount of money fixed as damages is so unreasonably large as to be a penalty. The first factor is the anticipated *or actual loss* caused by the breach. The second factor is the difficulty of proof of loss. If the difficulty of proof of loss is great, considerable latitude is allowed in that approximation of anticipated or actual harm. If, on the other hand, the difficulty of proof of loss is slight, less latitude if allowed in that approximation. *If, to take an extreme case, it is clear that no loss at all has occurred, a provision fixing a substantial sum as damages is unenforceable.*

§ 356 at comment b (emph. added).

The viability of a liquidated damages clause, thus, does not depend solely on the fixed amount for which the parties contracted; rather, all of the surrounding circumstances are important, those existing at the time of contracting, as well as those existing at the time of the breach, and they include consideration of the actual damages sustained. *See Baybank Middlesex v. 1200 Beacon Props., Inc.*, 760 F.Supp. 957 (D. Mass. 1991) ("In order to determine whether the liquidated damages provision is valid, this Court must examine the reasonableness of the liquidated damages provision, *both retrospectively, and at the time the parties agreed to it.*") (emph. added);

Lake Ridge Academy v. Carney, 66 Ohio St.3d 376 (1993) ("When a stipulated damages provision is challenged, the court must step back and examine it in light of what the parties knew at the time the contract was formed and *in light of an estimate of the actual damages caused by the breach*.") (emph. added). This is, in my view, the only way in which to be completely fair to both parties.

To be sure, the School is entitled to compensation for any and all damages it suffered as a result of the contract breach. When, however, considered retrospectively, it is determined that the School's recovery will be excessive, the liquidated damages clause that provides for that recovery is invalid and unenforceable. That simply means that the School will have to prove its actual damages as it would in any breach of contract action and will be required, moreover, to mitigate its damages, if the circumstances make that appropriate. . . .

Notes and Questions

1. <u>Who Was Right</u>? The dissent argued that the majority failed to consider whether the school suffered any harm; but is the dissent's assumption that there was no harm correct? Does the majority conflate the question of actual damages with mitigation of damages? Put another way, did the parents' lawyer do a bad job in distinguishing between the fact that no harm had occurred rather than the harm that had occurred was because of the failure of the school to mitigate?

2. <u>Discovery</u>. Recall that most courts ask whether *at the time of contracting* damages were difficult to determine and, at that time, the amount agreed upon had been a reasonable forecast. The amount of actual damages may be relevant to both issues. Consider that the party seeking to show that a liquidated damages clause is unenforceable bears the burden to prove it, and so evidence of actual damages usually is discoverable. *Trilegiant Corp. v. Sitel Corp.*, 272 F.R.D. 360 (S.D.N.Y. 2010) ("Documents that show actual damages are relevant to the determination of the enforceability of the liquidated damages clause because they bear upon both an evaluation of possible loss at the time of contracting and the difficulty of determining actual damages.").

3. <u>What If the LDC Is Triggered by Even a Minor Breach</u>? An LDC that permits recovery for even a trivial breach likely is unenforceable. *See Slinski v. Bank of Am., N.A.*, 981 F. Supp. 2d 19 (D.D.C. 2013). As a result, an LDC should either state it applies only to "material" breaches or specify the provisions that trigger it. If the LDC does not do so, the trend is for courts to presume the parties intended it to be triggered only by a material breach. *Cummings Properties, LLC v. Nat'l Commun. Corp.*, 869 N.E. 2d 617 (Mass. 2007) (sophisticated parties).

4. <u>What If Parties Expressly Agree Damages Are Difficult to Determine</u>? As the *Barrie School* opinion notes, courts are not bound by a contract's characterization, though it is a "factor." *Dean V. Kruse Foundation, Inc. v. Gates*, 973 N.E.2d 583 (Ct. App. Ind. 2012).

5. <u>Attacking an LDC as Too Low</u>. A court noted "it was unaware of any case where a liquidated damages clause was found unenforceable because the damages provided were disproportionately low in relation to the actual damage incurred." *Slinski v. Bank of Am., N.A.*, 981 F. Supp. 2d 19 (D.D.C. 2013) (collecting cases). Think about why such cases are rare.

3. Other Contractual Limitations on Remedies and Invalidating Them

Contracts often exclude certain types of damages. However, the freedom to do so is not unbounded. Generally, two "defenses" to enforcement to contractual terms limiting damages may be raised: unconscionability and, in the context of sales of goods, "failure of essential purpose."

Unconscionability allows a court to refuse to enforce all or a part of a contract. "The determination that a contract or term is or is not unconscionable is made in the light of its setting, purpose and effect. Relevant factors include weaknesses in the contracting process like those involved in more specific rules as to contractual capacity, fraud, and other invalidating causes." Restatement (Second) of Contracts § 208, cmt. a. Unconscionability is narrow, generally available only if "inequality of the bargain is so manifest as to shock the judgment of a person of common sense, and where the terms are so oppressive that no reasonable person would make them on the one hand, and no honest and fair person would accept them on the other." *Berent v. CMH Homes, Inc.*, 466 S.W.3d 740 (Tenn. 2015). "An unconscionable contract is one in which the provisions are so one-sided, in view of all the facts and circumstances, that the contracting party is denied any opportunity for meaningful choice." *Id.* Thus, a party seeking to avoid enforcement of a contractual limitation on damages has a very difficult burden.

Hearbest, Inc. v. Adecco USA
2014 WL 7183478 (W.D. Pa. Dec. 16, 2014) (Kelly, J.)

[Plaintiff HearBest, Inc., provided hearing aids and services to the hearing impaired. It needed a temporary employee, and retained Adecco USA to identify candidates for the position. As part of that agreement, Adecco agreed to perform a national criminal record file check on all candidates. The contract also contained two clauses limiting liability. Adecco sent a candidate, McKinney, to HearBest. Unbeknownst to HearBest, McKinney had a criminal record, and no check was run, and she embezzled $16,000 from HearBest. HearBest sought $200,000 in damages for breach of contract. Adecco moved for summary judgment.]

HearBest seeks an award of damages in the amount of $200,000, sustained as a result of Adecco's failure to conduct the national criminal record file check before referring McKinney for employment. This amount represents the $16,000 embezzled, additional amounts HearBest contends it incurred as a result of McKinney's conduct in orchestrating a cover-up of her theft, costs related to retaining an accountant to examine and reconcile accounts after discovering the theft, costs related to fees paid to Adecco, and lost sales and expenses related to Medicare re-credentialing, which it contends would not have been required if McKinney did not gain employment by HearBest. Adecco seeks the entry of judgment in its favor as to certain of HearBest's claimed damages, which Adecco contends exceed an express limitation of damages clause.

The contract provides that "each party's liability under this Agreement; if any, is limited to direct damages and to the risks and responsibilities inherent in that party's business or activity." Elsewhere, the contract provides an "Associate Guarantee," which states: "if for any reason you are dissatisfied with an Associate's qualifications and notify Adecco within the first 8 hours of the assignment, you will not be charged for the hours worked by the Associate and Adecco will make reasonable efforts to provide a replacement. This guarantee is your sole remedy for dissatisfaction with an Associate's qualifications, performance or conduct." Not surprisingly, Adecco contends that this "guarantee" limits HearBest's recovery to McKinney's salary for eight hours. The Court rejects reliance upon the Associate Guarantee for a number of reasons.

First, in unambiguous language, the Terms and Conditions of the contract broadly assume liability for "direct damages" and the "risks and responsibilities inherent in [Adecco's] business or activity." This assumption of liability conflicts with the nominal damages afforded by the "Associate Guarantee."

Pennsylvania law provides that contracts are best read as a whole and clauses seemingly in conflict should be construed, if possible, as consistent with one another. Terms in one section of the contract should not be interpreted in a manner which nullifies other terms. Reconciling the "Associate Guarantee" in light of the much broader acceptance of liability for breach does not require a far reach. The Associate Guarantee is triggered upon performance of Adecco's primary obligation to perform a national criminal record file check before referring McKinney as an "Associate." Once a properly vetted candidate is referred, the agreement provides the employing party eight hours to determine if the candidate is qualified for the assignment. Here, however, given Adecco's undisclosed and willful failure to perform the promised criminal background check when it supplied McKinney, the Associate Guarantee is not triggered. Instead, giving meaning to the broader and unambiguous liability clause, Adecco is liable for all "direct damages and to the risks and responsibilities inherent in its business or activity." This interpretation harmonizes and gives effect to all of contract provisions.

Second, while it is true that contractual limitations on remedies and damages are enforceable under Pennsylvania law, resort to such clauses is not unlimited. As discerned by the United States Court of Appeals for the Third Circuit in *Valhal Corp. v.*

Sullivan Associates, Inc., 44 F.3d 195 (3d Cir. 1995), the Pennsylvania Supreme Court has held that a willful or malicious omission under a contract will render a limitation of liability unenforceable:

> For example, in *Behrend v. Bell Tel. Co.,* 242 Pa.Super. 47 (1976), (*Behrend I*), a business subscriber sued a telephone company for lost profits because the telephone company omitted the subscriber's paid Yellow Pages advertisement. The advertising contract contained a provision limiting the telephone company's liability for an advertising omission to the monthly charge for each month omitted. The court stated that the issue was one of first impression, but concluded "we elect to join the majority of jurisdictions in upholding tariff limitations." The court then cautioned: "however, the limitation in the tariff is not enforceable if the damage is caused by willful or wanton conduct by Bell. The weight of authority supports interpreting the tariff limitations to extend only to acts of ordinary negligence and exclude conduct found to be willful, malicious or reckless." *Behrend,* 363 A.2d at 1166. The court then ordered that the matter be remanded to determine if the omission was willful or malicious. "If appellant Bell's acts are found not to be willful or malicious, damages must be limited to a maximum of the amount specified in the limitation in the applicable tariff provision." *Id.*

The Court of Appeals further observed that while limitation of liability clauses "are a way of allocating 'unknown or undeterminable risks,' "damage caps will not be enforced where they are unreasonable or "so drastic as to remove the incentive to perform with due care." *Id.* In *Valhal,* the Court of Appeals found that a limit of liability of $50,000 was not so nominal "as to negate or drastically minimize the breaching party's concern for the consequences of a breach of its contractual obligations." *Id.*

In this case, however, it is clear that Adecco accepted a substantial payment for its "standard pricing," to include a national criminal background check it knew it would not conduct. Thus, a limitation of liability to McKinney's salary for eight hours not only minimizes Adecco's concern for the consequences of its anticipatory breach, but it also serves to reward Adecco for nonperformance of its contractual obligations. Under these circumstances, Pennsylvania law would not give effect to the "Associate Guarantee."

Tokyo Ohka Kogyo Am., Inc. v. Huntsman Propylene Oxide LLC

35 F. Supp. 3d 1316 (D. Or. 2014) (Simon, J.)

[Plaintiff Tokyo Ohka Kogyo America, Inc. ("TOK"), made chemicals used to manufacture semiconductors. Pertinent here, it mixed propylene glycol ("PG") with other chemicals to create a mixture that TOK then sold to its semiconductor manufacturing customers. It had been purchasing PG from a supplier who, in turn, purchased it from Huntsman Propylene Oxide LLC.

TOK wanted to cut out the middleman and purchase directly from Huntsman. In response to TOK's inquiry, Huntsman asked TOK to submit a credit application. A one-page document titled "Huntsman General Terms and Conditions of Sale" ("Huntsman General Terms") was attached to the Credit Application signed by TOK. Immediately above the line for TOK's signature, the Credit Application stated:

> THE SIGNATORY BELOW HEREBY ATTESTS APPLICANT'S FINAN-CIAL RESPONSIBILITY, ABILITY AND AGREEMENT TO PAY ALL SUMS PROPERLY DUE AND OWING PURSUANT TO HUNTSMAN INVOICES. IN CONSIDERATION FOR HUNTSMAN'S AGREEMENT TO EVALUATE APPLICANT'S CREDITWORTHINESS, APPLICANT HEREBY ACKNOWLEDGES RECEIPT OF AND AGREES THAT ANY PURCHASE BY APPLICANT OF HUNTMAN [*sic*] PRODUCTS WILL BE MADE PURSUANT TO THE GENERAL TERMS AND CONDITIONS GOVERNING SALE ATTACHED HERETO.

> THE ABOVE INFORMATION IS PROVIDED BY APPLICANT FOR THE PURPOSES OF OBTAINING CREDIT AND IS WARRANTED TO BE TRUE, CORRECT AND COMPLETE. APPLICANT HEREBY AUTHO-RIZES HUNTSMAN TO INVESTIGATE THE INFORMATION AND TRADE AND BANK REFERENCES LISTED ABOVE PERTAINING TO APPLICANT'S CREDIT AND FINANCIAL RESPONSIBILITY. ALL DECI-SIONS MADE BY HUNTSMAN WITH RESPECT TO THE EXTENSION, CONTINUATION OR DISCONTINUATION OF CREDIT TO APPLI-CANT SHALL BE MADE PURSUANT TO HUNTSMAN'S DISCRETION.

The Huntsman General Terms include a limitation of liability clause ("Limitation Clause"):

> LIMITATION OF LIABILITY. Seller's maximum liability for any breach of this Agreement, or any other claim related to the Product, shall be limited to the purchase price of the Product or portion thereof (as such price is set forth on the first page of Seller's invoice) to which such breach or claim pertains. IN NO EVENT SHALL SELLER BE LIABLE FOR ANY CON-SEQUENTIAL, INCIDENTAL, SPECIAL OR PUNITIVE DAMAGES, INCLUDING BUT NOT LIMITED TO ANY DAMAGES FOR LOST PROF-ITS OR BUSINESS OPPORTUNITIES OR DAMAGE TO REPUTATION.

After Huntsman approved TOK's credit application, TOK informed Huntsman that it would mix Huntsman's PG with other chemicals to sell to semiconductor makers. TOK informed Huntsman that the PG had to meet both TOK's and its Customers' approval process, which included product and process specifications and inspection and approval of the Huntsman plant.

TOK began to purchase PG in August 2008. Because of the precise and demand-ing nature of TOK's customer's manufacturing needs and processes, the customer insisted on the right to approve all suppliers, vendors, chemicals, and components involved in its supply chain. TOK and Huntsman engaged in lengthy negotiations regarding PG specifications, and TOK worked to get Huntsman approved by the customer. In June 2010, TOK inspected and audited Huntsman's manufacturing plant. In August 2010, TOK and Huntsman agreed to an initial written procurement specification for the manufacture and sale of PG from Huntsman to TOK. As part of this agreement, Huntsman was required to notify TOK of any changes to its process.

Things went well for a while, but then in late 2012 the customer reported to TOK that semiconductor wafers were demonstrating defects well above acceptable levels. The three worked together to identify the specific issue and concluded that the PG was the problem. TOK then learned that Huntsman had modified its process without notice, and the modification caused the problems.

TOK sued Huntsman. Each moved for summary judgment on the issue of whether the limitation on liability on the credit application applied and so precluded recovery of most of TOK's damages. This is the court's opinion.]

Section 2-719 of the UCC establishes that parties may agree to limit the measure of damages available for a breach of contract and may limit the available remedies, subject to certain conditions. This section provides:

(1) Subject to the provisions of subsections (2) and (3) of this section and of the preceding section on liquidation and limitation of damages,

(a) the agreement may provide for remedies in addition to or in substitution for those provided in this Article and may limit or alter the measure of damages recoverable under this Article, as by limiting the buyer's remedies to return of the goods and repayment of the price or to repair and replacement of non-conforming goods or parts; and

(b) resort to a remedy as provided is optional unless the remedy is expressly agreed to be exclusive, in which case it is the sole remedy.

(2) Where circumstances cause an exclusive or limited remedy to fail of its essential purpose, remedy may be had as provided in this Act.

(3) Consequential damages may be limited or excluded unless the limitation or exclusion is unconscionable. Limitation of consequential damages for injury to the person in the case of consumer goods is prima facie unconscionable but limitation of damages where the loss is commercial is not.

U.C.C. § 2-719. The official comments to this provision further clarify the ability of parties to limit remedies and the check on that ability created by Section 2-719(2)–(3), stating:

1. Under this section parties are left free to shape their remedies to their particular requirements and reasonable agreements limiting or modifying remedies are to be given effect. However, it is of the very essence of a sales contract that at least minimum adequate remedies be available. If the parties intend to conclude a contract for sale within this Article they must accept the legal consequence that there be at least a fair quantum

of remedy for breach of the obligations or duties outlined in the contract. Thus any clause purporting to modify or limit the remedial provisions of this Article in an unconscionable manner is subject to deletion and in that event the remedies made available by this Article are applicable as if the stricken clause had never existed. Similarly, under subsection (2), where an apparently fair and reasonable clause because of circumstances fails in its purpose or operates to deprive either party of the substantial value of the bargain, it must give way to the general remedy provisions of this Article.

2. Subsection (1)(b) creates a presumption that clauses prescribing remedies are cumulative rather than exclusive. If the parties intend the term to describe the sole remedy under the contract, this must be clearly expressed.

3. Subsection (3) recognizes the validity of clauses limiting or excluding consequential damages but makes it clear that they may not operate in an unconscionable manner. Actually such terms are merely an allocation of unknown or undeterminable risks. The seller in all cases is free to disclaim warranties in the manner provided in Section 2-316.

In addition, courts have explained Section 2-719(2) in the following terms:

The exclusive remedy provision is not concerned with arrangements which were oppressive at their inception, but rather with the application of an agreement to novel circumstances not contemplated by the parties. Although an arm's length contract between sophisticated commercial parties, such as in this case, should not be readily upset by a court, where a party is deprived of the substantial value of its bargain by reason of the exclusive remedy, the contract remedy will give way to the general remedy provisions of the U.C.C.

Viking Yacht Co. v. Composites One LLC, 2007 WL 2746713 (D.N.J. Sept. 18, 2007) (*"Viking I"*), *aff'd,* 385 Fed.Appx. 195 (3d Cir. 2010) (*"Viking II"*).

Courts struggle with defining what it means for a limited remedy to "fail of its essential purpose." Conceptually, cases invoking Section 2-719(2) are more easily analyzed when they involve a repair-or-replace remedy for a specific product, because it can more readily be determined that the product is not as promised, has not been sufficiently repaired or replaced, and thus the remedy has failed of its purpose. The analysis is more nuanced when a refund remedy is at issue, although courts have found that a refund remedy can also fail of its essential purpose, such as when a seller conceals relevant facts or there is a latent defect.

Comment 1 to Section 2-719 offers guidance on how to analyze whether a remedy limitation fails in its essential purpose. Understanding that the word "its" refers to the remedy limitation, Comment 1 instructs that when a limitation "fails in its purpose or *operates to deprive either party of the substantial value of the bargain,* it must give way to the general remedy provisions of this Article." (emph. added). Courts analyzing whether limiting a remedy to a refund of the purchase price fails of its essential purpose generally focus on the requirement that a party should not be deprived of "the substantial value of the bargain" as opposed to otherwise defining what it means for a limitation to fail in its purpose. Additionally, many courts note that if a case involves a latent defect that is not discoverable upon reasonable inspection, then a limitation, including a limitation to a refund of the purchase price, necessarily fails of its essential purpose.

The determination under Section 7-219(2) of whether "circumstances have caused an exclusive or limited remedy to fail of its essential purpose" or whether the limitation has "operated to deprive either party of the substantial benefit of the bargain" requires consideration of the bargain made at the time the contract was entered into and whether, after breach and based on the circumstances of the breach, the limitation is operating to deprive either party of that bargain. A court should attempt to discern the essential purpose of the exclusive or limited remedy when it was first agreed-upon by the parties—the bargain of the parties with respect to their allocation of risks and remedies. *See Held v. Mitsubishi Aircraft Int'l,* 672 F.Supp. 369 (D. Minn. 1987) (noting that a court should "first determine what the bargain was before deciding whether any party has been deprived of it") (citing Jonathan A. Eddy, *On the "Essential" Purposes of Limited Remedies: The Metaphysics of UCC Section 2-719(2),* 65 Cal. L.Rev. 28 (1977) (hereinafter "Eddy, *Metaphysics* ")). The Court should not concern itself, at least under Section 7-219(2), with whether the agreed-upon limitation on remedy was wise, fair, or oppressive at the time of contract formation, but simply ask what was the limitation's essential purpose at that time.

A court must also focus on the circumstances surrounding the alleged breach of contract and resulting harm to discern whether the harm is one caused by novel circumstances not contemplated by the parties and involved a risk not allocated by the parties. *See Viking I,* 2007 WL 2746713 ("The exclusive remedy provision is not concerned with arrangements which were oppressive at their inception, but rather with the application of an agreement to novel circumstances not contemplated by the parties."). Where the circumstances involved were foreseeable by the parties, at least as a possibility, and the risk was allocated, the limitation on remedy properly can be seen to reflect the parties' agreed-upon allocation of anticipated risks. Where the circumstances surrounding the alleged breach of contract and resulting harm were not part of the bargained-for allocation of risk, then one party has been deprived of the substantial value of its bargain, the limitation on remedy fails of its essential purpose, and Section 7-219(2) operates to void that limitation.

This case involves a latent defect that was not discoverable upon reasonable inspection. The mere existence of such a latent defect, however, does not end the Court's analysis. It may be that the parties bargained for an allocation of risk relating to latent defects. Accordingly, the Court looks to the bargain between the parties, including determining the bargained-for allocation of risk and whether it included allocating the risk for the type breach committed by Huntsman and the type of latent defect that occurred. *See Held,* 672 F.Supp. at 382 ("The crucial question is whether the parties were knowingly allocating risks of latent or undiscoverable design defects to the purchaser after the expiration of the warranty period, or whether the eventuality of a design defect represents novel circumstances not contemplated by the parties.").

There is no evidence that in June 2008, when TOK signed the Credit Application, incorporating by reference the Huntsman General Terms, the parties consciously intended that the Limitation Clause would allocate the risk to TOK of an undiscoverable defect caused by Huntsman's breach of its obligation timely to notify TOK of any change in Huntsman's manufacturing process. To the contrary, this type of allocation could not possibly have been intended at that time because Huntsman's obligation to notify TOK of any change in the manufacturing process did not even arise until the 2010 specification contract. Additionally, during the two years that the parties engaged in testing and incremental orders and during the negotiations for the 2010 and 2011 specification contracts, the Limitation Clause was never mentioned.

The facts here are on point with the "extreme case of imbalance between the parties' relative ability to avoid the specific risk in issue" discussed at length in Eddy, *Metaphysics, supra,* at 57, in addressing the *Neville Chemical* case. TOK, like Neville Chemical, "very conscious of bearing the risk of nonconforming goods, appropriately limited its exposure by a slow process of testing and incremental orders. Only after the completion of a thorough risk assessment did" TOK agree to larger volume purchases. Eddy, *Metaphysics* at 55. Additionally, as in *Neville Chemical,* if the PG, "with no change in its composition, later proved defective, [TOK] alone would have borne the risk." *Id.* The Court agrees with Professor Eddy's conclusion that "the risk that the contract did not place upon purchaser, however, was that seller would change its production process without notice, potentially rendering purchaser's extensive testing useless." *Id.* at 56. Notably, the facts in this case are more compelling than those in *Neville Chemical* analyzed by Eddy, because Eddy only inferred from the contract in that case that Union Carbide should have provided notice to Neville Chemical if it changed its manufacturing process, whereas in this case there is an express contractual provision requiring Huntsman to notify TOK if Huntsman changes its manufacturing process.

The parties stipulate that they have entered into multiple agreements and that there are multiple documents that relate to the manufacture and sale of the PG by Huntsman to TOK, including the Credit Application, purchase orders sent by TOK, invoices sent by Huntsman, and the 2010 and 2011 technical specification contracts. These documents show that the bargain of the parties included the following allocations of risk: (1) TOK assumes the risk if there is no change in the manufacturing process, the PG complies with TOK's technical specifications, and the Customer's product later fails; (2) TOK assumes the risk if there is no change in the manufacturing process, the PG fails to comply with TOK's technical specifications, TOK still uses the PG in the mixture, and the Customer's product later fails; (3) TOK assumes the risk of losing some of its purchase price if the PG does not comply with TOK's technical specifications and TOK returns the PG to Huntsman, because TOK is only entitled to whatever amount Huntsman obtains in reselling the PG; (4) TOK assumes the risk if Huntsman timely discloses any change in its manufacturing process, TOK uses the PG, and the Customer's product later fails; but (5) TOK does *not* assume the risks created by Huntsman failing timely to disclose a change in its manufacturing process because this information is within the sole knowledge of Huntsman and TOK has no way of discovering any latent defects caused by a change in Huntsman's manufacturing process, thereby rendering the two years of testing useless. Such a breach was a novel circumstance not contemplated by the parties in 2008 when TOK signed the Credit Application.

There is a debate both in the case law and in the academic commentary about whether a seller's "good faith" is relevant to the analysis under Section 2-719(2). Many courts have concluded that a seller's good faith and due care will not be sufficient to save a limitation on remedy that otherwise fails of its essential purpose. Few courts, however, ask whether a seller's "bad faith" is relevant to this analysis. In comparison, however, some courts have held that a buyer's misbehavior, such as conduct that deprives the seller of the chance to repair or replace a nonconforming product or conduct in which a buyer has made unauthorized modifications to a product before asking the seller to make repair, is relevant to whether a limited remedy fails of its essential purpose. By the same reasoning, it would not be inappropriate to consider a seller's misbehavior in deciding whether a limited remedy fails of its essential purpose. Here, TOK was willing to assume certain inherent risks in accepting Huntsman's PG, and the parties did not agree that Huntsman would be a guarantor for the success of TOK's efforts. There is no indication, however, that TOK was willing to assume the risk of Huntsman's misbehavior, (indeed, Huntsman's arguable "bad faith") in intentionally failing to comply with its contractual obligation timely to inform TOK of changes in Huntsman's manufacturing process, of which only Huntsman could be aware and control.

Because the Court finds that TOK and Huntsman did not allocate to TOK the risk of an unknown, latent defect caused by Huntsman's breach of its obligation timely to notify TOK of a change in manufacturing, the Court also finds persuasive the reasoning of cases that find that refund-only remedies fail of their essential purpose when there are latent defects that were only discovered after the defective product was either integrated into something else or was otherwise put to use in a way that rendered it non-returnable, thus resulting in significantly greater damages than the original purchase price.

Parties may allocate the risk of an unknown latent defect on a buyer and limit damages, even when the limitation results in an inadequate remedy. Such a limitation is, however, subject to the requirements of UCC Section 2-719 that the remedy not fail of its essential purpose and that the limitation not operate in an unconscionable manner.

As discussed above, in this case there is no evidence that TOK and Huntsman intended to allocate the risk to TOK of a latent defect caused by Huntsman's breach of its obligation timely to notify TOK of any manufacturing process change. The evidence is that TOK was not aware of the Limitation Clause and intended and agreed to the limited remedy of a return of the purchase price, or even less than the purchase price, for nonconforming goods because TOK could test the delivered PG to ensure that it conformed to TOK's technical specifications and return nonconforming goods before using them. TOK attempted to reduce the risk of undetectable defects in the PG by taking two years to ensure that the PG and Huntsman's manufacturing process resulted in a workable chemical mixture and by requiring Huntsman timely to notify TOK of any change in Huntsman's manufacturing process. As in *Viking I* the undetectable defect, caused by information solely in Huntsman's possession and avoidable solely by Huntsman, resulted in significantly greater damages than the purchase price of the PG. These damages include transporting the defective PG and defective chemical mixture, the cost of the chemicals that were mixed with the defective PG and rendered unusable, and the cost of the hazardous waste disposal of the defective chemical mixture. Limiting TOK to damages of only the purchase price of the PG does not provide a "fair quantum of remedy" for Huntsman's breach of its obligation timely to notify TOK of any manufacturing change of which only Huntsman would be aware.

Whether a limitation fails of its essential purpose is generally an issue of fact for the jury. Here, however, the parties have stipulated to certain facts, and these facts establish as a matter of law that the Limitation Clause fails of its essential purpose under the circumstances presented because it deprives TOK of the substantial value of both its bargain regarding risk allocation and its bargain obligating Huntsman timely to notify TOK of any change in Huntsman's manufacturing process. Accordingly, the Court finds that the Limitation Clause fails of its essential purpose and grants TOK's motion for partial summary judgment on the issue that the limitation to a remedy of only the purchase price of the PG is unenforceable.

In addition to limiting TOK's remedies for a breach of contract by Huntsman to only the purchase price of the PG, the Limitation Clause also contains a limitation avoiding consequential and incidental damages. TOK asserts that the limitation barring consequential and incidental damages automatically fails because the exclusive purchase price remedy fails of its essential purpose, and, in the alternative, fails because the damages limitation is unconscionable. Deciding whether a damages limitation is unconscionable is an issue of law for the Court, and the burden of proof is on the party alleging unconscionability.

Courts are divided as to whether a limitation on consequential damages is automatically unenforceable when an exclusive remedy limitation is found to fail of its essential purpose. Many courts find that if the remedy limitation fails of its essential purpose then the buyer may receive any remedy available under the UCC, including consequential damages, notwithstanding that consequential damages also may have been specifically excluded under the contract. Other courts, however, find that a contractual waiver of consequential damages, particularly if it is in a separate clause from the exclusive remedy limitation, survives a remedy limitation failing of its essential purpose and requires a separate analysis of unconscionability. Finally, some courts take a case-by-case approach and look at the circumstances in the particular case to determine whether the exclusive remedy and damage exclusions are separable elements of risk allocation or 'inseparable parts of a unitary package of risk-allocation.

Neither Oregon nor Texas state courts have addressed the issue of whether when an exclusive remedy provision fails of its essential purpose a consequential damages exclusion also necessarily fails. The Court, however, need not reach the issue of whether Texas or Oregon would find that a consequential damages limitation automatically fails if an exclusive remedy provision fails of its essential purpose because the Court finds that under the circumstances of this case, the consequential damages limitation operates in an unconscionable manner and is unenforceable, even if it survives the exclusive remedy provision failing of its essential purpose and is analyzed independently.

Most cases analyze unconscionability under UCC Section 2-302, which expressly involves unconscionability of a contract "at the time it was made." U.C.C. § 2-302(1). UCC Section 2-719(3), however, does not include the specific language included in Section 2-302 that unconscionability under 2-719(3) be at the time the contract was made. To the contrary, Section 2-719(3) "makes it clear that clauses limiting consequential damages may not *operate* in an unconscionable manner." U.C.C. § 2-719 cmt. 3. A provision does not "operate" in an unconscionable manner at the time of formation. Thus, for purposes of analyzing unconscionability under Section 2-719(3), the Court is not limited to evaluating the provision at the time the contract was made, but must consider how the provision operated and evaluate the provision after the contract has been breached.

Under both Texas and Oregon law, an agreement may be procedurally or substantively unconscionable. Generally speaking, procedural unconscionability refers to the circumstances surrounding the adoption of the provision at issue and substantive unconscionability concerns the fundamental fairness of the provision itself.

Under Oregon law, procedural unconscionability focuses on the factors of oppression and surprise. Oregon courts explain these factors as:

> Oppression exists when there is inequality in bargaining power between the parties, resulting in no real opportunity to negotiate the terms of the contract and the absence of meaningful choice. Surprise involves the question whether the allegedly unconscionable terms were hidden from the party seeking to avoid them.

Livingston v. Metro. Pediatrics, LLC, 234 Or.App. 137 (2010). Procedural unconscionability may also involve deception, compulsion, or genuine lack of consent.

Under Texas law, procedural unconscionability is similarly analyzed, with courts considering factors such as:

> (1) the presence of deception, overreaching, and sharp business practices by part of the stronger party; (2) the absence of a viable alternative; (3) the

relative acumen, knowledge, education, and financial ability of the parties involved; (4) knowledge of the stronger party that the weaker party will be unable to receive substantial benefits from the contract; and (5) knowledge of the stronger party that the weaker party is unable reasonably to protect his interests.

U.S. v. Reed, 2014 WL 462620 (N.D.Tex. Feb. 5, 2014). A court must consider all of the circumstances surrounding the formation of the contract with respect to the allegedly unconscionable provision, including the parties' bargaining process, the conspicuousness of the provision, whether the buyer was on notice of the limitation, and whether each party had a reasonable opportunity to understand the language at issue.

Here, considering the factors relevant to both Oregon and Texas's evaluation of procedural unconscionability, the Limitation Clause is unenforceable under both states' analysis.

This is an unusual, perhaps *sui generis* case, in which a boilerplate damages limitation is attached to a Credit Application without any bargaining or discussion, without the seller calling the buyer's attention to the clause, and after the execution of which more than two years of sample purchases and extensive testing are conducted, the manufacturing process is inspected and audited by the buyer, additional contracts are extensively negotiated, including another damages limitation clause, and the seller breaches an expressly negotiated clause in a manner that was solely within the seller's knowledge and ability to avoid the resultant harm.

Although parties to a contract are presumed to have read its terms, the Court has serious concerns about Huntsman's attaching to a Credit Application a purportedly far-reaching damages limitation clause governing all future sales between the parties without drawing TOK's attention to the clause. These concerns are compounded by the fact that Huntsman negotiated with TOK for more than two years, including specifically negotiating another damages limitation clause, and yet still failed to mention the Limitation Clause to TOK. Then, when Huntsman changed its manufacturing process that had been extensively vetted by TOK, which Huntsman knew could alter the chemical makeup of the PG and result in the chemical no longer performing as required and which Huntsman knew it was required to disclose, Huntsman failed to disclose the manufacturing change to TOK. Under the circumstances of this case, this is a sufficient presence of deception, overreaching, or sharp business practice to rise to the level of unconscionability.

Analogously, where the seller knows of a latent defect and fails to disclose it to the buyer, any limitations may be unconscionable. Here, although Huntsman did not know about the specific defect in the PG, Huntsman knew that it had changed its manufacturing process, knew that knowledge of a change in its manufacturing process was essential to TOK, and failed to disclose that manufacturing change to TOK. Under these circumstances, Huntsman's failure to disclose the known manufacturing change renders the Limitation Clause unconscionable.

Huntsman's failure meaningfully to communicate the Limitation Clause to TOK is also fatal to the enforceability of the clause in these circumstances. The Limitation Clause was inconspicuous and unfairly surprising to TOK. TOK and Huntsman did not negotiate any of the terms of the Huntsman General Terms, including the Limitation Clause, and Huntsman did not bring the Limitation Clause to TOK's attention. Instead, Huntsman remained silent for years, and now attempts to enforce a provision to avoid paying damages for harm that only Huntsman could have avoided. In these circumstances, TOK was not provided effective notice, and enforcing the Limitation Clause would result in unfair surprise.

Although the parties are both commercial entities with roughly equal bargaining power and business acumen, in the circumstances of this case, Huntsman was the party with the knowledge that, if the Limitation Clause is effective, TOK would not receive the benefit of its bargain in the allocation of risk and the requirement that Huntsman timely notify TOK of any manufacturing change. Huntsman also knew that TOK could not protect itself from a breach by Huntsman of its obligation timely to notify TOK of a manufacturing change if the change resulted in a latent defect in the PG. Without such notice by Huntsman and if the PG otherwise passed TOK's tests, TOK did not have the knowledge or ability to avoid the resultant harm. "If there is a type of risk allocation that should be subjected to special scrutiny, it is probably the shifting to one party of a risk that *only* the other party can avoid." Eddy, *Metaphysics,* 65 Cal. L.Rev. at 47 (emph. in original). Under Huntsman's argument, that would be the effect of the Limitation Clause, and such a shifting of risk fails under the scrutiny of procedural unconscionability.

There also was no genuine consent on the part of TOK to the Limitation Clause acting as a damages limitation in the event Huntsman breached its obligation timely to notify TOK of any change in Huntsman's manufacturing process. The parties negotiated that obligation by Huntsman two years after the Credit Application was signed, and in those negotiations the parties agreed to limit Huntsman's liability for nonconforming goods for which TOK could test. There is no evidence of TOK's consent to shift the risk of harm that only Huntsman could avoid—a breach of Huntsman's obligation timely to notify TOK of any manufacturing change and a resultant undiscoverable defect.

If the Limitation Clause were evaluated as of the time the Credit Application was executed, there is little doubt that it would not be substantively unconscionable. Commercial parties regularly limit liability for consequential damages.

Huntsman argues that for cases involving only economic damages, the Court must evaluate unconscionability for purposes of Section 2-719(3) at the time the contract was formed, and that post-formation facts are only relevant in cases involving personal injury. Huntsman's reading of Section 2-719(3) is misguided. The only difference between economic injury and personal injury in an unconscionability analysis under Section 2-719(3) is that a limitation of consequential damages where there is an injury to the person is prima facie unconscionable, whereas a limitation of damages where the loss is commercial is not prima facie unconscionable.

Nothing in the language of Section 2-719(3) or its official comments supports the argument that post-formation facts are only relevant to an unconscionability analysis where there is a personal injury. The analytical difference between personal and economic injury established in Section 2-719(3) involves merely the burden of proving a prima facie case of unconscionability, not the relevant timeframe or facts that a court should consider.

Huntsman also argues generally that under Section 2-719(3) a court is constrained to only look to the facts at the time of contract formation. The genesis of Huntsman's argument is a conflation between Section 2-719(3) and Section 2-302(1), which expressly states that unconscionability under that section is considered "at the time [the contract] was made." U.C.C. §2-302(1). Section 2-302(1) is a broad provision establishing the test for considering whether any clause in a contract is unconscionable. Section 2-719(3), however, is a specific provision applying only to a limitation of consequential damages and does not contain the requirement contained in Section 2-302(1) that the unconscionability analysis be as of the time of the contract's formation. If the requirement that unconscionability for limitations on consequential damages be analyzed at the time of contract formation was intended, the same language used in Section 2-302(1) could easily have been included in Section 2-719(3). The Court gives meaning to the difference in language between the two provisions, and to the official comment explaining that Section 2-719(3) "makes it clear" that clauses limiting or excluding consequential damages "may not operate in an unconscionable manner." U.C.C. §2-719 cmt. 3.

The Court finds that in the context of Section 2-719(3), the Court is instructed by the UCC to consider whether the damages limitation *operates* in an unconscionable manner, which requires consideration of post-formation facts. Limiting TOK's damages for Huntsman's breach of its obligation timely to notify TOK of any manufacturing changes would operate in such an unconscionable manner.

Because the knowledge and ability to avoid the harm caused by a change by Huntsman in its manufacturing process was solely Huntsman's and the parties did not expressly and consciously allocate that risk to TOK, it is fundamentally unfair to enforce the Limitation Clause. Additionally, because the Court has found that a refund of the purchase price deprives TOK of the substantial value of its bargain and does not provide an adequate remedy under the specific circumstances presented, "the exclusion of incidental and consequential damages renders the available damages unconscionably low." *Viking Yacht I* at *7. Accordingly, the Limitation Clause, under the specific circumstances of this case, operates in a substantively unconscionable manner.

Notes and Questions

1. <u>Courts Rarely Find Commercial Contracts Unconscionable.</u> Don't be fooled by *TOK*: "In fact, agreements involving commercial parties on both ends have only been found unconscionable in context of extreme, blatant, unavoidable inequities, such as those where damages are limited even where a contract is wholly unperformed,

and those where parties are given no opportunity to review or read an agreement before signing it." *Whirlpool Corp. v. Grigoleit Co.*, 713 F.3d 316 (6th Cir. 2013).

2. Consumer Contracts. Consumers are arguing that agreements that require only one party to arbitrate its claims are unconscionable. *See Taylor v. Butler*, 142 S.W.3d 277 (Tenn. 2004) (contract that required consumer, not business, to arbitrate was unconscionable); *Lagrone Const. LLC v. Landmark, LLC*, 40 F. Supp. 3d 769 (N.D. Miss. 2014) (similar contract, between two businesses, was not unconscionable). Many companies require consumers to agree to arbitrate even claims brought as part of a class action. *See Epic Sys. Corp. v. Lewis*, 138 S. Ct. 1612 (2018) (holding such agreements generally enforceable).

3. Courts Uphold Disclaiming Liability for Personal Injury. Contracts that release claims for personal injury are generally enforceable, unless they release injuries caused by reckless or intentional conduct. *See Perrine v. E.I. du Pont de Nemours and Co.*, 694 S.E.2d 815 (W. Va. 2010) (collecting cases). In *Hojnowski v. Vans Skate Park*, 868 A.2d 1087 (N.J. Super. Ct. 2005), a mother sued for injuries to her child, who was injured at a skateboard park, but the defendant pointed to the release the mother had signed. The court held it void against public policy, but noting courts have split. The dissent wrote:

> Public policy is not hostile to the enforcement of pre-tort releases that are given in similar circumstances. The pre-tort release in question — if executed by an adult for the adult's use of the skateboarding facility — would undoubtedly be deemed valid. Such pre-tort releases are normally invalidated only when their execution is demanded in exchange for the released party's providing of a necessary service or commodity of great import, where the released party is under a public duty to exercise care, or where the parties are in grossly disproportionate bargaining positions. In this sense, a court should not enforce a pre-tort release when, for example, it is demanded by a hospital prior to treating a patient, or when included in a residential apartment lease by a landlord possessing superior bargaining power.

> Here, the pre-tort release was requested of Anastasia in exchange for permitting Andrew to use Vans' facility. The right to skateboard in a privately-owned facility is not a "necessity" nor may any patron seeking admittance be assumed to be in a grossly disproportionate bargaining position. Patrons that do not approve of such an agreement's terms may simply depart and skateboard elsewhere. As a result, the courts of most states, including this State, have upheld exculpatory agreements of various types when executed in connection with a person's participation in sporting activities, so long as the operator does not seek to insulate itself from a standard of care imposed by statute or regulation. I would conclude that this pre-tort release would be enforceable if applied to a claim based on an adult's injuries. Indeed, the point need not be belabored since I do not understand my colleagues to suggest otherwise.

Instead of following the principles set forth above, the majority concludes that the present circumstances differ because the injured suitor is a child and not an adult. While this fact may require consideration, I would nevertheless enforce a pre-tort release executed by a parent in this and other similar circumstances. That is, I disagree with my colleagues because I believe insufficient weight has been given to a parent's right to make decisions regarding the upbringing of a child.

4. <u>Courts' Approaches to Disclaiming Liability for Fraud and Misrepresentation and Related Claims</u>. Courts hold that limitations on liability cannot cover fraud claims, but split on whether they bar Section 552 negligent misrepresentation claims. *Puro v. Neil Enter., Inc.*, 987 A.2d 935 (Vt. 2009) (collecting cases holding fraud claim not barred by limitation of liability claim); *Sound Techniques, Inc. v. Hoffman*, 50 Mass. App. Ct. 425 (2000) (exculpatory clause defeated negligent misrepresentation claim). In *Airfreight Exp. Ltd v. Evergreen Air Ctr., Inc.*, 158 P.3d 232 (Ct. App. Ariz. 2007), the court collected cases holding that while a contract may limit liability, "a provision is not effective, however, if that party acts fraudulently or in bad faith."

5. <u>Limited Release</u>. In *Shipwash v. United Airlines, Inc.*, 28 F. Supp. 3d 740 (E.D. Tenn. 2014), the plaintiff was on a flight from Los Angeles to Hawaii when the flight attendants announced that for $7.99 a passenger could watch DirectTV. Plaintiff used his credit card but learned that only a few movies were available, and so asked the flight attendant for a refund, which she promised. When he showed up for his return flight at 7:00 p.m. a week later, it was delayed, and the airline allegedly gave false reasons for why this was so, eventually forcing the passengers out of the airport at 2:00 a.m. He sent letters to the defendant asking for a refund but was offered a $500 voucher to use in the future and $25 as a refund for the $7.99 charge. He refused, and filed suit alleging eight claims. The defendant moved to dismiss any claim for damages exceeding those permitted by the "Contract of Carriage," which is a part of all airline tickets. In response, the plaintiff asserted the limitations were part of a contract of adhesion and so against public policy. The court wrote:

> Parties to a contract are free to construct their own bargains, even limiting liability for future damages, subject, however, to some exceptions. One exception to this general rule is where an exculpatory clause adversely affects the public interest.

> Here, plaintiff argues that the clause in defendant's Contract of Carriage is void as against public policy because it affects the public interest. As an initial matter, this Court must determine whether the provision at issue qualifies as an exculpatory clause. "An exculpatory clause is one which deprives one party to the agreement of the right to recover damages for harm caused by the other party's negligence. Upon review, the Court finds that the provision in question is not an exculpatory clause. Defendant's Contract of Carriage does not purport to deprive plaintiff of damages

under the contract; rather, it merely limits what damages plaintiff is entitled to and the manner in which those damages can be enforced. Because the Court finds that the provision in defendant's Contract of Carriage is not an exculpatory clause, the Court does not further analyze whether the contract affects public interest or is void against public policy.

Plaintiff also argues that the Contract of Carriage is an adhesion contract and should, therefore, be unenforceable Under Tennessee law, an adhesion contract has been defined as a standardized contract form offered to customers of goods and services on essentially a 'take it or leave it' basis, without affording the customer a realistic opportunity to bargain and under such conditions that the customer cannot obtain the desired product or service without acquiescing to the form of the contract. The essence of an adhesion contract is that bargaining positions and leverage enable one party to select and control risks assumed under the contract so that the weaker party has no realistic choice as to its terms.

A contract is not rendered unenforceable solely by virtue of it being an adhesion contract; rather, enforceability generally depends upon whether the terms of the contract are beyond the reasonable expectations of an ordinary person, or oppressive or unconscionable. Tennessee courts have typically found provisions of adhesion contracts unenforceable when they purport to limit the weaker party's available remedies or provide an exclusive remedy for the weaker party that the leveraging party is not bound by.

Here, there is little doubt that the Contract of Carriage is an adhesion contract. The Contract of Carriage appears to be a standardized contract that defendant offers its passengers without creating any opportunity for bargaining by the passenger. The Court's inquiry, however, does not stop here. The Court is still required to clearly scrutinize the contract to determine if it includes terms that are unconscionable or oppressive. Plaintiff has not specifically argued that these terms are unconscionable or oppressive, and the Court fails to find so here. The Contract of Carriage provides that "the sole and exclusive remedy for a passenger who has a claim under this Rule shall be the express amenities provided in this Rule. The passenger shall have no other claims or [sic] law or equity or actual, compensatory, or punitive damages." This provision merely limits the damages that plaintiff can recover from defendant and the manner in which plaintiff can assert those damages. Such provisions limiting an airlines' potential liability are not unconscionable or oppressive, but are valid and binding on passengers as part of the contract of carriage where the passenger receives notice thereof either on or with the passenger's ticket.

4. Defenses to Specific Performance

A. Unreasonable Delay and Laches

A court has discretion to deny specific performance even if plaintiff's delay would be insufficient to bar all equitable relief through laches. *LLB Realty, L.L.C. v. Core Laboratories, LP*, 123 F. App'x 490 (3d Cir. 2005). Specific performance must be sought promptly or the right to it can be waived. *In re Corbett*, 2018 WL 832885 (Bankr. D. Mass. 2018) ("Specific performance, being an equitable remedy, must be asserted promptly unless there are circumstances which would excuse prompt action.").

EMF Gen. Contracting Corp. v. Bisbee

774 N.Y.S.2d 39 (N.Y. App. Div. 1st Dept. 2004) (Saxe, J.)

[This case is discussed in Chapter 8: during the five-year delay between the agreement to buy and plaintiff's request for specific performance, the land had appreciated significantly. Defendant sought to avoid specific performance based upon undue delay.]

Unconscionable delay in prosecuting one's rights is also a ground for denying equitable relief, when the defendant was prejudiced thereby (*see Eastern Shopping Cts. v Trenholm Motels*, 33 AD2d 930 [1970]). The plaintiff in *Eastern Shopping Centers* had sold property to the defendant with an option to purchase the property back for the contract price if the defendant did not start construction of a motel and restaurant on the property by January 1, 1965. Because the plaintiff waited over 3½ years, knowing that construction had not begun, while the defendant meanwhile expended substantial sums on the development and improvement of the property — and while the property increased in value — the Court found that the defense of laches was established.

The delay at issue in the present case was neither so long nor so "unconscionable." When we factor in the reasonable attempts to resolve the boundary issue involving a nonparty to the transaction, the period attributable to unexplained inaction is limited to eight or nine months, a period short enough to be explained by the parties' attention being focused on other business matters. Moreover, unlike the defendant in *Eastern Shopping Centers*, Bisbee presented no evidence to show that he was prejudiced by EMF's delay in seeking enforcement of the contract. He merely showed that the value of the property appreciated substantially by the time of trial; this alone does not constitute such prejudice.

While a substantial increase in value combined with an unreasonable delay has also been held to warrant denying specific performance on grounds of laches, the delay here does not warrant application of that reasoning. In *Groesbeck v Morgan* (206 NY 385 [1912]), specific performance was denied because the purchaser took no action to seek enforcement of his rights under the contract until almost five years from the time all hurdles to conveyance had been removed by the seller. It is interesting to note that in *Groesbeck*, it took the seller 15 months after entering into the contract to actually acquire the fee (when he entered into the contract, he merely had a lien) and to clear all other liens and encumbrances on the property; this portion of the delay between the contract date and the action's commencement date was not considered by the Court. However, the buyer's failure to take action to enforce his rights under the contract, once aware that the seller had acquired clear title, for an additional four years and nine months, during which time the value of the property had increased from $2,750 to $15,000, was considered proper grounds for denying specific performance.

Here, as in *Groesbeck*, a portion of the delay between contract and commencement of the action is irrelevant because it is attributable to attempts to clear title. The relevant portion of the delay in this case is just the eight or nine months in which nothing was done. We have already determined that this same nine-month delay does not constitute an abandonment such as would create a dissolution of the contract. We now conclude that it does not establish a laches defense.

Groesbeck reiterated the centuries-old common-law equitable defense of laches, that "when the lapse of time is occasioned or accompanied by a refusal or a failure to claim or act under the contract, and is *so great or of such characteristics as to amount to a waiver or abandonment of the contract*, the party who comes not into court until after such delay, will have forfeited all claim to equity." However, there is a vast difference between the nine-month delay here and the four-year-and-nine-month delay in *Groesbeck*: the nine-month delay is simply too short to be "so great or of such characteristics as to amount to a waiver or abandonment of the contract," as *Merchants' Bank* defines the defense. The defense of laches was not established here.

As to the enormous increase in value between the contract date in March 1998 and the January 2003 valuation date, we decline to rely upon it *alone* as a proper basis for denying specific performance. While specific performance will not be granted where it would result in injustice or inequity, the increase in market value of the property does not in itself create injustice or inequity.

Indeed, many treatises explain that an increase in value of the property between the time the contract is entered into and the time when specific performance is sought, in and of itself, would not normally be sufficient ground for denying specific performance, although such an increase, taken together with a delay or default on the part of the purchaser, may justify equity in refusing to aid him," especially where "the delay was a speculative one occasioned by the hope of just such an increase Having already determined that the relatively minor delay on plaintiff's part was not a speculative one and did not justify a refusal of equitable relief, we are left only with what is admittedly an enormous increase in value by January 2003.

As between the two parties, it is EMF, as the contract vendee, that is entitled to benefit from the increase in the value of the property. This is so since the vendee in a contract to sell real estate is viewed by the law as the equitable owner of the property, while the vendor is viewed as holding title merely as security for the payment of the agreed purchase price.

That plaintiff waited some eight or nine months before taking action to enforce the contract, notwithstanding the encroachment problem, does not successfully establish an equitable defense. There is no adequate remedy at law in this case, in light of the fluctuating market values and the unique nature of this real estate, to remedy EMF's loss of the benefit of its bargain. Therefore, we reverse the IAS court and find that EMF has established a right to specific performance.

B. Election of Monetary Damages in Lieu of Specific Performance

Ross U. Sch. of Med., Ltd. v. Brooklyn-Queens Health Care, Inc.

2013 WL 1334271 (E.D.N.Y. Mar. 28, 2013) (Matsumoto, J.)

A court may order specific performance along with a money award for damages that naturally flow from the breach, are within the contemplation of the parties, and can be proven to a reasonable degree of certainty. A non-breaching party may not, however, obtain an order of specific performance compelling the breaching party to fulfill its obligations under a contract and also recover money damages that would put the nonbreaching party in the position it would have been in had the contract never been breached.

Additionally, although a party may "plead inconsistent theories of recovery," because a summary judgment motion is "the procedural equivalent of a trial in New York, a litigant must elect among inconsistent positions upon seeking expedited disposition." *Jones Lang Wootton USA v. LeBoeuf, Lamb, Greene & MacRae,* 243 A.D.2d 168 (1st Dep't 1998); *Unisys Corp. v. Hercules, Inc.,* 224 A.D.2d 365 (1st Dep't 1996) (noting in context of breach of contract action that "even where a plaintiff may seek recovery on alternative theories, he must make an election of remedies at trial or upon submission of a motion for summary judgment, the grant of which is the procedural equivalent of a trial").

Here, notwithstanding the fact that Ross' Second Amended Complaint seeks specific performance of the Agreement as well as incidental and consequential damages, Ross moved this court for an order of summary judgment entitling it to money damages for the full extent of its alleged injuries, including damages for the Future Replacement Costs. (See Pl. SJ Mem. at 4–8 (requesting total sum of $20,089,052 in damages for its three categories of claimed damages).) Although Ross was entitled under New York law to seek inconsistent theories of recovery at the pleading stage, Ross chose to pursue money damages as its full measure of recovery in its motion for summary judgment, thereby constituting its election of damages for its future loss over future specific performance of the Agreement.

Ross' summary judgment motion further demonstrates that legal damages are adequate for its past and future harms incurred from BQHC's breach of the

Agreement: Ross asserts, based on its damages expert's report and sworn testimony, that $20,089,052 is the total amount of its three components of claimed damages, and that the Future Replacement Costs are ascertainable in the specific amount of $12,738,735. Indeed, Ross' request for specific performance of the Agreement (by either or both defendants) covers the same subject matter as its request for the Future Replacement Costs, because any specific performance of the Agreement ordered by this court would necessarily occur in the future, and such an order would necessarily entail a reduction of the Future Replacement Costs as defined and calculated by Ross. (See Pl. SJ Mem. at 6 (defining "Future Replacement Costs" as the projected future costs that Ross will likely incur in replacing clerkship rotations throughout the future life of the Agreement).) New York law does not permit Ross, however, to obtain an order of specific performance compelling the breaching party to fulfill its obligations under a contract and also recover money damages that would put it in the same position it would have been in had BQHC never breached the Agreement. Accordingly, the court grants defendants' motion for summary judgment seeking dismissal of Ross' requests for specific performance as to both BQHC and Wyckoff.

C. Impossibility and Hardship

"The reason impossibility is a defense to the remedy of specific performance is that a court of equity will not order an impossible act." *Ash Park, LLC v. Alexander & Bishop, Ltd.*, 853 N.W.2d 618 (Wis. App. 2014), *aff'd*, 866 N.W.2d 679 (Wis. 2015). "However, the fact that specific performance is not an available remedy based on equity principles does not mean the underlying contract is unenforceable." *Id.*

Fazzio v. Mason

249 P.3d 390 (Idaho 2011) (Burdick, J.)

[The defendant real estate developer, Mason, had agreed to buy plaintiff's farmland. To do so, plaintiff allowed a city to annex his land. The real estate market tanked and the buyer refused to close, but they settled by entering an agreement that permitted either party to demand specific performance and to perform by a certain date. The plaintiff-seller demanded specific performance but the defendant failed to close. The plaintiff sued and the trial court ordered specific performance. Defendant appealed.]

According to Mason, it is a well-established rule that a court should not order an equitable remedy, including specific performance, which is not feasible. Mason asserts that it is undisputed that he does not have the approximately $3.5 million needed to close on the Properties, and therefore, the award of specific performance is futile. Mason argues that when the district court was presented with this argument, it mistakenly analyzed a different legal doctrine—the defense of impossibility of performance—despite Mason's efforts to explain the difference between the two doctrines.

Mason is correct that the defense of impossibility of performance is distinct from the various equitable doctrines which concern whether an award of specific performance is appropriate. The defense of impossibility is a complete defense that excuses the defendant from performing. Whereas equitable doctrines that preclude, or warn against granting, equitable relief provide no defense for breaching a contract and leave the plaintiff with a remedy at law, such as damages.

Mason, however, misconstrued the equitable doctrine upon which he relies. Mason's argument concerns whether specific performance is appropriate where it is difficult or impossible for the defendant to comply. Mason has not made an argument concerning the court's ability to enforce the order of specific performance in this case. Even if Mason had made an argument concerning the feasibility of the court's enforcement, these contracts were for cash sales, and this Court has determined that cash sales for land are easily enforceable.

The Restatement (First) of Contracts § 368 (1932) provides, "specific enforcement will not be decreed if the performance sought is impossible", and explains in Comment A that this equitable doctrine of impossibility applies in instances of both subjective and objective impossibility. The district court, on the other hand, relied on *Christy v. Pilkinton*, 224 Ark. 407 (1954), where the Arkansas Supreme Court limited the equitable doctrine of impossibility of performance to instances of objective impossibility in a case with facts very similar to the facts of this case. In *Christy,* the seller of real estate sought specific performance, but the buyers put forth evidence showing that they did not have and could not borrow the unpaid balance of the purchase price. The Arkansas Supreme Court nevertheless awarded specific performance and explained:

> Proof of this kind does not establish the type of impossibility that constitutes a defense. There is a familiar distinction between objective impossibility, which amounts to saying, "The thing cannot be done," and subjective impossibility—"I cannot do it.". The latter, which is well illustrated by a promisor's financial inability to pay, does not discharge the contractual duty and is therefore not a bar to a decree for specific performance.

We agree that a buyer's financial inability to pay is not a complete bar to specific performance in a case involving the breach of an agreement to purchase land. While the defendant's subjective ability to comply with the award of specific performance is a relevant equitable factor to be considered, the district court acted within its discretion in dismissing Mason's impossibility argument. The district court considered the difficulties Mason faced in obtaining financing but concluded "we cannot find that the present case presents a situation where performance is so unlikely and impossible that it would render the order futile." Mason's affidavits show that he has been unable to obtain financing, despite many attempts to do so, and that liquidating his assets to close on the deal may be imprudent, given the current real estate market and given that the majority of his assets are real property serving as collateral on bank loans for most of which Mason owes more than the appraised property value. While the imprudence of liquidating one's assets may be a relevant factor in determining whether specific performance is appropriate in a given case, imprudence is not impossibility. Even if Mason had no assets that could be liquidated, his inability to obtain financing up to the time of the decision does not show impossibility, because he may still be able to obtain financing. Thus, it was within the district court's discretion, upon considering Mason's ability to perform, to award specific performance.

Notes and Questions

1. <u>Defaulting Buyers</u>. Does it make sense to allow the seller to obtain specific performance when money damages are, it seems, an adequate remedy and specific performance requires an unwise financial move by the buyer? Suppose the property was a condominium with a readily ascertainable market value. Same result?

2. <u>Don't Confuse Impossibility with Unenforceability</u>. Impossibility means specific performance is not available, but the contract is not unenforceable. *Ash Park, LLC v. Alexander & Bishop, Ltd.*, 853 N.W.2d 618 (Wis. App. 2014), *aff'd*, 866 N.W.2d 679 (Wis. 2015). So, if a buyer breaches a contract, the seller may seek actual damages.

3. <u>Defense to Contempt?</u> In *Hampton Island, LLC v. HAOP, LLC*, 731 S.E.2d 71 (Ct. App. Ga. 2012), the trial court had ordered a buyer to specifically perform an agreement to buy land. The buyer failed to close, and the seller moved for contempt. The trial court concluded the buyer's failure to perform was caused by its lack of financial resources to do so, and that was a defense to contempt. As a result, it converted the order of specific performance to a money judgment.

D. The Statute of Frauds

Ficke v. Wolken

868 N.W.2d 305 (Neb. 2015) (Cassel, J.)

[Plaintiff Gerald Ficke began in early 2000 to work for defendant Gilbert Wolken as an on-call "hired hand" on Wolken's cattle ranch, performing various manual labor 40 to 60 hours a week. His starting pay was $7.50/hour but was increased to $14.75, and Wolken properly paid for overtime. Wolken also paid Ficke an annual bonus, ranging from $500 to $2,000. Ficke asserted that sometime in 2002 or 2003, as they were driving in Wolken's truck, Ficke looked down at his muddy shoes and said, "There's the only ground I'll ever own." Wolken responded: "After working ten years for me, I will give you 80 acres," which, Wolken explained, were the first 80 acres he had purchased on what had become his very large cattle ranch. Ten years passed, during which time the men remained close friends.

Nine months after that, Wolken fired Ficke. Ficke then sued Wolken for specific performance of the oral contract to convey the 80-acre parcel. After a bench trial, the court found for Ficke, and found that but for Wolken's promise, Ficke would not have fulfilled the 10 years of employment, which he had completed, and ordered specific performance. The court of appeals affirmed, and defendant Wolken appealed.]

Ficke testified that he considered Wolken to be a "father figure." As to his reaction to Wolken's promise, Ficke testified that he was overwhelmed and that he "didn't really know how to take it." Ficke told Wolken that he did not have to give Ficke the land, but Wolken insisted. And Ficke indicated that Wolken raised the matter many times. Wolken would mention the promise "every so often" and would remind Ficke, usually in January, that Ficke had only "another year or two years," depending on the year. And Ficke iterated that Wolken's promise was a significant factor for his continued employment.

According to Ficke, on January 10, 2010, Wolken told him that he had completed the 10 years of employment and that the 80 acres belonged to Ficke. Although Wolken never signed over the 80 acres, Ficke described one instance when Wolken treated the 80 acres as belonging to Ficke. During harvest season, all of the wheat from the 80 acres was kept separate and Wolken instructed the cooperative to pay Ficke 40 percent of the profit from the wheat. Additionally, before Ficke's employment was terminated, Wolken offered to purchase a house for Ficke in exchange for the 80 acres. Ficke agreed to the proposal, but the purchase offer was not accepted and the deal "fell through." And after Ficke's employment was terminated, Wolken discussed the 80 acres with Ficke and mentioned that he was attempting to determine how he could purchase the 80 acres from Ficke with minimal tax consequences.

Wolken confirmed the existence of the promise. Wolken testified that he promised Ficke "eighty acres of land if Ficke fulfilled his job." And Wolken stated that in order to fulfill his job, Ficke was required to "act like a decent man." Wolken explained that he wanted to give Ficke a "better attitude on the job." But Wolken did not believe that Ficke had fulfilled his obligations.

According to Wolken, Ficke's temper was an issue and Ficke would argue with Wolken's wife and call Wolken names. Wolken testified that Ficke "was dangerous to be around," and he described one instance in which Ficke had intentionally set fire to bales of straw and another in which Ficke had thrown a telephone at the windshield of Wolken's vehicle.

Additionally, the district court received testimony from Wolken's sister. Wolken's sister testified that after Wolken had fired Ficke, Wolken told her that he had promised Ficke the 80 acres and that Ficke had completed the 10-year period.

In his petition for further review, Wolken does not challenge the Court of Appeals' conclusion that Ficke met his burden of proving the existence and terms of the oral contract by clear, satisfactory, and unequivocal evidence. Thus, we restrict our analysis to Wolken's specific assignments of error, both of which address the Court of Appeals' conclusion that Ficke's performance was referable solely to the oral contract.

An exception to the statute of frauds authorizes specific performance of an oral contract in cases of part performance. A party seeking specific performance of an oral contract for the sale of real estate upon the basis of part performance must prove an oral contract, the terms of which are clear, satisfactory, and unequivocal, and that the acts done in part performance were referable solely to the contract sought to be enforced, and not such as might be referable to some other or different contract, and further that nonperformance by the other party would amount to a fraud upon the party seeking specific performance.

The Court of Appeals determined that Ficke had satisfied the part performance exception for two reasons: (1) Ficke continued his employment for the 10-year period and (2) Ficke's testimony indicated that his continued employment was referable solely to the promise of the 80 acres and not to some other contract or relationship.

We first address the Court of Appeals' reliance upon Ficke's testimony as to his intent. In determining that Ficke's continued employment was referable solely to the oral contract, the Court of Appeals cited the portion of Ficke's testimony quoted above—that Ficke had thought about quitting, but that the promise of the 80 acres was "something that a person works for." The Court of Appeals determined that this testimony established the part performance exception, because it proved that the "sole reason Ficke continued his employment was to attain the land that was promised."

We disapprove of this reliance upon the above testimony as the sole basis for the part performance exception. The part performance exception entails an onerous burden of proof—a plaintiff must prove not only that the alleged performance is referable to the oral contract, but also that the performance cannot be accounted for on any other reasonable hypothesis. Multiple courts have recognized that in satisfying this high burden, the alleged acts of performance must speak for themselves.

We find the evidence received by the district court sufficient to support its conclusion that Ficke would not have continued his employment but for the promise of the 80 acres and that he did so with the 80 acres as his direct view. In doing so, we give weight to the fact that the district court heard Ficke's testimony and found it credible. Ficke testified that he "worked constantly" and was always "on-call," that he had no family life or health insurance, and that he always believed he "could do better."

Additionally, the district court received evidence of Wolken's own statements and conduct admitting that Ficke had fully performed his obligation and that Ficke was entitled to the 80 acres. Wolken's sister testified that Wolken had told her that Ficke had completed the 10-year period. And Wolken granted Ficke payment for a portion of the wheat harvested from the 80 acres and had attempted to purchase a house for Ficke as a substitute for the 80 acres.

Giving no consideration to Ficke's testimony as to his intent, we find the evidence regarding Ficke's acts—particularly Wolken's admissions by statements and conduct—is sufficient to establish that his continued employment for the 10-year period was referable solely to the oral contract. Thus, although for different reasons from those stated by the Court of Appeals, we agree that Ficke's claim as to the 80 acres was enforceable under the part performance exception to the statute of frauds.

LaRue v. Kalex Const. and Dev., Inc.

97 So. 3d 251 (Fla. Ct. App. 2012) (Rothenberg, J.)

[In 2005, Rosa LaRue left her former employer to accept a job with Kalex Construction and Development, Inc. She asserted that, in addition to salary and benefits, she and Kalex had orally agreed that after three years she would receive a 25% ownership interest in Kalex. She worked for Kalex from February 2006 to December 2009, but was fired. She sued, seeking specific performance of the oral agreement to convey that 25% ownership interest. The trial court granted summary judgment to Kalex, and she appealed.]

Section 725.01, Florida Statutes (2010) ("the statute of frauds"), provides in pertinent part:

> No action shall be brought upon any agreement that is not to be performed within the space of 1 year from the making thereof unless the agreement or promise upon which such action shall be brought, or some note or memorandum thereof shall be in writing and signed by the party to be charged therewith or by some other person by her or him thereunto lawfully authorized.

The statute of frauds was enacted to prevent fraud and the enforcement of claims based on loose verbal statements made faulty by the lapse of time, and should be strictly construed.

The statute of frauds grew out of a purpose to intercept the frequency and success of actions based on nothing more than loose verbal statements or mere innuendos. To accomplish this, the statute requires that all actions based on agreements for longer than one year must depend on a written statement or memorandum, signed by the party to be charged. The statute should be strictly construed to prevent the fraud it was designed to correct, and so long as it can be made to effectuate this purpose, courts should be reluctant to take cases from its protection.

Where the contract is for the sale of land and the relief sought is for specific performance or other equitable relief, partial performance may remove an oral agreement from the statute of frauds. However, the doctrine of partial performance does not remove the bar of the statute of frauds for actions seeking damages based on the breach of an oral contract. Full performance of an oral agreement, however, *may* remove the agreement from the statute of frauds if the agreement is capable of being performed within a year and was, in fact, performed within one year.

In applying these principles to the instant case, it is clear that the trial court correctly determined that LaRue's claims were barred by the statute of frauds. It is undisputed that LaRue's complaint was based on an alleged oral employment agreement, and the agreement and the intent of the parties was that LaRue would receive a 25% ownership interest in the company if she worked for the company for three years. Because the alleged agreement was incapable of being performed in one year, her claim is barred by the statute of frauds.

Notes and Questions

1. <u>The Cases</u>? If Ms. LaRue had been promised 25% of Blackacre, under Florida's approach would she have obtained specific performance? Conversely, if Mr. Ficke had lived in Florida, would he have been awarded specific performance? Why are there differences? Why do the courts require that performance be "referable only" to the alleged contract?

2. <u>Paying Money</u>. Courts generally hold that payment of money is insufficient evidence of performance because "the purchaser normally may have restitution of the consideration paid so that his predicament does not warrant the application of an equitable doctrine designed to prevent the statute of frauds itself from becoming an engine of fraud. Consistent with this rationale, this court also long has recognized that recovery may be had for money paid or services performed even in the absence of a contract that complies with the statute of frauds on a theory of implied contract." *Drelich v. Musser,* 2018 WL 710039 (Conn. Super. Jan. 8, 2018). *See Sanchez v. Aurora Loan Services, LLC,* 2014 WL 12589660 (C.D. Cal. June 10, 2014) ("The payment of money is not sufficient part performance to take the oral agreement out of the statute of frauds, for the party paying money under an invalid contract has an adequate remedy at law.")

3. <u>Partial Performance to Estop Reliance on the Statute of Frauds</u>. Some courts recognize that partial, not full, performance may be used to estop a party seeking to avoid specific enforcement from relying upon the statute of frauds, but only when allowing the party to rely on the statute of frauds would "work a fraud upon the other party." *Soccer Connection, Inc. v. Nike USA, Inc.,* 12018 WL 3827371 (D. Utah Aug. 10, 2018). Even then, it should be "applied with great care so as not to eviscerate the statute of frauds" and only to prevent that statute from "being made the means of perpetrating a fraud." *Id.*

E. Other Public Policies Barring Specific Enforcement

When the "subject or purpose of a contract concerns the doing of an illegal act or is against the public policy of the state, the contract will not be enforced by the courts." *Rischer v. Helzer,* 473 S.W.3d 188 (Mo. App. W. Dist. 2015). Only a strong, clear basis for invalidity or unenforceability will prevent specific enforcement:

- An "agreement designed to bring about and promote a divorce." *Murray v. Murray,* 293 S.W.2d 436 (Mo. 1956).

- In *In re Visitation of K.M.,* 2017 WL 657641 (Ill. Cir. Ct. Feb. 17, 2017), the plaintiffs were the biological family of a child they gave up for adoption to the defendants. They sought specific performance of an alleged oral agreement to permit post-adoption visitation. The trial court dismissed the complaint, holding that "Illinois public policy . . . does not recognize agreements for post-adoption visitation. Petitioners alleged that they entered into a preadoption contract for post-adoption visitation. This oral agreement is plainly contrary to the established public policy as it erodes the stability and certainty provided by the adoption proceedings and undermines the adoption judgment which completely severed petitioners' bundle of rights. Thus, the alleged agreement is void as contrary to public policy; the court properly dismissed the visitation petition."

- An agreement to arbitrate in a lawyer-client fee agreement that violated public policy as expressed in rules of professional conduct. *Sheppard, Mullin, Richter & Hampton, LLP v. J-M Mfg. Co., Inc.*, 2018 WL 4137013 (Cal. Aug. 30, 2018).

Johnson v. Nelson

861 N.W.2d 705 (Neb. 2015) (Stephan, J.)

[Chad Johnson rented farmland from Stewart Minnick and his sister, Mary Nelson, who owned it jointly. The two decided that Johnson could buy the land after Minnick died. Johnson did not have the funds to do so, so he asked his cousin, an insurance agent, who advised him that Johnson could obtain a life insurance policy on Minnick and use the proceeds on Minnick's death to acquire the property, and to enter into a written buyout agreement to do so.

As a result, a written buyout agreement signed by Johnson and Minnick provided that Johnson would buy the farmland from Minnick's sister for a specified price using proceeds of the life insurance policy. Johnson and Minnick both signed the $500,000 life insurance policy, which named Johnson as the beneficiary. After Minnick died and Johnson received those proceeds, he tendered them to the estate's representative, Minnick's sister, Nelson. She refused to convey the property. Johnson sought specific performance, but the estate asserted the buyout agreement was against public policy because Johnson lacked an insurable interest in Minnick's life. The courts below denied specific performance, and Johnson appealed.]

At common law, life insurance policies issued to a party not having an insurable interest in the life of an insured are considered a wager on the life of another and therefore void as being against public policy. In contract and insurance law, public policy is that principle of the law which holds that no subject can lawfully do that which has a tendency to be injurious to the public or against the public good, the principles under which the freedom of contract or private dealings are restricted by law for the good of the community. A contract which is clearly contrary to public policy is void. The determination of whether a contract violates public policy presents a question of law.

In Nebraska, an "insurable interest," in the matter of life and health insurance, exists when the beneficiary because of relationship, either pecuniary or from ties of blood or marriage, has reason to expect some benefit from the continuance of the life of the insured. Johnson and Minnick were not related by blood or marriage, so the question of whether Johnson had an insurable interest in Minnick's life turns on their "pecuniary" relationship.

This court has not decided the type of pecuniary or economic relationship which may form the basis of an insurable interest in the context of life insurance. Some courts have held that one business partner may have an insurable interest in the life of another business partner where there is an expectation of pecuniary benefit from the continued life of the insured partner. But Johnson acknowledged that he and Minnick were not business partners. Courts have also held that a business entity may have an insurable interest in the life of a key employee whose death would adversely affect the business. But there was no employment relationship between Johnson and Minnick. Under some circumstances, a creditor has been held to have an insurable interest in the life of a debtor. But the record reflects no such relationship between Johnson and Minnick.

At the time the policy issued, the relationship between Johnson and Minnick was that of (1) landlord and tenant under an oral farm lease and (2) parties to the buyout agreement, which could be performed only after Minnick's death.

We need not decide whether a landlord-tenant relationship with respect to agricultural property could ever form the basis of an insurable interest. We conclude only that in this case it did not. The agent who procured the policy for Johnson described the insurable interest as "guaranteeing a buyer for Minnick and his sister at a price agreeable to both parties, while at the same time ensuring Johnson and his family the opportunity and resources to purchase this farm property essential to continuing their farm business." But this does not meet the requirement of § 44-103(13)(b) that for there to be an insurable interest, the beneficiary must have "reason to expect some benefit from the continuance of the life of the insured." Johnson had no reason to expect any pecuniary benefit from the continuance of his landlord's life. As long as Minnick lived and was willing to rent the land to Johnson, Johnson would remain a tenant on the land. The only difference in the relationship after the execution of the buyout agreement was that Johnson had the financial obligation to pay premiums on the life insurance policy. The longer Minnick lived, the more premiums Johnson had to pay to keep the policy in force. Under this arrangement, Johnson's pecuniary interest would not benefit from the continuation of Minnick's life; to the contrary, it would benefit from Minnick's death before additional premiums came due. In effect, Johnson was gambling that Minnick would die sooner rather than later. This is precisely the reason why an insurance policy on the life of one in whom the owner and beneficiary of the policy lacks an insurable interest is void as against public policy.

The insurance policy on Minnick's life was an integral component of the buyout agreement which Johnson sought to enforce after Minnick's death. The agreement was the reason for the policy, and the policy was the exclusive financing mechanism for the agreement. The power of courts to invalidate contracts for being in contravention of public policy is a very delicate and undefined power which should be exercised only in cases free from doubt. We are satisfied that this is one of those cases. We conclude that the buyout agreement was void as against public policy because it incorporated a financing mechanism consisting of a life insurance policy in which the owner and beneficiary lacked an insurable interest in the life of the insured. We therefore agree with the district court that the buyout agreement was not specifically enforceable as a matter of law.

Notes and Questions

1. <u>Better Drafting</u>? How could an agreement accomplish the goals of the parties?

2. <u>Johnson versus His Cousin</u>? Consider what claims Johnson may have against his cousin, who suggested the buyout agreement would work. Would a claim for negligent misrepresentation under Section 552 (discussed below) be tenable?

Problems

1. <u>Sue If an LDC Is a Penalty</u>? Your client became a member of Zipcar, a service that gives its members access to cars. The agreement she entered required her to reserve specific time slots and return the car promptly or pay a late fee, stated to be for liquidated damages, starting at $50 for the first hour and doubling for each hour thereafter, up to $500 per hour. Your client kept her car for 10 hours longer than she had reserved it for. Zipcar has sent her a demand letter to collect several thousand dollars in fees. Your client wants you to file suit and assert a claim for damages. Assume that the law as expressed in *Barrie School* applies. What advice will you give your client?

2. <u>Drafted Well Enough</u>? You represent a client negotiating a lease for a classmate who is about to rent a room from a homeowner. The homeowner has proposed a short lease, which states as follows:

1. Rent is due on the first day of each month or, if a weekend or holiday, by 8:00 a.m. on the first day afterward.

2. Rent is $500 per month.

3. Tenant is responsible for paying one-third of utility bills within 24 hours of receiving them, which will be by email.

4. Landlord agrees to keep the premises in reasonable condition and to address reasonable concerns or complaints promptly.

5. In the event of any material breach of this agreement, tenant shall, as the sole and exclusive remedy, pay $500 in liquidated damages, and not as a penalty.

With respect to paragraph 5, what would you suggest if the law as described in *Barrie School* applies?

3. <u>Bidder Backs Out</u>. Your client is a city government. It routinely requests proposals from businesses for services it needs to provide. As part of the process to

register to bid, the city requires a bidder to provide a certified check, payable to your client, for 10% of the bid amount with a cap of $20,000, as a guarantee of performance. The bidder must also agree that, if it wins the bid, it will execute a formal contract within 10 days of being notified it was the successful bidder or forfeit the 10% guarantee. Recently, a bidder—GCA Services—paid $20,000 and was the low bidder on a two-year contract to provide custodial services to city buildings. GCA Services refused to execute the contract, however, and the city had to award the work to the next highest bidder, ABC Company, and the difference between the cost to the city of the GCA Services contract and the price the city had to pay ABC Company was $740,000. The city has GCA Services' $20,000 check but wants to sue for the additional $720,000. What additional information would you need, if any, and how will you advise it?

4. <u>Trailer Rent Term</u>. You are a judge preparing for an oral argument involving an appeal of a jury verdict in favor of the defendant on a counterclaim for reformation. The plaintiff had signed a lease-purchase agreement for a mobile home owned by the defendant. Under it, plaintiff paid $375 a month for lease payments. The plaintiff asserted the lease had always required payments for 10 years, and then gave a one-year option to purchase, but the defendant contended that when she had signed the lease, the term of years was blank and the parties had agreed it would be five years. Defendant stated she noticed the 10-year term just after starting the lease, more than five years before plaintiff filed the suit. Defendant added the counterclaim for reformation in her answer. The jury found for the defendant, finding that the parties had orally agreed to a five-year term, but the plaintiff had falsely induced defendant to sign the blank form, and later put a 10-year term in. Based on those findings, the trial court reformed the agreement to reflect a five-year term.

Chapter 17

General Defenses

The prior chapter discussed defenses that are only available against contract claims. Some defenses in this chapter apply to every claim, but certain ones apply only to certain tort claims, and still others apply differently depending not on the claim, but on the relief sought. Thus, and as with the meaning of "damage" for each claim, whether a particular defense applies turns on a claim-by-claim basis.

1. Unclean Hands

Unclean hands can be used against many claims to bar money damages as well as equitable relief. *See* T. Leigh Anenson, *Limiting Legal Remedies: An Analysis of Unclean Hands*, 99 Ky. L.J. 63 (2011). "The doctrine demands that a plaintiff act fairly in the matter for which he seeks a remedy. He must come into court with clean hands, and keep them clean, or he will be denied relief, regardless of the merits of his claim." *Biller v. Toyota Motor Corp.*, 668 F.3d 655 (9th Cir. 2012). Typical requirements were recently summarized in *Merisant Co. v. McNeil Nutritionals, LLC,* 515 F. Supp. 2d 509 (E.D. Pa. 2007): clear and convincing evidence of "egregious misconduct" by the defendant that has a "close nexus" to the plaintiff's claim.

Hicks v. Gilbert
762 A.2d 986 (Md. Spec. App. 2000) (Sonner, J.)

[Cindy Gilbert was living with Thomas Hicks when they acquired real property as joint tenants in 1989. In 1991, Hicks faced severe financial problems and was concerned his creditors could attach their property. To avoid this, he and Gilbert transferred the property to Gilbert and her parents. No liens were ever placed on the property. Hicks testified that, at that time, Gilbert and her parents agreed to pay Hicks if the property was ever sold, and throughout the time, until he and Gilbert separated in 1998, he improved and maintained the property. In 1998, their relationship ended and Hicks asked Gilbert to reimburse him for his contributions to the property. She refused and instead she and her parents transferred the property to Gilbert's brother for $50,000. Hicks sued the Gilbert family members, asserting various claims including unjust enrichment and constructive trust. The trial court granted the Gilberts' motion for summary judgment, holding Hicks' claims were barred because of the 1991 transfer to avoid possible creditors. Hicks admitted he had transferred the property to avoid potential creditors, but had paid them, thus "purging" any misconduct. Hicks appealed.]

Hicks does not challenge the nexus between the misconduct and the relief he sought by his complaint. Instead, he distinguishes *Manown v. Adams*, 89 Md. App. 503 (1991), *rev'd on other grounds*, 328 Md. 463 (1992) from the circumstances of this case and criticizes the trial court for "reviewing *Manown* in isolation" of earlier precedent. The plaintiff in *Manown* was involved in an extramarital relationship while he was separated from his wife. During the course of the relationship, he transferred assets to his girlfriend, with whom he shared a home and a business. He did not disclose these assets to his wife in the divorce action that ensued, nor did he disclose the assets to the bankruptcy court when he filed for bankruptcy soon after the divorce. The relationship ended, and the plaintiff sued his former girlfriend to recover the funds he had transferred to her. The girlfriend moved for summary judgment based on the unclean hands doctrine. The trial court denied the motion, but we reversed. The Court of Appeals then affirmed our analysis of the unclean hands doctrine, but reversed on the ground that the real party in interest was not joined in the suit.

Hicks distinguishes *Manown* because the plaintiff in that case actually filed bankruptcy to avoid his debts and creditors and the evidence that the Plaintiff acted in a fraudulent manner seemed overwhelming because clearly he was under no illusion as to the nature of his conduct. Essentially, Hicks argues that his conduct was not as bad or as blatant as the plaintiff's conduct in *Manown*. To his credit, that appears to be true, but the trial judge was still entitled to find Hicks's behavior bad enough to invoke the unclean hands doctrine.

As he did before the trial court, Hicks also refers us to *Sherwood Co. v. Sherwood Distilling Co.*, 177 Md. 455 (1939). That case involved a trademark dispute. The defendant attempted to bar plaintiff's claim because plaintiff's whiskey products bore a misleading label for a period of time. Following a change in the law, however, plaintiff promptly modified the label. The Court of Appeals declined to invoke the unclean hands maxim since plaintiff purged the impropriety. The maxim

> has nothing to do with retribution or punishment, or with disapproval of the character or past behavior of the applicant, but only with the effect of his present application. Consequently, when there has been a question of the propriety of conduct of an applicant in the past, but the applicant has corrected any alleged mistake and complied with the suggestions of the Court, his impropriety should be considered as closed and should not debar him from relief.

Sherwood merely confirms the central purpose of the unclean hands doctrine; we are not concerned with the party's impropriety, but with cloaking that misconduct in legitimacy. Where the impropriety has been corrected, or where it is unrelated to the claim before the court, we can rest assured that judicial resources will not be exerted to perpetuate fraud or inequity. In this case, the conveyance formed the basis of Hicks's claim.

Notes and Questions

1. <u>Defendants with Unclean Hands</u>? What if Gilbert or her brother had been part of the plan? Consider whether they might have been estopped to assert unclean hands.

2. <u>Nexus</u>. Abhorrent behavior without a relationship to the claim does not preclude equitable relief. As one court explained: "While unclean hands generally prevents the court from even considering the merits of plaintiff's claims, the unclean hands doctrine does not attach to all prior bad acts made by the plaintiff bringing suit. There must be a direct relationship between the allegations comprising the complaint and the acts giving rise to the unclean hands." *Functional Products Trading, S.A. v. I-Grain, LLC*, 2012 WL 13013592 (N.D. Ga.), *rep. adopted*, 2012 WL 13015081 (Aug. 10, 2012). If a court determines that the plaintiff has engaged in egregious conduct that is "immediately related" to the relief sought, it may *sua sponte* deny some or all relief in order to prevent the court from furthering the misconduct. *In re Everett*, 364 B.R. 711 (Bankr. D. Ariz. 2007) (denying entry of judgment in favor of plaintiffs as to ownership of stock in part because they had misrepresented their ownership interests to the public).

3. <u>Unclean Hands or Not</u>? The court in *Vt. Small Bus. Dev. v. Fifth Son Corp.*, 193 Vt. 185 (2013), held unenforceable a clause in a lease that provided that even if eviction had been wrongful, the tenant had to pay the remaining rent:

> We can find no precedent that would allow collection of future rent based on a wrongful eviction because of language in a lease, particularly language allowing recovery of future rent as liquidated damages. There are, however, cases to the contrary. *See Bryan v. Vaughn*, 579 S.W.2d 177 (Mo. Ct. App. 1979) ("The lease ended by the wrongful act of plaintiffs, constituting an eviction, and in such circumstances plaintiffs are in no wise entitled to liquidated damages."); *Cox's Bakeries of N.D., Inc. v. Homart Dev. Corp.*, 515 S.W.2d 326 (Tex. Ct. App. 1974) ("We are not overlooking the provision in the lease to the effect that the tenant's default could give rise to a termination of his right of possession without relieving him of his obligation for unaccrued rentals. However, reliance by the landlord upon this lease provision cannot be justified unless it be shown that he was not guilty of wrongful eviction."). As the trial judge observed, allowing liquidated damages when a landlord unlawfully terminates a tenancy "would give Lessor the unilateral right to terminate at any time for any reason regardless of any default *and* impose a large penalty on Lessee." Such a result would be unjust in any case; it is particularly unjust where the lessor terminates the tenancy by denying access to the business property and thereby prevents the lessee from earning income to pay the rent.

Is this unclean hands, or something else?

2. Buyer in the Ordinary Course

A defendant's status as a buyer in the ordinary course is an affirmative defense to several claims, including conversion and replevin. *Inland Bank and Tr. v. ARG Intl. AG,* 2018 WL 3543905 (S.D.N.Y. May 3, 2018), *report adopted,* 2018 WL 3542844 (S.D.N.Y. July 23, 2018). The status can arise under common law or UCC Article 2. *Arthur Glick Truck Sales, Inc. v. Stuphen E. Corp.,* 965 F. Supp. 2d 402 (S.D.N.Y. 2013), *aff'd,* 577 F. App'x 11 (2d Cir. 2014). A buyer of goods in the ordinary course of business takes free of a perfected security interest in the goods created by the seller. A "buyer in ordinary course of business" is defined by the UCC to mean:

> a person that buys goods in good faith, without knowledge that the sale violates the rights of another person in the goods, and in the ordinary course from a person, other than a pawnbroker, in the business of selling goods of that kind. A person buys goods in the ordinary course if the sale to the person comports with the usual or customary practices in the kind of business in which the seller is engaged or with the seller's own usual or customary practices. A person that sells oil, gas, or other minerals at the wellhead or minehead is a person in the business of selling goods of that kind. A buyer in ordinary course of business may buy for cash, by exchange of other property, or on secured or unsecured credit, and may acquire goods or documents of title under a preexisting contract for sale. *Only a buyer that takes possession of the goods* or has a right to recover the goods from the seller under Chapter 1302 of the Revised Code may be a buyer in ordinary course of business. "Buyer in ordinary course of business" does not include a person that acquires goods in a transfer in bulk or as security for or in total or partial satisfaction of a money debt.

Hockensmith v. Fifth Third Bank

79 UCC Rep. Serv. 2d 176 (S.D. Ohio 2012) (Beckwith, J.)

[Plaintiff Randall Hockensmith bought and sold vintage cars. Often he would buy a car and use Performance Plus Motor Sports, Inc., to restore or customize a car before reselling it. Performance Plus often retained a portion of the profits and titles to vehicles that were held in its name for matters of convenience.

Fifth Third Bank provided floor financing to Performance Plus under an agreement that gave Fifth Third a security interest in all goods owned, or acquired by, Performance Plus, including all new and used cars, "whether held for sale or lease, or furnished or to be furnished under any contract for service/" Hockensmith purchased several valuable, vintage Corvettes and Performance Plus was working on them when it notified Hockensmith that Fifth Third was "systematically putting it out of business" over its floor plan. Hockensmith asked Performance Plus to move the cars and title them in his name. Title was immediately changed to Hockensmith's name, but—four months later—they were still at Performance Plus when the sheriff entered Performance Plus's property and seized all property to satisfy Fifth Third's judgment against it.

Plaintiff sued Fifth Third, asserting claims for conversion and replevin. Fifth Third asserted in response that it had a perfected security interest and so had been entitled to sell the Corvettes to apply the proceeds to the debt owed to it by Performance Plus. In reply, Hockensmith asserted he had been a buyer in due course and moved for summary judgment on that ground. The court held that the fact that title was in Hockensmith's name was not dispositive and that a reasonable jury could find Fifth Third had had a perfected security interest. It then turned to whether summary judgment was proper in that Hockensmith had been a buyer in due course.]

There are three problems with Plaintiff's contention that he was a buyer of the Corvettes in the ordinary course of business. First, although Plaintiff adduced evidence showing wire transfers of cash to Performance Plus, at least two of the certificates of title indicate $0 as the purchase price of the car. In order to be a buyer in the ordinary course of business, however, the purchaser must give some value for the goods. Viewing the record in the light most favorable to Fifth Third, these certificates of title indicate that Plaintiff did not give value for at least two of the Corvettes. Additionally, as Fifth Third points out in its memorandum in opposition, Plaintiff has not adduced any bills of sale evidencing a purchase of the Corvettes from Performance Plus. A reasonable juror could conclude from these facts that Plaintiff did not give value to Performance Plus for the Corvettes.

Second, as Fifth Third correctly points out, Plaintiff never took possession of the Corvettes-indeed, he has never actually even seen them. Therefore, Plaintiff's failure to take possession of the Corvettes arguably disqualifies him from being a "buyer in the ordinary course of business." *But see Ace Equip. Sales, Inc. v. H.O. Penn Mach. Co., Inc.*, 88 Conn.App. 687 (2005) (buyer was buyer in the ordinary course of business, despite failure to take physical possession of rock crusher, because custom of the industry was not to take physical possession of heavy equipment because of prohibitive cost of transportation); In re Havens Steel Co., 317 B.R. 75 (Bkrtcy. W.D. Mo. 2004) (constructive possession sufficient to confer "buyer in the ordinary course of business" status).

Third, a buyer in the ordinary course of business only takes free of a security interest created by his seller. In this case, while the evidence shows that Performance Plus created the security interests in the Corvettes, Plaintiff did not buy the Corvettes from Performance Plus. Rather, the evidence shows that Performance Plus located sellers of Corvettes for Plaintiff and bought or traded for Corvettes from third-parties on his behalf. Stated another way, Performance Plus acted as Plaintiff's purchasing agent for the Corvettes. Plaintiff's affidavit in fact states that he bought Corvettes through Performance Plus and not from Performance Plus. Thus, the record shows that the actual sellers of the Corvettes to Plaintiff were third parties, not Performance Plus. Since Performance Plus, and not the actual sellers of the Corvettes, created the security interests in the Corvettes, Plaintiff was not a buyer of the Corvettes in the ordinary course of business from Performance Plus. *See United States v. Continental Grain Co.,* 691 F.Supp. 1193 (W.D. Wis. 1988) ("The buyer loses this protection buyer in the ordinary course of business where the buyer purchases farm products from a person engaged in farming operations, or where the buyer's seller did not create the security interest in the goods sold."). While Plaintiff might be a buyer of the Corvettes in the ordinary course of business vis-à-vis the third parties, a reasonable juror could find that he was not a buyer of the Corvettes from Performance Plus in the ordinary course of business.

3. Mitigation: Post-Injury Reasonable Care by Plaintiff

A. Reducing Damages If Plaintiff Failed to Mitigate Damages

As shown in Chapter 12, a plaintiff has a duty to mitigate damages and reasonable expenses incurred in meeting that 'duty' are recoverable damages. As a defense, mitigation permits a defendant "to show the damages award should be limited because the plaintiff failed to take reasonable measures to mitigate its loss." *VICI Racing, LLC v. T-Mobile, USA, Inc.,* 763 F.3d 273 (3ᵈ Cir. 2014). Analyzing what the plaintiff should have done after the harm requires the fact-finder to consider "whether mitigation was feasible, what measures to limit damages were reasonable under the circumstances, and whether the plaintiff took sufficient measures to mitigate." *Id.* For example, if the plaintiff seeks lost wages, the defendant can reduce damages by showing the plaintiff could have, but did not take, a similar available job. *Id.* The plaintiff must have acted reasonably and the defendant can avoid loss the plaintiff "could have avoided without undue risk, burden or humiliation." *Id.*

Ordinarily, a plaintiff's failure to mitigate does not bar recovery, but precludes recovery of damages to the extent they were caused by the plaintiff's lack of reasonable care *after the injury.* A plaintiff punched by a defendant can recover damages for the punch, but if the defendant shows that the plaintiff's failure to follow a doctor's orders and care for the wound led to infection, the plaintiff cannot recover for damages that reasonably could have been avoided. While courts state that an injured plaintiff has a "duty" to mitigate, there is no *claim* for "breach" of the duty to mitigate. *E.g., Route 40 Holdings v. Tony's Pizza & Pasta Inc.,* 2010 WL 2161819 (Del. Super. Ct. May 27, 2010) (dismissing counterclaim for failure to mitigate, recognizing that "courts often refer to this concept as a 'duty to mitigate,' but technically it is not a duty because there are no damages for breach of the duty" and holding it must be pled). Further, it does not bar all recovery, unlike "statute of limitations, absence of proper parties, res judicata, usury, a release, prior award, infancy, bankruptcy, denial of partnership, bona fide purchaser, and" the like. *New Dimensions, Inc. v. Tarquini,* 743 S.E.2d 267 (Va. 2013).

Monahan v. Obici Med. Mgt. Serv., Inc.

628 S.E.2d 330 (Va. 2006) (Agee, J.)

[Plaintiff Lawrence Monahan was at work when he told his supervisor he felt ill and had double vision. The supervisor noted Monahan "wasn't moving quite right," had a co-worker drive Monahan to Wakefield Medical Center for a medical evaluation and called Monahan's wife and let her know he was ill. (Obici Medical Management Services, Inc., owned Wakefield.) Upon arrival at Wakefield, Monahan was told Wakefield was closed for lunch, but the office manager, Anita Curl, let him into the building and to an examination room because he was sweaty, walking slowly, and looked unsteady. At 1:00 p.m., Carol Wiggins, a physician's assistant, determined his blood pressure was "200 over 95." The nurse concluded he was having a "hypertension crisis" and gave him samples of a blood pressure medicine and told him to rest for a few days and to come back in two weeks to have his blood pressure check, but to come back the next day if his condition did not improve.

Monahan went to the pharmacy next door, and Curl saw him there, and noticed he seemed "very sick" and was "walking like somebody that was drunk and dizzy." She went in to Wakefield and told Wiggins, and Wiggins then found Monahan leaning against the building and talked to him further and prescribed a medication for dizziness. Wiggins testified she told Monahan to go to the emergency room, but in response he said he would wait for his wife. Wiggins admitted she gave Monahan the option of awaiting his wife or going to the emergency room. Wiggins testified she told Monahan he might be having a stroke, but Monahan denied this.

About 90 minutes after he arrived at Wakefield, a nurse called Monahan's wife, telling her Monahan was ready to be taken home. At home, Monahan told his wife that Wiggins had told him to get in bed and return on Friday. Mrs. Monahan left the bedroom briefly, but returned to find he had fallen out of bed. She called Wakefield, but no one answered, so she put him in their car and headed toward Riverside Hospital. En route, she called Wakefield and spoke to Curl. Curl testified she told her to stop and call emergency rescue, but then the cell signal dropped. At 3:00 p.m. they arrived at Riverside and Monahan was diagnosed with having had a stroke.

Monahan sued Wakefield, alleging it failed to properly diagnose his stroke, seeking $1.6 million in damages. At trial, experts testified the additional 20 minutes that Monahan's wife spent did not cause the stroke or increase its severity or consequences. Even so, over Monahan's objection, the trial court gave Obici's requested instruction to the jury: "The plaintiff has a duty to minimize his damages. If you find that the plaintiff did not act reasonably to minimize his damages and that, as a result, they increased, then he cannot recover the amount by which they increased." The jury found for Monahan and awarded $215,000. Monahan appealed.]

A patient's duty to mitigate damages after receiving negligent medical care is a specific application of the general requirement that:

> One who is injured by the wrongful or negligent acts of another, whether as the result of a tort or of a breach of contract, is bound to exercise reasonable care and diligence to avoid loss or to minimize or lessen the resulting damage, and to the extent that his damages are the result of his active and unreasonable enhancement thereof or are due to his failure to exercise such care and diligence, he cannot recover.

Lawrence v. Wirth, 226 Va. 408 (1983). A mitigation of damages instruction is thus appropriate when the evidence shows that a plaintiff failed to mitigate his damages by neglecting his health following his physician's negligent treatment.

In the case at bar, the record is insufficient to sustain the mitigation of damages instruction because it does not reflect any act of neglect by Monahan following Wiggins' treatment. The uncontradicted evidence shows that Monahan chose one of the options his health care provider, Wiggins, offered to him: he had someone drive him home and went to bed. After his wife arrived home, his condition had worsened, and he was taken to an emergency room, as Wiggins had suggested. Because Wiggins gave Monahan the alternative course of action of either going to the emergency room or going home, and because Monahan complied with that advice by electing to go home, his decision cannot be the basis for a mitigation of damages instruction. Monahan did not act contrary to the advice given to him by his health care provider, but followed one of the courses offered. Therefore, no act of negligence supporting a failure to mitigate damages can be attributed to him based on his following the course of action offered by Wiggins. Obici points to no other evidentiary basis for the instruction.

The trial court thus erred in granting Obici's instruction on mitigation of damages, as there was no evidentiary basis to support it. If an issue is erroneously submitted to a jury, we presume that the jury decided the case upon that issue. Accordingly, we cannot say that the trial court's error in instructing the jury on the plaintiff's duty to mitigate his damages was harmless. We must presume the jury's consideration of damages was affected by the improperly given mitigation instruction.

Obici did not assign cross-error to the trial court's judgment that it was negligent. Upon retrial, the finding of liability is binding upon Obici, and Monahan will not be required to establish that Obici was negligent. We will also affirm that portion of the trial court's judgment that Obici was not required to specifically plead mitigation of damages as a condition precedent to asserting that defense. However, we will reverse the trial court's judgment as to damages because it was error to give the instruction on mitigation of damages and not to grant the motion to strike the evidence concerning the decision to drive Monahan to Riverside Hospital. We will therefore remand the case for a new trial limited to the issue of damages.

Notes and Questions

1. <u>When Does the Obligation to Mitigate Begin?</u> In *Brigham Young Univ. v. Pfizer, Inc.*, 2012 WL 1029116 (D. Utah March 26, 2012), the court stated that the "duty to mitigate damages does not arise until the promisee learns that the contract has been breached."

2. <u>Liquidated Damages Clauses</u>. Recall that failure to mitigate does not reduce the damages set in a liquidated damages clause. *NPS, LLC v. Minihane*, 451 Mass. 417 (2008) ("When parties agree in advance to a sum certain that represents a reasonable estimate of potential damages, they exchange the opportunity to determine actual damages after a breach, including possible mitigation, for the peace of mind and certainty of result afforded by a liquidated damages clause. In such circumstances, to consider whether a plaintiff has mitigated its damages not only is illogical, but also defeats the purpose of liquidated damages provisions.").

3. <u>Pleading</u>. Perhaps because mitigation does not cut off liability, courts split on whether mitigation of damages as a defense must be pled. Federal courts generally require it be pled or it is waived. *VICI Racing, LLC v. T-Mobile, USA, Inc.*, 763 F.3d 273 (3ᵈ Cir. 2014).

4. The Collateral Source Rule

A. Applicability to Torts at Common Law

By 1876, it was "well settled that the reception of the amount of the loss from the insurers is no bar to an action subsequently commenced against the wrong-doer to recover compensation for an injury occasioned by a collision." *The Atlas*, 93 U.S. 302 (1876). The term "collateral source" arose from *Harding v. Town of Townshend*, 43 Vt. 536 (1871), which characterized insurance proceeds received by the plaintiff as "collateral" to any recovery from the wrongdoer or its insurer:

> The policy of insurance is collateral to the remedy against the defendant and was procured solely by the plaintiff and at his expense, and to the procurement of which the defendant was in no way contributory. It is in the nature of a wager between the plaintiff and the third person, the insurer, to which the defendant was in no measure privy, either by relation to the parties, or by contract, or otherwise. It cannot be said that the plaintiff took out the policy in the interest or behalf of the defendant, nor is there any legal principle which seems to require that it be ultimately appropriated to the defendant's use and benefit.

Eventually, every state adopted some form of the rule, which is generally stated in Section 920A of the Restatement (Second) of Torts:

(1) A payment made by a tortfeasor or by a person acting for him to a person whom he has injured is credited against his tort liability, as are payments made by another who is, or believes he is, subject to the same tort liability.

(2) Payments made to or benefits conferred on the injured party from other sources are not credited against the tortfeasor's liability, although they cover all or a part of the harm for which the tortfeasor is liable.

The collateral source rule has both a substantive and evidentiary aspect. Substantively, it prohibits reducing a plaintiff's recovery by benefits from sources unrelated to the defendant, as a comment to the Restatement explains:

Payments made or benefits conferred by other sources are known as collateral-source benefits. They do not have the effect of reducing the recovery against the defendant. The injured party's net loss may have been reduced correspondingly, and to the extent that the defendant is required to pay the total amount there may be a double compensation for a part of the plaintiff's injury. But it is the position of the law that a benefit that is directed to the injured party should not be shifted so as to become a windfall for the tortfeasor. If the plaintiff was himself responsible for the benefit, as by maintaining his own insurance or by making advantageous employment arrangements, the law allows him to keep it for himself. If the benefit was a gift to the plaintiff from a third party or established for him by law, he should not be deprived of the advantage that it confers. The law does not differentiate between the nature of the benefits, so long as they did not come from the defendant or a person acting for him. One way of stating this conclusion is to say that it is the tortfeasor's responsibility to compensate for all harm that he causes, not confined to the net loss that the injured party receives.

Thus, the tortfeasor is held responsible for the harm he caused, not merely the "net loss" of the injured party.

The evidentiary aspect is simply a corollary of the substantive law: because a plaintiff's recovery should not be reduced by collateral benefits, evidence that a plaintiff received them should be excluded. Comment *c* to Section 920A relates to the evidentiary component of the collateral source rule. This comment lists the type of benefits precluded by the collateral source rule: (1) insurance policies, whether maintained by the plaintiff or a third party, (2) employment benefits, either gratuitous or arising out of contract, (3) gratuities, and (4) social legislation benefits, such as Social Security benefits, welfare, and pensions. *Id.* § 920A cmt. c.

ML Healthcare Serv., LLC v. Publix Super Markets, Inc.
881 F.3d 1293 (11th Cir. 2018) (Carnes, J.)

[Plaintiff slipped and fell at defendant's store. She sued, and defendant discovered that her treating physicians had a financial relationship with ML Healthcare under which the physicians sold debt to ML Healthcare at a discount, but it retained the right to recover the full cost of care out of any settlement or judgment she obtained. During the eight-day trial, defendant introduced evidence of the discounts over plaintiff's objection to exclude it under the collateral source rule. The jury returned a verdict for defendant, and plaintiff appealed.]

When a tort plaintiff has been compensated by her health insurer, or other non-defendants, for injuries that have been caused by the defendant, the question arises whether the plaintiff can recover those expenses for which she has already been reimbursed. The collateral source rule provides that the plaintiff is entitled to recover those already-reimbursed expenses. Georgia follows the collateral source rule, which gives a plaintiff the right to recover damages undiminished by collateral benefits. It refuses credit to the benefit of a tortfeasor of money or services received by the plaintiff in reparation of the injury or damage caused which emanate from sources other than the tortfeasor.

The collateral source rule, stated simply, is that the receipt of benefits or mitigation of loss from sources other than the defendant will not operate to diminish the plaintiff's recovery of damages. If a windfall must be had, it will inure to the benefit of the injured party rather than relieve the wrongdoer of full responsibility for his wrongdoing.

Given this prohibition against a credit to the defendant for expenses already recovered by the plaintiff, it follows that evidence of collateral benefits is inadmissible if the only proposition for which it is offered is in reduction of damages, because it is then offered to help prove a proposition which is not a matter in issue. On the other hand, the Georgia Supreme Court has recognized that there may be another issue in a case to which evidence of collateral benefits is material. When that happens and the evidence is admitted for that other purpose, the court should nonetheless charge the jury that collateral benefits shall not reduce damages the tortfeasor is otherwise liable to pay. Indeed, Georgia appellate courts have recognized that evidence of collateral benefits received by the plaintiff may be admissible for impeachment purposes when a witness gives false evidence relating to a material issue in the case. In short, under Georgia law, evidence of collateral benefits is not typically admissible in a personal injury tort case unless that evidence serves a valid evidentiary purpose other than just revealing to the jury those benefits. When that occurs and the evidence is admitted, the trial court should instruct the jury about the limited purpose of the evidence and, in particular, remind the jury not to consider the collateral payments to reduce its award of reasonable and necessary medical expenses.

Plaintiff and ML Healthcare argue that the collateral source rule was violated in this case as a result of the district court's orders requiring ML Healthcare to produce—and admitting at trial—evidence concerning payments made by ML Healthcare to Plaintiff's treating doctors. As noted, the district court denied the motion, in part, ruling that this evidence could be admitted for only two limited purposes: (1) to attack the credibility of the causation opinions proffered by Plaintiff's doctors and (2) to challenge the reasonableness of Plaintiff's claimed medical expenses.

Defendant asserted a theory of bias in this case stemming from ML Healthcare's business model and the incentives it creates for the treating doctors who testify on behalf of their patients. As explained above, ML Healthcare matches injured, uninsured plaintiffs who have viable tort claims with treating doctors. It then purchases at a discounted rate the medical bills these doctors generate. To recoup its investment and make a profit, its contract with the plaintiffs permits ML Healthcare to recover the full amount of these bills from any tort damages recovered by the plaintiffs. The contract also provides that the referred plaintiffs will personally repay ML Healthcare the full amount of the bills if they recover no damages or if there are insufficient damages to cover the bills. In short, the contract allows ML Healthcare to recover the difference between the discounted bills it pays treating doctors and what those doctors say is the full value of those medical services: either from the plaintiffs themselves or from any tort recovery the plaintiffs receive. Nonetheless, a plaintiff who recovers insufficient damages to pay back ML Healthcare may be unable or unwilling to repay her debt, meaning that, absent a recovery by the plaintiff in such cases, ML Healthcare will be out not only its investment, but also any hoped-for profit. Thus, for its business model to flourish, ML Healthcare needs the plaintiffs whom it subsidizes to win their lawsuits.

The district court did not abuse its discretion in crediting this argument, and thus permitting evidence of ML Healthcare's payment arrangement to be admitted for the limited purpose of showing bias on the part of the doctors who testified in this case. First, the evidence was relevant. Indeed, proof of bias will typically be relevant. The fact that the evidence also implicates the collateral source rule does not render it irrelevant for impeachment purposes.

With Plaintiff's full outstanding liability explained, there is no reason to think the jury would find it unnecessary to compensate Plaintiff because a portion of her medical bills had been paid by ML Healthcare. The purpose of the collateral source rule is to ensure that a tortfeasor is not allowed to benefit from its wrongful conduct simply because a plaintiff's bills have been paid by some other party. The jury presumably understood that plaintiff's bills were still due in full, and that any damages award should therefore not be reduced as a result of ML Healthcare's payments.

Finally, the district court properly instructed the jury about the collateral source rule and directed the jury not to reduce any damages it might award on account of ML Healthcare's payments. Few tenets are more fundamental to our jury trial system than the presumption that juries obey the court's instructions. Indeed, the presumption that juries follow their instructions is necessary to any meaningful search for the reason behind a jury verdict. This presumption is, therefore, almost invariable. In short, the district court's jury instruction was sufficient to ensure that the ML Healthcare evidence admitted to show bias on the part of Plaintiff's doctors would not be used in an unfairly prejudicial manner in violation of Georgia's collateral source rule.

Russell v. Haji-Ali

826 N.W.2d 216 (Ct. App. Minn. 2013) (Rodenberg, J.)

[Defendant ran a red light and injured the plaintiff, who had an underinsured motorist policy. Her damages exceeded the $50,000 policy held by the defendant. Before trial, she had incurred $43,000 in medical bills. During pre-suit mediation, plaintiff settled with her insurer, receiving $50,000 in exchange for release of her UIM claim. The insurer did not obtain subrogation rights. The case was tried and the jury returned a verdict of $102,974. Defendant moved to reduce damages by the $50,000 payment. The trial court denied the motion and defendant appealed.]

The common-law collateral-source rule provided that payment for some of the plaintiff's personal injury costs by a source other than the defendant may not be used to reduce the plaintiff's damage award against the defendant. This rule allowed injured claimants to recover damages from a tortfeasor even when the claimant received a double recovery as a result of having previously received payment from a collateral source.

In 1986, the Minnesota legislature partially abrogated the common-law rule by adopting Minn.Stat. § 548.251, the collateral-source statute. This statute requires courts, upon timely motion, to reduce a civil judgment by "amounts of collateral sources that have been paid for the benefit of the plaintiff." The statute defines "collateral sources" as "payments related to the injury or disability in question made to the plaintiff up to the date of the verdict, by or pursuant to: health, accident and sickness, or *automobile accident insurance* or liability insurance that provides health benefits or income disability coverage." *Id.* (emph. added).

The collateral-source statute enumerates specific sources that, on motion, operate to reduce the judgment. For all other collateral sources, the common-law rule continues to apply, and those sources do not result in a reduction of the judgment.[1] At issue in this case is whether "automobile accident insurance," as enumerated in the collateral-source statute, includes UIM benefits.

Here, the statute requires courts to reduce a damages award in a personal-injury case by the amount of any payments that are defined as collateral sources in the statute. The statute plainly provides that "automobile accident insurance" payments "related to the injury or disability in question made to the plaintiff up to the date of the verdict" constitute a statutory collateral source. As UIM benefits are a form

---

1. For example, under the common-law rule, collateral sources include gifts from third parties and family members. *See Swanson v. Brewster*, 784 N.W.2d 264 (Minn. 2010). By excluding such gifts from the definition of "collateral sources" under the statute, the legislature intended the common-law rule to continue to apply to such gifts, meaning that judgments will not be reduced by those amounts.

of "automobile accident insurance" payments "related to the injury or disability in question," and as the payments in this case were made to respondent prior to the verdict, the UIM benefits here are a collateral source under the plain language of the statute.

We are mindful that, in practice, the timing of payment as between the two coverages may differ. A claimant may generally obtain UM benefits (subject to subrogation rights) without first suing the uninsured tortfeasor. *See, e.g., State Farm Mut. Auto. Ins. Co. v. Galloway*, 373 N.W.2d 301 (Minn. 1985) (noting that injured claimants commonly collect UM benefits, subject to the insurer's subrogation rights, before commencing an action against the uninsured motorist). In contrast, because UIM coverage depends upon the tortfeasor's liability insurance being insufficient to cover a claimant's damages, a UIM claim does not mature until *after* liability and damages have been established. *See, e.g., Emps. Mut. Cos. v. Nordstrom*, 495 N.W.2d 855 (Minn. 1993) (holding that an injured claimant may not compel arbitration of UIM coverage until after the tortfeasor's liability and damages have been determined).

Additionally, because UIM benefits are generally not paid until after the tort action has been tried, UIM benefits are not a collateral source in the usual case. *See* § 548.251, subd. 1 (defining "collateral sources" to include only payments made "up to the date of the verdict"). In the normal course, a UIM claimant is limited to recovery of those items of damages not covered by the tortfeasor's liability insurance. As the amount of UIM benefits properly payable is based on the verdict or other recovery from the tortfeasor, a claimant in such situations usually recovers only the damages sustained in excess of the tortfeasor's liability insurance (and up to the contractual UIM limit) with no resulting possibility of any double recovery.

In this case, if respondent had refrained from presenting or settling her UIM claim until after the verdict, the UIM benefits would not be a collateral-source payment under the statute. By electing to settle the UIM claims *before* liability or damages had been determined, respondent brought those payments within the scope of the statute, essentially converting what would in the typical case have been excess coverage into a collateral-source payment. Her decision to settle the UIM claim prior to the verdict triggered the broad statutory definition of "automobile accident insurance" as a collateral source.

In sum, because respondent was paid UIM benefits before the verdict, that payment was a collateral-source payment under § 548.251, subd. 1. The district court erred in denying appellant's motion to reduce the jury award accordingly.

Notes and Questions

1. <u>Good Incentives</u>? Under *Russell*, if a plaintiff settles after verdict with her own insurance company, defendant's liability will not be reduced. What incentives does that rule create?

2. <u>Medical Bills</u>. Was the discount in *ML Healthcare* a collateral source? Further, consider that—whether by practice or discounts negotiated with insurance

companies—health care providers commonly write down the "actual" cost of care. Is this a "collateral source?" The court in *Dedmon v. Steelman*, 535 S.W.3d 431 (Tenn. 2017) discussed the approaches:

> Under the common law, courts in other jurisdictions have developed a variety of approaches to the role of the collateral source rule in awarding damages in personal injury lawsuits. These approaches have been grouped into three categories: (1) actual amount paid, (2) benefit of the bargain, and (3) reasonable value.

> A minority of courts follow the "actual amount paid" approach urged by the Defendants in this appeal. The "actual amount paid" approach limits a plaintiff's recovery to the amount actually paid to the medical provider, either by insurance or otherwise. Courts following this approach generally seek to avoid allowing plaintiffs any so-called "windfall" from tortfeasors. They take the position that limiting plaintiffs' recovery to the amount paid to the medical provider is not contrary to the collateral source rule because the rule is not implicated. When insurance payments are used to compensate the plaintiff's medical providers, they reason, limiting the plaintiff's recovery to only the amount actually paid by the insurance company to the medical provider simply permits the plaintiff to recover no more than he has expended.

> The next approach, the "benefit-of-the-bargain" approach, permits recovery of full, undiscounted medical bills, including the negotiated rate differential, only where the plaintiff paid consideration for the insurance benefits. Under this approach, when the plaintiff is privately insured, the negotiated rate differential is considered to be as much of a benefit for which the plaintiff paid consideration as are the actual cash payments made by his health insurance carrier to the health care providers. However, courts that follow this approach do not allow plaintiffs to recover the amount of their full bills if they did not pay for the benefit of discounted rates and write-offs. The "benefit of the bargain" approach seeks to encourage the purchase of insurance and reward those who exercise prudence and pay for an insurance policy.

> The third general approach may be called the "reasonable value" approach, with a proviso that courts have defined "reasonable value" in different ways. Under the reasonable value approach, plaintiffs may recover the "reasonable value" of their medical expenses, regardless of whether the plaintiff is privately insured. Of the courts that use the "reasonable value" approach, a minority defines "reasonable value" as the actual amount paid, while a majority holds that the "reasonable value" can be the plaintiff's full, undiscounted medical bills. A few courts use a "hybrid" method, allowing the trier of fact to consider both the actual amount paid and the full bill

in determining the "reasonable value" of medical services provided to the plaintiff.

Can you articulate the pros and cons of each approach, and why legislatures have not resolved the issue, but have largely left this to the courts? Does the presumption that juries follow instructions suggest which approach is correct?

3. <u>Gratuitous Medical Services</u>. Many states do not permit defendants to show services were provided for free, but instead instruct juries to award "reasonable" expenses. Why? Consider also *Rodriguez v. GPI MS-N, Inc.*, 2017 WL 2835749 (S.D. Miss. June 1, 2017), which held the plaintiff could recover for medical bills that he had not paid, even though any claim for payment by the healthcare providers was likely time-barred.

B. Inapplicability to Contract Damages

Hormel Foods Corp. v. Crystal Distrib. Serv., Inc.

2012 WL 1119885 (N.D. Iowa Apr. 3, 2012) (Scoles, J.)

[Hormel had a contract with Crystal for Crystal to store Hormel's products. Contrary to the agreement, Crystal stored products in a low warehouse floor, which flooded. Hormel lost $4 million in damaged products. With only contract claims remaining in the case, plaintiff Hormel moved to exclude evidence that its insurers had covered just over $3 million of those losses.]

Application of the collateral source rule in contract actions has not been widely discussed. One commentator has suggested that areas in other man tort law, "it has led little more than a shadow existence." John G. Fleming, *The Collateral Source Rule and Contract Damages*, 71 Cal. L.Rev. 56 (1983). Many cases reflexively suggest that a plaintiff in a contract action cannot recover for losses reimbursed by an insurer.

More recently, courts have considered whether the collateral source rule applies in contract actions when the collateral source has a right to subrogation. *See, e.g., Metoyer v. Auto Club Family Ins. Co.*, 536 F.Supp.2d 664 (E.D. La. 2008). The collateral source rule may not apply when "even though the action was termed a breach of contract, the action had elements of tort" because the plaintiff had to prove negligence. *Id.* Here, Hormel claims that Crystal breached paragraph 12 of the Warehouse Agreement, which requires Crystal to indemnify Hormel for any loss or damage to products resulting "from the negligence of Crystal, its employees and agents." When there is no danger of a double recovery or windfall because of a subrogation right, it is suggested that evidence of the collateral payment may be excluded.

Judge McManus has previously determined that the collateral source rule does not apply in this case. Accordingly, Hormel concedes that Crystal will be permitted to offer evidence regarding payments by Hormel's insurers. The fighting issue is whether Hormel's recovery is limited to unreimbursed losses, or if it may also recover reimbursed losses for which there is a right of subrogation. Hormel will not receive a double recovery and Crystal is not subject to a subsequent action by the insurers. Under the circumstances presented in this case, the Court concludes that a jury may award Hormel the full amount of its loss, provided Hormel is able to prove the insurers' rights to subrogation.

Notes and Questions

1. <u>Tort or Contract?</u> In *Miller v. St. Farm Mut. Auto. Ins. Co.*, 993 A.2d 1049 (Del. 2010), the Millers were injured in an accident when defendant King collided with their car. The Millers had a policy with State Farm for underinsured motorists. (In this jurisdiction, State Farm was a defendant, but the trial would be about liability of King and damages.) Before trial, King's insurer paid the $50,000 policy limits. One plaintiff's workers' compensation carrier accepted $24,000 of the $50,000 as settlement of its reimbursement right. The Millers were proceeding against State Farm and they moved to exclude reference to the workers' compensation payment. The trial court ruled that, because the collateral source rule did not apply to contract claims, it would admit the workers' compensation payment but instruct the jury that the Millers were required to repay it. This court reversed, stating that "State Farm's contractual obligation to pay the Millers is derived from King's liability in tort," and "Miller's entitlement to recover from King would not have been diminished by payments Miller received from a collateral source."

5. Comparative Fault, Preexisting Conditions, and Apportionment

The need to apportion damages arises only when two (or more) parties' conduct harms the plaintiff in an indivisible way. If two drivers both collide with plaintiff's car, at common law unless one driver could persuade the jury that it caused only some of the harm, each defendant was jointly and severally liable for the entire harm. Likewise, at common law, a plaintiff could choose which of those two drivers to sue for causing that single injury, and ordinarily that defendant would be unable to join the other driver as defendant. The single defendant would be held liable for all of the damages but have the right to sue the unnamed driver for contribution. This put the risk of insolvency on defendants: a plaintiff could pick who to sue or collect a judgment from, and let that defendant pursue contribution from the other wrongdoers.

State legislatures changed much of this, but in different ways. The statutes create bizarre questions, such as whether a defendant whose security system's failure allowed a defendant to rape a plaintiff can apportion damages to the rapist. This section explores those common issues. State legislatures have altered the common law approach as to whether, and to what extent, the defendants sued by the plaintiff can be held entirely responsible for the harm, even if others, including the plaintiff, contributed to the harm. Three clear majority approaches exist.

First, states have eliminated "contributory negligence"—under which a defendant could avoid all liability by showing the plaintiff had been slightly at fault—and replaced it with "modified comparative fault," under which a plaintiff can recover damages not caused by its own negligence, so long as the plaintiff was not more than 50% at fault (or 50% or more at fault, depending on the statute). Second, most states permit defendants to notify plaintiffs that third parties—not sued by the plaintiff—are responsible for all or a part of plaintiff's damages, and a jury will apportion fault to these non-parties. (Unless sued by the plaintiff, these are so-called "empty chair" defendants.) Third, most states have abolished, in large measure, joint and several liability. Instead of each defendant being liable for an entire judgment, each is liable only for its proportion of fault. While this means that a defendant cannot be forced to pay more than its "share" of damage, the risk of insolvent defendants falls on the plaintiff.

Beyond those basic statements, the legislative "solutions" to joint and several liability are varied, inconsistent, and driven by the statutory text. This section addresses several common issues and the different state legislatures' "solutions" to them. Issues in this chapter often turn on particular statutes. For example, a particular apportionment statute may not apply to breach of contract claims and so not permit comparative fault for breach of contract, *see L-3 Communics. Corp. v. E.R. Lewis Transp., Inc.,* 2005 WL 3591987 (D. Utah. Dec. 30, 2005); and some have been construed to permit apportionment of purely economic harm, at least in tort. *See Fed. Dep. Ins. Corp. v. Loudermilk,* 305 S.E.3d 558 (Ga. 2019) (concluding financial losses caused by bank directors were "injury" to "person or property").

A. Comparative Fault and Apportioning Tort Damages

I. Comparative Fault and Preexisting Conditions

Moore v. Fargo Pub. Sch. Dist. No. 1

815 N.W.2d 273 (N.D. 2012) (Sandstrom, J.)

[Fifteen-year-old plaintiff, M.M., the son of the other plaintiff, Thomas Moore, was seriously injured while practicing a bicycle stunt for a class in the school auditorium. The plaintiffs sued the school district and history teacher. The trial court refused the school district's request to instruct the jury to apportion fault to Moore. The jury awarded $285,000 for past medical expenses for care to M.M. to Moore. It apportioned 30% of the fault to the teacher, Hart, and district employees, and 70% to M.M. The court denied Moore's motion to enter judgment for $85,500—30% of the $285,000—because the state apportionment statute barred recovery if the fault of the person seeking to recover—here, M.M.—exceeded the fault of all others who had contributed to the harm to M.M. Moore appealed.]

North Dakota's modified comparative fault statute provides:

> Contributory fault does not bar recovery in an action by any person to recover damages for death or injury to person or property unless the fault was as great as the combined fault of all other persons who contribute to the injury, but any damages allowed must be diminished in proportion to the amount of contributing fault attributable to the person recovering. The court may, and when requested by any party, shall direct the jury to find separate special verdicts determining the amount of damages and the percentage of fault attributable to each person, whether or not a party, who contributed to the injury. The court shall then reduce the amount of such damages in proportion to the amount of fault attributable to the person recovering. When two or more parties are found to have contributed to the injury, the liability of each party is several only, and is not joint, and each party is liable only for the amount of damages attributable to the percentage of fault of that party, except that any persons who act in concert in committing a tortious act or aid or encourage the act, or ratifies or adopts the act for their benefit, are jointly liable for all damages attributable to their combined percentage of fault. Under this section, fault includes negligence, malpractice, absolute liability, dram shop liability, failure to warn, reckless or willful conduct, assumption of risk, misuse of product, failure to avoid injury, and product liability, including product liability involving negligence or strict liability or breach of warranty for product defect.

N.D.C.C. § 32-03.2-02.

Enacted in 1987, the modified comparative fault provisions of N.D.C.C. ch. 32-03.2 significantly revised tort liability in North Dakota and shifted the focus from traditional tort doctrines to the singular inclusive concept of 'fault.' Under the modified comparative fault law, negligence is included in the concept of fault, and the fault of two or more parties is compared so that each party is liable only for the amount of damages attributable to the percentage of fault by that party. By enacting N.D.C.C. § 32-03.2-02, the Legislature clearly intended to replace joint and several liability with several allocation of damages among those who commit torts in proportion to the fault of those who contributed to an injury. Although the modified comparative fault law significantly revised tort law in North Dakota, some former contributory negligence concepts remain viable.

Section 32-03.2-02 does not create an independent basis of tort liability, but deals only with the allocation of damages among those already at fault. The modified comparative fault laws are silent regarding whether a parent without fault may recover medical expenses for a child's injuries in proportion to the defendant's fault when the child's fault exceeds the defendant's fault. Considering the circumstances under which the statutes were enacted, however, we note the statutes were part of "tort reform" legislation believed necessary to lower insurance rates and improve the business climate within the state.

Generally, it is well-established that a parent's claims for medical expenses paid on behalf of an injured child are derivative, and the negligence of the injured family member is attributed to the person with the derivative claim. This result follows the view that the comparative-negligence statute was not intended to alter the judge-made law concerning derivative causes of action. *See also* Restatement (Second) of Torts § 494 ("The plaintiff is barred from recovery for an invasion of his legally protected interest in the health or life of a third person which results from the harm or death of such third person, if the negligence of such third person would have barred his own recovery."); Restatement (Third) of Torts § 6(a) (2000) ("When a plaintiff asserts a claim that derives from the defendant's tort against a third person, negligence of the third person is imputed to the plaintiff with respect to that claim.").

Moore recognizes the weight of authority does not favor his position, but argues barring his recovery because of M.M.'s negligence violates the plain language and purpose of § 14-09-21, which provides "neither parent nor child is answerable as such for the act of the other." Moore argues the statute precludes M.M.'s negligent acts from being "attributed" to Moore simply because they are parent and child. However, the statute uses the term "answerable," which means "subject to being called to account; responsible." *Webster's New World Dictionary* 57 (2nd College ed. 1980). As this Court said in *Peterson v. Rude*, 146 N.W.2d 555 (N.D. 1966), § 14-09-21 means "a parent is not *liable* for the negligent acts of a minor child merely because of such relationship." (Emph. added.) The statute codifies the common law rule. Attributing M.M.'s fault to Moore does not impose liability upon Moore.

Because Moore's claim for past medical expenses derives from M.M.'s injuries, and M.M. was denied recovery under our modified comparative fault laws, we conclude the district court correctly dismissed Moore's claim for M.M.'s medical expenses.

McLaughlin v. BNSF Ry. Co.

300 P.3d 925 (Ct. App. Colo. 2012) (Jones, J.)

[Plaintiff McLaughlin was injured when a train handbrake allegedly malfunctioned when he was releasing it. The defendant asserted that the injuries had not been caused by the handbrake, but he had preexisting conditions and the jury should have been, but was not, instructed to apportion between those and the harm caused by the handbrake. The jury found plaintiff had not been comparatively at fault and awarded $1,830,000. Defendant appealed.]

Evidence presented at trial showed that Mr. McLaughlin had pre-existing back and hernia conditions. Regarding his back conditions, Mr. McLaughlin testified that, after the handbrake incident, his doctors had diagnosed him with pre-existing degenerative disc disease and other age-related deteriorating back conditions. He also said, however, that he had not experienced any back pain or problems before the incident. One of his treating doctors confirmed that Mr. McLaughlin had not felt "any significant ongoing pain, prior to the injury, that was acute or chronic in nature, other than the sort of typical things that most people have, which is an occasional backache or something like that." He and another doctor also testified that most people who have such preexisting back conditions do not have persistent symptoms. The railroad did not show that Mr. McLaughlin's back conditions had been symptomatic immediately before the incident.

As to the hernia, Mr. McLaughlin testified that although he had suffered a hernia on his right side when he was seven or eight years old, the hernia was treated at that time, and he had not experienced any problems related to the hernia until after the incident. Both parties presented evidence that Mr. McLaughlin was born with a so-called indirect, or congenital, hernia, which is a weakness in the abdominal wall that may result in a sac or small, forming hernia that makes a person more susceptible to a symptomatic hernia. However, it was undisputed that this hernia was asymptomatic before the handbrake incident. It was also undisputed that there was no way to know whether the hernia would have become symptomatic had the incident not occurred.

At the close of evidence, the district court gave the following eggshell instruction, over the railroad's objection:

> In determining the amount of plaintiff's actual damages, you cannot reduce the amount of or refuse to award any such damages because of any physical frailties, conditions or diseases of the plaintiff that may have made him more susceptible to injury, disability or impairment than an average or normal person.

The court also gave the jury the following aggravation instruction:

> If you find for plaintiff Thomas F. McLaughlin, you should compensate plaintiff for any aggravation of an existing disease or physical defect resulting from such injury.

> If you find that there was an aggravation you should determine, if you can, what portion of plaintiff's condition resulted from the aggravation and make allowance in your verdict only for the aggravation. However, if you cannot make that determination or if it cannot be said that the condition would have existed apart from the injury, you should consider and make allowance in your verdict for the entire condition.

In deciding to give both instructions, the court reasoned that although the degenerative disc disease was a pre-existing condition warranting the aggravation instruction, the hernia was a congenital weakness for which an eggshell instruction was appropriate.

The court declined the railroad's request to give the jury a special verdict form asking it to specify what percentage of Mr. McLaughlin's damages was attributable to a pre-existing condition. Instead, it gave a verdict form which provided, in relevant part: "What amount do you find, if any, will fairly and adequately compensate the Plaintiff for all injuries and damages he sustained? Do not include any amount you find to be capable of apportionment to any pre-existing condition of Plaintiff."

The district court has a duty to instruct the jury correctly on the law applicable to the case. We review the district court's finding that sufficient evidence exists to give an instruction for an abuse of discretion. If the district court's decision to give an instruction was correct, we may affirm it on any grounds supported by the record.

A court errs by giving an instruction that misleads or confuses the jury. The court also generally errs by giving contradictory instructions.

The court's erroneous provision of an instruction is reversible error only if the error prejudiced a party's substantial rights. Such prejudice occurs where the jury might have returned a different verdict had the court not given the improper instruction. But there is no prejudicial error to the defendant in giving an instruction which states a rule more favorable than the defendant was entitled to have.

The eggshell doctrine provides that a tortfeasor takes its victim as it finds him. Thus, a tortfeasor is fully liable for any damages resulting from its wrongful act even if the victim had a pre-existing condition that made the consequences of the wrongful act more severe for him than they would have been for a person without the condition. Put differently, the tortfeasor may not escape or reduce liability because the victim's pre-existing condition made him more susceptible of injury from the tortfeasor's conduct.

However, a tortfeasor cannot be held liable for damages that it did not actually cause. Consequently, the aggravation doctrine provides generally that, notwithstanding the eggshell skull rule, a defendant is liable only for the extent to which the defendant's conduct has resulted in an aggravation of the pre-existing condition, and not for the condition as it was. The doctrine makes a tortfeasor liable for damages to the extent the tortious conduct has increased the severity of a pre-existing condition of the plaintiff.

The two doctrines thus may appear to conflict as to the amount of damages properly awardable where a plaintiff has a preexisting condition: the eggshell doctrine suggests that all damages are awardable despite the condition, whereas the aggravation doctrine indicates that only the damages resulting from aggravation of the condition are awardable. Nonetheless, we conclude that the doctrines are not necessarily mutually exclusive. Rather, instructions on both doctrines may be appropriate in certain circumstances, depending on whether there is evidence that the pre-existing condition was symptomatic before the incident giving rise to the plaintiff's claim.

The Restatement (Third) of Torts explains that "when a person has a preexisting condition or injury *that has already caused or is causing harm of some degree,* the actor is only liable for any enhancement of the harm caused by the tortious conduct." §31 cmt. c (emph. added). An illustration to this section provides:

> Gino, who worked as a concessionaire at a sports stadium, negligently collided with Maddy, a fan attending the game, and knocked her to the ground. Maddy had an asymptomatic herniated disc that resulted in her suffering

serious back injury and pain as a result of Gino's negligence. All of Maddy's harm is within Gino's scope of liability for his negligence, as a matter of law.

Id. cmt. b, illus. 1. However, under the same facts of this illustration

except that at the time Gino collided with Maddy, she had a mild level of chronic back pain and after the accident with Gino, Maddy suffered severe back pain, Gino is subject to liability for the enhanced injury to Maddy; he is not liable for the pain from which Maddy was suffering at the time of the accident.

Id. cmt. c, illus. 5. Consequently, according to the Restatement, a defendant is liable for all damages caused by its negligence where the plaintiff had an asymptomatic pre-existing condition: the aggravation doctrine does not apply in that circumstance. The aggravation doctrine does apply where the plaintiff had a symptomatic pre-existing condition that had already caused pain or disability.

A number of federal cases have also suggested that although apportionment of damages is appropriate where the plaintiff had a previously symptomatic condition, a plaintiff's damages cannot be reduced due to an asymptomatic pre-existing condition. *Johnson v. Cenac Towing, Inc.,* 599 F.Supp.2d 721 (E.D. La. 2009) (a jury may award damages for activation of a pre-existing latent condition); *see also Evans v. United Arab Shipping Co. (S.A.G.),* 790 F.Supp. 516 (D. N.J. 1992) (aggravation damages are for "the *increased and augmented suffering and disability* which was the proximate result of the defendant's act").

This is not to say, however, that giving instructions on both doctrines is necessarily improper where the pre-existing condition was symptomatic.[8] In *Waits v. United Fire & Casualty Co.,* 572 N.W.2d 565 (Iowa 1997), the Supreme Court of Iowa considered whether the trial court erred by providing both eggshell and aggravation instructions. The court began by determining the circumstances in which a trial court may properly give each instruction. Regarding the aggravation instruction, it reasoned that

a defendant is liable only for injuries caused by the defendant's fault, and not for pain or disability resulting from other causes. Thus, if a plaintiff had a prior back injury that caused pain and a ten percent disability *before* the injury inflicted by the defendant occurred, the defendant would not be responsible for the disability and pain that predated the current injury, but only for any *additional* pain and disability caused by the current injury.

---

8. This conclusion has also been reached by a number of state courts. *See, e.g., Montalvo v. Lapez,* 77 Hawai'i 282 (1994) (defendant could be held liable for all damages caused by the incident if the plaintiff had a dormant or latent preexisting condition or had fully recovered from the pre-existing condition before the incident; however, the jury should apportion damages if the condition was not dormant, latent, or fully resolved); *Lalim v. Debrobander,* 2003 WL 23811601 (Minn. Dist. Ct. Feb. 17, 2003) (the distinction between the eggshell and aggravation doctrines is the distinction between asymptomatic and symptomatic pre-existing conditions).

Under these circumstances, an aggravation instruction is appropriately submitted to the jury.

Conversely, when the pain or disability arguably caused by another condition arises *after* the injury caused by the defendant's fault has lighted up or exacerbated the prior condition, an eggshell instruction is appropriate because the mere existence of a prior nondisabling, asymptomatic, latent condition is not a defense. A tortfeasor whose act, superimposed upon such a condition, results in an injury may be liable in damages for the full disability. In these cases the injury, and not the dormant condition, is deemed to be the proximate cause of the pain and disability.

The court then indicated that both instructions could properly be given in two scenarios. First, either instruction could apply because there is evidence that the pre-existing condition was dormant, nondisabling, and asymptomatic (making an eggshell instruction appropriate); and there is conflicting evidence that the pre-existing condition had already caused symptoms or disability (making an aggravation instruction appropriate). Second, both instructions could apply because there is a factual basis for the jury to believe that the prior condition has caused some disability or pain that is aggravated by the second injury and at the same time the additional harm resulting from the second injury is greater than it would have been in the absence of the prior injury.

We are persuaded by the *Waits* court's reasoning. Therefore, we conclude that giving an eggshell instruction is appropriate where there is evidence that the plaintiff had a dormant or asymptomatic pre-existing condition. Giving an eggshell instruction is also appropriate where a pre-existing condition was symptomatic, if there is evidence that the harm resulting from the defendant's negligence is greater than it would have been in the absence of the pre-existing condition. Giving an aggravation instruction is not appropriate where the pre-existing condition was asymptomatic, but is appropriate where there is evidence that the plaintiff had previously suffered pain or symptoms from the condition, and the condition allegedly was aggravated by the incident. Depending on the evidence presented, one or both instructions may be appropriate. If both are given, an instruction clarifying for the jury how both should be applied should also be given.

Here, as noted, the district court gave both eggshell and aggravation instructions. The railroad contends that the court erred by providing the eggshell instruction because it was not arguing that Mr. McLaughlin should not be compensated due to his "frailty," but rather that the jury should apportion damages based on his pre-existing conditions. An eggshell instruction may be appropriate, however, where the defendant attempts either to eliminate or *to reduce* its liability based on the plaintiff's preexisting condition. Moreover, based on our analysis above, we conclude that the instruction was appropriate here because (1) there was no evidence that Mr. McLaughlin had suffered any pain or symptoms from his back conditions or hernia before the handbrake incident; and (2) there was evidence that his pre-existing conditions were made symptomatic or exacerbated by the incident.

In contrast, the evidence did not support giving the aggravation instruction. In *Waits*, the court concluded that an aggravation instruction was proper where the plaintiff had previously suffered a herniated disc that was resolved before the incident at issue, but which the incident reinjured. It did so in part because the previous injury made the plaintiff more susceptible to reinjury. Here, however, there was no evidence that the handbrake incident reinjured a previous injury. Nor, as noted, was there evidence that Mr. McLaughlin experienced symptoms before the incident that were aggravated, such that apportionment would have been appropriate.

Consequently, we conclude that the district court did not abuse its discretion by finding that the evidence supported giving the eggshell instruction, but did abuse its discretion by finding that the evidence of pre-existing degenerative disc disease warranted the aggravation instruction. It follows that the court did not abuse its discretion by rejecting the railroad's tendered special verdict form (allowing the jury to apportion damages attributable to pre-existing conditions by percentage), but did abuse its discretion by providing a modified verdict form telling the jury not to include "any amount you find to be capable of apportionment to any pre-existing condition of the Plaintiff."

However, the railroad does not argue that giving the aggravation instruction or modified verdict form was error. And, in any event, the errors were harmless because they did not affect the railroad's substantial rights. Giving the aggravation instruction and modified verdict form inured to the railroad's benefit because they told the jury to reduce the amount of damages based on Mr. McLaughlin's pre-existing conditions, thereby allowing the jury to reach a result that the evidence and the law did not warrant.

Notes and Questions

1. <u>The Cases</u>. What if M.M. had been 30% at fault? 50%? 51%? What if the teachers had conspired to harm M.M.? Consider also: who has the burden to uncover preexisting conditions? To come forward with evidence the condition was symptomatic?

2. <u>Preexisting Conditions</u>. As one of the principal cases explains, some courts treat preexisting conditions similar to comparative fault: if the defendant asserts some of the harm was preexisting, the defendant has the burden to prove what proportion preexisted the injury. *See Bouchard v. United States*, 501 F. Supp. 2d 200 (D. Me. 2007). Asymptomatic injuries create difficult issues. Suppose that before an accident, a plaintiff had no symptom of any back injury, but afterward plaintiff had back pain, but the medical evidence shows she had a preexisting, asymptomatic (or "latent") back injury. Courts split on whether apportionment is proper. In *Harris v. ShopKo Stores, Inc.*, 308 P.3d 449 (Utah 2013), the appellate court had held that if the preexisting injury had been asymptomatic, then an apportionment instruction was improper, but the state supreme court reversed:

> That the court of appeals would adopt this approach is certainly understandable given that other jurisdictions have followed a similar

approach, but we decline to adopt it. We conclude that our case law—which recognizes the central role proximate cause must play in tort law—is inconsistent with such a narrow, bright-line approach.

In *Brunson v. Strong*, 17 Utah 2d 364 (1966), we recognized that "one who injures another takes him as he is." Thus, a plaintiff is entitled to recover for all harm that is proximately caused by the defendant's negligence, "even if a given plaintiff is more vulnerable to injury than others." But this principle, commonly known as the eggshell plaintiff doctrine, in no way bars consideration of other relevant potential sources of a plaintiff's pain in determining the extent of damage proximately caused by the defendant.

Indeed, we further recognized in *Brunson* that although an injured party is taken "as he is, nevertheless the plaintiff may not recover damages for any pre-existing condition or disability she may have had *which did not result from any fault of the defendant.*" And while "she is entitled to recover damages for any injury she suffered, including any aggravation of such a preexisting condition," she may only do so to the extent that the aggravation *"was proximately caused by the defendant's negligence."* Moreover, in *Tingey v. Christensen,* 199 UT 68, we stated that "if the jury can find a reasonable basis for apportioning damages between a preexisting condition and a subsequent tort, it should do so."

These cases highlight the fundamental aim in deciding damages: to restore the injured party to the position he would have been in had it not been for the wrong of the other party. Proximate cause plays a central role in determining the precise extent of the defendant's liability and, in turn, what the plaintiff's position would have been absent the defendant's negligence.

The eggshell plaintiff doctrine does not alter this aim. It has never required tortfeasors to compensate plaintiffs for damages that the tortfeasors' negligence did not proximately cause. In our view, however, the court of appeals' narrow, bright-line approach to the eggshell plaintiff doctrine is inconsistent with this aim of awarding damages. An asymptomatic preexisting condition may well be an independent contributor to a plaintiff's pain and injury, which was also proximately caused to some degree by a tortfeasor's negligence. But the court of appeals' approach would prevent the jury from apportioning damages between the preexisting condition and the negligence simply because the preexisting condition was not symptomatic on the date of the accident. In our view, this result is potentially arbitrary and risks holding defendants liable for more than they proximately caused in damages. We accordingly conclude that whether a preexisting condition is symptomatic or asymptomatic on the date of the accident is not the determinative factor in granting an apportionment instruction.

While we reaffirm the jury's duty to apportion damages if the evidence supports doing so, we recognize that it is rarely easy to determine the causal contribution of a preexisting condition to a plaintiff's pain and injury. The objective symptoms and the physical basis of ailments are often difficult to discover, analyze and demonstrate to others. If the preexisting condition is asymptomatic at the time of the tortious conduct, the analysis will be even more difficult. But the evaluation and the conclusion to be drawn from the evidence is peculiarly within the province of the jury. Indeed, proximate cause — although often a thorny issue — is generally a question of fact for the jury to decide.

We are also confident that our case law already provides sufficient protection for eggshell-type plaintiffs even without the court of appeals' bright-line approach. In *Tingey*, we recognized that "a tortfeasor should bear the burden of uncertainty in the amount of a tort victim's damages." We accordingly held that while a jury should apportion if it can, it should find that the tortfeasor is liable for the entire amount of damages" if it "finds it impossible to apportion. Thus, the burden is on the defendant to demonstrate that apportionment is possible where there is any uncertainty.

Finally, we emphasize that our decision today is not an invitation for tortfeasors to dredge up every physical injury or defect a victim has ever had in an attempt to reduce liability. Evidence of preexisting conditions must be relevant to the pain or injury at issue and must also overcome other pertinent evidentiary hurdles in order to be admissible. If there is no evidence that a particular preexisting condition is relevant to the plaintiff's pain or injury, evidence of that condition should not be admitted.

3. Near-Simultaneous Injuries. In *Biazzo v. Parker*, 2014 WL 3407818 (N.J. Super. App. Div. July 15, 2014), the defendant was rear-ended twice in one afternoon and the court held: "plaintiff was not obliged to present proof apportioning the damage between the two collisions, as an essential element of his claim. We recognize that the accidents in this case were separated by a couple of hours. But, the similarity of the type of accident — rear-end collision with minor property damage, and the similarity of plaintiff's body areas affected by both collisions, warrant excusing plaintiff of the burden, otherwise borne by a tort plaintiff, to prove the damages caused by the respective defendants." How would a New Jersey jury in be instructed on the facts of *McLaughlin*?

II. Apportioning Damages for Harm Caused by a Non-Party

At common law, a plaintiff could obtain full recovery from any defendant(s) it chose to sue, leaving it (or them) to pursue contribution or indemnity from unnamed tortfeasors. Many apportionment statutes now permit defendants to notify plaintiffs of nonparties who may be wholly or partially liable for the plaintiff's harm. *E.g., Crandall v. Am. Family Mut. Ins. Co.*, 2013 WL 5819283 (D. Utah

Oct. 29, 2013) (where a Utah statute required notice within a reasonable time after discovery or 90 days before trial, court struck notice to apportion damages because, while filed more than 90 days before trial, defendant had unreasonably delayed).

Erdelyi v. Lott

326 P.3d 165 (Wyo. 2014) (Kite, J.)

[Plaintiff Erdelyi brought a fraud claim against her deceased mother's financial advisor, Lott. The trial court gave the jury a comparative fault instruction even though the claim was for economic harm and pled an intentional tort. The jury found for the defendant. Plaintiff appealed. After quoting the controlling apportionment statute in § 1-1-109, the court examined whether it required apportioning fault between a negligent and intentional wrongdoer.]

In *Board of County Comm'rs of Teton Co. v. Bassett,* 8 P.3d 1079 (Wyo. 2000), a negligence action, this Court held that Wyo. Stat. Ann. § 1-1-109 requires that "all species of culpable conduct" be compared in assessing fault. There, the plaintiffs were injured when a suspect fleeing from law enforcement ran a roadblock and crashed into their vehicle at a high rate of speed. Prior to the crash, law enforcement had waved the plaintiffs through the roadblock and onto the highway in front of the suspect without warning them that the suspect was speeding down the highway toward them. The plaintiffs brought an action against the officers alleging they were negligent for failing to warn them about the approaching vehicle. The issue was whether the suspect, a non-party actor, should be included on the verdict form so that his willful conduct could be compared with the officers' negligence.

In holding that the suspect must be included on the verdict form, the Court concluded that by using the word "fault" rather than negligence in § 1-1-109 and including strict and products liability, the legislature intended to broaden the scope of the statute to include willful conduct. The Court further concluded that the adoption of § 1-1-109 and the elimination of joint and several liability showed the legislature's intent to limit a tortfeasor's exposure to liability for the misconduct of other tortfeasors. The Court said:

> To leave an actor such as the fleeing suspect out of the apportionment calculation exposes the remaining defendants to the possibility that they will be held to answer for his misconduct. The legislature has clearly opted to relieve joint tortfeasors of liability beyond that for which they bear proportional fault.

Bassett, 8 P.3d at 1084. Thus, under *Bassett,* a joint tortfeasor who acts willfully is properly included as an actor on a verdict form in a negligence case so that the jury can compare the defendant's negligence and the non-party actor's willful conduct and apportion liability.

More recently, in *Strong Constr., Inc. v. City of Torrington*, 2011 WY 82 (Wyo. 2011), the Court held comparative fault was not applicable in a breach of contract action because the comparative fault statute applies to tort claims where a party is seeking personal injury or property damages caused by the fault of another, and breach of contract is not a tort claim.

The holding in *Bassett* must be placed in context. There, the issue was whether, under the comparative fault statute, the culpable conduct of a non-party tortfeasor must be compared with that of the defendants in a *negligence case. Bassett* did not address whether, in an *intentional tort case,* the negligence of a non-actor should be compared with the willful conduct of the defendant. More significantly for purposes of the present case, Bassett did not address whether in an *intentional tort case* any *negligence on the part of the claimant* should be compared with the *willful act of the defendant.* Confined to its facts, *Bassett* addressed only whether a non-party actor whose willful acts were a proximate cause of the claimants' injuries should be compared with the defendants' negligence to apportion fault and liability. In that context, it makes sense to include the non-party actor because it ensures the negligent defendants are not held liable for the intentional acts of another. In that context, it seems clear the legislature sought to ensure negligent defendants would not be held accountable for the intentional acts of another. We are not persuaded the legislature intended negligence on the part of a fraud victim to be compared with the intentional acts of the perpetrator so as to reduce the perpetrator's liability based upon any percentage of fault apportioned to the victim.

Some courts have declined to apply comparative fault principles when to do so would be inconsistent with public policy. *Otero v. Jordan Rest. Enters.*, 122 N.M. 187 (1996). Concluding it would be against public policy to allow the perpetrator of fraud to profit from his conduct, these courts have held comparative fault inapplicable in fraud cases. *Id. See also Tratchel v. Essex Group, Inc.*, 452 N.W.2d 171 (Iowa 1990) (holding that instruction on comparative fault of plaintiff was properly denied to defendant guilty of fraud); *Cruise v. Graham*, 622 So.2d 37 (Fla. Ct. App. 1993) (holding that denial of comparative fault instructions in fraud action was not error); *cf. Neff v. Bud Lewis Co.*, 89 N.M. 145 (Ct. App. 1976) (holding contributory negligence was not a defense to a claim for negligent misrepresentation by building owner against real estate broker and salesmen having fiduciary relationship to plaintiff); *Estate of Braswell v. People's Credit Union*, 602 A.2d 510 (R.I. 1992) (holding comparative negligence principles inapplicable in action for negligent misrepresentation against credit union).

Unlike this Court's holding in *Bassett*, some of these courts have held that comparative fault does not apply in *any* intentional tort case. Despite this difference, we find their reasoning persuasive in the context of a fraud claim. One who has committed fraud should not be allowed to escape liability for his wrongful conduct by shifting the responsibility to the victim. Such a result is contrary to public policy.

Absent clear statutory language showing the legislature intended the negligence of a fraud victim to be compared to the conduct of the perpetrator, thereby potentially reducing the latter's liability for his intentionally wrongful acts, we decline to hold that §1-1-109 is a proper matter for a jury instruction in a fraud case. The district court erred in instructing on comparative fault and negligence so as to allow the jury to compare Mr. Lott's willful act with any negligence of Ms. Erdelyi in this constructive fraud case. The district court further erred in providing a verdict form requiring the jury to compare Mr. Lott's constructive fraud and any negligence of Ms. Erdelyi.

In reaching this result, we note also that the legislature has provided a mechanism for relieving the perpetrator of fraud from liability for his conduct when a jury finds that the victim did not use due diligence to discover the fraud. The statute of limitations for fraud actions [in §1-3-106] is triggered when a claimant knows or could have discovered the fraud in the exercise of due diligence. If a jury finds that a claimant knew or could have discovered the fraud more than four years before filing the action, the perpetrator of the fraud is relieved from any liability. Thus, any "negligence" of the claimant in not discovering and timely pursuing a fraud claim is addressed in §1-3-106. There is no need for a separate instruction allowing a jury to compare a claimant's negligence or comparative fault with the willful act of the perpetrator in a fraud case.

On remand, the jury should not be instructed on negligence as to Ms. Erdelyi. The jury also should not be instructed on comparative fault as between Ms. Erdelyi and Mr. Lott.

Notes and Questions

1. Comparing Defendant's Negligence to a Third Party's Intentional Act. The principal case explains it "makes sense" to compare a negligent defendant with an intentional act by a third party. Many courts disagree, particularly if the defendant's negligence is what permitted the intentional harm to occur. Should a negligent landowner be able to shift its liability onto a criminal, who harmed someone on their land, when the intentional act was the foreseeable result of the defendant's negligence? The court in *Schoeff v. R.J. Reynolds Tobacco Co.*, 232 So. 3d 294 (Fla. 2017), reasons that the success of a negligence claim, when an intentional tort by a third party is the basis of the claim (such as when a parking lot owner knows of crime in the area, but does not take reasonable care, and the plaintiff is raped or beaten by an unknown third party), it is circular to permit apportionment: but for the defendant's negligence, the intentional tort would not have occurred. *See Martin v. Prime Hospitality Corp.*, 345 N.J. Super. 278 (N.J. Sup. Ct. 2001) (hotel could not apportion damages to non-party who sexually assaulted plaintiff). *Schoeff* also held that, because the statute prohibited apportioning damages caused by an intentional tort, it prohibited apportioning damages where a single harm was caused by both the defendant's negligent and intentional wrongdoing.

2. <u>Why Not Compare Defendant's Intentional Act with Plaintiff's Negligence?</u> The principal case suggests this is improper, but why not? Is it because fraud requires reasonable reliance, and so if the reliance was not reasonable, there is no claim? But what if plaintiff was reasonable, but only 49% so? The prevailing view is that apportionment does not apply to intentional tort claims. *See Garcia v. Gordon*, 136 N.M. 394 (2004) (holding that because jury was instructed false imprisonment could result from merely "unreasonable" detention, jury properly apportioned damages); *Le v. Nitetown, Inc.*, 72 So. 3d 374 (Ct. App. La. 2011) ("the trial court erred as a matter of law in reducing plaintiff's damages where the defendant is found liable for intentional tort.") One court explained:

> Negligent and intentional torts are different in degree, in kind, and in society's view of the relative culpability of each act. *Turner v. Jordan*, 957 S.W.2d 815 (Tenn. 1997). See, also, *Welch v. Southland Corp.*, 134 Wash.2d 629 (1998) (recognizing negligent and intentional torts are of "wholly different legal realm"); *Merrill Crossings Assocs. v. McDonald*, 705 So.2d 560 (Fla. 1997) (negligent acts are "fundamentally different" from intentional acts); *Veazey v. Elmwood Plantation Assocs., Ltd.*, 650 So.2d 712 (La. 1994) (recognizing intentional torts are of "fundamentally different nature" than negligent torts). Because of these differences, allowing allocation of damages between negligent and intentional tort-feasors presents practical difficulties. Fact finders are likely to allocate most, if not all, of the damages to the intentional tort-feasor due to the higher degree of social condemnation attached to intentional, as opposed to negligent, torts. Thus, allocation of a percentage of the damages to an intentional tort-feasor reduces the negligent party's incentive to comply with the applicable standard of care. Furthermore, it would be irrational to allow a party who negligently fails to discharge a duty to protect to reduce its liability because there is an intervening intentional tort when the intervening intentional tort is exactly what the negligent party had a duty to protect against.

Brandon ex rel. Est. of Brandon v. County of Richardson, 624 N.W.2d 604 (Neb. 2001). Yet another court held that because the state statute clearly required apportionment among intentional and negligent actors, arguments against doing so "would be more appropriately addressed to the legislature than to the judiciary." *Rodenburg v. Fargo-Moorhead Young Men's Christian Ass'n.*, 632 N.W.2d 407 (N.D. 2001). *See Graves v. North Eastern Serv., Inc.*, 345 P.3d 619 (Utah 2015) (statute required apportioning between employer who negligently retained an employee who sexually assaulted child-plaintiff); *Couch v. Red Roof Inns, Inc.*, 729 S.E.2d 378 (Ga. 2012) (apportionment between assailant and hotel whose negligence permitted assailant to assault hotel guest).

3. <u>Proof of Intent Defeats Apportionment</u>. In *Domke v. Alyeska Pipeline Serv. Co.*, 137 P.3d 295 (Alaska 2006), the plaintiff prevailed in an intentional interference with contract claim, which required establishing the defendant had not been

privileged to interfere. The court reasoned that apportionment was improper: "The definition of the cause of action does not allow a finding that the harm [defendant] caused was partly justified."

4. <u>Ohio</u>. Ohio Rev. Code Ann. § 2307.22(a)(3) states: "In a tort action in which the trier of fact determines that two or more persons proximately caused the same injury or loss to person or property or the same wrongful death and in which the trier of fact determines that fifty per cent or less of the tortious conduct is attributable to any defendant against whom an intentional tort claim has been alleged and established, that defendant shall be jointly and severally liable in tort for all compensatory damages that represent economic loss." In the case of the negligent parking lot owner where a plaintiff is intentionally harmed, if the plaintiff sues both defendants, what result? Indiana provides that if a defendant is convicted "based on the same evidence" used to show an intentional tort, the plaintiff may recover 100% of the damages from that defendant. Ind. Code § 35-51-2-10. Does that help in the typical negligent landowner case?

5. <u>Intentional Torts and Contribution</u>. Many states permit a defendant found liable to seek contribution from others if the defendant paid more than its proportionate share of damages to a plaintiff. However, a defendant found to have committed an intentional tort ordinarily may not do so. *See Joe Hand Promotions, Inc.*, 2013 WL 12145860 (W.D. Mo. July 26, 2013).

B. Comparative Fault or Apportionment of Contract Damages

At common law, "comparative negligence" or "contributory negligence" did not apply to contract actions. One court recently noted that "applying comparative fault principles in breach of contract actions would create havoc of unprecedented proportions" and so had "no place" in them. *L-3 Communics. Corp. v. E.R. Lewis Transp., Inc.*, 2005 WL 3591987 (D. Utah. Dec. 30, 2005) (collecting cases); *see Lifeline Youth & Family Serv., Inc. v. Installed Bldg.*, 996 N.E.2d 808 (Ct. App. Ind. 2013) ("No one disputes the assertion that comparative fault does not apply to a breach of contract claim.").

Likewise, at common law, damages were not apportioned among parties that caused the harm. Instead, under the doctrine of concurrent breach of contract, "where A and B owe contract duties to C under separate contracts, and each breaches independently, and it is not reasonably possible to make a division of the damage caused by the separate breaches closely related in point of time, the breaching parties, even though they acted independently, are jointly and severally liable." *Insure-One Indep. Ins. Agency, LLC v. Hallberg*, 976 N.E.2d 1014 (Ct. App. Ill. 2012). Put another way, "when two defendants independently breach separate contracts, and it is not 'reasonably possible' to segregate the damages, the defendants are jointly and severally liable." *Id. See Duluth Superior Erection, Inc. v. Concrete Restorers, Inc.*,

665 N.W.2d 528 (Ct. App. Minn. 2003) ("joint-and-several liability for damages in contract actions applies only where two persons independently and unintentionally breach separate contracts, closely related in point of time, to the same person, and it is not reasonably possible to make a division of the damages caused by the separate breaches.").

Apportionment statutes may alter the common law approach, but most seemingly would not. Breach of contract is not a tort, does not require proof of fault, and ordinarily causes only economic loss, not injury to person or property. In contrast, apportionment statutes often: (a) expressly apply only to tort claims, (b) require apportioning "fault," or (c) limit apportionment to "injury" to "person" or "property"—or are limited in one or more of these ways. *See Cathay Logistics, LLC v. Gerber Plumbing Fixtures, LLC,* 2016 WL 3912011 (C.D. Cal. July 19, 2016) ("Actions in contract do not allow an affirmative defense of comparative fault. Fault, comparative or otherwise, generally does not matter under the law of contracts. What matters, rather, is performance. Hence, performance with fault is sufficient, and nonperformance without fault is not enough."); *Leno v. K&L Homes, Inc.,* 803 N.W.2d 543 (N.D. 2011) (holding "fault and modified comparative fault do not apply where the cause of action arises solely out of the contract between the parties and the damages sought are for the loss of the expected bargain only."); *Kentucky Farm Bureau Mut. Ins. Co. v. Ryan,* 177 S.W.3d 797 (Ky. 2005) (statute "limits itself to tort actions"); *Pavlo v. Slattery,* 2004 WL 2165180 (Super. Ct. Conn. Aug. 30, 2004) (even though plaintiff pled defendant had negligently performed contract, apportionment statute did not apply because it was limited to "negligence" claims).

Trishan Air, Inc. v. Dassault Falcon Jet Corp.

532 F. App'x 784 (9th Cir. 2013) (Per Curiam)

[Plaintiff bought an airplane from defendant, and it crashed. Plaintiff sued for breach of warranty. The jury was instructed to apportion damages, based on plaintiff's alleged negligence, and its $3.5 million award reflected assigning 70% of the fault to plaintiff. Plaintiff appealed.]

We next consider whether the district court erred in reducing Plaintiffs' award on the breach of express warranty claim by the amount of Plaintiffs' comparative fault for the crash. When interpreting state law, we follow decisions of the state's highest court unless the state's highest court has not spoken on the issue, in which case we determine what result the state's highest court would reach based on state appellate court opinions, statutes and treatises.

The California Supreme Court has not expressly decided whether comparative fault applies to breach of express warranty claims such as the one at issue here. California Supreme Court decisions can be read to support both sides of the argument.

Regardless of whether the California Supreme Court would apply comparative fault in all cases of breach of express warranty, we conclude that because the contract-based claim at issue here is essentially an equivalent, alternative method of pleading the same basic theory of liability as the tort claims, the California Supreme Court would have applied comparative fault in this case. *See Brown v. Superior Court*, 44 Cal.3d 1049 (1988) (considering the overlap between claims and holding that if strict liability does not permit recovery, implied and express warranty claims are also barred); *see also Milwaukee Elec. Tool Corp.*, 19 Cal.Rptr.2d at 29 (noting that two separate causes of action, for strict products liability and breach of express and implied warranties, could be treated as "equivalent, alternative methods of pleading the same basic theory of liability" under the circumstances).

Notes and Questions

1. <u>Exception Swallows Rule</u>? If the *Trishan* plaintiff had a claim for breach of contract and for conversion (suppose defendant had sabotaged the plane), and prevailed on both, what result? *Compare Trishan* and *Avis Budget Car Rental, LLC v. JD2 Environmental, Inc.*, 2017 WL 3671554 (E.D.N.Y. Aug. 22, 2017) (holding state statute applied to negligence claims that "paralleled" breach of contract claim) *with Laethem Equip. Co. v. Deere & Co.*, 485 F. App'x 39 (6th Cir. June 13, 2012) (holding trial court properly did not reduce damages for plaintiff's fault where one of the three claims on which jury found for plaintiff was not subject to apportionment). What should courts do with "tort claims in a contractual wrapper?" Michael Ley, *Application of the Pro Rata Liability Statute to "Tort Claims in a Contractual Wrapper,"* 45-June Colo. L. 37 (2016) (stating "both lines of reasoning have their virtues").

2. <u>Why Not Apportion Pure Contract Claims of Economic Loss</u>? The text of a state statute could require apportionment, but many do not (or are not interpreted that way). Why would a legislature make that distinction? In considering that question, consider the explanation from *Strong Const., Inc. v. City of Torrington*, 255 P.3d 903 (Wyo. 2011), for not recognizing "common law" apportionment in breach of contract claims:

> We have been presented with no cogent argument or pertinent authority suggesting that the tort concept of fault has a counterpart in a breach of contract action, or that contractual damages should be similarly apportioned. Rather, as one recent decision from California explains, contract damages are generally awarded on an all-or-nothing basis:
>
> > In order to recover for breach of contract, the nonbreaching party must prove that it has substantially performed the conditions of the breaching party's performance (or that performance was excused). If it fails to do so, it obtains no recovery. If it does establish this predicate, it is entitled to recover all damages foreseeably caused by the other party's breach. See Rest.2d *Contracts*, § 235, com. b, p. 212 ("when performance

is due, anything short of full performance is a breach, even if the party who does not fully perform was not at fault and even if the defect in his performance was not substantial"); III Farnsworth on Contracts (3d ed. 2004) § 12.8, pp. 195–196 ("contract law is, in its essential design, a law of strict liability".) Thus, contract damages normally are awarded on an all-or-nothing basis. While the breaching party is liable only for damages foreseeably caused by its breach, there is no apportionment of that amount even if less than perfect performance of the conditions by the nonbreaching party contributed in some measure to the loss.

Stop Loss Ins. Brokers, Inc. v. Brown & Toland Medical Group, 143 Cal. App.4th 1036 (Ct. App. Cal. 2006). The Court of Appeals of New York has also noted the reasons that apportionment of damages does not translate to the realm of contract law:

> Nor are we persuaded that we should create a common-law right of contribution in contract actions. The need to liberalize the inequitable and harsh rules that once governed contribution among joint tort-feasors—are not pertinent to contract matters. Parties to a contract have the power to specifically delineate the scope of their liability at the time the contract is formed. Thus, there is nothing unfair in defining a contracting party's liability by the scope of its promise as reflected by the agreement of the parties. Indeed, this is required by the very nature of contract law, where potential liability is determined in advance by the parties.

Board of Ed. v. Sargent, Webster, Crenshaw & Folley, 71 N.Y.2d 21 (N.Y. 1987). Because we have been presented with no rebuttal to the principles expressed in these authorities, we find no basis in common law to extend apportionment of damages to breach of contract actions.

3. <u>Offset for Settling Defendants.</u> A defendant can reduce its damages by settlements received by the plaintiff. *E.g., Advanced Recovery Sys., LLC v. Am. Agencies, LLC,* 2017 WL 4862775 (D. Utah Oct. 26, 2017) (holding comparative fault statute did not apply to breach of contract action, but defendant could offset damages by amounts other parties paid to plaintiff).

4. *In Pari Delicto.* Under this equitable doctrine, if a contract plaintiff is in equal fault with the defendant, a court may bar or reduce damages. The court in *Adams Fin. Partners, L.P. v. Patke Assocs. Ltd.,* 2017 WL 3236584 (W.D. Wash. July 31, 2017), explained, however, that the doctrine does not apply to tort claims, which were subject to the apportionment statute:

> Comparative fault is the standard for the former; *in pari delicto* is applicable to the latter. *Compare* Wash. Rev. Code § 4.22.005 (establishing comparative fault in actions "seeking to recover damages for injury or death to person or harm to property"), *and ESCA Corp. v. KPMG Peat Marwick,* 959 P.2d 651 (Wash. 1998) (applying the comparative fault statute in a tort case), *with Golberg v. Sanglier,* 639 P.2d 1347 (Wash. 1982) (discussing *in*

pari delicto doctrine in contract case). Since the comparative fault statute was adopted in 1973, Washington courts have discussed the *in pari delicto* doctrine in tort cases only as it applies to indemnity between joint tort-feasors—not as a bar to a plaintiff's recovery. Thus, the *in pari delicto* doctrine would be inapplicable to Plaintiffs' negligence claim, but could bar their contract claim.

C. Conceptual Problems Created by Apportionment

J.S. Searcy v. United States

2018 WL 3733646 (W.D. Mo. Aug. 6, 2018) (Laughrey, J.)

[Plaintiff Jamie Searcy was pregnant and doctors allegedly committed malpractice, causing severe brain damage to her child, J.S., during birth. In response to a suit by her, her husband, and J.S., defendant raised the "defense" of comparative negligence and apportionment. Plaintiffs moved to strike it.]

In essence, Defendant seeks to reduce or bar the claims of all plaintiffs, including J.S. and Nathan Searcy, based on the alleged negligent conduct of Plaintiff Jamie Searcy. Comparative fault calls for the apportionment of fault amongst all parties to a tort claim. Under Missouri's pure comparative fault system, the fault of a plaintiff reduces the liability of the defendant in proportion to the plaintiff's share of the fault. The underlying theory is that a defendant is not forced to bear an unfair burden.

The parties' briefing raises three issues relevant to Plaintiffs' motion to strike: i) whether the fault of Jamie Searcy is imputed to co-plaintiffs J.S. and Nathan Searcy for the purpose of reducing their recovery; ii) whether the fault of Jamie Searcy can be applied to reduce her recovery on her derivative claim for medical expenses; and iii) whether, even if Jamie Searcy's fault is not imputed to her co-plaintiffs, apportionment of fault amongst the parties is otherwise required under pure comparative fault principles.

Plaintiffs argue that Jamie Searcy's alleged negligence cannot be used to reduce or bar recovery for J.S.'s claims because a parent's negligence cannot be imputed to a child. *See Profit v. Chicago G.W.R. Co.*, 91 Mo. App. 369 (1902) ("The rule of imputing negligence of the parent on the infant child does not prevail in this State. The child, however young and helpless, and however dependent upon the parent for care and protection, is nevertheless a separate entity.").

In response, Defendant asserts that "if J.S.'s injury was derivative of the injury to Jamie Searcy, Jamie Searcy's fault is chargeable to J.S. in her claim," and that *Kowalski* and *Profit* are not determinative. Defendant argues that J.S.'s injuries are derivative of the injury to Jamie Searcy because the hypoxia suffered by J.S. resulted from Jamie Searcy's uterine rupture, and any duty owed by Dr. Nielsen to Jamie Searcy's unborn child was "entirely derivative of and intertwined with his duty to

Jamie Searcy." Defendant analogizes J.S. to a third-party beneficiary to a contract between Jamie Searcy and Dr. Nielson such that J.S.'s rights vis-à-vis Dr. Nielsen are derivative of her mother's and generally subject to the same defenses Defendant would have against Jamie Searcy.

However, Defendant's derivative argument conflates case law regarding derivative claims with notions of derivative injury. In the cases cited by Defendant in support of its derivative argument, the fault of the injured or primary party reduced the recovery of the derivative party seeking to assert a derivative claim. *See Thompson v. Brown & Williamson Tobacco Corp.*, 207 S.W.3d 76 (Mo. App. 2006) (affirming reduction of wife's loss of consortium claim by the comparative fault percentage assessed to her husband); *Littleton v. McNeely*, 2007 WL 3027578 (W.D. Mo. 2007), *rev'd in part on other grounds*, 562 F.3d 880 (8th Cir. 2009) (reducing loss of consortium damages by percentage of fault allocated to injured spouse).

Here, however, J.S. is the primary injured party. The claims of Jamie and Nathan Searcy for medical expenses are derivative of, *i.e.*, arise out of, J.S.'s primary claim of injury. In other words, the question is not whether Minor J.S.'s hypoxia was derivative of Jamie Searcy's uterine rupture, but whether J.S.'s legal claim for personal injury is derivative of Jamie Searcy's legal claim for medical expenses. It is not. Thus, while J.S.'s fault, if any, could diminish Jamie Searcy's recovery for medical expenses, there is no legal basis for permitting Jamie Searcy's fault to reduce J.S.'s recovery or Nathan Searcy's recovery. Jamie Searcy's fault cannot be imputed to J.S. or Nathan Searcy.

Jamie Searcy's comparative fault may, however, be used to reduce her recovery by the percentage of fault allocated to her for claims raised in her individual capacity for past and future medical expenses. This is because comparative fault principles require the Court to diminish proportionately the amount awarded for an injury attributable to the claimant's own comparative fault, regardless of the nature of her claim. This result is consistent with Missouri precedent. *See e.g., Lester v. Sayles*, 850 S.W.2d 858 (Mo. 1993) (affirming judgment reducing mother's recovery for derivative claims by the percentage of comparative fault allocated to her); *Berry v. St. Louis, M. & S.E.R. Co.*, 214 Mo. 593 (1908) ("If parents sue in their own right to recover damages for injury to their child, a negligent defendant may defend by proving their concurrent negligence."); *Neff v. City of Cameron*, 213 Mo. 350 (1908) ("It is not too strongly put, to say that the doctrine of this court is settled that negligence of the parent cannot be imputed to an infant where the infant sues in its own right for a wrong done. If the parent sues in his own right, a radically different situation is presented.").

Defendant also argues that its comparative fault defense is valid as to all Plaintiffs even if Jamie Searcy's fault is not imputed, because under Missouri comparative fault principles Defendant is entitled to an apportionment of fault between Dr. Nielsen and Jamie Searcy on all claims. Section 2(a)(2) of the UCFA provides that percentages of fault are to be allocated across "all of the parties" to each claim; apportionment of fault is not limited to a single plaintiff. Plaintiffs' counter that a "defendant may not limit the recovery of one plaintiff based on the negligent conduct of a fellow plaintiff." The case law, however, appears to permit apportionment of fault against any party to the action, so long as comparative fault is alleged. *See Walley v. La Plata Volunteer Fire Dep't*, 368 S.W.3d 224 (Mo. App. 2012) ("comparative fault requires the jury be given the responsibility of assessing the relative fault of *the parties*") (emph. added); *Kansas City Power & Light v. Bibb & Assoc., Inc.*, 197 S.W.3d 147 (Mo. App. 2006) ("fault is only to be apportioned among those at trial"); *Coleman v. Mantia*, 25 S.W.3d 675 (Mo. App. 2000) (finding improper the reduction of plaintiff's damages by percentage of fault assigned to fellow plaintiff where defendant failed to plead principles of comparative fault and those issues were not tried by consent).

While Jamie Searcy's status as Next Friend [*i.e.,* guardian for J.S.] does not make her a party to the action, she has raised claims for recovery of past and future medical expenses individually. Defendant's affirmative defense provided Plaintiffs with adequate notice that it was seeking apportionment of fault under Section 2 of the UCFA. Because Jamie Searcy is a party to the action in her own right and her comparative fault has been alleged, her fault may be considered for apportionment. Thus, although Jamie Searcy's negligence is not imputed to all Plaintiffs, Defendant is entitled to an apportionment of fault amongst all the parties. The question of whether apportionment will result in a reduction of collectable damages, however, remains dependent upon the percentages of fault allocated as dictated by Missouri's joint and several liability statute. Plaintiffs' Motion to Strike or, in the alternative, for partial judgment with respect to affirmative defense twelve is denied because the law forecloses the first request and a dispute of facts precludes the second request.

Williams v. McCollister

671 F. Supp. 2d 884 (S.D. Tex. 2009) (Hacker, J.)

[P.A.M. Transport, Inc., employed defendant McCollister when he collided with plaintiff Danny Williams with his truck. Plaintiff asserted negligent retention by P.A.M. and negligence by McCollister. P.A.M. admitted that McCollister was operating in course and scope, and so it was vicariously liable. It then sought summary judgment on the negligence claims against it.]

Under the doctrine of *respondeat superior,* an employer will be held vicariously liable for the negligence of its employee regardless of any allegation of fault on the part of the employer. In contrast, direct claims such as negligent hiring, supervision, training, and retention are based on the employer's own negligent conduct in creating an unreasonable risk of harm to others. Thus, causes of action for negligent hiring, supervision, training, and retention are another means to make an employer liable for the negligence of an employee.

In the instant case, P.A.M. has stipulated that Mr. McCollister was acting within the course and scope of his employment at the time of the accident at issue. As such, P.A.M.'s liability for any negligence on the part of Mr. McCollister that was a proximate cause of the accident in question has been established under the doctrine of *respondeat superior*. Therefore, the question at hand is whether P.A.M.'s admission of vicarious liability precludes it from liability for its own negligence in hiring, failing to properly train, and negligently supervising.

With regard to this issue, Texas courts have underscored that, in matters involving only ordinary negligence, a direct liability claim (such as negligent hiring or entrustment) and a claim resulting in vicarious liability under *respondeat superior* could be mutually exclusive modes of recovery. This occurs only when a plaintiff pleads ordinary negligence (versus gross negligence) against an employer and employee, and the employer's liability for its employee's negligent acts has been established through a stipulation of vicarious liability. In other words, if vicarious liability is not contested, the employee's competence and the employer's own negligence in hiring, failing to properly train, or negligently supervising become irrelevant, as long as a plaintiff pleads ordinary negligence.

In contrast, where a plaintiff alleges ordinary negligence against the employee and gross negligence against the employer, the direct claims against the employer (*i.e.*, negligent hiring, negligent supervision, etc.) are treated as independent and separate grounds of recovery against the employer for purposes of punitive damages. What distinguishes gross negligence from ordinary negligence, and justifies the imposition of exemplary (punitive) damages, is the mental attitude of the defendant. *McDorman ex rel. Connelly v. Texas-Cola Leasing Co.*, 288 F.Supp.2d 796 (N.D. Tex. 2003). Thus, in addition to derivative liability for an employee's acts, "an employer may be liable for gross negligence in hiring an employee if the employee was unfit and the employer was reckless in hiring him." *Id.* (noting that where only ordinary negligence is alleged, negligent hiring and *respondeat superior* are mutually exclusive modes of recovery, while, on the other hand, a claim of grossly negligent hiring will preclude the owner from stipulating to vicarious liability for its employee's negligent acts so as to escape independent liability). And finally, it is well settled that an employer may be subject to derivative liability for punitive damages resulting from the acts of its employee if the employer authorized the manner of the act, the employee was employed in a managerial capacity and acting within the scope of his employment, or the employer ratified or approved the act.

In his complaint, Plaintiff does not allege a gross negligence claim against either P.A.M. or Mr. McCollister—nor does Plaintiff's complaint request punitive damages. Moreover, Plaintiff's attorney specifically stated during the deposition of its expert witness that Plaintiff has not pled a claim for gross negligence. In fact, on July 2, 2009, the Court held a hearing at which Plaintiff's attorney admitted, on the record, that Plaintiff is not seeking a claim for gross negligence. Further, Plaintiff does not allege that P.A.M. authorized, ratified, or approved the act or manner of the act or that Mr. McCollister was employed in a managerial capacity and acting within the scope of his employment when he ran over Plaintiff. Since Plaintiff has pled only ordinary negligence in his complaint, and P.A.M. has stipulated that Mr. McCollister was acting within the course and scope of his employment at the time of the accident, P.A.M. will be held responsible for any negligence assessed against its employee. As such, Texas law supports the Court granting P.A.M.'s partial summary judgment motion, dismissing the claims pertaining to negligent hiring, supervision, training, and retention of Mr. McCollister.

In its response, Plaintiff contends that P.A.M. is ignoring current Texas law and has erroneously based its argument on *Estate of Arrington,* an opinion rendered before the adoption of Chapter 33 of the Texas Civil Practices and Remedies Code ("Chapter 33"). Under the apportionment of responsibility scheme set forth in Chapter 33, the trier of fact must determine the negligence of each defendant. Specifically, Chapter 33 provides:

> The trier of fact, as to each cause of action asserted, shall determine the percentage of responsibility, stated in whole numbers, for the following persons with respect to each person's causing or contributing to cause in any way the harm for which recovery of damages is sought, whether by negligent act or omission, by any defective or unreasonably dangerous product, by other conduct or activity that violates an applicable legal standard, or by any combination of these:
>
> (1) each claimant;
>
> (2) each defendant;
>
> (3) each settling person; and
>
> (4) each responsible third party who has been designated under Section 33.004.

Tex. Civ. Prac. & Rem.Code Ann. § 33.003 (Vernon 2008).

For the purposes of Chapter 33, "defendant" is defined to include "any person from whom a claimant seeks recovery of damages." Although the language of the statute itself indicates a clear legislative preference for apportionment of responsibility in all tort actions, it is equally clear that an apportionment scheme is not proper in certain cases. Specifically, the Texas courts have held that where an employer's responsibility is based solely on vicarious liability, it would be improper to include the employer's negligence in the apportionment question. This is so because under vicarious liability, such as a theory of *respondeat superior,* the employer's liability is based solely on the negligence of its employee, and it may be held responsible even if it is entirely free of fault.

However, a closer question is presented as to whether liability should be apportioned under Chapter 33 between the party who is directly liable and a person whose liability is derivative, rather than purely vicarious. While derivative claims such as negligent hiring and negligent entrustment involve distinct acts of negligence on the part of the employer, the employer's liability for these acts is entirely dependent for causation upon the negligent actions of the employee who directly caused the accident. Because of this dependency, negligent entrustment and negligent hiring claims are similar to claims based on vicarious liability, which are excluded from Chapter 33's apportionment scheme.

Thus, in general, Texas courts addressing the interaction between Chapter 33 and theories of derivative liability, such as negligent hiring and negligent entrustment, have held that the hiring or entrusting employer's negligence should not be submitted for apportionment. In reaching this conclusion, the courts reason that once negligent hiring or entrustment is established, liability for the employee's negligent operation of the vehicle is passed on to the employer, and the employer's acts are of no consequence in determining its degree of responsibility.

Here, P.A.M.'s liability for any negligence on the part of Mr. McCollister in connection with the accident at issue has already been established through its stipulation of vicarious liability. Put simply, by assuming liability for Mr. McCollister's alleged negligence, P.A.M. has assumed all responsibility for the accident, and any negligence on its own part that may have contributed to the accident is irrelevant. If Mr. McCollister's negligent conduct is found to be the proximate cause of Plaintiff's injuries, questions regarding Mr. McCollister's competence as an employee and whether he received proper supervision and training become irrelevant for purposes of assessing liability. The logical approach under Chapter 33 would appear to be to apportion fault among only those directly liable for the accident at issue, and to hold the employer liable for the amount of fault apportioned to its employee. . . . For the reasons stated above, P.A.M.'s motion for summary judgment on Plaintiff's claims for negligent hiring, supervision, training, and retention of Mr. McCollister should be GRANTED.

6. The Workers' Compensation Exclusive Remedy Bar

Ordinarily, an employee's claim against an employer for harm is barred by state workers' compensation laws, even for intentional harm caused by a worker. *See, e.g., Doe v. Purity Supreme, Inc.*, 422 Mass. 563 (1996) (holding that the state's workers' compensation act barred the plaintiff's common law claims because "the assistant store manager is alleged to have raped an employee during work hours on the employer's premises" and noting that "the Legislature has provided employees with a separate remedy for sexual harassment"). Further, if a co-employee intentionally harms another employee, the employer did not act intentionally, and negligent hiring claims are barred. *E.g., Powell v. Ashland Hosp. Corp.*, 2014 WL 796205 (Ky. Ct.

App. Aug. 1, 2014) (claims by plaintiff who had been intentionally kicked by co-worker for negligent supervision and vicarious liability barred by workers' compensation law). A common exception permits claims for the *employer's* "intentional" wrongdoing, which this case examines.

Mead v. W. Slate, Inc.

848 A.2d 257 (Vt. 2004) (Johnson, J.)

[Plaintiff Martin Mead had been employed by Western Slate, Inc., as a mechanic, sawyer, and driller for several years. Defendant Jeffrey N. Harrison is the co-owner of Western, an experienced slate quarry operator, and generally in charge of mining operations at the time of the incident. Plaintiff noticed that a rock fall had occurred and reported it to Harrison. He was not instructed to stop working, however. As he was doing so, another rock fall occurred, injuring him. He obtained workers' compensation benefits and sued WSI and Harrison.

The jury was instructed that the plaintiff had the burden to prove defendants had the "specific intent to injure him," but that such intent could be established in one of two ways: that defendants either "had the purpose or desire to cause him injury or that although the Defendants lacked such purpose or desire they knew to a substantial certainty that their actions would bring about his injury." The jury returned a special verdict in favor of plaintiff, finding that although neither defendant had a specific purpose or desire to injure him, both knew to a substantial certainty that their actions or inactions would injure plaintiff. The jury found Western liable for medical expenses of $3,044, pain and suffering of $40,000, and lost wages of $14,176, and Harrison liable for medical expenses of $9,134, and pain and suffering of $50,000. Defendants appealed.]

We turn first to defendants' contention that the court erred by allowing plaintiff to prove a "specific intent" to injure based on a showing that defendants knew to a "substantial certainty" their conduct would result in injury to plaintiff.

Subject to certain limited exceptions, Vermont's workers' compensation statute provides the exclusive remedy for workplace injuries. The statute represents a public policy compromise in which the employee gives up the right to sue the employer in tort in return for which the employer assumes strict liability and the obligation to provide a speedy and certain remedy' for work-related injuries.

Like most other jurisdictions, we have recognized an exception to the exclusivity rule for intentional injuries committed by the employer. We stress, however, that the policy trade-off underlying the workers' compensation law was best served by allowing the remedial system which the Legislature has created a broad sphere of operation. Hence nothing short of a specific intent to injure falls outside the scope of the Act. Even wilful and wanton conduct leading to a sudden but foreseeable injury is within the scope of the Act.

A growing number of jurisdictions have broadened the definition of specific intent to include instances where the employer not only intends to injure the worker, but engages in conduct with knowledge that it is substantially certain to cause injury or death. On the continuum of tortious conduct, substantial certainty has been described as just below the most aggravated conduct where the actor intends to injure the victim; it is more than mere knowledge and appreciation of a risk, beyond gross negligence, and more egregious than even mere recklessness in which the actor knows or should know that there is a strong probability that harm may result. Thus, the substantial certainty standard has been variously described as tantamount to an intentional tort, a surrogate state of mind for purposefully harmful conduct, and a substitute for a subjective desire to injure.

The standard is not uniform. Some states that have modified their specific-intent exception have opted for a stricter test than substantial certainty, requiring a showing of knowledge by the employer that injury is certain or virtually certain to occur. Other states have enacted specific statutes codifying relatively stringent intent-to-injure exceptions in response to more expansive court decisions. *See, e.g.,* Mich. Comp. Laws § 418.131(1) (intentional tort exception applies where employer "had actual knowledge that an injury was certain to occur and willfully disregarded that knowledge," modifying Beauchamp v. Dow Chemical Co., 427 Mich. 1 (1986), which adopted substantial certainty test).

A number of state courts have also rejected invitations to adopt the "substantial certainty" standard, choosing instead to retain the strict requirement that the employer harbor a specific intent to injure an employee. Courts adopting the substantial certainty standard have also drawn harsh criticism from some commentators for altering the balance of interests within the workers' compensation system, employing a vague and ill-defined standard, and impinging upon the policy prerogatives of the legislative branch.

Even those courts that have adopted the substantial-certainty test have stressed that it is intended to operate as a very narrow exception, intended for the most egregious employer conduct, and hence is to be strictly construed. The line between negligent or reckless conduct on the one hand and intentional wrong on the other must be drawn with caution, so that the statutory framework of the Act is not circumvented simply because a known risk later blossoms into reality.

Viewed in light of this standard, the evidence shows—at most—that Harrison directed plaintiff and his co-workers to continue to work in the quarry knowing that a rock fall had recently occurred and that it represented a dangerous situation that required attention. Plaintiff's expert, a former inspector for the federal Mine Safety and Health Administration, also opined that another fall was substantially certain to follow the first, and that allowing the drilling to proceed violated at least two federal safety regulations. He offered no testimony, however, tying a second rock fall to any particular time-frame. All that the evidence shows, therefore, is a substantial risk of second fall, but there is no evidence that it was substantially certain to occur within a few hours, or a day, or a month. Nor was there any evidence presented of prior falls leading to injuries under similar circumstances at the Western quarry or elsewhere within defendants' knowledge. Thus, the evidence cannot support a reasonable inference that defendants knew to a substantial certainty that the decision directing plaintiff to continue to work until Harrison returned from his errand would result in plaintiff's injury. Indeed, neither Harrison nor anyone else on site — including plaintiff — expected the accident to occur. Even as he waited for word from Harrison as to how to proceed, plaintiff — an experienced quarry worker in his own right — voluntarily commenced to complete the drilling that he had started the day before, and later expressed surprise at the occurrence of the second fall. The evidence thus belies any rational inference that Harrison knew to a substantial certainty that directing plaintiff to work until he returned to inspect the area would result in plaintiff's injury.

This is not a case where an employer, for example, knowingly orders workers to expose themselves to dangerous fumes or toxic materials that are a constant and unavoidable presence in the workplace, or instructs an employee, over his objection and at the risk of termination if he refused, to operate a table-saw knowing that other employees had previously suffered injuries because of the lack of a safety guard which the employer had willfully removed to improve production speed. Here, there is little doubt that defendants were negligent in exposing plaintiff to the known risk of a subsequent rock fall, but unlike these other cases there is no evidence from which a jury could reasonably infer that defendants *knew* the injury to plaintiff was *substantially certain* to occur. This conclusion is buttressed by the trial court's own ruling that plaintiff failed to adduce sufficient evidence to submit the question of punitive damages to the jury, a standard which may be satisfied either where the defendant's wrongdoing has been intentional and deliberate, or by conduct showing a *reckless* or *wanton* disregard of one's rights. We agree, and conclude, *a fortiori*, that the evidence also failed to demonstrate misconduct by defendants evidencing a knowing and willful disregard of risks that made injury to plaintiff a substantial certainty.

While their standards may vary, decisions from other states that have adopted the substantial certainty test uniformly hold that the exception must be reserved for the exceptional case, where it can be said that the employee's injury — viewed in light of the risks known to the employer at the time — was not truly an accident. This is not such a case. We hold, therefore, that the evidence was insufficient as a matter of law to support the jury's finding that defendants knew to a substantial certainty their actions would result in injury to plaintiff. Accordingly, the judgments in favor of plaintiff and against defendants must be reversed.

Notes and Questions

1. <u>Does It Matter</u>? The verbal formulations are all variations on the same thing: horrific conduct. Should courts draw a line at one extreme, or the other, and invite legislative correction, rather than leaving it an amorphous middle?

2. <u>Who Is the "Employer"</u>? Courts limit the intentional tort exception by limiting whose intent matters to only high-level managers, but there is no clear rule, perhaps because the exception is so narrow. *See Pickett v. Colonel of Spearfish*, 209 F. Supp. 2d 999 (D.S.D. 2001) (knowledge of "foremen, managers and supervisors" was insufficient). The *Berkel & Co. Contractors, Inc. v. Lee*, 543 S.W.3d 288 (Ct. App. Tex. 2018), court suggested that when actions are taken by a "vice-principal of a corporation, those acts may be deemed to be the acts of the corporation itself." Another court rejected the argument by the employee, Ms. Helf, that "collective knowledge" applied in this context:

> Ms. Helf urged the district court to aggregate the knowledge of various Chevron employees to determine whether the requisite knowledge to support an intentional tort claim could be imputed to Chevron. The court rejected this collective knowledge theory and concluded that the expectation that an injury was virtually certain to occur had to be found in the mind of at least one individual. The district court further concluded that only the knowledge of the night-shift supervisor was relevant in this case because he was the Chevron manager who instructed Ms. Helf to perform the neutralization process.
>
> We agree with the district court's first conclusion that Ms. Helf must produce evidence that at least one individual with the authority to direct her actions had the required knowledge or expectation that she would be injured. Although we have never addressed this question, other courts have held that the collective knowledge of multiple employees cannot establish the state of mind requisite to the commission of an intentional tort of a corporation. Put simply, intent to commit tortious acts cannot be imputed to a corporation on the basis of disconnected facts possessed by various employees or agents of that corporation, where there is no evidence that any employee possessed the requisite state of mind. *Accord Woodmont, Inc. v. Daniels*, 274 F.2d 132 (10th Cir. 1959) ("While in some cases, a corporation may be held constructively responsible for the composite knowledge of all of its agents we are unwilling to apply the rule to fix liability where, as here, intent is an essential ingredient of tort liability as for deceit."); *see also Chaney v. Dreyfus Serv. Corp.*, 595 F.3d 219 (5th Cir. 2010) ("As a general rule, where an essentially subjective state of mind is an element of a cause of action we have declined to allow this element to be met by a corporation's collective knowledge, instead requiring that the state of mind actually exist in at least one individual.").

Although it may be possible that the collective knowledge of the agents of a corporation may be relevant in other legal contexts, we agree that for the purposes of proving that a corporation is liable for an intentional tort, a plaintiff must prove that at least one agent of the corporation had all of the requisite knowledge to support the claim. Inventing a corporate consciousness with the capacity to possess the state of mind necessary for an intentional tort is inconsistent with the principles of tort law. Therefore, the district court correctly concluded that at least one Chevron agent must have all of the knowledge necessary to support liability under an intentional tort theory.

The district court erred, however, in concluding that only the state of mind of Ms. Helf's direct supervisor could be relevant. If a more senior Chevron manager with the authority to direct Ms. Helf's actions knew or expected that workers would be injured during the neutralization process and either instructed the night-supervisor to order a worker to neutralize the pit or knew that the routine neutralization process would occur absent the manager's order to halt the process, then the knowledge of the more senior manager would be sufficient to support an intentional tort claim. Employers are not shielded from liability if a manager with the knowledge that an injury is virtually certain to occur simply orders another manager without this knowledge to instruct a worker to perform the dangerous task. Furthermore, if a manager knows or expects that a routine task will result in injury because of changed conditions, an employer does not avoid liability if that manager passively permits the worker's direct supervisor to instruct the worker to perform the task. Otherwise, employers would be encouraged to compartmentalize knowledge about dangerous conditions in order to insulate themselves from liability in situations where a more senior supervisor knows that an injury is virtually certain to occur but the direct supervisor does not have this knowledge.

Ms. Helf argued below and before this court that the knowledge of two of Chevron's senior managers was also relevant to the question of Chevron's liability. Ms. Helf produced evidence that both the area supervisor of the portion of the refinery where she worked and the emergency response team coordinator knew that reinitiating the neutralization process would be dangerous. The district court erred by not considering whether Ms. Helf produced sufficient evidence that either of these individuals (1) knew that an injury was virtually certain to occur if a worker neutralized the pit, (2) had the authority to halt the neutralization process or direct the pit operator's actions, and (3) either ordered the routine neutralization process to continue or knew that a worker would neutralize the pit during the night shift and failed to stop it or require additional safety precautions.

Helf v. Chevron U.S.A. Inc., 361 P.3d 63 (Utah 2015). Why such a high bar?

7. After-Acquired Evidence

Suppose in a wrongful termination case the defendant discovers facts that would have led it to fire the plaintiff, or never have hired him in the first place. Should this "after-acquired evidence" reduce or eliminate damages?

Ingwersen v. Planet Group, Inc.

2011 WL 2623501 (D. Neb. Apr. 22, 2011) (Camp, J.)

[The employment agreement between Plaintiff David Ingwersen and Planet Group, Inc., limited Planet's ability to fire Ingwersen "for cause," which was defined as "an uncured violated or breach of the terms and conditions of" a related agreement—called "the SPA"—and required Planet to first notify Ingwersen in writing of its intent to fire him, state why, and give him 30 days to cure. Planet notified Ingwersen he was being terminated *without* cause and offered him a severance package. The parties could not agree on its terms. Ingwersen sued for breach of contract. Planet counterclaimed, asserting that, after it had fired him, it learned that he had breached the SPA in various ways that constituted cause sufficient to terminate him. Planet moved for summary judgment on the ground that this after-acquired evidence defeated his claim that he was fired without cause.]

Planet argues that evidence acquired of Ingwersen's alleged pre-termination misconduct after Ingwersen's termination supports a termination-for-cause under the Employment Agreement. In support of this assertion, Planet cites *O'Day v. McDonnell Douglas Helicopter Co.*, 959 P.2d 792 (Ariz. 1998), which held that "after-acquired evidence of employee misconduct is a defense to a breach of contract action for wages and benefits lost as a result of discharge if the employer can demonstrate that it would have fired the employee had it known of the misconduct." The Arizona Supreme Court stated that the "overwhelming majority of courts holds that if an employer can demonstrate that it would have fired an employee had it known of prior misconduct, then the employee's claim for breach of contract is barred or, put differently, the prior misconduct excuses the employer's breach." The court also noted that this "result in contract merely reflects the private bargain between the parties." . Conversely, the court stated that "if the employee can demonstrate that the employer knew of the misconduct and chose to ignore it, then he will defeat the employer's attempted use of the after-acquired evidence and defense of legal excuse."

The Court acknowledges that under *O'Day*, an employer may use after-acquired evidence of misconduct as a defense to a breach-of-contract action for wages and benefits, if the employer can show that it would have fired the employee had it known of the misconduct. However, the ruling in *O'Day* is inapplicable to the present case for at least two reasons. First, Planet has not clearly established that evidence of Ingwersen's breach of the SPA was acquired after Ingwersen's termination. Thus, there is a question of fact as to whether Planet knew of the alleged breaches, and chose to ignore them. Second, because Planet's defense is based on the Employment Agreement, Planet is also bound by its provisions.

To trigger the legal-excuse defense with after-acquired evidence, Planet must demonstrate that it learned of Ingwersen's misconduct *after* his termination without cause. The timing of the discovery of this evidence is crucial because, if Planet knew of Ingwersen's misconduct before termination and chose to ignore it, the defense arising from after-acquired evidence does not apply. That is, the discovery of at least one of Ingwersen's alleged breaches of the SPA must have occurred post-termination. Further, Planet must show that had it known of the breach, Ingwersen would have been terminated. The manner in which Planet discovered evidence of Ingwersen's misconduct is not clear from the record.

Even assuming Planet has after-acquired evidence of misconduct by Ingwersen, supporting its defense of legal excuse, it still must comply with its obligations under the Employment Agreement. As the Arizona Supreme Court stated in *O'Day*, the result of the after-acquired evidence rule is one in contract, and "merely reflects the private bargain between the parties." *Id.* The court also stressed that the legal-excuse defense based on after-acquired evidence only excuses the employer from its *post-termination* duties under the contract. In other words, although after-acquired evidence of Ingwersen's termination may justify a "for cause" dismissal under the Employment Agreement, it did not excuse Planet's obligations under the contract that would arise prior to termination.

Planet does not request the Court to evaluate the sufficiency of whether it could terminate Ingwersen for cause. Planet's Motion is based on the narrow proposition that "if this Court determines that Ingwersen breached the Share Purchase Agreement in any manner that is outlined in Planet's original Brief, Planet Group has post-termination acquired evidence that can support a 'for cause' termination of Ingwersen and the Employment Agreement." This Motion relates solely to Paragraph 4 of the Employment Agreement which states that termination for cause includes "an uncured violated or breach of the terms and conditions of" the SPA. However, Paragraph 4 also requires that: "if termination is made the Company must first *notify* the Employee in writing and give the Employee at least thirty (30) days to *cure such breach. Id.* (emph. added).

Compliance with the notice and right-to-cure provisions of Paragraph 4 of the SPA were required before termination for cause arising out of Ingwersen's breach of the SPA. This provision was part of the parties' agreed-upon exchange, namely that Ingwersen could not be terminated for cause without notice and the opportunity to cure any breach of the SPA. It would be inequitable, and contrary to the parties' own agreement, to require Planet to furnish Ingwersen notice of a breach of the SPA if evidence had been discovered before termination, but release Planet from these obligations for evidence of breach discovered post-termination. To the extent Planet seeks to excuse its termination of Ingwersen based on his alleged breach of the SPA, it has not shown that he was given an opportunity to cure any alleged breach.

Planet has not identified any other language in the Employment Agreement or in case law that would excuse its obligation to provide notice and an opportunity to cure. Accordingly, even if post-termination evidence of pre-termination wrongdoing could excuse Planet's termination of Ingwersen without cause, the Court cannot conclude as a matter of law that Planet would also be excused from its corresponding pre-termination obligations under the Employment Agreement.

Problems

1. Employment Application. You are drafting employment questionnaires for potential employees for your client. In light of the doctrine of after-acquired evidence, what might you include?

2. Christmases Past. You are a mediator being paid by the parties to a suit to settle it. After a long day, the facts and damages have become clear, and the parties have asked you for a mediator's figure: what should both sides accept? The plaintiff, Paper Magic Group, Inc., makes greeting cards. It had a contract with Target Stores, Inc., to deliver Christmas cards in October 2017. Paper Magic hired J.B. Hunt Transport, Inc., to ship some of these cards from Pennsylvania to a Target in Wisconsin. Paper Magic had long used Hunt, and an agreement between them stated that Hunt's liability if a shipment was "lost, damaged, or destroyed" was "the price charged by the Shipper to its customer" with reasonable salvage value of any damaged goods deducted from the price paid. The invoice value of the shipment was $130,080.48. Ordinarily, shipments like this are delivered in about four days, but this one was lost in the shuffle. In February 2018, Hunt found it. Hunt offered to deliver the cards to Target, which refused, and then to Paper Magic, which also refused because they were "private label" Target cards and so had no value to it. In June 2018, Hunt was able to sell the goods at salvage for $49,645.96, and offered it in full payment. Paper Magic refused, demanding $130,080.48. In mediation, Hunt admitted that delayed delivery was effectively nondelivery, but has stated Paper Magic's refusal to accept the cards breached its duty to mitigate, yet there is no evidence Paper Magic could have obtained more than Hunt did for the cards. What are Paper Magic's general damages? What is the likely result if summary judgment motions are filed?

3. Your State's Approach to Collateral Source? Does your state apply the collateral source rule to contract actions? Does it permit plaintiffs to exclude evidence of gratuitous services, or write-offs due to insurance or other benefits?

4. Why Not a Presumption? Prepare to argue a court should presume it is reasonable for a party to refuse to mitigate damages by dealing with the party who breached a contract with it, and that the presumption is stronger if the breaching party offers to perform only with additional, or different, conditions.

Chapter 18

The Boundaries and Frontiers of Remedies

If a plaintiff does not experience the type of harm required by a particular claim, no recovery for that claim is available. For example, regardless of the anguish felt by the plaintiff, some courts permit familial loss of consortium damages, while others do not. The courts denying familial consortium presumably do not believe that only a spouse can feel anguish from injury to another spouse, but instead arbitrarily draw a boundary. Courts draw such boundaries in delineating whether, for example, "physical manifestation" is required, or someone must witness, or come quickly upon, injury to a family member to recover for distress damages.

Those boundaries limit remedies by defining the "damage" required by a claim. The courts in this chapter perhaps illustrate the truth of the proposition that there is "no hard and fast test that courts apply when determining whether to recognize" a new claim. *Byrne v. Avery Ctr. for Obstetrics and Gynecology, P.C.*, 175 A.3d 1 (Conn. 2018). Consider whether a legislature should step in where these courts have decided not to tread. *Cf. See Gordon v. Chipotle Mexican Grill, Inc.*, 2018 WL 3653173 (D. Colo. Aug. 1, 2018) (discussing courts' struggle with whether a plaintiff can recover after a merchant's electronic database has been hacked for fear of future identity theft).

Plowman v. Ft. Madison Community Hosp.

896 N.W.2d 393 (Iowa 2017) (Waterman, J.)

[Plaintiffs Pamela and Jeremy Plowman were married and Pamela was expecting. During an ultrasound, the radiologist detected a severe abnormality with the fetus's head but the doctor told her "everything was fine" with the baby's development and she was never informed "that the radiologist had found any abnormalities, or that the ultrasound was in any way abnormal." No further testing was done to follow up on the ultrasound results as recommended in the report.

Two months after an uneventful delivery, she had concerns about the development of her son, Z.P. Soon, he was diagnosed with small corpus callosum, which plaintiffs contend relates to the head circumference as shown in the ultrasound. The boy suffers from cerebral palsy, microcephaly, intellectual disability, cortical visual impairment, and seizure disorder. He requires frequent visits to numerous doctors in Iowa City and Keokuk. Physical therapists come to his home one to two times

731

weekly. He is on daily medication for seizures and reflux. Doctors have been unable to determine the exact cause of Z.P.'s disabilities. It is unlikely Z.P. will ever walk or speak.

The parents filed suit, claiming that had they been informed of the radiologist's conclusion, the wife would have had an abortion. They sought damages for: (1) the cost of past, present, and future extraordinary care required for Z.P. as a result of his disabilities; (2) the cost of ordinary care raising the child; (3) Pamela's mental anguish; and (4) Pamela's loss of income. Jeremy filed a separate action, mirroring Pamela's claims. No claim was made on behalf of Z.P.; rather, the parents sue for their own individual injuries and costs attributable to Z.P.'s disabilities. Meanwhile, Pamela and Jeremy divorced but share physical custody of their children, including Z.P. Z.P. does not walk or talk and is frequently sick; however, Pamela also noted that when he is not sick, he is "really happy" and "a good baby." Pamela testified she "really enjoys spending time with Z.P. and gets a lot of happiness from him." The trial court granted defendants' motion for summary judgment. Plaintiffs appealed.]

We begin by defining terms. Courts categorize three distinct types of claims. "Wrongful pregnancy" is a medical negligence action brought by the parents of a healthy, but unplanned, child against a physician who negligently performed a sterilization or abortion. "Wrongful birth" is an action brought by parents of a child born with birth defects. "Wrongful life" is a claim brought by the child suffering from such birth defects. One court discussed use of the term "wrongful" as follows:

> These labels are not instructive. Any "wrongfulness" lies not in the life, the birth, the conception, or the pregnancy, but in the negligence of the physician. The harm, if any, is not the birth itself but the effect of the defendant's negligence on the parents' physical, emotional, and financial well-being resulting from the denial to the parents of their right, as the case may be, to decide whether to bear a child or whether to bear a child with a genetic or other defect.

Viccaro v. Milunsky, 406 Mass. 777 (1990).

In *Nanke*, we addressed whether parents could recover for wrongful pregnancy in Iowa after a failed abortion procedure led to the birth of a healthy child. 346 N.W.2d at 521 ("The factual situation involved in this case would more accurately be depicted as a claim for 'wrongful pregnancy.'"). We held the parents could not recover, noting "a parent cannot be said to have been damaged or injured by the birth and rearing of a normal, healthy child because the invaluable benefits of parenthood outweigh the mere monetary burdens as a matter of law." *Id.* at 522. *Nanke* is distinguishable, as we expressly limited its holding to deny recovery for the costs of raising a "normal, healthy" child:

> Our ruling today is limited to the unique facts of this case and the narrow issue presented. We hold only that the parent of a *normal, healthy* child may not maintain an action to recover the expenses of rearing that child from

> a physician whose alleged negligence in performing a therapeutic abortion permitted the birth of such child.

Id. at 523 (emph. added). We now address the separate question of whether parents of a child born with severe disabilities can sue for wrongful birth.

In a wrongful-birth action, parents of a child born with a detectable birth defect allege that they would have avoided conception or terminated the pregnancy but for the physician's negligent failure to inform them of the likelihood of the birth defect. The injury to the parents results from the loss of the opportunity to make an informed decision about whether to avoid or terminate the pregnancy.

A majority of states recognize wrongful-birth claims. At least twenty-three states recognize the claim by judicial decision. Maine allows wrongful-birth claims by statute. A minority of jurisdictions decline to do so. Three state supreme courts have refused to allow wrongful-birth claims. Twelve states have enacted legislation barring wrongful-birth claims. Three of those states had allowed wrongful-birth claims by judicial decision before the legislature barred them.

Two developments help explain the trend toward judicial acceptance of wrongful birth actions. First, advancements in prenatal care have resulted in an increased ability of health care professionals to predict and detect the presence of fetal defects. This raises the importance of genetic counseling for expecting parents. Indeed, prenatal testing is extremely prevalent and is widely accepted, and will likely become more common in the future.

Second, *Roe v. Wade* and its progeny established as a matter of federal constitutional law that a woman has a right to choose whether to terminate her pregnancy free from state interference before the fetus is viable. 410 U.S. 113 (1973). As a result, today it is possible for prospective parents (1) to know, well in advance of birth, of the risk or presence of congenital defects in the fetus they have conceived; and (2) to decide to terminate the pregnancy on the basis of this knowledge. Accordingly, courts have held physicians who perform prenatal care and testing have an obligation to adhere to reasonable standards of professional performance.

Against this backdrop, we turn to whether Iowa law allows a cause of action for wrongful birth. In *Dier v. Peters*, we addressed whether Iowa tort law allows a cause of action for paternity fraud. 815 N.W.2d 1 (Iowa 2012). We considered three factors to decide whether to recognize the right to sue: (1) whether the action is consistent with traditional concepts of common law, (2) whether there are prevailing policy reasons against recognizing such a cause of action, and (3) whether Iowa statutes speak to the issue. Because paternity fraud fit within traditional notions of common law fraud and was not contrary to a law or policy expressed by the general assembly, we determined the father could maintain the claim. We use the *Dier* three-factor test to decide whether to recognize a wrongful-birth claim.

From our vantage point, a wrongful-birth claim "fits comfortably within the traditional boundaries of negligence law." We join the majority of other jurisdictions in concluding wrongful-birth claims fall within existing medical negligence principles.

The traditional elements of a medical negligence action are (1) an applicable standard of care, (2) a violation of this standard, and (3) a causal relationship between the violation and injury sustained. A physician owes a duty to his patient to exercise the ordinary knowledge and skill of his or her profession in a reasonable and careful manner when undertaking the care and treatment of a patient. This duty is based on privity, arising from the contractual relationship between the two. Although this contractual physician-patient relationship is sufficient to establish a duty, it is not required. To establish a deviation from the standard of care, plaintiffs need to prove that a reasonably competent physician would have observed the abnormalities from the ultrasound or other procedure and reported the results to the parents. Ordinarily, evidence of the applicable standard of care—and its breach—must be furnished by an expert. As to causation, plaintiffs must prove if the procedure had not been performed negligently or delayed and the parents had been timely informed of the impairment, they would have chosen to terminate the pregnancy. Finally, the resulting injury to the parents lies in their being deprived of the opportunity to make an informed decision to terminate the pregnancy, requiring them to incur extraordinary expenses in the care and education of their child afflicted with a genetic abnormality.

Courts declining to allow wrongful-birth claims have questioned the elements of causation and injury. One judge who dissented from a decision allowing a wrongful-birth claim concluded the physician "cannot be said to have caused" the child's genetic abnormality:

> The disorder is genetic and not the result of any injury negligently inflicted by the doctor. In addition it is incurable and was incurable from the moment of conception. Thus the doctor's alleged negligent failure to detect it during prenatal examination cannot be considered a cause of the condition by analogy to those cases in which the doctor has failed to make a timely diagnosis.

Becker, 386 N.E.2d at 816 (Wachtler, J., dissenting in part). By contrast, in traditional medical negligence actions seeking recovery for a child's disabling injuries, the disability was allegedly inflicted by the defendant doctor. *See, e.g., Asher v. OB-Gyn Specialists, P.C.*, 846 N.W.2d 492 (Iowa 2014) (affirming jury verdict awarding damages to parents for their baby's brachial plexis injury and broken clavicle caused by physician's negligence during delivery), *overruled on other grounds by Alcala v. Marriott Int'l, Inc.*, 880 N.W.2d 699 (Iowa 2016).

Yet we have previously allowed patients to sue for a physician's negligent failure to *diagnose* health problems the physician did not cause. In *DeBurkarte v. Louvar*, a physician failed to timely diagnose breast cancer. 393 N.W.2d 131 (Iowa 1986). The defendant argued there was insufficient evidence to hold that his failure to properly diagnose the cancer probably caused [the plaintiff's] injuries. Although it was undisputed that the physician did not "cause" the plaintiff's cancer, we allowed recovery for the plaintiff's lost chance of survival. We reasoned that the physician's negligent failure to diagnose, in combination with the preexisting condition, increased the risk of harm to the plaintiff who otherwise could have obtained timely treatment. Any other rule would subvert the deterrence objectives of tort law by denying recovery for the effects of conduct that causes statistically demonstrable losses.

Causation "takes on a markedly more complex character in those cases in which alleged negligence combines with a preexisting condition to cause the ultimate harm to the plaintiff. *See also Greco v U.S.*, 111 Nev. 405 (1995) ("Even though the physician did not *cause* the cancer, the physician can be held liable for damages resulting from the patient's decreased opportunity to fight the cancer, and for the more extensive pain, suffering and medical treatment the patient must undergo by reason of the negligent diagnosis."). Here, it is undisputed the physicians did not cause Z.P.'s birth defects. But the parents testified they would have terminated the pregnancy, and thereby avoided the costs of Z.P.'s disability, had the physicians informed them of the ultrasound results.

Courts disallowing wrongful-birth claims reject the view "that the existence of a human life can constitute an injury cognizable at law." *Azzolino v. Dingfelder*, 315 N.C. 103 (1985) ("We are unwilling to say that life, even life with severe defects, may ever amount to a legal injury."). We said as much in *Nanke* as to a healthy child. 346 N.W.2d at 523 ("That a child can be considered an injury offends fundamental values attached to human life.") However, under the wrongful-birth theory, the relevant injury is not the resulting life, but the negligent deprivation of information important to the parents' choice whether to terminate a pregnancy. Courts disallowing wrongful-birth claims "conflate the claimants' injury allegation with their ultimate claim for damages." *Grubbs ex rel. Grubbs v. Barbourville Family Health Ctr., P.S.C.*, 120 S.W.3d 682 (Ky. 2003) (Keller, J., concurring in part). A dissenting justice saw this "analytical flaw" in the majority's rejection of a wrongful-birth theory:

> While both the majority and concurring opinions attempt to frame the relevant issue as whether the child's *life* can constitute a legal injury in the context of a prima facie case for medical malpractice, we need not find that life, even life with severe defects,' constitutes a legal injury in order to recognize the claim for relief" because "the resulting injury to the plaintiff parents lies in their being deprived of the opportunity to make an informed decision to terminate the pregnancy. Although one facet of a plaintiff's compensable *damages* in such cases may consist of extraordinary costs associated with the care and education of a child with birth-defect-related disabilities, those damages are available only because they are the result of a physician's violation of the patient's right to make an informed procreative decision.

The compensable injury in a wrongful-birth claim is the parents' loss of the opportunity to make an informed decision to terminate the pregnancy. This is analogous to a claim for medical negligence based on lack of informed consent.

Both types of claims arise out of "the unquestioned principle that absent extenuating circumstances a patient has the right to exercise control over his or her body by making an informed decision." *Pauscher v. Iowa Methodist Med. Ctr.*, 408 N.W.2d 355 (Iowa 1987). "The patient's right to make an intelligent and informed decision cannot be exercised when information material to that decision is withheld." *Id.* To make an informed decision regarding continuation of a pregnancy, the patient has the right to expect the information reasonably necessary to that process will be made available by the physician.

We are persuaded by the New Jersey Supreme Court's analysis comparing informed-consent and wrongful-birth actions:

> In sum, the informed consent and wrongful birth causes of action are similar in that both require the physician to disclose those medically accepted risks that a reasonably prudent patient in the plaintiff's position would deem material to her decision. What is or is not a medically accepted risk is informed by what the physician knows or ought to know of the patient's history and condition. In both causes of action, the plaintiff must prove not only that a reasonably prudent patient in her position, if apprised of all material risks, would have elected a different course of treatment or care. The test of proximate causation is satisfied by showing that an undisclosed fetal risk was material to a woman in her position; the risk materialized, was reasonably foreseeable and not remote in relation to the doctor's negligence; and, had plaintiff known of that risk, she would have terminated her pregnancy.

Canesi ex rel. Canesi v. Wilson, 158 N.J. 490 (1999); *see also Bader v. Johnson*, 732 N.E.2d 1212 (Ind. 2000) (stating physician providing prenatal care has a duty to disclose "material facts relevant to the patient's decision about treatment," and while "discussion of this duty has generally arisen in cases involving informed consent and the doctrine of fraudulent concealment, the underlying premise is still the same").

An action in tort for a negligently performed or delayed medical diagnostic procedure lies within the common law of negligence. We decline to compound or complicate our medical malpractice jurisprudence by according this particular form of professional negligence action some special status apart from presently recognized medical malpractice. Without altering traditional rules of negligence, we acknowledge a newly recognized compensable event to which those traditional rules apply. The parents have alleged a well-recognized civil wrong without contorting any of the elements to conform to the facts. We conclude that a claim for wrongful birth is consistent with traditional common law principles of medical negligence, and we move on to the second *Dier* factor.

Defendants contend that recognition of a wrongful-birth action would contravene Iowa public policy. Public policy is not predicated on this court's generalized concepts of fairness and justice. Rather, "we must look to the Constitution, statutes, and judicial decisions of this state, to determine our public policy and that which is not prohibited by statute, condemned by judicial decision, nor contrary to the public morals contravenes no principle of public policy.

In *Nanke*, we confronted whether the parents of a "normal, healthy child" could recover for costs associated with raising the child after a negligently performed abortion. We concluded they could not because the invaluable benefits of parenthood outweigh the mere monetary burdens as a matter of law." We stated,

> The bond of affection between a child and parent, the pride in the child's achievement, and the comfort, counsel and society of a child are incalculable benefits, which should not be measured by some misplaced attempt to put a specific dollar value on a child's life.

Id. We also highlighted the "awkwardness that would inevitably surface under the application of the Restatement (Second) § 920 'benefits' approach," which offsets damages incurred by a benefit obtained. We noted parents would have to show that they did not want the child and the child was of minimal value to them to minimize the offset. We refused to sanction this type of argument.

The defendants contend the same reasoning applies here. They argue a contrary holding would stigmatize the disabled community, encourage abortions, increase the cost of prenatal care, and result in fraudulent claims. We are not persuaded those concerns warrant closing the courthouse door to parents harmed by medical negligence.

First, we distinguish the policy concerns expressed in *Nanke*. In a wrongful-birth claim, the injury is not the resulting life of a healthy child as in *Nanke*, but rather is the parent's deprivation of information material to making an informed decision whether to terminate a pregnancy of a child likely to be born with severe disabilities. Our informed-consent caselaw rests on the patient's right to exercise control in making personal medical decisions.

The legislature also has made a policy choice to help ensure a woman makes an informed decision whether to terminate or continue her pregnancy. Iowa Code section 146A.1(2) states that as a prerequisite to an abortion, a woman must be "provided information regarding the options relative to a pregnancy, including continuing the pregnancy to term and retaining parental rights following the child's birth, continuing the pregnancy to term and placing the child up for adoption, *and terminating the pregnancy*." (Emph. added.) To make an informed decision whether to proceed with the pregnancy, the woman must be informed of all material facts, including the likelihood the child will be born with a severe birth defect.

Nanke relied in part on an offset rule. 346 N.W.2d at 523. Under the Restatement (Second) of Torts, "when the defendant's tortious conduct has caused harm to the plaintiff and in so doing has conferred a special benefit to the interest of the plaintiff that was harmed, the value of the benefit conferred is considered in mitigation of damages." Restatement (Second) of Torts § 920. We noted in *Nanke* that a strict application of this rule to the ordinary costs of raising a normal, healthy child would require the parent to prove the child was of minimal value to them. In contrast, the *Lininger* court pointed out that in wrongful-birth cases involving a severely disabled child, "the extraordinary financial burden the Plaintiffs claim to have suffered, and will continue to suffer, is sufficiently unrelated to the pleasure they will derive from raising the disabled child as to preclude operation of the benefit rule, at least to the extent that it would require some offset against those particular damages." 764 P.2d at 1207. Imagine the case of a woman carrying a healthy fetus injured during the delivery because of a failure to diagnose a birthing issue, such as an umbilical cord wrapped around the neck. In that circumstance,

> we would have no problem assessing damages. More importantly we would not even consider the theory that the joy of parenthood should offset the damages. Would anyone in their right mind suggest that where a healthy fetus is injured during delivery the joy of parenthood should offset the damages? There is no more joy in an abnormal fetus come to full term than a normal fetus permanently injured at delivery. Both are heartbreaking conditions that demand far more psychological and financial resources than those blessed with normal children can imagine.

Atlanta Obstetrics & Gynecology Grp. v. Abelson, 260 Ga. 711 (1990) (Smith, J., dissenting). Pamela testified she "really enjoys spending time with Z.P. and gets a lot of happiness from him." But "that pleasure will be derived in spite of, rather than because of, the child's affliction." *Schroeder v. Perkel*, 87 N.J. 53 (1981). We decline to monetize the joy of raising a severely disabled child to offset the costs of raising him.

Defendants argue that allowing wrongful-birth claims will stigmatize the disabled community. That concern does not warrant closing the courthouse door to these parents. We fail to see how the parents' recovery of extraordinary medical and educational expenses, so as to minimize the detrimental effect of the child's impairment, is outweighed by any speculation about stigma that he might suffer. Parents make the difficult decision to sue for wrongful birth because they want to recover costs in order to ensure that their child would have the best possible medical care. For example, damages from a wrongful-birth claim were used by one family to "pay for some of the expenses of raising their child, including prostheses, wheelchairs, operations, attendants, and other healthcare needs. Defendants argue the disabled child may later be emotionally traumatized upon learning his or her parents would have chosen to abort. But given Z.P.'s severe cognitive disabilities, there is nothing in the record to indicate he will someday understand his parents sued over their lost opportunity to avoid his birth.

Defendants also contend that allowing a right to sue for wrongful birth will increase the cost of prenatal care by encouraging physicians to practice "defensive medicine" and that increased disclosure of risks will lead to more abortions. We disagree that these concerns justify closing the courthouse door.

> A physician need not, indeed should not, advise a patient on whether to abort a child. A physician's responsibility is simply to exercise due care to provide the information necessary for the *patient* to make an informed decision. If physicians do this, they need not fear a lawsuit if parents bear a child of one sex rather than the other, or even a child with congenital defects. The physician will not be liable for the patient's informed decision on the abortion question. To deny any remedy for a physician's negligently withholding information or negligently providing misinformation so immunizes the physician as to encourage the physician himself, in effect, to make the abortion decision.

Azzolino, 337 S.E.2d at 538 (Exum, J., dissenting). There are limitations on a physician's liability for a failure to disclose, or a negligent disclosure, already inherent in the common law negligence standard. As in informed-consent cases, a physician will only be liable when he or she has failed to disclose a *material* fact relevant to the decision to continue or terminate the pregnancy. *See Pauscher*, 408 N.W.2d at 361 ("Materiality may be said to be the significance a reasonable person, in what the physician knows or should know is his or her patient's position, would attach to the disclosed risk or risks in deciding whether to submit to surgery or treatment.") The applicable standard of care represents another limitation: a physician will only be liable for failure to discover a risk if a physician of reasonable care and skill in good standing under like circumstances would have discovered it.

Finally, defendants argue that recognition of wrongful-birth claims will lead to fraudulent claims. The Missouri Supreme Court declined to allow lawsuits for wrongful birth, noting that in the wrongful birth action, the right to recovery is based solely on the woman testifying, long after the fact and when it is in her financial interest to do so, that she would have chosen to abort if the physician had but told her of the risk of genetic abnormality. Although proof of causation will depend on a "counterfactual," or what the plaintiffs *would have done* if they had been properly informed by their physicians, this is the standard of proof in every informed-consent case. We favor placing trust in Iowa juries and our adversary system to root out fraudulent claims, rather than the alternative of closing the courthouse door to victimized parents with legitimate claims.

We must consider the public policy implications of an opposite ruling. Declining to recognize a claim for wrongful birth would immunize those in the medical field from liability for their performance in one particular area of medical malpractice, namely, prenatal care and genetic counseling. The defendants in this case have identified no other common law decision apart from *Nanke* in which we immunize physicians from liability for their negligence, and we decline to do so here. Conversely, recognition of wrongful-birth actions will encourage more accurate prenatal testing. Allowing recovery is also consistent with a goal of tort law—to compensate an injured party with damages in order to attempt to make them whole. On balance, we conclude public policy favors allowing wrongful-birth actions. If the legislature disagrees with our decision, it is free to enact a statute precluding wrongful-birth claims. No such statute is currently on the books.

Turning to the last *Dier* factor, defendants argue Iowa should not recognize a wrongful-birth claim because Iowa Code section 613.15A and Iowa Rule of Civil Procedure 1.206 limit parents' ability to recover medical expenses for a child's injuries. Iowa Code section 613.15A provides,

> A parent or the parents of a child may recover for the expense and actual loss of services, companionship, and society resulting from injury to or death of a minor child and may recover for the expense and actual loss of services, companionship, and society resulting from the death of an adult child.

Iowa Rule 1.206 states, "A parent or the parents, may sue for the expense and actual loss of services, companionship and society resulting from injury to or death of a minor child."

Both Fla. Stat. § 613.15A and rule 1.206 by their plain language apply to parents seeking to recover expenses resulting from the "*injury* of a minor child." (Emph. added.) To pursue a claim under those provisions, a parent must establish that the child's injury was wrongfully or negligently caused. "Actions brought under rule 1.206 are not for the injury to the child but for the injury to the parent *as a consequence of the injury to the child*." *Wardlow v. City of Keokuk*, 190 N.W.2d 439 (Iowa 1971) (emph. added). "The gist of a rule 1.206 action is a wrong done to the parent *in consequence of injury to his child* by the actionable negligence of another." *Dunn v. Rose Way, Inc.*, 333 N.W.2d 830 (Iowa 1983) (emph. added).

Here, as the defendants note, "there is no allegation that Defendants negligently caused Z.P.'s injuries." There is no injury to the child; rather, the injury is to the *parents*—specifically their right to make an informed choice whether to continue or end a pregnancy. Rule 1.206 and section 613.15A do not govern a wrongful-birth claim. We conclude the Iowa legislature has not statutorily barred wrongful-birth claims.

The Iowa legislature, however, has by statute expressed its policy preference for medical informed-consent procedures and accurately informing a woman regarding her options for continuing or terminating a pregnancy. Allowing a cause of action here furthers this legislative purpose without contravening section 613.15A or rule 1.206. Thus, we conclude that an action for wrongful-birth is cognizable under Iowa law.

The parents must prove the defendant's negligence deprived them of the opportunity to *lawfully* terminate the pregnancy in Iowa. *OB/GYN Specialists of Palm Beaches, P.A. v. Mejia*, 134 So.3d 1084 (Fla. Dist. Ct. App. 2014) (requiring plaintiff in wrongful-birth claim to prove she was deprived of the opportunity to lawfully obtain an abortion within the time permitted under the forum state's law, regardless of the plaintiff's ability to obtain a lawful late-term abortion in another state). We conclude Iowa public policy would not permit recovery for wrongful birth if the abortion in question would be illegal. To the contrary, the public policy codified in section 707.7 precludes such a recovery. The Plowmans' claims arise from the allegedly misinterpreted ultrasound during the second trimester of Pamela's pregnancy with Z.P.

The right to sue for wrongful birth belongs to parents who were denied the opportunity to make an *informed* choice whether to lawfully terminate a pregnancy in Iowa. It is not this court's role to second-guess that intensely personal and difficult decision. Parents of children with disabilities may find their lives enriched by the challenges and joys they confront daily. But under our tort law, financial compensation should be paid by the negligent physician if liability is proven.

The Plowmans seek damages for (1) their cost of ordinary care raising the child; (2) their cost of extraordinary care required for Z.P.'s life as a result of his disabilities; (3) their own pain, suffering, and mental anguish; and (4) their loss of income. They are not claiming any damages for loss of their child's consortium or services or for Pamela's labor and delivery of Z.P.

Because the district court granted defendants' motion for summary judgment on liability, it did not decide which damage claims can be submitted to the jury. A supreme court is "a court of review, not of first view." *Cutter v. Wilkinson*, 544 U.S. 709 (2005). The defendants did not file motions for partial summary judgment on particular elements of damages. On this sparse appellate record, we decline to decide what damages are recoverable. On remand, the district court must determine which types of damages may be submitted to the jury under the factual record made by the parties.

Tomlinson v. Metro. Pediatrics, LLC

412 P.3d 133 (Or. 2018) (Brewer, J.)

[T, a child, was born with severe birth defects. The parents filed suit against healthcare providers who failed to spot the defects, alleging that, had they known of them, the mother would have had an abortion. They pled negligence, seeking economic losses, mental anguish damages for themselves, and noneconomic losses for T. The trial court dismissed the appeal, the appellate court affirmed the dismissal of claims for T's damages, and plaintiffs appealed.

After holding that the parents, although not the patients of the physician, could assert a negligence claim against him, and noting that plaintiffs could recover the medical expenses and economic losses for T through age 18 (and on T's behalf after that date), the court turned to the parents' request for emotional distress damages and T's claim for mental distress, or wrongful birth.]

Generally, when a plaintiff establishes a cognizable negligence claim, damages are recoverable to the extent necessary to make the plaintiff whole. Thus, although emotional distress is not always a sufficient injury to establish a negligence claim, if the plaintiff establishes a negligence claim based on physical injury or the invasion of some other legally protected interest, then, generally speaking, the pain for which recovery is allowed includes virtually any form of conscious suffering, both emotional and physical. In this case, the parents have alleged facts that, if proved, could establish a legally protected interest in receiving information from defendants that, based on M's genetic condition, implicated the parents' reproductive choices.

Despite that broad rule, some courts have prohibited the recovery of emotional distress damages even while recognizing a parent's claim against a health care professional for allegedly negligent conduct that prevented the parent from avoiding or terminating a pregnancy that resulted in the birth of a disabled child. The reasoning of those decisions does not persuade us.

Some courts have disallowed damages for emotional distress on the ground that parenthood should not be viewed as emotional harm. *See, e.g.,* B*ecker v. Schwartz*, 46 N.Y.2d 401 (1978) ("While sympathetic to the plight of these parents, this court declined for policy reasons to sanction the recovery of damages for their psychic or emotional harm occasioned by the birth and gradual death of their child."). But allowing a parent to seek emotional distress damages does not require ignoring the emotional benefits that a parent may obtain from having a child. Instead, the jury may offset an award for emotional distress damages by the extent to which a parent receives emotional benefit from a child who resulted from a pregnancy that, but for the defendant's negligence, would have otherwise been avoided or terminated. Thus, most courts appear to be more than willing to award damages for the parents' emotional distress, subject to offsets for emotional benefits the parents may gain in having the child. In considering the emotional benefits of parenthood, a jury might determine that the benefits more than offset the emotional distress, and award no emotional distress damages at all. But that is a fact issue for the jury and not a reason to prevent the parents from seeking such damages.

Other courts that have disallowed damages for emotional distress have relied on principles created to limit recovery for emotional distress, such as the physical-impact rule or the zone-of-danger rule. *See, e.g., Bader v. Johnson*, 732 N.E.2d 1212 (Ind. 2000) (allowing mother to recover emotional distress damages, but not father, because mother satisfied the physical-impact rule). Those rules, however, have no logical bearing on the parents' wrongful birth claim. In such a claim, the parents do not assert a freestanding emotional distress claim, but merely assert emotional distress as an item of damages for a personal tort. For these reasons, the physical manifestation and zone-of-danger rules offer no occasion to reject mental distress damages in wrongful birth cases any more than they would do so in the case of libel or invasion of privacy." *See Kush v. Lloyd*, 616 So.2d 415 (Fla. 1992) ("There can be little doubt that emotional injury is more likely to occur when negligent medical advice leads parents to give birth to a severely impaired child than if someone wrongfully calls them liars, accuses them of unchastity, or subjects them to any other similar defamation."); *Naccash v. Burger*, 223 Va. 406 (1982) ("Furthermore, we believe it would be wholly unrealistic to say that the parents were mere witnesses to the consequences of the tortious conduct involved in this case.").

In short, we agree with the majority of courts that have addressed the issue and conclude that the parents should be allowed to seek such damages in this case....

T's claim is based on the factual premise that, if defendants had not acted negligently, then T would not have been born. The vast majority of courts that have considered the question have refused to recognize such claims. And most courts that have refused to recognize such claims have done so after confronting the imponderability of comparing life to nonexistence. That position, succinctly stated, is:

> Our finding of such a wrongful life injury would require first, that we value the child's present station in life; second, that we ascertain the value to the child of his not having been born; and finally, that we determine that the latter value is greater than the former. Because we find it impossible to complete those steps in any rational, principled manner, we cannot find that the child has suffered an injury sufficient to support a claim for relief.

Lininger v. Eisenbaum, 764 P.2d 1202 (Colo. 1988).

Courts rejecting such claims have emphasized the difficulty in determining whether a plaintiff has been harmed at all by a defendant's negligence when, but for that negligence, the plaintiff would not have been born in the first place. *See id.* ("The difficulty that besets the child's complaint is not merely that damages are inherently too speculative to assess. While the discussion above compels that conclusion, the more fundamental problem is that we cannot determine in the first instance that [the child] has been injured."). In this case, the Court of Appeals rejected T's claim on similar grounds after concluding that T had alleged that his existence itself is an injury and that it is impossible to calculate damages based on a comparison between life and nonexistence.

On review, T primarily argues that the Court of Appeals erred by defining his injury as life itself rather than as the impairment that accompanies his life. T remonstrates that he has not sought damages whose calculation would require a comparison between life and nonexistence. Instead, he argues, he seeks damages based on a comparison between his impaired life and a nonimpaired life. T notes that, although such damages may be difficult to measure, juries are routinely asked to make similar calculations in cases involving prenatal injuries to a child that resulted in permanent disabilities. *See, e.g., Klutschkowski v. PeaceHealth,* 354 Or. 150 (2013) (permanent injury to child during delivery).

A threshold difficulty with T's argument is that it puts the damages cart before the liability horse; that is, T's argument blurs the line between the identification of a cognizable injury and the determination of damages resulting from the injury. The general rule in Oregon in assessing damages has been that a plaintiff should recover only such sums as will compensate a plaintiff for the injury suffered as a result of a defendant's wrong. We must therefore first determine whether T has suffered a cognizable injury caused by defendants' negligence. Only then would T be entitled to have a finder of fact determine the damages needed to compensate that injury.

Contrary to T's argument, the comparison between life and nonexistence is inherent in determining both whether T suffered any harm as a result of defendants' conduct and whether any such harm constitutes a cognizable legal injury — that is, whether T's claimed injury is subject to legal protection against defendants' negligent conduct. As we now explain, those problems persist regardless how T frames the damages that he seeks.

To adequately state a negligence claim, a plaintiff must allege facts that would allow a reasonable factfinder to determine that the defendant's negligence caused the plaintiff harm. As alleged in the complaint, T was born and was born with DMD as a result of defendants' conduct. The question remains, however, whether being born and being born with DMD constitutes harm that defendants caused.

Central to determining causation of harm is a comparison between what actually happened and what would have happened if the defendant had not engaged in the allegedly negligent conduct. T contends that he can establish that defendants' conduct caused him harm without comparing the value of life to the value of non-existence. According to T, the harm that defendants caused him is analogous to a prenatal injury to a fetus, which requires no comparison to nonexistence.

In the case of a prenatal injury resulting in disability, the plaintiff can establish harm based on a comparison between his or her life with the disability and his or her life without the disability, because the defendant actually caused the alleged disability. As a result, establishing harm from a prenatal injury does not require comparing life to nonexistence. For example, in *Mallison v. Pomeroy*, 205 Or. 690 (1955), a defendant negligently caused a traffic accident that resulted in the plaintiff being born with a disability. In that case, but for the defendant's negligence, the plaintiff would have been born without the disability. The defendant, therefore, caused the plaintiff harm.

T's claim, however, is not analogous to a prenatal injury. It is true that, like the plaintiff in *Mallison*, T has alleged that defendants' negligence caused him to be born with a disability. But unlike the plaintiff in *Mallison*, T has not alleged that, but for defendants' negligence, T would have been born without the disability. Instead, as noted above, T has alleged that, "had defendants, and each of them, timely diagnosed M's DMD, the parents would not have produced another child suffering from Duchenne's muscular dystrophy." In short, as alleged, the alternatives for T were that he would be conceived and born with DMD or that he would not be conceived and born at all.

The comparison is not avoided merely because T has alleged that defendants caused him economic and emotional burdens. The role of nonexistence in that analysis is different depending on whether the damages that T seeks are deemed to be components of damages resulting from a physical injury or whether those burdens themselves constitute economic and emotional injuries. That distinction is highlighted by T's analogy to prenatal injuries. For a plaintiff who suffers a permanent impairment resulting from a prenatal injury, the impairment is a physical injury, and the financial and emotional burdens resulting from living with that impairment are components of damages needed to compensate for the physical injury.

Using that comparison to establish harm creates a problem for T. Framing T's argument in that way does not *avoid* a comparison between life and nonexistence, as T contends. Instead, it *enables* a comparison between life and nonexistence by asserting at least a partial conception of what nonexistence is like—namely, a state of being in which one experiences no economic or emotional burdens.

Notes and Questions

1. <u>In Kansas</u>. In response to the Kansas Supreme Court recognizing the tort of "wrongful birth"—the person sues for being alive, rather than having been aborted—its legislature enacted a statute to bar such claims. *See Tillman v. Goodpasture,* 424 P.3d 540 (Kan. App. 2018) (upholding statute against challenge it was unconstitutional under state law). Where the claim is allowed and pain and suffering of the child is recoverable, proof the child can, or did, feel pain and suffering is required. *E.g., Ng-Wagner v. Hotchkiss,* 2018 WL 2277803 (Md. Spec. App. May 18, 2018) (affirming jury award of pain and suffering for baby that was born very premature and died after 21 days without scientific proof of capacity for such feeling).

2. <u>Not in Kansas</u>. Maine's "wrongful birth" statute provides:

> No person may maintain a claim for relief or receive an award for damages based on the claim that the birth and rearing of a healthy child resulted in damages to him. A person may maintain a claim for relief based on a failed sterilization procedure resulting in the birth of a healthy child and receive an award of damages for the hospital and medical expenses incurred for the sterilization procedures and pregnancy, the pain and suffering connected with the pregnancy and the loss of earnings by the mother during pregnancy.

In *Doherty v. Merck & Co.,* 2017 WL 3668415 (D. Me. Aug. 24, 2107), the plaintiff used defendant's birth control device, but it failed. She had a healthy child. She sued for damages. The court held her claim barred and this statute constitutional. An intended result?

3. <u>Fetus, Sign Here</u>? A physician who fails to disclose to a patient the material risks of a procedure can commit battery. What if the doctor fails to disclose a risk to the mother—does the unborn child have its own battery claim? The court in *Jones v. MetroHealth Med. Center,* 89 N.E.2d 633 (Ct. App. Ohio 2017), held yes, and collected cases holding the physician owes a duty of disclosure to a fetus: "Assuming the injury occurred [after birth] at an age where the child lacked the legal ability to consent, it would be the child's parent or guardian who gave consent. But in all events, it would be an injury done to the child."

Problems

1. <u>Pros and Cons</u>. Although the issues in this chapter are in some ways profound and metaphysical, they implicate issues previously addressed. For example,

why should filial and other loss of consortium claims not be allowed when spousal claims are? Why is marriage sufficient? Required?

2. <u>Your State's Approach?</u> Has your state decided whether to recognize these claims? If so, what are the requirements and measure of damage?

3. <u>What Should the Remedy Be for Wrongful Life</u>? Think about what you would write as a jury instruction and ask yourself how you would argue a case to a jury.

4. "<u>Fear of</u>" Claims. Wrongful life and wrongful birth in some ways are distant from whether, as discussed here and earlier, courts should permit recovery for "fear of" becoming ill with a disease as a result of defendant's acts, or instead of awarding "medical monitoring" damages to earlier detect those harms. Yet they present the same issue and lead back to the beginning of this book: each claim has a "trigger harm" and, particularly with negligence, courts struggle to define it. Consider a client who contends that the defendant's negligence, occurring nearly two years ago, has put it in fear of identity theft when a hacker breached a bank's computer system. Which claim, or claims, discussed in this book might be most likely to lead to a recovery against the hacker? Against the bank? If the claim is extended to reach that harm, is any award of damages by a jury meaningfully reviewable?

Index